LAW AND GLOBAL HEALTH

Law and Global Health

Current Legal Issues

VOLUME 16

Edited by
MICHAEL FREEMAN FBA
Emeritus Professor of English Law
University College London

SARAH HAWKES
Reader in Global Health
Institute of Global Health
University College London

and

BELINDA BENNETT
Professor of Health Law
Queensland University of Technology
Australia

OXFORD
UNIVERSITY PRESS

OXFORD
UNIVERSITY PRESS

Great Clarendon Street, Oxford, OX2 6DP,
United Kingdom

Oxford University Press is a department of the University of Oxford.
It furthers the University's objective of excellence in research, scholarship,
and education by publishing worldwide. Oxford is a registered trade mark of
Oxford University Press in the UK and in certain other countries

First Edition published in 2014
Impression: 1

Published in the United States of America by Oxford University Press
198 Madison Avenue, New York, NY 10016, United States of America

British Library Cataloguing in Publication Data
Data available

Library of Congress Control Number: 2013957466

ISBN 978–0–19–968899–9

Printed in Great Britain by
CPI Group (UK) Ltd, Croydon, CR0 4YY

Preface

Law and Global Health is the product of an international, interdisciplinary colloquium held in UCL on 2 and 3 July 2012. It is the 16th such colloquium, all linking law with another discipline, and stretching back to Law and Science in 1997. The first editor of this volume has masterminded the series, and deeply regrets that this is likely to be the last one. The volumes have been at the cutting edge of interdisciplinary studies.

As is this one. Global Health is a growth area: it feeds on works and insights from a number of disciplines, which are well represented in this volume, and for obvious reasons resonates with scholars and policy-makers from low-, middle-, and high-income countries. A paper included in this collection is from Chad—not a common source for research papers. In fact there are contributions from eleven countries and from at least six disciplines—one cannot be precise since disciplines in this area especially are porous rather than discrete.

It remains to acknowledge and to thank those who supported this project: the UCL Grand Challenge of Global Health and Institute for Global Health, and Laws alumna Laura Devine offered vital financial assistance. As ever, the smooth running of the colloquium needed and got the administrative support of Lisa Penfold and Liz Carter. Jacqui Bennett, who will have retired by the time this volume is published, juggled her roles of PA and Lady Mayoress, and helped to organize an assortment of papers into, what we hope is, a coherent book. Last but not least, our gratitude is owed to Natasha Flemming, who rushed out a contract overnight, when, horror of horrors, it was discovered at the point of delivery that there *was* no contract!

Michael Freeman
Sarah Hawkes
Belinda Bennett
6 April 2013

Contents

List of Abbreviations

ACA	Affordable Care Act (US)
ACRWC	African Charter on the Rights and Welfare of the Child
ACTA	Anti-Counterfeiting Trade Agreement
ADI	acceptable daily intake (food safety)
AHED	Association for Health and Environment Development (Egypt)
AHRC	Australian Human Rights Commission
ALCJS	Arab Council for Judicial and Legal Studies
AMDD	Averting Maternal Death and Disability Program
APA	American Psychological Association
APHRC	African Population and Health Research Center
ART	antiretroviral therapy
ARVs	anti-retroviral drugs
ASEAN	Association of Southeast Asian Nations
ASH	Action on Smoking and Health
ATL	Tunisian Association for the Fight against STIs and AIDS
AVAAZ	an online campaigning organization
BGH	bovine growth hormone
BINGOs	business interest NGOs
BSCT	Behavioral Science Consultation Teams (or 'Biscuits') (US)
CBD	Convention on Biological Diversity
CCFAC	Codex Committee on Food Additives and Contaminants
CDS	Center for Development Services (Cairo)
CEDAW	Convention on the Elimination of all Forms of Discrimination against Women
CERD	Committee on the Elimination of Racial Discrimination
CESCR	Committee on Economic, Social and Cultural Rights
CIOMS	Council for International Organisations of Medical Sciences
CJD	Creutzfeld-Jakob Disease
CMHF	Cape Metro Health Forum
CMV	cytomegalovirus
Codex	Codex Alimentarius Commission
ComDT	community-directed treatment
CP	civil and political rights
CRC	Convention on the Rights of the Child 1989
CRPD	Convention on the Rights of Persons with Disabilities 2006
CRR	Center for Reproductive Rights
CSO	civil society organization
CV	circoviruses
DALYs	disability-adjusted life years
DFID	Department for International Development (UK)
DG-SANCO	Directorate General for Health and Consumer Protection
DH	Department of Health (UK)
DHHS	Department of Health and Human Services (US)
DNDi	Drugs for Neglected Diseases Initiative
DoD	Department of Defense (US)
DPAS	Global Strategy on Diet, Physical Activity, and Health (WHO)
DPOs	disabled persons organizations
EBRD	European Bank for Reconstruction and Development

ECCLR	Egyptian Council for Civil and Legislative Reform
ECD Centres	Early Childhood Development Centres
ECDC	European Centre for Disease Prevention and Control
ECOWAS	Economic Community of West African States
ECSR	European Committee of Social Rights
ECT	Energy Charter Treaty
EFSA	European Food Safety Authority
EIPR	Egyptian Initiative for Personal Rights
EmOC	emergency obstetric care
ESC	economic, social, and cultural rights
ESHRE	European Society of Human Reproduction and Embryology
FAO	Food and Agriculture Organization (UN)
FCA	Framework Convention Alliance (tobacco negotiations)
FCGH	Framework Convention on Global Health
FCN	friendship, commerce and navigation (treaties)
FCTC	Framework Convention on Tobacco Control
FDA	Food and Drug Administration (US)
FDI	foreign direct investment
FiTs	feed-in tariffs
FOIA	Freedom of Information Act
FPL	federal poverty level
FTA	free trade agreement
FWCW	Fourth World Conference on Women (1995)
GAD	Global Alcohol Database (WHO)
GAVI	Global Alliance for Vaccines and Immunization
GEF	Global Environment Facility (UN)
GFATM	Global Fund to Fight AIDS, Tuberculosis and Malaria
GNI	gross national income
GOARN	Global Outbreak Alert and Response Network (WHO)
GPHIN	Global Public Health Information Network (Canada)
HAI	Health Action International
HARPAS	HIV/AIDS Regional Programme in the Arab States (UNDP)
HCCRA	Health Care Conscience Rights Act (US)
HRC	Human Rights Council
ICBL	International Campaign to Ban Landmines
ICCPR	International Covenant on Civil and Political Rights
ICERD	International Convention on the Elimination of all Forms of Racial Discrimination
ICESCR	International Covenant on Economic, Social and Cultural Rights
ICF	WHO International Classification of Functioning, Disability and Health
ICPD	International Conference on Population and Development (1994)
ICSID	International Center for Settlement of Investment Disputes
ICTSD	International Centre for Trade and Sustainable Development
IDC	International Disability Caucus (UN)
IDLO	International Development Law Organization
IDM	informed decision-making
IERG	Independent Expert Reference Group
IFPMA	International Federation of Pharmaceutical Manufacturers and Associations
IGO	intergovernmental organization
IIMMHR	International Initiative on Maternal Mortality and Human Rights
IMPACT	International Medical Products Anti-Counterfeiting Task Force
INB	intergovernmental negotiating body

INFACT	Infant Formula Coalition
IPE	intellectual property enforcement
IPR	intellectual property rights
IRS	Internal Revenue Service (US)
IVF	in vitro fertilization
IXA	International Xenotransplantation Association
JALI	Joint Action and Learning Initiative on National and Global Responsibilities for Health
JECFA	Joint Expert Committee on Food Additives (joint WHO-FAO)
JMPR	Joint Meeting on Pesticide Residues (joint WHO-FAO)
KAM	Kenya Association of Manufacturers
KCAEM	Kenya Coalition for Access to Essential Medicines
KEI	Knowledge Ecology International
KIPI	Kenyan Industrial Property Institute (formerly Office)
LMICs	low- and middle-income countries
LN	Learning Network for Health and Human Rights
MAAN	National Council for Justice and Social Peace (Egypt)
MAI	multilateral agreement on investment
MDGs	Millennium Development Goals
MENA	Middle East and North Africa
Mercosur	Mercado Común del Sur (Common Market of the South)
MFN	most-favoured-nation
MIPAA	Madrid International Plan of Action on Ageing
MMR	maternal mortality ratio
MSF	Médecins Sans Frontières
NAFTA	North American Free Trade Agreement
NAMs	National Association of Manufacturers (US)
NCDs	non-communicable diseases
NCQA	National Committee for Quality Assurance (US)
NEL	no effect level (food safety)
NGO	non-governmental organization
NHRI	national human rights institutions
NIAA	National Institute on Alcohol Abuse and Alcoholism (US)
NIMHD	National Institute on Minority Health and Health Disparities (US)
NOAEL	no observed adverse effect level (food safety)
NPA	National Partnership for Action (US)
NTBs	non-tariff barriers to trade
OAU	Organization of African Unity
OECD	Organisation for Economic Co-operation and Development
OEWG	Open-Ended Working Group (on ageing)
OHCHR	Office of the United Nations High Commissioner for Human Rights
OPALS	Pan-African organization to Fight AIDS (Morocco)
PCMV	porcine cytomegalovirus
PD	Political Declaration
PDPs	product development partnerships
PEEREA	Protocol on Energy Efficiency and Related Environmental Aspects (part of the ECT)
PEPFAR	US President's Emergency Plan for AIDS Relief
PERVs	porcine endogenous retroviruses
PEEREA	Protocol on Energy Efficiency and Related Environmental Aspects
PHC	primary health care
PHEIC	public health emergency of international concern

PHLR	public health law research
PHR	Physicians for Human Rights
PINGOs	public interest NGOs'
PLWHA	people living with HIV/AIDS
PMNCH	Partnership on Maternal, Newborn and Child Health
PPACA	Patient Protection and Affordable Care Act (US)
PPB	Pharmacy and Poisons Board (Kenya)
PPPs	public-private partnerships
PSA	prostate specific antigen
R&D	research and development
rBST	recombinant bovine somatotropin
REFLECT	Regenerated Freirian Literacy through Empowering Community Techniques
SADC	Southern African Development Community
SCAHAW	Scientific Committee on Animal Health and Animal Welfare
SCVMPH	Scientific Committee on Veterinary Measures relating to Public Health (European Commission)
SDH	Social Determinants of Health (US)
SDM	shared decision-making
SERE	Survival, Evasion, Resistance, and Escape
SET	single embryo transfer
SF	safety factor (food safety)
SPF	specific pathogen free
SPS	Agreement on Sanitary and Phytosanitary Measures (WTO)
STIs	sexually transmitted diseases
TAC	Treatment Action Campaign (South Africa)
TFI	Tobacco Free Initiative (WHO)
TRIMs	Agreement on Trade-Related Investment Measures (WTO)
TRIPS	Agreement on Trade Related Aspects of Intellectual Property Rights (WTO)
TTCs	transnational tobacco companies
TWC	The Women's Circle (South Africa)
UDHR	Universal Declaration of Human Rights
UNAIDS	United Nations Programme on HIV/AIDS
UNCCD	Convention to Combat Desertification in those Countries Experiencing Serious Droughts and/or Desertification, Particularly in Africa
UNCITRAL	UN Commission on International Trade Law
UNCTAD	United Nations Conference on Trade and Development
UNDP	United Nations Development Programme
UNESCO	United Nations Educational, Scientific and Cultural Organization
UNFCCC	United Nations Framework Convention on Climate Change
UNFPA	United Nations Population Fund (formerly the United Nations Fund for Population Activities)
UNGA	United Nations General Assembly
UNGASS	United Nations General Assembly Special Session on HIV/AIDS
UNHRC	United Nations Human Rights Council
UNICEF	United Nations Children's Fund
UNIDO	United Nations Industrial Development Organization
UNOS	United Network for Organ Sharing
USCEA	US Cigarettes Export Association
USTR	Office of the United States Trade Representative
WFP	Women on Farms Project (South Africa)
WHA	World Health Assembly
WIPO	World Intellectual Property Organization

Notes on Contributors

Obijiofor Aginam is Senior Academic Officer at the United Nations University's Institute for Sustainability and Peace, Tokyo, and concurrently an Adjunct Research Professor of Law, Carleton University, Ottawa, and Visiting Professor at the University of Tokyo. He has been a tenured Associate Professor of Law at Carleton University, and Global Health Leadership Officer at the World Health Organization, Geneva. He holds a PhD from the University of British Columbia.

George J. Annas is William Fairfield Warren Distinguished Professor at Boston University, is Chair of the Department of Health Law, Bioethics & Human Rights of Boston University School of Public Health, and Professor at the Boston University School of Medicine, and School of Law. He is the co-founder of Global Lawyers and Physicians, a transnational professional association of lawyers and physicians working together to promote human rights and health. He is the author or editor of nineteen books on health law and bioethics, including *Worst Case Bioethics: Death, Disaster, and Public Health* (OUP, 2010).

Jacquineau Azétsop trained in social and religious ethics at Boston College and in public health at Johns Hopkins University. Currently, he lectures on bioethics and public health at the Faculté des Sciences de la Santé of N'djaména University in Chad. He also lectures in the Master Program in Public Health and HIV/AIDS Management at the Faculdade de Ciências de Saúde of the Catholic University of Mozambique. His main research interests are at the interface of ethics, public health challenges, and social policy.

Belinda Bennett is Professor of Health Law at Queensland University of Technology in Brisbane, Australia. Prior to joining QUT in 2014, she was Professor of Health and Medical Law at the University of Sydney. She researches on legal regulation of biomedicine and on the impact of globalization on health law. She is the author of *Health Law's Kaleidoscope: Health Law Rights in a Global Age* (Ashgate, 2008); editor of *Health, Rights and Globalisation* (Ashgate, 2006); and co-editor with George Tomossy of *Gobalization and Health: Challenges for Health Law and Bioethics* (Springer, 2006).

Hazel Biggs is Professor of Law at the University of Southampton. She is the author of *Healthcare Research Ethics and Law* (Routledge-Cavendish, 2009).

M. Gregg Bloche is Professor of Law at Georgetown University,

Paula Braveman is Professor of Family and Community Medicine and Director of the Center on Social Disparities in Health at the University of California, San Francisco. For over twenty-five years, Dr Braveman has studied and published extensively on health inequalities and health equity and has actively engaged in bringing attention to these issues in the US and internationally. Her research has focused on measuring, understanding, and addressing socio-economic and racial/ethnic inequalities in health, particularly in maternal and infant health.

Judith Bueno de Mesquita is a Lecturer in the School of Law, and a Member of the Human Rights Centre, at the University of Essex. From 2009 to 2011, she was a consultant on human rights and sexual and reproductive health at the Department of Reproductive Health and Research, of the World Health Organization. From 2001 to 2008, she was a Senior Research Officer at the Human Rights Centre, University of Essex, where she worked in support of the mandate of the Special Rapporteur on the Right to Health. She has worked as a consultant for, among others, the OHCHR, DFID, UNICEF, and PMNCH.

Scott Burris is Professor of Law at Temple University. He directs the programme in Health Care Law, Policy and Practice. He has published over a hundred books, chapters in books, and articles, many on HIV-related questions. His current research focus includes health governance.

Kent Buse is a political economist with expertise in health policy analysis. He serves as Chief, Political Affairs and Strategy, UNAIDS. Kent taught at Yale University and at the London School of Hygiene and Tropical Medicine. His books include *Making Health Policy* (McGraw-Hill, 2006), *Health Policy in a Globalizing World* (CUP, 2002), and *Making Sense of Global Health Governance and Health Systems: Policy, Finance and Organization* (Academic Press, 2008).

Terry Carney is Emeritus Professor of Law at the Faculty of Law, University of Sydney (where he was a long-serving Director of Research and past Head of Department) and Visiting Research Professor at the University of Technology, Sydney. A Fellow of the Australian Academy of Law, he is a past President (2005–07) of the International Academy of Law and Mental Health, and chaired Commonwealth bodies such as the National Advisory Council on Social Welfare and of the Board of the Institute of Family Studies.

Geoffrey B. Cockerham is an Associate Professor in the Department of History and Political Science at Utah Valley University in Orem, Utah. His research interests include international cooperation, international institutions, and global health governance. He is co-author of *Health and Globalization* (Polity Press, 2010) and has had recent publications in *International Politics, East Asia*, and *Social Science and Medicine.*

William C. Cockerham is Distinguished Professor of Sociology and Chair of the Department of Sociology at the University of Alabama at Birmingham. Recent books include *Social Causes of Health and Disease* (2nd edn, Polity Press, 2013), *Medical Sociology on the Move: New Directions in Theory* (Springer, 2013), and *Sociology of Mental Disorder* (9th edn, Pearson Prentice-Hall, 2013).

John Coggon is Reader in Law at the University of Southampton. His research focuses on legal, moral, and political theory, particularly with regard to human health and welfare. His principal area of interest is public health. Among his publications on the subject is the book *What Makes Health Public?* (CUP, 2012).

Kim Crow is a Research Associate at the ANU College of Law, Australian National University.

Dr Sylvie Da Lomba is a lecturer in the Law School of the University of Strathclyde. She researches in the areas of immigration, asylum, and human rights. She has a particular interest in social rights for irregular migrants and has published extensively on irregular migrants' right to health care. Her current research is concerned with the interface between immigration status, membership, and protection in the social sphere.

Shereen El Feki is the author of *Sex and the Citadel: Intimate Life in a Changing Arab World* (Random House, 2013). With a doctorate from the University of Cambridge, Shereen is a former immunologist turned healthcare journalist with *The Economist* and Al Jazeera. Most recently, she was Vice-Chair of the UN's Global Commission on HIV and the Law. Her writing and advocacy focuses on women, sexuality, and HIV in the Arab region.

Michal Engelman is Assistant Professor of Sociology at the University of Chicago. She is a demographer and gerontologist, studying the dynamics of population ageing and the determinants of longevity and health at older ages. Her work explores the factors that differentiate individual health trajectories and shape population trends over time, with particular attention to ageing in the context of economic and social change.

Tom A. Faunce is an Australian Research Council Future Fellow and Professor, ANU College of Law and College of Medicine, Biology and The Environment, at the Australian National University. He serves on the Board of Directors of the Energy Change Institute at the ANU. He has been awarded four Australian Research Council competitive Discovery Grants and published over a hundred refereed articles and over twenty-five book chapters in the field of health technology regulation. His most recent book is *Nanotechnology for a Sustainable World* (Edward Elgar, 2012). His main research interest is in the globalization of artificial photosynthesis as a combined energy security and climate change solution.

Charles Foster is a Fellow of Green Templeton College, University of Oxford. Recent books include *Medical Law: A Very Short Introduction, Human Dignity in Bioethics and Law* (OUP, 2013), and *Choosing Life, Choosing Death: The Tyranny of Autonomy in Medical Law and Ethics* (Hart, 2009).

Sara Fovargue is a Senior Lecturer in Law and Co-Director of the Centre for Bioethics and Medical Law at Lancaster University. Her research has considered the regulation of biotechnology and reproduction, clinical research, consent and capacity, risk, and the relationship between law and ethics. Her book, *Xenotransplantation and Risk: Regulating a Developing Biotechnology*, was published by Cambridge University Press in 2012. She is an Associate Editor of the Medical Law Review and of *Clinical Ethics*.

Michael Freeman is Professor Emeritus of English Law at UCL. He is Editor of this series, editor of the International Journal of Children's Rights, and author of *The Ethics of Public Health* (Ashgate, 2010). He is a Fellow of the British Academy.

Eric A. Friedman is Project Leader, Joint Action and Learning Initiative on National and Global Responsibilities for Health at the O'Neill Institute for National and Global Health Law, at Georgetown University Law Center in Washington, DC. Before joining the O'Neill Institute, Eric was Senior Global Health Policy Advisor at Physicians for Human Rights, where he focused on the right to health.

Lawrence O. Gostin is University Professor in Global Health Law at Georgetown, Faculty Director of the O'Neill Institute for National and Global Health Law, and Director of the World Health Organization Collaborating Center on Public Health Law & Human Rights. He has chaired numerous National Academy of Sciences committees and served on the WHO Director's Ad Hoc Advisory Committee on Reforming the WHO.

John Harrington is a Professor of Law at Cardiff University. Currently he is also a Senior Research Fellow at the British Institute in Eastern Africa and a Visiting Fellow at the African Population and Health Research Centre, both in Nairobi. He has published widely on health law issues in the UK, Europe, and Eastern Africa. Recent publications include *Global Governance of HIV/AIDS: Intellectual Property and Access to Essential Medicines* (Edward Elgar, 2013) (with Aginam and Yu) and *Global Health and Human Rights: Legal and Philosophical Perspectives* (Routledge, 2010) (with Stuttaford). His work develops a rhetorical critique of legal materials, academic commentary, and campaigning interventions. This method informs his current research project—a study of the 'globalization' of health law in Kenya.

Sarah Hawkes is Reader in Global Health at the Institute for Global Health, UCL, and a Wellcome Trust Senior Fellow in International Public Engagement. She specializes in looking at the link (or lack thereof) between evidence and policies to improve sexual health and rights, with a special focus on sexual health in South Asia and the Middle East.

Mark Henaghan is Dean and Professor of Law at the University of Otago. He specializes in family law and is a Barrister and Solicitor of the High Court of New Zealand. He is the sole author of *Health Professionals and Trust* (Routledge, 2012). He is on the editorial boards of Child and Family Law Quarterly and The International Journal of Human Rights and was the principal investigator of the Human Genome Project—Ethical and Legal Implications—funded by the New Zealand Law Foundation.

Jonathan Herring is a fellow in law at Exeter College, Oxford University and Professor of Law at the Law Faculty, Oxford University. He has written on family law, medical law, criminal law, and legal issues surrounding old age. He has written over forty books including: *Caring and the Law* (Hart, 2013); *Older People in Law and Society* (OUP, 2009); *European Human Rights and Family Law* (Hart, 2010) (with Shazia Choudhry); *Medical Law and Ethics* (OUP, 2010); *Criminal Law*, (4th edn, OUP, 2012); and *Family Law: A Very Short Introduction* (OUP, 2014).

Kristen Hessler is an Assistant Professor at University at Albany, She received her PhD from the University of Arizona. Her research focuses on political philosophy (especially issues in global justice, human rights, and international law) and bioethics (with a focus on environmental and agricultural issues). She has published articles on human rights law, international justice, and ethical issues concerning biotechnology in agriculture. She teaches courses in ethics, applied ethics, political philosophy, and feminist philosophy.

Stephen Holland is a Senior Lecturer in the Departments of Philosophy and Health Sciences at the University of York. He is the author of *Bioethics: A Philosophical Introduction* (Polity Press, 2003) and recently edited a bioethics anthology, *Arguing about Bioethics* (Routledge, 2012). He also wrote *Public Health Ethics* (Policy Press, 2007), a second edition of which is due out in 2014.

Caroline Jones is Senior Lecturer in Law at the University of Southampton.

Damaris Kiewiets is Chairperson of the Cape Metro Health Forum and is a Community Liaison Officer, University of the Western Cape. She assists students and communities to understand the role of the University in the surrounding communities. Damaris is a former nurse with a track record as an activist for the right to health and chairs a number of NGOs. She is completing her diploma in Adult Education, University of Cape Town.

Meri Koivusalo is a senior researcher at the National Institute of Health and Welfare, Helsinki, Finland. Her research has its focus on environmental health, international health policy, and the relationship between trade and health policies. She has provided advice and consultancy for the Finnish government, the European Commission, and the World Health Organization.

Leslie London is a public health specialist and Professor in the School of Public Health and Family Medicine, University of Cape Town and head of the School's Health and Human Rights Programme. His research includes work on the right to health, dual loyalties and human rights, and environmental justice issues. He serves as Theme Coordinator on health rights for the Network on Equity in Health in Southern Africa (EQUINET), and currently coordinates the Learning Network for Health and Human Rights.

Florencia Luna is Professor of Bioethics at the University of Buenos Aires. She is Research Adjunct at CONICET, and an adviser to the World Health Organization and CIOMS. She is the Editor of Perspectivas Bioeticas.

Gwendolyn Roberts Majette is an Assistant Professor of Law at the Center for Health Law and Policy at Cleveland-Marshall College of Law. She has Capitol Hill experience. She was a fellow with the Health Subcommittee of the Ways and Means Committee of the United States House of Representatives and was a member of the Health Subcommittee of the Senate Finance Committee.

Hadii M. Mamudu obtained his PhD from West Virginia University and had postdoctoral training at the University of California, San Francisco. Currently, he is an Assistant Professor in the College of Public Health at East Tennessee State University, where he conducts research into tobacco use and control with the focus on global health governance issues, including the WHO FCTC, trade/investment-public health relations, and NCDs.

Colin McInnes is Director of the Centre for Health and International Relations and was formerly Head of the Department at Aberystwyth University. He was Chair of the British International Studies Association; a member of the ESRC's Strategic Research Board and International Advisory Committee; a member of the WHO's expert group on Global Health Diplomacy; and Director of the UK Research Councils' Security Research Forum. He sits on a range of advisory panels covering various aspects of international relations, and is member of a variety of editorial boards.

Benjamin M. Meier is Assistant Professor of Global Health Policy, University of North Carolina at Chapel Hill, US.

Erik Millstone is a Professor of Science Policy at the University of Sussex. He is also joint leader of the STEPS Centre's work on Agriculture and Food policy. STEPS is the acronym for Social, Technological and Environmental Pathways to Sustainability. Since 1974 he has been researching the causes, consequences, and regulation of technological change in the food and chemical industries.

Khadija Moalla PhD is a Tunisian international law, gender, and human rights expert. She has more than twenty years of experience in development, including seven years in senior leadership positions at the United Nations. Her repertoire includes extensive expertise in international law and human rights, gender equality, civil society organizations, and HIV/AIDS. She has been a leadership development expert and facilitator in twenty Arab countries, and a speaker in more than sixty countries. As UNDP HIV Practice Team Leader in the Arab States, 2003–11, Dr Moalla coordinated initiatives with religious leaders, legislators, media, and NGO leaders which catalyzed the enactment of progressive laws, nation-wide training, and top level policy change in Morocco, Yemen, and other countries. Dr Moalla has had an in-depth involvement with governments, international organizations, the CSO, the media, and the private sector in twenty Arab countries, including all GCC members. She was recently chosen as one of the most influential 500 personalities of the Arab region.

Wendy Nefdt is the Regional Director of Epilepsy South Africa, Western Cape, a non-profit organization that provides developmental services to people with disabilities. Wendy is also a part-time PhD student, University of Cape Town. The topic of her research is 'The Role of Social Capital in the Integration and Implementation of Health and Human Rights Programmes Amongst Civil Society Organisations in Cape Town, South Africa'.

James Orbinski is a globally-recognized humanitarian practitioner and advocate, as well as a leading scholar in global health. He is Research Chair in Global Health at the Balsillie School of International Affairs, and is Director of the Africa Initiative, at the Centre for International Governance Innovation (CIGI). He is professor of International policy and governance at Wilfrid Laurier University, and professor of medicine at the Dalla Lana School of Public Health at the University of Toronto. After extensive field experience, he was international Council President of Médecins Sans Frontières (1998–2001) when it received the 1999 Nobel Peace Prize. He co-chaired the establishment of the Drugs For Neglected Diseases initiative, and co-Founded Dignitas international. Dr Orbinski sits on several global health-related boards, and is currently developing a research and policy agenda around the health impacts of global warming in Africa.

David Patterson is a graduate of Sydney University (BSc) and UNSW (LLB). Postgraduate studies include an LLM in human rights (McGill) and MSc in public policy and management (London), and certificates in community health (University of Montreal) and international development evaluation (World Bank & Carlton). As Head of the Social

Development Programs Unit at the International Development Law Organization (IDLO), he has managed IDLO's programme on HIV and law in the Middle East North Africa region since 2009.

Kerry Petersen is an Associate Professor at La Trobe University, Australia. She has published extensively in the fields of health law and human reproduction law. She has also collaborated with scholars from public health, the biological sciences, and bio-ethics on interdisciplinary and international research projects. She is the lawyer on the Melbourne IVF Human Research Ethics Committee.

Vanessa Reynolds joined the Women's Circle in 2006 as a community member and became a Community Circle Coordinator before taking up her current position as Programme Manager. Her experiences within her local community motivate her to provide access to tools and opportunities that lead to self empowerment and assist communities in overcoming poverty. She has a Diploma in Adult Education and is currently studying towards an Advanced Certificate in Adult Education, University of Cape Town.

Glynis Rhodes is the Women's Health and Empowerment Programme Coordinator, Women on Farms Project. She has a degree in Social Work from the University of the Western Cape and a Master of Education from Manchester University, UK. Glynis is a gender activist with extensive experience in the promotion of gender equality and women's rights in the Western Cape, serves on the Board of Management of the Western Network on Violence Against Women and on the South African National AIDS Council's Women's Expert Group.

Anne Roemer Mahler is a Lecturer at the Department of International Relations and a Research Fellow at the Centre for Global Health Policy at Sussex University. Her research examines the role of the pharmaceutical industry in shaping global health governance, and she has published in a variety of journals, including the Review of International Political Economy and Business and Politics.

Maya Sabatello is a Postdoctoral Research Fellow at Columbia University's Center on Research of Ethical, Legal, and Social Implications of Psychiatric, Neurologic and Behavioral Genetics. A lawyer with a PhD in political science, she previously litigated cases of medical malpractice and has worked as a legal adviser to national and international NGOs to promote health-related human rights. As a Permanent Representative for an NGO at the United Nations, she participated in the drafting of the Convention on the Rights of Persons with Disabilities. Since 2006, she has been teaching at NYU's Center for Global Affairs and Columbia University's Institute for the Study of Human Rights. She was appointed a Visiting Research Fellow at Columbia University Law School (2012–13) and a Research Fellow in Medical Ethics at Harvard Medical School (2011–13).

Lulama Sigasana is the Health and Nutrition Manager, Ikamva Labantu, and is involved in developing community-appropriate educational tools and capacity building, food security, and primary health care. She has a BSc in Dietetics from the University of the Western Cape and while specializing in nutrition, has a track record of working across disciplines with both government and non-government agencies. Lulama serves on various provincial platforms and contributes to postgraduate teaching at the University of Stellenbosch.

Daniel Sperling is a Senior Lecturer in the Federmann School of Public Policy and Government and Braun School of Public Health & Community Medicine, at the Hebrew University of Jerusalem where he teaches courses on bioethics, public health law, and health policy.

George P. Smith, II has taught and written extensively in the fields of bioethics and health law since 1977 at The Catholic University of America School of Law, Washington, DC. He is well regarded as an international lecturer and, since 1984 when he received a Fulbright Foundation fellowship to the University of New South Wales in Australia, has been a frequent return visitor to the Australian Continent and held research appointments at various major universities in Europe and in America. His bibliography includes 200 entries and his latest book is, *Law and Bioethics: Intersections along the Mortal Coil* (Routledge, 2012). He is the founding editor of the Journal of Contemporary Health Law and Policy.

Maria Stuttaford is a Senior Research Fellow, at Warwick Medical School, University of Warwick and Honorary Senior Lecturer, School of Public Health and Family Medicine, University of Cape Town. Her research interests include the right to health, public health, and health inequalities. She is involved in participatory action research and uses a range of research methods in multidisciplinary research in Southern Africa and Europe.

Anton Wasson is a Research Associate at the ANU College of Law, Australian National University. Anton has worked as a Post-Doctoral Fellow at CSIRO Plant Industry, where he studied the root architecture of wheat, and at the John Innes Centre in the UK, in a project to make cereal plants engage in a nitrogen-fixing symbiosis. His research interests include food security, international environmental law, international trade law, and international development.

Nicola Watt is a UK civil servant working at the Department for International Development, after several years at the Department of Health. She is a visiting Research Fellow at the European Centre on Health of Societies in Transition at the London School of Hygiene and Tropical Medicine.

Global Health

An Introduction

Michael Freeman

The concern of Global Health is with the improvement of health worldwide, the reduction (and ultimately the elimination) of disparities, and protection against global threats that disregard national borders.[1] It has been defined as the area of study, research, and practice that places priority on improving health and achieving health equity for all people worldwide.[2] The roots of global health are in public health.[3]

Public health envisages a philosophy of interventions, the object of which is the protection and promotion of the health of a population.[4]

Efforts to promote health and prevent disease were undertaken by some of the earliest civilisations.[5] Religion shared a common ground with medicine.[6] There is also archaeological evidence that ancient civilisations, for example the Egyptians and the Incas, appreciated the significance of sanitation and urban planning.[7] There were further developments with the Greeks: Hippocrates tried to explain ill-health and offer recommendations for avoiding disease.[8] The Romans, too, were aware of the health implications of the environment and developed methods of purifying water supplies.[9]

With the decline of the Roman Empire and the decay of its system of public health, the knowledge accumulated by the classical civilisation was lost. Thus, when the Black Death struck in 1347–51,[10] killing a third of Europe's population,[11] interpretations as to its causes were diverse, speculative, and also rooted in prejudice. Thus, a common belief was that Jews were to blame—they had poisoned the wells.[12] Physicians put the emphasis on individual treatment. They had no power to effect public health measures.

1 See J.P. Koplan, T.C. Bond, M.H. Merson et al, 'Towards A Common Definition of Global Health' (2009) 373 *Lancet* 193.

2 See S.B. Macfarlane, M. Jacobs, and E.E. Kaaya, 'In The Name of Global Health: Trends in Academic Instruction' (2008) 29(4) *Journal of Public Health Policy* 383.

3 On public health see J. Coggon, *What Makes Health Public?* (Cambridge: CUP, 2012). See also M. Verweij and A. Dawson, 'The Meaning of "Public" in "Public Health"' in A. Dawson and M. Verweij (eds), *Ethics, Prevention and Public Health* (Oxford: OUP, 2008).

4 See C.E.A. Winslow, 'The Untilled Fields of Public Health' (1920) 31 *Science* 23.

5 G. Rosen, *A History of Public Health* (Baltimore, MD: Johns Hopkins University Press, 1993).

6 See as an example *Deuteronomy* 18: 15, 21–2.

7 See B. Inglis, *A History of Medicine* (London: Weidenfeld and Nicolson, 1965).

8 See E.D. Phillips, *Greek Medicine* (London: Thames and Hudson, 1993).

9 See R. Porter, *The Greatest Benefit to Mankind* (London: Harper Collins, 1977).

10 A good account of which is P. Ziegler, *The Black Death* (New York: Harper Torchbooks, 1969).

11 See J. Kelly, *The Great Mortality* (London: Perennial, 2006); O.J. Benedictow, *The Black Death 1346–1353* (Woodbridge: Boydell Press, 2004).

12 See N. Cantor, *In The Wake of the Plague* (New York: NYU Press, 2001).

This was the province of the magistrate. Venice tried quarantine methods. Milan sealed in the occupants of affected houses, leaving them to die.[13] In Florence, a committee of eight was given dictatorial power: they ordered the culling of cats and dogs—they did not know the disease was being carried by rats. Throughout Italy, leper houses beyond the city limits were established.

In the centuries following the Black Death there was rarely any systematic response to disease. Only gradually were the causes of diseases examined, and this led to, or at least coincided with, public health interventions. James Lind (1716–91), a Scottish naval surgeon, noted that armies lost more men by sickness than 'by the sword'. He demonstrated, using the world's first controlled clinical trial, that scurvy was caused by an inadequate diet and could be prevented by issuing fresh fruit rations.[14]

By the close of the eighteenth century (in England) public health was being taken more seriously. Some municipal corporations began to tackle problems like polluted water supplies. Manchester even established a Board of Health (in 1796). The prison reform movement also awakened public health concerns.[15] The stage was set for the Victorian Revolution. The public health movement became a moral crusade to eliminate the visible signs of filth, since physical cleanliness and good health were viewed as a precondition for both social and spiritual progress.

The medical profession was not in the vanguard of public health reform. The medical colleges never gave an impetus, and the organized medical profession played a 'surprisingly secondary and desultory role in the vast expansion of Victorian state provision'.[16] And vested interests, business generally and water companies, were often resistant to public health reform. A key figure in the Victorian Sanitary revolution was Edwin Chadwick (1800–90).[17] It was his view that much poverty was due not to fecklessness, but to disease. The social costs of sickness converted Chadwick to the 'sanitary idea'—to prevention. Poverty could not be abolished but poverty which was the result of preventable disease could be. Chadwick used Poor Law medical officers' reports as data for his 'Report on the Sanitary Condition of the Labouring Population of Great Britain' of 1842.[18] This charts the prevalence of disease and poverty through maps, vital statistics, and descriptions of streets, dwellings, refuse, privies, sewers, drainage, and odours. His work led to Britain's first Public Health Act in 1848. This created the General Board of Health. Within five years, 103 towns had adopted the Act. But there was resistance from vested interests championing 'local autonomy'. *The Times* supported the opposition: it had described cholera as the 'best of all sanitary reforms'.[19]

The General Board ceased to operate in 1854. Chadwick's bureaucratic model was replaced by one based on medicine and run by a doctor. John Snow's cholera investigations in 1849[20] were a watershed: he argued that cholera was linked to contaminated drinking water. Better drainage and sewerage systems were gradually installed. There was significant new legislation. This included the Sanitary Act 1866 (which gave local authorities new powers to provide clean water supplies) and the

[13] Porter, *The Greatest Benefit to Mankind* (n 9) 125.

[14] S.R. Brown, *Scurvy: How a Surgeon, a Mariner, and a Gentleman Solved the Greatest Medical Mystery of the Age of Sail* (New York: St Martin's Press, 2003).

[15] Most influential was John Howard, *The State of the Prisons* (1777).

[16] R. Porter, *Disease, Medicine and Society in England 1550–1860* (Cambridge: CUP, 1993) 59.

[17] On Chadwick, see S.E. Finer, *The Life and Times of Sir Edwin Chadwick* (London: Methuen, 1952). Chadwick had been Jeremy Bentham's secretary.

[18] The circulation of this was enormous: 20,000 copies were sold within two weeks.

[19] Quoted in Porter, *The Greatest Benefit to Mankind* (n 9) 412.

[20] See M. Pelling, *Cholera, Fever and English Medicine* 1825–1865. (Oxford: OUP, 1978) 132–40.

Vaccination Act 1867 (which increased penalties for failure to vaccinate infants).[21] Vaccinations were opposed on civil liberties grounds.[22] This opposition was successful, and compulsory vaccination was rescinded in 1909.[23]

Similar battles were fought over communicable diseases. Sexually transmitted diseases began to attract attention in the second half of the nineteenth century: the impact on the army at the time of the Crimean War stirred concern. The first Contagious Diseases Act in 1864 targeted prostitutes working in the ports and garrison towns.[24] Prostitutes were required to undergo a physical examination: if found to be infected, they would be detained for up to three months and compulsorily treated. There was also legislation providing for the regular inspection of 'known prostitutes'. There was opposition from civil libertarians and feminists, as well as from the medical profession, and the legislation was short-lived.[25]

Tuberculosis also attracted public health legislation.[26] Bacteriology demonstrated that it was an airborne disease. There were campaigns to stop spitting in public places, and in Britain and France[27] in the 1890s there were demands for the compulsory detention of contagious cases. This did not happen, but the sanitoria which the poor were 'encouraged' to enter were custodial institutions in all but name. By 1910 there were forty-one public sanitoria in England, mostly run through the Poor Law. The sanitoria were 'nominally preventive or therapeutic',[28] but in reality they were 'dustbins', where the dying would never again infect family or workmates. The sanitorium functioned as a 'segregative' institution, protecting society from the 'degeneratives' within it.[29]

It is not surprising that medicine can expand its category of 'degenerates'. Nor was it long before the dangers of allowing such people to reproduce were perceived. The eugenics movement was a misguided product of the nineteenth-century initiative to improve public health. It led to policies of forced sterilization in a number of countries, and not just in Nazi Germany, the country with which it is particularly associated.[30]

The US developed medically-based immigration controls.[31] The target, initially at least, was the infectious disease, but mental abnormality assumed increasing importance as eugenics established itself. The US Supreme Court was prepared to legitimate this movement and its practices, including forced sterilization. Mr Justice Holmes famously proclaimed that 'three generations of imbeciles were enough'.[32] Carrie Buck, the victim of sterilization in this case, was subsequently shown to have above average intelligence.[33]

21 Compulsory vaccination against smallpox had been introduced in 1853.

22 The Anti-Compulsory Vaccination League was founded in 1874.

23 The debate continues. See M. Verweij, 'Individual and Collective Considerations in Public Health Influence Vaccination' (2001) 15 *Bioethics* 536.

24 See J. Walkowitz, *Prostitution and Victorian Society* (Cambridge: CUP, 1982).

25 It was repealed in 1886. See F. Mort, *Dangerous Sexualities* (London: RKP, 1987).

26 See F.B. Smith, *The Retreat of Tuberculosis* (London: Croom Helm, 1988).

27 See D.S. Barnes, *The Making of a Social Disease: Tuberculosis in Nineteenth Century France* (Berkeley, CA: University of California Press, 1995).

28 Porter, *The Greatest Benefit to Mankind* (n 9) 423.

29 Porter, *The Greatest Benefit to Mankind* (n 9).

30 In relation to England, see S. Trombley, *The Right To Reproduce* (London: Weidenfeld and Nicolson, 1988). See also M. Freeman, 'Sterilising The Mentally Handicapped' in M. Freeman, *Medicine, Ethics and Law* (London: Stevens, 1988) 55.

31 Between 1892 and 1934 over 12 million immigrants were medically inspected. Only 2% were denied entry.

32 In *Buck v Bell* 274 US 200 (1927). And see D. Kevles, *In The Name of Eugenics* (Cambridge, MA: Harvard University Press, 1995).

33 See S.J. Gould, *The Mismeasure of Man* (Harmondsworth: Penguin, 1974) 323–36.

Until the twentieth century, the health problems of the industrialized world and those of the rest of the world (much of which it had colonized) could be split. Colonization had not been good for the health of the 'Third World'.[34] Roy Porter explained why:

> Epidemiological link-ups between previously isolated regions, the movement of fleets and armies, of millions of slaves and indentured labourers, the spread of diseases by ecological change and social dislocation, the misery bred by shanty-towns—all have been implicated in the hail of death that European rule brought. The good that western medicine did was marginal and incidental.[35]

The twentieth century brought new problems. One of the early effects of globalization was to bring health problems from different parts of the world together. This was seen dramatically in 1918 when the most lethal and mobile pandemic ever to strike the world—not even rivalled by HIV/AIDS—killed over 25 million people in six months, to be followed by an epidemic of encephalitis lethargica; and a further wave of killer influenza two years later. A side-effect of the First World War, it killed about three times the number who died in the war.[36]

The flu pandemic was the worst pestilence since the Black Death, nearly 600 years earlier. Nothing of its intensity has happened since, though it may be feared that HIV/AIDS might kill as many. Whether this is pure chance or because of better medicine and better health measures is uncertain. Better international structures had been put in place after the cholera pandemic in the middle of the nineteenth century, and International Sanitary Conferences were held.[37] It was at the seventh of these—in Venice in 1891—that agreement was reached on the quarantining of westbound ships with cholera on board. In fact, by then, cholera had virtually disappeared.

In 1907, twenty-three European countries set up the Office International d'Hygiène Publique. This collected and disseminated information on a variety of diseases: cholera, plague, yellow fever, malaria, typhoid. It acted as a forum to discuss issues such as sanitation, immunization, and isolation. The League of Nations, established after the First World War, set up its own health body, the Health Organisation of the League of Nations. The United Nations was established after the Second World War. The World Health Organization (the WHO) was set up and, unlike its predecessor, was given a status independent of its parent body. The WHO's goal was a 'state of complete physical, mental and social well-being and not merely the absence of disease or infirmity'. The WHO initiates programmes of immunization for the world's children—targeting diphtheria, polio, tuberculosis, tetanus, whooping cough, and measles. It has also promoted the training of para-health personnel, such as China's barefoot doctors.

The world health movement had some outstanding successes, notably the worldwide eradication of smallpox.[38] When Bangladesh became free of this disease in 1974, the world's press was able to proclaim the end of smallpox, though ironically a British photographer caught and died of the disease in Birmingham four years later. Today, the virus only exists (at least officially) in two laboratories. There is, however, concern that it may constitute one of the biological weapons held in reserve by one or more of the irresponsible so-called 'rogue states'. The WHO has been less successful with other

[34] See S. Watts, *Epidemics and History: Disease, Power and Imperialism* (New Haven, CT: Yale University Press, 1997).

[35] Porter, *The Greatest Benefit to Mankind* (n 9) 482.

[36] See G. Kolata, *Flu* (Basingstoke: Macmillan, 2000).

[37] The first was in Paris in 1851.

[38] See I. Glynn and J. Glynn, *The Life and Death of Smallpox* (London: Profile Books, 2004).

major childhood diseases. India manages to immunize only half of its children born each year against measles and polio, and immunization rates in Central Africa are even lower. It is also now recognized that diseases unknown in the richer, developed world have been neglected or targeted inappropriately. An example is diphtheria, which went virtually unnoticed in the West until US personnel succumbed to it in the Philippines during the Second World War. Bilharzia is the second most socio-economically devastating parasitic disease after malaria, and it particularly affects children.

This was of little concern in the West. It was many years before war, poverty, famine, and population displacement were recognized as aggravating features in this developing world. For too long the pharmaceutical industry ('Big Pharma') were more concerned with erectile dysfunction in Western men than killer diseases in the developing world. Malaria has not been eradicated: indeed; more people are infected by it today than in 1960. And anyway, as Roy Porter pointed out, 'the parasite changes its genetic makeup more rapidly than the pharmaceutical industry can produce new and tested drugs'.[39] In addition, diseases once in retreat are returning, and not just in poor nations. Tuberculosis is becoming more common. It is on the increase in the US and in Europe, but the increase in prevalence in parts of Africa is much greater. More than 3 million people a year die from TB, 95 per cent of them in low and middle income countries. Cholera has also returned. It broke out in Indonesia in 1961, and spread through Asia and Africa, attacking twenty-nine countries in two years. In 1993 a new strain erupted in India and Bangladesh, and spread to South East Asia.

Old diseases re-emerge—diphtheria in the former Soviet Union and its empire is one example and cholera is another—and new ones emerge. AIDS was first noticed in 1981 and the HIV virus was discovered in 1983. It was HIV/AIDS, more than any other disease, which stimulated thinking about the ethics of Public (Global) Health. In the early 1980s, before the causes of AIDS were fathomed, we were able to hear pronouncements reminiscent of Biblical times—it was the wrath of God wreaked upon the gay. Even today there are some—the former President of South Africa is a prominent example[40]—who deny the causal role of HIV. Conflict rages, if a little more muted, over the policies of many companies, particularly the impact of these in the developing world. It is in sub-Saharan Africa where HIV/AIDS is most prevalent.[41]

Concern that there would be a worldwide AIDS pandemic forced governments to take sexual health more seriously (and more positively). In Britain it was the Thatcher era. Family values were pushed by the government, even if members of her government did not always practise this.[42]

There was a reluctance to promote sexual health. In the UK it was 1988 before the dangers of AIDS were proclaimed in a national advertising campaign. Things did improve: a Cabinet committee on AIDS was created. The medical profession and public health experts were given the task of devising a strategy.[43] The successor to Thatcher, John Major, heading the government for two-thirds of the 1990s, did not have a coherent policy on sexual health, but HIV/AIDS was proclaimed as one of the government's target areas. However, this did not stop it from instigating legislation to

[39] Porter, *The Greatest Benefit to Mankind* (n 9) 488.

[40] Thabo Mbeki. His Health Minister recommended beetroot! There were other dissenting voices.

[41] 69% of HIV sufferers and 70% of AIDS deaths are in Sub-Saharan Africa. See 'UNAIDS Report on Global AIDS Epidemic' (2012).

[42] On family values, see M. Freeman, 'Family Values and Family Justice' (2000) 56 *Current Legal Problems* 136.

[43] See M. Durham, *Sex and Politics: The Family and Morality in the Thatcher Years* (Basingstoke: Macmillan, 1991).

permit parents to withdraw their children from sex education classes.[44] Major's Health Minister ordered the withdrawal of a booklet on sexual health, and at the end of its thirteen years in government, the party stopped the AIDS awareness campaign, which cost all of £6.2 million a year. A later Conservative government (in 1996) cut funding for AIDS prevention and treatment.

During this period (and thereafter), HIV infection has continued to rise, though at a rate much less than was predicted in the early 1980s.[45] It is estimated that there are 33.4 million people living with HIV today, 3.4 million of whom are children under 15. Ninety-one per cent of these live in Sub-Saharan Africa.[46] The majority are women.[47] In 2011, about 1.1 million people in the world died of AIDS: about one-sixth of them were children under 15.[48] There are large numbers of AIDS orphans.[49] In the years since the pandemic was discovered, more than 25 million people have died as a result of AIDS. Most people in developing countries who could benefit from AIDS drugs have no access to these drugs. We were warned in 2008 that we may never find a vaccine for AIDS;[50] questions have therefore been raised as to whether it might be better to focus spending on prevention, for example on safe-sex campaigns, and on testing rather than on treatment.[51] The WHO designated 2006 the 'Year of Acceleration of HIV Prevention in the African Region', and made HIV testing its priority.[52] There is mandatory pre-marital HIV testing in Nigeria, Botswana, and the Democratic Republic of Congo.[53] In the US, two states, Illinois and Louisiana, imposed such a requirement but soon abolished it when couples moved to neighbouring states to marry.[54] The requirement is also on Missouri's statute book. In Europe, the only country to contemplate mandatory pre-marital testing (and prohibit marriage for those with HIV or AIDS) was Albania,[55] but it capitulated when many organizations, including international ones, voiced serious objections. There are problems with treatment too: high percentages of patients do not comply with their treatment regime.[56]

There was very little discussion of the ethical issues involved in global health questions until the emergence of AIDS,[57] but ethical issues in relation to HIV/AIDS began to be debated almost as soon as this pandemic was recognized.[58] Only more

44 Education Act 1993.

45 The number of AIDS-related deaths in Sub-Saharan Africa was 33% less in 2011 than in 2005. See further J. Iliffe, *The African AIDS Epidemic: A History* (Oxford: James Currey, 2006).

46 Most acquire HIV from mothers during pregnancy, birth, or breastfeeding. Early intervention can bring the infection rate down to 2%, but the drugs needed may not be available in most resource-limited countries where the burden of HIV is highest.

47 Women make up 60%. The population of women living with HIV has been increasing in the last 10 years or so. See further WHO, 'Women and Health: Today's Evidence, Tomorrow's Agenda' (2009).

48 A total of 3.4 million children have HIV/AIDS; 91% per cent of them live in Sub-Saharan Africa.

49 On the problems of orphans see J. Todres, 'Rights, Relationships and the Experience of Children Orphaned by AIDS' (2007) 41 *UC Davis Law Review* 417.

50 By David Baltimore: see *The Guardian*, 15 February 2008.

51 See E. Pisani, *The Wisdom of Whores: Bureaucrats, Brothels and the Business of AIDS* (London: Granta, 2008).

52 See K. De Cock, 'Unfinished Business—Expanding HIV Testing in Developing Countries' (2006). 354 *New England Journal of Medicine* 440.

53 See S. Rennie and B. Mupenda (2008) 8 *Developing World Bioethics* 126.

54 See M. Closen, R. Gamath, and D. Hopkins, 'Mandatory Premarital HIV Testing: Political Explanation of the AIDS Epidemic' (1994) 69 *Tulane Law Review* 71.

55 See Amnesty International, 'Albania: Disability and the Right to Marry' (2004).

56 According to S.C. Kalichman and D. Rompa: see 'HIV Treatment Adherence and Unprotected Sex Practices in People Receiving Antiretroviral Therapy' (2003) 79 *Sexually Transmitted Infections* 59.

57 See U. Schüklenk, *AIDS: Society, Ethics and the Law* (Aldershot: Ashgate, 2001).

58 eg R.D. Mohr, 'AIDS, Gays and State Coercion' (1987) 1 *Bioethics* 35; M. O'Brien, 'Mandatory HIV Testing Policies: An Ethical Analysis' (1989) 3 *Bioethics* 273.

recently, with the publication of the journal *Developing World Bioethics* in particular (but also other periodical literature), have the ethical issues come sharply into focus. And this has coincided with an appreciation of the impact of globalization on the world, and also with the rise of human rights.[59] Alison Brysk has pointed out that 'assaults on fundamental human dignity continue and the very blurring of borders and rise of transnational sectors that facilitates the development of a global human rights regime may also be generating new sources of human rights abuse'.[60] This may shock. After all, as Brysk also points out, a 'more cosmopolitan and open international system should free individuals to pursue their rights, but large numbers of people seem to be suffering from both long-standing state repression and new denials of rights linked to transnational forces'.[61]

The concept of global health only began to be discussed relatively recently.[62] It is uncertain when the expression was first used. John Rawls wrote of the 'law of peoples' in 1999.[63] But it had no egalitarian distributive principle of any kind. He was committed to a laissez-faire global economic order. In this international context Rawls' concept of justice is little different from that of Robert Nozick.[64] Why should representatives prefer an egalitarian law of peoples over more egalitarian alternatives? He may have been right to believe that the 'great social evils in poorer societies are likely to be oppressive governments and corrupt elites'.[65] But, as Thomas Pogge has responded, 'relative poverty breeds corruptibility and corruption', and it is 'by no means entirely home-grown'.[66]

Despite Rawls, global health was about to ignite the public imagination. Explaining why is not easy. McInnes and Lee suggest the following.[67] It was a response to real world change: 'as the world has become more globalised, so too has health'.[68] A second explanation can be found in the call for a 'paradigm shift'[69] in response to how human health is affected in many new ways by 'global interconnectedness',[70] such as the emergence of novel infections, increased drug resistance, new geographical distributions of disease vectors. They argue that the emergence of global health was presented as a 'natural response to changes in the material world'.[71]

Reference is often made to Laurie Garrett's book *The Coming Plague*.[72] Writing in 1994, she predicted 'recurrent eruptions of newly discovered diseases',[73] epidemics of diseases migrating to new areas, among others. The WHO was similarly alarmist—we were on the 'brink of a global crisis in infectious diseases' and could no longer afford to

59 On which see K. Sellars, *The Rise and Rise of Human Rights* (Stroud: Sutton Publishing, 2002).

60 A. Brysk, 'Introduction' in, *Globalisation and Human Rights* (Berkeley, CA: University of California Press, 2002) 1.

61 Brysk, 'Introduction' (n 60) 1–2.

62 See J. Youde, *Global Health Governance* (Cambridge: Polity Press, 2012).

63 J. Rawls, *The Law of Peoples* (Cambridge, MA: Harvard University Press, 1999). And see G. Brock, *Global Justice* (New York: OUP, 2009) ch 2.

64 R. Nozick, *Anarchy, State and Utopia* (New York: Basic Books, 1974).

65 Rawls, *The Law of Peoples* (n 63) 77.

66 T. Pogge, 'An Egalitarian Law of Peoples' (1994) 23 *Philosophy and Public Affairs* 195, 213, 214.

67 C. McInnes and K. Lee, *Global Health and International Relations* (Cambridge: Polity Press, 2012).

68 McInnes and Lee, *Global Health* (n 67) 7.

69 See T. Kuhn, *The Structure of Scientific Revolutions* (Chicago: University of Chicago Press, 1970).

70 McInnes and Lee, *Global Health* (n 67) 8.

71 McInnes and Lee, *Global Health* (n 67) 9–10.

72 L. Garrett, *The Coming Plague: Newly Emerging Diseases in a World out of Balance* (New York: Farrar, Straus and Giroux, 1994).

73 Garrett, *The Coming Plague* (n 72) 12.

ignore their threats. The WHO's Director-General warned in 1996 that no country was safe.[74]

The media played a role too. But what the media perceives to be the highest risk to health contrasts sharply with what actually poses the greatest risk. Harrabin, Coote, and Allen wrote: 'The news media tend to focus on stories about health services. Only rarely do they publish stories about public health—that is measures to improve health, prevent illness or reduce health inequalities.'[75] Rather than discussing obesity[76] or smoking[77] or alcohol,[78] unusual hazards such as SARS[79] can dominate headlines for weeks.[80]

This leads to the obvious question: what is global health? It is concerned with the health of the population in a global context. It transcends the perspectives of individual nations. It has been defined as 'an area for study, research and practice that places a priority on improving health and achieving health equity for all people worldwide'.[81] It is about the worldwide improvement of health, the reduction of disparities, and protection against global threats that disregard national boundaries.

At a UN Summit in 2000, member states declared eight Millennium Development Goals, reflecting major challenges which confronted human development globally. These goals were to be met by 2015. Three of the goals focus explicitly on health. Across all goals there are eighteen targets, supported by forty-eight health indicators. In 2012 the United Nations reported that several of the targets have been met ahead of the 2015 timeline.

The main diseases and health conditions prioritized by global health initiatives are often grouped under the term 'diseases of poverty' and 'diseases of affluence'. However, the impacts of globalization increasingly blur such a distinction.

Many low-cost, evidence-based healthcare interventions for improved health and survival are now known. For example, priority global targets for improving maternal health include increasing coverage of deliveries with a skilled birth attendant.[82] Interventions for improved child health and survival include the promotion of breastfeeding and vaccination. In malaria-endemic regions, the use of insecticide-treated bedmats and intermittent pharmacological treatment can reduce mortality.

Based on such studies, lists of treatments and intervention measures have been drawn up that could potentially save several million lives each year.[83]

[74] World Health Report 1996, 'Fighting Disease, Fostering Development' (Geneva: WHO, 1997) Introduction by Hiroshi Nakajima.

[75] R. Harrabin, A. Coote, and J. Allen, *Health in the News: Risk, Reporting and Media Influence* (London: King's Fund, 2003) 1.

[76] On childhood obesity see T. Lobstein, 'Child Obesity and the Junk Food Marketeers' in J. Wild (ed), *Exploiting Childhood* (London: Jessica Kingsley, 2013) 49.

[77] On the slow progress towards control see E.K. Ong and S.A. Glantz (2000) 355 *Lancet* 1253. But there is now a Framework Convention on Tobacco Control (2003).

[78] Anon, 'Let's be Straight Up About the Alcohol Industry' (2011) 8(3) *PLoS Medicine.*

[79] On SARS see F. Fleck, 'How SARS Changed the World in Less than 6 Months' (2003) 81(8) *Bulletin of the World Health Organization*, 625.

[80] See Macfarlane, Jacobs, and Kaaya, 'In The Name of Global Health' (n 2).

[81] Namely, reduce child mortality, improve maternal health, and combat HIV/AIDS, malaria, and other major diseases.

[82] According to the World Health Organization's 'World Health Report 2005', poor maternal conditions are the fourth leading cause of death for women worldwide, after HIV/AIDS, malaria, and tuberculosis.

[83] Z.A. Bhutta, T. Ahmed, R.E. Black, et al, 'What works? Interventions for maternal and child undernutrition and survival' (2008) 371 *Lancet* 417.

It is recognized that, to be most effective, interventions need to be sensitive to the local context, as well as timely and equitable. They must also achieve maximum coverage of the target population. Thus, for example, immunization programmes with partial coverage often fail to reach those at greatest risk of disease.

Even though there are health intervention programmes in place, they may not make a difference. There is a 'critical group': some populations have access to medical treatment and others do not. This may be the result of the absence of a sustainable infrastructure. Many external factors can influence how effective a programme can be.

There are many funds available. But funds do not always translate into positive outcomes. Focus on one particular disease—perhaps because of the interest of the donors—can lead to ignoring other children's diseases.

Investments have increased substantially in recent years. Attention is also being paid to imbalances in health systems and in health workforces. In 2006, the WHO estimated a shortage of almost 4.3 million doctors, midwives, nurses, and support staff worldwide, but mainly in Sub-Saharan Africa. Fifty-seven countries face severe shortages, partly because their doctors, etc are employed on higher salaries in the richer, developed world.[84]

When global health is discussed there is a tendency to focus on HIV/AIDS, malaria, TB, malnutrition, etc. But the range of issues is now expanding to embrace tobacco control,[85] obesity,[86] terrorism,[87] and global warming.[88] The latest health question to fire the global imagination is violence against women. It is easy to forget that it was only in the 1970s that domestic violence was recognized as a social problem.[89] Since one in five women worldwide are the victims of domestic violence, and its health consequences are manifest, it is surprising that initiatives to tackle its health implications have been so slow in coming. Within 'domestic violence' is embraced not just battering, but the sexual abuse of children, rape including marital rape, forced marriage, female genital mutilation,[90] and other traditional practices harmful to women, drug-induced violence, sexual harassment, inside the domestic setting and in the public space, for example at work, forcing a woman into prostitution, etc. The health issues include more than just physical injury, for example depression, and drug and alcohol abuse.

With many of the Millennium Development Goals having been met, and real progress achieved in several of the others, focus has shifted to the realization of 'sustainable development'.[91] This is defined as 'development that meets the needs of the present without compromising the ability of future generations to meet their own needs'. Human health is thus embodied within an ecological context of sustainable

84 The World Health Assembly adopted a Global Code of Practice in 2010 to facilitate the strengthening of health workforces with skills relevant to population needs.

85 See now the Framework Convention on Tobacco Control (2003). It is estimated that 200,000 children die each year as a result of exposure to secondhand smoke. See J. Heymann and K. McNeill, *Children's Chances* (Harvard University Press, 2013) 105.

86 Obesity is associated with numerous chronic diseases including cardiovascular conditions, diabetes, stroke, cancers, and respiratory diseases. About 16% of the global burden of disease, measured as DALYs, has been accounted for by obesity. In low-income countries the number of individuals with diabetes is expected to increase from 84 million to 228 million by 2030.

87 See J. Moreno, *In The Wake of Terror: Medicine and Morality in a Time of Crisis* (Cambridge, MA: MIT Press, 2003).

88 P. Haggett, *The Geographical Structure of Epidemics* (Oxford: OUP, 2000) is an early discussion of the association.

89 See E. Pizzey, *Scream Quietly or the Neighbours Will Hear* (Harmondsworth: Penguin, 1974).

90 See E. Dorkenoo and S. Elworthy, *Female Genital Mutilation* (London: Minority Rights Group, 1992).

91 'Our Common Future—Report of the World Commission on Environment and Development' (United Nations, 1987) (the Brundtland Report).

development: all aspects of human ecology fundamentally dependent on the quality of the natural environment, such as clean water, clean air, wholesome nutrition, and recreation.[92] This duly recognized, the challenges encountered in sustainable development for health not only include environmental and social determinants but are also substantively influenced as well by organizational and technological systems.[93]

For example, major reductions in the burden of malaria have been achieved by improved prevention and treatment. Yet, such success cannot be taken for granted: tuberculosis control is now threatened by the emergence of multiple antibiotic-resistant strains. While this disease has social and environmental determinants, it is a health systems and technological challenge as well. Similarly, whilst health promotion and primary prevention are critical in combating the non-communicable disease (NCD) pandemic,[94] they are much less than 100% effective: hundreds of millions of people are developing NCDs, most of them poor. Affordable technologies must be made accessible to assist in their management. The world must respond to this challenge as well, this is now being addressed by the WHO, in a new Global Action Plan for the Prevention and Control of Non-Communicable Diseases 2013–20.[95]

92 'Bringing human health and wellbeing back into sustainable development' in, *IISD Annual Report 2011–12.*

93 F. White, L. Stallones, and J.M. Last, *Global Public Health: Ecological Foundations* (Oxford: OUP, 2013).

94 Non-communicable diseases are caused by different factors such as environment, heredity, or nutrition and lifestyle habits. According to the WHO, non-communicable diseases account for 60% of deaths worldwide.

95 World Health Organization, Global Action Plan for the Prevention and Control of Non-Communicable Diseases 2013–2020 (Updated revised draft, 15 March 2013).

Keynote Address

Justice and Global Health

James Orbinski

The nexus of global health and law and justice has long held my interest, if only because I am primarily interested in what I know little about. . . . Hopefully, that won't put you off—too much—from what I am about to discuss!

I have worked as a humanitarian doctor in famine, in war, in situations of epidemic and pandemic disease, and in genocide—all catastrophic and apparently hopeless situations. This gives me a very particular perspective; one that has learned that human suffering does not take place in a political vacuum—or without causes and conditions. Global health is not simply a humanitarian question—or simply one of seeing the dignity of the other and acting for the immediate relief of human suffering. It was Kant who wrote in *Metaphysics of Morals*: 'Humanity in his person, is the object of the respect, which he can demand from every other human being.'[1] Kant's 'humanity in his person' is the basis of our conception of dignity which underlies our human rights conceptions and law—But does this make it true that all human beings have certain rights simply by virtue of being human?[2] In practice, not always, but the possibility exists, and law—and most especially its formulation and prescription—can make this possibility true.

Global health and law are intimately tied to national and global governance, to institutions like the WTO and their concrete practices around, for example, trade law and access to medicines; to health and security, to governance of communicable diseases for example through the International Health Regulations (IHR), and the governance of non-communicable diseases through, for example, the Framework Convention on Tobacco Control. Global health and law is also intimately tied to international humanitarian law—most especially in war—and to human rights law, in, for example, grappling with the HIV/AIDS pandemic. Yes, the Framework Convention on Tobacco Control 2005 is a significant achievement in GH law. And this is despite the self-interest and very real power of the tobacco industry, which made its best efforts to conceal, distort, and manipulate the evidence that tobacco causes many forms of cancer. And so too are the new international health regulations a significant achievement in GH law. And this despite the efforts of states such as China and Canada that sought to protect their domestic economies as a matter of priority over any alleged risk that may have existed because of SARS. But all of this is self-evident. More importantly,

[1] I. Kant, *The Metaphysics of Morals* (Cambridge: CUP, 1999) 434–5.

[2] D. Schroeder, 'Human Rights and Human Dignity An Appeal to Separate the Conjoined Twins' *Ethical Theory and Moral Practice* (2012) 15: 323. On dignity see M. Rosen, *Dignity* (OUP, 2011) and G. Kateb, *Human Dignity* (Harvard: HUP, 2011).

what is not self-evident is the process, which binds law and global health, and the ends to which that process aims. It is this that I want to explore in this address.

Our conceptions of global health have not caught up with the global political challenges that we face. Thinking around global health is too often still caught in a techno-charity mindset, one that does not easily see beyond the desire to do good, to examine critically and engage the political realities of making real this intention. To be clear, good intentions are not good enough in themselves—to bring us to the next step in developing a framework of law that both enables and governs the achievement of global health.

Global health, in its broadest conception, connotes a well-being in a state of justice. These are decidedly universalist claims and ends, and if global health is to be something other than an ideal beyond our grasp, it requires a framework rooted in fact, law, and a common sense of morality. This framework is typically called politics, and it both contains and shapes the plural forces, factors, and actors that define its content and outcomes.

With every respect to Jeremy Bentham—who may be present, but cannot vote—law is not simply made in the positivist doings of Aristotle's tripartite divisions of the Executive, the Legislature and the Judiciary. Rather, as Harold Lasswell argued—and I think correctly—lawmaking is a process of communication in which policy content, authority, and control intention are modulated both to create and sustain expectations. This is an inherently imperfect, and ongoing political process. Global health is also a deeply political process. And I am hopeful—deeply hopeful—and particularly about the power of law—as it is and can be—and most especially about the communicative stories and values that law can both capture—and sustain. Albeit incrementally, these can literally change the world. But how quickly?

We are today in the midst of converging global crises in food, fuel, climate, economy, and governance. Each of these crises has both local and global causes, is interdependent, and, as we know all too clearly, has highly contagious global consequences. We are at a moment in our human story where we must squarely face the unavoidable complexity, interdependency, and fragility of our human condition. We have become our own geological epoch, the *Anthropocene*, where human pressures on the planet are at risk of triggering abrupt and irreversible changes with potentially catastrophic outcomes for human societies. We have already crossed three of nine planetary boundaries—or tipping points—and risk triggering non-liner, abrupt environmental change within continental and planetary biospheric systems.[3] As crises converge and ramify in unexpected ways, policy spheres can no longer be distinct. The microbiologist, Louis Pasteur, said some 150 years ago that, 'the microbe is nothing, its terrain everything'. The implications of this context for global health are staggering to say the least. Are these matters of misfortune, or are they matters of justice?

If it is true, as Judith Shklar wrote, 'civilization advances when what is commonly perceived as misfortune becomes considered injustice',[4] then, global health is far more than a technical domain of knowledge primarily aimed at reducing avoidable morbidity

[3] J. Rockstrom et al, 'Planetary Boundaries: Exploring the Safe Operating Space for Humanity' *Ecology and Society* (2009) 14(2): 32.

[4] J.N. Shklar, *The Faces of Injustice* (New Haven, CT: Yale University Press, 1990), quoted in Harvard Law School Human Rights Program, Economic and Social Rights and the Right to Health: Session II: Defining the Right to Adequate Health (Cambridge, MA: Harvard Law School Human Rights Program, 1995) 30.

and mortality. In my view, global health is public health writ large. It is about the pursuit of better health for all, and it is necessarily about the pursuit of justice, and this necessarily involves law. There is of course a distinction between law and justice. Justice in its original classical meaning of Justitica, is one of the four cardinal virtues on which the well-being of a civilized society hinges.[5] Catherine Lu, a political philosopher at McGill University, argues:

> Justice is the hallmark of human society. . . . (and that) like all virtues and vices, [it] is particular to humanity. While we may metaphorically use the language of justice to define acts of the gods, or fate or nature, in the end, it is only human beings who can be just or unjust. . . . Justice is an ideal which requires no superhuman efforts for its attainment, but [that] cannot be effected without human will or effort, and these are most lacking when injustice is done.[6]

Despite the limits of law, it is sometimes the mere possibility of justice that is the only source of hope for so many. And that possibility is sometimes expressed in the stories—our human stories—that can give birth to pragmatic action, and sometimes to law that both enables and protects that action. I put it to you that the stories that law can *contain, reflect or derive from*—and their communicative power—are central to this advance from misfortune to justice. And that story is most powerful when the high ideals of humanity—compassion, common morality, and the notion of the common good—are overtly among its key themes. Stories matter, and matter a lot, and as human beings, we all have stories. As with justice, nature does not tell stories, we do. We find ourselves in them, choose ourselves in them, make ourselves in them. Stories can be revolutionary, and show that hope is not a fools' choice.

In Rwanda, in 1994, I was DWB/MSF's (Médecins Sans Frontières/Doctors Without Borders) Head of Mission in Kigali—the country's capital city. I was there as a humanitarian doctor. It was a place with a very particular politics—the criminal politics of genocide. It was a brutal, horrible time—a place of rational and state-planned evil. Over a million people—virtually all Tutsi's—were butchered in fourteen weeks. Bodies filled the streets of the capital city, and the gutters alongside a hospital that we managed to keep open literally ran red with blood. One night, after many long hours of surgery, a girl of about 9 told me how she escaped murder at the hands of the killing squads. Through an interpreter, the little girl told me—and I quote—'my mother hid me in the latrine. I saw through the hole. I watched them hit her with machetes. I watched my mother's arm fall into my father's blood on the floor, and I cried without noise in the toilet'.

Throughout the country, parents often paid to have their children shot in open pit latrines, rather than see them murdered by being hacked to death with a machete. For years before the genocide, the French government trained and armed the Rwandan soldiers. And, all the way through the genocide, the French supplied them with arms, mercenaries and military intelligence. DWB/MSF and others repeatedly called for UN military intervention. But the International Community—including my own country Canada—failed to act, and Belgium, France, and the United States actively worked to paralyze the UNSC, which abandoned the UN Peacekeeping Force that was already on the ground. Each of these countries knowingly pursued their foreign policies through

5 '"Cardinal" from the latin cardo, meaning "hinge". The other three cardinal virtues of antiquity are prudence, temperance, and fortitude, to which the theological virtues of faith, hope, and love/charity were later added.' As quoted in: Ursula Franklin. *The Ursula Franklin Reader: Pacifism as a Map* (Toronto: Between the Lines, 2006) 196.

6 See further M. Freeman, 'Speaking About The Unspeakable: Genocide and Philosophy' *Journal of Applied Philosophy* (1991) 8(1): 3.

genocide. The genocide was politics as we can choose to live it. But is that the end of the story?

How do you have hope in the face of genocide? How do you see possibility? It does not lie in naive utopian dreams, but in what we do. Hannah Arendt—one of the greatest political philosophers of the twentieth century, and a Jew who as a young woman escaped the Nazi Reich to France and then to New York—said, 'The first political act is to speak'. Many have described genocide and similar human cruelties as unspeakable.[7] But these are as unspeakable as they are undoable. As human beings, we do genocide. Doctors cannot stop this crime. The little girl had no voice, and we had a responsibility to speak out against what we knew. And we did speak. We spoke with a clear intent to rouse the outrage of public consciousness around the world, and to demand a politics that pursues justice by putting the dignity of the victim at its centre. Eighteen years ago when the genocide ended, there was no such thing as an International Criminal Court. In 2002 the ICC came into being. It has since issued many arrest warrants for alleged war criminals, and has had several significant convictions. Three years ago, it issued an arrest warrant for Omar Al Bashir, the president and sitting Head of State for Sudan. He is charged with intentionally directing attacks against civilians in Darfur; with pillage, murder, extermination, forcible transfer of civilians, torture, and rape as a weapon of war.[8] The creation of the ICC is a seminal—and imperfect—human achievement. Now, for the first time in human history, those individuals who violate the laws of war can be held to account if their own governments fail to do so.

The ICC emerged because of the outrage of citizens like you and me who listened to what was spoken by organizations like DWB/MSF, Oxfam, Amnesty International, and thousands of others in churches, schools, community clubs and on university campuses like this at UCL, around the world. They acted: they organized, bringing together academics, jurists, and some of the best political and legal minds in the world. The ideas of an apparently obscure preparatory committee that had been working in the margins for years suddenly became relevant as the central policy content. They focused their mind, their time, and their energy, engaged in debate and policy analysis, and explored alternatives in that messy and imperfect process called politics. All spoke, listened, and demanded a better politics, and they sought out courageous politicians who came to the point where it was impossible to ignore the voice and choice of citizens. Against all odds, against all naysayers, and against all pessimists, as human beings we did invent the ICC. And now, even with its current imperfections that must be corrected—including the fact that China, India, Russia, and the United States have not yet signed its statutes—it is clear that no one, not even a sitting head of state, can claim to be above the law.

The first act of justice is recognizing the victim. In January of 2000, I was in South Africa at a DWB/MSF AIDS clinic. I was examining a 20-year-old man. If he were here in London or virtually anywhere in the Western world, he would be just starting his life. But there his life was nearly over. He had AIDS and weighed less than a hundred pounds. Patented drugs to treat AIDS were available in the Western world. But at a cost of more than US$13,000 a year for treatment, there wasn't a hope in hell that anyone

7 International Criminal Court (2009) *The Prosecutor v Omar Hassan Ahmad Al Bashir* Int. Legal Materials, vol. 49, no. 3 (2010), 9-922-933.

8 UNAIDS, 'Global Report on the AIDS Epidemic' (Geneva, 2010) 7.

in the developing world would get them. The young man had an AIDS-related pneumonia, and was so weak that his mother and grandmother had to help him on to the examining table. As he lay gasping for air, he asked me some very simple questions—questions that get to the heart of inequity around the HIV/AIDS pandemic. He asked me: 'Why do you come here with only kindness when what I need is medicine to stop this AIDS? Your kindness is good but it will not help this AIDS. They have such medicine in your countries, why not here in South Africa for people like me?' As you know, AIDS is a fully treatable disease—as treatable as diabetes. Yet, today, 28 million have died of the disease worldwide, over 34 million people live with HIV, and under current global infection rates, at least 24 million[9] more will be infected by 2020.[10] And almost all live in the developing world.

How do you have hope in the face of an epidemic like AIDS? How do you see possibility when charity is simply not good enough? At that clinic in South Africa, in a public act of civil disobedience—DWB/MSF together with TAC, was about to begin treatment by publicly and illegally importing AIDS drugs into South Africa.

It was in listening and in seeing the dignity of people like this young South African man that DWB/MSF began its Access to Essential Medicines Campaign. As then-president of DWB/MSF, I had the privilege of launching the campaign. It was a challenge to a failing politics. We acted, and we were not alone. It was a similar process that others had used to create the ICC: as one among many actors, we established a plural grounding in multiple processes. We brought together some of the best like-minded scientific, business, political, and legal scholars and practitioners in the world. We focused our mind, time, and energy, applied rigorous policy analysis, and debated the meaning and limits of the law. We engaged in pragmatic action to challenge law and test its applications—in this case the CL and PI provisions of the TRIPS agreement, designed in theory to protect the public good. We explored alternatives, while simultaneously beginning treatment programmes in the developing to world to show not only that we believe all people have a right to treatment, but that treatment is possible even when health infrastructure is a little less than dismal. We mobilized a coalition of citizen-groups from around the world. We mounted a global campaign that publicly shamed pharmaceutical companies and governments that supported the privilege of profit over people's right to exist. We stood up to the challenge of the pharmaceutical industry in the South African courts, and we challenged them in the courts of public opinion. This litigation was not an end-point increasing access to ARVs, but a critical communicative act that challenged the moral legitimacy of the law as it was being interpreted.[11] Hours before the case was to be heard, the pharmaceutical industry dropped the case. We also pooled our purchasing power and bought generic versions of AIDS drugs. By 2001, we had brought the market price for the treatment of AIDS down from over US$13,000 for patented versions to less than $200 for generic versions of the same drugs.[12] Today, the cost is less than US$64. Against all odds, against all naysayers, and against all fatalists who dismissed apparent misfortune as a consequence of human nature, there are today more than 6 million on full treatment for

[9] L. Forman, '"Rights" and wrongs: What utility for the right to health in reforming trade rules on medicines?' *Health and Human Rights Journal* (2008) 10(2): 37.

[10] DWB/MSF, 'Briefing Document for the International AIDS Conference' (Toronto, 2006).

[11] Third World Network, 'Use TRIPS flexibilities to reduce HIV drug prices, urge UN bodies' (18 March 2011), available at <http://www.twnside.org.sg/title2/health.info/2011/health20110305.htm> (accessed 21 March 2011).

[12] UNAIDS, 'Global Report on the AIDS Epidemic' (n 8) 7.

HIV in the developing world.[13] And despite the most dire of predictions, the pharmaceutical industry did not collapse.

The problem that we were confronting was not only about access to existing drugs for AIDS. Some 15 million people die every year from largely treatable or neglected diseases, and over one billion people suffer from neglected tropical diseases for which there is virtually no drug R&D.[14] The problem—in the simplest of terms—is that the needs of poor people, who by definition have very little purchasing power, do not translate into a return on investment for pharmaceutical corporations.[15] This is both a failure of the market, and a failure of public policy. Again it was a similar process—we brought together academics, the best scientific, business, and political and legal scholars in the world. They focused their mind, time, and energy, applied rigorous analysis, explored alternatives, and experimented with options. We created the DNDi—the not-for-profit Drugs for Neglected Diseases initiative. The DNDi was launched in 2003, and its first drug—an FDC anti-malarial—was released in partnership with Sanofi Avenits, in March 2007. A second FDC was released in 2008, a new treatment for African sleeping sickness was released last year—among a total thus far of six new treatments that are now available for NTDs. And the DNDi has seventeen other drugs under development.[16] How did this happen? In the first instance, we saw the dignity of our patients. We refused to accept the unacceptable. We saw possibility, and against all naysayers, we acted to create an alternative. With rigorous attention to governance—its board is made up of exclusively public sector institutions and MSF, all committed by statute to the public good—and using existing IPR law creatively, for example, sub-licensing agreements—DNDi demonstrates that real alternatives are possible.

Both the Campaign and the DNDi—together with others—have also engaged in the communicative process of creating the enabling circumstances for relevant law to emerge. Ten years ago, both created a rationale and continued to push for the WHO to create a commission on the impact of IPR on public health. At the same time, both explored and pushed for the emergence of the concept and practice of patent polling. Most recently, in 2012 the WHO passed a resolution in favour of a Framework for Global Health Research & Development. The Campaign, the DNDi, and other initiatives like it in recent years, have changed global health—and our conception of what is possible—forever.

Hannah Arendt wrote also that 'we are not born equal: equality and equity are the result of choice and of human organization'.[17] For billions today, the lack of equity is a politically determined choice. Today, in Canada, life expectancy is 81 years and rising. In sub-Saharan Africa, average life expectancy is 46 years, and falling.[18] In our world of

13 UNAIDS, 'UN Secretary-General outlines new recommendations to reach 2015 goals for AIDS response', Press Release, 31 March 2011, available at <http://www.unaids.org/en/resources/presscentre/pressreleaseandstatementarchive/2011/march/20110331prsgreport/>.

14 WHO (2008) WHO global burden of disease: 2004 update' (2008), available at <http://www.who.int/healthinfo/global_burden_disease/2004_report_update/en/index.html> (accessed 21 March 2011).

15 WHO, 'Working to Overcome the Global Impact of Neglected Diseases' (2010) iii.

16 Of the more than 1,500 new drugs brought onto the market between 1975 and 2004, just over 1% were for tropical diseases, and of this 1%, half were for malaria and TB—diseases that affect Western travellers: P. Chirac and E. Torreele, 'Global Framework on Essential Health R&D' *Lancet* (2006) 367: 1560.

17 E. Chatelain and J.R. Ioset, 'Drug discovery and development for neglected diseases: the DNDi model' *Drug Design, Development and Therapy* (2011) 5: 175.

18 UN News Centre (2006) 'Life expectancy in sub-Saharan Africa is lower now than 30 years ago: UN index' (2006).

7 billion people, *3.8 billion*—or more than half of all people on the planet—live on less than US$2 a day.[19] In 2009, more than a hundred million were added to the already 900 million—making a total of one billion people—one in seven on the planet—who now go to bed hungry every night.[20] In 2008, hungry people deposed the prime minister of Haiti, a year before the devastating earthquake. In 2008, hungry people rioted in at least sixty countries. The director of the UN Food and Agriculture Organization, Jacques Diouf, said recently: 'One thousand million empty bellies accuse and shame us . . . And are a threat to world peace and security.'[21] He is right on both counts. This is our world, and for more than half of us on the planet, life truly is nasty, brutish, and short.

A few months ago, I was back in Malawi with Dignitas International, a new organization that I and another Canadian—James Fraser—started in 2004. It is focused on creating an alternative model of care for AIDS, TB, and non-communicable diseases (NCDs) using primary health care (PHC) for people in the developing world. Why PHC? Because by working with the MOH and supporting people with HIV, TB, and other PHC needs, individuals and communities can face their health needs on their own terms. We have trained hundreds of nurses, clinical officers, doctors, community health workers, and home-based care volunteers. We are supporting women's groups, groups of orphans, and groups of people living with HIV. We now have 20,000 children, women, and men on full treatment for AIDS, and thousands more HIV+ people under our medical care. We have published what is recognized as some of the best HIV research in the world. And our pilot programme is so successful that we are scaling up this year to offer the programme to a population base of 3 million people. Eight short years ago, when we started this organization from inside SMH at the University of Toronto, entire villages had collapsed in the despair and hopelessness of rampant disease. Ninety percent of hospital admissions were HIV+, and people literally languished and died in the shade of trees surrounding the hospital. Now villages are back at work, and peoples' primary concern—as it should be—is the education of their children.

That said, riots across Malawi in 2011 left eighteen dead, as people demanded better governance in the management of currency exchange rates, and in the face of rising fuel and food costs and food shortages. Why is this happening? The most immediate or proximate cause is the ongoing effects of the international financial crisis. Donor dollars have plummeted, currency valuations have fluctuated more down than up, and fuel and food commodity prices have fluctuated more up than down, creating political instability and, with it, massive civil society protests, and a new president. But just behind this immediate proximate economic cause is the reality of what the UN FAO recognizes as a pattern of severe and prolonged droughts that could become

[19] According to the US Census Bureau, the global population as of 23 March 2011, was 6,907,615,144; S. Benatar et al, 'Making progress in Global Health: the Need for New Paradigms' *International Affairs* (2009) 85(2): 347. People living on between US$1 and $2 per day number 2.6 billion, and an additional 1.3 billion live on less than $0.25 per day. That is 39 billion people—58%—or more than half of all the people in the world. See The World Bank, 'Poverty Analysis—Overview' (PovertyNet, 2001) 30 April 2007. <http://web.worldbank.org/WBSITE/EXTERNAL/TOPICS/EXTRPOVERTY/EXTPA/0,,contentMDK:20153855~menuPK:435040~pagePK:148956~piPK:216618~theSitePK:430367,00.html>.

[20] WFP, 'The State of Food Insecurity in the World' (Rome, 2010) 8.

[21] J. Diouf, 'Food And Agriculture Organisation. A Roadmap for global food security', G8 (Italy, 2009) 132. And see D. Maxwell et al, 'Fit For Purpose?' *Food Policy* (2010) 35: 91.

permanent due to climate change.[22] Climate change—or what I prefer to identify as global warming—is also a critical factor in the famine that last year left 13 million people at risk in Somalia and the greater Horn of Africa, and that threatens the Sahel region of Africa today. A mere ten years from now, crop yields in some parts of Africa are expected to drop by 50 percent and water stress could affect as many as 250 million Africans.[23] Exactly the same process is true for Central America and South East Asia. There is no amount of humanitarian assistance—as we organize it today—that can cope humanely and equitably with such massive need. In North America, West Nile virus, never seen before 2000, has infected more than 21,000 and killed more than 800 people in the United States and Canada.[24] The Canadian government has warned that the country might eventually experience yellow fever and malaria. Lyme disease has moved north up through the United States, and Dengue fever is following, all because of global warming. Indeed, the *Lancet* has recognized that global warming (climate change) is the greatest global health threat of the twenty-first century.[25] We come full circle when we realize that in Darfur, Sudan, it is global warming that drives competition for access to water and arable land and that leads today to war crimes, crimes against humanity, and slow-motion genocide.[26]

'Simply letting climate change rip and tidying up the damage as it occurs is not an enviable strategy... In poor countries, higher temperatures will mean an increased risk of hardship and societal collapse, and rich countries will be forced to respond.'[27] That was said, not by me, but by an Editorial in the *Financial Times*. Global warming is a matter of justice. Its health effects and implications have had little attention from climate scientists and governments. If there is 'fault' here, there is failure among those concerned with global health—a failure thus far to engage in a communicative process around global warming—that includes pragmatic action—and that can shape the emergence of both practice and law. In June 2102, Jerome Singh, from the University of KwaZulu-Natal in Durban, South Africa, correctly argued that human health and health ethics considerations must be a core—and not a peripheral—focus, and must be given equal status to economic considerations in future climate change deliberations.[28] And furthermore, that the health community, led by health ministers and the World Health Organization, must play a central role in climate change deliberations.

Before I close, let me note that I have told you a series of stories of engaging the world as it is, so as to shape it to what it can be. Each of these challenges I have touched on are complex, are fed by interdependent crises, are local and global in their causality and scope, and are—without a doubt—formidable. And yet I know that as human

22 J. Vidal and T. Radford, 'One in Six Countries Facing Food Shortage', *The Guardian*, 30 June 2005.

23 M.A. Novicki, 'Improving Africa's Water Supply: Special Initiative Seeks Greater Access for Farmers and the Poor' (1997), available at <http://www.un.org/ecosocdev/geninfo/afrec/vol11no2/special3.htm>.

24 A. Costello, M. Abbas, A. Allen, S. Ball, S. Bell, and R. Bellamy et al, 'Managing the Health Effects of Climate Change' Lancet and University College London Institute for Global Health Commission, *Lancet* (2009) 373: 1693.

25 'Climate change is the greatest global health threat of the 21st century', A. Costello et al, 'Managing the Health Effects of Climate Change' *Lancet* (2009) 373: 1693. See further C. Armstrong, *Global Distributive Justice* (Cambridge: CUP, 2012) ch 7.

26 J. Sachs in CIDA, 'Report on International Cooperation Days: The Millennium Development Goals Moving From Consensus to Momentum', 1–3 November 2004, Ottawa, at 6, available at <http://www.acdi-cida.gc.ca/INET/IMAGES.NSF/vLUImages/International%20Cooperation/$file/ICD-Final-Report-e.pdf> (accessed 29 March 2009).

27 Editorial, 'Learning to Live in A Changing Climate', *Financial Times*, 2 July 2012, 10.

28 J. Singh, 'Why Human Health and Health Ethics Must Be Central To Climate Change Deliberations' *PLOS Medicine* (2012) 9(6): doi:10.1371/journal.pmed.1001229.

beings, we are capable of extraordinary and yet always imperfect things. Whether it is justice in the face of genocide, equitable access to life-saving medicines, new research for neglected diseases, addressing hunger or the ongoing and new challenges facing the AIDS community, PHC, or climate change, the right kind of change is possible, and law as a communicative process, can be—and is—central.

The JALI initiative—or the Joint Action and Learning Initiative on National and Global Responsibilities for Health—is a potentially powerful initiative that seeks 'health for all, and justice for all'.[29] Koskenniemi, in his book, *The Gentle Civilizer of Nations: The Rise and Fall of International Law 1870–1960*, cautioned against an excessive positivism or instrumentalism. My sense is that JALI has taken this to heart, and is open to law as a communicative process. I hope it will avoid the pitfalls that have beset the NCD Initiative. Here, for example, despite ample data evidencing the need for such a framework, as an 'elites' initiative, it lacks a dialogic top-down bottom-up communicative process, as well as a coherent unifying clarion call. In contrast, the JALI initiative is full of possibility.

And how does one see possibility? As I said earlier, it does not lie in naive utopian dreams, but in what we do. The most innovative and politically transformative ideas—ideas in the pursuit of greater equity—of the last two hundred years have been driven by engaged citizens who acted—however imperfectly—to explore and create alternatives. The abolition of the slave trade, the emergence of labour, children's and women's rights, civil rights for African Americans, reform of the post-World War II and the post-Cold War rules of war, the environmental movement, and the global health movement, are each examples of transformative ideas rooted in notions of justice.

These have not led to law that has been created simply through self-evident necessity, but rather law that has emerged and is emerging is a long-time process and context of evidence gathering, political engagement, contestation, and confrontations of power in the pursuit of justice. Each began as an apparently lost cause, and—however imperfectly—has achieved practical outcomes that surpass those of the prior world.

The law can be, and now often is, central to such transformations. Here, to be effective, as Michael Reisman describes in an elaboration of Lasswell, law must be a communicative process that inculcates itself as a normative standard by which sustaining intentions and tensions within a polity can be guided, so that (law) 'contributes optimally to human dignity'.[30] For example, the legal authority of the ICC itself or its trials, their control intention and their policy content are three strands of a 'coaxial cable' that both harnesses and contains these sustaining intentions and tensions. The normative communicative process entails an ongoing redefinition or reshaping of the community's constitutive principles and objectives, and this makes the wrong of, for example, genocide both publicly and privately acknowledged for both perpetrator and victim.

I hope that I have argued that global health in its broadest conceptualization connotes well-being in a state of justice. I hope I have shown that the use and construction of law as a communicative process is central to reducing injustice and enhancing global health, I hope, too, that I have shown that GH law is most effective when it has a plural grounding in pragmatism, the high ideals of humanity, human rights, and the pursuit of the public good. I have argued for a conception of law in

[29] L. Gostin, 'A Framework Convention on Global Health' *Journal of the American Medical Association* (2012) 307(19): 2087.

[30] W.M. Reisman, *International Law-Making: A Process of Communication* (New Haven, CT: Yale University Press, 1981) 120.

relation to global health that is beyond positivism (which holds that law is only made by the legislature), to one that sees law as most powerful when it is a function of a communicative process over time that at least allows the possibility—but not the certainty—of justice.

Edmund Burke said that society 'is a partnership not only between those who are living, but between those who are living, those who are dead, and those who are to be born'.[31] As I said a few moments ago, in our human imperfection, stories and how we live them can be revolutionary, and show that hope is not a fools' choice. With the right kind of engagement, with the right kind of doing, with the right kind of story—we can be hopeful. The belief in authentic hope—is radical. A belief that people are not inherently evil and stupid, not consigned merely to live out pre-determined roles, is radical. The willingness to act publicly on that hope and that belief is radical. It is based on a faith in something common to us all, a capacity that is difficult to name, but which is perhaps best summed up by a phrase once used by the Brazilian educator Paulo Freire. Our task, simply put, Freire said, is 'to change some conditions that appear . . . as so obviously against the beauty of being human'.[32]

31 J.C.D. Clark (ed), Edmund Burke: *Reflections on the Revolution in France: A Critical Edition* (Cambridge: CUP, 2001) 25: 'Edmund Burke was an Irishman, born in Dublin but in an age before "Celtic nationalism" had been constructed to make Irishness and Englishness incompatible: he was therefore free also to describe himself, without misrepresentation, as "an Englishman" to denote his membership of the wider polity. He never attempted to disguise his Irishness (as some ambitious Scots in eighteenth-century England tried to anglicize their accents), did what he could in the Commons to promote the interests of his native country and was bitterly opposed to the Penal Laws against Irish Catholics' (at 261).

32 M. Horton and P. Freire, *We Make the Road by Walking* (Philadelphia, PA: Temple University Press, 1990) 131.

PART A

RIGHT TO HEALTH

1

What is Health?

Charles Foster and Jonathan Herring

1. Introduction

How are you? Unwell we hope. Certainly according to some common definitions of health. Here is the *Oxford English Dictionary*. Health is:

The state of being free from sickness, injury, disease, bodily conditions; something indicating good bodily condition.

Webster's Dictionary of Health:

The state of being hale, sound, or whole, in body, mind, or soul; especially the state of being free from physical disease or pain.[1]

The Youth of Scotland:

Males tended to think of health as to do with body building, muscles and obtaining a 'six-pack' and weight gain whereas females tended to look upon health as beauty, eating disorders, weight loss and contraception.[2]

And then there is the World Health Organization's infamous definition:

Health is a state of complete physical, mental, and social well-being and not merely the absence of disease or infirmity.[3]

Much has been written about this definition. It has been heavily criticized. It begs many questions.[4] Is the claim normative?[5] Does the definition depend on an individual's evaluation of her own health, or is it objective?[6]

For some the WHO definition is idealistic. One commentator rather facetiously suggested that the state of well-being it describes is only achieved at mutual orgasm.[7]

1 See <http://www.webster-dictionary.org/definition/health>.

2 Health Scotland, *Young People, Health and the Internet* (Edinburgh: Health Scotland, 2012) 3.

3 World Health Organization, *The Constitution of the World Health Organization* (Geneva: WHO, 1947).

4 See, for instance, R. Gillon,'On Sickness and on Health' (1986) 292 *British Medical Journal* 318; L. Breslow, 'A Quantitative Approach to the World Health Organization Definition of Health: Physical, Mental and Social Well-Being' (1972) 1 *International Journal of Epidemiology* 347; S. Katz, 'The Science of the Quality of Life' (1987) 40 *Journal of Chronic Diseases* 459–63; J. Ware, 'Standards for Validating Health Measures: Definition and Content' (1987) 40 *Journal of Chronic Diseases* 473; R. Saracci, 'The World Health Organization Needs to Reconsider its Definition of Health' (1997) 314 *British Medical Journal* 1409.

5 C. Boorse, 'Health as a Theoretical Concept' (1977) 44 *Philosophy of Science* 542.

6 If it is just a disvalued physical or mental condition it can be baldness or bushy eyebrows. For a view that it is a matter of public opinion, see the discussion in K. Sadegh-Zadeh, 'Fuzzy Health, Illness and Disease' (2000) 25 *The Journal of Medicine and Philosophy* 605.

7 Peter Skrabanek, quoted by R. Smith, 'The End of Disease and the Beginning of Health', available at <http://blogs.bmj.com/bmj/2008/07/08/richard-smith-the-end-of-disease-and-the-beginning-of-health/>.

We will not comment, but most people cannot realistically expect to inhabit the described state for most of the time. Raanon Gillon observes that, by that definition[8] 'none of us is, has ever been, or is ever likely to be healthy'. If that's what health is, doctors seeking to make patients healthy may as well give up. It is easy to understand why, for some, it is attractive to see health as the absence of disease.[9]

Another problem with the definition is that it fails to distinguish between the role of medicine and the role of social and political programmes designed to benefit the welfare of the population.[10] According to the definition the production of high quality television programmes is as much promoting health as is polio vaccination.

We will not explore further the difficulties with the WHO definition, nor the attempts at redefinition. In this chapter we first explore and dispute three assumptions that underpin much of the discussion of health. These are:

First: that it makes sense to see ourselves as atomistic, static entities.

Second: that health is an entirely personal, subjective quality.

Third: that the desirable norm is a capacitous, invulnerable human, and accordingly that incapacity and vulnerability are pathological.

We then go on to consider, in relation to three areas of healthcare law (resource allocation, confidentiality, and organ donation/use of body parts and materials), how our account of health should change legal analysis.

2. Assumption 1: It Makes Sense to See Ourselves as Atomistic, Static Entities

The ubiquity and insidiousness of this assumption is best illustrated by reference to the way the law works. We consider that later, in the sections where we discuss resource allocation, confidentiality, and the ownership of body parts.

For now we restrict ourselves to observing that the assumption is plainly untrue. We do not create ourselves. Our autonomy had no part in the fusion of the two gametes that formed the zygote that became us. We did not choose our parents or the genetic bequest that determines so much of our destiny. We had no control over the processes of differentiation and growth. In utero we received our nutrients and our oxygen from our mother's blood via the placenta. As children if our parents chose not to feed us, we would have starved. At the end of our lives we are likely again to be in a state of complete physical dependence. Even as supposedly capacitous adults we consistently over-represent our independence. If an oncogene is switched on by something in the environment over which we have no control, we will get cancer. Some genes will inevitably express themselves, however benevolent the environment. Our neuronal wiring (and hence our personalities and abilities) is determined by what happens around us. Even the most expensive school (for which, of course, we won't have paid

[8] R. Gillon,'On Sickness and on Health' (n 4).

[9] C. Boorse, 'On the Distinction Between Disease and Illness' (1975) 5 *Philosophy and Public Affairs* 49; C. Boorse, 'Origins of Indeterminacy Thesis' (1975) 72 *Journal of Philosophy* 369; C. Boorse, 'What a Theory of Mental Health Should Be' (1976) 6 *Journal of Theory of Social Behavior* 61; C. Boorse, 'Wright on Functions' (1976) 85 *Philosophy Review* 70; C. Boorse, 'Health as a Theoretical Concept' (1977) 44 *Philosophy of Science* 542.

[10] D. Callahan, 'The WHO Definition of "Health"' (1973) 1 *Hastings Center Report* 77; A. Cribb, *Health and the Good Society: Setting Healthcare Ethics in Social Context* (Oxford: Clarendon Press, 2005) 22.

ourselves) can't guarantee benign companions, congenial lessons, and immunity from road traffic accidents. As individuals we have, even in the most enlightened Western democracies, almost no control over the really big decisions that affect our lives. When we get ill (as we will: bacteria, viruses, and cancers haven't read John Stuart Mill) there will, for all the vaunted importance of autonomy in healthcare law, be a massive element of luck, paternalism, and downright mystery. Even if you choose your doctor, you will not know all his technical foibles and philosophical prejudices. Even if you do, you will have no control over his own personal life, which might make his hands tremble just as his scalpel approaches your thoracic aortic aneurysm. What he tells you about the complications of the procedure or the medication will depend on what he knows, what he thinks (perhaps entirely wrongly) you want to know, and on how badly he wants to catch the 6.14 from Paddington.

We talk about ourselves as immutable entities, but how true is that? It is true that consciousness confers on us (or perhaps *is*) a conviction that there is some sort of continuity between the 'me' that was a child several decades ago and the 'me' that is writing this chapter. But even if there is some truth behind the conviction, and there is indeed a persisting 'me', the continuity is fairly tenuous. My views differ significantly from those I held as a 7 year old. They have been moulded by circumstance. If you could look at the neuronal connections in my brain you would see that they are vastly different. My social, geographical, and medical circumstances are very different. The friends, relatives, and communities central to my self-understanding have passed away, moved on, or themselves changed beyond recognition. Even my physiological and anatomical hardware is very different. I have now very, very few of the cells that I had when I was a 7 year old. Indeed my intestine is lined with an entirely different set of cells from those that did the job two days ago.[11]

There is no clear distinction between me and others. My body does not stop at my skin. It leaks into the rest of the world, and the rest of the world leaks into me. If this doesn't happen, something is badly wrong. That's real pathology.

3. Assumption 2: Health is an Entirely Personal, Subjective Quality

Health, both subjectively and objectively, is an inevitably social notion. We make this point in two ways: first, by drawing on the powerful work of those writing from a disability perspective; and second, by arguing for the wider, more general proposition, that health must be understood in communitarian terms.

Much of the writing from a disability perspective has shown that it is often the social environment in which the disabled person has to live that makes a physical difference a disadvantage.[12] Liz Crow tells us:

> [The] social model of disability ... gave me an understanding of my life ... what I had always known, deep down, was confirmed ... It wasn't my body that was responsible for all my difficulties, it was external factors, the barriers constructed by the society in which I live.[13]

11 See J. Herring and P.-L. Chau, 'My Body, Your Body, Our Bodies' (2007) 15 *Medical Law Review* 34.

12 A. Silvers, 'Reprising Women's Disability: Feminist Identity Strategy and Disability Rights' (1998) 13 *Berkeley Women's Law Journal* 81.

13 L. Crow, 'Including All of Our Lives: Renewing the Social Model of Disability', in C. Barnes and G. Mercer (eds), *Exploring the Divide: Illness and Disability* (Leeds: Disability Press, 1996) 56.

We do not suggest that the impact of all disability is a consequence of the social environment. Even with all the institutional and attitudinal changes imaginable some impairments will still confer a disadvantage.[14] But the environment certainly matters profoundly. The terminology of 'disabled people' is therefore appropriate: they are disabled by the fact that social spaces, services, and provisions are modelled around certain kinds of bodies, to the disadvantage of others.[15] This is not limited to the lack of provision of physical equipment. Social expectations label certain children as having 'learning disabilities' because they lack selected skills[16] or because we do not value the skills they do have.[17]

This illustrates a further truth: health and well-being cannot be seen in an individualistic way. There is great wisdom in the National Aboriginal Health Strategy Working Party:

> Aboriginal health is not just the physical well being of an individual but is the social, emotional and cultural well being of the whole community in which each individual is able to achieve their full potential thereby bringing about the total well being of their community. It is a whole-of-life view and includes the cyclical concept of life-death-life.[18]

So, we cannot seek to promote the health of individuals without promoting the health of their communities. It is in, with, and through our communities that we understand ourselves and understand our health.[19] The person living alone on an island might have the most wonderful physique, but have no sense of self or health. This is because our identity is found in our relationship with others, from our beginning to our end and beyond—in the memories and other legacies we leave. We will argue shortly that vulnerability and dependency are central, essential, defining aspects of humanity. It follows that caring for others is a central, essential, defining human task. In caring, the division between 'you' and 'me' becomes lost. The vulnerability of the one becomes the vulnerability of the other; the disability of the one becomes the disability of the other.[20]

4. Assumption 3: That the Desirable Norm is a Capacitous, Invulnerable Human, and Accordingly that Incapacity and Vulnerability are Pathological

Much writing on health assumes, without discussion, what is normal. It then sees health as a departure from the 'norm'.[21] It is common, for example, to find a discussion

[14] J. Leach, *Disability Bioethics: Moral Bodies, Moral Difference* (Lanham, MD: Rowman and Littlefield, 2008).

[15] J. Morris, 'Impairment and Disability: Constructing an Ethics of Care that Promotes Human Rights' (2001) 16 *Hypatia* 1.

[16] V. Leiter, '"Nobody's just normal, you know": The Social Creation of Developmental Disability' (2007) 65 *Social Science and Medicine* 1630.

[17] C. Foster, 'My son's dyslexic and I'm glad', available at <http://www.charlesfoster.co.uk/?p%20=%20590>.

[18] National Aboriginal Health Strategy Working Party, 1989, quoted in P. Boddington and U. Raisanen, 'Theoretical and Practical Issues in the Definition of Health: Insights from Aboriginal Australia' (2009) 34 *Journal of Medicine and Philosophy* 49.

[19] R. Saltonstall, 'Healthy Bodies, Social Bodies: Men's and Women's Concepts and Practices of Health in Everyday Life' (1993) 36 *Social Science and Medicine* 7.

[20] S. Whitney, 'Dependency Relations: Corporeal Vulnerability and Norms of Personhood in Hobbes and Kittay' (2011) 26 *Hypatia* 544.

[21] S. Wood-Daughinee and I. Williams, 'Reintegration to normal living as a proxy to quality of life' (1987) 40 *Journal of Chronic Diseases* 491.

of the extent to which an individual has reached or can reach the standard of 'normal living'.[22] Look at what was considered 'unhealthy' in the past: it included everything from the wish of a slave to be free, to sexual desire in women. No doubt many of the things we currently deem 'illness' will not be seen as such in the future.[23]

It is difficult, if not impossible, to separate the question of what health is from that of how one thinks life should be lived.[24] As Foucault has so powerfully shown, to define disease in a particular way can amount to an exercise of power.[25] If one is 'ill' one needs the state's protection and therapy. A failure to recognize one's illness is further evidence that you are ill. Yet under the WHO definition we are all ill.

Turner[26] writes:

> Put simply, the doctor has replaced the priest as the custodian of social values: the panoply of ecclesiastical institutions of regulation (the ritual order of sacraments, the places of vocational training, the hospice for pilgrims, places of worship and sanctuary) have been transferred through the evolution of scientific medicine to a panoptic collection of localised agencies of surveillance and control. Furthermore, the rise of preventive medicine, social medicine and community medicine has extended these agencies and regulation deeper and deeper into social life.

As diets have replaced religious mortification, and gyms monasteries, clerics have been supplanted by doctors.[27]

Take one of the most plausible understandings of health—that developed by Sridhar Venkatapuram,[28] building on the writing of Lennart Nordenfelt and Martha Nussbaum. They argue that health should be seen as based around an ability to achieve 'vital life goals'—certain key capabilities. Nussbaum lists them as follows:

1) being able to live a normal length of lifespan;
2) having good health;
3) maintain bodily integrity;
4) being able to use senses, imagination, and think;
5) having emotions and emotional attachments;
6) possess practical reason to form a conception of the good;
7) have social affiliations that are meaningful and respectful;
8) express concern for other species;
9) able to play; and
10) have control over one's material and political environment.

We have noted already that much writing on health starts with an assumption about 'normal health'. The typically 'normal' person will be able-bodied, autonomous, rational, adult, and, very often, male.[29] Yet there is no reason to start with that assumption. There is every reason to doubt that that is either realistic or desirable.

22 Wood-Daughinee and Williams, 'Reintegration to normal living' (n 21).

23 R. Hamilton, 'The concept of health: beyond normativism and naturalism' (2010) 16 *Journal of Evaluation in Clinical Practice* 323.

24 Hamilton, 'The concept of health' (n 23).

25 M. Foucault, *Madness and Civilization* (London: Vintage, 2006 (1964)). The medicalization of pregnancy is a powerful example: see F. Ebtehaj, J. Herring, M. Johnson, and M. Richards (eds), *Birth Rights and Rites* (Oxford: Hart, 2011).

26 B. Turner, *Medical Power and Social Knowledge*, (London: Sage Publications, 1995) 35–6.

27 L. Koppelman and J. Moskop, 'The Holistic Health Movement: A Survey and Critique' (1981) 6 *Journal of Medicine and Philosophy* 209.

28 S. Venkatapuram, 'Health, Vital Goals, and Central Human Capabilities' (2013) 27 *Bioethics* 271. See also S. Venkatapuram, *Health Justice* (Cambridge: Polity Press, 2011).

29 L. Bondi and E. Burman, 'Women and Mental Health: A Feminist Review' (2001) 68 *Feminist Review* 6.

Eva Feder Kittay's daughter, Sesha, has cerebral palsy. She is profoundly cognitively and physically impaired. She will always be dependent on others for life's basics. Eva Kittay is not given to sentimentality, still she writes:

> Sometimes I wonder if Sesha is a special being sent to us from elsewhere, for there is an impossible-to-articulate sweetness, graciousness, and emotional openness about her—qualities we rarely find in others.[30]

On any conventional definition of health, Sesha would be found unhealthy, but do not her sweetness, graciousness, and openness demonstrate a rare health?[31] We elevate the capacity for logic, rational thought, and autonomy over the capacity for wonder, gentleness, and warmth, but perhaps the first set of qualities make for a better person than the other.

We need to accept that the orthodox images of illness are deceptive. They do not reflect the truth about the human condition. Smith argues 'Health for doctors is a negative state—the absence of disease. In fact, health is an illusion. If you let doctors get to work with their genetic analysis, blood tests, and advanced imaging techniques then everybody will be found to be defective—"dis-eased." '[32]

The extent of departure from the autonomous ideal within the adult population is easily underestimated. While not suggesting that the following groups are necessarily vulnerable, the next list indicates how common are departures by adults from the autonomous hyper-competent man who is the benchmark of much of the law:

- Seventy-five per cent of the population have an IQ of less than 110.[33]
- One in four people will experience some kind of mental health problem in the course of a year.[34]
- During 2011–12, in England, 1.5 million people received adult social care services.[35]
- Prior to interview in 2011–12, 35 per cent of men drank over 4, and 28 per cent of women drank more than 3 units of alcohol on at least one day in the week prior to interview in 2011–12. The average weekly alcohol consumption for all adults was 15.9 units for men and 7.6 units for women—26 per cent of men reported drinking more than 21 units in a typical week; 17 per cent of women reported drinking more than 14 units in a typical week. In 2010–11, there were 1,168,300 alcohol-related admissions to hospital based on the broad measure.[36]
- In 2010, just over a quarter of adults (26 per cent of both men and women aged 16 or over) in England were classified as obese (BMI 30kg/m2 or over). For the same period, around three in ten boys and girls (aged 2 to 15) were classed as either overweight or obese (31 per cent and 29 per cent respectively).[37]
- Total unemployment stood at 2.53 million for the three months to October 2012.[38]

[30] E.F. Kittay, 'Forever Small: The Strange Case of Ashley X' (2011) 26 *Hypatia* 610.

[31] L. Carlson, *The Faces of Intellectual Disability: Philosophical Reflections* (Bloomington, IN: Indiana University Press, 2009).

[32] R. Smith, 'The End of Disease and the Beginning of Health', available at <http://blogs.bmj.com/bmj/2008/07/08/richard-smith-the-end-of-disease-and-the-beginning-of-health/>.

[33] G. Boeree, *Intelligence and IQ* (Shippenberg, PA: Shippenberg University Press, 2009).

[34] Mental Health Foundation, 'Statistics on Mental Health' (London, 2012).

[35] NHS, 'Community Care Statistics 2011–12' (London: NHS, 2012).

[36] NHS, 'Statistics on Alcohol, England' (London: NHS, 2012).

[37] NHS, 'Statistics on Obesity' (London: NHS, 2012).

[38] Office of National Statistics, *Labour Market Statistics* (London: ONS, 2012).

The population of the UK is ageing. There are 10.3 million people aged 65 and over in the UK. This is an 80 per cent increase over six decades, from 5.7 million in 1951.[39]

- There are over 11 million people with a limiting long-term illness, impairment, or disability in Great Britain.[40]
- In 2012, around a third of children live in poverty, that is 3.6 million children.[41]

We noted previously how vulnerable we are, and how little autonomy we really have. The rhetoric of politics in a Parliamentary democracy, and of law in most Western countries, is that we are the authors of our destinies, But the truth about autonomy is fair less grand and rather more disturbing. As Martha Fineman observes:

> One way to begin to dismantle the existing facade of autonomy is to show the privilege and advantage that have been unequally distributed through society and its institutions and this has consequences and implications for the way we should think about equality. Turning our critical attention to issues of privilege and advantage must accompany and complement inquiry into discrimination and oppression. While we must continue to consider how some individuals and groups are uniquely disadvantaged, rendered unequally and oppressively vulnerable, by the structures and ideological predispositions of our system, the inquiry cannot stop there. We must also explore why and how some—often only a few but also frequently a majority—are and have been advantaged and privileged by that system.

Autonomy is used not only to disguise our own vulnerability, but also to justify the inequalities in society. The rich and powerful like to claim they reach that by their own hard work or gifts or wise choices. In fact they have been helped by the very systems that create the inequalities for others.

We praise ourselves when we make 'accommodations' for the 'disabled people', overlooking the many accommodations that the able-bodied give themselves. In a powerful article, Kate Lindemann contrasts the emphasis on disability-minimizing accommodations for disabled people, with the lack of appreciation of how much accommodation there is for the able bodied:

> Colleagues, professional staff members, and other adults are unconscious of the numerous accommodations that society provides to make their work and life style possible. ATM's, extended hours in banks, shopping centres and medical offices, EZpass, newspaper kiosks, and elevators are all accommodations that make contemporary working life possible. There are entire industries devoted to accommodating the needs of adult working people. Fast food, office lunch delivery, day time child care, respite care, car washing, personal care attendants, interpreters, house cleaning, and yard and lawn services are all occupations that provide services that make it possible for adults to hold full time jobs.[42]

We highlight the facilities used to deal with the vulnerabilities of others, while overlooking the accommodations *we* need to deal with our vulnerabilities. It's all about maintaining the fable of our own invulnerability.[43]

Not only is the image of the norm of the capacitous autonomous individual not the norm; it is not desirable. The medical model of health is not what people want. We

39 T. Rutherford, 'Population Ageing Statistics' (London House of Commons Library, 2012).

40 Office for Disability Issues, 'Disability Facts and Figures' (London, Department for Work and Pensions, 2012).

41 Barnardo's, 'Child Poverty: Facts and Statistics' (London: Barnardo's, 2012).

42 K. Lindemann, 'The Ethics Of Receiving' (2003) 24 *Theoretical Medicine and Bioethics* 501.

43 J. Herring, 'Vulnerability, Children and the Law' in M. Freeman (ed), *Law and Childhood Studies* (Oxford: OUP, 2012).

often need a lutist not a phlebotomist; a hot air balloon not an aspirin; a cuddle not a counsellor. What is forgotten is that people may have a host of things that are stopping them being the person they want to be: these may be health concerns, but they be family worries or social concerns. Being vulnerable is an aspect of many of the great values. Relationships; intimacy; care; all of these things necessarily make us vulnerable.[44] Dependency should not be something to be afraid of or ashamed of.

Susan Dodds also argues that we need a legal and social system which is premised not on individualistic conceptions of autonomy but an acceptance of our vulnerability:

> A vulnerability-centered view of the self and of persons is better able to capture many of our moral motivations and intuitions than can be captured by an autonomy-focused approach. We are all vulnerable to the exigencies of our embodied, social and relational existence and, in recognizing this inherent human vulnerability, we can see the ways in which a range of social institutions and structures protect us against some vulnerabilities, while others expose us to risk. We do not have to view our obligations towards those who lack the capacity to develop or retain autonomy as having a different source from our obligations towards those whose autonomy is made vulnerable due to a degree of dependency. It may be easier to recognize the social value of provision of care if it is viewed as something on which we all have been dependent and on which we are all likely to be dependent at different points in our lives, rather than altruistic behaviour extended to those who lack 'full personhood.'[45]

We have quoted a good deal of modern literature in support of our propositions. But the (currently unfashionable) insights we are urging have a long ancestry.

The Homeric world valued individual heroism. Achilles, Odysseus, and the rest were the pin-up boys of the Bronze Age. They were, by and large, and with some notable exceptions, interested more in their own glory and the view of them that posterity would have, than in the welfare of their battle-mates. A large part of their celebrity lay in their relative autonomy: they made their own decisions. But the gods always had the final word. The sponsoring deities on Olympus smiled on their chosen ones, applauding them for their audacity. But they also frowned on the favourites of other gods. The politics of Olympus ultimately determined the fates of the heroes. And so, even in the Homeric Golden Age, a hero was particularly heroic if he looked the fates squarely in the face—if he acknowledged his own contingency and vulnerability.

The evolution thereafter was, until the Enlightenment, in the direction of increased acknowledgement of the fact that humans are quintessentially social animals. After Homer there was intense and increasing interest in the business of politics, which assumes that humans need to be socially embedded. Socrates' enquiries into the nature of the good life were indistinguishable from his ponderings about the nature of a good society. In *The Republic*, Plato's main concern was to show how the components of the soul could relate to each other, and he demonstrated this by examining the components of a well-functioning city-state. The fact that he chose a political metaphor for such an important endeavour indicates that he thought good government was foundational.

For Aristotle, in the *Nichomachean Ethics*, the object of human existence is happiness, in the sense of *eudaimonia*. A crucial part of that is concern for others, demonstrated by doing as one would be done by, and hence by cooperation and sympathy.

We find ourselves standing alongside the Stoics. They held that each has an intimate connection to the other, which mandates a duty of service. And, famously, they

[44] G.W. Harris, *Dignity and Vulnerability* (Berkeley, CA: University of California Press, 1997).

[45] S. Dodds, 'Depending On Care: Recognition of Vulnerability and the Social Contribution of Care Provision' (2007) 21 *Bioethics* 500, 507.

emphasized the importance of acknowledging our own precariousness and dependence. Here is Epictectus, reported by Arrian in the *Enchiridion*: 'Some things are up to us and some things are not up to us . . . Our bodies are not up to us, nor are our possessions, our reputations, or our public offices . . . ' Knowing this, said the Stoics, releases us from the delusory hopes that make us miserable pawns of fate.

So far as interconnectedness is concerned, we cannot improve on Marcus Aurelius, who taught that the universe is an organism: everything in it is related to everything else. The flourishing of one cannot be viewed in isolation from that of the others. And, further, in a leap to the normative that will upset many, that whatever happens 'in accordance with nature' is good. Grayling puts it this way: 'Consider the example of disease: to the good person disease is simply a natural occurrence, and as such something to be calmly accepted.'[46] We pick up this point again shortly.

5. So What?

'The whole world', said Rabbi Nachman of Braslav, 'is a very narrow bridge. And the main thing is not to be afraid'.

As an expression of our ontological vulnerability, we agree with this. Anyone who fails to see the precariousness of the extraordinary project that we call our life isn't seeing things properly. Unless everything else about us (and importantly our philosophy, out theology and our relationships) is expressly conditioned by the knowledge of its essential transience and imminent extinction, our philosophy, theology, and relationships will be wrong. That is the contention of the first part of this chapter.

The Rabbi could have noted something else. In his other writings he did. Although the bridge is narrow, by some mysterious physical law it gets less narrow the more people accompany you across it. All the great mystics have noticed that true maturity (which goes under many names, including Enlightenment and Realization), consists in one's acknowledgement of and intimate participation in the interrelatedness of things. When you wake up and realize that the boundary between you and the rest of the world is illusory, you'll have woken up for the first time since you were a child (when you instinctively knew it anyway).

That is the contention of the second part of this chapter.

Eastern philosophy has never forgotten that atomism is a naive, deadly fallacy. Western philosophy has not only forgotten it, but has made a virtue of the forgetting, and repudiation of the forgotten insights an axiom. Law, which is a conservative creature, has meekly followed where the philosophers lead.

Law ought to be about the business of human thriving. It should be the quest to answer the question: 'How can people be made as fully human as possible?' If it is doing that job properly, it will start from the right premises. We've suggested two of those premises: vulnerability and interrelatedness. Get those wrong, and however sophisticated and heavily footnoted the rest of your thesis, you'll get bad law. As we have.

These observations are true for every part of law. They are particularly obviously and intimately true for health law, because of its obvious and intimate connection with human thriving.

Unless we see that vulnerability is part of the business of being alive as a human, we will fear and stigmatize vulnerability. That's bad in itself, but it is widely repercussive, since it establishes as the yardstick of our legal and philosophical norms an entirely

46 A.C. Grayling, *What is Good? The Search for the Best Way to Live* (London: Phoenix, 2007) 60.

mythical creature—the disease-free, unageing, immutable, immortal man. He doesn't exist, and if he did he'd be very boring.

Unless we see that we are defined in terms of our relationships, the unit of our philosophical and legal currency will be an icily independent man (and he necessarily would be a *man*) who took no advice, shed no tears, and had neither friends nor influences. He doesn't exist either, and if he did, he'd be in some sort of secure unit.

What does this mean for our healthcare law? Many things. We highlight three of them here. First, we contend that there are some obvious consequences for healthcare resource allocation. Second, we call for an approach to confidentiality that more accurately reflects our 'leakiness'. And third, we argue for a similar liberality in relation to organ donation and, more generally the use that can be made of body parts and human tissue.

5.1 Making the 'leakiness' principle work: general considerations

Broadly, we contend that healthcare decision-making should be determined by an appropriately weighted audit of the effect of the proposed decision on the thriving of all the stakeholders (as opposed to the effect only on the patient).[47] This is a sort of utilitarian calculus, but the way in which 'thriving' is determined would bemuse the traditional utilitarian. It would acknowledge that a terminally ill person might be thriving, or that a gold-medal winning Olympic athlete was not.

More narrowly, it would mean that we would strive less to ensure that patients conformed to the illusory and delusional yardsticks. We would have less active, interventional healthcare, and (since we acknowledge that there is, for embodied creatures, a link between bodily integrity and true thriving) more education about how to avoid doctors altogether. We would encourage people to take control of themselves—a concomitant of which is that they bear the consequences of their decisions. That might mean more pain, but it would also mean more integrity. We'd outsource ourselves less, and so be more ourselves. Being ourselves is a necessary prerequisite of thriving. Only if I'm X can I enjoy the fruits of X's thriving. Most people engage almost from birth in a Faustian bargain with the world whereby we surrender our tastes to advertisers and our principles to pop philosophers. We'd outlaw TV and encourage whatever anarchy was needed to produce again a nation of shabby, happy, self-possessed mavericks. Such people live better and die better.

They also die more cheaply. That's a good thing for everyone.

5.2 Healthcare resource allocation

We would fund:

- Health education of all kinds.
- Obstetric services: these permit people to start running the human race—to start being persons. And birth is necessary for the creation of the family relationships which, at best, are excellent examples of the relationships which make humans what they are.
- Much existing paediatric care, for the same reasons as we'd support obstetric services. The death or disability of a child is an obscenity in a way that the death or disability of an adult is not.

[47] C. Foster, *Human Dignity in Bioethics and Law* (Oxford: Hart, 2011).

- Palliative care: although pain might be ennobling, we don't see it as kind to use the thumbscrews of biology to force people to confront and utter truths about themselves. There's a real distinction between mitigating the pains of terminal cancer with medication (a mitigation which would enable reflection, stock-taking, and the restoration of crucial relationships), and the pains of an osteoarthritic hip by way of a hip replacement. We can see no real distinction between much advanced surgical treatment (such as joint replacement) and enhancement. We oppose enhancement on the grounds that it is expressly designed to cause a person to be less themselves: the objective of proper medicine and the law that regulates medicine is to help people to be *more* themselves.

We acknowledge that cases can be made, using our principles, for the funding of other types of healthcare, but we choose to leave the list there. By doing so we hope to encourage questioning about what the point of medicine really is.

Debates about healthcare resource allocation are fraught because the attempt to introduce the governing ethical principles comes too late in the analysis. If one starts from the premise that all possible healthcare is in itself a good thing, one runs into nightmarish difficulties in deciding who should be entitled to this assumed 'good'. Our analysis avoids the political and legal difficulties inherent in the conventional analysis by introducing the relevant principles earlier. We do not indiscriminately brand all medical possibilities as 'good': on the contrary, some things that can be done to some people (and which they might actively desire), are not good at all. Redefine 'health' by reference to the way that humans actually are, rather than by reference to what the atomistic model says that they are, and the QALY (quality-adjusted life-year) is redundant.

One of the important facts about humans is that they die. The old Stoics saw as good that which is natural. It enabled them to look death squarely in the eye: it was not the dark spectre that modern medical technology seeks to exorcise with its mechanical ventilators and percutaneous endoscopic gastrostomies. For them, as for us, vitalism is an evil:. There is no place in their or our philosophy (or in any sane healthcare budget), for vitalism's denial of the basic biological fact of our always imminent extinction. Few modern doctors see themselves as vitalists. But, in their often obsessive concern with the preservation of life at all costs (whether emotional, financial, or otherwise), they're not so far away from the Vatican's most dogmatic.

Our neo-Stoicism takes us close to Sandel's famous 'giftedness',[48] but close too to some old Eastern ideas. They have always been Stoical there. In Japan, for instance, humans are regarded as part of nature. It is not the proper function of medicine (or of any other rightly conceived human venture) to seek to frustrate the natural. Ryuichi Ida observes:

> It should be remembered that oriental medicine does not stand on the same footing as Western medicine. Oriental medicine has as its basic principle the re-establishment of the balance of body and soul. All the diseases come from the imbalance of the patient. It is true that this type of medicine does not practice big operations, like organ transplants, or brain operations. Oriental medicine sees the conditions that might call for such interventions as natural, simply a consequence of human mortality, and it accordingly sees such a patient as entering a stage of returning to nature, ie dying.[49]

[48] M. Sandel, 'The Case Against Perfection' (2004) 293 *Atlantic Monthly* 51.

[49] R. Ida, 'Should We Improve Human Nature? An Interrogation from an Asian Perspective' in J. Savulescu and N. Bostrom (eds), *Human Enhancement* (Oxford: OUP, 2009) 65.

If vulnerability to death is a crucial part of the human condition, and thriving consists in embracing that condition, we won't necessarily want that heroic cardiac surgery. But on the other hand we might: our interrelatedness might mandate our survival. A woman with small children might well express the significance of her interrelatedness by feeling an obligation to stay alive for them. And her clinicians will be properly motivated if they are sensitive to those feelings.

Our comments later about confidentiality and organ donation/body parts are without prejudice to our contentions about the justification for epic medical or surgical intervention. It follows from the points we have just made that we would have some misgivings about, for instance, sophisticated organ transplantation procedures and some genetic manipulations (especially if those manipulations were personality-transforming).

5.3 Leaky humans, leaky confidences

Although many types of language are used to describe the law of confidentiality (rights, duties in tort/contract/quasi-contract, trusteeship, and so on), the picture the language seeks to describe is essentially one of an isolated individual who has a right to remain anonymous, unprobed, and undiscussed. True, 'his' right (or whatever it is) to confidentiality sometimes has to give way to the rights of others. The trumping power of society is embodied in cases such as *W v Egdell*[50] and, most clearly, in the fact that individual rights under Article 8(1) of the ECHR are subject to the wider societal considerations in Article 8(2). But the way that the juxtaposition of the individual and the society is described serves to underline the assumption that the individual is something distinct from society. They are in a stand-off: if one wins, the other loses.

We have already contended that this is factually wrong and, since getting facts right is rather important to ensuring a correct legal result, it is legally dangerous.

Consider the following facts: X has a child with a serious genetic condition. X's sister, Y, is trying to get pregnant. Z is a genetic counsellor, Both X and Y have sought advice from him. He therefore knows X's child's history, and hence that X carries the gene for the disability. Suppose that technology exists whereby that gene can be modified in an embryo so that the disability is avoided. The only way in which it can be discovered whether Y is a carrier of the same gene (and therefore the only way in which medicine could help to modify the gene) is if Y can be persuaded to have a highly specific test for the gene. The only thing that would make her have the test is knowledge that X's child is affected and that X is therefore a carrier. X, despite Z's best efforts, refuses to allow disclosure of that information.[51]

Is the information really X's/X's child's own?[52] All humans are intimately genetically related to one another (and fairly intimately genetically related to higher and not-so-high primates too). X and Y may share the gene because they shared parents. They drew their DNA from the same pool. We all share parents if one goes back a surprisingly few number of generations.

50 [1990] Ch 359.

51 Based on an example given by M. Parker and A.M. Lucassen, 'Talking About Paternity in the Genetic Clinic: Some Ethical Considerations' (2001) 357 *Lancet* 1033. See also A.M. Lucassen and M. Parker, 'Confidentiality and Serious Harm in Genetics—Preserving the Confidentiality of One Patient and Preventing Harm to Relatives' (2004) 12 *European Journal of Human Genetics* 93–7.

52 See also J. Herring, *Caring and the Law* (Oxford: Hart, 2013).

One can break through the impasse by simply wielding *Egdell* or Article 8, but is it not more satisfactory to say that the crucial information is held in a joint account? One might then argue about who should be the signatories to that account. We contend that it makes biological sense to say that everyone potentially should. It does not follow that all signatories should have equal access: there is a good deal to discuss there, and it might well be said that the devil is in the detail. But there is a better chance of the detail being right if the starting premises are correct.

5.4 Leaky skins and shared parts

John Moore famously objected to his spleen cells being used to create a cell line that proved to be of great financial value.[53] It is not clear whether he would have objected, or objected so passionately, if the cell line had not had such value. Perhaps he was really upset not so much at not being enriched himself, but at the enrichment of the cell line developers. But in any event both his (unsuccessful) submissions and the *ratio* of the case itself represent the same view of the relationship of individual and society that we saw when we looked at the law of confidentiality. The Human Tissue Act 2004 has the same philosophy at its heart: 'This is mine [or my relative's]. And we have a right to do with it what we please.' In the context of organ donation, whether one is in an opt-in or opt-out jurisdiction, the message is the same: 'My heart can be food for worms if I choose. My choice is supreme. No matter if the heart would have saved another. That other is other: there's only a connection between us if I say that there can be a connection. That connection can only be forged by a gift. I can give my heart because it is mine.'

If we are right, this is wrong. As we have argued elsewhere, acting altruistically is a necessary part of thriving.[54] This proposition can be justified in several ways—for instance as an axiom of virtue ethics[55] (and hence virtue jurisprudence)[56] or, (as has been our focus in this chapter) as a corollary of the basic biological and sociological fact of interconnectedness. It doesn't matter for present purposes if the thriving is really a consequence of mutual back-scratching reciprocal altruism, or whether it is normatively good in itself.

This means that John Moore would get no remedy other than a solatium to represent his outrage at his exploitation. It would be a small solatium, since he would have to give credit for the satisfaction that right-thinking hairy leukaemia sufferers would feel at the thought that their cells might benefit other people in the collective of which they are a part. Similarly, organ donation should be assumed to be a privilege that everyone who acknowledges properly their place in the collective should want.

Does this sound like medico-legal communism? It's not far off.

53 See *Moore v Regents of the University of California* 793 P 2d 479 (Cal 1990).

54 J.J.W. Herring and C. Foster, 'Welfare Means Relationality, Virtue and Altruism' (2012) *Legal Studies* 480.

55 See, for instance, G. Anscombe, *Intention* (Oxford: Basil Blackwell, 1957); M. Nussbaum, 'Non-relative Virtues: an Aristotelean Approach' in M. Nussbaum and A. Sen (eds), *The Quality of Life* (New York: OUP, 1993).

56 See C. Farrelly and L. Solum (eds), *Virtue Jurisprudence* (London: Palgrave Macmillan, 2008); C. Cimino 'Private Law, Public Consequence and Virtue Jurisprudence' (2010) 71 *University of Pittsburgh Law Review* 279.

6. Conclusion

The top five NHS tips for health are: sleep more; drink milk; eat more fruit and vegetables; try new activities; and eat a hearty breakfast (ideally porridge). How sad. You cannot hug yourself. A lithe body can encase a dreary, sad soul. Health involves accepting our vulnerability and our changing bodies—bodies that are exhilaratingly different from other bodies, yet interact meaningfully with them.

2

Pathways Towards a Framework Convention on Global Health

Political Mobilization for the Human Right to Health

Kent Buse, Lawrence O. Gostin, and Eric A. Friedman

1. Decade of Global Health: Progress Marred by Persistent Inequalities

The 'Decade of Global Health'[1] brought major progress in reducing premature death. Maternal deaths fell to 287,000 in 2010 from 546,000 in 1990.[2] Child deaths decreased by 5 million during the same time period, from 12 million to 6.9 million.[3] Where a decade ago only 50,000 Africans received treatment for AIDS, by 2010, more than 5 million were on life-saving drug regimens.[4] Globally, antiretroviral therapy (ART) has added an estimated 14 million life-years in low- and middle-income countries globally since 1995—more than 9 million of these in sub-Saharan Africa. The trajectory and magnitude of these changes mean millions of lives saved, a tremendous testament to what committed communities working through social movements with the support of global solidarity can achieve.

Despite progress, much more needs to be done to bend the arc of history, to borrow a phrase from Martin Luther King. For behind these welcome headlines is the all too familiar news of the lives lost—the 7 million children, the more than a quarter-million women dying from causes related to pregnancy or child birth. Fully 66 percent of the 28.6 million people eligible for HIV treatment still lacked access to it in 2013.[5] The vast majority of these lives could be saved. And representing an unconscionable injustice, nearly all of these premature deaths occur in developing countries. To live in a poor society—or to be poor in a rich one—or to be marginalized or discriminated

[1] M. Dybul, P. Piot, and J. Frenk, 'Reshaping Global Health' (1 June 2012) 173 *Policy Review*, available at <http://www.hoover.org/publications/policy-review/article/118116>.

[2] World Health Organization, UNICEF, UNFPA and World Bank, 'Trends in Maternal Mortality: 1990 to 2010' (Geneva: WHO, 2012) 19, available at <http://whqlibdoc.who.int/publications/2012/9789241503631_eng.pdf>.

[3] UNICEF, World Health Organization, World Bank, and United Nations, 'Levels and Trends in Child Mortality, Report 2012, Estimates Developed by the UN Inter-agency Group for Child Mortality Estimation' (New York: UNICEF, 2012) 10, available at <http://www.unicef.org/media/files/UNICEF_2012_IGME_child_mortality_report.pdf>.

[4] World Health Organization, UNAIDS, and UNICEF, 'Global HIV/AIDS response: Epidemic update and health sector progress towards universal access, progress report 2011' (Geneva: WHO, 2011) 89, available at <http://whqlibdoc.who.int/publications/2011/9789241502986_eng.pdf>.

[5] UNAIDS, 'AIDS by the Numbers' (Geneva, 2013) 6, available at <http://www.unaids.org/en/media/unaids/contentassets/documents/unaidspublication/2013/JC2571_AIDS_by_the_numbers_en.pdf>. World Health Organization, 'HIV treatment reaching 6.6 million people, but majority still in need' News release of 3 June 2011, available at <http://www.who.int/mediacentre/news/releases/2011/hivtreatement_20110603/en/index.html>.

against on the basis of gender, sexual orientation, or drug use, for example, is to be much more likely to suffer from poor health and early death,[6] even as health is an equally and universally shared right.

The burden of non-communicable diseases (NCDs), and the proportion of the burden in developing countries, will grow.[7] These diseases will interact with the existing health challenges in these settings, creating the 'double burden' of, for example, hunger sitting beside obesity. The intersection of infectious and non-communicable diseases is mutually reinforcing in resource-poor settings. Pathogens cause one in six cancers worldwide, with infections being almost five times more likely to be responsible for cancer in Africa than in high-income countries (33 percent compared to 7 percent).[8] A growing and disproportionate burden of morbidity and mortality is traffic-related—a consequence of unpaved roads, jam-packed and old vehicles, and lack of enforcement of traffic safety rules. People in developing countries suffer 91 percent of traffic fatalities even though only 48 percent of the world's registered vehicles travel their roads.[9] Similarly, more than 90 percent of deaths from unintentional injuries occur in developing countries.[10]

Climate change, too, is taking its toll, responsible for at least 140,000 deaths in 2004, and according to perhaps the most comprehensive research on the health impacts of climate change, likely to be responsible for more than double this number annually.[11] Again it is the poorest—who live in makeshift housing most likely to collapse in storms, whose livelihoods hinge on fresh water that is now turning salty, who have no air-conditioning to protect them from heat waves—who suffer most.

These, and many other global health inequities cannot overshadow the equally vast domestic disparities. At the close of the 1990s, the under-5 mortality rate was nearly 150 deaths per 1,000 children for Indians in the poorest quintile and less than fifty in the richest.[12] At the extremes, the disparities are even more pronounced. Also in the late 1990s, under-5 mortality rates in Nairobi ranged from 254 in one slum area to less than fifteen in a high-income area of the city.[13] Similarly, as the Commission on Social

6 R.G. Wilkinson and K.E. Pickett, 'Income Inequality and Socioeconomic Gradients in Mortality' (April 2008) 98(4) *American Journal of Public Health* 699.

7 See <http://www.who.int/mental_health/management/depression/definition/en> (accessed 6 February 2012).

8 G. Danaei, 'Global Burden of Infection-Related Cancer Revisited' (June 2012) 13(6) *Lancet Oncology* 564.

9 World Health Organization, 'Global Status Report on Road Safety: Time for Action' (Geneva, 2009). The cited statistics are based primarily on data from 2007.

10 R. Norton et al, 'Unintentional Injuries' in D.T. Jamison et al (eds), *Disease Control Priorities in Developing Countries* (Washington, DC: World Bank, 2006) 737.

11 World Health Organization, 'Climate Change and Health': Fact Sheet No 266 (Geneva: WHO, 2010), available at <http://www.who.int/mediacentre/factsheets/fs266/en/index.html>. Global Humanitarian Forum Geneva, 'Human Impact Report: Climate Change—The Anatomy of a Silent Crisis' (Geneva, 2009), available at <http://www.eird.org/publicaciones/humanimpactreport.pdf>. J. Vidal, 'Global Warming Causes 300,000 Deaths a Year, Says Kofi Annan Thinktank', *The Guardian*, 29 May 2009, available at <http://www.guardian.co.uk/environment/2009/may/29/1> (accessed 6 February 2012).

12 Commission on Social Determinants of Health, 'Closing the Gap in a Generation: Health Equity Through Action on the Social Determinants of Health', Final Report of the Commission on Social Determinants of Health (Geneva: WHO, 2008), available at <http://whqlibdoc.who.int/publications/2008/9789241563703_eng.pdf>.

13 N. MacFarquhar, 'Wider Disparity in Life Expectancy is Found Between Rich and Poor', *New York Times*, 17 October 2008, available at <http://www.nytimes.com/2008/10/17/world/17briefs-WIDERDISPARI_BRF.html>; World Health Organization, '2008 World Health Report: Primary Health Care (Now More Than Ever)' (Geneva, 2008), available at <http://www.who.int/whr/2008/en/index.html>; African Population and Health Research Center, 'Population and Health Dynamics

Determinants of Health reported, life expectancy in Glasgow, Scotland, ranges from 52 years in a deprived neighborhood to 82 years in a well-off one.[14] Life expectancy for Native Americans in the Pine Ridge Indian Reservation in South Dakota is in the upper 40s.[15]

From child and maternal mortality and death due to AIDS to diabetes and the effects of climate change, neither the present burden nor the inequities—between and within countries, between privileged and marginalized populations and along a social gradient—are inevitable. The interventions are well known. They include ensuring everyone enjoys the basic underlying determinants of health, such as clean water and nourishing food, hygiene and sanitation, the benefits of proven public health strategies in such areas as tobacco reduction and vector control, and high quality and equitable health systems.

Beyond these highly effective health interventions is the more complex set of social interventions to reduce inequalities throughout societies. These interventions include: (1) improving living conditions; (2) tackling the inequitable distribution of power, money, and resources; and (3) measuring and understanding inequity and assessing the impact of actions to address it. Reducing socio-economic disparities could further reduce the health gap and transform global health.[16] From reductions of internal disparities in Brazil[17] to countries that have far exceeded global progress on reducing maternal and child mortality,[18] improvements in health and health equity on a national scale exist, demonstrating what is possible.

Given the potential to dramatically reduce the global burden of ill-health and early death and reduce global and domestic inequalities in health, the failure to address these inequities is unconscionable and has dire consequences. By one measure, comparing life expectancy in high-income countries to that in low-and middle-income countries, health inequalities have cost close to 20 million deaths each year from 1990 through 2008. That is one in three deaths globally.[19]

2. The Joint Action and Learning Initiative on National and Global Responsibilities for Health

Faced with these clashing realities of progress and potential on the one hand and inequalities and injustice on the other, a coalition formed to promote a legally binding global agreement, a Framework Convention on Global Health (FCGH). Such a treaty could forge a pathway towards global health justice.

in Nairobi's Informal Settlements' (Nairobi, 2002), available at <http://www.aphrc.org/insidepage/page.php?app=downloads&articleid=285>.

14 Commission on Social Determinants of Health, 'Closing the Gap in a Generation' (n 12).

15 N.D. Kristof, 'Poverty's Poster Child', *New York Times*, 10 May 2012, available at <http://www.nytimes.com/2012/05/10/opinion/kristof-povertys-poster-child.html>.

16 Commission on Social Determinants of Health, 'Closing the Gap in a Generation' (n 12).

17 Z.A. Bhutta et al, 'Countdown to 2015 Decade Report (2000–10): Taking Stock of Maternal, Newborn, and Child Survival' (2010) 375 *Lancet* 2032, 2040.

18 World Health Organization and UNICEF, 'Countdown to 2015: Maternal, Newborn and Child Survival: Building a Future for Women and Children. The 2012 Report' (Washington, DC, 2012) 14–16, available at <http://www.countdown2015mnch.org/documents/2012Report/2012-complete-no-profiles.pdf>.

19 J. Garay, 'Global health (GH)=GH equity=GH Justice=Global Social Justice: The Opportunities of Joining EU and US Forces Together' (Winter 2012) *Newsletter of the European Union of Excellence at the University of California, Berkeley*, available at <http://eucenter.berkeley.edu/newsletter/winter12/garay>.

The global initiative—the Joint Action and Learning Initiative on National and Global Responsibilities for Health (JALI)—posed several questions that capture the major conditions required for good health, the responsibility for ensuring these conditions, and the national and global norms, structures, and processes needed to realize these conditions.[20]

These questions, as well as their answers, are organized around a human rights approach to health. Human rights offer a legally binding framework that has received universal support. These rights encompass the right to the highest attainable standard of physical and mental health ('right to health'), which is driven by the same concerns of equity and equal human dignity that underlie global health justice. JALI is organizing a global research network to address a plethora of issues related to a progressive vision of the right to health, including the specific content of the FCGH. Considered broadly, these issues are all elements of the following four critical questions.

2.1 What are the services and goods guaranteed to every person under the human right to health?

A central challenge is to specify the essential health services and goods that make up the right to health. Answers would guide national efforts to provide universal health. The right to health framework militates against a narrow definition of 'key' services. Rather, the essential services and goods should encompass: (1) *health systems and services*—quality-assured, affordable, accessible, and equitable health systems and services across the lifespan; (2) *essential vaccines and medicines*—universal access to cost-effective vaccines and medicines to prevent and treat all illness and disease, as well as pain relief; and (3) *fundamental human needs*—public health measures and the underlying determinants of health, which are vital to maintaining good health. These include sanitation and sewage, vector control, clean air, potable water, diet and nutrition (neither under- nor over-nutrition), and tobacco and alcohol reduction.[21]

2.2 What responsibilities do states have for the health of the populations residing in their jurisdiction?

States hold primary responsibility for upholding the right to health for their inhabitants. This requires states, within their capacity, to provide the funding for and the delivery of all the essential goods and services guaranteed to every human being and progressively to achieve the highest attainable standard of health. The state's duties include at least providing adequate health resources within its capacity. Although a fair standard will have to be agreed upon, African Heads of State pledged, in the 2001 Abuja Declaration, to commit at least 15 percent of their government budgets to the health sector[22]—a pledge reaffirmed at their 2010 summit.[23] This is an important

20 L.O. Gostin et al, 'The Joint Action and Learning Initiative: Towards a Global Agreement on National and Global Responsibilities for Health' (2011) 8 *Plos Medicine* 5, available at <http://www.plosmedicine.org/article/info%3Adoi%2F10.1371%2Fjournal.pmed.1001031>.

21 L. O. Gostin, 'Meeting the Survival Needs of the World's Least Healthy People: A Proposed Model for Global Health Governance' (2007) 298 *Journal of the American Medical Association* 225.

22 Organization of the African Union, 'Abuja Declaration on HIV/AIDS, Tuberculosis and Other Related Infectious Diseases', Organization of the African Union Doc OAU/SPS/ABUJA/3, 24–27 April 2001.

23 Organization of the African Union, 'Actions on Maternal, Newborn and Child Health and Development in Africa by 2015', Organization of the African Union Assembly/AU/Decl.1 (XV), 25–27 July 2010.

starting point for determining a proper standard, which would need to encompass funding as well for those underlying determinants of health not funded through the health sector. Public officials who exercise authority over resources and make policy also have a duty of *stewardship*—a responsibility to act in the interests of those they serve. Sound governance is *honest*, in that it is avoids corruption. It is *transparent*, in that institutional processes and decision-making are open and comprehensible to the people. It is *deliberative*, in that government engages stakeholders and the public in a meaningful way. Good governance is also *accountable*, in that leaders give reasons for decisions and assume responsibility for successes or failures. Good governance enables states to formulate and implement sound policies, manage resources efficiently, and provide effective services.

2.3 What duties do states owe to people beyond their borders in securing the right to health?

The duty of states is not limited to caring for all their residents, but extends to fostering a functioning, inter-dependent global community, in which everyone recognizes that good health and survival is a matter of common concern. This responsibility includes—but goes far beyond—containing health threats that endanger other countries and regions. It is imperative to find innovative ways of holding states accountable for a certain level of international assistance, as agreed in the International Covenant on Economic, Social and Cultural Rights.

The Commission on Macroeconomics and Health calculated that affluent states would need to devote approximately 0.1 percent of Gross National Income (GNI) to international development assistance for health, while other estimates suggest more is needed,[24] and again additional funding beyond the health sector. Yet in 2008, Official Development Assistance (ODA) for health care from traditional donor countries was slightly below 0.05 percent of GNI, or less than half of what is required by this measure.[25]

International health financing, moreover, remains short-term, conditional, and too often siloed into discrete programs or diseases, with funding that is volatile and unreliable. The short-term nature of assistance makes states reluctant to invest it in recurrent costs, creating an obstacle to overcoming one of the major health constraints many low- and middle-income countries face—the severe shortages of health workers.

Financial assistance that is not based on mutual responsibility, and is unreliable in the long run, is an inefficient expenditure of resources, as it is limited in its ability to improve the provision of health-related goods and services. This alone should be

24 MDG Africa Steering Group, 'Achieving the Millennium Development Goals in Africa: Recommendations of the MDG Africa Steering Group, June 2008' (UN, 2008), available at <http://www.mdgafrica.org/pdf/MDG%20Africa%20Steering%20Group%20Recommendations%20-%20English%20-%20HighRes.pdf>.

25 Official development assistance for health was $18.7bn in 2008, excluding water and sanitation, which were not part of the estimate from the Commission on Macroeconomics and Health. Total official development assistance in 2008 was $119.8bn and represented 0.30% of the GNI of members of the OECD's Development Assistance Committee. Thus, the $18.7 billion for health care was approximately 0.047% of GNI for these countries. For further information see: Organization for Economic Cooperation and Development (OECD), 'Development Aid at its Highest Level Ever in 2008', available at <http://www.oecd.org/document/35/0,3343,en_2649_34447_42458595_1_1_1_1,00.html> (accessed 25 June 2012); and J. Kates et al, *Donor Funding for Health in Low- & Middle Income Countries, 2001–2008* (Washington, DC: Kaiser Family Foundation, 2010), available at <http://www.kff.org/globalhealth/7679.cfm> (accessed 25 June 2012).

sufficient reason to consider a global agreement on norms that clarify the national and global responsibilities for health, transforming ineffective short-term financial assistance into effective sustained funding.

2.4 What kinds of global governance for health are needed to ensure that all states live up to their mutual responsibilities?

The preliminary answers to the questions in the heading of this section should be sufficient to convey that better global governance for health is needed. The paradigm shift to genuine shared responsibility and global solidarity for global health that is grounded in the right to health will require more than an agreed-upon set of responsibilities and principles. It will also require constructing a more forceful, purposeful, efficient, and accountable set of institutions and arrangements.

A global governance structure that can at last make 'health-for-all' a reality will have to successfully address critical dysfunctions that exist within the global health landscape, including:[26] (1) *the lack of global health leadership* to mobilize, coordinate, and focus a large and diverse set of actors around a clear mission, common objectives, effective approaches, sustained action, and mutual accountability—all areas in which the WHO has been found to be deficient;[27] (2) *the need to harness the creativity, energy, and resources of diverse actors for global health*, particularly the imperative of engaging civil society, with its ability to reach and represent disadvantaged populations, advocate, and hold governments accountable; (3) *the lack of collaboration and coordination among multiple players*—today's global health landscape is marked by 'fragmentation' and 'duplication', with a proliferation of actors, in a tangled web of initiatives and programs; (4) *the need for accountability, transparency, monitoring, and enforcement*—although it is changing, the global health field is marked by a paucity of detailed targets and concrete plans to achieve them, along with an overall lack of accountability; and (5) *the need to engage multiple sectors and regimes*—national and global health cannot be achieved by health systems and services alone, so it is vital to engage with all of the key drivers of a healthy or unhealthy population, such as agriculture, energy, industry, trade, and the environment.

Mutual responsibilities can be expected to deliver reciprocal benefits. The global South would benefit from increased respect for its strategies; greater and more predictable funding from more accountable development partners; reform of international regimes that harm health, such as trade and agriculture; and improved health for its populations—leading to enhanced personal security and dignity as well as to enhanced economic productivity and social stability. The global North would benefit from greater confidence that development assistance is spent effectively; the prospect of reduced financing over time, as host countries build sustainable health systems; and better protection from global public health threats for their own populations. Developed and emerging countries would also acquire the diplomatic benefits that would come from enhancing their role in improving global health. All would benefit from lessons on successfully addressing shared health challenges and from the economic,

[26] L.O. Gostin and E.A. Mok, 'Grand Challenges in Global Health Governance' (2009) 90 *British Medical Record* 7–18; D. Sridhar, 'Seven Challenges in International Development Assistance for Health and Ways Forward' (2010) 38(3) *Journal of Law, Medicine and Ethics* 459.

[27] Department for International Development, 'Multilateral Aid Review: Ensuring Maximum Value for Money for UK Aid through Multilateral Organizations' (March 2011), available at <https://s3-eu-west-1.amazonaws.com/media.dfid.gov.uk/multilateral_aid_review_full_linked.pdf>.

educational, environmental, and security benefits that come from improved global health. And all would experience a sense of shared satisfaction from participating in a historic venture to make unprecedented progress towards global health equity.

JALI aims to harness the power of civil society and emerging powers to create change even as it contributes to an FCGH. Among other things, JALI is engaging advocates, academics, and practitioners to forge a common understanding of the critical global health challenges described previously—generating analysis that will clarify and enforce the right to health, and sharing lessons on effective strategies. Recognizing the importance of expanding its base of support, JALI catalyzed the formation of an inclusive global Platform for an FCGH, which will be open to all, from civil society advocates to governments. The Platform will build a more united and stronger social movement around the right to health to support networking and mutual support among civil society organizations. Late in 2013, JALI and initial members of the Platform for an FCGH launched a consultation process on a Framework for an FCGH,[28] which outlines the need for the framework convention and the key principles underlying it (see Box 2.1 for the key principles). Now is the time for strategic thinking on how to harness collective action to move forward to a Convention that can crystallize thinking and responsibilities for global health, as the world considers responsibilities and approaches to sustainable development post-MDGs in 2015.

JALI's goal is to reveal in vivid detail the yet untapped potential of human rights to redress the dire state of global health today, including through an FCGH. Above all, innovations in global governance for health are necessary to bring an end to stubbornly persistent health inequalities based on the happenstance of one's birth.

Box 2.1 Key Principles of a Framework Convention on Global Health (as of February 2014)

The . . . shortcomings [with respect to global health] create a risk of that health inequities will persist, with health underclasses forming, from impoverished and marginalized populations to the whole populations in the most fragile countries. Yet with great failings come great opportunities for change, through a renewed and reinforced commitment to health and other human rights.

Building on international treaties, national constitutions, civil society proclamations, and global declarations and other key instruments and commitments, grounded in the right to health and aimed at closing health inequities, and in the spirit of global solidarity, an FCGH should:

[Universal] Equitable health systems

a) Set standards for all countries to achieve [universal] equitable health systems to meet the physical and mental health needs of the whole population. Such health systems should:
 i) Be based upon robust standards for health systems and a comprehensive core of health services to which all people are immediately entitled, expeditiously building

(*continued*)

[28] 'Platform for a Campaign for a Framework Convention on Global Health', Draft, 12 December 2013, available at <http://www.jalihealth.org/documents/Framework.pdf,> (accessed 1 February 2014).

Box 2.1 (Continued)

towards [universal] equitable health systems, ones that serve people of all socio-economic and other statuses and comprehensively meet the health needs of the whole population. Such systems should avoid access to health services or facilities that differs based on ability to pay, but instead incorporate policies to enable marginalized and vulnerable populations to fully benefit.

ii) Aim to achieve equality through equity, recognizing that the right to health should enable all people in all countries to receive high quality health care and eliminate avoidable health disparities. Policies and strategies should promote human rights, human security, and address health inequities across the social gradient, with the greatest focus on people subject to the greatest inequities.

iii) Provide health care across the life course and continuum of care, including health promotion and disease prevention, care (including palliative), treatment, rehabilitation, and support services (including for people with disabilities), while ensuring integrated care, gender perspectives (both women and men), non-discrimination and equal access, accountability, participation, and other elements of a human rights approach to health systems.

iv) Be developed through equitable processes at local and national levels that promote social justice and empowerment; build on local knowledge, priorities, and processes, and; include informed participation of civil society and marginalized and affected populations.

v) Encompass public health services, including safe water, hygiene promotion, education, and supplies, sanitation, safe and nutritious food, housing, tobacco and vector control, alcohol and pollution reduction, and injury prevention, recognizing the joint roles and responsibilities of health and other sectors.

vi) Reduce the need for out-of-pockets payments on health and ensure that no one is impoverished by, or experiences catastrophic, health spending.

vii) Ensure access to medicines, health facilities, and equitably distributed, skilled, motivated, fairly compensated, and supported health workers with safe working conditions and who follow proper treatment protocols.

viii) Extend to areas of conflict and insecurity [, including through the necessary negotiation, international support, health worker incentives, and security measures].

ix) Protect patients' rights, including to safe health care, informed consent, confidentiality, and respectful treatment, and ensure sexual and reproductive health services and rights.

b) Empower governments to regulate corporate health actors based on evidence from health systems that are equitable, effective, efficient, and universal, with characteristics including removal of financial barriers, mandatory prepayment into financing mechanisms, large [where possible, national,] risk pools, and government financing, at least for people unable to afford full coverage.

Social determinants of health

c) Establish principles and [the mandate for health and other sectors to collaborate in establishing] standards to promote the positive determinants of health[, such as education and housing].

d) Effectuate Health in All Policies and policy coherence for health, such as through right to health assessments, comprehensive multi-sector public health strategies, and inter-sector and inter-country dialogue, while ensuring that policies of trade, energy, immigration, agriculture, transportation, the economy, and other sectors do not undermine the right to health.

e) Require needs-based planning and budgeting for determinants of health, developed through equitable and inclusive processes where all parts of the population can identify needs and solutions.

f) Ensure safe and healthy workplaces for all workers, without discrimination.

g) Regulate unhealthy products and practices of private actors that undermine health.

Funding for [universal] equitable health systems and the social determinants of health

h) Establish a national and global health financing framework with clearly delineated responsibilities that raises sufficient resources to achieve equitable and effective health systems, including public health services.

i) Raise additional resources for health through:
   i) Fair, progressive, effective, and transparent taxation and innovative forms of tax, such as on financial transactions, tobacco products, alcohol, unhealthy foods, and environmentally damaging processes.
   ii) Ensuring public benefit from, and transparent and accountable use of, state revenue from natural resources.
   iii) Increased global financing through increased state funding and innovative approaches.
   iv) Innovation and expansion in domestic financing for health including harnessing pooled funds and reducing out-of-pocket and other retrogressive forms of payment for health care services.
   v) Protecting resources for health through transparency and combating corruption, illicit financial transfers, tax havens, and misuse of public resources.

j) Equitably distribute financing within countries, including ensuring needed resources for underserved and marginalized communities and populations.

Human rights

k) Define state responsibilities for the health of all its inhabitants, on an equal basis, regardless of nationality, gender, race, age, sexual orientation, or socioeconomic, migration, disability, disease, or other status, and to promote equality through equity, ensuring equal access to quality and responsive health services, including by removing financial barriers and ensuring physical accessibility and dignified treatment of all patients.

l) Empower people to claim the right to health and other rights, including through effective enforcement and collective remedies; build capacities to realize this right among all stakeholders and sectors, including for the public, civil society, communities, and the media to hold governments to account; educate health workers, legal and judicial personnel, and government officials on the right to health and other human rights; require health accountability strategies at all levels, and; ensure community and civil society participation in all stages of health decision-making.

m) Ensure mechanisms to remedy individual and systematic violations of the right to health and the determinants of health, from legal procedures to structured community engagement, regular reporting on obstacles to implementing the right to health and these determinants, and plans of action to overcome these obstacles.

n) Affirm and ensure the immediate enforceability, including judicial enforcement, of the right to health in all states, including the obligations and understandings of the right

(*continued*)

Box 2.1 (Continued)

contained in the FCGH; create greater precision of the right's requirements, and; codify its principles.

o) Ensure respect for the right to health to protect against direct and indirect threats to health.

p) Define the responsibilities of states to the health of people beyond their borders, [as well as responsibilities of other entities,] including through sufficient funding, adequate investment in health research and development, and not harming the health of people in other countries (for example, as a result of pollution and climate change, impeding access to medicine, or actively recruiting health workers from countries facing shortages or agreeing to or engaging in other harmful trade in health services).

q) Remove all discrimination—both purposeful and in effect, both in law and in fact—and other barriers in law, policy, and practice that undermine the right to health; respond to specific health needs of women and other populations that are marginalized or have special needs, and; respond to gender-based violence.

r) Protect the rights of health workers and individuals seeking care in situations of conflict and insecurity, including providing access to care to all in need regardless of political or other affiliation, ensuring their security and unimpeded movement, and refraining from attacking or interfering with people seeking care and health personnel, facilities, and transport. States' right to health obligations continue during times of conflict and insecurity.

s) Strengthen global leadership on the right to health, including that of WHO.

Global governance for health

t) Empower WHO to effectively achieve its mandate of global health leadership.

u) Improve international health assistance harmonization and alignment with national health strategies and ensure that external funds contribute to health systems strengthening, country ownership, effective local and national governance, and mutual accountability.

v) Facilitate sharing lessons and evidence for implementing policies on effective approaches to improve health and health equity.

w) Enhance accountability for existing regional and global health frameworks.

Compliance with the FCGH

Ensure accountability including through timelines, indicators, benchmarks, and targets; rigorous reporting, monitoring, and evaluation including regular reporting on implementation and compliance, along with recommendations to state parties on specific actions to improve implementation and compliance; community participation in treaty monitoring; inclusive platforms that engage governments and other stakeholders to transparently implement actions to remedy non-compliance with provisions of the FCGH, and; effective incentives and sanctions. These might include an international mechanism for individual and groups to bring claims under the FCGH, peer review, citizen-based monitoring of adherence to FCGH obligations...

3. The Arduous Pathway for a Framework Convention: Strong Resistance Lies Ahead

Powerful vested interests are likely to vigorously contest the Framework Convention on Global Health, arguing that it is too ambitious and politically fraught. The Convention challenges long-held values and ideologies, with its transformational mission and binding norms. Critics may protest that it makes excessive claims on the state, with its significant redistributive aims, threatening powerful economic interests and the status quo. Practically speaking, it calls for changes to taxation, public sector priority setting, and resource allocation, curbing private sector actions as well as reforming development cooperation.

As a result, critics portray a Framework Convention as unrealistic and utopian—or, even worse, fiscally reckless in an era marked by 'the logic of austerity and the mantra of scarcity'. For ideological or self-interested reasons, some impugn the Framework for introducing 'socialism by stealth' or interfering in private affairs, fearful that it will diminish private sector wealth creation and foster a 'nanny-state'.

Critics will challenge the Framework's feasibility to define where the state's role ends and where personal responsibility begins, as well as what constitutes essential health services—both preventative and therapeutic. They will argue that the Framework blurs the boundaries between individual choice, agency, and personal responsibility for health and those factors that are structural and social in nature (for example gender, wealth, income inequality). This is so despite JALI's clear framing of the global health challenge as socio-economic as well as political, rather than a matter of personal responsibility and individual choice—a view firmly supported by the evidence.[29]

Although JALI aspires to model a truly global north-south partnership, ultimately driven by citizens of the global South, there may be challenges from the G77 countries—levelling charges of foreign interference and unwarranted intrusion on national sovereignty; an unwelcome cultural assault on traditional values as part of a western-liberal project. Some question why yet another treaty is required, given that the right to health is already enshrined in international law. And others may argue that treaties extend international responsibilities beyond reason or undermine national obligations.

The suggestion that the WHO should use its treaty-making authority for the Convention is likely to be questioned too, as the resource-strapped Organization should not assume another unfunded mandate; or that the Organization ought to be using existing resources to support Member States to meet existing obligations and priorities instead of creating new ones. Indeed, JALI itself has struggled with the decision of whether to strengthen the WHO by placing it at the centre of the FCGH or whether, given the multi-sectoral nature of such a treaty, the United Nations should adopt the Convention.

These are the daunting challenges demonstrating that the path to a Convention will not be an easy one. The Convention's ultimate adoption will be arduous and politically laden. What is certain is that the idea, and its movement, is changing the global discourse, bringing out great champions while also giving rise to a stinging backlash from entrenched interests.

[29] Commission on Social Determinants of Health, 'Closing the Gap in a Generation' (n 12).

4. Public Health and International Law: The Role of Transnational Advocacy Coalitions

Tensions, challenges, and opposition will inevitably surface as progressive public health goals are pursued through an instrument of international affairs. Indeed conflict has marked previous efforts with related, if different, ends—including the Framework Convention on Tobacco Control (FCTC), the Convention on the Rights of Persons with Disabilities, the Convention on the Prohibition of the Use, Stockpiling, Production and Transfer of Anti-Personnel Mines and on Their Destruction (Mine Ban Treaty) and the Agreement on 'TRIPS flexibilities'—particularly in the context of access to AIDS medicine. Even international 'soft law' codes and declarations, which carry many of the hallmarks of international law and human rights, have also incited political controversy, such as the International Code of Marketing of Breast-milk Substitutes and the UN Political Declarations on HIV/AIDS.[30]

All of these treaty and related processes have been marked by considerable contestation between blocs of Member States—often reflecting underlying struggles between coalitions of health and rights advocates and consumer groups on the one hand and industry and industry-related groups on the other. One can see these conflicts playing out in the geo-strategic power tensions between the traditional powers (for example Australia, Western Europe, and North America) and rapidly emerging powers (for example Brazil, China, India, Indonesia, Russia, and South Africa) in international negotiations on the treaties. While the outcomes of these treaties may not wholly reflect the aims of their progressive advocates, their very existence and relative successes have been a function of effective mobilization of broad social movements, often organized in transnational advocacy coalitions, which have been active over many years, preceding formal negotiations. These successes reflect the wider involvement of civil society in modern intergovernmental processes—involvement that, according to the United Nations, has become a 'key factor influencing intergovernmental and governmental priorities and actions . . . and is essential for effective action on global priorities'.[31]

The most critical force to achieve the dream of an FCGH and global health justice for all will be social movements that demand it. Here, the process of determining the content of the treaty is integrally related to developing a strong treaty, securing ratification, and ensuring compliance. While JALI, other FCGH Platform members, and other members of the global health community have outlined some central aspects of an FCGH around which health leaders, and civil society, are beginning to rally (see Box at the end of section 2.4), the contents must ultimately emerge chiefly from the communities with the most direct stake in the success of the treaty, and from civil society organizations working to advance the public's right to health.

The Convention must respond to people's perceived health needs, to how their right to health is being undermined, and to their demands. Only then will sufficient numbers of people be willing not only to support a treaty, but also to fight for it, and for its full implementation.

30 These Declarations have the hallmarks of international law—typically adopted with very few reservations and exceptional country reporting on implementation (186 out of 193 UN Member States in 2012).

31 United Nations, 'We the People: Civil Society, the UN and Global Governance: Report of the panel of immanent persons' (June 2004).

This link to communities and civil society will, in turn, require that FCGH Platform partners mobilize diverse social movements behind a Framework. The AIDS movement, maternal and child health advocates, those who are working on clean water and the right to food, labor and environmental movements, right to health campaigns—the support of these and more will be needed to overcome the resistance that a treaty with significant financial implications, that seeks to empower the dispossessed, is sure to face.

Successful collective action is by its nature highly dynamic. Past experience points to a range of strategies and tactics that can be considered and adapted to respond to evolving contexts. Indeed, the successful outcome of collective action in the intergovernment sphere demands continued mobilization long after any convention is ratified and enters into force because of the ongoing need to enable citizens to understand and claim their rights and hold countries accountable for becoming compliant with the treaty and its implementation.

The coalition for an FCGH will need to influence what is ultimately an intergovernmental process (as governmental negotiation is how international treaty law comes about). Hence its strategies need to focus on the various constituent parts that make up that process. This means working simultaneously at national, regional, and international levels to reinforce and amplify efforts at all three levels—what Keck and Sikkink refer to as a boomerang approach in international politics.[32] It also means linking the realities of the health experience and aspiration of communities to politics at the national level to negotiations at the international level. This is the glue that global advocacy coalitions can provide in connecting social movements and networks at each of these levels. Experience suggests that success depends on linkages from above and below, but that the real drivers of change need to be national actors with deep roots in their societies who require support from the international community to achieve their aims of health for all.[33] As the proposed Framework Convention seeks redress to health inequities in and among low-, middle- and upper-income countries, the scope of this project is truly universal.

This chapter now turns to look at some of the features that have marked effective coalitions for lessons they offer to the looming struggle for an FCGH.

5. Fomenting Change: The Role of Interests, Ideas, and Institutions

Using a conceptual framework borrowed from the policy sciences literature[34]—one which explains that policy change comes about through the on-going interactions among 'interests', 'ideas', and 'institutions'—this chapter considers how developments in each of these three streams may influence the kinds of strategies an FCGH Platform and the movements it fosters, supports, and allies itself with may adapt and adopt to influence any future intergovernmental negotiations on a Convention. There is no simple cookie-cutter strategy to achieving an effective and progressive FCGH, as what will be required will need to be tailored to engage and shape the interests, ideas, and institutions mobilized in support and opposition of the initiative.

[32] M.E. Keck and K. Sikkink, 'Transnational Advocacy Networks in International and Regional Politics' (March 1999) 51(159) *International Social Science Journal* 89.

[33] J. Gaventa and R. McGee, *Citizen Action and National Policy Reform: Making Change Happen* (London: Zed Books, 2010).

[34] P. John, *Analysing Public Policy* (London: Pinter, 1998).

5.1 Interests

Interests concern what affected actors wish to achieve—or stand to gain or lose from any change to the status quo. Given the sweeping breadth of the Framework Convention, as proposed in the FCGH Framework, a broad range of actors' interests will be affected. The treaty, of course, would benefit billions of the world's poor, but unless they are well organized and politically active they often have little power. Regrettably, their champions are often at odds with one another. As a result, the global health community sometimes pits particular 'deserving' diseases against others in an unproductive struggle for limited resources. Through a Framework Convention, global health advocates will come to see their specific interests met more through common cause than through fragmentation and competition.

While at this stage civil society, communities, and the wider public are at the heart of developing the proposed FCGH contents and building the constituencies to create and support action among states, eventually states will be at the maelstrom of the treaty process. The movement will need to treat states as both targets of advocacy and as essential collaborators for a Framework Convention. As such, the movement will need to appeal to the interests of states and influence those interests. This will require that civil society identifies and embraces reform-oriented and progressive officials from within the state. The strategies of these coalitions will therefore need to include both insider and outsider tactics. The South African Treatment Action Campaign provides a classic example—at times working with the government against the pharmaceutical industry while at other times engaging in civil disobedience to embarrass and cajole the government, as well as engaging in strategic litigation against government.[35]

Given the range of issues at play with the Framework Convention, a number of different ministries will need to be engaged. Ministries of health will need to be the key champions and allies of the Framework Convention. By the time the WHO took the decision to launch the negotiations process on the convention on tobacco control, more than fifty health ministers had indicated their support at the World Health Assembly.[36] A major and initial challenge for the movement is the need to identify supportive individuals and groups within the ministry of health to get the issues of the global health convention to be seen through the lens of local and national challenges that an international treaty can help to address. These champions will be required to get the Convention on agendas nationally.

Nonetheless, the ministry of health will need to work in concert with other, often more powerful, ministries. Ministries of foreign affairs are likely to exert a heavy influence over, if not lead, the negotiation—and hence any strategy needs to consider how to ensure capitals and missions in New York and Geneva (as there can be disjuncture between them) are on board. This is likely to require direction first from the President's office and subsequent heavy coordination with the ministry of health. The ministry of justice/interior has an important role to play because of the

35 N. Geffen, *Debunking Delusions: the Inside Story of the Treatment Action Campaign* (South Africa: 1st edn, Jacana Media, 2011).

36 Broadly speaking four categories of country actors were identified with different agendas in relation to the tobacco convention: (1) high income with strong tobacco control policies; (2) low and middle income with strong tobacco control policies—or considering; (3) low income with limited capacity for tobacco control and or major tobacco interests; (4) high income with transnational tobacco companies. As outlined in Wilkenfeld, 'Saving the World from Big Tobacco: A Case Study of NGO Coalition Building', Paper presented at the annual meeting of the International Studies Association, Hilton Hawaiian Village, Honolulu, Hawaii Online (2009).

Convention's goal of enabling people to claim the right to health effectively, including through the legal system. The ministry of trade would be likely to see its interests affected, as the treaty would seek to raise the priority of health within other legal regimes, including trade, and expand access to essential medicines, including by dismantling trade barriers. The ministry of finance/treasury would need to be engaged as the Convention envisions the establishment of funding targets and the redistribution of health-related funding. Beyond the executive branch, one envisions a role for parliamentarians as national champions by attracting attention to FCGH and pertinent issues through hearings—and by pushing on the executive branch through resolutions and, of course, laws that would ultimately implement aspects of an FCGH (indeed, parliament could implement FCGH-type measures even before or in the absence of an FCGH).

In light of the varied ministerial stakes, and the likely differing perceptions relating to the various elements of the Convention, there is likely to be a need for inter-ministerial discussions to arrive at consolidated Member State positions. These were seen as critical in the run up to, and during the negotiations on the tobacco convention.[37] These discussions benefit from both analysis and impetus provided by a supportive (and demanding) civil society. Inter-ministerial discussions will also serve to identify champions to recruit into a broad-based, national coalition in support of the Convention. Specific states emerge to assume leadership on international negotiations—and they do so for a variety of reasons. In the case of the tobacco control negotiations, Finland, Mexico, and Tanzania were the initial proponents. In the case of landmines, Canada exercised strong leadership, eventually taking the negotiations outside the UN system through a series of six consultations in different cities, which culminated in the Ottawa Charter. As early at 1987, Italy and Sweden proposed a convention on disabilities but this took until 2001, when Mexico formally called for negotiations in the United Nations General Assembly.[38] As noted earlier, it remains early days in the process of a global health convention, yet one could envision states such as Brazil, South Africa, and Thailand as natural champions—representing a powerful coalition of emerging economies—with Nordic support from the North. Nonetheless, much advocacy work remains to convince states that it is in their interest to take on this challenge.

National coalitions will need to go beyond state actors and civil society champions to include media, experts, and others to rally behind the cause. The South African Treatment Action Campaign (TAC) provides a powerful and successful example of such an advocacy coalition—with members coming from diverse realities. These included people living with HIV and leaders from the labour, science, medical, legal, and religious communities, who shared a core principled belief—in the right to treatment access (initially focusing on medicines to prevent mother-to-child transmission).[39] TAC was connected to international groups which shared this cause—indeed the TAC leadership recognized early on that the national campaign could not be effective without the support of a global campaign. The major march preceding the XIII International AIDS Conference was endorsed by over 250 organizations from

[37] H. Wipfli et al, 'Confronting the Tobacco Epidemic: Emerging Mechanisms of Global Governance' in M. McKee, P. Garner, and R. Stott (eds), *International Co-operation and Health* (London: OUP, 2001) 189.

[38] J.E. Lord, D. Suozzi, and A.L. Taylor, 'Lessons from the Experience of the UN Convention on the Rights of Persons with Disabilities: Addressing the Democratic Deficit in Global Health Governance' (2010) 38(3) *Journal of Law, Medicine and Ethics* 564.

[39] *Fighting For Our Lives: The history of the Treatment Action Campaign 1998–2010* (South Africa: Treatment Action Campaign, 2010).

around the world which reflected some of the links. TAC worked closely with a large number of international groups (including Consumer Project on Technology, MSF, Oxfam, Health Gap and the International AIDS Alliance, and individual activists, bureaucrats and diplomats) on a range of actions, including strategic litigation, science, and service delivery in a global moral coalition for social change.[40]

Intergovernmental and multilateral organizations are often critical to intergovernmental negotiations. The variety of support provided by the WHO to the development of the Framework Convention on Tobacco Control has been well documented. This included, among other things, financial support for an advocacy coalition, convening stakeholders—both formally through the Intergovernmental Negotiating Body (INB) as well as informally, marshalling scientific evidence (technical as well as political—the latter was particularly innovative in that it involved stakeholder analysis in tobacco producing and non-producing countries)[41] as well as strong leadership. In the case of this particular set of negotiations, the World Bank was also critical, in that it helped to influence perceptions of the economic costs of inaction through its well-respected analytical work.[42] The UN Secretary-General was an early supporter of a global health convention linking the historic gains of the AIDS movement to an eventual treaty: 'Let the AIDS response be a beacon of global solidarity for health as a human right and set the stage for a future United Nations Framework Convention on Global Health.'[43]

Regional political organizations, such as ASEAN, Mercosur, and the African Union, and sub-regional groupings, for example the SADC and ECOWAS, can play catalytic roles in treaty building. Building support regionally and among other governmental groupings can create a firm foundation for global action. And the smaller regional settings can enable a level of discussion, and attention to regional issues or other common concerns, that engages high-level officials in ways less possible at the global level. The regional blocs can also be instrumental in negotiations. For example, in advance of the 2011 UN High-Level Meeting on HIV/AIDS, the African Union developed a common position among its fifty-three Member States, which they brought as a bloc to the negotiations to advance positions on various issues and paragraphs of the text. Indeed the power of a similar bloc was described in personal detail by the South African negotiator in the second session of the Intergovernmental Negotiating Body of the tobacco framework negotiations:

> And I remember very clearly, clearing my throat, and then saying, I'm speaking... for South Africa, but I'm speaking on behalf of the 46 member states of the AFRO region. And I just felt the whole room become silent. And people's heads began to turn around. I just continued speaking but when I unpacked it afterwards I realized that if ever it came to a question of voting, there... were 191 at that stage, now there are 192 member states. So 46 of that is almost a quarter of the house. If we then could get consensus on the issues that were important to us, if ever it

[40] E. Grebe, 'Transnational Networks of Influence in South African AIDS Treatment Activism', AIDS2031 (no date), available at <http://www.aids2031.org/pdfs/workingpaper5-leadership-grebe.pdf> (accessed 28 October 2012).

[41] J.P. Vaughan, J. Collin, and K. Lee (eds), *Case Study Report: Global Analysis of the Political Economy of Tobacco Control in Low and Middle-Income Countries* (London: School of Hygiene and Tropical Medicine/Geneva: WHO Tobacco Free Initiative, 2000) 150.

[42] J. Collin and K. Lee, 'Globalization and the Politics of Health Governance: The Framework Convention on Tobacco Control' in A. Cooper and J. Kirton (eds), *Innovation in Global Health Governance: Critical Cases* (Aldershot: Ashgate, 2009).

[43] UN Secretary-General, 'Uniting for Universal Access: Towards Zero New HIV Infections, Zero Discrimination and Zero AIDS-Related Deaths': Report of the Secretary-General, UN Doc A/65/979 (March 2011), available at <http://www.unaids.org/en/media/unaids/contentassets/documents/document/2011/A-65-797_English.pdf>.

came to a vote, we felt that we would carry a great deal of power against other countries that perhaps were not looking for such stringent tobacco control as we were.[44]

Transnational civil society organizations have been the champions of most if not all progressive health-related international treaties and agreements. While they may or may not have direct access to the negotiating room—and if in the room are often only able to participate as observers (although, as noted later, there are precedents and not only through their participation as members of official national delegations)—they can lobby and influence delegations both at country level and in the negotiations themselves. In the case of the tobacco negotiations, the Framework Convention Alliance (FCA)—which became an alliance of over 180 NGOs from over seventy countries during the negotiation process[45]—undertook a number of, often creative, actions. These included publishing a daily bulletin with news and analysis, (free) luncheon briefings, media advocacy experts, expert witnesses, the provision of a 'death clock' for use by the WHO Director-General, letter writing campaigns, and more.[46] Allied organizations undertook complementary actions—for example ASH (Action on Smoking and Health) awarded a dirty ashtray award on a daily basis for the least constructive Member State and an orchid to those who moved things forward. Critically, the FCA provided funding to support the national work of some advocates and brought developing country NGO representatives to the negotiations. Critical to the success of a global health treaty will be a systematic approach to reaching out to diverse civil society constituencies whose aims would be furthered through recourse to a convention on the right to health and—as demonstrated earlier—this would be a broad church indeed. It is these constituencies, once mobilized, that will place political pressure on state representatives to act.

Civil society is far from homogenous and other, less progressive, elements of civil society often wish to influence international treaty and soft law. A major point of contestation in the run up to the 2011 UN High-Level Meeting on Non-communicable Diseases was the decision to include the for-profit private sector and its front organizations within the 'civil society hearings'. This conflict led to, among other things, the establishment of the Conflicts of Interest Coalition calling on the United Nations to differentiate between BINGOs (business interest NGOs) and PINGOs (public interest NGOs) in relation to engagement in the High-Level Meeting.[47] The Holy See has 'permanent observer' status to the United Nations and often assumes a highly proactive role in negotiations. This is particularly the case in the realm of sexual and reproductive rights (which it opposes as an attack on the 'natural family'), as exemplified in the lobbying and negotiation around the Programme of Action of the International Conference on Population and Development at Cairo, as well as in relation to the more recent UN Political Declarations on HIV/AIDS. The Vatican both spearheads an alliance with certain Islamic delegations and works with a range of religious civil society networks to advance its cause and block others within the UN negotiations.[48] These conservative views, which can lead to assaults on human rights,

44 The quotations are from an interview that Dr Otto gave to INFACT in preparation of the film 'Overcoming the Odds: A Story of the First Global Health and Corporate Accountability Treaty' (2004), as cited in Wilkenfeld, 'Saving the World from Big Tobacco' (n 36).

45 And has since grown to more than 350 organizations from over a 100 countries. For further information see <http://www.fctc.org/index.php?option=com_content&view=article&id=2&Itemid=277> (accessed 25 June 2012).

46 Wilkenfeld, 'Saving the World from Big Tobacco' (n 36).

47 Statement of Concern, available at <http://coicoalition.blogspot.com/2011/09/coi-coalition-statement.html> (accessed 28 October 2012).

48 C. Bob, *Global Right Wing and the Clash of World Politics* (Cambridge: CUP, 2012).

assume transnational links. The origin of a bill in Uganda that would have made homosexual behaviour a crime punishable by death has its roots in a visit of anti-gay American Christian activists.[49]

The experience with tobacco control also draws attention to the need to build relationships and coalitions within and between different relevant issue areas. The FCA thus brought together coalitions for health promotion, public health, consumer protection, women/gender, youth, and environment, among others, with scores of national organizations from each sector. As such, a major preoccupation of the Campaign for an FCGH is helping to build a more unified right to health movement. Consultations convened by JALI, before the Campaign's launch, included groups working on different health issues such as AIDS, TB, maternal and child health, malaria, NCDs, and treatment access, as well as linking to other sectors and related issues, such as tax justice, environment, food and nutrition, and water and sanitation, as well as labour. The global Platform for a Framework Convention on Global Health will help to broaden ownership of an FCGH across a wide range of movements.

A number of private for-profit sector actors may perceive their interests to be at risk if a Framework Convention is successfully agreed—particularly one which promotes more stringent and enforced regulations. These actors include national and transnational groups in the alcohol, tobacco, unhealthy foods, health insurance, and healthcare provision sectors, but also extractive and transport industries whose actions affect the well-being of people. The battle over the Framework Convention on Tobacco Control provides some insights into the strategies and tactics that industry may adopt to derail a progressive treaty outcome.[50] Yet, the tobacco industry strategies were somewhat limited by its widely perceived pariah status. Other accounts indicate that industry mobilizes highly successfully when it perceives that its interests are affected by intergovernmental processes—for example by effectively delaying the introduction of international legal instruments, blocking the adoption of instruments (for example the sugar industry concerning dietary guidelines), influencing the content of treaties (for example tobacco), or challenging the competence and mandate of international organizations with respect to relevant issues (for example the food industry initially attempted to block WHO involvement in NCDs).[51]

To summarize, the content and obligations of the Convention will potentially affect the interests of a range of actors. Many actors will need to be mobilized and encouraged to join national and transnational coalitions. Other actors will oppose the Framework using a variety of strategies and tactics to derail the efforts of FCGH supporters, and will need to be managed accordingly. Contentious issues require contentious politics.[52] The more contentious the issue; the more outsider and adversarial strategies that are required in order to hold their own against powerful interests—including the skilful and creative deployment of ideas.

[49] T. McVeigh, P. Harris, and B. Among, 'Anti-Gay Bigots Plunge Africa into New Era of Hate Crimes', *The Guardian*, 12 December 2009, available at <http://www.guardian.co.uk/world/2009/dec/13/death-penalty-uganda-homosexuals> (accessed 29 October 2012).

[50] Report of the Committee of Experts on Tobacco Industry Documents, 'Tobacco Company Strategies to Undermine Tobacco Control Activities at the World Health Organization' (WHO, July 2000); H.M. Mamudu, R. Hammond, S.A. Glantz, 'Project Cerberus: Tobacco Industry Strategy to Create an Alternative to the Framework Convention on Tobacco Control' (2008) 98 *American Journal of Public Health* 9.

[51] K. Buse and C. Naylor, 'Commercial Health Governance' in K. Buse, H. Hein, and N. Drager (eds), *Making Sense of Global Health Governance* (Basingstoke: Palgrave Macmillan, 2009) 187.

[52] J. Gaventa, 'Building Responsive States: Citizen Action and National Policy Change' (2008) IDS Policy Briefing 5, available at <http://www.ids.ac.uk/files/InFocus5.pdf>.

5.2 Ideas

Actors' interests are generally pursued through the deployment of ideas—whether expressed through evidence, argument, or narrative. Personal testimonies are particularly powerful to convey the human dimension of a problem or to provide legitimacy to a set of ideas that appear truthful, persuasive, and humane. Discourses, as well as emotive symbols and associations, are also 'ideas' deployed in the furtherance of policy goals. Indeed, there are those who argue that 'ideas and discourses can have a force of their own independently of particular actors'.[53] The point is that much of the policy battle involves policy argumentation: not simply the presentation of facts to decision-makers (which is of course a necessary role for champions of the Convention), but rather framing and conveying compelling stories (including the stories of the less powerful) that reflect specific contexts and specific audiences far beyond the technocratic arena.

Unsurprisingly, ideas are central to social justice campaigns. Covey has argued that: 'Framing a winning issue requires that the alliance define the debate in terms compelling to grassroots groups and which limit the opposition's ability to mobilize its own forces.'[54] The landmines campaign astutely shifted the terms of the debate from a concern with arms control to a humanitarian imperative—an imperative due to the indiscriminate nature and overwhelming impact on civilians. In so doing, it succeeded in reframing the issue to one which was at once 'media-friendly and morally unambiguous'.[55] This frame put pro-mine forces on the defensive and dealt a blow to the reputation of pro-mine states.[56] The Treatment Action Campaign (TAC) adopted a strategy of building a 'moral consensus' to tackle HIV—in the words of its co-founder 'revealing the government's "moral weakness"' and 'giv(ing) a sense of morality to politics'.[57] TAC's strategic use of morality and the principles of human rights resonated well and widely in post-Apartheid South Africa.

Earlier, we outlined some of the possible objections that might arise to a progressive FCGH. It is critical to note that the battle of ideas will be particularly complex in relation to this Framework—arguably much more complex than the more or less single-issue conventions relating to tobacco or breast-milk substitutes. Consider, for example, the body of evidence on the social and structural drivers of ill health. Despite the excellent work of the Commission on the Social Determinants of Health, the drivers are not widely understood and are extremely diverse. There is plenty of scope for contesting this complex body of knowledge—it is possibly more akin to the science around climate change than tobacco control—demonstrated by an overwhelming body of evidence and with near total consensus among scientists and researchers, but which nonetheless remains questionable in the eyes of certain publics—meaning the politics may be similar too.

53 F. Fischer, *Reframing Public Policy: Discursive Politics and Discursive Practices* (Oxford: OUP, 2003).

54 J.G. Covey, 'Accountability and Effectiveness in NGP Policy Alliances' (1995) 7(6) *Journal of International Development* 857.

55 N. Short, 'The Role of NGOs in the Ottawa Process to Ban Landmines' (1999) 4 *International Negotiation* 481, available at <http://faculty.maxwell.syr.edu/rdenever/IntlSecurity2008_docs/Short_NGOsOttawa.pdf>.

56 R. Price, 'Reversing the Gun Sights: Transnational Civil Society Targets Land Mines' (Summer 1998) 52(3) *International Organization* 613.

57 Mark Haywood quoted in S. Friedman, 'Gaining comprehensive AIDS treatment in South Africa: the extraordinary "ordinary"' in Gaventa and McGee, *Citizen Action and National Policy Reform* (n 33) 44.

Take the case of alcohol—the consumption of which is driven by social custom (including gender and perceptions of masculinity, etc) but is also linked to community customs governing social interaction as well as by factors including advertising, pricing, legal restrictions, and public education. Trying to get all those disparate forces to support the moderate consumption of alcohol in a context of potentially confusing and conflicting evidence about the health impacts of alcohol (is it cardio-protective or does it lead to strokes and at what level of intake?) and contested evidence about the impact of economic and legal restrictions will be challenging.

There are analogies from the world of climate change with, in the public mind—however unreasonably in the face of an overwhelming scientific consensus—a fairly contested body of evidence about the determinants of climate change and even more contest about what is going to make a difference to reverse and mitigate the impact of climate change. What the environmentalists seem to have done is to get across the argument that 'on the balance of probabilities' do we really want to take the risk of undermining the long-term viability of our planet? So too with alcohol, and some of the other social drivers of ill health that may be considered in the Framework. A reasonable line may be 'on the balance of probability, do we really need to wait for a meta-analysis of randomized control trials of alcohol policy, or should we accept that alcohol is responsible for a considerable global burden of disease and if we want to make the world healthier then we all need to face up to it together'.

The certainty of climate change and its human causes, like the certainty of today's devastating health inequities—as well as the strong evidence on how to redress them—stand in contrast to some more genuine questions. For example, how effective is educating health workers and communities on the right to health, or creating community mechanisms to hold local health services accountable to them, in improving health outcomes?

There is emerging evidence that these right to health strategies do make a measurable—and even major—difference. A study in Uganda, for example, found that one community-based health accountability strategy, using community scorecards of their local health services, led to a one-third reduction in child mortality.[58] But more research and understanding is required to better understand the connections and, most importantly, the best approaches to lead to the greatest change. The value of solid evidence cannot be understated. While resistance remains in some quarters, a plethora of studies that found that needle exchange programs reduce HIV infection without increasing drug use were the ammunition that advocates needed to lessen resistance and achieve the widespread rollout of these programs. The early success of Partners In Health at providing AIDS treatment in rural Haiti provided irrefutable evidence that AIDS treatment could succeed in even the world's most resource-scarce settings.

Meanwhile, the balance of probabilities approach could work here as well, even as firmer evidence on the direct links between these aspects of the right to health and health outcomes would be welcome. The desire for this evidence should not obscure the urgency and logic behind the premises that people have the right to know their rights and that governments must be accountable to their citizens. The logic is straightforward. If a government is failing in its right to health obligations and people have the genuine opportunity to hold their governments accountable, thus forcing that government to address its failings towards achieving the highest attainable standard of

58 M. Björkman and J. Svensson, 'Power to the People: Evidence from a Randomized Field Experiment on Community-Based Monitoring in Uganda' (2009) 124(2) *Quarterly Journal of Economics* 735, available at <http://people.su.se/~jsven/PtP_QJE.pdf>.

health, health and the strategies and services to achieve it will improve. The questions are about the most effective approaches towards accountability. Further, dignity demands that people have the opportunity to influence the nature of the health strategies, programs, and services that will have a central role in determining the course of their lives. There is little to lose and much to gain from facilitating efforts to hold governments to account, ranging from local to national levels.

Given the diversity of the ideas involved across the spectrum of issues the Framework hopes to tackle, and the likely opposition to certain elements, JALI proposed a 'protocol' approach to the Convention as a tactical move. Such a convention is inherently flexible, allowing states to agree to politically feasible obligations, saving the most contentious issues to subsequent protocols. Nonetheless, the process will still be marked by contestation. As such, the content of the Framework needs to include something for all parties. For example, consider the interests of the global North and South on the issue of development cooperation. In keeping with the Busan Partnership agreement, better, predictable, and longer-term international investments need to be part of the grand bargain in the Convention, in the context of shared responsibility and global solidarity. On the other side of the equation, enhanced commitments to increased domestic resource mobilization will reassure development partners.[59]

Success will require a proactive approach to defining and framing both the nature of the problems that the Framework seeks to resolve and the mechanisms through which it can do so as legitimate, as against those that would dispute them. Indeed the ultimate objective is to bring about the widespread acceptance and support of nation states for the treaty; in this case to create shared norms about responsibility of nation states and the international community for health for all. Finnemore argued that states are socialized to want certain things by international society.[60] They are socialized in a number of ways, including by how problems and their solutions are framed—to attract attention and appeal to different interests and resonate in different institutional venues and cultures.

Returning to frames with respect to campaigning on social issues, Deborah Stone argued that an issue needs to be translated into a 'causal story', among other things by conveying who bears responsibility or guilt.[61] This theme has featured throughout the work of George Lakoff in his analysis of US politics. One of the powerful examples revealed by Lakoff is the use of the term 'tax relief' by George W. Bush and his office when describing tax cuts for the affluent.[62] This was a deliberate choice of words to frame the problem and solution. As 'a relief' evokes the necessity of 'an affliction', an afflicted party, and a reliever who removes the affliction and is therefore a 'hero'. In this metaphor, taxation is the affliction, the President is the hero and all opposition to shifting the burden of financing from the state to the poor is simply bad.

Reflecting on previous treaties and agreements, it appears that it was relatively easy to vilify big tobacco and to garner support for the Nestlé boycott in light of its breaches of

[59] L.O. Gostin, E.A. Friedman, G. Ooms et al, 'The Joint Action and Learning Initiative: Towards a Global Agreement on National and Global Responsibilities for Health' (2011) 8 *PLoS Medicine* 5, available at <http://www.plosmedicine.org/article/info%3Adoi%2F10.1371%2Fjournal.pmed.1001031>.

[60] M. Finnemore, *National Interests in International Society* (Ithaca, NY: Cornell University Press, 1996).

[61] D.A. Stone, 'Causal Stories and the Formation of Policy Agendas' (1989) 104 *Political Science Quarterly* 281.

[62] G. Lakoff, H. Dean, and D. Hazen, *Don't Think of an Elephant! Know Your Values and Frame the Debate* (White River Junction, VT: Chelsea Green, 2004).

the International Code of Marketing of Breast-milk Substitutes which result, according to boycott organizers, in significant and unnecessary suffering and death of children. When the World Bank, on the basis of empirical evidence of the burden of disease, considered attempting to raise the salience of adult health, it engaged Michael Reich—a health policy guru from Harvard University—to provide some advice to support such a shift.[63] Reich emphasized the considerable difficulty facing the Bank—not only was child health an easier 'sell' symbolically (child health carried 'symbolic politics' which 'generat(e) sympathy and consensus' while the same imagery would not be possible for adult health), but it would also raise the question of who was responsible for adult ill-health—in short, industry activities or culpable men?). As argued previously, for too long the global health community has divided diseases and people into those that are deserving of our attention, and those that are not.

One aim of the Convention is to overcome this inequity by providing new, compelling frames related to the right to health—the right of all. Such frames may involve recasting health 'spending' as investments—and investing now to avert later treatment costs, reframing 'taxes' as 'innovative financing', and moving the outdated notion of donor/recipient to a more positive and empowering frame of shared responsibility and global solidarity. Such reframing would make the Convention not only more politically palatable but also begin the process of reformulating the expectations of states and the international community with respect to health. Such was the experience of advocates promoting the Convention on the Rights of Persons with Disabilities, who were partially successful in reframing the conceptualization of disability from a medical to social construction through the treaty negotiation process—thus demanding very different policy responses from the international community as well as Member States.[64]

Many of the treaties and agreements provided as examples in this chapter were negotiated before widespread access to the Internet and cell phones and, consequently, the advent of social media as a mechanism through which to organize and mobilize politically. Given the success of Iceland in crowdsourcing elements of its national constitution and of UNAIDS in using crowdsourcing to develop a strategy for its engagement with young people, it may be possible to move some of the machinery of international negotiations into the twenty-first century as well. Even if it is not possible to achieve such an ambition, it is certainly possible to use social media effectively to network and campaign on issues related to the FCGH. AVAAZ, for example, provides a ready mechanism to 'supercharge' transnational campaigns—'bringing people-powered politics to decision-makers world-wide'.[65] AVAAZ has a successful history of rapidly mobilizing tens of thousands of concerned citizens on progressive issues for a variety of actions and tactics—ranging from civil disobedience, to petitioning the Pope on condom policy (200,000 signatures), to petitioning the UN Secretary-General on the war on drugs (soliciting 600,000 signatures in a week). Social media can also be used to hold states accountable for the Treaty's implementation. Huduma, for example, provides an innovative media-based platform in Kenya to 'amplify citizen's concerns, displeasures, complaints and suggestions as a means to hold duty bearers to account'.[66] Citizens use their cell phones to notify authorities when services are found wanting—to prompt action and answerability.

63 M. Reich, 'The Politics of Agenda-Setting in International Health: Child Health Versus Adult Health in Developing Countries' (1995) 7(3) *Journal of International Development* 489.

64 Lord, Suozzi, and Taylor, 'Lessons from the Experience of the UN Convention' (n 38).

65 See <http://www.avaaz.org/en/> (accessed 25 June 2012).

66 See <http://huduma.info/> (accessed 25 June 2012).

The way that ideas are presented is critically important to advance the cause of those interests in favour of a Framework Convention. Lessons from previous global campaigns suggest that there is an ongoing need to calibrate and recalibrate the 'ask', not only in terms of its ability to win media coverage and mobilize constituencies but also to calibrate its 'ambition' with the extent of the mobilization of constituencies who can apply political pressure on decision-makers.[67] Given the Convention's bold nature—and its transformative potential—advocates must leverage ideas and narratives to inspire powerful civil society and gain state champions. The alternative, scaling back the Convention's aim, could undercut its raison d'être.

Having reflected on interests and ideas, we now turn to their interaction in different institutional domains.

5.3 Institutions

Institutions comprise both the rules of the game (how things are done—for example protocols governing representation and participation) in specific settings and the organizations that influence and/or make and enforce those rules (such as the World Health Assembly or the United Nations General Assembly).

Movements in support of a global health treaty will need to influence existing institutions and processes. Engaging with institutions such as national ministries, regional organizations and intergovernmental agencies, bilaterally and through networks and alliances, was discussed earlier. The central role of the WHO in the Framework Convention on Tobacco Control is incontrovertible. The Director-General threw her new leadership behind the initiative as one of her two corporate priorities—not least because she was looking to rehabilitate the Organization, which had lost much legitimacy during her predecessor's tenure.[68] Among other things, the WHO provided financial and other support to incubate and support a transnational advocacy coalition which would emerge as the FCA—a structured network of public health organizations, environmental activists, women's and children's groups, and more. The Alliance worked in partnership with the WHO throughout the process—influencing the ultimate positions of Member States. But context is critically important—the WHO may or may not be the institution of choice for the pursuit of a global health convention at this point in time.

The FCGH will need some legitimate institutional venue for its negotiation. The Ottawa Process (on landmines) illustrates the institutional flexibility inherent in such negotiations. A series of six sessions was held—in a number of different capital cities—and culminated in a final session in the United Nations General Assembly. The Canadian government assumed a leadership role—and was very sympathetic to the NGO communities—but the involvement of civil society in the process had to be brokered with other governments. Some of the sessions were 'closed' and only included two representatives of the ICBL (International Campaign to Ban Landmines) as non-voting delegates, while other sessions involved more NGO representatives and their outright participation. It is reported that civil society was able to influence the outcome text significantly. The ad hoc process was heralded as a 'model for cooperation' and a 'new form of diplomacy'.[69]

67 B. Cox, 'Campaigning for International Justice' (2011), available at <http://www.bond.org.uk/data/files/resources/52/Campaigning_for_International_Justice_Brendan_Cox_May_2011.pdf>.
68 Collin and Lee, 'Globalization and the Politics of Health Governance' (n 42).
69 Short, 'The Role of NGOs' (n 55).

The Human Rights Council provides another possible institutional forum to negotiate the Convention. It proved an amenable venue for the Convention on the Rights of the Child—in particular its use of a working group that included civil society.[70] The use of a similar process for an FCGH could be highly desirable, ensuring a civil society role in drafting the treaty and ensuring that human rights would be at the centre of the treaty. However, there is no guarantee that the Human Rights Council would endorse the FCGH—it has been less than enthusiastic on moving forward with a treaty to codify the right to development. And even the successful process in developing the Convention on the Rights of the Child had lasted a decade before the UN General Assembly adopted the treaty.

It has been said that movements use opportunities, flexibly seizing windows of opportunity to present their demands or reframe issues. Arguably, the advent of the birth control pill empowered women to demand the right to control their sexual and reproductive health. But civil society also creates opportunities for further progressive action. The involvement of civil society in the process of developing the Convention on the Rights of the Child—through the ad hoc NGO group—is said to have left a major imprint on the substantive articles of the treaty.[71] Equally importantly, it was successful in its efforts to influence procedural aspects. In particular, it gained a role for civil society in monitoring the implementation of the Convention through the invitation make contributions to and participate in the Committee on the Rights of the Child.[72] In this role, civil society has assumed critical functions—for example in drafting a subsequent protocol on children in armed conflict that had not advanced through the original framework process. As such, movements are critical to building and shaping new institutions, processes, and rules to move their agendas forward. For example, inter-ministerial consultations on national and international health obligations will be required to discuss the relevance and national interests to be gained from a Framework Convention at national level. There is likely to be a need for similar inter-agency processes across relevant UN agencies and programs, as is the norm, for example, in preparations for major conferences (for example the UN Task Team for the Advancement of the Post-2015 UN Development Framework, which fed into the Millennium Development Goals Review in 2013).

The movement for an FCGH should make full use of existing rules. For example, Member States may include representatives of civil society in official delegations to the United Nations during negotiations. Such was the case in the Ottawa Process—and this ought to be replicated in the case of the global health negotiations, but will require close and supportive relationships between some NGOs and government officials in the national coalitions.

The movement can also lobby to challenge or change existing rules. During the FCTC process, civil society worked hard to accelerate the process of accreditation of civil society organizations in official relations with the WHO so that more organizations could participate in some of the proceedings.[73] Similarly, in the months leading to the first governmental negotiations on the disability convention, disability groups

70 'United Nations Background Note: Children's Rights' (December 1995), available at <http://www.un.org/rights/dpi1765e.htm> (accessed 29 October 2012).

71 C.P. Cohen, 'The Role of Nongovernmental Organizations in the Drafting of the Convention on the Rights of the Child' (1990) 12(1) *Human Rights Quarterly* 137.

72 C. Breen, 'The Role of NGOs in the Formulation of and Compliance with the Optional Protocol to the Convention on the Rights of the Child on Involvement of Children in Armed Conflict' (2003) 25(2) *Human Rights Quarterly* 453.

73 Collin and Lee, 'Globalization and the Politics of Health Governance' (n 42).

'lobbied hard to achieve access to the meeting'[74] with their now familiar refrain 'nothing about us without us'. The United Nations established an *ad hoc* committee to draft the convention and it agreed that accredited NGOs were permitted to make statements and receive official documents, and it provided a space for their materials. Ironically, and fortuitously, the UN gallery, where observers were situated, was inaccessible for wheelchair users—resulting in the decision to locate such users on the floor of the committee itself. This permitted disability activists direct access to government delegates and participation in the proceedings—conferring on them considerable advantage.[75] Prior to that, the ad hoc committee had established a working group to draft the text—in addition to twenty-seven Member States, it included twelve disabled people's organizations.

As noted previously, the Ottawa Process challenged existing institutional mores of diplomacy by opening a major space for NGO representative participation. Yet perhaps more significant for the eventual outcome of the Treaty was the self-selection process for Member State participation. Only states that signed on to specific declarations were permitted to attend as full participants—the others as observers. This tactical approach ensured that only those states committed to a strong treaty could meaningfully participate—both framing the treaty and the extent of civil society involvement in its negotiation.[76]

The processes of developing UN Political Declarations on HIV/AIDS have, at the instigation of the AIDS movement, included 'informal' interactive civil society hearings presided over by the President of the General Assembly. The summaries of the hearings are issued as official documentation to the Assembly prior to the High-Level Meeting. Again, a useful precedent has been set, and can be emulated.

The Platform for an FCGH provides the preliminary institutional backbone of the global and national coalitions that are being nurtured, courted, and supported. The representativeness, legitimacy, and accountability of the Campaign are likely to be called into question—even when so doing lacks any meaningful justification. Strong links to affected communities represent the key to overcoming this critique. Recalling the experience with the Treatment Action Campaign, co-founder Mark Heywood remarked: '*TAC needed a leadership of black people who lived in the communities where TAC was organizing, if possible people living with HIV, and we needed to go out and create that leadership*' (emphasis in the original).[77] A consortium working closely with JALI, and sure to inform a Framework Convention, undertook dialogues in communities across nine countries in Africa, Asia, and Latin America concerning people's understanding of the right to health, what it entails, the responsibilities it creates, and how people can best assert and claim these rights.[78]

The FCGH Platform, in its formative stage, is governed by a steering committee of Southern and Northern organizations, academics, and practitioners, and intergovernmental organizations. Enhanced Southern capacity within the steering committee to provide Southern members dedicated time to work on the FCGH is critical. And the Platform will need

74 Lord, Suozzi, and Taylor, 'Lessons from the Experience of the UN Convention' (n 38).
75 Lord, Suozzi, and Taylor, 'Lessons from the Experience of the UN Convention' (n 38).
76 Short, 'The Role of NGOs' (n 55).
77 Mark Heywood, as quoted in Treatment Action Campaign, *Fighting For Our Lives* (n 39).
78 Go4Health Work Package 2, 'Community Consultations on the Post-2015 Global Health Agenda: A Demand for Dignity, Respect, Participation, and Accountability' (August 2013), available at <http://www.go4health.eu/wp-content/uploads/WP2-August-2013-FINAL-Light.pdf> (accessed 2 February 2014).

to strengthen links to social movements and involve more people in the development of the treaty. Experience gleaned from a review of eight international campaigns for international justice may hold lessons for the FCGH supporters as they seek to catalyze a social movement to advance the FCGH.[79] Among other things, the review suggested that success was more likely with a strong international coalition that sets a direction to which national coalitions align. Such an approach need not undermine the specificity of country demands on the content of the Convention or be at odds with diverse national-level actions. Strong individual leadership of an international campaign was also highlighted. The ICBL is exemplary of both of these characteristics. In this campaign, leadership was highly centralized in its coordinator, Judy Williams, in terms of its relationship to the primary governmental stakeholder (Canada) as well as the press, which enabled the campaign to speak with a unitary voice despite having a membership of around 1,000 organizations in over fifty countries. All this suggests that JALI was right to launch an international Platform for an FCGH.

6. Conclusions

Communities and civil society will be central to the Framework Convention—both in defining its content and mobilizing politically to ensure nation state support. Political mobilization has been central to realizing progressive health-related treaty outcomes. Mobilization needs to be grounded in country realities and linked to transnational coalitions. Proponents at all levels will need to develop specific strategies and tactics to address the interests, ideas, and institutions that emerge.

FCGH supporters will be challenged constantly to review and adapt their strategies in response to the tactics of the interests that work to undermine the Framework and thereby hold health for all ransom to the logic of the market, the mantra of austerity, and the lottery of one's life chances at birth. This will require creativity in terms of entering into new partnerships with a range of actors who are already, or who could be mobilized for a progressive health treaty—and playing politics with those interests which mount overt and covert opposition. Success will also demand the framing and reframing of the problems and solutions depending on the audience and prevailing discourses. Persistence and determination to identify and use all available institutional venues to shape the rules to support wide and deep engagement in an intergovernment process is a key to success. These are daunting propositions but there are many precedents that attest to the possibility of overturning the seemingly impossible when the goals are just and widely shared—from the end of Apartheid to treatment access for all—and what could be more just than the right to health.

79 Cox, 'Campaigning for International Justice' (n 67).

3

The Bloodless Ideological Supreme Court Battle over the Affordable Care Act and the 'Right to Health' in America

George J. Annas

On 21 January 2013, President Barack Obama delivered his second inaugural address. Many observed that his address had no memorable lines. But no one who has followed the health care debate in the US could miss the centrality of two paragraphs nestled in the middle of the speech:

> We the people still believe that every citizen deserves a basic measure of security and dignity. We must make the hard choices to reduce the cost of health care and the size of our budget. But we reject the belief that America must choose between caring for the generation that built this country and investing in the generation that will build its future. For we remember the lessons of our past when twilight years were spent in poverty and parents of a child with a disability had nowhere to turn.
>
> We do not believe that in this country freedom is reserved for the lucky, or happiness for the few. We recognize that no matter how responsibly we live our lives, any one of us at any time may face a job loss, or a sudden illness, or a home swept away in a terrible storm. The commitments we make to each other through Medicare and Medicaid and Social Security, these things do not sap our initiative, they strengthen us. They do not make us a nation of takers; they free us to take the risks that make this country great.

The politics of the 'right to health' in America has been intense ever since Barack Obama was first elected President in 2008, and it if anything intensified after his successful struggle with Congress to pass the Affordable Care Act (ACA). It was widely hoped that politics would finally take a backseat to law and constitutional interpretation when the ACA was challenged as unconstitutional before the US Supreme Court. But this was not to be; in fact, rather than lowering the political debate about whether the US should move to provide health care insurance to more of its citizens, the Supreme Court challenge intensified it. That the Supreme Court ultimately pulled back from *de facto* becoming a third political branch of the federal government was due entirely to the very late decision by Chief Justice Roberts to 'save' the ACA, albeit in a decision that was more political than legal in its approach. This chapter tells the story of an overly-political US Supreme Court faced with examining a major step in the direction of a federal 'right to health', and the opinions of four members of the Court who believe they have more legitimacy to determine national health care insurance policy than the President and Congress.

A week after his Solicitor General began his three-day defense of the ACA in the US Supreme Court, President Barack Obama offered a spirited defense of the Act, emphasizing its positive impact on the lives of real people. He noted, for example, that under the ACA, 2.5 million young people were already covered by their parents' health insurance, and millions of elderly people pay less for their prescription drugs. He continued: 'This is not an abstract argument. People's lives are affected by the lack of availability of health care, the unaffordability of health care, or their inability to get health care [insurance] because of preexisting conditions . . . I hope that's not forgotten in the political debate.' He also suggested that the Court should show 'judicial restraint' and 'not overturn a duly constituted and passed law'.[1]

In theory the Supreme Court is above politics, but in practice it is not. When combined with the politics of health care, high drama was anticipated when the Supreme Court met the ACA. As Paul Starr noted at the beginning of his own history of the ACA: 'Among the rich nations of the world, the United States stands out for the virulence of its political battles over health care.'[2] Passed by an ideologically-split Congress, most commentators and legal scholars nonetheless predicted that the 'virulent battle' would end with a solid, affirmative blessing of the ACA by the Court.[3] However, after the three days of oral arguments before the Court in late March 2012, the mood changed and no one could reasonably predict how the Court would rule.[4] Many people were asking after the oral arguments, What went wrong in the Court? This is a good question, and President Obama was not the only one asking it.

In theory, the ACA debate in the Supreme Court was exclusively about the limits of federal power. In practice, however, it was about what kind of country the US is with regard to providing health care to those who need it. The US stands out among developed countries as not having a right to health or a right to health care (outside of prisons and emergency departments), and what was at stake in the ACA debate was a limited right to access to health insurance (the abolition of insurance refusals based on 'preexisting conditions'), and subsidies to purchase insurance for some. In addition, those who could afford it were required to purchase health insurance, and those who could not were expected to benefit from a great expansion in the Medicaid programs. The strategy question for the administration was how to defend this very limited national health care compromise plan before the Supreme Court.

In my view, the Obama administration would have had a much stronger performance in both their written and oral arguments before the Court had it more explicitly explained how the ACA would affect the lives of real Americans. This factual approach was, of course, critical to getting the ACA enacted in the first place, as President Obama consistently used stories of real people whose lives have been devastated because of their lack of health insurance.[5] The health care act really is different from most, if not all, of the statutes reviewed by the Supreme Court. Even explicitly recognizing that the ACA has serious policy flaws, it is a once-in-a-half-century statute, on a par with Social Security, and Medicare. A sole focus on its constitutionality under the Commerce Clause not only makes the debate seem abstract and bloodless, it permits the opposition to position themselves as defenders of 'liberty', without taking into account the

[1] M. Landler, 'President Confident Health Law Will Stand: Warns High Court on Judicial Activism', *New York Times*, 3 April 2012, A17.

[2] P. Starr, *Remedy and Reaction: The Peculiar American Struggle over Health Care Reform* (New Haven, CT: Yale University Press, 2011).

[3] M.A. Hall, 'Supreme Court Arguments on the ACA—A Clash of Two World Views' (2012) 366 *New England Journal of Medicine* 1462, available at <http://www.nejm.org/doi/full/10.1056/NEJMp1201848>; J. Bravin, 'Justices Question Health Law', *Wall Street Journal*, 28 March 2012, A1.

[4] T.A. Jan, 'Grilling by Court's Conservatives over Health Care Law's Mandate', *Boston Globe*, 28 March 2012, A1.

[5] G.J. Annas, 'The Two-eyed Cyclops: Metaphor and Narrative in American Medical Research Policy' (2011) 44 *Genre* 393.

suffering and deaths of Americans who lack health insurance, and thus access to most health care.

Every law student knows that appellate courts, especially the Supreme Court, review law, not facts. The theory that the Supreme Court should be above politics is correct as a constitutional matter. But the argument that this particular Supreme Court is not political is difficult to defend. Most of the justices were appointed during an era when one's view on *Roe v Wade*[6] was critical to his or her nomination to the Court. Even more centrally, the Court itself decided it was appropriate for them to determine the outcome of the presidential election in *Bush v Gore*,[7] and more recently, in *Citizens United*[8] to decide that corporations could give unlimited amounts of money to political campaigns.

We can deplore the infection of politics in today's Court, but it is pointless to pretend it does not exist. That is why the bloodless framing of the legal debate as simply one about the authority Congress has under the Commerce Clause fed the worst instincts of the justices to revert to default Republican/Democratic positions, between helping citizens in need and promoting 'big government' and interfering with individual liberty. Framed in this ideological way, those arguing to the Court implicitly agreed to begin with a four-to-four split and vie for what they thought would be the 'swing' vote of Justice Anthony Kennedy.

1. Could the Argument have Gone Better?

Two basic issues dominated the two-hour argument over the 'minimum coverage provision' (termed the 'individual mandate' by its opponents, this requires individuals who can afford it to purchase health insurance):

(1) Does the federal government have authority under the Commerce Clause to require uninsured persons to purchase health insurance, and does it matter whether the relevant market is for health care or for health care insurance?

(2) If the Court accepts that Congress has power under the Commerce Clause to require individuals to purchase health insurance (or pay a penalty), what is the 'limiting principle' that would prevent the federal government from regulating anything that affects the US economy?

Solicitor General Donald Verrilli began his defense of the 'minimum coverage provisions' with what could have been his strongest point: 'Insurance has become the predominant means of paying for health care in this country.' He tried to explain that everyone is in the health care market. This is because we will virtually all get sick at unpredictable times, and need very costly care at that point. Therefore, the federal government should be able to require individuals who do not have health care insurance to enter arguably another part of the health care market, the health insurance market, to avoid the cost-shifting problem of making everyone who is insured pay for the health care of uninsured people who get care in emergency departments when they need it.

Several justices, who are almost universally described as 'conservatives', jumped in with hypothetical scenarios to refute the proposition that there is something that makes the health care industry unique. Chief Justice Roberts, for example, suggested that all

6 *Roe v Wade* 410 US 113 (1973). 7 *Bush v Gore* 531 US 98 (2000).

8 *Citizens United v Federal Election Commission* 130 S Ct 876 (2010).

emergencies have the same nature, and could justify the federal government to require that everyone purchase a cell phone so 'you can just dial 911 no matter where you are'. Roberts continued: 'You don't know when you're going to need police assistance. You can't predict the extent [of] emergency response that you'll need. But when you do, the government provides it.' When Verrilli asserted that health insurance played a unique role in paying for health care, Justice Alito responded with his own analogy: burial insurance. Alito suggested that since death is inevitable and most people don't have burial insurance, we'll all be stuck with the bill so Congress should be able to require young people to get insurance to subsidize the elderly. Justice Ginsburg quickly pointed out: 'If you're going to have insurance, that's how insurance works.' Thereafter, Justice Kennedy made the statement that has been extensively commented on:

> Assume for a moment that this is unprecedented, *this is a step beyond what our cases have* allowed, the affirmative duty to act to go into commerce. If that is so, do you not have a heavy burden of justification? I understand that we must presume laws are constitutional, but, even so, *when you are changing the relation of the individual to the government in this, what we can stipulate is, I think, a unique way, do you not have a heavy burden of justification to show authorization under the Constitution*? (emphasis added)[9]

Verrilli responded by repeating his opening argument, prompting Justice Scalia to wonder out loud about the nature of the health care market itself:

> Health care. It may well be that everybody needs health care sooner or later, but not everybody needs a heart transplant, not everybody needs a liver transplant . . . *everybody has to buy food sooner or later, so you define the market as food, therefore, everybody is in the market; therefore, you can make people buy broccoli.* (emphasis added)

Verrilli reasonably responded that this case would not provide a precedent for these examples because the health care market is unique. He also distinguished the two markets on the basis that the food market 'is not a market in which your participation is often unpredictable and often involuntary . . . [or a market in which when you seek a product or service] you will get it even if you can't pay for it.' This leads Justice Scalia to ask what has become the central question in the entire case, and certainly the one bothering Justice Kennedy: what is the limiting principle, if the Court accepts the argument that Congress can require individual citizens to purchase health insurance, is there anything Congress cannot require its citizens to do?

Justice Scalia adds another analogy, asking if Congress could make you purchase environmentally-friendly mufflers for your car. Justice Kennedy almost immediately asks: 'Can you identify for us some limits on the Commerce Clause?' Hearing an unconvincing response, Kennedy pressed him again: 'If Congress says that interstate commerce is affected, isn't, according your view, that the end of the analysis?' Verrilli answered that the muffler and broccoli cases are cases in which Congress is creating commerce, rather than trying to regulate the effects of existing commerce.

Again, Justice Ginsberg stepped in:

> I thought a major, major point of your argument was that the people who don't participate in this market are making it much more expensive for the people who do; that is . . . a good number of them will get services that they can't afford at the point where they need them, and the result is

[9] This and all other quotations from the oral argument are taken from *Department of Health and Human Services v Florida*, 11–389, United State Supreme Court Official Transcript, 27 March 2012, available at <http://www.supremecourt.gov/oral arguments/argument_transcripts/11-398-Tuesday.pdf>.

that everybody else's premiums get raised. So . . . it's not your free choice just to do something for yourself. What you do is going to affect others, affect them in . . . a major way.

Verrilli, asked yet again to state his limiting principle, provided the kind of answer that law professors have made and would accept, but which seemed weak and unconvincing when made to the Court:

We got two and they are different. Let me state them. First, with respect to the comprehensive scheme. When Congress is regulating—is enacting a comprehensive scheme that it has the authority to enact [under the Commerce Clause] that the Necessary and Proper Clause gives it the authority to include regulation, including a regulation of this kind, if it is necessary to counteract risks attributable to the scheme itself that people engage in economic activity that would undercut the scheme . . .

With respect to the [second] considering the Commerce Clause alone . . . our position is that Congress can regulate the method of payment by imposing an insurance requirement in advance of the time . . . the service is consumed when the class to which that requirement applies either is or virtually is most certain to be in that market when the timing of one's entry into that market and what you will need when you enter that market is uncertain and when you will get care in that market, whether you can afford to pay for it or not and shift costs to other market participants.

2. The Argument against the Mandate

Former Solicitor General Paul Clement, who represented the twenty-six states challenging the ACA, opened his attack with a direct and concise statement:

The mandate represents *an unprecedented effort by Congress to compel individuals to enter commerce in order to better regulate commerce.* The Commerce Clause gives Congress the power to regulate existing commerce. It does not give Congress the far greater power to compel people to enter commerce to create commerce essentially in the first place. Now, *Congress when it passed the statute did make findings about why it thought it could regulate the commerce here, and it justified the mandate as a regulation of the economic decision to forego the purchase of health insurance. That is a theory without a limiting principle.* (emphasis added)

To clarify the argument, Clement agreed that the federal government could require payment or purchase of insurance at the point of use, for example at the emergency department, because the individual would then have entered commerce. He also argued that even so, the issue was not just a matter of 'timing' of the purchase of health insurance; rather it was a way to 'capture' the young, healthy people, who 'are essentially the golden geese that pay for the entire lowering of the [health insurance] premium'. The questioning of the Solicitor General was dominated by Chief Justice Roberts, Justice Scalia, and Justice Kennedy; the questioning of the two lawyers arguing against the mandate was dominated by the four 'liberal' justices, Justices Breyer, Ginsburg, Sotomayor, and Kagan.

No one can predict the outcome of a case from the oral argument alone. Nonetheless, it seems fair to conclude that everyone should have been prepared to argue the reach of the Commerce Clause authority as a basis for federal regulation of the national economy. Likewise, everyone should have expected the basic federalism argument: does the modern Commerce Clause jurisprudence amount to a federal police power over US citizens, or is there some limiting principle that permits Congress to regulate the health care industry (including the insurance mandate), but bars it from requiring citizens to do other things, like buy broccoli or gym memberships, to decrease the cost of health care insurance?[10]

Another way of approaching a limiting principle is to ask when and how an individual enters a particular market. Justice Breyer, for example, suggested that a person could be considered to be in the health care market 'by virtue of being a human being'. The third advocate of the day, Michael Carvin, who represented an industry group in opposing the law, responded: 'If being born is entering the market, then I can't think of a more plenary power Congress can have, because that literally means they [the federal government] can regulate every human activity from cradle to grave. I though that's what distinguished the plenary police power from the very limited commerce power.' In other words, being human is not a useful limiting principle.

3. What about People Who Need Health Care?

Almost all of these Commerce Clause-based arguments proved to be too abstract to defend the constitutional challenge to the ACA. A clear limiting principle is what the justices wanted, and it was a mistake not to provide one in the administration's briefs. In the absence of a limiting principle, the uniqueness of the health care system could be argued best, I think, by using actual examples of the negative impact of the dysfunctional US health care system on tens of millions of Americans, and explaining how the mandate makes guaranteed insurance issue possible, and thus will change their lives for the better. In electoral politics this is, of course, noncontroversial. Both President Obama and then Senator Hillary Clinton, for example, recognized the power of individual stories of people whose lives had been dramatically and negatively affected by our current nonsystem on the campaign trail. And after his election, President Obama continued to rely on the stories of real people, including his mother and grandmother, to support the ACA. It is even fair to say that the law, which just barely survived, would not have been passed at all were it not for the transformative 25 February 2010 health care summit President Obama hosted at the White House. At this summit, stories of individuals and their often heartbreaking interactions with the health care insurance industry greatly outweighed more abstract arguments about cost and socialized medicine.[11]

Appellate courts are not supposed to care; but in this case at least an attempt should be made to convince them (or at least to convince Justice Kennedy) that they should. Real people did not figure in the oral arguments on the mandate, even as examples to explain how the health care market and its financing method, the health insurance market, actually work in the real world. Nonetheless, at the end of his arguments on the third and final day, in the context of the expanded Medicaid program, and with only a minute or so left in his presentation, Solicitor General Verrilli made the point I think he could have usefully led with, that the ACA solves 'problems in the economic marketplace that have resulted in millions of people not having health care because they can't afford insurance'. Verrilli continued, echoing the health and human rights mantra (that

10 W.K. Mariner, G.J. Annas, and L.H. Glantz, 'Can Congress Make You Buy Broccoli? And Why That's a Hard Question' (2011) 364 *New England Journal of Medicine* 201.

11 Kaiser Health News, Transcript: White House Health Summit, 25 February 2010, available at <http://www.kaiserhealthnews.org/Stories/2010/February/25/health-care-reform-transcript.aspx>.

health and human rights are 'inextricably linked')[12] in a country without a 'right to health':

> There is an important connection, a profound connection between that problem and liberty. And I do think it's important that we not lose sight of that... [because of the Medicaid expansion] there will be millions of people with chronic conditions like diabetes and heart disease, and as a result of the health care they will get, they will be unshackled from the disabilities that those diseases put on them and have the opportunity to enjoy the blessings of liberty. And the same will be true for the husband whose wife is diagnosed with breast cancer and who won't face the prospect of being forced into bankruptcy to try to get care for his wife and face the risk of having to raise his children alone, and I can multiply example after example after example. (emphasis added)[13]

The Solicitor General then aptly and succinctly summarized the administration's case that health care is unique, and upholding the ACA does require granting Congress unlimited power under the Commerce Clause. How to deal with the national problem of 50 million people with very limited access to health care because they have no health insurance is, he concluded, 'a judgment of policy that democratically accountable branches of this government made by their best lights' and that the Court (nonelected, unaccountable, and way right of center (left unsaid)) should respect; a point very similar to the one the president made a week later.

The Solicitor General may well have tried to drag the tens of millions of uninsured Americans before the Court in an act of desperation. As a general rule, facts should not substitute for arguments about constitutional doctrine. Unfortunately, constitutional arguments only matter to neutral, nonpolitical, judges. Those adjectives do not describe this Court. In the case of a once-in-a-half-century statute, that was passed to improve the lives and health of real people, to leave the people on the steps of the US Supreme Court building was a political, if not a legal, misjudgment. The uninsured people of the US are a necessary, if not sufficient, supplement to constitutional doctrine in the context of a constitutional challenge to a Congressional attempt to provide access to health care for all.

4. The Supreme Court Rules

The Court's final decision upholding most of the Affordable Care Act and its insurance coverage requirement was surprising, but much less surprising than the identity of its architect, the Chief Justice.[14] Chief Justice Roberts, not Justice Kennedy, turned out to be the 'swing' vote.

The original vote in conference was 4 to 4. Since the Chief Justice voted last, he could decide the case, and he assigned it to himself. It is reported by Jeffrey Toobin that his initial thought was to go with the conservative block and strike down the mandate under the Commerce Clause—but this was not enough for the four who wanted to kill off the entire law. In Toobin's words, they 'overplayed their hand... [prompting

[12] All quotations are from *National Federation of Independent Business v Sebelius* 132 S Ct 2566 (2012).

[13] *Florida v Department of Health and Human Services*, 11–400, United States Supreme Court Official Transcript, available at <http://www.Supremecourt.gov/oral_arguments/argument_transcrpts/11-400.pdf>.

[14] The remainder of this chapter is adapted from W.K. Mariner, L.H. Glantz, and G.J. Annas, 'Reframing Federalism: The Affordable Care Act (and Broccoli) in the Supreme Court' (2012) 367 *New England Journal of Medicine* 1154.

Roberts] to look for some kind of middle ground'.[15] Because of the 4 to 4 split, Chief Justice John Roberts was able to write the lead opinion that commanded five votes (his and four others) for whatever outcome he determined was constitutional.

It was widely assumed that the Court's interpretation of the Commerce Clause would determine whether the constitution authorized Congress to require individuals to purchase a product from private companies, something Congress had never done before and, therefore, something the Court had never considered. It was not surprising that the Chief Justice found no Commerce Clause authority for the individual mandate. The surprise was that he saved the individual mandate by determining that it was a constitutional tax. The Chief Justice got support for each of these conclusions from two different 4-justice groups, sometimes referred to as the liberal and conservative wings of the Court. Perhaps most unexpected, seven justices voted to limit the power of the federal government to impose conditions on federal funding allocated to the states.

5. The Commerce Clause

The Commerce Clause has historically been interpreted to grant the federal government broad power to regulate matters of interstate commerce, as well as activities that affect interstate commerce. Examples include the manufacture and sale of legal and illegal drugs, consumer products, air and water pollution, workplace safety, and discrimination in employment. Nonetheless, the Chief Justice concluded that the Commerce Clause did not include the power to impose the mandate on individuals who were not already buying health insurance. Justices Antonin Scalia, Anthony Kennedy, Clarence Thomas, and Samuel Alito, in a jointly written dissent, agreed with the Chief Justice on the Commerce Clause. In the majority's view on this issue, the federal government's power to require or regulate behavior only applies to people who are actively engaged in commerce. As the Chief Justice put it: 'The Framers gave Congress the power to *regulate* commerce, not to *compel* it....'[16] These justices accepted the argument that individuals who are not currently seeking or under the care of physicians or other health professionals 'are not currently engaged in any commercial activity involving health care'. They rejected the government's argument that the fact that virtually everyone is or will be in the health care market at some stage empowers Congress to regulate how they pay for their care. Instead, the Chief Justice distinguished the health insurance market from the health care market, concluding that they 'involve different transactions, entered into at different times, with different providers'.

The decisive issue for these five justices was their view of federalism, specifically how to distinguish federal authority to regulate commerce from the state's inherent authority ('police power') directly to regulate individuals, such as by requiring immunizations, school attendance, and regulating marriage. If the Commerce Clause allowed the federal government to regulate people who are not engaged in commerce, they worried, then the federal government would have the same power that states have to regulate individual behavior, because almost anything anyone does or does not do can affect the national economy. Congress can regulate a great deal of what people do, but these five justices drew the line at inactivity, lest the Commerce Clause 'give Congress the

15 J. Toobin, *The Oath: The Obama White House and the Supreme Court* (New York: Doubleday, 2012) 289.

16 All quotations are from *NFIB v Sebelius* (see n 12).

same license to regulate what we do not do, fundamentally changing the relation between the citizen and the Federal Government... That is not the country the Framers of our Constitution envisioned'. In the Chief Justice's words: 'Every day individuals do not do an infinite number of things... Any police power to regulate individuals as such, as opposed to their activities, remains vested in the states.'

Justice Ruth Bader Ginsburg dissented on the Commerce Clause interpretation. The Ginsburg opinion was joined by Justices Sonia Sotomayor, Stephen Breyer, and Elena Kagan, together comprising the remaining four justices on the Court. They accepted the government's view that health insurance is simply a method of paying for health care, along with self-payment (or self-insurance) and reliance on charity. Virtually everyone in the country uses health care, so they are necessarily health care consumers. More than 86 percent of national personal health care expenditures are paid through insurance. Thus, Justice Ginsburg concluded, the mandate regulates people who are or will be active in the health care market and Congress can regulate the terms on which they pay for their care: 'Persons subject to the mandate must now pay for medical care in advance (instead of at the point of service) and through insurance (instead of out of pocket).' The Ginsberg opinion characterized the uninsured as getting a 'free ride', a term often used as a major justification for the individual mandate, as former Massachusetts Governor Mitt Romney used it in signing the Massachusetts Health Care Act (the model for the ACA).

Justice Ginsburg concluded that health care (and its financing) was unique, and that therefore finding Commerce Clause authority for the individual mandate would not result in an unrestrained expansion of federal power. She specifically rejected the conclusion that finding the individual mandate valid under the Commerce Clause would mean that the federal government could require people to purchase healthy vegetables, including broccoli, which she characterized as the 'broccoli horrible'. She argued that broccoli purchases could be easily distinguished, and in any event, that the claim that broccoli or vegetable purchases would have a substantial effect on health care costs required a 'chain of inferences' that prior Commerce Clause cases had rejected.

6. Federal Power to Tax

Chief Justice Roberts (remarkably) saved the individual mandate by finding that the payment for non-compliance is a tax (rather than a penalty) which Congress has authority to impose under its Taxing Power, an enumerated power distinct from the Commerce Clause. With the members of the Ginsburg opinion, the Chief Justice had a 5 to 4 majority for this unlikely conclusion. The ACA calls the payment a 'penalty' for violating a mandate, but the Court is not bound by this label. The Chief Justice reasoned that the payment functions like a tax. The ACA does not prescribe any punishment for failing to have coverage. Instead, the Internal Revenue Service collects the payment with federal income taxes. The IRS is authorized to withhold the payment from any refund due the taxpayer, but it is barred from imposing criminal prosecution or additional penalties for nonpayment. Moreover, the payment amount is a small percentage of taxable income, and is capped at the amount of a very basic level health insurance premium. Thus, the failure to have coverage is not unlawful; it is simply taxable. The Joint Dissent argued that the Court should take Congress at its word in calling the payment a 'penalty', asserting that upholding the mandate as a tax amounted to rewriting, rather than interpreting, the statute.

7. Indirect Federal Regulation via Conditional Federal Spending

The ACA amends the Medicaid statute by adding a new category of eligible recipients: persons under 65 years of age with incomes below 133 percent of the Federal Poverty Level (FPL, $14,170 for an individual; $23,050 for a family of four). The federal government will pay 100 percent of the cost of the newly eligible beneficiaries up to 2016, and 90 percent after 2020, instead of the 50 to 83 percent it now pays for currently eligible categories. One of the possible sanctions for a state's noncompliance with Medicaid eligibility rules is forfeiture of federal funding for the state's entire Medicaid program. In the most unexpected result, seven justices concluded that the ACA's new category of eligibility for Medicaid could not be imposed on the states as a condition of continuing to receive federal Medicaid funds for their existing Medicaid programs. Congress's spending power is an important source of power in areas where the federal government does not have direct regulatory authority. Since states are free to accept or reject federal funds and the conditions that come with them, the Court has never found that a condition on federal funding is an impingement on state sovereignty.

The Court, nonetheless, agreed with the twenty-six states challenging this provision of the ACA that, in practice, the states have no choice but to accept the 'new', expanded eligibility category and amend their state Medicaid laws accordingly. They reasoned that if a state refused to accept this 'new' Medicaid expansion, the federal government could 'penalize' the state by terminating its participation in—and all federal funding for—the 'old' Medicaid program. The Court found that this 'penalty' made the offer of new federal funding 'coercive', such that the federal government was 'forcing' the states to accept it. In their opinion, federal coercion of states violated the core principle of federalism.

The Chief Justice also emphasized that the Medicaid expansion was intended to complete the construction of an overarching federal program: 'It is no longer a program to care for the neediest among us, but rather an element of a comprehensive national plan to provide universal health insurance coverage.' Medicare covers those aged 65 and over, and the ACA will allow all those under 65 to buy federally regulated health insurance on a federally regulated exchange, with federal subsidies for those with incomes between 100 and 400 percent of FPL. The Medicaid expansion, if adopted by all states, would bring everyone else into a federally regulated system, something that both the Chief Justice and Joint Dissent Justices appear to have found objectionable.

8. Federalism

The three opinions present strikingly different views of the authority of the federal government in relation to individuals and to the states. The Chief Justice and the Joint Dissent emphasized that the Constitution only grants Congress specifically enumerated powers, leaving all other sovereign powers to the states. They focus on how the Framers might have understood 'commerce', with the Joint Dissent quoting eighteenth-century dictionary definitions as authority for their interpretation. The Joint Dissent argued that if Congress could regulate people who do nothing other than 'breathe in and out', then it becomes, in the words of Alexander Hamilton in *The Federalist* No 33, 'the hideous monster whose devouring jaws . . . spare neither sex nor age, nor high nor low, nor sacred nor profane'. Their language suggests alarm at the prospect of an all-powerful national government, which they believe the Founders shared.

In contrast, the Ginsburg Opinion viewed the federal government as one designed to craft solutions to national problems that the states cannot solve by themselves. The Joint Dissent disparaged this view as treating 'the Constitution as though it is an enumeration of those problems that the Federal Government can address', rather than granting the federal government only specific, enumerated powers. The Ginsburg opinion replied that their views 'bear a disquieting resemblance to [the Court's] long-overruled decisions' that struck down early twentieth-century federal legislation requiring minimum wages and maximum hours for employees. The different perspectives are reminiscent of disagreements over New Deal legislation. This seems to be why the Ginsburg opinion compared the ACA to the Social Security Act, noting that although Social Security was unprecedented when first enacted, the Court found it a permissible exercise of Congress's power to tax and spend for the general welfare. They also expressed a disagreement over the nature of health care, which Justice Ginsburg argued is unique and critical to life, in other words, a public good; and the majority of justices saw as just another market good.

9. Unanswered Questions

By limiting Congress's power to directly regulate individuals under the Commerce Clause, while allowing Congress to indirectly regulate individuals by taxation, the Court permits the federal government to influence individuals by taxing them for not having health insurance. This is now a constitutional way to regulate people who are doing nothing. It is also precisely the type of expansion of federal power the Chief Justice said would redefine the relationship of the federal government to individuals. Yet nothing in the opinions appears to limit the use of this power. Given the number of things that 'people do not do', the taxing power is now remarkably broad. Future questions may include whether a federal tax on failing to use public transportation or failing to maintain a normal BMI would be constitutional. As for the 'broccoli horrible', this opinion arguably supports Congressional power to tax people for not buying broccoli.

The most unsettling aspect of the Court's decision is the limit on the federal government's authority to impose conditions on how its money is used. The Court had never before found a federal spending program to be coercive, and most scholars believed coercion to be a toothless standard that the Court would not apply. It is remarkable that the Court could conclude that states have no choice but to accept the new Medicaid conditions with their Medicaid funding. While federal funding provides an incentive for states to participate in a federal program, it is hardly a 'gun to the head', as the Chief Justice called it. The ACA made the new Medicaid funding generous in order to entice the states to participate, and Congress expected all states to do so. But, that expectation was based on the fact that the offer was so generous that no rational decision-maker would refuse it, not because it was coercive.

Because the coercion rationale seems so weak, it is perhaps not surprising that the opinions fail to explain what counts as coercion. The leading case on the spending power, *South Dakota v Dole*, held that it was not coercive for the federal government to withhold 5 percent of federal highway funds from states that failed to enact a state law raising the minimum age for drinking alcohol to 21 years.[17] In the ACA case, the Court found that it was coercive to withhold 100 percent of federal Medicaid funds.

[17] *South Dakota v Dole* 483 US 203 (1987).

However, the Court did not attempt to draw any principled line between coercive and non-coercive payments, so it is unclear whether withholding anything between 5 and 100 percent of funding could qualify as unconstitutionally forcing states to accept a federal program.

10. The Near Future

Remarkably, given all the political and constitutional commentary about the importance of this case to the future authority of the federal government, none of the opinions made any attempt to limit the broad power to regulate interstate commerce that the federal government currently possesses. Rather, the Court seems to have expanded federal power to tax people for 'doing nothing', the primary fear that brought this case to court. It is hard to believe that this power is as expansive as the Chief Justice suggested, but his opinion did not discuss limitations. The current taxing power certainly would permit an increased income or payroll tax to expand Medicare or create a new federal substitute for Medicaid. However, the limits of the taxing power probably will not be tested soon. It is the power that Congress is least likely to exercise in an era of federal deficits and widespread antipathy to tax increases.

The lack of health care for the poor is a national problem that the federal government was trying to fix, and one that only the federal government can fix. States cannot solve national problems. With health insurance exchanges open to all legal residents and Medicare covering elderly adults, the ACA's addition of all low-income, non-elderly adults to Medicaid would give virtually the entire population access to affordable health insurance. The Court's decision allowing the states to reject the Medicaid expansion, however, creates a significant gap in the ACA's comprehensive coverage design. Months after the opinion, it is still not clear how many states will reject Medicaid expansion. Such states will leave their uninsured populations doubly burdened. They will deny their citizens in poverty the coverage that the federal government was willing to finance, and also leave many (above the tax filing threshold) subject to the new tax on the uninsured. These individuals will remain subject to the charity of safety net providers, which is the very problem the ACA was designed to solve.

The broad significance of this case can be found in the justices' views of the proper roles of the state and federal governments, and not just in what they ruled about the ACA itself. Its immediate effect was to return the constitutionally-blessed ACA to the political realm, where it has always belonged. It was the centerpiece of Obama's campaign to be re-elected, and his re-election insures that the ACA will be implemented. Nonetheless, because the Republicans retained their majority in the House of Representatives, we are likely to see continued sparring over the funding of many of the provisions of the Act, and some states continue to actively or passively oppose various portions of the ACA, including the establishment of a state insurance exchange system. We are still a long way from agreeing that health care is a right in the US.

This is what makes the words the president chose to say about health care in his inaugural address of such interest. He did not specifically discuss the ACA, but did specifically pledge no retreat on previously existing programs of Medicare, Medicaid, and Social Security—there will be no trading 'old' programs for new ones. Moreover, Justice Roberts seems to have made peace with the President, comfortably swearing him in twice (once officially on the date prescribed by the Constitution, 20 January, and then publically on 21 January for the ceremonial swearing in), making a total of four times that he has sworn in Barack Obama (the first swearing, in 2009, saw Roberts mangling the words, so it was repeated in the White House soon thereafter). On the other hand, Justice Scalia seems to have grown even more bitter and strange, attending the swearing-in ceremony wearing a Thomas More-style cap that suggested that he had a religious conflict with the president, and that history would judge him to be on the side of God.

This seems highly unlikely. As the President put it near the end of his address:

> Our journey is not complete until all our children, from the streets of Detroit to the hills of Appalachia, to the quiet lanes of Newtown, know that they are cared for and cherished and always safe from harm. That is our generation's task – to make these words, these rights, these values of life and liberty and the pursuit of happiness real for every American . . . [In pursuing this task] we cannot mistake absolutism for principle, or substitute spectacle for politics, or treat name calling as reasoned debate. We must act, knowing that our work will be imperfect. We must act, knowing that today's victories will be only partial and that it will be up to those who stand here in four years and 40 years and 400 years hence to advance the timeless spirit once conferred to us in a spare Philadelphia hall.

4

Conceptualizing Implementation of the Right to Health

The Learning Network for Health and Human Rights, Western Cape, South Africa

*Maria Stuttaford, Damaris Kiewiets, Wendy Nefdt, Vanessa Reynolds, Glynis Rhodes, Lulama Sigasana, and Leslie London**

1. Introduction

There is a legal requirement, set out in international law, for states to respect, protect, and fulfil the right to health. While work will continue on further defining the right to health and how to monitor the right to health, it is vital that attention is given to implementation. International, regional, and national judicial systems have an important part to play in this. However, to see the right to health gain meaning for the majority, we need to extend implementation of the right to health outside the judicial system, while working with established international, regional, and national frameworks that provide the added value of human rights-based approaches. It is through civil society organization (CSO) action that a platform is provided to complement judicial approaches to rights[1,2] and this synergistic approach forms the basis for the work presented in this chapter.

The Learning Network for Health and Human Rights (LN) is a participatory action research programme established in 2008 to explore how CSOs implement a rights-based approach to health. In the LN we have initially focused on the action element of the research, with less attention to developing a conceptual framework. Here we attempt to draw together some conceptual elements to build a stronger basis for collective action on the right to health—outside the 'juridical model in which [a theory of human rights] is frequently incarcerated'.[3]

* A draft of this chapter was presented at the 'International Interdisciplinary Colloquium on Law and Global Health', University College London Laws, 2–3 July 2012, convened by Emeritus Professor Michael Freeman, Dr Sarah Hawkes, and Professor Belinda Bennett and we thank participants for comment and feedback. Kanya Mdaka, Ziyanda Ndzendze, and Nicolé Fick provided administrative assistance in bringing the contributors together. Members of the Cape Metropolitan Health Forum, Epilepsy South Africa Western Cape, Ikamva Labantu, The Women's Circle and Women on Farms Project continue to contribute to the Learning Network. Funding for the Learning Network is provided by the National Research Foundation South Africa, IDRC, and EuropeAid.

1 L. London, '"Issues of Equity are also Issues of Rights": Lessons from Experiences in Southern Africa' (2007) 7 *BMC Public Health* 4.

2 J. Perelman and L.E. White, 'Stones of Hope: Experience and Theory in African Economic and Social Rights Activism' in L.E. White and J. Perelman (eds), *Stones of Hope: How African Activists Reclaim Human Rights to Challenge Global Poverty* (Stanford, CA: Stanford University Press, 2011) 149.

3 A. Sen, 'Elements of a Theory of Human Rights' (2004) 32(4) *Philosophy and Public Affairs* 319.

While important work defining the right to health in national, regional, and international law provides a framework for state accountability and for guiding duty bearers as they develop and implement policies and programmes, a purely legal approach to the right to health is limited, since civil society action is also required to ensure implementation of the right to health. An often-cited example is that of the case brought by a public interest organization in 1998 on behalf of Irene Grootboom and 900 others who were living in an informal settlement area outside Cape Town but were threatened with eviction by municipal authorities.[4] The Constitutional Court ruled that the Cape Town local authorities had a constitutional obligation to provide shelter to homeless people and could not evict them until alternative accommodation was secured. In spite of the ruling, no formal housing was ever constructed for the community. Although the case was subsequently used to argue for the justiciability of socio-economic rights, a number of sobering lessons are evident arising from the case: if rights are to be used to implement social change, communities need to be aware of their rights; legal advice and assistance is needed to assist communities in enforcing their rights; and, most importantly, it is necessary for 'communities to become socially mobilized, structurally organized and actively involved'.[5] In other words, to transfer legal victories into reality, both state and civil society action is necessary—state action commensurate with its responsibilities and civil society action to hold the state to account.

Community action for health rights can engage not only with the state, but also with others as duty bearers. In *Minister of Health v Treatment Action Campaign 2002*, the TAC challenged the government limitation of access to the antiretroviral drug Nevirapine for the prevention of mother-to-child transmission of HIV: 'Far from litigation leading social movements strategy, the political approach TAC adopted involved the two shaping each other.'[6] In the subsequent Constitutional Court case, the court supported 'judicial collaboration with civil society organizations, on one hand, and government, on the other'. Civil society action and advocacy were promoted together with 'the courts keeping the civil society-state exchanges and negotiations open and vital, and prodding and compelling the state when it falls short of its procedural or substantive constitutional duties and commitments'.[7] Before the High Court ruling in TAC's favour, much work had been done outside the courts. This not only involved civil society action, for example demonstrations and media interviews, but also pressuring health departments to equip public facilities, encouraging doctors to vocalize their desire to prescribe treatment to patients, and pressuring pharmaceutical companies to lower the cost of treatments. In that regard, the TAC also supported government as *amicus curiae* in challenging the pharmaceutical industry's opposition to medicine pricing regulations.[8]

[4] *Government of the Republic of South Africa and ors v Grootboom and ors* 2001 (1) SA 46 (CC).

[5] G. Marcus and S. Budlender, *A Strategic Evaluation of Public Interest Litigation in South Africa* (The Atlantic Philanthropies, 2008) 67.

[6] W. Forbath with Z. Achmat, G. Budlender, and M. Heywood, 'Cultural Transformation, Deep Institutional Reform, and ESR Practice' in L.E. White and J. Perelman (eds), *Stones of Hope: How African Activists Reclaim Human Rights to Challenge Global Poverty* (Stanford, CA: Stanford University Press, 2011) 63.

[7] Forbath with Achmat, Budlender, and Heywood, 'Cultural Transformation' (n 6) 65.

[8] M. Heywood, 'Debunking "Conglomo-talk": A Case Study of the *amicus curiae* as an Instrument for Advocacy, Investigation and Mobilisation' (2001) 5(2) *Law, Democracy and Development* 133.

It is through procedural rights that civil society is able to hold duty bearers to account.[9] Orbinski[10] reminds us of Hannah Arendt's observation that the 'the first political act is to speak'. Rights do not enforce themselves and procedural rights enabling participation are as important as substantive rights.[11,12] As the example of the Grootboom and TAC cases demonstrates, human rights activists, 'use litigation but do not privilege it... they engage multiple public actors in every domain of state power... they engage both private and state actors'.[13] Legal pluralism emerges from the recognition of the limits of litigation and the recognition of legal activism and progressive politics.[14] To accommodate such pluralism, a diversity of contexts and forms of participation need to be recognized. One such form is the action research programme of the LN.

The aim of this chapter is to develop a conceptual framework to begin theorizing the LN as an example of local, collective action on implementing the right to health. Human rights, including the right to health, have been criticized for being insufficiently theoretically robust.[15] Building on an evolving participatory action research project, we re-visit theoretical concepts on which we have drawn over time and weave them together to propose an overarching conceptual framework for the assemblage of CSOs and universities which the LN comprises. In doing so, this chapter seeks to contribute to a deeper understanding of collective action by civil society for the right to health.

2. Conceptual Framework

Civil society has a crucial role to play in ensuring that the right to health is achieved,[16] particularly in terms of advocacy, developing policies and programmes, monitoring state obligations, and addressing violations of the right to health.[17] Mechanisms for participation and accountability are key principles of the right to health and provide the means by which civil society influences the implementation of the right to health. Non-discrimination is another key principle and collectives are not passive recipients of human rights, but are actors influencing the implementation of the right to health. Such action is taken in particular spaces, here referred to as sites for health rights.[18] Before action can be taken, it may be necessary to raise the consciousness[19] of civil society, state, private sector, and other actors through an adult education approach

9 M. Heywood, 'Making Sense of Section 27: Is a Rights-Based Budget Possible Within South Africa's "Available Resources"?', Paper presented at the International Interdisciplinary Colloquium on Law and Global Health, University College London Laws, London, 2–3 July 2012.

10 J. Orbinski, 'Justice and Global Health', this volume, 11–20.

11 L. Forman, 'Justice and Justiciability: Advancing Solidarity and Justice Through South Africans' Right to Health Jurisprudence' (2008) 27 *Medicine and Law* 661.

12 London, 'Issues of Equity' (n 1).

13 Perelman and White, 'Stones of Hope' (n 2) 150.

14 Perelman and White, 'Stones of Hope' (n 2).

15 Sen, 'Elements of a Theory of Human Rights' (n 3).

16 J. Thomas and L. London, *Towards Establishing a Learning Network to Advance Health Equity Through Human Rights Strategy: Final Project Report to the Center for Civil Society* (School of Public Health and Family Medicine, University of Cape Town, 2006).

17 L. London, 'Can Human Rights Serve as a Tool for Equity?', EQUINET Discussion Paper 14, EQUINET, Harare and University of Cape Town (2003).

18 M. Stuttaford, G. Lewando Hundt, and P. Vostanis, 'Sites for Health Rights: the Experience of Homeless Families in England' (2009) 1(2) *Journal of Human Rights Practice* 276.

19 P. Freire, *Pedagogy of the Oppressed* (Harmondsworth: revd edn, Penguin, 1996).

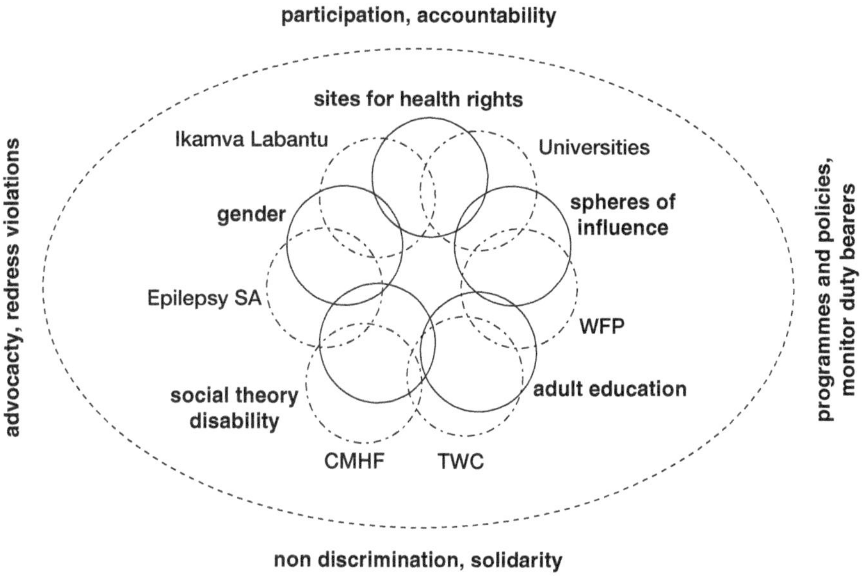

Fig. 4.1 Conceptualizing implementation of the right to health in the Learning Network

based on a dialogue of co-learning.[20] The conceptual framework presented here is one developed to support the sustainability and growth of the LN. It is not presented as a generalizable framework for the right to health, but to identify learning potentially applicable for other contexts. Each conceptual thread is examined in turn and woven into a framework (Figure 4.1). The application of the framework to the Learning Network is then discussed as a way to illuminate the on the ground implementation of the right to health.

We begin with the thread of sites for health rights. The right to health is established in national, regional, and international law and upheld in courts of law and the judicial system. States are held to account through various accountability mechanisms.[21] However, the actual implementation of the right to health takes place outside courts—for example in clinics that are physically and economically acceptable, that are available at convenient times, and that deliver appropriate, quality services; and through the availability of safe water, housing, education, and other determinants of health. Rights must be exercised somewhere. Spaces that fulfil and protect the right to health are therefore sites for health rights (for example courts of law but also places outside the judiciary such as fruit stalls, community centres, mobile clinics).[22] Moreover, because physical space is socially created and reflects power,[23,24] the spaces in

[20] M. Stuttaford, L. London, and G Glattstein-Young, 'Dialogue, Review and Reflect: A Spiral of Co-learning and Co-research to Surface Knowledge on the Right to Health' (2012) 5 *Gateways International Journal of Community Research and Engagement* 115.

[21] H. Potts, *Accountability and the Right to the Highest Attainable Standard of Health* (Human Rights Center, University of Essex, 2008).

[22] Stuttaford, Lewando Hundt, and Vostanis, 'Sites for Health Rights' (n 18).

[23] H. Lefebvre, *The Production of Space* (Oxford: 1991 trans, Blackwell, 1974).

[24] H.P.M. Winchester, L. Kong, and K. Dunn, *Landscapes: Ways of Imagining the World* (London: Pearson Prentice Hall, 2003).

which the right to health is upheld and implemented are spaces of social and political power that may need to be created.[25]

Civil society has the potential (where civil and political rights allow) to influence the creation of spaces in which to hold the state to account and to create spaces in which the right to health can be achieved. For example, Forman[26] demonstrates how, in 2001, litigation combined with social action by the TAC on the right to medicine and trade rules, led to a 'norm cascade' in which there was a shift in policies by state and non-state actors towards the right to medicines. Viewing this through the lens of sites for health rights, it is possible to see how civil society initiated the cascade of norm change by creating spaces, such as street demonstrations, media publicity, and policy positions, in which violations of human rights were challenged. The norm cascade subsequently led to the provision of ARVs at clinics, transforming the clinic space from a site where rights were violated, to sites where rights are implemented. Civil society therefore influences the sites in which the right to health is implemented[27] through advocacy, the development of policies and programmes, monitoring the state, and redressing violations.[28]

In order to influence spaces and hold duty bearers to account, local actions emerge that 'are the results of an assemblage of activists, institutions, organizations, legal and institutional frameworks, symbolic places, strategic sites, material resources'.[29] Assemblages are 'composites of place-based social movements which exchange ideas, knowledge, practices, materials and resources across sites.'[30] Rosen and Yoon[31] identify 'vernacularizers' as part of the 'human rights assemblages that emerge from the encounter between global concepts of human rights and localized practices'. They go on to explain how vernacularizers play a crucial role in translating social issues into human rights concerns, thereby making it possible to invoke the added value of national and international human rights norms. In order to act as vernacularizers, an 'empowered citizenry' is required in which 'Literacy Practitioners' can provide people with training on how to take action related to the right to health.[32] Thus, before collectives can take action, people may need their consciousness raised[33] and training on what their rights are, how to claim rights, and where to claim rights.[34] Many CSOs working in the field of health and human rights involve adults and there is a need to better understand adult learning. Approaches such as REFLECT (Regenerated Freirian Literacy through Empowering Community Techniques) are concerned with strengthening individual and collective skills to enhance participation and accountability on the

25 D. Mitchell, *The Right to the City: Social Justice and the Fight for Public Space* (New York: Guildford Press, 2003).

26 L. Forman, 'Rights and Wrongs: What Utility for the Right to Health in Reforming Trade Rules on Medicines?' (2008) 10(2) *Health and Human Rights* 44.

27 Stuttaford, Lewando Hundt, and Vostanis, 'Sites for Health Rights' (n 17).

28 London, 'Can Human Rights Serve as a Tool for Equity?' (n 16).

29 F.J. Bosco, 'Emotions that Build Networks: Geographies of Human Rights Movements in Argentina and Beyond' (2007) 98, 5 *Tijdschrift voor Economische en Sociale Geographie* 550.

30 C. McFarlane, 'Translocal Assemblages: Space, Power and Social Movements' (2009) 40 *Geoforum* 562.

31 M.Ş. Rosen and D.H. Yoon, '"Bringing Coals to Newcastle"? Human Rights, Civil Rights and Social Movements in New York City' (2009) 9(4) *Global Networks* 508.

32 M. Heywood, 'South Africa's Treatment Action Campaign: Combining Law and Social Mobilization to Realize the Right to Health' (2009) 1(1) *Journal of Human Rights Practice* 30.

33 Freire, *Pedagogy of the Oppressed* (n 19).

34 Marcus and Budlender, *A Strategic Evaluation* (n 5).

implementation of the right to health.[35] Experiential learning has a transformative element in which concepts are derived from and modified by experience and through reflection and action, individuals learn through testing knowledge and interacting with the environment.[36] Experiential learning leads to wider action[37] and influences the socio-political landscape as well as the physical landscape. In other words, learning will lead to influencing sites for health rights.

One of the limitations of participation is that people may become 'voices without influence'[38] or people may seek to influence the encouragement of 'uncivil' society.[39] Individuals and collectives need the skills to both speak and listen. As adult learners, there will be different motivations for gaining such skills.[40] Civil society will be motivated by different reasons for learning to speak and influence and duty bearers will need to be motivated to learn to listen. Influencing may take place as concentric circles, for example Dahlgren and Whitehead's[41] model of the determinants of health comprising individual characteristics in the inner circle followed by lifestyle, social networks, living and working conditions, and the outer circle of socio-economic, cultural, and environmental context. Or influencing may take place as overlapping, intertwining, and multilevelled spheres, for example as in Gaventa's[42] heuristic of a power cube operating across global, national, and local levels, across spaces that are created, closed, and invited and that represent different forms of power. CSOs are situated at the intersection of different forms of power, spheres of influence, and levels of actions and policies. In this way, CSOs translate the right to health to the local context and act as vernacularizers, creating sites for health rights across spheres of power and influence. The outcome of influencing may result in, for example, norm change, as identified by Forman,[43] or more concrete local applications, for example advocacy, monitoring duty bearers, programmes, and policies and redressing violations.[44] However, in order to be able to influence the substantive right to health, procedural rights of information, participation, and accountability need to be functioning.[45] This relates to the indivisibility of rights. In order for civil society to hold state and non-state actors to account, civil and political rights and a legal framework needs to be in place.

Participation assumes that procedural rights such as judicial reviews, national commissions, human rights impact assessments, parliamentary committees, and public hearings are in place and that people have the information and skills to hold duty bearers to account. Gender impacts on the different experiences people have of the right to health as a result of the local context in which they live, work, and socialize and have

35 D. Archer and S. Cottingham, 'REFLECT Mother Manual' (2008), available at <http://www.reflect-action.org/sites/default/files/u5/Reflect%20Mother%20Manual%20-%202012.pdf> (accessed 22 May 2012).

36 D. Kolb, *Experiential Learning* (New Jersey: Prentice Hall, 1984).

37 Archer and Cottingham, 'REFLECT Mother Manual' (n 35).

38 A. Cornwall and J. Gaventa, 'Bridging the Gap: Citizenship, Participation and Accountability' (2001) 40 *PLA Notes* 32.

39 D. Mosse, '"People's Knowledge", Participation and Patronage: Operations and Representations in Rural Development' in B. Cooke and U. Kothari (eds), *Participation: The New Tyranny?* (London: Zed Books, 2001) 16.

40 Archer and Cottingham, 'REFLECT Mother Manual' (n 35).

41 G. Dahlgreen and M. Whitehead, 'Policies and Strategies to Promote Social Equity in Health', Background document to WHO—Strategy Paper for Europe, Institute for Future Studies, Copenhagen (1991).

42 J. Gaventa, 'Finding the Spaces for Change: a Power Analysis' (2006) 37(6) *IDS Bulletin* 23.

43 Forman, 'Rights and Wrongs' (n 26).

44 London, 'Can Human Rights Serve as a Tool for Equity?' (n 17).

45 London, 'Issues of Equity' (n 1).

an effect on vulnerability to poor health outcomes, perceptions of health and health seeking behaviour, access and availability of appropriate and quality health services, and social determinants of health. In other words the intersectionality of gender is illustrative of the indivisibility of the right to health. A gender perspective and women are highlighted as special topics in General Comment 14 on the right to health.[46] While this provides an instrument for non-discrimination, such conventions have been criticized for emphasizing too heavily the maternal and reproductive rights of women and failing to take into account the wider determinants of health.[47] Bell[48] goes further to argue that international conventions alone are insufficient to ensure the attainment of human rights for women. Women have a particular role to play in influencing state policies and programmes related to the right to health, monitoring state implementation, and engaging with local action linking ideals of equality and social justice to legal frameworks.[49] While marginalized women may not have access to courts of law, and when they do, their experiences may be different to those of men,[50] they may be able to create other sites of resistance and influence by organizing for advocacy and addressing violations of the right to health. In this way, women may create the spaces and procedural rights for influencing programmes, polices and norms.

As with gender, it is important to recognize the intersectionality of disability and how it links with other determinants of inequality set out in General Comment 14.[51] Similarly to rights-based approaches, a social interpretation of disability seeks equitable access to appropriate and quality services and is based on non-discrimination and the right to participation. A social interpretation of disability takes account of the social context—including poverty, development, and power—and shifts challenges from individuals to society.[52,53] However, in the same way as individual notions of disability have limitations, so do collective, social interpretations that conceive of all disabled people as homogenous,[54] a problem which will be partly addressed by ensuring the participation of disabled people in policy-making and programme development.[55] Legal redress is insufficient alone and sites for individual and collective participation and accountability are necessary in order to ensure that the rights of people who are disabled are realized.[56]

In this section, we have sought to introduce and define each of the concepts to be used for framing the action of CSOs in the LN. Civil society has a vital role to play in

46 United Nations, UN General Comment 14 on the Right to Health (2000), available at <http://www.unhchr.ch/tbs/doc.nsf/(symbol)/E.C.12.2000.4.En> (accessed 2 September 2010).

47 A.E. Yamin, 'Promising but Elusive Engagements: Combining Human Rights and Public Health to Promote Women's Well-Being' (2004) 8(1) *Health and Human Rights* 62.

48 D. Bell, 'Considering Gender: Are Human Rights for Women, Too? An Australian Case' in A.A. An-Na'Im (ed), *Human Rights in Cross-Cultural Perspectives: A Quest for Consensus* (Philadelphia, PA: University of Pennsylvania Press, 1992) 339.

49 S.E. Merry, M. Şerban Rosen, P. Levitt, and D.H. Yoon, 'Law from Below: Women's Rights and Social Movements in New York City' (2010) 44(1) *Law and Society Review* 101.

50 Yamin, 'Promising but Elusive Engagements' (n 47).

51 UN General Comment 14 on the Right to Health (n 46).

52 M. Priestley, 'Constructions and Creations: Idealism, Materialism and Disability Theory' (1998) 13(1) *Disability and Society* 75.

53 B. Watermeyer, L. Swartz, T. Lorenzo, M. Schneider, and M. Priestley, *Disability and Social Change: A South African Agenda* (Cape Town: Human Sciences Research Council, 2006).

54 Priestley, 'Constructions and Creations' (n 52).

55 M. Heap, T. Lorenzo, and J. Thomas '"We've Moved Away from Disability as a Health Issue, It's a Human Rights Issue": Reflecting on 10 Years of the Right to Equality in South Africa' (2009) 24 (7) *Disability & Society* 857.

56 Priestley, 'Constructions and Creations' (n 52).

overcoming discrimination and health inequalities, especially where there are multiple levels of marginalization based on gender and/or disability. A human rights-based approach to health provides CSOs with a legal basis for action to redress violations and develop programmes. In the following sections it will be shown how action by CSOs utilizes concepts of gender, social interpretation of disability, adult education, spheres of influence, and sites for health rights to engage with state and non-state duty bearers. Moreover, through the solidarity of the LN, CSOs are able to learn from each other to strengthen participation and hold duty bearers to account.

3. The Learning Network

The LN is an assemblage of five civil society organizations (CSOs) working with marginalized communities in the urban and rural Western Cape, South Africa and four universities.[57] It was initiated in recognition of the need for CSOs to build capacity to implement the right to health.[58] The LN is governed by an Executive Committee (Exco), which meets quarterly and devolves responsibility for research coordination, budgeting, and leading funding applications to one of the academic partners, the University of Cape Town (UCT). Annual Strategic Planning Meetings are held, at which research goals are set jointly by all member organizations. Review and Reflection Workshops are held quarterly, designed around active participation by LN member organizations and their constituents. Additionally, the university-based researchers have monthly team meetings, open to CSO members, which include both operational discussions and a theoretically-based seminar.

The LN has undertaken several research and practice-based interventions designed to enhance and extend the implementation of the right to health.[59] The LN works outside the judicial system, utilizing international, regional, and national frameworks to advocate for the right to health, develop policy and programmes, monitor the state, and address human rights violations. The CSOs are 'positively' constituted in that they are characterized by working for equity and seek to operate in an accountable way in consultation with constituents and members. For the purposes of this chapter, a CSO is understood to be any organization that is outside the state and private sector. Such a broad definition of CSO is equally inclusive of, for example, NGOs with a formal constitution and board of directors and a member-led community-based organization that is informally constituted. The organizations making up the LN are as follows:

- Cape Metro Health Forum (CMHF)[60] is a consensus-oriented body and coordinates the eighty-six local Health Committees and eight health Sub Districts and engages with City Health and the City Health Portfolio Committee and Provincial Health and the Provincial Health Portfolio Committee. It partners and works with ten different CSOs which also have a rights-based approach.
- Epilepsy South Africa Western Cape[61] is a rights-based organization that provides social and economic development services to people with epilepsy and other disabilities. The purpose is to promote and protect the rights of people with

[57] See <http://salearningnetwork.weebly.com/index.html>.

[58] Thomas and London, *Towards Establishing a Learning Network* (n 16).

[59] L. London, N. Fick, K.H. Tram, and M. Stuttaford, 'Filling the Gap: A Learning Network for Health and Human Rights in the Western Cape, South Africa' (2012) 14 *Health and Human Rights* 1.

[60] See <http://www.facebook.com/cmhfsa>.

[61] See <http://epilepsy.org.za/wcape/>.

epilepsy and other disabilities and to provide services that are equitable and appropriate in keeping with the needs of the community.

- Ikamva Labantu's[62] vision is that every human being has the right to a dignified life. The organization's mission is to enable communities to be self-reliant because they have hope, information, support, and resources. Its values are for community ownership and drive—work is always driven and owned by actively involved community members.
- The Women's Circle's mission is to provide access to information and to orientate and equip women, men, and youth to address the challenges they face. The objectives of the community-based network are to enable groupings (Learning Circles) of women, men, and youth to take action on community issues in order to improve their living conditions and recognize and address violations of human rights.
- The coordinator of the LN is based at UCT[63] and provides financial accountability for the Network, as well as academic and strategic leadership alongside the LN Exco. Further academic partners are based at the Universities of Maastricht, Warwick, and Western Cape and are a multi-disciplinary team including public health, occupational health, nursing, psychology, anthropology, geography, and law specialists.
- The Women on Farms Project (WFP)[64] is a feminist organization that promotes the human rights of women who live and work on farms. The vision of WFP is one of a society where the farm women live lives of dignity and respect and they are able to claim their socio-economic and human rights and justice.

The principles underlying the work of the LN are that:

- empowerment implies knowledge, assertiveness, critical engagement, and collective action;
- health is a state of wellbeing, determined by access to health care and healthy social conditions; and
- networking for rights must be based on a partnership of mutual respect, benefit and equality (Report Strategic Planning Meeting 26/02/10).

In addition, four roles of the LN have been identified to support delivery of the previously mentioned objectives:

(a) a research role documenting and analysing best practices in realizing the right to health;

(b) an informational role to ensure communities are better informed about rights to health;

(c) a capacity-building role to promote access to learning opportunities for member organizations; and

(d) an action role to use the learning gained by member organizations to support services and advocacy around health (Report Strategic Planning Meeting 26/02/10).

62 See <http://ikamva.org.za>.
63 See <http://salearningnetwork.weebly.com/collaborations.html>.
64 See <http://www.wfp.org.za/content/XID1-home.html>.

The following two tables summarize the activities undertaken by the LN from inception. The design of the LN, based on a spiral of review, reflection, and dialogue, means that the co-learning and co-research elements are intertwined.[65] The representation of co-research activities (in Table 4.1) as separate from other activities (in Table 4.2) is therefore a representational convenience to highlight role (a) alongside roles (b) to (d) listed previously.

Rooted in critical theory, the LN research programme has followed a participatory action research design and has evolved by responding to learning and research objectives jointly identified by CSOs and academics. The research programme adopts a mix of methods including surveys, interviews, focus groups, observations, and auto-photography. This chapter follows that approach, particularly in trying to surface the voices of CSO participants, who are often excluded from formal academic writing. Having identified the opportunity to present a paper at the *Law and Global Health* conference, the first author (MS) canvassed LN members to participate in writing the conference paper and this chapter. Members of the LN had previously attended three writing workshops but no joint writing between the Exco had ever been undertaken, so this was a watershed development for the LN. The conceptual framework around which the paper was elaborated emerged for the first time in a LN Exco discussion in January 2012. MS drafted an outline of the paper and invited each co-author to write a short reflective piece about their organizations, which are presented in the discussion section. MS then edited the contributions into a coherent paper and invited iterative comments from other co-authors using email and Skype, until a final draft was agreed. MS led the incorporation of referee comments, with feedback from co-authors.

4. Discussion

We now explore the concepts of gender, disability, spheres of influence, adult education, and sites for health rights, together with human rights principles of participation, accountability, solidarity, and non-discrimination in relation to the activities of the Learning Network. Through this analysis, we aim to support the development not only of the LN, but of a better understanding of CSO action for the right to health.

4.1 Sites for health rights

We begin exploring where the right to health is implemented and the activities that take place in particular spaces. Ikamva Labantu has built and created various centres focused on improving health and social care—through service delivery but also through education about health care and about the right to health more broadly. Ikamva Labantu centres are spaces that are open to the community and partner NGOs to engage with each other on learning and advocacy on topics of mutual interest. Early Childhood Development (ECD) Centres (day care centres for children 0–6 years old) were developed by Ikamva Labantu and local community members in response to the self-identified need for safe, caring, and stimulating environments for children. Ikamva Labantu assisted communities in accessing government subsidies for the establishment of the ECD Centres. Linked to one of the ECD Centres is the kwaKhanya Early Childhood Learning Centre. The kwaKhanya Centre provides training using experiential learning for ECD teachers and parents involved with the

65 Potts, *Accountability* (n 21).

Table 4.1 Co-research activities undertaken within the Learning Network

Research activity	Description
Questionnaire organizational profiles	Basic demographic information on all the LN organizations
Questionnaire knowledge and practices	LN organizations at baseline and 3 years
In-depth interviews	CSO understanding of health rights and perceptions of LN activities
Mixed methods exploring organization learning for health and human rights	The impact of LN participation among member organizations
Photo voice	CSO members taking photos about health and human rights, which are used as a basis for focus groups and in-depth interviews
Case studies	In-depth interviews regarding health violations; used for training and advocacy
Toolkit on the right to health	Development and piloting of a toolkit on the right to health as a training and advocacy tool; monitoring and evaluation of roll-out; adapting for use in Southern and East Africa
Mixed methods evaluation: community participation through health committees	Community health committees as vehicles for community participation in advancing the right to health
Audit of health committees	Study of the capacity building needs of health committees and barriers to participation
Documenting health team development	Following the development of a health team in a rural farming region
Language as a component of the right to health	An exploration of how language acts as a barrier to realizing the right to health; based on data from experiences of deaf persons using sign language and Xhosa-speaking patients
Qualitative evaluation of LN pamphlets	Assessing coverage and effectiveness
Documentary review and key informant interviews	Policy study analysing the provincial draft policy on community participation and health committees
Qualitative study on disability and human rights	The understanding of human rights by people with disabilities
Qualitative reflection on the process of co-learning and knowledge creation	Reflecting on how the LN undertakes research
Literature review exploring the contribution of African philosophy to conceptualizing the right to health	An annotated bibliography; theoretical analysis of the traditional value of 'Ubuntu' as being expressed in the rights concept of dignity; rights explored as collective entitlements
Mixed methods research to explore the process of knowledge generation through rights-based research processes	Power and trust in the context of University-CSO engagement
Development and evaluation of modules for in-service training on the right to health for health care providers	Health care provider training
Mixed methods research on social capital	An exploration of the role of social capital in the integration and implementation of the right to health among CSOs

Source: Adapted from London et al, 'Filling the Gap: A Learning Network for Health and Human Rights in the Western Cape, South Africa' (2012) 14 *Health and Human Rights* 1.

Table 4.2 Co-learning activities undertaken within the Learning Network

Training area	Focus	No. of activities
The right to health	General information on what is meant by the right to health and how to hold government accountable	14
	Piloting of toolkit on the right to health	8
	Training of trainers on the toolkit	2
	Disability and the right to health	3
	Rights advocacy	1
	Community participation as key to the right to health	2
Engaging state services	Accessing basic services—advocacy with provincial and municipal authorities	
Community development tools	Participatory community mapping as an action research method	1
	Alternative methods for community decision-making in social structures	1
	Leadership training	1
Re-theorizing the right to health based on our experience	What do African theories and philosophies say about human rights, individual and collective rights, and the right to health?	2
	Culture as obstacle and opportunity	1
Writing skills	Building the capacity of LN members	2

Source: Adapted from London et al, 'Filling the Gap: A Learning Network for Health and Human Rights in the Western Cape, South Africa' (2012) 14 *Health and Human Rights* 1.

ECD Centres. The focus of the training includes the right to health and the wider, indivisible rights of the child. This is an example of how a self-identified need in the community for healthy spaces for children has led to not only addressing that need through the development of services, but also a Centre for adult education that includes rights entitlements. In this way, sites for rights have been constructed.

A different way of constructing sites for rights relates to spaces in which rights are violated and then transformed by LN CSOs. The Women on Farms Project (WFP) transforms spaces in which occupational health rights are violated into sites in which rights are upheld. This is an example of the importance of having a legal framework and social action working in conjunction to achieve accountability. State obligations to ensure the right to health is protected lead to laws being established around, for example, occupational health, which enshrine occupational health rights and place obligations on the private sector and non-state actors. When women farm workers who had no access to toilets in the vineyards and orchards were asked 'what happens when you need to go to the toilet', they replied that they 'just go in the bushes'. Once they became aware that they had the right to sanitation, and that a number of laws existed that place obligations on employers for health and safety, women workers and WFP launched a campaign demanding that toilets be made available to them in the place of work. This campaign was successful and most farmers now comply with regulations and make portable water closets available. This is an example of how legislation, coupled with adult education and community action, can influence the transformation of sites violating rights in the private sector, to sites for rights.

4.2 Gendered approaches

South Africa ratified the Convention to Eliminate all Forms of Discrimination against Women (CEDAW) and WFP uses a multi-level approach that integrates international, regional, and national conventions[66] combined with local action. In addressing the right to health, WFP uses a holistic perspective on gender and raises awareness about women's position in society and what systems and structures oppress them. WFP values the equality contained within the South African Constitution but is keenly aware that equality assumes a homogeneity that is not realized in practice when addressing issues of health. Masculine hegemony, capitalism, and patriarchy seek to perpetuate dominance in all spheres of life. In contrast, a rights-based approach addresses the needs and rights of all citizens and makes non-discrimination a key principle. By addressing health in a gendered approach, people become aware of gender inequality. For example, women farm workers face discrimination in terms of access to health care, in exposure to occupational hazards, and in gendered power relations in the household. Moreover, in rural farming areas women are generally responsible for ensuring that all the determinants of health are met. For example, they collect water and firewood, cook meals, and maintain general hygiene. Yet, in performing these basic tasks, women are at risk of violence and health hazards. Through its interventions with women on farms, WFP has found that women are attacked and raped when collecting water and fuel and often go hungry in order to ensure children and the elderly are fed. A rights-based approach incorporates addressing the intersection of multiple aspects of inequalities and frames civil society action that is gender sensitive. The approach to development taken by WFP is that improving the situation of women on farms will improve the situation of the family, the community, and the countryside and enhance equality. Thus, by addressing gender imbalances in the provision of and access to health and health care services, health status in South Africa will improve.

4.3 Spheres of influence

The objectives of the Cape Metro Health Forum (CMHF) include seeking consensus on strategies aimed at improving health and health care, promoting and monitoring the implementation of health care services, and ensuring services are equitable, accessible, affordable, appropriate and available. The CMHF has worked at the intersection of civil society and government, influencing both Health Committees and local and provincial government, seeking to influence the implementation of procedural rights. For example, the CMHF has ensured that Health Committees are trained on knowing what their rights are and work with primary health care facilities to establish formal complaints processes for the redress of violations. The CMHF and Health Committees have also influenced the provision of government services. For example, one of the Health Committees successfully influenced the Provincial Department to construct a Midwifery Obstetrics Unit next to a community health facility, and the CMHF successfully lobbied for the establishment of a new youth friendly service.

4.4 Adult learning

The previous examples illustrate the importance of consciousness-raising[67] coupled with learning about rights so that collectives can influence the physical landscape and

66 Gaventa, 'Finding the Spaces for Change' (n 42).
67 Freire, *Pedagogy of the Oppressed* (n 19).

landscapes of power to transform sites against rights into sites for rights. All LN member organizations engage in advocacy, training, and adult education. For example, Universities run train-the-trainers courses, WFP advocates with women, Epilepsy SA trains employers, and Ikamva Labantu provides primary health care education and training on the right to health at the Enkululeweni Wellness Centre. Adult education is central to The Women's Circle (TWC) and is seen as key to enabling collective action. The approach of TWC is one of emancipatory learning, with the purpose of developing understanding and knowledge of the nature and the root causes of people's circumstances, and guiding them, through a process of collaboration, to change these circumstances. All of the issues focused upon have a direct link to the right to health. TWC uses adult education and experiential learning to assist participants to engage in critical reflection, which in turn leads to conscientization and it is through the development of critical consciousness that transformation occurs. When participants are well informed, aware of the social, political, and cultural relations in society and take action, transformation is more likely to occur. This approach has assisted people in re-defining the right to health for their particular context. For example, in one community, there was a storm water pond that was used as a dumping ground for refuse and it became an area of high criminal activity. Children were also at risk by swimming and playing in the pond. The community lodged a complaint with the municipality that led to a clean-up of the area to make it safer. Since then, community members have been monitoring the situation to ensure that the municipality continues to maintain the area. This example demonstrates how once members of a community become aware of their rights, they are enabled to take action to improve their environment and their health. However, it also highlights the importance of having procedures in place through which communities can act to redress violations and monitor implementation. As Heywood[68] points out, rights do not enforce themselves, people enforce rights. Procedural rights to participation and accountability need to be in place for this to happen, as demonstrated by the TWC example.

4.5 Social explanation of disability

Adult education, training, and consciousness-raising is vital for rights holders. However, similar education and training is important for the whole of society, including health care professionals and health policy-makers.[69] Epilepsy South Africa Western Cape works with employers and service providers to develop their understanding of the rights of people who have additional needs. From a social explanation of disability, services to people with disabilities should be integrated and take cognizance of their social reality. Epilepsy SA addresses the intersection of inequality, unemployment, development, and poverty over the life course through: early intervention strategies, promotion of inclusion into mainstream education, and entry into various forms of employment. This is done through awareness raising campaigns for the general public, disability sensitization, and epilepsy management training in early childhood centres, schools, health care centres, the workplace, and other sectors of society. Epilepsy SA has a strong link with the Department of Health and the Disability Directorate and actively involves the Directorate through skills sharing as well as providing epilepsy awareness and management training to over fifty health centres. In addition, the

68 Heywood, 'Making Sense of Section 27' (n 9).

69 M.A. Stein, P.J.S. Stein, D. Weiss, and R. Lang, 'Health Care and the UN Disability Rights Convention' (2009) 374 *Lancet* 1796.

epilepsy counselling services at health centres provide a platform to guide clients and to advocate for change with, and on their behalf. An outcome of these services is awareness of the right to health and how to access appropriate services that would improve their overall quality of life. A key element to the success of this work has been the inclusion of duty bearers in consciousness raising.

4.6 Weaving the concepts together in the Learning Network

At certain times, CSOs work in partnership as 'insider' groups,[70] assisting duty bearers to fulfil obligations to the right to health—for example the Enkululekweni Wellness Centre. At other times, CSOs will act as 'outsider' interest groups[71] holding duty bearers to account for violations—for example the maintenance of a storm water pond. At the time of writing, CMHF is shifting from being an insider group working with local government and Health Committees, where CMHF received funding from local government to coordinate and represent Health Committees, to the role of an outsider group, where local government have withdrawn their recognition of CMHF.[72] CMHF has now registered as a not-for-profit organization and is re-positioning itself to continue to work in a way that holds local government to account. Local governments recognize the expertise, partnerships, and influence of individuals working with CMHF and are seeking to engage with them individually; a move which CMHF is resisting. CMHF is seeking to continue influencing local government by drawing on international conventions as well as national legislation and by creating new spaces in which to interact, a strategy not dissimilar to that put forward by WFP and Gaventa.[73] CMHF is influencing local government through the creation of new spaces, for example by joining university-based partnerships of which local government are already members, leading a local health summit, and strengthening the use of local media.

Solidarity is inherent in human rights instruments such as the South African Constitution[74] and an inclusive citizenship 'stresses that the relationship *between* citizens is at least as important as the more traditional "vertical" view of citizenship as the relationship between the state and the individual'.[75] While it is recognized that civil society can also be 'uncivil',[76] solidarity and an inclusive citizenship empowers CSOs and marginalized groups to hold the state to account on its obligations, and guards against CSOs simply accepting state transfer of responsibilities. There is a balance between holding the state to account on respecting, protecting, and fulfilling the right to health,[77] and civil society taking on these responsibilities. The health system in South Africa is strained and it may be necessary to balance the minimum core obligations of the state with the progressive realization of the right to health. In order for the right to health to be enforced through the judiciary, there needs to be an

70 G. Walt, *Health Policy: An Introduction to Process and Power* (Johannesburg: Witwatersrand University Press, 1994).

71 Walt, *Health Policy* (n 70).

72 B.M. Meier, C. Pardue, and L. London, 'Implementing Community Participation Through Legislative Reform: a Study of the Policy Framework for Community Participation in the Western Cape Province of South Africa' (2012) 12 *BMC International Health and Human Rights* 15.

73 Gaventa, 'Finding the Spaces for Change' (n 42).

74 C. Himonga, 'The Right to Health in an African Cultural Context: the Role of Ubuntu in the Realisation of the Right to Health with Special Reference to South Africa' (2013) 57(2) *Journal of African Law* 165.

75 N. Kabeer, *Inclusive Citizenship: Meanings and Expressions* (London: Zed Books, 2005) 23.

76 Mosse, 'People's Knowledge, Participation and Patronage' (n 39).

77 UN General Comment 14 on the Right to Health (n 46).

acknowledgement by a fully-functioning judiciary of the importance of socio-economic rights. As Forman[78] points out, judicial enforcement alone is insufficient and the right to health needs to be internalized within individual and collective expectations, discourse, and action. The Enkululekweni Wellness Centre was built by Ikamva Labantu, with local partners, because of the urgent need to engage communities on primary health care. Collective action through partnerships and collaboration has enabled Ikamva Labuntu to influence the physical environment through the construction of the centre, improving access and availability to health care. Ikamva Labantu has also engaged with partners on the determinants of health, such as partnering with the Social Justice Coalition, an organization that leads on sanitation issues, to hold government accountable for access to clean and safe toilets. The partnership involved an open seminar to which the mayor was invited, and the compilation of short- and long-term resolutions. One of the short-term resolutions was the appointment of janitors to maintain the condition of the toilets in the identified areas. The commitment entailed the release of funds which has been effected. The sanitation situation in schools was also examined in collaboration with the Department of Health Environmental Health Services, the Department of Education, and an NGO known as Equal Education. Through these partnerships, Ikamva Labantu has facilitated constructive solutions and practical plans with clear roles and responsibilities.

However, Ikamva Labantu found many challenges in actioning partnerships. The municipality outsourced garbage removal in the area to a private sector small or medium enterprise (SME), with the provision that the SME would employ local people. However, employment of local people has not happened in a way acceptable to the local community. As a result, the local community has refused to place garbage at agreed collection points in protest. To date, Ikamva Labantu has struggled to gain access to and influence the responsible SME in the same way as the CSO has engaged with local government. In this local setting, accountability mechanisms for engaging with private sector duty bearers, such as effective Service Level Agreements, are not yet established, unlike the case of the WFP, which was able to use legislation to influence the private sector actions to provide portable water closets on farms. Even more complex is the need for Ikamva Labantu to work with individuals as well as collectives in the community. Vandalism is responsible for damage to toilets and the dumping of rubble in drainage canals, leading to sanitation problems for the wider community. Ikamva Labantu is seeking to work with the individuals responsible to underscore the collective rights of the community. Nonetheless, Ikamva Labantu's work is driven by and owned by actively involving community members and addresses social determinants in collaboration with partners. Through several years of working at a local level, they have earned the trust of partners and are able to influence them. Ikamva Labantu believes that it is critically important to network in and develop partnerships. Memorandums of understanding have been signed with partners that assist the organization in meeting the needs of the community.

Collective action and collaborative partnerships can assist in supporting programmes working at the intersection of inequalities, and solidarity of collective action is demonstrated not only within CSO programmes but also in assemblages such as the LN. For example, a child with epilepsy living in conditions of poverty in a remote

[78] L. Forman, 'What Future for the Minimum Core: Contextualising the Implications of South African Socioeconomic Rights Jurisprudence for the International Human Right to Health' in J. Harrington and M. Stuttaford (eds), *Global Health and Human Rights: Legal and Philosophical Perspectives* (London: Routledge, 2010) 62.

rural area required medication for her seizure management. The closest health care facility stopped dispensing the medication and informed the parents that medication would only be available at another facility that would incur prohibitive transport costs. Epilepsy SA and CMHF jointly intervened to ensure redirection of the medication back to the closest health care facility. Furthermore, the case was used as a way to raise the awareness of relevant service providers of rights of people with disability. Through collaboration horizontally within the LN, the assemblage was able to action rights on the ground, illustrating how a clinic can become a site for rights.

If the first political act is to speak,[79] then how do we ensure there is genuine participation in which state and non-state duty bearers are listening and committing to action? By opening spaces for dialogue, researchers and activists can listen and build evidence to influence. The difference between the LN and other networks is that it is primarily a research network of academics and activists, whose action research provides the strategic direction of the network. In this situation, learning goes beyond 'pamphlet knowledge' to sharing underlying concepts and theories.[80] Working with the LN has enabled CSOs to engage with new communities in new ways. For example, based on research with the network, the LN has developed several pamphlets and a toolkit on the right to health and, while these were mutually agreed at the development phase, during training workshops CSOs have taken the toolkit and adapted it, or vernacularized it, for their own particular needs and purposes.[81] Whereas previously people would accept poor quality service at clinics or lack of sanitation in the workplace, people now know what their rights are and how to take action to ensure they are implemented. The LN is not simply about doing things together, but doing things *differently* together. This discussion has sought to show how CSOs—through influencing state and non-state actors—have created sites for health rights, defined by participation, accountability, and non-discrimination. Furthermore, they have demonstrated an inclusive citizenship, working across LN partners, to achieve this.

5. Conclusions

Building on empirical data gathered with the LN, this chapter has sought to develop a conceptual framework to support the ongoing development of the LN and to suggest opportunities for a deeper understanding of how collective action by civil society is a critical element for realizing the right to health. This chapter has also provided CSO co-authors the opportunity to write collaboratively for the first time for an academic audience. While the chapter draws solely on CSOs that are positively constituted in terms of a rights-based approach, future work may explore how the conceptual framework presented here might be translated to other types of organizations. Future work may also consider capturing the voices of the state, the private sector, and constituents of the CSOs. In addition, to date, there has been no formal evaluation of the Learning Network, though such an evaluation is in progress.[82] This evaluation

[79] Orbinski, 'Justice and Global Health' (n 10).

[80] L.T. Smith, *Decolonizing Methodologies: Research and Indigenous Peoples* (London: Zed Books, 1999).

[81] M. Strecker, M. Stuttaford, and L. London, 'Health rights pamphlets: critical literacy and inclusive citizenship, South Africa' (2012) Health Promotion International, doi: 10.1093/heapro/das067.

[82] W. Nefdt, 'The Role of Social Capital in the Integration and Implementation of Health and Human Rights Programmes Among Civil Society Organisations in Cape Town, South Africa', presentation to African Working Group, University of Utrecht, The Netherlands (2011).

may provide lessons for ensuring the sustainability of the Network and preparing for succession planning as individual and organizational membership evolves. Most evident in the findings is the fact that reliance solely on a legal approach will not achieve the right to health. Rather, action that builds on CSO engagement and that transforms state and CSO spaces into sites for rights is critical. Thus, learning, influencing, and transformation of the social-political and physical landscape are at the heart of what the LN strives to achieve. The intersectionality of gender and disability underpins the importance placed on the individisibility of the right to health. Particularly, but not limited to, resource-poor contexts, where access to legal processes is constrained, CSOs are able to translate, or vernacularize, the right to health to have meaning for the local context. The conceptual framework has extended our understanding of how the LN operates alongside a national and international legal framework, drawing on it to influence the implementation of the right to health, but at the same time utilizing rights to address local health challenges.

5

Access to Essential Medicines in Kenya

Intellectual Property, Anti-Counterfeiting, and the Right to Health

*John Harrington**

1. Introduction

This chapter considers the conflict between the right to health, increasingly given specific recognition in national constitutions, and the worldwide move to strengthen intellectual property enforcement (IPE) in the context of access to essential medicines. It takes as its focus a 2012 decision of the Kenyan High Court which found that anti-counterfeit legislation was unconstitutional having regard to the right to health enshrined in the country's new constitution. The chapter charts the background to the case, tracking the development of the struggle for access to essential medicines in Kenya over time. It focuses on the legislative process and litigation as two key and interrelated sites of this struggle. Drawing on theories of global health governance, it treats parliament and the courts as powerful 'nodes' capable of being enrolled to their ends by interested groups using the diverse material, legal, and rhetorical resources available to them. Combining this model with theories of adjudication in relation to social and economic rights, including the right to health, it argues that the Court's ruling was justified by oversights and exclusions in the process of parliamentary deliberation which lead to the passing of the legislation. These meant specifically that the vital health interests of many Kenyans were not adequately considered. The chapter concludes by considering whether the decision offers evidence of the socially and politically transformative effect of the new Kenyan constitution.

2. Access to Medicines in Kenya: Need and Governance

Kenya has been a particularly important site of struggle between access to medicines campaigners, including local and international non-governmental organizations (NGOs), and proponents of strong protection of intellectual property rights (IPR), particularly multinational pharmaceutical companies. For one thing, it is the biggest economy in East Africa and, therefore, a relatively large market for drugs. In 2008, Kenyan pharmaceutical imports were valued at US$240 million.[1] Kenya is the third

* I am grateful to Hugh Lamarque and Alasdair O'Hare for outstanding research assistance, to Edga Sichangi for help with materials, and to the interviewees who generously shared their insights and experiences. Thanks also to Vishwas Devaiah and Ambreena Manji, and to the reviewers, for comments on previous drafts. An earlier version was presented to a seminar of the African Population and Health Research Centre, Nairobi, on 3 October 2012. All responsibility for errors and infelicities is mine alone.

[1] United Nations Industrial Development Organization, 'Pharmaceutical Sector Profile: Kenya' (Vienna, 2010) 4.

largest African market for generic drugs from India, with sales valued at US$70 million in 2008.[2] It is also a key transport hub for Eastern and Central Africa, including for the distribution of medicines, both generic and branded.

There are between 1.3 and 1.5 million Kenyans living with HIV out of a total current population of approximately 43 million.[3] Although levels of infection among adults have fallen from around 14 per cent in the late 1990s, prevalence remains relatively high at over 7 per cent.[4] Moreover the disease accounts for nearly 10 per cent of all child deaths under the age of 5.[5] A further 1.2 million children have been orphaned by the disease.[6] Kenya is also marked by relatively high levels of poverty with 20 per cent of the population living on under US$1.25 per day.[7] Government spending on essential medicines is massively augmented by support from the US President's Emergency Plan for AIDS Relief (PEPFAR) and, to a lesser extent, from the Global Fund to Fight AIDS, Tuberculosis and Malaria (GFATM).[8] Nonetheless it remains the case that 52 per cent of Kenyans in advanced stages of HIV infection and 27 per cent of infected pregnant women still go without crucial anti-retroviral (ARVs) drugs.[9]

Legislators responded to these acute needs in 2001, when Kenya was obliged to reform existing intellectual property legislation to comply with its obligations under the World Trade Organization's (WTO) Agreement on Trade Related Aspects of Intellectual Property Rights (TRIPs). Notwithstanding the pressure exerted on developing country states by the major pharmaceutical manufacturers and their governments, Kenya was able implement the so-called 'flexibilities' contained in TRIPs in an expansive manner which tended to promote access to essential medicines, including imported generic medicines.[10] More recently Kenya and East Africa more generally have been a focus of the worldwide 'anti-counterfeiting' campaign backed by major IPR holders in pharmaceuticals and other industries, a campaign which resulted in dedicated legislation on the topic. As will be seen, it was widely argued by scholars and activists that this legislation tended to restrict access to essential medicines.[11] These struggles over access to essential medicines took place within a wider context of democratization in Kenya. After a number of thwarted initiatives, Kenyan voters approved a new constitution for the republic in 2010. The Bill of Rights includes a comprehensive catalogue of justiciable social and economic rights, including the right

[2] B.P. Mey, 'Unfettered Consumer Access to Affordable Therapies in the Post-TRIPS Era: A Dead-End Journey for Patients? Kenya and India Case Studies' (2010) 13 *Journal of World Intellectual Property* 403, 406.

[3] UNICEF, 'Kenya—Statistics', available at <http://www.unicef.org/infobycountry/kenya_statistics.html> (accessed 27 November 2012).

[4] National Aids Control Council, 'Kenya Aids Strategic Plan 2009/10–2012/13. Delivering on Universal Access to Services' (Nairobi, 2009) 5.

[5] World Health Organization, 'World Health Statistics Part II: Global Health Indicators' (Geneva, 2011).

[6] Kenya National Bureau of Statistics and ICF Macro, 'Kenya Demographic and Health Survey 2008–9' (Calverton, MD, 2010).

[7] UNICEF, 'Kenya—Statistics' (n 3).

[8] See UNIDO, 'Pharmaceutical Sector Profile: Kenya' (n 1).

[9] World Health Organization, 'World Health Statistics Part II: Global Health Indicators' (Geneva, 2011).

[10] B. Sihanya, 'Patents, Parallel Importation and Compulsory Licensing of HIV/AIDS Drugs: the Experience of Kenya' in P. Gallagher, P. Low, and A.L. Stoler (eds), *Managing the Challenges of WTO Participation: 45 Case Studies* (Cambridge: CUP, 2005) 264.

[11] J. Von Braun and P. Munyi, 'New Enforcement Mechanisms Challenge the Legality of Generics in the Name of Public Health: The Emergence of Anti-Counterfeiting Legislation in East Africa' (2010) 18 *African Journal of International and Comparative Law* 238.

to health. This right was relied upon by the Kenyan High Court in its decision in *P.A. O. v Attorney General*[12] (*P.A.O.*) of April 2012 to rule that key provisions of the Anti-Counterfeit Act 2008 were invalid in so far as they impeded access to essential medicines, including generics.

The dimensions of this ongoing struggle and the significance of the High Court decision in *P.A.O.* will be analysed with reference to the theory of 'nodal governance' developed by Burris, Drahos, and Shearing.[13] Put briefly, on this account, governance nodes are sites which seek 'to manage a course of events'.[14] They include private companies and NGOs, but also state bodies, such as courts and parliament. The governing potency of a given node depends on: (1) its institutional structure; (2) the material resources available to it; (3) the technologies which it can use to exert influence, such as publicity, but also its legal powers and rights; and (4) its characteristic 'mentality', ie how it frames problems and communicates the importance of solving them.[15] Each of these attributes influences the capacity of a node to enrol other nodes and, thus, to harness their distinctive resources and technologies to its own governance objectives. As will be seen in the following sections, enrolment may occur when, say, a well-funded industry association uses intensive lobbying to persuade parliament that a particular problem faced by business is of such social importance as to require new legislation and extended law enforcement.

State institutions are, thus, 'critical nodes' in governance networks, though as the model indicates they are governed as much as they govern.[16] This suggests that nodal governance cannot simply be equated with a democratic diffusion of decision-making. On the contrary, as Burris, Drahos, and Sheaing note, it may be associated with 'unaccountable concentrations of power', whereby even formally democratic nodes, such as parliament, are accessible to only a few and respond chiefly to their interests.[17] These normative concerns can be addressed by regulating significant nodes to provide for increased accessibility and improved deliberation.[18] The law is central to this task, for example through mandating public participation in legislative proceedings or widening standing to take legal action. As Rosalind Dixon has argued, entrenched social and economic rights too can be understood to function in this way.[19] Thus, it will be seen that the effect of the right to health as deployed in *P.A.O.*, was to remedy 'democratic failures' of nodal governance in relation to anti-counterfeiting and access to essential medicines.[20]

3. Implementing TRIPs Flexibilities: Industrial Property Act 2001

The Industrial Property Act 2001, which defines the substantive rights of patent holders, forms the baseline for the subsequent attempts to reform the law on IPE in

12 [2012] eKLR, HC Nairobi (*per* Ngugi J).

13 S. Burris, P. Drahos, and C. Shearing, 'Nodal Governance' (2005) 30 *Australian Journal of Legal Philosophy* 30.

14 Burris, Drahos, and Shearing, 'Nodal Governance' (n 13) 37.

15 Burris, Drahos, and Shearing, 'Nodal Governance' (n 13) 37–9.

16 Burris, Drahos, and Shearing, 'Nodal Governance' (n 13) 54.

17 Burris, Drahos, and Shearing, 'Nodal Governance' (n 13) 58.

18 Burris, Drahos, and Shearing, 'Nodal Governance' (n 13) 54–5.

19 R. Dixon, 'Creating Dialogue About Socio-Economic Rights: Strong-Form Versus Weak-Form Judicial Review Revisited' (2007) 5 *International Journal of Constitutional Law* 391.

20 K.L. Scheppele, 'A Realpolitik Defense of Social Rights' (2004) 82 *Texas Law Review* 1921, 1926.

Kenya. Its passage can also be seen as the first phase in recent struggles over access to essential medicines. The legislative process was marked by the formation of the Kenya Coalition for Access to Essential Medicines by local and international NGOs working with people living with HIV/AIDS (PLWHA).[21] The Coalition urged MPs to avoid offering patent protection in excess of TRIPs obligations and instead to use the flexibilities in the Agreement to widen access to affordable essential medicines.[22] They succeeded to a surprising degree in this task of enrolment.[23] Specifically the Coalition managed to win over leading officials of the Kenyan Industrial Property Office (now Institute) (KIPI) and key administrators in the Ministry of Trade.[24] Most importantly, perhaps, they received considerable support from the Minister of Trade, Mr Nicholas Biwott MP, a close ally of President Moi.[25]

The means used by the Coalition were essentially two-fold. The first can be seen as a deployment of 'legal technology'. Coalition experts developed a detailed technical analysis of the original reform Bill, as well as a set of precise proposals for widening access.[26] These were widely circulated, and several key proposals were taken up in Parliament, forming part of the Act as passed.[27] Significantly these legal arguments did not draw on the human right to health, which was not recognized by the Constitution then in force. In its place, the Coalition offered a starker political message. 'MPs should think about the plight of their people' argued Dr Chris Ouma of Action Aid, as 'they now have the power to alleviate their suffering'.[28] Parliament should 'put life before profit'.[29] This message helped to produce a 'general atmosphere' of 'public outrage'.[30] For instance, Professor Sam Ongeri, who moved the Bill as Health Minister, specifically criticized the multinational pharmaceutical companies for their defence of strong intellectual property rights in the face of pressing access needs on a number of occasions.[31] The Coalition complained furthermore that corporate lobbying was secretive and lacked transparency.[32] By contrast, industry arguments that distribution problems and corruption were greater obstacles to drug access than the patent law regime were less influential.[33]

21 The Coalition comprised 15 NGOs and medical organizations, including the Kenya Treatment Action Movement, Kenya Medical Association, Médecins Sans Frontières, Action Aid, Care International, and Health Action International, see Anon, 'Lobby Launches AIDS Bill Drive', *Daily Nation*, 30 May 2001.

22 R. Lewis-Lettington and S. Musungu, *In Defence of Kenya's Health: Proposed Amendments to the Industrial Property Bill 2000. Report from the Kenya Access to Essential Medicines Coalition* (Nairobi, 2000) (copy on file with author).

23 Lewis-Lettington and Musungu, *In Defence of Kenya's Health* (n 22) 9.

24 Interview with Robert Lewis-Lettington, Legal Consultant, 9 May 2012.

25 Interview with Robert Lewis-Lettington, Legal Consultant, 9 May 2012; Interview with James Kamau, Co-ordinator for Kenya Treatment Action Movment, 12 September 2012.

26 Lewis-Lettington and Musungu, *In Defence of Kenya's Health* (n 22).

27 Interview with Robert Lewis-Lettington, Legal Consultant, 9 May 2012.

28 Quoted in Sihanya, 'Patents, Parallel Importation and Compulsory Licensing' (n 10) 272.

29 See 'Lobby Launches AIDS Bill Drive', *Daily Nation*, 30 May 2001; M. Nyambala, 'Enforce Bill, Government Urged', *The Standard*, 26 November 2001.

30 R. Lewis-Lettington and P. Munyi, *Willingness and Ability to use TRIPS Flexibilities: Kenya Case Study* (London: Department for International Development, 2004) 9.

31 V. Bwire, 'Minister Accuses Drug Firms', *The Standard*, 8 February 2002; N. Ford, 'Patents, Access to Medicines and the Role of Non-Governmental Organisations' (2004) 1 *Journal of Generic Medicines* 142.

32 See Sihanya, 'Patents, Parallel Importation and Compulsory Licensing' (n 10) 272. Members of key parliamentary committees were lobbied on the content of the Bill by executives of drug multinationals at a Mombasa hotel in May 2001: D. Onyango, 'Firms Lobby Against Bill', *Daily Nation*, 9 May 2001.

33 O. Gruduah, 'Bruising Intellectual Property Rights Wars', *The Standard*, 26 November 2001.

The Coalition's success was surprising given that from independence in 1963 Kenyan governments had closely identified with the interests of international business. They had also set themselves firmly against any substantive view of social justice as a principle of government policy.[34] However, by the late 1990s Kenya's formerly close relationship with the Western powers had deteriorated greatly. President Moi's government had already been subject to a decade of international pressure to introduce political and economic reforms.[35] In resisting these dictates leaders were receptive to 'nationalist' or 'populist' arguments which opposed vulnerable and needy Kenyans to profit-oriented foreign companies and by implication their home governments.[36] The mentality of the Coalition node resonated with that of the government, making successful enrolment more likely. The years preceding the passage of the 2001 Act were also marked by an increase in struggles for access to essential medicines internationally.[37] As head of the Kenyan delegation to the WTO Ministerial Conference held at Seattle in December 1999, Minister Biwott would have seen at first hand the conflict over intellectual property and other trade issues both within the conference hall and on the streets of Seattle.[38] Moreover, Kenyan access campaigners highlighted the abandonment, in April 2001, by pharmaceutical manufacturers of litigation challenging the incorporation of TRIPs flexibilities into South African law.[39]

As finally passed, the Industrial Property Act 2001 is marked by 'an aggressive public health focus'.[40] It includes generous provisions on government use,[41] voluntary licensing,[42] compulsory licensing,[43] and the 'early working' or 'Bolar' exception.[44] Each has the potential to extend access to locally produced generic medicines. However, manufacturing capacity in the indigenous pharmaceutical sector was, and remains limited.[45] Moreover, compulsory licensing of Kenyan producers would require considerable state involvement with the attendant risk of obstruction and corruption.[46] Consequently the terms on which drugs could be imported to Kenya was a key focus for access campaigners and their legal advisers.[47]

34 D. Branch, *Kenya. Between Hope and Despair, 1963–2011* (New Haven, CT: Yale University Press, 2011) 54.

35 Branch, *Kenya. Between Hope and Despair* (n 34) 296.

36 This mentality is also manifest in the leading role taken by Kenya in the 'African group' which pressed for reform of TRIPs (especially Art 31(f)) to facilitate the export of generic drugs, see Sihanya, 'Patents, Parallel Importation and Compulsory Licensing' (n 10) 268.

37 See generally, D. Matthews, *Intellectual Property, Human Rights and Development. The Role of NGOs and Social Movements* (Cheltenham: Edward Elgar, 2011).

38 Interview with Peter Munyi, Partner Sisule, Munyi, Kilonzo and Associates, Advocates, 16 May 2012; Interview with James Kamau, Coordinator for Kenya Treatment Action Movment, 12 September 2012.

39 Anon, 'Ignore the Patents to Save Human Life', *Daily Nation*, 22 April 2001. On the South African controversy, see A. Lanoszka, 'The Global Politics of Intellectual Property Rights and Pharmaceutical Drug Policies in Developing Countries' (2003) 24 *International Political Science Review* 181, 192 et seq.

40 Mey, 'Unfettered Consumer Access to Affordable Therapies' (n 2) 424.

41 Industrial Property Act 2001, s 80.

42 Industrial Property Act 2001, s 69.

43 Industrial Property Act 2001, ss 76–78.

44 Industrial Property Act 2001, s 54(2).

45 UNIDO, 'Pharmaceutical Sector Profile: Kenya' (n 1) 3.

46 Interview with Robert Lewis-Lettington, Legal Consultant, 9 May 2012. No compulsory licences have been issued in Kenya since the passing of the 2001 Act. The voluntary licensing provisions have been used on two occasions, both for the production of ARVs, see L. Makutsa Opati, 'Intellectual Property Rights in Health-Impact on Access to Drugs' in B. Sihanya and M. Wekesa (eds), *Intellectual Property Rights in Kenya* (Nairobi: Konrad Adenauer Stiftung, 2009) 14.

47 Interview with Robert Lewis-Lettington, Legal Consultant, 9 May 2012.

Under the previous legislation, these terms were set by the operation of a 'national' regime of patent exhaustion.[48] Put briefly, this meant that branded drugs marketed more cheaply elsewhere by the patent holder could not be imported and sold at a lower price than that being asked for in Kenya, without the consent of the patent holder. This effectively barred parallel importation as a strategy for reducing the price of essential drugs, allowing patent holders to charge monopoly prices for ARVs and other drugs. However, TRIPs does not mandate a specific patent exhaustion regime for member states.[49] Perhaps the greatest practical victory of the Coalition was achieved when Parliament exploited this flexibility, adopting a broadly framed 'international' regime of patent exhaustion in section 58(2) of the Industrial Property Act 2001. This provided that: 'The rights under the patent shall not extend to acts in respect of articles which have been put on the market in Kenya or in any other country or imported into Kenya.'[50] Importation and marketing of cheaper branded products and generics, even where a Kenyan patent was in force, would henceforth be lawful.

This was not the end of the matter, however. In June 2002, just after the Act came into force, section 58(2) was subject to an amendment which added the qualification that the products have been originally marketed, in Kenya or abroad 'by the owner of the patent or with his express consent'.[51] The effect of this addition was to allow parallel importation of branded products, but to block the importation of generic versions of drugs save where these had been produced under a voluntary licence obtained from the patent holder. In particular generics produced in India, where no such licence was required, because of the pre-TRIPs patent law, could not be lawfully imported to Kenya without the consent of the patent holder. Significantly this amendment was passed in a hurried late-night sitting of parliament with few MPs present and as a part of an omnibus bill to amend several quite diverse pieces of legislation.[52] Suspicion focused on the connections between government legal offices and certain law firms, representing international drug companies during the legislative process, though this was never confirmed.[53] Activists responded swiftly to the June amendment, again gaining the support of Minister Biwott.[54] In August 2002 parliament voted to restore the version of section 58(2) originally passed and quoted earlier.[55] The effect of the Coalition's ultimate success in relation to parallel importation was rapid and dramatic, with the price of ARVs to the Kenyan patient falling by between 40 and 65 per cent almost overnight.[56]

48 Industrial Property Act 1989, s 36(a)(i).

49 TRIPs, Art 6. This is confirmed by para 5(d) of the Doha Declaration on the TRIPS Agreement and Public Health.

50 Industrial Property Act 1989, s 58(2) must be read with Rule 37 of the Industrial Property Regulations 2002 which requires that drugs have been '*legitimately* put on the market' in another country (emphasis added). Thus sub-standard generics which had not gained marketing approval in, say, India could not be lawfully imported to Kenya under s 58(2).

51 Lewis-Lettington and Munyi, *Willingness and Ability to use TRIPS Flexibilities* (n 30) 19.

52 Lewis-Lettington and Munyi, *Willingness and Ability to use TRIPS Flexibilities* (n 30) 19.

53 Lewis-Lettington and Munyi, *Willingness and Ability to use TRIPS Flexibilities* (n 30) 19, fn 54.

54 Interview with Robert Lewis-Lettington, Legal Consultant, 9 May 2012.

55 Two further attempts were made to restore the 'national regime of exhaustion' in 2005 and 2007, both unsuccessful: see J.I. Muthoni Nyaga, *Implementing Parallel Importation and Licensing Mechanisms to Increase Access to Medicines in Kenya* (Thesis Submitted for Master of Science in Law, Stanford University, 2009) 43.

56 Lewis-Lettington and Munyi, *Willingness and Ability to use TRIPS Flexibilities* (n 30) 17. Industry sources estimated that by 2008 parallel imports accounted for between 30 and 35% of the Kenyan drug market: see J.I. Muthoni Nyaga, *Implementing Parallel Importation and Licensing Mechanisms* (n 55) 48.

In summary, it can be said that a distinctive conjuncture of legal technologies and political mentalities meant that the Coalition was able to enrol key state nodes and, thus, to secure TRIPs flexibilities which promoted access to essential medicines. The attempt to undo these gains by enrolling rival state nodes was successfully resisted. However, such gains are always provisional only. Negotiations, as Peter Drahos has observed, can never be regarded as finally closed.[57]

4. The Intellectual Property Enforcement Agenda

The Kenyan Anti-Counterfeit Act 2008 forms the next stage in the ongoing domestic struggle over access to essential medicines and intellectual property rights. The Act can also be seen as a specific realization, at national level, of the 'enforcement agenda' being promoted worldwide by IPR holders and their representative associations.[58] Biadgleng and Munoz Tellez argue that the aim of the IPE agenda is 'to make enforcement of IPRs cheaper, easier and more secure and to put industries in a better position to earn profits from the export of their IPR-based products'.[59] The strategy for enhanced IPE includes the creation of dedicated legal regimes at international, regional, and national levels.[60] This section briefly examines the major initiatives in this campaign and considers the manner in which the issues in anti-counterfeiting have been framed. As will be seen in later sections, these practical and rhetorical features were also evident in the campaign for dedicated legislation in Kenya.

Most prominent among recent international initiatives has been the controversial Anti-Counterfeiting Trade Agreement (ACTA), finalized by a group of mainly OECD states in 2011. When in force the Agreement will oblige ratifying states to provide for severe sanctions, as well as execution measures, against the manufacturers of counterfeit and pirated products, their suppliers, and distributors, whether domestically or abroad.[61] The operation of the Agreement will be supervised by a dedicated ACTA Committee. Health care activists have claimed that these provisions of ACTA would have a significant chilling effect on the supply of generic medicines.[62] They also charge that ACTA was developed and negotiated in a highly secretive fashion. For example, while major corporations and industry bodies were kept abreast of negotiations, civil society organizations were not included; the negotiating text was released to the public on only two occasions; and venues for negotiation were kept secret until the last minute.[63] Moreover, the negotiations were kept away from multilateral fora such as

57 P. Drahos, 'Four Lessons for Developing Countries from the Trade Negotiations over Access to Medicines' (2007) 28 *Liverpool Law Review* 11, 35.

58 S.K. Sell, 'The Global IP Upward Ratchet, Anti-Counterfeiting and Piracy Enforcement Efforts: The State of Play' (2008) 4, available at <http://www.twnside.org.sg/title2/intellectual_property/development.research/SusanSellfinalversion.pdf> (accessed 30 January 2014).

59 E.T. Biadgleng and V. Munoz Tellez, *The Changing Structure and Governance of Intellectual Property Enforcement* (Geneva: South Centre, 2008) 20.

60 A. Rens, 'Collateral Damage: The Impact of ACTA and the Enforcement Agenda on the World's Poorest People' (2010–11) 26 *American University International Law Review* 783, 785.

61 See B.K. Baker, 'ACTA—Risk of Third Party Enforcement for Access to Medicines' (2010–11) 26 *American University International Law Review* 579.

62 Médecins sans Frontières, 'A Blank Cheque for Abuse. The Anti-Counterfeiting Trade Agreement (ACTA) and its Impact on Access to Medicines' (2012) 3, available at <http://www.msfaccess.org/content/acta-and-its-impact-access-medicines> (accessed 27 November 2012).

63 D.M. Quinn, 'A Critical Look at the Anti-Counterfeiting Trade Agreement' (2011) 17 *Richmond Journal of Law and Technology* 16, 23; 'EU Leak On ACTA Shows Path To Completion', IP Watch, 9 November 2010, available at <http://www.ip-watch.org/2010/11/09/eu-leak-on-acta-shows-path-to-completion/> (accessed 3 April 2013).

the World Intellectual Property Organization (WIPO) and the WTO which would have provided for greater transparency and allowed developing countries to exert influence in an area of great concern to them.[64] With the European Parliament's rejection of ACTA in 2012, the European Union will not be in a position to ratify the Agreement.[65] Nonetheless, ratification is proceeding in a number of other signatory states. African states were not among the latter. ACTA may nonetheless reduce their 'domestic policy space' where its standards are included in free trade agreements with, say, the United States or Japan.[66]

Of specific significance in the context of access to medicines is the work of the International Medical Products Anti-Counterfeiting Task Force (IMPACT). IMPACT was established under the auspices of the WHO Secretariat in 2006 and is a collaborative venture between the World Customs Organization, Interpol, the WTO, WIPO, the European Commission, OECD states, pharmaceutical industry bodies, and others.[67] It focuses on promoting national legislation and infrastructure to combat the trade in counterfeit medicines, as well as developing useful technology and risk communication systems.[68] Rather like ACTA, IMPACT proposes stringent criminal sanctions and border enforcement measures, equivalent to those for 'drug trafficking', in its Draft Principles and Elements for National Legislation against Counterfeit Medical Products.[69] Its definition of 'counterfeit medical product' has been influential in national debates on anti-counterfeit legislation, including in Kenya, as will be seen in the next section.[70] This definition has been criticized as being drawn so widely as to capture legitimate trade in generics.[71] Critics of IMPACT also point to insufficient transparency and inclusiveness in its proceedings, as well as a lack of accountability to WHO member states.[72]

At the regional level, East Africa has been an important focus for the IPE agenda. As well as the Kenyan Act, dedicated legislation is in force in Tanzania and bills on anti-counterfeiting are currently under consideration in the Ugandan parliament and the East African Legislative Assembly.[73] These measures have been the focus of considerable lobbying by both official bodies, such as the European Commission, and by private

64 S. Flynn and B. Madhani, 'ACTA and Access to Medicines' (2011) 22, PIJIP Research Paper Series 7–10, available at <http://digitalcommons.wcl.american.edu/cgi/viewcontent.cgi?article=1024&context=research> (accessed 26 November 2012).

65 W. New and M Ermert, 'European Parliament Rejection Puts ACTA Future In Doubt', IP Watch, 4 July 2012, available at <http://www.ip-watch.org/2012/07/04/european-parliament-rejection-puts-acta-future-in-doubt/> (accessed 3 April 2013).

66 E. Katz and G. Hintze, 'The Impact of the Anti-Counterfeiting Trade Agreement on the Knowledge Economy: The Accountability of the Office of the U.S. Trade Representative for the Creation of IP Enforcement Norms Through Executive Trade Agreements' (2009) 35 *Yale Journal of International Law* 24, 26–7.

67 Sell, 'The Global IP Upward Ratchet' (n 58) 8–11.

68 Biadgleng and Munoz Tellez, *The Changing Structure and Governance* (n 59) 28.

69 IMPACT, 'Principles and Elements for National Legislation Against Counterfeit Medical Products' (2008), available at <http://www.who.int/impact/events/FinalPrinciplesforLegislation.pdf> (accessed 27 November 2012).

70 Interview with William Mwatu, Medical and Regulatory Affairs Director, East Africa, GlaxoSmithKline, 19 September 2012.

71 South Centre and CIEL, 'Intellectual Property Update: Counterfeit Medical Products Need for Caution Against Co-opting Public Health Concerns for IP Protection and Enforcement', First Quarter 2009, 2–5.

72 Third World Network, 'WHO's "Counterfeit" Programme Legitimises IP Enforcement Agenda, Undermines Public Health': Briefing Paper No 2 (Geneva, 2010) 12.

73 Von Braun and Munyi, 'New Enforcement Mechanisms' (n 11) 239.

sector representatives.[74] Specific legislative models have been promoted and key political and administrative figures recruited to the cause of anti-counterfeiting.[75] These interventions are complemented by a number of international and bilateral initiatives aimed at capacity building, both among law enforcement officers and the judiciary.[76] Between 2008 and 2010 IMPACT, Interpol, and East African states, including Kenya, combined in 'Operation Mamba', a series of coordinated raids directed at trafficking in counterfeit medicines.[77] Training programmes in anti-counterfeiting for law enforcement staff and the judiciary have been supported by Interpol and the United States.[78] More coercive unilateral measures have also been deployed. Thus, in 2003 the United States threatened to put Kenya on its 'special 301' Watch List, with the risk of a withdrawal of trade preferences, on the basis that it was not affording adequate protection to US IPRs over software.[79] Finally, it should be noted that the IPE agenda has been promoted through billboard and newspaper advertising, and through a series of publicity campaigns seeking to promote popular mobilization around the issue of counterfeiting.[80] World Anti-Counterfeit Day has been marked in Kenya, for example, with demonstrations, the ritual burning of fake products, and well-publicized raids on suspected distributors.[81]

The shift to enforcement represents a change of focus from the campaign to globalize substantive IPRs which resulted in the TRIPs agreement.[82] The essential objective remains the same since, as critics have noted, more stringent enforcement measures will lead to a *de facto* expansion in substantive rights.[83] Indeed Sisule Musungu suggests that the agenda seeks precisely to recoup the negotiating losses sustained by branded producers when developing countries, like Kenya, legislated to exploit TRIPs flexibilities.[84] The IPE agenda has been advanced through the establishment of new governance

74 A. Mullard, 'EU Implicated in Controversial Counterfeiting Bill' (2010) 375 *Lancet* 1335; Interview with William Mwatu, Medical and Regulatory Affairs Director, East Africa, GlaxoSmithKline, 19 September 2012.

75 The Conservative politician, Baroness Lynda Chalker, who served as UK Minister for Overseas Development from 1989–97, has featured prominently in these campaigns, see L. Chalker, 'Declaring War on Counterfeiters and Pirates' (2007) 335 *African Business* 46.

76 There is an increasing trend for developed countries to focus aid on technical assistance for IP enforcement: Biadgleng and Munoz Tellez, *The Changing Structure and Governance* (n 59) 17–19.

77 M. Haman, 'Africa Rising to the Anti-Counterfeiting Challenge' (2010) 5(5) *Journal of Intellectual Property Law and Practice* 344, 347.

78 US Embassy Dar es Salaam, 'Outcomes of the Counterfeit Medicines Workshop Dar es Salaam', 10 March (2010), available at <http://www.africamatters.com/site_content_files/files/anti_counterfeit_medicine_event_summary_dar_march_2010.pdf> (accessed 27 November 2012); Interview with Stephen Mallowah, Executive Director, Kenya Anti-Counterfeit Agency, 21 September 2012.

79 B. Sihanya, 'Combating Counterfeit Trade in Kenya' in B. Sihanya and M. Wekesa (eds), *Intellectual Property Rights in Kenya* (Nairobi: Konrad Adenauer Stiftung, 2009) 205, 217.

80 J. Kariuki, 'Lobby to Launch Campaign Against Counterfeits', *The East African*, 6 September 2008; J. Muchangi, 'Chaka Chaka Launches Anti-Counterfeit Campaign in Kenya', *The Star*, 28 October 2011.

81 Anti Counterfeit Agency, 'World Anti-Counterfeit Day (WACD) in Kenya' (2012), available at <http://www.aca.go.ke/index.php?option=com_content&view=article&id=156:world-anti-counterfeit-day-wacd-in-kenya&catid=88&Itemid=503> (accessed 27 November 2012).

82 See R. Weissman, 'Long, Strange Trips: The Pharmaceutical Industry Drive to Harmonize Global Intellectual Property Rules, and the Remaining WTO Legal Alternatives Available to Third World Countries' (1996) 17 *University of Pennsylvania Journal of International Economic Law* 1069.

83 Health Action International, 'ACTA and Access to Medicines: A Flawed Process, Flawed Rationale and Flawed Agreement' (2012) 1, available at <http://haieurope.org/wp-content/uploads/2012/02/27-Feb-2012-HAI-Europe-Policy-Brief-ACTA-and-Access-to-Medicines.pdf> (accessed 27 November 2012).

84 Quoted in M. Wambi, 'EU Supports Law Threatening Access to Medicines', *IPS News Agency*, 15 March 2010.

nodes, most notably IMPACT, the ACTA Committee, and national anti-counterfeit agencies. Each has a stable institutional base, a specific set of powers, dedicated resources, and a clear conception of the problem posed by counterfeiting. These nodes have themselves been created by enrolling existing nodes at international and national level. The WHO, Interpol, and the World Customs Organization, for example, have all developed a specific focus on counterfeiting. The different levels are of course not fully separate. Rather nodes enrolled, or specifically created for IPE at international level, will then be capable of enrolling nodes in national jurisdictions and influencing their governance output in a manner favoured by IPR holders. International treaty obligations, obliging states to act at national level, but monitored and enforced at international level, form an important technology used to effect this enrolment. The expertise and prestige of agencies with global reach, such as the WHO, also function as important rhetorical supports for this effort.[85]

These institutional developments support a distinctive framing of the pro-enforcement campaign.[86] Whilst industry lobbyists in the period leading up to the TRIPs agreement identified IPR infringement with theft and piracy, this association has been eclipsed somewhat by the elaboration of two new frames. On the one hand, counterfeiting is represented as a security threat, with links to organized crime and international terrorism.[87] On the other, it figures as a public health crisis, with fake products, including medicines, killing and injuring thousands worldwide.[88] As noted, these frames are underwritten by the authority and expertise of nodes such as Interpol and the WHO. Taken together they enable counterfeiting to be represented as a global emergency, calling for a dramatic and urgent response from law-makers and administrators.[89] As will be seen in the next section, these frames were prominent in the debates which lead to the passing of the Kenyan Anti-Counterfeit Act 2008.

5. Implementing the Enforcement Agenda: Anti-Counterfeit Act 2008

5.1 Overview of the Act

The Anti-Counterfeit Act 2008 was the fruit of a long campaign by manufacturers for more effective enforcement of IPRs in Kenya. Weak civil remedies, insufficiently harsh criminal penalties, and a lax attitude to counterfeiting among law enforcement officers were cited as reasons for this campaign.[90] There was particular dissatisfaction with the Pharmacy and Poisons Board (PPB), which approves medicines for sale in Kenya.[91] Pharmaceutical industry leaders claimed that the Board was not policing the parallel importation of drugs with sufficient rigour, allowing counterfeit and unsafe products to enter the market.[92] This section of the chapter outlines the key provisions of the Act,

85 Third World Network, 'WHO's "Counterfeit" Programme' (n 72) 12.

86 P. Loughlan, '"You Wouldn't Steal a Car . . .": Intellectual Property and the Language of Theft' (2007) 29 *European Intellectual Property Review* 401.

87 Sell, 'The Global IP Upward Ratchet' (n 58) 4.

88 A. Attaran, R. Bate, and M. Kendall, 'Why and How to Make an International Crime of Medicine Counterfeiting' (2011) 9 *Journal of International Criminal Justice* 325, 326.

89 See Attaran, Bate, and Kendall, 'Why and How to Make an International Crime of Medicine Counterfeiting' (n 88) 340–4.

90 Sihanya, 'Combating Counterfeit Trade in Kenya' (n 79) 217.

91 Interview with William Mwatu, Medical and Regulatory Affairs Director, East Africa, GlaxoSmithKline, 19 September 2012.

92 See S. Mbogo, 'Why We Are Losing the War Against Fake Drugs', *Business Daily*, 1 May 2008.

before reviewing the process by which it was passed and the manner in which the arguments for legal change were posed and resisted by different interest groups.

The Act defines 'counterfeiting' as the manufacture, packaging, re-packaging, or labelling of goods which are identical to, substantially similar to, or calculated to be confused with goods subject to an IPR.[93] It is an offence under the Act to possess, manufacture, sell, distribute, import, export, or tranship counterfeit goods.[94] Harsh penalties are laid down: up to fifteen years' imprisonment and a fine of five times the retail value of the goods in the case of second and subsequent offences.[95]

The Act also establishes the Kenya Anti-Counterfeit Agency, which is tasked with combating counterfeiting and educating the public on the problem.[96] On reasonable suspicion, the Agency's inspectors are empowered to inspect premises, close manufacturing facilities, and seize goods and to search, detain, and arrest suspects without warrant.[97] Seized goods may be destroyed, or, where imported, returned to their country of origin by court order.[98] Equivalent powers are extended to customs officers.[99] The Act confers extensive rights to initiate complaints and to be informed of the details of investigations on IPR holders.[100] The latter need only satisfy the Agency or customs on a *prima facie* basis that the goods are counterfeits and that they hold the relevant IPRs.[101] By contrast, a party seeking compensation for wrongful enforcement or recovery of seized goods bears the burden of proving that the complainant did not hold the relevant IPRs.[102]

There are several respects in which the Act is 'TRIPs-plus', in that it offers protection to IPR holders in excess of what is required by that Agreement.[103] It extends the definition of counterfeiting beyond the areas of trademarks and copyright to infringements of other intellectual property rights, including patents.[104] It provides for border measures in cases of patent infringement, though these are not required under the Agreement, which only refers to trademark and copyright.[105] The imposition of criminal penalties in cases of patent infringement also exceeds TRIPs, which mandates these only in cases of 'wilful trademark counterfeiting and copyright piracy on a commercial scale'.[106] In addition, it contradicts the 'territorial' nature of the international patent system by allowing enforcement measures to be taken whether the intellectual property rights claimed to be infringed are recognized by Kenyan law or by the law of another jurisdiction.[107]

5.2 The legislative process

The Kenya Association of Manufacturers (KAM) exercised a decisive influence over the passage of the Anti-Counterfeit Act 2008. The Association represents over 700

93 Anti-Counterfeit Act 2008, s 2.
94 Anti-Counterfeit Act 2008, s 32.
95 Anti-Counterfeit Act 2008, s 53(1).
96 Anti-Counterfeit Act 2008, ss 3(1), 5(b), 5(a).
97 Anti-Counterfeit Act 2008, s 23(1),(3).
98 Anti-Counterfeit Act 2008, s 27(1)(a).
99 Anti-Counterfeit Act 2008, s 22 (3).
100 Anti-Counterfeit Act 2008, ss 33, 25.
101 Anti-Counterfeit Act 2008, s 33(2), (3)(b).
102 Anti-Counterfeit Act 2008, s 26(5).
103 Von Braun and Munyi, 'New Enforcement Mechanisms' (n 11) 247–8.
104 Anti-Counterfeit Act 2008, s 2. This exceeds the requirements of fn 14 to TRIPs, Art 51.
105 See respectively, Anti-Counterfeit Act 2008, ss 32(f), 23, 22(3) and TRIPs, Art 51.
106 TRIPs, Art 61.
107 Anti-Counterfeit Act 2008, s 2. On the principle of territoriality in patent law, see F.M. Abbott, 'Seizure of Generic Pharmaceuticals in Transit Based on Allegations of Patent Infringement: a Threat to International Trade, Development and Public Welfare' in O. Aginam, J. Harrington, and P.K. Yu (eds), *Global Governance of HIV/AIDS. Intellectual Property and Access to Essential Medicines* (Cheltenham: Edward Elgar, 2013) 131.

members and has been campaigning for dedicated legislation since the early 2000s.[108] After the failure to pass two earlier Bills, KAM established an Anti-Counterfeit and Illicit Trade committee which conducted an intensive campaign of lobbying and briefing throughout 2008.[109] The legislation was sponsored by the Ministry of Trade and Industrialization and its provisions were drafted in consultation with stakeholders, among whom KAM was most prominent.[110] Civil society groups such as Health Action International (HAI) Africa and Kenya Treatment Action Movement strongly criticized the TRIPs-plus aspects of the original Bill and its harsh enforcement provisions as likely impediments to the importation of generic medicines to Kenya, undoing the gains for access made in the Industrial Property Act 2001.[111] Concerns in this regard had also been raised by the PPB.[112] The Minister for Industrialization, Henry Kosgey, supported by KAM, sought to meet these complaints by adding two provisions to the definition of 'counterfeit' in section 2. The first provision defined counterfeiting in relation to medicine as 'the deliberate and fraudulent mislabelling of medicine with respect to identity or source, whether or not such products have correct ingredients, wrong ingredients, have sufficient active ingredients or have fake packaging'. As its proponents emphasized, this reproduces the definition of counterfeit medicines proposed by the WHO in 1992 and later adopted by IMPACT.[113] The second provision stated that 'nothing in this paragraph shall derogate from the existing provisions under the Industrial Property Act 2001'. Civil society groups were unconvinced, however.[114] Whatever the discrete meaning of the new provisions, they had to be read in the context of the rest of the Act, which retained its strong emphasis on IPE. There was no guarantee that these tensions would be resolved in favour of access to medicines. Activists thus argued that medicines should be categorically exempted from the scope of the Act.[115] But this was rejected, both by industry representatives and by government, who felt they had done enough to secure the interests of needy Kenyans living with HIV/AIDS and other diseases.[116]

KAM's success in getting the 2008 Act passed and in resisting the challenge from civil society is in marked contrast to the outcome of debates over the use of TRIPs

108 Interview with Joseph Wairiuko, Assistant Executive Officer, Kenya Association of Manufacturers, 10 September 2012.

109 Interview with William Mwatu, Medical and Regulatory Affairs Director, East Africa, GlaxoSmithKline, 19 September 2012.

110 Interview with Joseph Wairiuko, Assistant Executive Officer, Kenya Association of Manufacturers, 10 September 2012; Interview with William Mwatu, Medical and Regulatory Affairs Director, East Africa, GlaxoSmithKline, 19 September 2012.

111 See M. Kamau, 'Anti-Counterfeit Bill Debate Rages On', *The Standard*, 21 October 2008.

112 Interview with Gichinga Ndirangu, Regional Coordinator, Health Action International Africa, 29 October 2012.

113 Mr Kosgey MP, Minister for Trade and Industrialization, Kenya National Assembly Official Report, 30 October 2008, 3188; Interview with Joseph Wairiuko, Assistant Executive Officer, Kenya Association of Manufacturers, 10 September 2012; Interview with William Mwatu, Medical and Regulatory Affairs Director, East Africa, GlaxoSmithKline, 19 September 2012. The WHO/IMPACT definition can be found at <http://www.who.int/medicines/services/counterfeit/faqs/count_q-a/en/index.html> (accessed 27 November 2012).

114 Interview with James Kamau, Coordinator for Kenya Treatment Action Movement, 12 September 2012.

115 Interview with Gichinga Ndirangu, Regional Coordinator, Health Action International Africa, 29 October 2012; Interview with James Kamau, Coordinator for Kenya Treatment Action Movement, 12 September 2012.

116 Mr Murungatana MP, Assistant Minister for Medical Services, Kenya National Assembly Official Report, 10 December 2008, 4041; Interview with William Mwatu, Medical and Regulatory Affairs Director, East Africa, GlaxoSmithKline, 19 September 2012.

flexibilities during the passage of the Industrial Property Act 2001. As will be seen in the rest of this section, this success was significantly due to the manner in which KAM was able to represent the key issues at stake for legislators. First and foremost, it framed the Act as a matter of promoting economic growth. Without adequate enforcement of IPRs Kenya would fail to attract foreign investment and existing businesses would relocate elsewhere, leaving many 'ordinary hardworking Kenyans' unemployed.[117] Fakes, it claimed, already cost industry KSh 50 billion (US$585 million) in lost sales and the government KSh 19 billion (US$222 million) in lost taxes.[118] These arguments were all the more effective given that they were addressed initially to the Ministry of Trade and Industrialization which was sponsoring the Bill and latterly to the Parliamentary Committee on Trade which considered it closely. As might be expected, KAM has enjoyed long-running and close relations with the Ministry.[119] Its ability to state its case in terms of the national interest contrasts with the perception that civil society activists are 'noisemakers' pursuing merely sectoral concerns.[120] MPs, thus, easily agreed on the economic threat posed by counterfeiters.[121] Admittedly, the Health Committee of Parliament also considered the Bill, hearing the concerns of activists regarding access to generics.[122] However, it had a relatively marginal influence on the content of the legislation, given that counterfeiting was primarily framed as a trade issue.[123]

This specific framing also meant that industry representatives retained the power of initiative throughout the debate. Civil society activists felt they had to campaign in the face of the widespread assumption that, 'if you are against the Anti-Counterfeiting Act, you must be for counterfeiting' and therefore against the national interest.[124] By contrast with 2001, it was no longer possible simply to defend the health of vulnerable Kenyans against profit-hungry, foreign-owned companies seeking stronger IP protection. For one thing, KAM repeatedly acknowledged the need for low-cost medicines and affirmed that it was not its intention to stop the supply of genuine generics.[125] For another, it boldly seized the rhetorical ground usually occupied by activists in defining counterfeiting itself as a threat to the health of ordinary Kenyans. KAM's publicity material included dramatic vignettes of patients dying after being treated with

117 Kenya Association of Manufacturers, 'Anti-Counterfeit Bill: We Count on Legislators to Act Rightfully' (Nairobi, 2008) (copy on file with author); Kenya Association of Manufacturers, 'Press Release on the Anti-Counterfeit Bill' (Nairobi, 2008) (copy on file with author).

118 Quoted in Sihanya, 'Combating Counterfeit Trade in Kenya' (n 79) 216.

119 S. Mbatiah, 'Pharmaceutical Companies Pushing Anti-Counterfeit Law', IPS News Agency, 14 June 2010; Interview with Joseph Wairiuko, Assistant Executive Officer, Kenya Association of Manufacturers, 10 September 2012.

120 Interview with Gichinga Ndirangu, Regional Coordinator, Health Action International Africa, 29 October 2012; Interview with Stephen Mallowah, Executive Director, Kenya Anti-Counterfeit Agency, 21 September 2012.

121 See Mr Kosgey MP, Minister for Trade and Industrialisation, Kenya National Assembly Official Report, 30 October 2008, 3187; Mr Muriithi MP, Assistant Minister for Industrialisation, Kenya National Assembly Official Report, 30 October 2008, 3198.

122 Interview with William Mwatu, Medical and Regulatory Affairs Director, East Africa, GlaxoSmithKline, 19 September 2012.

123 Interview with Gichinga Ndirangu, Regional Coordinator, Health Action International Africa, 29 October 2012.

124 Interview with Christa Cepuch, Regional Pharmacist, East Africa, Médecins Sans Frontières, 4 June 2012; Interview with Gichinga Ndirangu, Regional Coordinator, Health Action International Africa, 29 October 2012.

125 Kenya Association of Manufacturers, 'Anti-Counterfeit Bill' (n 117); B. Maina, 'Looking Forward to MPs Acting in National Interest', *Daily Nation*, 11 September 2008.

counterfeit medicines.[126] Pharmaceutical members had originally taken the lead within KAM in pushing for greater IPE.[127] Their expertise, in emphasizing the threat of increasing resistance to anti-malarials, for example, was now used to lend authority to the health case for the Act in the media and before the Parliamentary Committee on Trade.[128] These interventions, which aimed to change perceptions of counterfeiting as a 'victimless crime', resonated widely.[129] MPs accepted that 'innocent lives were being lost' as a result of the use of fake products, and Minister Kosgey affirmed that protection of the public's health was an important aim of the Bill.[130]

Activists were thus left with the difficult task of highlighting the complexity and ambiguity of the Bill, including the amendments dealing with medicines, and its potential for misuse by corporate interests.[131] In particular, they had to distinguish sub-standard medicines, which posed quality and safety issues, from counterfeits, which merely raised questions of intellectual property rights.[132] Moreover, they were divided internally as to the most appropriate response to the legislation.[133] Some wanted to 'kill the bill' outright. Others, recognizing the momentum behind it, sought to reform it to protect access to generics.[134] These difficulties were compounded by the relatively modest resources available to civil society organizations and by the speed at which the legislation was passed.[135] Admittedly, each of the relevant constitutional requirements was complied with. It is notable, however, that the legislation was not preceded by any evident policy decision or statement from the government and that less than a month and a half passed between the second and third readings, the period for detailed scrutiny by parliamentary committees.[136] This sense of urgency was due in part to the impatience of industry representatives who had been campaigning for the best part of a decade.[137] But it was also actively created by rendering the economic and health concerns, discussed previously, in terms of national security. Rather like proponents of the IPE agenda at the international level, KAM emphasized, without proving, the links between counterfeiting and organized crime.[138] It added that the national territory was being 'penetrated', 'infiltrated', 'flooded', and 'pervaded' by

126 See eg Kenya Association of Manufacturers, 'Anti-Counterfeit Bill' (n 117).

127 Mbatiah, 'Pharmaceutical Companies Pushing Anti-Counterfeit Law' (n 119).

128 See K. Mugambi, 'Law Against Counterfeits Gets Backing', *Daily Nation*, 25 October 2008.

129 Interview with William Mwatu, Medical and Regulatory Affairs Director, East Africa, GlaxoSmithKline, 19 September 2012.

130 Mr I.E. Mohammed MP, Minister for Development of Northern Kenya and Other Arid Lands, Kenya National Assembly Official Report, 30 October 2008, 3195; Mr Kosgey MP, Minister for Trade and Industrialisation, Kenya National Assembly Official Report, 30 October 2008, 3187.

131 See D. Kimani, 'Anti-Fakes Bill Threatens Access to Generics', *The East African*, 6 September 2008.

132 Health Action International Africa, *The Anti-Counterfeit Bill 2008. Concerns on Access to Medicines for Kenyans* (Nairobi, (no date)) (copy on file with author).

133 Interview with Christa Cepuch, Regional Pharmacist, East Africa, Médecins Sans Frontières, 4 June 2012.

134 Interview with Gichinga Ndirangu, Regional Coordinator, Health Action International Africa, 29 October 2012; Interview with James Kamau, Coordinator for Kenya Treatment Action Movement, 12 September 2012.

135 Interview with Christa Cepuch, Regional Pharmacist, East Africa, Médecins Sans Frontières, 4 June 2012.

136 Von Braun and Munyi, 'New Enforcement Mechanisms' (n 11) 243, 246.

137 Interview with William Mwatu, Medical and Regulatory Affairs Director, East Africa, GlaxoSmithKline, 19 September 2012; Interview with Joseph Wairiuko, Assistant Executive Officer, Kenya Association of Manufacturers, 10 September 2012.

138 Kenya Association of Manufacturers, 'Anti-Counterfeit Bill' (n 117) 4.

fake goods.[139] This spatial idiom was adopted by MPs who worried that other countries 'were dumping their substandard goods' in Kenya, noting the specific vulnerability of the coastal region and the border with Somalia.[140] In passing the Anti-Counterfeit Act 2008, parliamentarians proved themselves receptive to KAM's call for a 'total war' on counterfeits 'in which everyone must join hands'.[141]

6. Asserting the Right to Health: *P.A.O. v Attorney General*

6.1 Fundamental rights review and standing under the new Constitution

Almost immediately upon the Anti-Counterfeit Act 2008 coming into force in July 2009, it was subject to a constitutional challenge by three Kenyans, each of whom had been living with HIV/AIDS for between eight and nineteen years. Two were in receipt of first line ARVs provided free through programmes run by the government of Kenya and Médecins Sans Frontières. The third was not taking medication, but her 5-year-old son, also infected with HIV, was receiving ARVs free of charge. The petitioners were joined by the Kenya AIDS Law Project as an interested party. They argued that the definitions, enforcement powers, and criminal penalties provided for in the Act threatened their right to life as guaranteed by Sections 70 and 71 of the Constitution then in force. That Constitution did not recognize social and economic rights, including the right to health, as such. However, more recent case law had seen an incrementally expansive interpretation of the right to life, beyond mere freedom from elimination to include social factors influencing quality of life.[142] The petitioners were also able to invoke statutory provisions committing the state to endeavour to provide affordable medicines to PLWHA and recognizing the right of children to health and medical care.[143]

In April 2010, the High Court granted interim orders suspending the operation of the Act as regards the importation of generic medicines.[144] Justice Rosalyn Wendoh found that there was a real threat that the Act would be used to seize shipments of generic drugs, putting the petitioners at risk of 'irreparable harm', namely loss of life through inability to access ARVs. Before the full hearing of the case, the legal landscape changed dramatically with the adoption by referendum of a new Kenyan Constitution in August 2010. By contrast with its predecessor the new Constitution includes an extensive catalogue of enforceable social and economic rights. Consequently, the petitioners amended their plea, arguing that the provisions of the 2008 Act, outlined earlier, threatened their rights to life, dignity, and health, protected under Articles 26(1), 28, and 43(1) respectively of the new Constitution.

139 Kenya Association of Manufacturers, 'Anti-Counterfeit Bill' (n 117) 1, 4.

140 Mr Murungatana MP, Assistant Minister for Medical Services, Kenya National Assembly Official Report, 30 October 2008, 3189; Mr Affey MP, Kenya National Assembly Official Report, 30 October 2008, 3194.

141 Kenya Association of Manufacturers, 'Press Release on the Anti-Counterfeit Bill' (Nairobi, 2008) (copy on file with author); Kenya Association of Manufacturers, 'Anti-Counterfeit Bill' (n 117) 4.

142 See C. Mbazira, 'The Judicial Enforcement of the Right to the Highest Attainable Standard of Health under the Constitution of Kenya' in J. Biegon and G. Musila (eds), *Judicial Enforcement of Social and Economic Rights under the New Constitution: Challenges and Opportunities for Kenya* (Nairobi: Konrad Adenauer Stiftung, 2012) 113, 128–9.

143 HIV and AIDS Prevention and Control Act 2006, s 19(2); Children Act 2001, s 9.

144 *P.A.O. v Attorney General* [2012] eKLR, HC Nairobi (*per* Ngugi J at para 56).

While fundamental rights review had been developed in the last decade of the old Constitution, this had an uncertain basis and was resisted by many conservative members of the judiciary.[145] By contrast, the new Constitution states explicitly that laws which are inconsistent with its provisions, including the Bill of Rights, are void to that extent.[146] It gives the High Court jurisdiction to determine claims that a right or fundamental freedom has been denied, violated, or infringed, or is threatened.[147] Equally, a faltering and incremental extension of standing in human rights cases under the old constitution has been reinforced and given textual basis in its successor.[148] As recently as 1988 the High Court had held that proceedings seeking enforcement of the constitutional rights of individuals were impermissible in the absence of relevant procedural rules.[149] Such rules were subsequently made by the Chief Justice and relied on by the petitioners in *P.A.O.*[150] They have now been given constitutional force in Article 22(1). The standing of parties 'acting in the public interest' had been similarly resisted under the old regime. Kenyan courts followed the traditional common law rule that parties had to show a sufficient personal interest in the matter to have standing.[151] Only in the decade before the new Constitution did the courts begin to consider applications on grounds of public interest.[152] Again the new Constitution built on these incremental developments, entrenching broad rules of standing for interested parties, such as the Kenya AIDS Law Project, in Article 22(2)(c). Moreover, the United Nations Special Rapporteur on the Right of Everyone to the Highest Attainable Standard of Physical and Mental Health, Anand Grover, was able to appear as an *amicus curiae* under Article 22(3)(e). He submitted a lengthy and detailed brief on relevant aspects of both Kenyan and international human rights law. As will be seen, this exerted considerable influence on the reasoning of the judge.

6.2 Content of the right to health

In her decision of April 2012, Lady Justice Mumbi Ngugi held that the rights to life, dignity, and health invoked by the petitioners were 'inextricably bound' with one another.[153] However, the greater part of her analysis focused on the scope and implications of the constitutional right to health. This is guaranteed by Article 43(1)(a) which states that: 'Every person has the right to the highest attainable standard of health, which

145 See J. Biegon, 'The Inclusion of Social and Economic Rights in the 2010 Constitution: Conceptual and Practical Issues' in J. Biegon and G. Musila (eds), *Judicial Enforcement of Social and Economic Rights under the New Constitution: Challenges and Opportunities for Kenya* (Nairobi: Konrad Adenauer Stiftung, 2012) 13, 31–3.

146 Constitution of Kenya (2010) Art 2(4).

147 Constitution of Kenya (2010) Art 165(3)(b).

148 E.Z. Ongoya, 'The Law, the Procedures and the Trends in Jurisprudence on Constitutional and Fundamental Rights Litigation in Kenya' (2008–10) 2 *KLR Journal*, available at <http://www.kenyalaw.org/klr/index.php?id=809> (accessed 27 November 2012); B.J. Mwimali, 'Public Interest Litigation and the Judicial Enforcement of Socio-Economic Rights: Prospects and Challenges under the Constitution of Kenya' in J. Biegon and G. Musila (eds), *Judicial Enforcement of Social and Economic Rights under the New Constitution: Challenges and Opportunities for Kenya* (Nairobi: Konrad Adenauer Stiftung, 2012) 247, 248–51.

149 *Gibson Kamau Kuria v Attorney General*, HC Nairobi, Civil Application No 550 of 1988.

150 They had originally joined the action as 'an interested party' under s 12 of the Constitution of Kenya (Supervisory Jurisdiction and Protection of Fundamental Rights and Freedoms of the Individual) High Court Practice and Procedure Rules, 2006.

151 *Wangari Maathai v Kenya Times Media Trust Ltd*, HC Nairobi, Civil Case No 5403 of 1989.

152 Mwimali, 'Public Interest Litigation' (n 148) 252–7.

153 *P.A.O. v Attorney General* [2012] eKLR, HC Nairobi (*per* Ngugi J at para 56).

includes the right to health care services, including reproductive health care'. In addition Article 53(1)(c) provides that every child has the right, *inter alia*, to basic health care.

In giving content to Article 43(1)(a), Ngugi J noted that she was bound by Article 2(6) which provides that any 'treaty or convention ratified by Kenya shall form part of the law of Kenya'.[154] On this basis she had regard to Article 12 of the International Covenant on Economic, Social and Cultural Rights (ICESCR), ratified by Kenya in 1972, which similarly recognizes 'the right to the highest attainable standard of health'.[155] Drawing on General Comment 14 of the Committee on Economic, Social and Cultural Rights (CESCR), she held that the right to health included 'a whole range of socio-economic factors and conditions including access to medication required to stay healthy'.[156] Moreover, as the CESCR had reasoned, the requirement of accessibility entails that medication be affordable.[157] This justified the judge in considering the broader social and policy context of the case and in particular those factors influencing the cost of medicines in Kenya. She noted the relatively high level of infection in the general population and among children and that the epidemic had received the government's special attention in the National AIDS Strategic Plan for 2004–09.[158] She recalled the effect of the Industrial Property Act 2001, discussed earlier, in dramatically reducing the price of anti-retroviral therapies and thus in greatly widening access for poor Kenyans living with HIV/AIDS.[159]

6.3 Threat to the right to health

Lady Justice Mumbi Ngugi held that access to affordable medicines was threatened by the uncertainty surrounding the definition of counterfeits in section 2 of the Act.[160] As noted previously, section 2 includes among the category of counterfeits 'deliberately or fraudulently mislabelled' medicines even where 'such products have correct ingredients' or 'sufficient active ingredients'. Given that legitimate generics are identical copies of originator drugs, they could be captured by this definition, according to the *amicus* brief of the Special Rapporteur, which the judge quoted approvingly.[161] The problems

154 *P.A.O. v Attorney General* (n 153) *per* Ngugi J at para 55. Under the previous Constitution international law instruments had to be specifically incorporated in order to form part of domestic Kenyan law. In recent years, however, the courts had shown some willingness to use international law in interpreting constitutional provisions, see G. Musila, 'Testing Two Standards of Compliance: A Modest Proposal on the Adjudication of Positive Socio-Economic Rights Under the New Constitution' in J. Biegon and G. Musila (eds), *Judicial Enforcement of Social and Economic Rights under the New Constitution: Challenges and Opportunities for Kenya* (Nairobi: Konrad Adenauer Stiftung, 2012) 55, 62–5.

155 *P.A.O. v Attorney General* [2012] eKLR, HC Nairobi (*per* Ngugi J at paras 60–63). The short period since the passing of the Constitution has seen a significant increase in the use of international human rights law in Kenyan cases: see eg *Satrose Ayuma v Registered Trustees of the Kenya Railways Staff Retirement Benefits Scheme* [2011] eKLR, HC Nairobi (Musinga J) (UN Basic Principles and Guidelines on Development-Based Evictions and Displacement A/HRC/4/18); *Re the Matter of Zipporah Wambui Mathara* [2010] eKLR, HC Nairobi (Koome J) (International Covenant on Civil and Political Rights, Art 11).

156 *P.A.O. v Attorney General* [2012] eKLR, HC Nairobi (*per* Ngugi J at paras 61, 63). See Committee on Economic, Social and Cultural Rights, General Comment No 14 (22nd Session 2000) The Right to the Highest Attainable Standard of Health E/C.12/2000/4, para 11.

157 Committee on Economic, Social and Cultural Rights, General Comment No 14 (22nd Session 2000) (n 156) para 12(b).

158 *P.A.O. v Attorney General* [2012] eKLR, HC Nairobi (*per* Ngugi J at paras 44–49).

159 *P.A.O. v Attorney General* (n 158) *per* Ngugi J at para 51.

160 *P.A.O. v Attorney General* (n 158) *per* Ngugi J at paras 73–75.

161 *P.A.O. v Attorney General* (n 158) *per* Ngugi J at para 76. See Written Submissions of UN Special Rapporteur on the Right of Everyone to the Highest Attainable Standard of Health, Mr Anand Grover, Amicus Curiae, 15 February 2011, paras 28, 32 (copy on file with author).

posed by this expansive definition were compounded by the fact that the inspectors and customs officers charged with enforcing the Act lacked training in the detail of intellectual property law. Unable to distinguish between generics and counterfeits, they were likely to apply the law too broadly.[162]

The combination of harsh criminal sanctions, broad enforcement powers, and ambiguous definitions would, she held, have a significant chilling effect on the production, importation, and distribution of generic versions of essential medicines.[163] The judge referred in this connection to cases where the Dutch authorities had seized and returned (or in some cases destroyed) generic drugs transiting from India to other developing countries through Schiphol airport.[164] These provided evidence of the 'manifest danger' presented by the Act.[165] The risk of seizure would lead generic producers to withdraw from the Kenyan market. With only branded medicines available there was likely to be a significant rise in price, rendering essential drugs unaffordable and, thus, inaccessible to many citizens.[166] She agreed with the Special Rapporteur's assessment that this 'posed a real threat to the petitioners' right to life, dignity and health under the Constitution'.[167]

The judge did take account of the proviso to the definition in section 2 of the Anti-Counterfeit Act 2008, which purported to save the provisions of the Industrial Property Act 2001.[168] However, as she pointed out, the 2008 Act being later in time would prevail over the 2001 Act in case of incompatibility.[169] In any case she found that the terms of the proviso were also vague. This too was unacceptable. As she put it, there could be 'no room for ambiguity' where the fundamental rights of Kenyans were at stake.[170]

6.4 Limitation of constitutional rights

The social and economic rights recognized in Article 43 of the new Constitution, including the right to health, are subject to two important qualifications. First, Article 21(2) adopts the terminology of the ICESCR in identifying the state's duty as one of 'progressive realization' only, including adopting policy measures and setting standards.[171] Second, Article 20(5)(c) provides that in considering a claim made under Article 43, a court 'may not interfere with a decision by a state organ concerning the allocation of available resources, solely on the basis that it would have reached a different conclusion'. These limitations were not, however, applicable in *P.A.O.*, since the case was not an attempt to enforce a positive claim, ie to force the state to rearrange or increase budgets in order to secure the right to health. Rather, as the judge recognized, the applicants were seeking to enforce a 'negative duty', ie to compel the state to refrain from taking legislative measures which would abrogate existing access to

162 *P.A.O. v Attorney General* (n 158) *per* Ngugi J at para 84.

163 *P.A.O. v Attorney General* (n 158) *per* Ngugi J at para 78.

164 *P.A.O. v Attorney General* (n 158) *per* Ngugi J at para 75. See further, Abbott, 'Seizure of generic pharmaceuticals' (n 107) 131.

165 *P.A.O. v Attorney General* (n 158) *per* Ngugi J at paras 75, 77.

166 *P.A.O. v Attorney General* (n 158) *per* Ngugi J at para 66.

167 *P.A.O. v Attorney General* (n 158) *per* Ngugi J at para 78. See Written Submissions of UN Special Rapporteur on the Right of Everyone to the Highest Attainable Standard of Health, Mr Anand Grover, Amicus Curiae, 15 February 2011, para 35 (copy on file with author).

168 *P.A.O. v Attorney General* (n 158) *per* Ngugi J at para. 83.

169 *P.A.O. v Attorney General* (n 158) *per* Ngugi J at para 85.

170 *P.A.O. v Attorney General* (n 158) *per* Ngugi J at para 84.

171 See International Covenant on Economic, Social and Cultural Rights, Art 2(1).

affordable generic ARVs, as provided for by the Industrial Property Act 2000.[172] This distinction between positive and negative duties is supported by the text of Article 21 (1) which requires the state, on the one hand, 'to observe, respect [and] protect' and, on the other hand, to 'promote and fulfil the rights and fundamental freedoms in the Bill of Rights'.[173]

As a result the state could, in effect, only rely on the general clause for the limitation of rights contained in Article 24(1) which allows a considerably narrower margin of appreciation to the state.[174] It requires the authorities to show that restrictions upon constitutionally protected rights are 'reasonable and justifiable in an open and democratic society' with reference, *inter alia*, to: the nature of the right or fundamental freedom; the importance of the purpose of the limitation; the nature and extent of the limitation; and whether there are less restrictive means to achieve the purpose. Moreover, Article 24(2)(c) provides that legislative measures 'shall not limit the right or fundamental freedom so far as to derogate from its core or essential content'. Though Ngugi J did not explicitly refer to Article 24, her reasoning can be read in terms of the pattern of analysis laid down there.

The petitioners in *P.A.O.* argued that that access to life-saving medicines formed part of the non-derogable core of the right to life, an argument which is supported by General Comment 14 as regards the right to health.[175] Moreover, according to the Special Rapporteur, the likely effect of the Anti-Counterfeit Act 2008 in limiting importation of generics would constitute a retrogressive measure.[176] As the CESCR has argued, however, there is a strong presumption against such measures in international law.[177] In response, the state offered a public health justification for the Anti-Counterfeit Act 2008, similar to that put forward by industry lobbyists discussed earlier, namely that it sought to vindicate the rights of the petitioners through protecting them from the harmful effects of counterfeit medicines.[178] Ngugi J accepted that counterfeits were a real problem for Kenya.[179] However, she held that the chief objective of the Act was not to promote public health, but 'to bolster protection of IPRs by providing criminal sanctions for infringement'.[180] This was supported by a close reading of the provisions of the Act which referred consistently to the 'course of trade' and the holders of 'intellectual property rights'.[181] By contrast, had 'the primary intention been to safeguard consumers from counterfeit medicine,

172 *P.A.O. v Attorney General* [2012] eKLR, HC Nairobi (*per* Ngugi J at paras 66, 52).

173 This broadly replicates the typology of duties elaborated in Committee on Economic, Social and Cultural Rights, General Comment No 14 (22nd Session 2000) (n 156) para 33; see further, Musila, 'Testing Two Standards of Compliance' (n 154) 83.

174 The differential application of such limitation clauses in the context of social and economic rights protected in the South African Constitution is discussed in S. Liebenberg, *Socio-Economic Rights. Adjudication Under a Transformative Constitution* (Claremont: Juta Law, 2010) 215.

175 Committee on Economic, Social and Cultural Rights, General Comment No 14 (22nd Session 2000) (n 156) para 40.

176 Written Submissions of UN Special Rapporteur on the Right of Everyone to the Highest Attainable Standard of Health, Mr Anand Grover, Amicus Curiae, 15 February 2011, para. 44 (copy on file with author).

177 Committee on Economic, Social and Cultural Rights, General Comment No 3 (5th Session 1990) 'The Nature of the States Parties Obligations (Art. 2 Para. 1 of the Covenant)', E/1991/23, para 9.

178 *P.A.O. v Attorney General* [2012] eKLR, HC Nairobi (*per* Ngugi J at para 69).

179 *P.A.O. v Attorney General* (n 178) *per* Ngugi J at para 70.

180 *P.A.O. v Attorney General* (n 178) *per* Ngugi J at para 70.

181 *P.A.O. v Attorney General* (n 178) *per* Ngugi J at paras 79–81; see Anti-Counterfeit Act 2008, ss 32, 33(1), 34(1).

then the Act should have laid greater emphasis on standards and quality'.[182] There was no such emphasis in the legislation.[183] In sum, she held that the protection of the public was at best a 'collateral issue' for the proponents of the Act.[184]

The tension between IPRs and the rights to life, health, and dignity could not be finessed away, either by the inclusion of ambiguous supplementary definitions and provisos or by repackaging the purpose of the Act. Once the conflict was acknowledged, the international law materials which she had been considering led the judge to hold that the rights of IPR holders 'must give way to the fundamental rights of citizens'.[185] She quoted the view of the CESCR in General Comment 17 that 'intellectual property is a social product and has a social function'.[186] Given this, states had a duty to avoid situations where the protection of intellectual property rights led 'to unreasonably high costs for access to essential medicines . . . contrary to the rights to life and health'.[187] On this basis she granted each of the three declarations sought. The decision not having been appealed within the permitted time, the operation of the Anti-Counterfeit Act 2008 is now permanently suspended in so far as it affects affordable and essential medicines, including generic medicines.

7. Remedying Democratic Failures: Justifying *P.A.O. v Attorney General*

The ongoing struggle to secure or overturn legislation recognizing and enforcing IPRs in Kenya can be viewed as a series of more or less successful attempts to enrol powerful state nodes. As was suggested previously, these struggles have a crucial normative dimension given that different nodes dispose of unequal technologies and resources. 'All nodes are not created equal', as Burris, Drahos, and Shearing put it, and this inequality may lead to governance outcomes which exacerbate existing social and political inequalities.[188] The substantive effect of *P.A.O.* is to secure the current level of availability of affordable medicines in Kenya. But the decision also demonstrates the role of social and economic rights, including the right to health, in overcoming the 'democratic failures' of nodal governance. The specific manner in which it does so can

182 *P.A.O. v Attorney General* (n 178) *per* Ngugi J at para 82.

183 Such an emphasis would have justified the state in pleading Art 46 of the Constitution which, *inter alia*, obliges the state to protect the health of consumers and their right to goods of reasonable quality. The CESCR has also reasoned that the quality of medical products is an essential element of the right to health, Committee on Economic, Social and Cultural Rights, General Comment No 14 (22nd Session 2000) (n 156) para 12(d). However, neither of these sources was raised by the state.

184 *P.A.O. v Attorney General* [2012] eKLR, HC Nairobi (*per* Ngugi J at para 83).

185 *P.A.O. v Attorney General* (n 184) *per* Ngugi J at para 86. Note that the Constitution also commits the state to promote, respect, and support 'the intellectual property rights of the people of Kenya' (Arts 11(2)(c), 40(5)). However, this commitment appears not to have been raised by the state and was not considered by the judge. For a subtle analysis of how these rights might be balanced with the right to health, see P.L. Yu, 'Reconceptualizing Intellectual Property Interests in a Human Rights Framework' (2007) 40 *UC Davis Law Review* 1039.

186 *P.A.O. v Attorney General* [2012] eKLR, HC Nairobi (*per* Ngugi J at para 86), quoting Committee on Economic, Social and Cultural Rights, General Comment No 17 (35th Session 2005) 'The Right of Everyone to Benefit from the Protection of the Moral and Materials Interests Resulting from any Scientific, Literary or Artistic Production of which He or She is the Author', E/C.12/GC/17, para 35.

187 *P.A.O. v Attorney General* [2012] eKLR HC Nairobi (*per* Ngugi J at para 86) quoting Committee on Economic, Social and Cultural Rights, General Comment No 17 (35th Session 2005) (n 186), para 35.

188 Burris, Drahos, and Shearing, 'Nodal Governance' (n 13) 39.

be outlined with reference to the work of Rosalind Dixon on 'dialogic constitutionalism'.[189] Dixon seeks to determine the proper basis and scope of judicial power to override the judgment of parliament and the executive as regards social policy, given concerns rooted in the doctrine of separation of powers. The task of judges, she argues, is not directly to rewrite policy or to transfer resources between different areas. Rather, their proper role is to sustain the legitimacy of the constitutional system as a whole by correcting for 'blockages'—'blind spots' and 'burdens of inertia'—in the operation of the other branches of government.[190] The latter are often constituted by a failure to afford adequate participation to poor and vulnerable groups of citizens and an omission of their concerns from political deliberation. Courts do the work of correction in allowing such citizens and their representative groups to challenge statutes and other measures on the basis that their social and economic rights have been infringed, in reasoning on the scope and implication of such rights in relation to other legal and policy measures and in providing suitable remedies where such claims are upheld. The rest of this section interprets *P.A.O.* as addressing the 'blind spots' and 'burdens of inertia' which marked the legislative process leading to the Anti-Counterfeit Act 2008.

Dixon identifies the three possible blind spots: of 'application', 'perspective', and 'accommodation', each of which is considered here.[191]

(1) '*Blind spots of application*' are constituted where parliament fails to recognize that the enforcement of a given law is likely to infringe fundamental rights.[192] In the case of the Anti-Counterfeit Act 2008 it has been seen that MPs were substantially swayed by the arguments of KAM and others to the effect that the most serious health threat at issue was that posed by counterfeit products. They failed to take sufficiently seriously the likely negative effect of the Act upon access to essential medicines. Ngugi J was able to correct for this blind spot by adopting a position of some scepticism towards the declared purposes of the Act. She made clear that the Act itself posed a significant threat to the health of Kenyans: namely the risk that it would allow seizure of supplies of generic medicines, leading to a rise in price and a decline in access.

(2) '*Blindspots of perspective*' arise when legislators fail to appreciate the viewpoints of rights claimants with very different lives and viewpoints from their own.[193] As has been seen, consultation and debate on the Anti-Counterfeit Act 2008 was weighted in favour of industry representatives. Health activists had more limited access to MPs and ministers and as a result the perspectives and views of PLWHA were relatively marginalized. By way of remedy, the presence of a justiciable right to health in the new Constitution opened up the courts as an alternative forum within which PLWHA could give voice to their distinctive needs. Moreover, widened rules of standing permitted the activist legal groups and the Special Rapporteur to join the litigation, enhancing the quality of information available to the Court as regards the practical situation and normative entitlements of affected groups.[194] Their contribution was reinforced by

[189] R. Dixon, 'Creating Dialogue about Socio-Economic Rights: Strong-Form versus Weak-Form Judicial Review Revisited' (2007) 5 *International Journal of Constitutional Law* 391.

[190] Dixon, 'Creating Dialogue about Socio-Economic Rights' (n 189) 393.

[191] Dixon, 'Creating Dialogue about Socio-Economic Rights' (n 189) 402.

[192] Dixon, 'Creating Dialogue about Socio-Economic Rights' (n 189) 402.

[193] Dixon, 'Creating Dialogue about Socio-Economic Rights' (n 189) 402.

[194] Note, although these rules would equally have permitted industry groups as such to join the proceedings, they did not in fact do so. However, the Attorney General's case in defence of the Act was

Article 2(6) which allowed Ngugi J to draw on international human rights materials in reasoning about the rights of the applicants and the duties of the state.

(3) Finally a '*blindspot of accommodation*' arises where, through a restricted policy focus, legislators overlook feasible alternatives for reconciling statutory objectives with the protection of fundamental rights.[195] Given the manner in which the issues were framed and the haste with which the Anti-Counterfeit Act 2008 was passed, realistic strategies for dealing with the real social problem of fake products which also respected the need for access to essential medicines were not considered. As the judge found in *P.A.O.*, such concessions as had been made by the Bill's proponents did not provide for an effective accommodation in this regard. In any case, as critics had pointed out, existing Kenyan law and administrative structures already provided the means to deal with the trade in counterfeit medicines and the threat which they posed to consumer welfare.[196] Whilst Ngugi J did not directly propose alternative means of tackling the problem of counterfeit medicines, the effect of her decision was to require the state to do just this.

Of the *burdens of inertia* identified by Dixon as justifying judicial review of legislation on the basis of social and economic rights, the most important for present purposes are '*priority-driven*' burdens.[197] These arise where the legislature fails to address rights claims because other tasks appear to be more pressing. As was seen, MPs debating the Anti-Counterfeit Act 2008 identified the promotion of national competitiveness as the overriding task of government. This priority, of course, reflected the particular interests of local and multinational businesses. But it also expressed the dominant economic orthodoxy which pits countries against each other in a vital struggle to attract and retain foreign investment. This aspect of neo-liberal common sense is so well anchored at national and international level as to amount to a structural constraint or a burden of inertia on the political process.[198] Its purchase is strengthened further in developing countries as a result of the difficult history of structural adjustment and the ongoing vigilance of donor countries and the Bretton Woods institutions.[199] Ngugi J dealt with this burden of inertia by effectively reasoning that the rights and needs of all Kenyans, particularly those who are poor and vulnerable, cannot simply be reduced to the interests of commerce. The constitution demands that they are considered discretely and, where necessary, prioritized over competing interests.[200]

based in part on an affidavit of the Chairman of the Anti-Counterfeit Agency, see *P.A.O. v Attorney General* [2012] eKLR HC Nairobi (*per* Ngugi J at para 38).

195 Dixon, 'Creating Dialogue About Socio-Economic Rights' (n 189) 402.

196 Mey, 'Unfettered Consumer Access to Affordable Therapies' (n 2) 448–50.

197 The others are 'coalition-driven' and 'compound burdens of inertia', see Dixon, 'Creating Dialogue About Socio-Economic Rights' (n 189) 403.

198 See S. Gill, 'Globalisation, Market Civilisation and Disciplinary Neo-Liberalism' (1995) 24 *Millennium, Journal of International Studies* 399.

199 K.L. Scheppele, 'A Realpolitik Defense of Social Rights' (2004) 82 *Texas Law Review* 1921.

200 See P. O'Connell, 'Human Rights and Health in an Age of Market Hegemony' in J. Harrington and M. Stuttaford (eds), *Global Health and Human Rights. Legal and Philosophical Perspectives* (London: Routledge, 2010) 190.

8. Conclusion: Towards a Transformative Constitution

The *P.A.O.* case ensured continued access to lower priced generic medicines for ordinary Kenyans. But the significance of the decision for the IPE agenda internationally and in other jurisdictions was also widely noted. Commentators, including the Executive Director of UNAIDS, noted that Ngugi J's ruling showed the potential use of entrenched social and economic rights in defending intellectual property law reforms which promote access to essential medicines.[201] From an industry point of view the IPE agenda can, thus, be seen as being specifically vulnerable at national level. Pro-access activists beyond Kenya welcomed the decision in just these terms.[202] They also highlighted the substantive affinity between the impugned provisions of the Kenyan Anti-Counterfeit Act 2008 and the terms of international agreements such as ACTA.[203] *P.A.O.* is furthermore of specific significance in the East African region. For one thing, as noted earlier, Kenya is an important transit point for generic drugs which are distributed in neighbouring countries. The terms of the Anti-Counterfeit Act 2008 raised the possibility that this important supply route could be interrupted. In addition, Kenyan activists noted a demonstration effect whereby any amendment made to the Act to reflect the terms of the judgment could be taken up and used to modify anti-counterfeiting legislation elsewhere in the region.[204]

P.A.O. also showcases the 'transformative' nature of the new Kenyan Constitution, which has been widely seen as marking a break with the autocratic, undemocratic, and socially unjust regimes that have dominated Kenya in the colonial and post-colonial periods.[205] The extensive consultations which preceded the passing of the Constitution revealed a popular desire that poverty be alleviated and basic needs met.[206] This 'expectation of better lives' has already been given normative weight by the High Court in its interpretation of Article 43.[207] The guarantees contained in the latter, it has held, represent 'a commitment to transform Kenya from a society based on social and economic deprivation to one based on equal and equitable distribution of resources'.[208]

201 Anon, 'UNAIDS Welcomes Kenya High Court Judgment on Anti-Counterfeit Law', UNAIDS, Geneva, 20 April 2012, available at <http://www.unaids.org/en/resources/presscentre/pressreleaseandstatementarchive/2012/april/20120420pskenya/> (accessed 4 April 2013); see also Anon, 'Landmark Decision on Medicines and Anti-Counterfeiting Law by Kenyan High Court', *Don't Trade Our Lives Away*, 24 April 2012, available at <http://donttradeourlivesaway.wordpress.com/2012/04/24/landmark-decision-on-medicines-and-anti-counterfeiting-law-by-kenyan-high-court/> (accessed 4 April 2013).On equivalent case law from India, see D. Matthews, *Intellectual Property, Human Rights and Development. The Role of NGOs and Social Movements* (Cheltenham: Edward Elgar, 2011) 53.

202 S.P. Barooah, 'Kenyan Court holds Anti-Counterfeit Act Unconstitutional', SpicyIP, 26 April, 2012, available at <http://spicyipindia.blogspot.ie/2012/04/kenyan-court-holds-anti-counterfeit-act.html> (accessed 4 April 2013).

203 G. Moody, 'Kenya's High Court Rules Anti-Counterfeiting Law Is Unconstitutional Because It Threatens Access To Generic Drugs', *techdirt*, 24 April 2012, available at <http://www.techdirt.com/articles/20120421/04274218595/kenyas-high-court-rules-anti-counterfeiting-law-is-unconstitutional-because-it-threatens-access-to-generic-drugs.shtml> (accessed 4 April 2013).

204 Interview with James Kamau, Coordinator for Kenya Treatment Action Movement, 12 September 2012.

205 See Musila, 'Testing Two Standards of Compliance' (n 154) 57–59.

206 As recorded in Constitution of Kenya Review Commission, 'The Final Report of the Constitution of Kenya Review Commission' (Nairobi, 2005) 63, 65, 103.

207 *Satrose Ayuma v Registered Trustees of the Kenya Railways Staff Retirement Benefits Scheme* [2011] eKLR HC Nairobi (*per* Musinga J at 7).

208 *John Kabui Mwai v Kenya National Examination Council* [2011] eKLR HC Nairobi (*per* Gacheche, Dulu, Muchelule JJ at 3).

This view has also been emphatically endorsed by Kenya's Chief Justice, speaking extrajudicially.[209]

Transformation is not simply a matter of allocating material resources, however. The passage of the Anti-Counterfeit Act 2008 suggests that the enjoyment of social and economic rights may be significantly compromised by institutional arrangements and political processes. The success of industry lobbyists in getting the Act passed was linked with shortcomings in the process of legislative deliberation. *P.A.O.* corrects for these 'democratic failures' by effectively requiring Parliament to give more adequate consideration to the issues should it wish to extend the Anti-Counterfeit Act 2008 to essential medicines. Moreover, the Act created a new governance node, the Anti-Counterfeit Agency, benefiting from dedicated resources, enhanced legal technologies, and a 'mentality' chiefly focused on addressing problems faced by business. The High Court can also be said to have disrupted this harnessing of public power to private interests by subjecting the powers and purposes of the Agency to close scrutiny in the light of Article 43(1)(a).

These aspects of the decision are consistent with the agenda for political, as well as social and economic transformation which is central to the new dispensation.[210] The consultation exercise, referred to earlier, found that 'representative democracy is widely thought to have been fundamentally a failure' in Kenya.[211] This is unsurprising given the allegations of duplicity, corruption, and bias repeatedly made against Kenyan MPs.[212] Article 118(1)(b) of the new Constitution responds by obliging Parliament and its committees to 'facilitate public participation and involvement in legislative and other business'. This purpose has been taken up in two recent cases where the High Court held that Parliament acted unconstitutionally in shortening the period of publication of a Bill and in failing to consider fully the criteria for making a statutory appointment.[213]

The final mode of transformation exhibited by *P.A.O.* concerns the judiciary itself. Kenyan judges were traditionally accused of being overly deferential to the Executive, functioning from colonial times as 'part of the state machinery which perpetuated human rights violations'.[214] These deficiencies were compounded in many cases by an excessive formalism which frustrated genuine litigants and in some cases by straightforward corruption.[215] To this extent the judicial decision-making itself has also been subject to 'blind spots' and 'burdens of inertia'. These concerns have been addressed by a refurbishment of the technologies available to the courts. As has been seen, the new

209 Speech by Dr Willy Mutunga, D Jur, SC, EGH, Chief Justice/President of the Supreme Court of Kenya at the launch of the publication of ICJ Kenya's Judicial Watch Report Series, Vol 10, at Serena Hotel, Nairobi/Kenya on 22 March 2012 (copy on file with author).

210 A.L. Bannon, 'Designing a Constitution-Drafting Process: Lessons from Kenya' (2007) 116 *Yale Law Journal* 1832.

211 Constitution of Kenya Review Commission, 'The Final Report of the Constitution of Kenya Review Commission' (Nairobi, 2005) 157.

212 See further, J. Harrington and A. Manji, 'Satire and the Politics of Corruption in Kenya' (2013) 22 *Social and Legal Studies* 3–23. It should be noted that there is no proof of corruption as regards the passage of the Anti-Counterfeit Act 2008.

213 See respectively, *Ladama Olekina v Attorney General* [2011] eKLR HC Nairobi (Ang'awa J); and *Trusted Society of Human Rights Alliance v Attorney General* [2012] eKLR HC Nairobi (Ngugi, Ogunga and Ngugi JJ).

214 Biegon, 'The Inclusion of Social and Economic Rights in the 2010 Constitution' (n 145) 31.

215 See the remarks of the Chief Justice: W Mutunga, 'Building a Progressive Kenya: The Judiciary and the Transformation Agenda within the Context of the New Constitution', in Kenya National Dialogue and Reconciliation, *Building a Progressive Kenya* (Nairobi, 2011) 17 (copy on file with author).

Constitution increases the capacity of ordinary citizens and interested parties to enrol the courts in defence of their fundamental rights. Judges themselves, the courts' chief resource, are currently subject to an extensive and rigorous process of vetting which has seen many disqualified.[216] The 'mentality' of the judiciary, too, is undergoing a process of transformation. In place of deference has come a growing appreciation that the Constitution, not Parliament or the Executive, is now supreme within the Kenyan system and that it is for the courts to uphold this supremacy.[217] Article 10 binds the courts to 'national principles' of inclusiveness, transparency, equity, and the protection of the marginalized, among others. In seeking to realize these values and the promise of the Bill of Rights, the High Court in *P.A.O.* has shown the 'new confidence and sense of purpose' typical of a transformed judiciary.[218]

216 D. Wanjala, 'Delayed Justice Robs Top Judges of Seats on the Bench' (2012) 3(8) *Nairobi Law Monthly* 34.

217 This principle is laid down in Art 2(1); see *Trusted Society of Human Rights Alliance v Attorney General* [2012] eKLR HC Nairobi (*per* Ngugi, Ogunga and Ngugi JJ at para 71).

218 See Anon, 'Editorial' (2012) 3(11) *Nairobi Law Monthly* 2.

PART B

VULNERABLE POPULATIONS

6

Vulnerability

An Issue for Law and Policy in Pandemic Planning?

*Belinda Bennett and Terry Carney**

The 2009 H1N1 'swine flu' pandemic was the first influenza pandemic of the twenty-first century. Unlike the first influenza pandemic of the twentieth century, the so-called 'Spanish flu' which killed millions of people worldwide, the 2009 pandemic was relatively mild. While the mildness of the 2009 pandemic meant that the world was spared from the impact of a high-mortality event that would cause widespread social and economic disruption, the 2009 pandemic did provide an opportunity to road-test pandemic readiness. In other work we have assessed Australia's pandemic plans and emergency management legislation, finding that both provide flexible and adaptive forms of regulation that are capable of adapting to the scale and severity of a pandemic or other public health emergency.[1] In this chapter we consider whether pandemic planning adequately addresses the needs of vulnerable individuals and groups, both within countries and between them. Central to this is the question of whether vulnerability is itself a useful concept for both law and policy, and if so, the implications of expressly incorporating the concept of vulnerability into pandemic planning.

1. Pandemics and Vulnerability

The constant minor genetic changes in influenza viruses, known as antigentic drift, mean that the influenza virus is able to effectively slip past the defences of the human immune system.[2] Sometimes, however, an influenza virus may swap genes with another influenza virus. This process, known as antigenic shift, leads to the creation of a new influenza sub-type to which there will be little or no immunity.[3] Our susceptibility to a particular strain of influenza, both individually and communally, will depend then on whether it is a strain to which we have had some previous exposure and therefore the possibility of some immunity.

In their comparison of three twentieth-century influenza pandemics in 1918, 1957, and 1968, Miller, Viboud, Balinka, and Simonsen identify the following features of influenza pandemics:

* Research for this chapter is supported by an Australian Research Council grant (DP0987239).

1 T. Carney, R. Bailey, and B. Bennett, 'Pandemic Planning as Risk Management: How Fared the Australian Federation?' (2012) 19 *Journal of Law and Medicine* 550; B. Bennett, T. Carney, and R. Bailey, 'Emergency Powers and Pandemics: Federalism and the Management of Public Health Emergencies in Australia' (2012) 31 *University of Tasmania Law Review* 37.

2 WHO, 'Avian Influenza: Assessing the Pandemic Threat' (World Health Organization, 2005) 10.

3 WHO, 'Avian Influenza: Assessing the Threat' (n 2) 10.

> ...a shift in the virus sub-type, shifts of the highest death rates to younger populations, successive pandemic waves, higher transmissibility than that of seasonal influenza, and differences in impact in different geographic regions.[4]

During an influenza pandemic we will all be at risk, at least to some degree. Some groups are, however, likely to be at particular risk from influenza. In a typical influenza season the very young, the elderly, and those with compromised immune systems[5] are likely to experience greatest mortality from influenza. In a pandemic, this traditional risk pattern may alter, placing other groups in the community at particular risk. For example, during the 1918 influenza pandemic, this traditional U-shaped pattern of mortality was reversed, with the highest rates of mortality occurring amongst young, previously healthy adults, with relatively low rates of mortality amongst the elderly, as Barry and others explain. John M. Barry noted in his book on the 1918 influenza pandemic that even the figures indicating that the pandemic killed between 50 and 100 million people 'understates the horror of the disease... [for] in the 1918 pandemic roughly half of those who died were young men and women in the prime of their lives, in their twenties and thirties'.[6] In twentieth-century pandemics, 'more and more older people were affected, but young age groups were still at a higher risk', hypothesized to be due either to acquired immunity as one ages, or the 'collateral damage', such as to lung tissue, caused by immune system response in the young.[7] This pattern, of higher risk for younger groups, was also evident during the 2009 H1N1 pandemic, with younger patients most affected and lower rates of infection amongst the elderly.[8]

Age was not the only factor relevant to risk during the H1N1 pandemic in 2009. Pregnant women and indigenous communities were also at risk. During the 2009 pandemic, pregnant women were at increased risk of serious illness and admission to intensive care from H1N1 during pregnancy.[9] The experience from Australia,[10] New Zealand,[11] Canada,[12] the Americas, and the Pacific[13] showed that indigenous populations were also at high risk during the H1N1 pandemic.

4 M.A. Miller et al, 'The Signature Features of Influenza Pandemics—Implications for Policy' (2009) 360 *New England Journal of Medicine* 2595, 2595.

5 T. Ulrichs, 'Airborne Transmission: Influenza and Tuberculosis' in A. Krämer, M. Kretzschmar, and K. Krickeberg (eds), *Modern Infectious Diesease Epidemiology: Concepts, Methods, Mathematical Models, and Public Health* (Dordrecht: Springer, 2010) 279, 279; K.M. Kunisaki and E.N. Janoff, 'Influenza in Immunosuppressed Populations: A Review of Infection Frequency, Morbidity, Mortality, and Vaccine Responses' (2009) 9 *Lancet Infectious Diseases* 493.

6 J.M. Barry, *The Great Influenza: The Epic Story of the Deadliest Plague in History* (New York: Viking Penguin, 2004) 4.

7 Ulrichs, 'Airborne Transmission' (n 5) 280.

8 M. Baker, H. Kelly, and N. Wilson, 'Pandemic H1N1 Influenza Lessons from the Southern Hemisphere' (2009) 14 *Euro Surveillance* pii=19370.

9 ANZIC Investigators and Australasian Maternity Outcomes Surveillance System, 'Critical Illness due to 2009 A/H1N1 Influenza in Pregnant and Postpartum Women: Population Based Cohort Study' (2010) 340 *BMJ* doi:10.1136/bmj.c1279; A.M. Siston et al, 'Pandemic 2009 Influenza A(H1N1) Virus Illness among Pregnant Women in the United States' (2010) 303 *Journal of the American Medical Association* 1517.

10 S.M. Flint et al, 'Disproportionate Impact of Pandemic (H1N1) 2009 Influenza on Indigenous People in the Top End of Australia's Northern Territory' (2010) 192 *Medical Journal of Australia* 617.

11 A. Verrall et al, 'Hospitalizations for Pandemic (H1N1) 2009 among Maori and Pacific Islanders, New Zealand' (2010) 16 *Emerging Infectious Diseases* 100.

12 A. Kumar et al, 'Critically Ill Patients with 2009 Influenza A(H1N1) Infection in Canada' (2009) 302 *Journal of the American Medical Association* 1872.

13 G. La Ruche et al, 'The 2009 Pandemic H1N1 Influenza and Indigenous Populations of the Americas and the Pacific' (2009) 14 *Euro Surveillance* (pii=19366).

These figures show that risk is spread unevenly and that some groups may be at greater risk of serious illness and even death in the event of a pandemic. While there had been calls even before the 2009 pandemic for pandemic planning to pay increased attention to pregnancy, to the needs of indigenous communities,[14] and to the needs of other vulnerable groups such as immigrant communities and people with disabilities,[15] the experience of H1N1 serves as a reminder of the importance of vulnerability and disadvantage in pandemic planning.

Vulnerability and risk are also relative between countries, with the world's poorest countries bearing the greatest burden of both communicable and non-communicable diseases. Murray et al used data from the 1918 pandemic to estimate excess mortality and extrapolated this to estimate mortality from a similar pandemic based on world population figures in 2004.[16] They found that there was a 30-fold variation in mortality between countries and that a large proportion of this variation was accounted for by per-head income. They found that had a 1918-type pandemic occurred in 2004 that it would have killed an estimated 62 million people, and that 96 per cent of deaths would occur in developing countries.[17]

2. Vulnerability and Disadvantage

Of central importance here is the need to conceptualize vulnerability in ways that go beyond a medical understanding and that include social and economic disadvantage. As Sharona Hoffman notes:

> [Often disregarded in disaster plans are] the special needs of vulnerable populations. During and after a catastrophic event, vulnerable populations may include individuals with disabilities, pregnant women, children, the elderly, prisoners, ethnic minorities, people with language barriers, and the impoverished... According to the United States Census Bureau, in 2006, 41.3 million noninstitutionalized Americans over the age of five had disabilities. Many more may have physical or mental impairments that may impact their welfare during an emergency but are not deemed to be serious enough to constitute reportable disabilities. In 2006, approximately 35.5 million individuals were sixty-five years of age or older and 38.8 million Americans were living in poverty. Children constitute approximately twenty-five percent of the United States population... Some subset of each of these groups will almost certainly have special needs during disasters.[18]

Despite the large number of individuals likely to have special needs during a pandemic or other public health emergency, social vulnerability tends to receive less attention in pandemic planning than medical risk. One review of thirty-seven pandemic plans published from 2000 to 2006 in fifteen high-income, eighteen middle income, and

[14] See eg S.A. Rasmussen, D.J. Jamieson, and J.S. Bresee, 'Pandemic Influenza and Pregnant Women' (2008) 14 *Emerging Infectious Diseases* 95; A.V. Groom et al, 'Pandemic Influenza Preparedness and Vulnerable Populations in Tribal Communities' (2009) 99 *American Journal of Public Health* S271.

[15] See eg V.A. Campbell et al, 'Preparing for and Responding to Pandemic Influenza: Implications for People with Disabilities' (2009) 99 *American Journal of Public Health* S294; B.I. Truman et al, 'Pandemic Influenza Preparedness and Response among Immigrants and Refugees' (2009) 99 *American Journal of Public Health* S278; S.S. Hutchins et al, 'Protection of Racial/Ethnic Minority Populations During an Influenza Pandemic' (2009) 99 *American Journal of Public Health* S261.

[16] C.J.L. Murray et al, 'Estimation of Potential Global Pandemic Influenza Mortality on the Basis of Vital Registry Data from the 1918–20 Pandemic: A Quantitative Analysis' (2007) 368 *Lancet* 2211.

[17] Murray et al, 'Estimation of Potential Global Pandemic Influenza Mortality' (n 16).

[18] S. Hoffman, 'Preparing for Disaster: Protecting the Most Vulnerable in Emergencies' (2009) 42 *UC Davis Law Review* 1491, 1493–5.

four low income countries, found that vulnerable individuals or groups were discussed in twenty plans, but that 'in all instances, the reference was to individuals or groups at *increased biological or medical risk* of succumbing to or transmitting pandemic influenza'.[19] Social disadvantage was recognized in some pandemic plans from high-income countries, but as the authors point out, the fact that social disadvantage was only addressed in pandemic plans from high-income countries is itself a cause for concern, 'as these countries are more likely than low- and middle-income countries to have and to enforce human rights protections'.[20]

Garoon and Duggan argue that:

> Failure to address social as well as biological vulnerability thereby poses the danger of repeating the differential trends in mortality observed in 1918—meaning individuals and groups disadvantaged in the *status quo ante* would suffer a significantly disproportionate force of mortality. Thus, the plans' apparently uncontroversial aim of minimizing morbidity and mortality should in fact raise critical questions: *Whose* illness? *Whose* deaths?[21]

The relative lack of attention given to social disadvantage rather than medical risk is not surprising. In their review of pandemic plans, Garoon and Duggan identified six discourses within the plans: 'scientific, political, legal, cultural, social, and ethical'.[22] However, not all of these discourses figure equally in the plans, with Garron and Duggan observing:

> Within the ordered universe of discourse in which the plans operate, the former three discourses clearly dominate the latter trio. The scientific, political, and legal discourses are not only more prominent in the plans, but also frame the terms in which the plans consider the social, cultural, and ethical.[23]

While legal discourses do have a strong normative element that can sometimes trump other discourses, as we have argued elsewhere, cultural and ethical factors are important aspects of pandemic planning.[24] Furthermore, history has shown that infectious diseases can compound existing disadvantage, as is evident in the burning of witches in the Middle Ages,[25] by the stigmatization of Chinese Americans when cases of plague where detected in San Francisco's Chinatown in 1900,[26] by the portrayal of HIV/AIDS as an African disease, and of SARS as a Chinese disease.[27]

As the stigmatization of these diseases shows, the issues of marginalization and disadvantage have also intersected with the construction of risk to further heighten disadvantage. As Alison Bashford and Carolyn Strange have noted:

19 Lori Uscher-Pines et al, 'Planning for an Influenza Pandemic: Social Justice and Disadvantaged Groups' (2007) 37 *Hastings Center Report* 32, 35 (emphasis in original). For discussion, see also Hoffman, 'Preparing for Disaster' (n 18) 1494.

20 Uscher-Pines et al, 'Planning for an Influenza Pandemic' (n 19) 36.

21 J.P. Garoon and P.S. Duggan, 'Discourses of Disease, Discourses of Disadvantage: A Critical Analysis of National Pandemic Influenza Preparedness Plans' (2008) 67 *Social Science and Medicine* 1133, 1135–6.

22 Garoon and Duggan, 'Discourses of Disease' (n 21) 1135.

23 Garoon and Duggan, 'Discourses of Disease' (n 21) 1135.

24 B. Bennett and T. Carney, 'Law, Ethics and Pandemic Preparedness: The Importance of Cross-Jurisdictional and Cross-Cultural Perspectives' (2010) 34 *Australian and New Zealand Journal of Public Health* 106.

25 M. Aaltola, *Western Spectacle of Governance and the Emergence of Humanitarian World Politics* (New York: Palgrave Macmillan, 2009) 138.

26 C. McClain, 'Of Medicine, Race, and American Law: The Bubonic Plague Outbreak of 1900' (1988) 13 *Law and Social Inquiry* 447.

27 Aaltola, *Western Spectacle of Governance* (n 25) 138.

People already marginalised on the grounds of their race, class, gender or religion have been seen historically more as risks than as being at risk, with the result that governing authorities have managed them primarily as 'sources' instead of sufferers.[28]

Mika Aaltola has recently pointed to a tension between the containment and distancing narratives characteristic of pandemic management and the usual compassion extended to victims of emergencies.[29] Rather than 'mobilized empathy' for victims of an emergency, he suggests that: 'The momentum of pandemic emergencies is towards *disengagement* with the suffering *distant other*.'[30]

3. Vulnerability: a Useful Concept?

As is clear from the previous discussion, certain groups within society will be particularly vulnerable in the event of a pandemic. For this reason it seems logical to incorporate vulnerability expressly into our pandemic planning. Vulnerability does resonate with health and bioethics as it has a long history within bioethics.[31] The development of the Nuremburg Code following the Nazi experiments during the Second World War,[32] and the recommendations of the Belmont Report in the US in the 1970s, led to a focus on the need to protect vulnerable groups who may be subjects in human research[33] and which is reflected in contemporary international declarations including the Declaration of Helsinki[34] and the Universal Declaration on Bioethics and Human Rights.[35]

Although the concept of vulnerability has been used as a way of identifying individuals, groups, or even countries potentially in need of special protection in the

28 A. Bashford and C. Strange, 'Thinking Historically about Public Health' (2007) 33 *Medical Humanities* 87, 89.

29 M. Aaltola, *Understanding the Politics of Pandemic Scares: An Introduction to Global Politosomatics* (London: Routledge, 2012) especially ch 2.

30 Aaltola, *Understanding the Politics of Pandemic Scares* (n 29) 1 (emphasis added).

31 W. Rogers, C. Mackenzie, and S. Dodds, 'Why Bioethics Needs a Concept of Vulnerability' (2012) 5(2) *International Journal of Feminist Approaches to Bioethics* 11, 14. See also, M.M. Lange, W. Rogers, and S. Dodds, 'Vulnerability in Research Ethics: A Way Forward' (2013) 27(6) *Bioethics* 333, 334.

32 Rogers, Mackenzie, and Dodds, 'Why Bioethics Needs a Concept of Vulnerability' (n 31); Lange, Rogers, and Dodds, 'Vulnerability in Research Ethics' (n 31). See also, G.J. Annas and M.A. Grodin (eds), *The Nazi Doctors and the Nuremberg Code: Human Rights in Human Experimentation* (New York: OUP, 1992).

33 Rogers, Mackenzie, and Dodds, 'Why Bioethics Needs a Concept of Vulnerability' (n 31); Lange, Rogers, and Dodds, 'Vulnerability in Research Ethics' (n 31); C. Levine et al, 'The Limitations of "Vulnerability" as a Protection for Human Research Participants' (2004) 4 *American Journal of Bioethics* 44, 45. See also, G.F. Tomossy, 'Vulnerability in Research' in I. Freckelton and K. Petersen (eds), *Disputes and Dilemmas in Health Law* (Sydney: Federation Press, 2006) 534, 534.

34 Rogers, Mackenzie, and Dodds, 'Why Bioethics Needs a Concept of Vulnerability' (n 31); World Medical Association, 'Ethical Principles for Medical Research Involving Human Subjects (Declaration of Helsinki)', 59th World Medical Association General Assembly, as amended October 2008, para 9 states:

> Medical research is subject to ethical standards that promote respect for all human subjects and protect their health and human rights. Some research populations are particularly vulnerable and need special protection. These include those who cannot give or refuse consent for themselves and those who may be vulnerable to coercion or undue influence.

35 UNESCO, Universal Declaration on Bioethics and Human Rights, Art 8 states:

> In applying and advancing scientific knowledge, medical practice and associated technologies, human vulnerability should be taken into account. Individuals and groups of special vulnerability should be protected and the personal integrity of such individuals respected.

context of research,[36] the concept itself has been criticized in recent years as being both 'too broad and too narrow'.[37] Levine et al argue that, 'so many categories of people are now considered vulnerable that virtually all potential human subjects are included'.[38] Yet, at the same time as the concept of vulnerability is seen as so broad as to be 'too nebulous to be meaningful',[39] it is also seen as too narrow. Levine et al argue that:

> An almost exclusive emphasis on group characteristics that ostensibly undermine or eliminate the capacity to give consent can divert attention from features of the research itself, the institutional environment, or the social and economic context that can put participants in harm's way.[40]

Finally, Levine et al argue that 'the concept of vulnerability stereotypes whole categories of individuals, without distinguishing between individuals in the group who indeed might have special characteristics that need to be taken into account and those who do not'.[41] Indeed, as Henderson et al argue, the label of vulnerability 'resembles the disfavored legal category of "status crimes" like vagrancy or homelessness', which stigmatize individuals.[42] In response to agreement over the limits to the concept of vulnerability, suggestions have therefore been made for vulnerability to be understood in relational ways that see vulnerability as vulnerability *to influence*;[43] for the development of criteria that would specify certain research protocols as in need of 'special scrutiny' because of the particular ethical challenges they pose;[44] and for a revision of the Declaration of Helsinki to 'invoke a broader conception of vulnerability that recognizes both individual and contextual factors'.[45]

All of us are vulnerable in the event of a pandemic. Indeed, as Margaret Battin et al remind us, each one of us can be both a 'victim and a vector'.[46] In this sense of the duality, vulnerability is generic, universal, and shared. Martha Fineman has argued 'that vulnerability is—and should be understood to be—universal and constant, inherent in the human condition'.[47]

If all of us, as human, are vulnerable in a variety of ways, and if 'vulnerability' is simultaneously both too broad and too narrow a concept, does 'vulnerability' still retain value in the context of bioethics and in its potential to inform pandemic planning? It is argued here that the concept does retain value and that what is needed in order to move beyond the too broad/too narrow problem is greater specificity in the categories of

36 R. Macklin, 'Bioethics, Vulnerability, and Protection' (2003) 17 *Bioethics* 472. See also, Rogers, Mackenzie, and Dodds, 'Why Bioethics Needs a Concept of Vulnerability' (n 31) 13; Levine et al, 'The Limitations of "Vulnerability"' (n 33) 45.

37 Levine et al, 'The Limitations of "Vulnerability"' (n 33) 46; Rogers, Mackenzie, and Dodds, 'Why Bioethics Needs a Concept of Vulnerability' (n 31) 15.

38 Levine et al, 'The Limitations of "Vulnerability"' (n 33); Rogers, Mackenzie, and Dodds, 'Why Bioethics Needs a Concept of Vulnerability' (n 31) 15–16.

39 Levine et al, 'The Limitations of "Vulnerability"' (n 33); Rogers, Mackenzie, and Dodds, 'Why Bioethics Needs a Concept of Vulnerability' (n 31).

40 Levine et al, 'The Limitations of "Vulnerability"' (n 33); Rogers, Mackenzie, and Dodds, 'Why Bioethics Needs a Concept of Vulnerability' (n 31) 15.

41 Levine et al, 'The Limitations of "Vulnerability"' (n 33) 47; Rogers, Mackenzie, and Dodds, 'Why Bioethics Needs a Concept of Vulnerability' (n 31) 15–16.

42 G.E. Henderson, A.M. Davis, and N.M.P. King, 'Vulnerability to Influence: A Two-Way Street' (2004) 4 *The American Journal of Bioethics* 50, 50.

43 Henderson, Davis, and King, 'Vulnerability to Influence' (n 42).

44 Levine et al, 'The Limitations of "Vulnerability"' (n 33) 48.

45 L.A. Eckenwiler et al, 'Hopes for Helsinki: Reconsidering "Vulnerability"' (2008) 34 *Journal of Medical Ethics* 765, 766.

46 M.P. Battin et al, *The Patient as Victim and Vector: Ethics and Infectious Disease* (New York: OUP, 2009).

47 M.A. Fineman, 'The Vulnerable Subject: Anchoring Equality in the Human Condition' (2008) 20 *Yale Journal of Law and Feminism* 1, 1.

vulnerability. While traditional categories of vulnerability in health research have focused on lack of decision-making capacity or the potential for unequal relationships and coercion, as the authors discussed earlier argue, there is a need for broader understandings of vulnerability that also take account of vulnerability to risks of research, and differences in vulnerability *within* groups.

Florencia Luna has argued that defining vulnerability in terms of subpopulations fails to take account of the different ways that vulnerabilities can intersect and overlap.[48] Luna argues that vulnerability needs to 'be understood dynamically and relationally'.[49] Luna conceptualizes vulnerability in terms of 'layers', a concept that allows for more nuanced understandings of the ways that we may be vulnerable, and of the relationship between vulnerability and context:[50]

> The metaphor of a layer gives the idea of something 'softer,' something that may be multiple and different, and that may be removed layer by layer. It is not 'a solid and unique vulnerability' that exhausts the category; there might be different vulnerabilities, different layers operating. These layers may overlap: some of them may be related to problems with informed consent, others to social circumstances. The idea of layers of vulnerability gives flexibility to the concept of vulnerability.[51]

Carl Coleman has also proposed alternative ways of seeing vulnerability so as to avoid its potentially stigmatizing effect. He proposes three categories of vulnerability: (1) 'consent-based vulnerabilities', in which concerns arise about the adequacy of informed consent by research participants; (2) 'risk-based vulnerabilities', where there are particular risks associated with the research in question; and (3) 'justice-based vulnerabilities', which raise concerns about the distribution of the benefits and burdens of research.[52] According to Coleman, there are several advantages to conceptualizing vulnerability in these ways. First, it allows us to move beyond seeing vulnerability as either entirely individual or entirely group-based. As Coleman argues: 'Consent- and risk-based vulnerabilities make more sense conceptualized as individual issues, but justice-based vulnerabilities are hard to understand as anything other than a population-based concern.'[53] In addition, Coleman argues that distinguishing between the three different categories of vulnerability allows for an appreciation of the fact that 'the relationship between vulnerability and consent is not the same in all situations'.[54] As Coleman points out, not all forms of vulnerability arise from concerns about consent, and the more nuanced understanding of vulnerability proposed by Coleman 'avoids the stigmatizing implication that vulnerable subjects are necessarily incapable of making decisions for themselves'.[55]

48 F. Luna, 'Elucidating the Concept of Vulnerability: Layers Not Labels' (2009) 2 *International Journal of Feminist Approaches to Bioethics* 121, 123–4. See also, Rogers, Mackenzie, and Dodds, 'Why Bioethics Needs a Concept of Vulnerability' (n 31) 16; Lange, Rogers and Dodds, 'Vulnerability in Research Ethics' (n 31) 334–5.

49 Luna, 'Elucidating the Concept of Vulnerability' (n 48) 128.

50 Luna, 'Elucidating the Concept of Vulnerability' (n 48) 129.

51 Luna, 'Elucidating the Concept of Vulnerability' (n 48) 128.

52 C.H. Coleman, 'Vulnerability as a Regulatory Category in Human Subject Research' (2009) 37 *Journal of Law, Medicine and Ethics* 12, 15. For further discussion of vulnerability and justice, see Rogers, Mackenzie, and Dodds, 'Why Bioethics Needs a Concept of Vulnerability' (n 31) 18–19.

53 Coleman, 'Vulnerability as a Regulatory Category' (n 52) 17.

54 Coleman, 'Vulnerability as a Regulatory Category' (n 52) 17.

55 Coleman, 'Vulnerability as a Regulatory Category' (n 52) 17.

Although Coleman uses the example of research in developing countries to illustrate his category of justice-based vulnerability, one can also see how the idea of justice-based vulnerability can be applied in the context of pandemic planning. For when vulnerability is understood in terms of justice, as Coleman suggests, vulnerability becomes a valuable lens that can focus attention on disadvantage *between* groups in society, as well as on disadvantage *within* groups. Thus, a justice-based vulnerability analysis of pandemic planning could assess whether proposed planning adequately addresses the needs of all groups in society. Justice-based vulnerability also allows pandemic planning to be evaluated in terms of whether it addresses disparities *within* groups, such as where indigenous communities, immigrant populations, or those with disabilities may be at greater risk from the social disruption during a pandemic.[56]

When vulnerability is understood as layers, as suggested by Luna, and in terms of justice, as suggested by Coleman, it is possible to transcend the debate of vulnerability as both too broad and too narrow. Instead, we can conceptualize vulnerability as part of the human condition as suggested by Fineman. In this sense any of us can be vulnerable and, indeed, as Fineman argues, our vulnerability is inherently linked with our embodiment, which 'carries with it the ever-constant possibility of dependency as a result of disease, epidemics, resistant viruses, or other biologically-based catastrophes'.[57] However, despite the universality of vulnerability, the concept of vulnerability also requires consideration of what Luna refers to as the 'context' of vulnerability, or what Fineman refers to as the 'particular' nature of vulnerability: 'it is experienced uniquely by each of us and this experience is greatly influenced by the quality and quantity of resources we can possess or command'.[58]

4. Reconceptualizing Public Health Law

As argued previously, vulnerability does remain a useful concept provided we understand it in nuanced ways that adequately address issues of diversity, specificity, and the context of human vulnerability. As also argued earlier, vulnerability, certainly when understood in these broader ways, remains valuable in terms of our pandemic planning. Yet this broader understanding of vulnerability leads us to ask about the implications for public health law and policy generally. Drawing upon feminist approaches to law and bioethics, we argue here that there are three elements to be considered: first, the need to conceptualize law and bioethics in relational terms; second, to understand public health in terms of embodiment; and finally, the practical measures that can be implemented in a relational approach to pandemic planning.

Law and bioethics both have strong traditions based on individualism and rights. These individualist traditions are contested in at least three different ways in the case of pandemics: (1) on a theoretical plane by feminist/communitarian frames; (2) at a conceptual level by the shift from a litigational/clinical to a public interest/public health perspective; and (3) by the duality of individuals as both 'victim' and 'vector'.

Feminist approaches to law and bioethics have challenged the traditional individualistic and rights-oriented approach to human interaction, arguing that people are inherently relational and that even the principle of autonomy, which in many ways is

56 See also the discussion in Rogers, Mackenzie, and Dodds, 'Why Bioethics Needs a Concept of Vulnerability' (n 31).

57 Fineman, 'The Vulnerable Subject' (n 47) 9.

58 Fineman, 'The Vulnerable Subject' (n 47) 10.

the pinnacle of individualism, should instead be conceptualized as relational, thus expressly recognizing the social nature of society.[59] As Jennifer Nedelsky argues:

> If we ask ourselves what actually enables people to be autonomous, the answer is not isolation but relationships—with parents, teachers, friends and loved ones—that provide the support and guidance necessary for the development and experience of autonomy.[60]

Public health for its part, is at its heart about the relationships between individuals within the communal context of contemporary society. But as Nedelsky points out, a relational understanding of the self means more than simply that we live with others. Instead, a relational view is concerned with the fact that 'each individual is in basic ways constituted by networks of relationships of which they are a part'.[61] The inherently communal context of public health provides a natural framework for relational perspectives on public health law.[62] Battin et al argue that we need to see our relational nature not only in terms of social relations, but also in terms of biological connections: 'not just the biological ties of family, ancestry, and reproduction, but the interrelationships of contagion and vulnerability to contagion—as well as the non-biological ties of society and culture'.[63] It is this relational viewpoint that allows us to move beyond ideas of rights and autonomy based on separation from others, and towards a public health law and ethics built on connection and relatedness. Battin et al recognized that it is in the relational context of public health that each of us can be both 'a victim and a vector', but as Azétsop and Rennie observe, standard bioethical models do not readily accommodate the relational aspect.[64]

It is also as a 'vector' (or potential vector), however, that a third challenge is mounted to patient agency, reprising the utilitarian liberal justification for overriding individual choice, about, say, vaccination or acceptance of anti-virals as a prophylactic, on the basis either of advancing the 'best interests' of individuals, or protection of others from actual or predicted risk of harm. Although individual rights and communal interests are often seen as conflicting in the context of public health, relational perspectives on public health allow us to transcend this division. As one of us has argued previously:

> By starting with a focus on relationships, public health is no longer about either individuals or communities but rather about the ways in which they are mutually constitutive and the

59 See eg Rogers, Mackenzie, and Dodds, 'Why Bioethics Needs a Concept of Vulnerability' (n 31) 23–4; A. Donchin, 'Understanding Autonomy Relationally: Toward a Reconfiguration of Bioethical Principles' (2001) 26 *Journal of Medicine and Philosophy* 365; L.C. McClain, '"Atomistic Man" Revisited: Liberalism, Connection, and Feminist Jurisprudence' (1992) 65 *Southern California Law Review* 1171; C. Mackenzie and N. Stoljar, *Relational Autonomy: Feminist Perspectives on Autonomy, Agency and the Social Self* (New York: OUP, 1992).

60 J. Nedelsky, 'Reconceiving Autonomy: Sources, Thoughts and Possibilities' (1989) 1 *Yale Journal of Law and Feminism* 7, 12.

61 J. Nedelsky, *Law's Relations: A Relational Theory of Self, Autonomy and Law* (New York, 2011) 19.

62 W. Rogers, 'Feminism and Public Health Ethics' (2006) 32 *Journal of Medical Ethics* 351; F. Baylis, N.P. Kenny, and S. Sherwin, 'A Relational Account of Public Health Ethics' (2008) 1 *Public Health Ethics* 196.

63 Battin et al, *The Patient as Victim and Vector* (n 46) 78.

64 Bioethical models of respect for autonomy and patient agency need to recognize that 'the ideal of the autonomous agent will remain a fiction unless the social context of the patient's vulnerability is also considered.': J. Azétsop and S. Rennie, 'Principlism, Medical Individualism, and Health Promotion in Resource-Poor Countries: Can Autonomy-Based Bioethics Promote Social Justice and Population Health?' (2010) 5 *Philosophy, Ethics, and Humanities in Medicine* 1, 4.

complementary, intersecting and overlapping rights and duties that arise in the shared space of contemporary society.[65]

For feminist scholars the subject of law and bioethics is also an inherently embodied subject,[66] with this embodiment understood as inessential and particular, rather than essential and universal.[67] The embodied subject of public health law and ethics is a subject who is situated within a social, economic, and cultural context, which in turn leads back to the need to consider the vulnerability of the embodied subject, and the context and 'layers' of that vulnerability. This link between embodiment and vulnerability is important, for as Bashford and Strange have noted, 'management of infectious disease entails weighing the risks and costs of individual freedoms against public safety. But the weighing of individuals has differed radically between categories of people and was often based on criteria other than disease status'.[68]

Finally, then, there is the question of how best to respond to embodied vulnerability. This is where there are more questions, and fewer entirely convincing answers. Put very simply, the duality of citizens as both victims and vectors appears to us to greatly compound the challenge of operationalizing the place of embodied vulnerability. Certainly there is a superficial attractiveness to the UN Siracusa principles, designed to presumptively preserve individual rights subject to least restrictive necessary and proportional limitations for the duration of a genuine emergency; until it comes to concrete examples.[69] As Baylis et al argue, the New Zealand National Ethics Advisory Council's ethical guidance is one which does largely reflect relational, communal, and reciprocal principles.[70] But there are competing rationales for public health pandemic planning decisions, including the previously mentioned utilitarianism, as well as virtue ethics (voluntary or noble sacrifices),[71] along with the notion of an expressive ethics (such as prioritizing the vaccination of children, in the absence of a scientific rationale).[72] While relational ethics could be said to weight for solidarity, utilitarianism favours scientific management (at the risk of public confidence), virtue ethics privileges sacrifice (benefiting those who make little or no sacrifice), and expressive ethics arguably cleaves to media-friendly rankings (that the well told injustice of one or a few, outranks mass injustice however egregious).

These are not abstract academic choices, but real life ones. For example, under relational ethics should an infected lone person be more liable to involuntary interventions or orders simply because no close member of their family is available to assume the risk? Or conversely to have their wishes respected because they have rich networks? Under this or a virtue ethics analysis, is it ethically acceptable to presumptively accept all offers of home quarantine made by apparently willing and able family or friendship networks, without inquiring about or protecting members especially vulnerable to infection? Should the utilitarian ethic implicitly underpinning resource allocation

65 B. Bennett, *Health Law's Kaleidoscope: Health Law Rights in a Global Age* (Aldershot: Ashgate, 2008) 93.

66 See eg Fineman, 'The Vulnerable Subject' (n 47); Rogers, 'Feminism and Public Health Ethics' (n 62); Baylis, Kenny, and Sherwin, 'A Relational Account of Public Health Ethics' (n 62).

67 Fineman, 'The Vulnerable Subject' (n 47) 10. See also, R. Fletcher, M. Fox, and J. McCandless, 'Legal Embodiment: Analysing the Body of Healthcare Law' (2008) 16 *Medical Law Review* 321.

68 Bashford and Strange, 'Thinking Historically' (n 28) 89.

69 Carney, Bailey, and Bennett, 'Pandemic Planning as Risk Management' (n 1).

70 Baylis, Kenny, and Sherwin, 'A Relational Account of Public Health Ethics' (n 62) 199.

71 A. Slowther, 'Planning for and Managing Pandemic Influenza' (2009) 4 *Clinical Ethics* 116, 117.

72 R. Pierce, 'The Expressive Function of Public Health Policy: The Case of Pandemic Planning' (2011) 4 *Public Health Ethics* 53.

priorities of most contemporary pandemic plans be maintained in the face of significant friction with principles of disability discrimination law?[73]

5. Practical Measures

There are practical measures that can be included in our pandemic planning to help to address the issue of vulnerability. The Bellagio Group has recommended that traditionally disadvantaged groups and groups 'likely to be disproportionately affected by preparations for a pandemic, responses to a pandemic, and by a pandemic itself' be identified, included in the planning process, and that their needs are specifically identified and addressed in recommendations and policies for pandemic planning.[74] Communication strategies will also be important to ensure that information can be disseminated effectively during to a pandemic to disadvantaged groups.[75]

Once a pandemic arrives, there is a range of practical measures that becomes important. New Zealand's National Ethics Advisory Committee report on ethical issues in pandemic planning, *Getting Through Together*,[76] uses the concept of 'neighbourliness' as part of considering community responses to a pandemic. This concept of 'neighbourliness' fits in well with relational theories of public health and expressly recognizes the relationships that form the communities in which we live. As the report points out, our neighbours are not only those living next door, but also those who live further away with whom we have relationships, and this also extends to the relationships between cities, countries, and governments.[77] It also recognizes that in a pandemic, many people who are not health professionals will be involved in caring for others: family, friends, neighbours, and that it will be important for people who are caring to be supported by providing them with information about how best to care for others 'while still protecting themselves from infection'.[78] The New Zealand report also includes discussion of reciprocity, in terms of providing support for health professionals who provide care during a pandemic, and the value of unity:

> The success with which a pandemic is managed may depend on the degree to which people, organisations and countries help each other and assume shared responsibility. It is important to maintain commitment to managing our way through any pandemic together.[79]

The report recognizes that good communication and transparent decision-making are important aspects of fostering public trust.[80]

Pandemics also have a financial impact on many parts of our communities. Individuals, families, and businesses can suffer loss of income due to the social distancing—both formal and informal—that occurs during a pandemic, raising issues of whether

[73] L.E. Wolf and W.F. Hensel, 'Valuing Lives: Allocating Scarce Medical Resources During a Public Health Emergency and the Americans with Disabilities Act' (2011) *PLoS Currents* 3: RRN1271 (doi: 1210.1371/currents.RRN1271), available at <http://ssrn.com/abstract=2033869>.

[74] Uscher-Pines et al, 'Planning for an Influenza Pandemic' (n 19) 33.

[75] C. Lee, W.A. Rogers, and A. Braunack-Mayer, 'Social Justice and Pandemic Influenza Planning: The Role of Communication Strategies' (2008) 1 *Public Health Ethics* 223.

[76] National Ethics Advisory Committee, 'Getting Through Together: Ethical Values for a Pandemic', Ministry of Health, Wellington (2007). See discussion in Baylis, Kenny, and Sherwin, 'A Relational Account of Public Health Ethics' (n 62).

[77] NEAC, 'Getting Through Together' (n 76) 41.

[78] NEAC, 'Getting Through Together' (n 76) 41–2.

[79] NEAC, 'Getting Through Together' (n 76) 47.

[80] NEAC, 'Getting Through Together' (n 76) 48.

financial compensation should be provided to those affected.[81] At times we may decide to use coercive social distancing measures such as quarantine and isolation. Yet as Michael Selgelid has pointed out, coercive measures are only justified if they result 'in net benefits to society as a whole'.[82] Selgelid argues: 'Some of these benefits should be returned to the victims of coercive measures. In the absence of compensation, those coerced would suffer a disproportionate share of the burdens required to benefit society, and this would be unfair.'[83] Compensation measures are also likely to be particularly important in developing countries, where culling of poultry or livestock may have a devastating impact on families.[84] The World Bank has recognized these issues and has developed recommendations for compensation schemes for those affected by culling of poultry to control highly pathogenic avian influenza.[85]

Community, relationships, and reciprocity will all be important and necessary values during a pandemic. Yet as we consider the role of community in supporting the vulnerable, we must also remember human history, where community has served as a boundary between the group and the 'other'. As Aaltola argues:

> People look for security in their perceived communal strength and traditional perceptions of communality. What come about are outbursts of customs, family values, nationalism, and ethnicity. The essential elements connected with one's sense of belonging to a group are highlighted and strongly expressed.
>
> The other side of these outbursts, which bring out the essential elements, is that they repulse the unessential as harmful and suspect. People are marginalized and stigmatized. As stated, in plague-ridden Europe, the normal communal responses to plague included the building of churches, giving of alms, pilgrimages, burning of witches (mainly young women), and the killing of Jews and other 'foreign' groups. Large segments of the population were forced into the roles of 'plague spreaders' or 'well poisoners.'[86]

This ugly side of human history should serve as a reminder that our understandings of community must go hand-in-hand with understandings of vulnerability.

6. Conclusion

We remain attracted to a relational accommodation of vulnerability within pandemic planning, whether for the citizen as an actual or prospective victim of infection or as a 'vector' for its spread to others. While there are practical challenges associated with this approach, ultimately by conceptualizing public health law and ethics in terms of nuanced understandings of vulnerability, and in terms of the relationships that make us who we are, we will have richer understandings and firmer foundations for our pandemic planning.

81 T. Ly, M.J. Selgelid, and I. Kerridge, 'Pandemic and Public Health Controls: Toward an Equitable Compensation System' (2007) 15 *Journal of Law and Medicine* 296, 299.

82 M.J. Selgelid, 'Pandethics' (2009) 123 *Public Health* 255, 258.

83 Selgelid, 'Pandethics' (n 82).

84 Ly, Selgelid, and Kerridge, 'Pandemic and Public Health Controls' (n 81) 301.

85 World Bank, 'Enhancing Control of Highly Pathogenic Avian Influenza in Developing Countries Through Compensation: Issues and Good Practice' (2006).

86 Aaltola, *Western Spectacle of Governance* (n 25) 138–9.

7

Legally Vulnerable

What is Vulnerability and Who is Vulnerable?

Hazel Biggs and Caroline Jones

In this chapter we examine the conceptualization of vulnerability in particular health care situations and consider how useful it is in a regulatory context. Vulnerability, and potential exploitation, are often used as justifications for the imposition of legal restrictions to protect the rights of those thought to be susceptible to harm. This is particularly evident in criminal law,[1] but is also relevant with regard to vulnerable adults, most obviously under the Mental Capacity Act 2005, the High Court's inherent jurisdiction,[2] and the Mental Health Act 1983.[3] We will use the examples of assisted suicide and surrogacy to explore some ways in which constructions of vulnerability operate to underpin legislative prohibitions in relation to cross-border health care. These areas were selected purely as two examples that represent the global health impacts of using vulnerability as a basis for legal regulation. The chapter begins with a brief theorization of the nature of vulnerability to determine whether it can be understood as a universally applicable concept in health care law, before focusing on the ways in which it has an impact on the provision of health care. The discussion will centre on whether it is possible always to characterize specific individuals or groups as inherently vulnerable, or whether instead a more nuanced understanding is required if the law is to succeed in protecting vulnerable individuals.

1. What is Vulnerability in Relation to the Law and Legal Approaches?

Vulnerability may stem from particular types of social disadvantage, based on factors such as young or old age, illness, disability, and poverty.[4] Although these factors provide an environment within which a person might be vulnerable they will manifest themselves in disparate ways in each person's life, and will consequently be experienced

[1] See further S. Ost, *Child Pornography and Sexual Grooming: Legal and Societal Responses* (Cambridge: CUP, 2009) 6–20, for an insightful discussion of some of the 'critical tensions' that arise when children are constructed as being inherently vulnerable.

[2] On the exercise of the inherent jurisdiction see further Munby J (as he then was) in *Re SA (Vulnerable adult with capacity: marriage)* [2005] EWHC 2942 (Fam), [2006] 1 FLR 867, paras 37 and 79.

[3] As amended by the Mental Health Act 2007. See further J. Herring, 'Protecting Vulnerable Adults' (2009) 21 *Child and Family Law Quarterly* 498 for an interesting analysis of the extent of the inherent jurisdiction with regard to vulnerable adults. Herring also notes, but does not discuss, the role of the defence of necessity in this context; see eg *Re F (Mental Patient: Sterilisation)* [1990] 2 AC 1.

[4] eg Florencia Luna usefully highlights the potential impact of gender, poverty, literacy, migrant status, and ethnic origins; F. Luna, 'Elucidating the Concept of Vulnerability: Layers Not Labels', (2009) 2(1) *International Journal of Feminist Approaches to Bioethics* 120, 128.

differently according to each individual's personal circumstances. Vulnerability is therefore defined in a variety of ways depending on the context. With regard to health care research, for example, the Council for International Organisations of Medical Sciences (CIOMS) refers to:

> ... a substantial incapacity to protect one's own interests owing to such impediments as lack of capacity to give informed consent, lack of alternative means of obtaining medical care or other expensive necessities, or being a junior or subordinate member of a hierarchical group.[5]

These factors are reflected in most ethical guides pertaining to medical research.[6] Other definitions of vulnerability contain similar elements, with impaired decision-making capacity, social disadvantage, or marginalization due to economic factors, and relationships of power being common factors.[7] Unsurprisingly, the criminal law includes many definitions of vulnerability in relation to various crimes. For example, under section 5(6) of the Domestic Violence, Crimes and Victims Act 2004 a '"vulnerable adult" means a person aged 16 or over whose ability to protect himself from violence, abuse or neglect is significantly impaired through physical or mental disability or illness, through old age or otherwise'.[8]

Various recent cases have attempted to provide typologies of vulnerability. However, the judges have been reluctant to introduce actual definitions for fear of being overly restrictive. In his highly significant first instance decision in *Re SA (Vulnerable adult with capacity: marriage)*,[9] Munby J (as he then was) 'characterized' (as opposed to defined)[10] vulnerability thus:

> In the context of the inherent jurisdiction I would treat as a vulnerable adult someone who, whether or not mentally incapacitated, and whether or not suffering from any mental illness or mental disorder, is or may be unable to take care of him or herself, or unable to protect him or herself against significant harm or exploitation, or who is deaf, blind or dumb, or who is substantially handicapped by illness, injury or congenital deformity. This, I emphasise, is not and is not intended to be a definition. It is descriptive, not definitive; indicative rather than prescriptive.[11]

5 CIOMS, 'International Ethical Guidelines for Biomedical Research Involving Human Participants' (2002) 10, available at <http://www.cioms.ch/images/stories/CIOMS/guidelines/guidelines_nov_2002_blurb.htm.>

6 See eg World Medical Association, 'Ethical Principles for Medical Research Involving Human Subjects (Declaration of Helsinki)', 59th World Medical Association General Assembly (2008) para 9. See further H. Biggs, *Healthcare Research Ethics and Law: Regulation, Review and Responsibility* (Abingdon: Routledge-Cavendish, 2009).

7 eg the Safeguarding Vulnerable Groups Act 2006, s 59 provides an extensive list of relevant factors to identify those deemed vulnerable 'in the context of the setting in which they are situated or the service they receive'; as outlined in the *Explanatory Notes* for the Safeguarding Vulnerable Groups Act 2006, para 158.

8 See also J. Collins, 'The Contours of "Vulnerability"' in J. Herring and J. Wallbank (eds), *Vulnerabilities, Care and Family Law* (Oxford: Routledge, 2013); and Ost, *Child Pornography and Sexual Grooming* (n 1) 140, for a consideration of vulnerability (and exploitation) in the context of some sexual offences.

9 *Re SA*, see n 11; since approved by the Court of Appeal in *DL v A Local Authority* [2012] EWCA Civ 253, paras 63 and 68, *per* McFarlane LJ.

10 We are grateful to John Coggon for this point.

11 *Re SA (Vulnerable Adult With Capacity: Marriage)* [2005] EWHC 2942 (Fam), [2006] 1 FLR 867, para 82. This description was proffered despite Munby J's earlier caution that it would be both 'unwise' and 'inappropriate' for him to define who might fall within the category of 'vulnerable adult' for the purposes of exercising the inherent jurisdiction (at para 77).

This case concerned the proper role of the inherent jurisdiction of the High Court.[12] Munby's judgment resulted in the concept of vulnerability being extended to adults who do not lack decision-making capacity—and thereby do not fall under the auspices of either the Mental Capacity Act 2005 or the Mental Health Act 1983—through the inherent jurisdiction. In effect, therefore, he created a new category of legal subject: the 'vulnerable' adult.[13]

In *Re SA*, and similarly in *Re SK (Proposed Plaintiff) (An Adult by way of her Litigation Friend)*,[14] autonomous decisions were thought to be likely to be constrained by the circumstances within which the women in question would be required to make their decisions about whether to marry, even though neither lacked mental capacity; ie a type of undue influence situation.[15] Through cases such as these the High Court (primarily in the Family Division, but latterly the Court of Protection too) has played a major role in determining individual cases, and has indeed been criticized in relation to its approach because in effect it has disregarded, even overridden, decisions made by adults who seem to have decision-making capacity if those individuals are regarded as in some way vulnerable to exploitation.[16] The implication is that despite apparently having decision-making capacity a person might need to be protected from exploitation arising from the situation or environment within which they find themselves, in this case relating to cultural pressures around arranged marriage.

Traditionally, based upon definitions like these, the concept of vulnerability has been regarded in law as indicating a need to protect specific susceptible individuals or groups from exploitation. The characteristics of the individual are central to the determination that they are at risk of exploitation, either because of their inherent weaknesses or because of the environment within which they find themselves. More specifically an individual may be inherently disadvantaged or they may be rendered less able to protect their interests because of external factors. These distinctions have been described as *etic*, 'an externally evaluated risk' approach based upon the inherent characteristics of individuals belonging to specific groups; or *emic*, situating vulnerability 'in a psycho-social-cultural context' and pertaining to an individual's experiences of external factors that can render them vulnerable regardless of their own characteristics.[17] The 1997 Government White Paper on mental capacity took an *etic* approach, and formulated a definition of vulnerability based upon the inherent characteristics of

12 See further *Re SA* (n 11) para 37, where Munby J states that the nature of the inherent jurisdiction is 'for all practical purposes indistinguishable from its well-established *parens patriae* or wardship jurisdiction in relation to children'; see also paras 79–80 on the exercise re 'vulnerable adults' (as opposed to 'incapacitated' ones). The former point is considered further by J. Herring and M. Dunn, 'Safeguarding Children and Adults: Much of a Muchness? *A Local Authority v A and B* [2010] EWHC 978 (Fam)' (2011) 23 *Child and Family Law Quarterly* 528, 528–9. See also J. Herring, 'Vulnerability, Children, and the Law' in M. Freeman (ed), *Current Legal Issues in Law and Childhood Studies*, Vol 14 (Oxford: OUP, 2012) 243, 260.

13 *Re SA* (n 11) para 79, *per* Munby J. See also M. Dunn, I.C.H. Clare, and A. J. Holland, 'To Empower or to Protect? Constructing the "Vulnerable Adult" in English Law and Public Policy' (2008) 28 *Legal Studies* 234, 238. Dunn et al argue that this definition closely reflects that provided by the Law Commission and Lord Chancellor's Department in the mid-1990s; see Law Commission, *Mental Incapacity: Law Commission Report 231* (Law Commission, 1995); Lord Chancellor's Department, *Who Decides? Making decisions on behalf of 'mentally incapacitated' adults* (London: The Stationery Office, 1997).

14 [2004] EWHC 3202 (Fam), [2005] 2 FLR 230—a case decided by Singer J, not Munby J.

15 However, in *Re SK* the plaintiff was located overseas, she subsequently returned to the UK and confirmed that she did not want the proceedings to continue, see *Re SK* (n 14) para 15, *per* Singer J.

16 See further Dunn, Clare, and Holland, 'To Empower or to Protect?' (n 13) 247–51.

17 J. Spiers, 'New Perspectives on Vulnerability using emic and etic Approaches' (2000) 31(3) *Journal of Advanced Nursing* 715, 716, 718.

individuals belonging to a specific group. Thus, a vulnerable adult was defined as 'someone over the age of 18 who is or may be in need of community care services by reason of mental or other disability, age or illness and who is or may be unable to take care of him/herself or unable to protect him/herself against significant harm or exploitation'.[18] On this basis vulnerable people are safeguarded according to generalizable characteristics that apply to all those who fall within a defined grouping.[19]

Etic perspectives epitomize the ways in which the law usually seeks to protect vulnerable groups. Under such an approach assumptions are made about the risk of harm based upon an 'external evaluation of relative danger'[20] that is beyond the control of the vulnerable person. By contrast, an *emic* view revolves around the individual, rather than the characteristics of a group, and is based on the experiences of the person. The distinction between the two approaches reflects the tension between objective risk, of the type addressed in the passage from the *Making Decisions* White Paper (cited earlier), and the subjective experience of the individual herself, which is enshrined in the focus on autonomy prominent in much of health care law.

Health care law generally is underpinned by the desire to protect those who are regarded as vulnerable while simultaneously respecting decision-making autonomy. The Mental Capacity Act 2005 exemplifies this approach with regard to safeguarding those who lack mental capacity.[21] This is not unique to health care law, however, and other areas of law, including criminal law, family law, and tort, among others, also operate to limit the effect of vulnerability. By way of example, commentators have posited that vulnerability is the 'golden thread' of the tort of negligence,[22] and capable of 'enriching' the duty of care framework in English negligence law.[23] Whereas, in the context of housing law, vulnerability has long been defined as occurring when one is 'less able to fend for oneself so that injury or detriment will result and a less vulnerable man will be able to cope without harmful effects'.[24] In each of these examples the legal focus tends to be on protecting those who are designated as vulnerable because of their particular circumstances. However, more contemporary understandings, such as that proposed by Martha Fineman, suggest that 'vulnerability is—and should be understood to be—universal and constant, inherent in the human condition';[25] ie a global concept.

Fineman argues that vulnerability should be foregrounded as the basis upon which social policy should be developed, rather than what is known in the US as the equal protection doctrine and in the UK as anti-discrimination. These mechanisms, based upon formal notions of equality and treating individuals as the same are, for Fineman, intrinsically flawed in their ability to address and correct social inequalities,[26] which

18 Lord Chancellor's Department, *Who Decides?* (n 13).

19 See also the Safeguarding Vulnerable Groups Act 2006 (n 7).

20 Spiers, 'New Perspectives' (n 17) 715.

21 P. Bartlett, *Blackstone's Guide to The Mental Capacity Act 2005* (Oxford: 2nd edn, OUP, 2008) 2.

22 J. Stapleton, 'The Golden Thread at the Heart of Tort Law' (2003–04) 24 *Australian Bar Review* 135, 142, cited in C. Stychin, 'The Vulnerable Subject of Negligence Law' (2012) 8 *International Journal of Law in Context* 337, 345–6.

23 Stychin, 'The Vulnerable Subject of Negligence Law' (n 22) 351.

24 *R v Waveney DC, ex p Bowers* [1983] QB 238, *per* Waller LJ at 244–5. For a contextual analysis of risk and the 'situational vulnerabilities' of older homeowners see L. Fox O'Mahony, *Home Equity and Ageing Owners: Between Risk and Regulation* (Oxford: Hart Publishing, 2012).

25 M. Fineman, 'The Vulnerable Subject: Anchoring Equality in the Human Condition' (2008) 20(1) *Yale Journal of Law and Feminism* 1, 1.

26 See M. Fineman, *The Illusion of Equality: the rhetoric and reality of divorce reform* (Chicago, IL: Chicago University Press, 1991) 46.

means that 'the "vulnerable subject" must replace the autonomous and independent subject asserted in the liberal tradition'.[27] She regards vulnerability as 'a universal, inevitable, enduring aspect of the human condition'[28] that should be regarded as a *positive* attribute through which obligations could be developed that would better guarantee equality. Fineman categorizes autonomy as a product of social policy that is always compromised by human frailty and consequently incapable of underpinning 'true' equality. She contends that understanding vulnerability as constant and common to all offers the potential to overcome the inadequacies of jurisprudence founded upon formal equality and thereby protect individual interests and human flourishing.

Fineman's perspective that 'everyone is vulnerable' has been embraced by Jonathan Herring, who argues that whilst the law appropriately characterizes children as vulnerable, it is deficient in failing to recognize the vulnerability of adults.[29] He goes further than Fineman in querying whether it is possible even for adults in their 'prime' to have the type of capacity and autonomy argued for by the traditional liberal approach.[30] Similarly, he argues that a focus on autonomy, as is prominent in much of health care law, can fail to reveal vulnerabilities relating to the context within which individuals are located, so that a person's rights and medical needs ought to be 'considered in a situational context'.[31] Clearly that context might involve a relational approach to autonomy whereby the decision-maker takes account of the needs and preferences of others when opting for particular options.[32] However, that process does not necessarily negate autonomy or render the decision-maker more vulnerable, it is merely the context within which they make their decision. It is of course almost inevitable that decisions will be influenced by concerns for others in a world where people live in societies based on emotional interactions, but that does not always render those decisions less autonomous or less reliable.[33]

In contrast, Florencia Luna conceptualizes vulnerability rather differently and argues for an understanding 'based on the idea of "layers of vulnerability"'.[34] She interrogates the concept of vulnerability in the context of medical research, where women are frequently typified as a vulnerable group. Much of the ethical guidance that governs medical research labels women, the sick, and the elderly as vulnerable and locates them within groupings that require special protection.[35] However, on closer scrutiny it is apparent that individuals within those groupings may not themselves actually be vulnerable, and that they, and indeed potentially the entire sub-population, might even be disadvantaged by being so characterized. Individuals who are capable of exercising autonomy through the mechanism of a legally valid consent can protect their own interests by deciding whether or not they wish to participate in research so

27 Fineman, 'The Vulnerable Subject' (n 25) 2.

28 Fineman, 'The Vulnerable Subject' (n 25) 8.

29 Herring, 'Vulnerability, Children, and the Law' (n 12) 244.

30 Herring, 'Vulnerability, Children, and the Law' (n 12) 251–3.

31 Herring, 'Vulnerability, Children, and the Law' (n 12) 262.

32 See further J. Herring, 'Relational Autonomy and Family Law' in J. Wallbank, S. Choudhry, and J. Herring (eds), *Rights, Gender and Family Law* (Oxford: Routledge, 2010) 257; also J. Bridgeman, *Parental Responsibility, Young Children and Healthcare Law* (Cambridge: CUP, 2007); and R. Gilbar, 'Family Involvement, Independence and Patient Autonomy in Practice' (2011) 19 *Medical Law Review* 192.

33 See H. Biggs, 'A Pretty Fine Line: Life, Death, Autonomy and Letting It Be' (2003) 11 *Feminist Legal Studies* 291.

34 Luna, 'Elucidating the Concept of Vulnerability' (n 4) especially 127–32.

35 See eg the Declaration of Helsinki; CIOMS, 'International Ethical Guidelines' (n 5) 64, Guideline 13; and the Belmont Report.

long as the formalities involved permit them to do so, which is generally the case under research governance procedures. Undoubtedly some, perhaps many, who fall within these groups will be capable of making their own decisions; therefore preventing entire groups from participating in research on the basis of vulnerability is an affront to their autonomy and dignity. In addition, it might mean that the evidence base for specific kinds of medical treatment, particularly pharmaceutical developments, may be inadequate if they are used in populations that have been excluded from participating in research because of stereotypical assumptions about vulnerability.[36] Despite its shortcomings, however, Luna argues that vulnerability remains a useful concept in relation to research ethics so long as a sufficiently nuanced approach is adopted.

This chapter evaluates the value of vulnerability as a legal concept by exploring these alternative ways of theorizing it. A better understanding of vulnerability will enable us to determine whether it is a useful mechanism upon which to develop the law, particularly in relation to health care. Alongside the assessment of vulnerability generally, our analysis will focus on whether the law can offer best protection by adopting an *etic* or an *emic* approach. We seek to argue that the law ought properly to focus on individuals, rather than attempting to protect groups or classes of people. Imposing 'blanket' protection to all in a sub-population, including those who are not actually vulnerable means that some people may find their choices and actions inappropriately restricted[37] or may paradoxically be rendered more vulnerable.[38] Luna has identified similar consequences in relation to ageing, leading her to conclude that 'when vulnerability is used as a fixed label on a particular sub-population, it suggests a simplistic answer to a complicated problem'.[39] It is important that vulnerability is properly conceptualized[40] if law is to be effective and avoid discriminatory tendencies in its attempt to protect those who might be vulnerable to exploitation.[41]

The law includes a number of different ways of protecting the interests of those who might be vulnerable. For example, as noted previously, the Mental Capacity Act 2005 revolves around identifying those who have capacity to make decisions, in order to protect those who lack capacity from making dangerous, or legally invalid decisions, whilst simultaneously focusing on enhancing the autonomy of those who might ultimately be assisted to make safe autonomous decisions. Conversely, the Suicide Act 1961 is based upon assumptions that a decision to be assisted to die is never safe and should not be condoned. Likewise, surrogacy regulation actively discourages decisions to become a surrogate mother on the understanding that it is normatively an undesirable practice (and this approach does not take account of others, such as the commissioning parents and the resulting children, who might also be vulnerable in cross-border surrogacy arrangements).

36 C. Levine, R. Faden, C. Grady, D. Hammerschmmidt, L. Eckenwiler, and J. Sugarman, 'The Limitations of "Vulnerability" as a Protection for Human Research Participants' (2004) 4 *American Journal of Bioethics* 44.

37 Diane Pretty provides a clear example of a situation where the person involved was not personally vulnerable, but she was prevented from exercising her preferred choice because vulnerable others might be disadvantaged as a consequence (discussed further at 139).

38 We have discussed elsewhere the ways in which children born of cross-border surrogacy arrangements might be rendered more vulnerable because of the law; see H. Biggs and C. Jones, 'Tourism: A Matter of Life and Death in the UK' in I.G. Cohen (ed), *The Globalization of Health Care* (New York: OUP, 2013).

39 Luna, 'Elucidating the Concept of Vulnerability' (n 4) 123.

40 J. Collins makes a similar point in the context of Family Law, see n 8.

41 See Biggs and Jones, 'Tourism' (n 38); S. Wilkinson, *Bodies for Sale: Ethics and Exploitation in the Human Body Trade* (London: Routledge, 2003).

2. Who is Vulnerable?

These differing theoretical approaches demonstrate that vulnerability is to some extent a socially constructed concept the understanding of which differs depending upon the context. It is therefore difficult to identify who exactly might be vulnerable since some people are vulnerable because they are socially or intellectually disadvantaged, and others because of the environment within which they find themselves or the relationships they encounter. Goodin has identified a number of reasons why a person might be vulnerable in the ways that they interact with others.[42] They may, for example, compete on unequal terms in situations where the so-called victim of exploitation deliberately does not seek to gain an advantage themselves in their interaction with the person who exploits them, or they may be disadvantaged by diminished bargaining power in relation to their exploiter. Alternatively, the exploited person may lack the capacity to protect themselves, or the exploitative party may gain from the 'vulnerable' person's misfortune.

From this it is clear that those considered vulnerable by others may have different perceptions or understandings of whether or not they feel vulnerable based upon their personal or lived experiences. Hence none of the accounts considered so far seems to provide a sufficiently nuanced understanding of vulnerability to offer an approach that is capable of application in the law. Consequently we now turn to examples of specific cases where vulnerability has been central to legislative and judicial reasoning to assess its value in relation to global health. The case studies we selected relate to cross-border health care: specifically in relation to assisted dying and reproduction. They raise concerns about whether the 'blanket' application of legal prohibitions on assisted suicide and commercial surrogacy do in reality protect those who are considered to be vulnerable.

3. Assisted Suicide

The legal prohibition of assisted suicide in England and Wales is governed by the Suicide Act 1961[43] and based upon assumptions about vulnerability that imply that a person who is assisted to commit suicide is vulnerable to abuse, and that anybody who assists does so with the intention of exploiting them. Stereotypical examples of situations where the vulnerable might be exploited include the greedy relative(s) who stand to benefit from the death of the suicide, or the worn-down carer who can no longer cope with the rigours of caregiving and persuades the cared for person to kill themselves. As a consequence the law takes an *etic* approach to the risk of harm to which a person who is assisted in suicide is exposed, and imposes a blanket prohibition to protect the entire group rather than assessing the specific characteristics of the members of the group. *Pretty* provides an illustration of this *etic* approach, when in the House of Lords it was stated that:

> The object of section 2(1) of the 1961 Act is to avoid an abuse which would put the lives of the weak and vulnerable at risk. In this way it seeks to preserve life. I would be willing to give full weight to Mrs Pretty's assertion that she is not weak or vulnerable in this sense—that she has sufficient mental strength not to be vulnerable to pressure to commit suicide. I can appreciate her

[42] R. Goodin, 'Exploiting a Situation and Exploiting a Person' in A. Reeve (ed), *Modern Theories of Exploitation* (London: Sage Publications, 1987).

[43] Suicide Act 1961, s 2.

objection that vulnerability should not be imposed upon her simply because her physical condition prevents her from doing so. But this does not meet the Director's argument. It is not unreasonable for him to think that, if he were to sanction one act of assisted suicide, this might lead to requests from others less well equipped to stand up to the unscrupulous.

And:

The condition of terminally ill individuals, like Mrs Pretty, will vary. The majority will be vulnerable. It is the vulnerability of the class of persons which provides the rationale for making the aiding and abetting of suicide an offence under section 2(1) of the 1961 Act. A class of individuals is protected by section 2(1) because they are in need of protection. The statutory provision does not therefore treat individuals in a discriminatory manner. There is no unequal treatment before the law.[44]

Similar comments were made in the European Court of Human Rights in relation to the purpose of the law, which is:

. . . designed to safeguard life by protecting the weak and vulnerable and especially those who are not in a position to take informed decisions against acts intended to end life or to assist in ending life. Doubtless the condition of terminally ill individuals will vary. But many will be vulnerable and it is the vulnerability of the class which provides the rationale for the law in question.[45]

The Lords effectively sacrificed Diane Pretty's autonomy to protect others who might be vulnerable. The European Court of Human Rights did the same when it concluded that Article 8(2) applied to ensure 'the protection of health or morals, or the protection of the rights and freedoms of others who might be vulnerable' whose protection should be 'paramount'. This despite earlier comments implying that Diane Pretty herself was not vulnerable because she had the capacity to act autonomously and a right to privacy and self-determination under Article 8(1) of the European Convention on Human Rights.

If we adopt an *emic* approach however, it is clear that vulnerability results from very specific factors arising from individual experiences at the end of life. For instance, Hoffmaster explains that vulnerability can mean different things to different people and that 'what is most important about vulnerability is . . . the loss of power that vulnerability . . . signifies, and the attendant loss of control that ensues. We fear vulnerability most immediately because of the particular harms we seek to avoid. But we fear vulnerability most profoundly because of the power we seek to retain'.[46] In this context claims about who is vulnerable should, as Luna argues,[47] be properly substantiated, rather than merely labelling minority groups like the dying as homogeneously vulnerable. Indeed, with regard to the prohibition on assisted suicide this was referred to in *Purdy* as 'the context in which Lord Pannick QC makes his argument that the blanket ban is not, without more, "in accordance with the law"'.[48] The reference here was to the lack of transparency in the determination of whether and when a prosecution might be brought following an assisted suicide, which formed the basis of the appeal in *Purdy*.

Debbie Purdy mounted her legal challenge as the prohibition of assisted suicide in England was witnessing a stream of Britons journeying to the *Dignitas* clinic in Zurich to be assisted to end their lives. Statistics indicate that the number availing themselves of the service has remained fairly consistently in the low twenties each year, while the

44 [2001] UKHL 61, paras 64 and 96.
45 *Pretty v UK* (App 2346/02) [2002] 35 EHRR 1, para 74.
46 B. Hoffmaster, 'What Does Vulnerability Mean?' (2006) 36 *Hastings Centre Report* 38, 41.
47 Luna, 'Elucidating the Concept of Vulnerability' (n 4).
48 *R (on the application of Purdy) v DPP* [2009] UKHL 45, para 75.

number of British members of *Dignitas* rises steadily.[49] Those who achieve the assisted death they desire in this way have retained control over their independence and might be regarded as having been empowered. Yet it must be remembered that these people will have to travel while still sufficiently physically fit to do so, and hence their lives may be shortened because the law in the UK does not facilitate assisted suicide. Similarly, those who wish to be assisted but are not physically and mentally fit enough to travel to Switzerland, or do not have the financial resources to do so will experience vulnerability in the sense described by Hoffmaster earlier. Because they are unable to travel they must either expose a domestic assistant to potential prosecution or endure a death which they sought to avoid.

From this it seems evident that not everyone who contemplates assisted suicide is vulnerable, but that otherwise competent people can be made vulnerable by a law which denies them autonomy and limits their power. This was seen in the past in relation to abortion where, prior to the enactment of the Abortion Act 1967, large numbers of women sought out unsafe and unhygienic backstreet abortions and became vulnerable as a result. It is not likely that those who wish to have an assisted suicide will seek out the kind of back street assistance offered by illegal abortionists in the 1950s and 60s, but they are quite likely to consider travelling to a jurisdiction where assisted suicide is permissible.

Accordingly, the criminal law, which allegedly 'is there as a tool to protect the vulnerable',[50] can have the opposite effect. The injustice of this position is heightened when one considers that no prosecutions have yet resulted from cross-border assisted suicide, which leaves the law itself 'in an even more vulnerable, dangerous and ambiguous position'[51] after the publication of the *Policy for Prosecutors in Respect of Cases of Encouraging or Assisting Suicide*.[52] The validity of a law that is not used is always open to challenge, although some commentators argue that 'although it has rarely been used in this context, Society is better protected by having it there'.[53] Nevertheless, while failing to enforce the law by turning a blind eye to death tourism does little to enhance the authority of the law, it does nothing to protect those who are perceived as vulnerable. Furthermore, it is possible that some people could be more likely to be exploited in an environment where it is routine not to uphold the law. As Sheila McLean has argued in a different context, 'transparency and accountability in decision-making offer a better chance of protecting the vulnerable, and validating the rights of people to make their own life choices than does a hidden unaccountable practice'.[54] Similar issues arise in relation to cross-border surrogacy.

49 M. Beckford, '14% increase in British Members of Dignitas', *The Telegraph online*, 23 January 2012, available at <http://www.telegraph.co.uk/news/uknews/law-and-order/9028651/14-rise-in-British-members-of-Dignitas.html> (accessed 26 January 2013).

50 John Cooper QC, quoted in T. Hennessey, 'Assisted Suicide: Protecting the Vulnerable' *Halsbury's Law Exchange*, 20 July 2011, available at <http://www.halsburyslawexchange.co.uk/assisted-suicide-protecting-the-vulnerable/> (accessed 27 January 2013).

51 S. Reidy, 'English Law on Assisted Suicide: A Dangerous Position' [2012] *Medico-Legal Journal of Ireland* 68.

52 CPS, 'Policy for Prosecutors in Respect of Cases of Encouraging or Assisting Suicide' (2010), available at <http://www.cps.gov.uk/publications/prosecution/assisted_suicide_policy.html> (accessed 24 January 2013).

53 John Cooper QC (n 50).

54 S.A.M. McLean, *Assisted Dying: Reflections on the Need for Law Reform* (Abingdon: Routledge-Cavendish, 2007) 74.

4. Surrogacy

In 1986 Michael Freeman presciently suggested that surrogacy 'is here to stay and criminal legislation cannot defeat it'.[55] Commercial surrogacy was prohibited in the UK under domestic legislation,[56] but provisions were subsequently made for (what are often termed) 'commissioning parents' to regularize their legal status in relation to any resulting children without recourse to adoption.[57] However, in the current global health context, the availability of commercial arrangements in other jurisdictions has led to an increase in prospective parents (who can afford to do so) seeking and utilizing cross-border reproductive care, including surrogacy.[58]

Surrogacy has been the subject of a vast number of commentaries, and we have engaged with some of that literature elsewhere.[59] Our concern here, however, lies with the characterization(s) of vulnerability in this context, with specific observations on cross-border arrangements. We seek to interrogate law's insensitivity to the range of potential vulnerabilities around the practice(s) of surrogacy, which 'blanket' policies at best conceal, and at worst exacerbate.

5. Who is Vulnerable?

5.1 Surrogates

As Emily Jackson notes, traditionally the 'principal' vulnerable parties have been identified as the surrogate mothers and the children.[60] Concern has been expressed as to the potential for women to be exploited;[61] for abuse with regard to the trafficking of 'economically or socially vulnerable women';[62] the potential for gender, race, 'class, status and education bias' to operate against surrogates,[63] with the 'double bind' that

55 M.D.A. Freeman, 'After Warnock—Whither the Law?' (1986) 39 *Current Legal Problems* 33, 44.

56 Surrogacy Arrangements Act 1985, s 2.

57 Originally under the Human Fertilisation and Embryology Act 1990, s 30, since repealed and replaced by the Human Fertilisation and Embryology Act 2008, s 54. See further C. Jones, 'The (Im)Possible Parents in Law' in C. Lind, H. Keating, and J. Bridgeman (eds), *Taking Responsibility: Law and the Changing Family* (Aldershot: Ashgate, 2011) 201; J. McCandless and S. Sheldon, 'The Human Fertilisation and Embryology Act (2008) and the Tenacity of the Sexual Family Form' (2010) 73 *Modern Law Review* 175.

58 The European Society of Human Reproduction and Embryology (ESHRE) responded by setting up a dedicated Taskforce on Cross-Border Reproductive Care; see further their initial research findings in F. Shenfield, J. de Mouzon, G. Pennings, A.P. Ferraretti, A. Nyboe Andersen, G. de Wert, and V. Goossens, 'Cross Border Reproductive Care in Six European Countries' (2010) 25 *Human Reproduction* 1361.

59 Biggs and Jones, 'Tourism' (n 38).

60 E. Jackson, *Regulating Reproduction. Law, Technology and Autonomy* (Oxford: Hart, 2001), 262.

61 M. Warnock (Chair) 'Report of the Committee of Inquiry into Human Fertilisation and Embryology' (London: HMSO, 1984) paras 8.17–8.18; but note the 'Expression of dissent: A. Surrogacy', in 'Report of the Committee of Inquiry into Human Fertilisation and Embryology' (London: HMSO, 1984) 87, para 3. See also M.D.A. Freeman, 'Is Surrogacy Exploitative?' in S. McLean (ed), *Legal Issues in Human Reproduction* (Aldershot: Dartmouth, 1990) 164; M. Brazier (Chair) *Surrogacy: Review for Health Ministers of Current Arrangements for Payments and Regulation* (Department of Health, Cm 4068, 1998), and Wilkinson, *Bodies for Sale* (n 41) 134–81.

62 BMA, *Changing Conceptions of Motherhood. The Practice of Surrogacy in Britain* (BMA Publications, 1996) xii.

63 Freeman, 'Is Surrogacy Exploitative?' (n 61) 168, fn 79, re the decision of the New Jersey Supreme Court, *In the Matter of Baby M* (1988) 537 A 2d 1227; see also D. Farquhar, *The Other Machine. Discourse and Reproductive Technologies* (London: Routledge, 1996).

commercial surrogacy could 'create hard choices for poor women'.[64] Inevitably this is a non-exhaustive list, drawn from selected commentaries.

Both the Warnock and Brazier Reports adopt an *etic* approach with regard to women as surrogate mothers, ie they will be vulnerable to exploitation if 'payment' is permitted, without consideration of their subjective lived experiences. Yet, as Freeman argues, with very few exceptions, we simply do not know if women are (non-)altruistic in their motivation, nor if they feel exploited, and cannot credibly extrapolate evidence from a few reported legal decisions. He cites Kim Cotton, Kirsty Stevens, and Mary Stewart as (then) three high profile surrogates who did not consider themselves exploited; but also notes Mary-Beth Whitehead's experience as a counter-example.[65] Although he does not adopt the language of '*emic* vulnerability' per se, Freeman's attention to the 'psycho-social-cultural context' is clear, as are the drawbacks of utilizing an *etic* approach to evaluating the risks for women in entering into surrogacy arrangements[66]—not all surrogates are or consider themselves to be vulnerable.

Both Freeman and Wilkinson have convincingly addressed the 'exploitation' arguments often used in this context, and so we will not revisit them here.[67] Rather, for our purposes, we have identified two key points of interest: statements regarding the potential emergence of a niche market and health matters.

5.2 Is a niche market emerging?

Some interesting obiter remarks have been made by Hedley J as to the possible emergence of a niche market in *unmarried* surrogate mothers in cross-border arrangements (to avoid issues in Anglo-Welsh law as to who is recognized as the child's father):

> The unmarried surrogate mother may be *more vulnerable*, more prey to exploitation and be more likely to be motivated principally by material considerations.[68]
>
> Less obviously, but importantly, is the fact that the present law (at least as understood by this court) might encourage the less scrupulous to *take advantage of the more vulnerable, unmarried surrogate mothers* and to be less than frank in the arrangements that surround foreign surrogacy arrangements.[69]

According to Hedley J's analysis, an unmarried woman entering into a surrogacy arrangement may be more vulnerable to the influence of unidentified unscrupulous others (as noted previously, similar comments have been made with regard to assisted suicide). Presumably she is 'single' and therefore in need of protection? She is also constructed as being more commercially driven. The latter quotation is reminiscent of the MP David Amess' controversial comments in the 1980s:

> If commercial surrogacy were allowed, it is inevitable that we should create a class of women who would be seen simply as breeding machines. It is doubtful such women, attracted by the lure of money, would be aware of and able to cope with the inherent difficulties that stem from surrogacy.[70]

64 M.J. Radin, 'Market Inalienability' (1987) 100 *Harvard Law Review* 1849. See also eg N. Smith 'Inside the Baby Farm', *Sunday Times Magazine*, 9 May 2010.

65 Freeman, 'Is Surrogacy Exploitative?' (n 61) 168–9.

66 Freeman, 'Is Surrogacy Exploitative?' (n 61) 175: 'Surrogacy does have dangers, but they are not inevitable consequences of the practice and they can be guarded against.'

67 Freeman, 'Is Surrogacy Exploitative?' (n 61); Wilkinson, *Bodies for Sale* (n 41).

68 *Re X and anor (Foreign Surrogacy)* [2008] EWHC 3030 (Fam), para 15, *per* Hedley J (emphasis added).

69 *Re X* (n 68) para 29 (emphasis added).

70 *Hansard*, HC vol 77, col 46, cited in Freeman, 'After Warnock' (n 55) 42.

Freeman rightly critiques this typification of women as 'irrational' (and cites it as evidence of Amess' failure to accept that exploitation is part of capitalism:[71] should it matter that these women might be motivated, even in part, by money?).

Both Amess' and Hedley's observations about potentially *more* vulnerable women are made without any evidence base whatsoever, and—in Hedley's judgment—are couched simply with the caveat that they 'may' be so. Yet the possibility that they might be *less* vulnerable, less subject to another person's influence, for example, is not even countenanced. The *etic* approach to vulnerability here—where it is assumed that a type of surrogate mother is especially vulnerable due to their unmarried (and therefore assumed single) status—is clearly problematic. We simply do not know if unmarried or single women are more or less vulnerable to exploitation or indeed any other risks in the global surrogacy market.[72] It would, in our view, be preferable to adopt Luna's conceptualization based on 'layers of vulnerability' in this context—this would provide a more nuanced, grounded approach to the potential (but manageable) risks raised by surrogacy in discrete cases.

5.3 Health matters

The second example we can address more briefly. It concerns the potential health risks with regard to the safety of the cross-border reproductive care women receive. It is accepted that multiple birth rates are associated with significant health risks for both the mother and resulting children.[73] In the UK, the Human Fertilisation and Embryology Authority imposes clear limits on embryo transfers,[74] and the latest research strongly supports single embryo transfer (SET).[75] However, anecdotal evidence suggests that clinics in some jurisdictions are transferring greater numbers of embryos per cycle, thereby increasing the likelihood of multiple births, with the attendant risks.[76] In some instances this practice has led to the use of selective reduction.[77]

ESHRE's published guidance clearly stipulates that SET 'is the only acceptable option' in surrogacy,[78] but there is no legislation to regulate the global surrogacy market.[79] Furthermore, prospective parents may regard the potential risks associated

71 Freeman, 'After Warnock' (n 55) 42.

72 See eg the 'double bind' argument outlined by Radin, 'Market Inalienability' (n 64).

73 'The single biggest risk of fertility treatment is multiple pregnancy' is the strap-line for the professionally-led website <http://www.oneatatime.org.uk/index.htm>, see also <http://www.oneatatime.org.uk/37.htm> re risks to mother, and re risks to the child(ren) <http://www.oneatatime.org.uk/38.htm> (accessed January 2013).

74 See <http://www.hfea.gov.uk/ivf-embryo-transfer.html> (accessed January 2013).

75 See <http://www.oneatatime.org.uk/485> (accessed January 2013).

76 See eg comments made by speakers at the Progress Educational Trust's conference on 'Passport to Parenthood: The Evidence and Ethics Behind Cross Border Reproductive Care', 24 November 2010, London, UK; for a published summary by Dr V. Raper, in *Bionews* (No 586, 29 November 2010) see <http://www.bionews.org.uk/page_83165.asp>. Also, S.K. Templeton, 'Health Warning for "Embryo Tourists"', *The Sunday Times*, 8 February 2009, 14.

77 Carol Hobson's treatment in India, aged 58; reportedly six embryos were transferred during a single cycle, leading to triplets and the selective reduction of one foetus: <http://www.dailymail.co.uk/femail/article-1367749/What-I-Single-mother-58-asks-giving-birth-IVF-twins.html#>. See also 'octo-mum', Nadya Suleman, where twelve embryos where reportedly transferred in one cycle leading to eight children (in the US).

78 F. Shenfield et al, 'ESHRE's Good Practice Guide For Cross-Border Reproductive Care For Centers And Practitioners' (2011) 26 *Human Reproduction* 1625.

79 See further K. Trimmings and P. Beaumont, 'International Surrogacy Arrangements: An Urgent Need for Legal Regulation at the International Level' (2011) 7 *Journal of Private International Law* 627.

with transferring multiple embryos as more acceptable than the prospect of failing to achieve a pregnancy.

We found only a single reported case where the numbers of embryos implanted in the surrogate mother was discussed (in the context of parental order applications). In *A and anor v P and ors*[80] it was noted that five embryos were transferred to the surrogate mother in one cycle (two created with Mrs A's oocytes, three from donor oocytes). Perhaps unsurprisingly there was no discussion as to the potential health risks to the surrogate mother.[81] Interestingly, in this context an *etic* approach to vulnerability might prove both useful and justifiable. It is feasible to evaluate the relative risks women, in general, face with a multiple pregnancy,[82] and although not all of these risks will eventuate in every surrogacy arrangement, it is entirely appropriate to manage 'known' risks such as these on a 'blanket' policy basis.

5.4 Children

Children are the other traditionally recognized 'primary' vulnerable group. The commodification, harm, welfare, and exploitation arguments have been well rehearsed elsewhere and will not be revisited here.[83] At first glance it seems potentially justifiable to adopt an *etic* approach to children born of surrogacy arrangements insofar as they are unable to make their own representations and are therefore dependent on others to act in their best interests; and utilizing externally evaluated risk factors for very young children seems unproblematic. In the interests of brevity we will address two key areas: an unforeseen event[84] and nationality.

The Warnock Report noted the potential for several 'unforeseen events' to arise in surrogacy arrangements, but interestingly did not directly address the possibility of neither party wishing to keep the child.[85] There is no known recorded data on such incidents in the UK and we do not wish to be alarmist. For such children born in the UK, responsibility for their care would ultimately fall on the state, which has a comprehensive system in place (note we did not say 'perfect'!). However, in inter-jurisdictional arrangements it is less clear which state should be responsible; which may be compounded in jurisdictions where surrogates (and, if relevant, their partners) are divested of any legal responsibilities for the child(ren) in question,[86] and further still where the state care provision is minimal or even non-existent.

There is no question that in such instances these children are potentially vulnerable. However, rather than adopting an *etic* approach, we suggest that—in the global health context with which we are concerned—Luna's conceptualization of 'layers of

80 [2011] EWHC 1738 (Fam).

81 This absence might be more surprising re the children, given the fact that child welfare considerations in this area are now 'paramount', see Biggs and Jones, 'Tourism' (n 38).

82 See eg the information provided by One at a Time (n 73).

83 eg the Warnock Report (n 61); Freeman, 'After Warnock' (n 55) 46: on the 'potential dangers' for children: 'There is no evidence that commissioning parents are anything other than good loving parents well able to take care of the child's needs and welfare'; Freeman, 'Is Surrogacy Exploitative?' (n 61); Brazier Report (n 61); Wilkinson, *Bodies for Sale* (n 41) especially 134–81.

84 Unforeseen events concerning the commissioning parents' situation will be addressed separately later, though in practice these too may well have an impact on the child(ren), eg if a parental order cannot be made (in the UK context).

85 But see P. Singer and D. Wells (1984) *New Ways of Making Babies: The Reproduction Revolution* (Oxford: OUP, 1984), cited in I. Kennedy and A. Grubb, *Medical Law Text with Materials* (London: 2nd edn, Butterworths, 1994) 822.

86 *Re X and Y (Foreign Surrogacy)* [2008] EWHC 3030 (Fam), para 8.

vulnerability' is more appropriate, as the relevant risk factors need to be determined on a case-by-case basis. A child born in a jurisdiction in which she or he has identifiable legal parents or, if not, at the very least a potentially good state care package, faces a rather different potential future from one that has neither in place; evaluations of vulnerability, therefore, should be appropriately nuanced to the child's particular circumstances.[87]

This brings us to the issue of nationality. Cross-border arrangements can lead to conflict of laws issues where the two national approaches are mutually exclusive, as seen in *Re X and Y (Foreign Surrogacy).*[88] This case concerned an agreement between a married UK couple and a married woman in the Ukraine. Under Ukrainian law, the UK applicants were the parents for all purposes; but under Anglo-Welsh law the children did not have any British parents, and hence no right of entry into the UK: 'The effect of all this was of course that *these children were effectively legal orphans and, more seriously, stateless*'; described as 'marooned stateless and parentless'.[89] Following DNA tests that confirmed the male applicant was the biological father, the children were granted discretionary leave to enter the UK 'outside the rules',[90] and a parental order was eventually given.

While children have consistently been posited as (one of) the most vulnerable groups in need of protection from commercial surrogacy markets, the current domestic legislation is resulting in situations where children are potentially being 'marooned stateless and parentless', and whose status can only be regularized when discretionary executive decisions permit their entry into the UK.[91] Quite how such an approach either promotes child welfare or minimizes the vulnerability of children is difficult to discern. Until a dedicated international convention on surrogacy is devised to establish an appropriate framework for inter-jurisdictional cooperation, akin to the Adoption Convention, these vulnerabilities will continue.[92] Accordingly, despite Herring's[93] observation that law rightly characterizes children as vulnerable, but fails to recognize the vulnerabilities of adults (discussed previously), this differential emphasis seems justifiable in a global surrogacy context where we need to consider whose vulnerabilities matter most in devising appropriate legal responses and regulation. That must be so even when those legal rules will improve one person's position whilst heightening the risk(s) to which another person is exposed.[94]

5.5 Commissioning parents

Would-be parents have not always been viewed as vulnerable, perhaps due to the assumption that they have a higher socio-economic status relative to surrogate mothers. Nevertheless, some potential vulnerability has traditionally been highlighted with regard to third party involvement in the marriage,[95] including claims made by the

87 Whereas an *emic* approach focusing on lived experience and autonomy is clearly inappropriate for very young children.

88 *Re X and Y* (n 86).

89 *Re X and Y* (n 86) paras 9–10, *per* Hedley J (emphasis added).

90 See Biggs and Jones, 'Tourism' (n 38).

91 For further details see Biggs and Jones, 'Tourism' (n 38).

92 Trimmings and Beaumont, 'International Surrogacy Arrangements' (n 79); also K. Trimmings and P. Beaumont, *International Surrogacy Arrangements. Legal Regulation at the International Level* (Oxford: Hart, 2013).

93 Herring, 'Vulnerability, Children, and the Law' (n 12) 244.

94 We are grateful to John Coggon for this point.

95 Similar comments have been made in the context of donor-assisted conception.

surrogate against the father for maintenance.[96] Further, where surrogacy is being used as a last resort due to infertility[97] there is clear potential for psychological or emotional vulnerabilities which may be exacerbated by the lack of enforceability of surrogacy contracts in the UK. Cross-border agreements do *not* however create a specific vulnerability around the contract issue. Nonetheless, other difficulties might arise which render them 'legally vulnerable',[98] unable to gain or exercise rights and responsibilities over the children in question, under the domestic legal regime. For example, the vicissitudes of life might result in the death of one of the parties[99] prior to a parental order being granted,[100] or the relationship breaking down;[101] or other aspects of the statutory requirements might not be met, for example lack of valid consent provided by the surrogate,[102] or an application outside the strict six-month limit.[103]

It would seem that the *etic* policy assumption that would-be parents are not especially vulnerable, combined with legislation aimed at discouraging involvement in surrogacy, has resulted in greater uncertainty and increased potential vulnerability for these parties. Some parties may be able to evade the domestic prohibition on commercial surrogacy, but this is subject to both their ability to pay and willingness to participate in the global market. Nevertheless, when they wish to regularize their legal parental status they are subject to the outmoded statutory requirements, which might be their undoing.[104]

6. Conclusions

In relation to assisted suicide and surrogacy the law is designed to protect the vulnerable from behaviour that might cause harm on the basis that society owes a moral duty to safeguard those who cannot defend their own interests. However, the protections put in place fail to acknowledge that not everyone who is potentially vulnerable actually requires protection, or that the protections put in place might instead be disadvantageous to individuals or groups.

96 eg in the Warnock Report it was observed that fathers 'may be vulnerable to a claim by the carrying mother for an affiliation order if she keeps the child' (ie as a pre-cursor to seeking maintenance); see Warnock (n 61) para 8.9. Affiliation orders were abolished under the Family Law Reform Act 1987, s 17; but under the current domestic law such fathers still may be exposed to child maintenance claims.

97 As opposed to 'convenience' arrangements undertaken for social reasons.

98 A term we have used elsewhere, see Biggs and Jones, 'Tourism' (n 38).

99 Only 'couples' can apply for parental orders, see further the Human Fertilisation and Embryology Act 2008, s 54; Jones, 'The (Im)Possible Parents in Law' (n 57).

100 As occurred in *A and anor v P and ors* [2011] EWHC 1738 (Fam), where an order was nevertheless granted by Theis J for the reasons outlined at para 31.

101 In *G v G* [2012] EWHC 1979 (Fam) the husband unsuccessfully sought to have the parental order set aside, due to the wife's alleged deceit (ie that she had always intended to separate from him and be a lone parent).

102 See *D and L (Minors Surrogacy)* [2012] EWHC 2631 (Fam), whereby, following an arrangement with an Indian clinic, the surrogate could not be found and the need for her consent was dispensed with by the court.

103 Natalie Gamble has expressed concern as to the non-extendable period during which an application must be made, see <http://www.nataliegambleassociates.co.uk/page/Why-surrogacy-law-needs-reviewing/39> (accessed January 2013). In contrast the court has a well-established discretion to retrospectively approve payments under the Human Fertilisation and Embryology Act 2008, s 54(8), see further Biggs and Jones, 'Tourism' (n 38).

104 See eg *Re G (Surrogacy: Foreign Domicile)* [2007] EWHC 2814 (Fam), also discussed in Biggs and Jones, 'Tourism' (n 38).

The vulnerable in society should be protected from activities and conduct that will disadvantage them, and in certain circumstances it is proper that this should become a legal responsibility. But in order to ensure that each person's interests are properly safeguarded it is important that the law operates according to a properly constructed understanding of what it means to be vulnerable and who is vulnerable under this definition. The examples we have discussed demonstrate that a blanket, or *etic* approach that decrees that, with the possible exception of the regulation of multiple embryo transfer which carries quantifiable risks, treating every member of a particular sub-population as inherently vulnerable is problematic. One result is that the law exhibits a paternalistic attitude that constrains choices and prevents those involved from exercising their individual autonomy. Both assisted suicide and surrogacy demonstrate how this can work in practice. Worse than this, however, is the very real possibility that people who are deemed worthy of protection within protected groups can instead be rendered more vulnerable. Our analysis shows that those who seek assisted suicide but are denied it because of the legal prohibition can become more vulnerable due to the loss of autonomy and control over the timing and method of their dying. Similarly, children who are the product of some cross-border surrogacy arrangements can find themselves stateless and parentless because of the application of statutory provisions that were, ironically, designed to safeguard their welfare.

This possibility of creating more harm is a damning indictment of law's insensitivity to the range of potential layers of vulnerability created by the global health market. Decisions need to be made as to whose vulnerability(ies) are to be prioritized and the law reformed accordingly. The current approach is clearly unfit for purpose: 'blanket' approaches to vulnerability are simply not working in this context. Nevertheless, vulnerability *can* be a useful legal concept provided that it is used to take account of the specific vulnerabilities of individuals or groups based on evidence of genuine susceptibility and understanding of the scope of the potential harms that might ensue. An *emic* or nuanced layered approach might be preferable.

8

The ECHR, Health Care, and Irregular Migrants

Sylvie Da Lomba

1. Introduction

For more than a decade, deep concern has been expressed over the plight of irregular migrants in Europe, notably over their poor access to basic social rights.[1] This period, however, has also witnessed an unprecedented problematization of irregular migration.[2] Consequently, calls for greater protection of irregular migrants' basic rights have remained largely unanswered.[3] It remains the case that irregular migrants have rights; international human rights law predicates rights on humanity and as such confers basic social rights on this group regardless of their immigration status.

Health care provision for irregular migrants brings to the fore the tension that exists between the universal premise of international human rights law and states' right to control immigration. Health care is a basic necessity and as such is recognized as a basic human right.[4] Irregular migrants' immigration status, however, significantly constrains their access to health care. Irregular migration covers a range of situations which include: clandestine arrival in the host state, staying beyond the permitted period of residence, or working without a permit or in a manner inconsistent with one's immigration status.[5] The term irregular migrant also applies to foreign nationals who enter on false papers, refused asylum seekers who have exhausted their appeal rights and can no longer remain in the host state, and regularized migrants who fall back into an irregular situation.[6] Because they have breached immigration laws, the realization and

1 R. Cholewinski, 'Study on Obstacles to Effective Access of Irregular Migrants to Minimum Social Rights' (Strasbourg: Council of Europe Publishing, December 2005).

2 See eg B.A. Vollmer, 'Policy Discourses on Irregular Migration in the EU—"Number Games" and "Political Games"' (2011) 13(3) *European Journal of Migration and Law* 317.

3 See eg: E. van Thijn, 'Report on Human Rights of Irregular Migrants', Doc 10924, 4 May 2006, Committee on Migration, Refugees and Population, Parliamentary Assembly, Council of Europe; and Parliamentary Assembly, Council of Europe, 'Human rights of irregular migrants', Resolution 1509 (2006).

4 The right to health care is a core component of the right to health. It is enshrined in a number of international human rights instruments. The 1966 International Covenant on Economic, Social and Cultural Rights, Art 12 provides the most authoritative articulation of the right to health. See also the 1979 Convention on the Elimination of All Forms of Discrimination against Women, Art 12 and the 1989 Convention on the Rights of the Child, Art 24. On irregular migrants' right to health care, see eg S. Da Lomba, 'Immigration Status and Basic Social Human Rights: A Comparative Study of Irregular Migrants' Right to Health Care in France, The UK and Canada' (2010) 28(1) *Netherlands Quarterly of Human Rights* 6, 15–22.

5 E. Guild, 'Who is an Irregular Migrant?' in B. Bogusz, R. Cholewinski, A. Cygan, and E. Szyszczak (eds), *Irregular Migration and Human Rights: Theoretical, European and International Perspectives* (Leiden and Boston: Martinus Nijhoff, 2004) 3.

6 R. Cholewinski, 'Identifying and Clarifying Concepts on "Irregular Migration"', Paper presented at the 10th IOM Regional Conference on Migration, Singapore, 2006.

protection of irregular migrants' right to health care are set against the exercise of the government immigration power.

The Parliamentary Assembly of the European Council has highlighted the need to protect irregular migrants' human rights, including their right to health care,[7] and the role that the European Convention on Human Rights (ECHR) may play in this regard.[8] Although the ECHR does not guarantee the right to health care, its contribution to protection in the field of health care must not be overlooked. First, while the rights enshrined in the ECHR are in the main civil and political, the Convention can apply to socio-economic conditions.[9] Second, the ECHR is central to the European human rights system. Finally and importantly, irregular migrants present in States Parties to the ECHR fall within the personal scope of the Convention.[10] This is critical, as irregular migrants largely fall outside the protection of the law, including human rights instruments, due to their immigration status.[11]

With this in mind, I examine the extent to which the ECHR may protect irregular migrants in the area of health care. To this end, I consider the application of the ECHR to the social sphere with an emphasis on health care. Having established that the Convention can give rise to health care obligations, I examine the case law of the European Court of Human Rights (ECtHR) on the expulsion of the seriously ill. I then discuss the implications of the Court's case law for the protection of irregular migrants in the field of health care.

2. The ECHR and Protection in the Social Sphere: the Case of Health Care

The ECHR 'guarantees, for the most part, civil and political rights'.[12] However, in *Airey v Ireland*, the ECtHR stressed that there was 'no water-tight division' between civil and political rights and social and economic rights.[13] On this basis, the Court held 'that the mere fact that an interpretation of the Convention may extend into the sphere of social and economic rights should not be a decisive factor against such an interpretation'.[14] It follows from the Court's judgment in *Airey v Ireland* that the ECHR can apply to socio-economic conditions;[15] this is often referred to as the Court's integrated approach to interpretation.[16]

7 Resolution 1509 (n 3).

8 Van Thijn, 'Report on Human Rights of Irregular Migrants' (n 3).

9 *Airey v Ireland* (App 6289/73), 9 October 1979, para 26.

10 Article 1 ECHR, Art 1 provides that: 'The High Contracting Parties shall secure to everyone within their jurisdiction the rights and freedoms . . . [set out in the ECHR].'

11 eg the 1990 International Convention on the Protection of the Rights of All Migrant Workers and Members of their Families confers basic rights on all migrants, but only bestows enhanced rights on regular migrants (Parts III and IV). Accordingly, equality of treatment with nationals in respect of general access to health care services only applies to regular migrants (Part IV, Art 43(1)(e)).

12 R.C.A. White and C. Ovey, *The European Convention on Human Rights* (Oxford: OUP, 2010) 8. However, there are exceptions; for example, Arts 1 and 2 of the First Protocol to the ECHR protect property rights and the right to education, respectively.

13 *Airey v Ireland* (n 9) para 26.

14 *Airey v Ireland* (n 9) para 26.

15 *Airey v Ireland* (n 9). See also eg *M.S.S. v Belgium and Greece* (App 30696/09), 21 January 2011 (GC).

16 See eg V. Mantouvalou, '*N v UK*: No Duty to Rescue the Nearby Needy?' (2009) 72(5) *Modern Law Review* 815, 820.

In line with its integrated approach, the ECtHR has held that Articles 3, 2, and 8 ECHR[17] could give rise to obligations in the field of health care. For example, the Court has developed a substantial case law on detainee medical care and constantly held that the authorities' failure to provide prisoners with adequate medical assistance violated Article 3 when the ensuing harm attained the requisite level of severity.[18] The Court has also accepted that health care standards in Contracting States could give rise to complaints under Article 2.[19] Article 2(1) 'enjoins the State not only to refrain from the intentional and unlawful taking of life, but also to take appropriate steps to safeguard the lives of those within its jurisdiction'.[20] On this basis and in keeping with its integrated approach, the ECtHR has, for instance, found that 'Article 2 . . . may impose an obligation on a Contracting State to make available a certain standard of health care'.[21] Article 2 may also be engaged 'where it is shown that the authorities . . . put an individual's life at risk through the denial of health care which they have undertaken to make available to the population generally'.[22] Article 8 ECHR may also beget health care obligations. For example, in *Pentiacova and ors v Moldova*, the Court held that 'Article 8 was applicable to . . . complaints about insufficient funding of treatment'.[23] In this instance, however, the Court observed 'that the applicants had access to the standard of health care offered to the general public' and that health care reform had improved their situation and declared their Article 8 complaint manifestly unfounded.[24]

The Court's integrated approach to interpretation, however, has not caused ECHR rights to morph into socio-economic rights and 'the Convention cannot serve as a proxy or stand-in for an enforceable set of socio-economic rights'.[25] Accordingly, the Court has constantly held that: 'the Convention does not guarantee, as such, socio-economic rights, including the right to charge-free dwelling, the right to work, *the right to free medical assistance*, or the right to claim financial assistance from a State to maintain a certain level of living'.[26] Moreover, the ECtHR has been cautious not to 'impose an impossible or disproportionate burden' on states when determining the

17 Art 3: prohibition of torture; Art 2: right to life; and Art 8: right to respect for private and family life.

18 eg in *Keenan v United Kingdom*, the Court found that the lack of adequate medical treatment for a prisoner suffering from schizophrenia amounted to degrading treatment ((App 27229/95), 3 April 2001, para 116). Likewise in *Khudobin v Russia*, the Court found that the applicant, a prisoner who was HIV positive and suffered from several chronic diseases, had not received the medical assistance he needed, in violation of Art 3 ((App 59696/00), 26 October 2006). See also eg *McGlinchey v United Kingdom* (App 50390/99), 29 April 2003; *Mouisel v France* (App 67263/01), 14 November 2002; and *Kudla v Poland* (App 30210/96), 26 October 2000 (GC).

19 See eg *Nitecki v Poland* (App 65653/01), 21 March 2002; and *Pentiacova and ors v Moldova* (App 14462/03), 4 January 2005.

20 *LCB v United Kingdom* (App 23413/94), 9 June 1998, para 36; and *Kontrová v Slovakia* (App 7510/04), 31 May 2007, para 49.

21 *Cyprus v Turkey* (App 25781/94), 10 May 2001, para 219.

22 *Cyprus v Turkey* (n 21) para 219.

23 *Nitecki v Poland*; and *Pentiacova and ors v Moldova* (n 19).

24 *Nitecki v Poland*; and *Pentiacova and ors v Moldova* (n 19).

25 C. O'Cinneide, 'A Modest Proposal: Destitution, State Responsibility and the European Convention on Human Rights' (2008) 5 *European Human Rights Law Review* 583, 586. For example, in *Botta v Italy*, the Court found that '[t]he rights asserted by the applicant were social in character' and as such 'went beyond the concept of legal obligation' under Art 8(1) (*Botta v Italy* (App 21439/93), 24 February 1998).

26 *Pancenko v Latvia* (App 40772/98), 28 October 1999 (emphasis added). See also eg *O'Rourke v United Kingdom* (App 39022/97), 26 June 2001; and *Marzari v Italy* (App 36448/97), 4 May 1999.

scope of their Article 8 and 2 obligations.[27] Consequently the scope of health care obligations that the ECHR may place on states is limited. For example, whilst Article 2 may give rise to obligations pertaining to medical care, this provision does not place an obligation on states 'to provide an effective system of healthcare'.[28] Likewise Article 8 does not entail a right to particular forms of medical treatment or to a certain standard of health care.[29] In *Sentges v The Netherlands*, the Court found the applicant's complaint that the authorities' refusal to provide him with a robotic arm violated Article 8 to be manifestly ill-founded.[30]

The margin of appreciation that states enjoy under Article 8 further limits the range of health care obligations that the ECHR can beget. Article 8 allows states to balance individuals' right to respect for private and family life against the interest of the community as a whole. The balance struck between these competing interests, however, must be fair[31] in that states remain under the obligation 'to secure the practical and effective protection of [Convention] rights'.[32] The Court has constantly held that states' margin of appreciation is wider in the social and economic spheres.[33] Importantly, in *Pentiacova v Moldavia*, the Court emphasized that the margin of appreciation enjoyed by states in the social and economic spheres was '*even wider* when . . . the issues involve[d] *an assessment of the priorities in the context of the allocation of limited resources*',[34] in this instance health care resources.[35] The Court opined that national authorities were better placed than an international court to undertake this kind of assessment because they were familiar with the demands made on national health care systems and the resources available to meet those demands.[36] The Court did not question the applicants' assertion that they could not afford necessary treatment and medication that was not provided free of charge by the state,[37] but considered 'that the applicants' claim amount[ed] to a call on public funds which, in view of the scarce resources, would have to be diverted from other worthy needs funded by the taxpayer'.[38] The Court added that:

> While it is clearly desirable that everyone should have access to a full range of medical treatment . . . the lack of resources means that there are, unfortunately, in the Contracting States many individuals who do not enjoy them, especially in cases of permanent and expensive treatment.[39]

27 See eg *Kontrová v Slovakia* (n 20).

28 O'Cinneide, 'A Modest Proposal' (n 25) 590.

29 *Pentiacova and ors v Moldova* (n 19). This is also implicit in *Nitecki v Poland* (n 19).

30 *Sentges v The Netherlands* (App 27677/02), 8 July 2003.

31 See eg *Pentiacova and ors v Moldova* (n.19). On the fair balance principle, see eg A. Mowbray, 'A Study of the Principle of Fair Balance in the Jurisprudence of the European Court of Human Rights' (2010) 10(2) *Human Rights Law Review* 289.

32 See eg Kontrová *v Slovakia* (n 20) para 51.

33 *Connors v United Kingdom* (App 66746/01), 27 May 2004, para 82. See also eg *Budayeva and ors v Russia* (Apps 15339/02, 21166/02, 20058/02, 11673/02, and 15343/02), 20 March 2008, para 135. States' margin of appreciation is also wide in the technical sphere (*Budayeva and ors v Russia*, para 135).

34 *Pentiacova v Moldavia* (n 19) (emphasis added).

35 See also *Sentges v The Netherlands* (n 30).

36 *Pentiacova v Moldavia* (n 19). In *Connors v United Kingdom*, the Court stressed that 'in spheres such as housing, which play a central role in the welfare and economic policies of modern societies, it will respect the legislature's judgment as to what is in the general interest unless that judgment is manifestly without reasonable foundation' (n 33) para 82). In *James and ors v United Kingdom*, the Court emphasized that 'the margin of appreciation available to the legislature in implementing social and economic policies should be a wide one' (*James and ors v United Kingdom* (App 8793/79) 21 February 1986, para 46). For a critique of 'some of the assumptions that underpin judicial reluctance to engage with health social care policies' (O'Cinneide, 'A Modest Proposal' (n 25) 605), see eg J.A. King, 'The Pervasiveness of Polycentricity' [2008] *Public Law* 101.

37 *Pentiacova v Moldavia* (n 19).

38 *Pentiacova v Moldavia* (n 19).

39 *Pentiacova v Moldavia* (n 19).

On this basis, the Court found that the respondent state had struck a fair balance between the applicants' Article 8 rights and the community's interests.

Health care obligations under the ECHR are also constrained by the high threshold of severity required to engage Article 3.[40] Whether the minimum severity threshold is attained 'depends on the circumstances of the case, such as the duration of the treatment, its physical or mental effects and, in some cases, the sex, age and state of health of the victim'.[41] The high severity threshold means that health care complaints under Article 3 will only be upheld in exceptional cases. For example, in *Khudobin v Russia*, the ECtHR found that:

> ...the absence of qualified and timely medical assistance, added to the authorities' refusal to allow an independent medical examination of [the applicant's] state of health, created such a strong feeling of insecurity that, combined with his physical sufferings, it amounted to degrading treatment within the meaning of Article 3.[42]

It follows from the ECtHR's case law that, while the ECHR cannot offer a substitute for the right to health care, it can give rise to health care obligations and therefore provide some protection to individuals within the jurisdiction of Contracting States in this area.

3. ECtHR's Case Law on the Expulsion of the Seriously Ill

In a number of cases, the ECtHR has assessed whether the expulsion of seriously ill persons would engage the ECHR, and especially Article 3. In these cases, the ECtHR has generally taken the view that complaints under Articles 8 and 2 did not raise any separate issues from Article 3 complaints, and for this reason did not assess whether deportation would violate these provisions.[43] The Court's approach was challenged by the dissenting judges in *N v United Kingdom*; while they could understand why the Court did not investigate the Article 8 complaint, they regretted the Court's laconic wording;[44] the majority simply stated that: 'It [was] not necessary... to examine [the Article 8] complaint.'[45] The dissenting judges further opined that a non-violation finding in respect of Article 3 did not exclude the possibility of a breach of Article 8.[46] They stressed that the majority 'should... have examined closely and carefully the situation of the applicant and of her illness under Article 8'[47] and added that: 'Faced with the situation of a person who will, without doubt, be sent to certain death, we

[40] See eg *Kafkaris v Cyprus* (App 21906/04), 12 February 2008 (GC) para 95; *Mouisel v France* (App 67263/01), 14 November 2003, para 37; and *Poghossian v Georgia* (App 9870/07), 24 February 2001, para 47.

[41] See eg *Ireland v United Kingdom* (App 5310/71), 18 January 1978, para 162; *Mouisel v France* (n 18) para 37; and *Poghossian v Georgia* (n 40) para 47.

[42] *Khudobin v Russia* (n 18) para 96. See also eg *McGlinchey and ors v United Kingdom* (n 18).

[43] eg in *D v United Kingdom*, the Court held that the Art 2 complaint was 'indissociable from the substance of the complaint under Article 3' (*D v United Kingdom* (App 30240/96), 2 May 1997, para 59). In *D v United Kingdom* and *N v United Kingdom*, the Court took the view that the Art 8 complaint overlapped with the Art 3 complaint (n 43) para 64; and *N v United Kingdom* (App 26565/05), 27 May 2008 (GC) para 53).

[44] *N v United Kingdom* (n 43), Joint Dissenting Opinion of Judges Tulkens, Bonello, and Spielmann Dissenting Opinion, para 26.

[45] *N v United Kingdom* (n 43) para 53.

[46] *N v United Kingdom* (n 43), Joint Dissenting Opinion of Judges Tulkens, Bonello, and Spielmann Dissenting Opinion, para 26.

[47] *N v United Kingdom* (n 43), Joint Dissenting Opinion of Judges Tulkens, Bonello, and Spielmann Dissenting Opinion, para 26.

think that the Court could neither legally... nor morally confine itself to saying "[no] separate issue arises under Article 8 of the Convention".'[48] In light of the centrality of Article 3 to the ECtHR's case law on the expulsion of the seriously ill, the focus of this section is on this provision.

The first case to consider is *D v United Kingdom*.[49] The applicant claimed that his expulsion to St Kitts, his home country, upon completion of his prison sentence for drug trafficking, would violate Article 3.[50] In keeping with its approach in immigration cases,[51] the ECtHR started by asserting the right of states 'to control the entry, residence and expulsion of aliens'.[52] The Court emphasized that the expulsion of a drug trafficker was 'a justified response to [the] scourge that was [drug trafficking]'.[53] The Court, however, reiterated that the exercise of the government immigration power was subject to states' 'treaty obligations including the Convention'.[54] The Court reaffirmed that 'Article 3... prohibits in absolute terms torture or inhuman or degrading treatment or punishment and that its guarantees apply irrespective of the reprehensible nature of the conduct of the person in question.'[55] The Court, however, held that *D v United Kingdom* should be distinguished from other Article 3 cases in that the respondent state could not be held responsible, directly or indirectly, for the risk of ill-treatment.[56] In this instance, the risk of harm arose from the lack of adequate health care provision in the receiving state. The ECtHR, however, unanimously held that, given the importance of Article 3 to the ECHR system, 'sufficient flexibility' was required in the application of this provision and that: 'To limit the application of Article 3... in this manner would be to undermine the absolute character of its protection.'[57] Having established that Article 3 could apply to wider contexts, the Court found that 'the conditions of adversity which await[ed] [the applicant] in St Kitts [would] further reduce his already limited life expectancy and subject him to acute mental and physical suffering'.[58] In light of the applicant's 'very exceptional circumstances', the Court found that the applicant's expulsion to St Kitts would violate Article 3.[59] Three factors were decisive in the ECtHR's characterization of the applicant's circumstances as 'very exceptional' and ensuing finding that removal would engage Article 3. First, the applicant was terminally ill. Second, the Court noted that: 'Any medical treatment which he might hope to receive [in St Kitts] could not contend with the infections which he may possibly contract on account of... [living conditions in St Kitts].'[60] Finally, the Court observed that the applicant would have no 'moral or social support' in the receiving country.[61]

To date, *D v United Kingdom* is the only judgment where the ECtHR has found that the expulsion of a seriously ill person would violate Article 3. In subsequent cases, the

48 *N v United Kingdom* (n 43), Joint Dissenting Opinion of Judges Tulkens, Bonello, and Spielmann Dissenting Opinion, para 26.

49 *D v United Kingdom* (n 43). The European Commission on Human Rights had examined in an earlier case whether the expulsion of the seriously ill would breach the ECHR. In *Tanko v Finland*, the Commission found that the removal of a national of Ghana who suffered from an eye condition did not engage Art 3 (*Tanko v Finland* (App 23634/94), 19 May 1994.

50 The applicant also claimed that his removal to St Kitts would breach Arts 2, 8, and 13 (right to an effective remedy) *D v United Kingdom* (n 43) paras 56, 61, and 66).

51 See eg *Chahal v United Kingdom* (App 22414/93) 15 November 1996, para 73; and *Boultif v Switzerland* (App 54273/00), 2 August 2001, para 46.

52 *D v United Kingdom* (n 43) para 46.

53 *D v United Kingdom* (n 43) para 46.

54 *D v United Kingdom* (n 43) para 46.

55 *D v United Kingdom* (n 43) para 47.

56 *D v United Kingdom* (n 43) para 49.

57 *D v United Kingdom* (n 43) para 49.

58 *D v United Kingdom* (n 43) para 52.

59 *D v United Kingdom* (n 43) para 53.

60 *D v United Kingdom* (n 43) para 52.

61 *D v United Kingdom* (n 43) para 52.

Court held that the applicants' circumstances should be distinguished from *D*'s in that they were not 'very exceptional'.[62] The Court noted that the applicants' illness had not yet reached an advanced stage.[63] The Court also observed that medical treatment was 'in principle' available in receiving states, although access could not be guaranteed in practice owing to the considerable cost of treatment and limited national resources.[64] The Court also noted that applicants had relatives in the receiving country.[65] In *B.B. v France*, however, the European Commission of Human Rights found that the deportation of an AIDS patient to the DRC would violate Article 3 because: his illness had reached an advanced stage; it was highly probable that he would not have access to necessary treatment in the receiving country; and he would have no family support there.[66] The case was referred to the ECtHR but was struck out of the list following the French government's undertaking not to deport the applicant.[67]

The ECtHR's judgment in *D v United Kingdom* marked a significant development in that it broadened the scope of Article 3 protection. However, the Court's willingness to apply Article 3 to contexts where the respondent state could not be held responsible for the risk of ill-treatment was set against concerns over placing overly onerous obligations on states. The Court stressed that:

> Aliens who ha[d] served their prison sentences and [were] subject to expulsion [could not] in principle claim any entitlement to remain in the territory of a Contracting State in order to benefit from medical, social and other forms of assistance provided by the expelling State during their stay in prison.[68]

In *N v United Kingdom*, however, concerns with regard to overstretching the scope of Article 3 obligations in the area of welfare gained significance in that they were extended to 'aliens without a right to stay' and led the Court to depart from principles central to the ECHR system.[69]

In *N v United Kingdom*, the Grand Chamber found that the removal of an HIV patient to her country of origin, Uganda, would not constitute a violation of Article 3.[70] The decisive factor in the Court's assessment that *N*'s circumstances should be distinguished from those of the applicant in *D v United Kingdom*[71] lay with her health status: unlike *D*, she was not on her 'death bed'. I posit that the Court's approach in *N v United Kingdom* is not sustainable as it undermines the absolute nature of

62 *S.C.C. v Sweden* (App 46553/99), 15 February 2000; *Bensaid v United Kingdom* (App 44599/98), 6 February 2001; *Arcila Henao v The Netherlands* (App 13669/03), 24 June 2003; *Ndangoya v Sweden* (App 25629/04), 22 June 2004; *Amegnigan v The Netherlands* (App 25629/04), 25 November 2004; *N v United Kingdom* (n 43); and *Yoh-Ekale Mwanje v Belgium* (App 10486/10), 20 December 2011. See also *Karara v Finland* (App 40900/98) European Commission of Human Rights, 29 May 1998. In *Tatete v Switzerland*, the applicant claimed that her deportation would breach the ECHR, but a friendly settlement was concluded and the case was struck out of the list (*Tatete v Switzerland* (App 41874/98), 6 July 2000).

63 *Bensaid v United Kingdom* (n 62); *Arcila Henao v The Netherlands* (App 13669/03) (n 62); *Ndangoya v Sweden* (n 62); *Amegnigan v The Netherlands* (n 62); *N v United Kingdom* (n 43); and *Yoh-Ekale Mwanje v Belgium* (n 62). See also *Karara v Finland* (n 62).

64 *Ndangoya v Sweden* (n 62); *S.C.C. v Sweden* (n 62); *Arcila Henao v The Netherlands* (n 62); *N v United Kingdom* (n 43); and *Yoh-Ekale Mwanje v Belgium* (n 62).

65 *Ndangoya v Sweden* (App 25629/04) (n 62); *S.C.C. v Sweden* (n 62); *N v United Kingdom* (n 43); and *Yoh-Ekale Mwanje v Belgium* (n 62).

66 *B.B. v France* (App 30930/96) Reports 1998-VI.

67 *B.B. v France* (App 47/1998/950/1165), 7 September 1998.

68 *D v United Kingdom* (n 43) para 54.

69 *N v United Kingdom* (n 43). For a case comment, see Mantouvalou, '*N v UK*: No Duty to Rescue the Nearby Needy?' (n 16).

70 *N v United Kingdom* (n 43) para 51.

71 *D v United Kingdom* (n 43).

Article 3,[72] retreats from its integrated approach to interpretation, and ultimately subject states' ECHR obligations to the government immigration power.

The Grand Chamber's approach in *N v United Kingdom* is inconsistent with the absolute nature of Article 3 on two accounts: it introduces a higher severity threshold and balances the right not to be subjected to ill-treatment against resource and immigration control considerations. The Grand Chamber stressed that the applicant was not 'critically ill at the present time'[73] and that she was 'fit to travel'.[74] However, it follows from the Court's judgment in *D v United Kingdom* that other circumstances such as 'a lack of medical and palliative care as well as a lack of psychological support, in the home country, might be equally relevant to the finding of a separate violation of Article 3'.[75] Such circumstances were present in *N*. It was established that without the necessary medication the applicant's 'condition would rapidly deteriorate and she would suffer ill-health, discomfort, pain and death within a few years'.[76] Moreover, there was serious doubt as to whether the applicant would have any form of support in Uganda. The Grand Chamber simply noted that: 'It appear[ed] that that she ha[d] family members in Uganda, although she claim[ed] that they would not be willing or able to care for her if she were seriously ill.'[77] Treatment was available in Uganda,[78] but access was uncertain.[79] It is true that the Court's assessments in this type of case have always entailed a degree of speculation, especially in respect of access to treatment and medication.[80] However, the Court's findings that applicants had family and social networks in the receiving state were less speculative.[81] The Grand Chamber, however, emphasized that:

> The rapidity of the deterioration she would suffer and the extent to which she would be able to obtain access to medical treatment, support and care, including help from relatives, involved a certain degree of speculation, particularly in view of the constantly evolving situation as regards the treatment of HIV and AIDS worldwide.[82]

It is true that the Court's assessments always entail a degree of speculation, especially in respect of access to treatment and medication.[83] However, the Court's assessments of whether applicants have family and social networks in the receiving state rest on greater certainty.[84] I concur with the dissenting judges that the distinction between *N* and *D*'s

72 See eg S. Palmer, 'A Wrong Turning: Article 3 ECHR and Proportionality' (2006) 65(2) *Cambridge Law Journal* 438.

73 *N v United Kingdom* (n 43) para 50.

74 *N v United Kingdom* (n 43) para 47.

75 *N v United Kingdom* (n 43), Joint Dissenting Opinion of Judges Tulkens, Bonello, and Spielmann Dissenting Opinion, para 21. See *D v United Kingdom* (n 43) para 53.

76 *N v United Kingdom* (n 43) para 47.

77 *N v United Kingdom* (n 43) para 48. The Court's assessment displayed the same degree of speculation in a subsequent case. In *Yoh-Ekale Mwanje v Belgium* (n 62), the Court observed that the applicant had a potential social and family network in the receiving country (at para 84).

78 *N v United Kingdom* (n 43) para 48.

79 *N v United Kingdom* (n 43) paras 19 and 48.

80 *Ndangoya v Sweden* (n 62); *S.C.C. v Sweden* (n 62); *Arcila Henao v The Netherlands* (n 62); *N v United Kingdom* (n 43); and *Yoh-Ekale Mwanje v Belgium* (n 62).

81 eg in *Arcila Henao v The Netherlands*, the ECtHR noted that the applicant's father and six siblings resided in Columbia (n 62); in *S.C.C. v Sweden*, the Court observed that the applicants' children as well as other family members lived in Zambia (n 62); and in *Ndangoya v Sweden*, the Court stressed that the applicant had maintained links with relatives who might be able to help (n 62).

82 *N v United Kingdom* (n 43) para 50.

83 *Ndangoya v Sweden* (n 62); *S.C.C. v Sweden* (n 62); *Arcila Henao v The Netherlands* (n 62); *N v United Kingdom* (n 43); and *Yoh-Ekale Mwanje v Belgium* (n 62).

84 eg in *Arcila Henao v The Netherlands*, the ECtHR noted that the applicant's father and six siblings resided in Columbia (n 62); in *S.C.C. v Sweden*, the Court observed that the applicants'

circumstances is 'misconceived'.[85] They pointed out that '[t]here [was] no doubt that in the event of removal to Uganda the applicant [would] face an early death after a period of acute physical and mental suffering' [86] and, on this basis, opined that the applicant's deportation would constitute a violation of Article 3.[87] I also agree with the dissenting judges that the majority's approach amounts to applying a higher threshold of severity, although there is no basis for increasing the severity threshold 'where the harm stems from a naturally occurring illness and a lack of adequate resources in the receiving country'.[88]

The higher severity threshold applied in *N v United Kingdom* sought to further circumscribe the conventional obligations that could be placed on states in respect of 'aliens without a right to stay' in the field of health care.[89] In *N v United Kingdom*, the Grand Chamber stressed that: 'Advances in medical science, together with social and economic differences between countries, entail[ed] that the level of treatment available in the Contracting State and the country of origin may vary considerably.'[90] On this basis, the majority held that to find the respondent state in breach of Article 3 would have amounted to requiring states 'to alleviate such disparities through the provision of free and unlimited health care to all aliens without a right to stay within its jurisdiction'.[91] This, in the majority's opinion, would have imposed 'too great a burden on the Contracting States'.[92] I posit that the Grand Chamber's reasoning equates to a balancing exercise. The Court balanced the applicant's right not to be subjected to ill-treatment against concerns over health care resources and medical immigration. Yet the absolute character of Article 3 rights means that they cannot be balanced against societal interests, no matter how legitimate these may be:[93] '[T]he alleged motivation for the ill-treatment is irrelevant: the ends can never justify the means.'[94] Yet, in *N v United Kingdom*, the Grand Chamber engaged in a balancing exercise in respect of Article 3.[95] In the dissenting judges' words, the majority were concerned that finding the respondent states in violation of Article 3 'would open up the floodgates to medical immigration and make Europe vulnerable to becoming the "sick-bay" of the world'.[96] The 'floodgate argument' is commonly used by governments to justify curtailments in welfare provision for irregular migrants and other 'undesirable' categories of migrants.[97] Yet there is a dearth of supportive evidence.[98] Significantly, in *N v United Kingdom*, the

children as well as other family members lived in Zambia (n 62); and in *Ndangoya v Sweden*, the Court stressed that the applicant had maintained links with relatives who might be able to help (n 62).

85 *N v United Kingdom* (n 43), Joint Dissenting Opinion of Judges Tulkens, Bonello, and Spielmann Dissenting Opinion, para 25.

86 *N v United Kingdom* (n 43), Joint Dissenting Opinion of Judges Tulkens, Bonello, and Spielmann Dissenting Opinion, para 23.

87 *N v United Kingdom* (n 43), Joint Dissenting Opinion of Judges Tulkens, Bonello, and Spielmann Dissenting Opinion, para 24.

88 *N v United Kingdom* (n 43) para 5.

89 *N v United Kingdom* (n 43).

90 *N v United Kingdom* (n 43) para 44.

91 *N v United Kingdom* (n 43) para 44.

92 *N v United Kingdom* (n 43) para 44.

93 eg in expulsion cases, the Court has always refused to balance individuals' Art 3 rights against states' concerns over national security and the threat of terrorism (see eg *Chahal v United Kingdom* (n 51)).

94 Palmer, 'A Wrong Turning' (n 72) 450.

95 *N v United Kingdom* (n 43).

96 *N v United Kingdom* (n 43), Joint Dissenting Opinion of Judges Tulkens, Bonello, and Spielmann Dissenting Opinion, para 8.

97 Da Lomba, 'Immigration Status and Basic Social Human Rights' (n 4) 14–15.

98 eg in 2010, the UK government recommended that overseas visitors' entitlements to free NHS health care be curtailed with a view to, *inter alia*, curbing health tourism; yet, in the same policy

dissenting judges pointed out that 'when one compares the total number of requests received (and those refused and accepted) as against the number of HIV cases, the so-called "floodgate" argument is totally misconceived'.[99] Moreover, 'it [is] not unusual for applicants to have been unaware of their HIV status when they arrived [in the respondent state]; this was the case in *N v UK* itself'.[100] Furthermore, '[irregular migrants] are often reluctant to pursue legal protections and remedies to which they are entitled, even when their most basic rights are at stake', for fear of coming to the attention of the authorities.[101] In support of its balancing exercise, the Grand Chamber referred to its judgment in *Soering v United* and emphasised that: 'Inherent in the whole of the Convention is a search for a fair balance between the demands of the general interest of the community and the requirements of the protection of the individual's fundamental rights.'[102]

In *Soering v United Kingdom*, however, the Court also stressed that 'the object and purpose of the Convention as an instrument for the protection of individual human beings require that its provisions be interpreted and applied so as to make its safeguards practical and effective'.[103] Yet the Court's approach in *N v United Kingdom* undermines the level of protection that the ECHR may afford 'aliens without a right to stay' in the field of health care.

Citing *Airey v Ireland*, the majority sought to further justify its approach by stressing that, whilst the ECHR could apply to socio-economic conditions, it was 'essentially directed at the protection of civil and political rights'.[104] The dissenting judges pointed out that this characterization of the ECHR was based on an incomplete statement.[105] Indeed, in *Airey v Ireland*, the Court stressed that there could be 'no water-tight division' between social and economic rights and civil and political rights.[106] O'Cinneide observes that: 'The minority are correct that incorporating a "social dimension" into the interpretation of the Convention is essential to maintain a coherent and responsive human rights jurisprudence...'[107], but opines that 'the majority's views [in *N v United Kingdom*] reflect the trajectory adopted by much of

document, the UK government admitted that only '[a] small proportion of visitors engaged in health tourism' (Department of Health, England, (February 2010) 'Review of Access to the NHS by Foreign Nationals, Consultation Proposals', 17, available at <http://www.dh.gov.uk/prod_consum_dh/groups/dh_digitalassets/@dh/@en/documents/digitalasset/dh_113243.pdf> (accessed 30 October 2012)). Overseas visitors are people who are not ordinarily resident (National Health Service (Charges to Overseas Visitors) Regulations 1989, SI 1989/306, reg 1(2)). See also V. Bettinson and A. Jones, 'The Integration or Exclusion of Welfare Rights in the European Convention on Human Rights: The Removal of Foreign Nationals with HIV after *N v UK* (App 26565/05; Decision of the Grand Chamber of the European Court of Human Rights, 27 May 2008)' (2009) 31(1) *Journal of Social Welfare and Family Law* 83, 87.

99 *N v United Kingdom* (n 43), Joint Dissenting Opinion of Judges Tulkens, Bonello, and Spielmann Dissenting Opinion, para 8.

100 Bettinson and Jones, 'The Integration or Exclusion of Welfare Rights' (n 98) 87.

101 J.H. Carens, 'The Rights of Irregular Migrants' (2008) 22(2) *Ethics and International Affairs* 163, 167.

102 *N v United Kingdom* (n 43) para 44, referring to *Soering v United Kingdom* (App 14038/88), 7 July 1989, para 89. See H. Battjes, 'In Search of a Fair Balance: The Absolute Character of the Prohibition of Refoulement under Article 3 ECHR Reassessed' (2009) 22(3) *Leiden Journal of International Law* 583.

103 *Soering v United Kingdom* (n 102) para 87.

104 *N v United Kingdom* (n 43) para 44, citing *Airey v Ireland* (n 9) para 26.

105 *N v United Kingdom* (n 43), Joint Dissenting Opinion of Judges Tulkens, Bonello, and Spielmann Dissenting Opinion, para 6.

106 *Airey v Ireland* (n 9) para 26.

107 O'Cinneide, 'A Modest Proposal' (n 25) 586.

the Court's case law'.[108] However, while it is true that the Court has often sought to circumscribe the 'social dimension' of the Convention,[109] it has also been willing to broaden it. In *M.S.S. v Greece and Belgium*, the Grand Chamber held that Article 3 was capable of having extraterritorial effect when applied to socio-economic circumstances.[110]

Further unease with the Court's approach in *N v United Kingdom* was expressed in *Yoh-Ekale Mwanje v Belgium*.[111] In line with its judgment in *N v United Kingdom*, the ECtHR found that the deportation of a foreign national in the advanced stages of HIV to her country of origin without certainty of appropriate medical treatment there would not violate Article 3. However, in a partly concurring opinion, six out of seven judges opined that 'this extreme severity threshold—to be close to dying' could not be easily reconciled with the letter and spirit of Article 3, which guarantees an absolute right inherent in human integrity and dignity.[112] These judges called on the Court to 'one day' reconsider its case law on this issue.[113] They explained that their decision to follow the Grand Chamber's approach in *N v United Kingdom* was intended to preserve 'legal certainty'.[114] In my view, *Yoh-Ekale Mwanje v Belgium* is a missed opportunity to develop a 'humane but reasonable approach'.[115] Such an approach was adopted by the European Commission on Human Rights in *B.B. v France*.[116] In this case, the Commission opined that deporting a person who was in the advanced stages of AIDS to the DRC without certainty of treatment there would breach Article 3.[117] The Commission emphasized the 'fundamental importance of Article 3 in the Convention system'[118] and reiterated that 'the object and purpose of the Convention as an instrument for the protection of individual human beings require[d] that its provisions be interpreted and applied so as to make its safeguards practical and effective'.[119] Accordingly the Commission found that:

> ... exposing a person to a real and substantiated risk to his health which is so serious as to amount to a violation of Article 3 on account of other factors in the receiving country, such as the lack of medical care and services, as well as social and environmental factors, are capable of engaging the responsibility of the State intending to expel the person.[120]

108 O'Cinneide, 'A Modest Proposal' (n 25) 586.

109 eg in *Pentiacova v Moldova*, the Court stressed that states enjoyed a particularly wide margin of appreciation in respect of the allocation of limited national resources (n 19).

110 The Grand Chamber found that the conditions of detention and subsistence of an asylum-seeker expelled from Belgium to Greece under the Dublin Regulation had violated Art. 3 *M.S.S. v Greece and Belgium* (n 15) paras 214–234. See G. Clayton, 'Asylum Seekers in Europe: M.S.S. v Belgium and Greece' (2011) 11(4) *Human Rights Law Review* 758.

111 *Yoh-Ekale Mwanje v Belgium* (n 62).

112 *Yoh-Ekale Mwanje v Belgium* (n 62), Partly Concurring Opinion of Judges Tulkens, Jočienė, Popović, Karakaş, Raimondi, and Pinto De Albuquerque, para 6.

113 *Yoh-Ekale Mwanje v Belgium* (n 62), Partly Concurring Opinion of Judges Tulkens, Jočienė, Popović, Karakaş, Raimondi, and Pinto De Albuquerque, para 6.

114 *Yoh-Ekale Mwanje v Belgium* (n 62), Partly Concurring Opinion of Judges Tulkens, Jočienė, Popović, Karakaş, Raimondi, and Pinto De Albuquerque, para 6.

115 This expression was used by the dissenting judges in *N v United Kingdom* to describe the approach of the European Commission on Human Rights in *B.B. v France* (n 43), Joint Dissenting Opinion of Judges Tulkens, Bonello, and Spielmann Dissenting Opinion, paras 16–17; and *B.B. v France* (n 66).

116 *B.B. v France* (n 66).

117 *B.B. v France* (n 66) paras 53–55.

118 *B.B. v France* (n 66) para 53. See also *D v United Kingdom* (n 43) para 49.

119 *B.B. v France* (n 66) para 54.

120 The case was referred to the ECtHR but was struck out of the list following the French government's undertaking not to deport the applicant (n 67).

In my opinion, the Commission's approach is 'humane' in that it does not erode protection standards under Article 3. However, it is also 'reasonable' in that the high threshold of severity required to engage this provision means that health care obligations in respect of 'aliens without a right to stay' will only arise in exceptional circumstances.

I posit that, in addition to undermining the absolute nature of Article 3 and the integrated approach to interpretation, the Grand Chamber's reasoning in *N v United Kingdom* departs from the well-established principle that the right of states to regulate immigration is subject, *inter alia*, to their ECHR obligations.[121] I contend that the Grand Chamber's approach does precisely the opposite: it subjects states' conventional obligations to their 'right to control the entry, residence and expulsion of aliens' at the expense of ECHR protection standards. This in turn has important implications for the protection of irregular migrants in the field of health care, which are discussed in the next section.

4. Implications for the Protection of Irregular Migrants in the Field of Health Care

The ECtHR's approach in *N v United Kingdom* was developed in the context of applications lodged by foreign nationals subject to removal.[122] Thus one could assume that the Court's approach is to be confined to this group. In *N v United Kingdom*, however, the Court uses the term 'aliens without a right to stay',[123] which is much broader in scope and covers most irregular migrants.[124] Crucially, 'there will always be a number of irregular migrants present in Europe, no matter the policies adopted by Governments to prevent their entry or to return them speedily'.[125] These migrants fall within the personal scope of the ECHR on account of their presence in States Parties to the Convention.[126] Yet the Court's approach *in N v United Kingdom* carries the risk of lowering protection standards for these migrants in the area of health care. The Court has upheld the conventional rights of irregular migrants, but its approach in *N v United Kingdom* intimates that their immigration status could inhibit their protection in the area of health care.

In immigration cases, the ECtHR has constantly maintained states' right to regulate immigration[127] and stressed that the ECHR does not guarantee the right to enter and reside in a state which is not the state of nationality.[128] Consequently, in immigration cases, effective protection[129] is set against the exercise of the government immigration power. This balancing exercise, however, is subject to states' ECHR obligations.[130] Accordingly the Court has protected irregular migrants' ECHR rights,

121 *N v United Kingdom* (n 43). 122 *N v United Kingdom* (n 43).

123 *N v United Kingdom* (n 43) para 44.

124 One category of irregular migrants who might fall outside the scope of this term are migrants who have the right to remain, but are working without a permit or in a manner inconsistent with their permit.

125 Parliamentary Assembly of the Council of Europe, Human rights of irregular migrants, 4 May 2006, Doc 10924, Draft Resolution A(4).

126 ECHR, Art 1.

127 See eg *Chahal v United Kingdom* (n 51) para 73; and *Boultif v Switzerland* (n 51) para 46.

128 *Sisojeva and ors v Latvia* (App 60654), 16 June 2005, para 99. See also *Al-Nashif v Bulgaria* (App 50963/99), 20 June 2002, para 114.

129 eg in *Hirsi Jamaa and ors v Italy*, the Court describes the ECHR as 'a treaty for the effective protection of human rights' ((App 27765/09), 23 February 2012 (GC) para 171).

130 See eg *Chahal v United Kingdom* (n 51) para 73; and *Boultif v Switzerland* (n 51) para 46.

whether absolute or qualified. For example, in *Siliadin v France*, the Court found that the respondent state had breached Article 4 because it had failed to afford effective protection against forced labour to a minor who was unlawfully present in its territory.[131] In *Mubilanzila Mayeka and Kaniki Mitunga v Belgium*, the applicants, a mother and daughter, claimed that the child's detention and subsequent deportation to the DRC violated, *inter alia*, their Article 3 and Article 8 rights.[132] The ECtHR found Belgium in breach of both provisions.[133] The Court stressed that the absolute nature of Article 3 was the 'decisive factor' and that 'it [took] precedence over considerations relating to the applicant's status as an illegal immigrant'.[134] Thus, in this case, states' right to control immigration was not the Court's starting point, which departs from the Court's well-established approach in immigration cases. The circumstances in *Mubilanzila Mayeka and Kaniki Mitunga v Belgium*, however, were exceptional in that the irregular migrant was a 5-year-old child.[135]

In a series of Article 8 cases, the ECtHR found that the respondent states had failed to strike a fair balance between the applicants' Article 8 rights and their right to regulate immigration, and held that, in certain circumstances, the ECHR could give rise to an obligation to regularize an *illegal* stay.[136] In *Slivenko v Latvia*, the Court considered, *inter alia*, whether the applicants' removal from Latvia pursuant to the 1994 Treaty on the Withdrawal of Russian Troops breached their Article 8 rights.[137] The Court found that the applicants' removal violated their right to respect for private life as it could not be regarded as necessary in a democratic society.[138] In *Sisojeva and ors v Latvia*,[139] the Court found that the Latvian authorities' prolonged refusal to recognize the applicants' right to permanent residence on the basis of the 1994 Treaty violated Article 8, as the interference with their right to respect for private life could not be justified under Article 8(2).[140] The case, however, was referred to the Grand Chamber at the request of the respondent state. The Grand Chamber recognized that the applicants had endured a period of insecurity and legal uncertainty, but opined that they did not face 'any real and imminent risk of deportation' and observed that they had failed to make any attempt to regularize their status in spite of the authorities' recommendations.[141] On this basis, the Grand Chamber held that the options offered by the authorities to the applicants to regularize their immigration status had been 'adequate and sufficient' to remedy their Article 8 complaint.[142] The Grand Chamber accepted that the ECHR

[131] *Siliadin v France* (App 73316/01), 26 July 2005. The applicant had worked for years for a couple, without respite, against her will, and without being paid. The couple maintained her fear of being arrested and led her to believe that her status would be regularized.

[132] *Mubilanzila Mayeka and Kaniki Mitunga v Belgium* (App 13178/03), 12 October 2006, paras 64 and 88.

[133] *Mubilanzila Mayeka and Kaniki Mitunga v Belgium* (n 132) paras 66–71 and 75–91. In addition, the Court found that Art 5(1) and (4) had also been breached in respect of the daughter (*Hirsi Jamaa and ors v Italy* (n 129) paras 95–105 and 109–114).

[134] *Mubilanzila Mayeka and Kaniki Mitunga v Belgium* (n 132) para 55.

[135] *Mubilanzila Mayeka and Kaniki Mitunga v Belgium* (n 132). The child's mother had been granted refugee status in Canada where she resided.

[136] See D. Thym, 'Respect for Private and Family Life under Article 8 ECHR in Immigration Cases: A Human Right to Regularize Illegal Stay?' (2008) 57 (1) *International and Comparative Law Quarterly* 87.

[137] *Slivenko v Latvia* (App 48321/99), 9 October 2003 (GC).

[138] *Slivenko v Latvia* (n 137) paras 113–129. The Court found that the applicants' removal did not violate the applicants' right to respect for family life as removal did not break up the family.

[139] *Sisojeva and ors v Latvia* (n 128).

[140] *Sisojeva and ors v Latvia* (n 128) paras 99–111.

[141] *Sisojeva v Latvia* (App 60654/00), 15 January 2007 (GC) paras 100–101.

[142] *Sisojeva v Latvia* (n 141) para 102.

could beget an obligation to regularize an unlawful stay in particular circumstances, but at the same time sought to avoid a 'substantive overstretch of Article 8 ECHR which the earlier chamber judgment... might have entailed'.[143] In *Rodrigues Da Silva and Hoogkamer v The Netherlands*, the ECtHR considered a more 'typical' case of irregular immigration.[144] The Court had to determine whether the deportation of an irregular migrant breached this person's as well as her daughter's Article 8 rights. The mother shared the care of her daughter with her former partner, a Dutch national. The Court found that it was in the child's best interests to allow her mother to stay and stressed that 'the economic well-being of the State [did] not outweigh the applicants' rights under Article 8', regardless of her unlawful residence.[145] These immigration cases do not signify a shift in the ECtHR's approach to balancing effective protection against states' right to regulate immigration in that the latter remains the Court's starting point, save where children's ECHR rights are at stake.[146] What these cases show, however, is that irregular immigration status does not act as a bar to protection. Yet the ECtHR's approach in *N v United Kingdom* suggests that protection standards can be eroded in the field of health care on account of irregular migrants' immigration status.

The use of the term 'aliens without a right to stay' potentially broadens the scope of the ECtHR's approach in *N v United Kingdom*[147] in two ways. First, it makes it applicable to *all* migrants with the exception of children.[148] Second, it makes the Court's approach applicable to contexts where the state may be held responsible for the risk of harm. What set cases on the expulsion of the seriously ill apart from other Article 3 cases was not the applicants' immigration status, but the fact that the risk of ill-treatment did not emanate, directly or indirectly, from the state.[149] However, not all irregular migrants are subject to removal orders and many live clandestinely in Contracting States. These migrants can avail themselves of the protection of the ECHR with the consequence that states could be held responsible for harm caused by inadequate health care provision for irregular migrants present in their territory. The Grand Chamber's use of the term 'aliens without a right to stay',[150] however, intimates that protection standards for irregular migrants in the field of health care could be lowered in contexts where the state is responsible.

In stark contrast with the ECtHR, the European Committee of Social Rights (ECSR) has brought irregular migrants within the protection of the Revised European Social Charter, notwithstanding its more limited personal scope. Indeed the Appendix (point 1) to the Charter provides that rights are conferred on 'foreigners only in so far as they are nationals of other Parties lawfully resident or working regularly within the territory of the Party concerned'.[151] In *FIDH v France*, however, the Committee

143 Thym, 'Respect for Private and Family Life' (n 136) 98.

144 *Rodrigues Da Silva and Hoogkamer v The Netherlands* (App 50435/99), 31 January 2006.

145 *Rodrigues Da Silva and Hoogkamer v The Netherlands* (n 144) para 44.

146 *Mubilanzila Mayeka and Kaniki Mitunga v Belgium* (n 132); and *Rodrigues Da Silva and Hoogkamer v The Netherlands* (n 144).

147 *N v United Kingdom* (n 43).

148 The Court has prioritized effective protection over immigration status considerations in cases involving migrant children in an irregular situation (*Mubilanzila Mayeka and Kaniki Mitunga v Belgium* (n 132); and *Rodrigues Da Silva and Hoogkamer v The Netherlands* (n 144)). It is debatable whether the term 'aliens without a right to stay' could apply to migrants who work without a permit or in a manner inconsistent with their immigration status.

149 *D v United Kingdom* (n 43).

150 *N v United Kingdom* (n 43).

151 1996 Revised European Social Charter, Appendix, point 1. The European Social Charter has the same personal scope (1961 European Social Charter, Appendix, point 1).

opined that the condition relating to lawful residence was only relevant to equal treatment with nationals.[152] The Committee emphasized that the Charter was a human rights instrument and as such embraced universal values such as dignity and solidarity.[153] Referring to the Vienna Declaration of 1993, the Committee recalled that 'all human rights are universal, indivisible, interdependent and interrelated'.[154] On this basis, the Committee held that 'the Charter must be interpreted so as to give life and meaning to fundamental social rights' and that restrictions on rights must consequently 'be read restrictively'.[155] The Committee found that reforms to health care provision for irregular migrants in France breached Article 17, which enshrines the right of children and young persons to social, legal, and economic protection, by depriving the children of irregular migrants of immediate access to health care save in emergency cases.[156] The Committee emphasized that health care was a prerequisite for the preservation of human dignity.[157] Thus its reasoning sought to affirm the universality and fundamental character of respect for human dignity.[158] Significantly, the Committee did not refer to states' right to control immigration. This, however, should not be interpreted as a challenge to the government immigration power, but should be construed as an affirmation of humanity as a source of basic social rights. The decision in *FIDH v France*, however, was not unanimous. Dissenting members, whilst they deplored irregular migrants' predicament, opined that their inclusion in the personal scope of the Charter went against the letter of the Appendix.[159] In this respect, the Parliamentary Assembly of the Council of Europe observed that: 'The reasoning underlying the Committee's decision [did] not completely neutralise the exclusion of foreign nationals provisions of the Appendix'.[160] The Assembly stressed that these provisions were only overridden 'in one particular circumstance, namely when their

[152] *International Federation of Human Rights Leagues (FIDH) v France*, 7 October 2004, Collective complaint No 14/2003, paras 26–32.

[153] *FIDH v France* (n 152) para 27.

[154] *FIDH v France* (n 152), referring to the Vienna Declaration and Programme of Action, World Conference on Human Rights, Vienna, 14–25 June 1993, UN Doc A/CONF.157/23, para 5.

[155] *FIDH v France* (n 152) para 29.

[156] *FIDH v France* (n 152) paras 33–34. Barriers on children's and adolescents' access to health care were subsequently lifted by the French government (Circulaire DHOS/DSS/DGAS, No 2005-141 of 16 March 2005 relative à la prise en charge des soins urgents délivrés à des étrangers résidant en France de manière irrégulière et non bénéficiaires de l'aide médicale de l'Etat, Bulletin officiel du ministère chargé des affaires sociales n° 2005/4, 170–2). The Committee, however, found that France had not breached Art 13 because irregular migrants were not deprived of all entitlement to medical assistance (*FIDH v France* (n 152) paras 35–37). Two Committee members found that France had also violated Article 13 (n 152), Dissenting Opinion of Mr Tekin Akillioğlu and Dissenting Opinion M Jean-Michel Belorgey).

[157] *FIDH v France* (n 152) para 31.

[158] The reasoning of the ECSR is resonant with the approach of the German Federal Constitutional Court in its judgment of 18 July 2012 (1 BvL 10/10, 1 BvL 2/11). The Constitutional Court held that cash benefits paid to asylum seekers under the Asylum Seekers Benefits Act to secure their existence were unconstitutional. The Court ruled that the provisions governing basic cash benefits in the Act were incompatible with the fundamental right to a minimum existence, protected as human dignity in Art 1(1) in conjunction with Art 20(1) of the Basic Law. The Committee's reasoning is also reminiscent of the well-established approach of the Inter-American Court of Human Rights. See eg *Juridical Condition and Rights of the Undocumented Migrants*, Advisory Opinion OC-18, Inter-American Court of Human Rights Series A No 18 (17 September 2003).

[159] *FIDH v France* (n 152), Dissenting Opinion of Mr Stein Evju joined by Mrs Polonca Koncar and Mr Lucien François and Dissenting Opinion of Mr Rolf Birk.

[160] J.F. Akandji-Kombe, 'Memorandum on the European Social Charter and Protection of Illegal Immigrants', Committee on Migration, Refugees and Population, AS/Mig/Inf (2005) 17, 28 September 2005, 9.

application could have consequences that are incompatible with human dignity'.[161] In line with its approach in *FIDH v France*, the Committee found that The Netherlands' denial of access to adequate housing to children unlawfully present in its territory breached Articles 31(2) and 17 of the Revised European Social Charter.[162] In this case, the Committee explicitly affirmed the government immigration power, but this did not cause the Committee to retreat from its approach in *FIDH v France*.[163] In contrast with the ECtHR's approach, the Committee's reasoning reconciles the exercise of the government immigration power with states' human rights obligations, thereby upholding humanity as a source of basic social rights for irregular migrants.

5. Conclusion

The ECHR bestows rights on irregular migrants who are within the jurisdiction of Contracting States. The Convention does not enshrine the right to health care, but can nonetheless give rise to limited health care obligations. Thus the ECHR can contribute to protecting irregular migrants in the field of health care. Yet rather than bringing irregular migrants within the protection of the Convention in line with ECHR provisions and principles, the ECtHR's approach in *N v United* Kingdom undermines protection for this group in the area of health care. This, however, is not the only consequence of the Court's approach. In my view, the latter has broader and deeper implications.

I posit that the significance that the ECtHR attaches to irregular migrants' immigration status gives credence to states' objections to health care provision and, more broadly, to social rights for irregular migrants.[164] I do not dispute that health care provision for irregular migrants raises complex issues pertaining to resource allocation and immigration; nor do I suggest that these considerations can have no bearing on the range of health care obligations the ECHR may place on states. What I take issue with, however, is the ECtHR's failure to achieve a fair balance between effective protection and states' right to regulate immigration. In my opinion, in addition to constraining protection for irregular migrants in the social sphere, the Court's approach also has far-reaching consequences for humanity as a source of basic social rights. In stark contrast with the ECSR, the ECtHR does not put respect for human dignity at the heart of its reasoning and makes migrants' protection in the field of health care contingent on their immigration status. I contend that the Court's approach does not sit well with the universal premise of international human rights law and undermines humanity as a source of basic social rights for irregular migrants.

161 Akandji-Kombe, 'Memorandum on the European Social Charter' (n 160) 9. The Assembly's comment is not quite in line with the Committee's reasoning in that the Committee construed the inclusion of irregular migrants as a matter of interpretation (*FIDH v France* (n 152) paras 26–29).

162 *Defence for Children International (DCI) v The Netherlands*, 20 October 2009, Collective complaint No 47/2008. The Revised Social Charter, Art 31(2) provides that: 'With a view to ensuring the effective exercise of the right to housing, the Parties undertake to take measures designed... to prevent and reduce homelessness with a view to its gradual elimination.'

163 *FIDH v France* (n 152) paras 33–34.

164 See S. Da Lomba, 'Irregular Migrants and the Human Right to Health Care: A Case-Study of Health-Care Provision for Irregular Migrants in France and the UK' (2011) 7(3) *International Journal of Law in Context* 379.

9

Rights-based Approaches to HIV in the Middle East and North Africa Region

*David Patterson, Shereen El Feki, and Khadija Moalla**

There are about 300,000 people living with HIV in the Middle East and North Africa (MENA) region.[1] Although most countries have low overall HIV prevalence (0.2 per cent or less of the general population is living with HIV), there are significant epidemics in all countries, concentrated in so-called 'key affected populations'.[2] These populations include men who have sex with men, injecting drug users, and sex workers; groups which are the least likely to have their rights respected because these behaviours are generally illegal. This makes them more vulnerable to HIV infection, and less likely to seek testing for HIV, or then treatment which can both limit the progress to AIDS *and* reduce the risk of onward HIV transmission. Because of the long latency period of HIV infection, during which people can be symptom-free for many years, there are also strong public health imperatives for addressing HIV-related discrimination, and encouraging people to know their status and seek treatment if appropriate.

Approximately 40 per cent of people with HIV in the region are female. Women are also directly affected—as injecting drug users or sex workers—or as the sexual partners of clients, of injecting drug users, or men who have sex with men. In some countries the majority of women living with HIV have been infected by their husbands.[3] Although still at the early stages, the emerging HIV/AIDS epidemic in MENA already bears distinctly female features.

The MENA region is one of only two where new infections, and AIDS-related deaths, continue to rise. Although the MENA region is not the poorest region of the world, it has the lowest coverage of treatment for people living with HIV—a regional average of 15 per cent.[4] The lack of access to consistent, quality treatment for HIV infection is another disincentive to HIV testing.

* An early version of the paper which forms the basis of this chapter was presented in November 2011 at the conference, 'Family, the Millennium Development Goals and HIV in the Middle East Region: Linkages, Challenges and Opportunities', with the financial support of the Qatar Foundation and UNAIDS. Research assistance was provided by Mr Ahmed Shehata, IDLO Legal Consultant. The views expressed in this article are the views of the authors and do not necessarily reflect the views or policies of IDLO or its Member Parties.

1 'UNAIDS Report on the Global AIDS Epidemic' (UNAIDS, 2012); 'Middle East and North Africa Regional Report on HIV/AIDS 2011' (UNAIDS, 2011). UNAIDS defines the MENA region as: Algeria, Bahrain, Djibouti, Egypt, Iran, Iraq, Jordan, Kuwait, Lebanon, Libya, Morocco, Oman, Occupied Palestinian Territories, Qatar, Saudi Arabia, Somalia, South Sudan, Sudan, Syria, Tunisia, United Arab Emirates, and Yemen.

2 There are generalized epidemics, where the predominant mode of transmission is heterosexual sexual intercourse, in Djibouti, Somalia, and South Sudan. In South Sudan and parts of Djibouti and Somalia, women account for more than half of reported cases of HIV. 'Standing Up Speaking Out: Women and HIV in the Middle East and North Africa' (UNAIDS, 2012).

3 'Standing Up Speaking Out' (n 2).

4 'UNAIDS Report on the Global AIDS Epidemic' (n 1) 51.

It is also a region of great economic, social, religious, cultural—and legal—diversity. MENA contains least developed countries (such as South Sudan) and the high-income countries of the Arabian Gulf. It is religiously diverse, with Islam predominating. Male circumcision, which is protective against HIV infection, is a common cultural practice. All countries are socially conservative. Female genital mutilation Type III, which can facilitate HIV transmission to women and girls, exists in Sudan, Djibouti, and Somalia. Literacy levels are much lower among women than men in some countries, which also increases women's vulnerability to HIV infection, as do discriminatory laws and practices regarding women's political, economic, and social rights. Gender-based violence is a fact of life for millions of women across the region, also heightening their risk of HIV.[5] Many countries are struggling economically, and unemployment and underemployment are high, particularly among the young. Access to non-state media including through satellite TV is widespread, even where this is illegal, and also through social networking sites, such as Facebook.

The political upheaval in the MENA region started in Tunisia in 2011 and has since spread to Egypt, Yemen, Bahrain, Libya, and Syria. Many people had hoped these changes would lead to more economic opportunities for the poor, less corruption, and greater respect for human rights. However, the election of conservative religious governments in Egypt and Tunisia put into question the status of women and minorities that existed in these countries before their respective revolutions. Both countries saw the conservative Muslim brotherhood in Egypt and Al-Nahdha in Tunisia along with the Salafist religious movement emboldened under the governments elected in 2011.

In 2013 the Morsi government in Egypt was ousted through a military intervention following mass demonstrations. The succeeding crackdown on press freedom and freedom of assembly, in the name of combatting terrorism, swept up not only the Muslim Brotherhood, but also secular critics of the interim military government, and did little to reassure Egyptians that the principles of the pro-democratic uprising of 2011 would be realized in the foreseeable future. In Tunisia, in 2014, Al-Nahdha ceded power to an interim government, pending new elections. On 27 January 2014, a new Constitution was adopted by the vast majority of the country's National Constituent Assembly. The new Constitution has been welcomed as a landmark document in the region, not only for its progressive approach to religion and the State, but also its strong commitment to human rights and the promotion of gender equality, marking this a historic moment for Tunisia.

The future can go either way. Following the Arab Spring revolutions, new attitudes towards women and key affected populations may emerge. These may be based on human rights and public health principles and inspired by the democratic aspirations of the revolution, or they may reflect the conservative attitudes of populist Islamic fundamentalists.

This chapter will briefly present the human rights-based approach to HIV, and then explore relevant regional and national initiatives, including the provision of legal services to people with HIV and key affected populations. Promising initiatives from six countries in the region are noted, and then conclusions and recommendations for continuing rights-based responses to HIV in the region.

[5] 'HIV and the Law: Risks, Rights & Health' (Global Commission on HIV and the Law, 2012).

1. Human Rights-Based Approaches to HIV, the Enabling Legal Environment, and HIV-Related Legal Services

It is over half a century since the UN General Assembly adopted the International Covenant on Economic, Social and Cultural Rights (ICESCR), which recognizes the right of everyone to 'the enjoyment of the highest attainable standard of physical and mental health'.[6] The importance of protecting and promoting human rights in the context of HIV has been endorsed by the global community at the highest level—in resolutions adopted unanimously by the United Nations General Assembly—and is reflected in the technical guidance provided by the Joint United Nations Programme on HIV/AIDS (UNAIDS), the UN Development Programme (UNDP), the International Development Law Organization (IDLO), and other international organizations.[7] Every country in the MENA region has ratified most of the international human rights treaties which are relevant to the response to HIV in those countries (albeit with reservations in some cases). Every country in the MENA region has endorsed the United Nations General Assembly resolutions on HIV, which include multiple and specific references to the importance of protecting the rights of people living with HIV and key affected populations, including by law.[8]

This is often referred to as the 'enabling legal environment' for the response to HIV. The legal environment includes laws, of course, and also the application of these laws: the practices of the police, the legal profession, and the courts. For example, unless the police cooperate in the operation of needle and syringe distribution programmes for drug users to prevent needle-sharing, these programmes will be largely ineffective. In other words, the legal framework—laws, government policies, and the practices of state actors—should enable (not undermine) the national response to HIV.

Although appropriate laws and policies are important, an often overlooked component of an enabling legal environment is quality, affordable, and accessible legal services. HIV-related legal services are 'legal services for people living with HIV, people affected by HIV and key populations that directly relate to legal issues that affect their vulnerability to HIV and/or increase the impact of HIV in their lives'.[9]

There is now substantial international experience in designing and delivering HIV-related legal services. The following section explores why legal services are recognized as

6 ICESCR, Art 12.1 The Convention has 160 State Parties, including many countries in the Middle East North Africa region. A list of countries which have ratified or otherwise agreed to be bound by the ICESCR and other human rights treaties is available at <https://treaties.un.org> (accessed 20 April 2013).

7 See eg International Guidelines on HIV/AIDS and Human Rights (UNAIDS, OHCHR, 2006). The Guidelines were first published in 1998, and have since been updated. Available at <http://data.unaids.org/Publications/IRC-pub07/jc1252-internguidelines_en.pdf> (accessed 20 April 2013). See also Key Programmes to Reduce Stigma and Discrimination and Increase Access to Justice in National HIV Responses (UNAIDS, 2012) Guidance Note, available at <http://www.unaids.org/en/media/unaids/contentassets/documents/document/2012/Key_Human_Rights_Programmes_en_May2012.pdf> (accessed 6 February 2014).

8 United Nations General Assembly (UNGA) Declaration of Commitment on HIV/AIDS 2001; UNGA Political Declaration on HIV/AIDS 2006; UNGA Political Declaration on HIV/AIDS 2011. Periodic country reports on the implementation of the commitments in these resolutions can be found at <http://www.unaids.org/en/dataanalysis/knowyourresponse/countryprogressreports/2012countries/> (accessed 6 February 2014).

9 'Toolkit: Scaling Up HIV-related Legal Services' (IDLO, UNAIDS, UNDP, 2009), available in Arabic, Chinese, English, French, Russian and Spanish at <http://www.idlo.int/healthlaw> (accessed 6 February 2014).

a central component of the national response to HIV, and then considers the experience of the MENA region.[10]

1.1 Legal services providing access to justice

Legal services are often essential to access justice systems. Informing people of their rights, while failing to provide ways to realize them can be demoralizing and counter-productive. Many programs include human rights education for people living with HIV and key affected populations. We also need to offer concrete, practical, and affordable ways to address the human rights abuses faced by people living with and vulnerable to HIV.

In the MENA region, today, there is a strong focus on civil and political rights. Following the revolutions first in Tunisia, then in Egypt, Yemen, and Libya, many have noted the high expectations among a large section of the population that civil and political rights, and also economic, social, and cultural rights, will be more widely respected. This is particularly true of younger and more educated people who have access to international and social media. However, others have cautioned that aspirations for greater political freedoms do not necessarily equate with liberal social or cultural values.[11] The Member States of the United Nations have often repeated that all human rights are universal, indivisible and interdependent and interrelated.[12] However it makes little sense to inform people living with HIV and key affected populations that they have the 'right to health' under international law, without also providing the means to claim that right through enacting national laws and other national processes, such as court action.

1.2 Law reform

Law reform to protect people living with and affected by HIV and AIDS is often a long-term goal, particularly in conservative cultural and religious contexts, while legal services can often improve peoples' lives right now. Even in a hostile legal environment, lawyers can get better results for clients than if they are left to deal with employers, landlords, health authorities, and the justice sector on their own. Lawyers can intervene with police and other public authorities to achieve changes in the ways laws are implemented, such as guidelines on the discretion to prosecute.

This is certainly true in the MENA region, where the criminal law still penalizes sex between men, sex work, and drug use in many (but not all) countries in the region. In a 2009 review of legal frameworks and human rights in relation to sexual diversity, out of fourteen states surveyed in the MENA region, six were highly repressive and seven were moderately repressive. Only one was regarded as neutral.[13]

10 See 'Ten Reasons why legal services must be central to a rights-based response to HIV' (two-page brochure) translated into Arabic, Chinese, English, French, Spanish, and Russian, available at <http://www.idlo.int/healthlaw> (accessed 6 February 2014). The author, David Patterson, is a member of the UNAIDS working group on programming (a sub-committee of the UNAIDS Reference Group on HIV/AIDS and Human Rights), which reviewed an early draft of the Guidance Note on Key Programmes to Reduce Stigma and Discrimination and Increase Access to Justice in National HIV Responses (see n 7). 'Legal services' is the second key programme addressed in the Guidance Note.

11 S. El Feki, *Sex and the Citadel: Intimate Life in a Changing Arab World* (Pantheon, 2013).

12 World Conference on Human Rights, 1993, Vienna Declaration and Programme of Action, Art 5.

13 C. Caceres et al, 'Review of Legal Frameworks and the Situation of Human Rights related to Sexual Diversity in Low and Middle Income Countries' (UNAIDS, 2009), available at <http://data.

A 2011 study on law and homosexuality in the Arab region noted that legislation was often vague, moralistic in tone, and subject to wide interpretation. The study cites a 2005 incident in Dubai in which men wearing women's clothing were arrested at an inn and subsequently convicted of 'homosexuality', even though there was no evidence given of sexual activity at the time of the arrest and no law banning men from wearing women's clothes.[14] Lawyers may also face harassment for defending the rights of vulnerable populations, and it can be difficult to find lawyers with the skills and courage to take on such cases.

In many countries in the region, the law is unclear or misunderstood, and police harass and detain people unjustly. In Egypt, for example, in one study more than 70 per cent of sex workers had been arrested at some point, and 12 per cent reported sexual abuse at police stations during arrest.[15] Whatever the law, the outcome is almost certainly better for the client if he or she has competent legal representation. For a drug user in Lebanon, for example, this could include referral to rehabilitation services rather than imprisonment. A 2011 study of legislation relating to drug abuse in the Arab region noted that judges have discretion in most Arab countries to order treatment instead of punishment.[16] However, judges need guidance on such sentencing options, particularly when the relevant laws may have been recently reformed. In Iran, for example, in 2005 harm reduction approaches to drug use became official policy, and courts and judicial authorities were instructed by the head of the judiciary to support methadone and needle exchange.[17]

In every jurisdiction, police exercise discretion in the decision to arrest and lay charges. In Morocco, as noted later, police training on the public health implications of their work has been undertaken. Such guidelines have been adopted in other jurisdictions to clarify the role of the police in promoting public health.[18]

1.3 Taking legal action

Taking legal action can empower individuals by affirming their right to recognition everywhere as a person before the law. Whatever the outcome, legal support empowers individuals and groups to understand the legal context in which they live. Legal

unaids.org/pub/Report/2009/20091215_legalframeworks_sexualdiversity_en.pdf> (accessed 6 February 2014).

14 W. Ferchichi, 'Law and Homosexuality: Survey and Analysis of Legislation Across the Arab World' (2011), Working Paper prepared for the Middle East and North Africa Consultation of the Global Commission on HIV and the Law, 27–29 July 2011, available at <http://www.hivlawcommission.org/index.php/working-papers> (accessed 6 February 2014).

15 I. Kabbash, I. Abdul-Rahman, and Y. Shehata, 'Looking Beyond Legality: Understanding the Context of Female Sex Workers in Greater Cairo, Egypt' (2013) 19(1) *Eastern Mediterranean Health Journal* 24.

16 F. Al-Shazly, (2011), 'How to Best Reach HIV-Vulnerable Groups in Arab States: Drug Abuse in International Laws and Arabic Legislations' (2011), Working Paper prepared for the Middle East and North Africa Regional Consultation of the Global Commission on HIV and the Law, 27–29 July 2011, available at <http://www.hivlawcommission.org/index.php/working-papers> (accessed 6 February 2014).

17 T. Rosenberg, 'An Enlightened Exchange in Iran', *New York Times*, 29 November 2010, available at <http://opinionator.blogs.nytimes.com/2010/11/29/an-enlightened-exchange-in-iran/> (accessed 20 April 2013).

18 See eg Crown Prosecution Service (UK), 'Drug Offences, incorporating the Charging Standard', available at <http://www.cps.gov.uk/legal/d_to_g/drug_offences/> updated September 2010 (accessed 22 January 2012).

empowerment approaches also affirm dignity and self-esteem, which have other positive health and social benefits.

This is an area which deserves much more research. The very fact of being a client in consultation with a lawyer, ie as a rights-holder seeking to claim his or her rights, can be empowering, irrespective of the final result of the legal complaint:

> For a person experiencing HIV-related stigma and discrimination, a legal empowerment approach affirms and restores his or her humanity and citizenship, and supports psychological wellbeing, essential dimensions to overall welfare and health. It describes a truly holistic approach to HIV.[19]

In Egypt, HIV infection in men is often equated with homosexuality, and men identified as homosexual have faced involuntary HIV testing and forced anal examinations. Men who are HIV positive have been convicted of the criminal offence under Egyptian law of 'habitual debauchery', and received prison sentences of from one to three years.[20]

Yet being HIV positive is not illegal in any MENA country, nor is sexual attraction to the people of the same sex, being a drug user, or a sex worker. Rather, the law penalizes sexual activity between people of the same sex, selling sex, and drug use.[21] Further, the police must follow prescribed processes when arresting and detaining anybody. Under the Mubarak regime in Egypt, police often acted outside the law and with impunity. For example, in Egypt men identified as homosexual were arrested only because of how they looked or acted, in the absence of any ground in Egyptian criminal law. After the revolution many hoped these practices would change, though recent reports suggest that widespread police abuse continues.[22]

1.4 Legal services can also help outside courts

Lawyers and paralegals can use a range of legal and non-legal ways to solve problems, including by working with traditional legal systems and community leaders. Formal justice systems can be slow, expensive, and unpredictable. Lawyers and paralegals can use alternative dispute resolution mechanisms and facilitate access to traditional legal structures, such as mediation by community leaders.

Since 2004, UNDP has supported a dialogue in twenty Arab states with religious leaders, which included a discussion of the application of *shari'a* to HIV and AIDS. Religious leaders are a key influence in the Arab region, shaping social norms

[19] D. Stephens and M. Urbano, 'HIV and Legal Empowerment' in S. Golub, *Legal Empowerment: Practitioners' Perspectives* (Rome: IDLO, 2010) 287, available at <http://www.idlo.int> (accessed 6 February 2014).

[20] 'Combating HIV/AIDS Related Stigma in Egypt: Situation Analysis and Advocacy Recommendations' (Egyptian Initiative for Personal Rights, Cairo, undated) 16, available at <http://eipr.org/sites/default/files/reports/pdf/stigma_report_en.pdf> (accessed 6 February 2014). See also 'Document—Egypt: HIV arrests: Policing in Ignorance and Fear: Doctors failing in their Medical Responsibility' (Amnesty International, May 2008), available at <http://www.amnesty.org/en/library/asset/MDE12/009/2008/en/5d2cc203-362f-11dd-9db5-cb00b5aed8dc/mde120092008eng.html> (accessed 6 February 2014).

[21] N. Al-Riahi, 'Prostitution in the Arab World: A Legal Study of Arab Legislation' (2011), Working Paper prepared for the Middle East and North Africa Regional Consultation of the Global Commission on HIV and the Law, 27–29 July 2011; Ferchichi, 'Law and Homosexuality' (n 14).

[22] 'State Crimes Remained Unpunished: the Interior Ministry is Above the Law and the Public Prosecution is Missing in Action' (EIPR, 2013).

and values and influencing public attitudes and national policies related to HIV and AIDS.

Mobilizing religious leaders to address stigma, taboos, and condemnation was thought to be an impossible task; however, since 2004 there has been an evident change in religious discourse related to HIV and AIDS in the region, moving from punitive pronouncements to compassionate human rights-based messaging, supported by scripture from the Koran and the Bible. This was reflected in the 2004 'Cairo Declaration of Religious Leaders in the Arab States in Response to the HIV/AIDS Epidemic' (Cairo Declaration), which was written and signed by eighty prominent Christian and Muslim religious leaders from nineteen Arab countries.[23] In Yemen, advocates for a progressive law on HIV included religious leaders, in partnership with Yemeni people living with HIV, parliamentarians and nongovernmental organizations (NGOs). The law was enacted by the Yemeni Parliament in September 2009.

Through this initiative, religious leaders from across the Arab region had a unique opportunity to work with key affected populations. As Dr Khadija Moalla, who initiated the religious leaders' dialogue in the region, has since noted:

> The imams and priests were more receptive to dealing with the issue of homosexuality when it was presented in the context of HIV prevention, framing it as a public health issue and a way of protecting those we care about . . . Similarly, we found it helpful to approach the issue of LGBT [lesbian, gay, bisexual, transgender] rights through the notion of privacy. In both Christianity and Islam the right to privacy is respected. Thus, it was argued that the lifestyle practiced by two adults, in a private sphere, and with their consent, is their personal life and this should be respected.[24]

1.5 Courts can provide an open, structured forum to resolve conflict

Legal action requires all parties to state their case in an open, structured forum. Many issues, such as discrimination in employment and health care, are complex. Employers (for example restaurants, airlines) complain about customer preference and safety. Medical personnel complain they lack basic resources, such as latex gloves and sterilization equipment to prevent workplace infection. Legal action permits an open examination of these claims, and can allow for public policy and public health evidence as well.

In the MENA region, as in other regions, there are still many misconceptions about HIV, particularly as they relate to the means of HIV transmission. The courts, in many countries, have yet to affirm unequivocally that HIV is not transmitted through casual contact, and therefore there can be no public health reason to limit the participation of people living with HIV in all aspects of public life. In the absence of clear government guidance on this issue, legal action can force employers to recognize the scientific evidence on HIV transmission. Discrimination in access to health services is of concern, as portrayed in the excellent Egyptian film, *Asmaa*, about a woman living with HIV.[25]

[23] 'Compassion and AIDS in the Arab World' *Al-Ahram Weekly Online*, 20–26 October 2005, available at <http://weekly.ahram.org.eg/2005/765/sc9.htm> (accessed 6 February 2014). Related publications, including a review of religious texts in the context of HIV, are available from the UNDP Regional Office in Cairo. See <http://arabstates.undp.org/content/rbas/en/home/ourwork/hiv_aids/overview.html> (accessed 6 February 2014).

[24] K. Moalla, 'Transformational Leadership in the Arab Region' (2012) 16 *Kosmos* 6.

[25] A. Morrow and S. Nabih, 'Combating HIV/AIDS Related Stigma in Egypt: Situation Analysis and Advocacy Recommendations', Egyptian Anti-Stigma Forum, Cairo (2012).

As such legal cases are often reported in the media, legal action can have a wider positive social impact.

1.6 Data on complaints and outcomes can support policy reform

Law and policy reform must be based on local realities as well as international law and best practice. Legal services can collect data on complaints and outcomes and provide these to policy-makers, thus assisting the reform process.

However, HIV-related legal services in the MENA region, where they exist, are often ad hoc, inadequate, and poorly documented. The lawyers involved rarely keep comprehensive records of complaints and outcomes, nor do they share them routinely to inform law and policy reform. Yet without these data, governments are unlikely to adopt measures which reflect local realities. It is essential that this 'policy loop' be closed—ie that governments and policy-makers are informed of the impact of current laws and policies as evidenced by legal complaints and outcomes. This includes both quantitative and qualitative data.

1.7 Working within the legal system can strengthen the rule of law

Involving the legal profession and the courts in resolving HIV-related issues and disputes also strengthens the rule of law and good governance. In contexts where the rule of law is weak, public protest may be the only way to bring crucial issues to the attention of governments. Strengthening the ability of the legal profession and the courts to deliver sound decisions on HIV-related issues also contributes to social harmony.

The rule of law is perceived to be weak in many countries in the MENA region. Yet the rule of law was weak in other countries, such as South Africa, which have since transitioned to more robust legal environments. South African courts have delivered HIV-related decisions based on law and science which have had an enormous impact on the response to HIV in that country, and sometimes around the world. These decisions have in turn strengthened the independence and credibility of South African courts.[26] This opportunity also exists in the MENA region, through strengthening the capacity and independence of the legal profession and the courts.

1.8 Legal services can be delivered in multiple ways

Legal services can be delivered in multiple ways, including by engaging law students and peer counsellors, and by using paralegals and other community educators for referral. Different models for providing HIV-related legal services include:

(1) stand-alone HIV-specific legal services;

(2) HIV legal services integrated into the government's legal aid agency;

(3) HIV legal services integrated into an HIV organization or harm reduction organization;

[26] Issues include access to programs to prevent mother to child transmission, access to medicines for HIV infection, and discrimination against people with HIV in employment in the airline and other industries. See 'Courting Rights: Case Studies in Litigating the Human Rights of People Living with HIV' (UNAIDS and Canadian HIV/AIDS Legal Network, 2006), available at <http://data.unaids.org/pub/Report/2006/jc1189-courtingrights_en.pdf> (accessed 6 February 2014).

(4) HIV legal services provided through community outreach;
(5) HIV legal services integrated into an organization with a broader human rights focus;
(6) HIV legal services provided by private sector lawyers on a *pro bono* basis;
(7) HIV legal services provided by private lawyers on retainer to community-based organizations; or
(8) HIV legal services provided by a university law school.[27]

In the MENA region, legal services have often been provided by a lawyer working with an AIDS service organization or by a private sector lawyer on a *pro bono* or fee for service basis. The role of paralegals and peer educators as outreach workers is particularly important to reach key affected populations. To be effective, these outreach workers must be protected from police harassment. Education, training, and improved police discipline are urgently needed.

1.9 HIV-related legal services can also be mainstreamed

The integration of HIV-related legal issues into existing access to justice and legal aid programs provides opportunities to mainstream the response to HIV for long-term sustainability.

Although HIV-specific legal clinics may be appropriate in some contexts, scale-up can most often be achieved through the integration of HIV concerns into mainstream legal aid programs. Legal aid programs may be government run, or supported by the legal profession or other sources. Government legal aid services are rare in the MENA region.[28]

1.10 Strategic litigation can lead to policy reform

Strategic litigation involving legal challenges combined with social mobilization can achieve policy reform and educate communities in ways which can have a huge impact nationally, and even globally.

The revolution in drug pricing for developing countries since 2000 was largely driven by strategic litigation in South Africa. Not only have prices for anti-retroviral therapies dropped globally, but pricing for medications for other diseases of public health significance in developing countries is now under examination. This is a huge contribution to global health and development.

Strategic litigation is legal action designed to achieve a wider social good, beyond the satisfactory resolution of the legal issue facing the individual complainant(s). However, people with HIV and members of key affected populations are often afraid to engage in court action that will reveal their identity to their families and communities. Therefore, mechanisms for closed proceedings, which ban publication of the names of the complainants, must be clarified, and courts must be encouraged to grant such orders.

27 'Toolkit: Scaling Up HIV-related Legal Services' (n 9).

28 In 2007, the Arab Council for Judicial and Legal Studies (ALCJS), which is based in Amman, hosted a policy dialogue entitled 'Access to Justice: Legal Aid and its Future in the Arab World'. The ALCJS has also published 'White Paper on Access to Justice and Legal Aid in the Arab World', available at <http://acjls.org/?page_id=337&lang=en> (accessed 6 February 2014). The paper does not mention HIV or AIDS, however.

Social mobilization is also an essential component, which requires strong civil society organizations of people living with HIV and key affected populations, such as women's organizations. However, freedom of speech and association, which are guaranteed by international law, remain fragile in many countries in the MENA region.

2. Rights-based Initiatives on HIV in the MENA Region

Although civil and political rights are limited in all countries in the region, the rule of law still exists to a greater or lesser extent, and it is in this space that progress can be made in protecting and promoting the rights of people living with HIV and key affected populations.

2.1 Regional level

In 2012, the League of Arab States endorsed the 'Arab Convention on HIV Prevention and Protection of People Living with HIV', which is now open for signature by Member States. To achieve this breakthrough, from 2008 the UNDP HIV/AIDS Regional Programme in the Arab States (HARPAS) worked to secure the endorsement of the League of Arab States. A working paper draft of the convention was prepared and discussed in a one-day preparatory meeting in the League of Arab States headquarters with members of the Arab Parliament representing delegates from all member countries. The draft was provisionally endorsed, with a further decision to take it to all committees of the League's Parliament, followed by a more extensive discussion in conjunction with a follow-up meeting of the Parliament in Damascus, Syria in 2008. The draft was further developed at this meeting, and ready to be voted upon and endorsed by the League's Parliament. However, political events led to the postponement of the vote until 2011, when it was finally approved at the Heads of States Summit. This is a significant step towards upholding the rights of people living with HIV in the region, and a great achievement of the new Arab League Parliament.

In addition, UNDP has conducted extensive national legal reviews, developed a model law on HIV/AIDS, and engaged with religious leaders on the need for reform.[29]

IDLO has hosted annual regional consultations on HIV-related legal services and rights in Egypt since 2010, bringing together lawyers and representatives of people living with HIV.[30] In April 2011 the Global Commission on HIV and the Law and UNDP hosted a regional consultation in Cairo, which informed the final report of the Commission.[31] An online legal database and discussion forum on issues relating to HIV and AIDS in Arabic, English and French is available at www.aidslex.org. In 2012 IDLO and UNAIDS published a survey of HIV-related legal services in the MENA region.[32]

29 See <http://arabstates.undp.org/content/rbas/en/home/ourwork/hiv_aids/overview.html> (accessed 6 February 2014).

30 Reports are available in English and Arabic. See <http://www.idlo.int/healtlaw> (accessed 6 February 2014) or contact <HIVlaw@idlo.int>. The consultations in 2011 and 2012 were organized by the Center for Development Services (CDS), Cairo.

31 The Final Report of the Commission is available at <http://www.hivlawcommission.org> (accessed 6 February 2014).

32 'Report on Best Practices of HIV-related Legal Services in the MENA Region' (Rome: IDLO, 2012) English, Arabic, available at <http://www.idlo.int/healthlaw> (accessed 6 February 2014).

2.2 National level

Details in the following section are based on work done by IDLO and UNAIDS.[33]

Algeria

Association for Information on Drugs and AIDS 'AIDES Algérie'

The Association for Information on Drugs and AIDS is one of the few organizations which support people living with HIV in Algeria. The Association also provides HIV training programs for judges, and security personnel. HIV-related legal issues addressed by the Association include:

Confidentiality: the Association intervenes with the relevant authorities and services to ensure respect for confidentiality.

Access to HIV medicine: the Association advocates with the relevant authorities regarding treatment access. Support is provided by El Hayet Association, an NGO supporting people living with HIV, especially women.

Children's rights: Information is given to a child living with HIV, adapted to his or her age and capacity to understand. Treatment for the child is suggested to the parents and, if they refuse it, the Association's lawyers take legal action to ensure the child is cared for.

Gender-related violence: This includes violence against women or sexual minorities. In such cases AIDES will denounce cases of violence, especially those involving underage individuals, and inform women who are victims of violence of their rights. AIDES also provides support for access to other services such as dental care, health screening for people living with HIV, and migrant populations, and also legal support to fight discrimination.

Groups supported by the Association: Support is given to people living with HIV, migrants, and mobile populations, to inform them about their right to access to treatment and HIV prevention.

Legal services offered by the Association: Legal information is provided, for example, through the drafting of brochures on rights related to HIV infection, and there is wide distribution to affected populations. In terms of legal education, the Association offers training for judges and security personnel, and participates in international forums on people living with HIV and rights. The Association also provides legal aid for people living with HIV.

Experience in providing HIV-related legal services:

Case 1: A woman living with HIV was expelled from her house by her husband after their separation. *Action*: The case was referred to Court; with the support of the Association's legal team, the Court found in her favour and ordered that she could continue to live in the house. The husband left the house after the Court's decision.

Case 2: A woman living with HIV lost custody of her child when her former husband discovered her HIV status. *Action*: A member of the Association's legal team wrote to the Court to explain that woman has the right to keep her child and that, as HIV is

[33] Based on the IDLO and UNAIDS regional survey, and work supported by IDLO under a grant from the Ford Foundation 2012–2014.

not contagious, she does not risk infecting her child. *Result:* Custody of the child was returned to the mother.

The Association uses community outreach to inform the public about HIV-related rights and to strengthen their implementation. The main challenge has been the mobilization of resources to carry out studies and research, and to intensify local work to promote the rights of people living with HIV.

Aniss

In 2011 the NGO Aniss undertook an analysis of relevant laws and on legal issues related to HIV in prison settings. The organization also hosted a national consultation and stakeholder mapping for legal services.

Egypt

Al Shehab Foundation

The Al Shehab Foundation started activities in 2001. The Foundation provides legal services for people living with HIV and the groups most vulnerable to HIV, and in particular within squatter camps and poor urban areas. The Foundation also provides legal support to sex workers who are exposed to violence, whether in the family, in the community, or by law enforcement officials. Al Shehab aims to reduce the suffering faced by sex workers, to create a space for freedom of choice, and to enable the enjoyment of social, economic, civil, and political rights. The foundation seeks equality for all persons within Egypt and subject to its jurisdiction, without distinction of any kind, such as of race, colour, ethnic origin, sex, language, religion, political or other opinion, national or social origin, property, birth or other status, economic or otherwise. Al Shehab believes clients should have effective legal representation in all cases where the interests of justice require it, and without the payment of fees if they do not have sufficient means to cover these expenses. Al Shehab also conducts research to identify the needs of such groups.

The Foundation aims to provide all types of legal services for sex workers, including legal advice to prevent legal problems. An important function is providing services related to civil status, such as relating to birth records or national identification cards. These assist clients to gain legal employment. They can also gain access to benefits such as social security, and avoid police harassment for not carrying their identification cards.

Al Shehab also assists in matters such as alimony, divorce, and child custody, and also prosecution for sex work (termed 'incitement to debauchery'). Known sex workers are subject to random arrest simply due to their presence on the street or in public places, without any legal justification or evidence of crime. The Al Shehab Legal Unit includes both male and female lawyers, in order to achieve better communication with the clients. Al Shehab also works with human rights organizations, whether local, regional, or international, especially in the use of law to limit the spread of HIV and enable vulnerable groups and people living with HIV to enjoy their rights. Legal support is offered throughout the day, seven days a week.

Al Shehab has prepared a training manual for field researchers working with vulnerable groups and people living with HIV for the purpose of monitoring the violations faced by both the legal field researchers and the vulnerable groups. The manual also discusses how to provide legal support to these groups. In 2012, the Foundation commenced a joint project with the Association for Health and Environment Development (AHED) to improve access to health services for people living with

HIV. Also in 2012, Al Shehab commenced an initiative with the Center for Development Services (CDS) to address the low rate of treatment access for HIV in Egypt. This will include government-civil society dialogue, sharing experiences from other MENA countries, and building capacity on relevant legal issues such as the application of the national intellectual property law.

New Generation Organization—Justice and Freedom Program

The Justice and Freedom Program, implemented by the New Generation Organization, is a legal rights program in eight governorates of Egypt. The main objectives include supporting religious freedom and rights, freedom of expression and thought, and the rights of key populations (sex workers, men who have sex with men, injecting drug users, people living with HIV), women, children, and victims of persecution.

In 2009, the Egyptian Initiative for Personal Rights (EIPR) undertook a needs analysis of HIV-related legal services in Egypt.[34] Based on the results of this research and discussions with people living with HIV and affected communities, in 2010, New Generation Organization commenced a legal services project for people living with HIV and key populations. The project included the development of a curriculum for lawyers on HIV and law, capacity building of lawyers, and the provision of legal services. Justice and Freedom conducted a four-day training course for nineteen lawyers in October 2010, followed by a second training course for the same group. In April 2011, the project conducted a workshop on HIV and law for civil society organizations. Representatives from eleven NGOs and people living with HIV networks attended the workshop. During the project period twenty-two cases were referred to the project lawyer. Issues addressed included inheritance, blackmail, child custody, drug-related offences, hospital administration, and sentencing. In 2012, the program published a legal training manual on HIV for lawyers.[35] Also in 2012, New Generation Organization commenced a joint project with the Windows of Blessing charitable organization, which works with injecting drug users, to provide coordinated legal and health services.

Caritas and Women and Development Association

This joint initiative commenced in 2012 and brought together legal and public health professionals and people living with HIV to improve access to health care services for people living with HIV in Alexandria.

The National Council for Justice and Social Peace (MAAN) and the Egyptian Council for Civil and Legislative Reform (ECCLR)

This joint initiative commenced in 2012 and, similarly to the CDS/Al Shehab project noted earlier, also focuses on improving access to treatment for people living with HIV. The project includes government-civil society dialogue, the engagement of religious leaders, and the production of communications materials on rights and access to treatment.

34 'Needs Assessment to Strengthen and Expand HIV-related Legal Services in Egypt' Egyptian Initiative for Personal Rights (2009), available at <http://www.idlo.int/healthlaw> (accessed 6 February 2014). Also available in Arabic.

35 'HIV Training Manual for Lawyers' (New Generation, Cairo, 2012). In Arabic, available at <http://www.idlo.int/healthlaw> (accessed 6 February 2014).

Jordan

The NGO the Jordanian Commission for Human Culture was founded in 2003 in Amman. It provides support and legal advice for people living with HIV, including through the print and broadcast media, and social networking via the internet.[36]

HIV-related issues addressed by the Commission include inheritance rights and access to treatments for HIV or related diseases, for example sexually transmitted infections. The Commission cooperates with the Jordanian Government through the National AIDS Programme under the umbrella of the Ministry of Health to secure anti-retroviral treatment for people living with HIV. The Commission also addresses HIV-related discrimination, for example in access to health care or work. Since 2008, the Commission has used local media, international workshops, and lectures to increase the level of legal and human rights awareness and to reduce stigma and discrimination against people living with HIV. The Commission also provides legal advice to resolve legal problems informally, and advocates for relevant political and legal reforms.

In November 2011, the Commission, in collaboration with IDLO, held a training workshop on law and HIV, with Jordanian lawyers and local and international associations. It addressed issues such as the lack of work and inability to access treatment. The Commission has also intervened to address discrimination against prisoners living with HIV regarding prison work opportunities.

Case records form the basis for case studies for capacity building for lawyers and law students. The Commission has experience in working with government legal aid providers on HIV-related legal issues. The Commission has held workshops to educate people living with HIV about their legal rights, in collaboration with the National AIDS Programme under the Ministry of Health. Furthermore, the Commission uses social networking websites to provide HIV-related legal services, for example the website 'people living with HIV', as well as outreach via Facebook and Twitter. In 2012, the Commission commenced an initiative to inform law students in Jordanian universities about HIV and law, and to document the HIV-related cases in other countries in the MENA region.

Lebanon

Skoun Association

Skoun is a non-profit, non-political, and non-sectarian organization. Established in 2003, it is the first walk-in outpatient therapeutic facility in Lebanon to offer prevention, awareness, and psychological treatment to drug users and society at large. The core activity of Skoun is treatment. Supplementary activities are prevention, social reintegration, information, research, and legal advocacy.

Since 2007, Skoun, in cooperation with its legal counsel and its medical unit, has sought to ensure that drug users receive treatment and rehabilitation instead of prosecution and imprisonment. This began with dialogues with judges, stressing the importance of treatment over prosecution and foundations for such an approach, as well as stressing the vital leadership of judges in devising solutions to overcome

36 See eg the interview with Mr Mohamed El Nasser, a legal consultant with the Commission, on the Roya channel, Jordanian television, 26 February 2013. The interview includes a locally produced video about HIV and discrimination, and includes telephone calls from PLHIV describing how legal services have helped them to address HIV-related discrimination, available at <http://www.youtube.com/watch?v=EhRiS7-aT8Y&feature=share> (accessed 6 February 2014).

obstacles and fill in the gaps in the law (the AFKAR 2 project with funding from the European Union, 2007–09). Skoun then participated in consultations with civil society to propose amendments to the national Drugs Act (the Midnit Project, in collaboration with the Bambido Center 2010–11). This was followed by an assessment of the treatment needs of addicts (the Midnit Project, in collaboration with the Bambido Center 2010–11), and recommendations whereby drug users are more easily referred to NGO treatment centres (funded by the Open Society Institute, 2010–11). In 2010, Skoun undertook a study of court judgments relating to drug users to identify trends in approaches to sentencing.

In 2011, Skoun conducted a needs assessment of the rights of persons charged under the Drugs Act of 1998. The study examined the opportunity under the existing law to avoid sending convicted persons who use drugs to prison (and hence avoid the risk of HIV transmission in prison), and also to increase access to treatment for drug addiction. The research will support legal action to assist the development of jurisprudence to reinforce the principle of treatment as an alternative to punishment. Skoun has drafted model pleadings to assist the legal representatives of persons charged with drug offences, requesting the court to consider rehabilitation rather than imprisonment, as both options are provided by Lebanese law. This resource will be published in 2013, with examples of cases in which the pleadings were used, and the outcomes.

Morocco

Pan-African organization to Fight AIDS (OPALS)

The Pan-African organization to Fight AIDS (OPALS) was founded in Rabat in 1994, and is one of the few organizations in Morocco to address the legal needs of people living with HIV. The organization has two lawyers and five staff members.

HIV-related legal issues addressed by OPALS include: breaches of confidentiality, for example regarding HIV status, sexual practices, or drug use; gender-related violence, such as violence against women or sexual minorities; and issues related to criminal prosecution, for example in sexual contact or drug abuse. A training program was organized for counsellors at centres which receive women and girls who are victims of violence, including those who have suffered sexual assault. The training includes information on HIV and AIDS and on human rights and gender approaches. OPALS has addressed illegal police practices such as extortion and violence, as well as the rights of children, for example regarding access to adequate information on HIV. Several meetings were organized for the benefit of school children, and a publication was developed on the rights of children living with HIV.

The organization also provides legal services to sex workers and undocumented migrants. Services for people living with HIV and their families include the provision of legal information, advice, and representation. Legal information includes the distribution of printed materials. Legal representation includes assistance in registering in schools, in gaining access to medical care, and in the settlement of disputes through informal dispute resolution mechanisms. OPALS also makes recommendations and proposals for legislative reform. This was done through meetings with women parliamentarians and others who attended a training course organized by OPALS in 2010, which resulted in the formation of a forum for female elected representatives on sexual and reproductive health and HIV.

In 2011, the organization conducted a field study on the legal needs of people living with HIV and vulnerable groups. The results were presented in public forums, including associations of people living with HIV and vulnerable groups; human rights organizations; lawyers and law professors; and representatives of the National Council for Human Rights. This was followed by a discussion about the establishment of procedures to ensure legal support for people living with HIV and vulnerable groups. OPALS has also held several public forums and meetings to raise awareness and encourage recognition of the importance of community outreach to address the challenges resulting from this disease.

The following examples demonstrate the operation of OPAL's HIV-related legal services:

> *Example 1*: Sex workers were detained by police for carrying condoms in their bags. OPALS intervened with the police and the Court for their release. This was followed by an invitation to the police to discuss the importance of encouraging sex workers to use condoms. In December 2011, OPALS was invited to participate in a meeting organized by the Administration of National Security—the police—to educate students at the Institute of Police on the importance of HIV prevention.
>
> *Example 2*: OPALS operated a voluntary HIV testing program for prisoners, and refused to provide the results to the prison administration. As a result, OPALS came under pressure to cease its voluntary testing services. In parallel, the organization launched an advocacy campaign to support the rights of prisoners regarding HIV testing, while ensuring confidentiality.

The organization has agreements with some government departments, such as a partnership agreement with the Minister of Justice to cooperate on HIV-related issues. In one case, the organization intervened to support the school registration of an HIV positive student. The school had refused to register him for the fear of complaints from the parents of other students. In 2013, OPALS initiated a telephone hotline to provide HIV-related legal advice.

Tunisia

The Tunisian Association for the Fight against STIs and AIDS (ATL)

ATL provides legal support to people living with HIV, as well as promoting HIV awareness and access to treatment. In Tunisia, as in much of the MENA region, HIV is often transmitted from husband to wife after marriage, and the husband often dies first.[37] The most common legal and social issue faced by the wife of the deceased is the denial of inheritance. The husband's family often refuses to allow a widow to inherit what is due to her (sometimes wrongly believing that she caused the death of her husband). HIV-related legal issues addressed by the Association also include breaches of confidentiality.

ATL also supports prisoners, and the relatives of people living with HIV and persons who are close to them. The association provides advice and guidance on how to live with the disease and how to deal with social issues faced by the person living with HIV and his or her family. ATL provides legal advice in person, or by telephone. In some cases the association intervenes in cases related to work or housing, by legal representation in courts, or through informal dispute resolution mechanisms.

The association also helps people living with HIV and their families to obtain support from the government to finance small projects to increase their income and

[37] See 'Middle East and North Africa Regional Report on HIV/AIDS 2011' (n 1).

access medical care. ATL provides legal advice on how to access funding from the Ministry of Social Affairs to set up micro-enterprises for the benefit of the people living with HIV, for example sheep breeding projects.

However, ATL suffers from a lack of funding and human resources. Other challenges are related to expertise and technical support. In 2011, ATL undertook research on cases and issues related to HIV. There are three hundred persons living with HIV who are associated with ATL and another seven hundred from vulnerable groups. The project will identify and store the case records for advocacy for law and policy reform. ATL also plans to develop a training manual for lawyers offering services *pro bono* to people living with HIV and key affected populations.

3. Conclusion

Much is happening across the MENA region to promote and protect the rights of people living with HIV and key affected populations. However, these initiatives are still largely ad hoc, poorly funded, largely undocumented, and not evaluated for impact. At the same time, there are emerging opportunities to strengthen the rule of law and empower vulnerable communities across the region. HIV will continue to spread in the MENA region unless the enabling legal environment is strengthened.

Early experience in the region demonstrates that, even where the rule of law is weak, legal services can make a difference in the lives of people living with HIV and key affected populations who have access to them. Peer outreach is key to expanding legal services. Religious leaders can be engaged in a dialogue on HIV prevention, particularly when privacy and public health arguments are made. More research is needed on police practices and motivations for supporting rights-based public health approaches, which can then support training and improve discipline. Research is also needed on the impact of legal empowerment approaches on self-esteem and behaviour change among key affected populations. Legal barriers to increased access to HIV treatments need to be urgently addressed.

All of these initiatives would benefit from increased collaboration between the legal and public health disciplines, in collaboration with government and civil society. There is as yet no common understanding of the role of the law in protecting and promoting the right to health. The projects and initiatives noted earlier demonstrate the protective role of the law in addressing HIV. The lessons learned from these experiences will be invaluable in addressing other health issues in the region, such as hepatitis and also the growing burden of non-communicable diseases.[38]

The MENA region is rich in human and material resources. There are opportunities to engage with religious authorities on the public health arguments for proven responses to HIV, such as community education and outreach with HIV prevention commodities (condoms, sterile injection equipment), as well as non-judgmental engagement with people living with HIV and key affected populations. By strengthening legal services for people living with HIV and key affected populations, we can begin to address the legal and social obstacles to HIV prevention, care, treatment, and support. This way we can more effectively work towards UNAIDS's global goal of zero new infections, zero discrimination, zero AIDS-related deaths.

[38] See 'Strengthening the Legal Environment to Reduce Disability and Early Death through Noncommunicable Diseases in the Middle East and North Africa Region: Overweight, Obesity and Diabetes' (Center for Development Services, Ain Shams University, IDLO, 2013), available at <http://www.idlo.int/healthlaw> (accessed 6 February 2014).

10

Indigenous People, Emerging Research, and Global Health

*Mark Henaghan**

1. Introduction

We are living in an ever increasingly global world. To improve health on such a global scale requires an increased understanding of how the human body works. Scientific research is crucial to increasing this knowledge. Health research relies on the goodwill of research participants, who place themselves in the trust of the researcher. Historically, the trust research participants placed in some health researchers was significantly betrayed. These betrayals of trust are particularly evident in some genetic research projects involving indigenous peoples from different corners of the globe. This chapter identifies some of these breaches and provides a more positive model for the future from a New Zealand case study.

2. Betrayals of Trust

There are many historical examples that illustrate what happens when trust is betrayed in relation to health-related research. This section provides several international case studies to demonstrate what can go wrong between researchers and research participants and discusses how and why these relationships frequently break down.

2.1 Havasupai Tribe v Arizona Board of Regents

An anthropology professor at the Arizona State University, John Martin, began studying the Havasupai Tribe in 1963.[1] The Havasupai Tribe live in the Supai Village at the bottom of the Grand Canyon in the State of Arizona in the United States.[2] Martin built a strong relationship with the Havasupai people. Work was carried out in collaboration with the Havasupai Tribe on education issues, community issues, community action, and development programs, and social and environmental studies. In 1989 a member of the Havasupai Tribe asked Martin to do some research into what was seen as an 'epidemic' of diabetes among members of the Havasupai Tribe.[3] Martin hypothesized that the high levels of diabetes the Havasupai Tribe was experiencing were related to genetics and diet. Arizona State University Genetics Professor Therese Markow agreed to undertake the research, which was called a 'diabetes-centred

* Thank you to Ruth Ballantyne, Professional Practice Fellow, Faculty of Law, University of Otago, Dunedin, New Zealand for her research and editorial assistance with this chapter.

1 *Havasupai Tribe v Arizona Board of Regents and ors* 22 Ariz 214 204 P 3d 1063 (Ariz 2008) 1066.
2 *Havasupai Tribe v Arizona Board of Regents* (n 1) 1066.
3 *Havasupai Tribe v Arizona Board of Regents* (n 1) 1066.

project'.[4] Markow wanted to add research into schizophrenia as part of the project. Martin told her the Havasupai Tribe would not be interested in such an extension to the study, but did not totally rule out such a possibility.[5] Without discussing it with the Havasupai Tribe, Markow successfully applied for a research grant to study schizophrenia among the members of the Havasupai Tribe.[6]

Two hundred Havasupai people signed informed consent forms to give their blood for what they believed was research on diabetes within their Tribe. The researchers concluded that diabetes was developing too quickly among tribal members for it to be relevant to genetics.[7] Markow published a paper in 1991 that reported that there was too little variation among the Havasupai peoples' genetics to 'conclude the incidence of the disease among them was genetics-related'.[8]

Unbeknown to the members of the Havasupai Tribe, without any consultation whatsoever, the researchers at Arizona State University and elsewhere, including the University of Arizona, continued to perform research and publish articles based on the blood samples taken from the Havasupai Tribes' members.[9] Four doctrinal dissertations and a number of academic papers were published using evidence obtained from the blood samples.[10] The publications dealt with a variety of issues totally unrelated to the original informed consent given. They dealt with evolutionary genetics, 'schizophrenia, inbreeding and theories about ancient human population migrations from Asia to North America'.[11] Theories concerning ancient human population migrations from Asia were directly contrary to the Havasupai Tribe's belief that they originated from the Grand Canyon.[12] It was particularly upsetting to the Havasupai people to have such information released without their consent.

In 2002, Martin found out that non-diabetes research was continuing on the samples.[13] In 2003, the Havasupai Tribe asked Arizona State University for information on what had happened to their samples.[14] Eventually, after the researchers were banned from the Havasupai Reservation, the University commissioned an agreement with the Havasupai Tribe for an independent report to look into:

> . . . the circumstances surrounding the collection of blood samples and other research data from members of the Havasupai Tribe and any and all subsequent uses of the sample or their derivatives and other research data for research or other purposes.[15]

Unsuccessful settlement meetings followed before the matter proceeded to trial. The Havasupai Tribe claimed $50 million from the University, alleging breach of fiduciary duty, lack of informed consent, fraud, misrepresentation, fraudulent concealment, intentional infliction of emotional distress, conversion, violation of civil rights, negligence, and gross negligence.[16]

4 *Havasupai Tribe v Arizona Board of Regents* (n 1) 1066.
5 *Havasupai Tribe v Arizona Board of Regents* (n 1) 1066.
6 *Havasupai Tribe v Arizona Board of Regents* (n 1) 1067.
7 *Havasupai Tribe v Arizona Board of Regents* (n 1) 1067.
8 *Havasupai Tribe v Arizona Board of Regents* (n 1) 1067.
9 *Havasupai Tribe v Arizona Board of Regents* (n 1) 1067.
10 *Havasupai Tribe v Arizona Board of Regents* (n 1) 1067.
11 *Havasupai Tribe v Arizona Board of Regents* (n 1) 1067.
12 *Havasupai Tribe v Arizona Board of Regents* (n 1) 1067.
13 *Havasupai Tribe v Arizona Board of Regents* (n 1) 1067.
14 *Havasupai Tribe v Arizona Board of Regents* (n 1) 1067.
15 *Havasupai Tribe v Arizona Board of Regents* (n 1) 1067–8.
16 *Havasupai Tribe v Arizona Board of Regents* (n 1). 1068–70.

The University, after spending $1.7 million fighting the claims in Court (which further highlighted the University's aggressive approach), eventually settled with the tribe for $700,000 and issued a public apology.[17] The University agreed to return the blood samples they still had, and collaborate with the Havasupai Tribe on matters such as health, education, and economic development, and to create a scholarship program for tribal members.[18]

The breach of trust was deeply personal. The Havasupai Tribe were upset that Markow and others had used their blood samples in a way to which Havasupai people had never consented. The Havasupai Tribe gave their blood samples to the researchers in an effort to understand the epidemic of diabetes that their people were experiencing over generations. However, as stated previously, the researchers went on to use the Havasupai Tribe's blood samples to research schizophrenia, inbreeding, and the ancestral origins of the Havasupai Tribe, which are totally different areas of research.

In interviews with the *New York Times*, members of the Havasupai Tribe expressed deep feelings of betrayal, particularly by Arizona State University putting their blood through genetic testing to link the origins of the Havasupai people to Asia. The Havasupai people had a long tradition of stories that linked their origins to the Grand Canyon itself. As Rex Tilousi, a Havasupai Tribe member, states: 'It hurts the elders who have been telling these stories to our grandchildren.'[19] This new information went to the very core of their identity, without giving the Havasupai people any opportunity to say whether they wanted such an inquiry. Carletta Tilousi, a member of the Havasupai tribal council, said: 'I'm not against scientific research . . . I just want it to be done right. They used our blood for all these studies, people got degrees and grants, and they never asked our permission.'[20]

As Hank Greely, Director of the Centre for Law and the Biosciences at Stanford University, states, this kind of behaviour 'sows distrust . . . And researchers cannot do their research unless people are willing to trust them.'[21] Mary Pember described the Havasupai case as 'an example of the paternalism that has dominated the relationship between academic researchers and tribes for generations.'[22] Dr Sonya Alalay, a member of the Anishinabe tribe and an Assistant Professor of Anthropology at Indiana University, said: 'There continues to be a sense that Western ways of knowing and understanding are more important and therefore give researchers the right of way in understanding the world.'[23] When researchers adopt this attitude, they fail to equalize power with those they are carrying out research with, and thus they fail to build trust and become trustworthy. Such an attitude gives researchers a sense of entitlement, of might is right, and of individual careers coming before a whole people's sense of well-being. The Arizona State University researchers had no sense of mutual obligation to the people who had given their blood samples for research.

In a formal public apology to the tribe, Ernest Calderon, President of the Arizona Board of Regents, said: 'The Board of Regents has long wanted to remedy the wrong

17 M. Pember, 'American Indians Grow Wary of Genetics Research', *Diverse: Issues In Higher Education*, 23 June 2010.

18 Pember, 'American Indians Grow Wary' (n 17).

19 A. Harmon, 'Indian Tribe Wins Fight to Limit Research of Its DNA', *The New York Times*, 21 April 2010.

20 Harmon, 'Indian Tribe Wins Fight' (n 19).

21 A. Harmon, 'Havasupai Case Highlights Risks in DNA Research', *The New York Times*, 21 April 2010.

22 Pember, 'American Indians Grow Wary' (n 17).

23 Pember, 'American Indians Grow Wary' (n 17).

that was done. This solution is not simply the end of a dispute but is also the beginning of a partnership between the universities, ASU and the Tribe.'[24] Dr Daniel Wildcat of the Muscogee Tribe, a Professor of American Indian Studies at Haskell Indian Nations University, puts the University's apology in its context: 'They had no choice . . . but to settle if they expected to work with any Indian communities in the future.'[25]

2.2 The Hagahai People of Papua New Guinea

The Hagahai people are a group of approximately 260 indigenous people in Papua New Guinea.[26] The US National Institute of Health filed a patent application for a cell line formed from a member of the Hagahai people's blood. A blood sample from a Hagahai individual was used to develop a cell line that was infected with a local variant of HTLV-I.[27] The purpose was to develop vaccines and diagnostic tools to screen and treat Melanesian people infected with the HTLV-I virus. In 1995, a US patent was granted over the cell line 'in spite of objections from the Papua New Guinea government'.[28] In 1996, after extensive pressure from indigenous people and the international community, the patent on the human cell line of the Hagahai indigenous person was withdrawn by the US National Institute of Health.[29] Alejandro Argumedo of the Canada-based Indigenous Peoples' Biodiversity Network said: 'I hope this is the end of what is arguably the most offensive patent ever issued.'[30] Neth Dano, of the South East Asia Regional Institute for Community Education in the Philippines, pointed out the contradiction in the US government's responses to this particular patent. As Dano said:

> If, as the US State Department said, the Hagahai patent was 'for their benefit', why did the US not even bother to contact the Hagahai when it gave up the patent? Why does NIH blame a researcher in Papua New Guinea for the US Government's own patent? The Papua New Guinea Institute for Medical Research has said that it followed NIH's lead.[31]

Aroha Mead of the Māori (the indigenous people of New Zealand) Congress sums up the feelings of indigenous people after the Hagahai patent was withdrawn thus:

> While the US may have now disclaimed the Hagahai patent, a trail of trauma and mistrust has been left behind . . . The patent deeply affected indigenous peoples of the Pacific. It sent a message to Pacific communities that researchers cannot be trusted and it will take a long time to convince them otherwise. While the Hagahai patent is dropped, which unsuspecting community will it be tomorrow?[32]

Breach of trust features strongly in the indigenous peoples' reactions to what happened with the Hagahai people. The indigenous Hagahai individual who provided his cells for

24 Pember, 'American Indians Grow Wary' (n 17).

25 Pember, 'American Indians Grow Wary' (n 17).

26 D. Posey and G. Dutfield, *Beyond Intellectual Property: Towards Traditional Resource Rights for Indigenous Peoples and Local Communities* (Ottawa: International Development Research Centre, 1996) 27.

27 Posey and Dutfield, *Beyond Intellectual Property* (n 26) 27.

28 Posey and Dutfield, *Beyond Intellectual Property* (n 26) 27.

29 ETC Group: Action Group on Erosion, Technology and Concentration, 'US Government Dumps the Hagahai Patent' (1996), ETC Group <http://www.etcgroup.org/en/node/461> (accessed 10 February 2014).

30 ETC Group, 'US Government Dumps the Hagahai Patent' (n 29).

31 ETC Group, 'US Government Dumps the Hagahai Patent' (n 29).

32 ETC Group, 'US Government Dumps the Hagahai Patent' (n 29).

the research was not treated as an equal by either the researcher, or by the US National Institute of Health. The Hagahai individual was a means to the end of creating a cell line, that was then quickly turned into the property of the US National Institute of Health by the lodging of the patent. The Hagahai individual was not seen as an equal collaborator in the research, but rather, as a convenient set of cells that could be used for financial gain. The US government argued that it had the informed consent of the Hagahai people and the approval of the Papua New Guinea government for the patent, but produced nothing to substantiate these claims.[33] This is a classic example of using someone else as a means to one's own ends, without any consideration of their feelings or their rights.

2.3 The Guaymi Patent Claim

Type II of the rare human T-cell lymphotrophic viruses (HTLV), is known to be the causative agent of adult T-cell leukaemia and a neurological disease.[34] Infection with HTLV type II is common among the Guaymi of Panama, as well as other Amerindian peoples in North and South America.[35] A research project carried out by the Centre for Disease Control of the US Department of Health and Human Services and the National Institute of Health, in collaboration with Panamanian scientists, was designed to look into why infection with HTLV led to cell leukaemia.[36] The President of the General Congress of the Guaymi people, Isidro Acosta, is quoted as saying:

> Doctors came to the communities of Pandilla in small groups and started to collect indigenous blood, pretending that the indigenous people were suffering from a mortal disease and that the blood study was necessary to investigate the malformation or type of disease they suffered. Participants were given a small pill to compensate for the loss of blood.[37]

It was discovered that one of three Guaymi women suffering from leukaemia had an unusual ability to resist the disease.[38] A patent application was filed by the US National Institute of Health for a T-cell line infected with HTLV-II developed from blood donated by the Guaymi people. The Centre of Disease Control of the US Department of Health claimed that the purpose of the patented cell line was to make the line available to researchers.[39] The patent application was filed without any notification to the Guaymi woman who had the capacity to resist leukaemia, or any other Guaymi people.[40] The Panamanian government and the collaborative researchers from that country were not told about the patent application until after it had been filed, 'first in the United States and later worldwide under the Patent Cooperative Treaty (an international agreement that makes it possible for a single patent application to be filed in several countries in which patent protection is desired)'.[41]

When the World Council of Indigenous Peoples and the General Congress of the Ngobe-Bugle (Guaymi) found out about the patent application, and the circumstances in which it was obtained, they publicly condemned it.[42] Isidro Acosta, President of the

33 ETC Group, 'US Government Dumps the Hagahai Patent' (n 29).
34 Posey and Dutfield, *Beyond Intellectual Property* (n 26) 26.
35 Posey and Dutfield, *Beyond Intellectual Property* (n 26) 26.
36 Posey and Dutfield, *Beyond Intellectual Property* (n 26) 26.
37 Posey and Dutfield, *Beyond Intellectual Property* (n 26) 26.
38 Posey and Dutfield, *Beyond Intellectual Property* (n 26) 26.
39 Posey and Dutfield, *Beyond Intellectual Property* (n 26) 26.
40 Posey and Dutfield, *Beyond Intellectual Property* (n 26) 26.
41 Posey and Dutfield, *Beyond Intellectual Property* (n 26) 26.
42 Posey and Dutfield, *Beyond Intellectual Property* (n 26) 26.

General Congress of the Ngobe-Bugle (Guaymi), wrote to both the United Nations Secretary of Commerce and the Patents and Trademarks Office to reject the patent application.[43] At the General Agreement on Tariffs and Trade (GATT) Secretariat, Isidro Acosta said that to patent living cells was to patent private property and that it was 'against all Guaymi traditions and laws'.[44]

Ultimately, the patent application was withdrawn, allegedly due to the high cost of pursuing it.[45] However, Darrell Posy and Graham Dutfield suggest that: 'It seems more likely that the real reason the claim was abandoned was the international outcry.'[46]

The actions of the US researchers demonstrate a belief that their endeavours were more important than the people from whom the blood samples were taken. The researchers' right to try to solve the pathways of adult T-cell leukaemia was seen as more important than the sensitivities and beliefs of the people whose cells had made their research possible. There was no attempt to equalize power with the Guaymi people. They were simply seen as a means to the ends of the US medical researchers. No thought was given to the dignity and equality of the indigenous people.

2.4 The Solomon Islands Patent Claims

A woman from the Solomon Islands, with a history of hepatitis contracted through a blood transfusion, and a man with an enlarged liver and spleen, provided cells which contained a local HTLV-I viral strain from which a T-cell line was developed and a patent lodged by the US National Institute of Health.[47] The researchers claimed that the Solomon Islanders gave their informed consent to the samples being taken.[48] Officials from the Solomon Islands were very concerned about the patent application and did not want the patent to be granted.[49] The Solomon Islands United Nations ambassador wrote a letter of protest to the US Department of Commerce about the patent application. Former Department of Commerce Secretary, Ron Brown, stated in response:

> Under our laws, as well as those of many other countries, subject matter relating to human cells is patentable and there is no provision for considerations relating to the source of the cells that may be the subject of a patent application.[50]

Ultimately, the US National Institute of Health withdrew the patent application for the Solomon Islands cell line in 1994.[51] The reason for this withdrawal was not because of the protest by Solomon Islands officials, but rather 'because it appeared that the demand for commercial products that might be produced from this cell line was low'.[52]

So-called informed consent does not mean much if it is not fully understood and where those obtaining it have a wider financial motivation. Without trust, informed consent is an empty shell. All the case studies discussed above had as a common

43 Posey and Dutfield, *Beyond Intellectual Property* (n 26) 26.
44 Posey and Dutfield, *Beyond Intellectual Property* (n 26) 26.
45 Posey and Dutfield, *Beyond Intellectual Property* (n 26) 26.
46 Posey and Dutfield, *Beyond Intellectual Property* (n 26) 26.
47 Posey and Dutfield, *Beyond Intellectual Property* (n 26) 27.
48 Posey and Dutfield, *Beyond Intellectual Property* (n 26) 27.
49 Posey and Dutfield, *Beyond Intellectual Property* (n 26) 27.
50 K. Ching, 'Indigenous Self-Determination in an Age of Genetic Patenting: Recognizing an Emerging Human Rights Norm' (1997) 66 *Fordham Law Review* 700.
51 A. Bhat, 'The National Institutes of Health and the Papua New Guinea Cell Line', *Genes, People and Property* (1996) 20, available at <http://www.cultural survival.org>.
52 Bhat, 'The Papua New Guinea Cell Line' (n 51).

denominator researchers' desires to obtain new knowledge, which is not an inherently bad thing. But all of the researchers failed to fully collaborate with and involve the people from whom the samples were taken. Only part of the story was shared with the indigenous peoples involved. The full implications of commercializing their cell lines and using them for other purposes was consistently kept in the background.

3. The Importance of Trust

Scientific research is one of the keys to improving global health. All the case studies mentioned show fundamental breaches of the rights of the indigenous peoples concerned to control information about their own bodies. But if we are going to improve global health by working with indigenous people to discover the causes of certain conditions, we need to go beyond a rights analysis, to a trust analysis. The key to building an environment of trust is to communicate clearly and accurately what one's expectations are. Even if nothing is being said, expectations are forming. The expectations may be in sync, or they may be miles apart.

Annette Baier, in her work *Moral Prejudices*, says: 'When I trust another, I depend on her goodwill toward me.'[53] As a consequence, 'Trust... is accepted vulnerability to another's possible but not expected ill will (or lack of goodwill) toward one.'[54] There is inevitably an element of subjectivity to trust. The truster and the trusted may well have different views of what goodwill is. The truster may have very high expectations of what should happen, whereas the trusted may have a lower standard in mind. Expectations are relevant to the sphere of influence for which trust is given. In the context of indigenous peoples providing cell lines and genetic material for research, there is a legitimate expectation that the indigenous peoples' interests will be fully considered.

Baier argues that trust 'is reliance on others' competence and willingness to look after, rather than harm, things one cares about which are entrusted to their care'.[55] Baier proposes a test whereby trust is 'morally decent' when the continuation of the trust relationship 'need not rely on successful threats held over the trusted or on her successful cover up of breaches of trust'.[56] Baier goes on to say that to be 'morally decent' a trust relationship must be 'able to survive awareness by each party to the relationship of *what* the other relies on in the first to ensure their continued trustworthiness or trustingness'.[57]

Accordingly, Baier explains that a 'trust relationship is morally bad to the extent that either party relies on qualities in the other which would be weakened by the knowledge that the other relies on them'.[58] If researchers who work with indigenous peoples to find genetic causes of diseases and illness can only be trusted to share the fruits of their research with the research participants because of fear of legal action, the trust relationship between the respective parties is unstable. In these circumstances, the trusted person is only trusted because of a particular weakness, namely fear of consequences. The trusted person is therefore likely to try to cover up their weaknesses.[59] This increases the potential for the trusted person to cover up breaches of trust because the truster is not aware of them, or persuade the truster to forgive any breach relying on the good nature of the truster.

53 A. Baier, *Moral Prejudices: Essays on Ethics* (Cambridge, MA: Harvard University Press, 1994) 99.
54 Baier, *Moral Prejudices* (n 53) 99.
55 Baier, *Moral Prejudices* (n 53) 128.
56 Baier, *Moral Prejudices* (n 53) 123.
57 Baier, *Moral Prejudices* (n 53) 128.
58 Baier, *Moral Prejudices* (n 53) 123.
59 Baier, *Moral Prejudices* (n 53) 123.

Over time, once there is knowledge of a cover-up, and repeated reliance on the good nature of the truster, this is likely to lead to breakdown of trust depending on the patience of the truster. Not many people would like to think that a researcher would only treat them properly because they were worried about external repercussions if they do not. That would not be a relationship of trust, but a relationship of fear. No one can live or work in fear for long periods. It saps human spirit and initiative. In an ideal moral world:

> [A trust relationship] where each relies on the other's love, concern for some common good, or professional pride in competent discharge of responsibility, knowledge of what the other is relying on need not undermine but will more likely strengthen those relied-on features.[60]

More ethics committees and greater scrutiny does not necessarily create more trust. Ethics committees have their own agendas, one step removed from the researcher/ research participant relationship.

Trust is a fragile value that can be pulled in different directions. As Baier says, 'Over-willingness to excuse untrustworthiness, like undue distrust, may not merely deprive me of a good but destroy a mini-system, a little network of mutually beneficial expectations'.[61] By way of contrast: 'Demanding one's rights belligerently is certainly one way to destroy trust, but never standing up for them or not bothering to find out if they are being ignored is an equally effective destroyer of a network of trust.'[62] Giving rights out, without their corresponding duties, is a sure-fire way to create a climate of belligerent insistence on rights. A right to informed consent not only places a duty on researchers to give clear and accurate information, it also places a duty on research participants to listen to that information and assess it.

Baier says we can only really measure trust on a case-by-case basis and tentatively puts forth the general thesis that:

> . . . trust is appropriately placed in those who, for whatever motives, welcome the equalization of power, who assist the less powerful and renounce eminence of power, who, when they ask us to delay the accounting of their use of discretionary power, do so for reasons that we will eventually see to have been good (as good parents correctly tell their young children 'one day you will understand, but not yet. And it is so that you will one day understand, and be my equal, that I ask you now to trust me').[63]

A welcoming of the equalization of power is the central idea to Baier's proposal for when trust is most likely to thrive. Actual equalization of power is difficult to measure and may be impossible to achieve. Using Baier's analysis, the most trustworthy attitude is to strive to equalize power as best as one can, regardless of the circumstances, rather than simply exercising power over another. In the research context, whilst the researcher has superior scientific understanding, they can, by sharing that knowledge with the indigenous research participant via good communication, demonstrate an attitude of power equalization. The research participants have some power, in their knowledge of their own bodies. By listening to this information, the researcher cultivates a climate of trust which is much more likely to lead to accurate research results.

Care, empathy, and respect for the other is necessary to equalize power and thereby foster trust. Care in the sense of doing what is best for the other, empathy in trying to understand how the other may feel, and respect in the sense that the other is an equal as a human being.

60 Baier, *Moral Prejudices* (n 53) 123–4.
61 Baier, *Moral Prejudices* (n 53) 150.
62 Baier, *Moral Prejudices* (n 53) 151.
63 Baier, *Moral Prejudices* (n 53) 180–1.

At the heart of trust is the balance between belief that another has goodwill toward me, and the risk that I am vulnerable to their ill will. Ideally, trust thrives in an environment where there is love and care for the other. Such environments are not easy to find in the modern world of external measures, performance indicators, and the need to demonstrate research outputs. These environments often start from the premise of distrust of the individual's ability to make their own decisions.

Richard Wilkinson and Kate Pickett show in their book *The Spirit Level*, that the greater income inequality in a society, the less trust there is between members of that society.[64] This is often the case between researchers and indigenous research participants. As the authors say: 'Imagine living somewhere where 90 per cent of the population mistrusts one another and what that must mean for the quality of everyday life—the interactions between people at work, on the streets, in shops, in schools.'[65]

As Baier is quoted as saying so eloquently, trust depends on 'goodwill' in the sense of doing what is best for one another.[66] Trust is morally decent and it 'does not rely on successful threats held over the trusted' or on 'successful cover-ups of breaches of trust'.[67] Human nature is infinitely flexible and adaptable. If we expect the worst in people, then it should come as no surprise that we will receive the worst. If we expect the best in human nature, then we may just receive the best. The destiny of sustaining successful health research is in the hands of researchers themselves: no one else can do it for them. Just as individuals can increase their trustworthiness over time, so too can health researchers.

4. The Warrior Gene Story—a Catalyst for Building Trust

A headline, 'Warrior Gene Blamed for Māori Violence', was breaking news around the world in August 2006.[68] An Australian scientist, Dr Rod Lea, who was working in New Zealand, said that Māori men have a 'striking over-representation' of the monoamine oxidase gene that is 'strongly associated' with risk-taking and aggressive behaviour—'it definitely predisposes people to be more likely to be criminals'.[69] Dr Tony Merriman, a genetic scientist at University of Otago, New Zealand, was of the view that Dr Rod Lea's claims did not stack up scientifically.[70] Dr Merriman and his colleague, Dr Vicky Cameron, found longitudinal studies that showed the crucial fact was whether or not the person had been severely mistreated as a child, and that 'high' monoamine oxidase-A (MAO-A) alleles were protection against anti-social behaviour even where there had been severe maltreatment.[71]

64 R. Wilkinson and K. Pickett, *The Spirit Level: Why More Equal Societies Almost Always Do Better* (London: Allen Lane, 2009).

65 Wilkinson and Pickett, *The Spirit Level* (n 64) 54.

66 Baier, *Moral Prejudices* (n 53) 99.

67 Baier, *Moral Prejudices* (n 53) 123.

68 '"Warrior gene" Blamed for Māori Violence', *The Age*, 8 August 2006, available at <http://www.theage.com.au/news/National/Warrior-gene-blamed-for-Maori-violence/2006/08/08/1154802879716.html>.

69 '"Warrior gene" Blamed for Māori Violence' (n 68). See also, R. Lea and G. Chambers, 'Monoamine Oxidase, Addiction, and the "Warrior" Gene Hypothesis' (2007) 120 *New Zealand Medical Journal* 5, where Rod Lea retreats from the inferences drawn by the media.

70 T. Merriman and V. Cameron, 'Risk-Taking: Behind the Warrior Gene Story' (2007) 120 *New Zealand Medical Journal* 59.

71 Merriman and Cameron, 'Risk-Taking' (n 70) 59–61. See also A. Caspi et al, 'Role of Genotype in the Cycle of Violence in Maltreated Children' (2002) 297 *Science* 851; J. Kim-Cohen et al, 'MAOA, Maltreatment, and Gene-Environment Interaction Predicting Children's Mental Health: New

Many Māori were rightfully upset by the findings that appeared to say they had a gene that made them more likely to be criminals. With Māori making up a high proportion of those in prison in New Zealand, the warrior gene headline furthered a stereotype that some sections of New Zealand society wanted to believe anyway.[72] The gap between the headline and the realities of the longitudinal studies potentially disempowered Māori people in New Zealand.

The balance of power between indigenous communities and researchers is out of sync in all the case studies discussed in this chapter. The book *Genes, Society and the Future: Vol 1* recommends that test results should be reported back to the indigenous research participants' community and that: 'Genetic samples should be considered "on loan" to the researchers for the specific purposes for which consent was obtained.'[73] Some researchers will say that this gives too much power to the community. But if the researcher builds a good relationship with the community then, from that trust, the researcher is more likely to have access to successful research results.[74]

Because Dr Rod Lea lived within the community on which he was carrying out his research, and because he had set up a wide range of health benefits for their participation in his study, the Rakaipaaka people he was working with continued to trust him even after the warrior gene headline burst into the media. The Rakaipaaka people could see the immediate health benefits they were gaining from their participation in Lea's study. The study was wide ranging, looking at all aspects of the 3,000 strong communities' well-being and encouraging healthy eating and habits. The release to the media of the warrior gene idea sharpened the community's awareness of what was at stake when genetic research is carried out.

The community took control of the research project. Te Iwi o Rakaipaaka (the New Zealand Māori Tribe involved in the research) entered into an agreement in 2005 with the Institute of Environmental Science and Research, a Crown Research Institute set up by the New Zealand government.[75] A comprehensive consultation and negotiation process was carried out over several months before the agreement was signed. Local people welcomed the genetics-based healthcare research. One Rakaipaaka individual said:

> I felt excited at the time; it was one way of getting health services coming to our people in Nuhaka, to start looking at the ways we need to make ourselves well, to address concerns of health that were taking our people beyond the veil before their time.[76]

The research agreement between the Institute of Environmental Science and Research and the Rakaipaaka people stated that 'the genetic information from this project cannot

Evidence and a Meta-Analysis' (2006) 11 *Molecular Psychiatry* 903; C. Spatz Widom and L. Brzustowicz, 'MAOA and the "Cycle of Violence": Childhood Abuse and Neglect, MAOA Genotype, and Risk for Violent and Antisocial Behavior' (2006) 60 *Biological Psychiatry* 684.

72 New Zealand Department of Corrections, 'Annual Report 1 July 2004–30 June 2005', Wellington: Department of Corrections (2005) 18. People who identify as Maori constitute only 14.5% of the general population of New Zealand but those who identify as Maori make up 50% of the prison population.

73 M. Henaghan, *Genes, Society and the Future: Vol I* (Dunedin: Human Genome Research Project, 2007) 17.

74 See eg P. Guilford et al, 'E-cadherin Germline Mutations in Familial Gastric Cancer' (1998) 392 *Nature* 402.

75 B. Tipene-Matua and the Rakaipaaka Health and Ancestry Study Management Team, 'Part Four: The Rakaipaaka Health and Ancestry Study: An Alternative Indigenous Response to Genetic Research' in M. Henaghan (ed), *Genes, Society and the Future: Vol III* (Wellington: Brookers, 2009) 202.

76 Tipene-Matua et al, 'The Rakaipaaka Health and Ancestry Study' (n 75) 202.

be used for secondary studies without the express permission of Ngāti Rakaipaaka [the Rakaipaaka people]'.[77]

Participants in the study were provided with access to a General Practitioner of Medicine (GP), free health screening, and health care planning. The Rakaipaaka people live in a rural area where there is a major shortage of health care services.[78] The purpose of the research is to identify the 'serious diseases and conditions common amongst the Rakaipaaka community, and analyse the potential for underlying genetic-based explanations for the conditions'.[79] The study investigated how the genetic explanations interact with lifestyle and environmental factors. Some of the Rakaipaaka people suffer from conditions such as cancer, diabetes, and strokes at disproportionately higher rates than those of the standard population.[80]

If the research leads to the discovery of a particular genetic marker being able to be used in a new way to help predict future diseases, then the Rakaipaaka people themselves will take out the patent.[81] The research moves at a pace that the Rakaipaaka people are comfortable with. As a spokesman for the people said:

> We want to be a Māori organisation or Māori people that can say we've instigated this because we feel this is the way we want and we're going to do it the way we feel is more comfortable for us to do. For instance, instead of a non-Māori organisation that's going to drive this, it's going to be us. We're going to drive this in the way we want it to be driven. These are the benefits, only Māori can realise that they are the only ones who can be the architects of their own development to reach their full potential... This is one way we can show ourselves that we can do it. We're looking at sharing with other communities that this could happen to.[82]

The potential for the Rakaipaaka people to take out patent protection over genetic data collected from its members raised considerable ethical issues for them. In particular, questions were raised about the right of an Iwi (a New Zealand Māori Tribe) to take out a life patent on genetic markers, that are not only common to Rakaipaaka, but are associated with the wider Polynesian population.[83] For the members of the Iwi the most important thing was that their whakapapa (their ancestral lineage) was not going to be abused or commercialized by others.

5. Conclusion

Research into improving human health is essential for global health to flourish. Indigenous peoples are often participants in this health research. In order for such research to be morally and ethically sound it is essential that researchers work with indigenous peoples to ensure that trust and equalization of power is at the core of the researcher/participant relationship. A research model based on power equalization and trust will not inhibit new discoveries, but will ensure that both researchers and research participants are treated fairly in the quest to enhance the health of our global village.

77 Tipene-Matua et al, 'The Rakaipaaka Health and Ancestry Study' (n 75) 202.
78 Tipene-Matua et al, 'The Rakaipaaka Health and Ancestry Study' (n 75) 202.
79 Tipene-Matua et al, 'The Rakaipaaka Health and Ancestry Study' (n 75) 203.
80 Tipene-Matua et al, 'The Rakaipaaka Health and Ancestry Study' (n 75) 203.
81 Tipene-Matua et al, 'The Rakaipaaka Health and Ancestry Study' (n 75) 203.
82 Tipene-Matua et al, 'The Rakaipaaka Health and Ancestry Study' (n 75) 205–6.
83 Tipene-Matua et al, 'The Rakaipaaka Health and Ancestry Study' (n 75) 216.

11

Human Trafficking and Organ Trade

Does the Law Really Care for the Health of People?

Daniel Sperling

1. Introduction

Transplantation surgeries are remarkable medical interventions that save, prolong, and improve the quality of the lives of thousands of people throughout the world. Yet, transplantation is becoming a victim of its own success with demand for organs that far exceeds supply. In Western Europe, as of 2006, nearly 40,000 people were on waiting lists and mortality rates while waiting for a heart, liver, or lung transplant usually range from 15 to 30 percent.[1] In the US, at the end of 2008, 100,597 people were registered on waiting lists.[2] A significant increase in the registration of people on those lists can be observed throughout the years. While in 1999, 21,002 people were waiting for transplantable kidneys, in 2008 there were 33,051 people waiting.

Under these circumstances, desperate patients seek strategies to obtain organs from outside their home countries. Figures collected by the WHO based on questionnaires answered by ninety-eight countries representing about 82 percent of the world population demonstrate that in 2005, 66,000 kidney transplants were performed, 60 percent of which in industrialized countries. Of the more than 21,000 liver transplants and 6,000 hearts transplants, 75 percent were performed in industrialized and emerging economies. According to these reports, transplant tourism, defined by the United Network for Organ Sharing (UNOS) as 'the purchase of a transplant organ abroad that includes access to an organ while bypassing laws, rules, or processes of any or all countries involved'[3] accounts for 10 percent of global transplantation practices.[4] Between 5 and 10 percent of the kidney transplants performed annually throughout the world has its source in organ trafficking. In 2006 alone, 11,000 transplants were performed in China from executed prisoners.[5] In Pakistan, about half of kidney transplantation undertaken prior to 2007 was on foreign patients.[6] Current estimates refer to 2,000 illegal kidney transplants occurring in India each year.[7] Countries that

1 See European Commission, 'Special Eurobarometer: Europeans and Organ Donation' (May 2007) 3, available at <http://ec.europa.eu/public_opinion/archives/ebs/ebs_272d_en.pdf>.

2 See US Department of Health & Human Services, 'OPTN/SRTR Annual Report: Transplant Data 1999–2008' (2009) ch 1, available at <http://optn.transplant.hrsa.gov/ar2009/>.

3 See D.A. Budiani-Saberi and F.L. Delmonico, 'Organ Trafficking and Transplant Tourism: A Commentary on the Global Realities' (2008) 8(5) *American Journal of Transplantation* 925.

4 See World Health Organization, 'WHO Proposes Global Agenda on Transplantation' (2007).

5 See Budiani-Saberi and Delmonico, 'Organ Trafficking and Transplant Tourism' (n 3).

6 See S.A.A. Naqvi et al, 'A Socioeconomic Survey of Kidney Vendors in Pakistan' (2007) 20(11) *Transplant International* 934.

7 See M. Raza and J. Skordis-Worrall, 'Pakistan's Kidney Trade: An Overview of the 2007 "Transplantation of Organs and Tissues Ordinance" To Donors: To What Extent Will it Curb the Trade?' (2012) 62(1) *Journal of Pakistan Medical Association* 85.

have facilitated organ trafficking mostly include Pakistan, the Philippines, Egypt, and India, although brokering, trade, and offering monetary compensation are also evidenced in developed countries, including ones which have a specific ban on organ sales, like the US[8] or the Netherlands.[9] Moreover, in the US, for example, health insurance companies acknowledge the benefit of outsourcing transplants in Third World countries and occasionally encourage subscribers to bring their own 'legitimate donor with a desire to donate'.[10]

Although the first accounts of organ trade date from the late 1980s, it was not until the beginning of the twenty-first century that evidence for organ trafficking came to light.[11] Indeed, organ trafficking is a major global issue.[12] As Nancy Scheper-Hughes puts it, 'the spread of transplant capabilities into new areas has created a global scarcity of organs at the same time that the processes we call globalization have released an exodus of displaced persons and a voracious appetite for foreign bodies to do the shadow work of production and to provide "fresh" organs for medical consumption'.[13] Other than serious health implications, which will be discussed in more depth later, organ trafficking has financial effects as well. As of 2011, it was estimated by a Washington Institute, Global Financial Integrity, that the illicit organ trade generates between $600 million and $1.2 billion per year.[14]

Literature review on commercial organ donors suggests that these people decide to sell their organs out of desperation deriving from poverty, debts, or familial obligations. Organ vendors report feeling victimized by the hospital and medical professionals, suffering humiliation and torment by the community, and rejection by their families.[15] A study of 210 unrelated-living kidney donors in Iran, for example, explored that most of them had low or mid socioeconomic status, 10 percent were illiterate and 67 percent of them had education to less than high-school level. A cross-sectional study conducted in India revealed that almost all kidney donors (96 percent) sold their kidneys to pay off debts.[16]

Studies also show that ethnic and cultural ties between patients and their destination countries significantly explain transplantation tourism. It follows from these studies that minority ethnic groups who are usually less likely to receive a transplant in their home country are more likely to travel to their country of origin or to a close country where they may have better familiarity and trust with the health care system to receive

8 See D. Tao, 'Worldwide Market Fuels Illegal Traffic in Organs', *The New York Times*, 29 July 2009, available at <http://www.nytimes.com/2009/07/30/nyregion/30organs.html?pagewanted-all&r=0>.

9 See M.C. Van Buren et al, 'For Love or Money? Attitudes Toward Financial Incentives Among Actual Living Kidney Donors' (2010) 10(11) *American Journal of Transplantation* 2488.

10 See F. Ambgatsheer, D. Zaitch, and W. Weimar, 'The Battle for Human Organs: Organ Trafficking and Transplant Tourism in a Global Context' (2013) 14(1) *Global Crime* 1, 7–8.

11 See Ambgatsheer, Zaitch, and Weimar, 'The Battle for Human Organs' (n 10).

12 See A. Ginzel, M. Kraushaar, and S. Winter, 'Vera's Kidney, Walter's Money: Desperation, Greed and the Global Organ Trade', *Der Spiegel*, 30 July 2012, English translation available at <http://www.spiegel.de/international/world/the-illegal-trade-in-organ-is-fueled-by-desperation-and-growing-a-847473.html>.

13 See N. Scheper-Hughes, 'Parts Unknown: Undercover Ethnography of the Organs-Trafficking Underworld' (2004) 5(1) *Ethnography* 29, 34.

14 See Ambgatsheer, Zaitch, and Weimar, 'The Battle for Human Organs' (n 10).

15 See A. Tong et al, 'The Experiences of Commercial Kidney Donors: Thematic Synthesis of Qualitative Research' (2012) 25(11) *Transplant International* 1138.

16 See M. Goyal et al, 'Economic and Health Consequences of Selling a Kidney in India' (2002) 288(13) *Journal of the American Medical Association* 1589.

an organ.[17] Other reasons for transplantation tourism involve language barriers,[18] and a feeling of alienation and discrimination in the home country.[19]

The debate relating to financial incentives to donors or their family members more generally raises serious moral objections and evokes weighty sentimental responses.[20] Some questions include the following: Is one really free to sell his or her liver or heart? Is payment not an undue or unjust inducement?[21] Are potential vendors of organs truly autonomous?[22] Do financial incentives not lead to exploitation of the poor who will sell their organs in order to survive? Do they not express disrespect for the dignity of humanity and the treatment of others merely as means?[23] Will these incentives not result in broadening the social gaps in society and increase injustice and inequality in access to health?

2. Health Risks

A central perquisite of living donations is that the donor would not be harmed beyond the organ retrieval. Yet, as suggested by the literature, living donations, most notably kidney donations, are associated with many risks in the short and long term. Mortality of living kidney donors is between 0.2 and 0.4 percent.[24] A meta-analysis of seventy-five studies on living kidney donations found a complication rate of 3 to 30 percent.[25] A survey of 1,022 living donations performed between 1997 and 2008 explored major complications in 3 percent (re-operation, hematoma), and minor complications in 18 percent (urinary tract infection, wound infection, pneumonia).[26] In the long term, studies show that 2 to 20 percent of donors experience long-term pain, about 70 percent a reduced glomerular filtration rate, and 5 to 30 percent develop arterial hypertension.[27]

Health risks associated with transplantation also involve donor-transmitted infection, such as hepatitis or tuberculosis and donor-transmitted malignancy. Reviewing health outcomes of recipients and donors grouped by country of origin and donor's hospitals reveals that patient and graft survival was generally inferior to the data obtained from UNOS. A higher incidence of unconventional and life-threatening

17 See A.J. Cronin et al, 'Solving the Kidney Transplant Crisis for Minority Ethnic Groups in the UK: Is Being Transplanted Overseas the Answer?' in W. Willem, M.A. Boss, and J. Bussbach (eds), *Organ Transplantation: Ethical, Legal and Psychological Aspects. Expanding the European Platform* (Lengerich: Pabst, 2011) 62.

18 See Ambgatsheer, Zaitch, and Weimar, 'The Battle for Human Organs' (n 10) 16.

19 See S. Berglund and S. Lundin, '"I Had to Live": Making Sense of Buying a Kidney Abroad' in M. Gunnarson and F. Svenaeus (eds), *Sodertorn Studies in Practical Knowledge* (Huddinge, 2012) 321.

20 See J.S. Taylor, *Stakes and Kidneys: Why Markets in Human Parts are Morally Imperative* (Aldershot: Ashgate, 2005); and S. Wilkinson, *Bodies for Sale: Ethics and Exploitation in the Human Body Trade* (New York: Routledge, 2003).

21 See S.D. Halpern et al, 'Regulated Payments for Living Kidney Donation: An Empirical Assessment of the Ethical Concern' (2010) 34(6) *Annals of Internal Medicine* 358.

22 See P.M. Hughes, 'Constraint, Consent and Well-Being in Human Kidney Sales' (2009) 34(6) *Journal of Medicine and Philosophy* 606.

23 See S.J. Kerstein, 'Autonomy, Moral Constraints and Markets in Kidneys' (2009) 34(6) *Journal of Medicine and Philosophy* 573.

24 See M. Giessing, 'Living Donor Nephrectomy: Quantifying the Risk for the Donor' (2012) 44(6) *Transplantation Proceedings* 1786.

25 See F. Greco et al, 'Laparoscopic Living-Donor Nephrectomy: Analysis of the Existing Literature' (2010) 58 *European Urology* 498.

26 See G. Mjoen et al, 'Morbidity and Mortality in 1022 Consecutive Living Donor Nephrectomies: Benefits of Living Donor Registry' (2009) 88(11) *Transplantation* 1273.

27 See Giessing, 'Living Donor Nephrectomy' (n 24).

infections such as malaria, invasive fungal infections, pneumonia, HIV, and hepatitis has been observed. Researchers also found a markedly increased incidence of post-operative surgical interventions in recipients.[28] A meta-analysis of odds ratios comparing the risks of participating in kidney transplant abroad to the risks associated with domestic kidney transplant re-demonstrated that individuals transplanted domestically were less likely to experience cytomegalovirus, hepatitis B, HIV, post-transplantation diabetes mellitus, and wound infection. Domestic transplant was also associated with a greater likelihood of one-year graft and patient survival. The study estimates that an average of 4.1 percent of those transplanted abroad return with HIV, 7.1 percent with hepatitis B, and 8.6 percent with wound infection. Similarly, mean one-year graft and patient survival rates of those transplanted abroad are 86.8 percent and 92.8 percent, respectively.[29] In addition to the health risks that are more prominent in transplant tourism, such a phenomenon prevents countries of organ recipients' origin from developing expertise in performing organ transplantation from which other residents and citizens could benefit. This creates additional health risks and burden on those not opting for transplant tourism.

Finally, there is much evidence showing that hypothetical markets will result in an equilibrium price which is very high,[30] and that existing markets in nations such as India have failed and did not result in increased successful transplants as a result of poor organ conditions. To the contrary, studies show that participants in organ sales report deterioration in their health status after, for example, nephrectomy.[31] A study was conducted comparing the health status and renal function of living-unrelated kidney vendors with a matched group of living-related donors.[32] The study found a high prevalence of hepatitis C (25 percent) and liver dysfunction in the vendors as compared to controls. This finding is very important when the reported positivity in the general population is 3 percent for HCV and 5.8 percent for HbSAg. Hypertension was found in 17 percent of vendors as compared to 9 percent in the control group. Post-nephrectomy complaints and complications, such as urinary tract symptoms and hypertension, were significantly higher among vendors as opposed to the control group. The authors conclude that vendors were at high risk of developing long-term chronic kidney disease and nearly a third of them may have failed selection as donors if guidelines were followed.[33]

3. Legal Regulation

The existence of a commercial market for organs is usually located within a human trafficking framework.[34] Advocating for financial incentives to donors may not be

28 See I. Sajjad et al, 'Commercialization of Kidney Transplants: A Systematic Review of Outcomes in Recipients and Donors' (2008) 28 *American Journal of Nephrology* 744.

29 See A.E. Anker and T.H. Feeley, 'Estimating the Risks of Acquiring a Kidney Abroad: A Meta-Analysis of Complications Following Participation in Transplant Tourism' (2012) 26(3) *Clinical Transplantation* E232.

30 See A.J. Wellington and J.B. Whitemire, 'Kidney Transplants and the Shortage of Donors: Is A Market an Answer?' (2007) 25(2) *Contemporary Economic Policy* 131.

31 See Naqvi et al, 'A Socioeconomic Survey' (2007) (n 6); and see Goyal et al, 'Economic and Health Consequences' (n 16).

32 See Naqvi et al, 'Health Status and Renal Function Evaluation of Kidney Vendors: A Report from Pakistan' (2008) 8 *American Journal of Transplantation* 1444.

33 See Naqvi et al, 'Health Status' (n 32).

34 See S. Yea, 'Trafficking in Part(s): The Commercial Kidney Market in a Manila Slum, Philippines' (2010) 10(3) *Global Social Policy* 358.

practical within legal systems already prohibiting commerce in organs, for example the National Organ Transplant Act 1984 and the Uniform Anatomical Gift Act 2003 in the US, although some attempts to reimburse donors have already been made, for example in Pennsylvania[35] and Israel.[36]

While trafficking was identified as an international legal issue more than a century ago, only over the past decade did the international community make clear that it is important enough to be the subject of detailed rules. The first definition of human trafficking was made only in December 2000.[37] According to Article 3(a) of the Protocol to Prevent, Suppress and Punish Trafficking in Persons, Especially Women and Children (supplementing the UN Convention against Transnational Organized Crime) (also known as the Palermo Protocol), 'Human trafficking' is defined as:

> ... the recruitment, transportation, transfer, harbouring or receipt of persons, by means of the threat or use of force or other forms of coercion, of abduction, of fraud, of deception, of the abuse of power or of a position of vulnerability or of the giving or receiving of payments or benefits to achieve the consent of a person having control over another person, for the purpose of exploitation.

Under this article, 'Exploitation' could include, at a minimum, the 'exploitation of the prostitution of others or other forms of sexual exploitation, forced labour or services, slavery or practices similar to slavery, servitude or the *removal of organs*'.[38] The Protocol aims at preventing and combating trafficking in persons (especially women and children), protecting and assisting victims of such trafficking, and promoting cooperation among state parties to realize these objectives.[39] It calls state parties to such legislative and other measures as necessary to establish as criminal offences the conduct set forth in the Protocol. However, the protocol does not prohibit organ sales for profit or for other forms of compensation and its main focus is on the prohibition of trafficking, understood as a form of organized crime involving force, exploitation, or coercion.

In 2004, the WHO called on member states to take measures to protect the poorest and most vulnerable groups from transplant tourism and the sale of tissues and organs and to pay attention to the wider problem of human trafficking.[40] To address these problems a summit meeting of more than 150 experts from around the world was held in Istanbul, Turkey. Following this meeting and many consultations thereof, the Declaration of Istanbul ('the Declaration')—which is the major international regulation on the subject—was issued in 2008.

Two major premises of the Declaration are set forth in its preamble. The first is that unethical practices (specifically human trafficking) are, in part, an undesirable

[35] See J.T. Sanford and J.T. Rocchiccioli, 'Cash for Kidneys: The Use of Financial Incentives for Organ Donation' (2003) 4(4) *Policy, Politics and Nursing Practice* 275.

[36] See A. Meranda, 'Knesset Approves Organ Donation Law' (25 March 2008), available at: <http://www.ynetnews.com/articles/0,7340,L-3523461,00.html>; and D. Sperling and G. Gabriel, 'Factors Encouraging and Inhibiting Organ Donation in Israel: The Public View and the Contribution of Legislation and Public Policy' (2012) 9 *Bioethical Inquiry* 479.

[37] See A.T. Gallagher, *The International Law of Human Trafficking* (Cambridge: CUP, 2010).

[38] See UN Office on Drugs and Crime, 'United Nations Convention against Transnational Organized Crime and the Protocols Therto' (2004) Annex II, available at <https://www.unodc.org/documents/treaties/UNTOC/Publications/TOC%20Convention/TOCebook-e.pdf>.

[39] See UN Office on Drugs and Crime, 'United Nations Convention against Transnational Organized Crime' (n 38).

[40] See World Health Assembly, 'Resolution 57.18, Human Organ and Tissue Transplantation' (22 May 2004), mentioned in the Declaration of Istanbul (2008).

consequence of the global shortage of organs for transplantation. This is why the Declaration calls on state members to ensure that 'programs to prevent organ failure are implemented and meet the transplant needs of residents from donors within each country population or through regional cooperation', and to increase and remove obstacles to deceased organ donations. The second premise of the Declaration is that the life and health of the donor are no less important than those of the organ recipient. Hence, 'for a transplant with a live donor to be regarded as a success means that both the recipient and the donor have done well'.

Applying the definition of the Protocol for human trafficking discussed earlier, the Declaration holds as one of its principles that the primary purpose of transplant policies and programs should be optimal short and long-term medical care to promote the health of both donors and recipients (Principle 4). Principle 6 of the Declaration holds that organ trafficking and transplant tourism violate the principles of equality, justice, and respect for human dignity and should be prohibited. According to the Declaration, prohibitions on these practices should include a ban on all types of advertising, soliciting, or brokering for transplant commercialization, organ trafficking, or transplant tourism, and they should also include penalties for acts, such as medically screening donors or organs or transplanting organs that aid, encourage, or use the products of organ trafficking or transplant tourism.

To fulfil the foregoing principle, the Declaration recommends that the act of donation be regarded as heroic and honoured as such by representatives of the government and civil society organizations. It also states in its Proposals part, that the care of organ donors, including those who have been victims of organ trafficking, is a critical responsibility of all jurisdictions that sanction organ transplants utilizing such practices. Additionally, it permits and legitimizes comprehensive reimbursement of the actual documented costs of donations and suggests additional expenses that may be reimbursed when documented.[41]

Another document that regulates organ trade is 'The WHO Guiding Principles of Human Cell, Tissue and Organ Transplantation'. In Principle 5, it is stated that 'Cells, tissues and organs should only be donated freely, without any monetary payment or other reward of monetary value. Purchasing, or offering to purchase, cells, tissues or organs for transplantation, or their sale by living persons or by the next of kin for deceased persons, should be banned'. However, the Principle holds that the prohibition on sale or purchase of cells, tissues, and organs does not preclude reimbursing reasonable and verifiable expenses incurred by the donor, including loss of income, or paying the costs of recovering, processing, preserving, and supplying human cells, tissues, or organs for transplantation. It is further held that the ban on paying for organs applies to all individuals, including recipients who attempt to circumvent domestic regulations by travelling to places where such prohibitions are not enforced.

In the commentary to Principle 5, it is also stated that incentives that encompass essential items which donors would otherwise be unable to afford, such as medical care or health insurance coverage, raise concerns.[42] The justification for this principle lies in

41 These costs include the cost of medical and psychological evaluations of potential living donors who are excluded from donation; costs associated with the pre-, peri-, and post-operative phases of the donation process, such as telephone calls, accommodation, travel and other expenses; medical expenses incurred for post-discharge care of the donor; and lost income in relation to donation.

42 See World Health Organization, 'Guiding Principles on Human Cell, Tissue, and Organ Transplantation' (2008) (endorsed in May 2010, in Resolution WHA63.22). On this issue see eg M. Quigley, L. Wright, and V. Ravitsky, 'Organ Donation and Priority Points in Israel: An Ethical Analysis' (2012) 93(10) *Transplantation* 970.

the proposition that payment for organs is likely to take unfair advantage of the poorest and most vulnerable groups, undermines altruistic donation, and leads to profiteering and human trafficking. No mention of the serious health risks to donors and recipients associated with paid donations is made.

Common to the international and national regulation of human trafficking is the focus on human dignity and the prevention of exploitation and coercion of vulnerable people. The justification for the prohibition against human trafficking from a global perspective is the global injustice of 'using a vulnerable segment of a country or population as a source of organs', while vulnerability is defined in terms of social class, gender, or ethnicity.[43] The fact that the practice of organ trade is understood and legally reformulated under the umbrella of human trafficking results in much emphasis on the breach of human dignity and freedom, and little weight is given to the serious health risks of organ vendors and organ recipients participating in these problematic transactions. As will be argued, the legal regulation of global organ trade provides the means to escape responsibility or serious punishment when no strong proofs exist to support the conclusion that the trade involved a breach of human dignity or voluntariness amounting to trafficking in persons. The next section will provide a detailed description of the legal response to organ trade in countries where most of this trade is made and the prosecution of people who are involved in the trade in countries where paid donations took place, or from which brokers originated.

4. The Legal Response to and Management of Organ Trade under the Trafficking Framework

4.1 Legislation in countries with most trafficking

4.1.1 Pakistan

In Pakistan, a new law was introduced in 2007 superficially prohibiting donation of organs or tissues by a living person unless they are genetically or legally related to the patient. The Transplantation of Human Organs and Tissues Ordinance further states that donation by Pakistani citizens shall not be permissible to citizens of other countries, while punishment for the breach of this provision is ten years' imprisonment and a fine of one million rupees.[44] However, when there is donor non-availability, the law allows donation by a non-close relative but only if entirely voluntarily determined by a hospital evaluation committee. Along with these changes, the Pakistani government declared organ donation an act of merit in line with Islamic scholars and organizations, with the hope that reframing postmortem donation would result in more donations.

Due to the short time that has elapsed since the new law came into effect it is not yet possible to tell whether it has been successful in eradicating organ trade in Pakistan.[45] Yet, some data suggest that it has led to important changes in this area. Between the introduction of this new law in September 2007 and until June 2010 only 6.2 percent of kidney donations were living-unrelated. Moreover, while prior to the law there had been only two deceased organ donations, as of May 2008, there had already been four such donations. According to media reports, the number of kidney tourists visiting

43 See Budiani-Saberi and Delmonico, 'Organ Trafficking and Transplant Tourism' (n 3).

44 See Raza and Skordis-Worrall, 'Pakistan's Kidney Trade' (n 7).

45 See F. Moazam, 'Pakistan and Kidney Trade: Battles Won, Battles to Come' (2013) 16(1) *Medicine, Healthcare and Philosophy* 19.

Pakistan since the law was introduced has dropped dramatically, from 500 a month to ten to thirty per month.[46] However, other reports suggest that organ trafficking in Pakistan is still relatively widespread. The fact that the law still permits donation by a non-close relative upon the approval of an institutional committee that can be deceived or bribed by foreign brokers, and that the only evidence that needs to be presented to this committee is that the 'donor' consented freely to donation may not sufficiently deter or prevent such harmful practices.

4.1.2 India

In India, the Transplantation of Human Organs Act 1994 prohibited payment for organ donation, and allowed only donation for immediate family members. However, as in Pakistan, the law also permitted donation to a non-relative for reasons of affection and attachment to the recipient upon the approval of a special committee. As a result, poor organ vendors are still recruited by brokers. They are dressed and photographed with recipients so that committee members will falsely believe they have close relations with recipients. It is clear that the law has been unsuccessful in eradicating organ trafficking. It has simply made it go underground.[47] Along with this loophole within the law, other reasons, such as lack of enforcement, a low percentage of legal cases that have been concluded, and corruptive measures of committee members explain the failure of the law[48] and the continued organ trade in India.[49]

4.2 Criminal procedures where trafficking is carried out and in traders' countries of origin

4.2.1 Kosovo

On 2 March 2011 an indictment against six medical doctors and an economist was assessed and confirmed by a single Judge (Vitor Hugo Pardal) at the District Court of Pristina, Kosovo, *in the Matter of Lufti Dervishi et al.*[50] In this leading case, some or all of the accused were prosecuted for trafficking in persons, organized crime, unlawful exercise of medical activity, and abusing official position in connection with at least twenty surgical procedures which took place at the Medicus Clinic between 2004 and 2008—some of which were transplants of organs—an unlawful act in Kosovo at that time, along with organized activity aimed at facilitating such operations, recurring systematically amongst foreigner donors and recipients, and involving trade payments.

Analyzing the evidence, the court concluded that it could not be proved that the victims were recruited due to their acute vulnerability and through the use of coercive offers of cash payments in order to gain consent for the removal of organs, as is necessary for the prohibition against human trafficking under the local law (article 139 CCK). The court also could not conclude that all the monetary promises were not fulfilled, which would have rendered them fraudulent. For example, while discussing

46 See Raza and Skordis-Worrall, 'Pakistan's Kidney Trade' (n 7) 87–8.

47 See Raza and Skordis-Worrall, 'Pakistan's Kidney Trade' (n 7).

48 See Raza and Skordis-Worrall, 'Pakistan's Kidney Trade' (n 7).

49 See M. Moniruzzaman, '"Living Cadavers" in Bangladesh: Bioviolence in the Human Organ Bazaar' (2012) 26 *Medical Anthropology Quarterly* 71.

50 *In the Matter of Lufti Dervishi et al* (The District Court of Pristina) KA 278/10, P 309/10, KA 309/10, P 340/10 <http://www.eulex-kosovo.eu/en/judgments/CM-District-Court-of-Pristina.php> (Kosovo).

the testimony of the donor Y.A., who was given a promise of $20,000 in cash by someone called Ismail, stating 'I needed the money, had a lot of depts [should be debts], and thought of a better life', the court commented that Y.A., however, 'has never said that Ismail was aware of these thoughts, reasons, or of his personal and financial situation; he never mentioned that Ismail used any pressure or any of the means mentioned on article 139, paragraph 8 KCC'. The court further referred to a statement by Y.A. that 'because I was caught by the police I lost money that I was promised to get and the kidney'.[51] Moreover, the court was not convinced from Y.A.'s statement that 'Ismail told me it was not legal in Turkey but it was legal in Kosovo' that it reflected a means of deception by which the charge of human trafficking could be proven. The court held that this statement was the only one on this issue and was not supported by other evidence. In addition, the court held that an 'illegal activity' may be different than a 'criminal activity'.[52] Therefore, the court dismissed the count of trafficking in persons as not being well grounded.

The court then went on to dismiss the offence of organized crime under paragraphs 1 and 3 of article 274 CKK, holding that the criminal offence of organized crime demands the existence of a serious crime. Since such a serious crime was lacking, it was held that the count of organized crime was also not well-grounded. On the other hand, the court found from the evidence presented that the criminal offence of unlawful exercise of medical activity (paragraph 1 of article 221 CKK), referring to the performance of human transplants at the Medicus clinic, without authorization from the Ministry of Health at that time, could be substantiated at that stage of proceedings, although it would still need to be verified and evaluated at the main trial.

An appeal of the prosecutor and of counsel for one of the accused, dated 7 March 2011, was heard and decided by three judges (Presiding Judge Malcolm Simmons) at the District Court of Pristina on 27 April 2011. Revising the ruling of Judge Pardal, the court held that

> The persons who had come to Kosovo to donate their organs did not do so to assist a family member or for any of the usual reasons that people in a civilized society [choose] freely to donate their organs. They did so because of their acute position of vulnerability. To suggest that persons would travel to a foreign country, endanger their health through such an invasive procedure on the say so of a stranger runs (if they were not in a position of vulnerability) contrary to common sense.

The court held that Y.A.'s statement according to which he 'needed the money, and had a lot of debts', and the fact he was approached in a park in Turkey, along with the time that had elapsed since his operation to him being taken to the airport, are sufficient to show he was in a vulnerable position. Important to the discussion of this chapter, the court inferred that if Y.A. was not in a vulnerable situation he would have at least been able to demand better aftercare and choose whether or not to travel in his weakened physical state. The court also referred to Y.A.'s lack of contract and the absence of any lawful enforcement mechanism to obtain payment despite having donated a kidney as other evidence to support his vulnerability. It was held that being involved in the transplant surgery contributes substantially to the commission of the offense. It also followed from the evidence on trafficking in persons that there was a well-grounded suspicion with regard to the commission of organized crime under the CKK. Having approved the prosecution, the main trial of the case began in October 2011 and is still ongoing.

[51] *In the Matter of Lufti Dervishi et al* (n 50).
[52] *In the Matter of Lufti Dervishi et al* (n 50).

4.2.2 South Africa

In November 2010, Netcare Kwa-Zulu (proprietary) Ltd,[53] the parent company of St Augustine Hospital in Durban, South Africa (the company), along with its CEO, four transplant doctors, a nephrologist, two administrative coordinators, and a translator pleaded guilty to counts related to charges in connection with 109 illegal kidney transplant operations, which took place between June 2001 and November 2003. The charges were laid under the South African Human Tissue Act 1983 prohibiting the purchase of tissue, such as kidneys,[54] and the Prevention of Organized Crime Act 1998. The kidneys at stake were first supplied from Israeli citizens and later on from Romanian and Brazilian citizens. The broker, Ilan Perry, who was not South African and has not been charged, charged recipients between US$100,000 and $120,000 while paying the suppliers of kidneys $20,000, and later on $6,000. Prospective kidney suppliers and recipients who were found compatible for transplant surgery were 'accommodated and chaperoned'. They were also given documents falsely attesting to their relatedness. This is how a Ministerial committee approved 'donations'. While the hospital was paid upfront for participating in these illegal surgical procedures, kidney suppliers were paid after the fact and in cash.

In addition to the national legislation, the Department of Health of South Africa issued a policy holding that donor organs must be used primarily for South African Citizens and permanent residents. The policy also requires a written approval from the Minister of Health before any person who is not a South African citizen or a permanent resident is accepted on to the transplantation program. According to this policy, transplantation of unrelated living donors must be approved by a ministerial committee.[55]

Reviewing the agreement between the company and the state reveals very little reference to the wrong that is done through the practices of illegal transplants in the territory of South Africa. The only interest that the agreement holds that it seeks to promote and secure is that 'the prosecuting authorities and the Department of Health will not tolerate breaches of the code of conduct and standards of ethics and compliance with the law required in a civil society' (paragraph 21). No mention of the serious health risks and harms that are associated with such a practice is made under the agreement.

The agreement between the parties sets out a confiscation order of 3,800,000 Rand, amounting to the benefit of the company derived from the offenses, and a sentence of 4,020,000 Rand (£293,108) amounting to fines for each of the counts to which the company pleaded guilty. The nephrologist, who acted as the liaison at the hospital, was fined 150,000 Rand. As of January 2011, the two hospital administrators and four transplant surgeons were awaiting trial.[56] No other reports have been issued on this case.

The court approved the agreement that includes very little wording on the seriousness of these practices. No imprisonment of any of the people involved was set, and the fines that were determined for such a large number of transplants involving serious

[53] *The State v Netcare Kwa-Zulu (Proprietary) Ltd*, Commercial Crime Court, Regional Court of Kwa-Zulu Natal, Durban, South Africa, case no 41 (3 September 2010), unpublished report, mentioned in J. Allain, 'Commentary: Trafficking of Persons for the Removal of Organs and the Admission of Guilt of a South African Hospital' (2011) *Medical Law Review* doi:10.1093/medlaw/fwr001.

[54] Counts 1–5 involved the use of five minors as kidney suppliers, also contrary to the Act.

[55] See Allain, 'Commentary: Trafficking of Persons' (n 53).

[56] See Allain, 'Commentary: Trafficking of Persons' (n 53).

health risks were relatively small and un-proportional. Moreover, the company escaped charges, most notably for assault with intent to do grievous bodily harm.

4.2.3 Israel

In recent years, Israel has had few criminal cases, especially against brokers, that have gone to court. The first case which came to court is *The State of Israel v Genadi Mishkis et al.*[57] This case involved the recruitment of immigrants to Israel from the former Soviet Union as kidney vendors outside the country. After a few meetings at Court, the state attorney declared that it was experiencing some difficulties in proving its case, and due to the evidentiary obstacles requested to withdraw prosecution. According to media reports, one of the three accused, Albert Chernov, fled from Israel and some of the witnesses refused to cooperate with the State Attorney. The court approved this request in 2004 and cancelled the prosecution.

The first substantial decision on the issue was reached in the case of *State of Israel v John (Jath) Ellen (Mohamed) and Hassan Zachalka*,[58] reported in 2007. Mr Ellen, occasionally also with the help of Zachalka, published advertisements in two Arab newspapers in which the first sought to recruit kidney vendors in the guise of 'kidney donor of any blood type'. In his advert, Ellen used an MD title and a faked name. Indeed, the accused managed to convince five innocent Israeli Arabs to give away their kidneys, and after several physical examinations, to have them fly to Ukraine where the transplant surgery took place under Dr Michael Zis. Dr Zis charged organ recipients between $125,000 and $135,000 which was paid directly to the accused. The kidney sellers were told that they would receive $7,000 for their efforts.

In one case, a single parent aged 32, who initially agreed to sell her kidney, changed her mind, but the accused forced her to continue. She was made to stay at the house of the first accused, he prevented her from 'running away' from this house, and held her passport. Not only did this woman receive only half of the price she was promised, but she still suffered from physical pain and was left with a 30 cm scar. In another case, a single 21-year-old man, who suffered from emotional distress and did not fully understand Hebrew, was paid only $500 for the kidney removal. When this person asked for the remaining payment the accused refused to pay him and threatened him that he would get hurt when caught by police. This person believed the accused and did not even go to the health fund to receive treatment for the wounds caused by his surgery. At the time of conviction, his mental state had deteriorated and he considered suicide.

The two accused were prosecuted under sections of the Penalty Act 1977, most notably section 377a(a)(1), which was added to the Act in 2006. This section holds that anyone who trades in another person and puts him in danger for the purpose of extracting an organ from his body is liable to up to 16 years of imprisonment. 'Trade in another person' includes the buying or selling of a person or making another 'deal' in connection with a person, whether for a consideration or not. At court, the state attorney argued that since it was the first time that it had made use of this section, some evidentiary and interpretation questions could be raised, and given that the accused admitted the charges against them, they should receive a lighter punishment than the one set by law. The fact that part of the evidence and some of the witnesses had

[57] *State of Israel v Genadi Mishkis et al* 40225-03 (Israel).

[58] *State of Israel v John (Jath) Ellen (Mohamed) and Hassan Zachalka* 4044-07 (District Court of Haifa) (2007).

to come from Ukraine created an additional burden on the state to prove beyond reasonable doubt all charges.

The court held that the agreement between the state and the accused should be enforced. Given the various possible interpretations of this new offense the court stated that the parties should not be forced to face a full trial, which would be extremely complicated, and involve many items of evidence. In its decision, the court also referred to the fact that the accused had pleaded guilty at the beginning of the trial, that Dr Zis was arrested in Ukraine and was awaiting trial, and that the agreement between the parties also included compensation for the victims. The court therefore approved the punishment agreed to by the parties, according to which the first accused would be imprisoned for four years and would compensate each of the victims with the sum of 15,000 NIS (US$3,750). Due to a lesser responsibility, it was held that the second accused would be imprisoned for 20 months only.

Another case, reported in 2011, involved the prosecution of five Israeli citizens under the Transplantation Act 2008. In *State of Israel v Michael Glov et al*,[59] the accused pleaded guilty to charges concerning organ trade and assistance in the extraction of organs from Israeli citizens contrary to the Transplantation Act. According to the agreement between the parties, which was approved by the court, all of the accused deposited a total sum of 1,200,000 NIS (US$30,000) for the compensation of the victims. Three of the five accused were also sentenced to periods of three to six months of imprisonment but in the form of work for the benefit of the public. This work included being a volunteer at a police station, a nursing home, and a private ambulance company. In a hearing for the sentences, the court heard a retired Major General who testified in favor of one of the accused who had an impressive military record. The court decision did not include any statements concerning the health status of the victims affected, but briefly mentioned that the monetary compensation should be appropriate.

Another case, which is still being heard (*State of Israel v Sami Ben-Michael, Shemtov*),[60] involved the recruiting of kidney vendors from Israel and abroad and the unlawful match between them and potential kidney recipients who underwent transplant surgery in Panama, Ecuador, and the Philippines. The major accused, a retired coordinator who worked in the medical data department at Hadassah Ein-Kerem hospital, cooperated with a lawyer who falsely presented their acts as lawful, and managed to escape the law in thirteen different cases between 2006 and 2010. In an agreement recently reached between the state and the accused, it was held that the state will ask for no more than thirty-eight months' imprisonment along with monetary compensation to all victims. This agreement has not yet been approved by the court.

4.2.4 Singapore

In 2008, the first criminal case on illegal purchase of organs was *Public Prosecutor v Wang Chin Sing*,[61] heard in Singapore. The case involved the prosecution of a broker, Wang Chin Sing, who coordinated the buying of kidneys from living donors for Singaporean and Indonesian men. The donors were a garbage collector in Indonesia who earned less than 140 SGD ($110) per month and who lost his job, and an Indonesian laborer who earned 120 SGD ($95) per month who also lost his job.

59 *State of Israel v Michael* TPH 10-10 (District Court of Nazareth) (2011).

60 *State of Israel v Sami Ben-Michael, Shemtov* P 26647-08-10 (District Court of Jerusalem).

61 *Public Prosecutor v Wang Chin Sing* SGDC 268 (2008), available at <http://www.unodc.org/cld/caselaw/sgp/2008/wang_chin_sing_v_public_prosecutor.html>.

While Sing charged 300,000 SGD ($237,125) for a kidney, he paid the donors around 23,700 and 29,290 SGD ($18,737 to $23,150). Sing also instigated and coached both donors into making false statutory declarations before a commissioner and in an application for authorization by an ethics committee. Since the law in Singapore at that time did not make a distinction in terms of criminal culpability or punishment between the various parties to the organ trade, the kidney vendors and the kidney purchaser in Singapore were also brought to trial.[62]

Sing was convicted under the Human Organ Transplant Act and Regulations and the Oath and Declarations Act. He was sentenced to fourteen months' imprisonment. The kidney purchaser was also convicted under the aforementioned Acts and regulations, but due to his ill health and the fact the he needed a daily regimen of treatment he was sentenced to one day of imprisonment[63] and fined $7,000. As for the kidney sellers, both were convicted under the Acts and regulations. One was sentenced to two weeks' imprisonment and fined $1,000;[64] the other, who was a runner for an organ-trafficking syndicate and sold his kidney to an Indonesian woman, was sentenced to three months' imprisonment and fined $2,000. In both cases, the court took into account the fact that these kidney sellers were approached and exploited by a syndicate seeking to sell their organs.

In order, perhaps, to justify its judicial mercy toward the kidney purchaser, the District Judge found that this person did not intend to exploit the donor, and that there was no evidence that the donor was coerced or subject to duress. However, one should then question why the donor's culpability in the same transaction should have been mitigated on the basis that he had been exploited and why the broker should have been given a harsher sentence than either the donor or purchaser on the basis that he had exploited both of them in order to make a profit.[65]

In an appeal to the Supreme Court of Singapore brought by Sing, the court upheld the lower court decision, holding that 'sentences must firmly deter other individuals from contemplating acting as middlemen in organ trading. As such the role played by the middleman should be accorded prominence as a matter of sentencing policy'. In validating the sentence decided by the District Judge, the court held that it articulates the message that trafficking will not be tolerated in Singapore.

5. From Transplantation Tourism and Organ Trade to Human Trafficking: The Small Effect of the Law

What do the foregoing legal responses teach us about the shift from transplant tourism and organ trade to human trafficking? The rulings of the single judge in Kosovo and the

62 In November 2008, the Act was amended with the intention of imposing a heavier penalty on 'middlemen' and organ trading syndicates than on the donor or recipient (P. Tan, 'Case Comment: Judicial Mercy and Its Limits': *Public Prosecutor v. Tang Wee Sung* [2008] SGDC 262' (2009) 9(1) *Oxford University Commonwealth Law Journal* 185, 189, fn 19). The changes in the law focused on four major issues: widening of the pool of organ donors by removing the prohibition against harvesting organs of a dead person over 60 years old; allowing paired living donor organ transplant arrangements and removing doubts as to whether or not such arrangements constitute inducement; allowing comprehensive reimbursement of costs and expenses incurred by a living donor; and enhancing the penalties for intermediaries in organ trading. See C.A.C. Lim, 'Life and Death: A Decade of Biomedical Law Making 2000–2010' (2010) 22 *Singapore Academy of Law Journal* 868.

63 It should be clarified that an offence under the Oaths and Declarations Act required a mandatory term of imprisonment.

64 This person could not pay the fine and was consequently imprisoned for another week.

65 See Tan, 'Case Comment: Judicial Mercy and Its Limits' (n 62).

one in Singapore demonstrate the problematic association between organ trade and human trafficking. In these cases, in order to determine if a criminal liability could, indeed, be proved, the court analyzes the question of whether organ vendors/donors were, in fact, forced, coerced or exploited. Paying a great deal of attention to segments of accused and victims' statements at court and to anecdotal circumstances surrounding the case, the court may come to conclude that despite the strong evidence for transplant tourism, especially involving racial minorities, poor, unemployed, or otherwise vulnerable people, and the money transactions involved, no criminal offence has been made. The *Genadi Mishkis* and *Ellen & Zachalka* Israeli cases further reveal the evidentiary difficulties usually associated with proving criminal offences that involve actors in various countries, some of whom are difficult to locate. These difficulties may lead to the quashing of prosecutions or a preference for an agreement with the accused (rather than letting the court trial run its course), and as a result, asking for by-far lighter punishments for the accused. At most, these punishments include several months of imprisonment, when the maximum punishment in Israel, for example, is sixteen years' imprisonment. The *Michael Glov* Israeli case is perhaps an extreme example, where having found the accused guilty the court gives a sentence of imprisonment in the form of work for the public benefit. There should be particular scrutiny of this unsatisfactory sentence in light of the fact that the work chosen involved—once again—interaction with the most vulnerable sections of the population (the elderly, the sick, and people who attend police stations). The *Wang Chin Sing*[66] Singaporean case also attests to the symbolic punishment of those who are involved with commerce in humans for the purpose of organ extraction. In addition, the South African case, in common with most other cases, assumes that monetary compensation to victims should be an appropriate replacement for a harsher punishment, including fines and imprisonment. Importantly, none of the cases or agreements discussed in these cases includes statements concerning the health status of the victims at stake. Nor do they refer to the serious risks to organ vendors and recipients, as strongly suggested by the literature.

Analysis of the legislation established in countries where organ trade mostly takes place also reflects the fact that as long as the law does not prohibit living donation to non-relatives who are not residents in these countries, and defers the discretion in these cases to institutional committees, a lack of enforcement, fraud, and the corrupt measures of committee members will prevent the law from succeeding in its attempt to combat the organ trade. As such, the legal regulation of the organ trade, and especially the re-formulation of these illegal practices under the criminal offence of human trafficking, has proved insufficient and ineffective, and does not pay serious attention to the harm, especially bodily harm, that may be associated with such offenses.

One can offer several reasons for the relatively small effect that the criminal law has had in the area of trade in organs. First, patients who go abroad for organ transplants are not reported or registered. Unless they seek immediate post-transplant treatment or financial reimbursement, and for many other reasons, they are not known and cannot be monitored.[67] Also, because most of the recipients who travel abroad for an organ are highly stigmatized in their home country, it is highly unlikely that they would tell their story truthfully.[68] For this reason, the organ trade is under-reported and receives less attention from the police and legal authorities. As a result, the development of

66 *Wang Chin Sing v Public Prosecutor* SGHC 215 (2008), 1 SLR(R) 870 (2009), available at <http://www.unodc.org/cld/caselaw/sgp/2008/wang_chin_sing_v_public_prosecutor.html>.

67 See Ambgatsheer, Zaitch, and Weimar, 'The Battle for Human Organs' (n 10) 10–13.

68 See Berglund and Lundin, 'I Had to Live' (n 19).

knowledge and expertise in relation to the legal management of these complex cases has been slow and inadequate.

Second, while the purchase of organs is illegal in most states, it is punishable only under the law of the state within which it is carried out and not the law of the state in which the purchaser resides.[69] In other countries, for example Israel, a person who purchases or sells an organ is exempted from criminal procedures, although the action itself is prohibited by law. Additionally, even if criminalization is possible, in many of the cases it may be difficult to prove that an organ transplanted abroad was in fact purchased for money, since the medical records attesting to such transplants reveal little information, if any, as to the source of the organ and the circumstances (especially any costs) surrounding transplantation. If some information about the donor is included in these records, it usually refers to general biographical and medical characteristics and, as evidenced from a number of empirical studies, in most cases, states that the donor is related to the recipient.[70]

Another reason for law's negligible effect is that the law in many states, particularly the criminal law, does not distinguish between commercialism in organs and coercing or exploiting someone into selling organs (trafficking). To this one should add the major characteristic of transplant tourism, which, as the UNOS definition presents, essentially involves the bypass of the law and does not refer to a legitimate form of medical practice. It follows that in order to succeed in these cases, the state attorney must demonstrate beyond reasonable doubt that a violation of the free will of the vendor/donor has occurred. Although many of the cases will include circumstances from which such coercive action could be inferred, this may not necessarily suffice as a standard in criminal procedure.

Finally, the ethical debate concerning the trade in organs is still ongoing and a consensus has not been reached. At times, the prohibition against the organ trade is accused of being ethnocentric, regarding the world primarily from the perspective of Western culture.[71] It is also not entirely clear whether the organ trade is wrong in itself, or whether what is wrong is the circumstances under which such a practice occurs or the circumstances to which it leads. Also, the harm that is evidenced with regard to organ trafficking mostly occurs in unregulated markets for organs, and so it is still difficult to assert that the organ trade would be as bad in regulated markets. State attorneys, judges, and other people who may be potential witnesses and victims take part in this realm of ideas and ethical queries. They also have different views on the organ shortage problem, on people's right to enhance their personal situation (including financially), on people's right to own their bodies, and on whether people should hold any duties toward residents of other nations. These views affect their being active and participatory in the enforcement of the legal regulation of organ trade. Although the law usually shapes and strengthens ethical views mediated by the idea of rights,[72] in the case of an ongoing ethical controversy like the selling of organs, it may be that law's contribution is severely limited.

69 See Ambgatsheer, Zaitch, and Weimar, 'The Battle for Human Organs' (n 10) 12.

70 See Ambgatsheer, Zaitch, and Weimar, 'The Battle for Human Organs' (n 10) 12–13.

71 See R.W. Evans, 'Ethnocentrism Is an Unacceptable Rationale for Health Care Policy: A Critique of Transplant Tourism Position Statements' (2008) 8 *American Journal of Transplantation* 1089.

72 See D. Sperling, 'Law and Bioethics: A Rights-Based Relationship and Its Troubling Implications' (2008) 11 *Current Legal Issues* 52.

6. Conclusions

The organ trade and trafficking in humans for the purpose of extraction of organs is an increasing illegal and ethically disturbing phenomenon characterizing not only developing countries, but also ones that hold specific bans on commerce in organs. Beside the disrespect and exploitation that are reflected in such a phenomenon, it raises serious health risks both to organ sellers and organ recipients, and has a considerably larger effect on the health systems of the societies from which sellers and recipients originate. Analysis of the legal regulation of the organ trade, as well as the legal response to it by legislation and case law in various countries, reveals that the law and especially the reformulation of such illegal practice under the criminal offence of human trafficking has proved insufficient and ineffective and does not pay serious attention to the physical harm that may be associated with it.

No matter how effective the laws in the developing countries where most of organ trafficking takes place and from which most of recipients and vendors originate are, developed countries which cooperate and participate in this phenomenon should also take responsibility and address the problem of organ shortages through the consideration of various mechanisms, including, but not limited to, revising the rule of consent for organ retrieval (from opt-in to opt-out systems), compensating and reimbursing the costs of living donations done locally, allowing directed donations, expanding after-death donations, and improving the enforcement of the criminal prohibitions set on members of their states who are involved in this unfortunate trend. These other measures need to be seriously considered and use needs to be made of more powerful legal institutions to enforce the prohibition on the illegal trade in organs, since the law on human trafficking alone is inadequate to the task of protecting those caught up in the organ trade worldwide.

12

Cross Border Commercial Surrogacy

A Global Patchwork of Inconsistency and Confusion

*Kerry Petersen**

Lest it be overlooked, irrespective of how State law views the application's actions, *the children have done nothing wrong.*

Ellison and anor and Karnchanit[1]

1. Introduction

The practice of commercial surrogacy, where a woman receives payment for gestating, giving birth, and surrendering a child to the intended parents is very controversial. Altruistic surrogacy, where a woman receives reimbursement only for expenses, is less controversial and it usually involves an arrangement between a surrogate mother and a friend or relative. It is often noted that surrogacy is not a new practice and goes back to Biblical times.[2] However, the impact of reproductive technologies has taken surrogacy into the realm of what was once regarded as science fiction.

Commercial surrogacy has been condemned, discouraged, and criminalized in many jurisdictions on the grounds that it is immoral, it leads to the commodification of children, and exploits poor women and their families. However, there are human rights involved in these surrogacy arrangements which are generally overlooked. For example, it is discriminatory *not* to treat children born as a result of a surrogacy in the same way as other children. As well, Articles 7 and 8 of the United Nations Convention on the Rights of the Child 1989 (CRC) set out key rights which include a child's right to acquire a nationality and, as far as possible, to be cared for by his or her parents—as well as a right to identity:

Article 7

1. The child shall be registered immediately after birth and shall have the right from birth to a name, the right to acquire a nationality and[,] as far as possible, the right to know and be cared for by his or her parents.

2. States Parties shall ensure the implementation of these rights in accordance with their national law and their obligations under the relevant international instruments in this field, in particular where the child would otherwise be stateless.

* I would like to thank Mr Dennis Warren the Law Librarian at La Trobe University for his expertise and assistance; and Professor Emily Jackson for her generosity in sending information and material regarding British legal developments.

1 [2012] Fam CA 602, para 92, *per* Ryan J.

2 R. Lee, 'New Trends in Global Outsourcing of Commercial Surrogacy; a Call for Regulation' (2009) 20 *Hastings Women's Law Journal* 275, 294.

Article 8

1. States Parties undertake to respect the right of the child to preserve his or her identity, including nationality, name and family relations as recognized by law without unlawful interference.

2. Where a child is illegally deprived of some or all of the elements of his or her identity, States Parties shall provide appropriate assistance and protection, with a view to re-establishing speedily his or her identity.

In *Ellison and anor and Karnchanit*,[3] the Australian Human Rights Commission (AHRC), acting as an intevenor, added that 'children born of surrogacy arrangements should not be subjected to a disadvantage or detriment as a result of any difference in legal status conferred on their parents or guardians'.[4]

Both the Warnock Report[5] and Brazier Report[6] were opposed to commercial surrogacy. The Warnock Report noted that the weight of public opinion at that time was against surrogacy because it was inconsistent with human dignity as well as an 'attack on the value of the marital relationship'.[7] The Warnock Report recommended that all surrogacy arrangements should be unenforceable and that agencies which recruited women to act as surrogate mothers should be criminally liable. The Brazier Report recommended that payments to surrogate mothers other than those expenses genuinely associated with the pregnancy should be prohibited and the practice of surrogacy should not be encouraged. The Brazier Report met with considerable criticism from two medical law scholars.[8] One of Freeman's criticisms concerned reproductive autonomy rights. As he said: 'We cannot stop women exercising their autonomy, nor can we persuade them that being paid aggravates their exploitation, when common sense tells them the reverse.'[9]

More recently, a report published by the Law Commission of India also expressed reservations about commercial surrogacy. The Law Commission noted that these 'moral issues . . . are pretty obvious, yet of an eye-opening nature'.[10] However, the Law Commission also found that basic human rights issues tend to be overlooked in the surrogacy debate, and reminded us that Article 16.1 of the Universal Declaration of Human Rights 1948 states that men and women 'have a right to marry and found a family'.[11]

In the latter decades of the twentieth century, the public imagination about the iniquity of surrogacy was ignited by futuristic science fiction novels and films. In *The Handmaid's Tale*,[12] most adults in the fictional Republic of Gilead were barren due to pollution and radiation. Fertile women were forced to be 'Handmaids' (slaves) with one sole function—to breed. Each handmaid was handed over to a Master and she acted as

3 [2012] FamCA 602.

4 Summary of Argument of Australian Human Rights Commission (AHRC), File No (P)SYC 1924 of 2011 in *Ellison and anor and Karnchanit* [2012] FamCA 602, para 23.

5 Department of Health and Social Security, 'Report of the Committee of Inquiry into Human Fertilisation and Embryology' (London: HMSO, 1984) Cmnd 9314 (Warnock Report).

6 M. Brazier, A. Campbell, and S. Golombok, 'Surrogacy: Review for Health Ministers of Current Arrangements for Payments and Regulation' (London: HMSO, 1998) Cmnd 4068 (Brazier Report).

7 Warnock Report (n 5) para 8.10.

8 See M. Freeman, 'Does Surrogacy Have a Future after Brazier?' (1997) *Medical Law Review* 1; see also E. Jackson, *Regulating Reproduction Law, Technology and Autonomy* (Oxford: Hart, 2001) 284–91.

9 Freeman, 'Does Surrogacy Have a Future after Brazier?' (n 8) 10.

10 Law Commission of India, 'Need for Legislation to Regulate Assisted Reproductive Technology Clinics as well as Rights and Obligations of Parties to a Surrogacy', Report No 228 (2009) 11.

11 Law Commission of India, 'Need for Legislation' (n 10) 11–12.

12 M. Attwood, *The Handmaid's Tale* (McClelland and Stewart, 1985).

a surrogate for the Master's barren wife. This novel has been commonly interpreted as a warning from Attwood about the evils of surrogacy.

However, recent research has found that the experiences of contemporary surrogate mothers in Britain and the United States are quite different from the story told in *The Handmaid's Tale*. Busby and Vun found that:

> The empirical research focusing on surrogate mothers in Britain and the United States does not support concerns that they are being exploited by these arrangements, that they cannot give meaningful consent to participating, or that the arrangements commodify women or children. Money is a motivator for some participants, but for most the decision to participate comes out of a desire to help a childless couple, to do something unusual or to make a unique contribution.[13]

Lee endorses the claims that financial considerations are not the only or primary motivator for American women agreeing to become gestational surrogates; and that problems are most likely to arise when women are not given adequate information or advice before deciding to enter into a surrogacy contract.[14] It must be emphasized that the respondents in these studies were not from undeveloped countries where the main reason for the surrogate mother entering into a contract is most likely to be financial. Moreover, in India, many women are under pressure from husbands and families and their experience of surrogacy will be determined by the ethical values of the clinic they attend.[15]

The thriving industry of cross border surrogacy and the increase in the number of parental applications demonstrates that laws banning commercial surrogacy are virtually unenforceable in the global context of the twenty-first century. Furthermore, it is argued that the legitimacy of these laws is questionable as they are antithetical to public policy goals. Rather than promoting the best interests of children and respecting their rights, they expose children born as a result of cross border surrogacy to a range of the risks, including becoming stateless orphans and victims of trafficking. They also encroach on reproductive rights by prohibiting socially and biologically infertile people from being parties to a commercial surrogacy contract and having a family.

2. Surrogacy Developments

Advances in reproductive technologies have revolutionized contemporary surrogacy. A traditional or partial surrogacy refers to a pregnancy where a surrogate mother's egg is fertilized by artificial insemination with sperm from the intended father or a donor and she gives birth to a child for the intended parents. The development of in vitro fertilization (IVF) in the twentieth century paved the way for gestational surrogacy where the surrogate mother has no genetic relationship with the child and which provides more options for people 'who have been denied the blessings of reproduction'.[16] This procedure refers to a pregnancy where eggs from the intended mother or an anonymous donor are fertilized through IVF with sperm from the intended father or an anonymous source and where another woman carries the fetus and gives birth. Gestational surrogacy is used in most commercial surrogacy arrangements to avoid

[13] K. Busby and D. Vun, 'Revisiting the Handmaid's Tale: Feminist Theory Meets Empirical Research on Surrogate Mothers' (2010) 26 *Canadian Journal of Family Law* 80.

[14] Lee, 'New Trends in Global Outsourcing of Commercial Surrogacy' (n 2) 276.

[15] A. Pande, 'At Least I am Not Sleeping with Anyone: Resisting the Stigma of Commercial Surrogacy in India' (2010) *Feminist Studies* 292.

[16] D. Spa, 'Where Babies Come From' (2006) Harvard Business Review 133.

relinquishing issues and legal problems. One Australian study found 'evidence to suggest that where the surrogate mother has no genetic link to the child, the potential for disputes between parties is reduced'.[17]

There has been a noticeable change in the attitudes of the courts towards surrogacy over the last few decades. In one of the first surrogacy cases, *A v C*,[18] the surrogate mother changed her mind at the birth and the biological father of a child born as a result of artificial insemination was denied custody of the child but granted access on the welfare principle. All three judges in the Court of Appeal condemned the arrangement, describing it as a form of 'baby-farming'. In the high profile English *Baby Cotton* case,[19] a child welfare agency intervened and prevented the surrogate mother from relinquishing the baby to the intended parents. Latey J characterized the surrogacy arrangement as bizarre and unnatural.[20] He noted that the commercial aspect of the surrogacy arrangement raised difficult moral and ethical questions but decided that these were questions for 'others', not for the wardship court. In his view, the first and foremost consideration for the wardship court was the best interests of the child.

Across the Atlantic in the New Jersey case *The Matter of Baby M*,[21] the Court ruled that a commercial surrogacy contract was invalid because it was in conflict with the law and public policy of the State of New Jersey. Chief Justice Wilentz found the surrogacy arrangement between the biological mother and the biological father was potentially degrading to women because of the payment of money. He classified the surrogacy contract as a form of 'baby-bartering' and thus illegal if not criminal, because it was against the law to pay or accept money for a private adoption placement. Nevertheless, he awarded custody of the child to the intended parents because he found it was in the best interests of the child.

The application of the welfare principle in these early cases has influenced contemporary cases where the intended parents apply for parental orders. *Re L (A Minor)*[22] was a case involving a British couple who entered into a commercial surrogacy agreement made in the State of Illinois. When considering their application for a parental order, Hedley J took the view that the current law which incorporates the paramountcy principle into the decision to grant parental orders means that 'welfare is no longer merely the court's first consideration but becomes its paramount consideration... It must follow that it will only be in the clearest case of an abuse of public policy that a court will be able to withhold an order if otherwise, welfare considerations support its making.'[23] This would appear to make the prohibition on commercial surrogacy in Britain virtually ineffective.

The welfare principle has also been central to cross border surrogacy decisions in the Family Court of Australia, where judges have expressed more concerns about evidentiary issues, consent, and the effect of an illegal contract on parenting orders rather than moral questions.[24] The welfare principle has become entrenched in these cases and has contributed a degree of legitimacy to the practice of both traditional and commercial surrogacy.

17 P. Trowse, 'Surrogacy: Is it Harder to Relinquish Genes?' (2011) 18 *Journal of Law and Medicine* 614.

18 [1985] FLR 445. This case was decided in 1978 and reported seven years later.

19 *Re C (A Minor) (Wardship: Surrogacy)* [1985] FLR 846.

20 [1985] FLR 846.

21 109 NJ 396; 537 A 2d 12(1988).

22 [2010] EWHC 3146 (Fam).

23 [2010] EWHC 3146 (Fam) para 10.

24 *Ellison and anor and Karnchanit*; *Denis and anor and Pradchaphet* [2011] FamCA 123; *Dudley and anor and Chedi* [2011] FamCA 502.

3. Global Commercial Surrogacy

The continuing advances in reproductive technologies have contributed to the growing market in commercial surrogacy, which in turn has led to less social stigma. Such advances have also made it possible for single people and homosexual couples to be biological or social parents, and this development has contributed to many changes in contemporary family formation, family households, and definitions of parenthood.[25]

The commercial surrogacy market emerged in the United States in the late 1970s with some 'unregulated States'[26] offering these services—followed later by countries such as India and Ukraine building reputations 'as international surrogacy meccas providing quality medical care at a low cost and by attempting to provide the most comprehensive legal protection for intended parents.'[27] Cross border commercial surrogacy is a 'booming global business' which in India is estimated to be worth US$400 million a year.[28] Another source estimates that 'the industry in India is worth up to '1.5 billion each year and growing'.[29] Cross border commercial surrogacy involves intended parent(s) entering into a financial agreement with the surrogate mother in another jurisdiction to conceive, gestate, and give birth to a baby with the intention of relinquishing the baby to the intended parents to raise the child in their home jurisdiction.[30]

As predicted, the demand for surrogacy worldwide has increased, not diminished.[31] There are no reliable statistics, but the growing number of parenting applications being made to the courts indicates that cross border traffic in surrogacy is not only increasing but is fraught with legal problems. The growth of the international surrogacy market can be attributed to various causes. There is a growing demand for babies because the incidence of infertility has increased in developed countries and the number of babies available for adoption has diminished. Across the world there are many children who are waiting to be adopted and many people wishing to adopt them, but the extensive waiting periods and bureaucratic hurdles make surrogacy an appealing option. Furthermore, the global regulation of surrogacy is a patchwork of prohibitive and permissive jurisdictions with considerably lower costs in some of the permissive jurisdictions. According to the Report of the Law Commission of India, 'the usual fee is around $25,000 to $30,000 in India which is around a third of that in developed countries like the USA'.[32] The acceptability of modern travel, combined with access to information offered by the internet, makes border crossing to a cheaper or more permissive

25 R. Cook, 'Donating Parenthood: Perspectives on Parenthood from Surrogacy and Gamete Donation' in A. Bainham, S. Day Sclater, and M. Richards (eds), *What is a Parent?: A Socio-Legal Analysis* (Oxford: Hart, 1999) ch 7.

26 B.A. Patton, 'Buying a Newborn: Globalization and the Lack of Federal Regulation of Commercial Surrogacy Contracts' (2010–11) 79 *University of Missouri-Kansas City Law Review* 507.

27 S. Mohapatra, 'Stateless Babies and Adoption Scams: A Bioethical Analysis of International Commercial Surrogacy' (2012) 30 *International Commercial Surrogacy* 412, 413.

28 Hague Conference Permanent Bureau, 'Private International Law Issues Surrounding the Status of Children. Including Issues Arising from International Surrogacy Agreements', Preliminary Document No 11 of March 2011 for the attention of the Council of April 2011 on General affairs and Policy of the Conference, 6–7. (Hague Conference, 2011).

29 J. Ware, 'Britons paying up to £25,000 for Indian Surrogate Babies' *BioNews*, 6 June 2012, available at <http://www.bionews.org.uk/page_148622.asp> (accessed 29 September 2012)

30 Standing Committee of Attorneys-General Australian Health Ministers' Conference (A Joint Working Group), 'A Proposal for a National Model to Harmonise Regulation of Surrogacy' (2009) 2.

31 M. Freeman, 'Is Surrogacy Exploitative?' in S. McLean (ed), *Legal Issues in Human Reproduction* (Ashgate: Dartmouth, 1989).

32 Law Commission of India, 'Need for Legislation' (n 10) 11.

jurisdiction a very attractive and feasible choice for many people. As examples of the flow of international surrogacy traffic: US citizens travel from prohibitive domestic States to clinics in permissive States such as California, or they go to countries such as India or Thailand where these services are unregulated and relatively cheap; Europeans from prohibitive jurisdictions travel to clinics in Eastern Europe, India, Thailand, and California; and Australians generally travel to clinics in California, India, and Thailand.[33]

The narratives underpinning many reported cases demonstrate that there are health risks for surrogate mothers and the new born babies, particularly for twins and triplets, when intended parents have to travel to another jurisdiction to have a child through surrogacy. One particular concern is the use of multiple IVF embryo transfers, which pose higher health risks to the surrogate mother and the baby than single transfers. This practice seems to be relatively common given the number of the surrogacy cases involving twins, presumably because the children will have a biological sibling and it is more efficient. The reported cases also suggest there is high degree of medical intervention such as induction of pregnancy and caesareans, which may not necessarily be for the benefit of the surrogate mother or the baby.[34] Also, when intended parents face passport and citizenship problems and these families are stranded in a foreign country with their newly born child or children—they may not have access to appropriate health facilities.

4. Global Regulation

At one end of the international regulatory spectrum there are jurisdictions where commercial surrogacy is illegal; and at the other end there are jurisdictions where it is legal. However, the legality of the surrogacy arrangement is only one side of the coin. The other side concerns the consequences of illegality, covering matters such as citizenship rights, child support, succession rights, and entitlements to subsidized medical treatment and passports. In *Dudley and anor and Chedi*, Watts J refused to recognize that the biological father was a legal parent but granted an order giving both intended parents equal, shared parental responsibility for the children.[35] In most cross border cases the courts have prioritized the welfare of the child on the basis that it would not be in the interests of these children to be classified as orphans and 'non-citizens' if parental orders were not granted. At the same time, it can be acknowledged that granting parental orders in the context of an illegal surrogacy contract partially subverts 'at least the spirit of the law ... in relation to commercial surrogacy'.[36] In *Dudley and anor and Chedi*, Watts J noted that to grant an order giving the applicants parental responsibility could be 'perceived as a means of sanctioning illegal acts which were illegal in Queensland at the relevant time and which were against public policy'.[37] These developments have resulted in a legal checkmate of policy objectives in countries such as Australia. As can be expected, these issues are less complex in regimes such as Israel, where commercial surrogacy is permitted and regulated.

Commercial surrogacy is not legal in jurisdictions such as Australia, France, Germany, Italy, Japan, Spain, Turkey, Britain, and some states in the United States, with varying

[33] Lee, 'New Trends in Global Outsourcing of Commercial Surrogacy' (n 2) 276–7.
[34] *Dudley & Chedi* [2011] FamCA 502.
[35] *Dudley & Chedi* [2011] FamCA 502, para 41.
[36] *Ellison and anor and Karnchanti* [2012] FamCA 602, para 87, *per* Ryan J.
[37] *Dudley & Chedi* [2011] FamCA 502, para 37, *per* Watts J.

degrees of latitude and state intervention in each jurisdiction. In the federation of Australia, for example, the regulation of surrogacy is a state matter and it is a criminal offence in every state for a 'surrogate mother' to receive a material benefit or advantage as a result of a surrogacy agreement, other than reimbursement for costs related to the treatment. As well, the publication or advertisement of surrogacy services is a crime and commercial surrogacy contracts are legally unenforceable.[38] It is also a crime in the Australian Capital Territory but not in the Northern Territory. Furthermore, in the Australian Capital Territory, New South Wales and Queensland have passed extra-territorial laws which make it an offence for residents to be involved in a commercial surrogacy arrangement in another country. Residents from the Australian Capital Territory, New South Wales, and Queensland who engage in an international commercial surrogacy arrangement risk facing criminal charges and jail. So far no laws have been passed banning extra-territorial commercial contracts in the remaining States.

In contrast, the United States has not passed a federal law regulating surrogacy and each state has its own surrogacy policy. Mohapatra notes that:

> Some states specifically prohibit gestational surrogacy. Other states only recognize surrogacy that is noncommercial or "altruistic". Some states allow commercial surrogacy, i.e. where surrogates may be paid compensation over and above medical expenses. Finally, numerous states have yet to address surrogacy agreements in either case law or by statute. In these states it is unclear precisely how surrogacy contracts would be handled in a legal dispute.[39]

Mohopatra adds that within this legal patchwork, 'California is the capital of commercial surrogacy in the United States'.[40] Lee notes that 'the confusing state of the law in the U.S. combined with expensive legal costs to deal with surrogacy contracts are... likely contributors to the heightened demand for fertility tourism in India'.[41]

British law is riddled with ambiguity and complexity. The Surrogacy Arrangements Act 1985 prohibits commercial involvement in the process of organizing and negotiating a surrogacy agreement and advertising surrogacy services. However, non-profit organizations are allowed to charge reasonable fees in order to cover their expenses. It is not an offence to enter into a surrogacy contract, but they are not enforceable and therefore none of the parties is bound by the agreement.[42] Describing Britain's complex surrogacy laws, Hedley J observed in *X and Y (Foreign Surrogacy)* that 'whilst commercial surrogacy is unlawful, surrogacy itself is not, but no surrogacy agreement is legally enforceable as such'.[43] The courts can also retroactively authorize payments that have been made in a commercial arrangement even if the amount paid is more than the expenses—if it is in the child's best interests.[44] In *Re L (a minor)*,[45] Hedley J made it clear that legislative changes to the welfare test mean that the welfare of a child is the paramount consideration in these cases. In both *X and Y (Foreign Surrogacy)* and *Re L (a minor)*, Hedley J pointed out that if Parliament intends to control commercial surrogacy arrangements that take place in other jurisdictions effectively, these controls should operate at the point of admission to Britain.

38 See eg Assisted Reproductive Treatment Act 2008 (Vic), ss 44 and 45.
39 Mohapatra, 'Stateless Babies and Adoption Scams' (n 27) 424–5.
40 Mohapatra, 'Stateless Babies and Adoption Scams' (n 27) 426.
41 Lee, 'New Trends in Global Outsourcing of Commercial Surrogacy' (n 2) 290.
42 Surrogacy Arrangements Act 1985 (UK), s 1B.
43 *X and Y (Foreign Surrogacy)* [2008] EWHC 3030 (Fam) para 3.
44 See *Re X (Children) (Parental Order: Retrospective Authorisation of Payments)* [2011] EWHC 3147 (Fam).
45 [2010] EWHC 3146 (Fam).

The Australian and British approaches to regulating surrogacy 'pass the buck' to other countries to deal with problems associated with commercial surrogacy while standing aside and allowing their own citizens to exercise their reproductive choices. They also delegate the responsibility for deciding the fate of these children to the family courts. As a result, judges have to make decisions which would have challenged the wisdom of the biblical King Solomon.

Commercial surrogacy is legal in countries such as India, Ukraine, Israel, and (as already noted) in some US states. In India, commercial surrogacy is lawful and unregulated. Infertility in India is regarded as a major problem because kinship and family ties are dependent on progeny. On the one hand, hiring a surrogate mother has been embraced by Indian people as a solution to infertility, but on the other hand there is a degree of social stigma attached to surrogate mothers. It has been reported that the Indian government encourages surrogacy practice with concessions and tax breaks for hospitals that treat international patients, and world-class medical facilities with low costs for fertility tourists.[46] The incidence of surrogacy in India has increased in the last few years and it is estimated that a third of the people entering into surrogacy arrangements are foreign parents who hire Indian woman as surrogates.[47]

The Law Commission of India recommended legislative intervention into the surrogacy industry and the Assisted Reproductive Technologies (Regulation) Bill and Rules 2008 should be presented to the Parliament in the near future.[48] For the time being, clinics are expected to comply with professional Guidelines published by the Indian Council of Medical Research.[49] These Guidelines are designed to protect the interests of intended parents rather than surrogate mothers and are not legally enforceable.[50] Furthermore, the requirement to obtain informed consent indicating that the surrogate mother understands the nature of the contract is not mandatory under the Guidelines.[51] The websites and popular press articles on India suggest that the clinics 'do not strictly adhere to the Guidelines'.[52] There is no national registry providing reliable information on the number of clinics in India but it has been reported that: 'There are up to 1,000 fertility clinics in [India] with many specialising in international surrogacy arrangements.'[53] The Law Commission of India's Report sums up the situation as follows: 'It seems that wombs in India are on rent which translates into babies for foreigners and dollars for Indian surrogate mothers.'[54]

California has not passed legislation banning or regulating surrogacy, with the result that contractual disputes, gestational matters and parentage issues are resolved by the courts. The costs are very high in California, but clinics are experienced and can operate in an established legal framework.[55] In the US patchwork of different surrogacy regimes, California is an example of a laissez faire state with a thriving

46 Mohapatra, 'Stateless Babies and Adoption Scams' (n 27) 433.

47 Mohapatra, 'Stateless Babies and Adoption Scams' (n 27) 433.

48 Law Commission of India, 'Need for Legislation' (n 10) 16–17.

49 Indian Council of Medical Research and the National Academy of Medical Sciences (NAMS) National Guidelines for Accreditation, Supervision and Regulation of ART Clinics in India (2005) <http://icmr.nic.in/art/art_clinics.htm> (accessed 14 January 2013).

50 Mohapatra, 'Stateless Babies and Adoption Scams' (n 27) 434.

51 U.R. Smerdon, 'Crossing Bodies, Crossing Borders: International Surrogacy between the States in India' (2008–09) 39 *Cumberland Law Review* 15, 41.

52 Smerdon, 'Crossing Bodies, Crossing Borders' (n 51) 30.

53 Ware, 'Britons paying up to £25,000 for Indian Surrogate Babies' (n 29).

54 Law Commission of India, 'Need for Legislation' (n 9) 11.

55 Y. Ergas, 'Babies Without Borders, Human Rights, Human Dignity, and the Regulation of International Surrogacy' (2013) 27 *Emory International Law Review* 117, 123.

surrogacy industry which attracts large numbers of international clients and people from other US states with prohibitive regimes.

Israel, unlike India, has introduced an effective legal framework regulating gestational commercial surrogacy which is supported by cultural traditions, a pro-natalist state policy and a pragmatic approach to the social importance of the family.[56] As well, Israel has 'invested large amounts of money into developing reproductive technologies' and 'national health insurance funds IVF treatments both to married women and single women for up to two successful births'.[57]

In 1996, Israel passed legislation which permits and controls the practice of surrogacy.[58] The legislation requires that approvals for surrogacy contracts must be obtained from a statutory body called the Approvals Committee. This well organized regulatory system aims to protect state interests in regulating human reproduction and also to respect personal autonomy and privacy rights. The Approvals Committee 'is responsible for judicial review and formal approval of surrogacy contracts, ensuring all parties' interests are protected in a balanced way'.[59] The regulatory scheme provides safeguards for the surrogate mother by ensuring: '(1) her suitability for the role (2) that her consent is voluntary and fully informed (3) protection for her physical and mental health (4) protection of her rights to privacy and (5) financial protection'.[60] Children's interests are protected by the Approvals Committee requiring both the intended parents and the surrogate mother to undergo medical checks, and imposing age conditions on the intended parents. The intended parents must also give an undertaking to make provision for a child who is born with disabilities and if the marriage breaks down. As well, a sole legal guardian must be appointed as soon as the child is born and the intended parents must apply for a parentage order within seven days of the child's birth.

There is no payment scale in Israel and the Approvals Committee does not interfere with the financial side of the agreement; however, the amount being paid to the surrogate mother is transparent. The interests of the intended parents are protected by rules denying the birth mother the right to renege without a court order. It is claimed that there have not been any reneging incidents to date and this is probably due to the initial screening process.[61] Initially only heterosexual couples were eligible for surrogacy. However, in 2012 *BioNews* reported that a public health commission in Israel has recommended that 'Gay men' should be allowed to engage a surrogate to have a family.[62]

5. Commercial Surrogacy Arrangements and Interests: Consent

Consent is the core of reproductive autonomy and therefore there are serious concerns about the voluntariness of many women from poor backgrounds making a free choice to enter into a commercial surrogacy. One of the reasons for prohibiting commercial surrogacy in Queensland appears to be a concern that surrogate mothers may be subject

56 D. Spurling, 'Commanding the "Be Fruitful and Multiply" Directive: Reproductive Ethics, Law and Policy in Israel' (2010) 19 *Cambridge Quarterly of Healthcare Ethics* 363.

57 Lee, 'New Trends in Global Outsourcing of Commercial Surrogacy' (n 2) 295.

58 The Embryo Carrying Agreement (Agreement Authorisation and Status of the Newborn Child), 1996, Statute Book 176.

59 Lee, 'New Trends in Global Outsourcing of Commercial Surrogacy' (n 2) 296.

60 Lee, 'New Trends in Global Outsourcing of Commercial Surrogacy' (n 2) 296.

61 Lee, 'New Trends in Global Outsourcing of Commercial Surrogacy' (n 2) 296.

62 S. Gray, 'Israel Gives Gay Men the Right to Conceive Children Via a Surrogate' *BioNews*, 6 June 2012 <http://www.bionewhs.org.uk/page_148599.asp> (accessed 8 January 2013).

to 'coercion, undue influence or exploitation'.[63] However, as cases such as *Ellison and anor and Karnchanit* demonstrate, if people are denied access to surrogacy in jurisdictions such as Queensland they will go to countries such as Thailand, where the surrogacy industry is flourishing and where it appears the concept of an informed consent is barely a consideration.

The Hague Permanent Bureau notes that the claims about women who live in poverty being forced to become surrogates are real and cites a 2011 BBC programme[64] which covered a report about a Taiwanese-run surrogacy agency, which, it was alleged, 'in some cases, forced Vietnamese to become surrogate mothers'.[65] The Bureau also suggests that even in some routine cases it is not clear that women are choosing freely to become surrogate mothers.[66] The lack of free choice may be attributed to coercion but also to a lack of power due to illiteracy and a limited general education. Mohapatra concludes that 'it is unlikely that surrogates in places like India may freely negotiate the terms of their surrogacy arrangements because of the financial need of the surrogate and their relative lack of legal sophistication'.[67] These concerns are compounded by the fact that the children are born in foreign jurisdictions and the applications for parental orders take place in the legal domicile of the intended parents—where it is unlikely that a surrogate mother from a country such as India or Thailand will be available to give evidence in person. This situation limits the ability of courts to test the veracity of the evidence.

In *Ellison and anor and Karnchanit*, the AHRC submitted that:

> In assessing evidence of the consent given by a surrogate mother to proceedings of this nature (particularly where the surrogate mother is not available to give evidence in person), the Commission submits that it is important for independent evidence (including, for example, from a family counsellor) to be obtained of her views so that the court can be satisfied that her expressed consent is free and informed consent.[68]

The AHRC added:

> If reliance is placed solely on evidence given by a surrogate mother in the form of an affidavit prepared by the solicitors for the applicants, over time such affidavits may be prepared in a pro forma way and may not be sufficiently robust for the Court to satisfy itself of matters relating to consent (both to the surrogacy agreement itself and to the parenting orders sought).[69]

In *Ellison and anor and Karnchanit*,[70] the applicants brought their two 8-week-old children from Thailand to Australia on 18 March 2011. The intended parents paid $7,350.00 to the birth mother, the respondent, Ms Karnchanit. They resided in Queensland where extra-territorial surrogacy is illegal, and initially provided the court with scant evidence supporting the application to mask the illegality of the commercial surrogacy agreement. Ryan J observed that there 'was a paucity of evidence

63 Queensland Parliament, Report, 'Investigation into Altruistic Surrogacy Committee', October 2008, available at <http://www.parliament.qld.gov.au/work-of-committees/former-committees/IASC/inquiries/past-inquiries/Surrogacy> 15, 33, and 41 (accessed 13 January 2013).

64 <http://www.bbc.co.uk/news/world-asia-pacific-12575566> (accessed 11 January 2013).

65 Hague Conference 2011, 'Private International Law Issues' (n 28) para 34.

66 Hague Conference 2011, 'Private International Law Issues' (n 28) para 34; see also J.A. Gupta, 'Towards Transnational Feminisms: some Reflections and Concerns in Relation to the Globalisation of Reproductive Technologies' (2006) 13 *European Journal of Women's Studies* 23.

67 Mohapatra, 'Stateless Babies and Adoption Scams' (n 27) 446.

68 Summary of Argument of AHRC (n 4) para 7.2.

69 Summary of Argument of AHRC (n 4) para 40.

70 [2012] FamCA 602.

presented by the applicants in support of their application . . . the evidence was so poor it was difficult to see how the applicants' unchallenged evidence provided an evidentiary foundation for the orders sought'.[71] In order to ensure that the 'Court could get to the truth, each applicant was granted a certificate pursuant to s.128 of the Evidence act 1995 (Cth). They were thus able to speak freely and be confident that their evidence could not be used in other courts'.[72]

In this case, Ryan J emphasized the need for 'close attention to ensure [that the birth mother] has given free and informed consent and has not been subject to exploitation, coercion or undue influence and that her rights have been adequately protected'.[73] She also emphasized the need for a thorough investigation to be made regarding the children's identity so that the possibility of child trafficking would be ruled out. On the identity issue Ryan J said:

> Lest it be thought the Court's concerns are fanciful, writing ex judicially Chief Federal Magistrate Pascoe recently drew together various international reports about the extent and methods used in international baby selling and trafficking. From UNHCR and other credible reports he highlighted international concern about the extent of international baby trafficking and '. . . the ability of traffickers to become legal guardians of [trafficked] babies without any record to prove otherwise'. Not infrequently this involves the trafficker declaring himself the biological father of the child and the birth mother refuting her parental rights. In the same paper the Chief Federal Magistrate explained how coercion may be used and that discrimination against women and poverty are major reasons why some women see no option other than to abandon or sell their babies. These are compelling reasons why it is incumbent upon agencies (including courts) to be satisfied to a high level that babies brought to this country are who it is claimed they are, about the circumstances of their birth and that the subject children have not been wrongfully taken from their parents.[74]

Ryan J also recommended a number of 'Best Practice Principles' (based on recommendations submitted by the AHRC and the Independent Children's Lawyer (ICL)) to be followed by courts in all surrogacy cases. These recommendations include the need for independent evidence regarding the identification of the child, which would include the surrogacy contract; a certified copy of the child's birth certificate; parentage testing; and evidence of Australian citizenship—if granted. The recommendations also include the need for independent evidence confirming that the surrogate arrangement was 'made with the informed consent of the surrogate mother'[75] and 'the views of the birth mother, in particular her consent to the proposed parenting orders'.[76]

In Britain, a court cannot grant a parenting order under section 54(1) of the Human Fertilisation and Embryology Act 2008 (HFEA 2008) unless the court is satisfied that the surrogate mother and any other person (other than the intended father) who is the child's parent 'freely, and with full understanding of what is involved, agreed unconditionally to the making of the order'.[77] Evidence is provided to the court via affidavits and surrogacy contracts which contain consent clauses; however, the actual consent to relinquish the child cannot be given by the surrogate mother before six weeks after the birth unless the mother is missing or incompetent.[78]

71 [2012] FamCA 602, para 6.
72 [2012] FamCA 602, para 3.
73 [2012] FamCA 602, para 132.
74 *Ellison and anor and Karnchanit* [2012] FamCA 602, para 5; see J. Pascoe, 'How Trafficking in Expectant Women Affects the Rights of the Child', 5th World Congress on Family Law and Children's Rights, Nova Scotia, August 2009.
75 [2012] FamCA 602, para 137(d).
76 [2012] FamCA 602, para 138(f).
77 See *A and A v P, P and B* [2011] EWHC 1738.
78 HFEA 2008, s 54(7).

6. Children's Interests and Birthrights

Birthrights and heritage are not usually a problem where family members are related through marriage, biology, or adoption. The formal process of recording information about identity and personal history commences with birth registration. Once born, a child is registered and a birth certificate is issued with information about the child's parents. However, when a surrogate mother in an international commercial cross border arrangement gives birth to a child, the information on the birth certificate will depend on the laws concerning surrogacy and the status of children in that jurisdiction.

Most of the cross border cases coming before the courts involve problems concerning the establishment or recognition of a 'child's legal parentage and the legal consequences which flow from such a determination', which include the child's nationality, immigration status, and who has the parental responsibility and duty to maintain the child.[79] In countries such as Australia, France, Germany, and Thailand, and in the UK there is an irrebuttable presumption that the birth mother is the legal mother and that her husband or *de facto* partner will be the legal father—unless and until the parental status is relinquished. In India, the surrogate mother is not considered to be the legal mother and the birth certificate is made in the name of the genetic parents.[80] In the United States, courts in some states have attempted to define motherhood according to the intent of the parties when the conception took place. In California, for example, the definition of the legal mother is determined by the circumstances of conception if the court decides this is in the best interests of the child.[81]

The intended mother can be the biological mother if she provides the egg; otherwise, a donor is the biological mother. Similarly, the intended father can be the biological father if he provides the sperm; otherwise a sperm donor will be the biological father. In commercial cross border contracts donors are usually anonymous and the children will never be able to obtain information about their genetic heritage.

The following cases provide examples of the legal complexities and legal conflicts that face courts in some of the surrogacy cases. In *Re X&Y (Foreign Surrogacy)*,[82] a professional couple from England entered into a gestational surrogacy agreement with a Ukrainian woman who had her own children. The surrogate mother was implanted with an embryo conceived in vitro with donor eggs fertilized by the intended father's sperm, and gave birth to twins. Under English law, the Ukrainian woman was the sole legal mother of the twins and her husband was the sole legal father. However, under Ukrainian law, once the surrogate mother had given birth to the twins and delivered them to the intended couple they were free of all obligations to the children. As a result, the children were not entitled to a Ukrainian passport, or Ukrainian nationality. Furthermore, the children were initially refused British passports because under English law the surrogate woman and her husband were the parents of the children. As a result of these conflicting laws the children were legal orphans, and stateless. Eventually, and after DNA tests established that the male applicant was the biological father, the children were given *discretionary leave* to enter the UK 'outside the rules', for the parents to regularize the status of the twins under English law. Hedley J granted the intended parents a Parental Order on the welfare principle.

79 Hague Conference, 2011 'Private International Law Issues' (n 28) para 3.
80 Law Commission of India, 'Need for Legislation' (n 10) 14.
81 *Johnson v Calvert* 851 P 2d 776 (Cal 1993).
82 [2008] EWHC 3030 (High Court).

The oft cited case of *Baby Manji Yamada v Union of India*[83] is another legal saga concerning parentage. In this case a Japanese couple entered a gestational surrogacy agreement with a surrogate mother in India. The intended father was the biological father but the egg was obtained from a donor. A month before the baby, Manji, was born the intended parents got divorced. Under the surrogacy contract the surrogate mother's role terminated once the baby was born. The intended father wanted the child but his wife did not want to raise her and refused to accompany him to India to get the child. He had to return to Japan because his visa expired and even though the child became very ill he could not take her back to Japan because Japanese law did not permit single fathers to adopt baby girls. The child was a stateless orphan. The child's paternal grandmother flew to India to take care of the child and she filed a petition in the Supreme Court seeking a parenting order. Subsequently, baby Manji was taken to Japan by her genetic father and grandmother.

In Australia, children born overseas as a result of a commercial cross border arrangement 'are not the legal children of their Australian intended parent(s) regardless of genetic link and regardless of any provision in a foreign birth certificate or court order to the contrary'.[84] It is not even clear that these children are entitled to Australian citizenship by descent. However, citizenship is usually granted if one intended parent can prove a genetic link through DNA testing 'and evidence is presented of both the legality of parentage for at least one intended parent and the relinquishment of parental rights by the birth mother in the foreign jurisdiction'.[85] On the other hand, if the parties are both infertile it would appear to be very difficult for them to comply with these requirements.

If the intended parents are not eligible for a state transfer of legal parentage order because of the extra-territorial laws in the Australian Capital Territory, New South Wales and Queensland, they may apply to the Family Court of Australia for a parental order which gives the intended parents equal parental responsibility for making decisions on both day-to-day and long-term issues in relation to the children. However, these orders do not confer the status of legal parent on the intended parents.[86]

The traditional laws dealing with the ascription of parenthood are not designed to deal with the issues that arise in cross border surrogacy arrangements. As has already been noted in this chapter, these conflicts may constitute breaches of various Articles of the CRC.

7. Conclusion

The developments in global surrogacy discussed in this chapter have shown that there is a demand and market for surrogate mothers to be paid to gestate and give birth to a child for the benefit of the intended parents. Commercial surrogacy is very controversial and there are many legal and ethical issues which need to be publicly debated, however, more restrictive laws are likely to drive the practice underground. Surrogacy laws are struggling to keep up with continuing advances in reproductive technologies and the continuing evolution of family formation. As a result, there is a patchwork of

83 JT 2008 (11) SC 150.

84 J. Millbank, 'The New Surrogacy Parentage Laws in Australia' (2011) 35 *Melbourne University Law Review* 165, 200.

85 Millbank, 'The New Surrogacy Parentage Laws' (n 84) 201.

86 *Dennis and anor and Pradchapet* [2011] FamCA 123; and *Dudley and anor and Chedi* [2011] FamCA 5002.

global surrogacy laws and a thriving 'off shore' surrogacy industry in countries such as India, Thailand, and Ukraine. In this global 'jurisdictional chaos' the critical issues concern the welfare of children, the risk of exploiting women who act as surrogates, and the right to 'found a family'. The domestic courts play an important role in granting parental orders when the intended parents bring the children back to their domestic domicile. This has been achieved by courts placing their focus on the welfare of the children and requiring and assessing independent evidence regarding the identity of children and also independent evidence that the surrogate mother has given her informed consent to the surrogacy contract and the proposed parenting orders. However, in prohibitive countries, such as Australia, the criminal laws can act to obfuscate the ability of the courts to assess the true circumstances of these children in genuine cases, as well as child trafficking cases. Admittedly, there is no consensus on this issue of commercial surrogacy. The empirical findings reported in the Busby and Vun study[87] are most important because they strongly suggest that many of the early ethical concerns about commercial surrogacy can be overcome if criminal laws are repealed and substituted with permissive regulation. The findings also remind us that there is a dearth of much needed research about the experiences of people involved in commercial surrogacy arrangements in jurisdictions where commercial surrogacy has been banned.

More recently it seems that the authorities in India are taking some steps to limit access to surrogacy. It has been reported that intending parents seeking to employ a surrogate mother in India are now required to apply for medical visas which are only available to heterosexual couples who have been married for at least two years.[88] It is difficult to ascertain how strictly this new condition is enforced. If this intervention is successful in controlling access, it is most likely that the clinics will establish facilities in other undeveloped countries such as Thailand where the laws are not restrictive.

Instead of 'passing the buck' to undeveloped countries, it would be a wiser and more intelligent approach for developed countries to address the reasons why people risk entering into foreign surrogacy contracts. Also, action needs to be taken in order to introduce regulatory models permitting and controlling commercial surrogacy in the developed countries—taking into account a country's cultural mores, costs, reproductive liberties, and changing family patterns. This approach could be the first step to the more ambitious solution of introducing a 'multilateral, legally binding instrument that would establish a global, coherent and ethical practice of international surrogacy'.[89] However, in the short term, the surrogacy laws in Israel are an example of a successful model which is tailored for that particular country. With political will, it could be adapted to serve the needs of all the parties involved in cross border contracts in other jurisdictions.

87 Busby and Vun, 'Revisiting the Handmaid's Tale' (n 13).

88 N. Hyder, 'India Limits Surrogacy to Married Couples', *Bio News*, 21 January 2013, available at <http://www.bionews.org.uk/page_242618.asp>; R. Carr, 'India to Enforce Visa Restrictions on Those Seeking Surrogacy', *Bio News*, 4 November 2013, available at <http://www.bionews.org.uk/page_359997.asp>; see also <http://boi.gov.in/content/surrogacy> (accessed 17 November 2013).

89 K. Trimmings and P. Beaumont, 'International Surrogacy Arrangement: An Urgent Need for Legal Regulation at the International Level' (2011) 7 *Journal of Private International Law* 628, 633.

13

Maternal Mortality and Human Rights

From Theory to Practice

Judith Bueno de Mesquita

1. Introduction

In 2010, 287,000 women died worldwide during pregnancy and in, or following, childbirth.[1] Almost all of these deaths could have been prevented.[2] Maternal mortality reduction has been a key international development and public health commitment since the 1980s. Most notably, the reduction of the maternal mortality ratio (MMR) by 75 per cent between 1990 and 2015 is number five of the eight Millennium Development Goals (MDGs), agreed by the international community in 2000 and the centrepiece of the global development agenda. However, the international community, and many developing countries in particular, are off-track to meet MDG5: maternal deaths have reduced by 47 per cent since 1990.[3]

Although preventable maternal deaths occur in significantly greater numbers than other human rights violations such as torture or enforced disappearances,[4] until recently, the issue was marginalized by the mainstream international human rights community. However, in the past five years, some of the key global human rights bodies and mechanisms have placed the issue firmly at the heart of their agendas: since 2009, the Human Rights Council (HRC) has adopted four resolutions on *preventable maternal mortality and morbidity and human rights*;[5] the Office of the United Nations High Commissioner for Human Rights (OHCHR) has written three reports on the subject;[6]

1 WHO et al, 'Trends in Maternal Mortality: 1990 to 2010 WHO, UNICEF, UNFPA and The World Bank Estimates' (Geneva, 2012).

2 World Health Organization, Fact Sheet No 348: 'Maternal Mortality' (Geneva, May 2012).

3 WHO, 'Trends in Maternal Mortality' (n 1).

4 United Nations Human Rights Council, 'Report of the United Nations Special Rapporteur on the right to the enjoyment of the highest attainable standard of physical and mental health', 17 January 2007, A/HRC/4/28.

5 United Nations Human Rights Council resolution (2009) 11/8, 'Preventable Maternal Mortality and Morbidity and Human Rights' (11th Session) A/HRC/Res/11/8; United Nations Human Rights Council resolution (2010) 15/17, 'Preventable Maternal Mortality and Morbidity and Human Rights: Follow-up to Council resolution 11/8' (fifteenth session) A/HRC/15/L.27; UN Human Rights Council resolution (2011) 18/2, 'Preventable Maternal Mortality and Morbidity and Human Rights' (eighteenth session) A/HRC/18/L.8; UN Human Rights Council resolution (2012) 21/6, 'Preventable Maternal Mortality and Morbidity and Human Rights' (twenty-first session) A/HRC/21/6.

6 UN Human Rights Council, 'Report of the Office of the United Nations High Commissioner for Human Rights (OHCHR) on preventable maternal mortality and morbidity and human rights' (15th session) 16 April 2010, A/HRC/14/39; UN Human Rights Council, 'Report of the OHCHR on Practices in Adopting a Human Rights-based Approach to Eliminate Preventable Maternal Mortality and Human Rights' (eighteenth session) 8 July 2011, A/HRC/18/27; UN Human Rights Council, 'Report of the OHCHR on Technical Guidance on the Application of a Human Rights-based Approach to the Implementation of Policies and Programmes to Reduce Preventable Maternal Morbidity and Mortality' (twenty-first session) 2 July 2012, A/HRC/21/22.

the Committee on the Elimination of Discrimination Against Women (CEDAW Committee) adopted the first international decision on maternal mortality, *Alyne da Silva Pimentel v Brazil*;[7] and the first Special Rapporteur on the right to the highest attainable standard of health ('right to health'), Paul Hunt, presented several reports to the HRC and the General Assembly (GA) on maternal mortality, including a report on an official mission to India that focused on this issue.[8] These developments are important because human rights can support maternal mortality reduction.

In this chapter, I analyse how maternal mortality evolved from a development to a leading human rights issue, and assess how human rights have been used to enhance maternal mortality reduction. Section 2 highlights that maternal mortality became a mainstream human rights issue as long as two decades after it emerged as a prominent development concern. I argue that this lengthy delay was part of a broader neglect of economic, social, and cultural (ESC) rights by the human rights community. Key developments that precipitated the trajectory of maternal mortality towards the centre of the international human rights agenda include a greater focus on ESC rights by the international human rights community, the development of a reproductive health and human rights agenda, and catalytic roles played the UN Special Rapporteur on the right to health and civil society in galvanizing attention to the issue from a wide variety of actors. Section 3 is devoted to assessing the different strands of work on maternal mortality and human rights by researchers and practitioners. It examines important conceptual analysis of the relationship between maternal mortality and human rights and finds several contrasting approaches, which have subsequently underpinned practice. Moving from theory to practice, I argue that the three main ways that human rights have been used to support maternal mortality reduction are: as an authoritative and powerful framework for research and advocacy; to enhance accountability for maternal mortality through engaging international and domestic human rights machinery; and through their integration into development and public health policies, programmes, and strategies.[9] However, the use of human rights is still the exception rather than the norm in maternal mortality reduction efforts. Where human rights have been integrated, this has sometimes been on paper without full implementation in practice. Moreover, the contribution of human rights has not been consistently evaluated. In section 4, I argue that these shortcomings need to be addressed if human rights are to play a prominent role and fully realize their potential in maternal mortality reduction efforts.

2. Maternal Mortality: from Development to Human Rights

2.1 Where and why do women die as a result of pregnancy and childbirth?

Globally, 800 women die from pregnancy and childbirth-related causes every day.[10] Of these deaths, 99 per cent occur in developing countries, more than half in Sub-Saharan

[7] Committee on the Elimination of Discrimination against Women (CEDAW Committee), Views: Communication No 17/2008 (forty-ninth session) 11–29 July 2011, CEDAW/C/49/D/17/2008.

[8] UN Human Rights Council, 'Report of the United Nations Special Rapporteur on the right to the enjoyment of the highest attainable standard of physical and mental health: Addendum—Mission to India', 15 April 2010, A/HRC/14/20.Add.2.

[9] A tripartite contribution of advocacy, accountability, and rights-based approaches was first identified by Mindy Roseman. See M. Roseman, 'Bearing Human Rights and the Promises of ICPD' in L. Reichenbach and M. Roseman (eds), *Reproductive Health and Human Rights: the Way Forward* (University of Pennsylvania Press, 2009) 91.

[10] WHO, 'Trends in Maternal Mortality' (n 1).

Africa, and almost one-third in South Asia.[11] Whilst the maternal MMR in developed countries is 16 per 100,000 births, in developing countries it is 240 per 100,000 births. Within countries, there are large disparities, including between wealthy and impoverished women, and rural and urban women, reflecting a range of inequalities that affect access to maternal health.

A maternal death is defined by the World Health Organization (WHO) as 'the death of a woman while pregnant or within 42 days of termination of pregnancy, irrespective of the duration and site of the pregnancy, from any cause related to or aggravated by the pregnancy or its management but not from accidental or incidental causes'.[12] The four major causes of maternal deaths, accounting for 80 per cent of the total, are: severe bleeding, mostly after childbirth; infections, usually after childbirth; high blood pressure during pregnancy; and unsafe abortion. Other leading causes of death include infection, including with malaria and AIDS, during pregnancy.

Almost all maternal deaths are avoidable through well-known healthcare interventions to prevent or manage complications. Antenatal care during pregnancy, skilled care during childbirth, and care and support in the weeks after childbirth are critical to the prevention of maternal mortality.[13] Of these, skilled care during childbirth is particularly important. This is reflected in MDG5, which is monitored by two indicators—the MMR and the proportion of births attended by skilled health personnel.

In high-income countries, nearly all women receive the recommended care in pregnancy and during and after childbirth. However, in low-income countries, only 46 per cent of women benefit from skilled attendance at childbirth, and only a third have the recommended four antenatal appointments.[14] Among the barriers to these women are poverty, distance from services, a lack of information, poor quality services, and cultural practices,[15] as well as underlying contributory problems such as gender inequality and its various manifestations such as the status of women in the family and society, and early marriage and pregnancy.

2.2 The emergence of maternal mortality in the international public health and development agendas

The consensus document of the Third World Conference on Women (1985) raised the profile of maternal mortality in the international community, calling for a reduction to a 'minimum level' by 2000.[16] However, subsequently maternal mortality remained neglected in the development priorities of governments and funding priorities of donors.[17] In 1985, in a seminal article, Allan Rosenfield and Deborah Maine argued that although maternal and child health had received increased attention, programmes tended to focus on infants/children. They pointed out that specific initiatives for maternal health—where they existed—tended to focus on high-technology subspecialities, whereas different interventions were required to reduce maternal mortality,

11 WHO, 'Trends in Maternal Mortality' (n 1).

12 WHO, 'International Statistical Classification of Diseases and Related Health Problems' (Geneva, 2010).

13 WHO, 'Trends in Maternal Mortality' (n 1).

14 WHO, 'Trends in Maternal Mortality' (n 1).

15 WHO, 'Trends in Maternal Mortality' (n 1).

16 Report of the World Conference to Review and Appraise the Achievements of the United Nations Decade for Women: Equality, Peace and Development, 15–26 July 1985, Nairobi. A/CONF.116/28/Rev.1, para 155.

17 Family Care International, 'Safe Motherhood: A Review' (New York, 2007).

notably to promote ready access to maternity care. The authors argued that it was 'difficult to understand why maternal mortality receives so little serious attention from health professionals, policy makers and politicians'.[18]

From this point, international attention to maternal mortality increased. The Safe Motherhood Initiative, launched in Nairobi in 1987, aimed to raise awareness of maternal mortality and galvanize commitment from governments, UN agencies, and other stakeholders.[19] The Initiative set a target of halving global maternal mortality by 2000.[20] The meeting led to the formation of the Inter-Agency Group for Safe Motherhood, which aimed to maintain international focus on the issue, and organized a series of national and regional meetings. Despite increased focus, by the late 1990s, there was renewed scrutiny of the absence of large programmes focusing directly on maternal mortality in developing countries, as well as a failure to reduce maternal mortality in practice.[21]

Global commitments to reduce maternal mortality by 50 per cent by the year 2000 were reaffirmed by global leaders at the 1990 World Summit for Children. The 1994 International Conference on Population and Development (ICPD), and the 1995 Fourth World Conference on Women (FWCW) affirmed this commitment and called for a further halving between 2000 and 2015, a target taken up by the MDGs.

Despite the increasing centrality of maternal mortality to public health and development, progress towards meeting the MDG5 commitment remains off-track. In 2010, the United Nations Secretary General launched a 'Global Strategy for Women's and Children's Health' to mobilize governments, international organizations, civil society, the private sector, research institutions, and foundations to accelerate progress towards meeting MDGs 4 (on reducing child mortality) and 5. The Strategy sets out the need for support of country-led health plans, a comprehensive and integrated package of essential services, integrated care, health system strengthening, health workforce capacity building, and coordinated research and innovation. At a meeting to launch the Strategy, stakeholders committed a staggering $40 billion in resources to women's and children's health.[22]

2.3 The emergence of maternal mortality as a human rights issue

The Universal Declaration on Human Rights (1948) provides that 'motherhood and childhood are entitled to special care and protection' (Article 25). The Convention on the Elimination of Discrimination Against Women (CEDAW: 1979) makes direct reference to maternal health, requiring that 'States Parties shall ensure to women appropriate services in connection with pregnancy, confinement and the post-natal period, granting free services where necessary, as well as adequate nutrition during pregnancy and lactation' (Article 12(2)). Despite these references and the raised profile of maternal mortality in the development and public health communities since the mid-1980s, it was not until several years into the new millennium that the issue began

[18] A. Rosenfield and D. Maine, 'Maternal Mortality—A Neglected Tragedy: Where is the M in MCH?' (1985) 2 *Lancet* 83.

[19] Family Care International, 'Safe Motherhood' (n 17).

[20] Family Care International, 'Safe Motherhood' (n 17).

[21] D. Maine, and A. Rosenfield, 'The Safe Motherhood Initiative: Why has it Stalled?' (1999) 89(4) *American Journal of Public Health* 480.

[22] UN Department of Public Information, 'Global Strategy Launched by United Nations Millennium Development Goals Summit Draws More than $40 Billion to Save the Lives of 16 Million Women and Children', Press Release, 22 September 2010.

to attract widespread attention within the mainstream international human rights community. Why was this the case?

Three interconnecting and concurrent factors in the fields of maternal health, sexual and reproductive health and human rights, and international human rights law, paved the way for the emergence of maternal mortality as a key human rights issue during the 1990s.

First, until the 1990s, the human rights community had predominantly focused its attention on civil and political (CP) rights, and had neglected ESC rights, including the right to health. Whilst maternal mortality is linked to CP rights, including the right to life, it has a particularly close relationship with ESC rights, particularly the right to health. By the time of the World Conference on Human Rights (1993), the international consensus on ESC rights had shifted to the extent that the Conference outcome document stated that: 'All human rights are universal, indivisible and interdependent and interrelated. The international community must treat human rights globally in a fair and equal manner, on the same footing, and with the same emphasis.'[23] More analysis and attention was being divested in ESC rights monitoring and analysis, including on health.[24] In 1999, the CEDAW Committee, which monitors implementation of the CEDAW, adopted General Recommendation 24 on Women and Health. In 2000, the Committee on Economic, Social and Cultural Rights (CESCR), which monitors implementation of the International Covenant on Economic, Social and Cultural Rights (ICESCR) adopted General Comment 14 on the Right to the Highest Attainable Standard of Health.[25] The documents elaborate conceptual frameworks which help to clarify the meaning of CEDAW and ICESCR articles on health and resulting obligations on States parties. This framework has subsequently been applied to specific health issues, including to maternal mortality. A decision of the then Commission on Human Rights in 2002 to appoint a Special Rapporteur on the right to health, another consequence of increasing attention to ESC rights, was also important in the sense that the Special Rapporteur was to become an influential proponent of addressing maternal mortality as a human rights issue.

Second, during the 1990s, the human rights community also began to address a number of other health issues, including HIV/AIDS, mental health, and other related sexual and reproductive rights issues, including abortion and violence against women. The focus on maternal mortality was a natural, although not inevitable extension of this field of work.

Third, the ICPD Programme of Action made explicit conceptual links between maternal mortality and human rights, as it placed maternal health within a broader reproductive health context, which was in turn grounded in a reproductive rights framework. The ICPD also provided a stage for the confluence of the safe motherhood movement with the reproductive health and human rights movement.[26] Until this point, these movements had largely worked in parallel, but henceforth human rights

23 Vienna Declaration and Programme of Action, adopted by the World Conference on Human Rights on 25 June 1993, A/CONF.157/23.

24 P. Hunt, J. Bueno de Mesquita, J.-Y. Lee and S.-A. Way, 'Implementation of Economic, Social and Cultural Rights' in N. Rodley and S. Sheeran (eds), *Routledge Handbook on International Human Rights Law* (Routledge, 2013).

25 CEDAW Committee, General Recommendation No 24: 'Article 12 (Women and Health)' (20th session) (1999) A/54/38/Rev.1; Committee on Economic, Social and Cultural Rights, General Comment No 14: 'The Right to the Highest Attainable Standard of Health' (11 August 2000) E/C.12/2000/4.

26 Roseman, 'Bearing Human Rights and the Promises of ICPD' (n 9).

began to find its way into safe motherhood, and the reproductive health and human rights community began to address maternal mortality. For example, two years later, at a ten-year review of the Safe Motherhood Initiative, human rights were raised as a concept to reinvigorate its efforts.[27] In a keynote address, James Wolfensohn, then World Bank president stated: 'Safe motherhood is a human right... if the system lets a woman die, then the system has failed.'[28]

Against this backdrop, in the late 1990s, four leading reproductive health and human rights experts wrote influential articles arguing that human rights could assist maternal mortality reduction efforts. They articulated different strategies for doing so. Rebecca Cook demonstrated how existing human rights could be conceptually interpreted in the context of maternal mortality, and made the case for reproductive health and human rights activists to work more closely together.[29] Deborah Maine and Alicia Yamin analysed a set of health system indicators developed to monitor maternal mortality. They argued that this could be used to help monitor States parties' maternal health obligations under ICESCR Article 12 on the right to health.[30] Lynn Freedman argued that human rights, including principles of accountability, non-discrimination, and participation, could be used to guide the design and implementation of maternal mortality policies and programmes.[31] The varying approaches of these authors are worth noting not least because they are reflected in different strands of practice on maternal mortality and human rights that have developed since this time and which are elaborated later, in Section 3: forging conceptual links; use of human rights standards and mechanisms for accountability; and integrating human rights into maternal mortality policy-making and programmes. The analyses also collectively set the train in motion for maternal mortality to be taken up as a human rights issue by a range of actors in the development and human rights communities. Influenced by Freedman, Cook, and Yamin and Maine, a number of civil society organizations, international organizations, and donors began to make the links between maternal mortality and human rights in their work from around 2000.[32]

However, maternal mortality remained a peripheral issue for UN human rights bodies such as the Commission on Human Rights (CHR) and its special procedures (such as Special Rapporteurs), treaty monitoring bodies, as well as for regional human rights bodies and leading international human rights NGOs such as Amnesty International and Human Rights Watch. This was problematic because these bodies have some clout and the potential to influence governments and development actors to use human rights to reduce maternal mortality in practice. In response to this, in 2005, the Special Rapporteur on the right to health suggested that this community should be

27 Roseman, 'Bearing Human Rights and the Promises of ICPD' (n 9).

28 Quoted in Roseman, 'Bearing Human Rights and the Promises of ICPD' (n 9).

29 R.J. Cook, 'Human Rights Law and Safe Motherhood' (1998) 5 *European Journal of Health Law* 357.

30 A.E. Yamin and D. Maine, 'Maternal Mortality as a Human Rights Issue: Measuring Compliance with International Treaty Obligations' (1999) 21 *Human Rights Quarterly* 563.

31 L. Freedman, 'Using Human Rights in Maternal Mortality Programs: From Analysis to Strategy' (2001) 75 *International Journal of Gynecology and Obstetrics* 51.

32 Averting Maternal Death and Disability (AMDD), 'AMDD Program Report 1999' (New York, 2006); Physicians for Human Rights, 'Maternal Mortality in Herat Province, Afghanistan' (Cambridge, MA, 2002); J. Dasgupta, 'Ten Years of Negotiating Rights Around Maternal Health in Uttar Pradesh, India' (2011) 11 *Biomedical Central Health and Human Rights*; Department for International Development (DFID), 'Reducing Maternal Deaths: Evidence and Action' (London, 2004).

challenged to mount a global campaign against maternal mortality.[33] He argued that the community must be urged to 'remonstrate and demonstrate' against maternal mortality as loudly as it complains about CP rights violations such as disappearances and torture, and noted the experience of identifying domestic violence as a human rights violation in the 1990s, which helped this global movement gain momentum. For his part, the Special Rapporteur's 2006 report to the General Assembly elaborated the right to health dimensions of maternal mortality.[34] His 2007 report to the HRC (which replaced the CHR) re-emphasized the importance of the human rights community addressing the issue.[35] The Special Rapporteur's oral remarks delivered to the Assembly and HRC to present these reports also focused on maternal mortality. This was the first time that maternal mortality was raised in a relatively sustained and detailed way by a part of the UN's human rights machinery.

Also at this time, the Special Rapporteur, together with other leading players such as the Center for Reproductive Rights and the Averting Maternal Death and Disability Program (AMDD) at the Mailman School of Public Health, created an NGO partnership, the International Initiative on Maternal Mortality and Human Rights (IIMMHR). In turn, the IIMMHR helped to coordinate civil society advocacy and research on maternal mortality as a human rights issue.

As a result of the Special Rapporteur's efforts and lobbying by civil society, including by NGOs involved in the IIMMHR, in 2009, the HRC adopted a resolution (without a vote) on *preventable maternal mortality and morbidity and human rights*.[36] This was the first time that the HRC officially recognized that maternal mortality is a human rights matter. Co-sponsored by over seventy states, the resolution indicated widespread recognition among states that their obligations under international human rights law include duties to reduce maternal mortality and morbidity. The HRC has since adopted three further resolutions on the issue, in 2010, 2011, and 2012.[37] The resolutions legally reinforce the political commitments to reduce maternal mortality contained in the ICPD, FWCW, and the MDGs among others, which is important given that many states have failed to meet these commitments.

Maternal mortality also became more prominent on the agenda of other important human rights bodies. In 2011, the CEDAW Committee adopted the first international decision on maternal mortality, *Alyne da Silva Pimentel v Brazil*.[38] The case, which was brought by the family of Alyne, who were supported in this endeavour by the Center for Reproductive Rights and Advocaia Cidadã pelos Direitos Humanos, confirmed that maternal mortality is a human rights violation. The case concerned a Brazilian woman of African descent who died from pregnancy-related causes after her local health centre misdiagnosed her symptoms and delayed providing her with emergency obstetric care. Her mother took the case to the CEDAW Committee, arguing that national authorities had made no effort to establish professional responsibility and that she had been unable to obtain justice in Brazil. The Committee found violations of the right to access

[33] P. Hunt, 'Health Rights, Women's Lives: Challenges and Strategies for Movement Building', Valedictory Address at the 10th International Women and Health Meeting, New Delhi, 21–25 September 2005.

[34] UN General Assembly, 'Report of the Special Rapporteur on the right of everyone to the enjoyment of the highest attainable standard of physical and mental health', 13 September 2006, A/61/338.

[35] UNHRC, 'Report of the United Nations Special Rapporteur on the right to the enjoyment of the highest attainable standard of physical and mental health' (n 4).

[36] See n 5. [37] See n 5.

[38] CEDAW Committee, Views: Communication No 17/2008 (n 7).

healthcare and effective judicial protection in the context of non-discrimination. The HRC's resolutions and the Alyne case have been used as authoritative legal and political reference points as regards the relationship between maternal mortality and human rights and have encouraged development actors to treat maternal mortality as a human rights issue.[39]

Reinforcing international developments, regional human rights mechanisms have also begun to address maternal mortality. For example, in 2010, the Inter-American Commission on Human Rights published a thematic report on 'Access to Maternal Health Services From a Human Rights Perspective'. Moreover, as is further elaborated later, maternal mortality also found its way on to the research and advocacy agendas of key human rights NGOs, such as Amnesty International and Human Rights Watch. Now addressed by the HRC, treaty bodies, the Special Rapporteur on the right to health, international organizations, donors, and diverse civil society actors, maternal mortality as a human rights issue has come of age.

3. The Theory and Practice of Maternal Mortality and Human Rights

Over the past decade, maternal mortality has been firmly established as an issue on the international human rights agenda. But how have human rights been used to address maternal mortality in practice? In this section, I identify four main strands of work on maternal mortality and human rights, the first being theoretical and the following three practical: conceptual analysis, research and advocacy, litigation, and policy and programme work. I highlight the key characteristics of each of these strands and consider their contribution to maternal mortality reduction.

3.1 Conceptualizing maternal mortality as a human rights issue

Drawing on the early work of Cook, Freedman, and Yamin and Maine, the General Comment and Recommendation, and public health and development analysis, a range of organizations and commentators have sought to clarify the conceptual links between maternal mortality and human rights. This body of analysis has refined theoretical foundations for the application of human rights as a practical tool to reduce maternal mortality.

Some commentators have explored the links between maternal mortality and a range of human rights. In 2001, a WHO occasional paper by Rebecca Cook and Bernard Dickens identified four major clusters of rights relating to safe motherhood: rights to life, survival, and security; rights relating to maternity and health; rights to non-discrimination and due respect for difference; and rights to information and education.[40] Also adopting a multi-rights approach, in its first resolution on 'preventable maternal mortality and morbidity and human rights', the HRC identified that preventing maternal mortality required the effective promotion and protection of the rights of women, notably 'their rights to life, to be equal in dignity, to education, to be free to seek, receive and impart information, to enjoy the benefits of scientific progress, to freedom from discrimination, and to enjoy the highest attainable standard of

[39] UN Secretary-General, 'Global Strategy for Women's and Children's Health' (New York, 2010).

[40] R. Cook and B. Dickens, 'Advancing Safe Motherhood Through Human Rights: WHO Occasional Paper' (Geneva, 2001).

physical and mental health, including sexual and reproductive health'.[41] In a report prepared in the follow-up to this resolution, the OHCHR fleshed out these rights and how they apply to maternal mortality. The analysis was based on the international legal framework, particularly the jurisprudence of UN treaty monitoring bodies such as the CEDAW Committee, including their General Comments and Concluding Observations on States parties' periodic reports on their implementation of treaties.[42] This multi-rights approach has been used in practice as a framework for many human rights-based policies and programmes on maternal mortality.

By contrast, the 2006 report to the General Assembly of the Special Rapporteur on the right to health applied the framework for unpacking rights to health norms and obligations developed by the CESCR—particularly in its General Comment 14—and other actors to the issue of maternal mortality. Drawing on concepts elaborated in this General Comment, the report explored the implications of the General Comment's requirements that maternal healthcare should be *available, accessible, acceptable*, and of *good quality*. It also explored how obligations of *progressive realization*, the use of *maximum available resources*, and *international assistance and cooperation* under Article 2.1 of the ICESCR apply to the right to health in the context of maternal mortality. The report highlighted the valuable role of other rights to health norms, such as non-discrimination, participation, and accountability in policies and programmes to reduce maternal mortality.[43] Perhaps reflecting the particular conceptual relevance of the right to health to maternal mortality, many civil society and academic analyses have likewise focused in on the right to health,[44] whilst a finding of a violation of Article 12 of the CEDAW on health was central to the CEDAW Committee's decision *Alyne da Silva Pimentel v Brazil*. As such, the right-to-health approach has been useful in advocacy and research, and litigation.

Another key strand of conceptual development has been interdisciplinary analysis to marry the evidence of the causes of maternal mortality and interventions to prevent it within the framework of international human rights law. The primary rationale for this work was explained by Yamin and Maine:

> As valuable as the rights perspective is, however, it is not sufficient. Without a sound understanding of the epidemiology of maternal mortality (and therefore, the interventions that can prevent it), the concept of a human right to be free from avoidable death during pregnancy and childbirth will remain meaningless. Without a clear understanding of the causal chain leading to maternal mortality (and how to break it), programs intended to reduce maternal deaths are likely to be ineffective.[45]

A related reason why this type of approach has been important is the historic lack of direct international and domestic jurisprudence on maternal mortality. The approach has a particular precedent in human rights responses to HIV/AIDS, which have often

41 United Nations Human Rights Council resolution (2009) 11/8, 'Preventable Maternal Mortality and Morbidity and Human Rights' (n 5) para 2.

42 Report of the OHCHR on preventable maternal mortality and morbidity and human rights, A/HRC/14/39 (n 6).

43 UNGA, 'Report of the Special Rapporteur on the right of everyone to the enjoyment of the highest attainable standard of physical and mental health' (n 34).

44 See eg Physicians for Human Rights, 'Deadly Delays: Maternal Mortality in Peru—A Rights-Based Approach to Safe Motherhood' (Cambridge, MA, 2007); A. Yamin, 'Toward Transformative Accountability: a Proposal for Rights-Based Approaches to Fulfilling Maternal Health in the MDGs and Beyond' (2010) 7(12) *Sur: An International Journal* 95; Amnesty International, 'Out of Reach: The Cost of Maternal Health in Sierra Leone' (London, 2009).

45 Yamin and Maine, 'Maternal Mortality as a Human Rights Issue' (n 30).

been reasonably specific in terms of policy, medication, and other evidence-based requirements for countering the pandemic, and have led to important developments in some countries, including policy changes.[46]

Prior to the mid-1990s, there were misconceptions about how to effectively reduce maternal mortality, among them that improving socio-economic conditions in general, and the importance of prediction and prevention of obstetric complications through a focus on antenatal care and traditional birth attendants, were central strategies.[47] However, the four key interventions for reducing maternal mortality are now widely understood to be: family planning, skilled birth attendance, effective referral networks, and emergency obstetric care (EmOC).[48] The critical role of health systems in reducing maternal mortality is also better understood.[49] This evidence-based consensus provides a more concrete framework upon which to construct a human rights or right-to-health analysis. In relation to EmOC, for example, as put by Lynn Freedman, 'if the human right in question is the right not to die an avoidable death in pregnancy and childbirth, then the first line of appropriate measures that will move progressively toward the realization of the right is the implementation of EmOC. In a human rights analysis, EmOC is not just one good idea among many. It is an obligation.'[50] More recently, the Special Rapporteur on the right to health stated that: 'Universal access to EmOC is an integral part of the right to the highest attainable standard of health'.[51] Likewise, in *Alyne da Silva Pimentel v Brazil*, the CEDAW Committee's recommendations focused on, among others, the obligation of Brazil to ensure women's right to safe motherhood and EmOC.

Of course, in different countries or localities the balance of what is required may vary. Moreover, over time, new evidence may emerge which either refines or shifts priorities. Human rights analysis must be based on the evidence, undertaken on a case-by-case basis, and continue to adapt if our understanding of maternal mortality and its prevention evolves. For example, in 2011, the Partnership on Maternal, Newborn and Child Health (PMNCH) published the results of a global review of the key interventions related to reproductive, maternal, newborn, and child health, which outlined evidence-based key interventions for reducing maternal mortality, among others.[52] This provides even more specific guidance for the human rights community to use and refine its approach: the commodities and interventions could be used as a point of reference for litigation, in any future relevant General Comments or reports by Special Rapporteurs, in human rights-based policy and programme design, or research and advocacy. This would be similar to the existing use of the WHO Model List of Essential Drugs by many actors, including the CESCR, as a normative human rights reference point to facilitate access to drugs including those for HIV/AIDS. Drawing on this approach, human rights could now also be used in a similar way to help facilitate access to misoprostol to treat post-partum haemorrhage. The drug, which has remained

46 Most famously in *Minister of Health and ors v Treatment Action Campaign and ors*, decision CCT9/02 of the Constitutional Court of South Africa, 5 July 2002.

47 Maine and Rosenfield, 'The Safe Motherhood Initiative' (n 21).

48 Millennium Project, Task Force on Child Health and Maternal Health, 'Who's Got the Power? Transforming Health Systems for Women and Children' (New York, 2005).

49 See eg 'Who's Got the Power?' (n 48); G. Backman and P. Hunt, 'Health Systems and the Right to the Highest Attainable Standard of Health' (2008) 10(1) *Health and Human Rights* 81.

50 Freedman, 'Using Human Rights in Maternal Mortality Programs' (n 31).

51 P. Hunt, 'Supplementary Note on the United Nations Special Rapporteur's Report on Maternal Mortality in India' (Colchester, 2010).

52 Partnership on Maternal, Newborn and Child Health, 'Essential Interventions, Commodities and Guidelines for Reproductive, Maternal, Newborn and Child Health' (Geneva, 2011).

unavailable in many countries due to a range of misperceptions, was added in 2011 to the WHO Model List of Essential Drugs for the prevention of post-partum haemorrhage, and has also recently been added to other international and national clinical guidelines.[53]

Whilst drawing on public health evidence, another feature and contribution of human rights analyses has been the emphasis given to maternal mortality issues that were being given limited attention by the public health community and where evidence is sometimes patchy. Three such issues are unsafe abortion; gender equality, women's empowerment and non-discrimination; and accountability.

In many countries, there are legal restrictions on access to abortion, the principal effect of which has been to force women to seek unsafe abortion, which increases pregnancy-related mortality and morbidity. The international development and public health agenda has not faced the problem of unsafe abortion head-on, due to political, social, and religious sensitivities. Women's rights have provided a key analytical framework to challenge restrictive abortion laws. UN treaty monitoring bodies such as the CEDAW Committee, and regional and national courts, have a growing jurisprudence which requires that states ensure that abortion is legal in cases where the health and life of the woman is at risk; amend laws that criminalize medical procedures needed only by women and/or that punish women who undergo those procedures; and provide rapid access to post-abortion care regardless of the legal permissibility of abortion.[54]

Gender equality, women's empowerment, and non-discrimination are not new issues in the context of maternal mortality, and in the ICPD framework they were integrally linked through the broader sexual and reproductive health and rights paradigm. Yet development and public health interventions have tended to focus on the healthcare interventions required to reduce maternal mortality, paying less attention to the broader relationship of gender inequality and maternal mortality. This is reflected in the MDG approach to maternal mortality, with its process indicator focused on skilled birth attendance. This approach has been criticized by women's rights activists. Of course, if a woman is experiencing obstetric complications then her first and potentially life-saving priority is to reach appropriate healthcare in a timely fashion, and this is well-recognized within the field of human rights. However, in the longer term, empowerment of women and addressing gender discrimination and discrimination facing particular groups of women can also play an important role in ensuring legal and policy change to reduce maternal mortality. Underlying gender equality issues—for example early marriage and pregnancy, low education levels of women and girls, women's status in the family, and women's lack of power—are a starting point, together with health systems issues for some (but not all) human rights analyses of maternal mortality.[55]

As regards the 'human rights principle' of accountability, Lynn Freedman proposed that this could help to inform mechanisms of community participation in improving the responsiveness and functioning of health facilities—a principle which she referred to as 'constructive accountability'. The idea was less to apportion blame and mete out punishment, and more to encourage a partnership between rights-holders and duty

[53] A. Starrs and B. Winikoff, 'Misoprostol for Postpartum Hemorrhage: Moving from Evidence to Practice' (2012) 116(1) *International Journal of Gynecology and Obstetrics* 1.

[54] E. Kismodi, J. Bueno de Mesquita et al, 'Human Rights Accountability for Maternal Death and Failure to Provide Safe, Legal Abortion: The Significance of Two Ground-Breaking CEDAW Decisions' (2012) 20(39) *Reproductive Health Matters* 31.

[55] See eg Amnesty International, 'Giving Life, Risking Death: Maternal Mortality in Burkina Faso' (London, 2009).

bearers to create high-quality services.[56] In this vein, within the field of public health, maternal death audits have been given increasing attention as a means to counter under-reporting, establish causes of death, and as a tool for reform of policy and practice to prevent future deaths.[57] The Commission on Information and Accountability for Women's and Children's Health, set up to make recommendations in the wake of the Secretary General's Global Strategy on Women's and Children's Health, highlighted that strengthening accountability is an essential but neglected strategy for improving women's and children's health and reducing maternal mortality. In linking accountability with human rights, the Commission built its accountability framework on the right to health, equity in health, and gender equality.[58]

3.2 Using human rights as a framework for maternal mortality research and advocacy

A 2002 Physicians for Human Rights (PHR) report on maternal mortality in Herat Province, Afghanistan,[59] was one of the first pieces of NGO human rights-based research into, and advocacy on, maternal mortality. Since then, there has been a large increase in the number of such NGO reports. Traditional and influential human rights organizations, such as Amnesty International and Human Rights Watch, have importantly expanded their primary focus from CP rights to ESC rights and have also enhanced their focus on sexual and reproductive rights, facilitating a focus on maternal mortality. The Center for Reproductive Rights (CRR) has also conducted important research on maternal mortality including in Mali, India, and Kenya, whilst PHR published an analysis of maternal mortality in Peru. Meanwhile, some NGOs that have a history of working on development and public health issues, such as SAHAYOG in India, have incorporated a human rights-based approach into their research and advocacy on maternal mortality.[60]

Many NGO reports combine traditional human rights research and advocacy methods, including fact-finding, naming and shaming, and witness testimony, with new tools and techniques that are being used to enhance effective monitoring and accountability for human rights, such as indicators and benchmarks, and budget analysis. Where relevant, reports not only make demands on the state as the primary duty bearer under international human rights law, but also call on other actors, including the private sector and the international community, to undertake action to reduce maternal mortality.

For example, the PHR report on Herat focused on documenting the extraordinarily high risk for women of dying in pregnancy or childbirth, as well as its causes. The study combined detailed qualitative interviews (testimonies) with a randomized population-based survey of over almost 4,500 women in Herat to estimate the MMR, as well as a survey of health facilities in the districts in Herat which were sampled for the survey. The report identified public health and human rights causes of maternal mortality, including inadequacies in the public health system as well as denials of civil and political

56 Freedman, 'Using Human Rights in Maternal Mortality Programs' (n 31).

57 WHO, 'Beyond the Numbers: Reviewing Maternal Deaths and Complications to Make Pregnancy Safer' (Geneva, 2004).

58 J. Bueno de Mesquita and E. Kismodi, 'Maternal Mortality and Human Rights: Landmark Decision by United Nations Human Rights Body' (2012) 90 *Bulletin of the World Health Organization* 79.

59 Physicians for Human Rights, 'Maternal Mortality in Herat Province' (n 32).

60 Dasgupta, 'Ten Years of Negotiating' (n 32).

rights, for example the right to be able to enter freely into marriage. Recommendations were addressed to both the donor community and the national government.[61]

Likewise, a report by Amnesty International on Burkina Faso combined investigations of more than fifty cases of women who died in pregnancy and childbirth, interviewing family and community members as well as healthcare staff, with a review of statistics and the national legal, policy, and budgetary frameworks, and analysed these from the point of view of the human rights framework. The report made a number of recommendations to the Government as well as to international donors, including that they support the Government of Burkina Faso with adequate and long-term predictable technical and financial assistance.[62]

Human rights can provide a powerful, legally grounded discourse for advocacy by civil society. The traditional human rights technique of naming and shaming can raise awareness of problems and prompt action by duty-bearers. Although it is difficult to identify a direct cause-effect relationship, since a 2009 Amnesty International report, 'Out of Reach: The Cost of Maternal Health in Sierra Leone', human rights language has found its way into government rhetoric on the issue, while the country is taking important steps in reducing maternal mortality. Likewise, the PHR report on Afghanistan received widespread coverage and maternal mortality in Afghanistan subsequently became a priority of a number of donors,[63] although, again, it is difficult to pinpoint this report as the cause of this change in priorities.

3.3 The use of traditional human rights mechanisms to enhance accountability for maternal mortality

An accountability deficit has been widely recognized by the public health and development communities as a major obstacle to maternal mortality reduction.[64] A significant albeit embryonic contribution of the human rights community has been the utilization of traditional human rights accountability mechanisms to address this problem.

In the 1990s, while leading commentators, notably Lynn Freedman, successfully advocated the benefits of 'constructive accountability', there was less appetite for litigation both within the health and development, and the human rights communities. However, the CRR and some national NGOs were interested at an early stage in litigation as a strategy to hold states to account for their obligations where alleged violations had occurred and been treated with impunity. In the past decade, burgeoning jurisprudence on ESCR and sexual and reproductive health and rights have provided precedents to support litigation. In the past three years, there have been ground-breaking national and international decisions on maternal mortality and human rights. There has also been increasing use of non-judicial human rights accountability mechanisms to enhance accountability for maternal mortality.

In India, there have been several interesting cases on maternal mortality. *Sandesh Bansal v Union of India and ors* was a public interest lawsuit brought by a public health activist in response to the extremely high levels of maternal mortality in Madhya Pradesh, caused by unaffordable healthcare, corruption, and poor quality of care, and the alleged failure of the Government to implement its health policies in the

61 Roseman, 'Bearing Human Rights and the Promises of ICPD' (n 9).

62 Roseman, 'Bearing Human Rights and the Promises of ICPD' (n 9).

63 Roseman, 'Bearing Human Rights and the Promises of ICPD' (n 9).

64 Commission on Information and Accountability for Women's and Children's Health, 'Keeping Promises, Measuring Results' (Geneva: WHO, 2011).

province.[65] The High Court of Madhya Pradesh held that a woman's right to survive pregnancy and childbirth is a fundamental right protected under Article 21 (the right to life) of the Indian Constitution. The court found that the provincial government had failed to implement its policies, and to provide timely access to maternal healthcare. The court called for improvements in staffing and infrastructure, vaccinations for pregnant women, and a system to ensure monitoring and patients' records. After the case was filed, as a result of interim orders, a blood bank was set up at one hospital and a well was constructed at a primary health centre.

Human rights litigation is not, however, always successful. For example, in 2012, Ugandan activists lost a maternal mortality case in the Ugandan Constitutional Court. In contrast to the approach of the Indian courts, the court held that as a result of the doctrine of separation of powers, it had 'no power to determine or enforce its jurisdiction on matters that require an analysis of the health sector government policies'.[66] Reportedly, the activists will challenge this decision in the Supreme Court.

The Ugandan decision highlights that some national courts are not always going to be strategic accountability mechanisms: much will depend on legal protections as well as judicial culture. Other human rights accountability mechanisms, including national human rights institutions (NHRIs), can also play an important role. NHRIs can raise awareness of maternal mortality as a human rights issue, follow up court decisions and complaints, undertake research, and make recommendations to government. For example, the Kenyan National Commission on Human Rights recently held a Public Inquiry into Violations of Sexual and Reproductive Health Rights in Kenya. The report of the Inquiry included a chapter on maternal health, which concluded that 'women continue to die or suffer disability due to preventable causes' as a result of health system factors, cultural barriers, restrictive laws, and a lack of policies and programmes on safe abortion. The report framed maternal mortality recommendations in four main areas: mitigating maternal mortality and morbidity; strengthening health systems; health education; and promoting safe abortion.[67] This example is not representative of NHRIs: many continue to focus primarily on traditional CPR issues. However, there is great scope for such innovation.

At the international level, the CEDAW Committee's 2011 *Alyne da Silva Pimentel v Brazil* decision (see earlier) is significant for a number of reasons. First, the rights recognized in the CEDAW are legally guaranteed in the 187 countries that are party to it, as well as by most countries' constitutions and laws. Cases of this kind, which concern common causes of maternal mortality, set precedents which furnish further opportunities for international and domestic accountability. Second, the decision included a number of recommendations which provide reasonably precise guidance about the sorts of actions that are required of states to reduce maternal mortality, and therefore what the CEDAW Committee might hold states to account for. The majority of the CEDAW Committee's recommendations to Brazil required national systemic actions, both reforms and the implementation of existing policies: (1) to ensure women's right to safe motherhood and affordable access to EmOC; (2) to provide adequate professional training for health workers; (3) to ensure that private healthcare facilities comply with national and international reproductive healthcare standards; (4) to implement its National Pact

65 *Sandesh Bansal v Union of India and ors* WP (C) No 9061/2008 (MP HC, 2008).

66 Constitutional Petition No 16 of 2011, *Centre for Health Human Rights and Development and ors v Attorney General*, Constitutional Court of Uganda decision of 5 June 2012, 25.

67 Kenya National Commission on Human Rights, 'A Report of the Public Inquiry into Violations of Sexual and Reproductive Health Rights in Kenya' (Nairobi, 2012).

for the Reduction of Maternal and Neonatal Mortality, which includes the establishment of more maternal mortality committees to monitor maternal deaths; and (5) to ensure women's access to effective remedies when their reproductive rights have been violated. The CEDAW Committee also recommended that Brazil provides reparation, including monetary compensation, to Alyne's family.

The UN treaty monitoring bodies have also been used to hold states to account through the State party reporting processes under core international human rights treaties. This process involves States parties periodically reporting on their implementation of a given treaty, and results in the issuing of Concluding Observations, including recommendations, to the state under review. Treaty monitoring bodies have addressed a large number of recommendations to States parties on matters related to maternal mortality, and some have found violations where states have not taken measures to prevent it.[68] The Independent Expert Reference Group (IERG), set up in 2011 by the WHO to monitor progress in relation to the UN Secretary-General's Global Strategy on Women's and Children's Health, recognized the particular role of treaty monitoring bodies and recommended that those which interface with health 'routinely incorporate the health of women and children, where appropriate, into their work'.[69]

Complementing the work of treaty monitoring bodies, the Special Rapporteur on the right to health has also held states to account for maternal mortality in reports on his official missions. Most notably, in 2007, he undertook a mission to India to examine maternal mortality through the lens of the right to health. The mission report focused on two issues: the right to health workforce and accountability.[70] Whilst commending the government for some initiatives, the report identified shortcomings, and importantly found India in breach of its international human rights obligations on a number of counts, including an inadequate number of skilled birth attendants and technical senior managers, the absence of health workforce strategies and plans of action, the low level of public health expenditure, and the lack of progress towards establishing an appropriate regulatory framework for the private health sector. The report made recommendations in relation to these and other issues.

3.4 Human rights-based approaches to maternal mortality policies and other interventions

In the first five years of the new millennium, many UN agencies, donors, and civil society organizations committed to 'human rights-based approaches' in development and public health policies and programmes, including those relating to maternal health.[71] More recently, some organizations have developed tools and guidance for implementing their human rights commitments, or to support states or other organizations to do so.

For example, the WHO's 2004 reproductive health strategy to accelerate progress towards the attainment of international development goals and targets, including on

[68] Center for Reproductive Rights, 'Bringing Rights to Bear: Preventing Maternal Mortality and Ensuring Safe Pregnancy' (New York, 2008).

[69] Independent Expert Review Group on Women's and Children's Health, 'Every Woman: Every Child—from Commitments to Action' (Geneva, 2012).

[70] UNHRC, 'Report of the United Nations Special Rapporteur on the right to the enjoyment of the highest attainable standard of physical and mental health' (n 8).

[71] L.-H. Piron and T. O'Neill, *Integrating Human Rights into Development: A Synthesis of Donor Approaches and Experiences* (London: Overseas Development Institute, 2005).

maternal mortality,[72] is 'guided by principles based on international human rights'. The strategy is intended to guide both the WHO and its partner governments. As regards guidance and tools, and taking another example from the WHO, its technical and policy guidance on safe abortion, first published in 2003 and revised in 2012, is also based on human rights.[73] The WHO 2003 technical guidance has been used as a tool in assessments by health ministries in twelve countries and in other efforts to improve access to and quality of abortion care, including in Colombia as a template for technical norms for legal abortion services following liberalization of the abortion law.[74] Recently, the WHO's Department of Reproductive Health and Research and the Harvard School of Public Health's Program on International Health and Human Rights have created a practical tool that uses human rights concepts and methods to strengthen government efforts related to sexual and reproductive health. The tool consists of a data compilation instrument on laws, regulations, policies, health systems, and health outcomes, which are mapped against a country's international and national human rights commitments. Maternal health is one of the key issues addressed in the tool. Through a multi-stakeholder government-led process, application of the tool assists governments to identify and analyse sexual and reproductive health legal, regulatory, and policy barriers with a view to modification.[75] The tool is a new instrument, and it remains to be seen how widely it will be used.

To take examples from another stakeholder, the UK Department for International Development (DFID) strategy for reducing maternal deaths recognized that women's rights were important for achieving equitable progress towards meeting MDG5.[76] In 2005, the DFID published a practical 'how to note' to help its advisers and programme managers working on maternal health to bring human rights and equity into their work with governments, civil society, and international development agencies.[77]

It is perhaps within civil society that human rights-based approaches have been most fully and widely implemented in maternal mortality projects and programmes. These have focused particularly on issues of empowerment, participation, non-discrimination, and accountability. Some have had positive outcomes. The AMDD Program undertook early pioneering work integrating human rights into its activities.[78] More recently, the IIMMHR supported three field projects by SAHAYOG in India, Family Care International in Kenya, and CARE in Peru. SAHAYOG's project, 'voices from the ground', documented the experience of poor women seeking institutional delivery. The project aimed to address the exclusion of women's voices and experiences from maternal mortality policy-making and programme design in Uttar Pradesh and in India more broadly. The research was presented at a national event in New Delhi, attended by many stakeholders including some from the Government, and also resulted in a policy brief and booklet which were launched by a Minister of Health in the presence of many new MPs in July 2009. Among other reported outcomes were increased voice,

72 WHO Department of Reproductive Health and Research, 'World Health Strategy to Accelerate Progress Towards the Attainment of International Development Goals and Targets' (Geneva, 2004).

73 WHO, 'Safe Abortion: Technical and Policy Guidance for Health Systems' (Geneva: 2nd edn, 2012).

74 J. Erdman, T. dePiñeres, and E. Kismodi, 'Updated WHO Guidance on Safe Abortion: Health and Human Rights' (2013) 120 *International Journal of Gynecology and Obstetrics* 200.

75 J. Cottingham et al, 'Using Human Rights for Sexual and Reproductive Health: Improving Legal and Regulatory Frameworks' (2010) 88 *Bulletin of the World Health Organization* 551.

76 DFID, 'Reducing Maternal Deaths' (n 32).

77 DFID, 'How to Reduce Maternal Deaths: Rights and Responsibilities—How to Note' (London, 2005).

78 Roseman, 'Bearing Human Rights and the Promises of ICPD' (n 9).

agency, and participation among local women leaders in two districts in Uttar Pradesh; and increased responsiveness of duty bearers, including to women's service requirements at the local level, and in terms of gaps in service design and accountability at the national and state levels.

The FCI's 'right to care' project in Kenya used meetings and tools with the Government, health facility staff, community leaders, and civil society partners to 'transform communities from passive recipients of government social services to engaged citizens able to claim their rights, and health staff from potentially or inadvertent abusers of women's right to maternal health into active protectors and guarantors of these rights'.[79] The outcomes of the project included increased knowledge and attention to women's rights as they relate to pregnancy and childbirth among health providers and community members. They also included supporting progress towards protective measures to ensure women's rights were not violated, mobilizing communities around the right to health.

CARE's 'no woman behind' project strengthened the capacity of local surveillance mechanisms to improve the quality of healthcare services in two provinces in Puno, Peru's region with the highest maternal mortality. The project trained *vigilantes* to visit healthcare centres regularly to monitor whether patients' rights were respected. On the basis of their findings, regular reports were produced that documented reasons why women were deterred from using the services, which were then discussed with the office of the local Ombudsperson, CARE Peru, and ForoSalud, a civil society network. Findings were then discussed with healthcare providers to agree commitments for improvement. Preliminary data indicated that there was increased satisfaction of rural women with health services provision, increased rates of childbirth in health facilities, and increased access to culturally appropriate delivery in facilities where surveillance was carried out. The programme was also influential in the development and launch of National Policy Guidelines to Promote Citizenship Surveillance by the Ministry of Health.[80]

Despite positive developments within specific organizations, the global maternal mortality agenda and policies and programmes in many countries have been slow to integrate human rights. The MDGs, which have been influential in many states, have a development, poverty-reduction, and technocratic focus. Some relevant sexual and reproductive health issues, including safe abortion and human rights, have become excluded from this central international development agenda. This orientation reflects a shift away from the sexual and reproductive health and rights approach of the ICPD. A range of factors contributed to this shift, including more conservative politics in the United States, where the Christian right had become increasingly powerful and pushed an anti-abortion agenda.

This has been criticized by women's rights and sexual and reproductive health and rights activists. Experts have worked to reinvigorate both human rights-based approaches to maternal mortality, as well as a broader sexual and reproductive health rights approach, in the global agenda and the policies and programmes of states. For example, in 2005, a report on MDG5 by the Millennium Project called for a human rights-based approach as being key to the realization of MDG5.[81] In 2005, a new MDG target was adopted as a result of activism by sexual and reproductive health and

79 International Initiative on Maternal Mortality and Human Rights, 'Human Rights-Based Approaches to Maternal Mortality Reduction Efforts' (New York, 2009).

80 IIMMHR, 'Human Rights-Based Approaches' (n 79).

81 'Who's Got the Power?' (n 48).

rights activists and the United Nations Population Fund (UNFPA). MDG5b focused on universal access to reproductive health, which included family planning targets.[82]

Further contributions were made by international human rights mechanisms, including the Special Rapporteur on the right to health, the HRC, and the OHCHR. The Special Rapporteur called for states and others to adopt a right-to-health approach to the health processes, mechanisms, and features that should be a part of governments' maternal mortality reduction efforts. He outlined how the right to health required, and provided guidance on how it could shape, a national strategy on maternal health, situational analysis, impact assessment, indicators and benchmarks, and accountability.[83] The HRC's 2009 and 2010 resolutions on maternal mortality and morbidity and human rights called for states to 'integrate human rights into maternal mortality and morbidity initiatives', while the 2010 resolution also called on the OHCHR to prepare a thematic study on preventable maternal mortality and morbidity and human rights, including options for better addressing the human rights dimension of preventable maternal mortality and morbidity through the UN system.[84]

Echoing the approach of the Special Rapporteur and other actors, the HRC and the OHCHR have also focused on developing tools and guidance to help states and others implement a human rights-based approach. The HRC's 2010 resolution requested the OHCHR to prepare a thematic report which identifies initiatives that exemplify good or effective practices in adopting a human rights-based approach to eliminating preventable maternal mortality and morbidity, how they succeed in reducing maternal mortality, and ways in which similar initiatives could give effect to a human rights-based approach.[85] The HRC's 2011 resolution requested the OHCHR to prepare technical guidance on the application of a human rights-based approach to the implementation of policies and programmes to reduce maternal mortality and morbidity, and to enhance human rights.[86] The technical guidance subsequently developed by the OHCHR identified how a human rights-based approach should influence all stages of the national public health policy cycle, namely: 'the initial situation analysis and design of a national public health strategy and plan of action, budgeting, programme implementation, monitoring and evaluation as well as the provision of effective remedies'.[87] This technical guidance was aimed at governments, which frequently do not follow human rights-based approaches to maternal mortality reduction.

These resolutions, as well as the corresponding reports by the OHCHR, have influenced the reintegration of human rights into the UN's mainstream development agenda on maternal mortality. Indeed, the UN Secretary-General's Global Strategy for Women's and Children's Health (2010) is based on the recognition of women's and children's health 'as a fundamental human right in treaties such as ICESCR, CEDAW and the Convention on the Rights of the Child' and also refers to the HRC's resolutions. The Strategy recommends that governments and policy-makers should 'introduce or amend legislation and policies in line with the principle of human rights'. The Commission on Information and Accountability for Women's and Children's Health, established by the WHO pursuant to the Global Strategy to determine

82 Yamin, 'Toward Transformative Accountability' (n 44).

83 P. Hunt, 'Supplementary Note on the UN Special Rapporteur's Report on Maternal Mortality in India' (Colchester, 2010).

84 See n 5. 85 See n 5. 86 See n 5.

87 A.E. Yamin, 'Sexual and Reproductive Health, Rights and MDG5: Taking Stock; Looking Forward' in M. Langford, A. Sumner, and A.E. Yamin (eds), *MDGs and Human Rights: Past Present and Future* (Cambridge: CUP, 2013).

institutional arrangements for reporting on the Strategy, proposed a framework which makes explicit links between accountability and human rights: the framework is built on the right to health, equity in health, and gender equality.[88] The IERG also used an accountability framework that has its origins in human rights practice, and comprises monitoring, review and remedy, and action. In its first report, the IERG not only reviewed progress, but also made recommendations, including that human rights tools and frameworks should be strengthened to achieve better health and accountability for women and children: as the report puts it, 'human rights-based approaches have a crucial, but neglected, part to play in the delivery of the Global Strategy'.[89]

4. The New Agenda: Implementation, Rolling-Out, Evidence

Maternal mortality reduction faces many challenges. Human rights norms and mechanisms can play an important role in addressing some of them such as a lack of accountability, inequitable access to care, access to commodities and interventions, inadequate financing, poorly functioning health systems, and disrespectful treatment of women. In order for human rights to realize their potential, a number of challenges need to be overcome.

Court and treaty monitoring body decisions, and human rights policy commitments mean little without implementation. Policy commitments can even be misused to perpetuate the status quo, for the repackaging of 'old wine in new bottles'.[90] Across the field of maternal mortality and human rights, implementation of human rights-based policy and programme approaches and remedies awarded in court decisions is a future milestone. That is not to say that implementation has not occurred at all so far. Some of the programmes described in this chapter—such as those of SAHAYOG, FCI Kenya, and CARE Peru—are positive examples where human rights-based approaches have genuinely been applied in practice and helped to create more favourable circumstances for maternal mortality reduction. Moreover, some cases, such as *Sandash Bansal v Union of India*, have led to the implementation of much needed interim measures. However, in relation to other recent landmarks for maternal mortality and human rights, implementation is the next step. For example, at the time of writing, the Government of Brazil has not yet fully outlined how it intends to implement the recommendations made to it in the *Alyne da Silva Pimentel* case, although it has commendably initiated a process of discussion. Likewise, the OHCHR's technical guidance must now be put into operation (and there are plans for this). It also remains to be seen how the global community will respond to the IERG recommendations to strengthen human rights tools and frameworks, and for wider adoption of a human rights-based approach.

However, the implementation of human rights can sometimes be a significant challenge. As is clear from the CEDAW Committee's recommendations in the *Alyne da Silva Pimentel* case, this may demand new policies and programmes as well as effective implementation of existing ones. Likewise, existing human rights legal protections must be respected; sometimes litigation or new laws may be required. Some measures demand structural change. They may require states and other actors to address questions of power, inclusion and exclusion, and equality and discrimination; resource

88 'Keeping Promises, Measuring Results' (n 64).

89 'Every Woman: Every Child' (n 69).

90 P. Uvin, 'On High Moral Ground: The Incorporation of Human Rights by the Development Enterprise' (2002) 17 *Fletcher Journal of Development Studies* 1.

generation, distribution, and redistribution; and accountability. This is a political challenge, and requires support from across government and notably from the ministries of health, finance, and justice, the executive and local government, as well as from civil society, health professionals, and the population. Potential opposition may arise from vested interests in any of these constituencies. Outside government, civil society, national human rights institutions, and other actors also have a critical role to play in ensuring this challenge is met. They can help to raise awareness, empower rights-holders to claim their rights, and demand accountability of duty bearers.

A second issue on the agenda is the rolling out of human rights-based approaches. There is great scope for actions from a much wider variety of actors in government, international organizations, civil society, and national human rights institutions. Linked to this is the need for the human rights community to continue to engage with health and development actors to ensure that human rights, including sexual and reproductive health rights, remain on the development and maternal mortality agenda, particularly as we near 2015 when new global development targets will be adopted.

As I argued earlier in this chapter, the application of human rights to maternal mortality was greatly facilitated by increased evidence and consensus in the public health and development communities about the key interventions required to reduce maternal mortality. If human rights-based approaches are to be fully integrated into policies and programmes, then, in turn, the human rights community will be asked to provide evidence back to the public health and development community demonstrating how human rights can advance maternal mortality reduction. Of course, human rights have an inherent *intrinsic* rationale, ie they should be respected, protected, and fulfilled because it is right to do so and to guarantee dignity. However, actors from the development and public health communities will also be interested to know about their *instrumental* value in terms of their contribution to existing development objectives. The bottom line is that many actors will be interested to know if they help to reduce maternal deaths or contribute to associated objectives in practice. Some human rights programmes and projects have begun to collect evidence,[91] or at least monitor impact, and some initial findings are positive,[92] although whether or not maternal deaths have been reduced by a human rights-based approach is less easy to say.

A general challenge for the human rights community will be to collect and present this evidence more systematically, and to highlight the vast range of ways in which human rights can be used successfully—for example to transform political priorities, to claim accountability through courts and other bodies, and to inform and strengthen programme and policy design in international, national, local, and clinical settings. A further challenge is that it is difficult to measure the impact of some of the issues human rights brings to the fore, for example underlying gender discrimination, cultural reform, legal protections, and accountability.

Keeping human rights on the maternal mortality agenda in the longer term, and keeping maternal mortality on the human rights agenda in the longer term, are important for implementation, rolling-out, and evidence, and will determine whether human rights are able to make a sizeable difference. This will depend on a host of political and policy considerations, including: the development and implementation of global human rights norms concerning the unacceptability of maternal death; the offer of financial and technical resources for human rights-based activities; the political force

[91] F. Bustreo and P. Hunt, *Women's and Children's Health: Evidence of Impact of Human Rights* (WHO, 2013).

[92] IIMMHR, 'Human Rights-Based Approaches' (n 79).

of human rights-based safe motherhood promoters; the presence of human rights champions for the cause, the availability of evidence of human rights dimensions of the problem, the organization of human rights forums to generate attention for the cause; the availability of clear human rights-based policy alternatives to demonstrate that the problem is surmountable; and policy environment factors, including political changes and the priority of other health issues.[93]

5. Conclusion

The links between maternal mortality and human rights have gone from being virtually unknown outside a small circle of practitioners fifteen years ago, to being endorsed at the highest level in the human rights, and the development and public health communities. Academic analyses, followed by advocacy, legal and policy approaches by civil society, international organizations and donors, and analysis and action by the Special Rapporteur on the right to health, have convinced bodies such as the Human Rights Council and the UN Secretary-General to address maternal mortality as a human rights issue.

High-level endorsement is recognition not only of the fact that maternal mortality is a human rights issue, but also that human rights are valuable for strengthening advocacy, accountability, and policies and programmes for maternal mortality reduction. Human rights have enhanced and provided a more nuanced understanding of considerations for reducing maternal mortality which are now broadly accepted within the public health community: empowerment of rights-holders, non-discrimination, and accountability. They have provided a legal grounding for key interventions such as EmOC and could be used to do so for other important evidence-based interventions, such as the use of misoprostol to prevent post-partum haemorrhage. They also have the potential to ensure that issues such as access to safe, legal abortion, and gender equality, are not neglected in the fight to reduce maternal mortality.

This high-level endorsement is important if human rights are going to be integrated into the policies and programmes of states as well as being reflected in the global development agenda in years to come. Human rights activists must continue to engage with development and public health actors, gather evidence of the positive effect of human rights on maternal mortality reduction, and continue to engage in litigation, policy development and programming, and advocacy to help ensure that global preoccupation with maternal mortality as a human rights issue is on-going rather than a phase. This will be vital for human rights to make a contribution to maternal mortality reduction in practice.

93 This analysis draws on research by Jeremy Shiffman on the factors that determined whether maternal mortality appeared on national policy agendas. See J. Shiffman, 'Generating Political Priority for Maternal Mortality Reduction in 5 Developing Countries' (2007) 97(5) *American Journal of Public Health* 796.

14

Disability, Human Rights, and Global Health

Past, Present, Future

Maya Sabatello

The past couple of decades have been characterized by a multitude of health and sexual health initiatives that address global health concerns. From nutrition to hygiene, from infectious diseases to access to medication, from reproductive health to sexuality and sexual-identity—the concept of health encompasses more than ever before. The HIV/AIDS pandemic, especially since the 1990s, has played a critical role in this development, taking the field by storm. Its devastating consequences on individuals, especially women (and children), communities, and entire nations demanded a global response. It also planted the seeds for the human rights approach to health.[1] This approach centralizes attention on the negative impact of discrimination, marginalization, stigmatization, and disrespect for human rights and dignity on the vulnerability of individuals and groups to exposure to diseases and to lack of access to basic, general, sexual, and reproductive healthcare. It calls attention to the notion of development—the underlying causes of global health crises, including the rates of poverty, illiteracy, unemployment, and deteriorating health—and it requires upholding the notion of justice, ie that legal recourse is available when the system fails. Indeed, it is because of these developments that contemporary initiatives to support and develop resolutions for health and sexual health crises increasingly target not only men, but also women, especially those in the Global South, and, more recently, also persons belonging to the lesbian, gay, bisexual, and transgender communities.

One group that is consistently denied these opportunities is persons with disabilities. Notwithstanding the increasing awareness within the international human rights community about the interconnectedness between societal dimensions, contexts, and health, studies show that persons with disabilities are often absent from the plethora of such health-related initiatives. The social, economic, and political marginalization of persons with disabilities and the common view of disability, and especially of women with disabilities, as negating cultural norms of sexual attractiveness and reproductive capacities, render them invisible in both national and international discourses on health and sexual health-related programmes. Thus, despite evidence demonstrating that persons with disabilities have at least the same needs for health and sexual health services as their non-disabled peers, the needs of most of them are rarely met.

This chapter explores the intersection between disability, human rights, and global health in light of the 2006 Convention on the Rights of Persons with Disabilities

[1] J.M. Mann et al, 'Health and Human Rights' in J.M. Mann et al (eds), *Health and Human Rights: A Reader* (New York and London: Routledge, 1999) 16–18.

(CRPD). The CRPD is the eighth core international human rights treaty, and it was adopted 'to promote, protect and ensure the full and equal enjoyment of all human rights and fundamental freedoms by all persons with disabilities, and to promote respect for their inherent dignity'.[2] It is a groundbreaking treaty in terms of the historical process of its adoption: it was characterized by the most extensive involvement and participation of civil society organizations, including in particular disabled persons organizations (DPOs) and individuals with disabilities, ever. Importantly, it is a groundbreaking treaty also in substance, in its approach to human rights. Although the CRPD was not intended to create new rights, the provisions enshrined in it certainly have innovative features. And more generally, it represents a shift in the conceptualization of human rights towards a more relational approach, as I believe human rights should be understood in the twenty-first century.

To be sure, the CRPD is not a perfect document. As any international law-making process, the final result is a compromise, and for political and advocacy-related reasons, some issues did not make it into the final text. The context of health and sexuality as an integral component of global health is most revealing in this regard. Furthermore, as with every international treaty, its adoption is only a beginning. Indeed, the CRPD's implementation is critical for persons with disabilities to realize their right to health and for the success of the international commitment, through the stipulated Millennium Development Goals (MDGs),[3] to reverse the grinding poverty, hunger, and disease affecting billions of people.

This chapter is structured as follows: I first briefly describe the phenomenon of disability and discuss why the CRPD was needed despite the previously stipulated human rights standards pertaining to health. In section 2 I discuss some of the major achievements of the CRPD and highlight more specifically those relating to health and sexual health. Section 3 raises some of the lost opportunities, proposals relevant to global health and sexual health that did not make it into the treaty, and discusses the reasons for these failures. Tracing the historical legislative process is valuable not only since it allows for a better appreciation of what has been achieved, but also as it illustrates the politics of human rights and the potential impact of global health initiatives on the inclusion of persons with disabilities. Section 4 considers the challenges in advancing the health-related rights of persons with disabilities. The arguments advanced are that global health and development cannot be achieved unless a disability rights perspective is recognized and adopted as part and parcel of the human rights approach to health. For that to occur, a multi-leveled address of the marginalization of persons with disabilities is needed to include appropriate legal reform, empirical and other studies, and a genuine so-called inclusive development approach. The final section draws some conclusions.

1. Disability and Human Rights

It is estimated that at least 15 percent of the world's population experiences some type of disability.[4] This includes physical, mental, developmental, intellectual, and multiple disabilities. In numbers, this estimate is translated into some 800 million to just over

2 CRPD, Art 1.

3 For information about the Millennium Development Goals, see <http://www.unmillenniumproject.org/goals/index.htm>.

4 World Health Organization and World Bank, 'World Report on Disability' (WHO, 2011) 25–32.

1 billion people worldwide currently classified as having a disability.[5] Of this number, 80 percent live in developing countries, and about 2.5 to 3.5 million of them are displaced.[6] Further, given the persistence of war, infectious diseases, environmental degradation, aging, lack of access to basic healthcare, including maternal health during and post-partum, it is unlikely that the phenomenon of disability will disappear or even significantly reduce in the immediate future. Indeed, this also resonates with the most unchallengeable characteristics of disability: it is a universal phenomenon. It exists in one form or another in all societies both across space and time;[7] it cuts across racial, ethnic, gender, and age divides; and it is an integral part of common human experience.[8] Thus, it is not only that today, one in four people has a person with disabilities in their immediate circle of friends and relatives,[9] but it is expected that most individuals will experience some sort of a disability themselves at some point in their life. Disability is therefore far more than something that is relevant to this minority group: it is a condition that actually touches upon all members of society.

Bearing these facts in mind, the need to create a new human rights treaty that is dedicated to persons with disabilities may seem odd. Indeed, previous efforts to draft such a convention have failed,[10] with some scholars and activists suggesting that it is unwarranted. After all, there are other human rights treaties on the international level, all of which have established committees to monitor states' compliance. As persons with disabilities are human, it has been argued that they are inherently covered by existing treaties and that over-theorization of rights would reduce the value of already stipulated rights.[11] Opponents of a new international convention further raised the concern that such a new instrument would duplicate the work of existing committees, and unnecessarily divert from their already constrained financial resources. Put differently, opponents were concerned that a new treaty would create procedural and substantive redundancy that could be rectified simply by improving the enforcement of existing treaties through the authorized bodies (committees under the treaties, general comments, special rapporteurs, etc).[12]

The context of health is reflective of this debate. Article 12 of the International Covenant on Economic, Social, and Cultural Rights (ICESCR) explicitly states 'the right of *everyone* to the enjoyment of the highest attainable standard of physical and mental health' (emphasis added). This obviously includes persons with disabilities. Article 12 additionally lists an array of measures that states are required to follow to fulfill their obligations under the ICESCR, including, *inter alia*, the reduction of the stillbirth-rate and of infant mortality; the improvement of all aspects of environmental

5 Depending on type of survey used: WHO, 'World Health Survey' of 2002–2004, and the WHO's 'Global Burden of Disease' study, 2004 update ('World Report on Disability' (n 4) 24–5).

6 The Women's Commission on Refugee Women and Children, 'Disabilities Among Refugees and Conflict-Affected Populations' (2008) 6.

7 A.D. Renteln, 'Cross-Cultural Perceptions of Disability: Policy Implications of Divergent Views' in S.S. Herr et al (eds), *The Human Rights of Persons with Intellectual Disabilities: Different But Equal* (OUP, 2003) 71.

8 A. Asch, L.O. Gostin, and D.M. Johnson, 'Respecting Persons with Disabilities and Preventing Disability: Is There a Clash?' in S.S. Herr et al (eds), *The Human Rights of Persons with Intellectual Disabilities: Different But Equal* (OUP, 2003) 323.

9 Handicap International, 'Disability: Key Figures 2008', available at <http://www.handigosolidaires.com/fileadmin/gallery/docs/Key_Figures.doc>.

10 UN Enable, at <http://www.un.org/esa/socdev/enable/dissre01.htm>.

11 UN Enable (n 10).

12 G. Quinn and T. Degener, 'Human Rights and Disability' (UN, Office of HCHR, 2003) ch 12, available at <http://www.ohchr.org/Documents/Publications/HRDisabilityen.pdf>.

and industrial hygiene; the prevention, treatment, and control of pandemic, endemic, occupational, and other diseases; and the creation of conditions which would assure to all medical service and medical attention in the event of sickness.

The monitoring bodies under the human rights treaties further provide relevant authoritative interpretation of this right. The Committee under the Convention on the Elimination of All Forms of Discrimination against Women (CEDAW) had emphasized that the right to health includes reproductive health as 'a basic right'.[13] In General Comment No 14 (2000), the Committee monitoring the ICESCR further adopted a broad understanding of the right to health and linked the achievement of this right to other socio-economic and civil and political rights, development, non-discrimination, and human dignity. Accordingly, it stipulated that the right to health includes a wide range of socio-economic factors and other rights that promote conditions in which people can lead a healthy life, and extends to the underlying determinants of health, such as food and nutrition, housing, access to safe and potable water and adequate sanitation, safe and healthy working conditions, and a healthy environment.[14] The Committee further interpreted the right to health to include the 'interrelated and essential elements' of *availability*, *accessibility*, *acceptability*, and *quality*:[15] ie that there is a sufficient quantity of functioning public health and healthcare facilities, goods, services, and programmes available in a State Party; that health facilities, goods, and services are accessible 'to everyone without discrimination'; that all health facilities, goods, and services are respectful of medical ethics and culturally appropriate; and that all health facilities, goods, and services are scientifically and medically appropriate and of good quality. Further, consistent with the interpretation of the Committee under CEDAW, the ESCR Committee gave special attention to the issue of sexual and reproductive health: it required, *inter alia*, the provision of access to family planning, pre- and post-natal care, emergency obstetric services, and access to information, as well as to resources necessary to act on that information.[16] The ESCR Committee also made explicit references to the HIV/AIDS pandemic, requiring that States Parties establish preventative and educational programmes for 'behaviour-related health concerns such as sexually transmitted diseases, in particular HIV/AIDS, and those adversely affecting sexual and reproductive health'.[17] Finally, the Committee emphasized that a non-discrimination, gender and age sensitive, and participatory approach to the implementation of the right are essential.[18]

Importantly, the Committee's interpretation of the requirements under the right to health is inclusive of persons with disabilities. First, the ESCR Committee clarified that the Covenant's prohibition of discrimination extends to include any discrimination in access to healthcare and underlying determinants of health, as well as to means and entitlements for their procurement, on the grounds of physical or mental disability.[19] Among states' core obligations is the requirement that they '*shall give particular attention to all vulnerable or marginalized groups*',[20] which naturally—and under the CEDAW

13 CEDAW, General Recommendation No 24 on article 12: Women and Health (1999) para 1.

14 CESCR, General Comment No 14 on article 12: the right to the highest attainable standard of health (2000) paras 3–4.

15 General Comment No 14 (n 14) para 12.

16 General Comment No 14 (n 14) para 14.

17 General Comment No 14 (n 14) para 16.

18 General Comment No 14 (n 14) paras 18–27.

19 General Comment No 14 (n 14) para 18.

20 General Comment No 14 (n 14) para 43(f).

Committee also explicitly[21]—includes persons with disabilities. The Committees further required that states ensure accessibility to health facilities, goods, and services; that health services are sensitive to the needs of persons and women with disabilities and are respectful of their human rights and dignity; and that children with disabilities are given the opportunity to enjoy a fulfilling and decent life and to participate within their community.[22] Additionally, the ESCR Committee issued General Comment No 5 that is dedicated in its entirety to persons with disabilities. In paragraphs 3 to 4 of this General Comment it stipulated the requirement that 'persons with disabilities, particularly infants and children, are provided with the same level of medical care within the same system as other members of society', and emphasized later on that compliance with the principle of non-discrimination in this context applies to both public health sector and private providers of health services and facilities.[23] Significantly, the ESCR Committee makes further links between the right to health and participation, highlighting the right of persons with disabilities to receive social and medical services, which 'enable persons with disabilities to become independent, prevent further disabilities and support their social integration'.[24]

As impressive as this web of standards—and rights—with respect to health and sexual health of individuals may be, however, decades of activism and some research have shown that existing human rights treaties have had only limited—if any—impact on the rights of persons with disabilities.[25] The stigmatized social construction of disability merely as inability has been translated into a view whereby persons with disabilities, especially women with disabilities, are perceived as objects and are assumed to be asexual, sexually inactive, or else, that their sexuality and fertility should be controlled.[26] Consequently, life with disabilities has been constructed not only as a life of misery[27] but as evil, bad, and cursed. Indeed, in some cultures women who give birth to a child with disabilities are blamed for the disability: the disability is seen as evidence of the woman's infidelity and sin.[28]

The confinement of the discussion about disability merely to the realm of medicine, too, has negatively impacted the health situation of persons with disabilities. Certainly, some connection between disability and health exists. For instance, low physical activity may increase the likelihood of developing secondary conditions such as obesity; some disabilities are associated with higher rates of other chronic health conditions (for example a person with developmental disabilities may experience higher blood pressure, diabetes, and others); and some persons with disabilities, such as autism and

21 General Recommendation No 24 (n 13) para 6.

22 General Comment No 14 (n 14) paras 12(b) and 22; General Recommendation No 24 (n 13) para 25.

23 General Comment No 5: Persons with Disabilities (1994) para 34; General Comment No 14 (n 14) para 26.

24 General Comment No 5 (n 23) para 34.

25 Quinn and Degener, 'Human Rights and Disability' (n 12).

26 M.L. Perlin, '"Everybody Is Making Love/Or Else Expecting Rain": Considering the Sexual Autonomy Rights of Persons Institutionalized Because of Mental Disability in Forensic Hospitals and in Asia' (2008) 83 *Washington Law Review* 481, 502; Nisha, 'Regulation of Disabled Women's Sexuality', 10, available at <http://www.iiav.nl/epublications//2004/Regulation_of_Disabled_Womens_Sexuality.pdf>. See also S. Buchanan, 'Surviving the System: One Woman's Experience of Disability and Health Care' in R.P. Marinelli and A.E. Dell Orto (eds), *The Psychological and Social Impact of Disability* (4th edn, Springer, 1999) 423, 425.

27 R.J. Hull, 'Cheap Listening?—Reflections on the Concept of Wrongful Disability' (2006) 20(2) *Bioethics* 59.

28 World Health Organization, 'Promoting sexual and reproductive health for persons with disabilities': WHO/UNFPA guidance note (2009) 10.

hyperactivity, are at higher risk of unintentional injury from road and car accidents, to falls, and to burns.[29] This overwhelming medical concentration has been problematic, however, first, because many persons with disabilities are in fact healthy; and second, because this medical-oriented concentration meant that the focus had been on one's deficiencies and impairments merely as a matter of personal trait that needs to be fixed. Conversely, very little emphasis was given to the societal aspects that are responsible for the deteriorating health that many persons with disabilities experience.[30]

These in turn have had significant ramifications for the rights of persons with disabilities. On the one hand, the pervasive stigma and confinement to medicine have translated into segregation policies and on-going discrimination against and exclusion of persons with disabilities in all spheres of life, from education to employment to political participation and to family life.[31] With regard to the latter context, the common assumptions are that persons with disabilities, and particularly women with disabilities, are incapable of engaging in intimate relationships and of raising children (regardless of the type of disability they have).[32] Subsequently, high rates of children with disabilities are sterilized (including in economically-developed countries such as Australia and the US),[33] and women with disabilities who get pregnant often encounter negative reaction from health professionals, family members, and the community at large.[34] This further reflects the double and triple levels of discrimination that some subgroups of persons with disabilities experience.

Moreover, because of the perception of persons with disabilities as non-marriageable and asexual objects, they are much more likely than non-disabled persons to be victims of physical and sexual abuse and rape.[35] This phenomenon of abuse is particularly evident in institutions and with respect to persons with intellectual disabilities. In the

29 World Health Organization and World Bank, 'World Report on Disability' (n 4) 59–60.

30 T. Shakespeare, 'Cultural Representation of Disabled People: Dustbins for Disavowal?' (1994) 9(3) *Disability and Society* 292; R. Olkin, *What Psychotherapists Should Know About Disability* (The Guilford Press, 1999) 10; H. Hahn, 'The Political Implications of Disability: Definition and Data' in R.P. Marinelli and A.E. Dell Orto (eds), *The Psychological and Social Impact of Disability* (Springer, 1999) 3, 5–6.

31 C. Barnes, *Disabled People in Britain and Discrimination: a Case for Anti-discrimination Legislation* (Hurst in Association with the British Council of Organisations of Disabled People, 1991); M. Oliver, *The Politics of Disablement* (Macmillan, 1990).

32 See generally C.H. Coleman, 'Conceiving Harm: Disability Discrimination in Assisted Reproductive Technologies' (2003) 50 *UCLA Law Review* 17, 19; see also references in n 26.

33 See Perlin, 'Everybody Is Making Love/Or Else Expecting Rain' (n 26) 499–500. In China, sterilization is regularly carried out against women with mental and intellectual disabilities. In other countries, including the US and Australia, sterilization of a woman with disabilities may be approved either by medical ethics committees or by courts. See C. Black, 'Children's Hospital Admits It Broke State Law With Girl's Surgery', *Seattle Post-Intelligencer*, 9 May 2007, available at <http://seattlepi.nwsource.com/local/314810_ashley09.html>; C. Trenwith, 'Parents Win Bid to Sterilise Daughter', *Brisbane Times*, 9 March 2010, available at <http://www.brisbanetimes.com.au/queensland/parents-win-bid-to-sterilise-daughter-20100309-ptlf.html> (describing the ruling of an Australian court approving a hysterectomy on a severely disabled 11-year-old girl). See also, 'Promoting sexual and reproductive health for persons with disabilities' (n 28) 4.

34 C. Begley et al, 'Women with Disabilities: Barriers and Facilitators to Accessing Services During Pregnancy, Childbirth and Early Motherhood', School of Nursing and Midwifery, Trinity College Dublin (2009), available at <http://www.nda.ie/cntmgmtnew.nsf/0/419BBFC356BC438A8025770 5003FA51D/$File/literaturereview.pdf> especially 118–24; R. Mykitiuk and E. Chadha, 'Site of Exclusion: Disabled Women's Sexual, Reproductive and Parenting Rights' in M.H. Rioux, L.A. Basser, and M. Jones (eds), *Critical Perspectives on Human Rights and Disability Law* (Martinus Nijhoff, 2011) 186–8.

35 HRW, 'Human Rights for Women and Children with Disabilities' (2010) 4–5.

US, for instance, persons with disabilities are at a four-to-ten times greater risk for general violence, and the prevalence is estimated to be higher for sexual violence.[36] And in some African countries, the presumption of asexuality of persons with disabilities has led to the development of 'virgin rape' as a cure for HIV. As women with disabilities are viewed as sexually inactive, they are prime targets of such sexual abuse.[37]

On the other hand, persons with disabilities have been strikingly invisible in the human rights arena. States' reporting on the prevalence of disability, particularly in developing countries, is significantly low: it averages 2.9 percent compared to 15.5 percent in high-income countries.[38] Considering the higher risk factors for disabilities in these countries, such as poverty, lack of healthcare, a damaged environment, and infectious diseases, however, this discrepancy should at least raise a red flag. Certainly, this may be at least partially attributed to the lack of a cross-cultural definition of disability.[39] For instance, in contrast to the traditional vision of persons with disabilities within American society as persons who use wheelchairs, in cultures such as China and Eastern Europe, disability applies predominantly to psychological conditions.[40] But the definitional issue does not fully capture the problem. Indeed, in some developing countries, children with disabilities are often not registered at all,[41] and generally, because of the associated stigma, individuals often also deny their disability when asked. For instance, in one study, no blind people were found to live in Egypt. The researchers found that the fear from stigmatization prevented individuals from going on the record as having vision impairment or being blind.[42] Furthermore, in some languages, such as the Massai and Somali, there is no formal term for the 'category' of disability.[43] Thus, how can disability be recorded if it is not classified?

Simultaneously, states' reports to the various human rights bodies consistently fail to include information about persons with disabilities,[44] and also when they do, they fail to provide a description of how their human rights are being upheld but focus on welfare. For instance, references to persons with disabilities under the right to found a family commonly do not deal with the question of whether and what are the rates of

36 WHO and World Bank, 'World Report on Disability' (n 4) 59. For an overview of studies about violence against children and persons with disabilities see D.K. Marge (ed), 'A call to action: preventing and intervening in violence against children and adults with disabilities: a report to the nation', Syracuse, State University of New York Upstate Medical University Duplicating and Printing Services (2003) 39–42, 49–51.

37 N. Groce and R. Trasi, 'Rape of Individuals with Disability: AIDS and the Folk Belief of "Virgin Cleansing"' (2004) 363 *Lancet* 1663.

38 M. Palmer and D. Harley, 'Models and Measurement in Disability: an International Review' (2011) 27(5) *Health Policy and Planning* 3, see also Table 1 at 4. For instance, in Vietnam the reported rate of persons with disabilities for 2004 was 6.4%, Bangladesh reported 5.6% for 2005, India reported 2.1% for 2002, and Thailand reported 1.7% for 2002 (compared to Australia, reporting 20% for 2003, Norway reporting 17.8% for 1995, the US reporting 15% for 1994, and the UK reporting 12.2% for 1991).

39 For further discussion on this issue, and the implications of lack of a universal definition of disability, see M. Sabatello, 'A Short History of the International Disability Rights Movement' in M. Sabatello and M. Schulze (eds), *Human Rights and Disability Advocacy* (Pennsylvania University Press, 2014).

40 M.T. Westbrook, V. Legge, and M. Pennay, 'Attitudes Towards Disabilities in a Multicultural Society' (1993) 36(5) *Social Science and Medicine* 620, 622.

41 R. De Silva de Alwis, 'Mining the Intersections: Advancing the Rights of Women and Children with Disabilities within an Interrelated Web of Human Rights' (2009) 18 *Pacific Rim Law and Policy Journal* 301.

42 Renteln, 'Cross-Cultural Perceptions of Disability' (n 7) 64.

43 Renteln, 'Cross-Cultural Perceptions of Disability' (n 7) 64.

44 See, for instance, CEDAW, General Recommendation No 18: disabled women (tenth session, 1991).

persons with disabilities who are married, but with what sort of welfare family measures were taken.[45]

The traditional Western human rights approach may be partially blamed for the neglect of disability rights. Since its inception, the traditional human rights approach has paid greater attention to negative rather than positive rights, and, respectively, on states' negative rather than positive obligations. As disability claims often ask for the provision of special services, they are seemingly outside the conventional human rights legal framework.[46] Moreover, historically, this approach viewed individuals as separate beings, autonomous decision-makers who exercise their rights independently.[47] Despite efforts by the feminist movement to reframe the human rights discourse to consider the contextual interdependency and responsibilities of individuals and which takes into account one's relationships,[48] the case of persons with disabilities stands out as different. The reliance of persons with disabilities on care-takers, in need of accommodation, of equipment, skills, and buildings, and issues of communication, seemingly sets them apart, and justifies different treatment.[49] This also explains the difficulties of persons with disabilities in accessing justice: their complaints about health-related discrimination and violence are not taken seriously, they are less likely to obtain police intervention, legal protection, or preventive care, and their testimonies and evidence when they are physically and sexually abused are often disregarded.[50]

Thus, notwithstanding some changes that have occurred in the past two decades with regard to persons with disabilities—from a shift in the terminology[51] to de-institutionalization and community-based approaches, to some national non-discrimination legislation addressing persons with disabilities,[52] and to the increasing number of international soft-law instruments such as General Comments and declarations that have been adopted[53]—in practice, much discrimination against and exclusion of persons with disabilities persists. The failure to accurately estimate how many persons

[45] Quinn and Degener, 'Human Rights and Disability' (n 12) 66.

[46] C. O'Cinneide, 'Extracting Protection for the Rights of Persons with Disabilities from Human Rights Frameworks: Established Limits and New Possibilities' in O.M Arnardottir and G. Quinn (eds), *The UN Convention on the Rights of Persons with Disabilities: European and Scandinavian Perspectives* (Martinus Nijhoff, 2009) 168–71.

[47] R.E. Howard, 'Dignity, Community and Human Rights' in A.A. An-Na'im, *Human Rights in Cross-Cultural Perspectives: A Quest for Consensus* (University of Pennsylvania Press, 1992) 82–3.

[48] M. Sabatello, *Children's Bioethics: The International Biopolitical Discourse on Harmful Traditional Practices and the Right of the Child to Cultural Identity* (Martinus Nijhoff, 2009) 169–70.

[49] O'Cinneide, 'Extracting Protection for the Rights of Persons with Disabilities' (n 46) 170.

[50] UN DESA, 'Some Facts about Persons with Disabilities', available at <http://www.un.org/disabilities/convention/facts.shtml>; S. Ortoleva and H. Lewis, 'Forgotten Sisters—A Report on Violence against Women with Disabilities: An Overview of Its Nature, Scope, Causes and Consequences', Northeastern University School of Law Research Paper No 104-2012, 21 August 2012, 2–8, available at <http://papers.ssrn.com/sol3/papers.cfm?abstract_id=2133332>.

[51] Certainly, the terminology used in the context of disabilities is culturally dependent. However, a linguistic examination shows a transformation from a charity framing ('handicap') to a medical/disability-focused ('disabled-person') to a language that positions the individual as the focal point, before the disability ('person with disabilities'); the latter also being the terminology used on the international level and in the CRPD.

[52] Such as the Americans with Disabilities Act (ADA) of 1990 (including changes made by the ADA Amendments Act of 2008) and the current Equality Act of 2010 in the UK that focus on persons with disabilities.

[53] See, for instance, 1975 Declaration on the Rights of Disabled Persons, which is the first rights-based international instrument on disability; declaring 1981 the International Year of persons with disabilities and 1983 the beginning of the UN Decade of Disabled Persons; and establishing the World Program of Action Concerning Disabled Persons. See also Standard Rules on the Equalization of Opportunities for Persons with Disabilities, UNGA Resolution A/RES/48/96, 85th Plenary Meeting,

with disabilities exist leads to policy-makers on local, national, and international levels commonly assigning lower priority to their needs. And whereas on the national level disability rights claims are often simply dismissed, the international human rights monitoring bodies only rarely included any actual recommendation to states as to how to implement the human rights of persons with disabilities.[54]

The context of health and sexual health is most illustrative of this reality of structural discrimination. One glaring example is the different application of the principles of autonomy and informed consent. Although these principles are considered to be core values embedded within the conventional human rights regime and leading ones in medical ethics, with regard to persons with disabilities they are often overlooked. Sterilization of women and girls with disabilities is an irreversible medical procedure that has been historically carried out without their consent, and, only more recently, has been accepted within the human rights bodies as a violation of women's right to bodily integrity, and even as torture.[55] Moreover, studies show that the limited application of these principles is not only relevant for persons with mental disabilities.[56] Rather, it reflects a more general experience of persons with disabilities in healthcare systems, including in economically-developed countries such as the US, Australia, and the UK. In one study, for instance, the researchers concluded that persons with disabilities in the US are more likely than non-disabled people to perceive that the physician does not listen to them, does not explain treatment so that they understand, does not treat them with respect, does not spend enough time with them, and does not involve them in treatment decisions.[57] Certainly, healthcare professionals' attitudes towards persons with disabilities are not necessarily the result of bad intention or any ingrained hostility: in all probability, it is out of lack of awareness.[58] Nonetheless, it is exactly this lack of knowledge that reflects the problem when it is translated to the human rights arena. Although the ESCR Committee interpreted the right to health (Article 12) as having a direct link to participation in society, with an emphasis on non-discrimination in access to treatment, human dignity, independence, and autonomy, states' reports suggest that they do not endorse it, and, in any case, that the Committee's follow up subsequent to states' omissions is limited at best.[59]

Beyond that: as the recent 'World Report on Disabilities' by the World Health Organization and the World Bank (2011) confirmed, the healthcare needs of persons with disabilities, both men and women, in both developed and developing countries,

20 December 1993; Committee under ICCPR, General Comment No 8, 'Liberty and Security of the Person' (1982); See also references for other General Comments/Recommendations (nn 13 and 14).

54 Quinn and Degener, 'Human Rights and Disability' (n 12) 66–77, 115–31, 163–4, 178–89, 208–16, 226–7, and 239–40.

55 UN Human Rights Council, 'Promotion and protection of all human rights, civil, political, economic, social and cultural rights, including the right to development: Report of the Special Rapporteur on torture and other cruel, inhuman or degrading treatment or punishment', Manfred Nowak, 15 January 2008, A/HRC/7/3, paras 38, 39; see also CEDAW Committee, 'Concluding observations of the Committee on the Elimination of Discrimination Against Women: Australia' CEDAW Forty-sixth session, 12–30 July 2010, CEDAW/C/AUS/CO/7, available at <http://www2.ohchr.org/english/bodies/cedaw/cedaws46.htm>.

56 For an interesting discussion on the autonomy-based rights approach to treat mental disorders, see M. Donnelly, 'From Autonomy to Dignity: Treatment for Mental Disorders and the Focus for Patient Rights' (2008) 26(2) International Trends in Mental Health Laws 37.

57 D.L. Smith, 'Disparities in Patient-Physician Communication for Persons with a Disability from the 2006 Medical Expenditure Panel Survey (MEPS)' (2009) 2 *Disability and Health Journal* 206.

58 T. Shakespeare, *Disability Rights and Wrong* (Routledge, 2006), 191–193.

59 Quinn and Degener, 'Human Rights and Disability' (n 12) 5, 94–7, and 116–30.

are often unmet.[60] Persons with disabilities are about twice as likely to be unable to afford the associated costs for physicians' visits and transportation; they are two to three times more likely to find the providers' skills and equipment inadequate for their needs; they are significantly less likely to know where to get healthcare; and overall, persons with disabilities are at least two to three times more likely to be treated badly by healthcare providers and more likely to be denied care altogether. These rates further increase with age: persons with disabilities over 60 years old are eight times more likely to be denied treatment altogether.[61]

It is against this background that disability rights activists launched the initiative for a new human rights treaty focusing on the rights of persons with disabilities. And, unlike previous efforts, once the international community convened in 2002 to consider this possibility, the drafting proceeded at a rather expeditious pace.

2. The CRPD in a Nutshell

As mentioned previously, the CRPD breaks ground in its approach to human rights. First, the drafters of the treaty opted for a comprehensive and holistic instrument to address disability rights. Accordingly, unlike the prototype human rights treaties, the CRPD includes civil and political rights, as well as economic, social, and cultural rights. The CRPD further establishes a right to development through its link between poverty and disability and the explicit requirement in Article 32 that 'international cooperation, including international development programmes, is inclusive of and accessible to persons with disabilities'.[62] The treaty further takes into consideration gender distinctions, and the entire life-span of persons with disabilities, from birth to majority to old age, along with tailored provisions that reflect the experience of persons with disabilities, such as accessibility and access to justice. Second, the CRPD unequivocally recognizes persons with disabilities as subjects rather than objects. This is encapsulated especially in the explicit reference to the right to legal capacity and in the shift towards supportive decision-making rather than guardianship (Article 12). In doing so, the Convention removes central philosophical and practical obstacles in the realization of persons with disabilities of their right to health and sexual health. It re-entrusted the power of medical decision-making, as has been long recognized and implemented for non-disabled individuals, in the hands of the individuals at stake.

Third, the treaty reflects a conceptual shift from a medical approach to a social-relational approach to disability. Instead of the previous focus on predominantly the individual's impairment in need of fixing, the CRPD explicitly views disability as an 'evolving concept', integrating factors of the physical impairment, the society, and the environment as disabling.[63] It lays down positive obligations on states and it expressly requires greater social responsibility in raising awareness of and respect for the rights and dignity of persons with disabilities (Article 8) as well as in eliminating the stigma and discrimination by any person, organization, or private enterprise (Article 4 General

60 WHO and World Bank, 'World Report on Disability' (n 4) ch 3. See also M.A. McColla, A. Jarzynowskab and S.E.D. Shorttc, 'Unmet Health Care Needs of People with Disabilities: Population Level Evidence' (2010) 25(2) *Disability and Society* 205.

61 WHO and World Bank, 'World Report on Disability' (n 4) 60–2.

62 See also M.A. Stein, C. McClain-Nhlapo, and J.E. Lord, 'Disability Rights, the MDGs and Inclusive Development' in M. Langford et al (eds), *Millennium Development Goals and Human Rights: Past, Present, and Future* (CUP, 2013) (on file with author).

63 CRPD, Preamble (e).

Obligations). Accordingly, although the CRPD does not provide a definition of a person with disabilities or of disabilities, the targeted group in Article 1 of the CRPD looks at the interaction between one's impairment and the various societal and environmental barriers that prevent one's full and effective participation in society.

The CRPD achievements further include more specific provisions with regard to health, sexual health, and sexuality. Some provisions follow existing standards. Following Article 12 of the ICESCR, the general right of one to achieve the highest attainable health 'without discrimination on the basis of disability' is stipulated in Article 25. Elimination of discrimination is broadly defined in Article 2 to include also lack of reasonable accommodation, and stipulated among the Convention's General Principles, and General Obligations, as well as in an additional provision on equality before and under the law (Articles 3, 4, and 5, respectively). In line with Articles 10 and 16 of CEDAW, specific reference to the elimination of discrimination is also explicitly mentioned in matters relating to marriage, family planning, parenthood, and relationships (Article 23).

Other health-related provisions are new: the requirement of accessibility, including access to medical facilities and to information (Article 9); a right to live independently in the community (Article 19); the requirement to uphold the equal right to privacy, including privacy of personal health information (Article 22); the right to free and informed consent in medical treatment is explicitly stipulated in Article 25(d) with respect to the requirement that health professionals provide care of the same quality to persons with disabilities as to others; and a new article on habilitation and rehabilitation (Article 26). This latter article requires States Parties to 'take effective and appropriate measures, including through peer support, to enable persons with disabilities to attain and maintain maximum independence, full physical, mental, social and vocational ability, and full inclusion and participation in all aspects of life', noting health among the most important areas of concern. Additionally, the CRPD stipulates provisions that are more specific to sexual health. It calls for the provision of age-appropriate information and reproductive and family planning education (Article 23);[64] protection from abuse including gender-based violence and abuse (Article 16), and importantly, the right of persons with disabilities, including children, to retain their fertility (Article 23). Further, for the first time in a human rights treaty, there is an explicit reference to states' obligation to provide persons with disabilities with, among other things, sexual and reproductive health and population-based public health programmes (Article 25(a)).

The combined effect of these provisions is significant. It positions the CRPD as the most comprehensive hard-law instrument thus far dealing with the right to health and sexual health with a requirement of global health initiatives. It further opens the door for the human rights approach to health, if properly adjusted, to amplify its impact. The negative impact of the persistent discrimination, inequality, marginalization, and stigmatization of persons with disabilities needs to be addressed through the landscape of human—transformed to disability—rights. The rates of poverty, illiteracy, and deteriorating health among persons with disabilities make the issue a matter of development. Achieving the MDGs—which range from halving extreme poverty to halting the spread of HIV/AIDS and providing universal primary education by 2015—will not be possible if persons with disabilities are not taken seriously into account.[65] Yet conspicuously, persons with disabilities are not mentioned at all in the 2000

64 cf CEDAW, Art 14: rural women.

65 'Mainstreaming Disability in MDG Policies, Processes and Mechanisms: Development for All', Report of the Expert Group Meeting (April 2009).

international pledge. The insensitivity of the legal system, including the UN human rights monitoring bodies, makes this a matter of justice. The human rights approach to health should thus too be interpreted *in lieu* of the CRPD. Furthermore, it is suggested that applying the disability rights approach to health should bear in mind other relevant health-related issues that, due to politics, did not make it into the final text. I now turn to consider three such issues.

3. Lost Opportunities

In the context of health and sexual health, three 'lost opportunities' merit consideration: disability and HIV/AIDS, a right to sexuality, and disability and sexual orientation.[66] While other issues that arose during the negotiations are relevant for health too (for instance the issue of abortion on the basis of disability, as discussed in connection with the right to life), the issues discussed in this section have a direct impact on the health and sexual health of *existing* persons with disabilities.

3.1 Disability and HIV/AIDS

The debilitating impact of HIV/AIDS has been well documented, and especially since the 1990s, there are on-going international initiatives to address the pandemic on both national and international levels. The opposite association, however, between populations with pre-existing disabilities and HIV/AIDS has hardly been explored.

In 2004, not long after the beginning of the treaty's negotiation, the World Bank and Yale University published a seminal report entitled, *Global Survey on HIV/AIDS and Disability*.[67] The goal of the survey was to assess the impact of the AIDS pandemic on persons with disabilities and to identify issues of access to information, services, and care specific to persons with disabilities. It received 1,000 responses from fifty-seven countries, portraying a devastating picture as to where the issue of HIV/AIDS and disability stands. The report revealed that persons with disabilities have higher risk factors due to stigma, lack of education, rates of poverty, and drug use. It further showed that because of stigma and the assumption of non-marriageability of persons with disabilities, they are prone to sexual abuse and rape, and that overall, persons with disabilities have higher rates of sexually transmitted diseases (STIs) than the general population. In one study in the US, for example, the rate of individuals who are deaf with HIV was found to be twice the rate of the hearing population, and another study found the disease to be a leading cause of death among women with mental disabilities in New York.[68]

A particular cause for concern were the report's findings about the lack of sexual education and preventative measures for persons with disabilities. As the researchers found, because of the view of persons with disabilities as asexual and the pervasive discrimination against them, they are often excluded from the provision of health and

[66] This section is based on my first-hand involvement in the UN drafting process of the treaty and on the CRPD's negotiation archives, available at <http://www.un.org/disabilities/default.asp?id=1423>. For another useful source, see M. Schulze, 'Understanding the UN Convention on the Rights of Persons with Disabilities' (Handicap International, 2010), available at <http://www.equalityhumanrights.com/uploaded_files/humanrights/unconventionhradisabilities.pdf>.

[67] N. Groce, *Global Survey on HIV/AIDS and Disability: Capturing Hidden Voices* (World Bank and Yale University, 2004).

[68] Groce, *Global Survey on HIV/AIDS and Disability* (n 67) 4.

sexual health promotion and prevention programmes.[69] Because persons with disabilities are often not enrolled and do not attend school,[70] they have very limited access to the most basic education and information about their bodies, health, and sexual and reproductive issues. Further, because health-related information is commonly not provided in an accessible format, such as Braille, simple language, pictures, and language interpreter, it was estimated that only 3 percent of persons with disabilities in the world receive information about HIV/AIDS.[71] This finding is especially a cause for concern for women and girls with disabilities whose global literacy rate is estimated to be as low as 1 percent.[72]

Subsequently, civil society representatives who participated in the drafting process made efforts during the CRPD's negotiations to include specific reference to persons with disabilities living with HIV/AIDS. Specifically, suggestions were made to include such a reference in the provision on states' General Obligations (Article 4) to provide accessible information or to promote the training of professional and staff working with persons with disabilities, as well as in the context of minimizing or preventing further disabilities within the article on the right to health (Article 25). Neither of these proposals made it into the final text, however. Although such a reference did not seem to raise much disagreement, it disappeared from the discussion—seemingly, given the multitude of other issues that were considered, and ultimately, due to insufficient advocacy for its inclusion.

3.2 A right to sexuality?

A second health-related issue that was raised and was hotly debated during the negotiations was whether the CRPD should stipulate an explicit right to sexuality. Aware of the attitude towards persons with disabilities as asexual and the subsequent risk of physical and sexual abuse, as well as to the cultural and legal non-marriageability of persons with disabilities,[73] a few proposals were submitted to include references to sexuality. The first included a stipulation in the article on awareness-raising (now Article 8) about changing negative perceptions and social prejudices towards persons with disabilities in all matters of sexuality, marriage, parenthood, and family relations. Another suggestion was to add to the provision on respect for home and the family the phrase that 'persons with disabilities are not denied the equal opportunity to experience their sexuality, have sexual and other intimate relationships, and experience parenthood'. This formulation follows the previously adopted—and significantly influential—Rule 9 of the Standard Rules on the Equalization of Opportunities of Persons with Disabilities (1993), which made possible the inclusion of this proposal in the first draft text of the CRPD that was circulated. A third proposal was more general, suggesting the inclusion within the scope of the right to family of a statement that, 'persons with disabilities have a right to sexuality and to form intimate relationships

69 Groce, *Global Survey on HIV/AIDS and Disability* (n 67) 10.

70 It is estimated that 90% of children with disabilities in developing countries do not attend school. UNESCO, 'Gendered Outcomes in Education: Why Girls Still Held Back' in Education for All Global Monitoring Report 2003/4 (2003) 131, available at <http://www.unesco.org/pv_obj_cache/pv_obj_id_5AE8EE78E881D08503D5D42C7049E295EB340500/filename/chapter3.pdf>.

71 Groce, *Global Survey on HIV/AIDS and Disability* (n 67) 10, 12.

72 UN DESA, 'Some Facts about Persons with Disabilities' (n 50).

73 A. Dhanda, *Legal Order and Mental Disorder* (Sage Publications, 2000) 182–7; Mykitiuk and Chadha, 'Site of Exclusion' (n 34) 178; see also M. Wates, 'Righting the Picture: Disability and Family Life' in J. Swain et al (eds), *Disabling Barriers—Enabling Environments* (Sage Publications, 2009) 135.

with others. This right includes the right of all men and women with disabilities who are of marriageable age to marry and to found a family'.

Both the wording and the issue in general, however, raised acute debates. While it was generally agreed that persons with disabilities should be able to experience their sexuality,[74] disagreement arose as to whether it should be stipulated as a right and as to the scope of any such interest or right. The Arab Group (including Morocco, Yemen, and Bahrain), for instance, advanced the proposition that any reference to sexuality would be reserved to be 'in accordance with the precepts of religion, convictions and various customs'. Others (such as the Holy See and Yemen) tied any reference to sexuality with marriage. They preferred having only a general right to family life and to found a family, without any explicit mentioning of sexuality. Finally, some states (such as the US and Iran) retracted to a more formal explanation to their opposition to a reference on sexuality and sexual life: the fact that such a right is not stipulated in any other international human rights treaty. They therefore expressed preference for using only terminology that already exists in other human rights instruments. Similarly, although Canada was in favour of one's 'right to express sexuality', it did not accept the wording of 'a right to sexuality', as it seemingly granted persons with disabilities a right that others do not have.

Certainly, this is an ironic—though unsurprising—argument. References to sexuality or to sexual and other intimate relationships are not found in other human rights conventions simply because the enjoyment of the opportunity to have such relationships has not been denied to other groups; it has been systematically denied, however, to persons with disabilities.[75] Indeed, regardless of how states' delegate framed their objections, it is the politicized nature of the issue of sexual relations that led to the contestation. This is further evident given that proposals to include sexuality and sexual orientation merely as prohibited grounds for discrimination were also rejected (discussed later). Additionally, the lack of sufficient activism may account for this failure. Although civil society organizations, especially through the organized International Disability Caucus (IDC), were a mobilizing force behind the CRPD and highly involved throughout the drafting process, at the end, the context of sexuality was not a priority. This may have been critical, particularly given that a few conservative NGOs that do not view sexuality outside of the marital institution as positive or desirable expressed their position from an early stage.[76] The result is nonetheless that sexuality was not elevated to the status of a right. Rather, the CRPD contains merely the conventional statement about equalization of rights in family life.

3.3 Disability and sexual orientation

Although the issue of disability and sexual orientation—just as the issue of disability and sexuality more generally—received only scant attention, there is no doubt that persons with disabilities express their sexuality in different ways. Studies suggest that homosexuality and bisexuality occur at the same rate among individuals with disability as among the non-disabled.[77] Simultaneously, there are stereotypes that often preclude

[74] eg see statements submitted by Norway, Iran, Australia, and the Philippines.

[75] See also statement by New Zealand's delegate.

[76] For instance, United Families International and the Society for the Protection of Unborn Children.

[77] Groce, *Global Survey on HIV/AIDS and Disability* (n 67) 10; N.E. Groce, 'HIV/AIDS and Individuals with Disability' (2005) 8(2) *Health and Human Rights* 217.

the societal recognition of sexual orientation other than the heterosexual one.[78] Subsequently, persons with disabilities who are gay often experience multiple layers of oppression and discrimination.[79] Furthermore, it has been suggested that they are excluded from the disability movement, where they may experience similar prejudice and homophobia.[80] Thus, from the beginning of the CRPD's negotiations, efforts were made to ensure that such groups are explicitly mentioned—and protected—under the treaty. In fact, with Canada and New Zealand at the forefront, the first draft text already included an explicit prohibition of discrimination on the ground of disability in conjunction with sexuality and sexual orientation within the scope of (now) Article 2.

Initially, this proposal received support, especially from the EU countries. By the end of the third session of the drafting process in June 2004, however, the specific reference to sexuality (among others) was omitted from the definition of equality and non-discrimination. The formal reason was a disagreement among states as to whether a list of prohibited grounds of discrimination should be retained at all. As is often the case in such legal deliberations, the concern raised is that once the instrument contains a list, it necessarily excludes some groups/issues that merit mentioning while including other groups/issues that should not be mentioned. Consequently, the drafters agreed to replace the list with the general statement, as adopted in Article 2, that the term 'discrimination on the basis of disability' shall mean any distinction, exclusion, or restriction that aims at or practically impairs or nullifies the equal human rights and fundamental freedoms of persons with disabilities 'in the political, economic, social, cultural, civil or any other field'.

This formal reason can—and should—be questioned, however. Other core international human rights instruments include some specific prohibited grounds for discrimination, such as race, colour, sex, language, religion, political or other opinion, national or social origin, property, birth, or other status.[81] The Convention on the Rights of the Child (CRC) further includes disability as a prohibited ground for discrimination.[82] It is thus hard to accept that updating the list of prohibited grounds of discrimination so that it reflects the contemporary world is wrong. This excuse for omitting the reference to sexuality is particularly questionable for another reason: an alternative proposal (raised by Canada, the EU, and Brazil) to incorporate a reference to sexual orientation in the Preamble's sub-paragraph that calls attention to aggravated discrimination[83] was rejected as well, although the sub-paragraphs of a preamble to a treaty do not have an operative and legally binding force. Thus, as with the right to sexuality, it is safe to conclude that the reasons for omission are rooted in international politics and, again, lack of sufficient activism or the ability to leverage sufficient external states' support for this position.

Undeniably, these aforementioned omissions do not mean that the process is over. The CRPD can be interpreted to include these issues as well through the authoritative interpretation of the Committee monitoring the CRPD's implementation. In fact, the issue of disability and HIV/AIDS has more recently received increasing attention. In January 2007, the African Campaign on Disability and AIDS was launched to collect

78 P. Cambridge, 'How Far to Gay? The Politics of HIV in Learning Disability' (1997) 12(3) *Disability and Society* 431.

79 J. Sinecka, '"I am Bodied," "I am Sexual." "I am Human." Experiencing Deafness and Gayness: A Story of a Young Man' (2008) 23(5) *Disability and Society* 477.

80 Mykitiuk and Chadha, 'Site of Exclusion' (n 34) 171.

81 See for instance ICCPR, Art 2 and ICESCR, Art 2.

82 CRC, Art 2.

83 CRPD, Preamble P. This is an innovative provision in a human rights treaty on its own.

and share good practice, research, challenges, and successes in African communities.[84] In the same year, the AIDS-Free World, an international advocacy organization that works virtually from a dozen locations in the US, Canada, Africa, the Caribbean, and Europe was established to collect information on this issue, to identify those responsible for creating problems and for solving them, and to hold both to account.[85] Disability and HIV/AIDS has also been recognized among the UN's key areas of work for persons with disabilities—not least because of the CRPD's explicit language of Article 25(a) that requires the provision of sexual and reproductive health and population-based health programmes—thus, overall, suggesting that it will not be lost in future health-related initiatives.[86] Existing provisions in the CRPD further allow for the revisiting of the issue of disability and sexuality.[87] For instance, in Canada, the issue of reproductive assistance has explicitly been extended to women with disabilities and it has also been suggested that access to, and accommodation in, care services so that persons with disabilities can enjoy intimate and sexual expression should be viewed as part of their right to equality.[88]

It is regrettable, however, that the treaty does not include any acknowledgement of a pandemic that has aggravated the discrimination of a subgroup of persons with disabilities and that prevention programmes have clearly failed to include. It is equally regrettable that the most up-to-date human rights treaty retains the notion of sexuality merely as heterosexual gender dichotomy and does not explicitly recognize individuals' continuum sexual citizenship. Indeed, these omissions are especially a cause for concern if they reflect unlearnt lessons. As the history of disability rights has shown, without an explicit reference it is hard to cross the barrier of invisibility. It is to be hoped that these omissions would not, even if unintentionally, maintain the status quo of the presumed asexuality of persons with disabilities.

4. Challenges Ahead

As successful as the CRPD may be, it is not a magic wand but is only the first step. This is especially so in the context of health and sexual health: there is a need to ensure that prevention and promotion programmes are disability-friendly. Yet the CRPD's implementation encounters three main challenges. The first is what I see as a 'traditional challenge' in the implementation of human rights treaties. This challenge concerns the question of universalism of human rights standards and the extent to which the stipulated norms can be applied across various religious and cultural settings. This is an old debate, and it is unlikely to be resolved in the disability context—all the more so given the multiple levels of stigma, prejudice, and cultural constructs that exist. The fact that the concept of health itself is perceived differently through diverse cultural prisms further complicates the issue.[89] Notwithstanding the scientific revolution, many societies remained religiously-oriented, and they maintained systems of medical

84 The African Campaign on Disability and AIDS, see <http://www.africacampaign.info/about-us/background-of-the-campaign.html>.

85 AIDS-Free World, see <http://www.aidsfreeworld.org/About-Us/What-We-Do.aspx>.

86 UN Enable, 'Priority Themes', available at <http://www.un.org/disabilities/default.asp?id=33>.

87 See also CRPD, Preamble P, which includes the phrase 'other status' in reference to persons with disabilities who are subject to multiple or aggravated forms of discrimination. See also General Comment 14 (n 14) paras 16 and 18.

88 Mykitiuk and Chadha, 'Site of Exclusion' (n 34) 174, 181–91.

89 Sabatello, *Children's Bioethics* (n 48) 2–7.

conduct, ethics, and beliefs that significantly differ from what the conventional health and sexual health-related programmes and human rights standards have had in mind.

The 'traditional challenge' also revolves around the need to create national legislation that incorporates the CRPD in a way that is effective and that reflects the life experiences of persons with disabilities and their needs. Many of the states that have ratified the treaty still do not have anti-discrimination laws in the context of disabilities.[90] Moreover, newly adopted national laws may become dead laws. One disturbing issue is the possibility that non-discrimination laws adopted in lieu of the CRPD may nevertheless envelope the medical and paternalistic approach to disability rather than the social and human rights one.[91] Another is that national disability laws that are adopted may not include any actual regulations for implementation (as has been the case, for instance, in Uganda and Zimbabwe).[92] And yet still another cause for concern is the possibility of reservations, where states that sign and ratify the CRPD enter a statement by which they will not be bound by certain provisions of the treaty.[93] Indeed, some worrying developments have already occurred, with Egypt and Syria, for instance, entering a reservation that the right to legal capacity would be interpreted to mean legal capacity to rights but not legal capacity to act.[94] While such a reservation does not immediately translate into the field of health and healthcare, it certainly may. For instance, if the right of persons with disabilities to give informed consent to medical treatment will be overridden by others, the stipulated right will have very little meaning. Reservations made to the right to health, especially the right to sexual and reproductive health (Article 25(a)) are similarly a cause for concern.[95] Such reservations reflect the debates during the treaty's negotiations, whereby some state delegates objected to the inclusion of 'sexual and reproductive health', as they equated it with abortion. Even if, given the politicization of the issue, a statement that sexual and reproductive health would not include abortion is acceptable, the potential rippling effect on other maternal health issues is worrying. Indeed, with over half a million women worldwide (99 percent of them in developing countries) dying every year from complications of pregnancy and childbirth, and with estimates that 75 percent of such mortality instances are preventable,[96] it is clear that the issue of women's sexual and reproductive health is already neglected and ignored.

A second set of challenges concerns the acute lack of up-to-date empirical and other research on the health needs of persons with disabilities. Considering the lack of cross-cultural definition of disability and the overall neglect over the years, there is insufficient data and statistics, particularly in a comparable form. Consequently, there are

90 As of 2008, only forty-five countries have passed such non-discrimiantion laws. UN DESA, 'Some Facts about Persons with Disabilities' (n 50).

91 T. Degener, 'Disability as a Subject of International Human Rights Law and Comparative Discrimination Law' in S.S. Herr et al (eds), *The Human Rights of Persons with Intellectual Disabilities: Different But Equal* (OUP, 2003) 175.

92 R. Lang et al, 'Implementing the United Nations Convention on the Rights of Persons with Disabilities: Principles, Implications, Practice and Limitation' (2011) 5 *European Journal of Disability Research* 212.

93 Reservations are allowed under the Vienna Convention on the Law of Treaties as long as they do not go against the purpose and object of the treaty (Arts 2 and 19–23).

94 UN Treaty Collection—CRPD, available at <http://treaties.un.org/Pages/ViewDetails.aspx?src=TREATY&mtdsg_no=IV-15&chapter=4&lang=en>.

95 See for instance reservations by Lithuania, Malta, Poland, and Monaco (UN Treaty Collection—CRPD (n 94)).

96 International Initiative on Maternal Mortality and Human Rights, available at <http://righttomaternalhealth.org/about-us/about>.

many gaps in the information that exists—from estimates of the prevalence of persons with disabilities living with HIV/AIDS, to epidemiological studies to figure out the direction of the connection between disability and health (for example how does pregnancy impact people with various pre-existing disabilities?), and to research about how the intersection between multiple stigmatized identities plays out (for instance, a member of the deaf community or of the 'Mad Pride' movement and sexual orientation). Similarly, developing best practices to allow for the mainstreaming of persons with disabilities into existing health and sexual health prevention and promotion programmes and assessment of the extent to which these programmes are responsive to persons with disabilities are only just beginning to emerge.[97] For instance, although there are a few HIV/AIDS interventions that have recently been made in Kenya, Uganda, Tanzania, and other countries,[98] almost none of them have been systematically monitored or evaluated.[99] Further, while recent HIV/AIDS projects in Kenya focus on deaf people and seem to be successful, how such programmes should be expended to other countries and types of disabilities so they respond to the specific localities, is less clear.[100]

The WHO International Classification of Functioning, Disability and Health (ICF)[101] provides an important and useful framework within which to consider the barriers to health of persons with disabilities. The ICF measures one's health and health-related needs and degree of impairment in a way that integrates the contextual and environmental factors, and it is valuable also for its request for multidisciplinary approaches to disability. There is much room for further utilization of the ICF, however, and it takes time to compile and develop such information. Nonetheless, empirical and other studies are critical in order to assess properly the needs of persons with disabilities and to create accurate human rights and health-related targets for the states to implement.[102] Indeed, it is in this vein that Article 31 of the CRPD explicitly requires the collection of appropriate information, including statistical and research data, on persons with disabilities so as to enable the formulation and implementation of policies that give effect to the Convention.

Finally, the third set of challenges is the need to break down the barriers. This is at the heart of a human rights approach to disability since it revolves around equity, non-discrimination, and participation. There are various barriers that need to be overcome, including physically accessible environment, economic (ensuring affordable transport and healthcare services), information/communication (needing to be in accessible formats and material such as Braille, large print, simple language, pictures, and lack of sign language), and institutional barriers (ensuring the removal of intentional and unintentional discrimination in legislation and policy-making). Perhaps the most

[97] See for instance the three-part typology developed in N.E. Groce, R. Trasi, and A.K. Yousafzai, *Guidelines for Inclusion of Individuals with Disability in HIV/AIDS Outreach Efforts* (Yale University, 2006), available at <http://globalsurvey.med.yale.edu/inclusion_guidelines_hivaids.pdf>.

[98] S. Shome and M. Tataryn, 'Challenges and Successes in Addressing the Exclusion of People with Disabilities from HIV Prevention, Testing and Treatment' (AIDS-Free World, 2008), available at <http://www.aidsfreeworld.org/Our-Issues/Disability/~/media/Files/Disability/Challenges%20and%20Successes.pdf>.

[99] Groce, Trasi, and Yousafzai, *Guidelines for Inclusion of Individuals with Disability* (n 97) 3, 14.

[100] Shome and Tataryn, 'Challenges and Successes in Addressing the Exclusion of People with Disabilities' (n 98) 6; Groce, Trasi, and Yousafzai, *Guidelines for Inclusion of Individuals with Disability* (n 97) 13.

[101] For further information about the ICF see <http://www.disabilitaincifre.it/documenti/ICF_18.pdf>.

[102] Lang et al, 'Implementing the United Nations Convention' (n 92) 214.

cardinal challenge is the need to remove the attitudinal and cultural barriers: the stigma and prejudice, including the wrong assumption about persons with disabilities being asexual and/or sexually inactive, along with real acceptance of the phenomenon of disability.[103] This barrier is as yet also the most pervasive one—from healthcare providers to human rights and humanitarian agencies to international bodies, to states and national policy-makers, to the general public—and in most likelihood, also out of mere lack of awareness and knowledge. Indeed, one of the clear characteristics of the drafting process of the CRPD is what I termed elsewhere 'diplomatic shortcoming', referring to state delegates' (and general human rights organizations') lack of the expertise, knowledge, and understanding of how to properly address the needs of persons with disabilities.[104] As legal reforms alone cannot bring about social change, removing this barrier requires building partnerships with all of the aforementioned actors on both national and international levels—a complicated task on its own.

Finally, there is a need to ensure that persons with disabilities are partners in the programming, planning, and implementation of health promotion and prevention programmes. While such inclusive development is now part and parcel of states' obligations under the CRPD,[105] it requires that significant effort is put into capacity-building. Despite the international success, at its heart, the disability rights movement is a grassroots movement. Many of those who attended the UN sessions came with no legal expertise or background and their encounter at the UN was their first with such an international process.[106] Further, many organizations of persons with disabilities in developing (as well as developed) countries remained welfare-oriented, taking a paternalist and charity-focused rather than human rights approach.[107] The extent—and pace—at which the disability rights movement can play the international field and carry its success from the protected area of the UN to the real world is yet to be seen.

5. Conclusions

Persons with disabilities have historically been excluded from human rights, development, and global health initiatives. The CRPD, which views persons with disabilities in whichever life-stage, gender, race, etc as subjects and as holders of all human rights is therefore a first step in the right direction to remedy this global wrong. The Convention unequivocally emphasizes that disability rights are human rights and that the various barriers are at the locus of the on-going stigmatization, exclusion, and discrimination. There is much to be done, however, and the international human rights and global public health communities have a critical role in doing so.

Given the history of disability rights, the human rights approach to health—adjusted to include the understandings of human rights as developed in the CRPD—is particularly appealing to address global health concerns in their regard. Revisiting pertinent issues of disability and HIV/AIDS, sexuality, and sexual orientation that were omitted during the negotiation process due to internal and international politics is too important.

103 CRPD, Art 3(d) includes among the treaty's General Principles: 'Respect for difference and acceptance of persons with disabilities as part of human diversity and humanity.'

104 M. Sabatello, 'The New Diplomacy' in M. Sabatello and M. Schulze (eds), *Human Rights and Disability Advocacy* (Pennsylvania University Press, 2014).

105 Arts 4 (General Obligations) and 32 (International Cooperation).

106 Sabatello, 'The New Diplomacy' (n 104); see also Lang et al, 'Implementing the United Nations Convention' (n 92) 213, making a similar point.

107 Lang et al, 'Implementing the United Nations Convention' (n 92) 213, 215.

Concerted advocacy work is essential to ensure that they are addressed through the authoritative work of the human rights bodies and implemented by states and others who are engaged in this field.

While challenges to the implementation of the CRPD certainly exist, establishing a body of data on the health and sexual health needs of persons with disabilities, the removal of societal barriers, striking real partnerships with persons with disabilities, and empowerment will enable rethinking of how exercising human rights can be done in ways that are more relational, dependent, and accepting of physical and mental differences as part of the human fabric. It is in this intersection that the creation of an inclusive society will be possible, not as a matter of welfare, but as a matter of rights and justice. Otherwise, persons with disabilities will remain at the bottom of the societal structure, making global health and development unachievable agendas.

15

What Can Human Rights Do for Women's Health?

Kristen Hessler

1. Introduction

Onora O'Neill has argued extensively that human rights must be translated into specific assignments of correlative duties to determinate actors before they can make any practical difference for rights-holders. In this chapter, I first explore how elements of O'Neill's framing of the problem of human rights have been taken up in the literature on women's human rights to health. I then argue that it is a significant defect of O'Neill's account that it ignores the role that women's human rights play in establishing women's equal moral standing with men in their social and political communities, which is best captured by Pogge's institutional account of human rights. Moreover, I draw on the literature on women's health and human rights to argue that establishing women's equal standing provides an institutional structure that fosters positive change in women's health. Finally, in the course of considering objections and clarifying my view, I argue that this view of human rights can be grounded in Kant's political philosophy, in particular the demand that we establish institutions that respect the equal freedom of individuals and avoid subordination.

2. O'Neill on Women's Human Rights

In a series of articles, Onora O'Neill has consistently argued for skepticism regarding the project of human rights in general, and in particular regarding welfare rights like the right to health. Her skepticism is grounded in the concern that, while human rights impose obligations on others, 'the rhetoric of rights . . . obscures what is really at stake by focusing on the rights rather than the obligations'.[1] Instead, she claims, 'if we want to establish intellectually robust norms for health policies it would be preferable to start from a systematic account of obligations rather than of rights'.[2] As O'Neill argues, traditional liberty rights (against assault, for example) are associated with well-defined, universal, and determinate obligations, even in the absence of institutions, while '[r]ights to goods and services' (or welfare rights), by contrast, are not:

> Rights to goods and services can be thought of only in the hazy way which the rhetoric of rights favours and allows until they are at least partly institutionalized. It may be possible to state what ought to be provided or delivered, but it will be impossible to state who ought to do the providing or delivering, and who can be called to account when deliveries are botched, or nothing is delivered, unless there are established institutions and well-defined special relationships.

[1] O. O'Neill, 'Women's rights: Whose obligations?' in *Bounds of Justice* (CUP, 2000) 97, 99.

[2] O. O'Neill, 'Public Health or Clinical Ethics: Thinking Beyond Borders', *Ethics and International Affairs* (2002) 16(2): 35, 42.

Rights to goods and services are easy to proclaim, but until there are effective institutions their proclamation may seem bitter mockery to those who most need them.[3]

This matters for women in particular, she argues, since 'as long as women still carry more of the real work of caring for true dependents (children, those who are ill, the elderly) and as long as they have fewer resources with which to do so, they will need rights to financial support and to relevant social services more often'.[4] In O'Neill's view, reliance on the framework of women's human rights threatens to shortchange women by distracting us from the real issue at stake regarding social policy, namely, ascertaining who ought to do what for whom—in particular, who ought to do what for women—and then (to the extent possible) ensuring that these obligations are met.

O'Neill's skepticism can be understood as an argument both about the theory of human rights, as well as about the practical implications of current human rights practice. Regarding human rights theory, O'Neill believes that if an account of obligations could be given instead of an account of rights, this would minimize the assertions of rights that really aren't rights:

. . . a focus on required action, rather than on entitlements to receive, makes it easier to spot incoherence. For example, it is easy and rather fetching (and regrettably common) to talk about a universal 'right to health,' but plain enough when one considers who has to do what for whom that universal health cannot be provided, so that there can be no such right.[5]

According to this theoretical strand of her argument, claimability is an existence condition of human rights. As a practical consideration, O'Neill argues that the inclusion of broad rights to goods and services in international human rights agreements threaten a number of adverse consequences, from providing the mere illusion of doing something positive in the world without actually making anyone better off, to encouraging what John Tasioulas calls 'a grasping recipient's perspective' on the part of rights-holders.[6] On O'Neill's account, then, there is very little to say on behalf of a human rights approach to women's health. Not only are 'rights to health' difficult to defend theoretically, but such an approach also has significant practical disadvantages.

Elements of O'Neill's framing of the problem characterize the literature on women's health and human rights, even if her broadly skeptical conclusions about human rights are not themselves widely shared. In a 2010 paper on women's reproductive health, for example, Sara Davies argues that the distinction between positive and negative rights has thrown up a stumbling block for the realization of women's human rights to health. As Davies notes:

There is a big difference between the insistence that 'all I have to do is not prevent people seeking the best health care they can afford,' which is a negative right based on the 'do no harm principle,' and a claim that 'I have a duty to ensure that every person is able to access the best health care possible,' which is implied by the positive rights approach. The distinction in understanding what a human right to health means is one between *access* (the right to seek care and not be prevented from doing so with no specific duty-bearer assuming responsibility for the provision of care) and *provision* (the right to be provided with the best care possible with a duty-bearer having an obligation to ensure that such a provision is made available).[7]

[3] O'Neill, 'Women's rights: Whose obligations?' (n 1) 105.

[4] O'Neill, 'Women's rights: Whose obligations?' (n 1) 106.

[5] O'Neill, 'Public Health or Clinical Ethics' (n 2) 42.

[6] J. Tasioulas, 'The Moral Reality of Human Rights' in T. Pogge (ed), *Freedom from Poverty as a Human Right* (OUP, 2007) 75, 98.

[7] S.E. Davies, 'Reproductive Health as a Human Right: A Matter of Access or Provision?' *Journal of Human Rights* (2010) 9: 387, 391.

Davies argues that the failure of relevant actors to specify and assign to determinate actors positive duties regarding the provision of women's health (as opposed to mere access) is to a significant degree responsible for the lack of substantive progress on improving women's health within a human rights framework. This critique echoes O'Neill's concerns about welfare rights in the absence of institutional frameworks that specify and assign correlative duties to specific agents.

Consider also the title of Ruth Macklin's paper, 'Global Inequalities in Women's Health: Who Is Responsible for Doing What?'[8] In this paper, Macklin analyzes the assignment of specific obligations regarding women's health to specific actors, based on the capabilities of the relevant agents. Importantly, unlike O'Neill, Macklin does not discredit a human rights approach to women's health generally. However, Macklin does attempt to assign specific obligations regarding women's health to states, the international community, and non-state actors (such as state-level or international NGOs), presumably on the premise that only such specific assignments of determinate duties will enable women to claim their human rights in any effective way.

In the remainder of this chapter, my aim is not so much to respond to O'Neill's critique of human rights (or these manifestations of it in the literature on women's health), but rather to explore what her perspective on human rights leaves out. In the next section, I argue that her focus on assigning determinate obligations to specific agents ignores an important institutional function of women's human rights: that of establishing women's equality in their social and political communities. In turn, this function of women's human rights contributes to the improvement of women's health status, since the social subordination of women contributes in multiple ways to their poor health.

3. Equality, Institutions, and Women's Human Rights

Women's human rights law emphasizes women's equality of standing with men in their social and political communities. As the United Nations Economic and Social Council argues: 'The equal right of men and women to the enjoyment of all human rights is one of the fundamental principles recognized under international law and enshrined in the main international human rights instruments.'[9] The Convention on the Elimination of all Forms of Discrimination Against Women (CEDAW) defines 'discrimination against women' as:

> ...any distinction, exclusion or restriction made on the basis of sex which has the effect or purpose of impairing or nullifying the recognition, enjoyment or exercise by women, irrespective of their marital status, on a basis of equality of men and women, of human rights and fundamental freedoms in the political, economic, social, cultural, civil or any other field.[10]

Article 5(a) of CEDAW assigns to states the obligation to 'take all appropriate measures to modify the social and cultural patterns of conduct of men and women, with a view to achieving the elimination of prejudices and customary and all other practices which are based on the idea of the inferiority or the superiority of either of the sexes or on

[8] R. Macklin, 'Global Inequalities in Women's Health: Who is Responsible for Doing What?' *Philosophical Topics* (2009) 37(2): 93.

[9] Committee on Economic, Social and Cultural Rights (CESCR), General Comment 16, 'Article 3: the equal right of men and women to the enjoyment of all economic, social and cultural rights' (34th session, 2005), UN Doc E/C.12/2005/3 (2005).

[10] CEDAW, Art 1.

stereotyped roles for men and women'.[11] And, importantly, in its General Comment on the equal rights of men and women, the Economic and Social Council argues that women are entitled to both formal equality with men, in the sense that laws and policies should not discriminate unfairly against women, and to substantive equality, in the sense that laws and policies must work to alleviate 'the inherent disadvantage' of women.[12]

These broad assertions of equality are not readily translatable into specific obligations borne by determinate actors, and they are not easily accounted for within the framework of positive and negative rights. Rather, these claims place demands on the institutional framework of states' laws and policies—in particular, the demand that these institutions treat the men and women subject to them as equals. As such, they illustrate Thomas Pogge's institutional understanding of human rights, according to which human rights are understood 'primarily as claims on coercive social institutions and secondarily as claims against those who uphold such institutions'.[13] By contrast, an 'interactionist' conception of human rights 'presents human rights as placing the treatment of human beings under certain constraints that do not presuppose the existence of social institutions'.[14] On this account of human rights, asserting a human right to X implies 'that any society or other social system, insofar as this is reasonably possible, ought to be so (re)organized that all its members have secure access to X, with "security" always understood as especially sensitive to persons' risk of being denied X or deprived of X officially: by the government or its agents or officials'.[15]

As Pogge notes, an accounting of whether specific human rights are violated will not suffice to inform us whether the institutional standard for human rights is met. To illustrate why not, consider the following contrasting cases:

> A person may fully enjoy X even while her access to X is insecure (as when persons relevantly like her, say blacks or vocal government opponents, are beaten or threatened). Conversely, a person may be temporarily deprived of X, through a crime by a rogue government official perhaps, in a society that is very effective in preventing crimes of the relevant type. Opposite to the interactional understanding, my institutional one regards only the first case as a human-rights problem.[16]

Pogge uses the term 'human rights problem' in his comparative analysis of these two cases because shifting to an institutional conception of human rights requires paying attention to whether human rights are fulfilled in the institutional order as a whole; information about the existence of discrete human rights violations will not suffice, on the institutional model, to establish the existence of a 'human rights problem'. As Pogge interprets the institutional account of human rights, therefore, it links 'human rights fulfillment with insecurity rather than violation':

> On the interactional understanding of human rights, governments and individuals have a responsibility not to violate human rights. On my institutional understanding, by contrast, their responsibility is to work for an institutional order and public culture that ensure that all members of society have secure access to the objects of their human rights.[17]

[11] CEDAW, Art 5(a). [12] CESCR 2005.

[13] T. Pogge, *World Poverty and Human Rights* (Polity Press, 2002; 2nd edn, 2008) 44–5. My explication of Pogge's view in this section, and my analysis of O'Neill in section 5.1, both draw from K. Hessler, 'Equality, Human Rights, and Political Legitimacy' in A. Follesdal, J. Karlsson Schaffer, and G. Ulfstein (eds), *The Legitimacy of International Human Rights Systems* (CUP, 2014) 117–40.

[14] Pogge, *World Poverty and Human Rights* (2002) (n 13) 44–5.

[15] Pogge, *World Poverty and Human Rights* (2002) (n 13) 64.

[16] Pogge, *World Poverty and Human Rights* (2008) (n 13) 71.

[17] Pogge, *World Poverty and Human Rights* (2008) (n 13) 71.

O'Neill's question about human rights ('who has to do what for whom?') cannot capture the institutional aspects of human rights, and therefore cannot recognize the role of women's human rights in establishing women's equality with men in their social and political communities. In the following section, I show how current literature on women's health and human rights suggests that the recognition of women's equal standing in their social and political communities is important for improving women's health. If this is right, then there is an important practical as well as theoretical significance to the fact that O'Neill's view fails to recognize the institutional elements of human rights.

4. Women's Human Rights and Global Public Health

The literature on global public health and human rights provides a close analysis of how ideologies of women's subordination in their social and political communities structures the material realities of women's and girls' day-to-day existence. Importantly, this literature connects the dots between culturally embedded traditions of women's subordination, on one hand, and health outcomes, on the other. For example, a 2008 report from the WHO's Commission on Social Determinants of Health (CSDH) notes that gender inequities worldwide 'influence health through, among other routes, discriminatory feeding patterns, violence against women, lack of decision-making power, and unfair divisions of work, leisure, and possibilities of improving one's life'.[18] It is the recognition that these material realities often result in poor health, combined with the public health mandate to improve health outcomes, that provide the motivation within this movement to research how to change the complex social determinants of women's status and health.

What has emerged thus far is that, while improving women's status is a complex and multifaceted process, it is not entirely mysterious. Indeed, broad strategies have begun to emerge in the public health and human rights literature on how to bring it about. The CSDH report recommends six broad strategies 'towards improving gender equity for health'.[19] These are:

(1) state-level legislation promoting gender equity;
(2) 'gender mainstreaming'—ie including likely impacts on gender equity in the analysis of policies, legislation, and institutions;
(3) measuring and accounting for unpaid, informal work in the household or community;
(4) improving and investing in education for women and girls;
(5) instituting policies aimed at promoting women's greater abilities to engage in paid work (including ensuring equal opportunity by law, pay equity legislation, and family-friendly legislation);
(6) realizing sexual and reproductive health rights for women.

More importantly, however, it is becoming clear that this program is not simply a list of distinct efforts that might work separately, but a coordinated platform for action that

[18] CSDH, 'Closing the Gap in a Generation: Health equity through action on the social determinants of health', Final Report of the Commission on Social Determinants of Health (Geneva: WHO, 2008) 16.

[19] CSDH, 'Closing the Gap in a Generation' (n 18) 147–54.

emphasizes gender equity at the highest levels of policy and law to provide the necessary context underwriting the effectiveness of any more targeted actions. Consider a background paper for the CSDH report, which assessed the literature in English on how to change gendered norms about women and girls at the household or community levels. The survey adopts a public health framework to classify interventions aimed at promoting gender equity: interventions are classified as 'downstream' if they focus on influencing individual behavior, and 'upstream' if they focus on populations as a whole. According to the literature review:

> Downstream strategies including the provision of basic primary health care are increasingly recognised as critical in addressing specific programs such as violence against women and general efforts to raise women's social status. However, social change occurs when downstream and midstream programs are conducted in the context of broader systemic (upstream) efforts to increase gender equity.[20]

Within any particular society, then, the public health and human rights movement suggests that moving toward a commitment to women's legal and social equality with men is an important step toward changing the material realities of women's daily lives through any more targeted policies. As the report concludes:

> Strategies for increasing the levels of education of girls or raising their access to health services will have little or no effect on lessening the gender gap between men and women, whether rich or poor, if they are not embedded in human rights frameworks that affirm, guide, and monitor violations of equal and universal rights.[21]

In summary, the lack of social standing of women in their political and social communities is itself a human rights problem that in turn has serious consequences for women's health. Part of the point of women's human rights, then, is to establish women's equal standing with men, not only as a human right in itself, but also, as the health and human rights literature suggests, as an essential structural feature of social institutions within which women's more concrete human rights (to health, for example) can be realized.

Inegalitarian social structures themselves causally influence women's poor health in ways that are difficult to capture by an accounting of who has done what for whom. Without investigating the social structures that assign women an inferior status in their social and political communities, we will lack an adequate causal account of women's poor health, and we will lack the theoretical resources and practical tools to improve it. In turn, this suggests that O'Neill's view that the theoretical import of human rights can be fully captured by assigning determinate obligations to identifiable duty-holders is radically incomplete. Human rights practices based upon an adequately institutional account of human rights proclaim women's equal status with men in their social and political communities, thereby creating political and social structures within which women's status can improve.

It is worth noting here that this view of human rights undermines O'Neill's extended critique of human rights, not just for their theoretical flaws and practical disadvantages, but also for the ways in which they situate agents as rights-holders or duty-bearers. Along these lines, O'Neill notes that one effect of being a right-holder is that one is put

20 H. Keleher and L. Franklin, 'Changing gendered norms about women and girls at the level of household and community: A review of the evidence', Background paper prepared for the Women and Gender Equity Knowledge Network of the WHO Commission on Social Determinants of Health (Geneva: WHO, 2007) 14–15.

21 Keleher and Franklin, 'Changing gendered norms about women and girls' (n 20) 15.

in a position to seek redress when the objects of one's rights are not fulfilled, or, failing that, to enjoy 'the dubious pleasures of casting blame':

> Those who cast blame can appropriate, enjoy and prolong their role and status as victims, can enjoy indignation and a feeling of superiority, even if they cannot quite identify or demonstrate the failings of others. If it proves impossible to identify a blameworthy culprit, they can at least blame the system, that is to say the institutional framework that is failing to achieve 'progressively the full realization of the rights recognized . . . by all appropriate means, including particularly the adoption of legislative measures'.[22]

Notice that O'Neill's concern about the moral psychology of rights assumes her account of rights as claims to be provided with specific goods or services (or to certain kinds of treatment by others). If we understand human rights instead as, at least in part, rights to equal status, then the moral psychology of recognizing oneself as a rights-holder looks very different, especially in social and political contexts characterized by subordination and oppression. In such situations, which are the reality for women in countless ways across many different social and cultural traditions, self-recognition as a rights-holder can be empowering in a much more dignified way than O'Neill's account admits.

5. Objections and Clarifications

If my argument in the previous section is correct, then women's rights in particular as well as human rights in general are at least in part grounded in the moral value of equal standing among those who share social and political communities. By contrast, O'Neill treats human rights as if they were discrete claims, which can be measured in interactionist terms by assessing who has to do what for whom. This analysis of the moral force of human rights—seeing moral human rights as serving the function of assigning specific obligations to specific actors—entirely overlooks the egalitarian element of human rights. Moreover, O'Neill ignores the role of human rights declarations of establishing women's status as equal rights-holders with men in their social and political communities, instead seeing the practical functions of human rights as limited to specifying and enforcing specific obligations for specific agents.

In this section, I consider four objections to my argument. First, one might note that O'Neill's criticism actually does assign to institutions a necessary role in specifying and assigning the counterpart duties to human rights. So, one might think that my argument that her view is insufficiently institutional is unfair. Second, one might object on various grounds to Pogge's institutional view of human rights. Third, one might be worried that the health and human rights movement is not really talking about human rights in any philosophically recognizable sense. Finally, and relatedly, the institutional view as well as the general orientation of the health and human rights movement might be said to be working with admirable conceptions of social justice, but ones that are too demanding to plausibly be conceptions of human rights, which are (it is generally supposed) more minimal moral demands than those of social justice. I consider each of these objections in turn.

22 O. O'Neill, 'The Dark Side of Human Rights', *International Affairs* (2005) 81(2): 427, 438.

5.1 How do institutions matter?

O'Neill's argument might seem to give a greater role to institutions than I give it credit for. After all, she argues that welfare rights acquire their correlative obligations (and therefore exist as rights) only when they are made claimable within some political institutional order. Here O'Neill ascribes an essential role to institutions in specifying the obligations correlative with human rights and assigning them to particular agents. However, and importantly for my purposes, this view does not regard political institutions as sources of moral obligations in their own right. Nor do institutions on this account play any role in generating the content of the moral obligations correlative to human rights in any substantive way. This ignores an important aspect of an institutional perspective on human rights, which is captured in the following description of the distinction between the institutional and interactional accounts of human rights:

> An *institutional* conception postulates certain fundamental principles of social *justice*. They apply to institutional schemes and are thus second-order principles: standards for assessing the ground rules and practices that regulate human interactions. An *interactional* conception, by contrast, postulates certain fundamental principles of *ethics*. These principles, like institutional ground rules, are first-order in that they apply directly to the conduct of persons and groups...[23]

Importantly, O'Neill's analysis does not associate human rights with standards for assessing shared practices that are mediated by political institutions. Rather, her account relegates institutions to the merely instrumental role of specifying and allocating the obligations determined by ethical theory to correlate with human rights. In Pogge's terms, institutions for O'Neill serve only to make first-order obligations determinate and actionable. Thus, the claim that her account is insufficiently institutional does not mean that her account does not mention institutions. Rather, it is that her account of human rights does not provide the tools to adequately analyze the moral and practical role that human rights to equality play in social and political institutions.

5.2 Objections to the institutional account

At this point, one might worry that the argument so far relies too heavily on the details of Pogge's institutional account, without adequately defending it. My ultimate reply to this objection is that, for my purposes in this chapter, I can simply set aside debate about the priority of institutional versus interactionist accounts. What matters for understanding women's health and human rights is that, in any adequate account of human rights, there must be a way to accommodate the egalitarian commitments of human rights doctrine, and that these particular commitments are best understood via an institutional account of human rights, according to which human rights are not simply discrete claims against some other actors, but also claims to equal standing in one's social and political communities. It is conceptually possible to find theories of human rights that draw on both institutional and interactionist conceptions (though I do not do that work here). All I need to do is to motivate an institutional account enough to justify its inclusion in theories of human rights as a way of articulating certain elements of moral and legal human rights, not to argue that the institutional account should replace interactionist ones.

23 Pogge, *World Poverty and Human Rights* (2002) (n 13) 170.

However, to clarify my view, I consider in this section a critique of Pogge's view from John Tasioulas, who argues specifically that finding O'Neill's account of human rights unsatisfactory need not (and should not) result in a turn to 'its institutional rival'. As Tasioulas notes, among the more controversial provisions of Pogge's institutional view is the provision that rights violations must be perpetrated by government officials. On this view, patterns of private (domestic) violence or deprivation do not count as human rights violations. Thus, Tasioulas's example of 'the man who habitually inflicts serious violence on his wife and children' is not (on Pogge's account) violating the human rights of his wife and children to physical security—but this seems unduly restrictive of the concept of human rights.[24]

In response, it is important to note that, on one hand, the word 'habitually' may be doing more work in Tasioulas's example than we might at first realize, insofar as it invokes the familiar scenario in which victims of domestic violence have little effective recourse, either to ensure their own safety or to prosecute the perpetrator. One horrific element in many accounts of domestic violence is the larger pattern of institutional influences which leave victims isolated, powerless, and facing tragic trade-offs between freeing themselves (and/or their children) from violence and maintaining custody of their children or the means of subsistence provided within the abusive relationship. The fact that Western liberal societies are still working their way out of the inheritance of such institutional realities might be one reason why domestic violence comes to mind as an example of a private human rights violation, rather than, say, a murder committed in the course of a bank robbery.[25] In a sense, then, the institutional account of human rights provides a powerful critique of much more than the actual violence. To the extent that the institutional conception of human rights incorporates a human right to equal standing in one's social and political communities, the domestic violence example is addressed by a positive obligation to ensure effective remedies for such violence within social and legal institutions.

The hard case, however, is one where the institutional requirements of effective recourse for victims of domestic violence are in place, but where it occurs anyway. One modification of the example would be that, presumably, given the safeguards provided by the institutions, such violence would not be 'habitual'—or if it was, this would not be due to structural flaws in the relevant institutions. Do isolated instances of domestic abuse under such circumstances constitute a human rights violation? If the institutional account implies that they are not human rights violations, Tasioulas's more general criticism against both O'Neill's and Pogge's theories of human rights is that they are both overly restrictive about what count as human rights.

However, recall that Pogge's later articulation of his institutional view distinguishes human rights *violations* from human rights *insecurity*. It is the latter that is the focus of his institutional account, according to which the primary obligation regarding human rights calls on governments and individuals to 'work for an institutional order and public culture that ensure that all members of society have secure access to the objects of their human rights'.[26] The institutional view can therefore accommodate the idea that isolated cases of domestic violence count as human rights violations, but still maintain that the primary obligation based on human rights is to establish a social and

24 Tasioulas, 'The Moral Reality of Human Rights' (n 6) 97.

25 Elizabeth Ashford makes the same argument regarding domestic violence in 'The Duties Imposed by the Human Rights to Basic Necessities' in T. Pogge (ed), *Freedom from Poverty as a Human Right* (OUP, 2007) 183, 185.

26 Pogge, *World Poverty and Human Rights* (2008) (n 13) 71.

political order within which such violations are both minimized and appropriately handled by social agencies and the law.

Moreover, returning to the domestic violence case, it is important that the institutional account has the advantage of better accounting for an important function of human rights discourse, which is to capture the sense that something rising to the level of what Charles Beitz calls 'international concern' is at stake in claims about human rights.[27] Impunity for perpetrators of widespread domestic abuse within a state would, intuitively, rise to such a level, while a single instance of domestic abuse within a state that has excellent resources for victims and aggressive prosecution of perpetrators would be more appropriately described as crime than in the language of human rights. Thus, there is a strong argument for developing theories of human rights that recognize these institutional elements.

5.3 Are we really talking about human rights?

Is it plausible to classify claims to equal standing in one's social and political communities as human rights? One way to answer this question affirmatively would be to consult the texts of human rights conventions. In addition to the broad claims on behalf of women's equality in CEDAW, the UDHR includes the claim that: 'Everyone is entitled to a social and international order in which the rights and freedoms set forth in this Declaration can be fully realized.'[28] These examples show that human rights law is not averse to including such broad institutional claims among these canonical lists of human rights.

These observations will not suffice to address the concern that we have a philosophically coherent account of human rights that justifies such claims. I do not have the space to develop such an account here. However, as a gesture in the general direction of such an account, consider once more Pogge's description of an institutional account of human rights as one that 'postulates certain fundamental principles of social *justice*'. One important avenue opened by institutional accounts of human rights, on this broad description, is that philosophical theories of justice (not just of morality) become relevant to articulating human rights standards. In that spirit, I suggest that an idea from Kant's political philosophy is a helpful framework for understanding human rights to equality.[29] Kant argued that the primary function of political institutions—ie the feature of political institutions that makes their creation morally mandatory—is to avoid the unjust subordination of some to others.[30] The moral prohibition on unjust subordination is, in a sense, a negative duty, as is Pogge's negative duty to avoid imposing on others a regime in which some lack secure access to the objects of their human rights. But importantly, both negative duties are not simple negative duties, but rather at the same time impose a complex set of positive duties (to reform the regime, if necessary, or to educate others regarding the subordinative effects of various policies, for example).

While the Kantian idea of equality as non-subordination nicely captures the basic idea behind the equality claimed for women in CEDAW and other elements of women's human rights doctrine, one need not be a Kantian to give equality a starring

[27] C. Beitz, *The Idea of Human Rights* (OUP, 2009) ch 7.

[28] UDHR, Art 28.

[29] I. Kant, *The Metaphysics of Morals* (ed, Mary Gregor) (CUP, 1996).

[30] I am indebted here to Jon Mandle's account of Kant in his 'Distributive justice at home and abroad' in T. Christiano and J. Christman (eds), *Contemporary Debates in Political Philosophy* (Wiley-Blackwell, 2009) 408.

role in a theory of political justice or of human rights. Many interest-based theories of human rights can develop an account of our basic interests in being treated as an equal in our social and political communities, for example. And some philosophers are pursuing other avenues of articulating the egalitarian component of human rights.[31] One advantage of attending to the institutional aspects of human rights is that it reveals the presence of this kind of value in human rights practice, and pushes us to think more carefully about the role that this kind of value should be playing in our theories.

5.4 Human rights and social justice

The main challenge of using this Kantian theoretical framework in connection with human rights is that it expands human rights claims to something very close to, if not identical with, social justice. Many theorists reject in principle any such account of human rights—indeed, many define human rights as requiring less than social justice, or even being in some way minimal claims of special urgency. In closing, I briefly mention two reasons to reconsider this at least as a definitional account of human rights. First, as my account of the health and human rights movement has shown, there is a strong and growing strand of international human rights practice that endorses a practical platform for action that mirrors closely the Kantian social justice account, as demanding as it is. Second, the point of the health and human rights movement's expansion to concerns of social and political justice is to point out that social justice concerns *are* urgent—both as a matter of people's everyday standing as moral agents and as structural conditions underlying what we recognize as human rights emergencies, such as current high levels of maternal mortality and other manifestations of women's poor health.

31 See A. Buchanan, 'The Egalitarianism of Human Rights', *Ethics* (2010) 120: 679.

16

Uvulectomy, Children's Rights and Public Health Challenges in Chad

Confronting Highly-Condoned Traditional Practice

Jacquineau Azétsop

1. Introduction

The practice of uvulectomy is widespread in Chad and engrained in local cultures. It is a common practice performed by a traditional healer or the local medicine person mainly on children and, on rare occasions, on adults. It is a procedure involving the cutting of the uvula[1] and sometimes the near-by structures such as the tonsils. For the latter treatment, a sore throat is the common symptom. The uvula is the fleshy lobe which hangs from the rear middle of the soft palate. It works together with the soft palate to coordinate the movement of air and food in the pharynx. Its role as a separate anatomical entity is unclear. Modern medical specialists today are concerned with this part of human anatomy only in cases of congenital defects such as bifid uvula and congenital clefts of the palate. Uvulectomy is often done as part of a combined procedure uvulo-palato-pharyngoplasty to ameliorate conditions like snoring. Biomedicine suggests treatment with antibiotics or other non-invasive treatment when the uvula is affected. In several middle-eastern and sub-Saharan countries as well as in the Maghreb, however, it is traditional for a part of the uvula to be cut away.[2]

The traditional practice of uvulectomy on children can result in serious complications that may endanger their health. The negative impacts of uvulectomy on children's health are well-known and documented by trained health professionals. Surveys and interviews carried out for this study revealed uncritical perceptions and acceptance of the harmful effects of this widespread practice. The practice of uvulectomy is condoned by most mothers we interviewed. Most of them clearly acknowledged its health benefits. Even though the medicine persons or traditional healers who performed this practice on their children have never been trained in human biology and anatomy, mothers perceive them as skilled health specialists trained in traditional medicine. In his 2004 socio-anthropological study, Ngoniri confirmed this high level of acceptance by mothers—including those who were educated and younger—all over Chad.[3] For 90 per cent of women interviewed by Ngoniri, uvulectomy is performed on children in

[1] The uvula is a small soft tissue that hangs down from the back of the mouth above the throat and between the two lymphoid tissues (tonsils). It helps to prevent choking during swallowing and is used in producing certain sounds necessary for language communication.

[2] A. Prual, Y. Gamatie et al, 'Traditional Uvulectomy in Niger: a Public Health Problem?' (1994) 8 *Social Science and Medicine* 1077.

[3] J.N. Ngoniri, *'Ablation de la Luette', in Tchad—Enquête Démographique de Santé* (Calverton, 2004) 159.

order to alleviate suffering or to fulfil a cultural duty.[4] Consequently, this practice does not violate children's dignity and rights to survival and harmonious development because its fundamental goal is nothing other than the best interests of children.

Even though modern medicine offers better and less invasive alternatives, the mothers we interviewed tended to accept what traditional society has established as a normal therapeutic procedure for their children's health. Their views were not accepted by medical professionals. Interviews with medical professionals and evidence found in existing literature clearly show that uvulectomy can be harmful to children in many ways. The health consequences of this practice vary from poor health to death.[5] Uvulectomy violates children's rights. Children's rights are grounded firmly in the fundamental human needs for life, growth, and development.[6] Quite aside from its ethical and moral force as well as the potential health benefits that its implementation can bring about, the Convention on the Rights of the Child (CRC) is a legal document which sets out standards, and assigns responsibility for ensuring these standards are met.[7]

This chapter seeks to demonstrate that the practice of uvulectomy raises both serious health and human rights challenges that need to be addressed concomitantly. Taken separately, legal approaches grounded in human rights may produce adverse effects while campaigns that focus solely on the health consequences of uvulectomy may lack the legal persuasion needed to change adults' perception of uvulectomy and children's rights. We believe that a collaborative approach to the public's education, including both health and legal aspects of uvulectomy, may progressively change people's perception of the usefulness of this practice. Interventions may, then, focus on the provision of human rights and health education understood as the core of eradication and the promotion of the child's best interests, the foundation of progressive prohibition. The inertia of civil society and the government is quite surprising, since available data show that uvulectomy is a widespread and health-damaging phenomenon performed under standards of care inferior to those prescribed by the CRC. Besides its violation of the rights to life and health, as well as its undermining of the principle of the best interests of the child, uvulectomy violates children's rights to non-discrimination, development to the fullest, and survival.

2. Methodology

We carried out research at the Dadouar healthcare centre in the Guera Region and the Chagoua healthcare centre located in the city of N'Djamena. We interviewed mothers who often bring their under-5-year-old children to the nutritional recuperation clinics in these centres. Our aim was to confirm what Ngoniri said in his 2004 paper about the acceptance level and knowledge of uvulectomy. We also surveyed three sites where uvulectomy is carried out near the Dadouar healthcare centre. Our main focus was to confirm what Ngoniri and other authors said about the hygiene conditions and the

4 Ngoniri, *'Ablation de la Luette'* (n 3) 162.

5 C.O. Eregie, 'Uvulectomy as an Epidemiological Factor in Neonatal Tetanus Mortality: Observations from a Cluster Survey' (1994) 13 *West African Journal of Medicine* 56; D.R. Nalin, 'Death of Child submitted to Uvulectomy for Diarrhoea' (1985) 325 *Lancet* 643; A.O. Olaosun, K.O. Ojemakinde, A.A. Raji, T.O. Adedeji, and S.O. Adebola, 'Death of Child with Leukaemia Subjected to Traditional Uvulectomy' (2007) 2 *The Internet Journal of Third World Medicine*.

6 The International NGO Council on Violence against Children, 'Violating Children's Rights: Harmful Practices Based on Tradition, Culture, Religion or Superstition' (2012), available at <http://www.crin.org/docs/InCo_Report_15Oct.pdf>.

7 United Nations Convention on the Rights of the Child (CRC), Art 24(3).

physical environment in which uvulectomy is performed. In addition, we organized focus groups both in N'djamena and Dadouar to understand the worldview that sustains this practice. Finally, we interviewed seven physicians in N'djamena to find out what they think about uvulectomy and its health consequences. The general aim of this research was essentially informative.

3. Uvulectomy as a Public Health Issue

The traditional practice of uvulectomy is found in sub-Saharan Africa (including Chad, northern Cameroon, Ethiopia, Niger, Nigeria, Mali, Kenya, Somalia, and Tanzania), in the Maghreb, and the Arabian Peninsula.[8] The statistics vary from 19.6 per cent in Niger to over 86 per cent in Ethiopia, where a considerable number of children under 5 years of age have undergone uvulectomy.[9] In Gondar, people believe that the uvula may cause airway obstruction. Ethiopians believe that if a baby has a uvula and a sore throat develops, the baby will suffocate.[10] Assefa et al noted that the 1998 study by the Ethiopian Committee on Harmful Traditional Practices established that uvulectomy was practised on 84 per cent of children and milk teeth extraction on 89 per cent of children.[11] Uvulectomy is commonly practised in northern Ethiopia but rarely seen in the Gambella region. The 1997 national survey showed that 84.3 per cent of the general population practise uvulectomy despite some 48.6 per cent of them being aware of its harmful effects, indicating an enormous need for health education.[12]

Prual et al found that 19.6 per cent of children in their survey in Niamey, capital of Niger, had undergone uvulectomy by the age of 5.[13] Despite the fact that healthcare centres are easily accessible to more than 93 per cent of the population of Saudi Arabia, folk medicine, manual tonsillectomy, and uvulectomy are still widely practised in the Kingdom.[14] Among the Bedouins in the south of Sinai, partial or total removal of the uvula is usually performed on both boys and girls during the first two years of life as a ritual custom.[15] Uvulectomy is performed as a ritual custom by tribes of Bedouins in the south of Sinai.[16]

In Chad, uvulectomy is a routine practice for children with sore throats (or any respiratory problem). The 2004 socio-anthropology study carried out by Ngoniri showed that almost one in two children (47 per cent) had undergone this procedure.[17] If we add to this the number of children whose mothers said they intended to get their child's uvula removed, the proportion of children who underwent this procedure

8 N.L. Johnston and P.J. Riordan, 'Tooth Follicle Extirpation and Uvulectomy' (2005) 4 *Australian Dental Journal* 269.

9 Johnston and Riordan, 'Tooth Follicle Extirpation and Uvulectomy' (n 8) 270.

10 R.M. Hodes, 'Cross-cultural Medicine and Ethiopians' (1997) 1 *Western Journal of Medicine* 31.

11 D. Assefa, E. Wassie, M. Getahun, M. Berhaneselassie, and A. Melaku, 'Harmful Traditional Practices', Ethiopia Training Public Health Initiative (2005), available at <http://www.cartercenter.org/resources/pdfs/health/ephti/library/modules/Degree/Mod_HTP_final.pdf>.

12 Assefa et al, 'Harmful Traditional Practices' (n 11).

13 Prual, Gamatie et al, 'Traditional Uvulectomy in Niger' (n 2) 1077.

14 M.A. Abdullah, 'Traditional Practices and other Socio-Cultural Factors Affecting the Health of Children in Saudi Arabia' (1993) 13 *Annals of Tropical Paediatrics* 228.

15 Johnston and Riordan, 'Tooth Follicle Extirpation and Uvulectomy' (n 8) 270.

16 Johnston and Riordan, 'Tooth Follicle Extirpation and Uvulectomy' (n 8) 270.

17 Prual, Gamatie et al, 'Traditional Uvulectomy in Niger' (n 2) 159.

may have reached 58 per cent.[18] Uvulectomy is performed all over the country. Its practice is predominant in N'Djamena (61 per cent), but lower in rural areas (44 per cent). Ethnicity tends to determine the ubiquity of the phenomenon. High prevalence of this phenomenon (72 per cent) is found in ethnic groups living in the region of Tandjilé, whilst in the region of Guera, only 39 per cent of Hadjarai practise it.[19] This traditional surgical operation is performed on young children (86.4 per cent) of less than 1 year by traditional healers (40.1 per cent), skilled people (men 42.5 per cent, women 14.2 per cent), sometimes friends or relatives. Uvulectomy is rarely performed by medical staff (1 per cent).[20] For 20 per cent of mothers interviewed by Ngoniri, this operation has no benefit, others feel that it is effective in reducing vomiting (53 per cent), and to prevent coughing (29 per cent) and angina (20 per cent).[21]

3.1 The standard of care

We visited and surveyed three places where uvulectomy is performed and talked to traditional healers who run the practice. These places are located in Dadouar and Barlo-Bagoua, two villages in the region of Guera in Chad. We discovered that uvulectomy was performed in a shed in one of the three locations and outdoors in the two others. The cleanliness and comfort of these places were inadequate. Traditional healers who operate at these places have never been to school; they have no concept of human anatomy or physiology. In these adjirai villages, uvulectomy is performed under unacceptable conditions and by unskilled individuals.

The information we gathered shows that these healers are poor compared to average persons in the village. They were dressed like anyone else during the operations. Their clothes were not clean enough, which suggested potential risk of infection due to the conditions under which the removal of uvulae was done. They all used an instrument that resembles a sickle curved edge. They cleansed it with water or a tissue. Moreover, the cleansing was done without disinfectant. Neither anesthesia nor antiseptic techniques and materials were used, which suggests the level of pain children experience during a uvulectomy. After the operation took place, these traditional healers disinfected the wounds of children with salted water. The procedures were carried out in unsanitary conditions, using unsterilized instruments.

The process started with the mother firmly holding the child. The child's tongue was pulled out and a flat piece of wood was placed in the mouth to prevent injury. The practitioner inserted the sharp instrument through a hollow stick in the mouth to trap the uvula, which was cut by pulling the strings or by the use of a sharp instrument. The same unsterilized instrument was also used on other children with the attendant risks of the spread of infections, including HIV, hepatitis, and other blood borne diseases.

3.2 A harmful traditional practice

The decision to bring a child to the traditional practitioner is often made by the parents or the parents' relatives. The mother is sometimes forced to obey the family, otherwise she may be accused of neglect by her in-laws should something bad happen to her child. Uvulectomy can be labelled 'traditional' because it is rooted in a way of thinking, of

18 Prual, Gamatie et al, 'Traditional Uvulectomy in Niger' (n 2) 159.
19 Prual, Gamatie et al, 'Traditional Uvulectomy in Niger' (n 2) 162.
20 Prual, Gamatie et al, 'Traditional Uvulectomy in Niger' (n 2) 162.
21 Prual, Gamatie et al, 'Traditional Uvulectomy in Niger' (n 2) 163.

doing, or of acting that is an inheritance from the past. The partial or complete removal of the uvula is a procedure considered almost obsolete in contemporary biomedicine. Antibiotic therapy is now accepted as the treatment of choice for most enlarged or infected uvulae. However, traditional practitioners continue to perform uvulectomy on children at the request of their parents and to claim safe alleviation of symptoms despite severe complications noted by physicians that we interviewed. Uvulectomy is based on false information and beliefs about child development and health. Uvulectomy places the child's physical and psychological health at risk. Although some children do well after the procedure, this unsupervised practice is potentially dangerous for their health. Numerous severe complications have been found in connection with the procedure. Tetanus is a serious complication found in Nigeria, where the association between neonatal tetanus, death, and traditional surgery was highly significant and uvulectomy was the most frequently performed traditional surgery.[22] Other complications of this unscientific practice include palatal palsy, cellulitis of the neck, eritonsillar and parapharyngeal abscesses, upper airway obstruction, and pharyngo-laryngocele with pneumothorax.[23] Prual et al demonstrated that severe complications of uvulectomy represented 7.8/1000 cases of hospitalization for children under 15 years of age in the capital of Nigeria.[24] Other complications include severe haemorrhage and anaemia, oropharyngeal infection, cellulites of the neck, septicemia, peritonsillar and parapharyngeal abscesses, aspiration with consequent upper airway obstruction, laryngocoele with pneumothorax, infant and child morbidity, and even death.[25]

4. Uvulectomy as a Human Rights Problem

What do human rights have to do with an age-old, widespread, and highly-condoned traditional practice such as uvulectomy? The practice of uvulectomy is a tragic human rights violation whose cultural roots run deep, making it difficult to combat. Uvulectomy is based on beliefs proven to be scientifically unsound. The rights perspective provides us with the moral and legal authority to legitimize advocacy efforts to progressively put an end to it. Beside the moral and legal authority, the rights approach provides the adequate language with which to name the shortcomings of such an outdated practice. This approach is based on international treaties, national constitutions, penal laws, and ethical norms of biomedical practice.

4.1 International instruments on the rights of the child

Despite its harmful nature and its violation of international human rights and Chadian laws, uvulectomy persists because it is not questioned. Uvulectomy inflicts both immediate and long-term pain on children. It violates a number of recognized human rights protected in international, regional, and national instruments and reaffirmed by international conference documents. These rights include the right to life and right to health.[26] The practice also violates the right to liberty and security of

22 Eregie, 'Uvulectomy as an Epidemiological Factor' (n 5) 56.

23 A. Olu-Ibekwe, 'Complications of the Treatment of Tonsillar Infection by Traditional Healers in Nigeria' (1983) 97 *The Journal of Laryngology and Otology* 845.

24 Prual, Gamatie et al, 'Traditional Uvulectomy in Niger' (n 2) 1077.

25 Eregie, 'Uvulectomy as an Epidemiological Factor' (n 5) 56.

26 UNHCHR, Fact Sheet No 23, 'Harmful Traditional Practices Affecting the Health of Women and Children', available at <http://www.unhchr.ch/html/menu6/2/fs23.htm>.

the person, which includes the right not to be subjected to violence and recognizes the need for children to receive special protection. Uvulectomy interferes with the right to freedom from inhuman or degrading treatment, which recognizes the inherent dignity of the person.

The following human rights treaties bind almost all countries and prohibit the toleration of harmful traditional practices by signatory countries: the Convention on the Rights of the Child (CRC),[27] and the International Covenant on Civil and Political Rights (ICCPR).[28] Children also benefit from provisions that protect their rights under various international covenants, conventions, and other instruments either jointly with adults or separately. For instance, they enjoy human rights under the Universal Declaration of Human Rights (UDHR).[29] The UDHR starts with a strong affirmation of the equality in dignity and freedom that all human beings enjoy and to which they are all entitled by virtue of being human.[30] This same document stresses the special need to protect motherhood and childhood. All children should enjoy special protection.[31] The International Covenant on Economic, Social and Cultural Rights (ICESCR) forcefully emphasizes the right to the highest attainable standard of physical and mental health.[32]

In addition to these, however, two international instruments make special provisions for children's rights. These are the United Nations CRC and the African Charter on the Rights and Welfare of the Child (ACRWC). In this chapter, we will focus essentially on the CRC and the ACRWC, and on the constitution of Chad and slightly less on other international human rights documents. Since the CRC is underpinned by four general principles, namely, the right to non-discrimination; the best interests principle; the right to life, survival, and development; and the right to respect for the views of the child, these provisions will be examined more closely with the aim of determining the impact of uvulectomy on children and addressing ethico-legal issues raised by this traditional phenomenon.

4.2 Social construction of the child's identity and the principle of non-discrimination

Most mothers we interviewed in N'djamena and Dadouar affirmed that uvulectomy was performed on their child in their best interests. Their conception of the child's best interests is essentially sustained by an understanding of the child as someone who needs to be cared for. There is no room for the child as a rights bearer and, to some extent, as an agent whose point of view can be sought and listened to. The idea of the child, as someone who needs to be cared for, can easily downplay the inherent dignity and rights that every child should enjoy as a human being. With such a construction of the child's identity, the question of consent is not a contentious issue because the 'care-for' approach to the child's identity overshadows the ethical and legal demands of parental consent. Parents who consent to a procedure that children should undergo ought to seek to promote their welfare. Parents should not seek to promote cultural practices

27 CRC, Arts 2, 6, 12, 19, 24, 27, and 28.

28 United Nations International Covenant on Civil and Political Rights (ICCPR), Art 7 <http://treaties.un.org/doc/Publication/UNTS/Volume%20999/volume-999-I-14668-English.pdf>.

29 United Nations Universal Declaration of Human Rights <http://www.un.org/en/documents/udhr/index.shtml>.

30 Universal Declaration of Human Rights (n 29) Arts 1 and 2.

31 Universal Declaration of Human Rights (n 29) Art 25(2).

32 International Covenant on Economic, Social and Cultural Rights, Art 12.

that promote the corporate identity of their social groups at the expense of their children's health.

The principle of non-discrimination is one of the most important human rights principles and not just in the CRC.[33] Underlying this principle is the affirmation of the dignity inherent in all human beings. Often, customary laws or those laws that draw heavily on cultural norms and customs discriminate on the basis of birth, age, sex, and marital status.[34] For children, such laws can be detrimental to their development and security as human beings. The principle of non-discrimination highlights what is most essential for all children as for all human beings irrespective of sex, age, ability, religion, ethnicity, or social status:[35] every child is a human being and should be treated as such. A rights-based approach to child caregiving and protection requires a paradigm shift towards respecting and promoting the human dignity and the physical and psychological integrity of children as rights-bearing individuals rather than perceiving them primarily as 'victims' or as 'care receivers'.[36] The principle of non-discrimination is tightly connected to the principle of dignity, which requires that every child is recognized, respected, and protected as a rights holder and as a unique and valuable human being with an individual personality, distinct needs, interests, and privacy.[37]

Information gathered from Dadouar and N'djamena revealed that parental rights over children allow the perpetration of a wide range of these sorts of practices, some by parents directly, others by other individuals with the parents' consent. Some of these practices include female genital mutilation, tooth removal, scarifications, and piercings. Parental consent is very important for child safety and welfare. Giving consent for health-enhancing procedures on behalf of a child who lacks the capacity to give consent or withhold consent is the duty of parents or caretakers.[38] However, this duty cannot be carried out at the expense of child health and welfare. Performing uvulectomy on children is simply incompatible with children's rights, since the CRC states that this practice falls under 'traditional practices prejudicial to the health of children'[39] and their overall well-being. What is required from parents to ensure that children's rights are respected is also to be required from the state. The idea of human rights presupposes that all human beings have rights because they are human beings. Children are endowed with a dignity no less than that of adults. As human beings, children's rights are inalienable.

Uvulectomy and many other harmful traditional practices are persistent because they are perpetrated with the approval of local communities and especially of their influential members. None of the perpetrators or practitioners of these unlawful practices has been questioned by civil or judicial authorities. This tacit approval is symptomatic of children's low status in Chad, where they are perceived as possessions of their parents and family rather than as individuals and rights-holders. Enforcing and implementing the CRC in Chad may spare children from the harmful effects of obsolete practices which are incompatible with modern biomedicine. The CRC astutely challenges

[33] CRC, Art 2.

[34] World Health Organization (South-East Asia Region), 'Towards a Better Tomorrow: Child Rights and Health', available at <http://www.searo.who.int/entity/child_adolescent/documents/child_rights/en/index.html>.

[35] WHO, 'Towards a Better Tomorrow' (n 34).

[36] International NGO Council on Violence against Children, 'Violating Children's Rights' (n 6).

[37] United Nations Committee on the Rights of the Child, General Comment No 13, 'The Right of the Child to Freedom from all Forms of Violence', Art. 3, available at <http://www2.ohchr.org/english/bodies/crc/docs/CRC.C.GC.13_en.pdf>.

[38] International NGO Council on Violence against Children, 'Violating Children's Rights' (n 6).

[39] CRC, Arts 16(1) and 24(3). Organization of African Unity, African Charter on the Rights and Welfare of the Child (ACRWC), Art. 21(1a), available at <http://www1.umn.edu/ . . . /africa/afchild.htm>.

parental rights over children to improve children's status in society. Those who drafted the CRC and the ACRWC replaced the concept of parental rights over children with that of parental responsibilities. They also equated the concept of 'the best interests of the child' with that of the 'parents' basic concern'.[40] This important move was dictated by the need to affirm strongly that children are persons like any other human beings and parents do not have a right as such over children. In order to protect the well-being of their children, parents ought to refrain from making decisions that conflict with children's rights. They do not have the right to consent to harmful practices on behalf of their children. The Chadian Constitution still clings to the concepts of the 'right of parents over their children' and of the 'best interests of the child'. The latter principle is set forth in article 38 of the Constitution, which states in substance that parents possess the natural right to raise their children. This right may be withdrawn if they fail in their duty.[41] The Chadian penal law stipulates that, even though parents have the natural right to supervise their children, protection of the best interests of the child is guaranteed by the courts. The term 'best interests' means everything that contributes to children's physical, mental, and social development in order to ensure the full and harmonious development of their personalities. Consequently, priority is given to ensuring that children receive protection and assistance in all circumstances. This consideration is taken into account in both civil and criminal legal proceedings.[42] Even though the penal code does not use the language of the CRC, its approach to child protection is quite close to that of the CRC. It is clear, then, that, in theory, as with the CRC, we can no longer develop care for children without at least nominally taking them into account as subjects of rights.[43] Cultural constructs that determine practices performed on children should be shaped by the realization that children are not simply passive objects of concern, or victims, but that they make important contributions to society. So far, the Chadian government and actors of civil society have failed to challenge attitudes that condone or legitimize uvulectomy. Where parents fail their children, states must intervene. The CRC places an active duty on the state to ensure parents are equipped with accurate information on child health and development.

The fact that the negative consequences of uvulectomy are known and the lack of effective commitment to eradicate this phenomenon challenges a human rights-minded individual to question the deep-seated philosophical and social underpinnings of the state's silence or inertia. Even though the state welcomed the CRC, most adult citizens still uphold a degrading and undermining approach to a child's identity. Children are viewed as 'becomings', who are less deserving of respect for their dignity. The concepts of equality and freedom cannot be applied to children because they are simply perceived as dependent 'becomings', dependent on their parents or kin. Human dignity is the underlying basis for children's rights, and thus provides the moral compass for rights-oriented practices and policies with regard to child protection. In this way, 'the concept of human rights helps to form a specific picture of our shared humanity and to communicate the idea that human beings possess a certain dignity that ought both to be protected and respected'.[44]

40 CRC, Art 18(1); ACRWC, Art 21.

41 République du Tchad, Constitution du 31 mars 1996 révisée, available at <http://www.presidencetchad.org/Constitution_Tchad.pdf>.

42 République du Tchad, Code de Procédure Pénal, available at <http://www.lexinter.net/PROCPEN/index.htm>.

43 J. Ennew, 'The History of Children's Rights: Whose Story?', available at <http://www.culturalsurvival.org/ourpublications/csq/article/the-history-childrens-rights-whose-story>.

44 I. Bonabom, 'The Human Rights Question in the HIV/AIDS Pandemic in sub-Saharan Africa' in P.A. Mombé, I.A. Orobator, and D. Vella (eds), *AIDS 30 Years Down the Line: Faith-based Reflections about the Epidemic in Africa* (Nairobi, 2013) 209.

4.3 The child's development and survival

Ensuring the maximum survival and harmonious development of every child appears to be the most important principle of the CRC.[45] The right to survival and development permeates the entire Convention. This right is a general principle of the CRC and therefore informs the interpretation of all the articles in the Convention. Consequently, a wide variety of rights and obligations in the CRC are related to the issue of survival—not just the articles relating to the right to the highest attainable standard of health. Hence, its realization is nothing other than a fundamental outcome of all initiatives that seek to successfully protect children's rights. In other words, the adequate protection of all the other rights necessarily leads to the fulfilment of the child's right to survival and harmonious development.

The CRC includes both the right to life and the right to survival and development, whilst the right to life can be understood as including the other. The right to life is a negative right; it requires non-interference and imposes an obligation to refrain from causing harm. In contrast, the right to survival and development captures the positive obligations of a state to create and promote an environment conducive to the maximum development of the child. The right to survival and development encompasses the obligation of the state to create an environment in which all children grow up in a healthy and protected manner, are free from fear and want, and develop their personalities and physical abilities to their fullest potential consistent with their evolving capacities. Thus, our obligations in meeting the right to healthy development demand that we create an optimal experience of childhood, an environment that builds resilience and conditions that nurture a positive future for each child.

Child survival is inextricably linked to child development. Child survival must be understood and approached within the broader context of children's overall development and well-being. The right to maximum survival and development speaks to a continuum that begins at maximum survival and progresses to an endpoint represented by the optimum development of the child.[46] Children, therefore, have the right to survive under conditions that enable them to develop to their full potential. There is a general tendency to narrowly interpret the concept of 'child survival'.[47] Even UN agencies and most NGOs design child survival interventions that cater essentially for the needs of children aged under 5. Survival initiatives take place within the biomedical framework that has under-5 mortality and morbidity measurements as means of intervention and evaluation.[48] Within this framework, child survival initiatives are dominated by the burden of disease, which includes communicable diseases, non-communicable diseases, and childhood trauma and injuries.[49] Child survival initiatives would then focus essentially on sick, malnourished, dying, and deceased children younger than 5 years old.

There have been more recent attempts to consider other contributory factors impacting on child survival, such as those involving the mother's and the child's socio-cultural environment.[50] It is common knowledge that the socio-cultural environment determines

45 CRC, Art 6.

46 M. Dutschke and K. Abrahams, 'Children's Right to Maximum Survival and Development', Child Survival Project, Children's Institute, University of Cape Town (2006).

47 Dutschke and Abrahams, 'Children's Right to Maximum Survival' (n 46).

48 Dutschke and Abrahams, 'Children's Right to Maximum Survival' (n 46).

49 Dutschke and Abrahams, 'Children's Right to Maximum Survival' (n 46).

50 WHO, 'Towards a Better Tomorrow' (n 34).

disease etiology and management.[51] Furthermore, political decisions and policy-making are important determinants of children's survival and health. Even though medical intervention is important to tackle the shortcomings and the harmful effects of traditional uvulectomy, the eradication of this phenomenon demands that individual adults and communities willfully accept the need to change some of their cultural practices. In addition to this solution, a nation-based solution rooted in the political commitment of decision-makers to address the cultural and socioeconomic drivers of uvulectomy is much needed to support efforts deployed by individuals and local communities that show willingness to end this practice. From a child rights perspective, a restricted focus on the biomedical framework alone is not sufficient to give full effect to the child's right to maximum survival and development.[52] The prevention and progressive eradication of uvulectomy should be conducted in a broader framework that includes yet surpasses the realm of biomedicine. The features of the cultural environment, individual behaviours, and public practices that sustain uvulectomy should be addressed in context because they are deeply entrenched in local cultures. Addressing the cultural drivers of uvulectomy does not undermine the rule of law but determines how the law can be applied.

The Chadian Constitution clearly states that 'no one shall be subjected to torture or to cruel, inhuman or degrading treatment' (article 18).[53] The right to life, survival, and development upheld by the CRC is taken up in article 17 of the Chadian Constitution. Article 17 stipulates that 'every individual shall have the right to life, to physical integrity, security, liberty and protection of his privacy'.[54] Under article 37 of the Constitution, the state and decentralized territorial communities are responsible for ensuring the well-being of the family. This responsibility also extends to requirements for the development and welfare of youth.[55] The specific care for children is the responsibility of parents. The Civil Code expressly stipulates that parental obligations include the obligation to provide for the upkeep of children and to look after their life, health, and education.[56] In the criminal sphere, the Penal Code criminalizes acts that jeopardize the survival and development of children. Some of these acts include infanticide (article 244); child neglect (article 250); malicious wounding, deprivation of food or care to the point of compromising the health of a child who is younger than 13 years (article 254); indecent assault (article 273); rape (article 276); removal, concealment, substituting a child for another or giving a child to a woman who has not given birth (articles 286–287); kidnapping or hijacking of minors (article 289); non-representation of children (article 295); abandoning one's family (article 295); and abortion (article 296).[57]

4.4 The child's best interests versus the right to culture

The 'child's best interests' is a general principle of the CRC. This principle is non-negotiable and cannot be undermined by the rights to culture and religion. The norms prevailing in a society determine what is regarded as best for the child. There can be a

[51] B. Link and J.C. Phelan, 'Social Conditions as Fundamental Causes of Disease' (1995) 35 *Journal of Health and Social Behavior* 82.

[52] Dutschke and Abrahams, 'Children's Right to Maximum Survival' (n 46).

[53] République du Tchad, Constitution du 31 mars 1996 révisée (n 41).

[54] République du Tchad, Constitution du 31 mars 1996 révisée (n 41).

[55] République du Tchad, Constitution du 31 mars 1996 révisée (n 41).

[56] République du Tchad, Code de Procédure civil, available at <http://www.cefod.org/legitchad/web/rechercher/Tchad/code/19?en_vigueur=on>.

[57] République du Tchad, 'Violences contre les Enfants, Réponses du Gouvernement Tchadien', available at <http://www2.ohchr.org/english/bodies/CRC/docs/study/ . . . /Chad.pdf>.

conflict between what may be seen as best for the child by the family, for example, and what the international community may consider as best for children.[58] The rights to culture and religion as well as the rights of minorities have often been invoked to give legitimacy to harmful traditional practices. Such arguments contradict the principles of equality in dignity and freedom that shape the UDHR.[59] These principles strongly affirm the inherent equality co-natural to our being-human regardless of the cultural or religious practices of particular communities. A human rights perspective affirms the universality of the rights of the child to physical and mental integrity, to freedom from discrimination, and to the highest standard of health. Cultural claims cannot be invoked to justify violations of these rights.[60] Cultural practices that interfere with the child's flourishing and dignity diminish our shared humanity. Respect for culture cannot be upheld at the expense of the child's welfare. It is unacceptable that the international community remains passive in the face of massive violations of human rights in the name of a distorted vision of multiculturalism. Human behaviours and cultural values have meaning and fulfil a function for those who practise them. However, culture is not static but in constant flux, adapting and reforming. People will change their behaviour when they understand the indignity of uvulectomy and when they realize that it is possible to give up harmful practices without giving up meaningful aspects of their culture.[61] Particular cultural practices do not represent a whole culture. When a practice is harmful, it does not serve the best interests of the child, no matter the socio-cultural explanation that gives legitimacy to its use. Those traditional practices that should be challenged and abolished are those which jeopardize the children's well-being. A culture is not bad in itself. However, harmful cultural practices cannot be validly legitimized by culture or claims of cultural diversity because the right to culture and children's rights are not antithetical. The protection of the best interests of the child should be guaranteed by the courts. The term 'best interests' means everything that contributes to children's development.[62] Consequently, priority should be given to ensuring that children receive protection and assistance in all circumstances. This consideration is also taken into account in both civil and criminal legal proceedings.[63]

5. Confronting uvulectomy

Strategies and programmes to reduce and progressively eradicate uvulectomy may benefit a great deal from the intrinsic and instrumental links that exist between human rights and public health.[64] Jonathan Mann and colleagues first suggested three ways of linking public health and human rights. Mann et al affirmed that 'Health and human rights are both powerful, modern approaches to defining and advancing human well-being.'[65]

[58] WHO, 'Towards a Better Tomorrow' (n 34).

[59] Universal Declaration of Human Rights (n 29) Art 1.

[60] Council on Violence against Children, 'Violating Children's Rights' (n 36).

[61] World Health Organization, UN Children's Fund and UN Population Fund, Joint Statement, February 1996, available at <http://www.policyproject.com/matrix/harmful%20trad%20practices.cfm>.

[62] The meaning of the best interests principle in international law is vague and unclear.

[63] Dutschke and Abrahams, 'Children's Right to Maximum Survival' (n 46).

[64] V. Iacopino, 'Teaching Human Rights in Graduate Health Education' in S. Gruskin, M.A. Grodin, G.J. Annas, and S.P. Marks (eds), *Perspectives on Health and Human Rights* (New York: Routledge, 2005) 550.

[65] J. Mann, 'Medicine and Public Health, Ethics and Human Rights' in J. Mann, S. Gruskin, M. Grodin, and G. Annas (eds), *Health and Human Rights: A Reader* (New York: Routledge, 1999) 444.

Mann later added to this earlier framework the view that human rights can be an ethics of public health.[66] Mann astutely asserted that:

> ...modern human rights, precisely because they were initially developed entirely outside the health domain and seek to articulate the societal preconditions for human well, seem a far more useful framework, vocabulary; and form of guidance for public health efforts to analyze and respond directly to the societal determinants of health than any inherited from the biomedical or public health tradition.'[67]

Public health policy that truly promotes the child's well-being cannot tolerate the persistence of harmful practices. Failure to enforce public health laws is, in itself, a violation of human rights.

The pain and unnecessary suffering resulting from this practice are simply unacceptable when it is well established that clinical medicine offers better alternatives and/or when uncritical and unscientific assumptions about diseases that justify this practice are simply wrong. The promotion of human rights and the practice of public health are complementary and indivisible approaches to protecting and advancing the well-being of people.[68] The two forms of interventions are ethical enterprises aiming at promoting children's well-being. A public health prevention intervention is a human rights intervention because uvulectomy cannot cause harm unless children's rights prescribed by the CRC are not respected. The public health interventions provide a context within which we can concretely promote children's rights while human rights give the adequate language and framework to name, analyse, and challenge the behavioural and structural underpinnings that have legitimized and sustained the practice of uvulectomy over time. For Mann: 'The modern human rights framework can provide a new movement of health professionals with the necessary instruments and modes of action to uncover and act upon the societal foundations for disease, disability, and death.'[69] Similarly, the implementation of human rights education programmes is a public health intervention because it ensures that children's rights are respected. It is then obvious why Mann suggested that human rights can serve as the ethics of public health. This is a deeper insight informed by his experience as a public health physician and interventionist working to understand the rapid spread of AIDS in some countries and within particular population groups. Mann viewed the human rights ethos as the conscience of public health because public health policies and programmes can infringe on human rights.[70] Mann viewed the human rights framework as a potential tool for protecting human dignity and assuring the respect due to every single human being. Treating individuals with dignity and respect is important for their health.

5.1 Making human rights and health education the core of eradication

With uvulectomy, we have a clear example of a clash between culture and human rights. Dealing with such a clash within specific contexts requires a pragmatic, open-minded, and multi-faceted approach, in order to attain a meaningful measure of

[66] J. Mann, 'Medicine and Public Health' (n 65) 442.

[67] Mann, 'Medicine and Public Health' (n 65) 444.

[68] J. Mann et al, 'Health and Human Rights' in J. Mann, S. Gruskin, M. Grodin, and G. Annas (eds), *Health and Human Rights: A Reader* (New York: Routledge, 1999) 11.

[69] Mann et al, 'Health and Human Rights' (n 68).

[70] L.O. Gostin, 'Public Health, Ethics, and Human Rights: A Tribute to the Late Jonathan Mann' (2001) 29 *Journal of Law, Medicine and Ethics* 121.

success. There cannot be a complete reliance on legal and constitutional measures, although these are still very important. With such a complex phenomenon, a purely legal approach to prevention and eradication may be ineffective without appropriate human rights and public health education programmes carried out both at the community and national level.

The N'Djaména Law is a good example of the failure to criminalize a practice which is deeply engrained in local culture. This law contains legal dispositions that aim at protecting people living with HIV/AIDS (PLWHA) against social discrimination. This anti-discrimination law narrowly portrays HIV infection as a problem pertaining to the individual whose rights need to be protected, while discrimination against infected and affected individuals is a widespread phenomenon. Although anti-discrimination laws may seem to be a reasonable way of protecting PLWHA from stigmatization and discrimination, we argue that bias and discrimination against PLWHA can be best addressed by reframing the risks for HIV infection and, by giving the salient importance of treatment as prevention, within an environmental perspective from which tools and strategies can be developed to address both the distal and proximal determinants of HIV infection. Reframing the risks for HIV infection from a public health perspective will give a comprehensive view of the causes and impacts of stigmatization and discrimination of PLWHA. Discriminating against PLWHA would not reduce risk of infection. Instead, it fuels risks by preventing PLWHA from having access to available treatment. The N'Djaména Law will not reach its goal without a broader societal change of attitude towards the disease itself.[71] Thus far, this law has not (and will not) reduce HIV risks or address structural drivers of infection and discrimination. Legal solutions do not really address bias, which is primarily an attitude and stigma that results from the internalization of societal discrimination. The public may not discriminate openly against a PLWHA but may develop subtle forms of discrimination, as has been done to women all over the world and to black people in the US. Laws that protect women, for example, have reduced the incidence of gender-based discrimination. However, these laws have not eradicated individual or structural violence against women. Laws prohibiting discrimination may not successfully prevent discrimination unless society reframes its understanding of HIV infection. Changing the negative attitudes of the general public in relation to sexuality will also be challenging. To start with, public education campaigns to counter HIV/AIDS stigma and discrimination and to promote acceptance of PLWHA need to be implemented.

Having said this, criminalizing uvulectomy may yield results contrary to the expected outcomes, since the law may merely push uvulectomy practitioners underground or even encourage the practice itself. Overcoming deeply-entrenched beliefs requires that communities be supplied with adequate education that will provide them with information about the feasibility and desirability of abandoning uvulectomy and turning to life-promoting practices.[72] This could be termed a form of positive deviation.[73] Reversing particular cultural practices is similar to reversing social conventions, and needs to be a carefully considered process that promotes

[71] UNAIDS, Rapport de la Situation Nationale à l'Intention de l'UNGASS (N'Djaména, Chad, 2009).

[72] G. Mackie and J. LeJeune, 'Social Dynamics of Abandonment of Harmful Practices: A New Look at the Theory', UNICEF Innocenti Working Papers, May 2009, available at <http://www.unicef-irc.org/publications/pdf/iwp_2009_06.pdf>.

[73] Mackie and LeJeune, 'Social Dynamics' (n 72).

human rights, whilst at the same time being respectful of the culture and values of particular communities.[74]

Human rights education can and does play an important role in building a culture of respect within which human worth is promoted and children are recognized as subjects of rights. The fundamental aim of human rights education is known to be the establishment of a culture where human rights are understood, respected, promoted, and translated into positive laws.[75] There has not been any attempt to provide either the elite or local communities with human rights education in relation to child health. There is still a significant need to educate the public and to create a wider awareness of the Bill of Rights and the processes and mechanisms of its enforcement if notable progress is to be made, and before more focused programmes can be designed and implemented. To be efficient, human rights education should focus on particular cultural and community contexts.[76]

Human rights and public health advocacy on violence against children is also critically important in eliminating practices that place child health at risk. The role of non-state actors cannot be neglected; rather, it is crucial. The traditional human rights law paradigm, which focuses essentially on the state, is typically inadequate for dealing with human rights abuses related to public health violations that take place in rural communities or remote neighbourhoods of major cities. These are places where culture, tradition, and customs are profoundly entrenched in people's behaviour.

Individual behaviour change is a part of the solution but in order to eradicate uvulectomy, intervention should take place at the level of the general population, and more specifically at the community level. NGOs and community-based associations in Chad can be instrumental in promoting and protecting children welfare. They can be instrumental in communicating the public health and human rights implications that result from the practice of uvulectomy to individuals and families. With the support of the state and its partners, these local institutions can also be empowered to design programmes and interventions that aim at changing communities' perception on the usefulness and relevence of uvulectomy.

5.2 Making the principle of 'the best interests of the child' the foundation of prohibition

The Chadian criminal law prohibits harmful practices against children. However, the law is not enforced. Enforcement of prohibition when parents and the community are passively or actively involved makes it hard to highlight the preventive function of the law.[77] Upholding the principle of the 'best interests of the child' while, at the same time, arguing for law enforcement is a challenge that law-makers and human rights activists should face up to because perpetrators are most often caregivers. What should come first, the need to highlight the preventive and didactic function of the law or the affirmation of the 'child's best interests' as a non-negotiable principle in child protection? It has been argued that 'the criminal law must be enforced in a way that is sensitive to the special nature of family relationships and children's dependence on their parents

74 Mackie and LeJeune, 'Social Dynamics' (n 72).

75 S. Manisuli, 'Culture and the Human Rights of Women in Africa: Between Light and Shadow' (2007) 1 *Journal of African Law* 45.

76 Manisuli, 'Culture and the Human Rights of Women' (n 75).

77 Council on Violence against Children, 'Violating Children's Rights' (n 36).

and family'.[78] If the law prohibiting harmful practices on children and the human rights obligations to prohibit these same practices were to be recognized and enforced, a significant proportion of the Chadian population would be prosecuted. Uvulectomy is so widespread that if all children who have undergone this practice and other harmful practices were removed from the custody of their parents there would not be enough institutions to provide care for them.

Will it ever be possible to develop measures that can challenge and end the active or passive condoning of uvulectomy without a serious state commitment to ensure that children are protected from harmful practices? The answer is no! Human rights education and health awareness of the effects of uvulectomy should accompany legal implementation, for 'it is obvious that law reform to prohibit harmful practices, while an essential foundation required by human rights, will not in isolation lead to the changes in attitude required to eliminate practices, which remain strongly supported by adults close to the child in their family and community'.[79] Even though intervention has to be contextual, we cannot help but reaffirm the power of law as an instrument for social and behavioural change.

5.3 Health education as a preventive intervention

The prevention of uvulectomy requires more than the education of the public and health professionals about the normal functioning of uvula and tonsils. It entails an intervention that brings to the forefront the need to respect the child's rights and promote the child's health. Education campaigns should target traditional healers as well as parents and local communities. Traditional healers need to be the main targets because they hold an important place in the neighbourhood where they carry out their practice. They are highly trusted and influential and their words are taken seriously by the members of their communities. The honour and respect attached to their function make them essential elements of any intervention that aims at preventing the health complications of this practice and, ultimately, at discouraging the practice itself. It is obvious that the likelihood that they will give up performing uvulectomies is quite low.

Without neglecting the role of penal law to repress inappropriate behaviour, legal arrangements that criminalize uvulectomy can be part of the human rights and public health education package. It is well known in the public health community that health law that banned public smoking in the US only gained popular approval after well-implemented public health campaigns both at the national and community levels. A vertical implementation of child protection laws might not be successful without the collaboration of local communities and traditional healers. In the short term, traditional healers will be the main target. A close collaborative programme of training for traditional practitioners is more likely to be effective in reducing the morbidity associated with their work and an overall improvement of the health outcome for patients. This training may focus on the sterilization of instruments, conflicts between traditional and modern medicine, and practices which are harmful to health and children's rights.

To sustain a long-term education campaign, the government should fulfil its obligation to protect children's rights by providing the leadership needed to eradicate uvulectomy. A well-designed education programme at all levels of society should be

[78] Council on Violence against Children, 'Violating Children's Rights' (n 36).
[79] Council on Violence against Children, 'Violating Children's Rights' (n 36).

embarked upon in which the traditional practitioners and the entire population will be adequately educated on the dangers of this practice, on children's rights, and legal arrangements that criminalize uvulectomy. The realization of children's rights places an active duty on the state to ensure that parents are equipped with accurate information on child health and development. Such information will enable parents to fulfil their responsibilities and protect their children against harmful treatments. Efforts to alter or eradicate such practices require the cooperation and understanding of community leaders, policy-makers, and the people who have experienced or witnessed the hardships this practice causes. Community education is critical to increasing public awareness of the negative consequences of these practices and changing societal norms. While respectful of tradition, advocacy can unite communities, reinforcing practices which benefit all members. Advocacy strategies should be grounded in the non-negotiable principle that no violence against children is acceptable.[80]

5.4 Clinical encounter as a site for human rights promotion and health education

Clinical encounters between clinicians and patients cannot be neglected because families often rely on healthcare institutions when they are faced with complications of uvulectomy. Interviews with patients revealed that clinicians dismiss the claims of patients too quickly. Being able to understand the sociocultural attitudes to ailments such as sore throats among children and the solutions with which traditional healers provide children's parents can better equip clinicians to discourage those who rely on unhygienic and harmful practices to solve medical problems. The clinical encounter presents an opportunity for human rights education and the prevention of harm that can be done to other children. Avoiding paternalism and patronizing attitudes for the sake of openness and listening attitudes may be the best position to adopt.

A clinician trained in human rights can provide parents with instruction on children's rights and on the health impacts of uvulectomy. For health practitioners to promote health and well-being, human rights concerns need to be integrated into health education so that clinicians can be better equipped to protect our shared humanity. When conceptualizations of health and human suffering are devoid of human rights concerns, clinicians may simply treat the consequences without going to the root causes of the problem. Clinicians may treat the health consequences of uvulectomy, but addressing the sociocultural etiology of these health consequences requires a set of skills that medical training does not necessarily offer.

6. Conclusion

Although Chad has ratified the CRC, most children do not always enjoy the full range of human rights to which they are entitled. The practice of uvulectomy violates children's rights in many ways. One child in two has undergone this traditional procedure. The magnitude of uvulectomy in Chad is highly significant. However, the Chadian government's inaction implicitly encourages and condones structures and practices that place children's lives at risk. Uvulectomy is a harmful practice that poses health and human rights challenges. These challenges are well known by health professionals and human rights activists. Attempts to eradicate this phenomenon

80 Council on Violence against Children, 'Violating Children's Rights' (n 36).

should take into consideration the intrinsic linkage that exists between health and human rights. It should also take into account the widespread ignorance of children's rights and these health consequences. Most mothers and traditional doctors we interviewed ignore the health consequences of uvulectomy. Furthermore, they have no notion of human rights, which makes eradication difficult. Ngoniri's 2004 socio-anthropological survey confirms this widespread ignorance. Hence, focusing solely on legal solutions may drive the practice underground, whilst passing on information on the health consequences of uvulectomy will lack the legal persuasion necessary for the eradication of this practice. Collaborative and community-based interventions that include education as the core of eradication and child best interests (child health and dignity) as the foundation of prohibition may stimulate the progressive eradication of this phenomenon.

PART C

ETHICAL ISSUES

17

Adding Nonideal Agents to Work Out a Pending Debt

Florencia Luna

Every year, 8 million children die before they reach the age of 5. More than 300,000 women die in pregnancy or childbirth and more than 4 million people die of AIDS, malaria, and tuberculosis.[1]

On the one hand, global health would appear to be a permanently irresoluble issue: an immutable pending debt. On the other, it reveals a complexity and variance that makes it a moving target.

In this chapter I will first present some empirical facts about global health. I will argue for a multiple strategy with a nuanced and context-specific solution. Secondly, I will outline possible responsible agents who should tackle global health. Because of partial compliance and practical obstacles to putting ideal theories into practice, I will consider a nonideal approach. I will defend the need to consider a plurality of responsible agents to ameliorate global health. Finally, I will analyze a real case and show how this proposal based on multiple strategies and various responsible agents is feasible and the best response.

1. Why is Global Health a MovingTarget?

Basic and fundamental public health policies can solve part of the problem of global health. However, these are structural modifications like sanitation, drinkable water, or a working electric system. Most of the developing countries are indebted to their inhabitants owing to the absence of such infrastructure. In addition to this public health infrastructure that is lacking in most developing countries, specific illnesses still present particular challenges (for example malaria, river blindness, Chagas, or dengue), some of which, the so-called neglected diseases, are infectious and strongly related to poverty, climate, and living conditions. In what follows I will focus on those diseases. Let me enumerate some of the challenges these diseases present and why their control or cure can be considered so complex.

A first challenge is the lack of an available cure for many of these illnesses and the ineffectiveness of existing treatments; many drugs also have side-effects or patients have built up a resistance to those drugs, making them less effective. Research is crucial. However, as these are the illnesses of the poorest, pharmaceutical companies show little interest in conducting research. This lack of interest is an enormous obstacle. Some solutions may come from a theoretical and innovative framework like the Health Impact Fund (HIF) proposed by Pogge and Hollis to incentivize

[1] L. Gostin et al, 'National and Global Responsibilities for Health' *Bulletin of the World Health Organization* (2010) 88: 719.

pharmaceutical firms.[2] It seeks to promote research in relevant illnesses (for example those killing a large number of persons) in order to develop and make drugs available at cost. It is based on a complex scheme of rewards depending on the impact the new drug has on the health of the people. Although this proposal is creative, interesting, and has the correct ethical insight, it is still very hard to implement. Less structural but supposedly more feasible alternatives are public-private partnerships (PPPs) with the leadership of international intergovernmental organizations, such as the World Health Organization (WHO), or non-governmental organizations (NGOs). But such partnerships can be more restrictive and sometimes difficult to achieve.[3]

A second challenge, once a cure or a possible medicine has been found, is the difficulty of deciding how this cure should be distributed, given that the poverty context can add further obstacles. Making the new drug or treatment accessible in hospitals is not without problems in itself. Hospitals need the resources to buy the drug and make it available to those in need. When the product is connected to an agency, such as the WHO, prior agreements can be made to implement price reductions or have the drug distributed cost free.[4] When this is not the case, the state will have to buy it and endorse the universal policy of providing the drugs to those patients. Should this not happen, NGOs can provide the treatment or help the population. But there is a long, steep, and winding road from the success of finding a new efficacious drug or treatment to the effective treatment of the population.

A third quite different challenge shows that some treatments cannot be reduced to a pill or a short treatment provided during hospitalization or a visit to the clinic. Many of these diseases have no 'magic bullets': just providing the drug does not necessarily mean the problem is over. Treatment may not be easy to adhere to or effective. For example, some cures can take months and are difficult to follow up on and enforce. Consider Chagas disease; this is a chronic disease that causes irreversible cardiovascular, gastrointestinal, and neurological problems and occurs in adult life. By the time the symptoms appear, it is too late to cure. An effective treatment exists for children with Chagas disease but it has to be taken daily for one month. The medication has side-effects. As there are no symptoms of the disease, the child appears to be healthy, making it difficult to ensure adherence to the full course of treatment. Another case is the treatment of tuberculosis, which takes even longer and generates high drop-out rates. This poses a serious threat to public health as it is extremely contagious, especially in the case of large families living together in a small room in large overpopulated cities.

The opposite situation is that of people living in rural or inaccessible areas. A lack of transport could mean hours of walking to reach the nearest village or hospital; no electricity means medicines cannot be kept cold. Thus, dealing with these circumstances calls for other strategies, other approaches. But as we can see, it is far from simple. If measures are going to be implemented as a public health policy, they should be carefully studied and this implies a different kind of research. How to achieve adherence or the effectiveness of treatment? Who is to fund this kind of research? No new drugs are involved. This public health research or implementation research poses new and different problems.

2 A. Hollis and T. Pogge, *The Health Impact Fund: Making New Medicines Accessible for All* (Incentives for Global Health, 2008).

3 Care should be taken about the drive of private partners to foster private interests and not public health.

4 As will be explained in Section 3, this was the case with ivermectin for onchocerciasis, which was donated by Merck.

The availability of drugs or treatments in hospitals is one of the challenges, but as mentioned previously, countless obstacles can give rise to other problems: treatment and provision alone does not suffice. Most illnesses are not merely 'biomedical'; there are psycho-social components in resilience and recuperation. In the case of the infectious diseases of poverty, these factors are even more relevant. Poverty itself largely explains why the elimination of these diseases is so complex. Different social determinants of health play a significant role.[5] Illness in these deprived economies is more devastating than in other societies, where labor laws protect the workers. The poorest of the poor are almost certainly the informal workers without any social protection. They depend on what they can produce and have a hand-to-mouth existence. These situations are so complex that it is hard to find a feasible answer.

Another fundamental issue for a cure is an accurate diagnosis to avoid overtreatment or undertreatment. But again, if we cannot access the physician or clinic easily, how can we manage the diagnosis? The 'standard way' to solve medical problems (reaching a clinic, being tested, and receiving an accurate diagnosis and treatment) will not follow. One example of this kind of situation arises with malaria. An effective treatment of malaria involves training and working directly with the communities or households. That implies a shift in the usual biomedical Western paradigm and illustrates how difficult it is not only to make the established drug available but also to provide for its effective use.

Hence, even if we can solve the second challenge of obtaining the resources, finding the desired cure, and making it available in hospitals or clinics, the target will move as it will not be easy to deliver the drugs efficaciously to many of the people that need them the most.

Fourth, a set of problems is related to the prevention and eradication of the causes of these illnesses. A number of these diseases have to do with climate and vectors such as insects. Chagas disease is transmitted by an insect that can be hosted in dogs and chickens. It is very hard to make people understand that bringing the pet dog into the house can pose a serious threat, that it should not enter, not to mention sleep in the house. Here again, it is not merely a question of introducing a cure or a drug... but the daunting task of changing life styles and educating the community so that they can modify their habits and customs. This goes well beyond the biomedical realm.

Some of the prevention tools are as simple and commonsensical as bed-nets, insect traps, or insecticides to prevent infected mosquito bites and to fight against the vectors of these illnesses. However, before these devices can be implemented as a public health policy by a poor government, they must be shown to be efficacious and relevant. One of the problems is that these studies are not very common and do not follow 'standard procedures'. Even though some manufacturers may find it profitable, they are not in the business of conducting the research trials (specific cluster randomized trials) that should be designed and put into practice.[6] Again, once their role in prevention and

5 For example, many of the people that fall sick are generally weak and suffer from bad health: they may not be able to rest and eat nutritious food for a quick recovery. The simple fact of 'not eating enough food' can hinder a proper absorption of the medication without incurring side-effects. Rest is a luxury they cannot access. In addition, just being sick introduces a vicious circle because illness generates more poverty. Not only is money spent on the cure but the illness also stops them from working.

6 For example, a first study in the Gambia showed a 63% reduction in child mortality owing to the use of bed-nets with insecticides, but when replicated with a design of cluster randomization in three countries, it found a 20% reduction in malaria. Hence, the final study showed a lower impact than the first. On the whole, however, it demonstrated that this was an effective tool to implement as a public health policy.

usefulness has been proven, a second step will be to provide these devices and educate the people in prevention behaviors.

Fifth, there are even more complex issues involving neighboring nations. This challenge is related to the mobility of people and migrations. Frontiers are permeable and negatively affect a country that has made efforts to eradicate one of the vectors and the illness (for example Chagas) because seasonal migrant workers may come back. Consequently, the vector and the disease will return year after year. Solving these kinds of problems signifies a regional rather than state policy that can be exceedingly difficult to implement.

In addition it is crucial to develop surveillance systems to gather and share data. And there is a further need to install strategic responses at global, regional, national, and local levels if changes are to be sustained[7]—another front of action.

The complexities described so far show conditions that are far from ideal and why one answer alone does not follow. So many and diverse obstacles are involved that multilevel answers have to be proposed. So many and diverse are these challenges that we are witness to a moving target. Once a cure is found, there is the provision issue, and when the isolation or adherence problems are overcome to achieve the effective cure, all these other peri-health issues regarding vectors, hosts, and regional strategies move it to a new level. Once again, the scenario changes because of new obstacles. Most of the answers in themselves prove partial and ineffective. But this partiality is not just a building-block system where the solution can be found in a step-by-step construction. It is not clear in these cases whether partial solutions will ultimately solve the problem. In most situations there is no lineal progress; this implies the need for a set of different approaches. That same partial solution may modify the problem and create a new one. Merely taking one step can give the impression of having implemented a policy without having resolved it, thus worsening the situation, discouraging and fostering a negative reaction towards the problem. A useful analogy for the situation is the incorrect use of an antibiotic.[8] Not only can an incorrect dosage or early abandonment not cure, but it may generate a resistance, as well as the subjective feeling that the medicine did not work.

Hence, without a systematic, coordinated, and efficient approach by different agents, stakeholders, and the community and the 'political will' at the national and international levels to implement changes, global health will still lag behind, conceived as a mere utopia. Social policies, human health (biomedical and public health), veterinary, environmental, and wildlife management expertise should join to formulate innovative and suitable strategies.

2. Who are the Responsible Agents?

Do the challenges and obstacles presented in the previous section imply that nothing can be done? I do not believe so. However, we must acknowledge challenges if we are to overcome them. As was said previously, the issues are very complex and, in consequence, we should seek out complex and diversified ways to solve them with different nontraditional tools. The primary goal is to ameliorate global health. In this section I will identify in political theory some of the responsible agents in order to evaluate their possible role in global health.

[7] World Health Organization (WHO), Special Programme for Research and Training in Tropical Diseases (TDR), *Global Report for Research on Infectious Diseases of Poverty* (Geneva: WHO/TDR, 2012) 32.

[8] I am grateful to Julieta Arosteguy for her comments and her suggestion of this analogy.

In recent years, a strong debate has emerged in the theoretical arena regarding ideal and nonideal theories, their relationship, merits, and problems.[9] These considerations are increasingly relevant to bioethics and the field of global health. Ethical and political theories designing institutions and attributing responsibilities assume an ideal world where people comply with their responsibilities and ethical requirements. The first and fundamental feature of an ideal theory is that it assumes 'strict compliance'. According to Rawls, an ideal theory presupposes that: '(Nearly) everyone strictly complies with... the principles of justice'.[10] The second feature is that it assumes favorable circumstances. These include 'historical, *economic*, and *social conditions*, such as *economic means*, education, or the main skills to run a democratic regime'.[11] Even if strict compliance can be distinguished from the moral compliance of a saint or a hero and even if Rawls is not considering the 'best possible circumstances', the situation seeking global health (the conditions described in the first part of this chapter) are far from strict non-heroic compliance or normal socio-economic contingencies.[12] Hence, I argue that the answer will not be found in ideal theories. A nonideal approach, by contrast, will suggest how to deal with noncompliance and unfavorable conditions.[13]

In an imperfect world with extreme conditions and scarcity, where the ideal responsible agents do not comply, a nonideal strategy should be designed. And this can be justified until fairer and more feasible conditions for justice and ideal agents' actions are in effect. The ideal theory may still have a place: it can take the role of a target or aspiration.[14] It may identify the objective at which to aim; it may help nonideal theories to become transitional theories, hence pursuing new ways of thinking. And this applies not only to principles and institutions but to responsible agents. Instead of only considering ideal responsible agents, a pluralistic nonideal approach may be better: researchers, states involved, rich states, and international corporations should have a role until the ideal responsible agent or agents can comply.

2.1 Ideal agents and compliance

In ideal theories, who are the responsible agents? Philosophers such as Peter Singer target *individual responsibility*: each affluent person has a moral obligation.[15] In Singer's

[9] J. Simmons, 'Ideal and Nonideal Theory' (2010) *Philosophy and Public Affairs* 38: 5. Z. Stemplowska and A. Swift, 'Ideal and Nonideal Theory' in D. Estlund (ed), *Oxford Handbook of Political Philosophy* (Oxford: OUP, 2012). A. Hamlin and Z. Stemplowska, 'Theory, Ideal Theory and the Theory of Ideals' *Political Studies Review* (2012) 10: 48.

[10] John Rawls was the first to introduce the distinction between ideal and nonideal theories regarding his own *Theory of Justice*, but his proposal can be applied broadly. J. Rawls, *Justice as Fairness: A Restatement* (Cambridge, MA: Harvard University Press, 2001) 13.

[11] Rawls, *Justice as Fairness* (n 10) 47 (emphasis added).

[12] It can be argued whether ideal theories are applicable to more 'normal' situations because in the real world, people do not generally comply with their obligations. Aside from this controversy, it is clear that in very scarce resource settings where global health is not achieved, conditions are unmistakably far from ideal.

[13] Rawls and others explain that nonideal comprises such topics as theory of punishment, doctrines of just war, and various ways of approving unjust regimes; Stemplowska and Swift, 'Ideal and Nonideal Theory' (n 9) 2. I think we can apply this nonideal approach more broadly to unfavorable situations and noncompliance.

[14] There is also a debate regarding this interaction. I think that the ideal theory might not be a prerequisite but should be on the horizon. A possible role is to guide nonideal strategies. See Stemplowska and Swift, 'Ideal and Nonideal Theory' (n 9).

[15] Singer is mainly considering affluent people from developed countries. See P. Singer, 'Famine, Affluence and Morality' *Philosophy and Public Affairs* (1972) 1(3): 229.

view, we ought to exercise our duty to assist the needy. This is currently quite easy. The world has changed and we can now use the internet to help distant persons. It is also true that if every person is committed to global health or global poverty, more possibilities and help will become available. This would also mean a wider exercise of values such as solidarity through moral obligations. Moreover, if the suffering of others, even distant and unknown individuals, truly mattered and a moral obligation to help others was felt, the world would be better and fairer. Civil society and every individual can become fundamental actors in a profound change. However, no matter how easy and achievable this proposal may seem, Singer had to reduce the amount of money to be given due to the refusal to help and noncompliance. Hence, it is difficult to meet Singer's proposal. But even more problematic is that even if individual help is needed and desirable; 'general' and harmonized policies performed by *collectives*[16] may be a better fit for sustainable global changes in health.

Philosophical positions, such as Thomas Pogge's, could be applied. For him, not only citizens from the rich countries—that is, individuals—but also elites from scarce resource countries and global institutions—that is, collectives—are morally responsible for the extreme condition of the global poor. This proposal also appeals to human rights, which is another interesting perspective worth pursuing.[17]

Human rights provide an important answer. However, while the human rights framework discourse and documents have mainly focused on the recipients, a relevant question is who should be responsible for providing them?[18] In this area, there are different analyses about the proper agents of justice. For example, 'traditional' or 'orthodox' interpretations hold each national state responsible for its citizens' access to health care.

Health obligations are typically carried out by national states. States, as primary agents, should care for their people. Access to health care could be developed through public hospitals and policies and national state policies are the best suited to do so. For example, when Gostin et al[19] propose a Joint Learning Initiative on National and Global Responsibilities for Health, one of the proposals they outline is governments' obligations to their inhabitants and they define what these essential health services and goods are. They explain that the World Health Organization estimates an annual cost of US$40 per person to cover these essential health services. In 2001 in Abuja, Nigeria, African heads of state pledged to devote at least 15 percent of their national budget to the health sector. Yet, in 2007, the average per capita allocation was US$34, an average of 9.6 percent of the budget.

16 It should be acknowledged that responsibility, as a moral concept, is typically attributed to individuals. People speak of the causal responsibility of moral agents for harm in the world and blame them for causing harm. This is based on the assumption that actions begin with intentions and moral blameworthiness requires the existence of intention. Nonetheless, it is also true that, in practice, groups are blamed and that people have emotional reactions to groups, such as anger, resentment, or moral indignation. Therefore, it can be argued that even if, in the strict sense, responsibility is attributed to individual persons, in a subsidiary sense the notion of collective responsibility as an intellectual construct is also used.

17 Regarding the human rights framework, the Universal Declaration of Human Rights, Art 25; the International Covenant on Economic, Social and Cultural Rights, Art 12; the Convention on the Rights of the Child; and the Convention on the Elimination of All Forms of Discrimination Against Women—among other human rights texts—all speak of the right to enjoy the highest attainable standard of physical and mental health. This includes medical care, treatment, and control of epidemic and endemic diseases, besides other issues.

18 O. O'Neill, 'Agents of Justice' in T. Pogge (ed), *Global Justice* (Oxford: Blackwell, 2001) 189.

19 L. Gostin et al, 'National and Global Responsibilities for Health' (n 1).

Can we infer that weak and poor states found this too difficult to achieve? There are at least two interpretations of this situation. The first and more benevolent one can be found in O'Neill's words:

> Weak states may simply lack the resources, human, material, and organizational, to do very much to secure or improve justice within their boundaries . . . They may fail to represent the interests of their citizens adequately in international fora and may agree to damaging or unsupportable treaties or loans. They may lack the capabilities to end or prevent rebellions and forms of feudalism . . .[20]

This may be true of the situation of some poor states. But there can also be a second less charitable interpretation suggesting that many of these states do not make the necessary investments and, regrettably, money is instead spent on corruption, wars, or unwise endeavors. However, even if the role and responsibility of these inefficient or corrupt governments is condemnable, the fate of the people suffering under them should be highlighted so that they are not punished even further. States as primary agents of justice can fail and, in fact, many of them do. And because of this, nonideal strategies can enter the picture. Thus, these reprehensible cases should not be ignored, however, other ways to end the detrimental consequences of the actions of such governments should be determined.

Another issue to consider is the responsibility of other states as bearers of global health obligations. These states vary in their ability to provide aid without suffering unreasonably high costs for their own population's quality of life and well-being.[21] That is, global health obligations increase in proportion to the agent's capacity to assist. The more resources they have, the larger funding commitments they can achieve. Therefore, rich European countries, for example, would seem to have a stronger duty to assist. Gostin et al, in exploring the responsibilities of all governments for the world's poor, also point out that high-income countries have not come close to fulfilling their pledges made in 1970 to spend 0.7 percent of their gross national product per annum on Official Development Assistance. Four decades later their average contribution stands at 0.31 percent. From a human rights positive law perspective, the United Nations Charter aims at international cooperation for the solution of economic, social, cultural, or humanitarian international problems. Articles 55 and 56 explicitly establish international cooperation, among other duties to health, as 'an obligation of all states'. In the same vein, international, interstate or intergovernmental agencies or programs such as the World Health Organization and UNAIDS can also be held responsible. They belong to the United Nations system and were created for this and similar purposes. The constitution of the World Health Organization, for example, as the coordinating authority on international public health, states as its objective 'the attainment by all people of the highest possible level of health'.

2.2 A nonideal approach

In an ideal ethical and political theory, states can be held responsible for the health of their people and richer states for international cooperation with disadvantaged countries. In an ideal theory, human rights agents are the responsible actors. This is also

[20] O'Neill, 'Agents of Justice' (n 18) 197.

[21] Lowry and Schüklenk also point this out. C. Lowry and U. Schüklenk, 'Two models in Global Health Ethics' *Public Health Ethics* (2009) 2(3): 276.

reflected in the international system of human rights through positive law.[22] However, due to the failures of poor states and a lack of general compliance of those ideal agents (we have just pointed out the partial or lack of compliance of poor states to their citizens and the partial or non-compliance of richer states), we should think of nonideal strategies as a sort of bridge.[23] These new strategies, then, should focus on a combination of agents (in addition to the previous ones) working together towards global health.

When discussing agents of justice, Onora O'Neill argues for a plurality of agents. She explains that primary agents (generally the national states) can construct other agents or agencies with specific competences, and they can assign powers or build institutions with certain powers and capacities to act. Secondary agents are thought to contribute to justice mainly by meeting the demands of primary agents, most evidently by conforming to any legal requirements they establish.[24] O'Neill holds international non-governmental organizations and, especially, transnational or multinational companies or corporations responsible. Regarding international non-governmental organizations, she argues that their typical mission is to contribute to specific transformations of states, governments, and policies—quite often to a single issue or objective.[25]

In response to the question of how transnational or multinational corporations could be concerned with justice, except insofar as justice requires conformity to law, O'Neill argues that what matters is what transnational or multinational corporations or companies *can or cannot do*: the capabilities they can or cannot develop.[26] She claims *capabilities are more important than motivations*: '. . . It is more important to consider the capabilities, rather than the (supposed) motivations of transnational companies.' Many transnational companies are evidently capable of throwing their considerable weight in the direction either of greater justice, of the status quo, or of greater injustice. 'Corporate power can be used to support or strengthen reasonably just states. Equally, they can accept the status quo, fall in with local elites and with patterns of injustice, and keep powers to keep things as they are—or indeed to make them more unjust.'[27]

I believe these considerations regarding the capabilities of certain agents can be more defensible and stronger from a nonideal approach than from an ideal perspective as O'Neill attempts.[28] What in the ideal system can be deemed as beneficent,[29] and where

22 Including interstate organizations, such as the World Health Organization responsible for public health as its mission.

23 I will provide some nonideal strategies. I will consider specifically the cases of states without the capacities to achieve global health. However, for other failures of poor states due to corruption or unwillingness to do the right thing, other strategies might be designed, such as the empowerment of citizens or international monitoring institutions.

24 O'Neill, 'Agents of Justice' (n 18) 189.

25 They may contribute to justice precisely because the states are too weak; they can act opportunistically and secure an unusual degree of access to some key players. O'Neill, 'Agents of Justice' (n 18) 199.

26 She takes this concept from Amartya Sen. She says an agent's capabilities are not to be identified with their individual capacities or with their aggregate power. An agent or agency, considered in the abstract, may have various capacities or abilities to act. Capabilities are, instead, the specific capabilities of agents and agencies in specific situations rather than the abstract capacities or their aggregate power. O'Neill, 'Agents of Justice' (n 18) 197.

27 O'Neill, 'Agents of Justice' (n 18) 201.

28 Although I endorsed O'Neill's proposal in a previous paper, I now think that her ideas can be better defended from a nonideal perspective. F. Luna, 'Pobreza en el mundo: obligaciones individuales, institucionales y Derechos Humanos' *Revista Latinoamericana de Filosofía* (2007) XXXIII(2): 293.

29 Although the classic idea is that for-profit corporations obtain benefits for their stockholders, is maximizing stockholders' benefits the sole legitimate purpose of corporations? There are arguments for a stronger obligation of beneficence from a stakeholder's perspective. E.R. Freeman *Strategic Management: A Stakehholder Approach* (London: Pitman, 1984).

no strong responsibility is felt; in a nonideal strategy these agents can be held responsible. Efforts are needed to complement partial compliance and failures, and a minimum standard should be established from which to move forward. A nonideal strategy also leaves aside the debate regarding human rights agents and the extent of their obligations,[30] introducing an independent and complementary layer of analysis and responsibility. However, I believe that to hold agents responsible, we should not only consider their capabilities—as O'Neill proposes—but also whether they are related in some relevant way to these populations and can make a reasonable difference without harming or destroying themselves. This is the case with major pharmaceutical companies regarding global health or of international companies based or working substantially in these lower resource countries.

In addition, we can endorse the rescue principle—a nonideal approach—to justify such obligations. Timothy Scanlon, for example, says: 'If you are presented with a situation in which you can prevent something very bad from happening or alleviate someone's dire plight, by making only a slight (or even moderate) sacrifice, then it would be wrong not to do so.'[31]

Although Scanlon is considering persons and reasons, this principle can easily be applied to corporations. Undoubtedly, the previous situation is so bad that providing medicines for some pharmaceutical companies is, at best, a slight sacrifice. Note that, for example, companies—especially major pharmaceutical ones—do have a policy of corporate social initiatives on which they spend millions of dollars to promote education, the sponsorship of art programs, etc.[32] Directing those funds or part of them to rescuing people from devastating preventable illnesses seems a slight sacrifice.

An additional and interesting argument is given by Thomas Dunfee,[33] regarding the role-based obligation of the pharmaceutical companies. He argues for a mandatory obligation to devote substantial resources towards rescuing victims of catastrophes.[34] He provides a stringent definition of catastrophe and points to firms that possess 'unique competencies' for rescue. His position might be narrower than mine, as he attributes obligations only to very specific pharmaceutical firms due to the 'uniqueness competency' criterion. However, we are both proposing a similar trend. Dunfee makes a case for some specific big pharmaceutical corporations in the Sub-Saharan Africa AIDS catastrophe, but I believe his arguments are easily applicable to some of the situations depicted earlier.

Hence, within this framework, not only should the usual ideal agents be responsible, but transnational and pharmaceutical corporations should also be committed to the improvement of health, for example by developing better health habits among their employees, promoting pro-health policies through their advertising strategies, supporting local hospitals or local efforts to provide better access to health, using their resources (their fleet of trucks and logistics) to distribute medicines or other health devices,[35] and

[30] M. Freeman, *Human Rights* (Cambridge: Polity Press, 2011) 81.

[31] T.M. Scanlon, *What We Owe to Each Other* (Cambridge: Belknap Press of Harvard University Press, 1998) 224.

[32] T. Dunfee, 'Do Firms with Unique Competencies for Rescuing Victims of Human Catastrophes Have Special Obligations? Corporate Responsibility and the AIDS Catastrophe in Sub-Saharan Africa' *Business Ethics Quarterly* (2006) 16(2): 200.

[33] Dunfee, 'Firms with Unique Competencies' (n 32).

[34] 'The minimum amount that firms should devote to rescue is the largest sum of their most recent year's investment in social initiatives, their five-year trend, their industry's average or the national average.' Dunfee, 'Firms with Unique Competencies' (n 32) 185.

[35] Coca Cola has delivered AIDS testing kits to hospitals in Nigeria, billboards for awareness campaigns in Kenya. Dunfee, 'Firms with Unique Competencies' (n 32) 189.

so on. Therefore, from a nonideal perspective, pharmaceutical companies and even transnational corporations can be held responsible.

3. Is It Feasible?

If a plurality of responsible agents can address different needs, a dynamic and flexible answer will be obtained. It is not just one agent but a multiplicity of them with different and appropriate levels of responsibilities.[36] Each of them can reinforce the other's action.

Let us consider a case: River blindness, or onchocerciasis, is a disease, transmitted by *Simulium* blackflies living near streams. It is endemic in more than thirty countries in Africa. Gradual progression to blindness often occurs in infected individuals and in the more forested central and eastern African regions; debilitating, itching, and disfiguring skin lesions are the primary symptoms.[37]

Recalling the 1970s, the Director of the Special Programme for Research and Training in Tropical Disease (TDR), a co-sponsored programme of UNICEF, UNDP, the World Bank and WHO, said:[38]

> The two drugs we had for onchocerciasis at the time were notorious poisons.... We were really desperately looking for a new drug. When we visited the major drug companies, it was clear they *were not interested in this disease.* No one was screening any compounds. We thought that perhaps there was a compound on the shelf that had not been discovered. The strategy put forward was to open a compound-screening network... We asked the industry to give us compounds to test and we would give them the results. We offered this free of charge and confidentially. We had thousands of compounds sent through small animal screens in the broader network.[39]

In July 1978, scientists at the pharmaceutical company Merck, who had been researching ivermectin for several years, sent the compound to the TDR-supported drug-screening facility at James Cook University in Australia. Such screening was regarded by scientists as the best predictor of how a compound would act against human onchocerciasis. Results showed the drug was 'highly effective' against the microfilariae, or infant larvae of the parasite, although it did not, in fact, seem to kill the adult worm.[40]

In analyzing this case, we should first note a typical situation: ineffective drugs and the need for research. In addition, drug companies were not interested in that disease. However, WHO-TDR, an intergovernmental organization, acting as a responsible agent of justice, began the interaction and research in 'non-interesting' compounds with drug companies to develop a suitable drug; it also created a compound screening network. This first action was biomedical.

Because of the good results obtained through the drug research, Merck had been negotiating with development and donor agencies over the purchase of ivermectin, but had received little response. TDR and WHO officials came ready to drive a hard bargain over pricing for developing countries.[41] Finally, in 1986, Merck offered to donate the drug. Large-scale trials were launched to determine the safety and effectiveness of mass

36 How to decide levels of responsibilities in this case is a relevant and important issue but goes beyond the scope of this chapter.

37 World Health Organization-Tropical Disease Research, 'Making a Difference. 30 Years of Research and Capacity Building in Tropical Diseases' (Geneva: WHO, 2007) 39–40.

38 Dr Lucas, director of TDR at that time.

39 WHO-TDR, 'Making a Difference' (n 37) 12–13 (emphasis added).

40 WHO-TDR, 'Making a Difference' (n 37) 12.

41 WHO-TDR, 'Making a Difference' (n 37) 12–13.

drug administration. Since then ivermectin (mectizan) has reached some 60 million of the 100 million people at risk in endemic areas in sub-Saharan Africa.

Continuing with the analysis of the case, another obstacle should be outlined—the difficulties of making the drug available. There was no interest or money on the part of poor states, or of donor agencies, to pay for the drugs. Millions of poor people were at stake and could not afford the drug. However, this time, Merck, acting as a responsible agent with strong capabilities—as the owner of the compound—acknowledged its responsibility and offered the drug at no cost. It provided the drug to the population at risk for more than twenty years.[42] Considering the arguments that claim that pharmaceutical companies should not be burdened, and that their only goal is to maximize profits; it is interesting to point out that giving this drug cost free to the population in need for such a long time was no threat to the survival or profits of the company. On the contrary, Merck is proud of its corporate responsibility as can be seen on its website, where the Merck Mectizan Donation Program is outlined as one of the longest and more successful public/private collaborations in the world.[43]

Given the nonideal approach I follow, which shows the lack of capabilities and failures of ideal agents and the difficulties in providing the drug, Merck (acting as a pharmaceutical company with an effective drug for a devastating illness) has a moral obligation to provide it. Merck can reduce the price to make it available or, as in this case, provide the drug at no cost. Merck, like many of the leading pharmaceutical companies, has the means to do so.[44] These corporations can make a substantial change in global health amelioration and their action does not seem to endanger their companies.

During the 1990s, results indicated that a combined strategy of vector control plus drug treatment would reduce the projected timeline to bring onchocerciasis under control and eliminate onchocerciasis as a public health problem in the Onchocerciasis Control Program in West Africa (OCP) region. However, the actual interruption in disease transmission might not be feasible in many hyper-endemic areas. In such areas, annual ivermectin treatment would have to be sustained almost indefinitely. This posed a significant challenge to disease control:[45]

> Eleven West African States, together with the World Bank, the Food and Agriculture Organization of the United States (FAO), the United Nations Development Programme (UNDP), and the WHO embarked on one of the largest and most comprehensive vertical vector control operations against onchocerciasis in West Africa. An area of about 1,300,000 km, with more than 50,000 km of rivers, was covered by the operation. The success of this intervention was due in large part to the enormous information infrastructure. . . . This drew on hydrology/seasonal river flows, information on vector habitats, parasite mapping, and information on population levels of infection and blindness.[46]

Here again, multiple agents interacted in order to solve the challenge. Many African countries acted responsibly as primary agents of justice. Note the necessary level of coordination whereby eleven countries acted together. The action of each single

42 Consider that in most cases the production of the drug in itself is not expensive, unlike the discovery process and the procurement of a patent through clinical trials and regulatory agencies requirements.

43 See <http://www.merckresponsibility.com> which deals with corporate responsibility and the role and programs of this company.

44 Not only because of the high profits that most pharmaceutical companies obtain, but also because they already devote substantial funds to corporate social activities.

45 WHO-TDR , 'Making a Difference' (n 37) 40–1.

46 WHO-TDR, 'Global Report for research on infectious diseases of poverty' (Geneva, 2012) 32.

country acting alone did not suffice; regional efforts had to be achieved (with the challenges this implied). Note also the action of stewardship and harmonization of United Nations international agencies, responding to their mandate and responsibilities. Also consider the different expertise involved (environmental, biological, veterinary, medical) working together. The drug or narrow biomedical knowledge was not enough.

Even though a substantial amelioration was achieved, obstacles persisted: the actual field distribution of the drug was still limited. Getting the drug to the people who needed it in remote areas year after year was a significant challenge. Some 80 percent of the population at risk of onchocerciasis lives outside of West Africa. In these other African regions, the disease exhibited different features and control presented different challenges.[47]

In 1994, a new framework for 'community-directed treatment' (ComDT) put communities directly in charge of ivermectin administration and health services were developed to provide the necessary training. This effort called for a different kind of research. It was demonstrated that ComDT has been feasible and effective and has led to greater treatment coverage since 1996.[48]

Again note how the strategy to make the drug available changed in light of this final challenge. Another kind of research was needed and new responsible agents appeared: the narrow biomedical approach was not enough. The people themselves and the communities were also responsible agents. In this case, they had to be trained and—mostly—empowered in order to obtain efficacious results.[49]

As the main agents in this case caution:

> The picture has never been all rosy. Serious problems were encountered in sustaining drug distribution when wars and instability struck various endemic countries. In October 2001, a detailed review of the African Programme of Onchocerciasis Control (APOC) and OCP experiences with onchocerciasis control concluded that while onchocerciasis was well under control as a public health problem in the 11 original OCP countries, it could not be eradicated using the currently available tools. The development of a drug that can kill or sterilize the adult onchocercal worm living inside infected individuals remains a top priority. Disease transmission cannot be permanently interrupted with ivermectin, and so annual treatment must continue for an indeterminate length of time, placing a considerable burden on health systems.[50]

Hence, even if many goals were achieved, river blindness as a health problem has not yet been resolved. New strategies and new research are pending. But we should also note that all this progress would not have been possible had we only targeted one particular agent (be it the national state, the pharmaceutical companies, the wealthy countries, or the actions of international agencies).

47 WHO-TDR, 'Making a Difference' (n 37) 40–1.

48 ComDT was adopted by OCP as its ivermectin delivery strategy and became the backbone of APOC operations in 1996. By 2007, ComDT had succeeded in extending the annual ivermectin coverage to more than 45 million people in Africa, out of an ultimate target population for treatment of approximately 70 million, in collaboration with APOC and local research institutions.

49 Even if we can appeal to the responsibility of the community, it is not the same situation as that in which international corporations have the means to make a change. Here we need to empower the populations and work closely with the communities, which are isolated, often illiterate, and have very few resources. Hence, a very different level of responsibility exists.

50 WHO-TDR, 'Making a Difference' (n 37) 73.

4. Conclusion

Global health presents itself as an immutable debt and as a moving target with a cluster of different challenges. Following ethics and political philosophy proposals, the states and the international human rights architecture are ideal agents of justice. However, because global health presents a combination of very little compliance by 'ideal' responsible agents and manifold obstacles exist, I argued for a joint effort appealing to the responsibility of multiple agents and actors aiming for a transitional strategy. Within this strategy, secondary agents of justice—in O'Neill's proposal—can be identified as responsible agents. This implies holding various institutions, pharmaceutical companies, and even transnational corporations responsible. Finally, I presented a real case where many different agents (intergovernmental agencies, states, international corporations, among others) interacted to fight onchocerciasis in Africa. Instead of defending a simple monistic answer, I consider a pluralistic and diversified view to be far richer and more constructive.

18

Global Ageing

Demographic and Ethical Challenges to Population Health and Development Policies

Michal Engelman

Population ageing is among the defining demographic developments of the past century. It is an outcome of improved living conditions, broader access to health and social services, and a myriad other human successes that have brought about longer and, for the most part, healthier lives. And yet, rather than being hailed as a triumph, the resulting age structure is more often portrayed as a threat that will overwhelm or radically alter social, economic, and political institutions. Policy analysts and popular writers describe population ageing as an 'old age crisis'[1] or a 'gray dawn',[2] and detail concerns about population decline, labour force shortages, and the endangered solvency of public pension and healthcare programs.[3]

Demographic factors such as population ageing are crucial in shaping social, economic, and political trends, but contrary to the popular 'demography is destiny' trope, population dynamics alone do not determine the course of human affairs. Population ageing calls for the reassessment of existing policies and programs and their realignment to fit both the new demographic reality and the ethical principles and social values that define intergenerational relationships. Aggregate statistics and generalizations about the burdens of ageing populations conceal considerable heterogeneity in the circumstances of older people both across and within countries. Some older people enjoy long periods of good health, well-being, and the capacity to contribute to their families and societies, while others are burdened by illness, disability, and dependency. Indeed, older people have long been described as a particularly heterogeneous population group and an interest in exploring variation, rather than averages, characterizes much of the research in gerontology.[4] Gerontologists have tended to discount age-based generalizations and instead argue against stereotyping older adults,[5] emphasize variation in trajectories of ageing and the distribution of physical, behavioural, and social characteristics in

1 World Bank, *Averting the Old Age Crisis: Policies to Protect the Old and Promote Growth* (Oxford and New York: OUP, 1994).

2 P.G. Peterson, 'Gray Dawn: The Global Aging Crisis' (1999) 78 *Foreign Affairs* 42.

3 D. Brooks, 'The Fertility Implosion', *The New York Times*, 12 March 2012.

4 G.L Maddox and E.B. Douglass, 'Aging and Individual Differences: A Longitudinal Analysis of Social, Psychological and Physiological Indicators' (1974) 29(5) *Journal of Gerontology* 555; D. Dannefer, 'Aging as Intracohort Differentiation: Accentuation, the Matthew effect, and the Life-course' (1987) 2(2) *Sociological Forum* 211; M. Engelman, V. Canudas-Romo, and E.M. Agree, 'The Influence of Increased Survivorship on Mortality Variation among Aging Populations' (2010) 36(3) *Population and Development Review* 511.

5 R.N. Butler, *Why Survive? Being Old in America* (New York: Harper & Row, 1974); B. Friedan, *The Fountain of Age* (New York: Simon & Schuster, 1993).

later life,[6] and caution against social policies that treat the older population as a homogeneous group.[7] However, as I show in the following, this recognition of diversity among older adults has not been well-reflected in policy and practice contexts, where older people tend to be perceived primarily as recipients of support, and their roles as care providers and engaged citizens are frequently overlooked.

Ageing was long considered a notable population issue mainly in high-income nations, but it is increasingly recognized as a global phenomenon with considerable relevance for low-income countries. In fact, older persons constitute the fastest growing population group in many low-income nations.[8] A 2004 United Nations policy paper reported that approximately half of the world's low-income nations cited population aging as 'a major concern',[9] given their constrained resources and many competing priorities. And yet, older people's needs for support as well as their capacities to contribute to their families and communities often remain unacknowledged in mainstream international development policies and programs. This is partially because ageing has traditionally been viewed as a social welfare issue, a perspective that situates older people as objects of charity who, particularly in low-income settings, must vie with younger vulnerable populations for scarce resources. The allocation of resources for the promotion of older people's well-being was further constrained by a view of older people as a less promising target for investment than other population groups. The conceptual challenge facing advocates involves countering the prevailing simplified and largely negative depictions of older people and of the societal implications of population ageing while at the same time raising awareness of the very real needs and vulnerabilities of many older people.

In the past decade, there has been growing recognition of the need for changes in attitudes, policies, and practices to ensure that older persons' contributions are recognized alongside their needs, that their rights are respected, and that they are included as active participants in and contributors to the cultural, social, and economic life of their communities. New reports produced by UN agencies and other international and national organizations are characterized by an increasingly optimistic tone about the protection of older people's rights and the promotion of their health, as well as the incorporation of ageing into the general international development agenda. This turn reflects the advocacy efforts of researchers and activists working to reshape the image of population ageing as a challenge or even a demographic dividend, rather than simply an impending crisis.[10]

6 G.L. Maddox and M.P. Lawton (eds), *Annual Review of Gerontology and Geriatrics 8: Varieties of Aging* (New York: Springer, 1988); D. Dannefer, 'Cumulative Disadvantage/Disadvantage and the Life Course: Cross-Fertilizing Age and Social Science Theory' (2003) 58(6) *Journal of Gerontology: Social Sciences* S327.

7 B. Neugarten, *Age or Need: Public Policies and Older People* (Beverly Hills, CA: Sage Publications, 1982); M.W. Riley, J. Riley, and A. Foner, 'The Aging and Society Paradigm' in V.L. Bengtsson and K.W. Schaie (eds), *Handbook of Theories of Aging: In Honor of Jim Birren* (New York: Springer, 1999) 327.

8 The categorization of countries as more or less developed is complicated and unsatisfactory, but a convenient tool for facilitating comparisons. See United Nations Statistics Division, 'Composition of macro geographical (continental regions) geographical sub-regions, and selected economic and other groupings' (2010), available at <http://unstats.un.org/unsd/methods/m49/m49regin.htm>.

9 United Nations Population Division, 'United Nations World Population Policies 2003', (New York, 2004).

10 A. Sidorenko, 'World Policies on Aging and the United Nations' in M. Robinson, W. Novelli, C. Pearson, and L. Norris (eds), *Global Health and Global Ageing* (San Francisco: Jossey-Bass, 2007) 3; A. Kalache, 'The World Health Organization and Global Aging' in Robinson et al (see previously) 31.

The shift in the discourse on global ageing happened within the context of changing notions about the relationship between human rights and development, in particular, the late twentieth-century process of redefining development in terms of the realization of individual needs and capabilities[11] and supplementing an exclusive emphasis on national economic growth with human rights as a framework and objective of development. Debates about the moral and instrumental nature of human rights[12] and about their alignment or alliance with development efforts[13] are ongoing. As I describe later, the positioning of human rights into the heart of international development discourses and activities has proven key for the evolution of responses to global ageing.

The changing emphasis in international aid, development, and advocacy circles has also brought health into sharper focus, with growing recognition of health's interconnections with social and economic rights and other components of well-being.[14] Attention to health has always been integral to the study of ageing and to the provision of care and services to older adults, but the focus has now expanded from biomedical concerns with specific diseases and declining physical functioning in later life to include the upstream social determinants of health and their cumulative effects throughout the life course. Data on older people in low-income countries is still too scarce, but preliminary studies have been central to documenting the vulnerability of older people as well as their exclusion from healthcare services and other aid programs. They have also, on the other hand, served to document their roles as caregivers. In the advocacy discourse, access to healthcare and health-promoting resources is positioned as essential for keeping older people productive and contributing, and also as a human right, thereby reflecting and instantiating the tension between older people's exceptionality and their commonality with others in the broader discussion of ageing and development.

Later, I review demographic and public health issues associated with global ageing, and argue that older populations across and within countries are increasingly heterogeneous, complicating attempts to treat 'the elderly' as a cohesive unit in policy and programmatic considerations. I then examine the transformation of the global ageing discourse, tracing the manifestations and evolution of economic and ethical perspectives in consensus statements designed to inform international and national policies. I show how the growing dominance of human rights frameworks as tools of social justice has come to shape advocacy efforts on behalf of older people in low-income and transitional countries, and explore the implications of critiques of these frameworks for the ethical and practical response of societies around the world to the ageing of their populations.

11 A. Sen, *Development As Freedom* (New York: Knopf, 1999).

12 M. Ignatieff, *Human Rights as Politics and Idolatry* (Princeton: Princeton University Press, 2001); A. Chowdhury, 'The Giver or the Recipient? The Peculiar Ownership of Human Rights' (2011) 5(1) *International Political Sociology* 35.

13 K. Manzo, 'Africa in the Rise of Rights-Based Development' (2003) 34(4) *Geoforum* 437; S. Hickey and D. Mitlin, 'The Potential and Pitfalls of Rights-Based Approaches to Development' in S. Hickey and D. Mitlin (eds), *Rights-Based Approaches to Development: Exploring the Potential and Pitfalls* (Sterling, VA: Kumarian Press, 2009) ch 12.

14 J.M. Mann, 'Medicine and Public Health, Ethics and Human Rights' (1997) 27(3) *Hastings Center Report* 6.

1. The Demography of Global Ageing

Population ageing is a result of two distinct but related demographic processes: declines in mortality during childhood and earlier adulthood which allow an increasing number of people to reach old age, and reductions in fertility that bring about a gradual increase in the relative proportion of older people relative to other age groups in the population.[15] Together, the dynamic patterns of mortality and fertility over time reshape the age composition of populations, turning classic pyramids that reflect populations largely composed of young individuals into more rectangular structures indicating an age distribution shifted to later ages.

The number of older[16] people in the world has been growing steadily for over a century, but their proportion relative to other age groups began to increase noticeably in the 1970s and 1980s. The trend has accelerated in the past twenty years, and is projected to continue in the decades ahead as approximately 880,000 persons reach older ages per month.[17] Approximately 810 million people were over 60 years old in 2012, and the number will reach 2 billion by 2050.[18] Globally, older people already outnumber children less than 5 years of age, and by 2050, they will outnumber those under 15.[19] While each country has its own particular historical, cultural, economic, demographic, and epidemiological history, ageing is an increasingly central characteristic of populations across diverse regions and socioeconomic circumstances.

In higher-income nations, older persons have constituted the fastest growing age group for several decades.[20] In most of these countries, population ageing happened slowly in the context of rising economic prosperity. In many low-income nations, however, population ageing is occurring quickly, often before the establishment and vetting of policies, programs, or healthcare systems prepared to meet the needs of older people. Though higher rates of fertility and mortality kept the pace of population ageing in low-income regions slower in the past, things in many nations are changing rapidly.[21] While industrialized nations have higher percentages of older people than most

15 While fertility and mortality are the only determinants of population ageing on a global scale, within national and local populations, migration can also play an important role in shaping the population age structure. For example, in settings such as the United States and some European countries, a substantial number of working-age immigrants with higher fertility than that of the native-born population may increase the number and relative proportion of younger people and thus slow population ageing. Conversely, in many rural regions throughout the world the out-migration of working-age individuals can yield a disproportionately older population. Indeed, the changing mobility of populations could make a substantial difference for the future dynamics of both fertility and ageing.

16 There is no universal definition of old age and classification varies between countries. In Europe and the United States, the retirement age, 65, has traditionally defined older status, though both retirement ages and markers of senescence are subject to change. In countries where much of the population works outside the formal sector, there is no expectation of retirement at a particular age. In addition to chronological age, an appropriate definition of old age could incorporate changes in social roles (including work patterns, the adult status of children, and loss of reproductive roles for women) and changes in physical functioning and mental capabilities. Following the United Nations' First and Second World Assembly on Ageing, I consider the category of older persons to include those aged 60 and over.

17 K. Kinsella and W. He, 'An Aging World: 2008', Current Population Reports P-95-09-1, (Washington, DC: US Census Bureau 2009).

18 United Nations Department of Economic and Social Affairs (UNDESA), 'Population Ageing and Development 2012', Wall Chart (New York, 2012).

19 UNDESA, 'World Population Prospects, the 2010 Revision' (New York, 2011).

20 See Maddox and Douglass, 'Aging and Individual Differences' (n 4).

21 K. Kinsella and V.A. Velkoff, 'An Ageing World: 2001', Current Population Reports P95/01-1 (Washington, DC: US Census Bureau, 2001).

low-income countries, the absolute number is greater in low-income countries and the rates of both absolute and relative increases are higher.[22] Today, 65 percent of people aged 60 and over live in low and middle-income countries; by 2050, 80 percent will.[23]

Different geographic regions are ageing at varied paces, reflecting heterogeneous histories of fertility and mortality change, as well as experiences with the diffusion of health advances.[24] Currently, older people make up 22 percent of the population in Europe, 19 percent in Northern America, 15 percent in Oceania, 11 percent in Asia, 10 percent in Latin America and the Caribbean, and 6 percent in Africa.[25] The United Nations projects that by 2050, the proportion of the population aged 60 years and over will reach 10 percent in Africa, 24 percent in Asia and in Oceania, 25 percent in Latin America and the Caribbean, 27 percent in North America, and 34 percent in Europe.

The gradual ageing of Europe and North America stands in contrast to the rapid pace of survival improvement and fertility decline (and thus, population ageing) in post-World War II Japan and several contemporary nations in Asia (for example China, India, South Korea, and Indonesia, among others) and Latin America (for example Brazil and Columbia). The nations of the former Soviet Union experienced drastic declines in both fertility and life expectancy during their transition to a market economy, a situation that led to population ageing as well as absolute declines in population size. Africa remains the region with the slowest rate of ageing due to persistently high rates of fertility and mortality (particularly from HIV/AIDS and other infectious diseases). Notably, the number of older people is growing substantially in Africa, too, but this growth has not yet translated into a more sizeable proportion of the total fast-growing population. It has, however, begun to attract more attention to the circumstances of older people in Africa.[26]

The older population is predominantly female, with the sex ratio (number of men per 100 women) declining sharply with age. Globally in 2012, there were 84 men per 100 women aged 60 and over, and only 61 men per 100 women among the oldest-old (aged 80 and over). The sex ratio at older ages is lower in high-income regions than in low-income ones (75 versus 89) because women outlive men by a wider margin in high-income regions. While women tend to live longer than men, they have greater levels of disability. Older men are more likely to be married than older women globally (81 percent versus 50 percent), and these gender differences in marriage are largest in least developed countries (85 percent of men versus 38 percent of women), where age differences between spouses tend to be higher and widowers are more likely than widows to remarry. Almost three-quarters of all older persons in high-income regions either live alone or only with a spouse, compared to only a quarter of older persons in less developed regions and just over 10 percent in the least developed regions.[27]

Old age tends to be characterized as a time of need, but many older people continue to support themselves and provide for members of their families and communities. The proportion of older persons who participate in the labour force is much higher in the

22 L.G. Martin, 'Demography and Ageing' in R.H. Binstock and L.K. George (eds), *Handbook of Aging and the Social Sciences* (Burlington, MA: 7th edn, Elsevier, 2011).

23 UNDESA, 'Current Status of the Social Situation, Wellbeing, Participation in Development and Rights of Older People Worldwide' (New York, 2011).

24 UNDESA, 'World Population Prospects, the 2008 Revision' (New York, 2009).

25 United Nations Population Fund (UNFPA) and HelpAge International, 'Ageing in the Twenty-First Century: A Celebration and a Challenge' (New York and London, 2012).

26 I. Aboderin, 'Development and Ageing Policy in Sub-Saharan Africa: Approaches for Research and Advocacy' (2007) 4(3) *Global Ageing* 7.

27 UNDESA, 'Population Ageing and Development' (n 18).

less developed regions (50 percent of older men and 22 percent of older women) than in higher-income regions (26 percent of older men and 15 percent of older women).[28] There is also growing evidence of the contributions older people make by using their pension funds to support other members of their families, for example by paying for grandchildren's school fees or relatives' medical care.[29] Unpaid care for grandchildren or other dependents, including sick relatives, is also widespread,[30] but, as with all work outside of formal economic institutions, hard to quantify in official statistics.[31]

The heterogeneous roles and lives of older adults have long been a theme in the study of ageing and the life course.[32] As members of any cohort age, the accumulation of exposures and experiences sets each person on a unique trajectory shaped by one's initial personal endowments as well as the historical, environmental, and social context. As individuals move through time, the accumulation of positive and negative experiences—based on their individual traits, starting circumstances, and opportunities for accessing resources—increases diversity and entrenches population patterns of advantage and disadvantage.[33] From this perspective, population ageing doesn't simply increase the number of people above a certain chronological threshold—it also creates a population structure characterized by more heterogeneity in social, economic, psychological, and cognitive characteristics. Because health both influences and is influenced by these diverse characteristics, summarizing the health of ageing populations is thus also not a simple matter.

2. Ageing, Health, and the Practice of International Development

The common discourse on population ageing tends to assume that older people are both unproductive economically and necessarily have expensive care needs that divert resources from other population groups. While the reduction of population subgroups to formal labour force participants or dependents is clearly oversimplified,[34] the assumption that the prioritization of the young over the aged is ethically and practically justifiable is rarely challenged by agencies working in global health and development. This perspective is enshrined in the 'dependency ratios' (the proportion of older people relative to those in the presumed economically-active 15 to 64 age range) calculated in economic demography[35] as well as in population health metrics like the widely-used disability-adjusted life years (DALYs),[36] which assign lower values to years of life lived by older adults or in a state of disability in cost-benefit analyses that inform the prioritization of healthcare investments.

Whether population ageing is understood as a burden or an opportunity for societies is primarily a function of whether individuals age in good health and maintain their

28 UNDESA, 'Population Ageing and Development' (n 18).

29 P. Lloyd-Sherlock, 'Simple Transfers, Complex Outcomes: The Impacts of Pensions on Poor Households in Brazil' (2006) 37(5) *Development and Change* 969; E. Duflo, 'Child Health and Household Resources in South Africa: Evidence from the Old Age Pension Program' (2000) 90 *American Economic Review* 339.

30 UNDESA, 'Population Ageing and Development' (n 18).

31 N. Folbre, *The Invisible Heart: Economics and Family Values* (New York: The New Press, 2001).

32 Dannefer, 'Aging as Intracohort Differentiation' (n 4).

33 Dannefer, 'Cumulative Disadvantage/Disadvantage' (n 6).

34 Folbre, *The Invisible Heart* (n 31).

35 Old-age dependency ratios for all nations are available at <http://data.un.org/Data.aspx?d=PopDiv&f=variableID%3A44>.

36 T. Arnesen and E. Nord, 'The Value of DALY Life: Problems with Ethics and Validity of Disability Adjusted Life Years' (1999) 319 *British Medical Journal* 1423.

independence and ability to contribute as long as possible, or age in poor health with physical or cognitive limitations that render them vulnerable and dependent on others. Health and reliable access to effective healthcare services are key to older people's well-being and therefore to their continued capacity to contribute to their families and participate in the social, economic, political, and cultural life of their communities. Some individuals reach older ages in excellent health, thanks to the benefits of a favourable genetic endowment or the combination of a consistently nutritious diet, a physically and mentally active lifestyle, and few exposures to environmental or behavioral hazards;[37] others reach the same chronological threshold with pre-existing burdens of disease and disability, the consequences of challenges they've faced over the life course.[38] As a result, individual trajectories of health at older ages proceed along markedly different paths within any population, reflecting the diverse living circumstances and experiences of individuals during the entire lifespan.[39] While some health declines at the end of life are inevitable, the type, timing, and duration of such declines are a function of multiple interacting factors leading to substantial heterogeneity in health status among older people within and across populations. Consequently, the broad health priorities for ageing societies include the prevention of disease and disability throughout the life course, the promotion of healthy lifestyles, and the provision of treatment and rehabilitation services to an increasingly heterogeneous older population.

Together with income security, health (and access to healthcare) is the major concern of older persons, as well as of policy analysts and governments serving ageing populations.[40] However, attention to the intersection of global health and population dynamics is new and still relatively thin. This is partially because much of the response of international agencies to ageing to date has focused on pension policies and the implications of ageing populations for economic development,[41] and partially because the global health agenda centers on responding to infectious diseases including AIDS, malaria, and tuberculosis, and on issues related to nutrition and maternal and child health.[42] Furthermore, in some countries (for example in slow-ageing sub-Saharan Africa), ageing is not yet recognized as a pressing issue, particularly given the standard timeframes of development projects, which tend to operate within five-year funding cycles rather than taking a longer-term view. While continued attention to infectious diseases and the health of the young is essential, there is little indication that policy, funding, or programmatic priorities related to health promotion in low-income countries have expanded to respond to the changing age composition of developing country populations.

For example, neither the United Nations' eight Millennium Development Goals (a collection of targets including halving poverty and hunger, providing universal primary education, reducing under-5 mortality by two-thirds, and reducing the maternal mortality ratio by three-quarters—all by 2015)[43] nor the Poverty Reduction

[37] J.W. Rowe and R.L. Kahn, 'Human Aging: Usual and Successful' (1987) 237 *Science* 143.

[38] L. Ferrucci et al, 'Progressive Versus Catastrophic Disability: A Longitudinal View of the Disablement Process' (1996) 51 *Journal of Gerontology: Medical Sciences* M123.

[39] S. Mavandadi, K.S. Rook, and J.T. Newsom, 'Positive and Negative Social Exchanges and Disability in Later Life: An Investigation of Trajectories of Change' (2007) 62B *Journal of Gerontology: Social Sciences* S361.

[40] UNDESA, 'Population Ageing and Development' (n 18).

[41] P. Lloyd-Sherlock, 'Ageing and International Development' in D. Dannefer and C. Phillipson (eds), *The Sage Handbook of Social Gerontology* (London: Sage Publications, 2010) 379.

[42] K. Hanson, K. Ranson, V. Oliveira-Cruz, and A. Mills, 'Expanding Access to Priority Health Interventions: A Framework for Understanding the Constraints to Scaling Up' (2003) 15(1) *Journal of International Development* 1.

[43] See <http://www.un.org/millenniumgoals/>.

Strategy Papers required by the International Monetary Fund and the World Bank from low-income countries seeking debt relief and other forms of aid[44] make any specific references to older people or chronic diseases. Older people are similarly absent from major plans and strategies for health: among forty-nine health intervention priorities identified for low-income countries by the World Health Organization's Commission on Macroeconomics and Health in 2001,[45] none specifically mentioned older people. Older people are likewise rarely included in national plans for primary healthcare interventions.

In poor settings, building a healthcare infrastructure that will integrate support for older people is a substantial challenge. Unlike interventions for mothers and children, which are viewed as an investment contributing to the social and economic development process, healthcare and welfare services for older people are often viewed as only a cost (and burden) to society's already constrained resources. Even when older persons needs are acknowledged, it is hard to adjudicate between their needs and those of multiple other vulnerable groups, such as mothers, children, and adolescents for an equitable allocation of limited public health resources.

Notably, while families and communities integrate children, working-age adults, and older people in a series of interdependent relationships, formal allocation decisions are often framed as trade-offs between groups competing for the same limited resources. Philosophers and bioethicists in the past decades have developed several justifications for the prioritization of the young over the aged in response to the rising prevalence (and spiraling cost) of life support procedures or aggressive interventions—such as organ transplants or extensive surgery—in later life. Some ethical arguments have built on utilitarian or communitarian reasoning to call for age-based rationing, while others have used social contract theory and arguments based on duties or definitions of vulnerability to justify limiting the resources devoted to elder care and prioritizing the needs of mothers and children.[46]

These rationing arguments are part of a larger debate regarding the ethical implications of extending life, not merely the preservation of basic health. But in resource-poor contexts, it is the lack of basic primary healthcare services for older adults and the obstacles that prevent them from accessing other forms of support that are the main concern of advocates for older people's rights.[47] While standard rationing arguments presume that older people have had sufficient opportunity to achieve their goals and life plans over their lifespan, the arguments fall flat in contexts characterized by resource scarcity, lack of infrastructure, and political instability. Many older people in low-income countries face old age—and its declines in capacity—with the added burden of a lifetime of poverty. Furthermore, structural inequalities including lack of access to education, employment, adequate nutrition, and healthcare throughout the lifespan are known to have adverse effects on well-being that are compounded and exacerbated by old age, leaving older people increasingly vulnerable.[48] The intergenerational justice

[44] See <http://www.imf.org/external/np/exr/facts/prsp.htm>.

[45] <http://whqlibdoc.who.int/publications/2001/924154550x.pdf>.

[46] J. Harris, *The Value of Life* (London and Boston, MA: Routledge & Kegan Paul, 1985); N. Daniels, *Am I My Parents' Keeper? An Essay on Justice between the Young and the Old* (New York: OUP, 1988); D.W. Brock, 'Health Resource Allocation for Vulnerable Populations' in M. Danis, C. Clancy, and L. Churchill (eds), *Ethical Dimensions of Health Policy* (Oxford: OUP, 2002) 283.

[47] B.A. Dodge, 'Primary Healthcare for Older People: A Participatory Study in Five Asian Countries', Chiang Mai: HelpAge International Asia/Pacific regional Development Center (2008).

[48] M. Engelman and S. Johnson, 'Population Aging and International Development: Addressing Competing Claims of Distributive Justice' (2007) 7(1) *Developing World Bioethics* 8.

dilemma in this context, therefore, is not about whether older people should be entitled to more resources than those allotted to the young but, rather, about whether it is justified to deny older people a basic level of care.

Responses to this distributive justice problem hinge on one's view of the social contract delineating rights and obligations between generations. Some see different age groups as engaged in a competition for resources and interpret intergenerational equity in terms of older people's obligation to refrain from burdening the young and using up resources that would be invested in future generations.[49] Others emphasize social cohesion and reciprocity, and call on younger people to take care of older people in recognition and return for their past contributions. Yet another perspective has relied on empirical data to show that older people's continued contributions and the documented downward flows of intergenerational supports in low-income countries[50] counteract the notion that older people are simply a drain on familial and public resources. While older people's capabilities may diminish with age, instrumental and social support can help prolong and enhance their independence and enable their continued contributions.

At the same time, the growth of the older population worldwide is quickly transforming population health profiles and disease burdens. The epidemiologic transition framework[51] describes a gradual shift in the major causes of death from infectious and acute diseases that primarily affect children to chronic and degenerative diseases that manifest in later life. A critical challenge for many resource-poor countries is what is known as the double burden of disease, or the need to address chronic and non-communicable diseases even as the prevalence of communicable diseases remains high. Indeed, for over a decade non-communicable diseases have been the dominant contributors to the burden of disease in all countries except those in sub-Saharan Africa.[52] In 2002, non-communicable diseases accounted for 85 percent of the burden of disease in high-income countries, and 44 percent of the burden in low and middle-income countries. By 2030, non-communicable diseases are projected to account for 54 percent of the disease burden in low and middle-income countries, with the share attributable to communicable diseases expected to decline to 32 percent. Notably, these diseases already form as much of the disease burden in low and middle-income countries as all communicable disease, maternal and perinatal conditions, and nutritional conditions.[53]

Worldwide, more than 46 percent of people aged 60 years and over have disabilities and more than 250 million older people experience moderate to severe disability. Ischaemic heart disease, stroke, and chronic lung disease are the most common causes of death in adulthood, and visual and hearing impairment, dementia, and osteoarthritis are the main sources of disability.[54] These conditions are associated with a greater burden of disease—as measured by years of life lost and years lived with disabilities—in

[49] S.H. Preston, 'Children and the Elderly: Divergent Paths for America's Dependents' (1984) 21 *Demography* 435.

[50] Lloyd-Sherlock, 'Simple Transfers, Complex Outcomes' (n 29); Duflo, 'Child Health and Household Resources in South Africa' (n 29).

[51] A.R. Omran, 'Epidemiological Transition: A Theory of the Epidemiology of Population Change' (1971) 49(4) *The Milbank Quarterly* 509.

[52] Lopez et al, 'Global and Regional Burden of Disease and Risk Factors, 2001. Systematic Analysis of Population Health Data' (2006) 367 *Lancet* 1747.

[53] National Institute on Aging, *Why Population Aging Matters: A Global Perspective* (Washington, DC: National Institutes of Health, 2007).

[54] World Health Organization, 'The Global Burden of Disease: 2004 update' (Geneva, 2004).

low-income countries relative to their higher-income counterparts.[55] For example, older people in low-income countries lose five times as many years from chronic lung disease and twice as many from stroke as in high-income countries. Older people in low-income countries also carry almost three times the burden of visual impairment as their counterparts in high-income nations. There are 32.5 million older people in low-income countries with significant visual impairment from cataracts, and 39.8 million with significant visual impairment from refractive errors. There are also over 40 million older people in low-income countries with significant hearing impairment.[56] These impairments can affect older people's independence as well as their ability to communicate with others, contributing to social isolation, anxiety, depression, and cognitive decline. While many vision and hearing impairments can be corrected or ameliorated at relatively little cost, there is a lack of health professionals trained in geriatric medicine, knowledgeable about chronic diseases, and able to provide appropriate long-term care.[57] Assistive technologies that could help older adults to remain independent longer are likewise scarce. More generally, there is a dearth of appropriate health and social provisions for older people in many low-income countries, including during natural disasters, military conflicts, or other crisis or emergency situations.[58]

Because of their often-marginalized status, older people in low-income countries are also less able to safeguard their own interests, facing economic, social, and political marginalization in addition to age-related health deficits.[59] Older people in developing regions are often excluded from healthcare, education, vocational training, and economic development opportunities due to age-based discrimination by members of their households and communities, as well as by public institutions and humanitarian agencies.[60] Age is thus an additional layer[61] of vulnerability that interacts with other personal and group characteristics (such as race or ethnicity, gender, and class) to increase or decrease susceptibility to adverse outcomes.

Common wisdom once held that in low-income countries, older adults whose health declines will be cared for by co-residing family members, and that norms of filial piety and respect for elders will obviate the need for formal or institutional eldercare services.[62] But such arrangements can no longer be counted on. As a recent UN report notes, 'informal support systems for older persons are increasingly coming under stress as a consequence, among others, of lower fertility, out-migration of the young, and women working outside the home'.[63] Throughout Africa, Asia, and other regions, young and middle-aged adults leave rural villages to pursue economic opportunities in

55 World Health Organization, 'Good Health Adds Life to Years: Global Brief for World Health Day 2012' (Geneva, 2012), available at <http://www.who.int/ageing/publications/whd2012_global_brief/en/index.html>.

56 World Health Organization, 'World Report on Disability 2011' (Geneva, 2011).

57 I. Keller et al, *Global Survey on Geriatrics in the Medical Curriculum* (Geneva: World Health Organization, 2002), available at <http://www.who.int/entity/ageing/publications/alc_tegeme_survey.pdf>.

58 G. Bramucci and S. Erb, 'An Invisible Population: Displaced Older People in West Darfur' (2007) 4(3) *Global Ageing* 23.

59 Report of the United Nations High Commissioner for Human Rights, 20 April 2012, E/2012/51, at 7.

60 HelpAge International, 'State of the World's Older People 2002' (London, 2002); HelpAge International, 'The Ageing and Development Report: Poverty, Independence and the World's Older People' (London, 2000).

61 F. Luna, 'Elucidating the Concept of Vulnerability: Layers not Labels' (2009) 2(1) *International Journal of Feminist Approaches to Bioethics* 120.

62 D.O. Cowgill and L.D. Holmes, *Aging and Modernization* (New York: Appleton-Century-Crofts, 1972).

63 UNFPA and HelpAge International, 'Ageing in the Twenty-First Century' (n 25).

cities, leaving older adults behind to take care of themselves and, often, to tend to their grandchildren, too. In countries with high rates of HIV/AIDS, a growing number of older people serve as primary caregivers to their adult children or other younger family members suffering from the disease.[64] Violence, substance abuse, and incarceration are additional factors contributing to older people's increasing caregiving responsibilities.

Health is thus an arena where the tension between seemingly contradictory images of older people as on the one hand, particularly vulnerable, and, on the other, productive and contributing members of families and societies becomes especially apparent. This tension is the result of real heterogeneity in the needs and capabilities of older people, but it also reflects the need of advocates to connect older people's experiences to the dominant dictates of development agendas.[65] Thus, older people's private caregiving roles are highlighted to showcase their ability to contribute to the welfare and capacity of younger generations in ways that promote neoliberal goals of continued economic growth and productivity, while their vulnerability to ill health, poverty, and exclusion from services are noted as grounds for interventions to promote human rights and social development. These competing yet complementary ideas about older people's roles reflect another broad tension about their exceptionality or commonality with other population groups. In the following sections, I discuss the ways in which these tensions have played out in policy responses to global ageing.

3. Early International Responses to Population Ageing

The first documented reference to older people's needs in the context of global development dates from 1948, when a 'Declaration of Old Age Rights' was proposed at the United Nations General Assembly.[66] The declaration was never ratified, and nearly thirty years passed until the next major discussion on the subject at the United Nations, reflecting the low priority placed on responding to global ageing at a time when high fertility and rapid population growth in poor countries were the main demographic concerns. The subject of ageing resurfaced in the 1970s, and Resolution 33/52 in 1978 called on the United Nations to convene a 'World Assembly on the Elderly' in 1982. The purpose of the assembly was 'to launch an international action program aimed at guaranteeing economic and social security to older persons, as well as opportunities to contribute to national development'.[67] In subsequent Resolution 35/129 in 1980, the General Assembly further indicated its desire that the planned World Assembly 'should result in societies responding more fully to the socioeconomic implications of the aging of populations and to the specific needs of older persons'.[68]

The dual concern with, on the one hand, the welfare of older individuals and, on the other, the societal implications of ageing populations, was central to the discussions at the 1982 World Assembly on Ageing, which took place in Vienna. The assembly

64 J. Knodel and C. Saengtienchai, 'Older Aged Parents: The Final Safety Net for Adult Sons and Daughters with AIDS in Thailand' (2005) 26(5) *Journal of Family Issues* 665; M.G. Merli and A. Palloni, 'The HIV/AIDS Epidemic, Kin Relations, Living Arrangements, and the Elderly in South Africa' in B. Cohen and J. Menken (eds), *Aging in Sub-Saharan Africa: Recommendations for Furthering Research* (Washington, DC: National Academies Press, 2006).

65 Lloyd-Sherlock, 'Ageing and International Development' (n 41).

66 M. Gorman, 'Development and the Rights of Older People' in HelpAge International (ed), *The Ageing and Development Report* (London: Earthscan, 1999).

67 See <http://www.undemocracy.com/A-RES-33-52>.

68 See <http://daccess-ods.un.org/TMP/7684242.72537231.html>.

culminated in the adoption of the Vienna International Plan of Action on Ageing, which enumerated sixty-two recommendations for research, data collection and analysis, training and education, as well as policies and programs important to the well-being of older individuals and populations.

With regard to older individuals, the Vienna Plan's stated aim was to guide the development and application 'at the international, regional and national levels . . . [of] policies designed to enhance the lives of the aging as individuals and to allow them to enjoy in mind and in body, fully and freely, their advancing years in peace, health and security'. The plan's recommendations thus focused on health and nutrition, protection of elderly consumers, housing and environment, family, social welfare, income security and employment, and education.

In discussing ageing on the population level, however, the tone was quite different, focusing on the negative impact of population ageing on national economies at a time when dependency ratios were growing. The Plan noted that:

> . . . the trend towards the successive aging of population structures is bound to be one of the main challenges to international and national planning efforts during the last decades of this century and well into the twenty-first . . . attention should be given to the vast and multifaceted impact which the aging of populations will have on the structure, functioning and further development of all societies of the world. The role of the public and private sectors in assuming responsibility for some of the functions now provided by the family in low-income countries will probably have to increase under such circumstances.

On the aggregate front, then, the focus on forthcoming economic burdens coexisted with a lack of accounting of older people's economic contribution. Notably, health, although mentioned as a priority area in the discussion of older individuals, received little mention in the context of global population ageing. Here, the discussion focused almost exclusively on the presumed negative economic consequences of demographic changes.

In the early 1980s, ageing was still considered mainly a rich-country phenomenon, and this was reflected in the Vienna Plan's concentration on pension and social security policies in developed countries with established welfare systems. The relatively brief consideration of ageing in low-income countries was heavily influenced by modernization and ageing theory.[69] This theory was developed in the 1960s[70] and 1970s[71] as a specific case of a more general modernization theory,[72] which posited a linear, uniform transition from 'traditional' to 'modern' societies, equated contemporary low-income nations with historical, pre-industrialized western ones, and presumed that after their inevitable eventual transformation, less developed countries would come to resemble their more advanced counterparts. Modernization and ageing theory focused on the demographic transition observed in Europe and North America, and anticipated a similar rise in the absolute number and proportion of older people in the populations of low-income countries. It also predicted the diffusion of secularism and individualistic values, leading to a gradual erosion of traditional family support structures. This was

[69] S. Neysmith and J. Edwardh, 'Ideological underpinnings of the World Assembly on Aging' (1983) 2 *Canadian Journal on Aging* 125.

[70] E.W. Burgess (ed), *Ageing in Western Societies* (Chicago, IL: University of Chicago Press, 1960).

[71] D.O. Cowgill, 'Ageing and Modernization: A Revision of the Theory' in J.F. Gubrium (ed), *Late Life* (Springfield, IL: Thomas, 1974) 123.

[72] W.W. Rostow, *The Stages of Economic Growth* (Cambridge: CUP, 1960); W.J. Goode, *World Revolution in Family Patterns* (New York: Free Press, 1963).

expected to result in a loss of support and security as well as a decline in social status for older people. Under this scenario, older people's knowledge would become obsolete in increasingly industrialized and technologically driven societies, and they would end up marginalized, abandoned by their families, and therefore increasingly dependent on the state or on charitable organizations. Poor nations, however, would not be able to provide adequate support for older people, given their limited resources and lack of formal welfare structures. Furthermore, the attempts to deal with the burden of an ageing population would potentially impede their continued economic development.

Theoretical critiques, beginning in the 1980s, exposed the fallacy of assuming and therefore predicting a uniform and inevitable course of development throughout the world, and empirical studies both historical and contemporary likewise challenged the dichotomy drawn between traditional societies that value their elderly and modern ones that discard them.[73] Contrary to premises of modernization theory, the past was neither so golden for older people nor the present so dire.[74] There is also, to date, no evidence indicating that population ageing itself undermines economic development.

Nonetheless, the bleak predictions of modernization theory and the focus on the negative economic consequences of population ageing continued to dominate discourse and practice for several decades. The Vienna Plan was thus an attempt to reconcile the protection of older individuals with the advancement of development programs, two goals then thought to be in conflict because population ageing was viewed as a fundamental economic and social problem. By embracing modernization and ageing theory, the plan implicitly discounted their existing and potential contributions and emphasized only their need for charity and assistance from governments and humanitarian organizations. In the global context, the plan's recommendations were driven by concern with the crisis that would unfold in low-income countries as family support systems failed in the absence of the formal care mechanisms that exist in industrialized countries. While the plan's recommendations laid out laudable policy goals for the protection of older people alongside the promotion of continued economic development, it did not offer specific legal mechanisms for accomplishing these goals and left much to be addressed by regional, national, and local administrations.

4. From Vienna to Madrid: Understanding Global Ageing

Since the first Assembly and the Vienna Plan, research in the social and health sciences has helped to create a more nuanced and less stereotypical portrait of ageing populations. In 1983, a group of NGOs dedicated to assisting older people in Canada, Colombia, Kenya, India, and the United Kingdom created HelpAge International, a network dedicated to supporting older people worldwide through research, advocacy, and partnerships with service-providers. HelpAge International now partners with organizations in sixty countries, and its advocacy arm has been instrumental in connecting the issue of global ageing—with a focus on low-income and transitional economies—to mainstream development agendas. It has also worked to shift prevailing

[73] Merli and Palloni, 'The HIV/AIDS Epidemic' (n 64); J. Treas and B. Logue, 'Economic Development and the Older Population' (1986) 12(4) *Population and Development Review* 645; I. Aboderin, 'Modernisation and Ageing Theory Revisited: Current Explanations of Recent Developing World and Historical Western Shifts in Material Family Support for Older People' (2004) 24 *Ageing and Society* 29.

[74] V.W. Marshall, S.H. Matthews, and C.J. Rosenthal, 'The Elusiveness of Family Life: A Challenge for the Sociology of Aging' (1993) 13 *Annual Review of Gerontology and Geriatrics* 39.

views of ageing as liability to a more positive sense of population ageing as both an opportunity and a challenge.

Bringing about this shift required the collection and presentation of data that, on one hand, described older people's poverty, vulnerability, and marginalization, and, on the other, highlighted their productivity and contributions to family and community. The results spoke to existing mainstream development goals, including the reduction of poverty and protection for the most vulnerable as well as the promotion of productivity and human capital.[75] Older people's vulnerability to poverty, poor health, and limited support from families and communities have been documented in a series of ongoing participatory studies with older individuals and focus groups in low-income countries and those, like members of the former Soviet Union, undergoing rapid economic and social changes.[76] These studies highlight age-associated physical, mental, and social changes as well as the impact of economic stress, dramatic sociocultural transitions, and crises such as natural disasters, epidemics, and armed conflict. They underscore the need for old-age economic security policies and also note the lack of appropriate health services and social supports for older people.[77] Additional evidence documents some older people's problems with violence and abuse in their own homes and in institutional settings, and the restrictions they face in making decisions about their personal finances, property, or medical care and accessing social security, health resources, work, food, and housing.[78]

Other studies have tracked older people's contributions across multiple domains. Economic analyses revealed that older people's income—whether from continued participation in the labour force or from pensions (including non-contributory or social pensions implemented in settings like South Africa and Brazil) is often used to the benefit of multiple generations in the family.[79] In particular, older people have been shown to use their money to pay for grandchildren's school fees and supplies—leading to increases in school enrolment and reductions in child labour. They also help to provide for other family members' healthcare needs, thereby reducing poverty and promoting the well-being of multiple generations.[80] Less formally, older people provide care for adult children or other close family members affected by HIV/AIDS, and increasingly serve as primary guardians for grandchildren whose parents have migrated for work or succumbed to the pandemic.[81] Older people thus continue to act as educators, homemakers, and caregivers, providing support to younger generations at a time in their lives when they previously might have expected to draw on the support of others. Research has also highlighted the persistence of family ties. Rather than breaking down, as predicted by modernization theory, families appear to be adapting to rapidly changing socioeconomic realities, with adult children remaining older people's

75 Folbre, *The Invisible Heart* (n 31).

76 HelpAge International, *Participatory Research with Older People: A Sourcebook* (London: HelpAge International, 2002).

77 M. Gorman and A. Heslop. 'Poverty, Policy, Reciprocity and Older People in the South' (2002) 14 *Journal of International Development* 1143; A Barrientos and P. Lloyd-Sherlock, 'Older and Poorer? Ageing and Poverty in the South' (2002) 14 *Journal of International Development* 1129.

78 United Nations, 'Situation of the Rights of Older People in all Regions of the World', Report of the Secretary General, A/66/173 (2011), available at <http://www.ohchr.org/EN/Issues/OlderPersons/Pages/Reports.aspx>.

79 HelpAge International, 'Age and Security: How Social Pension Can Deliver Effective Aid to Poor Older People and Their Families' (London, 2004).

80 Chowdhury, 'The Giver or the Recipient?' (n 12).

81 M. Ferreira, 'HIV/AIDS and Older People in Sub-Saharan Africa: Towards a Policy Framework' (2006) 4(2) *Global Ageing* 56.

primary sources of support and participating in a complex dynamic of intergenerational transfers.[82]

The challenge facing advocates thus involved countering the prevailing simplified and largely negative depictions of older people and of the societal implications of population ageing, while at the same time raising awareness of the very real needs and vulnerabilities of many older people. Advocates for older people have thus argued that governments must invest in older people both because of their duty to uphold their human and civil rights and because of their obligation to protect the vulnerable. As an added benefit, they point out, providing support to older people seems to also positively impact children and younger adults in the family.

Progress on the policy and programmatic side, however, was slow. In December 1990, the UN General Assembly passed Resolution 45/106, noting that the resources assigned to the UN Programme on Ageing were not sufficient for implementing its goals or raising the profile of global ageing as a priority issue, and that contributions to the Trust Fund for Ageing had declined since the Vienna Assembly in 1982. More optimistically, the resolution asserted, 'the elderly are an asset to society and can contribute significantly to the development process', and designated 1 October as 'International Day of Older Persons' to be commemorated annually.[83]

The next year, the United Nations passed Resolution 46/91 calling on governments to incorporate five *Principles for Older Persons* into their national programs on ageing. These *Principles* included independence (asserting older persons' rights to basic care as well as family and community support and access to education, work, or other income-generating opportunities, and safe and adaptable living environments); participation in society (including opportunities for informing policies, performing community service, and forming organizations); access to care from family and community in accordance with each society's cultural values (including health care, social and legal services, and, when needed, institutional care in humane and secure environments; self-fulfillment (including access to educational, cultural, spiritual, and recreational resources); and dignity (including freedom from exploitation, abuse, and prejudice). Signaling a deliberate change in rhetoric from one emphasizing costs to another emphasizing rights, the *Principles* specifically mentioned that older people should 'be valued independently of their economic contribution'.[84]

In 1992, the United Nations convened an international conference to commemorate the tenth anniversary of the Vienna Plan. The conference led to Resolution 47/5, which called for the observance of an *International Year of Older Persons* in 1999 'in recognition of humanity's demographic coming of age and the promise it holds for maturing attitudes and capabilities in social, economic, cultural, and spiritual undertakings, not least for global peace and development in the next century'.[85] This language signalled a change in attitude towards old people and the implications of population ageing, and the *Year* activities—ranging from academic conferences and policy meetings to cultural festivals and grassroots gatherings—were organized under the motto 'towards a society

82 A. Hashimoto, 'Family Relations in Later Life: A Cross-Cultural Perspective' (1993) 17 *Generations* 24; K.M. Yount, S.A. Cunningham, M. Engelman, and E.M. Agree, 'Gender and Material Transfers between Older Parents and Children in Ismailia, Egypt' (2012) 74(1) *Journal of Marriage and Family* 116.

83 See <http://www.un.org/documents/ga/res/45/a45r106.htm>.

84 Office of the United Nations High Commissioner on Human Rights (OHCHR), 'United Nations Principles for Older Persons', adopted by General Assembly Resolution 46/91 of 16 December 1991.

85 See <http://www.undemocracy.com/A-RES-47-5>.

for all ages',[86] calling for solidarity, respect, and exchanges between generations, pairing them in a joint venture rather than pitting them in competition. The *Year*'s activities were organized around four themes that would continue to shape ageing policy and program discourses in the years to come: individual lifelong development; multigenerational relationships; interrelationships between population ageing and development; and the situation of older persons. In 1995, the UN International Committee on Economic, Social and Cultural Rights released General Comment No 6 on 'the economic social and cultural rights of older persons', which explains that the omission of 'age' as an illegal ground of discrimination in the 1966 International Convention on Economic, Social and Cultural Rights was not intentional, but rather occurred because at the time of the adoption of these conventions 'the problem of demographic ageing was not as evident or pressing'[87] as it later became. In 2009, the same committee noted more decisively in General Comment No 20 that 'age is a prohibited ground of discrimination'.[88]

A similar change of orientation was taking place within the World Health Organization. In 1995, the WHO changed the name of its Health of the Elderly program to Ageing and Health, reflecting a perspective that recognizes the influence of early and mid-life events on well-being in later life and emphasizes disease prevention and health promotion throughout the life course as a key to healthy ageing. In 2000, the program name was changed again, to Ageing and the Life Course, highlighting the integration of ageing into a broader, developmental view of health and placing a greater emphasis on the concept of active ageing.[89] The WHO also created a Regional Adviser on Ageing position in each regional office, marking a greater commitment to understanding and addressing issues related to health and ageing in a variety of cultural, social, and economic contexts. These changes reflect ongoing efforts to recast policies and programs focused on older persons as part of, rather than challenges to, overall development strategies.

The influence of the accumulated research findings and advocacy efforts highlighting the heterogeneous experiences, contributions, and vulnerabilities of older adults was evident by the time the Second World Assembly on Ageing was convened in Madrid in April 2002 to review the progress since the Vienna Assembly and assess the impact of demographic, economic, and technological developments (for example demographic change in low-income countries, new geo-political and economic configurations, economies in transition, the information revolution and its resultant digital divide, and the HIV/AIDS epidemic) that shape and interact with population ageing.

The Second World Assembly brought together representatives from 156 nations and culminated in the adoption of updated international consensus documents on ageing, including a Political Declaration (PD) and the Madrid International Plan of Action on Ageing (MIPAA), expressly designed to refine and replace the1982 Vienna Plan.[90] The

[86] See <http://www.unac.org/iyop/>.

[87] Committee on Economic, Social and Cultural Rights (CESCR): General Comment No 6, 'The economic, social and cultural rights of older persons' (August 1995) para 11, available at <http://social.un.org/ageing-working-group/documents.shtml>.

[88] Committee on Economic, Social and Cultural Rights (CESCR): General Comment No 20, 'The economic, social and cultural rights of older persons' (June 2009) para 29, available at <http://social.un.org/ageing-working-group/documents.shtml>.

[89] A. Kalache, 'The World Health Organization and Global Aging' in M. Robinson, W. Novelli, C. Pearson, and L. Norris (eds), *Global Health and Global Aging* (San Francisco, CA: Jossey-Bass, 2007) 31.

[90] A. Sidorenko and A. Walker, 'The Madrid International Plan of Action on Ageing: From Conception to Implementation' (2004) 24(2) *Ageing and Society* 147.

PD highlighted three priority directions: issues related to older persons and development, the protection and promotion of health and well-being into old age, and the creation and maintenance of enabling and supportive environments. The MIPAA expands on the three priority directions by detailing a series of issues and objectives as well as 239 specific recommendations to guide both policy-making and program development. Together, the PD and MIPAA give particular prominence to ageing in low-income countries and economies in transition, emphasizing the challenge of simultaneously addressing ageing and poverty and highlighting the need to assure basic necessities (for example income and health), as well as providing opportunities for fulfillment, well-being, and empowerment. In doing so, the MIPAA takes up the position that population ageing and societal development are parallel processes (rather than countervailing ones, as implied in the Vienna Plan) that should be both compatible and, ideally, synergistic.[91]

While the Vienna Plan viewed the welfare of older people as a humanitarian issue, the PD and MIPAA replace what has been termed 'compassionate ageism'[92] with acceptance of older people's rights to equal treatment, self-determination, and inclusion. The Madrid documents state and affirm commitments to the elimination of age-based discrimination (along with violence, neglect, and abuse of older persons), the incorporation of older people's concerns into economic and social development policies, the recognition of older persons' dignity, and the protection of their human rights in general. Reflecting a more positive attitude towards ageing, the MIPAA asserts that 'persons, as they age, should enjoy a life of fulfillment, health, security and active participation in the economic, social, cultural and political life of their societies'.

While the financial concerns that dominated the Vienna Plan remain prominent,[93] the MIPAA is notable in explicitly linking ageing to social and economic development strategies[94] and articulating older people's rights to full social and political participation in both poor and rich countries. The MIPAA calls for the mainstreaming of ageing issues into major national policy domains and development efforts—including education, health, employment, and finance, among others, as well as attention to ageing-specific concerns including pensions, long-term care, and healthcare services. The plan further recommends international cooperation via research, training, and capacity-building projects, and calls for support of older people's grass-roots organizations and initiatives designed to promote security and dignity throughout the life course into older ages.

While signaling an important change in international responses to population ageing, the MIPAA is a non-binding document, and the scope and structure of its implementation is left entirely up to individual governments and the partnerships they might forge with civil society and private sector actors. Deliberately broad to allow for cross-country differences in economic development, historical and cultural traditions, political opinions, social diversity, and levels of population ageing, the plan was intended to guide implementation strategies developed by regional commissions, national governments, and local agencies as they work to influence the ways in which

91 Sidorenko, 'World Policies on Aging and the United Nations' (n 10).

92 Sidorenko and Walker, 'The Madrid International Plan of Action on Ageing' (n 90).

93 J.A. Vincent, 'Globalization and Critical Theory: Political Economy of World Population Issues' in J. Baars, D. Dannefer, C. Phillipson, and A. Walker (eds), *Aging, Globalization, and Inequality* (Amityville, NY: Baywood, 2006) 260.

94 United Nations, Report of the Secretary-General, 'Follow-up to the Second World Assembly on Ageing', A/58/160 (2003).

their societies view, interact with, and support their older citizens. Whilst the language of human rights is featured throughout, the MIPAA is thus more focused on general principles and aspirational goals than on enforceable rights or policies. In this, it is a 'soft law'—a document encoding norms that are broadly accepted by their signatories but which lacks mechanisms to assure the implementation of the commitments it states.[95]

5. Towards an International Convention on the Rights of Older People?

The change in rhetoric between the Vienna and Madrid plans reflects a paradigm shift in the broader worlds of development and global health practice. The shift to a new rights-based agenda for development took place in response to critics who urged a theoretical re-direction away from a reductionist focus on national economic growth towards a more holistic account of human capabilities, freedoms, and well-being,[96] as well as concerns about failures on the part of international development agencies to effect positive changes in low-income countries.[97] The alliance between development and human rights is apparent in the new terminology of development discourse, in the addition of human rights objectives to the goals and evaluation criteria of development agencies, and in the redefinition of development itself in human rights terms. Thus, rather than underscoring a tension between concern for human rights and economic development, the new paradigm positions development and the promotion of human rights as mutually reinforcing processes. The 1986 Declaration on the Right to Development embodied this new perspective in asserting that development itself is a human right to 'participate in, contribute to and enjoy economic, social and cultural and political development'.[98]

Human rights—moral rights possessed by all people—are inherently egalitarian in upholding the value and dignity of *all* human life. The universal nature of human rights means that they can neither be granted or denied, and they are international in scope, and not contingent upon a nation's economic status or the capacity of a given government to provide basic human needs to its citizens.[99] Whilst the international human rights community initially focused primarily on civil and political rights, there is growing attention to economic, social, and cultural rights, and an emerging recognition that all human rights—including the right to health, the right to a decent standard of living, and the rights to education, freedom, and participation—are interrelated and indivisible.[100] Human rights offer a useful framework for a discussion of global ageing, health, and justice because they both articulate and address the social determinants of health and because they cannot cease to apply after a certain age. An ethical framework founded on human rights has served as the basis for proposals for an age-integrated approach to resource allocation in low-income countries[101] and for advocacy at levels

95 M. Fredvang and S. Biggs, 'The Rights of Older Persons: Protection and Gaps under Human Rights Law', Brotherhood of St Laurence and the University of Melbourne Center for Public Policy, Social Policy Working Paper No 16, August 2012.

96 Sen, *Development As Freedom* (n 11).

97 Hickey and Mitlin, 'The Potential and Pitfalls of Rights-Based Approaches' (n 13).

98 See <http://www.un.org/documents/ga/res/41/a41r128.htm>.

99 L.O. Gostin. 'Beyond Moral Claims: A Human Rights Approach to Mental Health' (2001) 10 *Cambridge Quarterly of Healthcare Ethics* 264.

100 S. Gruskin, G. Annas, M. Grodin, and S. Marks, *Perspectives on Health and Human Rights* (New York: Routledge, 2005).

101 Engelman and Johnson, 'Population Aging and International Development' (n 48).

ranging from local programs to international guidelines for addressing population ageing.[102]

Advocates for the broader rights-based development movement argued that such an orientation will lead to greater accountability from governments and make development institutions more equitable as well as more effective. However, the precise meaning and implications of 'rights-based development' remain contested, with different international actors disagreeing over definitions and about the precise nature of the relationship between development and human rights: the World Bank, for example, views human rights as outcomes of development assistance (for example programs promoting education, health, nutrition, food security, housing, and gender equity, among others), while the United Nations and various NGOs argue that human rights are essential precursors for achieving development goals.[103]

The human rights movement also has its critics, who point out that human rights are often vague and rarely enforceable; that they are more symbolic than substantive; that they simplistically impose Western individual-centered notions of well-being rather than promoting broader, collaborative social justice measures; and that, while they were meant to protect individuals from states, their enforcement relies solely on states.[104] Most significantly for the rights-based development movement, critics have argued that human rights are simply a new form of liberal imperialism that allows existing powerful groups to occupy a moral high ground while pursuing their global capitalist agendas. They note that human rights are simply compatible with and subservient to contemporary neo-liberal development thinking, rather than an ethical framework that challenges it.[105]

Whilst acknowledging the moral force of many of these criticisms, defenders of human rights and their use in development contexts point out that the pragmatic value of the human rights approach lies in its ability to limit political violence, prevent suffering, and improve the security and well-being of ordinary people, thereby fostering a better and more sustainable human development.[106] Others note that changing the discourse of development to include human rights language is useful as a first step in a longer-term process of change by influencing perceptions and reshaping both incentive structures and the parameters of acceptable and unacceptable actions.[107] In the case of global ageing, the human rights perspective, as embodied in the MIPAA, has become a prevalent and largely uncontested point of departure, with both ethical and instrumental arguments marshaled by advocates in calling for more attention to the circumstances of older people in low-income countries. Advocates for older persons working within a human rights framework focus on promoting equality, security, and nondiscrimination, and call for the removal of barriers and the broadening of opportunities.[108]

102 UNDESA, 'Report of the Second World Assembly on Ageing', Madrid, 8–12 April 2002 (2002), available at <http://social.un.org/index/Ageing/MadridPlanofActionanditsImplementation/SecondAssemblyonAgeing.aspx>.

103 Manzo, 'Africa in the Rise of Rights-Based Development' (n 13).

104 Ignatieff, *Human Rights as Politics and Idolatry* (n 12); Chowdhury, 'The Giver or the Recipient?' (n 12); W. Brown 'The Most We Can Hope For . . .': Human Rights and the Politics of Fatalism (2004) 103(2/3) *South Atlantic Quarterly* 451.

105 P. Uvin, 'On High Moral Ground: The Incorporation of Human Rights by the Development Enterprise' (2002) 27 *Praxis: The Fletcher Journal of Development Studies* 1.

106 Ignatieff, *Human Rights as Politics and Idolatry* (n 12).

107 Uvin, 'On High Moral Ground' (n 105).

108 HelpAge International, 'Equal Treatment, Equal Rights' (London, 2001).

Perhaps unsurprisingly, the implementation of MIPAA recommendations in the aftermath of the Second World Assembly has been uneven.[109] Older people remain a low priority for governments, donors, and international development and aid agencies. Most legal systems have not recognized the rights of older people as such, and do not provide protection from age discrimination and lack of equal access to healthcare, social services, and income security. Furthermore, the few policies and programs that do exist tend to depict older people as passive recipients of benefits and services rather than promoting active ageing with full participation in society.[110] This is consistent with the usual framing of issues related to ageing via medical and welfare service lenses, rather than the broader lens of justice, dignity, and human rights. In response, advocates have called for a specific convention on the human rights of older people, hoping that international law can enhance the authority and influence of older people's claims against human rights violations. In 2009, the Human Rights Council Advisory Committee commissioned a study on the human rights of older persons, and in 2010 the UN General Assembly established the Open-Ended Working Group (OEWG) on Ageing, which is tasked with evaluating the current international human rights framework for older persons, identifying gaps in it, and suggesting ways of addressing them.[111]

Whilst the rights of older people can be deduced from existing human rights instruments such as the Universal Declaration of Human Rights (UDHR), the International Covenant on Civil and Political Rights (ICCPR), and the International Covenant on Economic, Social and Cultural Rights (ICESCR), advocates frequently note that there is a gap in the international human rights system concerning older people.[112] The three instruments, together known as the International Bill of Human Rights, offer general protection of cultural, economic, social, civil, and political rights. They cover rights that matter to older persons (such as rights related to work, social security, adequate standard of living, education, and highest attainable standards of physical and mental health), but despite the fact that these human rights treaties implicitly apply to older persons just as they do to others, there are no direct references to older persons in the three texts of the Bill, and little mention of older people in follow-up reports that monitor and evaluate states' concordance with the treaties.[113] While Article 25 of the UDHR—which also directly addresses motherhood and childhood—does guarantee the 'right to security in the event of... old age', it does not single out that phase of the life course as 'entitled to special care and assistance', as it does motherhood and childhood.[114] The ICESCR[115] echoes the UDHR's explicit protections of mothers and children, and the ICCPR[116] singles out children for special consideration repeatedly—but neither convention mentions old age or older populations.

Whilst other vulnerable groups, including women, children, migrant workers, and people with disabilities are all protected through special international conventions or standards, there is no similarly dedicated instrument for the protection of older people's

109 UNDESA, 'The Madrid International Plan of Action on Ageing: Guiding Framework and Toolkit for Practitioners and Policy Makers' (2008).

110 UN General Secretary's report, 'Follow-up to the Second World Assembly on Ageing', A/64/127 (2009).

111 For more information on the UN OEWG see <http://social.un.org/ageing-working-group>.

112 UNDESA, 'Current Status of the Social Situation, Wellbeing, Participation in Development and Rights of Older People Worldwide' (New York, 2011) 3.

113 Sidorenko and Walker, 'The Madrid International Plan of Action on Ageing' (n 90).

114 See <http://www.un.org/en/documents/udhr/index.shtml#a25>.

115 See <http://www2.ohchr.org/english/acprof:oso/cescr.htm>.

116 See <http://www2.ohchr.org/english/acprof:oso/ccpr.htm>.

rights and no specific international body with a mandate to focus on the rights of older people.[117] The concern of advocates, then, is that the needs of older people are likely to continue being overlooked within a broad human rights framework, requiring a separate Convention on the Rights of Older Persons.

The proposed convention raises both conceptual and operational challenges. The previously-mentioned tension between older people's heterogeneous portrayal as contributing members of society as well as particularly vulnerable individuals brings up questions about their need for protections beyond the universally applicable human rights. The former image suggests that older people are care providers and engaged citizens capable of advancing development goals and should not be treated differently from other adults simply because they have passed an arbitrary chronological threshold. If older people are sufficiently covered by existing guarantees, a new convention for yet another subgroup would simply fragment or dilute the universalism of human rights. On the other hand, the reality of ageism and discrimination based on older people's physical appearance, disability, and functional limitations suggest they do need special protections beyond those afforded to individuals not burdened by age-related stigma. Indeed, those arguing for more explicit attention to older people's rights note that old age on its own does not diminish older people's access to the basic resources guaranteed by existing treaties; rather, pervasive social ideas *about* old age lead to older people being denied the full enjoyment of their rights.[118]

Another objection warns that drawing added attention to older adults may erect new age barriers that increase their marginalization.[119] Negative attitudes towards old age and older people are deeply ingrained in many societies, but unlike many other forms of prejudice, ageism is rarely challenged and in fact is widely tolerated as unproblematic or even natural. This leads to discriminatory behaviours at both interpersonal and institutional levels, and results in older people's isolation and exclusion.[120] Old age interacts with other identity categories like race, gender, ethnicity, class, or disability status, but is not subsumed by them, and older people may thus experience distinct and disproportionate violations of numerous rights. Those arguing in favour of a convention note that it is the unique experiences of older people coupled with relative indifference to their circumstances by international and local organizations that warrants a more tailored response beyond the general protections of current international laws.[121] Indeed, advocates posit that the process of creating and disseminating a new convention (much like the process resulting in the Convention on the Rights of Persons with Disabilities) would bring greater visibility to the issues of population ageing and older people's special contributions and vulnerabilities, signaling that these issues merit attention and a greater degree of priority than they have received to date.[122]

In discussions about the feasibility of a new convention, representatives of nations including the United States, the European Union, China, and Russia, have argued that a stronger use of existing human rights instruments like the *Principles* and the MIPAA is

117 D. Rodriguez-Pinzon and C. Martin, 'The International Human Rights Status of Elderly Persons' (2003) 18 *American University International Law Review* 915.

118 I. Doron and I. Apter, 'The Debate Around the Need for an International Convention on the Rights of Older Persons' (2010) 50(5) *The Gerontologist* 586.

119 Fredvang and Biggs, 'The Rights of Older Persons' (n 95).

120 Report of the United Nations High Commissioner for Human Rights, 20 April 2012, E/2012/51, at 4.

121 F. Mégret, 'The Human Rights of Older Persons: A Growing Challenge' (2011) 11(1) *Human Rights Law Review* 37.

122 R.E. Morgan and S. David, 'Human Rights: A New Language for Aging Advocacy' (2002) 42 *The Gerontologist* 436.

more prudent than investing scarce resources, time, and energy into a convention that will (inevitably) lack the power of enforcement or sanction. They see a tradeoff between a superficial adoption of a new treaty and the implementation new service programs. Indeed, even advocates for a convention would like greater investment in ageing-related resources and more policies and programs targeting older people. However, there is an important distinction to be drawn between a service-based and a rights-based approach to addressing global ageing, and a major goal of advocates has been to shift the image of older people from passive charity recipients to holders of fundamental rights.

Advocates for a convention argue that drawing attention to older people will strengthen the struggle against ageism by confronting age-blindness (the exclusion of older people due to a lack of prioritization of their rights), and raise awareness of the prevalence and extent of age discrimination, neglect, and abuse. Though enforcement will certainly be a challenge, a convention would serve as a stimulus for change and go beyond the MIPAA's soft law to create more tangible obligations for states to establish legislation, procedures, and institutions to monitor, protect, promote, and ensure the rights of older people. In December 2012, the UN General Assembly considered Resolution 67/139, entitled 'Towards a comprehensive and integral international legal instrument to promote and protect the rights and dignity of older persons.' The recorded vote—54 in favour to 5 against, with 118 abstentions—clearly shows that a consensus position on a new Convention on the rights of older persons remains elusive.

6. Conclusion

Our understanding of the relationship between economic development processes and later-life experiences remains incomplete. Chronological thresholds can mean quite different things in the context of vastly disparate life experiences, and the rapidly changing circumstances of living arrangements, family formation, education, work and more broadly the life course in many low-income countries present challenges for the construction of informed and effective policies. Both globally and within a variety of national and local contexts, ageing populations require policies and institutions that will allow a dignified quality of life for those lucky enough to survive to old ages. Notably, doing this will require not only the allocation of substantial resources, but also a rethinking and potentially restructuring of current priorities in the fields of global health and development.

Alarmist generalizations and stereotypes are pervasive, but the realities of ageing are heterogeneous and nuanced. Early awareness of global population ageing triggered fears of economic collapse—or at least a slowing down of economic developments—but decades of research and advocacy have begun to shift the discourse towards ways of fostering the continued health, independence, and the social, economic, and civic participation of older people. While pension reform has dominated the discourse on global ageing and economic development, more attention to health promotion throughout the life course, disease prevention, and the postponement of disability in old age is essential for advancing the well-being of older people themselves and for their families and communities.

While population ageing poses challenges to existing (or in some cases, nascent) welfare and medical infrastructures, it may also serve as an impetus for shaping policies that encourage generations to live together more cohesively, recognize each others' vulnerabilities and contributions alike, and support each other to a fuller extent. The life course perspective inevitably leads advocates for older people to characterize their needs and contributions within a framework that includes all other age groups both in the family and in the broader community. Thus, public support for the old and the young may interact in mutually beneficial ways rather than in competition, because generations are interconnected.

Thoughtfully designed policies are essential both for realizing the generative potential inherent in the world's longevity revolution and for advancing health and well-being across the full life course. Whether or not the human rights perspective on global ageing is written into international law, the political influence of older people (and their advocates) is beginning to catch up to their constituent numbers, suggesting that attention to, and prioritization of, their concerns in all realms is likely to increase. Ideally, this will help narrow the persistent gap between the socioeconomic and epidemiological changes that produce population ageing and the age-stratified social structures, norms, and policies that have inflexibly lagged behind.

19

Libertarian Paternalism and Public Health Nudges

Stephen Holland

Libertarian paternalism has become an important approach to behaviour modification. In practice, libertarian paternalism amounts to employing behavioural techniques to nudge people to choose options that are in their own best interests, whilst keeping any cost of resisting a nudge very low. Advocates present this as a way of getting people to benefit themselves without restricting their freedom. This approach is discussed in theoretical and practical terms. Theoretically, the important challenges to libertarian paternalism are from a libertarian perspective. This chapter argues that standard libertarian objections—based on, for example, slippery slopes and redistributive effects—are not in themselves fatal to the approach but do raise a serious question: are public nudges compatible with the account of the just state presented by libertarianism? Regarding libertarian paternalism in practice, various applications of the approach to public health are critiqued with a view to teasing out some general constraints. It is argued that public health nudges are inappropriate where there is a distinctive sort of clinical uncertainty, where choice scenarios are governed by legal strictures, and where behaviour is addictive or otherwise compulsive.

1. Introduction

1.1 Public health paternalism

Public health is concerned with protecting and promoting the health of populations of people by collective action, as opposed to the encounter between individual patients and doctors which is the focus of clinical medicine. In practice, public health comprises specific interventions, underpinned by epidemiological research. These include established and ongoing preventive programmes of screening and testing, mass immunization, and health surveillance; health promotion efforts, such as health education campaigns and attempts to change health behaviour; and sporadic responses to unusual conditions and new health threats, notably, outbreaks of contagious diseases such as SARS.

A crucial ethical point about public health programmes is that, in order to be effective, they are intrusive in the lives of members of the target population. Programmes are liberty-limiting when they compromise individual rights, choice, and freedoms, and coercive when they force people to behave contrary to their preferences. This ethical tension is increased when public health programmes are devised and implemented by the state, and sanctioned by law enforcement agencies with legal powers. That public health is an exercise of state power raises central questions of political philosophy: what sort of state is just; what grounds the authority of the state; what sorts and extent of state intervention are legitimate? Such issues are addressed not in a vacuum but in the context of a political system, and it is assumed throughout this discussion that public health is practised in a political culture dominated by liberalism, broadly construed. Notwithstanding definitional disputes, all liberals emphasize the right of individuals to self-determination and are suspicious of state intrusion. So, the ethical problematic centres on the justifiability of state sanctioned, liberty-limiting public health programmes in a liberal context.[1]

Given this, it is natural to look for resources within the liberal tradition to justify intrusive public health programmes. Here there is an important distinction between interventions in terms of how they are intended to protect and promote the health of populations. The first sort of programme imposes on individuals for the sake of others; they are intended to get people to act in ways that will benefit, or refrain from acting in ways that will harm, others. For example, if an outbreak of a contagious disease is shown to be sufficiently dangerous, infected patients might be isolated; if herd immunity is threatened, policy might switch from an opt-in system of voluntary participation to mandatory vaccination. The second sort of programme protects and promotes the health of populations by imposing on people, not for the sake of others, but for the individual's own sake; they are intended to get people to act in ways that will benefit, or refrain from acting in ways that will harm, themselves. Health promotion activities are public health interventions of this latter sort; central to health promotion is behaviour modification, that is, getting people to behave in ways conducive to their own wellbeing.[2]

The major theoretical resource within the liberal tradition with which to justify state sanctioned, liberty-limiting, public health interventions is Mill's harm principle but the principle applies differently to each of the two sorts of public health programmes just distinguished. The principle asserts that the state is justified in coercing individuals in order to avoid third party harms (that is, to prevent harm to others): 'the only purpose for which power can be rightfully exercised over any member of a civilised community, against his will, is to prevent harm to others'.[3] This provides some justification for public health programmes (in the form of a necessary condition) of the first sort distinguished earlier, namely, those that impose on individuals in order to prevent harms to others. By contrast, the second sort of intervention distinguished previously constitutes state paternalism, that is, interference by the state to get people to benefit or

1 S. Holland, *Public Health Ethics* (Cambridge: Polity Press, 2007). Public health programmes are not always or inevitably liberty-limiting. On the other hand, this is not the only ethical problematic created by public health's population perspective. For example, surveying populations of people reveals inequalities in health status and access to health care services which are not apparent from individual clinical encounters. These raise issues of justice centring on health resource creation and allocation, and equitable access to health care. When the perspective taken on the population is global, a tranche of related issues arises. What are the obligations of wealthier nations to developing countries? How can global health inequalities be reduced? Are notions such as a right to health and health care, or global public goods, helpful in achieving global health goals?

2 Interventions of this second sort achieve population—and not merely individuals'—health goals because populations comprise individuals and were each member to act so as to benefit, or refrain from harming, him or herself, the net result would be population health gain.

3 J.S. Mill, 'On Liberty' in *Three Essays: On Liberty, Representative Government, The Subjection of Women* (London: OUP, 1975) 15. The principle is often interpreted more expansively because Mill endorsed state actions aimed at getting people to benefit—not just avoid harms to—others. For example, Mill states that one can be compelled to perform 'positive acts for the benefit of others' (see Mill, 16). Arguably, contemporary liberals should endorse this more expansive interpretation of the principle, not least because it is difficult to maintain the distinction between harming and benefiting. For example, should carriers be forcibly isolated during outbreaks because not doing so harms, or because doing so benefits, others? This interpretive issue can be put aside because even the more expansive interpretation of the principle does not justify state paternalism.

avoid harming themselves. Such programmes cannot be justified by appeal to the harm principle: 'His own good, either physical or moral, is not a sufficient warrant [for exercising power against someone's will].'[4]

The difficulty in seeing a liberal grounding for public health paternalism is intensified when liberalism segues into libertarianism. Again putting definitional disputes aside,[5] libertarianism is a comparatively extreme form of liberalism that emphasizes the value of personal liberty and an individual's right to self-determination, the only side constraint being the obligation to respect everyone else's equal right to the same. In particular, libertarians prefer the free market, as opposed to governments, to supply mechanisms for creating and distributing wealth, and making social choices. They are suspicious of more expansive interpretations of the harm principle which would allow the state to coerce individuals to benefit others, because they think that whether, how, and to what extent to benefit one's fellows is a matter of personal choice. And, because they are hostile to making people act so as to benefit oneself, welfare paternalism is anathema to libertarians.[6] The upshot is a dilemma: achieve public health goals by getting individuals to act in their own best health interests, but at the expense of liberal values; or preserve liberal values, but at the expense of public health gains that would be achieved by public health paternalism.[7]

1.2 Libertarian paternalism

Libertarian paternalism is intended to pass through the horns of this dilemma between getting people to act in their own best interests and respecting liberal principles such as the right to self-determination. Libertarian paternalism is the theoretical basis of 'nudge' which, in turn, has become an influential approach to public policy planning.[8] In their seminal argument for libertarian paternalism, Sunstein and Thaler claim that people tend not to make choices in their own best interests because they are subject to irrational influences on their decisions. Sunstein and Thaler report findings from the behavioural sciences, such as behavioural economics and psychology, to characterize these irrational influences. In particular, choosers are subject to various cognitive biases. Examples include default settings and the status quo bias: people tend to be influenced by the existing arrangement that confronts them, as opposed to ignoring this and

4 Mill, 'On Liberty' (n 3) 15. Paternalistic actions can be justified by appealing to subtle, indirect, or long-term harms to others. For example, seat belt laws are justified on liberal grounds because of the harms to society of having to deal with injured drivers who choose not to wear a belt. But this still invokes third party harms, as opposed to justifying paternalism per se by appeal to Mill's principle.

5 There are various versions of libertarianism (including right-leaning and left-leaning variants) see E. Mack and G.F. Gaus, 'Classical Liberalism and Libertarianism: The Liberty Tradition' in G.F. Gaus and C. Kukathas (eds), *Handbook of Political Theory* (London: Sage Publications, 2004). The argument of the present chapter relies on fundamental features of libertarian thinking but, where differences between versions of libertarianism are germane, this will be indicated in the text.

6 See P. Vallentyne, 'Libertarianism and the State' (2007) 24(1) *Social Philosophy and Policy* 187; although, as discussed later, state paternalism to protect and promote liberty is acceptable to some libertarians.

7 Rival political philosophies prominent in public health literature seem no more conducive to paternalism than is libertarianism. For example, communitarianism most obviously justifies getting people to act for their community's, as opposed to their own, sake; see D.E. Beauchamp, 'Community: The Neglected Tradition of Public Health' (1985) 15(6) *Hastings Center Report* 28.

8 R.H. Thaler and C.R. Sunstein, 'Libertarian Paternalism' (2003) 93(2) *The American Economic Review* 175. See also C.R. Sunstein and R.H. Thaler, 'Libertarian Paternalism Is Not an Oxymoron' (2003) 70(4) *University of Chicago Law Review* 1159; R.H. Thaler and C.R. Sunstein, *Nudge: Improving Decisions about Health, Wealth and Happiness* (London: revd edn, Penguin, 2009).

choosing the most rational option. Similarly, choosers are subject to various choice-framing effects; in particular, the way in which options are presented to choosers influences their decision. For example, a medical treatment that is presented as having a 90 per cent chance of success is more likely to be chosen than if it is presented as having a 10 per cent chance of failure.

Libertarian paternalists point out that irrational influences on choosers are unavoidable. For example, a choice scenario has to be arranged in some fashion and whichever way it is designed will influence choosers. Similarly with choice-framing: options have to be presented in some way or other; whichever way they are presented will influence a decision. Given this, it seems sensible to utilize these unavoidable influences to induce people to choose in their own best interests, that is, by getting them to benefit, or avoid harm to, themselves. Conversely, it seems perverse to allow these influences to motivate people to choose sub-optimally. Hence, planners should design the choice architecture so as to nudge people towards options that are in their bests interests. Whilst being paternalistic, this is not coercive because the cost of resisting the nudge is non-existent to very low (the paradigm recommended by libertarian paternalists is that it takes no more than the click of a computer mouse to choose contra-planner).

A well known example of a nudge, presented by Sunstein and Thaler, involves the layout of a cafeteria. Customers' food choices are susceptible to irrational influences, such as the order in which items are presented. For example, they are more likely to choose options placed closer to hand. The café has to be organized somehow so the influence of the layout is unavoidable. It seems sensible to utilize such influences to good effect by getting customers to choose in their own best interests, that is, by getting them to select healthy items. After all, the alternative—to prompt customers to choose unhealthy options, against their best interests—is perverse. Constructing the choice architecture so as to nudge people towards the healthy options is acceptable even to a libertarian because the cost of resisting the nudge is no greater than, say, having to walk a little further for unhealthy items.

One comment on Sunstein and Thaler's original argument concerns the relationship between the premise that features of choice settings inevitably influence choosers and the conclusion that planners plan paternalistically. The premise only entails that, however planners construct the choice architecture, choosers will be influenced; nothing follows about being paternalistic. To illustrate, suppose two planners, public health officials and an advertising agency, are invited to design a choice setting. They are equally adept at exploiting choice-framing effects. The public health planners will construct the choice architecture so as to nudge people towards healthy options whereas the advertising agency will do so in order to nudge people to buy whatever unhealthy product they are promoting. The former plans paternalistically, the latter not so. Since both plans are consistent with the premise that choice-framing effects are unavoidable, that premise does not entail that planners must plan paternalistically.

Perhaps what is meant to follow from the premise that features of choice settings inevitably influence choosers is normative: not that planners necessarily plan paternalistically, but that they ought to do so. This is supported by libertarian paternalists' appeals to intuition:

> ...consider three alternative strategies: (1) [the planner] could make choices she thinks would make the customers best off; (2) she could make choices at random; or (3) she could maliciously choose those items that she thinks would make the customers as obese as possible...would anyone advocate options (2) or (3)?[9]

9 Thaler and Sunstein, 'Libertarian Paternalism' (n 8) 175.

So now the argument is that normative intuition favours utilizing unavoidable influences in order to get people to choose in their own best interests. But there is a straightforward problem, centring on the alternatives Sunstein and Thaler have presented. Normative intuition might well support (1) paternalism as opposed to (2) randomness or (3) maliciousness but it is not nearly so obvious that normative intuitions support paternalistic planning when this is opposed by other popular values and goods, such as making money and enjoying pleasurable experiences, which are at odds with planners' assumptions about what is in people's best interests. Suppose, for example, that normative intuitions about whether to plan paternalistically, or in order to expand a business, or so as to enhance immediate pleasures, were elicited from a public health professional, a successful businessman, and a self-destructive hedonist. Presumably, their normative intuitions would differ as to which sort of plan to endorse. So, appealing to normative intuition does not validate the argument from the inevitability of irrational influences to paternalistic planning.

Neither the necessity claim that planners must be paternalistic nor the normative claim that planners ought to be paternalistic follows from the fact that choice-framing effects are unavoidable. But this does not derail libertarian paternalism. What follows from the premise is that a paternalistic planner *could* utilize such effects in order to get people to choose in their own best interests; in other words, paternalism is one of the options available to a planner given that choices are inevitably susceptible to irrational influences. The libertarian paternalist will press the point that such paternalistic planning is not coercive because agents remain at liberty to pursue goods and values other than those towards which they are being nudged. So, paternalistic planning of the envisaged kind is an appealing option, one that is available in public health.[10]

2. Objections to Libertarian Paternalism

The nudge agenda has generated an enormous literature but some familiar criticisms of the approach are not important. For example, the point is often made that libertarian paternalism is unoriginal because the influence of irrational factors on choices has long been known.[11] In particular, marketing companies and advertising agencies are adept at exploiting behavioural techniques to influence consumer choice.[12] This is not a weighty objection because it matters less that libertarian paternalism is original than

[10] One that has been enthusiastically adopted by governments, notably those of the UK and US. For example, the UK government's 'Behavioural Insights Team', known as the 'Nudge Unit', has been influential in forming health and other public policy: see Discussion Paper, 'Applying Behavioural Insight to Health' (London: Cabinet Office, 2010).

[11] T.M. Marteau, D. Ogilvie, M. Roland, M. Suhrcke, and M. Kelly, 'Judging Nudging: Can Nudging Improve Population Health?' (2011) 342 *British Medical Journal* 263: 'Nudging is not new. It builds on psychological and sociological theory dating back over a century that shows how environments shape and constrain human behaviour'. A theme throughout the health promotion movement is the attempt to structure environments to make it easier for individuals to choose freely healthier options: see eg The Ottawa Charter for Health Promotion (1986) 1(4) *Health Promotion International*; and the Public Health White Paper, *Choosing Health: Making Healthy Choices Easier* (London: Stationery Office, 2004). cf S. Vallgårda, 'Nudge—A New and Better Way to Improve Health?' (2012) 104 *Health Policy* 200, who discusses some advantages and drawbacks of the fact that 'nudge is a reinvention of the wheel'.

[12] J. Blythman, *Shopped: The Shocking Power of British Supermarkets* (London: Fourth Estate, 2004). Attempts to change health behaviour that pre-date the current interest in nudge interventions include social marketing in the health field; see eg J.C. Ling, B.A. Franklin, J.F. Lindsteadt, and S.A. Gearon, 'Social Marketing: Its Place in Public Health' (1992) 13 *Annual Review of Public Health* 341.

whether it is politically and ethically acceptable, and practicable.[13] Similarly, there has been considerable interest in whether 'libertarian paternalism' is a misnomer: 'A key conceptual question about paternalism is whether the interference with individual liberty must be against the person's will... If this feature is a necessary condition of paternalism, then libertarian paternalism is inappropriately titled.'[14] But the appeal of nudging is precisely that it gets people to change their behaviour for the better without contravening their will, so the permissibility of the approach is more important than verbal disputes over labels.

An equally familiar, but more interesting, set of objections centres on the charge that nudging is not effective.[15] A quick response is that the evidence is incomplete: for example, nudging might take longer than has thus far been allowed, planners might become more adept at utilizing behavioural techniques, new techniques might be devised, or nudging might be effective in untried choice scenarios.[16] But more interesting versions of this objection are based on the claim that the approach is of the wrong sort to be effective. Specifically, nudges are too 'shallow'. One variant of this is that nudges are only intended to influence people's actual choices as opposed to the motivational sets from which they emanate; people might be successfully nudged to eat less fatty foods on specific occasions but become no more 'body aware' or health conscious, hence quickly slip back into old habits.[17] Another version is that nudge interventions do not address, and might even mask, underlying structural determinants of unhealthy behaviour and resultant health inequalities, such as economic disadvantage and social constraints. In fact, it is argued, when all their ramifications are taken into account, nudges can have various sorts of negative effects.[18]

13 A related complaint is that it 'isn't clear how nudges are distinctive' given the plethora of non-coercive health behaviour modification techniques already employed; see C. Bonnell, M. McKee, A. Fletcher, P. Wilkinson, and A. Haines, 'One Nudge Forward, Two Steps Back: Why Nudging Might Make for Muddled Public Health and Wasted Resources' (2011) 342 *British Medical Journal* 241. But it is hard to see why these extant techniques do not constitute nudges, in which case the complaint is simply lack of originality again.

14 R. Faden and S. Shebaya, 'Public Health Ethics', in E.N. Zalta (ed), *The Stanford Encyclopedia of Philosophy* (Summer 2010 Edition). See also D.M. Hausman and B. Welch, 'Debate: To Nudge or Not to Nudge' (2010) 18(1) *Journal of Political Philosophy* 123: '[Thaler and Sunstein's] definition of paternalism is unsatisfactory', at 126.

15 See eg the year-long review of the approach by a subgroup of the UK House of Lords' Science and Technology Committee, led by Baroness Neuberger, which is pessimistic about the effectiveness of nudge: House of Lords, Science and Technology Select Committee Report (HL Paper 179), 'Behaviour Change' (London: Stationery Office, 2011).

16 Baroness Neuberger, in an interview with *The Observer*, Sunday 17 July 2011, commented that 'if you really want to change people's behaviour it takes a very long time... you have to look at a 20- to 25-year span before you get a full change of behaviour'. cf Marteau et al, 'Judging Nudging' (n 11) 263: 'Nudging certainly works. Shaping environments to cue certain behaviours is extremely effective, unfortunately often to the detriment of our health.' Marteau et al are noticeably less forthright about public health nudges: 'To date, few nudging interventions have been evaluated for their effectiveness in changing behaviour in general populations and none, to our knowledge, has been evaluated for its ability to achieve sustained change of the kind needed to improve health in the long term' (see Marteau et al, 264). See also A.R. Salazar, 'Libertarian Paternalism and the Dangers of Nudging Consumers' (2012) 23(1) *King's Law Journal* 51, who cites 'evidence that food nudging is working' before going on to criticize the approach's 'shortcomings'.

17 Salazar, 'Libertarian Paternalism' (n 16) 58–9: 'nudges may work for a while, influencing unintentional or automatic behaviours, but they are not capable of sustaining long-term behavioural change as nudges do not really change individuals' knowledge, attitudes, values or patterns of decision making in the reflective system'.

18 Suggestions include personal, socio-economic, and environmental negative effects. See Salazar, 'Libertarian Paternalism' (n 16); K. Wilcox, B. Vallen, L. Block, and G.J. Fitzsimons, 'Vicarious Goal Fulfilment: When the Mere Presence of a Healthy Option Leads to an Ironically Indulgent Decision'

The libertarian paternalist has at least two responses to this set of objections to the nudge agenda. First, the claim that nudging is practically inefficacious does not present a problem with the approach in principle. This leaves it open for proponents to suggest combining nudges with other sorts of interventions.[19] Libertarian paternalists are unlikely to be dismayed by this because no one advocates nudging as the only approach to behaviour modification. Second, the objection begs the question as to how 'deep' behaviour modification techniques should be. Proponents advocate nudge interventions precisely because they are 'shallow' in being aimed at specific behaviour in discrete choice settings. When critics advocate interventions that are aimed at something 'deeper', such as motivational sets or underlying social structures, they beg the question against the libertarian paternalist who is suspicious of allowing planners to employ behaviour modification techniques that go beyond designing choice architecture.[20]

To locate more telling objections it is best to look to responses by committed libertarians because, as Stevenson puts it, libertarian paternalists' arguments 'may not win over many hard-core libertarians (paternalists would probably find less that is objectionable)'.[21] Specifically, soft paternalists will not object to libertarian paternalism because nudging is a form of soft paternalism; hard paternalists already think it acceptable to coerce people to act in their own interests so their only objection will be that the approach does not go far enough, which is uninteresting because it ignores the requirement on planners to fully respect individual autonomy, which is central to libertarian paternalism.[22] Two objections by committed libertarians are discussed here, based on slippery slope arguments and the redistributive effects of nudges, respectively.[23] These objections are familiar, but the argument in this section is that neither of them is in itself convincing. Rather, close analysis reveals a shared theme: both objections allude to the fact that libertarian paternalism allows and encourages a certain role for the state. This is really what the libertarian objects to: not slippery slopes or

(2009) 36(3) *Journal of Consumer Research* 380; A. Chernev, 'The Dieter's Paradox' (2011) 21(2) *Journal of Consumer Psychology* 178.

19 'Behavioural change interventions appear to work best when they're part of a package of regulation and fiscal measures' (Baroness Neuberger (n 16)); 'evidence thus indicates that the use of a range of regulatory and non-regulatory interventions offers a better solution to the problem of unhealthy eating and obesity rather than excluding regulatory measures in order to rely solely on nudge interventions' (Salazar, 'Libertarian Paternalism' (n 16) 66). Of course, which combinations of interventions are efficacious is in itself an empirical question requiring further evidence.

20 A refinement of the charge that nudging is ineffectual focuses on the distinction Thaler and Sunstein draw between the 'automatic' and 'reflective' systems: Thaler and Sunstein, *Nudge* (n 8) 21–4. See O. Amir and O. Lobel, 'Stumble, Predict, Nudge: How Behavioral Economics Informs Law and Policy' (2008) 108(8) *Columbia Law Review* 2098, who suggest that biases caused by 'automatic' responses are easier to correct than those rooted in the 'reflective' system.

21 D. Stevenson, 'Libertarian Paternalism: The Cocaine Vaccine as a Test Case for the Sunstein/Thaler Model' (2006) 3(1) *Rutgers University Journal of Law and Urban Policy* 4. See, also, Vallgårda, 'Nudge—A New and Better Way' (n 11) 201–2.

22 Autonomy is often considered to be an independent value: 'One component of agency is deciding for oneself. Even if I constantly made a mess of my life, even if you could do better if you took charge, I would not let you do it. Autonomy has a value of its own.' J. Griffin, *Well-Being: Its Meaning, Measurement, and Moral Importance* (Oxford: Clarendon Press, 1986) 67. Recall that libertarian paternalism aims to respect autonomy because the cost of resisting the nudge is very low to non-existent.

23 Numerous objections presented on behalf of libertarians are less weighty than the two discussed in the main text. For example, Vallgårda, 'Nudge—A New and Better Way' (n 11) 201–2, rightly points out that the important critical perspective on libertarian paternalism is from libertarianism not paternalism, but none of the five ways in which libertarianism conflicts with libertarian paternalism suggested in that paper is compelling.

redistributive effects, per se, but the way the nudge agenda fosters a state other than the one advocated in libertarianism.[24]

2.1 Slippery slope arguments

Rizzo and Whitman present numerous slippery slope arguments; these are based on vagueness and gradients which are intrinsic to—in fact, they claim, created by—libertarian paternalism.[25] For example, nudges are supposed to be acceptable to libertarians because any cost of choosing contra-planner is low, but there is no bright line between costs low enough to preserve liberty and costs so high as to be objectionably coercive, so this distinction is vague. Given such features, Rizzo and Whitman argue, nudging is bound to create various slippery slopes. But it is hard to see how the slippery slope objection is supposed to work.[26] The general structure of slippery slope arguments is: action A may be permissible in itself but is at the top of a slippery slope to action B, which is impermissible. The two versions of this sort of argument relevant to libertarian paternalism differ as to what lies at the bottom of the slope: first, nudges are the top of a slippery slope to a myriad of further nudges; second, nudges are the top of a slippery slope to coercive interventions. But neither of these versions is convincing.

Regarding the former version, it is certainly plausible that nudges will proliferate. Planners may become psychologically predisposed to create more nudges as nudging becomes commonplace. Or the slope may be created in more subtle ways. For example, libertarian paternalists tend to think of cognitive biases as discrete when, in fact, they interact; hence, a nudge designed to address one sort of irrational influence on agents might well necessitate a further nudge to address a different irrational influence, and so on.[27] So, the problem with this version of the argument is not the plausibility of the slope. Rather, it is hard to see what is objectionable at the bottom, namely, the myriad of further nudges. The libertarian paternalist will point out that what is important is the sort, not the number, of interventions: provided it is in the interests of the agent but preserves their freedom to do otherwise, each of even a myriad of nudges is permissible.[28] In fact, it is ironic to criticize the approach on the grounds that it will result in a proliferation of nudges since this is precisely what the libertarian paternalist wants, namely, that their planning strategy is so successful that it is widely adopted.

According to the other version of the slippery slope argument, what lies at the bottom of the slope are interventions of the objectionable sort, namely, coercive interventions. For example, Rizzo and Whitman speculate:

[24] The inductive claim is that this argument extends to other libertarian objections to nudging: what is really going on is not the overt criticism in question but the covert hostility to the sort of state libertarian paternalists endorse.

[25] M.J. Rizzo and D.G. Whitman, 'Little Brother is Watching You: New Paternalism on the Slippery Slopes' (2009) 51(3) *Arizona Law Review* 685.

[26] For Rizzo and Whitman's reply to Sunstein and Thaler's response to slippery slope arguments, see Rizzo and Whitman, 'Little Brother is Watching You' (n 25) 735–7.

[27] Rizzo and Whitman, 'Little Brother is Watching You' (n 25) 706. Rizzo and Whitman distinguish two sets of slippery slopes: those discernible given that planners are fully rational and those discernible given that planners are subject to irrational influences. Slippery slopes due to bias interaction are in the former category.

[28] In this respect, nudges are analogous to laws. A piece of legislation governing, say, traffic might necessitate further legislation. For example, if mandating seatbelt use results in people driving faster, further legislation might be required to address speeding. But this proliferation of laws is not problematic so long as each one is justified.

> A fat tax helps the individual to improve his diet... However, he might also reduce his effort toward other subgoals, like exercise... As a result, policymakers have reason to intervene further—by increasing the fat tax, or subsidizing gym membership, or perhaps even resorting to food bans and exercise mandates.[29]

But this is not a fair criticism of libertarian paternalism because what lies at the bottom of this putative slope are interventions expressly ruled out by the approach.[30] Rizzo and Whitman appeal to features of libertarian paternalism, such as vagueness, to imply that the slide to coercive interventions is inevitable. But vague boundaries are still boundaries, and the interventions in the quoted list are on the coercive side of the grey area between nudging and coercion. This conceptual clarity provides a clear break on the putative slippery slope.

One response to this is that planners are insensitive to such a conceptual distinction or mischievously ignore it in favour of coercion. But *ad hominem* arguments against planners should be distinguished from slippery slope objections. That planners might prove to be poor implementers of libertarian paternalism is not a strong argument against the approach unless it can be shown that such ineptitude is inevitable.[31] An interesting *ad hominem* argument is that irrational influences on choosers are ubiquitous, so planners themselves must be subject to them. But it is easier to be impressed by this subtle shift to the meta-level of irrational planners than to see what objection to libertarian paternalism can be grounded on it. If planners are influenced by irrational factors to design a choice scenario contrary to libertarian paternalist principles—agents are coerced to choose in, or nudged to choose against, their best interests, say—then the plan is proscribed by the approach. If planners are influenced by irrational factors to design a choice scenario in accordance with libertarian paternalist principles—that is, people are nudged to choose in their best interests—then the plan is unobjectionable because choosers remain free to resist the nudge.[32]

To confirm that slippery slope objections to nudging are not strong, consider the contrast with more convincing slippery slope arguments. For example, it is often argued that cannabis should not be legalized because that puts us on a slippery slope to increased hard drug abuse.[33] Empirical evidence reveals a tendency for drug users to progress from soft to hard drugs, indicating that the slippery slope exists. What lies at

29 Rizzo and Whitman, 'Little Brother is Watching You' (n 25) 709.

30 In fact, what lies at the top of this putative slope is ruled out, too: Rizzo and Whitman repeatedly suggest that sin taxing is a libertarian paternalist strategy but sin taxes are economic (dis)incentives which are too strong to count as nudges. Admittedly, these waters are muddied by, for example, Thaler and Sunstein's endorsement of the 'dollar a day' programme to dissuade teenage mothers from further pregnancies: Thaler and Sunstein, *Nudge* (n 8) 234.

31 Rizzo and Whitman seem to confuse slippery slope arguments with *ad hominem* arguments at various points; this is particularly noticeable in their discussion of slippery slopes that they say arise given the assumption that planners are cognitively biased, and their rather dim view of policy-makers: Rizzo and Whitman, 'Little Brother is Watching You' (n 25) 737.

32 Two other responses are available to the libertarian paternalist. One is to utilize the fact that planners evince cognitive biases: since, *ex hypothesi*, it is unobjectionable to nudge ground level agents, why not nudge planners to plan according to libertarian paternalist principles? (Of course, this introduces a regress of planners nudging planners... etc, but the regress is not objectionable.) The other available response is to deploy the kinds of debiasing techniques to which libertarian critiques of libertarian paternalism appeal; see eg G. Mitchell, 'Libertarian Paternalism is an Oxymoron' (2005) 99 (3) *Northwestern University Law Review* 1245, 1255–7. Whilst it seems unfeasible to debias *everyone*—see n 42—perhaps it is plausible to insist that policy-makers undertake to be debiased as a matter of professional duty.

33 Of course, this argument is contentious and might well not be conclusive; it is used here only as a point of contrast.

the bottom of this slope—increased prevalence and abuse of hard drugs—is clearly undesirable. There are obvious explanations for the slipperiness of the slope, such as that users become inured to soft drugs so crave stronger effects; and the social pressures motivating people to use drugs are, if anything, exacerbated by their being users. The slide down a slippery slope can be a matter of either psychological or logical necessity;[34] in this case, the former is clearly important because typical drug users have addictive personalities and the substances in question have addictive qualities. By contrast, none of these features is typical of nudges. Conversely, there is a logical break in the putative slippery slope from nudges—provided by the clear conceptual distinction between what sits at the top of the slippery slope (nudges) and what is said to lie at the bottom (coercive interventions)—an equivalent to which is lacking in the drugs case.

Notwithstanding this scepticism, we see in the literature on slippery slopes a hint of what libertarians really object to about libertarian paternalism. Rizzo and Whitman point out that the 'main problem with [libertarian paternalism] ... is that it defines freedom of choice ... in terms of costs of exit, *without any attention to who imposes the costs and how*'.[35] In particular, they repeatedly advocate planners' maintaining important distinctions: 'One such bright-line rule is the distinction between public and private decision-making.'[36] By 'public actions' they mean state-sanctioned or governmental interventions, as opposed to private actions undertaken by non-governmental planners. This introduces the important libertarian objection to nudges: not that nudging creates slippery slopes but that libertarian paternalism encourages governments to undertake paternalistic behaviour modification. Before developing this further, consider another example of the same dialectic.

2.2 Redistributive effects

Libertarians point out that nudges can result in redistributions of resources from rational to irrational individuals. Mitchell illustrates: 'If the cafeteria director helps diners with low self-control gain some greater control over their impulses and eat less, then she may need to raise prices, meaning that diners with high self-control may now bear some of the cost of the libertarian paternalist policy.'[37] Libertarians find this objectionable. Before clarifying what is impermissible to libertarians about such a redistributive effect, consider two responses to this objection mentioned on behalf of the libertarian paternalist by Mitchell, a committed libertarian.[38]

First, 'the low self-control of diners who were overeating keeps the price of the foods eaten by the high self-control diners artificially low'. Mitchell does not pursue this but, presumably, the thought is that the redistributive effect of the nudge is acceptable to a libertarian because it results in the rational diner paying the correct—as opposed to artificially low—price. But what is the correct price? According to libertarians, this

34 D. Walton, *Slippery Slope Arguments* (Oxford: Clarendon Press, 1992).

35 Rizzo and Whitman, 'Little Brother is Watching You' (n 25) 698 (italics in the original).

36 Rizzo and Whitman, 'Little Brother is Watching You' (n 25) 738. A second 'bright-line rule' is between 'coercive and non-coercive intervention', but this begs the question by assuming precisely what is under discussion, namely, that there is a slippery slope from non-coercive to coercive interventions.

37 Mitchell, 'Libertarian Paternalism is an Oxymoron' (n 32) 1274. See also R. Korobkin, 'Libertarian Welfarism' (2009) 97(6) *California Law Review* 1651; A.C. Desai, 'Libertarian Paternalism, Externalities, and the "Spirit of Liberty": How Thaler and Sunstein are Nudging Us toward an "Overlapping Consensus"' (2011) 36(1) *Law and Social Inquiry* 263.

38 Mitchell, 'Libertarian Paternalism is an Oxymoron' (n 32) note 106.

should be left to the market and, if the market sets a price on rational choices lower than that charged after the nudge, they will continue to be exercised by the redistributive effect. The second rejoinder Mitchell suggests, on behalf of libertarian paternalists, is that 'the cafeteria owner may try only to redirect diners to healthier foods that are priced the same as unhealthy foods'. Such a nudge evades the objection because it has no redistributive effect. But, as Mitchell comments, it is 'unlikely' that nudges will have no effect on consumption and revenue. In fact, the most the libertarian paternalist can achieve here is a Pyrrhic victory: they want nudging to be successful and widespread, but the greater the number of people who are influenced by a nudge, the less plausible is the claim that it has no redistributive effect (the only nudges of which one can say with confidence that they will have no redistributive effects are unsuccessful ones).

So, successful nudges have redistributive effects and libertarians find this objectionable. But why? After all, libertarians cannot object to all redistributive effects. In particular, since they advocate the free market, libertarians are bound to accept redistributive effects brought about by market forces. For example, libertarians would not object if the redistributive effect described earlier in Mitchell's cafeteria illustration, was due to changes in consumer trends that have nothing to do with nudges. Libertarians cannot even object to all redistributive effects due to nudges. Specifically, they cannot object to redistributive effects due to privately initiated nudges. Referring again to Mitchell's cafeteria illustration, if the redesign is the personal project of a particularly health conscious proprietor, libertarians will think the proprietor is within their rights to change their business practices in this way, be happy to leave it to customers to decide whether to follow the nudge, and accept any resultant redistributive effect.

What explains the libertarian's objection to some, but not all, redistributive effects is that what the libertarian really objects to is not wealth redistribution per se—not even wealth redistribution due to nudging per se—but to redistributive effects of nudges resulting from governmental planning. It is not *takings* that are objectionable but *state-based* takings. This transgresses libertarian strictures on state interference to redistribute resources. Libertarianism allows the state to take resources in order, for example, to compensate losses incurred by involuntary contracts, but disallows the state from redistributing resources for other reasons, such as and notably, to promote welfare. Libertarians' preferred mechanism for redistributions of resources is the free market; redistributions due to state nudges are objectionable. This explains the libertarian's acceptance of redistributive effects due to market forces or privately initiated nudges: neither is the result of state action. It is when libertarian paternalism sanctions public nudges that the libertarian complains, because then the upshot is wealth redistribution by government. So, as was the case with slippery slope objections, arguments based on redistributive effects are somewhat misleading; in both cases, what the libertarian really finds objectionable is the role libertarian paternalism allows the state.[39]

[39] A challenge to this is that some versions of libertarianism allow a more expansive interventionist role for the state, one that includes a redistributive function. But the ways in which the state can redistribute resources according to these versions of libertarianism fall far short of allowing a government agenda which, if successful, would redistribute wealth from rational to irrational choosers. To illustrate, Vallentyne's discussion of state enforced redistributions permitted by libertarianism focuses on left-libertarianism. He agrees that the state endorsed by this sort of libertarianism is permitted to redistribute resources; for example, the 'state thus redistributes resources by taking from those who own natural resources but have not fully discharged their equality-promoting duties relative to the competitive rent owed for the rights they hold': Vallentyne,'Libertarianism and the State' (n 6) 201. Such redistributions are of a sort quite different from those brought about by successful nudges.

2.3 Nudge and the libertarian state

To summarize the discussion so far: the important thing about standard libertarian objections—based on, for example, slippery slope arguments and redistributive effects—is that they indicate a serious problem with libertarian paternalism concerning the role it allots to the state. To clarify this problem it is useful to emphasize that libertarianism is a political philosophy. Central to political philosophy is the just state, that is, the right account of the grounds and limits of state authority. So libertarians define the just state. The worry—indicated by, but not developed in, standard libertarian objections—is that nudging is at odds with this conception. Is a state that nudges the sort of state libertarians advocate?

This libertarian worry about the nudge agenda needs to be developed carefully. The founding idea of libertarian conceptions of the state is, as Wolff explains, hostility to the state's telling people how to live their lives: 'Libertarian theories start from the thought that, as far as possible, we should keep government out of individual lives. It is not for governments to tell us what we can do, provided we respect the rights of others.'[40] Hence, libertarians advocate a minimalist state which imposes as little as possible on individuals and prioritizes their freedom. Given this, one might think it obvious that public nudges are incompatible with the libertarian state. After all, nudges are paternalistic interventions and the libertarian is bound to be hostile to government intervention and state paternalism. But this is too quick because libertarians can allow the state to be both interventionist and paternalist.

For one thing, as has been mentioned a number of times, there are disparate versions of libertarianism; some of these allow a state that does not enjoy universal consent but still has a significant interventionist role. For example, Vallentyne argues that 'almost all minimally plausible forms of libertarianism are compatible with the justice of some kind of state, and some forms of left-libertarianism are compatible with a reasonably robust state'.[41] Nor does libertarianism rule out state paternalism—that is, allowing the state to implement policies, including nudges, that are intended to get people to choose in their own best interests—when confronted with unavoidable choice-framing effects.[42] In this respect, they seem to agree with libertarian paternalists, but there is a major difference between the two. When libertarians say that the state can plan paternalistically, they mean that the government can design choice architecture so as to protect and promote what they see as the crucial value, namely, individual liberty. By contrast, libertarian paternalists advocate state paternalism to promote what *they* see as of crucial value, namely individual agents' welfare. The dispute here is not about state paternalism per se but, rather, the values—liberty versus welfare—that paternalistic government interventions are intended to promote.[43]

40 J. Wolff, 'Economic Justice' in H. LaFollette (ed), *The Oxford Handbook of Practical Ethics* (Oxford: OUP, 2003) 434.

41 Vallentyne, 'Libertarianism and the State' (n 6) 205 (for limits on the state which libertarians of all stripes impose, see Vallentyne, 192–4).

42 Some libertarian commentators deny that choice-framing effects are insuperable or inevitable and advocate 'debiasing techniques' to 'inoculate' people against irrational influences; see eg Mitchell, 'Libertarian Paternalism is an Oxymoron' (n 32) 1248–60. But debiasing is not possible in all choice scenarios—this is implied by the empirical evidence, for example—so libertarian paternalism remains feasible for choice scenarios resistant to debiasing. And there is a general worry about how practicable it is to 'debiase' people.

43 Mitchell illustrates the difference in practice by reference to terminating employment contracts: libertarian paternalists would advocate a 'for-cause' default rule because this protects welfare, whereas libertarians would advocate an 'at-will' employment rule because it stops irrational people from

So, governmental nudges are not objectionable to libertarians simply in virtue of being a form of state intervention, nor simply in virtue of being paternalistic. Nonetheless, that nudging is compatible with the libertarian state remains questionable. Libertarians of all stripes disallow that it is in the remit of the state to devise and impose a conception of the good, where this is understood as a more or less comprehensive account of what is important in life and how it should be lived. This is because libertarians insist on each individual's right to devise and pursue their own conception of the good: 'Most importantly, the state does not impose any substantive notion of the good life but helps individuals retain freedom to determine their own preferred ends.'[44] Given this, the obvious thought is that a state that nudges is objectionable to libertarians because it transgresses their strictures on how a conception of the good is devised and pursued.

There are two obvious rejoinders here. The first is that state nudges are not based on anything as grand as a conception of the good. But this is debatable. What are state nudges based on if not an implicit conception of the good? Nudges cannot be based on how people actually behave because the point of an intervention is to change behaviour. Nor can they be based on how most people behave or on how they would choose if mandated to choose: the former would be a case of the tyranny of the majority; libertarian paternalists expressly reject the latter for most choice scenarios.[45] Thaler and Sunstein repeatedly insist that state planners base nudges on what makes people better off *as judged by themselves*. But there are epistemic problems with finding out whether people agree that a nudge makes them better off (when and how this is to be established, for example). And there is a dilemma here between how confident planners are that people want to be nudged, and the appropriateness of such a soft paternalist intervention. Suppose it is very obvious that people want to stop doing X and do Y instead: planners can be confident that people would think themselves to be better off for having changed their behaviour; but nudging is inappropriate because, presumably, people would not object to interventions too strong to count as nudges. On the other horn of the dilemma, it is unclear as to whether people want to change their behaviour: nudging would seem more appropriate than 'harder' paternalistic interventions; but planners cannot be confident that people will judge themselves to have been made better off by a nudge.

There are other accounts of how governments decide the direction in which to nudge people which avoid any implicit conception of the good. One is that state nudges are based on what people would choose if they were ideal deliberators, that is, had full knowledge, time, intelligence, etc.[46] But the sort of behavioural and lifestyle options to

curtailing their liberty regarding employment whilst allowing employees to enter voluntarily into more permanent or binding contracts; see Mitchell, 'Libertarian Paternalism is an Oxymoron' (n 32) 1263. Note that welfare and liberty are not the only two values which planners might aim to promote; for example, interventions might be intended to promote equality: M.A. Smith and M.S. McPherson, 'Nudging for Equality: Values in Libertarian Paternalism' (2009) 61(2) *Administrative Law Review* 323.

44 Mitchell, 'Libertarian Paternalism is an Oxymoron' (n 32) 1263.

45 C.R. Sunstein, 'Preferences, Paternalism, and Liberty' (2006) 59 *Royal Institute of Philosophy Supplement* 233: 'Perhaps the majority's choices would be insufficiently informed, or a reflection of bounded rationality or bounded self-control. Perhaps those choices would not, in fact, promote the majority's welfare'; and, 'there is a risk that [choices people are forced to make explicit] will be inadequately informed or will not promote welfare' (at 257–8).

46 See M. Qizilbash, 'Informed Desire and the Ambitions of Libertarian Paternalism' (2012) 38(4) *Social Choice and Welfare* 647. Qizilbash discusses the definition of welfare that underpins Sunstein and Thaler's approach; he suggests that they implicitly adopt a strong version of the informed desire

which people are nudged are contestable by ideal deliberators. For example, disputes about what to eat are not resolvable by having more knowledge, time to deliberate, etc, because they are grounded in different conceptions of how to live one's life, such as whether to be health conscious and prudent or hedonistic and riotous. Another account emphasizes interests: state nudges are intended to get people to choose in their own interests, and interests are independent of a conception of the good. But a similar point applies: apart from very basic interests that everyone has—which are not the subject of nudges—what is in one's interests will depend on one's conception of how to live one's life.[47] Conversely, there is something implausible about free-floating, discrete nudges that are entirely independent of a conception of the good. For example, is it really plausible that nudging people to eat more fruit and take more exercise is detachable from a more comprehensive account of what people should be like and how they should live their lives?

The second obvious rejoinder is that, even if state nudges are grounded in an implicit conception of the good, this is unobjectionable to a libertarian because people remain free to resist nudges that are at odds with how they want to live their lives. To recall a previous quotation from Mitchell, what the libertarian insists on is that 'the state does not *impose* any substantive notion of the good life'; since nudges are not *impositions* they escape the libertarian stricture. But, again, this is debatable. The libertarian objection here is to nudging in principle, on grounds of political philosophy: according to libertarianism, a government that nudges is the wrong sort of government, namely one that devises, and plans by reference to, an implicit conception of the good. Since this objection is theoretical, it is substantive and compelling even if nudges are liberty-preserving in that agents remain free to resist them. But the libertarian can go further because the objection is not only theoretical but has practical ramifications. For one thing, establishing the sort of government that pursues a nudge agenda makes the creation of the sort of state advocated by libertarians—one that has no remit to devise and promote a conception of the good—less likely. And furthermore, the libertarian will point out how implausible it is that, in practice, a nudging government will abide by libertarian strictures on other state activities, and limit itself to the only legitimate business of government, which is to maximize individual liberties.

So, it is suggested here that the important libertarian worry about libertarian paternalism is that it is at odds with their account of the just state.[48] A natural way for political philosophers to frame the discussion is in terms of neutrality versus perfectionism: libertarians advocate state neutrality but the nudge agenda is implicitly

view according to which welfare is the satisfaction of desires held by agents who are perfectly rational, fully informed, have perfect self-control, etc. Qizilbash points out that, if this view of welfare underpins the nudge agenda, there will be implementation problems because real-world planners have less than fully informed desires. But that libertarian paternalists do implicitly endorse such a strong version of the informed desire view is questionable.

47 Vallentyne's left-libertarianism includes an account of rights that refers to people's interests: 'A person has a claim-right against others that they not perform action X if and only if it is wrong for others to perform X when (1) she has validly *dissented* from their X-ing... or (2) she has *not validly consented* to their X-ing and their X-ing is *against her interests* (on some appropriate conception of interest)': Vallentyne, 'Libertarianism and the State' (n 6) 193. But it is clear that Vallentyne has in mind very basic interests such as to avoid being run over by a car.

48 'Libertarians value freedom of choice above all, including the freedom to make mistakes and cognitive errors... Although *Nudge* envisions that the choice of end goals will remain open because of an opt-out architecture, one must first recognize that the default itself conveys a normative message... The idea that the formation of norms and values is a task for government is antithetical to libertarian principles' (Amir and Lobel, 'Stumble, Predict, Nudge' (n 20) 2120–2).

perfectionist. Thaler and Sunstein have explicitly discussed objections to their approach that are grounded on neutrality.[49] But their discussion misses the point. First, they illustrate the 'constitutional right to government neutrality': incumbents should not be allowed to nudge voters by determining the order in which candidates are listed on ballots. But this is too narrow a sense of neutrality to capture what libertarians have in mind. Thaler and Sunstein seem to acknowledge this when they go on to discuss 'a more general question about neutrality' that goes beyond 'the context of constitutional rights'. But the question they consider 'extends to both the private and the public sectors' when, according to the suggestion being developed here, the neutrality problem is one specifically for governments. And the bulk of their discussion centres on the conditions that make the potential for successful nudges high (such as, 'choices are fraught and Nudgers have expertise'). Finally, for Thaler and Sunstein, the views of those who 'want government-sponsored nudging to be kept to a bare minimum' are based on assessments of government officials as 'incompetent and corrupt', as opposed to the libertarian worry expressed here that state nudges are at odds with the libertarian account of the role of government.

More generally, libertarian paternalists seem to have a blind spot regarding this sort of libertarian objection to nudge interventions. To illustrate, recall the foregoing discussion of slippery slope arguments in which Whitman advocates a bright-line distinction between state and private nudges. Thaler responds:

> I likewise do not understand the big distinction Whitman makes between government vs. private use of libertarian Best Guess.[50] If he would use Save More Tomorrow in his company, why shouldn't the government offer it to its employees, or utilize the concept in a partial privatization of Social Security? If one favors school choice, then wouldn't you want to help parents make better choices for their children, and especially encourage more parents of disadvantaged children to make good use of the choices being offered to them? . . . These are the kinds of policies for government that we propose in *Nudge*. . . . Does Whitman think [painting horizontal lines across the road near a dangerous curve on Lake Shore Drive] is bad because it was implemented by the government?[51]

In the light of what is presented here as the important libertarian objection to state nudges, Whitman's 'big distinction' is easy to understand and crucial.[52] State nudges are grounded in an implicit conception of the good, which is at odds with the libertarian account of the state. By contrast, nudges undertaken by non-governmental planners escape this objection, for at least two reasons. First, libertarians are concerned to define the just state, not other sorts of institutions, so there is no tension between libertarian political philosophy and the activities of, say, private companies (unless, of course, they infringe liberties). Second, private nudges tend to be based on specific goals, such as selling a particular product, which are not underpinned by a conception of the good.[53]

49 Thaler and Sunstein, *Nudge* (n 8) 246–8.

50 'Libertarian best guess' is simply an alternative label for libertarian paternalist planning, suggested by Thaler to placate opponents who are hostile to 'paternalism'.

51 R. Thaler, 'Cato Unbound, The Argument Clinic, The Conversation', posted 16 April 2010, available at <http://www.cato-unbound.org>.

52 To be fair, it is not surprising that libertarian paternalists find it hard to 'understand the big distinction Whitman makes' because—as argued earlier in the main text—he puts it in the context of distracting and unconvincing slippery slope objections.

53 That there is a blind spot here is suggested by the shortcomings of Thaler's quoted examples. (1) There's a difference between how a government treats its employees and how it treats its citizens; libertarians might allow a government, *qua* employer, to nudge its employees toward a particular

3. Public Health Nudges

The preceding discussion of what a committed libertarian should object to about libertarian paternalism leaves open the question as to whether nudging is appropriate in public health. This is because public health is not a libertarian endeavour. Public health practitioners and institutions are not 'neutralists' in wanting people to be maximally free to pursue 'their own preferred ends' but 'perfectionists' in that they work with and towards a conception of the good to which mental and physical health are central. In this sense, public health has an objective list theory of the good: mental and physical health, and conducive options and behaviour, are good for people whether or not they recognize or pursue them.[54]

How appropriate and useful is nudging in public health? Evidently, libertarian paternalism cannot be public health's sole conceptual basis. The problem libertarian paternalism addresses is narrow, namely, how to get people to choose in their own best interests without compromising their freedom. Libertarian paternalism is relevant to public health only to the extent that this problem arises in the field. But public health addresses other issues—including social and other non-individual determinants of health, and the social injustice of health inequalities—to which libertarian paternalism simply does not speak.[55] On the other hand, nudging scores well in dealing with standard worries about public health interventions. As clarified at the outset, a major theme in public health ethics is the tension between the pursuit of public health goals and individuals' liberty and autonomy. Nudging people to choose healthier options seems like a promising way to ease this tension because it steers people towards healthy options without coercing them. Similarly, public health is often criticized for prioritizing health at the expense of other components of well-being.[56] Again, this criticism is met by nudging because it leaves people free to choose whatever is more important to them than their health.

Furthermore, nudging might be invoked to justify public health interventions other than those with the paternalistic intention of getting people to choose in their own best interests. As discussed in the Introduction, many public health programmes impose on individuals to prevent harms to others. For example, an infected individual might be

pension scheme but baulk at nudging citizens towards certain lifestyle choices. (2) State education systems are justified on libertarian grounds by market failure (ie the market cannot be relied on to provide education). Thaler's example trades on differences in quality of schools; the government's responsibility here is to make sure all schools are good, not to nudge parents. (3) Speed limits are justified by the harm principle (speeding drivers endanger others) and so coercion in the form of legal sanctions is admissible (drivers should be made, not nudged, to slow down; see later for a discussion of nudging in the context of clear legal strictures).

54 This 'perfectionism' is the feature of public health that many find objectionably patronizing, as expressed, for example, by complaints of 'nannying'. But public health planners should be unashamed of aiming at pre-established goals and values provided they acknowledge that public health can be at odds with other complex programmes of activities designed to achieve alternative goals and values. This is true at both the institutional and individual levels: the public health lobby has to compete for public funds with other legitimate claimants whose main aims are not directly health related; and getting individuals to achieve health goals can be at odds with their other interests; see T.M. Wilkinson, 'Making People Be Healthy' (2009) 1(3) *Journal of Primary Health Care* 244.

55 And should not be criticized for not doing so; cf J.-F. Ménard, 'A "Nudge" for Public Health Ethics: Libertarian Paternalism as a Framework for Ethical Analysis of Public Health Interventions?' (2010) 3(3) *Public Health Ethics* 229.

56 'Health is important as a component of well-being . . . on any sensible view of [health and well-being] people trade off health against other goods': Wilkinson, 'Making People Be Healthy' (n 54) 245.

isolated to protect others from a communicable disease during an outbreak. Liberals can appeal to Mill's harm principle to justify such interventions. But it is harder for liberals to justify imposing on individuals to benefit, as opposed to avoid harming, others because the harm principle does not obviously apply to such actions. Nudging might be appropriate here because people who are nudged to help maintain and improve the health of their population or community remain free to do otherwise.[57]

It looks, then, as though nudging can be an appropriate and useful—albeit non-comprehensive—approach in public health. This is pursued in the rest of this chapter by criticizing some nudges proposed in the public health literature.[58] The focus is on applications that seem dubious, with a view to teasing out general constraints on public health nudges. Specifically, three conditions on public health nudges emerge from this discussion, centring on uncertainty (clinical and other), criminal actions, and addictive or compulsive behaviour, respectively.

3.1 Uncertainty: clinical and other

Public health is bedevilled by epistemic uncertainty despite its scientific grounding in epidemiology and the success of evidence-based medicine. Uncertainty arises at various points, including whether a programme will achieve its stated goals of, for example, reducing mortality rates or the incidence of disease; the extent to which a public health intervention contributes to a public health gain; and whether the benefits of a programme outweigh the costs (including opportunity costs) of funding the programme. It is natural to think that such uncertainties in public health will impact on the appropriateness of public health nudges.

To pursue this, consider Wheeler et al's application of libertarian paternalist strategies to prostate specific antigen (PSA) screening for prostate cancer.[59] They describe two current decision-making approaches, informed and shared decision-making (IDM and SDM, respectively), and suggest augmenting these with nudges to improve patients' decisions about, and ameliorate harms caused by, PSA screening. What makes this suggestion instructive is the uncertainty surrounding this screening programme. As Wheeler et al explain, uncertainty arises at both the population and individual levels. Regarding the former, the best evidence as to whether the programme reduces rates of mortality is unclear; regarding the latter, screening can result in overdiagnosis and overtreatment which, in turn, cause serious unnecessary harms to individual patients,

[57] In this respect, public health nudges are akin to nudging people to contribute more to charity: unobjectionable, provided any cost of resistance remains very low. Still, even here there could not be sole reliance on nudging because sometimes the stakes are simply too high to worry about avoiding coercion and preserving individual liberties. For example, one reason the Nuffield Council on Bioethics eschewed libertarian paternalism in favour of the 'stewardship model' is that individuals should be coerced to contribute to 'arrangements that benefit a larger group of people, and, importantly, where these benefits can only be sustainably achieved through collective efforts', such as mandatory taxation to fund the UK NHS: Nuffield Council on Bioethics, *Public Health: Ethical Issues* (London: Nuffield Council on Bioethics, 2007) 25.

[58] For illustrative lists of current and potential public health nudges see Marteau et al, 'Judging Nudging' (n 11) 263; O. Oullier and S. Sauneron, 'Improving Public Health Prevention with Behavioural, Cognitive and Neuroscience', Report by Centre D'analyse Stratégique, Paris (May 2010) 42–5; Cabinet Office Behavioural Insights Team, 'Applying Behavioural Insight to Health' (n 10).

[59] D.C. Wheeler, K.M. Szymanski, A. Black, and D.E. Nelson, 'Applying Strategies from Libertarian Paternalism to Decision Making for Prostate Specific Antigen (PSA) Screening' (2011) 11 *BMC Cancer* 148.

including incontinence and impotence. Is it appropriate to augment IDM and SDM with libertarian paternalist strategies given such uncertainty?

It would seem not but the point has to be put carefully. There are general epistemic concerns about libertarian paternalism, some of which have been discussed or alluded to already. For example, how can planners know that people will judge a nudge to have been in their best interests given that individuals differ as to what they value? And Thaler and Sunstein's condition on potentially successful nudges that 'nudgers have expertise' has been mentioned. But the clinical uncertainty surrounding PSA is of a different sort and degree to such general epistemic concerns. The clinical uncertainty in question persists despite clear consensus on values and goals, and impeccable medical expertise. Sometimes, medicine is simply too uncertain for anyone to know the best treatment plan. In a case such as PSA, clinical uncertainty renders it unclear as to what options are optimal: more screening, further testing, and treatment, or to decline screening, testing, and/or treatment. Given this, nudging is irrelevant for the simple reason that planners do not know which options to nudge patients towards.

This suggests a general constraint on public health nudges: nudging is inappropriate in the context of clinical uncertainty. There are complications. Wheeler et al discuss three libertarian paternalist strategies, namely defaults, framing, and timing. The last of these might seem to escape the point that clinical uncertainty makes nudging inappropriate. Timing amounts to allowing patients the opportunity to reflect on and make their choice which, if anything, is more important—obligatory, even—given the sort of clinical uncertainty surrounding PSA screening, and might well result in better decision-making. By contrast, the other two libertarian paternalist strategies—framing choices and setting defaults—seem clearly problematic in the light of the clinical uncertainty. So it might seem that Wheeler et al are at least right to suggest augmenting current decision-making approaches with the libertarian paternalist strategy of timing, though not with framing and defaults.

But this does not salvage Wheeler et al's suggestion. Consider paradigmatic uses of timing to nudge people. Suppose, for example, that skilful but unscrupulous salespersons trade on customers' gullibility and rashness to get them to buy a product. In response, planners invoke timing by requiring a 'cooling-off' period during which consumers can reconsider their purchase, based on evidence that customers tend to return items after some reflection. This is paradigmatic libertarian paternalism: getting people to act in their own best interests without coercing them. But in such cases planners know the optimal option—to return unwanted purchases, for example—and hope that consumers will choose it given time to reflect. This is not so in the PSA screening case because, to reiterate, clinical uncertainty renders it unclear as to what options are optimal. This is not to deny that patients should be allowed time to reflect. But any decision-making approach should give patients time to reflect. This is not exclusive to libertarian paternalism; it is perfectly possible—again, even obligatory—to build sufficient time for patients to reflect into any decision-making approach, including ISM and DSM which Wheeler et al describe as alternatives to libertarian paternalism. So, there are no grounds here for augmenting them with libertarian paternalist strategies.

Hence, the general constraint stands: public health nudges are not appropriate when clinical uncertainty makes it unclear as to what are optimal options. This constraint can be refined. Invoking libertarian paternalism in the case of PSA screening seems to be clearly inappropriate but other cases are not so clear-cut. This raises the question as to what sorts and degrees of uncertainty are compatible with nudges. For example, April focuses on HIV testing in sub-Saharan Africa.[60] He advocates shifting from an opt-in to an opt-out system of testing. This nudges people towards getting tested by reframing the choice—specifically, by resetting the default—whilst leaving them free to decline the test. April's application of libertarian paternalism seems very sound despite there being a good deal of uncertainty in this case. Why does uncertainty undermine Wheeler et al's application of libertarian paternalism to PSA screening but not April's suggestion?

An uncertainty shared by the two cases is that the seemingly optimal option might prove detrimental: for example, the PSA patient might suffer the consequences of unnecessary treatment; finding out one's HIV status might result in social exclusion. The crucial difference is this. In the latter case, the two testing strategies—opt-out versus opt-in—are equally uncertain because there is as much chance that nudging an individual to get tested will prove detrimental as there is that nudging an individual not to get tested will prove detrimental. For example, social consequences (notably, stigmatization) might outweigh the benefits of early diagnosis (treatment) for an individual nudged to get tested; but, equally, foregoing the benefits of early diagnosis might outweigh avoiding the social costs of a positive test result, for individuals nudged to avoid testing. When the options are balanced in this way, what decides the issue is the population perspective. There is clear evidence that opt-out testing achieves public health gains foregone by alternative testing strategies. So, the nudge is justified despite uncertainty at the individual level. By contrast, the uncertainty surrounding PSA is of a different sort. Not only is there clinical uncertainty as to what is in an individual patient's best interests, there is also no clear evidence at the population level as to which of alternative screening programmes and policies achieve public health gains. So, adverting to the population level will not resolve the uncertainty surrounding PSA.

3.2 Criminal behaviour

That public health is state sanctioned and governed by legal strictures and law enforcement raises another question about public nudges: is it appropriate to employ libertarian paternalist strategies in areas of public health governed by legislation? Stevenson's discussion of the cocaine vaccine is instructive here.[61] The vaccine works when the anti-cocaine agent injected into the bloodstream bonds with cocaine molecules to form a compound that is too big to pass through the blood-brain barrier; hence, it remains inert in the sense that it does not afford the user any pleasurable experiences. Given this, there is no point in buying cocaine and the drug is rendered non-addictive. Stevenson considers four applications of the cocaine vaccine: vaccinating parolees or those with a history of drug abuse; vaccinating welfare recipients; universal vaccination; vaccinating air traffic controllers. He pursues the research question as to whether the 'Sunstein/Thaler model' of libertarian paternalism is appropriate to each of these.

[60] M.D. April, 'Rethinking HIV Exceptionalism: The Ethics of Opt-Out HIV Testing in Sub-Saharan Africa' (2010) 88(9) *Bulletin of the World Health Organization* 703. cf D. Brewster, 'Science and Ethics of Human Immunodeficiency Virus/Acquired Immunodeficiency Syndrome Controversies in Africa' (2011) 47(9) *Journal of Paediatrics and Child Health* 646. Brewster comments that April, 'examines the issue from a deontological perspective of protecting individual rights, but where the right to autonomy can be infringed to protect others' welfare, which he calls the doctrine of libertarian paternalism'. This misrepresents both April and libertarian paternalism.

[61] Stevenson, 'Libertarian Paternalism: The Cocaine Vaccine' (n 21).

Stevenson seems to have in mind mandatory vaccinations of the various groups he discusses (parolees, welfare recipients, etc). A typical suggestion is that 'Sunstein/Thaler's model would allow for mandatory vaccinations for this group'.[62] There seems to be a category error here because the point of 'Sunstein/Thaler's model' is to get people to choose freely what is in their best interests as opposed to mandatory interventions. Libertarian paternalism in this context would advocate nudging people to get vaccinated whilst allowing them to remain free not to do so; this disallows 'mandatory vaccinations'. Similarly, some of the policies Stevenson considers make the cost of choosing the suboptimal option so high as to rule out calling them nudges.[63] For example, if the cost of refusing the cocaine vaccine is one's parole or welfare benefits, choosers are more than nudged to get vaccinated, and the strategy is no longer endorsed by libertarian paternalism.

Furthermore, at various points Stevenson seems to adopt approaches that are alternatives to libertarian paternalism. For example, he deploys 'utilitarian arguments', such as that utility would be maximized by inoculating young people against the attractions of drugs. And the harm principle is clearly at work. This is most notable in his discussion of vaccinating air traffic controllers, a 'somewhat randomly' selected example of professionals whose decisions involve 'high stakes... hundreds of lives may be at stake in each of [their] decisions'.[64] As this description suggests, policies such as compulsory drugs testing and mandatory vaccination are justified by the need to avoid third party harms, not by the need to get air traffic controllers to choose in their own best interests without coercing them. This is why '[h]ere again, the libertarian paternalist model gives little guidance':[65] it was never intended to justify coercive interventions to avoid third party harms.

Notwithstanding these criticisms, Stevenson's discussion is illustrative when it comes to devising further constraints on public health nudges. One thing that makes the applications of libertarian paternalist strategies to the cocaine vaccine contentious is that the principal options—purchasing, possessing, and using cocaine—are illegal. This is obviously dissimilar to paradigmatic nudges, such as choosing from a café menu and contributing to a pension plan, where all relevant options are legally permitted. Is it appropriate to deploy libertarian paternalist strategies in choice scenarios that are legally governed in the sense that principal options have been criminalized? Arguably not: the point of libertarian paternalism is to nudge people to choose certain options whilst remaining free to do otherwise; but where options are criminal, agents neither do nor should have this freedom. People are and should be coerced to abide by the law, not nudged in a way that leaves them at liberty to choose criminal options.

This suggests another general constraint on nudging: libertarian paternalist strategies are inappropriate when the choice in question is governed by public health law. A caveat is that some laws are so generally and universally broken as to be seen as *de facto* notional. For example, since everyone drives over 70 miles per hour on British motorways, it is tacitly assumed that the law is notional (hence recent discussion of bringing the law in line with established practice and changing the motorway speed

62 Stevenson, 'Libertarian Paternalism: The Cocaine Vaccine' (n 21) 10.

63 To recall the earlier critique of slippery slope arguments: notwithstanding vague boundaries and gradients, mandatory vaccinations are clearly in a different conceptual category to nudges.

64 Stevenson, 'Libertarian Paternalism: The Cocaine Vaccine' (n 21) 12.

65 Stevenson, 'Libertarian Paternalism: The Cocaine Vaccine' (n 21) 59.

limit to 80 miles per hour).[66] Such cases can be construed as exceptions to the general constraint. Since the prospects of, for example, coercing drivers to drive within a speed limit are so dim, perhaps the best thing to do is to employ behavioural techniques to nudge people to drive more slowly despite legal strictures.[67]

But this caveat does little to undermine the general constraint on nudging agents in legally governed choice scenarios. Very few laws have the ambiguous status of the British motorway speed limit. And the right response to those that have is either to change the law to bring it in line with established practice or re-establish legal strictures by getting people to abide by the law in question. Neither of these—legal reform or law enforcement—is relevant to the nudge agenda. So, the general constraint is reconfirmed: nudging is not appropriate in legally governed choice scenarios. By extension, public health nudges are not appropriate in cases covered by public health law.

3.3 Compulsive behaviour: addiction and mental health

A major theme in public health includes abstinence policies, cessation services, and harm reduction strategies aimed at unhealthy behaviour typically involving use of substances such as drugs, alcohol, and tobacco. Such substances are addictive so at least some of the unhealthy behaviour in question is compulsive. This raises another fairly obvious challenge to the application of libertarian paternalist strategies in public health: is nudging appropriate in the context of addictive or otherwise compulsive behaviour? One way of putting the challenge is that libertarian paternalist strategies simply will not work for substance users because the relevant behavioural techniques—choice framing, default setting, etc—are so subtle they will be overwhelmed by the urge to satisfy cravings which is characteristic of addictive behaviour. A more technical way of putting the point centres on autonomy. The point of libertarian paternalism is that it gets people to choose in their own best interests whilst respecting their autonomy; addiction compromises autonomy so libertarian paternalism is not an appropriate approach to the modification of the health behaviour of substance users.

How strong this challenge is to public health nudges depends on the nature of addiction. There are numerous competing models but let's assume that it is correct to construe addictive behaviour as rational, for the sake of the argument.[68] This might seem to salvage the libertarian paternalist approach to compulsive behaviour modification by suggesting that addicts retain sufficient autonomy to be appropriate targets of nudges. But, typically, models of rational addiction centre on claims such as that substance users display rationality by being price sensitive.[69] This might well ground

66 Relatedly, some laws are either so questionable or outdated as to make it inappropriate to deploy resources to enforce them.

67 These sorts of nudges—to drive more slowly or desist from soft drug use, for example—are not clear-cut cases of libertarian paternalism in action because they can be construed as other-regarding, as opposed to paternalistic, interventions. This is because the nudges are intended to avoid harms to others, such as road users and pedestrians and the victims of drug-related crime, as opposed to benefiting choosers themselves. But it is clearly also in the agents' own interests to avoid traffic accidents and the detrimental effects of drug abuse. So, the nudges in question are both other-regarding and paternalistic.

68 Stevenson's paper is again useful because cocaine is an addictive substance; he discusses the nature of addiction, concluding in favour of Heyman's model of rational addiction (Stevenson, 'Libertarian Paternalism: The Cocaine Vaccine' (n 21) 15–22). See, also, G.M. Heyman, 'Resolving the Contradictions of Addiction' (1996) 19(4) *Behavioral and Brain Sciences* 561.

69 See eg G.S. Becker and K.M. Murphy, 'A Theory of Rational Addiction' (1988) 96(4) *Journal of Political Economy* 675.

some approaches to addictive behaviour modification, such as heavily sin taxing a substance. But these are economic levers that exploit agents' economic rationality; they are expressly distinct from nudges which appeal to the non-rational part of people's natures and which can be resisted without significant (economic or other) costs. So the libertarian paternalist approach is not salvaged by endorsing rational addiction models.[70]

Furthermore, nudging is an inappropriate response to unhealthy addictive behaviour because other sorts of interventions are more important. People addicted to substances such as drugs, alcohol, and tobacco need complex and carefully constructed programmes drawing on disparate disciplines, including addiction studies and health psychology; nudging seems simply irrelevant to this. A similar comment applies to a cognate issue, namely, public health programmes aimed at maintaining and promoting mental health. The connection is that mental illness often manifests in compulsive behaviour. How appropriate are nudges to this part of the public health field? The same bipartite argument applies: nudges are ineffective and inappropriate ways of influencing behaviour; interventions other than libertarian paternalist strategies—ranging from pharmaceutical through cognitive-behavioural to 'talking therapies'—are altogether more important. The upshot is another general constraint: libertarian paternalist strategies are inappropriate when the choice setting involves addiction or other sorts of compulsive behaviour.[71]

4. Concluding Remarks

This chapter has pursued two questions about libertarian paternalism. The first is whether, and if so why, a libertarian should object to the approach. It was argued that standard libertarian objections are not compelling but do indicate a problem with government nudges. Public nudges are grounded in a more comprehensive account of how people should be, how they should live their lives. To the extent that this comprises a conception of the good, libertarians should be concerned that a nudging government is not of the sort endorsed by their political philosophy. This worry is not dispelled by the fact that people remain free to resist nudges: for one thing, the theoretical objection persists that, by libertarian lights, this is the wrong sort of state; for another, there are practical ramifications, such as that the creation of a libertarian state is made less likely by allowing governments a nudging role.

The second question pursued in this chapter is whether libertarian paternalist strategies are applicable to public health. It was argued that some of the public health nudges recommended in the literature are not appropriate. This gave rise to three sorts of constraints on applying libertarian paternalist strategies to public health, grounded in clinical uncertainty, legal restrictions, and addictive behaviour, respectively. This is

[70] A refinement here is that the argument in the main text is against nudging addicts but people use the relevant substances—such as drugs, alcohol, and tobacco—in various ways. Libertarian paternalist strategies may well be appropriate for more casual users of (non-criminalized sorts of) these substances. It might also be appropriate to nudge specific users in a targeted fashion; for example, nudging pregnant women to give up smoking.

[71] The strategy of identifying problematic public health nudges pursued in this section is, conversely, also a strategy for revealing acceptable public health nudges: if general constraints on applying libertarian paternalist strategies do not apply then a public health nudge is permissible. So, for example, if it is not the case that there is a good deal of uncertainty about the programme in question, and relevant choices are not governed by legal strictures or addictive behaviour, a public health nudge might well be appropriate.

non-comprehensive because there are more suggested applications of libertarian paternalism to public health than those pursued here and, doubtless, more general constraints on the approach than the three discussed; besides, there is more to a complete analysis of public health nudges than teasing out general constraints on the approach. Nonetheless, one sort of strategy for deciding when public health nudges are appropriate has been presented and pursued.

20

Interrogation Medicine?

M. Gregg Bloche

More than a dozen years have passed since the 9/11 attacks, and America's post-9/11 frisson with so-called 'enhanced interrogation' now seems a subject for historians, not those who follow current events. The practice of enhanced interrogation conducted on al-Qaeda prisoners has been repudiated by the US government and widely recognized as torture. In one of his first acts, US President Barack Obama proscribed enhanced interrogation and disowned the legal architecture devised to justify it.[1] He issued an executive order limiting military interrogators to a list of non-abusive tactics approved in the US Army Field Manual, which permits aggressive questioning and even some deception but forbids physical abuse.[2]

Yet the political and legal battles over enhanced interrogation have much resonance today. Less than six weeks before the 2012 Presidential elections, the *New York Times* observed that: 'The future of American government practices when interrogating high-level terrorism suspects appears likely to turn on the outcome of the election.' Republican presidential nominee Mitt Romney's legal advisers favored reversing President Obama's ban on enhanced interrogation.[3] Romney insisted that he opposed torture, but he said he did not believe waterboarding constitutes torture.[4]

As this chapter went to press, a new CIA Director, John Brennan, found himself caught between demands that Agency officials who conducted or countenanced enhanced interrogation be held accountable and insistence that the methods at issue were necessary and lawful. The film *Zero Dark 30*, which portrayed brutal interrogation as playing a role in the hunt for Osama Bin Laden, inflamed the debate. And a still-secret US Senate Intelligence Committee report on the CIA's post-9/11 interrogation program reportedly criticizes the program in scathing terms, setting the stage for renewed wrangling over interrogation policy if and when the report is released.[5] Brutal methods for breaking terror suspects remain a charged issue in American politics. Should a Republican win the White House in 2016 or thereafter, there is no small likelihood of a return to the legal interpretations that permitted these methods.[6]

1 See Executive Order 13491, 22 January 2009, available at <http://www.whitehouse.gov/the_press_office/EnsuringLawfulInterrogations>.

2 C. Savage, 'Election to Decide Future Interrogation Methods in Terrorism Cases', *New York Times*, 27 September, available at <http://www.nytimes.com/2012/09/28/us/politics/election-will-decide-future-of-interrogation-methods-for-terrorism-suspects.html>.

3 Savage, 'Election to Decide Future Interrogation Methods' (n 2).

4 Savage, 'Election to Decide Future Interrogation Methods' (n 2).

5 P. Zengerle, 'Senate Committee Approves Report on CIA Interrogations, Revives Torture Debate', Reuters, 13 December 2012.

6 S. Shane, 'C.I.A.'s History Poses Hurdles for an Obama Nominee', *New York Times*, 6 March 2013, available at <http://www.nytimes.com/2013/03/07/us/politics/cias-harsh-interrogations-pose-hurdles-for-john-brennan.html?hp&_r=0>.

Psychologists and physicians designed these methods, monitored their use, and, in some cases, carried them out.[7] Involvement by health professionals, moreover, played a central role in Bush Administration lawyers' efforts to rationalize these methods as compatible with legal prohibitions against torture.[8] Professional societies countenanced this involvement, condemning 'torture' but crafting ethical loopholes that allowed involvement without disciplinary consequence.[9] Though CIA and military operatives no longer practice enhanced interrogation (at least for now), the medicalization of national security interrogation is an enduring legacy of America's post-9/11 frisson with methods that at times crossed the border into torture.

Documents that Jonathan Marks and I have obtained via the Freedom of Information Act (FOIA) show that psychologists and psychiatrists now regularly advise, oversee, and train with military interrogators. Leaders in the behavioral sciences outside the armed forces serve on panels that guide the development of military interrogation practice. And the Pentagon has maintained a position on the ethics of interrogation practice that is at odds with the great weight of civilian medical ethics opinion: doctors who counsel interrogators, the military holds, do not act as health professionals and thus are not bound by the Hippocratic obligation to avoid harm. These developments have received minimal attention in the trans-national medical ethics literature. I address them here—and consider the ethical constraints that should apply—after first reviewing what we now know about the involvement of psychologists, psychiatrists, and other mental health professionals in harsh, post-9/11 interrogation.

1. Post-9/11 Transformation of Interrogation Practice

US Navy pilots downed and taken prisoner during the Korean War were subjected to brutal treatment by their Chinese and North Korean captors, resulting in false confessions of sensational crimes. Concerns about the propaganda value of these confessions (and public alarm over Chinese 'brainwashing') inspired a crash program of research into how the Chinese methods worked. Teams of psychiatrists, neurologists, and sociologists assembled by the Pentagon and the CIA concluded that the methods were designed to first reduce prisoners to the point of hopelessness and despair. Sleep deprivation, confinement in tiny spaces, and other cruel conditions worked not so much through raw force as by engaging prisoners in unwinnable struggles with their own fears and needs. Hopelessness and despair, the Pentagon and CIA researchers concluded, induced a state of compliance. Interrogators could then shape compliance (typically a 'confession' thought to have propaganda value) by offering modest relief from the miseries that inspired hopelessness.[10]

This research became the foundation for a Defense Department training program designed to prepare personnel at high risk of capture to resist abuse of the sort that Korean-War pilots suffered. In the program, known as SERE (for Survival, Evasion, Resistance, and Escape), trainees practiced wilderness survival and, upon 'capture', were confined and subjected to sleep deprivation, temperature extremes, physical abuse, and other harsh treatment, sometimes including waterboarding. Psychologists sequenced

[7] M. Gregg Bloche, *The Hippocratic Myth: Why Doctors Are Under Pressure to Ration Care, Practice Politics, and Compromise their Promise to Heal* (New York: Palgrave Macmillan, 2011) 119–57.

[8] Bloche, *The Hippocratic Myth* (n 7) 119–57.

[9] Bloche, *The Hippocratic Myth* (n 7) 159–80.

[10] Bloche, *The Hippocratic Myth* (n 7) 123–6.

these stressors—each modeled on the conduct of communist interrogators in Korea and, later, Viet Nam—to build trainees' confidence in their ability to resist.[11]

The enhanced interrogation program borrowed SERE stressors, remixing them to serve the original, spirit-crushing purpose that communist interrogators had in mind. Psychologists and psychiatrists did the remixing initially at clandestine CIA sites and, later, at Guantanamo, Abu Ghraib, and other military detention centers. 'Behavioral Science Consultation Teams' (BSCTs) or 'Biscuits', at these centers evaluated high-profile detainees and crafted individualized interrogation plans, employing both 'enhanced' and traditionally lawful techniques. Biscuits drew from the SERE experience and from the aforementioned studies of communist interrogation methods in North Korea and, later, Viet Nam. They also tapped the research literature on what psychologist Martin Seligman, who consulted to the enhanced interrogation program's CIA designers, called 'learned helplessness': the reduction of laboratory animals (and people) to a state of stress-induced immobility and despair.[12]

Physicians and other health professionals, moreover, frequently monitored the abuse, pursuant to a CIA Office of Medical Services memo that established guidelines for doing so. They kept notes on its clinical effects and at times intervened to set limits. The involvement of all of these professionals in designing and overseeing the abuse was invoked by Bush Administration lawyers to 'show' that it did not constitute torture. The memos these lawyers wrote conjured up medicine's clinical restraint and caring ethos. In turn, doctors who played roles in enhanced interrogation cited these memos to 'show' that the program was lawful—and that their activities were therefore ethical.[13]

2. Clinical Ethics and Present Pentagon Policy

Today, years after the end of the enhanced interrogation program and America's formal repudiation of the legal memos purporting to justify it, the role of psychologists, psychiatrists, and other physicians in national security interrogation remains a matter of much controversy. Statements by professional societies seem, on the surface, to proscribe personalized involvement in interrogations. But the post-9/11 revolution in participation by health professionals remains in place. The Department of Defense (DoD) has formalized the 'Biscuit'—indeed made it into an integral part of military interrogation practice. Biscuits no longer coach interrogators to violate international human rights or the laws of armed conflict (at least they are not supposed to), but interrogators are now trained to work with Biscuit psychologists and psychiatrists to develop interrogation plans. The DoD has even developed its own ethical rules and rationale for psychologists and psychiatrists who serve on Biscuits. This rationale is at odds with the weight of civilian ethics opinion, including the positions taken by medical societies; however, it has been accepted by the principal professional body representing America's psychologists.

In June 2005, an American Psychological Association (APA) panel (rather grandly called the 'Presidential Task Force on Psychological Ethics and National Security') issued a report on the ethics of psychologists' involvement in national security interrogations. The ten-person panel included six members who were military psychologists; five had taught, advised, or overseen interrogators at Guantanamo, Abu Ghraib, bases

11 Bloche, *The Hippocratic Myth* (n 7) 129.

12 Bloche, *The Hippocratic Myth* (n 7) 130.

13 Bloche, *The Hippocratic Myth* (n 7) 143–5.

in Afghanistan, or elsewhere.[14] They met for just two days, a few weeks before the report came out. Within a week of its issuance, their report was approved by the Association's board and became APA policy.[15]

The panel endorsed interrogation as a new 'area of practice' for psychologists. It concluded that the APA's ethical proscription against doing harm did not stand in the way, so long as psychologists disclosed their non-therapeutic role. 'Psychologists have a special responsibility', the panel said, 'to clarify their role in situations where individuals may have an incorrect impression that psychologists are serving in a health care provider role.'[16] The report sanctioned breaches of clinical confidentiality, as where Biscuit doctors had access to detainees' medical records and used clinical information to craft interrogation strategies, so long as: 'Psychologists take care not to leave a misimpression that information is confidential when in fact it is not.'[17] The only 'ethical obligation' psychologists have to 'individuals who are not their clients' (ie 'detainees'), the report said circularly, is to 'ensure that their activities . . . are safe, legal, and ethical'.[18] The APA task force, in essence, adopted the Pentagon's position that psychologists who advise and consult on interrogation do not act as health care providers and therefore are not governed by codes of clinical ethics.

Moreover, the task force rejected international law as the basis for defining torture, instead endorsing the Bush Administration's creative redefinition, which had been crafted by Administration lawyers to justify enhanced interrogation. The panel reassured more casual readers with boilerplate language barring participation in torture, and it announced: 'Psychologists do not engage in behaviors that violate the laws of the United States.'[19] But then came the bow to the Bush Administration's redefinition: 'Psychologists involved in national security-related activities follow all applicable rules and regulations that govern their roles. Over the course of the recent United States military presence in locations such as Afghanistan, Iraq, and Cuba [Guantanamo], such rules and regulations have been significantly developed and refined.'[20] The panel thus gave carte blanche to psychologists to participate in the CIA and military enhanced interrogation programs.

Over the next several years, the APA reversed the panel's rejectionist stance toward the ethical relevance of international law. Through petition drives, referenda, and other means, thousands of the group's members demanded that it do so. The Association endorsed international law's stricter approach to the definition of torture, barred psychologists from consulting to interrogators in settings that violate international law, and revised its code of ethics to require respect for 'human rights' even if at odds with national 'law, regulations, or other governing legal authority'.[21] Nevertheless, despite strong objections from its clinical members, the APA kept to the 2005 task force's position that consultation to interrogators is permissible—and beyond the reach of clinical ethics.

In 2006, the American Psychiatric Association announced what appeared to be a more restrictive interrogation ethics policy. However, the Association made this policy unenforceable against its members by issuing it as a 'Position Statement', not an ethical

14 Bloche, *The Hippocratic Myth* (n 7) 162.

15 Bloche, *The Hippocratic Myth* (n 7) 165–6.

16 Report of the American Psychological Association Presidential Task Force on Psychological Ethics and National Security (June 2005) 5.

17 Report of the American Psychological Association (n 16) 7.

18 Report of the American Psychological Association (n 16) 7.

19 Report of the American Psychological Association (n 16) 5.

20 Report of the American Psychological Association (n 16) 5.

21 Bloche, *The Hippocratic Myth* (n 7) 167.

rule. This, in turn, signaled to the Pentagon and CIA that the Association did not see the policy as obligatory. The policy prohibited psychiatrists' 'direct participation' in interrogations, including 'being present in the interrogation room, asking or suggesting questions, or advising authorities on the use of specific techniques of interrogation with particular detainees'.[22] It also barred disclosure of medical records or 'information derived from the treatment relationship' to interrogators.[23] The Association thus instructed psychiatrists to stay out of the business of giving advice on individual interrogations (or performing interrogations). However, the policy permitted psychiatrists to provide 'training' on 'the possible medical and psychological effects of particular techniques and conditions of interrogation, and on other areas within their professional expertise'.[24]

Pentagon policy has hewed to the psychology APA's position that doctors who advise interrogators—even doctors who help to plan individual interrogations—do not act as health care providers and are thus not governed by clinical ethics. There has been internal dissent; for example, an Army assistant surgeon general cautioned in 2005 (in a memorandum we obtained through FOIA) that the Geneva Conventions 'generally prohibit physicians from playing a direct role in interrogations'.[25] But for both psychologists and psychiatrists, the psychology association's role-separation stance prevailed. The DoD finessed the Geneva Conventions, which afford protected status to physicians and other health care providers as non-combatants, by treating doctors who serve on Biscuits as *combatants*, to the point of forbidding them from providing clinical care.

By 2005, the Biscuit had become formalized as a team of two SERE-qualified psychologists or psychiatrists (the former were preferred) and two 'psych technicians' (enlisted personnel with some psychiatry or psychology training).[26] Mental and other health care for detainees had to be provided by separate clinical teams.[27] In June 2005, the Assistant Secretary of Defense for Health Affairs issued Memo 05-006 (which remains in effect at the time of writing), governing the conduct of health care professionals involved in interrogations. Memo 05-006 states that only 'Health care personnel *charged with the medical care of detainees* have a duty to protect their physical and mental health and provide appropriate treatment.'[28] '*All* health care personnel', the memo adds, 'have a duty in all matters affecting the physical and mental health of detainees to perform, encourage and support, directly and indirectly, actions to uphold the humane treatment of detainees'.[29] In short, DoD mental health professionals who serve on Biscuits do not have a duty to protect the health of detainees, but must merely treat them 'humanely'.

22 American Psychiatric Association, Position Statement on Psychiatric Participation in Interrogation* of Detainees (May 2006).

23 American Psychiatric Association, Position Statement (n 22).

24 American Psychiatric Association, Position Statement (n 22).

25 Memorandum from Philip Volpe, Col, Assistant Surgeon General for Force Protection, for Commanders, MEDCOM Major Subordinate Commands, and Directors, OTSG/MEDCOM OneStaff, 'Interim Guidance on Detainee Medical Care', 24 May 2005, 2.

26 Air Force Background Paper on BSCTs to the Surgeon General of the Air Force (2005).

27 Air Force Background Paper on BSCTs (2005) (n 26), noting that the '[i]mportant distinction' between this separate team and the Biscuit is that they 'are not present during interrogations, but will respond initially to medical emergencies to stabilize the detainee until the Army [health care providers] can respond'.

28 Memorandum from William Winkenwerder, Jr, Assistant Secretary of Defense for Health Affairs for Secretaries of the Military Departments, 3 June 2005, available at <http://www.health.mil/libraries/HA_Policies_and_Guidelines/05-006.pdf> 2 (emphasis added).

29 Memorandum from William Winkenwerder, Jr (n 28) (emphasis added).

Memo 05-006 goes into considerable detail on the Pentagon's role-separation policy. Moreover, it extends this policy beyond the interrogation context to other settings in which health care professionals put their knowledge or skills to use for non-therapeutic purposes. The memo states: 'Health care personnel engaged in non-treatment activities, such as forensic psychology or psychiatry, behavioral science consultation, forensic pathology, or similar disciplines, shall not also engage in any professional provider-patient treatment relationship with detainees.'[30] These professionals, the memo holds, have no duty to the health of the people they evaluate. They are, moreover, severed from their separate medical chains of command (leading up to the Army, Navy, and Air Force Surgeon Generals—all physicians) and placed under the control of combatant commanders, typically military intelligence officers. By contrast, the clinical care-giving relationship with patients must be characterized by a sole purpose: 'to evaluate, protect, or improve their physical and mental health'.[31] (But even here, the memo imposes a constraint: whether medical professionals are acting in a therapeutic or a non-therapeutic role, it says, '[d]etainees shall not be given cause to have incorrect expectations of privacy or confidentiality', and medical information may be disclosed 'to prevent harm, to maintain public health and order in detention facilities, and any lawful law enforcement, intelligence, or national security activity [sic]'.[32] The memo thus leaves open the possibility of Biscuit team access to medical records for interrogation-planning purposes, on the ground that interrogation can 'prevent harm' and constitutes 'lawful... intelligence or national security activity'.[33])

Other regulations speak more specifically to involvement by medical professionals in individual interrogations. DoD guidelines on 'Medical Program Support for Detainee Operations', issued in 2006, authorize Biscuit medical personnel to perform assessments of individual detainees and to offer advice concerning their interrogations.[34] Biscuit psychologists and psychiatrists, moreover, 'may observe, but shall not conduct or direct, interrogations'.[35] They are 'authorized to make psychological assessments of the character, personality, social interactions, and other behavioral characteristics of detainees, including interrogation subjects, and, based on such assessments, advise authorized personnel performing lawful interrogations'.[36] The only constraints appear to be those that apply to interrogation personnel more generally: they must operate within the bounds of applicable law and cannot facilitate the use of health information that would result in inhumane treatment.[37]

The 'Medical Program Support for Detainee Operations' guidelines further develop the separation between health professionals' Biscuit and clinical care-giving roles. When assigned to Biscuits, the guidelines state, psychologists or psychiatrists 'shall not allow themselves to be identified to detainees as health care providers' and 'shall not provide medical care for staff or detainees' except in emergency circumstances.[38] 'BSCs [behavioral science consultants] shall not provide medical screening (which is a health

30 Memorandum from William Winkenwerder, Jr (n 28) 3.
31 Memorandum from William Winkenwerder, Jr (n 28) 2.
32 Memorandum from William Winkenwerder, Jr (n 28) 3.
33 See Memorandum from William Winkenwerder, Jr (n 28).
34 Department of Defense Instruction 2310.08E, 'Medical Program Support for Detainee Operations', 6 June 2006.
35 Department of Defense Instruction 2310.08E (n 34) Encl 2.
36 Department of Defense Instruction 2310.08E (n 34).
37 Department of Defense Instruction 2310.08E (n 34).
38 Department of Defense Instruction 2310.08E (n 34).

care function) to detainees, nor act as medical monitors during interrogation',[39] the guidelines say. In response to the Air Force's concern, raised in 2005, that there was '[n]o tracking mechanism to ensure these folks don't return to same locations in medical care capacity',[40] the guidelines mandate a minimum period of three years between deployment with a Biscuit and service as a clinical care-giver at the same location, '[a]bsent compelling circumstances'.[41]

The Army Surgeon General issued additional guidance on 'Behavioral Science Consultation Policy' in late 2006, after the American Psychiatric Association put out its 'Position Statement' proscribing participation in the planning of individual interrogations. Treating the 2005 American Psychological Association Task Force report as a reference (and disregarding the Psychiatric Association's prohibition), the Surgeon General said Biscuit members could and should counsel interrogators on the conduct of individual interrogations. The Biscuit mission, the Surgeon General wrote, is two-fold: to 'ensur[e] the humane treatment of detainees, prevention of abuse, and safety of US personnel, [and to] provide psychological expertise to assess the *individual* detainee and his environment and provide recommendations to improve the effectiveness of intelligence interrogations and detainee debriefing operations'.[42] To this end, the Surgeon General added, Biscuit team members should observe interrogations in order to 'evaluate the psychological strengths and vulnerabilities of detainees'.[43] '[M]aximizing the effectiveness of eliciting accurate, reliable, and relevant information' was the goal.[44]

The Army Surgeon General's guidance adds that Biscuit members must 'remain within professional ethical boundaries as established by their professional associations, their licensing State, and by the military [sic]'.[45] For psychiatrists, this would seem a contradiction in terms, since the American Psychiatric Association's 'Position Statement' on interrogation proscribes the consultation on individual interrogations that is at the heart of the Biscuit role. But some sleight of hand is involved here: a 'Position Statement' does not count, for the Psychiatric Association, as an ethical rule. Neither the Association nor state licensing bodies have enforced the 'Position Statement' on interrogation, leaving the military, and its psychiatrists, free to disregard it without consequence (aside from appearances). The Army Surgeon General's reliance on the American Psychological Association's 2005 report makes the sleight of hand complete: psychologists who served in the military or were DoD employees or contractors dominated the task force that authored it.[46]

Under President Barack Obama, the Pentagon has hewed to both the Biscuit model and the rationalizing ethic of role separation. An October 2012 DoD Directive on 'DoD Intelligence Interrogations, Detainee Debriefings, and Tactical Questioning' endorses both:

Behavioral science consultants are authorized to make psychological assessments of the character, personality, social interactions, and other behavioral characteristics of interrogation subjects and to advise authorized personnel performing lawful interrogations regarding such assessments in

39 Department of Defense Instruction 2310.08E (n 34).

40 Air Force Background Paper on BSCTs (2005) (n 26).

41 Department of Defense Instruction 2310.08E (n 34) Encl. 2.

42 Memorandum from Kevin C. Kiley, Lieutenant General, The Surgeon General, Department of the Army, for Commanders, MEDCOM Major Subordinate commands, 'Behavioral Science Consultation Policy', 20 October 2006, 5 (emphasis added).

43 Memorandum from Kevin C. Kiley (n 42) 10.

44 Memorandum from Kevin C. Kiley (n 42) 6.

45 Memorandum from Kevin C. Kiley (n 42) 6.

46 Bloche, *The Hippocratic Myth* (n 7) 162–6.

accordance with [the previously-cited DoD policy]. During assignments in which a health care provider delivers behavioral science consultant services, the provider may not supply medical care for detainees except in an emergency when no other health care providers can respond adequately.[47]

The 2012 policy included just one additional constraint—that Biscuits 'may not be used to determine detainee phobias for the purpose of exploitation during the interrogation process'.[48]

The military manages the contradiction between the Biscuit model and clinical ethics in part by construing the Geneva Conventions to permit designation of Biscuit members as combatants.[49] The Geneva Conventions are silent on this question. They strip doctors of their non-combatant status—and, thus, their immunity from attack—when they take up arms for purposes other than self-defense. But the Conventions do not contemplate the use of *clinical* knowledge and skills as means for waging war. Moreover, doctors assigned to Biscuits report that the distinction between care-giving and combatant roles is not so easy in practice. Based on interviews with doctors deployed to Biscuits during the program's early years, a Pentagon background memo reported that it was a '[c]onstant challenge to avoid being involved formally with personnel that need formal mental health care or support'.[50] Identity as a health professional evokes expectations that endure beyond disclosure that, as Scott Uithol, the first Biscuit psychiatrist at Abu Ghraib, put it: 'I'm with the guys with the guns.'[51]

3. Fort Huachuca: Training for a New Profession?

When Scott Uithol arrived at Abu Ghraib in November 2003, he told me much later, 'I didn't know what a Biscuit was'.[52] He had neither trained with interrogators nor received formal ethical or legal instruction about his role. Over the next decade, though, as Biscuit service became institutionalized, a formal training program evolved. In 2006, even as the Bush Administration began to back away from enhanced interrogation, the Army initiated a Biscuit training program. Previously, none had existed, or as an Air Force background paper we obtained through FOIA put it: 'Specific training regarding interrogations [wa]s OJT [on-the-job] or Ad Hoc.'[53] The first Biscuits had only SERE training to rely upon[54]—in the face of intense pressure from combatant commanders dissatisfied with traditional interrogation's results. The training program that began in 2006 consisted of two components, a 'distance learning' phase, followed by a twelve-day 'resident phase' at Fort Huachuca, Arizona, where Army interrogators had long learned their craft without the support of psychologists or psychiatrists. During the 'distance learning' phase, trainees (psychologists, psychiatrists,

47 Department of Defense Directive 3115.09, 'DoD Intelligence Interrogations, Detainee Debriefings, and Tactical Questioning', 11 October 2012, Encl 4.

48 Department of Defense Directive 3115.09 (n 47).

49 See Background Paper on BSCTs (December 2006). Note, however, that in 2005, a BSCT member was 'either a combatant or non-combatant', but '[c]annot change roles once in AOR [area of responsibility]'. Air Force Background Paper on BSCTs (2005) (n 26).

50 Background Paper on BSCTs (December 2006) (n 49).

51 Bloche, *The Hippocratic Myth* (n 7) 121.

52 Bloche, *The Hippocratic Myth* (n 7) 120.

53 Air Force Background Paper on BSCTs (2005) (n 26).

54 Senate Committee on Armed Services, 'Inquiry Into the Treatment of Detainees in U.S. Custody' (2008), 3–16.

and enlisted personnel known as 'mental health techs') studied written materials and videos, then responded to questions, including the following (which we obtained via FOIA) about their new role:

- 'Why is it important that Behavioral Science Consultants must not be confused with or portrayed as health care providers?'
- 'Can Behavioral Science Consultants ever use or facilitate, indirectly or directly, the use of medical, physical, or behavioral health information regarding any detainee?'
- 'What should Behavioral Science Consultants do if they encounter actual, suspected, or possible violations of law, regulations or policies at facilities where they are working? What should the Behavioral Science Consultant do if action is not taken on his/her report?'
- 'Can Behavioral Science Consultants ever provide medical care for detainees at the facilities [where] they do interrogation consultation?'
- 'We wondered if you had read any of the articles making accusations about healthcare providers['] involvement in maltreatment of detainees and, if so, what you thought about them.'
- 'What's your thinking about whether psychologists can ethically confer with interrogators and provide treatment at the same facility?'[55]

In 2007, enrollment was increased and the training program was intensified. Forty-one students—psychologists, psychiatrists, and mental health techs—from the Army, Navy, and Air Force participated between April 2006 and October 2007. The 'distance learning' segment grew to forty hours, and the resident phase—extended to sixteen days—was more closely integrated with the US Army Intelligence Center and School at Fort Huachuca.[56] The resident phase included 'practical exercises' and 'role playing scenarios' with military intelligence instructors, interrogators, lawyers, and interpreters.[57] The training program was, in the words of an Air Force briefing document, designed to help Biscuit assignees make 'a shift in role for medical personnel from noncombatant healthcare provider to combatant behavioral science consultant to interrogation and detention operations'.[58]

By 2008, curriculum development involved the several armed services, military lawyers, and the American Psychological Association's ethics director,[59] Steve Behnke, principal author of the Association's 2005 interrogation report. The 'distance learning' phase incorporated additional material on the laws of armed conflict and the Geneva Conventions' application to different legal categories of detainees (including both prisoners of war and unlawful combatants). And the curriculum had shed the Biscuit model's original connection to enhanced interrogation. Through 'role-playing scenarios' and other teaching approaches, Biscuit training emphasized 'the principles of persuasion as applied to the interrogation process'.[60]

55 Briefing on BSCT training, US Air Force.

56 Briefing on BSCT training, US Air Force.

57 Briefing on BSCT training, US Air Force.

58 Briefing on BSCT training, US Air Force.

59 Memorandum for Students in the Course, 'Enhancing Behavioral Science Consultation to Intelligence-Collection and Detention Operations', 5 February 2008.

60 'Enhancing Behavioral Science Consultation' (n 59).

4. A New 'Area of Practice': Permissible Roles for Psychologists and Psychiatrists?

Biscuit training at Fort Huachuca has continued to take its ethical cues from the American Psychological Association's controversial 2005 report embracing national security interrogation as a new 'area of practice'. The American Psychiatric Association's 2006 'Position Statement' opposing psychiatrists' participation in the planning of interrogations has not been explicitly rejected, but it has been, for practical purposes, disregarded. A 2008 memo to Biscuit trainees invokes the Psychological Association report as a lodestar, declaring that it 'frames the key ethical dilemma of being a BSC [behavioral science consultant]: "do no harm" versus "benefit to society."'[61] The 2012 DoD 'Directive' reaffirming this report's rationalizing ethic of role separation signals that change in this regard is unlikely in the near term.

The DoD's embrace of the role-separation argument continues to engender outrage, as does the Pentagon's reliance on the 2005 Psychological Association report. Dismay over use of the APA report is, in my view, justified. The panel that prepared it (made up mostly of DoD-affiliated psychologists, including several who had consulted to interrogators) had obvious interests in the outcome and produced a document that served these interests. This document gave short shrift to Hippocratic ideals and to the identity of medicine and psychology as caring endeavors: the disclaimer that 'I'm not your doctor' does not dispense with deeply-embedded social expectations that health professionals will act with compassion.

Not only do these expectations invite a sense of betrayal on the part of detainees; Biscuit doctors' breach of them undermines trust in clinical care-givers. This threat to trust is not susceptible to objective measurement, but skepticism about prison doctors' commitment to their patients' welfare is a common theme in detainees' accounts of their confinement. There is, moreover, an ironic twist: as Jonathan Marks has observed, *interrogators'* beliefs about doctors' benevolence can unleash them to treat detainees harshly, counting on doctors to set needed limits. In turn, Biscuit members eager to be part of the team can let these limits slip.[62]

For some critics of the Biscuit model, consultation to interrogators poses no ethical dilemma: it is simply wrong because it violates the 'do no harm' ideal. But this proposition claims too much. Health professionals put their skills and judgment to use on behalf of myriad public and other non-therapeutic purposes, and harm to individuals sometimes ensues.[63] Clinical diagnosis itself often has adverse social consequences, occupational and otherwise. Forensic psychiatrists routinely render judgments with disastrous consequences for the people they evaluate—including criminal punishment and loss of parental rights. The challenge for medical ethics, and for the law, is to draw lines between acceptable and impermissible uses of clinical skill and judgment for non-therapeutic purposes.

As medicine's capabilities expand, this challenge will grow greater. Physicians and psychologists will increasingly be asked to act for national security, criminal justice, performance enhancement, and other non-therapeutic purposes. It is, in my view, unrealistic to insist that they always say no. Medicine and psychology are, in many senses, self-governing professions, but their ethics are the product of ongoing 'negotiation'

61 'Enhancing Behavioral Science Consultation' (n 59).
62 J.H. Marks, 'Doctors of Interrogation' (2005) 35 *Hastings Center Report* 17.
63 Bloche, *The Hippocratic Myth* (n 7).

between the professions and society. Doctors are in no position, for example, to insist that all plausible treatments be provided regardless of cost; nor are they in a position to roll back cultural beliefs about the relationship between diagnosis and personal responsibility that have given psychiatric opinion a large role in the courts. But doctors are in a strong position—because of their patients' expectations—to assert the primacy of their care-giving role. This, in turn, empowers them to say no to non-therapeutic endeavors that undermine this role.

Is consultation to interrogators such an endeavor? A global conversation about this is urgently needed—a conversation that engages military and intelligence professionals as well as psychologists, physicians, and society writ large—and that takes the national security needs of human rights-respecting nations into account. My own view is that consultation to interrogators in the form of general advice about interviewing poses no threat to psychologists' and psychiatrists' care-giving role, as a matter of either popular perception or professional identity—if this advice comports with domestic and international law, robustly enforced. The same is the case, I think, for counseling on particular interrogations (here, I am more permissive than the Psychiatric Association 'Position Statement') so long as the psychologist or psychiatrist makes no personal connection with the detainees being questioned, plays no role in their clinical care, and does not review medical records or seek information from care-givers (this would turn clinicians into adjuncts of interrogators). Psychological profiling and interview coaching based on information from non-clinical sources, including the viewing of interrogation videos, offer potential national security benefits without the breach of faith that a relationship with an interviewee might entail.

I would draw the line, though, at the forming of any sort of personal connection between detainee and psychologist or psychiatrist acting as interrogation consultant. Because any such relationship is fraught with mixed messages arising from social expectations of health professionals (and their own sense of professional identity), it is a set-up for the experience of betrayal. The disclaimer, 'I'm not acting as your doctor', does not wash away these expectations; indeed a psychologist's warm smile, empathic tone, and insightful questions may feed them. Evaluative interviews—or even brief encounters—should thus be off-limits, as should any role in clinical care. Such interviews are ethically problematic for this reason when forensic psychiatrists conduct them,[64] but forensic evaluees have lawyers whom (in theory, at least) they can safely trust. National security interrogation lacks even this safeguard.

5. Conclusion

What is most disturbing about the emergence of national security interrogation as a new 'area of practice' is that it has happened behind the national-security veil. Our FOIA inquiries have revealed the secret emergence of a professional specialty, with ethical rules that disregard urgent concerns. The Biscuit ethic of role separation developed absent dialog with biomedical ethics scholars outside the armed services, and it was 'validated' in circular fashion by a professional association panel composed mainly of military members who were advocates for the new specialty. This specialty and ethic are the enduring, ill-scrutinized legacy of America's post-9/11 frisson

64 A.A. Stone, 'The Ethical Boundaries of Forensic Psychiatry: A View from the Ivory Tower' (1984) 12 *Bulletin of the American Academy of Psychiatry and the Law* 209.

with torture. So is the more general proposition that it is acceptable for a specialty and its practice norms to develop in secret.

Should another presidential election or terrorist attack swing American legal policy back to enhanced interrogation (as advisors to the most recent Republican presidential nominee urged), the Biscuit model will be available as an implementation tool. Advances in the neuroscience of stress, moreover, could open the way to 'enhanced interrogation 2.0', powered by pharmacological interventions to reduce detainees' mental resilience. Research that is today furthering our understanding of anxiety and depression could find a parallel use, as a basis for interfering with neural circuitry to aid in inducing learned helplessness.

Keeping discussion of this and other interrogation consultation possibilities secret will not do. If this 'area of practice is to win professional and public acceptance, it cannot remain closeted. Nor can its ethics be unilaterally imposed by government. Professional ethics arise from social negotiation among professional bodies, the rest of civil society, and the state. To reject this oft-contentious process on national security or other grounds is to foreclose, to an 'area of practice', the possibility of standing as a profession.

PART D

LEGAL RESPONSES

21

Global Health, Law, and Ethics

Fragmented Sovereignty and the Limits of Universal Theory

*John Coggon**

> The hard question is not whether law is practically or philosophically important to public health but whether the political conditions in which the body of public health law and its supporting philosophy must operate are conducive to governance progress in the protection of population health.
>
> D. Fidler, 'Global Health Jurisprudence: A Time of Reckoning'[1]

1. Introduction

The quotation that heads this chapter, taken from one of David Fidler's many contributions to debates on global health, captures the burden of my inquiry and the complexities that I wish to examine as a preliminary study of the roles and relationships of law and ethics in relation to global health. As Fidler makes clear, there is no difficulty in establishing that law is an important practical and normative tool in efforts to safeguard health (even whilst we should note that heated argument is inevitable on the legitimate bounds and basis of law's role in so doing).[2] The difficult matter in global health is not establishing that law (and other formalized modes of governance) would have a role to play in optimizing good health outcomes, ensuring greater equity internationally, protecting against abuses of power, and so on. Rather, it is in finding the legal or quasi-legal mechanisms that might be employed to afford law a practical role to play. As Fidler makes clear, that question can only be answered given an inquiry in politics.[3]

* For feedback on the ideas discussed in this chapter, I would like to express my thanks to audiences at the Hastings Center on 12 March 2012, The Kennedy Institute of Ethics at Georgetown University on 21 March 2012, and at the Law and Global Health Colloquium at University College London on 2–3 July 2012.

1 (2008) 96 *Georgetown Law Journal* 393, 407.

2 For a stark representation of such argument, see R. Epstein, 'Let the Shoemaker Stick to his Last: A Defense of the "Old" Public Health' *Perspectives in Biology and Medicine* (2003) 46(3): S138; R. Epstein, 'In Defense of the "Old" Public Health' *Brooklyn Law Review* (2004) 69(4): 1421; L. Gostin and M.G. Bloche, 'The Politics of Public Health: A Response to Epstein' *Perspectives in Biology and Medicine* (2003) 46(3): S160. See also M. Rothstein, 'Rethinking the Meaning of Public Health' *Journal of Law, Medicine and Ethics* (2002) 30: 144; M. Rothstein, 'The Limits of Public Health: A Response' *Public Health Ethics* (2009) 2(1): 84; J. Anomaly, 'Public Health and Public Goods' *Public Health Ethics* (2011) 4(3): 251; J. Coggon, *What Makes Health Public? A Critical Evaluation of Moral, Legal, and Political Claims in Public Health* (Cambridge: CUP, 2012) ch 8. In relation to global health, consider also the distinct aims of global health policy described in D. Stuckler and M. McKee, 'Five Metaphors about Global-Health Policy' *Lancet* (2008) 372: 95.

3 D. Fidler, 'Global Health Jurisprudence: A Time of Reckoning' *Georgetown Law Journal* (2008) 96: 393.

I have argued at length elsewhere that the analysis of national health law and policy similarly demands a study in politics, and that any normative inquiry into public health law and ethics will (or anyway should) ultimately be reducible to an exercise in political rather than moral philosophy.[4] The essence of my approach is the claim that to engage in public health law and ethics is to ask and answer the question 'what makes health public?'. In this sense, we sift out questions of 'purely moral' responsibility for health (or lack thereof), and find that our focus falls on the matters that are a shared concern amongst a people whose rights, duties, liberties, and so forth are filtered through, mediated by, and given effect by the State.[5] These questions may be informed by principled moral argument, but require examination too of such matters as 'coordination problems', and political, economic, and regulatory possibility.[6] Although the study will necessarily cover voluntarily-assumed responsibilities and the impact of 'private' actors, a scholar in public health law and ethics is ultimately interested in establishing and defending a claim about what role law and governance can and should play in relation to health and health-affecting behaviour and practices.[7]

In this chapter, my aim is to explore the potential application of such a mode of thinking to global health law and ethics. My concern is to address whether and how ethical argument can be brought to bear in a wider political analysis of health and governance. However, the project differs radically from an analysis of national public health law for an obvious reason: whilst the study of 'domestic' public health law enjoys the luxury of being framed within a 'central case' of law and governance, the study of global health necessarily falls outside such a frame. In what follows, therefore, I present two informative and widely-discussed branches of scholarly argument about how we should approach global health law, with a specific emphasis on the possible (or otherwise) inclusion and effect of ethical theory on our deliberations. As I do so, and in reflection of Fidler's framing of the subject, I find it important to distinguish what I would term the philosophical (or academic's) question—what makes health public?—and the political (or activist's) question—how can health be made public?

The analysis is in three main sections. First, I ask what academics, activists, practitioners, and others take public health and global health respectively to mean. Drawing on points of similarity and points of difference, I am able to examine how we might say that global health is or is not a 'public' issue. Given the conceptual and analytical points made, the study then moves to ethics. This analysis begins by looking at the place of ethics in global health, questioning its effectiveness, its constraints in a complex global system, and its limitations in explanatory potential and action-guiding power. I then move to consider arguments that would introduce ethics to global health agendas. This involves two stages of evaluation. First I explore critically the theory and practical proposals advanced in the work of Jennifer Prah Ruger. Ruger's analysis presents a theory of 'global health justice', whose imperatives would lead to the development of

4 See especially Coggon, *What Makes Health Public?* (n 2).

5 Contrast eg G. Dworkin, 'Taking Risks, Assessing Responsibility' *The Hastings Center Report* (1981) 11(5): 26; D. Wikler, 'Who Should be Blamed for Being Sick?' *Health Education and Behavior* (1987) 14(1): 11; H. Schmidt, 'Patients' Charters and Health Responsibilities' *British Medical Journal* (2007) 335: 1187; O. Golan, 'The right to treatment for self-inflicted conditions' *Journal of Medical Ethics* (2010) 36(11): 683.

6 These matters, which are discussed further later in the current chapter, are receiving increasing attention in the recent literature on public ethics. See eg J. Wolff, *Ethics and Public Policy: A Philosophical Inquiry* (Abingdon: Routledge, 2011); J. Montgomery, 'Reflections on the Nature of Public Ethics' *Cambridge Quarterly of Healthcare Ethics* (2013) 22(1): 9.

7 For a contrasting approach, see I. Brassington, *Public Health and Globalisation* (Exeter: Imprint, 2007).

formally designated and sovereign Global Health Institutions whose authority is established within a Global Health Constitution. Their legitimacy would derive from a universally shared commitment to her theory of justice. Following this critical engagement, I reconsider concerns about resignation to 'real world limitations' that speak against a role for ethics in global health governance. Whilst I suggest that we should accept serious constraints on the potential effect of philosophical ethics in this area, I also argue that we have sound reason to accept that ethical argument can impact productively. In conclusion, my aim is to have demonstrated some of the theoretical and practical questions that must be addressed in the development of a satisfactory study of global health law and ethics. In positive terms, I hope to have shown too that ethical theory is not a practically redundant component in discussions of global health law and governance.

2. Public Health and Global Health

2.1 Public health as a political agenda

Amongst the starker problems in the study of public health, and of public health, law, and ethics, is the uncertain meaning of 'public health' itself.[8] We see in the quotation from Fidler mention of public health's, or public health law's, 'supporting philosophy'. At once such reference opens a series of questions. What are public health and public health law that they can be said to have a supporting philosophy? As in other areas of law (for example torts, crime, human rights), we may find normative arguments about the proper purpose and use of the law, but it is not clear that we can find a consensus on *the* philosophy underpinning the law or its purpose.[9] What authority does this suggested philosophy have? How are the demands of this philosophy to be understood in the light of 'supporting philosophies' of other spheres of law and activity? What happens, for example, when 'the philosophy' of transnational commerce suggests one course of action, and 'the philosophy' of public health suggests another? Is it even meaningful to suggest that public health has a 'philosophy', or that public health law does?

These are not simply rhetorical questions. They bear exploration. Certainly, a good number of scholars, activists, and others do perceive a normative agenda in public health and public health law.[10] Consider the following two quotations from Lawrence Gostin, a leading and influential scholar in national and global health law. First, I present Gostin's definition of public health law itself, and second, a characterization that allows us to infer the normative agenda of public health practitioners, found in a paper co-authored by Gostin and Lesley Stone. Gostin defines public health law as:

> ... the study of the legal powers and duties of the state, in collaboration with its partners ... to ensure the conditions for people to be healthy ... and of the limitations on the power of the state to constrain for the common good the autonomy, privacy, liberty, proprietary, and other legally protected interests of the individual. The prime objective of public health law is to pursue the

[8] For a much fuller analysis than I can offer here, see Coggon, *What Makes Health Public?* (n 2) ch 3.

[9] See also the argument presented in J. Coggon, 'Morality and Strategy in Politicising Tobacco Use: Criminal Law, Public Health, and Philosophy' in A.M. Viens, J. Coggon, and A. Kessel (eds), *Criminal Law, Philosophy, and Public Health Practice* (Cambridge: CUP, 2013).

[10] For my part, I have argued that the normative agenda ought to be kept separate from our understandings and study of the subject (see Coggon, *What Makes Health Public?* (n 2) ch 5). Nevertheless, it is useful here to draw from the very influential accounts that do include in them the agenda that I describe.

highest possible level of physical and mental health in the population, consistent with the values of social justice.[11]

And Gostin and Stone state that 'public health communities take it as an act of faith that health must be society's overarching value'.[12] The commitment to health is drawn from a theory of human functioning that sees health as foundational to human well-being and social and political existence; they employ a theory of government that has the State's primary function as being to secure the population's health, safety, and welfare.[13]

These definitions and theories give clear echoes of C.E.A. Winslow's celebrated definition of public health as:

... the science and the art of preventing disease, prolonging life, and promoting physical health and efficiency through organized community efforts for the sanitation of the environment, the control of community infections, the education of the individual in principles of personal hygiene, the organization of medical and nursing services for the early diagnosis and preventive treatment of disease, and the development of the social machinery which will ensure to every individual in the community a standard of living adequate for the maintenance of health.

Public health conceived in these terms will be something vastly different from the exercise of the purely police power which has been its principal manifestation in the past.[14]

The characterizations presented in these quotations combine to make clear a view of the necessary role of government in securing people's health, and the links between public health as a profession and the State. They also hint at a normative purpose; they suggest a practical imperative. We do not simply find claims that 'public health might be conceived as X'. Nor do we see public health law as simply the detached study of a particular body of norms. Rather, public health denotes a political agenda. Human health is given as a socially, morally, and politically predominant value, such that it gives rise to a governmental mandate, and demands professional, legal, and institutional infrastructures to assure the conditions in which people can be healthy. And scholars in public health law are entreated to become part of this public health agenda.

2.2 Linking public health and global health

How, we must next ask, can the foregoing characterizations be brought to bear on global health? In their analysis of the 'public' in public health, Marcel Verweij and Angus Dawson present two meanings that can be found in the most noteworthy definitions of public health:

Firstly, ... it makes sense to talk about public health as the state of the health of the public; that is, the health of the population as [a] whole, or a population's 'collective health' ... Secondly, in talking of 'public health' we often refer, not to the state of health of the public, but to a practice or set of interventions aiming to protect the health of the public. The latter use is clear in most definitions, e.g. 'what we, as a society do ...' or '... through organised community efforts'. These interventions are in some way organised either by public institutions or they are carried out through collective effort.[15]

11 L.O. Gostin, *Public Health Law: Power, Duty, Restraint* (Berkeley, CA: University of California Press, 2008) 4.

12 L.O. Gostin and L. Stone, 'Health of the People: The Highest Law?' in A. Dawson and M. Verweij (eds), *Ethics, Prevention, and Public Health* (Oxford: OUP, 2007) 60.

13 Gostin and Stone, 'Health of the People' (n 12) 60.

14 C.E.A. Winslow, 'The Untilled Fields of Public Health' *Science* (1920) 51(1306): 23, 30.

15 M. Verweij and A. Dawson, 'The Meaning of "Public" in "Public Health"' in A. Dawson and M. Verweij (eds), *Ethics, Prevention, and Public Health* (Oxford: OUP, 2007) 21.

Verweij and Dawson's understanding here is clear, and well-distilled from a wide conceptual analysis of definitions of public health. In potential application to global health, we might immediately note that whilst there can be no principled problem with the population under consideration being international, or even entirely global, there is no straightforwardly accessible central point of reference for the second sense of public; something approximating the State, which can coordinate organized, collective efforts. It should be emphasized that Verweij and Dawson's thesis does not demand that collective efforts be organized only by public institutions (ie a central political government is not a necessary condition of this meaning). But even still, current global health practices are not, and clearly cannot as things stand, be organized through anything approximating to the sort of collective effort that might be found embodied in a single nation State.

Despite such a point about public health as it relates to government, the literature does point us to approaches that would include global health within the frame of public health as a political agenda. Consider, for example, Solomon Benatar and Ross Upshur's portrayal of global health as:

> ...the science and art of preventing disease, prolonging life and promoting physical and mental health through organized global efforts for the maintenance of a safe environment, the control of communicable disease, the education of individuals and whole populations in principles of personal hygiene and safe living habits, the organization of health care services for the early diagnosis, prevention and treatment of disease, and attention to the societal, cultural and economic determinants of health that could ensure the standard of living and education for all that is adequate for the achievement and maintenance of good health.[16]

And Lawrence Gostin and Allyn Taylor have provided a definition of global health law that has obvious links to public health (law), including a clear pro-health agenda, but which expands beyond the 'traditional confines of formal sources and subjects of international laws'.[17] They argue:

> Global health law is a field that encompasses the legal norms, processes, and institutions needed to create the conditions for people throughout the world to attain the highest possible level of physical and mental health. The field seeks to facilitate health-promoting behaviour among the key actors that significantly influence the public's health, including international organizations, governments, businesses, foundations, the media, and civil society. The mechanisms of global health law should stimulate investment in research and development, mobilize resources, set priorities, coordinate activities, monitor progress, create incentives, and enforce standards. Study and practice of the field should be guided by the overarching value of social justice, which requires equitable distribution of health services, particularly to benefit the world's poorest populations.[18]

Gostin and Taylor note that their definition 'is prescriptive as well as descriptive', and draw from it:

> ...five salient features, namely its: *mission*—ensuring the conditions for the public's health (meeting 'basic survival needs'); *key participants*—states, international organizations, private and

[16] S.R. Benatar and R. Upshur, 'What is Global Health?' in S.R. Benatar and G. Brock (eds), *Global Health and Global Health Ethics* (Cambridge: CUP, 2011). See also S.R. Benatar, 'Needs, Obligations and International Relations for Global Health in the 21st Century' in J. Coggon and S. Gola (eds), *Global Health and International Community* (London: Bloomsbury, 2013).

[17] L.O. Gostin and A.L. Taylor, 'Global Health Law: A Definition and Grand Challenges' *Public Health Ethics* (2008) 1(1): 53, 55.

[18] Gostin and Taylor, 'Global Health Law' (n 17) 55.

charitable organizations and civil society; *sources*—public international law; *structure*—innovative mechanisms for global health governance; and *moral foundations*—the values of social justice, which call for the fair distribution of health benefits to the world's most impoverished and least healthy populations.[19]

In Benatar and Upshur's definition of global health, and Gostin and Taylor's of global health law, the agenda is clear. There is also, arguably, a heightened emphasis on the ethical aspects of their perspective, reflective of a correspondingly complex, fragmented, and incomplete regulatory system that might achieve the desired goals. Thus, whilst we might see a logical association between national and global health from an activist's perspective, we might question how strong is the 'public' aspect of global health in its governmental (and ultimately legal) connotations.

3. How 'Public' is Global Health: Political Authorities, 'Us and Them', 'One World'?

The discussion so far has shown that it is possible to track the idea of global health onto those prevalent understandings of public health that conceive public health as a compellingly legitimate and driving political agenda; a social mission. However, it is also clear that (to put it mildly) the formal infrastructure is not present globally to institute a legal agenda that would radically support, push, strengthen, or enhance health goals in a manner equivalent to those available within 'developed' nation States (we can leave to one side here separate questions of whether and how well such formal infrastructures are in fact used to advance people's health within such states).[20] Before moving to substantive and practical ethical questions that would respond to this situation, it is informative to explore the question 'how public is global health?'. Doing so provides a theoretical backdrop that allows us to contrast the extent of the ethical commitments that different theorists in global health might espouse. This will work through two sub-sections. First, I present a short summary of an argument about 'private transnational governance' and its implications for our ideas about the concepts of law, public authority, and private actors in global health. I then briefly note the import of claims about health inequalities in arguments regarding global health, and outline two dominant, contrasting approaches to political morality: nation State politics, and cosmopolitanism.

3.1 'Private transnational governance', globalization, and public health

The effects of globalization on our ideas of public authority, national sovereignty, and the very idea of an integrated legal system have been profound. This chapter does not purport to review the range of important literatures that have been developed to conceptualize and explain economic, legal, and regulatory norms in the current global order. However, my analysis is assisted by brief reference to A. Claire Cutler's thesis concerning private actors and the role and effect of experts in contemporary debates on power, authority, and governance.[21] In her argument, Cutler suggests that we need to rethink our concept of 'public'. Her reasoning has important implications for how,

19 Gostin and Taylor, 'Global Health Law' (n 17) 55.

20 But see Benatar, 'Needs, Obligations and International Relations' (n 16).

21 A.C. Cutler, 'Private Transnational Governance and the Crisis of Global Leadership' in S. Gill (ed), *Global Crises and the Crisis of Global Leadership* (Cambridge: CUP, 2012).

globally, we might modify our conception of 'public' in the structural, coordinating, governmental sense alluded to previously, particularly in reference to Verweij and Dawson's analysis of the 'public' in public health.[22]

Cutler's idea is that scholars interested in questions concerning global leadership (amongst others) need to study the private actors who operate within transnational governance. In her words: '[T]he significance of private lawmaking is obscured by distinctions between *public* and *private* international law that ascribe political governance roles solely to the former, and not to the latter.'[23] Transnational governance, Cutler argues, 'is associated generally with the expansion of global capitalism and neoliberal principles that privilege the market as the template of "good governance" and "common sense"'.[24] As such, a focus that ignores powerful private actors, or accepts their claims that they operate within a system that is 'efficacious, democratic and universal',[25] accommodates their public impact whilst failing to account adequately for concerns for legitimacy and accountability.

In developing her thesis, Cutler first demonstrates the multiplicity of actors and matters that fall within global governance. She then goes on to argue that a common aspect across the range of modes within global governance is a central role for experts. With expertise, she suggests, comes (apparent) authority. Bringing this to bear on global health, we find resonance in various responses to questions that have been explored from a range of perspectives.[26] Of especial relevance is the need to look at the influence and governance roles of both State and non-State actors. The 'anarchic' system to which David Fidler has referred draws from, amongst other things, what he labels 'open-source anarchy'; the post-Westphalian order is not a 'governance space' only occupied by States, but is accessed and shaped also by non-State actors.[27] As Fidler emphatically puts it: 'governing Bill Gates may prove as challenging in its own way as governing the United States in terms of global health'.[28] Non-governmental organizations, philanthropies, and others are all engaged in global health governance, and in this sense are 'public' actors. So questions emerge concerning matters such as legitimacy, transparency, and establishing to whom (if anyone) these global health actors are answerable, and indeed on quite what terms. There is no 'overarching governance architecture'[29] to house the actors, even as their impact and activity would suggest many public interest type concerns.

Within this practical frame (such as it may be), we can begin to approach arguments concerning global health ethics. As stated earlier, the ethical theories that will interest us present responses to questions of political morality; concerns for ethically defensible institutional structures and practices, and attempts to address coordination problems in

22 Verweij and Dawson, 'The Meaning of "Public" in "Public Health"' (n 15).

23 Cutler, 'Private Transnational Governance and the Crisis of Global Leadership' (n 21) 57 (emphasis in original).

24 Cutler, 'Private Transnational Governance and the Crisis of Global Leadership' (n 21) 56–7 (reference omitted).

25 Cutler, 'Private Transnational Governance and the Crisis of Global Leadership' (n 21) 58.

26 This is evidenced in many of the works cited in the current chapter. For further perspectives see also eg S. Burris, 'Governance, Microgovernance and Health' *Temple Law Review* (2004) 77: 335; C. Thomas and M. Weber, 'The Politics of Global Health Governance: Whatever Happened to "Health for All by the Year 2000"?' *Global Governance* (2004) 10: 187; A.L. Taylor, 'Governing the Globalization of Public Health' *Journal of Law, Medicine and Ethics* (2004) 32(3): 500; R.S. Magnusson, 'Rethinking Global Health Challenges: Towards a 'Global Compact' for Reducing the Burden of Chronic Disease' *Public Health* (2009) 123: 265.

27 D.P. Fidler, 'Architecture amidst Anarchy: Global Health's Quest for Governance' *Global Health Governance* (2007) I(1): 2.

28 Fidler, 'Architecture amidst Anarchy' (n 27) 2.

29 Fidler, 'Architecture amidst Anarchy' (n 27) 3.

accordance with defensible norms. The literature is wide-ranging, and gives rise to competing arguments about how legitimacy is established.[30] A core aim of a theorist bringing ethics to global health, therefore, is to overcome normative disagreements. And more practically, it is widely argued in the global health ethics and governance literatures that we have a sub-optimal, wasteful, and even positively harmful system of governance.[31] So theories need also to be able properly to substantiate these criticisms and provide practical guidance on a response to them. Before moving to consider a good example of a moral theorist who has sought to address the situation, I will present two further, important questions that arise in the construction of an ethical framing of global health problems.

3.2 Global health inequalities, nation state politics, and cosmopolitanism

Arguments in global health ethics often begin with data that show the radical inequalities in health status internationally. Health inequalities abound across groups within countries, and across different nation States globally, and the extent of differences in mortality and morbidity is both staggering, and avoidable.[32] For many commentators, these inequalities of themselves demonstrate that the existing international order (or at least the way it is administered) is indefensible. For such a view to be theoretically robust, however, two questions need to be addressed.

The first of these is to ask whether health inequalities are in themselves a cause for concern. When we are faced with the sorts of statistics alluded to in the previous paragraph, this question will seem offensive even to ask. But it is not just a crass 'ivory tower' concern. An argument that holds health inequalities self-evidently to be indefensible leads to particular practical imperatives. If we should give priority to health above other potential candidate human 'goods', 'capabilities', 'functionings', or so forth (as, for example, *per* theories that place health as uniquely foundational to human functioning)[33] that means one thing. But without commitment to such a view—ie if health sits as perhaps just one amongst various equally important goods, or if we think that these matters are not straightforwardly commensurable—instances of ill-health can provide no more than an indication that there might be a need to change governance structures.[34] When exploring this issue, it is important to think not just about desirable outcomes but also the reasons for desiring them. As Stephen Latham argues:

> The theorist of global health justice will observe, for example, that women who lack reproductive autonomy are at considerable health risk from unwanted and ill-timed pregnancy. Health justice, then, will seem to require women's reproductive autonomy. But it requires reproductive

30 We might contrast, for example, the theories of political morality advanced in works such as N. Daniels, *Just Health* (Cambridge: CUP, 2008); A. Sen, *The Idea of Justice* (London: Penguin, 2009); P. Singer, *One World: the Ethics of Globalization* (New Haven, CT and London: 2nd edn, Yale University Press, 2004); T. Pogge, *World Poverty and Human Rights* (Cambridge: 2nd edn, Polity Press, 2008).

31 For a particularly powerful argument in this regard, see L. Garrett, 'The Challenges of Global Health' *Foreign Affairs* (2007) 86(1): 14.

32 See M. Marmot, 'Social Determinants of Health Inequalities' *Lancet* (2005) 365: 1099.

33 See eg Lawrence Gostin's theory of human functioning, which holds that health, 'among all the other form of disadvantage, is special and foundational' for individuals, and also 'a transcendent value' at a population and governmental level: L.O. Gostin, 'Meeting Basic Survival Needs of the World's Least Healthy People: Toward a Framework Convention on Global Health' *Georgetown Law Journal* (2008) 96: 331, 344.

34 See R. Ashcroft, 'Ethics and Global Health Inequalities' in J. Coggon and S. Gola (eds), *Global Health and International Community* (London: Bloomsbury, 2013).

autonomy for what immediately seems to be the wrong reason, or not the core reason; it requires reproductive autonomy for the sake of the woman's health, rather than on the more compelling ground that reproductive autonomy is what women, as persons, deserve. Similar difficulties will arise in connection with concerns for education, peace, job opportunities and so on: the global health theorist's concern for them will be based in health, because she is a health theorist; and that kind of concern for those important items will ring hollow.[35]

This tension is a matter that demands consideration in any ethical analysis of global health. If we are to be motivated just, or above all, by health, we need a sound set of reasons for being so. If we are to be motivated by matters other than (but perhaps including) health, we need the means of conducting an all-things-considered analysis to assure we work towards the best possible outcomes.[36]

The second question that needs to be explored before we can understand and accept a practical ethical imperative in global health debates derives from the on-going philosophical debates between defenders of a global order of separate State systems, and defenders of cosmopolitanism. In its essence, this dispute can be reduced to the question of whether the world should be viewed as rightfully comprising many discrete political communities, with their own internal political systems, or whether moral obligations are owed equally and universally regardless of political divisions of peoples. On the former view, there is something morally relevant in being based within a particular State, and the institutions of that State filter and mediate obligations within its jurisdiction with no (or very limited) regard having to be given to people elsewhere.[37] On the latter view, national institutions may serve defensible administrative purposes (ie be defensible on pragmatic grounds), but the fact of an international regime does not provide sound moral reason to treat your compatriots preferentially or with heightened moral concern.[38] It should be recognized that given real-world constraints, some might advocate for a view that is sympathetic with cosmopolitans' moral concerns whilst acknowledging, too, the practical reality and its bearing on political possibility.[39]

The disputes between cosmopolitans and statists have a profound effect on debates in global health. They are further problematized by the array and effect of 'private-public' actors involved in global health governance. The fact of globalization has implications for the tenability of purely State-based concerns, even as the fact of an international legal order speaks against the practical force of arguable imperatives based on cosmopolitanism. The crucial point here is that insofar as these are ethical questions, they require ethical responses. And insofar as they are practical concerns, action-guiding responses must be able to respond to the institutional realities that the world presents. I will now bring these, and the other issues presented previously, to bear directly on questions of ethics in global health.

35 S. Latham, 'On Some Difficulties for Any Theory of Global Health Justice,' in J. Coggon and S. Gola (eds), *Global Health and International Community* (London: Bloomsbury, 2013) 22.

36 See further Ashcroft, 'Ethics and Global Health Inequalities' (n 34).

37 See J. Rawls, *The Law of Peoples* (Cambridge, MA: Harvard University Press, 1999), and foundationally J. Rawls, 'The Law of Peoples' *Critical Inquiry* (1993) 20:1, 36. To be clear, Rawls emphasizes a 'distinction between the law of peoples and the law of nations, or international law' (at 43). This is made on the basis that he is not purporting to describe or justify the existing legal order, but to advance a theory of political morality. Acknowledging his distinction in terminology, I continue here to speak of nations, as I think that is more appropriate in this context.

38 Seminally, see C.R. Beitz, *Political Theory and International Relations* (Princeton, NJ: Princeton University Press, 1979).

39 See especially T. Nagel, 'The Problem of Global Justice' *Philosophy and Public Affairs* (2005) 33 (2): 113.

4. What Place for Ethics in Global Health?

4.1 How effective can ethical argument be?

If we are to take seriously any potential ethical argument as realistically *action-guiding*, as opposed to being an abstracted hypothesis regarding some 'utopian' situation, it is salutary to consider factors that militate against the efficacy of moral argumentation.[40] First of all, it is necessary to give due account to the real-world complexity presented in works such as Fidler's. For the purposes of refining a theory, we may abstract away issues of how realistic it is to introduce measures or coordinate activity, but if the theory is to be implemented such concerns must be addressed. These ideas demand an analysis in political realism, as advocated, for example, by Raymond Geuss.[41]

In short, if we are to understand what can be done, it is ineffective to ignore what actually motivates different people and agencies, or to attribute nebulous characteristics to global health actors. The abstracted persons of various celebrated moral theories are not reflected universally, and indeed the very idea of universality, of who is included within the whole, is not clear. An ethical argument will not always motivate, or even give cause for consideration. To the extent that that is the case, some modesty is required in an understanding of what ethics can achieve.[42] Furthermore, even insofar as we do find commitments to a moral agenda, there is radical disagreement on how moral norms are properly established and what they might indicate as imperative. So even if it is rejected on philosophical grounds, a theorist needs to be able to account for and respond to the practical truth presented by theorists such as Isaiah Berlin and John Gray concerning moral pluralism.[43]

In this regard it might be worth emphasizing the relative modesty found in arguments on global health ethics. Even moral cosmopolitans such as Peter Singer, who might be argued generally not to appear too willing to compromise in the face of practical bars to ethical action, exhibit a carefully considered degree of restraint in their ideas for global health governance.[44] This is not to suggest that such theorists lack ambition, or that their proposals should be considered less than revolutionary. Rather, it is to emphasize that their ambitions are tempered by recognition of what might be achieved. The lesson to carry into the following analysis is that whether approaching global health ethics from the academic's or the activist's perspective, it is crucial to give due consideration to the 'practical' in 'practical ethics'. With that by way of a preamble, I will now critically assess an impressive account of global health justice, before moving to a wider consideration of theory and strategy in global health ethics.

4.2 Health justice and a global health constitution

It is clear that there are radical moral disagreements between cosmopolitans and nationalists. Furthermore, the very fact of globalization across an international world

[40] I address such questions in greater detail in Coggon, *What Makes Health Public?* (n 2) especially in chs 7 and 10.

[41] R. Geuss, *Philosophy and Real Politics* (Princeton, NJ and Oxford: Princeton University Press, 2008).

[42] See also Gostin, 'Meeting Basic Survival Needs' (n 33); Latham, 'On Some Difficulties for Any Theory' (n 35).

[43] I. Berlin, 'Two Concepts of Liberty' in I. Berlin, *Four Essays on Liberty* (Oxford: OUP, 1969); J. Gray, *Two Faces of Liberalism* (Cambridge: Polity Press, 2000).

[44] See Singer, *One World* (n 30).

order means that in its application neither advocates for 'pure cosmopolitanism' nor advocates for 'pure State nationalism' could quite fully capture legal reality in their ideal governmental framework. For those who would aim to improve health globally, we might then explore what is brought with insights from ethically informed practical argument. To that end, I will in this section focus in detail on Jennifer Prah Ruger's theory of health justice and its implications for global health governance. Ruger posits her theory as one that accommodates the concerns of both nationalists and cosmopolitans. Rooted firmly in an ethical agenda, furthermore, it offers a practical proposal to improve health globally in a way that achieves morally required outcomes whilst respecting due side-constraints. As such, it is a useful example of an enterprise that would bring ethics to global health debates.

Ruger is a long-standing advocate for a moral theory that has its roots in Aristotelian notions of human flourishing. In an impressive and broad-ranging body of work, she has given sustained attention to questions in public health ethics through a prism of *health justice*.[45] In a mode that she explicitly contrasts with theories of justice *simpliciter*, she has consistently advocated that health is the foundational moral value that should underpin moral norms and practical governance. In regard to global governance and health, it is her position that there has been a dearth of literature giving due attention to the importance of 'global health justice'. For the purposes of the current chapter, I draw particularly on two of her papers that aim to address this problem. One gives special attention to her theoretical account of 'global health justice', and the other looks in more practical detail to the idea of 'global health governance as shared health governance'.[46]

For Ruger, the effect of externalities on health and the stark global inequalities in health status make apparent that the world is unjust. And this obvious injustice (which is substantiated according to her philosophical position) is its own call for a theory of global health justice that is currently lacking, but which would ground the individual, national, and international obligations to fix the problem.[47] The role of theory here, she argues, is crucial because global governance for health needs to be based on a sound moral bedrock.[48] Whilst it is clear that actors may be motivated towards ethical ends by non-moral concerns (for example self-interest), allowing a system that comprises a mesh of aims and motivations is counterproductive: maximization of self-interest conduces to skewed priorities and suboptimal outcomes.[49] In her argument, there is thus strong reason to acknowledge the need for a single, shared objective. Her '*one-goal, multiple actors* approach to [global health governance] contrasts with the *multiple-goals, multiple actors* approach of the current system'.[50]

Our interest here is in the role and potential effect of ethical reasons and reasoning in practical arguments about global health. In Ruger's project we can contrast two areas of concern (albeit that the two are inextricably linked in her analysis). The first is morally normative, and urges a particular moral outlook. The second relates to effective, practical developments. I will consider each in turn.

45 See especially J.P. Ruger, *Health and Social Justice* (New York: OUP, 2010).

46 J.P. Ruger, 'Global Health Justice' *Public Health Ethics* (2009) 2(3): 261; J.P. Ruger, 'Global Health Governance as Shared Health Governance' *Journal of Epidemiology and Community Health* (2012) 66(7): 653.

47 Ruger, 'Global Health Justice' (n 46) 262.

48 Ruger, 'Global Health Justice' (n 46) 262.

49 Ruger, 'Global Health Governance as Shared Health Governance' (n 46) 654–5.

50 Ruger, 'Global Health Governance as Shared Health Governance' (n 46) 657 (emphases in original).

Seeking to overcome the tensions between nationalists and cosmopolitans without resigning to claims about an anarchic world order, Ruger describes her position as one of 'provincial globalism'.[51] Her theory permits for special commitments locally (ie special duties held between people within the jurisdiction of a nation State), but also presents duties that are owed transnationally. Crucially, her theory posits health as a uniquely important basis for the capability for human flourishing; our shared obligations are derived from the need to assure 'central health capabilities'. A concern for 'health agency', however, demands constraints against a consequentialist position that would simply maximize human welfare. People and governments cannot ethically be *compelled* to guarantee everyone's health capabilities. Nevertheless, her theory is also not formed in a Kantian-type social contract framework. Its reach is not limited to the confines of a State, and it is not founded on theoretically established individual autonomous commitments. It is founded on obligations given the basic moral commitment to promote human flourishing. Her theory can be seen, therefore, to overcome the traditional conflict described earlier between nationalists and cosmopolitans. When people are persuaded by Ruger's position, they will acknowledge a shared commitment to a single goal of assuring health capabilities. On her analysis, these capabilities can be measured and prioritized. Thus, actors guided by provincial globalism have a theory of health justice that would direct them globally in allocating responsibilities, and in devising practical frameworks for ensuring that health needs are met at the most suitable level, be that through national or international governance.[52]

As indicated, if the obligations are to have practical effect, Ruger argues (on ethical and practical grounds) that they must be internalized. In other words, individuals, organizations, and States must voluntarily assume the obligations. Practical duties must not be simply imposed on or by governments, however compelling the reasons that support the duties may be. This, I would argue, potentially leaves us with something of a practical problem. For whilst Ruger shuns social contract theory, she seems to stipulate as essential for the legitimacy of her position a practical condition that is widely viewed as an unattained (and practically perhaps unattainable) requirement even within State-focused contractarian theories of justice:[53] namely a condition that governmental obligations can only be legitimately fulfilled with the *actual* consent of all the people. It is hard to know quite how literally to take Ruger's ideas here, but assuming that the internalization condition is to be taken seriously, there must be good reason to doubt the immediacy of a global order in which everyone would actually, actively assume obligations all given the same goal. Even scholars who recognize an imperative to 'make health the highest law' differ radically in their interpretation of that maxim.[54] And there are many scholars (and others) who argue on principled grounds that health is no business of government whatsoever.[55] In this regard, there is a weakness in

[51] Ruger, 'Global Health Justice' (n 46) 262.

[52] Ruger, 'Global Health Justice' (n 46) especially 266.

[53] See eg A.J. Simmons, *On the Edge of Anarchy: Locke, Consent, and the Limits of Society* (Princeton, NJ: Princeton University Press, 1993).

[54] eg consider the radically distinct implications found to be entailed in the maxim in O. O'Neill, 'Informed Consent and Public Health' *Philosophical Transactions of the Royal Society B* (2004) 359: 1133; Epstein, 'Let the Shoemaker Stick to his Last' (n 2); W. Parmet, *Populations, Public Health, and the Law* (Washington, DC: Georgetown University Press, 2009); Gostin and Stone, 'Health of the People' (n 12).

[55] See eg I. Illich, *Limits to Medicine—Medical Nemesis: The Expropriation of Health* (London: Marion Boyars, 1995 [1976]); P. Skrabanek, *The Death of Humane Medicine and the Rise of Coercive Healthism* (Bury St Edmunds: St Edmundsbury Press, 1994).

the practical utility of Ruger's ethics as compared with, say, the Kantian-type models based on institutions designed *as if* by rational, contracting agents, rather than an *actually consenting* populace.[56]

Nevertheless, Ruger takes her ideas forward from theory to consider how best to institute measures to secure sound global health governance. Given the multiplicity of actors involved in global health, Ruger describes a position of 'hyper-pluralism and fragmentation' that is often characterized 'as anarchic and requiring coordination and control'.[57] Within this situation: 'Public and private actors each pursue their own goals and preferences and not necessarily those of their "beneficiaries."'[58] Interestingly, part of Ruger's concern is that the absence of theory is a significant cause of the problem here: '*No dominant theory has emerged to elucidate current [global health governance] or to provide principles upon which a new approach might develop.*'[59]

So what Ruger is advancing is, it may be hoped, what will become the dominant theory that will direct the new approach. Whilst quite radical, her argument for 'shared health governance' does not aim to eradicate the pursuit of individual national interests, or the self-interest of non-governmental organizations. It does, however, aim to supplant the focus on power and particular interests with a commitment to the principles inherent in her theory of health justice.[60] The position is rooted in a normative commitment, which, as seen previously, requires internalization and voluntary assumption of duties. But in pragmatic terms, Ruger suggests that once individuals and institutions adopt the theory of health justice they will be more likely to meet the duties that, but for their failure in recognition, they would necessarily be meeting. In her words:

> Internalising a public moral norm of health equity is important because effective health governance requires *not just self- and national interest or even legal instruments* but individuals and groups willing to make choices to ensure health capabilities for all. This orientation in turn leads to domestic and global policies embracing health equity and measures to achieve it.[61]

So where does this move things practically? Ruger (for clear reasons) sees that a 'world health government with global authority and enforcement powers'[62] is unavailable, so formulates a means of achieving alternative governance structures that can be instituted to coordinate global health agendas. Her position is that the means to achieve this is through the production of a Global Health Constitution. This constitution would be founded on the theory of global health justice, and agreed to by parties who have recognized and internalized the norms. It would overarch the World Health Organization, give clear allocation of responsibilities, and set frameworks, standards, and principles. For Ruger, through interpretation of this instrument we would find clearly whether or not different global actors were meeting their duties. And the shared agenda would mean that coordination and resolution would be possible.

56 eg Rawlsian models brought to bear on health such as Daniels, *Just Health* (n 30). See also Peter Singer's critique of Rawlsian theory in Singer, *One World* (n 30) 172–9; and G. Ooms and R. Hammonds, 'Just Health, from National to Global: Claiming Global Social Protection' in J. Coggon and S. Gola (eds), *Global Health and International Community* (London: Bloomsbury, 2013).

57 Ruger, 'Global Health Governance as Shared Health Governance' (n 46) 653.

58 Ruger, 'Global Health Governance as Shared Health Governance' (n 46) 653.

59 Ruger, 'Global Health Governance as Shared Health Governance' (n 46) 653 (emphasis added).

60 Ruger, 'Global Health Governance as Shared Health Governance' (n 46) see especially 654 and 657.

61 Ruger, 'Global Health Governance as Shared Health Governance' (n 46) 657.

62 Ruger, 'Global Health Governance as Shared Health Governance' (n 46) 657.

In the next section, I will build on my critical presentation of Ruger's proposal for a global health constitution. In a shorter review of a wider literature, I aim to express reasons for being sceptical of how realizable her approach is, but also to ask whether there can still be a role for ethics in global health.

4.3 Political realism, optimality, and ethics

Ruger's thesis would unify global actors, give some space to conserving the status quo, but serve to overcome coordination problems and conflicting agendas through the universal adoption of a commitment to health. I have already expressed some reservations about some of the conditions imposed. In particular, I suggest we have reason to doubt the likely internalization of the justice-based commitment to global health, regardless of how strong Ruger's philosophical argument may be. Furthermore, I would argue that the idea of a global health constitution is theoretically effective, but that there is strong reason to doubt that it could be effected in practice (at least in the foreseeable future, and on the grounds that Ruger would advocate).

My views are clearly entrenched in a perspective of political realism. But do they give grounds for total pessimism in relation to ethically defensible, or at least ethically informed, global health governance? First, we might consider Ruger's argument that there is a need for a dominant new theory of justice. Practical innovations advanced by philosophers are a welcome, and indeed inspirational, component of debates in global health ethics.[63] But in a complex political climate, it might be regarded as strategically more efficacious to track substantive ethical argument onto existing, if perhaps as yet under-theorized, public ethical discourses.

Accordingly, in response to Ruger's concern that there is no existing, satisfactory theory, we might argue that there are two potential candidate 'dominant theories' on to whose discourse an effective theory might be built. Each has been espoused and promoted by the World Health Organization, as well as having received support in academic and wider literatures. First is the idea of stewardship.[64] Rather like Ruger's theory, stewardship is argued to track a 'middle way' path between competing concerns about efficiency and ethics. Although in some of its presentations there are reasons to doubt it as a robust theory,[65] it could certainly be developed as a dominant and analytically robust one, whose effect in health governance could operate both nationally and internationally.[66] In this sense, whilst it may be under-theorized, it does stand tall as a 'dominant theory'. Furthermore, insofar as it lacks theoretical content, this could be substantiated in accordance, for example, with Ruger's theory. Recent discussion on

63 eg consider the advocacy of Thomas Pogge and colleagues for a 'Health Impact Fund' to incentivize the development of accessible pharmaceutical innovations: A. Banerjee, A. Hollis, and T. Pogge, 'The Health Impact Fund: Incentives for Improving Access to Medicines' *Lancet* (2010) 375: 166.

64 World Health Organization, 'World Health Report 2000' (Geneva, 2000); R.B. Saltman and O. Ferroussier-Davis, 'The Concept of Stewardship in Health Policy' *Bulletin of the World Health Organization* (2000) 78(6): 732; Nuffield Council on Bioethics, *Public Health—Ethical Issues* (London, 2007).

65 See eg J. Coggon, 'Harmful Rights-Doing? The Perceived Problem of Liberal Paradigms and Public Health' *Journal of Medical Ethics* (2008) 34(11): 798; A. Dawson and M. Verweij, 'The Steward of the Millian State' *Public Health Ethics* (2008) 1(3): 193; J. Coggon, 'What Help is a Steward? Stewardship, Political Theory and Public Health Law and Ethics' *Northern Ireland Legal Quarterly* (2011) 62(5): 599.

66 See eg R. Brownsword, 'Responsible Regulation: Prudence, Precaution and Stewardship' *Northern Ireland Legal Quarterly* (2011) 62(5): 573.

morality, policy, and public ethics makes clear the importance of working from 'where we are': it speaks to the importance of accounting for status quo bias, and also of being able to track ethical argument onto language found in the current thinking of the audience an argument is hoped to influence.[67] Thus, rather than lament the lack of a robust theory, the philosopher's contribution in the activist's agenda may be to give intellectual content and support to existing but incomplete ideas. If an ethical theory of global health governance is not to be pure hypothesis (or subject to a charge of being too 'utopian'), this sort of terminological compromise may be well recommended.

We can take these thoughts further and look at a second candidate 'dominant theory' that is perhaps more obvious still than stewardship: the human right to health. Ruger gives explicit consideration to this, but expresses the concern that a 'vague, under-specified conception of a "right to health" and unclear, inadequate allocation of obligations to meet rights claims undermine this approach'.[68] As such, the human right to health provides an 'insufficient framework'.[69] Ruger's criticism has some force, and support for the view that the right has proven an inadequate framing device finds support, for example, in earlier works of Gostin, who nevertheless is now a prominent advocate for the right to health.[70] We may ask, however, whether rejection of the right to health is necessary, or whether it in fact provides an important point for building a sufficiently robust and practically realizable mechanism for global health governance.[71] Tracking the discourses between participants in what Bruce Jennings labels 'advocacy ethics' and 'critical ethics' in public health ethics,[72] we can clearly see the right to health as an important practical mechanism in both intellectual and governance developments.[73] As such, we see political philosopher Jonathan Wolff reflecting that, for reasons of philosophical scepticism and wariness of rights-based arguments, he was 'slow to come to the human rights party', but is nevertheless pleased to be 'here at last'.[74]

The indications here suggest that philosophical ethics can therefore have a role in global health, even if we do not share the ambitions of Ruger, whether on the basis of conflicting ethical concerns (ie we are not persuaded by her account of justice), or concerns based on real politics (for example if we are not persuaded that a World Health Constitution, as Ruger would have it, could be realistically devised and implemented). To conclude the analysis in this chapter, I draw brief attention to the work—both in his role as an activist and as an academic—of Lawrence Gostin. Like Ruger, Gostin works from a theory of human functioning in which health is foundational; his moral position could also well be cast as a theory of health justice.[75] For some years, Gostin has been advocating for radical global governance reforms, albeit ones that are more modest than Ruger's proposals outlined earlier. His participation in the development and launch of the Joint Action and Learning Initiative on National and Global Responsibilities for Health is directed to achieving 'a global agreement, such as a

67 See Wolff, *Ethics and Public Policy* (n 6); Montgomery, 'Reflections on the Nature of Public Ethics' (n 6).

68 Ruger, 'Global Health Governance as Shared Health Governance' (n 46) 653–4.

69 Ruger, 'Global Health Governance as Shared Health Governance' (n 46) 654.

70 See eg L. Gostin, 'Public Health, Ethics, and Human Rights: A Tribute to the Late Jonathan Mann' *Journal of Law, Medicine and Ethics* (2001) 29: 121.

71 Consider, eg J. Wolff, *The Human Right to Health* (New York and London: Norton, 2012).

72 B. Jennings, 'Frameworks for Ethics in Public Health' *Acta Bioethica* (2003) IX(2): 165.

73 For a crucial contribution to this debate, see J. Mann, 'Medicine and Public Health, Ethics and Human Rights' *Hastings Center Report* (1997) 27(3): 6.

74 Wolff, *The Human Right to Health* (n 71) 179.

75 Gostin, 'Meeting Basic Survival Needs' (n 33).

Framework Convention on Global Health, which sets priorities, clarifies national and international responsibilities, ensures accountability, and develops corresponding institutions, such as a Global Health Fund'.[76] As in the case of Ruger, the aim is to overcome sub-optimal outcomes and coordination problems with concerted efforts to address governance problems in the global order presented by scholars such as Fidler.

Yet whilst Gostin would tie the guiding idea to a theory of justice, he engages in his methods a multi-faceted approach to reasoning, wherein ethical argument is advanced but then to a great extent side-lined. Rather than rest his case merely on the strength (such as it would be) of moral reasons, he advances arguments framed in terms of matters such as national interest and prudence. In introducing his argument, he notes that positive global health activity is generally driven by narrow self-interest or humanitarian concern rather than a commitment to moral or legal obligation.[77] The legal and political situation, including regard to private actors, is in Gostin's argument (as in those of many others, including Ruger) found to be regrettably ineffective. He recognizes the difficulty of establishing a Framework Convention on Global Health, but sees it as the most realistic mechanism 'to engage States, the private sector, and civil society to find sustainable solutions to improve prospects for a healthier and longer life for the world's population'.[78] Despite presenting a robust (if necessarily contestable) moral theory, Gostin doubts the potential for ethics to provide the answer. However, he is clearly himself motivated by moral concerns, and recognizes the (albeit limited) importance of ethical argument in advancing global health ends and adding a level of persuasion to his advocacy.[79]

I am interested here to emphasize the manner in which Gostin chooses to frame his argument. He gives detailed consideration to the substance of his own moral position, to its relationship to other theories of justice (particularly ones that would support State-based spheres of moral concern), and to the practical and theoretical limitations of ethics in global health. The context and implications of his position are fascinating. It is hard to argue on their basis that ethics can or should be ignored. But Gostin's approach lends insight into practical strategy, and the potential for aligning the agendas of theorists and activists in global health. Building on arguments about the effects of globalization and transnational practices, a clear argument is made about causation of ill health globally, and its potential resolution. In seeking to advance reasons to address the matters he raises, Gostin frames an analysis on the basis of national interest (in protecting health, and wider interests such as economic and security concerns).[80] The Framework Convention is driven by an attempt to unify global health agendas, even if the motivations for participating in global health activities vary. This reworking of governance is crucial, because, in Gostin's words:

76 L.O. Gostin, E.A. Friedman, G. Ooms, T. Gebauer, N. Gupta, D. Sridhar, W. Chenguang, J.-A. Røttingen, and D. Sanders, 'The Joint Action and Learning Initiative: Towards a Global Agreement on National and Global Responsibilities for Health' *PLoS Medicine* (2011) 8(5): 1.

77 Gostin, 'Meeting Basic Survival Needs' (n 33) 334.

78 Gostin, 'Meeting Basic Survival Needs' (n 33) 335.

79 Whilst Gostin directs his efforts to looking beyond ethical argument, and explicitly concedes that his view on the limits of ethical reason will be lamented by theorists such as Ruger (see Gostin, 'Meeting Basic Survival Needs' (n 33) 347), we may reasonably infer that he sees both force and importance in ethical argument or else he would lack the motivation himself, and would also see little benefit in advancing the moral case to his readers.

80 Gostin, 'Meeting Basic Survival Needs' (n 33) 352–64.

In the currently fractured environment where states, NGOs, IGOs, and foundations all fund and prioritize different health interventions, establishing a global set of priorities and coordinating efforts is an overwhelming, but essential, task.[81]

Gostin's work in this area is exemplary for its detail and wide-range of analysis. But for present purposes, it is also exemplary for the manner in which it accounts simultaneously for the 'real world' concerns that would beset any attempt at global governance, whilst not surrendering a commitment to a moral agenda.

In the present chapter I have neither presented enough to refute Ruger's position, nor enough to persuade a sceptic of the force of Gostin's approach (the great detail of which I have not even hinted at). Within the foregoing discussion, however, there is, I hope, sufficient reason to suggest that Gostin's strategy is a practically and theoretically forceful example of how global health advocacy might work in practice, and what the work of ethical theory might lend to it. The important conclusion then, for the narrow purposes of this chapter, is that within such an approach there is a clear role for philosophical ethics in debates on global health, law, and governance.

5. Conclusions

My aim in this chapter has been to explore what, if any, place philosophical ethics has in debates on global health and law. Having explored what ethical inquiry brings to analysis of public health, I examined the links between public health and global health. When moving from national public health to global health, we see various, I would argue compelling, reasons to question the role, scope, and effectiveness of moral reasoning, and I have sought to test that thesis by challenging the position advanced by Jennifer Ruger. However, my position does not result in the belief that ethics has no role. Rather, in the closing section of the chapter I have hinted at how academic theorists can contribute to practical debates; uniting philosophical and political agendas. In particular, by drawing attention to contemporary arguments on public ethics, and the methods and reasoning of Lawrence Gostin's scholarship and activity in global health, I hope to have pointed to a process that is strengthened by the collaborative commitment and contributions of scholars in law and ethics.

81 Gostin, 'Meeting Basic Survival Needs' (n 33) 385.

22

International Human Rights Laws and Principles

Cornerstone for Defining Health Inequalities and Health Equity

Paula Braveman

1. Rigorous Definitions of Health Inequality and Equity are Needed to Guide Measurement and Resource Allocation

While the term 'health inequalities' has hardly become a household word, over the past twenty to twenty-five years the term has become increasingly familiar in public health circles in the UK, Europe, the US (as 'health disparities') and other affluent countries, and also has achieved wide recognition in many resource-scarce countries. Highly visible policy initiatives to reduce health inequalities have been launched at the global, regional, and national levels. Virtually everywhere except in the US, health inequalities are implicitly understood to refer primarily to health differences between social classes, groups characterized by different levels of access to or control over economic resources; the concept has been extended at times to include health differences by gender, nationality, and other social characteristics associated with social position. In the US, by contrast, socioeconomic advantage and disadvantage have for centuries been intimately entwined with racial or ethnic identification, and the myth of a classless society still prevails. For these reasons, the movement to reduce health disparities began with a clear focus on racial or ethnic differences and the term generally has been understood to refer implicitly to racial/ethnic differences in health, although, as elsewhere, it has at times been extended to encompass other social characteristics, including socioeconomic status/position, gender, disability status, and sexual orientation.[1]

The most eloquent and concise definition of health inequalities was articulated by Margaret Whitehead in the UK, who stated that health inequalities were differences in health that were avoidable, unfair, and unjust.[2] That definition conveys the essence of the concept and has been very useful in guiding efforts throughout the world. At times, however, challenges have arisen that have required the development of a more rigorous basis for defining the concept and grounding the definition in widely recognized principles. For example, in 2000, a proposal emerged that health inequalities should not be measured by comparing the health of rich and poor (or, by implication, the

[1] P. Braveman et al, 'Health Disparities and Health Equity: The Issue Is Justice' *American Journal of Public Health* (2011) 101 (Suppl 1): S149; US Department of Health and Human Services, Office of Disease Prevention and Health Promotion, 'Healthy People 2020', available at <http://www.healthypeople.gov/2020/about/disparitiesAbout.aspx>.

[2] M. Whitehead, 'The Concepts and Principles of Equity and Health' *International Journal of Health Services* (1992) 22(3): 429.

health of a disadvantaged racial/ethnic minority group versus that of the dominant racial/ethnic group), but by comparing the health of the healthiest and the sickest individuals, without regard to their social groups.[3] Advocates of this approach said that comparisons by *a priori* characteristics such as social class prejudge causality and therefore obstruct comprehensive inquiry into the causes of health differences.[4] Critics of that position questioned its usefulness and noted that it would remove social justice from the agenda for public health monitoring and policy.[5] Despite generating some initial interest, that proposal for defining and measuring health inequalities was soon buried. The traditional approach—measuring health differences between more or less disadvantaged groups—has continued to prevail globally, as illustrated by the work of the WHO's Commission on the Social Determinants of Health.[6]

Other challenges have arisen, however. Particularly during the 1990s in the UK, there was a period of intensive debate regarding whether to use the term 'health variations' rather than 'health inequalities'. Until recently, most US health agencies officially defined health disparities simply as differences in health between specific population groups, without specifying which groups or the criteria for identifying them.[7] More recently in the US, the creation of the National Institute on Minority Health and Health Disparities (NIMHD) within the National Institutes of Health has generated demands for a wide array of groups to be regarded as 'health disparity populations' and therefore to receive attention and resources on the agenda of the new institute and other federal agencies.

These challenges have required more guidance than that provided by intuitive definitions, because notions of what is avoidable, fair, and just vary widely. Some individuals may argue that any health difference that is avoidable is unfair, ie that if we can prevent suffering or death, it is unjust not to do so; this perspective would justify unlimited spending to prolong life by a day, for example, and would not provide guidance on setting priorities. Some individuals may believe that it is inevitable that the poor will have worse health than those better-off, and that poverty is inevitable. Furthermore, a particular health problem may be detected in one affluent neighborhood that is not found in other neighborhoods. Is that health difference unfair or unjust and therefore a health inequality to which funds designated for addressing health inequalities and health equity should be directed? In the US, women of European-American background (White) have higher rates of incidence of breast cancer than women of African-American (Black) background; should that difference receive attention on a health inequalities agenda, despite the fact that Black women have much higher mortality from breast cancer? And what if the causes of a given health

[3] C.J. Murray, E.E. Gakidou, and J. Frenk, 'Health Inequalities and Social Group Differences: What Should We Measure?' *Bulletin of the World Health Organization* (1999) 77(7): 537.

[4] C.J. Murray, E.E. Gakidou, and J. Frenk, 'Health Inequalities and Social Group Differences: What Should We Measure?' *Bulletin of the World Health Organization* (1999) 77(7): 538.

[5] C. Almeida et al, 'Methodological Concerns and Recommendations on Policy Consequences of the World Health Report 2000' *Lancet* (2001) 357: 1692; P. Braveman and S. Gruskin, 'Defining Equity in Health' *Journal of Epidemiology and Community Health* (2003) 57(4): 254; P. Braveman, N. Krieger, and J. Lynch, 'Health Inequalities and Social Inequalities in Health' *Bulletin of the World Health Organization* (2000) 78(2): 232; P. Braveman, B. Starfield, and H.J. Geiger, '*World Health Report 2000:* How It Removes Equity from the Agenda for Public Health Monitoring and Policy' *British Medical Journal* (2001) 323(7314): 678.

[6] Commission on Social Determinants of Health, 'Closing the Gap in a Generation: Health Equity through Action on the Social Determinants of Health. Final Report of the Commission on Social Determinants of Health' (Geneva: WHO, 2008).

[7] O. Carter-Pokras and C. Baquet, 'What Is a "Health Disparity"?' *Public Health Reports* (2002) 117(5): 426.

inequality are largely unknown? This is the case with the wide, persistent disparity between Whites and Blacks in rates of low birth weight and premature birth, which predict infant mortality, developmental problems in childhood, and adult chronic disease, and hence are very important in addressing racial disparities in health. How can we call a difference unfair or unjust if we do not know the causes? Individuals with autism (or other health conditions) clearly have worse health than individuals who do not; should that count as a health difference warranting part of the budget for the NIMHD? What about shorter life expectancy among men than among women? Or the fact that male newborns have a higher rate of neonatal mortality than females? The definitions of health disparities adopted by most US public health agencies would imply that all of these differences warrant attention on a health inequalities agenda. It should be noted that health inequalities are not the only important consideration that should drive public health efforts; a number of issues that are not health inequalities concerns deserve high priority—along with health inequalities issues—on an agenda for population health overall.

Another recurring debate has been that of the appropriate reference group to use when making health inequality comparisons—the population average or median, the healthiest group, or the most socially advantaged? An additional concern has been which risks to health should be considered in routine monitoring of health inequalities—lack of access to or quality of medical care only, or a wide range of social determinants of health as well?

Challenges to the concept or measurement of health inequalities constitute challenges to the concept and measurement of health equity, because the two concepts are inextricable. Health equity is the goal of and the motivation for reducing health inequalities, and reductions in health inequalities are the metric by which progress toward health equity can be assessed.

1.1 The relevance of ethics and human rights

Ethical principles, particularly the ethical principle of distributive justice, are an important resource for defining health inequalities and health equity. Distributive justice would dictate that because health is essential to the capacity to function in society, resources required for health should be distributed according to need, not privilege.[8] These concepts are useful, but there is considerable controversy about how to measure need, and about the other considerations that also should be taken into account, for example capacity to benefit. The thinking of the late philosopher John Rawls also makes a substantial contribution. He proposed that to decide which actions or policies are just or fair, we should imagine that we are deciding behind 'a veil of ignorance' that blinds us as to whether we were born rich or poor, of one racial group or another, or with any other attribute that shapes social advantage or disadvantage. If we could decide behind a veil of ignorance, that would indicate the just path to take; an obvious practical limitation is that those shaping policies are not acting behind a veil of ignorance. He also proposed that societies have an ethical obligation to give priority to maximizing the opportunities for well-being of those who are disadvantaged.[9] All of

[8] N. Daniels, 'Health-Care Needs and Distributive Justice' *Philosophy and Public Affairs* (1981) 10 (2): 146; N. Daniels, B.P. Kennedy, and I. Kawachi, 'Why Justice Is Good for Our Health: The Social Determinants of Health Inequalities' *Daedalus* (1999) 128(4): 215.

[9] J. Rawls, *A Theory of Justice* (Cambridge, MA: Belknap/Harvard University Press, 1971).

these ethical notions offer tremendously valuable conceptual guidance but do not provide adequate guidance for measurement.

Fortunately, international human rights laws, treaties, and principles help considerably to address the challenges to the concepts of health inequality and health equity. When human rights are mentioned, most people think of civil and political rights, such as freedoms of speech and assembly, and freedoms from torture and arbitrary imprisonment. International human rights, however, also include economic, social, and cultural rights. These include rights to health, education, a decent standard of living, to participate in the benefits of progress, to participate in society, and to develop one's potential. The right to health is defined as the right to achieve the highest attainable standard of health;[10] this concept has been widely criticized for its vagueness, its failure to consider available resources and trade-offs, and the difficulty of operationalizating it for the purposes of measurement.[11] Nevertheless, the acknowledgement of a right to health in human rights agreements has been an inspiration and an important point of reference in many social policy initiatives. Because all rights are considered interconnected and indivisible, violating economic or social rights is considered to violate civil and political rights, and vice versa. Ratifying human rights agreements obligates governments to progressively remove obstacles to all people realizing their rights, especially for those who face more obstacles; this latter phrase is of crucial importance for the field of health inequalities and health equity.

Non-discrimination and equality also are human rights principles with particular relevance for health inequalities. According to these principles, all persons have equal rights and should be able to realize all of their rights without experiencing discrimination. The concern is not only with overt, deliberate discrimination but also with *de facto* discrimination, ie structures and institutional processes that have discriminatory effects even if there is no intent to do so; human rights principles prohibit policies that have either the intent *or the effect* of discrimination. These principles justify affirmative action as necessary to achieve equal rights for all groups, particularly those who have historically been disadvantaged, that is to say, in human rights terms, those who have faced more obstacles to achieving their rights.

In addition to justifying affirmative action, the principles of non-discrimination and equality also provide guidance for defining and measuring health inequalities by specifying a number of socially vulnerable groups, including groups defined by race or ethnicity, skin color, religion, language, or nationality; socioeconomic resources or position (for example as measured by income, wealth, education, occupation); gender, sexual orientation or gender identity (often referred to as 'sexual minorities' in human rights documents); age; physical, mental or emotional disability or illness; geography; or political or other social affiliation.[12] Implicit in the discussion of the specified groups is

[10] UN General Assembly, 'International Covenant on Economic, Social and Cultural Rights', GA Resolution 2200a (Xxi), Art 12, available at <http://www.ohchr.org/EN/ProfessionalInterest/Pages/CESCR.aspx>.

[11] T. Goodman, 'Is There a Right to Health?' *Journal of Medicine and Philosophy* (2005) 30(6): 643; A. Hendriks and B. Toebes, 'Towards a Universal Definition of the Right to Health?' *Medicine and Law* (1998) 17(3): 319; J.P. Ruger, 'Health and Social Justice' *Lancet* (2004) 364: 1075.

[12] Committee on Economic, Social and Cultural Rights, General Comment No 20, Nondiscrimination in Economic, Social and Cultural Rights, Un Doc E/C.12/Gc/20 (2009) paras 19–35, available at <http://www.unhcr.org/refworld/docid/4a60961f2.html>; UN General Assembly, Universal Declaration of Human Rights. GA Resolution 217, UN GAOR, 3rd Session, 1948, available at <http://www.un.org/en/documents/udhr/>; International Covenant on Civil and Political Rights, GA Resolution 2200a (Xxi), UN GAOR, Supp No 16, UN Doc A/6316 (1966), 999 UNTS 171, 6 ILM 368 (entered into force 23 March 1976), available at <http://www1.umn.edu/humanrts/instree/b3ccpr.htm>.

that they are socially (including economically) disadvantaged and have experienced a history of discrimination, marginalization, social exclusion, or low social position, which have constituted obstacles to full realization of their rights.

2. Defining Health Inequality and Health Equity Based on Human Rights Principles

Based on these human rights concepts and principles, and consistent with ethical principles, a health inequality can be defined as a health difference closely linked with social/economic disadvantage (less wealth, influence, prestige, and/or acceptance in society). Health inequalities, furthermore, adversely affect groups of people who have systematically experienced greater economic and/or other social obstacles to health based on their: racial or ethnic group; religion; socioeconomic status/position; gender; physical or mental illness or disability; sexual orientation or gender identity; or other characteristics historically linked to discrimination or social exclusion.

Health equity is the goal that underlies a commitment to reduce health inequalities. Health inequalities are the metric by which we assess progress toward achieving greater health equity, which is fairness or justice with respect to health. Pursuing health equity means removing obstacles in the way of everyone—particularly those with the most economic or other social obstacles—achieving the highest attainable standard of health, given the resources of the society as a whole and due consideration of the trade-offs involved with respect to other societal investments.

Box 22.1 A rights-based definition of health inequalities and health equity

- A health inequality is a health difference closely linked with economic or other social disadvantage (lower wealth, influence, prestige, or acceptance in society). Health inequalities adversely affect groups of people who have systematically experienced greater economic or other social obstacles to health based on their: racial or ethnic group; religion; socioeconomic status/position; gender; physical or mental illness or disability; sexual orientation or gender identity; or other characteristics historically linked to discrimination or social exclusion.
- Health equity is fairness or justice with respect to health. It means removing obstacles in the way of everyone achieving the highest attainable standard of health, given the resources of the society as a whole. It is the goal that underlies a commitment to reduce health inequalities, which are the metric by which we assess efforts toward greater health equity.

Not all health differences—or even all health differences that warrant attention by public policies—are health inequalities. Health inequalities are a particular subset of health differences that raise concerns about social injustice. It must be plausible, based on current scientific knowledge, that the inequalities are avoidable; the burden of proof, however, is not to establish definitively that a given health inequality is avoidable, only that avoidability is plausible. Health inequalities must be systematic, not exceptions, and they must adversely affect a socially/economically disadvantaged group. Although a health inequality may reflect social/economic disadvantage, it is not necessary to prove that the inequality resulted from disadvantage, but only to demonstrate that it adversely affects a socially disadvantaged group. Health inequalities apply to social groups, not individuals, and not all individuals in a disadvantaged group are equally disadvantaged.

3. How Do These Definitions Address the Challenges?

The proposed approach makes it explicitly clear that the appropriate comparisons when considering health inequalities are between social groups that have different levels of underlying social (including economic) advantage and disadvantage: different levels of resources, power, and social inclusion or prestige. The human rights principles of non-discrimination and equality specify the groups to be compared, including socioeconomic, racial, ethnic, tribal, or religious groups, and groups based on gender, gender identity, or sexual orientation, mental or physical disability/illness, or geographic location. Referring to human rights principles, the criterion for considering a group as socially disadvantaged is that the group—as a group—faces heavy obstacles to its members achieving their rights and has experienced discrimination or marginalization. These criteria are measurable using credible sources of data, for example with respect to the distribution of wealth, education, power (for example which groups are under-represented in high political office or executive positions), or social inclusion (for example which groups have been victims of hate crimes, or have suffered slavery, denial of their civil rights, disproportionate rates of incarceration, or expropriation from ancestral lands).

This rights-based approach addresses the issues regarding the burden of proof of the causation of inequalities and their avoidability. The causes of many important health inequalities are unknown. Regardless of the causes, health inequalities are particularly unjust because they adversely affect groups already at underlying social disadvantage, and put them at further disadvantage with respect to their health, which is needed to escape disadvantage. Health inequalities reflect compound disadvantage—social disadvantage and health disadvantage. Framed in terms of human rights principles, health inequalities constitute further obstacles to disadvantaged groups realizing their rights, and therefore warrant special attention. As stated previously, the avoidability of a given health inequality must be plausible based on current scientific knowledge, but not proven.

Human rights principles also provide guidance for selecting appropriate reference groups for health inequality comparisons. They justify selecting the most socially privileged groups, ie those with the greatest power, wealth, or prestige, for example wealthy individuals, households, or neighborhoods, and the dominant racial/ethnic group (in the US and Europe, light-skinned persons of European background). Selecting the most socially privileged group as the reference group is indicated based on the description of the right to health as the right to the highest attainable standard of health. The health of the most socially privileged groups indicates what should be possible for everyone. According to this interpretation of the right to health, using the population average as a reference group for measuring health inequalities would reflect too low a standard. Particularly where large proportions of the population are highly disadvantaged, a group doing very poorly may not be much worse off than the average level, only because there are so many disadvantaged people; in such a case, inequalities would appear small despite a high level of injustice. It also may not be appropriate to choose the healthiest group as the comparison when measuring inequalities because the healthiest group may be healthiest for reasons that are unavoidable or not related to social injustice, for example age or genetic endowment.

A human rights framework also implies that when considering health inequalities, the full range of determinants of health, including social factors and medical care, must be considered; this is implied not only by the right to a standard of living necessary for health, but also by the inter-connectedness of the economic, social, and cultural rights with the civil and political rights, and the breadth of rights included under each of these major categories (for example the right to participation in the political[13] and cultural[14] life of one's society). Human rights agreements and principles call for the progressive removal of obstacles to the attainment of all rights, clearly calling for reducing inequalities in all of the determinants of health that can be shaped by policies in any sector, not just the medical care sector.

4. Final Remarks

Many of the challenges to the concepts of health equity and health inequalities have come from the US, where there has been a long-standing denial of class differences. In that context, the US 'health disparities' movement focused exclusively on race may have unwittingly tended to reinforce racialized notions of health which assume underlying biological and/or cultural differences across races or ethnic groups, while obscuring differences in resources, power, and social inclusion. In other affluent countries and in resource-poor nations, by contrast, social class differences are not denied and there is wide consensus that those class differences that result in health consequences are unfair; in those contexts the concept of health inequalities generally has required less hair-splitting conceptual rigor.

In the US more than elsewhere, there have been many attempts to reduce the concept of health inequalities to a purely technical notion. Epidemiology is the study of differences in health and in risk factors across different populations. Attempts to conflate the study of health inequalities with all of epidemiology fundamentally represent efforts—conscious or not—to remove the social justice content that has been at the core of the concept since it came into use two to three decades ago. It is likely that some proponents of doing this have not consciously intended to undercut the ability to monitor how the disadvantaged are doing; rather they have been intellectually fascinated with what they view as a novel idea and blind to the implications. One also can only conjecture about the motivations of leaders in government agencies whose definitions have removed the normative content from the definition of health inequalities. A likely explanation is a well-meaning fear of politicization and political conflict, which could make efforts for health equity the targets of conservative political opponents. Efforts to eliminate health inequalities by race or class imply affirmative action to redress historic injustice, whose existence is still denied by many; affirmative action in general has been on the defensive in the US for decades. Some well-meaning individuals have probably advocated for a technical rather than normative approach to defining health inequalities out of a desire to protect the limited resources available for health equity.

[13] International Covenant on Civil and Political Rights, GA Resolution 2200a (Xxi), UN GAOR, Supp No 16, UN Doc A/6316 (1966), 999 UNTS 171, 6 ILM 368 (entered into force 23 March 1976) Art 25, available at <http://www1.umn.edu/humanrts/instree/b3ccpr.htm>.

[14] International Covenant on Economic, Social and Cultural Rights, GA Resolution 2200a (Xxi), Art 15a, available at <http://www.ohchr.org/EN/ProfessionalInterest/Pages/CESCR.aspx>.

Box 22.2 Assessing health inequalities

Health inequalities or disparities are fundamentally normative concepts, grounded in principles from the fields of ethics and human rights. The ethical concept of distributive justice is of great relevance to health inequalities. The laws, other agreements, and principles of international human rights, however, which represent a global consensus on values and aspirations, uniquely provide a crucial and firm conceptual basis that can guide both conceptualization and measurement.

If one looks up health inequality or health disparity in a dictionary, one may find them translated simply as difference or variation, without any normative connotation, although some definitions convey a vague sense of concern about the difference. The movement for health equity, however, is not a movement to reduce all health differences. Nor is it a movement to reduce all important health differences that deserve public policy attention. Efforts to achieve health equity—ie to eliminate health inequalities—aim to reduce a very specific subset of differences in health that are particularly unfair because they put already socially—including economically—disadvantaged groups of people at further disadvantage based on their health. Health equity and health inequalities are fundamentally normative concepts, grounded in principles from the fields of ethics and human rights. The ethical concept of distributive justice is of great relevance to health inequalities; the laws, other agreements, and principles of international human rights, however, representing a global consensus on values and aspirations, uniquely provide a crucial conceptual basis that can guide both conceptualization and measurement.

23

Exposing the Limits of the Law?

Biotechnological Challenges to Global Health

Sara Fovargue

1. Introduction

In Steven Soderbergh's 2011 film *Contagion* a highly contagious and lethal unknown fictional virus spreads across the world and scientists and public health officials attempt to identify it, decode it, and control and prevent its spread. At the start of the film, Beth returns to the US after a business trip to Hong Kong. She stops en route for an extra-marital liaison with an ex-boyfriend, returns to her family and falls ill with what appears to be a cold. She collapses with severe seizures and dies in hospital two days later from what is thought to be a meningoencephalitis virus. Her son is sent home from school when he shows symptoms of a 'cold', and also dies; and her husband is then put into isolation. The virus spreads rapidly throughout the world but its source and origin are unknown. Is this a bioterrorist attack, a man-made disaster, or a zoonosis; an infectious disease transmitted between non-human and human animals? Scientists attempt to decode it to produce a vaccine, and the virus is named as Meningoencephalitis Virus One (MEV-1). MEV-1 is fictional but its origin and symptoms are based on the Nipah virus.[1] MEV-1 is transmitted via respiratory droplets and surfaces that infected individuals have come into contact with (fomites), and in the film nearly 26 million people are killed by it while scientists struggle to find a culture in which to grow it. When a potential live vaccine is eventually produced a researcher tests it on herself, and the vaccine is then mass-produced and allocated to survivors by random lottery, based on birth dates. This occurs for a year until every survivor has been inoculated.

Contagion deals with a zoonose which develops 'naturally', but some medical and scientific advances *may* inherently facilitate cross-species infection. Xenotransplantation is one such biotechnological development. Xenotransplantation involves 'the transplantation of living cells, tissues or organs of animal origin or of human material that has had *ex vivo* contact with these living, xenogeneic materials'.[2] The idea is that non-human animal organs can be used to address the perpetual shortage in human organs available for transplantation. Since the 1990s this has taken the form of genetically engineering pigs in order to minimize the rejection of their organs by humans. The initial immunological barriers to solid organ xenotransplants appear to have been negotiated via the development and use of genetically engineered pigs; however, other physiological and microbiological barriers have been identified but not yet

[1] This zoonotic virus was first recognized in pig farmers in Malaysia in 1998 and causes severe illnesses characterized by respiratory diseases or encephalitis. There is no cure or vaccine for it: World Health Organization, 'Nipah virus (NiV) Infection' (2014), available at <http://www.who.int/csr/disease/nipah/en/> (accessed 3 February 2014).

[2] World Health Organization, 'GKT4 Xenotransplantation' (2014), available at <http://www.who.int/transplantation/gkt/xenotransplantation/en/index.html> (accessed 3 February 2014).

addressed.[3] Some of the barriers remain because no genetically engineered solid non-human animal organ has been reported to have been (xeno)transplanted into a human, and so information is based on pre-clinical trials. Non-human primates have survived for fifty-seven days with a pig's heart in an orthotopic (life supporting) xenotransplant, eight days with a pig's liver, and for ninety days with a pig's kidney.[4] With regard to life supporting *non*-genetically engineered clinical xenotransplants, humans have survived for nine months with a chimpanzee's kidney, twenty days with a baboon's heart, and seventy days following the xenotransplant of a baboon's liver.[5] No solid organ non-human to human animal xenotransplant has been reported since 1993,[6] and a genetically engineered solid organ is yet to be xenotransplanted into a human. Nevertheless, pre-clinical research into genetically engineered solid organ xenotransplantation continues,[7] and it has been suggested that clinical trials of pig liver xenotransplants are imminent as a bridge to an allotransplant (human-to-human transplant),[8] and that a small number of xenotransplant clinical trials should be permitted to determine the nature and extent of the physiological and microbiological barriers that remain.[9]

With regard to global health, the most pressing concern raised by clinical xenotransplantation is the risk of transmitting infectious diseases across the species barrier, and then from the xeno-recipient to her close contacts (including involved health professionals) and the wider public. There is no consensus on the nature or degree of this risk and, although it is widely acknowledged to exist, 'it is impossible to make accurate predictions concerning the relative risks of infection . . . [or] their likely disease manifestations'.[10] Nevertheless, it is agreed that the human and non-human animals involved in xenotransplantation should be monitored pre- and post-xenotransplant, and in many countries surveillance regimes have been suggested or introduced.[11] The

3 See eg B. Ekser et al, 'Clinical Xenotransplantation: The Next Medical Revolution?' (2012) 379 *Lancet* 672.

4 C.G.A. McGregor et al, 'Preclinical Orthotopic Cardiac Xenotransplantation' (2009) 28 *Xenotransplantation* S224; P. Ramirez et al, 'Life-Supporting Human Complement Regulator Decay Accelerating Factor Transgenic Pig Liver Xenograft Maintains the Metabolic Function and Coagulation in the Nonhuman Primate For Up To 8 Days' (2000) 70 *Transplantation* 989; N. Baldan et al, 'Ureteral Stenosis in HDAF Pig-to-Primate Renal Xenotransplantation: A Phenomenon Related to Immunological Events?' (2004) 4 *American Journal of Transplantation* 475.

5 K. Reemtsma et al, 'Renal Heterotransplantation in Man' (1964) 160 *Annals of Surgery* 384; L.L. Bailey, S.L. Nehlsen-Cannarella, W. Concepcion, and J.B. Jolley, 'Baboon-to-Human Cardiac Xenotransplantation in a Neonate' (1985) 254 *Journal of the American Medical Association* 3321; T.E. Starzl et al, 'Baboon-to-Human Liver Transplantation' (1993) 341 *Lancet* 65.

6 A human *may* have received a pig heart in India in 1996 but no results have been published: K.S. Jayaraman, 'Pig Heart Transplant Surgeon Held in Jail' (1997) 385 *Nature* 378.

7 eg see the papers published in *Xenotransplantation*, available at <http://onlinelibrary.wiley.com/journal/10.1111/(ISSN)1399-3089/issues> (accessed 3 February 2014).

8 D.K.C. Cooper, 'A Milestone in Xenotransplantation Research' (2014) *Xenotransplantation* doi: 10.1111/xen.12079; B. Ekser et al, 'Clinical Pig Liver Xenotransplantation: How Far Do We Have To Go?' (2011) 18 *Xenotransplantation* 158.

9 A.S. Daar, 'Xenotransplantation: Three Questions to Advance the Discourse' (2000) *British Medical Journal*, available at <http://www.bmj.com/rapid-response/2011/10/28/xenotransplantation-three-questions-advance-discourse> (accessed 3 February 2014).

10 D.A. Muir and G.E. Griffin, *Infection Risks in Xenotransplantation* (London: Department of Health (DH), 2001), 118.

11 *Australia*—National Health and Medical Research Council (NHMRC), 'Discussion Paper—Xenotransplantation: A Review of the Parameters, Risks and Benefits' (2009), available at <http://www.nhmrc.gov.au/_files_nhmrc/file/about/committees/expert/gtrap/nhmrc_xeno_discussion_paper_website.pdf> (accessed 3 February 2014); NHMRC, Xenotransplantation Working Party (XWP), 'Guidelines for Clinical Animal-to-Human Transplantation (Xenotransplantation) Research DRAFT for NHMRC Consideration' (2004), accompanying NHMRC, XWP, 'Animal-to-Human Transplantation (Xenotransplantation): Final Report' (Canberra: NHMRC, 2004); *Canada*—Canada—Health

existence of these regimes indicates that although the risks of xenotransplantation are (and may continue to be) unquantifiable, they are not taken lightly.

In this chapter I explore law's response to zoonoses in situations where we may facilitate infectious disease transmission as a result of decisions made in order to meet other important health needs. I focus on xenotransplantation as an example of a biotechnology which may in seeking to benefit the health of the individual place global health in danger. I outline some of the key issues relating to xenotransplantation, and consider the xeno-surveillance regimes suggested or implemented to date, before considering the role of the law in protecting global health in this context. Legal involvement is essential because xenotransplantation requires the management of risks with a reach which may know no bounds, and extend beyond the intended beneficiary of the procedure. However, 'the global heterogeneity allows unregulated xenotransplantation activities to continue in countries with regulatory loopholes or weak health authorities'.[12] These regulatory loopholes are not explored here, but it is important to note that the different regulatory schemes (or lack thereof) could result in a fait accompli, as it will be impossible to prevent somebody somewhere from conducting a clinical xenotransplant.[13] Linked to this is the growing trend of health

Canada, 'Proposed Canadian Standard for Xenotransplantation' (Ottawa: Health Canada, 1999); *France*—Comité Consultatif National d'Ethique pour les Sciences de la Vie et de la Santé (CCNE), 'Opinion on Ethics and Xenotransplantation' (1999) No 61, 8, available at <http://www.ccne-ethique.fr/sites/default/files/publications/avis061en_0.pdf> (accessed 3 February 2014); *the Netherlands*—Health Council of the Netherlands, Committee on Xenotransplantation, 'Xenotransplantation' (Rijswijk: Health Council of the Netherlands, 1998), No 1998/01E; *New Zealand*—Human Research Council (HRC) Gene Technology Advisory Committee (GTAC), 'Guidelines for Preparation of Applications Involving Clinical Trials of Xenotransplantation in New Zealand' (2007), available at <http://www.hrc.govt.nz/sites/default/files/GTAC%20Guidelines%20for%20Preparation%20of%20Applications%20Involving%20Clinical%20Trials%20of%20Xenotransplantation%20in%20NZ.pdf> (accessed 3 February 2014); HRC GTAC, 'Process and Guidelines for Application for Approval of Proposals Involving Administration of Gene Products to Human Subjects in New Zealand' (2008), available at <http://www.hrc.govt.nz/sites/default/files/GTAC%20Process%20and%20Guidelines.pdf> (accessed 3 February 2014); 'National Health Committee's Advice on Living Cell Technologies Application for Xenotransplantation Clinical Trials in New Zealand' (2008), criterion 2, available at <http://nhc.health.govt.nz/system/files/documents/publications/nhc-living-cell-technologies-report-oct082.pdf> (accessed 3 February 2014). This advice relates to a specific application to conduct pig cell xenotransplants and the recommendations within have not translated into a specific xenotransplant surveillance scheme; *Norway*—I.L. Gjørv, 'Political Considerations of Controversial Medical Issues: Xenotransplantation and Society. A Presentation of the Work of the Norwegian National Working Group on Xenotransplantation' (2004) 45 (Suppl 1) *Acta Veterinaria Scandinavica* S53; *Spain*—'Recommendations for the Regulation of Xeno Activities in Spain—Extracted from the Report of the Xenotransplantation Commission of the National Transplant Commission' (1998) XVIII (Suppl 7) *Nefrologia* 35; *Sweden*—A Report by the Swedish Committee on Xenotransplantation, 'From One Species to Another—Transplantation From Animals to Humans: Summary and Statutory Proposals' (Stockholm: Swedish Committee on Xenotransplantation, 1999) Swedish Government Official Report No 1999, 120; *Switzerland*—Statement of Position of the SAMS (Swiss Academy of Medical Sciences), 'Medical-Ethical Principles of Xenotransplantation' (2001) 131 *Swiss Medical Weekly* 388; *the UK*—Department of Health, 'Xenotransplantation Guidance' (London: DH, 2006); United Kingdom Xenotransplantation Interim Regulatory Authority (UKXIRA), 'Draft Report of the Infection Surveillance Steering Group of the UKXIRA' (London: DH, 1999); *the US*—US Department of Health and Human Services (DHHS), Food and Drug Administration (FDA), 'PHS Guideline on Infectious Disease Issues in Xenotransplantation' (2001), available at <http://www.fda.gov/downloads/BiologicsBloodVaccines/GuidanceComplianceRegulatoryInformation/Guidances/Xenotransplantation/UCM092858.pdf> (accessed 3 February 2014).

12 L. Noel, 'Global Regulatory Requirements for Xenotransplantation Clinical Trials' (2012) 19 *Xenotransplantation* 71.

13 The xenotransplant regulatory schemes are discussed in S. Fovargue, *Xenotransplantation and Risk: Regulating a Developing Biotechnology* (Cambridge: CUP, 2012) ch 4.

tourism and there is no reason to think that this will not include xeno-tourism; thus, 'the best efforts at minimizing... risks in countries with appropriate regulatory oversight may be thwarted by the free travel of individuals undergoing unmonitored xenotransplantation in countries lacking such regulation'.[14] This is of especial concern because of the inherent risks involved in xenotransplantation.

If clinical genetically engineered solid organ xenotransplants are performed, an effective surveillance regime is vital to protect the health of the recipient and others. Such regimes are required at local, national, and international levels but will it be possible to devise, implement, and enforce them? If xeno-surveillance is not internationally enforceable then national claims of protecting public health via individual country-specific local and national schemes are rendered meaningless, but what role might law have in protecting global health? In some ways I am not discussing new issues; rather, I am highlighting existing problems relating to global infectious disease control and surveillance. What I am suggesting, however, is that a developing biotechnology such as xenotransplantation requires us to focus on these problems with some urgency and that if it is not possible to sufficiently and appropriately regulate, monitor, and control xeno-infection risks, we must ask whether clinical genetically engineered solid organ xenotransplants should be permitted.

2. The Threat(s) from Xenotransplantation

Pigs are the main source of xeno-organs because of, among other things, the similar size of their organs and their functions, their availability in large numbers, and the fact that pigs may be microbiologically 'safer' because the biological differences between the species may minimize the risk of transmitting infections.[15] Additionally, pigs can be bred and raised in specific pathogen free (SPF) environments, thereby further reducing the transmission possibilities.[16] Infections may be transmitted post-allotransplant but these are usually limited to the recipient,[17] whereas diseases that may be transmitted following a genetically engineered solid pig organ xenotransplant may have a wider reach moving from the xeno-recipient, to her close contacts, on to the wider public, and thereby endangering global health. Thus, in allowing an individual to *possibly* benefit from a xenotransplant the wider community *may* be put at risk. This is only a possibility, and much is unknown about what may be transferred and how, and detection methods are necessarily limited. Infections are common post-allotransplant because of the immunosuppressants the recipients require, but xeno-recipients may require extra levels of immunosuppression, genetically engineering the pigs may increase the risks of importing pig novel pathogens, and xenotransplantation bypasses the normal host defences.[18] Thus: '[v]ascularized xenografts create unique immunological niches in which bidirectional transmission of pathogens between donor and recipient may occur.'[19]

14 M. Sykes, M. Sandrin, and E. Cozzi, 'International Cooperation on Xenotransplantation' (2004) 10 *Nature Medicine* 119, 119.

15 J.M. Dobson and J.H. Dark, *The Physiology of Xenotransplantation* (London: DH, 2002) ch 1.

16 G. Mattiuzzo, L. Scobie, and Y. Takeuchi, 'Strategies to Enhance the Safety Profile of Xenotransplantation: Minimimizing the Risk of Viral Zoonoses' (2008) 13 *Current Opinion in Organ Transplantation* 184.

17 A-L. Millard and N.J. Mueller, 'Critical Issues Related to Porcine Xenograft Exposure to Human Viruses: Lessons from Allotransplantation' (2010) 15 *Current Opinion in Organ Transplantation* 230.

18 Mattiuzzo, Scobie, and Takeuchi, 'Strategies to Enhance the Safety Profile of Xenotransplantation' (n 16); C.A. Wilson, 'Porcine Endogenous Retroviruses and Xenotransplantation' (2008) 65 *Cellular and Molecular Life Sciences* 3399.

19 N.J. Mueller and J.A. Fishman, 'Herpesvirus Infections in Xenotransplantation: Pathogenesis and Approaches' (2004) 11 *Xenotransplantation* 486, 486.

2.1 What could be transmitted?

Some of the xeno-infection risks posed by pigs are well-known and include bacteria, parasites and viral pathogens which may be removed or reduced by early weaning, selective breeding, and breeding the pigs in SPF environments.[20] Since the 1990s the focus has mainly been on porcine endogenous retroviruses (PERVs), as it was discovered that these retroviruses could infect human cells *in vitro* and, under certain circumstances, actively infect human cells so that the retroviruses replicate and spread to other cells in the human.[21] Some types of these retroviruses are present in the genome of all breeds of pig, and it is unclear whether a vaccine may be effective or if they can be removed via genetic engineering and/or selective breeding, but SPF breeding will not assist.[22] Some types of PERVs have been found to infect pig cells and some human cell lines and primary cell cultures *in vitro*, while others only infect porcine cells.[23] Retroviruses are of concern because they may induce immunodeficiencies, neurodegeneration, and cancers of the blood system,[24] and it appears that numerous retroviral cross-species transmissions from non-human primates resulted in the viruses which cause AIDS.[25] Retroviruses inject themselves into human cells and if they insert themselves into germline cells the host's offspring will carry them. When they insert themselves into a cell's chromosomes they block infection by other retroviruses and any offspring is resistant to those viruses.[26] However, if those cells are transplanted into another species there is no resistance and the virus can infect the new host. Retroviruses can be passed to offspring over successive generations without causing harm, but may be lethal if transferred cross-species.[27] They may also recombine with viruses from the new host species and 'generate viruses with novel mechanisms of virulence'.[28]

Research continues into the nature, existence, and ability of PERVs to cause disease in humans, and although the RNA and DNA viruses which may pose an infection risk

[20] J. Denner, 'Infectious Risk in Xenotransplantation—What Post-Transplant Screening for the Human Recipient?' (2011) 18 *Xenotransplantation* 151.

[21] V. Specke, S. Rubant, and J. Denner, 'Productive Infection of Human Primary Cells and Cell Lines with Porcine Endogenous Retroviruses' (2001) 285 *Virology* 177; C. Patience, Y. Takeuchi, and R.A. Weiss, 'Infection of Human Cells by Endogenous Retrovirus of Pigs' (1997) 3 *Nature Medicine* 282.

[22] U. Fiebig et al, 'Neutralizing Antibodies Against Conserved Domains of p15E of Porcine Endogenous Retroviruses: Basis for a Vaccine for Xenotransplantation?' (2003) 307 *Virology* 406; J. Ramsoondar et al, 'Production of Transgenic Pigs That Express Porcine Endogenous Retrovirus Small Interfering RNAs' (2009) 16 *Xenotransplantation* 164.

[23] J.C. Wood, G. Quinn, and K.M. Suling, 'Identification of Exogenous Forms of Human-Tropic Porcine Endogenous Retrovirus in Miniature Swine' (2004) 78 *Journal of Virology* 2494; C.A. Wilson et al, 'Type C Retrovirus Released from Porcine Primary Peripheral Blood Mononuclear Cells Infects Human Cells' (1998) 72 *Journal of Virology* 3082; Y. Takeuchi et al, 'Host Range and Interference Studies of Three Classes of Pig Endogenous Retrovirus' (1998) 72 *Journal of Virology* 9986; P. Le Tissier et al, 'Two Sets of Human-Tropic Pig Retrovirus' (1997) 389 *Nature* 681.

[24] Mattiuzzo, Scobie, and Takeuchi, 'Strategies to Enhance the Safety Profile of Xenotransplantation' (n 16); B. Dieckhoff et al, 'Knockdown of Porcine Endogenous Retroviruses (PERV) Expression by PERV-Specific shRNA in Transgenic Pigs' (2008) 15 *Xenotransplantation* 36.

[25] Dieckhoff et al, 'Knockdown of Porcine Endogenous Retroviruses' (n 24); Muir and Griffin, *Infection Risks in Xenotransplantation* (n 10) 38.

[26] Mattiuzzo, Scobie, and Takeuchi, 'Strategies to Enhance the Safety Profile of Xenotransplantation' (n 16).

[27] Mattiuzzo, Scobie, and Takeuchi, 'Strategies to Enhance the Safety Profile of Xenotransplantation' (n 16).

[28] C. Moran, 'Xenotransplantation: Benefits, Risks and Relevance of Reproductive Technology' (2008) *Theriogenology* 1269, 1271.

to xeno-recipients have been listed,[29] these risks can only reliably be determined by xenotransplant clinical trials. Without such trials the effect of PERVs and their consequences will remain speculative; nevertheless, in the light of experiences with other retroviruses it is not unreasonable to expect more than influenza-like symptoms to result if PERVs are transmitted and cause infection post-xenotransplant. Indeed:

> Evidence from naturally occurring retroviral zoonosis and cross-species infections by animal retroviruses . . . provides a basis for reasoned speculation on the risk posed by PERVs. In a worst case scenario xenograft-related PERV transmission would be the starting point of a new viral disease resulting in a public health problem.[30]

Although the extent of the risk is currently unknown (a small risk to many or a high risk to a few), 'the risk of PERV infection following [xenotransplantation] will never be zero'.[31]

There are also other microbial pathogens which merit consideration;[32] for example, herpesviruses are DNA viruses which cause diseases in human and non-human animals, are difficult to detect, can be latent, and cause lifelong infections. Indeed, reactivating latent herpesviruses is one of the most common infectious complications post-allo-transplant,[33] with cytomegalovirus (CMV) the most significant infection. Herpes-viruses have been identified in xenotransplants, including porcine cytomegalovirus (PCMV) which may cause pneumonia, hepatitis, and have oncogenic and immuno-logical effects such as lymphoma and bacterial or fungal infections.[34] PCMV has been identified in pigs, and although it has not been shown to transmit to human cells *in vitro*,[35] baboon CMV and PCMV have been activated following pig-to-primate xeno-transplants because of the immunosuppression required.[36] Circoviruses (CV) are also of concern as some of these viruses affect pigs and wild boars, and can be transmitted via the placenta, porcine CV are capable of infecting human cells *in vitro*,[37] and are associated with immunodepressive and immunosuppressive diseases.[38] Importantly, Sykes has suggested that 'the greatest remaining risk comes from non-PERV unknown viruses that may be non-pathogenic in source animals but could adapt and become pathogenic in immunosuppressed humans'.[39] These could be viruses which newly emerge and were not previously known in humans, such as the Nipah virus and swine hepatitis E virus,[40] and emerging infectious diseases have recently been identified

29 Muir and Griffin, *Infection Risks in Xenotransplantation* (n 10) 5.

30 D. Louz et al, 'Reappraisal of Biosafety Risks Posed by PERVs in Xenotransplantation' (2008) 18 *Reviews in Medical Virology* 53, 60.

31 C. Patience, L. Scobie, and G. Quinn, 'Porcine Endogenous Retrovirus—Advances, Issues and Solutions' (2002) 9 *Xenotransplantation* 373, 373.

32 N.J. Mueller et al, 'Microbial Safety in Xenotransplantation' (2011) 16 *Current Opinion on Organ Transplantation* 201; Denner, 'Infectious Risk in Xenotransplantation' (n 20) 151.

33 Mueller and Fishman, 'Herpesvirus Infections in Xenotransplantation' (n 19) 487.

34 Mueller and Fishman, 'Herpesvirus Infections in Xenotransplantation' (n 19); N.J. Mueller et al, 'Activation of Cytomegalovirus in Pig-to-Primate Organ Xenotransplantation' (2002) 76 *Journal of Virology* 4734.

35 A.W. Tucker et al, 'Methods for the Exclusion of Circoviruses and Gammaherpesviruses' (2003) 10 *Xenotransplantation* 34.

36 Mueller and Fishman, 'Herpesvirus Infections in Xenotransplantation' (n 19); Mueller et al, 'Activation of Cytomegalovirus' (n 34).

37 K. Hattermann et al, 'Infection Studies on Human Cell Lines with Porcine Circovirus Type 1 and Porcine Circovirus Type 2' (2004) 11 *Xenotransplantation* 284.

38 F. Faurez et al, 'Replication of Porcine Circoviruses' (2009) 6 *Virology Journal* 60.

39 M. Sykes, '2007 IXA Presidential Address: Progress Toward an Ideal Source Animal: Opportunities and Challenges in a Changing World' (2008) 15 *Xenotransplantation* 7, 10.

40 Muir and Griffin, *Infection Risks in Xenotransplantation* (n 10) Table 4.1, 102. Also, S. Busby et al, 'Emerging Pathogens of Concern in Xenotransplantation' (2011) 18 *Xenotransplantation* 278.

in allotransplants.[41] Newly emerging viruses could be newly recognized viruses which have existed undetected for a long time or 'genuinely newly emerging ... as a result of variations of existing organisms'.[42] Thus, 'newly emerging or unrecognised organisms, as well as those that cannot be eliminated (currently endogenous retroviruses for example) continue to pose a potential threat'.[43]

2.2 Can xenotransplants transmit infections?

Since the mid-1990s it has been known that *in vitro* human cells are susceptible to PERV infection and that retroviruses have the *potential* to transfer from imported tissue to the human host and *might* be able to infect living human recipients.[44] To date there is no evidence that PERVs have been transmitted to living human recipients of pig cells or tissues,[45] but these studies have been criticized because the recipients had limited exposure time to those cells and tissues, were not long-term studies of immunosuppressed recipients, did not involve solid organs,[46] and it is questionable whether the results of pre-clinical trials between pigs and non-human primates can be extrapolated to the clinical situation.[47] On the other hand, it has been suggested that even if PERVs do infect human cells *in vivo* that infection may have limited clinical effects.[48] Furthermore, '[i]t is not possible to predict the precise behaviour of unidentified, animal-derived pathogens in human hosts or the range of clinical manifestations that may occur',[49] and it is also not known whether genetically engineered cell and solid organ xenotransplants present the same risks. Similarly:

> ... we have no data on infectivity ... or latency of PERV agents in either man or immunosuppressed man: indeed there are no clinical data indicating how such agents would affect a patient ... we know nothing of the ecological dynamics of PERV in relation to other porcine viruses or human endogenous retroviruses and other human infections.[50]

It will thus be difficult to predict *which* organisms may be pathogenic in humans, particularly as those organisms may not cause disease in their native hosts or may acquire new characteristics via genetic recombination in their new human hosts, and their virulence may increase as they adapt and pass into them.[51]

41 L. Scobie and Y. Takeuchi, 'Porcine Endogenous Retrovirus and other Viruses in Xenotransplantation' (2009) 14 *Current Opinion in Organ Transplantation* 175.

42 Muir and Griffin, *Infection Risks in Xenotransplantation* (n 10) 102.

43 Muir and Griffin, *Infection Risks in Xenotransplantation* (n 10) 118.

44 C. Patience, Y. Takeuchi, and R.A. Weiss, 'Infection of Human Cells by Endogenous Retrovirus of Pigs' (1997) 3 *Nature Medicine* 282; Le Tissier et al, 'Two Sets of Human-Tropic Pig Retrovirus' (n 23).

45 G. Nicuolo et al, 'Long-Term Absence of Porcine Endogenous Infection in Chronically Immunosuppressed Patients after Treatment with the Porcine Cell-Based Academic Medical Center Bioartificial Liver' (2010) 17 *Xenotransplantation* 431; R.B. Elliott et al, 'No Evidence of Infection with Porcine Endogenous Retrovirus in Recipients of Encapsulated Porcine Islet Xenografts' (2000) 9 *Cell Transplantation* 895; K. Paradis et al, 'Search for Cross Species Transmission of Porcine Endogenous Retrovirus in Patients Treated with Living Pig Tissue' (1999) 285 *Science* 1236.

46 Louz et al, 'Reappraisal of Biosafety Risks' (n 30); R.A. Weiss, 'Xenografts and Retroviruses' (1999) 285 *Science* 1221.

47 Louz et al, 'Reappraisal of Biosafety Risks' (n 30).

48 L.E. Chapman and E.T. Bloom, 'Clinical Xenotransplantation' (2001) 285 *Journal of the American Medical Association* 2304.

49 J.A. Fishman, L. Scobie, and Y. Takeuchi, 'Xenotransplantation-Associated Infectious Risk: A WHO Consultation' (2012) 19 *Xenotransplantation* 72, 73.

50 C. Michie, 'Xenotransplantation: Endogenous Pig Retroviruses and the Precautionary Principle' (2001) 7 *Trends in Molecular Medicine* 62, 63.

51 Fishman, Scobie, and Takeuchi, 'Xenotransplantation-Associated Infectious Risk' (n 49) 76.

2.3 Detecting transmitted infections

Although it is difficult to assess the risks of PERVs, diagnostic methods have been developed to screen xeno-recipients for retroviral infection,[52] but detecting unknown viruses and pathogens is obviously problematic. Nevertheless, certain types of viruses can be screened even though the virus has yet to be characterized.[53] The possibility of latent infections also makes it harder to detect transmitted diseases, and 'the HIV/AIDS pandemic demonstrates [that] persistent latent infections may result in person-to-person transmission for many years before clinical disease develops in the index case, thereby allowing an emerging infectious agent to become established in the susceptible population before it is recognized'.[54] If the risks are unidentifiable for some time, perhaps generations, any infection could have spread widely and undetected, and there is currently:

> ... no way of predicting when a virus may manifest itself. The expression of a virus could occur after only a few or perhaps thousands of xenotransplants have been performed. Almost certainly, we would have to perform xenotransplantation on humans to ascertain this risk. And only if a patient became infected would we be able to begin estimating the risk.[55]

Additionally, as xeno-recipients will be immunosuppressed it might be more difficult to recognize and identify signs of infection, and so 'animal-derived infections may go undetected against the high background incidence of infection in immunosuppressed transplant recipients'.[56] Nevertheless, it is widely recognized that xeno-recipients and some others need to be monitored pre- and post-xenotransplant in order to safeguard individual and global health.

3. Protecting Global Health: Infectious Disease Surveillance

While the virus in *Contagion* is fictional and the infectious risk(s) from xenotransplantation unclear, the importance of protecting and securing global health from infectious diseases has been highlighted by our experiences of zoonotic transmissions such as Ebola and new variant Creutzfeld-Jacob disease, and it has been suggested that the majority of emerging infectious diseases have been caused by zoonotic pathogens with a non-human animal cause.[57] Indeed, in 2011 it was reported that an adenovirus had crossed the species barrier from non-human to human animals, and had then infected other humans.[58] In the last fifteen years the world has also experienced zoonoses such as Severe Acute Respiratory Syndrome (SARS), avian influenza A (H5N1), and what is

52 Denner, 'Infectious Risk in Xenotransplantation' (n 20).

53 Health Canada, 'Report of the Xenotransplantation Surveillance Workshop—Infection Control Database and Sample Archiving' (2001) 27S1 Canada Communicable Disease Report, available at <http://www.collectionscanada.gc.ca/webarchives/20071207071354/http://www.phac-aspc.gc.ca/publicat/ccdr-rmtc/01pdf/27s1e.pdf> (accessed 3 February 2014).

54 US DHHS and FDA, 'PHS Guideline on Infectious Disease Issues in Xenotransplantation' (n 11) para 1.3.

55 F.H. Bach, A.J. Ivinson, and C. Weeramantry, 'Ethical and Legal Issues in Technology: Xenotransplantation' (2001) 27 *American Journal of Law and Medicine* 283, 286.

56 Fishman, Scobie, and Takeuchi, 'Xenotransplantation-Associated Infectious Risk' (n 49) 76.

57 K.E. Jones et al, 'Global Trends in Emerging Infectious Diseases' (2008) 451 *Nature* 990.

58 E.C. Chen et al, 'Cross-Species Transmission of a Novel Adenovirus Associated with a Fulminant Pneumonia Outbreak in a New World Monkey Colony' (2011) 7 *PLoS Pathogens* 1.

officially known as pandemic influenza A (H1N1) 2009 virus[59] (commonly known as swine influenza or H1N1). It is useful to explore the international response to these zoonoses to determine how (and whether) global health has been (and can be) protected, and whether, and how, law played a role in this. In so doing, the key role of the World Health Organization (WHO) with regard to infectious disease surveillance and control is evident. Indeed, the WHO established its Global Outbreak Alert and Response Network (GOARN) in 2000,[60] which 'contributes to global health security by combating the international spread of outbreaks, ensuring that appropriate technical assistance reaches affected states rapidly, contributing to long-term epidemic preparedness and capacity building'.[61] The WHO coordinates the response from GOARN, which has developed guiding principles on international alerts and responses to outbreaks,[62] but the WHO recognizes that: 'No single institution or country has all of the capacities to respond to international public health emergencies caused by epidemics and by new and emerging infectious diseases.'[63]

3.1 2003—SARS epidemic

SARS is an acute viral respiratory syndrome which belongs to the coronavirus family and is believed to originate in a non-human animal virus.[64] The first cases of this atypical pneumonia were reported in China in November 2001, and it was recognized as an epidemic[65] and a threat to global health during March 2003.[66] Over 1,800 patients were diagnosed with SARS in seventeen countries between 1 February and 31 March 2003,[67] and between November 2002 and July 2003, 8,096 people in twenty-six countries were suspected of contracting it. Ultimately, 774 people were recognized as having died of SARS,[68] and it 'travelled more widely, swiftly and lethally

59 WHO, 'Implementation of the International Health Regulations (2005)', Report of the Review Committee on the Functioning of the International Health Regulations (2005) in relation to Pandemic (H1N1) 2009, Report by the Director-General, A64/10, 5 May 2011, 61, available at <http://apps.who.int/gb/ebwha/pdf_files/WHA64/A64_10-en.pdf> (accessed 3 February 2014).

60 WHO, 'Global Outbreak Alert and Response', Report of a WHO Meeting, Geneva, Switzerland, 26–28 April 2000, WHO/CDS/CSR/2000.3, available at <http://www.who.int/csr/resources/publications/surveillance/WHO_CDS_CSR_2000_3/en/index.html> (accessed 3 February 2014).

61 WHO, Global Outbreak Alert & Response Network (GOARN), see <http://www.who.int/csr/outbreaknetwork/en/> (accessed 3 February 2014).

62 WHO, Global Alert and Response (GAR), 'Guiding Principles for International Outbreak Alert and Response', available at <http://www.who.int/csr/outbreaknetwork/guidingprinciples/en/index.html> (accessed 3 February 2014).

63 WHO, 'Global Outbreak Alert and Response Network—GOARN, Partnership in Outbreak Response', available at <http://www.who.int/csr/outbreaknetwork/goarnenglish.pdf> (accessed 3 February 2014).

64 F. Fleck, 'How SARS Changed the World in Less than Six Months' (2003) 81 *Bulletin of the World Health Organization* 625; R. Antia et al, 'The Role of Evolution in the Emergence of Infectious Diseases' (2003) 426 *Nature* 658.

65 An outbreak of a disease which spreads more extensively and quickly among a group of people than would normally be expected.

66 WHO, 'WHO Guidelines for the Global Surveillance of Severe Acute Respiratory Syndrome (SARS): Updated Recommendations October 2004' (2004) WHO/CDS/CSR/ARO/2004.1, at 6, available at <http://www.who.int/csr/resources/publications/WHO_CDS_CSR_ARO_2004_1.pdf> (accessed 3 February 2014).

67 J.L. Gerberding, 'Faster... but Fast Enough? Responding to the Epidemic of Severe Acute Respiratory Syndrome' (2003) 348 *New England Journal of Medicine* 2030.

68 WHO, 'Summary of Probable SARS Cases With Onset of Illness From 1 November 2002 to 31 July 2003' (2004), available at <http://www.who.int/csr/sars/country/table2004_04_21/en/index.html> (accessed 3 February 2014).

than any other recent new disease so far'.[69] Indeed, during the epidemic it was commented that:

> Many household contacts have become ill. Concern is mounting about the potential for spread in schools, the workplace, airplanes, and other crowded areas. New cases among travellers from affected areas continue to emerge and have led to infections in household contacts and health care personnel in many countries, including the United States and Canada.[70]

There was a high level of fear and panic surrounding SARS, which was a significant threat to health because it was efficient in transmitting from person-to-person. However, it was difficult to detect and diagnose because the symptoms were non-specific, acute respiratory infections and fevers are common, and the symptoms could be masked by existing conditions.[71] The reaction to SARS was further complicated by the fact that it 'took society back to a pretherapeutic era with no definitive diagnostic test, a nonspecific definition, and no effective vaccine or treatment'.[72] Mode(s) of transmission were unclear (face-to-face contact, airborne transmission, fomite transmission, increased susceptibility to transmission, resistant non-carriers), and there was a concern that: 'If SARS transmission evolves to mimic that of influenza, containment may well be impossible without vaccination, prophylaxis, or treatment.'[73]

Following the WHO's global alert on SARS,[74] the US Centers for Disease Control and Prevention initiated its emergency operations and joined with investigators from the WHO and teams from affected countries to discover and characterize the new coronavirus which had been isolated from SARS patients.[75] This was successfully achieved within a short period of time and accurate diagnostic tests were then developed and assessed, and an appropriate vaccine investigated.[76] The WHO reported that 'the last human chain of transmission' was broken in July 2003,[77] and during November 2002 and July 2003 a range of measures and approaches to protect health were adopted in the affected countries. These included name reporting, contact tracing for the ten days prior to when it was thought the symptoms had developed (Singapore), mandatory or voluntary taking of body temperatures (Singapore and Toronto), answering health questionnaires (Singapore and Toronto), wearing 'fever-free' stickers (Singapore), travel restrictions (issued by the WHO), and containment measures such as quarantine or isolation[78] (China, Hong Kong, Vietnam, Singapore, Canada, and the US).[79] In some countries the police or military were involved in tracing (Hong Kong

69 Fleck, 'How SARS Changed the World' (n 64) 625.

70 Gerberding, 'Faster . . . but Fast Enough?' (n 67) 2031.

71 WHO 'Guidelines for the Global Surveillance of SARS' (2004) (n 66) 7.

72 L.O. Gostin, R. Bayer, and A. L. Fairchild, 'Ethical and Legal Challenges Posed by Severe Acute Respiratory Syndrome: Implications for the Control of Severe Infectious Disease Threats' (2003) 290 *Journal of the American Medical Association* 3229, 3229 (reference removed).

73 Gerberding, 'Faster . . . but Fast Enough?' (n 67) 2031.

74 WHO, 'WHO issues a global alert about cases of atypical pneumonia', 12 March 2003, available at <http://www.who.int/mediacentre/news/releases/2003/pr22/en/> (accessed 3 February 2014).

75 CDC Investigative Team, A.T. Fleischauer, 'Outbreak of Severe Acute Respiratory Syndrome—Worldwide, 2003' (2003) 52 *MMWR* 226, available at <http://www.cdc.gov/mmwr/preview/mmwrhtml/mm5211a5.htm> (accessed 3 February 2014).

76 Gerberding, 'Faster . . . but Fast Enough?' (n 67) 2030.

77 WHO 'Guidelines for the Global Surveillance of SARS' (2004) (n 66) 5.

78 Quarantine restricts healthy individuals who have been exposed to infection during the relevant incubation period; whereas, known infected individuals are isolated to prevent or limit disease transmission.

79 Gostin, Bayer, and Fairchild, 'Ethical and Legal Challenges' (n 72) 3230–1. For further information on the measures adopted in Singapore, see WHO, 'Update 70—Singapore removed from list of areas with local SARS transmission' (30 May 2003), available at <http://www.who.int/csr/

and Singapore, respectively), while in others hospitals were responsible for these activities (Toronto).[80] Differences were also evident regarding the public naming of the infected 'superspreaders' (Singapore), and whether quarantine was viewed as voluntary (the US) or mandatory and enforceable (Singapore).[81] Despite these variances in response and practice, participants in the global consultation on SARS epidemiology agreed that 'early identification and isolation of patients, vigorous contact tracing, management of close contacts by home confinement or quarantine, and public information and education to encourage prompt reporting of symptoms' supported the WHO's view that SARS 'can be contained and driven back out of its new human host'.[82]

Given the relatively low death rate (nearly 10 per cent of those affected), they were right in this assessment. However, it has been suggested that epidemiologic investigations were delayed because China did not provide information on SARS in a timely manner;[83] although China was not legally obliged under the WHO's International Health Regulations (IHR)[84] or any other international law to report SARS cases. Regardless, the SARS epidemic indicated how international and national agencies *could* cooperate, coordinate, and work together aided by the internet so that 'almost instantaneous communication and information exchange . . . supported every aspect of the response'.[85] Fears about SARS were such that the World Health Assembly (WHA), the most important policy-making body of the WHO, adopted a resolution on SARS in May 2003 urging member states to take eleven different actions, including applying WHO recommended guidelines on surveillance, providing requested information and reporting cases promptly to the WHO, and exchanging information and enhancing collaboration with the WHO and other international and national organizations.[86] This 'underscores not only the SARS threat, but also the importance of international cooperation and the role of the WHO in global infectious disease efforts'.[87] Additionally, the WHA adopted a resolution on revising the IHR which, among other things, recognized 'the part played by animals in the transmission and pathogenesis of some diseases which occur in humans' and requested that non-governmental sources of

don/2003_05_30a/en/> (accessed 3 February 2014). For a compelling discussion of the surveillance required in the SARS crisis, the legal, social, psychological, and other effects on those subject to it, and the fact that such health surveillance is not straightforward in practice, see L.A. Jacobs, 'Rights and Quarantine During the SARS Global Health Crisis: Differentiated Legal Consciousness in Hong Kong, Shanghai, and Toronto' (2007) 41 *Law and Society Review* 511.

80 Gostin, Bayer, and Fairchild, 'Ethical and Legal Challenges' (n 72) 3230. Also, WHO, 'Update 70' (n 79).

81 Gostin, Bayer, and Fairchild, 'Ethical and Legal Challenges' (n 72) 3230–1. Also, WHO, 'Update 70' (n 79).

82 WHO, 'Update 58—First Global Consultation on SARS Epidemiology, Travel Recommendations for Hebei Province (China), Situation on Singapore', 17 May 2003, available at <http://www.who.int/csr/sars/archive/2003_05_17/en/> (accessed 3 February 2014).

83 Fleck, 'How SARS Changed the World' (n 64) 626; J.A. Fishman, 'SARS, Xenotransplantation and Bioterrorism: Preventing the Next Epidemic' (2003) 3 *American Journal of Transplantation* 909.

84 WHO, 'International Health Regulations (IHR)' (1969), amended 1977 and 1983.

85 Gerberding, 'Faster . . . but Fast Enough?' (n 67) 2030.

86 World Health Assembly (WHA), 'Severe Acute Respiratory Syndrome (SARS)', 28 May 2003, WHA56.29, available at <http://www.who.int/csr/sars/en/ea56r29.pdf> (accessed 3 February 2014). WHA Resolutions are not legally binding on member states.

87 D.P. Fidler, 'Developments Involving SARS, International Law and Infectious Disease Control at the Fifty-Sixth Meeting of the World Health Assembly' (2003) 7 *American Society of International Law Insights*, available at <http://www.asil.org/insigh108.cfm> (accessed 25 June 2012).

information on infectious diseases could be taken account of to validate reports of infection.[88]

3.2 1997, 2003 to the present—H5N1 pandemic?

As the threat from SARS diminished during 2003, another zoonosis took centre stage. Avian influenza is an infectious viral disease of birds and most avian influenza viruses do not affect humans but, in 1997, H5N1 viruses were identified in humans, and sixteen people were infected and six killed by it.[89] H5N1 re-emerged in humans in 2003 and between then and 4 June 2012 there have been 605 confirmed cases in fifteen countries, predominantly in Asia and North East Africa, and 357 people have died from this zoonosis.[90] H5N1 viruses are 'unusually aggressive' viruses in humans, those who contract them often deteriorate rapidly, and they have a high (59 per cent) mortality rate.[91] The incubation period of H5N1 is commonly between two and eight days, and symptoms include a high fever, other influenza-like symptoms, diarrhoea, vomiting, abdominal and chest pains, and breathing difficulties.[92] H5N1 needs to be treated promptly in hospital, and antiviral medication may be prescribed.[93] Infection appears to result from (direct or indirect) exposure to infected live or dead poultry or contaminated environments.[94]

The WHO describes H5N1 as having 'pandemic *potential*' because it is widespread in some poultry populations, humans are unlikely to have immunity to it, and it can cause severe disease and death.[95] However, it does not currently view H5N1 as a risk to human health because this virus has not yet been transmitted *between* humans, but it continues to monitor it.[96] Recent research involving altering the virus's genetic code suggests that H5N1 viruses have the potential to spread between humans;[97] thereby

[88] WHA, 'Revision of the International Health Regulations', WHA56.28, 28 May 2003.

[89] WHO, 'Avian Influenza: Fact Sheet' (2011), available at <http://www.who.int/mediacentre/factsheets/avian_influenza/en/index.html> (accessed 3 February 2014); M. Honigsbaum, 'Robert Webster: "We ignore bird flu at our peril"', *The Guardian*, 17 September 2011, available at <http://www.guardian.co.uk/world/2011/sep/17/bird-flu-swine-flu-warning?INTCMP=SRCH> (accessed 3 February 2014).

[90] WHO, 'Influenza at the Human-Animal Interface—Summary and Assessment as of 4 June 2012' available at <http://www.who.int/influenza/human_animal_interface/Influenza_Summary_IRA_HA_interface_04June12.pdf> (accessed 3 February 2014).

[91] WHO, 'Avian Influenza: Fact Sheet' (n 89). The mortality rate is, however, contested, see D. Butler, 'Death-rate Row Blurs Mutant Flu Debate' (2012) 482 *Nature* 289.

[92] WHO, 'Avian Influenza: Fact Sheet' (n 89).

[93] WHO, 'Influenza—FAQs: H5N1 Influenza' available at <http://www.who.int/influenza/human_animal_interface/avian_influenza/h5n1_research/faqs/en/index.html> (accessed 3 February 2014).

[94] WHO, 'Avian Influenza: Fact Sheet' (n 89).

[95] WHO, 'Avian Influenza: Fact Sheet' (n 89) (emphasis added).

[96] WHO, 'Influenza: Evolution of H5N1 Avian Influenza Virus Does Not Increase Risk to Public Health' available at <http://www.who.int/influenza/human_animal_interface/avian_influenza/h5n1-2011_08_30/en/index.html> (accessed 3 February 2014).

[97] Controversy surrounded the publication of the two papers detailing this work as there was concern that doing so could enable others to replicate the experiments in order to endanger global health: K.I. Berns et al, 'Policy: Adaptations of Avian Flu Virus are a Cause for Concern' (2012) 482 *Nature* 153; Y. Kawaoka, 'H5N1: Flu Transmission Work is Urgent' (2012) 482 *Nature* 155. The debate over publication can be followed in, for example, issues of *Nature* between January and April 2012; see also WHO, 'Influenza—FAQs: H5N1 Research Issues', available at <http://www.who.int/influenza/human_animal_interface/avian_influenza/h5n1_research/faqs_research/en/index.html> (accessed 3 February 2014). One paper was eventually published in May 2012: M. Imai et al, 'Experimental Adaptation of an Influenza H5 HA Confers Respiratory Droplet Transmission to a

creating forms of the virus that are more transmissible in mammals than the naturally occurring viruses.[98] The response to H5N1 is different from that to SARS because the threat is viewed as primarily between infected birds and humans rather than infected humans and other humans. Thus, H5N1 has resulted in a number of measures being adopted with regard to poultry, including affected flocks being killed and trade restrictions being imposed on importing poultry and poultry products.[99] As with SARS, the WHO has had a key role in developing diagnostic methods and therapeutic treatments, including vaccines.[100]

3.3 2009 to 2010—H1N1 pandemic

In contrast to both SARS and H5N1, H1N1 was recognized as a pandemic[101] during 2009 and 2010, and the first cases of it were identified in Mexico during March 2009.[102] Swine influenza viruses do not normally infect humans but are highly contagious respiratory diseases in pigs. The H1N1 virus had not previously been detected in pigs or humans and was a mix of pig, avian, and human influenza virus genes.[103] It was thought that transmission had occurred through direct or indirect contact with droplets from infected pigs.[104] By 29 April 2009, 148 cases of H1N1 were confirmed in nine countries,[105] and in April 2009, the WHO declared it a 'Public Health Emergency of International Concern (PHEIC)'[106] under the 2005 IHR.[107] By August 2010, when the WHO announced the transition from pandemic to post-pandemic, 18,500 deaths had been attributed to H1N1;[108] however: '[t]he true extent of deaths attributable to the pandemic virus could... be significantly higher, since many people died without being tested.'[109] H1N1 appeared to be spread in a similar manner to seasonal influenza (via droplets released when speaking, sneezing, or coughing), and shared some of the symptoms but also nausea, vomiting, and diarrhoea. Most patients recovered within a week without treatment, but some suffered severe or fatal

Reassortant H5 HA/H1N1 Virus in Ferrets' (2012) 486 *Nature* 420. The second paper was published in June 2012: S. Herfst et al, 'Airborne Transmission of Influenza A/H5N1 Virus Between Ferrets' (2012) 336 *Science* 1534. For a useful summary of the key 'puzzles' about this virus, see E. Yong, 'Influenza: Five Questions on H5N1' (2012) 486 *Nature* 456.

98 WHO, 'Influenza—FAQs: H5N1 Research Issues' (n 97).

99 World Organisation for Animal Health (OIE), 'Avian Influenza Portal: Rapid Response' available at <http://www.oie.int/animal-health-in-the-world/web-portal-on-avian-influenza/rapid-response/> (accessed 3 February 2014).

100 See WHO, 'H5N1 Research Issues', available at <http://www.who.int/influenza/human_animal_interface/avian_influenza/h5n1_research/en/index.html> (accessed 3 February 2014).

101 A disease or condition that affects many people in many different countries.

102 WHO, 'Implementation of the IHR (2005)' (n 59) 51.

103 WHO, '(Update) 30 April 2009, INFOSAN Information Note No 2/2009—Human-Animal Interface Aspects of Influenza A/H1N1: The Influenza Outbreak in Humans Caused by Influenza A/H1N1—Considerations at the Human-Animal Interface' (2009) 1, available at <http://www.who.int/foodsafety/fs_management/No_02_influenza_Apr09_en_rev1.pdf> (accessed 3 February 2014).

104 WHO, '(Update) 30 April 2009, INFOSAN Information Note No 2/2009' (n 103) 2.

105 WHO, 'Implementation of the IHR (2005)' (n 59) 55.

106 'an extraordinary event which is determined... (i) to constitute a public health risk to other States through the international spread of disease and (ii) to potentially require a coordinated international response': WHO, 'International Health Regulations (IHR)' (Geneva: 2nd edn, WHO, 2008), as amended in 2008, Art 1.

107 WHO, '(Update) 30 April 2009, INFOSAN Information Note No 2/2009' (n 103) 1.

108 WHO, Global Alert and Response (GAR), 'Pandemic (H1N1) 2009—Update 112', 6 August 2010, available at <www.who.int/csr/don/2010_08_06/en/index.html>, accessed 3 February 2014; WHO, 'Implementation of the IHR (2005)' (n 59) 49.

109 WHO, 'Implementation of the IHR (2005)' (n 59).

complications which were caused by viral pneumonia and resulted in severe lung damage, respiratory failure, and, sometimes, circulatory collapse and kidney failure.[110] Unusually, H1N1 affected younger age groups more than normally occurs with seasonal influenza, and pregnant women and women who had recently given birth were also at an increased risk of infection.

Following the declaration of a PHEIC, the first issued under the IHR (2005), temporary recommendations were issued in April 2009 to reduce or prevent the disease spreading globally.[111] Countries were recommended to 'intensify surveillance for unusual outbreaks of [influenza-like illness] and severe pneumonia' in humans, surveillance in pigs was to increase, but neither trade nor travel were restricted.[112] Temporary recommendations are not binding under the IHR, and countries are able to implement measures beyond those set out in those recommendations provided they are consistent with the IHR and are not more restrictive, invasive, or intrusive of trade and travel or to persons, and achieve the same or increased health protection as the WHO recommendations.[113] Thus, for example, in Hong Kong travel notices were issued warning against travelling to Mexico, in Japan air passengers arriving from affected countries were screened, and Russia banned pork products from Mexico and affected states in the US.[114] In August 2010, the WHO declared that the world was in a post-H1N1 pandemic period but that the virus was expected to 'circulate as a seasonal virus for some years to come'.[115] Thus, national health authorities are to remain vigilant, particularly as H1N1's behaviour as a seasonal virus 'cannot be reliably predicted',[116] respiratory diseases should continue to be monitored, and the WHO notified 'immediately' in certain situations, including under the IHR (2005), and vaccinations encouraged.[117]

4. The International Health Regulations (2005) and Global Health Surveillance

The H1N1 pandemic is important in the history of global surveillance and control of infectious diseases as it was 'a major test on how well WHO and its member states apply the IHR (2005) to a dangerous outbreak'.[118] Both SARS and H5N1 occurred

110 Writing Committee of the WHO Consultation on Clinical Aspects of Pandemic (H1N1) 2009 Influenza, 'Clinical Aspects of Pandemic 2009 Influenza A (H1N1) Virus Infection' (2010) 362 *New England Journal of Medicine* 1708.

111 WHO, *IHR* (2008) (n 106) Art 15.

112 WHO, '(Update) April 2009, INFOSAN Information Note No 2/2009' (n 103) 3–4.

113 WHO, *IHR* (2008) (n 106) Arts 1 and 43(1), respectively.

114 K. Bradsher, 'Hong Kong, Minding SARS, Announces Tough Measures in Response to Swine Flu', *New York Times*, 26 April 2009, available at <http://www.nytimes.com/2009/04/27/world/asia/27kong.html?_r=1&pagewanted=print> (accessed 3 February 2014); B. Harden, 'Japanese Health Inspectors Search Plane From Dulles for Cases of Swine Flu', *Washington Post*, 5 May 2009, available at <http://www.washingtonpost.com/wp-dyn/content/article/2009/05/05/AR2009050500817.html> (accessed 3 February 2014); BBC News, 'World "Well Prepared" for Virus', 27 April 2009, available at <http://news.bbc.co.uk/1/hi/8019566.stm> (accessed 3 February 2014).

115 WHO, 'WHO Recommendations for the Post-Pandemic Period—Pandemic (H1N1) 2009 Briefing Note 23' (2010), available at <http://www.who.int/csr/disease/swineflu/notes/briefing_20100810/en/index.html> (accessed 3 February 2014).

116 'WHO Recommendations for the Post-Pandemic Period' (n 115).

117 'WHO Recommendations for the Post-Pandemic Period' (n 115).

118 D.P. Fidler, 'The Swine Flu Outbreak and International Law' (2009) 13 *American Society of International Law Insights*, available at <http://www.asil.org/insights/volume/13/issue/5/swine-flu-outbreak-and-international-law> (accessed 3 February 2014).

under the first edition of the IHR, which only applied to three diseases (cholera, plague, and yellow fever);[119] whereas, H1N1 occurred after the revised Regulations came into force in 2007. The IHR (2005) are binding on 194 countries, which are required to report outbreaks of certain diseases and public health events to the WHO. The Regulations 'establish a regime for routine public-health protection functions and provide for the ongoing management of disease threats, both in countries and at their borders... [and] provide a framework for coordinated and proportionate responses to significant, urgent disease threats'.[120] They set out the rights and obligations of countries to report certain infectious diseases, require countries to strengthen their capacities for public health surveillance and response, and establish procedures for the WHO in order to 'uphold global public health security'.[121] The IHR (2005) now apply to any 'disease'[122] and 'public health emergencies of international concern' (PHEIC).[123] The IHR are intended to 'prevent, protect against, control and provide a public health response to the international spread of disease in ways that are commensurate with and restricted to public health risks, and which avoid unnecessary interference with international traffic and trade'.[124] A public health risk is 'a likelihood of an event that may affect adversely the health of human populations, with an emphasis on one which may spread internationally or may present a serious and direct danger'.[125]

State Parties retain the right to legislate their own health policies[126] and, with regard to surveillance, should 'develop, strengthen and maintain detection, assessment, notification and reporting capacity'.[127] They should notify the WHO within twenty-four hours of events[128] which may constitute a PHEIC; set out the health measures[129] implemented in response to this;[130] provide the WHO with 'all relevant public health information' on this event;[131] and consult and keep the WHO informed of events that are not notifiable because of insufficient information.[132] The WHO should 'collect information regarding events through its surveillance activities and assess their potential to cause international disease spread and possible interference with international traffic',[133] and may take into account reports from non-official sources.[134] It can share information about infectious disease threats with others if the affected country refuses international assistance, and can unilaterally declare a PHEIC if a country fails to cooperate with it.[135] The WHO should issue non-binding temporary

119 WHO, *IHR* (1969) (n 84) Art 1.

120 WHO, 'Implementation of the IHR (2005)' (n 59) para 22.

121 WHO, 'What are the International Health Regulations?' (2008), available at <http://www.who.int/features/qa/39/en/index.html> (accessed 3 February 2014).

122 'illness or medical condition, irrespective of origin or source, that presents or could present significant harm to humans': WHO, *IHR* (2008) (n 106) Art 1.

123 Defined in WHO, *IHR* (2008) (n 106). Art 12 determines whether an event is a PHEIC and the assessment criteria are set out in a decision instrument in Annex 2: is the public health impact of the event serious?, is the event unusual or unexpected?, is there a significant risk of international spread?, and is there a significant risk of international trade or travel restrictions?

124 WHO, *IHR* (2008) (n106) Art 2.

125 WHO, *IHR* (2008) (n 106) Art 1.

126 WHO, *IHR* (2008) (n 106) Art 3. See also, Art 43.

127 WHO, *IHR* (2008) (n 106) Art 5. The 'core capacity requirements for surveillance and response' at local and national levels are set out in Annex 1.

128 'a manifestation of disease or an occurrence that creates a potential for disease': WHO, *IHR* (2008) (n 106) Art 1.

129 'procedures applied to prevent the spread of disease or contamination; a health measure does not include law enforcement or security measure': WHO, *IHR* (2008) (n 106) Art 1.

130 WHO, *IHR* (2008) (n 106) Art 6.

131 WHO, *IHR* (2008) (n 106) Art 7.

132 WHO, *IHR* (2008) (n 106) Art 8.

133 WHO, *IHR* (2008) (n 106) Art 5

134 WHO, *IHR* (2008) (n 106) Art 9.

135 WHO, *IHR* (2008) (n 106) Arts 10–12.

recommendations following a PHEIC,[136] and may make non-binding standing recommendations 'for routine or periodic application'.[137] More specifically, the WHO can make recommendations to States Parties relating to people, including requiring medical examinations,[138] placing suspect[139] people under public health observation,[140] implementing contact tracing of suspect or affected[141] people, and implementing quarantine[142] of suspect people, or isolation[143] and treatment of affected people.[144] Health measures should be 'initiated and completed without delay, and applied in a transparent and non-discriminatory manner',[145] and State Parties should collaborate with and assist other State Parties and the WHO.[146]

The WHO has commented that '[t]he 2009 influenza pandemic shone a revealing light on the function of the Regulations', and noted that '[b]eyond testing the Regulations, the influenza pandemic exposed vulnerabilities in global, national and local public-health capacities, limitations of scientific knowledge, difficulties in decision-making under conditions of uncertainty, complexities in international cooperation and challenges in communication among experts, policy-makers and the public'.[147] In one respect the international responses to H1N1 can be viewed as successful because the pandemic was fairly quickly and effectively minimized, with the move to the post-pandemic period occurring sixteen months after the PHEIC was declared. However, the WHO's handling of the H1N1 pandemic has been criticized for a lack of transparency, accountability, and coherence.[148] In particular, the WHO's

136 WHO, *IHR* (2008) (n 106) Art 15. Also, Art 1: 'non-binding advice issued by WHO pursuant to Article 15 for application on a time-limited basis, in response to a public health emergency of international concern, so as to prevent or reduce the international spread of disease and minimize interference with international traffic'. Art 17 sets out the criteria for issuing, modifying, or terminating either of these recommendations.

137 WHO, *IHR* (2008) (n 106) Art 16. Also, Art 1: 'non-binding advice issued by WHO for specific ongoing public health risks pursuant to Article 16 regarding appropriate health measures for routine or periodic application needed to prevent or reduce the international spread of disease and minimize interference with international traffic'.

138 'the preliminary assessment of a person by an authorized health worker or by a person under the direct supervision of the competent authority, to determine the person's health status and potential public health risk to others, and may include the scrutiny of health documents, and a physical examination when justified by the circumstances of the individual state': WHO, *IHR* (2008) (n 106) Art 1.

139 'those persons . . . considered by a State Party as having been exposed, or possibly exposed, to a public health risk and that could be a possible source of spread of disease': WHO, *IHR* (2008) (n 106) Art 1.

140 'the monitoring of the health status of a traveller over time for the purpose of determining the risk of disease transmission': WHO, *IHR* (2008) (n 106) Art 1.

141 'persons . . . that are infected or contaminated, or carry sources of infection or contamination, so as to constitute a public health risk': WHO, *IHR* (2008) (n 106) Art 1. Infection is 'the entry and development or multiplication of an infectious agent in the body of humans and animals that may constitute a public health risk', and contamination is 'the presence of an infectious or toxic agent or matter on a human or animal body surface . . . that may constitute a public health risk': Art 1.

142 'the restriction of activities and/or separation from others of suspect persons who are not ill . . . in such a manner as to prevent the possible spread of infection or contamination': WHO, *IHR* (2008) (n 106) Art 1.

143 'separation of ill or contaminated persons . . . from others in such a manner as to prevent the spread of infection or contamination': WHO, *IHR* (2008) (n 106) Art 1.

144 WHO, *IHR* (2008) (n 106) Art 18.

145 WHO, *IHR* (2008) (n 106) Art 42.

146 WHO, *IHR* (2008) (n 106) Art 44.

147 WHO, 'Implementation of the IHR (2005)' (n 59) 6.

148 P. Flynn, Social, Health and Family Affairs Committee, Parliamentary Assembly, Council of Europe, 'The Handling of the H1N1 Pandemic: More Transparency Needed' AS/Soc (2010) 12, 23 March 2010, available at <http://assembly.coe.int/CommitteeDocs/2010/20100329_Memorandum Pandemie_E.pdf> (accessed 3 February 2014).

precautionary approach to H1N1 was condemned, and it was suggested that as 'numerous scientists had expected the outbreak of a new world-wide pandemic for a long time [they] were therefore extremely sensitive to the possible dramatic consequences of any new viruses'.[149] The WHO maintained this approach 'even when empirical evidence had *later* shown that the pandemic had been much milder than initially expected'.[150] (Note that the same comment could be made in relation to xenotransplantation because of the unknowns and uncertainty regarding the risks and, thus, the appropriate response(s) to them.) As such, 'the WHO and other public health institutions involved in public decisions on the pandemic, have "gambled away" some of the confidence that the European public has in these highly reputed organisations'.[151]

The WHO itself has also reflected on its response to the H1N1 pandemic and issued fifteen recommendations as a result, summarised in three conclusions.[152] The first related to global preparedness for public health emergencies, and links to the core capacity requirements for surveillance and response which are set out in Annex 1 of the IHR. These were to have been implemented by June 2012 (five years after the Regulations came into force); however, in summary conclusion one the WHO concluded that: 'The core national and international capacities called for in the IHR are not yet fully operational and are not now on a path to timely implementation worldwide.'[153] Furthermore, in summary conclusion three the WHO said that: 'The world is ill-prepared to respond to a severe influenza pandemic or to any similarly global, sustained and threatening public-health emergency.'[154] Nevertheless, the second summary conclusion was that the WHO had performed 'well in many ways' during the H1N1 pandemic, although 'systemic difficulties' and 'some shortcomings' were noted.[155] These included the lack of a 'consistent, measurable and understandable depiction of severity of the pandemic', and that the WHO might have contributed to 'confusion and suspicion' by not acknowledging inconsistent descriptions of a pandemic and lack of prompt disclosure of possible conflicts of interest among experts.[156]

5. Protecting (Global) Health?—Xenotransplantation Surveillance Regimes

Alongside these recent experiences of threats to global health from zoonotic infections sit the revised IHR (2005), which are designed to manage disease threats and protect public health. Given continuing research in the area, it is timely to consider how the infection risks of xenotransplantation have been and can be addressed before this developing biotechnology moves from the laboratory to the clinic. Although xeno-specific surveillance regimes for recipients, close contacts and, possibly, relevant health workers have been widely proposed,[157] the details differ and so it is important to explore how it is suggested that health is (and can be) protected via such regimes.[158]

149 Flynn, 'The Handling of the H1N1 Pandemic' (n 148) para 9.
150 Flynn, 'The Handling of the H1N1 Pandemic' (n 148) para 10 (emphasis added).
151 Flynn, 'The Handling of the H1N1 Pandemic' (n 148) para 45.
152 WHO, 'Implementation of the IHR (2005)' (n 59) paras 20–62.
153 WHO, 'Implementation of the IHR (2005)' (n 59) para 16.
154 WHO, 'Implementation of the IHR (2005)' (n 59) para 18.
155 WHO, 'Implementation of the IHR (2005)' (n 59) para 17.
156 WHO, 'Implementation of the IHR (2005)' (n 59) para 33.
157 See n 11.
158 For a summary of the 'general concepts' relating to xeno-surveillance, see Fishman, Scobie, and Takeuchi, 'Xenotransplantation-Associated Infectious Risk' (n 49).

Internationally, xenotransplantation has been a matter of concern since the 1990s and the need for, and importance of, surveillance and international cooperation and collaboration in this matter has long been recognized,[159] including by those working within the field.[160] In 2001, the WHO published guidance aimed at facilitating an international xeno-surveillance network and response,[161] and in 2004, the WHA urged member states to only allow xenotransplantation when 'effective national regulatory control and surveillance mechanisms overseen by national health authorities are in place', cooperate in formulating recommendations and guidelines to harmonize global practices, and support international collaboration and coordination for preventing and monitoring post-xenotransplant infections.[162] The Director-General of the WHO was requested to, among other things, 'facilitate communication and international collaboration' on xenotransplantation issues, and 'inform proactively Member States of infectious events of xenogeneic origin arising from xenogeneic transplantation'.[163] In order to implement the 2004 Resolution, the WHO 'encouraged' member states to, among other things, 'ensure that there are effective surveillance systems in place which would identify and manage events which pose a potential danger to public health. WHO should be notified about major public health problems'.[164] In collaboration

159 eg WHO, 'Ethics, Access and Safety in Tissue and Organ Transplantation: Issues of Global Concern', Madrid, Spain, 6–9 October 2003, Report (Madrid: WHO, 2003); Council of Europe, Recommendation Rec(2003)10 of the Committee of Ministers to member states on xenotransplantation and explanatory memorandum, Adopted by the Committee of Ministers on 19 June 2003 at the 844th meeting of the Ministers' Deputies; Council of Europe, 'Report on the State of the Art in the Field of Xenotransplantation', CDBI/CDSP-XENO (2003) 1, available at <http://www.coe.int/t/dg3/healthbioethic/activities/06_xenotransplantation_en/XENO(2003)1_SAR.pdf> (accessed 3 February 2014); OECD and WHO, 'OECD/WHO Consultation on Xenotransplantation Surveillance: Summary' (2001), WHO/CDS/CSR/EPH/2001.1, available at <http://whqlibdoc.who.int/hq/2001/WHO_CDS_CSR_EPH_2001.1.pdf> (accessed 3 February 2014); OECD, 'Xenotransplantation: International Policy Issues' (Paris: OECD, 1999); WHO, 'Xenotransplantation: Guidance on Infectious Disease Prevention and Management' (1998) WHO/EMC/ZOO/98.1, available at <http://whqlibdoc.who.int/hq/1998/WHO_EMC_ZOO_98.1.pdf> (accessed 3 February 2014); WHO, 'Report of WHO Consultation on Xenotransplantation', Geneva, Switzerland, 28–30 October 1997 (1998) WHO/EMC/ZOO/98.2, available at <http://whqlibdoc.who.int/hq/1998/WHO_EMC_ZOO_98.2.pdf> (accessed 3 February 2014); Council of Europe, Recommendation No R(97)15 of the Committee of Ministers to member states on xenotransplantation, Adopted by the Committee of Ministers on 30 September 1997 at the 602nd meeting of the Ministers' Deputies; OECD, 'Advances in Transplantation Biotechnology and Animal to Human Organ Transplants (Xenotransplantation) Safety, Economic and Ethical Aspects', OECD Working Papers, Vol IV, No 97 (Paris: OECD, 1996).

160 eg Fishman, Scobie, and Takeuchi, 'Xenotransplantation-Associated Infectious Risk' (n 49); E. Cozzi et al, 'The International Xenotransplantation Association Consensus Statement on Conditions for Undertaking Clinical Trials of Porcine Islet Products in Type 1 Diabetes—Chapter 1: Key Ethical Requirements and Progress Toward the Definition of an International Regulatory Framework' (2009) 16 *Xenotransplantation* 203; M. Sykes, A. d'Apice, and M. Sandrin, 'Position Paper of the Ethics Committee of the International Xenotransplantation Association' (2003) 10 *Xenotransplantation* 194; D.K.C. Cooper et al, 'Report of the Xenotransplantation Advisory Committee of the International Society for Heart and Lung Transplantation: The Present Status of Xenotransplantation and Its Potential Role in the Treatment of End-Stage Cardiac and Pulmonary Diseases' (2000) 19 *Journal of Heart and Lung Transplantation* 1125.

161 WHO, 'WHO Guidance on Xenogeneic Infection/Disease Surveillance and Response: A Strategy for International Cooperation and Coordination', WHO/CDS/CSR/EPH/2001.2 (2001), available at <http://whqlibdoc.who.int/hq/2001/WHO_CDS_CSR_EPH_2001.2.pdf> (accessed 3 February 2014).

162 WHA, 'Human Organ and Tissue Transplantation', 22 May 2004, WHA57.18, Section II, para 1, available at <http://apps.who.int/gb/ebwha/pdf_files/WHA57/A57_R18-en.pdf> (accessed 3 February 2014).

163 WHA, 'Human Organ and Tissue Transplantation' (n 162) Section II, para 2.

164 WHO, 'Statement from the Xenotransplantation Advisory Consultation, Xenotransplantation: Hopes and Concerns', Geneva, 18–20 April 2005, 2, available at <http://www.who.int/transplantation/XenoEnglish.pdf> (accessed 3 February 2014).

with the University of Geneva and the International Xenotransplantation Association (IXA), the WHO established a voluntary global xenotransplantation inventory of clinical xenotransplants in 2006. This has no surveillance remit, but collects 'minimal data on all types of human xenotransplantation practices'.[165] The WHO also organized, in collaboration with the Chinese Ministry of Health, the Central South University of China, and the IXA, a meeting on clinical xenotransplantation in 2008.[166] It acted as the Secretariat for this meeting, but the meeting's conclusions are not WHO policies.[167] Nevertheless, principles for clinical xenotransplants were compiled, and key recommendations set out for the WHO, member states, and investigators and proposers of such trials.

These 'Changsha principles' are not legally binding but Principle 7 sets out the need for xeno-recipients and their (undefined) 'close contacts' to comply with lifelong surveillance including pre- and post-xenotransplant monitoring and archiving of samples, and states that xeno-recipients should be registered on a database in order to link to the source of the xenotransplanted organ.[168] Under Principle 8, there should be 'a system in place for vigilance and surveillance with contingency plans to identify and respond to any indication of xenotransplantation-related infection in a timely manner', and 'a global system for exchanging information, preventing unregulated xenotransplantation, providing support for states and coordinating xenotransplantation vigilance, surveillance and response to suspected infections' is needed.[169] Furthermore, the WHO 'should have in place a system for the identification of and response to any xenotransplantation infectious disease outbreak in a timely manner',[170] and member states should 'ensure that public health officials are aware of the infection risks of xenotransplantation, including those associated with patients traveling to receive xenotransplantation products outside their territories and have plans in place to timely identify and respond to any such infection'.[171] Clinical trial researchers 'must have a comprehensive plan for post-transplant long-term patient follow up and timely identification, reporting, and management of possible xenotransplant-related infection episodes',[172] and must 'ensure storage of appropriate pre- and post-procedure specimens and maintain both the specimens and records in accordance with national regulatory guidelines (normally for 30 to 50 years)'.[173]

165 WHO, 'GKT4 Xenotransplantation' (n 2). For the inventory site, see IXA, Hôpitaux Universitaires de Genève, WHO, 'Inventory of Human Xenotransplantation Practices' (2012), available at <http://www.humanxenotransplant.org/home/index.php> (accessed 3 February 2014). The minimal information requested is the country and institution, the therapeutic purpose of the treatment, whether the treatment is part of a clinical trial, the non-human animal source, the type of cells/tissues/organs xenotransplanted, the source of information, whether the results have been presented at a scientific congress or published in a scientific journal.

166 D.K.C. Cooper, 'Global Consultation on Regulatory Requirements for Xenotransplantation in Clinical Trials, Conference held in Changsha, China, 19–21 November 2008' (2009) 16 *Xenotransplantation* 58.

167 'First WHO Global Consultation on Regulatory Requirements for Xenotransplantation Clinical Trials, Changsha, China, 19–21 November 2008' (2009) 16 *Xenotransplantation* 61.

168 'First WHO Global Consultation on Regulatory Requirements' (n 167) Principle 7.

169 'First WHO Global Consultation on Regulatory Requirements' (n 167) Principle 9.

170 'First WHO Global Consultation on Regulatory Requirements' (n 167) Key Recommendation 5 to WHO.

171 'First WHO Global Consultation on Regulatory Requirements' (n 167) Key Recommendation 2 to Member States.

172 'First WHO Global Consultation on Regulatory Requirements' (n 167) Key Recommendation 6 to Investigators and Proposers of Clinical Trials using Xenotransplantation Products.

173 'First WHO Global Consultation on Regulatory Requirements' (n 167) Key Recommendation 7 to Investigators and Proposers of Clinical Trials using Xenotransplantation Products.

Despite the long-standing interest in and discussion of xeno-infection risks, the international aspects of regulating xenotransplantation and its surveillance are largely absent from the surveillance regimes proposed in individual countries.[174] The first draft xenotransplant guideline (including surveillance) was published by the US Department of Health and Human Services (DHHS) in 1996,[175] and was revised in 2001.[176] Since then, xeno-surveillance has been considered (in differing levels of detail and depth) in a number of countries,[177] and there is a consensus that local and national surveillance are required and that information should be collected on and from the non-human animals, their workers, xeno-recipients, their contacts, and (possibly) relevant health workers. At the national level, some regimes recommend a national xeno-database or registry[178] and/or a xeno-biobank to hold relevant samples from those involved in or potentially affected by the procedure,[179] and it is widely accepted that xeno-recipients must consent to the xenotransplant *and* to lifelong or long-term post-xenotransplant surveillance, including physical examinations and the removal and retention of tissues and/or serum samples.[180] In contrast, there is no consensus as to what surveillance should entail at the local level but, commonly, an individual or team at the site where the xenotransplant is performed is to be responsible for surveillance and determine what information, samples, and tissues are to be taken and when.[181] A few regimes set out pre- and post-xenotransplant minimum testing schedules,[182]

174 Notable exceptions include *Australia*—NHMRC (2009) (n 11) para 9.1. International aspects were noted but not explored in detail in *New Zealand*—'National Health Committee's Advice' (n 11) 36; *Norway*—Gjørv (n 11) 54; *the UK*—DH (n 11) 1; UKXIRA (n 11) paras 1.1, 2.8.

175 US DHHS, Public Health Service, 'Draft Public Health Service (PHS) Guideline on Infectious Disease Issues in Xenotransplantation', 23 September 1996, 61 *Federal Register* 49920.

176 *The US*—DHHS and FDA (n 11).

177 See n 11. For details of the xeno-surveillance schemes, see Fovargue, *Xenotransplantation and Risk* (n 13) ch 6.

178 *Australia*—NHMRC (2009) (n 11) 19; NHMRC, XWP (n 11) Guideline 9; *Canada*—Health Canada (n 11) 31–2; *the Netherlands*—Health Council (n 11) para 5.3.2; *New Zealand*—Toi te Taiao, The Bioethics Council, 'The Cultural, Spiritual and Ethical Aspects of Xenotransplantation: Animal-to-Human Transplantation—Final Report' (Wellington: New Zealand, 2005) 34; *Norway*—Gjørv (n 11) 56; *Sweden*—A Report by the Swedish Committee (n 11) 16, 23–31; *Switzerland*—Statement of Position (n 11) 391; *the US*—US DHHS and FDA (n 11) para 5.1. Also, WHO, *Report of WHO Consultation* (n 159) para 3.3. A similar suggestion was made with regard to cellular xenotransplants in *New Zealand*—'National Health Committee's Advice' (n 11) criterion 2.

179 *Norway*—Gjørv (n 11) 56; *Sweden*—A Report by the Swedish Committee (n 11) 16, 27–31; *the US*—US DHHS and FDA (n 11) para 5.2. For a similar suggestion with regard to cellular xenotransplants in *New Zealand*, see 'National Health Committee's Advice' (2008) (n 11) criterion 2.

180 *Australia*—NHMRC, XWP (n 11) Guideline 7; *Canada*—Health Canada (n 11) 6, 33; *France*—CCNE (n 11) 8; *the Netherlands*—Health Council (n 11) para 5.3.2; *New Zealand*—HRC GTAC (2007) (n 11) Section 7; *Norway*—Gjørv (n 11) 56; *Spain*—'Recommendations for the Regulation' (n 11) 40; *the UK*—UKXIRA (n 11) paras 2.5, A5.2, A5.4; *the US*—US DHHS, FDA, Center for Biologics Evaluation and Research (CBER), 'Guidance for Industry: Source Animal, Product, Preclinical and Clinical Issues Concerning the Use of Xenotransplantation Products in Humans—Final Guidance' (2003), Sections VIII D, available at <http://www.fda.gov/downloads/BiologicsBloodVaccines/GuidanceComplianceRegulatoryInformation/Guidances/Xenotransplantation/ucm092707.pdf> (accessed 3 February 2014); US DHHS and FDA (n 11) paras 2.5.7, 4.1.1.1–4.1.1.2. Also, 'First WHO Global Consultation on Regulatory Requirements' (n 167) Principle 7; Council of Europe, Recommendation Rec(2003)10 (n 159) Art 13.

181 *Canada*—Health Canada (n 11) 29, 32–3; *New Zealand*—HRC GTAC (2007) (n 11) Section 7; *Spain*—'Recommendations for the Regulation' (n 11) 40; *Sweden*—A Report by the Swedish Committee (n 11) 17, 34; *the UK*—UKXIRA (n 11) paras 2.3, 2.6–2.7, Annex One and Three; *the US*—US DHHS et al, 'Guidance for Industry' (2003) (n 180) Section VIII F3 and G; US DHHS and FDA (n 11) paras 2.4 and 4.1.2.

182 *Spain*—'Recommendations for the Regulation' (n 11) 40; *the UK*—UKXIRA (n 11) para 2.6, Annexes Three-Four; *the US*—US DHHS et al, 'Guidance for Industry' (2003) (n 180) Section VIII F3; US DHHS and FDA (n 11) paras 2.4, 4.1.2.

with more requiring that provision is made for an untoward event, significant exposure, or when xenogeneic infectious agents are suspected or known to be in the xenotransplanted organ.[183] Under some regimes biological specimens are to be archived for fifty years post-xenotransplant,[184] while in others storage is required but the length of time is not set out.[185] Xeno-recipients are to remain contactable post-xenotransplant under some regimes,[186] and refrain from unprotected sex and procreation,[187] from donating organs, tissues, and other bodily parts and fluids post-xenotransplant,[188] and mandatory post-mortems are implied.[189] Recipients might also have to be informed that they might be confined, isolated, or placed in other specialized medical housing if hospitalized, and may need to undertake specific precautions on discharge.[190] The possibility of quarantine in the event of infection is noted in some regimes,[191] and the Health Council of the Netherlands has gone further:

> ... during the clinical experimentation phase at least, it would be necessary to restrict the number of people with whom a patient had contact... so as to keep the postoperative monitoring programme to tolerable proportions. As a result, the organ recipient's freedom of movement would need to be restricted.[192]

Additionally, under some of the regimes xeno-recipients must consent to their intimate/household/close contacts (variably defined)[193] being informed of the xenotransplant, the

183 *Canada*—Health Canada (n 11) 33, 35–7, Section F; *New Zealand*—HRC GTAC (2007) (n 11) Section 7; *Spain*—'Recommendations for the Regulation' (n 11) 40; *the UK*—UKXIRA (n 11) paras 2.5–2.6, 2.8, Section 3; *the US*—US DHHS and FDA (n 11) paras 4.1.1.2, 4.1.2.3, 4.2.2.

184 *New Zealand*—HRC GTAC (2007) (n 11) Section 7; *Norway*—Gjørv (n 11) 56; *the US*—US DHHS and FDA (n 11) paras 4.1.2, 4.1.2.1, 4.1.2.2.

185 *Canada*—Health Canada (n 11) 6–7, 32–3; *the UK*—UKXIRA (n 11) para 2.7.

186 *Canada*—Health Canada (n 11) 6; *New Zealand*—HRC GTAC (2007) (n 11) Sections 7–8; *the UK*—UKXIRA (n 11) A5.2; *the US*—US DHHS et al, 'Guidance for Industry' (2003) (n 180) Sections VIII J2a vi; US DHHS and FDA (n 11) para 2.5.8.

187 *Canada*—Health Canada (n 11) 6–7, 33; *New Zealand*—HRC GTAC (2007) (n 11) Section 8; *the UK*—UKXIRA, 'Third Annual Report September 1999–November 2000' (London: DH, 2001) 15; UKXIRA (n 11) A5.2; *the US*—US DHHS et al, 'Guidance for Industry' (2003) (n 180) Sections VIII J2a iii; US DHHS and FDA (n 11) para 2.5.12.

188 *Canada*—Health Canada (n 11) 7, 33; *New Zealand*—HRC GTAC (2007) (n 11) Section 8; *the UK*—UKXIRA (n 11) A5.2; *the US*—US DHHS et al, 'Guidance for Industry' (2003) (n 180) Sections VIII J2a i, ii; US DHHS and FDA (n 11) para 2.5.11.

189 *Canada*—Health Canada (n 11) 6, 33; *New Zealand*—HRC GTAC (2007) (n 11) Sections 7–8; *Norway*—Gjørv (n 11) 57; *Spain*—'Recommendations for the Regulation' (n 11) 40; *the UK*—UKXIRA (n 11) A5.2; *the US*—US DHHS et al, 'Guidance for Industry' (2003) (n 180) Section VIII F3, J2a viii; US DHHS and FDA (n 11) para 2.5.9.

190 *New Zealand*—HRC GTAC (2007) (n 11) Section 8; *the US*—US DHHS et al, 'Guidance for Industry' (2003) (n 180) Sections VIII J2b ii; US DHHS and FDA (n 11) paras 2.5.5, 2.5.6, 4.2.1.2.

191 *Canada*—Health Canada (n 11) 6; *France*—CCNE (n 11) 8. Also, WHO, *Xenotransplantation* (n 159) para 6.6.3.

192 *The Netherlands*—Health Council (n 11) para 5.3.2.

193 eg household/close contacts are defined in *the UK* as 'household members and sexual partners and others with whom the xenotransplant recipient may engage in activities in which bodily fluid may be exchanged': UKXIRA (n 11) para 2.5, Annex Seven; and in *the US* as 'other intimate contacts of recipients (e.g., persons with whom recipients repeatedly engage in activities that could result in intimate exchange of body fluids)': US DHHS et al, 'Guidance for Industry' (2003) (n 180) Section VIII F4, and '[i]ntimate contacts of xenotransplantation product recipients include persons who have engaged repeatedly in activities that could result in intimate exchange of body fluids, including blood or saliva, with a xenotransplantation product recipient. Examples of intimate contacts include, but are not limited to, sexual partners, household members who share razors or toothbrushes and health care workers or laboratory personnel with repeated percutaneous, mucosal, or other direct exposures': US DHHS et al, 'Guidance for Industry' (2003) (n 180) Section VIII J2a i. This definition has been adopted in *New Zealand*—HRC GTAC (2007) (n 11) Guideline 8.

possible side-effects for the xeno-recipient and symptoms in themselves,[194] and recipients might also have to identify possible contacts beyond known close contacts if there is an adverse event post-xenotransplant; or contacts could only be involved if there was an adverse event.[195] Some regimes require a xeno-recipient's intimate/household/close contacts to agree to similar health surveillance, archiving, and restrictions on post-xenotransplant behaviour, including donation, as is expected of the xeno-recipients.[196] Elsewhere, educating rather than monitoring contacts is preferred,[197] and some regimes deploy both education and monitoring.[198] The surveillance of relevant health professionals has also not been universally considered, but where it has been occupational health records and services play a central role,[199] and active surveillance is generally only required if there is an adverse event or significant exposure post-xenotransplant,[200] although in some countries pre-xenotransplant baseline blood samples are recommended, along with the archiving of samples.[201]

Despite this talk of the importance of and need for xeno-surveillance, there has been negligible concrete activity nationally and internationally or, importantly, linking human and non-human health surveillance.[202] Little has been done to set up or facilitate systems of notification and communication specific to xenotransplantation and, for example, no known specific xenotransplant-related infectious disease is listed as being the subject of surveillance on the European Centre for Disease Prevention and Control website.[203] This is notable, as the Centre is the EU agency which aims to

194 *Canada*—Health Canada (n 11) 6; *New Zealand*—HRC GTAC (2007) (n 11), Guideline 8; *Norway*—Gjørv (n 11) 57; *Switzerland*—Statement of Position (n 11) 391; *the UK*—UKXIRA (n 11) A5.2.

195 *The UK*—UKXIRA (n 11) A5.2; *Sweden*—A Report by the Swedish Committee (n 11) 17, respectively.

196 *Australia*—NHMRC, XWP (n 11) Guideline 8; *Canada*—Health Canada (n 11) 6, 7, and 33; *the Netherlands*—Health Council (n 11) para 5.3.2; *New Zealand*—HRC GTAC (2007) (n 11) Guideline 8; *Sweden*—A Report by the Swedish Committee (n 11) 17; *the UK*—UKXIRA (n 11) paras 2.5, 2.8, Annex Three, A5.2; *the US*—US DHHS et al, 'Guidance for Industry' (2003) (n 180) Sections VIII F4; US DHHS, FDA, CBER, 'Guidance for Industry: Precautionary Measures to Reduce the Possible Risk of Transmission of Zoonoses by Blood and Blood Products from Xenotransplantation Product Recipients and Their intimate Contacts—Draft Guidance' (2002), 2, 5, available at <http://www.fda.gov/downloads/biologicsbloodvaccines/guidancecomplianceregulatoryinformation/guidances/blood/ucm080375.pdf> (accessed 3 February 2014); US DHHS and FDA (n 11) para 2.5.11.

197 *Spain*—'Recommendations for the Regulation' (n 11) 41. This was initially the position in *the US*—US DHHS and FDA (n 11) paras 2.5.4, 2.5.8, see now US DHHS et al, 'Guidance for Industry' (2002) (n 196) Section VIII F4.

198 *New Zealand*—HRC GTAC (2007) (n 11) Section 7; *the US*—US DHHS, Secretary's Advisory Committee on Xenotransplantation (SACX), 'Informed Consent in Clinical Research Involving Xenotransplantation—Draft' (2004) 22, available at <http://mckinneylaw.iu.edu/instructors/orentlicher/Social%20Regulation/xenotransplantation_informed_consent.pdf> (accessed 3 February 2014); US DHHS et al, 'Guidance for Industry' (2003) (n 180) Section VIII F4, J2a i.

199 *Spain*—'Recommendations for the Regulation' (n 11) 41–3; *the UK*—UKXIRA (n 11) paras 2.5, 2.8, Annex Three; *the US*—US DHHS and FDA (n 11) paras 4.2.3–4.2.3.3.

200 *Canada*—Health Canada (n 53) 16; *Sweden*—A Report by the Swedish Committee (n 11) 17; *the UK*—UKXIRA (n 11) Annexes Three and Four.

201 *Spain*—'Recommendations for the Regulation' (n 11) 42; *the UK*—UKXIRA (n 11) para 2.5, Annex Three; *the US*—US DHHS et al, 'Guidance for Industry' (2003) (n 180) Section VIII F4; US DHHS and FDA (n 11) para 4.2.3.2.

202 On the latter see Committee on Achieving Sustainable Global Capacity for Surveillance and Response to Emerging Diseases of Zoonotic Origin, G.T. Keusch et al (eds), *Sustaining Global Surveillance and Response to Emerging Zoonotic Diseases* (The National Academies Press, 2009) 6.

203 European Centre for Disease Prevention and Control (ECDC), 'Health topics by disease group', available at <http://www.ecdc.europa.eu/EN/HEALTHTOPICS/Pages/health_topics_disease_group.aspx> (accessed 3 February 2014).

'[strengthen] Europe's defences against infectious diseases' and 'identify, assess and communicate current and emerging threats to human health posed by infectious diseases'.[204] While the WHO has laid much of the groundwork for an international xeno-surveillance system, it has been suggested that its role is now to be no more than a 'catalyst bringing together regular (annual or biennial) interaction between regulator and xenotransplantation subject matter experts, as appropriate to the level of contemporary xenotransplantation activity'.[205] However, without international surveillance, clinical xenotransplants will jeopardize global health (although the extent of the threat is unknown), and it is thus a cause for concern that no international xeno-specific surveillance system has been implemented given the continuing pre-clinical research and statements about its clinical use.

6. Moving Forward

The risks of xenotransplantation are such that xeno-specific surveillance regimes are necessary if this developing biotechnology is to move to the clinic; however, variances in the content, detail, and complexity of current regimes make it questionable whether effective surveillance regimes (can) exist. It may not be possible to monitor and control xenotransplantation risks because it is not known which, if any, diseases may be transmitted post-xenotransplant. It is therefore difficult to devise detection and diagnostic tests, respond to any infections by monitoring their existence and spread, or treat any infections; some of which may be latent, with the length of any latency period also unknown. A further complication is that the risks may go beyond the xeno-recipient. Xenotransplantation thus highlights the global nature of advances in health and the risks which may sit alongside them. International communication, cooperation, and action are thus vital as borders are irrelevant, decisions made in one country will affect behaviour in another, and it has been suggested that: 'Some promoters of xenotransplantation clinical trials have moved their activities from continent to continent, sometimes evidently taking advantage of weaknesses in the regulatory oversight.'[206] Collaboration is needed to minimize the risk of 'xeno-havens' developing (ie countries with little or no xeno-regulation or surveillance), with the accompanying xeno-tourism. These are dangerous because 'regulatory gaps among different legal systems as to public health protection . . . leave the worldwide normative landscape looking quite inadequate to cope safely with the new therapies'.[207] Indeed: 'In the contemporary international environment, one nation's failure in legal preparedness can affect global public health and, simultaneously, damage perceptions of that nation's ability to engage in cooperative disease control efforts and commitment to the protection of domestic civil rights.'[208] Nevertheless, international surveillance will not be easy because of varied histories and agendas, issues of accountability, and different legal and cultural norms; but if there is no such action then clinical xenotransplants may endanger everyone's health. Without an international infrastructure local and national country-specific

[204] ECDC, 'Mission', available at <www.ecdc.europa.eu/en/aboutus/Mission/Pages/Mission.aspx> (accessed 3 February 2014).

[205] Noel, 'Global Regulatory Requirements for Xenotransplantation Clinical Trials' (n 12) 71.

[206] Noel, 'Global Regulatory Requirements for Xenotransplantation Clinical Trials' (n 12) 71. Also WHO, 'GKT4 Xenotransplantation' (n 2).

[207] M. Tallacchini and S. Beloucif, 'Regulatory Issues in Xenotransplantation: Recent Developments' (2009) 14 *Current Opinion in Organ Transplantation* 180, 183 (reference removed).

[208] J.W. Sapsin et al, 'SARS and International Legal Preparedness' (2004) 77 *Temple Law Review* 155.

xeno-surveillance schemes will be rendered meaningless, and our experiences with SARS, H5N1, and H1N1 have shown that global surveillance may be difficult but not impossible and such surveillance is 'the primary tool of prevention'.[209] Additionally, global interconnectedness is one of the reasons why the IHR (2005) are required;[210] and, of course, 'diseases know no frontiers'.[211]

However, while global consensus and consistency is a laudable aim, one significant problem is securing compliance with a surveillance scheme; xeno-specific or otherwise. This is complicated with xenotransplantation where surveillance extends beyond the recipient to her contacts (however defined), possibly health professionals, and maybe even further. The regimes' requirements are lifelong, physically intrusive, and are such that traditional notions of consent and confidentiality are necessarily challenged.[212] Thus, well established and protected human rights will be infringed, limited, or suspended, and public health laws and measures can authorize compulsory treatment, detention, or isolation, and so engage and/or challenge rights such as those to life, liberty, security, and privacy. As such, those subject to these regimes may be reluctant to comply with all or any of the requirements. Regulatory authorities may similarly be averse to (or legally incapable of) compelling their citizens to comply with their national schemes. How likely is it, then, that they will enforce global requirements, especially if they do not agree with them? This is recognized in relation to the IHR (2005), which 'seek to balance the sovereignty of individual States Parties with the common good of the community, and take account of economic and social interests as well as the protection of health'.[213] Despite these difficulties, Gostin has argued that vertical governance (where international agencies set minimum health capacities at regional and national levels) is more likely to be effective at protecting global health than horizontal governance (where threats are regulated via bilateral state or regional agreements), because the former can '[set] uniform standards for national health surveillance and regulation based science'.[214] This is undoubtedly what the IHR (2005) seek to do, but while they are said to be binding on 194 countries there are no sanctions for non-compliance. In reality, their effectiveness to protect global health largely depends on, as the WHO itself recognizes, (fear of) political embarrassment, political will, and pressure.[215] These were in evidence during the SARS outbreak in 2003 but are they sufficient, especially where a threat to health has been consciously introduced; albeit as a side-effect of an attempt to benefit the health of some?

The WHO is undoubtedly well placed to implement a specific international xeno-surveillance regime; however, its inability to enforce the standards it sets makes it harder for national governments to protect their populations from transboundary threats. Parmet suggests that 'in times of crisis, the most potent variable distinguishing the community that survives a plague from that which does not is not a community's

209 House of Lords Select Committee on Intergovernmental Organisations, 'Diseases Know No Frontiers: How Effective Are Intergovernmental Organisations in Controlling Their Spread?', Vol I: Report HL Paper 143-I (2008) para 50.

210 WHO, 'What are the International Health Regulations?' (n 121).

211 Sapsin et al, 'SARS and International Legal Preparedness' (n 208).

212 Discussed further in Fovargue, *Xenotransplantation and Risk* (n 13) chs 5 and 6.

213 WHO, 'Implementation of the IHR (2005)' (n 59) para 12.

214 L. Gostin, 'The International Health Regulations: A New Paradigm for Global Health Governance?' in S.A.M. McLean (ed), *First Do No Harm: Law, Ethics and Healthcare* (Aldershot: Ashgate, 2006) 63.

215 WHO, 'Frequently asked questions about the International Health Regulations (2005)' (2009), Question VII, available at <http://www.who.int/ihr/about/FAQ2009.pdf> (accessed 3 February 2014).

degree of scientific knowledge but rather its legal system's responsiveness and stability'.[216] While this may be so, law has an important *but limited* role in protecting global health even though public health models regarding infectious diseases focus on ideas of 'legal preparedness'.[217] Law can create 'powers to act, but also responsibilities to respond, obligations to communicate, authority to intervene, formality of hierarchies of response, clarity of accountability, and mechanisms for resolution of conflicts when they arise'.[218] However, without enforceable international sanctions supporting such legal preparedness it is hard to see how health can be protected if genetically engineered solid organ xenotransplants leave the laboratory. A developing biotechnology such as xenotransplantation thus exposes the boundaries and limits of laws' reach in situations where in seeking to benefit individuals the health of others may be put at risk.

216 W.E. Parmet, 'Introduction: The Interdependency of Law and Public Health' in R.A. Goodman et al, (eds), *Law in Public Health Practice* (New York: 2nd edn, OUP, 2007) xxxi.

217 A.D. Moulton et al, 'What Is Public Health Legal Preparedness?' (2003) 31 *Journal of Law, Medicine and Ethics* 672, 672. Also, G.C. Benjamin and A.D. Moulton, 'Public Health Legal Preparedness: A Framework for Action' (2008) 36 (Suppl 1) *Journal of Law, Medicine and Ethics* 13.

218 G.T. Laurie and K.G. Hunter, 'Mapping, Assessing and Improving Legal Preparedness for Pandemic Flu in the United Kingdom' (2009) 10 *Medical Law International* 101, 102.

24

Global Health Law Norms

A Coherent Framework to Understand PPACA's Approach to Eliminate Health Disparities and Address Implementation Challenges

*Gwendolyn Roberts Majette**

It is time to refocus, reinforce and repeat the message that health disparities exist and that health equity benefits everyone.[1]

1. Introduction

The existence of health disparities for people of color is a persistent problem in the United States.[2] Health disparities are 'difference[s] in health or clinical outcomes that [are] not attributable to clinical appropriateness or patient preference'.[3] Absent significant intervention, health disparities will exacerbate given the Census Bureau prediction that in 2045 one half of the US population will be people of color.[4]

There are tremendous costs at the individual and societal level that underlie these disparities. They include the unnecessary loss of life, disabilities, and illness coupled with the imposition of significant, yet avoidable financial costs. One study estimated that over a nine-year period, 886,202 deaths could have been avoided if the mortality

* Many thanks to Professors Michael Freeman, Dr Sarah Hawkes, and Professor Belinda Bennett for putting together an outstanding colloquium on Law and Global Health. The author wishes to thank her husband, Mario Majette, MD, MPH, and Professors Browne Lewis, Ruquaiijah Yearby, Christopher Roberts, Lance Gable, Benjamin Mason Meier, and Sandy Han for their willingness to review drafts of this chapter or to discuss its concepts. She also wishes to thank the following individuals for their research assistance: members of the CM-Law library staff, especially Amy Burchfield, and her research assistant, Gordon Gantt.

1 K.G. Sebelius, Secretary of Health and Human Services, US Department of Health and Human Services, 'HHS Action Plan to Reduce Racial and Ethnic Health Disparities' (2011), 1, available at <http://minorityhealth.hhs.gov/npa/files/Plans/HHS/HHS_Plan_complete.pdf>.

2 Sebelius, 'HHS Action Plan' (n 1) 1; US Department of Health and Human Services, Agency for Healthcare Research and Quality, 2010 National Healthcare Disparities Report (2011) 1.

3 Institute of Medicine, 'Future Directions for the National Healthcare Quality and Disparities Report' (C. Ulmer et al (eds), 2010) 44. These differences in health status can be due to barriers to health care for people of color or other determinants of health like social and economic conditions; the physical environment; biology and genetics; and human behavior. G.R. Majette, 'Access to Health Care: What a Difference Shades of Color Make' (2003) 12 *Annals of Health Law* 121, 123–39; D. Satcher and E.J. Higginbotham, 'The Public Health Approach to Eliminating Disparities in Health' (2008) 98 *American Journal of Public Health* 400; D. Satcher, 'Our Commitment to Eliminate Racial and Ethnic Health Disparities' (2001) 1 *Yale Journal of Health Policy Law and Ethics* 1, 2; S. Isaacs and S. Schroeder, 'Class—The Ignored Determinant of the Nation's Health' (2004) 351 *New England Journal of Medicine* 1137.

4 Institute of Medicine, 'Future Directions' (n 3) 44.

rates between white and black individuals were equal in the United States.[5] The financial costs of disparities are equally startling; it is estimated that between 2003 and 2006 the combined costs of health inequalities and premature deaths in the United States was $1.24 trillion.[6] Elimination of health disparities for people of color can save lives, reduce disabilities, and help reduce health care costs in the United States.

The United States has taken some steps to eliminate health disparities for people of color. Over twenty-seven years ago, in 1985, the United States released the Report of the Secretary's Task Force on Black and Minority Health (Heckler Report) which first recognized that there were significant disparities in health for people of color. Another major step to address health disparities occurred in 1998, when President Clinton announced the Presidential Initiative to Eliminate Racial and Ethnic Disparities in Health. This was the first initiative designed 'to eliminate, not simply reduce disparities in health in six key areas: (1) cancer screening and management, (2) cardiovascular disease, (3) diabetes, (4) HIV/AIDS, (5) immunization rates, and (6) infant mortality'.[7] Subsequently, elimination of health care disparities became a goal of Healthy People 2010 and 2020, the nation's health-promotion and disease-prevention agenda.[8]

In 1999, Congress provided funding for a one-time Institute of Medicine study on the prevalence and impact of racial and ethnic bias in medicine. In 2003, the Institute of Medicine released the seminal report, 'Unequal Treatment: Confronting Racial and Ethnic Disparities in Health Care', which identified the extent of racial and ethnic differences in health care, potential causes, and interventions to eliminate them.[9]

Notwithstanding these and other initiatives, in 2010, a former Surgeon General, David Satcher, and the current Assistant Secretary for Health, Howard K. Koh, concluded that little progress has been made to reduce and eliminate health disparities.[10] A significant cause of the deficient progress in the reduction of health disparities for people of color is the lack of commitment of resources.[11]

The passage of the Patient Protection and Affordable Care Act (PPACA)[12] in 2010 provides the United States with a tremendous opportunity to eliminate health disparities for people of color. Eliminating health disparities for people of color in the United States is also a global concern. The seminal goal of the right to health is to 'alleviate

5 The nine-year time period was 1991–2000. M. Marmot and R. Bell, 'Action on Health Disparities in the United States: Commission on Social Determinants of Health' (2009) 301 *Journal of the American Medical Association* 1169, 1170.

6 T. LaVeist, D. Gaskin, and P. Richard, 'The Economic Burden of Health Inequalities in the United States' (Joint Center for Political and Economic Studies, 2009).

7 Satcher and Higginbotham, 'The Public Health Approach' (n 3) 400; Satcher, 'Our Commitment' (n 3); D. Satcher, 'The History of the Public Health Service and the Surgeon General's Priorities' (1999) 54 *Food and Drug Law Journal* 13, 19.

8 H.K. Koh, 'A 2020 Vision for Healthy People' (2010) 362 *New England Journal of Medicine* 1653, 1653.

9 Institute of Medicine, 'Unequal Treatment: Confronting Racial and Ethnic Disparities in Health Care' (B.D. Smedley et al (eds), 2003) 4.

10 E.J. Sondik et al, 'Progress Toward the Healthy People 2010 Goals and Objectives' (2010) 31 *Annual Review of Public Health* 271, 280; Koh, 'A 2020 Vision for Healthy People' (n 8) 1656.

11 Sondik et al, 'Progress Toward the Healthy People 2010 Goals' (n 10) 271. Other scholars argue that a major cause of persistent health disparities is racial discrimination. R. Yearby, 'Does Twenty-Five Years Make a Difference in "Unequal Treatment"?: The Persistence of Racial Disparities in Health Care Then and Now' (2010) 19 *Annals of Health Law* 57, 58; V. Randall, 'Racial Discrimination in Health Care in the United States as a Violation of the International Convention on the Elimination of All Forms of Racial Discrimination' (2002) 14 *University of Florida Journal of Law and Public Policy* 50.

12 Patient Protection and Affordable Care Act (PPACA), Pub L No 111–148, 124 Stat 119 (2010), *amended by* Health Care and Education Reconciliation Act of 2010, Pub L No 111–152, 124 Stat 1029.

human suffering and address inequality'.[13] Thus, health and human rights norms require governments to address inequality and discrimination.[14] Moreover, both the World Health Organization (WHO) and the Special Rapporteur for Health recognize the inequitable treatment of disadvantaged groups across the world as a pressing international issue. Scholars like Jennifer Prah Ruger and Vernellia Randall note that eliminating global health disparities requires both international and domestic legal and policy approaches.[15]

This chapter fills a gap in the legal scholarship by analyzing how global health law norms provide a coherent legal and policy framework to understand the multitude of diverse provisions within PPACA that have the potential to reduce health disparities for people of color in the United States. It also analyzes some of the barriers to implementation created by constitutional and political challenges to PPACA. Section 2 provides global health laws that impose an obligation on the United States to eliminate health disparities for people of color. Section 3 analyzes the framework that PPACA creates to protect the right to health and eliminate health disparities for people of color. Section 4 analyzes the constitutional challenge to PPACA in *National Federation of Independent Business, et al v Sebelius* and its potential threat to undermine the United States' efforts to reduce health care disparities for people of color. Sections 5 and 6 examine the continuing moral imperative to reduce health care disparities and ensure that the United States complies with global health law norms in light of the Supreme Court's *NFIB* decision and the United States' inconsistent history of addressing health and race matters.

2. Global Health Laws that Impose a Duty on the United States to Reduce or Eliminate Health Disparities

Scholars Larry Gostin and Allyn Taylor define global health law as:

> . . . a field that encompasses the legal norms, processes, and institutions needed to create the conditions for people throughout the world to attain the highest possible level of physical and mental health. The field seeks to facilitate health-promoting behavior among the key actors that significantly influence the public's health, including international organizations, governments, businesses, foundations, the media, and civil society. The mechanisms of global health law should (a) encourage investment in research and development, (b) mobilize resources, (c) [establish] priorities, (d) coordinate activities, (e) create incentives, and (f) enforce standards. The overall guiding principle is social justice.[16]

There are two critical aspects of this normative governance model: coordination and an emphasis on addressing global health inequities. The evolving area of global health law moves beyond activities of the government to protect health by seeking to influence a broad array of actors whose conduct impacts health. Global health law also reflects an important normative shift in global health policy to focus on health as an end itself to

13 J. Tobin, *The Right to Health in International Law* (OUP, 2012) 21.

14 P. Hunt, 'Missed Opportunities: Human Rights and the Commission on Social Determinants of Health', Address at the Closing the Gap in a Generation: Health Equity Through Action on the Social Determinants of Health Conference (6–7 November 2008), in *Global Health Promotion*, 8 April 2009, at 36, 37, available at <http://ped.sagepub.com/content/16/1_suppl/36.full.pdf+html>.

15 J.P. Ruger, 'Normative Foundations of Global Health Law' (2008) 96 *Georgetown Law Journal* 423, 425; Randall, 'Racial Discrimination in Health Care' (n 11) 45.

16 L.O. Gostin and A.L. Taylor, 'Global Health Law: A Definition and Grand Challenges' (2008) 1 *Public Health Ethics* 53, 55.

promote justice.[17] Thus, countries pursue a health agenda primarily to prevent the causes of disease and prevent domestic suffering. The leading framework in global health law that promotes global cooperation and addresses health inequalities is human rights.[18] Today, 'all countries have ratified one or more binding treaty that includes the right to health'.[19]

There are several global health laws that have a human rights focus that impose an obligation on the United States to eliminate health disparities for people of color. They include binding laws such as the global health governance documents of the WHO and the International Convention to Eliminate Racial discrimination (ICERD). The United States is a member of the WHO, whose constitution protects the right to health, and it has ratified ICERD. They also include non-binding aspirational laws like the International Covenant on Economic, Social and Cultural Rights (ICESCR), and reports of the Special Rapporteur for Health. While two presidents of the United States have urged ratification of the ICESCR, Congress has not provided its advice and consent.[20]

2.1 The right to health under the WHO Constitution and the International Covenant on Economic, Social and Cultural Rights (ICESCR)

'Human rights is the most developed and accepted normative framework in global health.'[21] It is a norm that provides legal accountability to protect human dignity.[22] Human rights principles protect the intrinsic value and worth of all human beings.[23] Thus it combines 'universally recognized moral values' with legal obligations.[24] It also provides legal force for various health movements like health equity and social determinants of health[25] which are particularly important concepts to reducing health care disparities for people of color.

The WHO broadly defines health as a 'state of complete physical, mental and social well-being and not merely the absence of disease or infirmity'.[26] The critical importance of protecting health is recognized by the WHO Constitution and ICESCR which both provide that health is a fundamental right. The WHO Constitution provides: 'The enjoyment of the highest attainable standard of health is one of the fundamental rights of every human being without distinction of race . . . economic or social

17 B.M. Meier, 'Global Health Takes a Normative Turn: The Expanding Purview of International Health Law and Global Health Policy to Meet the Public Health Challenges of the 21st Century', 10 available at SSRN.

18 Ruger, 'Normative Foundations of Global Health Law' (n 15) 427.

19 G. Backman, P. Hunt et al, 'Health Systems and the Right to Health: An Assessment of 194 Countries' (2008) 372 *Lancet* 2047.

20 E. Kinney, 'Recognition of the International Human Right to Health and Health Care in the United States' (2008) 60 *Rutgers Law Review* 335, 347–8

21 Meier, 'Global Health Takes a Normative Turn' (n 17) 22.

22 Meier, 'Global Health Takes a Normative Turn' (n 17) 22.

23 A. Chapman, 'Introduction' in *Health Care Reform: A Human Rights Approach* (Georgetown University Press, 1994) 5.

24 P. Hunt and S. Leader, 'Developing and Applying the Right to the Highest Attainable Standard of Health: The Role of the U.N. Special Rapporteur (2002–2008)', in J. Harrington and M. Stuttaford (eds), *Global Health and Human Rights: Legal and Philosophical Perspectives* (Routledge, 2010) 57.

25 Hunt, 'Missed Opportunities' (n 14) 39.

26 See World Health Organization, Constitution of the World Health Organization, 22 July 1946, Preamble 1, available at <http://apps.who.int/gb/bd/PDF/bd47/EN/constitution-en.pdf>.

condition.'[27] The ICESCR protects the right to health by requiring governments to prevent, treat, and control 'epidemic, endemic, occupational and other diseases'; and to create conditions to 'assure to all medical service and medical attention in the event of sickness'.[28] Given the comprehensive way in which the ICESCR defines the right to health, it is one of the most important treaties to the development of a country's health system.[29]

Conceptualizing a health care system through a right to health perspective facilitates development of a system that is effective, integrated, and accessible. Accordingly, the Special Rapporteur for Health defines the right to health as the 'right to an effective and integrated health system, encompassing health care and the underlying determinants of health, which is responsive to national and local priorities, and accessible to all'.[30] Unfortunately, the US health care system is not accessible to all. Instead, people of color encounter numerous barriers to care including: lack of financing or health insurance, insufficient individual and institutional providers within geographic reach, communication challenges due to cultural insensitivity or language differences, stereotyping, and discrimination.[31] The effectiveness of the US healthcare system is also questioned, when the Institute of Medicine concludes that it produces 'unacceptable outcomes' because the 'use of evidence based treatments and the quality of care vary by race and ethnicity'.[32]

2.2 The International Convention on the Elimination of all Forms of Racial Discrimination

The International Convention on the Elimination of all Forms of Racial Discrimination (ICERD) prohibits the United States from engaging in or supporting racial discrimination; requires it to take effective measures to review and revise policies, laws, and regulation that have the effect of creating or perpetuating racial discrimination; and requires it to prohibit others from engaging in racial discrimination.[33] In the context of the right to health, ICERD requires the United States to prohibit and eliminate 'racial discrimination in all its forms and guarantee the right to everyone, without distinction as to race, color, or national or ethnic origin to equality before the law, . . . in the enjoyment of the right to public health and medical care'.[34]

The convention does not impose an obligation on a country like the United States to protect the right to health, but instead establishes the parameters that govern economic,

27 WHO, Constitution of the World Health Organization (n 26) 1.

28 International Covenant on Economic, Social, and Cultural Rights, Art 12(2)(c), (d), 16 December 1966, 1966 UST 521, 993 UNTS 3.

29 Backman, Hunt et al, 'Health Systems' (n 19) 2047.

30 Special Rapporteur on the Right of Everyone to the Enjoyment of the Highest Attainable Standard of Physical and Mental Health, 'Economic, Social and Cultural Rights', para 4, Commission on Human Rights, Economic and Social Council, UN Doc E/CN.4/2006/48, 3 March 2006 (by Paul Hunt); see also United Nations, Economic and Social Council, Committee on Economic, Social and Cultural Rights, 'Substantive Issues Arising in the Implementation of the International Covenant on Economic, Social and Cultural Rights, General Comment No 14', UN Doc E/C.12/2000/4, 11 August 2000, para 4, explaining that the right to health includes a number of socioeconomic factors.

31 Majette, 'Access to Health Care' (n 3) 123–39, discussing the common barriers to care for people of color and proposing an interdisciplinary approach to eliminate those barriers that relies on the work of lawyers, physicians, business leaders, and health economists; Institute of Medicine, 'Unequal Treatment' (n 9) 1.

32 Institute of Medicine, 'Best Care at Lower Cost—The Path to Continuously Learning Health Care in America' (M. Smith et al (eds), 2012) 3–6 (prepublication copy: uncorrected proofs).

33 ICERD, Art 2(1)(a)(c)(d).

34 ICERD, Art 5 (e)(iv).

social, and cultural rights when a country chooses to provide them. ICERD explicitly rejects discrimination that arises out of 'any doctrine of superiority based on racial differentiation as scientifically false, morally condemnable, socially unjust and dangerous'.[35] The treaty further seeks to promote understanding, tolerance, and friendship among races.[36]

In 2008, the Committee on the Elimination of Racial Discrimination provided its concluding observations on the last report submitted by the United States. The CERD Committee commended the United States on some of the efforts that were undertaken to address 'persistent health disparities affecting low-income racial, ethnic and national minorities', including the Department of Health and Human Services creation of the National Partnership for Action to End Health Disparities for Ethnic and Racial Minority Populations in 2007.[37] It also provided recommendations to the United States on what it needed to do to improve its compliance with ICERD. In particular the CERD Committee concluded that the United States violated Article 5(e)(iv) of ICERD because a disproportionately large number of racial and ethnic minorities still lack health insurance and face numerous barriers to care like unequal distribution of health care resources, persistent discrimination, and poor quality care in public health care services.[38] Additionally, the CERD Committee concluded that the 'wide racial and ethnic disparities in sexual and reproductive health, . . . [especially] the high maternal and infant mortality rate' also suggest noncompliance with Article 5(e)(iv) of ICERD.[39] The CERD Committee concluded its recommendations on health matters by advising the United States to collect statistical data on the existence of disparities among racial and ethnic minorities and disaggregate the data by race, ethnicity, national origin, age, and gender and include the information in its next report due on 20 November 2011.[40] Unfortunately, the United States did not file its report on time. Instead it filed the report two years late on 12 June 2013.[41] Moreover, despite ICERD's laudable goals, US citizens are precluded from seeking enforcement for violations in US courts given the reservations, understandings, and declarations that accompanied the country's ratification.[42]

35 ICERD, Preamble. 36 ICERD, Preamble and Art 7.

37 UN Committee on the Elimination of Racial Discrimination, 72nd Session, Consideration of Reports Submitted by States Parties Under Art 9 of the Convention: Concluding Observations of the Committee on the Elimination of Racial Discrimination, United States of America, 2, para 8, UN Doc CERD/C/USA/CO/6 (May 2008).

38 CERD Committee 2008 Concluding Observations 11, para 32.

39 CERD Committee 2008 Concluding Observations 11, para 33.

40 CERD Committee 2008 Concluding Observations 11, para 32.

41 Periodic Report of the United States of America to the UN Committee on the Elimination of Racial Discrimination Concerning the International Convention on the Elimination of All Forms of Racial Discrimination, 12 June 2013. This report constitutes the seventh, eighth, and ninth report of the United States. The US has never filed its periodic reports to the CERD Committee every two years as the treaty requires nor when they are due. See ICERD, Art 9(1)(b). The US files a single report every five, seven, or six years from the first due date in 1995 or the date of the last report that it has submitted. Reports Submitted by States Parties Under Article 9 of the Convention, Third Periodic Reports of States Parties Due in 1999, Addendum, United States of America, UN Doc CERD/C/351/Add.1, 10 October 2000; Periodic Report of the United States of America to the UN Committee on the Elimination of Racial Discrimination Concerning the International Convention on the Elimination of All Forms of Racial Discrimination, April 2007.

42 G. McDougall, 'Domestic Relevance of International Efforts to Eliminate All Forms of Racial Discrimination' (1997) 40 *Howard Law Journal* 571, providing an in-depth analysis of the effect of the US reservations to ICERD.

2.3 Report of the United Nations Special Rapporteur for Health on Features that Strengthen a Health System to Protect the Right to Health and the *Lancet* Report on Right to Health Indicators

Scholars recognize that the development of a country's health care system is the product of that country's unique history, economic policy, and politics.[43] However, use of right to health features coupled with monitoring using right to health indicators provides a framework to help ensure that health systems are strong and reasonably equitable.[44] In 2008, the Special Rapporteur for Health filed a report with the Human Rights Council that identified seventeen features of a health care system that protects the right to health.[45] This soft-law global health standard is based on features in existing health systems, features recognized in international health instruments, features advocated for in the medical and public health literature, and consultations with stakeholders in eight countries. The United States was one of the seven developed countries where stakeholders were consulted.[46] There are three features that are relevant to the reduction of health disparities in the United States: Feature 5–Equity, Equality, and Non-Discrimination; Feature 7–Medical Care and Underlying Determinants; and Feature 10–Quality.

2.3.1 Three RTH features relevant to reducing health disparities in the United States

(a) Building a health care system that is consistent with social justice values

The concepts identified in Feature 5—equity, equality, and non-discrimination—reflect social justice principles. A significant difference among the concepts is that equity is a global health concept grounded in ethics[47] whereas equality and non-discrimination are principles of global health law that are incorporated into legally enforceable human rights treaties.

The meaning of equity is an evolving concept in the United States. In 2001, the Institute of Medicine defined equitable care as the provision of health care to all individuals in a manner that does not vary in quality because of personal characteristics such as gender, ethnicity, . . . and socioeconomic status.[48] More recently, in 2010, the Institute of Medicine increased the significance of equity as a guiding principle by reconceptualizing the quality framework to include equity as an overarching principle while simultaneously recommending that the United States include equity as a core principle in its national quality improvement agenda.[49] Globally, the WHO has sought

43 T. Jost, 'Global Health Care Financing Law: A Useful Concept' (2008) 96 *Georgetown Law Journal* 413, 416; W. Savedoff, D. de Ferranti, A. Smith, and V. Fan, 'Political and Economic Aspects of the Transition to Universal Health Coverage' (2012) 380 *Lancet* 924.

44 Backman, Hunt et al, 'Health Systems' (n 19) 2047–8.

45 Special Rapporteur on the Right of Everyone to the Enjoyment of the Highest Attainable Standard of Physical and Mental Health, 'Promotion and Protection of all Human Rights, Civil, Political, Economic, Social and Cultural Rights', paras 36–66, UNGA Human Rights Council, UN Doc A/HRC/7/11, 31 January 2008 (by Paul Hunt).

46 Special Rapporteur, 'Promotion and Protection of all Human Rights' (n 45) 6, note 5.

47 Hunt and Leader, 'Developing and Applying the Right to the Highest Attainable Standard of Health' (n 24) 46; A.R. Chapman, 'The Social Determinants of Health, Health Equity and Human Rights' (2010) *Health and Human Rights* 21–2.

48 Committee on Quality of Health Care in America, Institute of Medicine, 'Crossing the Quality Chasm: A New Health System for the 21st Century' (2001) 6.

49 Institute of Medicine, 'Future Directions' (n 3) 44.

health equity for people throughout the world using its Health for All agenda.[50] Health for All seeks to create opportunities for individuals to have a level of health to live a meaningful life. The agenda relies on health equity as a tool to 'eliminat[e] disparities in health and health's major determinants that are systematically associated with underlying social disadvantage within society'.[51] Thus, according to the Special Rapporteur for Health, an equitable health system provides access to health care based on need.[52]

Equality is a global health law concept that reflects principles found in Article 7 of the Universal Declaration of Human Rights (UDHR), Article 26 of the International Covenant for Civil and Political Rights (ICCPR), and the Preamble to the International Convention on the Elimination of Racial Discrimination. These treaties provide that 'all are equal before the law'.[53] The meaning of equality is rarely defined. Instead it is often viewed as the positive equivalent to nondiscrimination. Scholars like Gillian MacNaughton define positive equality as imposing a duty that countries treat everyone the same unless there is explicit justification to the contrary.[54] For health systems this means that the health facilities, goods, and services are available to all.[55]

Nondiscrimination is also a global health law concept that is found in several human rights treaties, including the ICERD and the ICESCR. The ICERD prohibits racial discrimination, which is defined as any racial distinction, exclusion, restriction, or preference based on prohibited grounds such as race, color, descent, national or ethnic origin, with the intent or effect of impairing enjoyment of a covenant right.[56] The ICESCR also prohibits racial discrimination by requiring countries to provide the treaty rights 'without discrimination of any kind as to race, color, ... language ... and other status'.[57] For health systems this means that the health facilities, goods, and services will be accessible to everyone, especially vulnerable and marginalized populations, without discrimination.[58]

(b) Building a health care system that broadly protects the right to health

Feature 7—Medical Care and Underlying Determinants of Health, reflects a broad concept of the right to health that includes medical care, public health, and social factors like race, ethnicity, and income that stratify society and result in social exclusion.[59] Feature 9 is derived from Article 12(2) and General Comment 14 of the ICESCR. General Comment 14 provides that:

> ... the drafting history and [text of ICESCR] article 12. 2 acknowledge that the right to health embraces a wide range of socio-economic factors that promote conditions in which people can lead a healthy life, and extends to the underlying determinants of health, such as food and

50 G. Luca Burci and C.-H. Vignes, *World Health Organization* (Kluwer Law International, 2004) 162.

51 WHO, '25 Questions & Answers on Health and Human Rights', Health & Human Rights Publication Series (2002) 24, available at <http://www.who.int/hhr/activities/en/25_questions_hhr.pdf>.

52 Special Rapporteur, 'Promotion and Protection of all Human Rights' (n 45) 43.

53 UDHR, Art 7; ICCPR, Art 26; ICERD, Preamble.

54 G. MacNaughton, 'Untangling Equality and Non-Discrimination to Promote the Right to Health Care for All' (2009) 11 *Health and Human Rights* 47–8.

55 Special Rapporteur, 'Promotion and Protection of all Human Rights' (n 45) 11.

56 ICERD, Art 1.

57 ICESCR, Art 2.

58 General Comment 14, para 12(b); Special Rapporteur, 'Promotion and Protection of all Human Rights' (n 45) 42.

59 Gostin and Taylor, 'Global Health Law' (n 16) 902; Special Rapporteur, 'Promotion and Protection of all Human Rights' (n 45) para 45.

nutrition, housing, access to safe... water and adequate sanitation, safe and healthy working conditions, and a healthy environment.[60]

(c) Building a health care system that ensures the provision of quality care

Feature 10 provides a global standard for the provision of quality care. This feature is mandated by General Comment 14, which requires that health care facilities, services, and goods are scientifically and medically appropriate.[61] General Comment 14 also requires that health care workers not only be skilled, but that they be polite and respectful to all patients.[62] This requirement coupled with the requirement that health care services be provided on a non-discriminatory basis precludes subjecting patients to provider bias.[63]

In the United States, quality health care is defined by the Institute of Medicine as 'the degree to which health services for individuals and populations increase the likelihood of desired health outcomes and are consistent with current professional knowledge'.[64] Thus, quality health care 'is based on scientific and medical evidence'.[65] Quality health care also has several components: it is safe, effective, patient-centered, timely, efficient, and accessible.[66] Furthermore, as discussed previously, equity is an overarching principle of quality assessment.[67]

Feature 10 is important to the health of Americans generally and people of color in particular. In the 2010 National Healthcare Disparities Report, the Agency for Healthcare Research and Quality notes, 'that Americans too often do not receive the care that they need, or they receive care that causes harm'.[68] The report further notes that while health care quality and access are suboptimal, quality is improving. However, access and disparities are not improving. Additionally, priority areas for quality improvement show disparities related to race, ethnicity, and socioeconomic status.[69]

2.3.2 Health care systems and right to health indicators

According to a 2008 report published in the *Lancet*, researchers have identified seventy-two right to health indicators which are divided into fifteen categories to monitor the progress of a health system towards protecting the right to health.[70] The list of health indicators is not exhaustive; it does not address all of the seventeen features of a right to health system identified in the previously discussed report of the Special Rapporteur for

60 General Comment 14, para 4; Special Rapporteur, 'Promotion and Protection of all Human Rights' (n 45) para 45.

61 General Comment 14, para 12(d); Special Rapporteur, 'Promotion and Protection of all Human Rights' (n 45) para 54.

62 General Comment 14, para 12(c), (d); Special Rapporteur, 'Promotion and Protection of all Human Rights' (n 45) para 54.

63 General Comment 14, para 12(b),(c).

64 NCQA, 'Crossing the Quality Chasm' (n 48) 232.

65 National Committee for Quality Assurance, 'The Essential Guide to Health Care Quality', 8, available at <http://www.ncqa.org/Portals/0/Publications/Resource%20Library/NCQA_Primer_web.pdf>.

66 NCQA, 'Crossing the Quality Chasm' (n 48) 6, 232; Institute of Medicine, 'Future Directions' (n 3) 46.

67 Institute of Medicine, 'Future Directions' (n 3) 42.

68 US Department of Health and Human Services, Agency for Healthcare Research & Quality, '2010 National Healthcare Disparities Report' (2011) 1.

69 '2010 National Healthcare Disparities Report' (n 68) 2.

70 Backman, Hunt et al, 'Health Systems' (n 19) 2048.

Health, and some indicators, like those that address access, need more development.[71] The indicators were created using best practices to identify additional and neglected features for health systems, not to rank countries.[72] Six categories are relevant to the reduction of health disparities for people of color: (1) *Legal Recognition of the right to health*—the number of treaties signed; (2) *Non-Discrimination*—the number of treaties signed and non-treaty laws that protect vulnerable groups from discrimination (ie ethnicity, race, color, language, national origin, and socioeconomic status); (3) *National Financing*—proportion of households with catastrophic health expenditures; (4) *Awareness raising about the right to health* with the public and health professionals; (5) *Health workers*—the existence of a national workforce strategy; and (6) *Monitoring, assessment, accountability, and redress*—this includes mortality and morbidity indicators as well judicial decisions on the right to health.[73] The right to health indicator report also reaffirmed the importance of collecting and disaggregating data by ethnicity and socioeconomic status to prevent and monitor discrimination.[74]

2.4 Global health governance—Commission on Social Determinants of Health

The Creation of the Commission on Social Determinants of Health (SDH) coupled with the release of its final report, 'Closing the Gap in a Generation', created a worldwide framework to address health equity as a tool to reduce disparities and improve population health. The concept of social determinants of health has old roots in social medicine and in the current work of social epidemiologists who study the pathologic social conditions that adversely impact health.[75]

Recognition of the social gradient in health: 'the lower the position in the social hierarchy, the worse the health' is also important to eliminating disparities among and within countries.[76]

The SDH Commission's Final Report is powerful, according to Burris and Evans, because it provides a conceptual framework that links the environment, social position, and health while simultaneously revealing the 'black box' of how these structures sort.

[71] Backman, Hunt et al, 'Health Systems' (n 19) 2056.

[72] Backman, Hunt et al, 'Health Systems' (n 19) 2053. The final indicators were externally reviewed by 'lawyers, human-rights professionals, clinicians, public-health practitioners, academics, and policy makers'. Special Rapporteur, 'Promotion and Protection of all Human Rights' (n 45) 2056.

[73] Backman, Hunt et al, 'Health Systems' (n 19) 2057–8.

[74] Backman, Hunt et al, 'Health Systems' (n 19) 2056.

[75] Meier, 'Global Health Takes a Normative Turn' (n 17) 15; S. Burris, 'From Health Care Law to the Social Determinants of Health: A Public Health Law Research Perspective' (2011) 159 *University of Pennsylvania Law Review* 1651.

[76] R. Bell, S. Taylor, and M. Marmot, 'Global Health Governance: Commission on Social Determinants of Health and the Imperative for Change' (2010) 38 *Journal of Law, Medicine and Ethics* 472. Income inequality can adversely affect social conditions that are important for good health. Among OECD countries, the US has the third highest poverty rate and the fourth highest disposable income inequality. M.G. Marmot and R. Bell, 'Action on Health Disparities in the United States: Commission on Social Determinants of Health'(2009) 301 *Journal of the American Medical Association* 1169, 1170. The higher rates of poverty and income inequality adversely affect the health of the entire population. Thus when cross-country comparisons are done between the US and OECD countries with less income inequality and poverty, the US population has worse health outcomes. For example, the life expectancy for men and women in the US is less than in the UK, Switzerland, and France. In fact, the US ranked 17th for men and 16th for women in life expectancy among 17 high-income countries. National Research Council and Institute of Medicine, 'U.S. Health In International Perspective: Shorter Lives, Poorer Health' 39 (S.H. Woolf and L. Aron (eds), 2013).

Thus the conceptual framework illuminates 'how injustice is bad for health'.[77] In addition to the conceptual framework, the Final Report provided three recommendations to countries on how to reduce health inequity. First countries should take steps to improve the daily living conditions of individuals (ie where people are born, grow, live, work, and age). This recommendation also includes creating a health system that values equity, disease prevention, and health promotion. The health system should provide universal coverage and equitable financing such that individuals have access to care regardless of ability to pay. Second, countries should tackle the inequitable distribution of power, money, and resources, the structural drivers of the conditions of daily living. Countries can address this recommendation by simultaneously making health equity a priority issue at the highest levels of government and adopting a health-in-all policies approach to promoting and protecting population health. Finally, countries should measure and understand the problem and assess the impact of action.

After release of the SDH Commission's Final Report, four SDH Commissioners provided specific recommendations to the United States on how to incorporate equity into health policy to reduce inequity and improve the health status of the American people. They include incorporating health equity into performance indicators to evaluate the US health care system; prioritizing health equity at the highest levels of government; and using community initiatives to address health equity.[78] Two American SDH Commissioners also advocated the incorporation of health equity and social determinants of health into any national health reform strategy.[79] Furthermore, all four of the SDH Commissioners agreed that shifting the health care system to focus more on social determinants of health instead of the disproportionate focus on the provision of biomedical care would save money, or at least not cost the system any more money.[80]

2.5 Global health governance—initiatives of the World Health Organization that continue the work of the SDH Commission

Once the Commission on Social Determinants of Health issued its Final Report, the WHO adopted the findings of the report in a resolution.[81] The WHO also agreed to provide support to countries to develop policies seeking to eliminate inequities based on social determinants of health.[82]

77 S. Burris and E. Anderson, 'A Framework Convention on Global Health: Social Justice Lite, or a Light on Social Justice?' (2010) 38 *Journal of Law, Medicine and Ethics* 582.

78 Marmot and Bell, 'Action on Health Disparities' (n 76) 1171.

79 G.R. Majette, 'PPACA and Public Health: Creating a Framework to Focus on Prevention and Wellness and Improve the Public's Health' (2011) 39 *Journal of Law, Medicine and Ethics* 371–2, describing Dr. Satcher's testimony before the US Congress on the impact of social determinants of health on population health and the need to adopt a public health approach that includes social determinants of health as part of health care reform legislation; G.R.Wilensky and D. Satcher, 'Don't Forget About the Social Determinants of Health' (2009) 28(2) *Health Affairs* w194, w194–5, w198.

80 Wilensky and Satcher, 'Don't Forget About the Social Determinants of Health' (n 79) w195; Marmot and Bell, 'Action on Health Disparities in the United States' (n 5) 1171.

81 WHO, World Health Assembly, 'Reducing Health Inequities Through Action on Social Determinants of Health', Resolution 62.14 62d Session, WHA Doc A62/VR8 (22 May 2009).

82 Bell, Taylor, and Marmot, 'Global Health Governance' (n 76) 477; WHO-Europe, 'Putting Our Own House in Order: Examples of Health-System Action on Socially Determined Health Inequalities' (2010) 2, available at <http://www.euro.who.int/__data/assets/pdf_file/0004/127318/e94476.pdf>.

2.5.1 World Conference on Social Determinants of Health and the Rio Political Declaration

Subsequently the WHO convened the World Conference on Social Determinants of Health on 19–21 October 2011, in Rio De Janeiro, Brazil.[83] The conference continues the work of the Commission on Social Determinants of Health. The World Conference on SDH was designed to bring together health leaders and policy-makers to discuss how to reduce health inequities between and within countries, and 'to forge a global vision for a coordinated international response'.[84] The conference was hosted by Brazil, with delegates from 125 member countries, representatives from the United Nations system, civil society, and technical experts.[85]

Both the discussion paper,[86] prepared before the World Conference on SDH, and the Rio Political Declaration, signed at the end of the conference, have five priorities.[87] The first priority is to improve governance at the national level for health and development issues. The governance should be transparent and inclusive. It should produce realistic and fair outcomes. Second, national policy-making and implementing processes should be participatory. Third, national health sectors should be 'further reoriented towards reducing health inequities'.[88] Fourth, 'global governance and collaboration should be strengthened' to address social determinants of health.[89] This can be done by encouraging multilateral organizations to emphasize social determinants of health in their norms and guidelines and facilitation of access to financial resources and technical support. Fifth, nations should include accountability measures to monitor their progress in reducing health inequities.[90]

2.5.2 World Health Assembly 2012

Additional action was taken on social determinants of health at the 65th World Health Assembly (WHA). The 65th WHA endorsed the Rio Political Declaration on Social Determinants of Health.[91] It also requested that the WHO Director General report to the 66th and 68th World Health Assemblies scheduled for 2013 and 2015 on the

83 WHO, 'Social Determinants of Health: Outcome of the World Conference on Social Determinants of Health: Report by the Secretariat', 65th WHA, Provisional agenda item 13.6, Doc A62.9 (22 March 2012).

84 WHO, World Conference on Social Determinants of Health, 'Conference Summary', 28 November 2011, 1, available at <http://www.who.int/sdhconference/background/news/WCSDH-summary-final.pdf>.

85 WHO, 'Social Determinants of Health' (n 83) para 4.

86 This document was created in a participatory fashion which included consultation with Member States, the advisory Group, UN bodies, civil society, academia, the Secretariat, and public web consultation. WHO, 'Social Determinants of Health' (n 83) para 5.

87 WHO, 'Closing the Gap: Policy Into Practice on Social Determinants of Health: Discussion Paper', World Conference on Social Determinants of Health, October 2011; World Conference on Social Determinants of Health, 'Rio Political Declaration on Social Determinants of Health', paras 11–15, Rio de Janeiro, Brazil, 21 October 2011.

88 'Rio Political Declaration' (n 87) para 13; WHO, 'Closing the Gap' (n 87) 24–5.

89 'Rio Political Declaration' (n 87) para 14; WHO, 'Closing the Gap' (n 87) 29–32.

90 'Rio Political Declaration' (n 87) para 15; WHO, 'Closing the Gap' (n 87) 35–9.

91 WHO, 'Outcome of the World Conference on Social Determinants of Health', *65th WHA, Agenda item 13.6, Doc WHA65.8* (26 May 2012), also requests that the WHO play a leading role in global health governance on addressing social determinants of health; and that there be international cooperation providing financial support and the transfer of technology, technical expertise, and scientific data to reduce health inequity worldwide).

progress in implementing the Rio Political Declaration on Social Determinants of Health.[92]

3. The PPACA Framework to Eliminate Health Disparities

General Comment 14 encourages countries that have ratified the ICESCR to develop a strategy to protect the right to health, to include benchmarks and indicators in that strategy, and to implement that strategy by adopting framework legislation.[93] While the United States has not ratified the ICESCR, in a previous article, I argued that the Patient Protection and Affordable Care Act (PPACA) constituted framework legislation designed to eliminate health disparities among people of color consistent with global health law norms that protect a right to health.[94] This section briefly reviews those arguments and provides additional supportive analysis.

With respect to eliminating disparities for people of color, PPACA constitutes framework legislation for seven basic reasons. First, PPACA makes health and health inequity priority issues at the highest level of government. For example, PPACA complies with the Commission on Social Determinants of Health priority requirement by reorganizing the Office of Minority Health by removing it from a subsidiary office and placing it within the Office of the Secretary for the Department of Health and Human Services.[95] The passage of PPACA also facilitated the creation of the first ever department-wide strategy to eliminate health disparities: the Health and Human Services Action Plan to Reduce Racial and Ethnic Health Disparities. The HHS Disparities Reduction Plan has five goals and twelve strategies. Four goals are worth highlighting. The plan seeks to 'transform health care' by reducing disparities for people of color in insurance coverage, access to care, and quality of care. It seeks to strengthen the US health workforce by increasing the diversity of personnel and by training health professionals to address disparities. It seeks to improve the health, safety, and well-being of people of color through community-based programs. Finally, it seeks to 'advance scientific knowledge and innovation' through data collection and research.[96]

Second, PPACA ensures that US health policy addresses health disparities and social determinants of health as recommended by the Final Report of the Commission on Social Determinants of Health and four commissioners' specific recommendations to the United States. There are many provisions within PPACA that explicitly mention disparities or social determinants of health. One example includes the requirement that the national quality strategy make reduction of disparities for vulnerable populations a priority issue.[97]

Third, PPACA complies with global health law norms articulated by the SDH Commission by adopting a multi-sectoral approach to health. The primary way this is accomplished is through the creation of the National Prevention, Health Promotion, and Public Health Council. The National Prevention Council is led by the Surgeon General, includes the Secretary of Health and Human Services, and is composed of

[92] WHO, 'Outcome of the World Conference on Social Determinants of Health' (n 91) para 5.5.

[93] General Comment 14, paras 53, 56.

[94] G.R. Majette, 'Global Health Law Norms and the PPACA Framework to Eliminate Health Disparities' (2012) 55 *Howard Law Journal* 887, 910–26, providing a comprehensive analysis of how the PPACA constitutes framework legislation that is consistent with protecting a right to health.

[95] PPACA § 10334 (a).

[96] Sebelius, 'HHS Action Plan' (n 1) 11.

[97] PPACA § 3011.

cabinet level officials for administrative agencies that impact health such as the Secretary of Transportation, Education, Agriculture, etc.[98] The National Prevention Council is tasked with providing leadership and coordination on national prevention activities throughout the federal government to improve public health and lower preventable disease and disability.[99] 'Each year the Council must provide a report to the President and Congress on the activities and efforts on prevention, health promotion, and public health, and the national progress toward these goals'.[100] The National Prevention Council has identified eliminating health disparities as a pressing national issue.[101]

The National Prevention Council is assisted by an Advisory Group composed of 25 non-federal, licensed health professionals. The Advisory Group's key areas of focus include (a) lifestyle-based chronic disease prevention and management, (b) integrative health care practices, and (c) health promotion.[102] One improvement that can be made to the National Prevention Council and Advisory Group is to reconstitute either one to include a lawyer with an understanding of health law, public health, and global health law norms. This insures that law, broadly defined to include practices and institutions, is considered as a social structure itself to be assessed as part of any comprehensive preventative solution.

Fourth, as discussed further in section 4, PPACA makes universal coverage, a key aspect of universal health care, a priority issue.[103] For example, PPACA creates marketplaces for individuals to purchase affordable insurance, provides subsidies to low-income individuals to purchase insurance, and expands eligibility for Medicaid. Expanding health insurance coverage also complies with a global health law norm, the most recent recommendations of the CERD Committee to the United States to address the disproportionate number of people of color that lack insurance.

Fifth, PPACA requires the US government to monitor social determinants of health and health equity as recommended by the Commission on Social Determinants of Health, the final report of the World Conference on SDH, and the Rio Political Declaration. PPACA contains a multitude of provisions that monitor progress on the elimination of health disparities for people of color through requirements that various councils and the Department of Health and Human Services file mandatory reports with Congress or the President on the progress made, coupled with provisions requiring the collection of data on disparities for people of color using standardized categories.[104]

Sixth, PPACA contains many quality provisions that provide additional tools to reduce and eliminate health disparities. Past and recent evaluations of the quality of

98 PPACA § 4001(g).

99 Majette, 'PPACA and Public Health' (n 79) 366, providing an insider's perspective on Congress's approach to public health during the drafting of the PPACA and in-depth analysis of how PPACA shifts the US health care system to focus on prevention, wellness, and public health consistent with IOM and human rights norms.

100 Majette, 'PPACA and Public Health' (n 79) 374.

101 National Prevention Council, Department of Health and Human Services, 'National Prevention Strategy: America's Plan for Better Health and Wellness' (2011) 26.

102 Majette, 'PPACA and Public Health' (n 79).

103 See section 4 of this chapter.

104 Majette, 'Global Health Law Norms' (n 94) 922–3. While the focus of this chapter is people of color, efforts flowing from PPACA take a broad approach to the reduction of health disparities targeting race, ethnicity, sex, primary language, or physical disability. Each of these vulnerable groups and more are addressed in the 2011 National Prevention Strategy published by the National Prevention Council. National Prevention Council, Department of Health and Human Services, 'National Prevention Strategy: America's Plan for Better Health and Wellness' (2011) 25.

care provided in the United States have concluded that the quality is poor. For example, the most recent report published by the Agency for Health Care Quality and Research described the quality of health care provided in the United States as suboptimal, especially for people of color.[105] Several global health law norms also specifically recognize the importance of providing care that is medically and scientifically appropriate—General Comment 14 and right to health feature ten on quality. PPACA complies with these norms, as discussed previously, by requiring the creation of a national quality strategy that must also address health disparities. Another example is the requirement that HHS identify clinical practice protocols that have been created pursuant to best practices.[106] The improved practice protocols can be used to set standards as to appropriate care and to evaluate whether the care provided to people of color meets those standards.

Finally, several PPACA provisions comply with right to health indicators that are designed to ensure compliance with global health law norms and eliminate health disparities. One right to health indicator assesses the existence of non-treaty based non-discrimination laws.[107] PPACA contains a provision expanding existing civil rights laws to cover private insurance companies that will receive new insurance customers as part of the plan to expand insurance coverage.[108] Another indicator examines whether a country has a national workforce strategy.[109] PPACA created the National Health Care Workforce Commission, a fifteen-member board with national expertise in health care labor market analysis. The Workforce Commission was designed to be a resource to Congress, the President, states, and localities on workforce priorities, goals, and policies. The Workforce Commission was also tasked with assessing the workforce needs of special populations, including people of color.[110] Unfortunately, while members have been appointed to the Commission, Congress has not funded it. Additionally, PPACA created the Commission on Key National Indicators that is designed to provide oversight for the creation of a national indicator system.[111] The Key National Indicator System is an independent public-private partnership implemented by the National Academy of Science and a non-profit, State of the USA.[112] This complies with the right to health indicator requiring countries to monitor and assess their compliance with health and human rights treaty obligations.[113] The Key National Indicator System is important because researchers have recommended that a non-government controlled source of data be available to provide an independent assessment of compliance.[114] While the indicator system is still in the process of being developed, several of the indicators recommended by the Institute of Medicine are relevant to reducing disparities for people of color. They include life expectancy at birth, infant mortality, insurance coverage, preventive services, and unmet medical, dental, and prescription drug needs.[115]

105 '2010 National Healthcare Disparities Report' (n 68) 2.

106 PPACA § 10303(c).

107 Backman, Hunt et al, 'Health Systems' (n 19) 2057.

108 PPACA § 1557.

109 Backman, Hunt et al, 'Health Systems' (n 19) 2058.

110 PPACA § 5101(a).

111 PPACA § 5605(b).

112 'Congress Appoints Key National Indicators', available at <http://www.stateoftheusa.org/content/commission-on-key-national-ind.php>.

113 Backman, Hunt et al, 'Health Systems' (n 19) 2058.

114 Backman, Hunt et al, 'Health Systems' (n 19) 2056.

115 H. Parnell, 'From Hundreds of Health Measures, 20 Seen as Key' (2009), available at <http://www.stateoftheusa.org/content/from-hundreds-of-health-indica.php>.

4. The Constitutional Challenge to PPACA—A Potential Threat to the US Efforts to Reduce Health Care Disparities for People Of Color

The Patient Protection and Affordable Care Act is comprehensive legislation. It not only expands insurance coverage, but it also addresses improving the health care delivery system in the United States and shifting the health care system to focus on public health, prevention, and wellness.[116]

On the same day that President Obama signed the Patient Protection and Affordable Care Act into law, Florida and several other states, filed suit in the Federal District Court for the Northern District of Florida challenging the constitutionality of several provisions of PPACA.[117] The original states were subsequently joined by thirteen more states, several individuals, and the National Federation of Independent Business. The country was split in half with two of the twenty-five states supporting and opposing the litigation, and twenty-five states affirmatively filing an *amicus* brief in support of the constitutionality of PPACA or taking no position in the litigation.[118]

Like the states, the Supreme Court was also closely split in its decision on the constitutionality of PPACA, deciding several of the core challenges by 5 to 4. The litigation and the Supreme Court opinion reflect competing goals and values in the United States on the propriety and means of moving towards universal insurance coverage. PPACA moves toward universal insurance coverage by limiting an insurance company's ability to set premiums based on health status. Since 1 January 2014, when the insurance rating provisions came into effect, health insurance has been guaranteed issue and premiums have been based on community rating.[119] The legislation also imposes a general requirement that individuals purchase health insurance (minimum coverage provision) or pay a penalty (shared responsibility payment).[120] PPACA also moves towards universal coverage through expansion of Medicaid to all non-elderly individuals below 133 percent of the federal poverty limit. Medicaid is a joint federal-state program that finances health care services to the poor. While states choose to participate in the overall program, PPACA imposed a mandatory change to beneficiary eligibility to expand coverage, and provided a financial incentive whereby the federal government would pay substantially all of the expansion costs.[121]

4.1 PPACA narrowly survives the constitutional challenges presented to the United States Supreme Court

The Supreme Court narrowly upheld the constitutionality of two of PPACA's provisions designed to move the United States toward universal coverage and refused to

116 Majette, 'PPACA and Public Health' (n 79) 366–7.

117 *National Federation of Independent Business et al v Sebelius* 132 S Ct, 2566, 2581 (2012).

118 The governors and attorneys general in Iowa and Washington took opposite positions. Kaiser Family Foundation, 'A Guide to the Supreme Court's Decision on the ACA's Medicaid Expansion' (August 2012) 3, available at <http://www.kff.org/healthreform/8347.cfm>.

119 PPACA § 1201 prohibits discrimination against individuals based on health status, medical condition, claims experience, receipt of health care, medical history, genetic information, evidence of insurability, disability. Insurance rating can only be based on age (limited to 1:3 for adults), tobacco use (limited to 1.5:1), geography, and family size. PPACA § 1201.

120 PPACA § 1501 (HCCRA §§ 10106, 1002).

121 PPACA § 2001.

strike the entire legislation despite some of its constitutional infirmities. The states argued that the minimum coverage provision was an unconstitutional exercise of Congress's power under the Taxing Clause and the Commerce Clause of the Constitution.[122] While the Court held that the minimum coverage provision was unconstitutional under Congress's power to regulate commerce among the states,[123] it upheld the provision under Congress's power to lay and collect taxes to provide for the General Welfare.[124] It found that the shared responsibility payment functioned as a tax because it was paid to the IRS, with one's income tax; was calculated like taxes; and raises some revenue.[125] The Court further found that the legislative label that the shared responsibility payment was a 'penalty' was not controlling. It was not a penalty since the amount was small, there were no criminal penalties, and non-purchase of minimum coverage insurance was not unlawful.[126] Thus, PPACA's minimum coverage provision and the shared responsibility payment are constitutionally permissible under Congress's power to tax. Individuals have a choice to purchase minimum coverage or pay a tax, the shared responsibility payment.

PPACA provided that the federal government would initially pay for 100 percent of the costs to the states for Medicaid expansion, dropping to 90 percent.[127] The existing Medicaid legislation authorized the Secretary of Health and Human Services to withhold State Medicaid funding for noncompliance with the federal requirements. However, the Secretary of Health and Human Services has never exercised this discretion to withhold a state's entire Medicaid funding.[128] Although the Court found that Congress exceeded its constitutional authority under the Spending Clause to condition states' expansion of the Medicaid program to non-elderly individuals under 133 percent of poverty on their existing Medicaid funding,[129] it also found that the Secretary's authority to withhold all existing funds could be severed from the legislation.[130] Thus the constitutional infirmity of PPACA's Medicaid expansion provision would be remedied by allowing states to choose whether to expand their Medicaid programs.

[122] *NFIB v Sebelius* 132 S Ct 2580–3. The commerce clause and tax and spend clause are both found in Art I, § 8 of the US Constitution.

[123] This was a 5 to 4 decision including the opinion of the Chief Justice Roberts combined with the Joint Dissent of Justices Scalia, Kennedy, Thomas, and Alito. *NFIB v Sebelius* 132 S Ct 2591(Chief Justice Roberts), 2644 (Joint Dissent). The Commerce Clause analysis is discussed in section 5.2 of this chapter.

[124] This was a 5 to 4 decision written by Chief Justice Roberts and joined by Justices Ginsburg, Breyer, Sotomayor, and Kagan. *NFIB v Sebelius* 132 S Ct 2595–6.

[125] *NFIB v Sebelius* 132 S Ct 2594–5.

[126] *NFIB v Sebelius* 132 S Ct 2595–7.

[127] PPACA § 2001 (a)(2).

[128] Brief for Health Law and Policy Scholars and Prescription Policy Choices in Support of Petitioners on the Constitutional Validity of the Medicaid Expansion, at 43, *State of Florida et al v United States Department of Health and Human Services* (No 11-400), 2012 WL 588459; S. Rosenbaum and T. Westmoreland, 'The Supreme Court's Surprising Decision on the Medicaid Expansion: How Will The Federal Government and States Proceed' (2012) 31 *Health Affairs* 1663, 1665.

[129] The Court found that the Medicaid expansion was textually unconstitutional by 7 to 2. The majority opinion was formed by the opinion of the Chief Justice joined by Justices Breyer and Kagan coupled with the Joint Dissent. *NFIB v Sebelius* 132 S Ct 2604–6 (Chief Justice), 2666 (Joint Dissent).

[130] A different composition of justices agreed to sever the unconstitutional provision authorizing the Secretary of Health and Human Services to withhold all of the state's existing funding. The 5 to 4 majority included the opinion of Chief Justice Roberts joined by Justices Breyer and Kagan, and the opinion of Justice Ginsburg joined by Justice Sotomayor. *NFIB v Sebelius* 132 S Ct 2607 (Chief Justice Roberts), 2642 (Justice Ginsburg).

4.2 Rhetoric in the health care reform opinions of the United States Supreme Court undermines some of the PPACA efforts to comply with global health law norms and reduce disparities in health care

4.2.1 Commerce clause

The commerce clause analysis of both the opinion of the Chief Justice of the United States Supreme Court and the Joint Dissent in *National Federation of Independent Business et al v Sebelius* reflects a commodification of health care approach which undermines PPACA's attempt to redistribute resources to achieve *global health equity*. As noted earlier, in section 3, PPACA makes universal coverage a priority issue. One of the significant mechanisms used to expand insurance coverage to the uninsured is to prohibit insurance companies, beginning in 2014, from using health status to issue insurance.[131] Thus, PPACA establishes a national standard for insurance coverage based on guaranteed issue and community rating.[132] PPACA also requires everyone in the United States to purchase insurance to spread the risk across a large risk pool.[133] Equitable and efficient risk pooling is a key tool used to achieve global health equity.[134]

Chief Justice Roberts implies that it is improper for Congress to impose a mandate on individuals to purchase insurance under the Commerce Clause because 'the mandate primarily affects healthy, often young adults' who 'as an actuarial class, incur relatively low health care costs that the mandate helps counter the effect of forcing insurance companies to cover others who impose greater costs than their premiums are allowed to reflect'.[135] He also states that guaranteed issue and community rating 'threaten to impose massive new costs on insurers, who are required to accept unhealthy individuals but prohibited from charging them rates necessary to pay for their coverage'.[136] Similarly, the Joint Dissent provides that 'government regulation typically imposes costs on the regulated industry—especially regulation that prohibits economic behavior in which most market participants are already engaging, such as "piecing out" the market by selling the product to different classes of people at different prices (in the present context, providing much lower insurance rates to young and healthy buyers)'.[137]

Chief Justice Roberts and the Joint Dissent's acceptance of the free market approach to pricing health insurance which segregates risks favoring the healthy, ignores the fact that the market does not allow some individuals to '"buy in"—the poor, the uninsured, the uninsurable'.[138] These individuals have higher premiums, more deductibles, or are excluded from coverage. Under the free market approach inequality is normalized and rationalized.[139] Thus one does not ask the moral question of whether actuarial fairness makes sense when higher premiums or exclusions are the result of illnesses that are unpredictable and often not voluntarily created. Moreover, it neglects the historical fact that the US health insurance industry began with a unified risk pool—Blue Cross Blue Shield, based premiums on community rating.

131 PPACA § 1201. 132 PPACA §1201.

133 PPACA §1501 (HCCRA §§ 10106, 1002).

134 Ruger, 'Normative Foundations of Global Health Law' (n 15) 432.

135 *NFIB v Sebelius* 132 S Ct 2566, 2590 (2012).

136 *NFIB v Sebelius* 132 S Ct 2585. 137 *NFIB v Sebelius* 132 S Ct 2645.

138 E.D. Pellegrino, 'The Commodification of Medical and Health Care: The Moral Consequences of a Paradigm Shift from a Professional to a Market Ethic' (1999) 24 *Journal of Medicine and Philosophy* 243.

139 P. O'Connell, 'The Human Right to Health in an Age of Market Hegemony' in J. Harrington and M. Stuttaford (eds), *Global Health and Human Rights: Legal and Philosophical Perspectives* (Routledge, 2010) 195, 202.

4.2.2 Medicaid expansion

Additionally, the Supreme Court's decision on PPACA's Medicaid expansion provision to cover all non-elderly individuals below 133 percent of poverty in 2014 undermines legislative and policy objectives to achieve global health equity by expanding coverage to the poorest citizens of the United States. By allowing states to choose whether to expand coverage,[140] there is no standardized floor or minimal level of insurance coverage provided in the United States. Instead a coverage gap occurs when states choose to exercise the power afforded to them by the Court to not expand their Medicaid programs. The most impoverished US citizens, those below 100 percent of poverty that are not within the original Medicaid categories are not entitled to Medicaid coverage or other financial assistance that PPACA provides through other federal mechanisms.[141] Moreover, failure to have 100 percent of the states expanding Medicaid will adversely affect people of color who will not have the same level of access to insurance coverage as part of PPACA's original framework to provide universal coverage.[142] It was predicted that the highest reduction in uninsured rates would occur among African Americans and Hispanics.[143] This will not occur if Medicaid is not expanded.

Prior to the Supreme Court decision in June 2012, it was estimated that 15.1 million individuals would be covered under the Medicaid expansion and 11.5 million would have incomes below 100 percent of the federal poverty level.[144] Failure to expand Medicaid would have a disproportionate effect on the poorest people of color, those 5.01 million individuals below 100 percent FPL, including Hispanic Americans (2 million), African Americans (2.2 million), and other groups of color (0.81 million).[145] This reduced level of coverage undermines the United States' forward progress on the CERD Committee 2008 recommendation that the United States continue to address

140 This is a 5 to 4 decision. The majority is formed by the opinions of Chief Justice Roberts joined by Justices Breyer and Kagan and the opinion of Justice Ginsburg joined by Justice Sotomayor. *NFIB v Sebelius*, 132 S Ct 2608 (Justice Roberts), 2642 (Justice Ginsburg).

141 Medicaid coverage prior to PPACA was categorical. It covered pregnant women, children, some needy families, the blind, the elderly, and the disabled. PPACA creates a new eligibility category, all non-elderly individuals under 133% of poverty. PPACA §§ 2001, 2002. This expansion would include, but is not limited to, childless adults. The other financial assistance provided by PPACA to aid low-income individuals is the provision of premium tax credits and cost-sharing subsidies through the insurance exchanges. However, the assistance is only provided to individuals between 100 and 400% of the federal poverty level. PPACA §§10105, 1401. It is likely that individuals between 100 and 133% of the FPL will have financial challenges obtaining coverage through the exchanges because they must pay a percentage of the insurance premium. For example, a family of four at 133% FPL would make $31,000 dollars and have to pay 2% of their income totaling $620. S. Rosenbaum and T. Westmoreland, 'The Supreme Court's Surprising Decision on the Medicaid Expansion: How Will the Federal Government and States Proceed?' (2012) 31 *Health Affairs* 1663, 1670.

142 Former Surgeon General of the United States, David Satcher, MD, PhD, and former member of the Commission on Social Determinants of Health, who is now founder and director of the Satcher Health Leadership Institute and Center of Excellence on Health Disparities at Morehouse School of Medicine, 'supports the expansion of Medicaid eligibility as a crucial step toward eliminating health disparities for low-income Americans and people of color'. Brief for David Satcher, MD, PhD et al as Amici Curiae Supporting Respondents at 18, *State of Florida et al v United States Department of Health and Human Services* (No 11-400), 2012 WL 588459.

143 L. Clemans-Cope, G. Kenney, M. Buettgens, C. Carroll, and F. Blaven, 'The Affordable Care Act's Coverage Expansions Will Reduce Differences in Uninsurance Rates by Race and Ethnicity' (2012) 31 *Health Affairs* 920, 926.

144 G.M. Kenney, S. Zukerman, L. Dubay, M. Huntress, V. Lynch, J. Haley, and N. Anderson, 'Opting in to the Medicaid Expansion under the ACA: Who Are the Uninsured Adults Who Could Gain Health Insurance Coverage' (Urban Institute, 2012).

145 Kenney et al, 'Opting in to the Medicaid Expansion under the ACA' (n 144) 2 (Table A).

'"persistent health disparities" among racial and ethnic minorities by continuing efforts to reduce barriers to care by increasing access to health insurance'.[146]

4.2.3 Implications for addressing Social Determinants of Health consistent with global health law norms

The Supreme Court decision presents contrasting positions on Congress's constitutional authority to address future social and economic issues. Justice Ginsburg's dissenting opinion analyzing the Commerce Clause provides that Congress has 'large authority to set the Nation's course in the economic and social welfare realm', provided it does 'not infringe [on] some constitutional prohibition'.[147] This recognition of Congress's power to legislate in the social welfare realm is supportive of federal efforts to promote social determinants of health.

In contrast, language in the Joint Dissent would undermine federal congressional efforts to promote social determinants of health through federal state programs. While the text of the Constitution provides that Congress may tax and spend to provide for the *general welfare*, the Joint Dissent takes an originalist position and argues that Congress's power under the Tax and Spend provision of the Constitution is too broad. It is beyond Madison's vision, which would limit the provision to enumerated powers.[148] Thus the Joint Dissent points out that today there exist large federal agencies like the Department of Education, the Department of Health and Human Services, and the Department of Housing and Urban Development which engage in activity beyond Congress's enumerated powers and are insufficiently economic to be encompassed within Congress's Commerce power.[149] Global health law norms articulated by The Commission on Social Determinants of Health, Resolutions of the World Health Organization, and the Final Report of the World Conference on Social Determinants of Health, all advocate prioritizing action on health, education, housing, and other conditions of daily living to reduce inequity and promote health.[150]

5. The Continuing Moral Imperative to Reduce Health Care Disparities in the US

While the Supreme Court largely upheld Congress's authority to enact the Patient Protection and Affordable Care Act, the decision on Medicaid creates a moral dilemma since the most economically vulnerable individuals will not have access to insurance coverage while those more economically secure will. This problem is sizable since twenty-one states have decided not to expand their Medicaid programs.[151] Moving

146 See section 2.2 of this chapter. 147 *NFIB v Sebelius* 132 S Ct 2609.
148 *NFIB v Sebelius* 132 S Ct 2643 (Joint Dissent).
149 *NFIB v Sebelius* 132 S Ct 2643 (Joint Dissent).
150 See section 2.5 of this chapter.
151 The degree of the problem is evolving. As time has passed, the number of states deciding not to participate has increased to twenty-one. In March 2013, fifteen states decided not to participate and three states were leaning towards not participating. The Advisory Board Co, 'Where Each State Stands on ACA's Medicaid Expansion', available at <http://www.advisory.com/Daily-Briefing/2012/11/09/MedicaidMap#lightbox/1>. Several of the non-participating states have some of the highest numbers of uninsured, including Texas (6.2 million), Florida (3.2 million), and Georgia (1.8 million). As of February 2014, Governors in twenty-five states and the District of Columbia are participating, and four states are leaning towards participating. The Advisory Board Co, 'Where Each State Stands on ACA's Medicaid Expansion', available at <http://www.advisory.com/daily-briefing/resources/primers/medicaidmap/> (accessed 7 February 2014).

forward, the United States must consider not only the Medicaid dilemma, but implementation more broadly in light of the moral imperative to work to reduce health disparities for people of color.

5.1 Moral imperative: PPACA and regulative global justice norms

Several regulative global justice norms impose a moral obligation on the United States to eliminate health disparities for people of color. Regulative justice norms are normative frameworks that shift global health policy to address global health inequalities.[152] Examples of those frameworks include global health laws like health and human rights and global health equity discussed earlier, in section 2 of this chapter.

Global health equity focuses not simply on equitable disparities between countries, but also disparities within countries.[153] PPACA complies with regulative global justice norms by facilitating the reduction of inequity within the United States as discussed previously, in section 3.

The American public has a familiar choice on which norms will guide future implementation of health care reform: human rights, the market, or cost. During the recent debate on health care reform in the United States, there were some policy discussions focusing on international models that could be used to develop aspects of health care reform, yet there was little public discourse on adopting a health and human rights approach to health care reform. As a Fellow with a Senator on the Health Subcommittee of the Senate Finance committee during the early conversation on health care reform, we did not discuss a human right to health, yet we did attend briefings discussing the health care systems of other countries such as the Netherlands, Germany, and Switzerland.[154]

This result is déjà vu of prior health care reform conversations. Health and Human Rights scholar, Professor Virginia Leary, critiqued previous health care reform proposals, such as President Clinton's health care reform plan, for its failure to adopt a human rights approach to protecting health.[155] She argued that the guiding principles should not be a cost or market approach, but instead emphasize the dignity of the individual, fairness, equity, and social justice.[156]

5.2 Perils of an undue focus on the market or cost paradigm

Some human rights scholars describe the last twenty years in global health as reflecting market hegemony. Market hegemony is an 'era in which all of the governments of the

152 Meier, 'Global Health Takes a Normative Turn' (n 17).

153 Marmot and Bell, 'Action on Health Disparities in the United States' (n 5) 1169.

154 See 'Lessons on Coverage from Abroad: How Do the Dutch, German and Swiss Health Care Systems Do It', Alliance for Health Reform & The Commonwealth Fund (14 November 2008). My conversations with staffers in leadership positions that occurred after the passage of PPACA revealed that 'human rights' language might have derailed the passage of health care reform legislation in Congress and with the public. This insight is consistent with the arguments made by Professor Christopher Roberts in a recent article. He asserts that recent and future polarizing conversations about health care reform are influenced by historical domestic and international debates about universal health care that ultimately resulted in splitting the Covenant on Human Rights into two treaties—the International Covenant on Civil and Political Rights, and the International Covenant on Economic, Social and Cultural Rights. C. Roberts, 'Dynamics of Healthcare Reform: Bitter Pills Old and New' (2012) 45 *Vanderbilt Journal of Transnational Law* 1341.

155 V.A. Leary, 'Defining the Right to Health Care' in A.R. Chapman (ed), *Health Care Reform: A Human Rights Approach* (Georgetown University Press, 1994) 87.

156 Leary, 'Defining the Right to Health Care' (n 155) 97.

world, whether through ideological commitment or under the pressures of market discipline, embraced and implemented . . . libertarian policy prescriptions'.[157] Libertarian policies range from the basic idea that the government should be small with limited functions that enforce contracts and protect citizens against force, theft, and fraud to policies that cause governments to shrink in size through fiscal austerity, privatization, and deregulation to free markets.[158] When courts and governments adopt libertarian values, it causes them to think in a binary oppositional manner which reflects a false dichotomy between government regulation and the market. Following this logic, there are only two types of government, an interventionist redistributive state and a non-interventionist state. In reality, all government action or inaction redistributes. The real question is who benefits from the distribution—the poor, the middle class, the wealthy, or a combination. The adoption of libertarian values also causes courts and governments to be reluctant to interfere with individual freedom, corporate freedom, and the market.[159]

The commerce clause analysis of both the opinion of the Chief Justice of the United States Supreme Court and the Joint Dissent in *National Federation of Independent Business et al v Sebelius* reflects *binary, libertarian* thinking that is harmful to a health and human rights perspective. For example, the Joint Dissent concludes by expressly stating the three guiding principles for the opinion—'caution, minimalism, and limited federal government'.[160] Both opinions express an overwhelming concern with the burden of regulation on insurance companies.[161] Moreover, these opinions fail to acknowledge that the insurance market has failed to cover all individuals seeking coverage; and some companies within the insurance market failed to readily pay for medically necessary care, continue to provide coverage when individuals become ill, or provide affordable coverage to individuals in the individual and small group market.[162] A right to health perspective would acknowledge and prioritize access to care concerns.

5.2.1 The market and regulation working together

PPACA is a legislative example that promotes health and rejects market hegemony. Consistent with the right to health, the US government should identify areas of collaboration with the private sector to protect the right to health.[163] PPACA adheres to this global health law norm. Justice Ginsburg's opinion in *NFIB v Sebelius* also accepts this collaborative norm. Her opinion reflects a balanced approach to the role of the government and the market in addressing access to care and the role of insurance. Justice Ginsburg does this by interpreting the commerce clause, the spending clause,

157 P. O'Connell, 'The Human Right to Health' (n 139) 195.

158 L. Forman, 'What Future for the Minimum Core? Contextualizing the implications of South African Socioeconomic Rights Jurisprudence for the International Human Right to Health' in J. Harrington and M. Stuttaford (eds), *Global Health and Human Rights: Legal and Philosophical Perspectives* (Routledge, 2010) 65.

159 Forman, 'What Future for the Minimum Core?' (n 158) 65.

160 *NFIB v Sebelius* 132 S Ct 2566, 2676.

161 *NFIB v Sebelius* 132 S Ct 2590 (Chief Justice), 2645 (Joint Dissent).

162 E.D. Kinney, 'For Profit Enterprise in Health Care: Can it Contribute to Health Reform?' (2010) 36 *American Journal of Law and Medicine* 422–3; L. Nichols, 'Government Intervention in Health Care Markets is Practical, Necessary and Morally Sound' (2012) 40 *Journal of Law, Medicine and Ethics* 553, notes that risk selection is a problematic way of doing business if the goal is to cover everyone by private insurance.

163 General Comment 14, para 56.

and the tax clause of the Constitution in a way that protects Congress's authority to preserve the role of insurance companies and the states in assuring access to care.[164]

The United States has a long history of using its regulatory power to protect health and create free market health care.[165] Some regulatory initiatives have improved the health of people of color. For example, Congress provided hospital funding through the Hill Burton Act which protected health by requiring hospitals to provide a certain amount of charitable care and to not discriminate based on race or national origin in exchange for construction dollars to build and expand hospitals across the United States.[166] Through the Medicare program, financing was provided for health care services to the elderly, and hospitals were desegregated across the United States to increase access to hospital services for people of color. At the same time, the Medicare program selected private insurance companies to serve as the third-party administrators for the program (claims processors).[167]

Similarly, PPACA protects the right to health by taking a balanced approach to meeting the coverage needs of uninsured and underinsured people of color. PPACA expands affordable coverage to low-income individuals by the creation of insurance exchanges and the provision of subsidies to purchase insurance and assist with the payment of cost-sharing obligations. The creation of the insurance exchange to facilitate the purchase of private insurance is a growth opportunity for the insurance industry.

PPACA as enacted also protects the right to health by providing coverage to the poorest of the poor, including people of color, by expanding Medicaid coverage to all individuals below 133 percent of poverty. The expansion of Medicaid is another attempt by Congress to address the access needs of the poor while simultaneously preserving the role of the private insurance industry. Many states use private insurance companies to operate Medicaid Managed Care programs that provide services to Medicaid beneficiaries.[168]

Economists recognize that government regulation is appropriate when market failure exists. Thus when the practices of businesses within the private health sector cause harm to the public, regulation is warranted. Prior to the implementation of PPACA millions of individuals were uninsured, ranging from 15.3 percent of the US population (45.7 million individuals) in 2007 to the highest level of 16.7 percent (50.7 million individuals) in 2009.[169] People of color represented a disproportionate share of the uninsured—53 percent in 2007 and 52 percent in 2009. This demonstrates market failure in the insurance market.[170]

164 *NFIB v Sebelius* 132 S Ct 2566, 2609–42.

165 R.I. Field, 'Regulation, Reform and the Creation of Free Market Health Care' (2011) 32 *Hamline Journal of Public Law and Policy* 301; see also Kinney, 'For Profit Enterprise in Health Care' (n 162) 405.

166 Hospital Survey and Construction Act, 42 USC § 291 (2006); 42 CFR § 124.603(a)(1) (2001) (the original act was amended in 1974 to impose a requirement to provide charitable care and prohibit discrimination based on race or national origin).

167 D. Smith, 'Addressing Racial Inequities in Health Care: Civil Rights Monitoring and Report Cards' (1998) 23 *Journal of Health Politics, Policy and Law* 83.

168 Kinney, 'For Profit Enterprise in Health Care' (n 162) 412; Kaiser Commission on Medicaid and the Uninsured, 'Medicaid Managed Care: Key Data, Trends, and Issues', 12 February 2012, available at <http://www.kff.org/medicaid/upload/8046-02.pdf>.

169 US Census Bureau, 'Income, Poverty, and Health Insurance Coverage in the United States: 2007' (August 2008) 22; US Census Bureau, 'Income, Poverty, and Health Insurance Coverage in the United States: 2009' (August 2010) 26.

170 See n 169.

A concern with use of a market model that relies on private insurance to provide access to health services is that the government will allow the purpose of the authorizing regulation to be marginalized and eventually abandoned.[171] Thus the Department of Health and Human Services, Centers for Medicaid and Medicare Services—Center for Consumer Information and Insurance Oversight, must strongly adhere to PPACA's coverage purposes and continue diligent oversight in the future. This includes paying attention to the insurance coverage needs of people of color by ensuring compliance with global health law principles of non-discrimination, equality, and global equity. Another concern with using the market model for health care is the idea that it will blunt the human rights perspective that health is an essential good. It also blurs the distinction that health and human rights is patient-centered while the market perspective focuses on the investor or is corporate centered.[172] The distributive principle also contrasts with the human rights focus on beneficence[173] (affirmatively doing good) in contrast to the market focus on non-maleficence (do no harm).[174]

Each of these concerns with a market perspective on health can be overcome if sufficient attention is paid to the warning that the market perspective can have a distorting effect that shuts out other values that are equally or more important.[175] As one scholar notes, using market principles to justify a reduction in health disparities can result in reinforcing the idea that the market, not reduction of health disparities, is the dominant idea.[176] Thus an economist must answer the question 'whether the [health care] market is work[ing] in socially desirable ways'[177] by tempering the normative focus on efficiency to incorporate a human rights focus addressing equity, equality, and the need to address human suffering.

5.2.2 PPACA and cost challenges to implementation

A common challenge made to health care policy based on moral imperatives, including human rights justifications, is that they should not be adopted because they are too costly.[178] Einer R. Elhauge's comparative paradigm analysis provides insight into this argument by identifying the chief strength and weakness of the moral paradigm. The strength of the moral paradigm is also its weakness: the paradigm provides care regardless of a patient's ability to pay.[179] Arguably this means an unlimited amount of resources can be spent on health care. However, a health and human rights perspective does not require spending an unlimited amount of resources. Instead, the

171 O'Connell, 'The Human Right to Health' (n 139) 199.

172 O'Connell, 'The Human Right to Health' (n 139) 199; Pellegrino, 'The Commodification of Medical and Health Care' (n 138) 254.

173 O'Connell, 'The Human Right to Health' (n 139) 199; Pellegrino, 'The Commodification of Medical and Health Care' (n 138) 258.

174 O'Connell, 'The Human Right to Health' (n 139) 199; Pellegrino, 'The Commodification of Medical and Health Care' (n 138) 254.

175 A. Okun, 'Equality and Efficiency: The Big Tradeoff' (The Brookings Institute, 1975) 6.

176 L. Ikemoto, 'Racial Disparities in Health Care and Cultural Competency' (2004) 48 *Saint Louis University Law Journal* 75.

177 P. Musgrove (ed), 'What is the Minimum a Doctor Should Know about Health Economics' in *Health Economist in Development* (World Bank Publications, 2003) 25, while he does not address human rights, the author does note that economic thought includes a long and deep tradition of thinking about ethical issues such as what constitutes a just society.

178 Tobin, *The Right to Health in International Law* (n 13) 71.

179 E. Elhauge, 'Can Health Law Become a Coherent Field of Law' (2006) 41 *Wake Forest Law Review* 383.

ICESCR provides that the right to health is limited and a government is only required to spend 'available resources'.[180] The definition of 'available resources' is determined by the country and at a minimum should provide minimum subsistence rights.[181]

After the passage of PPACA in the United States, cost concerns arose from citizens, the US House of Representatives, some states, and Presidential Candidate Mitt Romney. For two years the permanence of health care reform was in question. The republican-controlled House of Representatives was concerned about PPACA's impact on the deficit, even though the Congressional Budget Office showed that it would actually reduce the federal deficit in the long term.[182] The Republican-controlled House of Representatives voted at least thirty-three times to repeal or dilute PPACA before the 2012 federal elections.[183] Some states, given the recession and their shrinking budgets, were concerned about the financial strain of increasing eligibility for Medicaid. Presidential candidate Mitt Romney repeatedly promised to repeal health care reform if elected even though the president does not have this authority under the Constitution.[184]

These cost concerns would threaten the realization of the reduction of health disparities among people of color if health care reform, and the PPACA framework to eliminate health disparities, were repealed. The American public would decide whether health care reform implementation would continue. On 6 November 2012, the electorate voiced its decision that health care reform should remain by re-electing President Obama to a second term.

Despite President Obama's re-election, efforts have not stopped to repeal the health care reform legislation. On 19 December 2012, a bill was introduced in the House of Representatives to repeal PPACA. On 7 March 2013, a bill was introduced in the United States Senate to repeal PPACA.[185] The vote on the Senate bill was fairly close, at 52 to 45.[186] In 2014, the number of repeal votes taken by the House of Representatives reached a high of forty-eight.[187] As a result, during the State of the Union address, President Obama reconfirmed his commitment to implementing the health care reform law and highlighted its numerous benefits. He also admonished the House lawmakers to stop 'refighting old battles' and to set forth 'specific plans to cut costs, cover more people, and increase choice' in a way 'that the numbers add up'.[188]

180 ICESCR, Art 2(1); Tobin, *The Right to Health in International Law* (n 13) 70; V.A. Leary, 'The Right to Health in International Human Rights Law' (1994) 1 *Health and Human Rights* 46.

181 Leary, 'The Right to Health in International Human Rights Law' (n 180) 46.

182 'Elmendorf: Health Reform Will Reduce Deficit, Warns of Fiscal Crisis', 9 April 2010, available at <http://www.kaiserhealthnews.org/daily-reports/2010/april/09/cbo-weighs-in.aspx?referrer=search>.

183 L. Mascaro, 'House votes—again—to repeal "Obamacare"', *Los Angeles Times*, 12 July 2012, A15.

184 US Constitution, art I, § 1: 'All legislative Powers herein granted shall be vested in a Congress of the United States'.

185 Spending Reduction Act of 2012, HR 6684, 112th Cong (2012); Patient Choice Restoration Act, § 499, 113 Cong (2013).

186 'ACA Repeal Amendment Fails in the Senate', *American Health Lawyers Health and Life Sciences Daily*, 14 March 2013.

187 N. Tanden, 'If at First You Don't Succeed', *Politico Magazine*, 30 January 2014.

188 President Barack Obama's State of the Union Address, 28 January 2014, available at <http://www.whitehouse.gov/the-press-office/2014/01/28/president-barack-obamas-state-union-address>. President Obama concluded his remarks about the repeal strategy as follows: 'Let's not have another forty-something votes to repeal a law that is helping millions of Americans . . . The first 40 were plenty. We got it. We all owe it to the American people to say what we're for, not just what we're against.'

6. Securing Continuous US Compliance with Global Health Law Norms

There are many approaches to reduction of health disparities, but the use of 'rights' in the United States is a controversial tool. Civil rights and human rights are two bodies of laws—domestic and international—that are designed to address inequality and thus lead to a reduction of health disparities.

The US approach to addressing human rights and civil rights targeting racial inequality is also inconsistent. It waxes and wanes. With respect to human rights, the United States, through the work of Eleanor Roosevelt, was an integral player in the development of the Universal Declaration of Human Rights.[189] Additionally, several African American civil rights leaders, like W.E.B. Du Bois, Mary McLeod Bethune, Mordecai Johnson, and the NAACP participated in meetings discussing the founding of the United Nations and the UN Charter. The NAACP and Du Bois later filed petitions in the United Nations calling for an investigation of the United States for domestic racial discrimination, given the existence of *de jure* segregation.[190] This information was used by Communist countries to expose the United States' hypocrisy.[191] Later a coalition led by Senator Bricker attempted to secure a constitutional amendment requiring separate legislation to implement treaties as a mechanism to ensure that human rights treatys would not be used to advance the civil rights of African Americans.[192]

Under Presidents Johnson, Carter, and Clinton, civil rights and human rights were advanced.[193] During the Carter administration the International Covenant for Civil and Political Rights, the International Covenant on Economic, Social and Cultural Rights, and the Convention on the Elimination of all Forms of Racial Discrimination were all submitted to Congress for its advice and consent. the ICERD was ratified during the Clinton administration and President Clinton, like President Carter, urged ratification of the ICESCR.[194] Under President G.H.W. Bush, the International Covenant for Civil and Political Rights was ratified, but his administration did not support ratification of the ICESCR.[195]

In contrast, under President Reagan, some scholars argue that civil rights did not receive sufficient support from the executive branch, and the government focused on cost control to the exclusion of other worthy goals.[196] The official policy of the Reagan State Department was 'that economic rights were not human rights'.[197] During

189 McDougall, 'Domestic Relevance of International Efforts' (n 42) 587–90; Kinney, 'Recognition of the International Human Right to Health' (n 20) 346–7.

190 McDougall, 'Domestic Relevance of International Efforts' (n 42) 573–4.

191 McDougall, 'Domestic Relevance of International Efforts' (n 42) 575.

192 McDougall, 'Domestic Relevance of International Efforts' (n 42) 576; Kinney, 'Recognition of the International Human Right to Health' (n 20) 347.

193 Under President Johnson, the Civil Rights Act of 1964 was signed into law and the Medicare Program was used to desegregate hospitals. Field, 'Regulation, Reform and the Creation of Free Market Health Care' (n 165); McDougall, 'Domestic Relevance of International Efforts' (n 42) 576.

194 McDougall, 'Domestic Relevance of International Efforts' (n 42) 576.

195 Kinney, 'Recognition of the International Human Right to Health' (n 20) 347.

196 At least one scholar, Professor Randall, relying on reports from the US Civil Rights Commission, advocates that civil rights enforcement in the area of health has been neglected for a longer period, 1980–1999. Randall, 'Racial Discrimination in Health Care' (n 11). According to Professor Leary, the Reagan administration was not supportive of social and economic rights, including the right to health. Leary, 'Defining the Right to Health Care' (n 155) 90.

197 Kinney, 'Recognition of the International Human Right to Health' (n 20) 347–8.

Tommy Thompson's tenure as Secretary of the Department of Health, administrative officials ordered staffers to revise a legislatively mandated report on health disparities without the use of the term 'health disparities', and to delete the conclusion that health care disparities are pervasive.[198] Additionally, during President George W. Bush's term, the State Department questioned the scope of General Comment 14 as going beyond the text of the ICESCR.[199] The G.W. Bush administration also attempted to block the creation of the special rapporteur for health and block other countries from addressing the right to health.[200] So vehement was the Bush administration's opposition to the right to health that it 'had a deeply chilling effect, making it difficult for UN bodies, initiatives and reports to discuss right to health issues in an open, balanced, rational and constructive manner'.[201]

While President Obama has stated that health care should be a right, his administration did not urge Congress to ratify the ICESCR. Instead he made health care reform a signature initiative of his first term in office and included passage of PPACA in the health section of the Report of the United States Submitted to the UN High Commissioner for Human Rights in conjunction with the Universal Periodic Review and the belatedly submitted 2013 periodic report to the CERD Committee.[202]

The inconsistent and controversial history of 'rights' and the Supreme Court decision in *NFIB v Sebelius* raise the question, what can be done to secure the United States' continuous compliance with the encompassing global health law norms designed to reduce health disparities for people of color?

6.1 PPACA structures help to secure continuous US compliance with global health law norms

There are several tools that Congress can use when drafting legislation to allow it to continue to influence implementation of the law. PPACA reflects the use of two formal mechanisms of congressional oversight that strengthen the future implementation of PPACA in ways consistent with global health law norms. First, PPACA restructures and creates executive level offices and councils to address health disparities and social determinants of health. For example, PPACA restructured the organization of part of an administrative office within the executive branch,[203] the HHS Office of Minority Health. As discussed previously, consistent with global health law norms, PPACA prioritizes issues of minority health by moving these issues within the Office of the Secretary and by the creation of six additional offices of minority health within

198 M.G. Bloche, 'Healthcare and the Politics of Race' in R.A.Williams (ed), *Eliminating Healthcare Disparities in America: Beyond the IOM Report* (Humana Press, 2007) (The original report was leaked and during a congressional hearing Secretary Thompson said that the rewrite was a mistake. Professor Bloche also notes that since 1968 some conservatives have pandered to the working class by seeking to create racial and cultural resentment by sending political messages that (a) oppose affirmative action, (b) dispute claims of race-based disadvantage, (c) vigorously object to anti-discrimination measures, and (d) caricature concerns on racial disparities in health care.)

199 K. Gorove, 'Shifting Norms in International Health Law' (2004) 98 *American Society of International Law Proceedings* 18.

200 Hunt, 'Missed Opportunities' (n 14) 39.

201 The former Special Rapporteur for Health, Paul Hunt, recognized that the US did not have to champion the right to health, and advised the Obama Administration to take a 'more benign' approach which allows other countries to explore this fundamental right. Hunt, 'Missed Opportunities' (n 14) 39.

202 Report of the United States of America Submitted to the UN High Commissioner for Human Rights in Conjunction with the Universal Periodic Review (August 2010) 18–19; US Periodic Report to the CERD Committee (2013).

203 J. Beerman, 'Congressional Administration' (2006) 43 *San Diego Law Review* 61, 107–11.

HHS. Additionally, as discussed previously, PPACA creates the National Prevention, Health Promotion, and Public Health Council. This executive level council has the advisory power to shape the development of a health-in-all policies approach to health which can begin to address social determinants of health. These legislatively mandated structures cannot be removed by another Presidential administration.[204] However, another presidential administration can seek to influence the implementation of PPACA through the political appointments selected to lead the agencies. This means that while PPACA puts organizational structures in place and contains provisions to address health disparities and social determinants of health, these mechanisms can potentially be neutralized or minimized through political appointments of individuals not supportive of the statute's legislative purpose. The structures can also be minimized by the passage of subsequent legislation that reduces or eliminates funding. For example, the passage of the Middle Class Job Creation and Tax Relief Act of 2012, reduced the Public Health and Prevention Fund created in PPACA by one-third, from $15 billion dollars to $10 billion dollars.[205] The Public Health and Prevention Fund was the first fund created to provide mandatory funding to support public health and prevention efforts.[206]

Second, Congress can monitor implementation of enacted legislation by imposing reporting requirements on administrative departments. These reporting requirements are an effective way for Congress to get information from the agency, express its interest in the agency activity, and keep the agency acting within the scope of its authority as expressed in particular legislation.[207] PPACA adheres to global health law norms by containing accountability features that protect the right to health by requiring reporting on efforts to improve minority health and the quality of health care provided and to eliminate racial and ethnic disparities. For example, the Secretary of Health and Human Services must file a bi-annual report with the congressional committees that have jurisdiction over health, based on statutorily mandated reports from the newly created offices of minority health on their initiatives designed to improve minority health.[208]

Third, Congress can move beyond PPACA structures to influence implementation of legislation through hearings or informal contact with personnel of the administrative agencies. Congressional hearings not only provide information to Congress, but to the American people.

6.2 Integration of human rights treaty rules into federal and state bureaucracies can help secure continuous US compliance with global health law norms

To comply with the UN Treaty Monitoring Committees' concerns about human rights awareness, the United States Department of State made federal administrative agencies and state governors aware of the United States' human rights obligations. This occurred

204 Beerman, 'Congressional Administration' (n 203) 107–8, noting that 'it is largely Congress that decides what departments to create [and] how to organize those departments'.

205 Middle Class Job Creation and Tax Relief Act of 2012, Pub L No 112-96, 126 Stat 156. Prior to the passage of this act, the Prevention Fund had been under attack. Two bills passed the House of Representatives which would have defunded the entire fund created in PPACA § 4002(b). HR 1217, 112th Cong (1st Session 2011) (The Pitts Proposal passed the House on 13 April 2011); HR 4628, 112th Cong (2nd Session 2012) (The Biggert Bill passed the House on 27 April 2012).

206 Majette, 'PPACA and Public Health' (n 79).

207 Beerman, 'Congressional Administration' (n 203) 106.

208 See section 3 of this chapter (discussing OMH restructuring); PPACA §10334.

prior to the passage of PPACA. In electronic letters dated 17 December 2009 and 21 January 2010, the Legal Advisor to the Secretary of State, Harold Koh, reminded executive branch agencies and governors that the United States has obligations under several human rights treaties which the United States takes 'very seriously'.[209] The letter included links to copies of the treaties that the United States has ratified as well as human rights reports that the United States filed in compliance with the treaties from 2005 to 2008. As previously discussed, two treaties relevant to the elimination of health disparities for people of color include the International Covenant on Civil and Political Rights and the International Convention on the Elimination of All Forms of Racial Discrimination. Transmission of the treaties, coupled with the most recently submitted treaty monitoring reports of the United States, promotes treaty compliance by facilitating internalization of human rights norms like the ICCPR's non-discrimination and equality provisions and the ICERD's non-discrimination and affirmative obligation to take special measures to protect racial groups' rights to public health or medical care.[210] The Legal Advisor's letters further advised the federal agencies and state governors of the need to implement the treaties at all levels of government and the need to share this information with the public.[211]

Future compliance with global health law norms can be advanced by adopting a constructivist theorist perspective[212] that individuals and society interact to construct rules and institutions that regulate a country's conduct. Accordingly, the diffusion of human rights principles can be expanded by developing a strategy to coordinate and identify norm entrepreneurs that can advocate for a broad view of global health law norms that will move beyond mandatory hard law and focus on other regulative global justice norms.

The passage of PPACA shows the importance of norm entrepreneurs and rights discourse on shaping the priorities of US health policy. For decades Senator Ted Kennedy pushed for health care reform as 'the cause of his life'.[213] He believed that securing health care for every American was a fundamental right, because of his belief in social justice.[214] During his last few years in the Senate, Senator Kennedy worked with Senator Obama on health matters as members of one of the committees that has jurisdiction over health, the Health, Education, Labor, and Pension Committee. Later candidate and President Barack Obama became the 'catalyst norm entrepreneur' by making universal coverage, especially for the sick and vulnerable, a priority for his campaign, presidency, and re-election. During a presidential debate with John McCain in 2008, candidate Obama responded that he thought 'health care should be a right for every American' when asked, 'Is health care in America a privilege, a right, or responsibility?' As President Obama he stated several times *that health care was a moral imperative.*[215]

209 Memo from Harold Hongju Koh, Legal Adviser, US Department of State to Executive Branch Agencies (17 December 2009), available at <http://www.state.gov/documents/organization/137293.pdf>; Memo from Harold Hongju Koh, Legal Adviser, US Department of State to State Governors (20 January 2010), available at <http://www.state.gov/documents/organization/137292.pdf>.

210 ICERD, Arts 1, 2(2); ICCPR, Arts 2, 26.

211 Memo from Harold Hongju Koh (n 209).

212 Meier, 'Global Health Takes a Normative Turn' (n 17) 12; P.M. Haas, 'Choosing to Comply: Theorizing from International Relations and Comparative Politics' in D. Shelton (ed), *Commitment and Compliance—The Role of Non-Binding Norms in the International Legal System* (OUP, 2000).

213 Majette, 'PPACA and Public Health' (n 79) 376, note 37, discussing E.M. Kennedy, '"The Cause of My Life" Inside the Fight for Universal Health Care', *Newsweek*, 18 July 2009.

214 Kennedy, 'The Cause of My Life' (n 213).

215 5 March 2009 White House Forum on Health Reform; 11 June 2009 Remarks by the President in Town Hall Meeting on Health Care (Green Bay, WI).

6.3 Compliance with the recommendation of General Comment 14 to develop collaborative partnerships to protect the right to health helps to secure the United States' adherence to global health law norms

The evolving area of global health law moves beyond activities of the government to protect health by seeking to influence a broad array of actors whose conduct impacts health, including international organizations, civil society, and businesses. Pursuant to General Comment 14, a government can influence non-governmental actors like the private sector and civil society by making them aware of health and human rights legal requirements and collaborating on health promotion activities where possible.[216] Moreover these interactions also shape government behavior.

The National Stakeholders Strategy for Achieving Health Equity serves as a critical collaborative effort between the government, civil society, and private business to reduce health disparities and improve the health of the nation and its most vulnerable citizens.[217] The National Stakeholders Strategy was an initiative of the National Partnership for Action (NPA) which is a public-private partnership organized by the Office of Minority Health within the Department of Health and Human Services.

The National Stakeholders Strategy was released one year after passage of PPACA in April 2011 and is available on the internet. The Strategy has five goals: (1) to increase awareness of disparities and their adverse impact on health, (2) to develop a cadre of leaders to help eliminate disparities, (3) to change the health care system to address the needs of racial and ethnic populations, (4) to improve cultural competence, and (5) to ensure that data and research is available and disseminated to eliminate disparities.[218]

The Strategy explicitly internalizes human rights norms by defining health using language similar to the fundamental right language in the WHO Constitution and explicitly mentioning the seminal SDH Commission's Report, 'Closing the Gap in a Generation'.[219] It also sets forth the requirements of domestic non-discrimination laws, Title VI of the Civil Rights Act of 1964 which prohibits discrimination on the basis of race, color, and national origin in programs and activities that receive federal financial assistance. While noting that most hospitals and health care providers are covered by Title VI, it goes further and provides examples of discriminatory conduct such as denying a service or benefit, providing different services, or separately treating individuals because of their race, color, or national origin.[220] Use of human rights and civil rights language in a report that will have widespread dissemination among the public begins to normalize these concepts and creates a shared understanding that can facilitate future compliance with the human rights obligations of the United States.

Another mechanism to facilitate the continued compliance with global health law norms to reduce health disparities is through social learning. Social learning theory recognizes that the process of interaction and deliberation among political leaders, thought leaders, and ordinary citizens can create or confirm societal and political support for action.[221]

216 General Comment 14, paras 55, 56.

217 US Department of Health and Human Services, National Partnership for Action to End Health Disparities, National Stakeholder Strategy for Achieving Health Equity, available at <http://minorityhealth.hhs.gov/npa/templates/content.aspx?lvl=1&lvlid=33&ID=286> (hereinafter 'National Stakeholder Strategy').

218 National Stakeholder Strategy (n 217) 2.

219 See section 2 of this chapter.

220 National Stakeholder Strategy (n 217).

221 Ruger, 'Normative Foundations of Global Health Law' (n 15) 439; J. Checkel, 'Why Comply? Social Learning and European Identity Change' (2001) 55 *International Organization* 553.

When viewed through the lens of social learning, the United States' participation in the 2011 World Conference on Social Determinants of Health confirms the importance of equity as an incorporated global norm in US health policy. The United States played a role in preparing for and participating in the World Conference on SDH. A representative from the United States was part of the Advisory Group that helped the WHO plan the conference. Two case studies from the United States were selected to be part of the evidence base collected from member countries to document their experiences with efforts to address social determinants of health. The case studies were from the NPA and a university.[222] Additionally, the Secretary of the United States Department of Health and Human Services, Kathleen Sebelius, was one of the fifty high level conference speakers.[223] Secretary Sebelius' participation is also important because it sets a precedent for future HHS Secretaries on the importance of equity nationally and globally as a mechanism to eliminate health disparities.

An additional step that should be taken in the United States that is consistent with global health law norms is to comply with the right to health indicator that requires raising awareness among health professionals regarding a country's human rights obligations. Education about health and human rights is not part of the standard curriculum in medical schools in the United States.[224] Moving forward, health care professionals in the United States should be taught about the health and human rights obligations under ICERD at a minimum, and ideally under aspirational global health laws, as discussed in section 2 of this chapter. For example, health and human rights awareness raising education should begin in medical school and continue as part of continuing medical education. This type of information could be incorporated into existing cultural competence training.[225]

222 The US case studies were entitled: (1) 'A national partnership for action to end health disparities in the United States of America' and (2) 'How can we get the "social determinants of health" message on the public policy and public health agenda?'. The NPA case study was prepared by representatives from the Office of Minority Health; the Association for State and Territorial Health Officials; the National Association of State Offices of Minority Health; the National Rural Health Association; and the National Business Group (non-profit association of the largest US employers). WHO, Resources, 'Case Studies on Social Determinants of Health', available at <http://www.who.int/sdhconference/resources/case_studies/en>.

223 WHO, World Conference on Social Determinants of Health, 'Conference Summary' (n 84) 1.

224 Approximately 32% of the seventy-nine medical schools surveyed offer training on health and human rights even though a majority of the medical school deans thought that it was important to offer such courses. Health and human rights training is significantly more likely to occur in schools of public health as compared to medical schools. L.E. Cotter, J. Chevrier, W. El-Nachef, R. Radhakrishna, L. Rahangdale, S. Weiser, and V. Iacopino, 'Health and Human Rights Education in U.S. Schools of Medicine and Public Health: Current Status and Future Challenges' (March 2009) 4 Plos ONE e4916; V. Iacopino, 'Teaching Human Rights in Graduate Health Education' in S. Gruskin, M. A. Grodin, G.J. Annas, and S.P. Marks (eds), *Perspectives on Health and Human Rights* (Routledge, 2005) 549.

225 The US is starting to move in this direction by providing education on domestic civil rights laws that prevent discrimination. The US 2013 Periodic Report to the CERD Committee briefly mentions a model medical school curriculum for a two- to three-hour workshop developed in partnership with the National Consortium for Multicultural Education for Health Professionals, Stanford University Medical School, and the US Department of Health and Human Services—Office of Civil Rights. The workshop entitled, 'Stopping Discrimination Before it Starts: The Impact of Civil Rights Laws on Health Care Disparities', is designed to teach professionals to identify and address potential discrimination under the Civil Rights Act, Title VI. US Periodic Report to the CERD Committee (2013) 71, para 141.

6.4 Global Health Law norms should be conceived as providing a conceptual framework to continuously focus on the reduction of health disparities for people of color

Global Health Law norms should be viewed as providing a normative coordinating framework for non-binding hard law and soft law structures that are designed to reduce health disparities and inequality in the United States. In essence, global health law norms will serve as a tool to identify and coordinate existing and future national and international efforts to reduce such health disparities and inequality.

In section 2, I use global health law as a tool to identify and discuss the non-binding hard law (ICESCR) and soft law structures (reports of the RTH Special Rapporteur, report of the SDH Commission, WHO resolutions on SDH, and reports of the World Conference on SDH) that can be used to reduce health disparities and inequality in the United States. It is from this perspective that I conceptualized PPACA as framework legislation designed to eliminate health disparities and inequality for people of color. This perspective should also be applied to future legal norms.

For example, Professor Larry Gostin has proposed the creation of a Framework Convention on Global Health to meet the basic needs of the least healthy.[226] While the Framework Convention on Global Health is primarily focused on the health care systems in poor countries, it could be beneficial to continued progress on the elimination of health disparities for people of color in the United States. The existence of the treaty reaffirms the legal and moral imperative to address the health care needs of vulnerable populations, including people of color. The framework convention also ensures the provision of basic services such as access to essential medicines and vaccines and the creation of a functioning health system (public health and primary health care)[227] to prevent, detect, treat, and ameliorate disease, disability, and premature death.[228]

7. Conclusion

Significant health disparities exist for people of color in the United States, resulting in avoidable disability, disease, and death. In 2010, the United States passed comprehensive health care reform legislation, the Patient Protection and Affordable Care Act. This legislation, when viewed through the prism of global health law, creates a framework to eliminate health disparities for people of color. Global health law seeks to facilitate health promoting behavior among the key actors that impact health, like governments, international organizations, businesses, and civil society. Several global health law norms impose an obligation on the United States to eliminate health disparities for

226 L. Gostin, 'Meeting the Basic Survival Needs of the World's Least Healthy People: Toward a Framework Convention on Global Health' (2008) 96 *Georgetown Law Journal* 331. Professor Gostin has begun to actualize his scholarly proposal by creating the Joint Action Learning Initiative, which is a collaboration between civil society and academia designed to advocate and conduct research to support the creation of the Framework Convention. Towards a Framework Convention on Global Health: The Joint Action and Learning Initiative (November 2010), available at <http://www.law.georgetown.edu/oneillinstitute/global-health-law/jali.cfm>.

227 Primary Health Care does not include specialty or tertiary care. It would include counseling, maternal and child health, family planning, and medical treatment. Gostin, 'Meeting the Basic Survival Needs of the World's Least Healthy People' (n 226) 372.

228 Gostin, 'Meeting the Basic Survival Needs of the World's Least Healthy People' (n 226) 367–74.

people of color, including global health governance documents of the World Health Organization, the International Convention on the Elimination of all Forms of Racial Discrimination, the International Covenant on Economic, Social, and Cultural Rights, Reports of the Special Rapporteur for Health, and the Commission on Social Determinants of Health.

After PPACA was enacted, several impediments arose to its implementation. Opponents challenged the constitutionality of the legislation. While the Supreme Court opinion largely upheld the constitutionality of PPACA, the Court's decision to allow states to choose whether to expand Medicaid, the public insurance program for the poor, and rhetoric in the opinion undermines PPACA's efforts to eliminate health disparities for people of color. The decision creates a gap in insurance coverage that excludes segments of the most impoverished individuals, those below 100 percent of the federal poverty level, while providing financial assistance to individuals above the poverty line. The decision also creates barriers to Congress's use of the commerce clause and spending clause to solve future social problems. Second, tensions arose over whether the legislation would survive based on moral imperatives or succumb to market hegemonic and cost concerns.

Moving forward one must consider whether the country will continue to comply with global health law norms and eliminate health disparities for people of color. There are four recommendations that can facilitate the United States' continued compliance with global health law norms. First, PPACA structures and non-PPACA structures should be exploited to secure continuous compliance with global health law norms to eliminate health disparities for people of color. Second, integration of human rights treaty rules into federal and state bureaucracies can secure continuous US compliance. Third, efforts to collaborate with civil society, the private sector, and international organizations will help secure US compliance. Fourth, conceptualizing global health law norms as a normative coordinating framework for nonbinding hard law and soft law structures to eliminate health disparities for people of color facilitates continuous US compliance.

25

Global Health Law

Aspirational, Paradoxical, or Oxymoronic?

George P. Smith, II

1. The Gates Foundation as a Catalytic Force

The phenomenal success of the Bill and Melinda Gates Foundation is without parallel in both its aims and its action programs to enhance—globally—healthcare and reduce extreme poverty; secure sustainable ways to make water, sanitation, and hygiene services safer and more affordable; and—in America—expand educational opportunities and further enhance access to information technologies.[1] The Global Health Program of the Foundation is not only working toward the eradication of poliomyelitis, but makes grants for research and immunizations through its Global Alliance for Vaccines and Immunization, a Children's Vaccine Program, together with research monies specifically for HIV/AIDS research, tuberculosis, and malaria.[2] Through a Financial Access Initiative, millions of dollars have been dedicated to undertake field research and to respond to significant questions concerning *micro* finance and financial access in impoverished Third World states in the global community.[3] This response is recognition of the incontrovertible fact that before health care delivery systems can be operative, the oppressive poverty of the Third World must be reduced.

Both the challenge and the hope of the Gates Foundation is to create and maintain infrastructure within impoverished states which enable them to provide basic health protections to their citizens.[4] Nevertheless, concerns have been raised that the Foundation—by prioritizing medical needs for combating AIDS, for example—is effectively diverting health care resources and clinical staff from addressing more basic health needs such as nutrition and from developing public health delivery systems.[5] Even with these reservations, the Foundation is nonetheless seen as being in the vanguard of the 'philanthrocapitalism' revolution in global philanthropy and—as such—has become a catalyst for shaping new mediating social, economic, medico-legal, and political structures which, in turn, promote global health.[6]

Admirable though this path-breaking work of the Gates Foundation is, its immediate effect on structuring a *legal* framework for Global Health Law remains tenuous. This is the case—as will be seen—because of foundational issues in international law-making, and the infrastructures for the enforcement of normative standards globally. To be sure, incremental efforts are under way to secure global health law. Charting the

1 See <http://en.wikipedia.org/wiki/Bill_Gates_Foundation> (accessed 4 February 2013).

2 See n 1.

3 See n 1. See generally N.N. Levey, 'Less Affluent Nations Push to Provide Health Care for All', *Washington Post*, 14 May 2012, A11.

4 L. Garrett, 'The Challenge of Global Health' (2007) 86 *Foreign Affairs* 14.

5 Garrett, 'The Challenge of Global Health' (n 4).

6 'The Birth of Philanthrocapitalism', *The Economist*, 23 February 2006, 8.

actual success of these efforts remains, for the future, mired in geo-politics and economic vectors of force. Presently, a definitive body of enforceable global health law remains paradoxical and even oxymoronic as a contradiction in terms.[7]

2. Economic and Geopolitical Realities

In the United States, it is projected that the cost of health care will be $4.6 trillion in 2020, accounting for about $1.00 of every $5.00 in the economy.[8] In 2011, health care spending in the United States was approximately $2.7 trillion—which broke down to about $8,650.00 per capita.[9]

The World Health Organization (WHO) put a price tag on fatal non-communicable medical conditions at $11.4 billion dollars a year. These major conditions—high blood pressure, high cholesterol, high blood sugar, and obesity—result, significantly, from four behavioral issues: smoking, excessive drinking, inactivity, and unhealthy diets.[10]

A health care package designed to combat these weaknesses was set by the WHO which includes tobacco control, salt and fat reductions in processed food, basic generic drugs for heart patients, cervical cancer screening, and several other measures. It will cost less than $1.00 a year per person in the poorest countries and about $3.00 per person in richer countries. Sixty-three percent of deaths each year result principally from heart attacks, strokes, cancer, diabetes, and chronic lung conditions such as emphysema and asthma.[11]

Raising funds in order to meet the yearly costs of this package could be achieved, in part, it has been suggested, by countries raising taxes on cigarettes and alcohol. Reduction in tobacco and alcohol use is—by consensus—the most decisive way to combat the chronic health issues arising from their use. Consumer and commercial interests could—predictably—be strong opposition forces to strategies of this nature, however.[12]

Enhanced medical treatment of people with cardiovascular disease (or a high risk of it) necessitates drugs and expertise which are in very short supply in many impoverished countries.[13] The WHO package of medicines needed to combat fatal illnesses is modest in cost and generic (for example aspirin, statins, and the drug—metformin—to control diabetes). Yet, pharmaceutical companies are concerned that they may well be pressured to provide patented drugs at discounted prices, or to let offshore companies make them without paying royalties (as is the case with some AIDS drugs).[14] Interestingly, the WHO did not plead or request the global community to underwrite this health project on behalf of the poor countries. Lacking altruism and applying the standard of self-interest, it is very doubtful—given the state of the global economy—that the 'wealthy' countries will accept any health care responsibility for the less developed countries.[15]

7 A. Kennedy, 'Free Healthcare? That has to be the Greatest Oxymoron of Our Age', *The Guardian*, 4 September 2011, 7.

8 'Nation's Health Tab to Hit $4.6t in 2020', *Washington Examiner*, 29 July 2011, 12.

9 'Nation's Health Tab to Hit $4.6t in 2020' (n 8).

10 D. Brown, 'WHO Puts Price Tag on Preventing Fatal Illnesses', *Washington Post*, 29 September 2011, A3.

11 Brown, 'WHO Puts Price Tag on Preventing Fatal Illnesses' (n 10).

12 Brown, 'WHO Puts Price Tag on Preventing Fatal Illnesses' (n 10).

13 Brown, 'WHO Puts Price Tag on Preventing Fatal Illnesses' (n 10). But see V. Bajaj, 'India Weighs Providing Drugs at State-Run Hospitals', *New York Times*, 6 July 2012, B1.

14 Brown, 'WHO Puts Price Tag on Preventing Fatal Illnesses' (n 10).

15 Brown, 'WHO Puts Price Tag on Preventing Fatal Illnesses' (n 10). See generally E. Kinney, 'The International Human Right to Health: What Does This Mean for Our Nation and World?' (2001) 34 *Indiana Law Review* 1457.

3. Historical Glosses

As early as the fourth century BCE, Aristotle wrote reportedly of a citizen's absolute right to the measure of good health that society is able to give.[16] Over the course of time, the notion of a right to health, or health care as a human right, has gained some level of credence—this, because the right to health is sometimes considered as a corollary to the general duty and responsibility of states to advance the enjoyment of freedoms and entitlements considered as the rights of each human.[17] The battle for universal recognition and enforcement of health care rights has, nevertheless, been largely aspirational and unenforceable.[18] However, there is a framework for actuating this right, and it is that construct or framework that I wish to explore.

The modern genesis of human rights is to be found in the United Nations 1948 Universal Declaration of Human Rights,[19] together with the 1966 International Covenant on Civil and Political Rights[20] and the International Covenant on Economic, Social and Cultural Rights.[21] Human rights are, by their nature, however, inherent to all human beings by virtue of their very humanity and do not depend on the grace of the state for their existence, as opposed to their effective enjoyment.[22] This principle is confirmed in Article 1 of the Universal Declaration of Human Rights, which proclaims: 'All human beings are born free and equal in dignity and rights.'[23] The function of human rights, then, is to create state obligations, and not to create general ethics.[24] Human rights are minimum standards for acceptable governance and a means of empowerment against oppression by states.[25]

The very concept of a right to health care is of little practical value when health care policy-makers as well as legislators, physicians, and average citizens, confront the foundational question underlying the whole of this area: namely, how much medical care should be given to specific individuals or made available to particular groupings of people.[26] A plurality of values within contemporary society preclude the notion that a definitive answer can ever be forthcoming. With a multitude of ways of allocating limited health care resources, some will be perceived as just, others as unjust. Additionally, some priorities will be seen as essentially political, and others promoting a more progressive realization of a so-called 'right to health-related goods'.[27]

16 See generally G.P. Smith, II, *Human Rights and Bioethics* (The Hague: Kluwer, 2000); G. Smith, 'Human Rights and Bioethics: Formulating a Universal Right to Health, Health Care, or Health Protection?' (2005) 35 *Vanderbilt Journal of Transnational Law* 1295.

17 See generally G.P. Smith, II, 'Access to Health Care: Economic, Medical, Ethical and Socio-Legal Challenges' in D.N. Weisstub and G.D. Pintos (eds), *Autonomy and Human Rights in Health Care* (Dordrecht: Springer, 2008) ch 20.

18 Smith, 'Access to Health Care' (n 17).

19 UNGA Res 217A (III), 71, UN GAOR, 3rd Session, 1st plen mtg UN Doc A/810 (12 December 1948).

20 16 December 1966, 933 UNTS 3 (the US is not a party).

21 16 December 1966, 999 UNTS 171 (the US is a party, subject to several reservations, understandings, and declarations).

22 Smith, 'Human Rights and Bioethics' (2005) (n 16).

23 UNGA Res 217A (III) (n 19). See generally R. Glensy, 'The Right to Dignity' (2011) 43 *Columbia Human Rights Law Review* 65.

24 A. McBeth, 'Privatising Human Rights: What Happens to the State's Human Rights Duties When Services are Privatized?' (2004) 5 *Melbourne Journal of International Law* 133, 143.

25 McBeth, 'Privatising Human Rights' (n 24).

26 B. Brody, 'Why the Right to Health Care is not a Useful Concept for Policy Debates' in T.J. Bole, III, and W.B. Bondesen (eds), *Rights to Health Care* (Dordrecht: Springer, 1991).

27 J. Arras and E. Fenton, 'Bioethics and Human Rights: Access to Health-Related Goods' (2009) 39 *Hastings Center Report* 27, 33.

It appears as though contentious debate will continue over succeeding years to focus—nevertheless—on whether economic, social, and cultural rights are as pressing as civil and political rights. Some would seek to prioritize rights—arguing that there are varying moral weights attached to them. Others contend that no ranking can be made of fundamental rights and, indeed, none should be honored before others. Seeking universality in the application of human rights requires all states to respect a defined set or core of minimum standards of behavior or, as Belinda Bennett phrases it, 'a common ground of moral understanding'.[28] So long as they meet these standards, adjustments might, in turn, be allowed for differing legal, moral, and cultural value systems within each state.[29]

If, in due course, an international right to health is recognized, for it to have any meaning at all, requires the imposition of some implementing obligations on states and—furthermore—requires affirmative action to be taken by the states themselves.[30] At bottom, however, as will be seen, economic development and self-sufficiency are the determinants of the level of respect, protection, and enforcement of human rights—regardless of their derivation and regardless of whether a state has by treaty, or acquiescence, acknowledged them.[31]

Nobel Laureate, Amartya Sen, has correctly linked health—and especially public health—to freedom and economic development by observing that: 'Sometimes the lack of substantive freedoms relates directly to economic poverty, which robs people of the freedom to satisfy hunger, or to achieve sufficient nutrition, or to obtain remedies for treatable illnesses, or the opportunity to be adequately clothed and sheltered, or to enjoy clean water or sanitary facilities.'[32]

4. Definitional Uncertainties

Defining and enforcing civil and political rights in the world community has taken—and continues to take—tenacity and great patience. The record of achievement has, at best, been quite irregular. An even greater challenge is to be seen in shaping a meaningful, identifiable, operational, and enforceable right to health within the ambit of economic and social rights.

To make a right to health more than merely aspirational, a first step is to develop a workable definition of what precisely such a right includes. What, for example, does 'enjoyment of the highest attainable standard of health'—as used in the preamble of the World Health Organization's 1946 Constitution mean? Article 55 of the UN Charter dedicated the United Nations to promoting solutions for international health problems. What is the nature and scope of these problems? The Universal Declaration of

[28] B.J. Bennett, 'Globalising Rights? Constructing Health Rights in a Shrinking World' in B.J. Bennett, T. Carney, and I. Karpin (eds), *Brave New World of Health* (Sydney: Federation Press, 2008) 20.

[29] Smith, *Human Rights and Bioethics* (2000) (n 16) and Smith, 'Access to Health Care' (n 17). See T. Zewart, 'Using Local Culture to Further the Implementation of International Human Rights: The Receptor Approach' (2012) 34 *Human Rights Quarterly* 546.

[30] T. Faunce, 'Will Human Rights Subsume Medical Ethics? Intersections in The UNESCO Universal Bioethics Declaration' (2004) 31 *Journal of Medical Ethics* 173.

[31] Kinney, 'The International Human Right to Health' (n 15). See I. Brownlie, *Principles of Public International Law* (Oxford: 7th edn, OUP, 2008) 575–6, discussing the principle of marginal appreciation which recognizes a respondent state is best qualified to understand the necessity of a specific situation giving offense within its own jurisdiction. See also H.J. Steiner, P. Alston, and R. Goodman, *International Human Rights in Context: Law, Politics, Morals* (Oxford: 3rd edn, OUP, 2007) chs 4, 6, and 9.

[32] A. Sen, *Development as Freedom* (Oxford: OUP, 1999) 4.

Human Rights structures a right to enjoy 'a standard of living adequate for the health and well-being of individuals and their families' (Article 25). What are the requisites of health necessary for a state of well being?[33] Interestingly, the International Covenant on Economic, Social and Cultural Rights (ICESCR) does not define the right to health and treats it in general, rather than in specific, terms.[34]

Some rights within the Covenant are 'recognized',[35] while others need only be 'respected',[36] 'ensured',[37] or 'guaranteed'.[38] The highest ordering of state responsibility under the Covenant, then, is to be found under the terms, 'to ensure' and 'to guarantee'; for they are not subject to the standard of 'progressive realisation'.[39] While the right to the highest standard of health is, as seen, only 'recognized', this was done in the drafting of the Covenant to assure wider acceptability to states unwilling, initially, to assume specific responsibilities—it is, however, given a stronger ordering by the enumeration of various, non-exhaustive steps for realization.[40]

In actuality, a fundamental right to health suggests something that usually cannot be guaranteed at all—namely, perfect health. Not only does this state or condition vary from person to person, but from country to country, and is thus truly an indeterminate variable.[41] In the relevant international human rights instruments pertinent to shaping a right to health,[42] a right to health is seen as corresponding to a shorthand term for 'the right to the highest attainable standard of health'[43]—with the right to health care seen as an inherent part of the right to health.[44] Caution must always be taken to avoid broadening the scope of this right to include 'almost everything'.[45]

There is agreement, however, that there are basic underlying preconditions which influence health and indeed become part of a right to health. They include: adequate nutrition, safe drinking water, sanitation, safe working conditions or occupational health, and a healthy environment.[46] Without doubt, many of these preconditions

[33] L.O. Gostin and Z. Lazzarini, *Human Rights and Public Health In AIDS Pandemic* (Oxford: OUP, 1997) 27–31.

[34] Gostin and Lazzarini, *Human Rights and Public Health* (n 33). See P. Sieghart, *The Lawful Rights of Mankind* (Oxford: OUP, 1985) 13, acknowledging that the European Social Charter (Art 11), and the African Charter (Art 16), also recognize the rights of everyone to the enjoyment of the highest or best attainable standard of health—both physical and mental. See (1982) 21 *International Legal Materials* 58. See also M.C.R. Craven, *The International Covenant on Economic, Social and Cultural Rights* (Oxford: Clarendon Press, 1995).

[35] ICESCR, Art 12(1) right to health.

[36] See eg ICESCR, Art 13(3) liberty of parents regarding certain aspects of their children's education; Art 15(3) freedom of scientific research.

[37] See eg ICESCR, Art 3 (equal rights of men and women), Art 8 (trade union rights).

[38] See eg ICESCR, Art 2(2) nondiscrimination, Art 7(a)(1) prohibition of gender discrimination in employment.

[39] B.C.A. Toebes, *The Right to Health as a Human Right in International Law* (Cambridge: Intersentia, 1999) 293.

[40] Toebes, *The Right to Health* (n 39) 293–332.

[41] Toebes, *The Right to Health* (n 39) 16. See generally A. Moncrieff, 'The Freedom of Health' 159 (2011) *Pennsylvania Law Review* 2209.

[42] Toebes, *The Right to Health* (n 39) 28, passim 245–6. The instruments are: The WHO Constitution; The Universal Declaration of Human Rights; Convention on the Elimination of All Forms of Discrimination Against Women; and The Convention on The Rights of The Child (Toebes, 28).

[43] Toebes, *The Right to Health* (n 39) 293–332.

[44] Toebes, *The Right to Health* (n 39) 19.

[45] Toebes, *The Right to Health* (n 39) 259. The right to health is seen, essentially, as a right of access to health services. D.P. Fidler, *International Law and Public Health: Materials on and Analysis of Global Jurisprudence* (New York: Ardsley, 2000) 302–9.

[46] Toebes, *The Right to Health* (n 39) 122, 272. It has been argued that the right to health, as a social human right to health, is linked—perhaps inextricably—to 'the right to an adequate standard of

overlap with the Covenant for Economic and Cultural Rights.[47] They, in turn, complement and strengthen what has been termed 'core health care elements' such as safeguarding maternal and child health care (including family planning), immunizing against major infectious diseases, and the appropriate treatment of common diseases and injuries.[48]

Article 3 of the European Convention on Human Rights mandates equitable access to health care of appropriate quality.[49] This, of course, does not resolve in any manner the defining issue of what form of health care is accessible and appropriate.[50] Nor does this mandate allow for any recognition of the fact that the strength and availability of health care services depend upon, in reality, not only the resource bases available to those within domestic health care systems[51] but the social settings in which health demands arise.[52] Consequently, individual claims to appropriate health care are often seen as incompatible with communitarian obligations to preserve the general good.[53]

As seen, the Universal Declaration and the two Covenants can be understood—at best—as referencing the *right* to health as but an 'imperfect obligation'.[54] And, under the principle of cultural relativism, serious doubts remain as to whether all of the rights in the Declaration are encoded culturally in one context or are subject to differing applications within the varying world cultures themselves, especially since notions of right and wrong vary across transnational boundaries.[55]

4.1 Shaping a right to health care

Because of these profound uncertainties, it has been suggested that it is misleading to refer to a governmental obligation to guarantee a person's good health.[56] Rather, it is better and more accurate to refer to a right to health protection[57] which would include a right to health care and a right to live under healthy conditions.[58] Yet, it has been seen that a strong conceptual framework for both identifying and analyzing those essential

living and right to food'. M. Novak, *Introduction to the International Human Rights Regime* (London: Brill, 2003) 143.

47 Toebes, *The Right to Health* (n 39) 122, 272.

48 Toebes, *The Right to Health* (n 39) 284.

49 European Treaty Series No 164, 36 International Legal Materials 817 (1997). See A. Sweet and J. Matthews, 'Proportionality, Balancing and Global Constitutionalism' (2008) 47 *Columbia Journal of Transnational Law* 68, discussing a dominant technique of rights adjudication under the European Convention on Human Rights.

50 D. Giesen, 'Health Care as a Right: Some Practical Implications' (1994) 13 *International Journal of Medicine and Law* 285, 290.

51 R.A. Epstein, *Moral Peril: Our Inalienable Right to Health?* (Boston, MA: Basic Books, 1997) 417.

52 G.J. Annas, *Some Choices: Law, Medicine and The Market* (Oxford: OUP, 1998) 254.

53 E.B. Brody, *Biomedical Technology and Human Rights* (New York: Unesco, 1993) 29.

54 M. Kirby, 'The Right to Health Fifty Years On—Still Skeptical?', Paper, Bagnoud Center for Health and Human Rights, Harvard University School of Public Health, Cambridge, MA, 4 December 1998, 20.

55 Kirby, 'The Right to Health Fifty Years On' (n 54) 18; H.J. Steiner and P. Alston, *International Human Rights in Context: Laws, Politics, Morals* (Oxford: OUP, 1996) 192–4.

56 cf J.E. Childress, *Practical Reasoning in Bioethics* (Bloomington, IN: Indiana University Press, 1997) 241, arguing for equitable access to health care.

57 'Health, Human Rights and International Law' (1998) 82 *American Society of International Law Proceedings* 122.

58 V. Leary, 'The Right to Health in International Human Rights Law' (1994) 1 *Health and Human Rights* 25, 31. See generally E. Kinney and B. Clark, 'Provisions for Health and Health Care in the Constitutions of the Countries of the World' (2004) 37 *Cornell International Law Journal* 285, 291, 305–59, suggesting that 67.5% of the world constitutions have provisions covering health or health care, and then surveying them.

societal factors representing the conditions under which people can be healthy is lacking.[59] Others suggest a right to health does exist in the abstract but disagree as to the practical consequences of its recognition.[60] Consistent with all of these concerns, the WHO concluded recently that it made poor economic sense to provide comprehensive medical services for *everyone*. Accordingly, poorer countries should be helped to carry out low cost programs to tackle illnesses such as malaria, while wealthier countries should learn how to prioritize the care they offer. Again, the components of qualitative health care availability are seen as being shaped by a clear understanding of resource availability within each state.[61]

4.2 The ESCR Comment

The United Nations Committee on Economic, Social and Cultural Rights (ESCR) which is charged with monitoring the implementation of the ICESCR, issued—in 2000—General Comment No 14: The Right to the Highest Attainable Standard of Health.[62] While proclaiming health as 'a fundamental human right indispensable for the exercise of other human rights', the ESCR structures the right within broad norms, state obligations, violations, and implementations.[63]

Among these core state obligations determined by the ESCR Committee to be necessary to guarantee a minimal level of health are four: nondiscriminatory access to health services—especially for vulnerable or marginalized groups; adequate food sources that are enriched nutritionally; basic shelter which accommodates sanitation and potable water; and use of essential drugs.[64] The development of national public health strategies which seek to address health concerns regarding reproduction and maternal health, immunization, infectious disease control, and ready access to health information are of central importance.[65]

While impressive, General Comment 14 must surely be seen as more aspirational than determinative—for, the indisputable fact remains: these lofty (albeit noble) pronouncements on state obligations remain non-justiciable. As well, the harsh reality is that the members of the transnational community simply—by and large—refuse to invest the necessary economic capital to guarantee the components of the right to health as seen by the ESCR. Enforcement of such broadly defined and indeterminate rights are not thought practical nor sound geopolitical policy.

Since the United States has not ratified the CESCR, the General Comment has neither force nor effect on its international responsibilities. In point of fact, the United States may be seen as probably violating the right to health—surely not because it

59 J. Mann, 'Medicine and Public Health, Ethics and Human Rights' (1997) 37 *Hastings Center Report* 6, 8.

60 R. Beddard and D.M. Hill (eds), *Economic, Social and Cultural Rights: Progress and Achievement* (New York: Palgrave Macmillan, 1992) 201.

61 Brown, 'WHO Puts Price Tag on Preventing Fatal Illnesses' (n 10). See J.S. Bhandri and A.O. Sykes (eds), *Economic Dimensions in International Law* (Cambridge: CUP, 1998); G.P. Smith, II, *Distributive Justice and The New Medicine* (London: Edward Elgar 2008) ch 2.

62 General Comment 14, E/C 12/2000/4, 4 July 2000, available at <http://www.unhchr.ch/tbs/doc.nsg/>.

63 General Comment 14 (n 62). Sadly, Art 12(2) of the International Covenant is far too general to provide clear insight into concrete actions states parties need to take in order to be in compliance. D.P. Fidler, *International Law and Infectious Diseases* (Oxford: OUP, 1989) 188.

64 General Comment 14 (n 62).

65 General Comment 14 (n 62).

spends too little on health care and public health—but rather because its resources are distributed inequitably.[66]

5. Insurmountable Difficulties?

For any working definition of a right to health, health care, or health protection to have contemporary relevance, it must first include recognition of an obligation of the state 'to ensure the conditions necessary for the health of individuals'.[67] Even though the UN Committee on Economic, Social, and Cultural Rights has determined broadly what the core state obligations necessary to attain a standard of health are, there is no universal consensus on what minimal *conditions* are necessary for health[68]—this, because of the almost inextricable relation its recognition as a perfect or imperfect right has with the level of cultural and economic development of each state within the world community.[69] Inevitably, then, individual claims to health right protections must be balanced within a utilitarian construct against societal or communal needs.[70] The result of this often means that equity is forsaken for economic stability.

Organizationally, at the supranational level of administration, the internal weaknesses of the UN Security Council and the International Court of Justice for enforcing violations of human rights are compounded—in specific health policies—by the WHO's inability to assume a decisive leadership role. Indeed, the WHO has been reluctant to utilize its legal powers—or to adopt legal principles—which implement directly health care strategies. It has chosen instead to adopt a functional or technical approach to health care matters—thereby developing a well regarded and limited reputation for the collection of data and for technical standardization of international health regulations.[71]

Recommendations, resolutions, codes of conduct, and technical standards, then, make up the arsenal used by the WHO to impact health issues transnationally.[72] Whether this is viewed as an effective, systematic, and assertive approach to problem-solving is questionable. In the absence of the use of the treaty-making process, however,

66 L. Gostin, 'The Human Right to Health: A Right to the Highest Attainable Health' (2001) 31 *Hastings Center Report* 29, 30. Indeed, the WHO ranked performance of the US health care system 37th among all nations, due to disparities by race and income. See Kinney, 'The International Human Right to Health' (n 15). See also D. Orientlicher, 'Rights to Healthcare in the United States' (2012) 38 *American Journal of Law and Medicine* 326.

67 Gostin and Lazzarini, *Human Rights and Public Health* (n 33) 29.

68 Mann, 'Medicine and Public Health' (n 59).

69 Kirby, 'The Right to Health Fifty Years On' (n 54) 18.

70 Gostin and Lazzarini, *Human Rights and Public Health* (n 33) 4, 33–4; and Annas, *Some Choices* (n 52).

71 A. Lakin, 'The Legal Powers of the World Health Organization' (1997) 3 *Medical Law International* 23, 24. See generally Y. Arai-Takahashi, 'The Role of International Health and The WHO in The Regulation of Public Health' in R. Martin and L. Johnson (eds), *Law and the Public Dimension of Health* (London: Cavendish, 2001) ch 4; Steiner, Alston, and Goodman, *International Human Rights in Context* (n 31) ch. 9.

72 Lakin, 'The Legal Powers of the World Health Organization' (n 71) 24, 33–4. Revised International Health Regulations (IHL), which entered into effect in 2007, are a noble effort to effect a multilateral agreement geared at facilitating cooperation through information-sharing in disease control by prescribing (voluntary) obligations for WHO member states to meet. There is, however, no effective enforcement mechanism to ensure compliance with these regulations. The effectiveness of the work of the WHO is limited severely by this state-centered model of voluntary disease control. The enforcement powers of the WHO would be strengthened immeasurably if the World Trade Organization's dispute settlement system was to be adopted. D. Fidler et al, 'Strategies for Implementing the New International Health Regulations' (2008) 86 *Bulletin of the World Health Organization* 215.

it is feared that the leadership ability of the WHO and, for that matter, other international organizations, will remain limited—this, due inherently to the continuing domination of independent states.[73]

5.1 An uncertain future

Regardless of which approach is taken to resolving the complex definitional issues of human rights and their scope, the over-riding need is for more explicit implementation standards to be articulated and developed in order to reflect the dynamic quality of a modern human rights doctrine.[74] The very imprecision in problems of definition as well as measurement, monitoring, and enforcement have been roadblocks to applying useful economic, social, and cultural rights. Indeed, some consider them insuperable obstacles.[75] Until all countries ratify the ICESCR, establish the domestic capability to monitor the successful enjoyment of these covenant rights, and create a complaint and investigative process when allegations of human rights violations occur, no resounding progress or success will be recorded.[76]

Concrete steps have been taken to address many of these concerns. Central to this agenda for change has been the 11th Additional Protocol to The European Convention for the Protection of Human Rights and Fundamental Freedoms, which has streamlined a new complaint procedure for individual human rights complaints and interstate complaint procedures for all state parties.[77] As well, the Commission on Human Rights and other specialized agencies[78] provide a venue for individual human rights complaints. The current efforts of a Working Group of the UN Human Rights Commission to study and (it is hoped) resolve the issue of whether human rights are universal and, thus, should be enforced under one mechanism, can have nothing but a salutary effect on clarifying the issues of justiciability.[79] Prevailing authority holds that violations of both social and cultural rights generally, and violations of the right to health in particular, are not justiciable and are thus unsuitable as bases for judicial overview because of their indeterminancy.[80]

Whether justiciability of economic, social, cultural, and health rights is achieved (as it has been for civil and political rights)[81] in the future, depends in very large measure upon the willingness of the courts to recognize and enforce them. Perhaps as important is whether there is a demonstrable level of economic prosperity achieved nationally which accommodates a recognition, and a guarantee, of these rights.[82] Even though a

73 Lakin, 'The Legal Powers of the World Health Organization' (n 71) 24, 33–4.

74 Gostin and Lazzarini, *Human Rights and Public Health* (n 33) 35.

75 Gostin and Lazzarini, *Human Rights and Public Health* (n 33) 35.

76 Gostin and Lazzarini, *Human Rights and Public Health* (n 33) 35. cf A Harrington, 'Don't Mind the Gap: The Rise of Individual Complaint Mechanisms within International Human Rights' (2012) 22 *Duke Journal of Comparative and International Law* 153.

77 See Novak, *Introduction to the International Human Rights Regime* (n 46) 163–5. See also, Harrington, 'Don't Mind the Gap' (n 76).

78 M. Dennis and D. Steward, 'Justiciability of Economic, Social, and Cultural Rights: Should There Be an International Complaints Mechanism to Adjudicate The Rights to Food, Housing and Health?' (2004) 98 *American Journal of International Law* 462, 560.

79 Dennis and Steward, 'Justiciability of Economic, Social, and Cultural Rights' (n 78) 462–3.

80 Toebes, *The Right to Health* (n 39) 168.

81 Toebes, *The Right to Health* (n 39) 231, 232, 345. See Zewart, 'Using Local Culture' (n 29); and Steiner and Alston, *International Human Rights in Context* (n 55) 275–8.

82 Toebes, *The Right to Health* (n 39) 349.

discernible trend is seen toward such a recognition,[83] the fact remains that without a sustained level of economic stability, justiciability will not be validated for claims to either a right to health, health care, or health protection. To be remembered is the fact that Article 2(1) of the ICESCR allows the realization of rights set out within it by the state signatories 'progressively' *and* 'to the maximum of a State's available resources'. Thus, the principle of progressive realization has the very real effect of emasculating any concerted and sustained attempt to structure a universal right to health—this, because the justifiable differences among states (timely or otherwise) in this area of concern are based upon their varying respective degrees of political will and levels of economic resources.[84] So long as their compliance efforts move 'progressively' toward the goal of realizing the Article 12 right to health, no violations are registered.[85]

Perhaps the self-defeating weakness of the whole enforcement structure is its reliance upon a voluntary system of compliance and self-policing efforts by individual states. Inevitably, self-interest shapes and controls the ultimate response to a violation of human rights as well as health care protections which are an inherent part of those basic rights.[86]

6. Building a Global Framework for A New Constitutionalism

The 1988 Universal Declaration on Human Genome and Human Rights,[87] the 2003 International Declaration on Human Genetic Data,[88] and the 2005 Universal Bioethics Declaration[89] are pivotal to a new global effort to maintain a framework to advance a contemporary bioethics/human rights constitutionalism.[90] These three United Nations Declarations, together with, as seen, the Universal Declaration of Human Rights,[91] the International Covenant on Civil and Political Rights,[92] and the International Covenant on Economic, Cultural and Social Rights,[93] contain numerous principles and obligations that bear a direct relationship to norms of medical ethics.[94] Provisions requiring respect for human dignity and equality, the right to life, freedom from arbitrary interference with privacy, and the realization of a standard of living promotive of health and medical care, together with the right to share in scientific advancements and the right to be free from inhuman and degrading treatment, all underscore and, indeed, link, bioethics, medical ethics, and human rights[95] as a policy-making triad of potential force.

83 Toebes, *The Right to Health* (n 39) 349. See also B. Meir, 'Breathing Life into the Framework Convention on Tobacco Control: Smoking Cessation and The Right to Health' (2005) 5 *Yale Journal of Health Policy Law and Ethics* 137, 159; and Bhandri and Sykes, *Economic Dimensions in International Law* (n 61).

84 Toebes, *The Right to Health* (n 39) 349.

85 Gostin and Lazzarini, *Human Rights and Public Health* (n 33) 8, 9. See Arras and Fenton, 'Bioethics and Human Rights' (n 27) 32 and Steiner and Alston, *International Human Rights in Context* (n 55) 302–7.

86 See generally H. Koh, 'How Is International Human Rights Law Enforced?' (1999) 74 *Indiana Law Journal* 1397.

87 UNESCO, Final Report, B10-97 CONF 201/9 (22–25 July 1997).

88 UNESCO, 32/C Res 22 (16 October 2003).

89 See <http://www.unesco.org/new/en/social—and—human—sciences/themes/bioethics/bioethics—an_human_rights>.

90 See G. Smith, 'Bioethics and Human Rights: Toward a New Constitutionalism' (2011) 13 *Constitutional Law and Policy Review* 68.

91 UNGA Res 217A (III), UNGA Res 217A (III) (n 19).

92 16 December 1966, 933 UNTS 3 (the US is not a party).

93 16 December 1966, 999 UNTS 171 (the US is a party, subject to several reservations, understandings, and declarations).

94 Koh, 'How Is International Human Rights Law Enforced?' (n 86).

95 Smith, 'Human Rights and Bioethics' (2005) (n 16).

On 19 October 2005, UNESCO's member states adopted, by acclamation, the Universal Declaration on Bioethics and Human Rights.[96] Enunciating a Principle of Social Responsibility codified in Article 14, the Declaration directs decisions and practice in science and technology to advance 'the common good' by providing 'access to quality health care and essential medicines', providing 'access to adequate nutrition and water', improving living conditions, eliminating the marginalization of persons, and reducing poverty and illiteracy.[97] Building on this delineation of social responsibility, Article 15 directs the benefits of scientific research to advance, among other interests, 'access to quality health care' and 'support for health services'.[98]

Finally, again underscoring the responsibility of the state to promote and safeguard public health standards, Article 23 of the Declaration urges that proportionate measures designed to accord respect for 'human dignity, human rights and fundamental freedoms' be undertaken when there are 'threats of serious or irreversible damage to public health or human welfare'.[99] In this regard, the Declaration is to be seen as a bold effort to recognize—and thereby validate—the inextricable relationship between human dignity and human rights with access to health care.[100]

Although of marginal regulatory impact owing to its limited ratification, the European Convention on Human Rights and Biomedicine is another bold illustration of a direct overlapping of contemporary bioethics and medical ethics with the norms of international human rights. Within the scope of this Convention are found policies regulating equitable access to health care, informed consent, rights to information, and restrictions on the use of the human genome and scientific research, together with regulations on organ and tissue removal from living donors for transplantation.[101]

Some of the principles contained within this Human Rights and Biomedicine Convention (for example the right to life, to physical integrity and privacy, as well as the prohibition of inhumane or degrading treatment and all forms of discrimination) have, previously, been included in other international human rights treaties—such as the International Convention on Civil and Political Rights and the European Convention on Human Rights of 1950.[102] The significant achievement of this Convention is that—for the first time—these rights have been codified as a framework for action within one, single multilateral *binding* instrument devoted entirely to biomedical issues.[103] The importance of reaching an agreement on common standards in this field is that these standards serve as a tangible first step toward the development of regulating schemes at national levels which, in reality, is the primary level at which human rights are realized.[104]

96 UNESCO, Final Report (n 87).

97 UNESCO, Final Report (n 87).

98 UNESCO, Final Report (n 87).

99 See A. McHarg, 'Reconciling Human Rights and the Public Interest: Conceptual Problems and Doctrinal Uncertainty in the Jurisprudence of the European Court of Human Rights' (1999) 62 *Modern Law Review* 671.

100 E. Wicks, *Human Rights and Healthcare* (Oxford: Hart, 2007) 12–14, ch 4, observing that autonomy and dignity underlie modern human rights. See generally G. Dworkin, *The Theory and Practice of Autonomy* (Cambridge: CUP, 1988).

101 Smith, 'Human Rights and Bioethics' (2005) (n 16).

102 R. Andorno, 'The Oviedo Convention: A European Legal Framework at the Intersection of Human Rights and Health Law' (2005) 2 *Journal of International Biotechnology Law* 133.

103 Andorno, 'The Oviedo Convention' (n 102) 143.

104 Andorno, 'The Oviedo Convention' (n 102). See also Smith, 'Human Rights and Bioethics' (2005) (n 16); Toebes, *The Right to Health* (n 39) 293–332; and Steiner and Alston, *International Human Rights in Context* (n 55).

Noble though the spirit and the design of these United Nations Conventions and Declarations may be, the salutary effect they have as types of international constitutional frameworks or constructs for the New Age of Biotechnology, they remain inherently flawed. This defectiveness is seen when it is remembered that covenants, statutes, protocols, and conventions are legally binding *only* for those states that ratify or accede to them.[105] The extent to which international instruments are accepted and implemented is—as seen—determined by the economic, social, and cultural self-interests of each state.

Any effort to structure, and then enforce, a right to health, as a social or cultural right, is—as seen—subject to the standards of progressivity,[106] a flawed enforcement mechanism allowing states to remain immune from actual human rights violations *so long as* they can demonstrate that they are moving progressively (or at least measurably) towards the realization of these rights.[107] Ultimately, then, economic self-interest and survival determine at what level of recognition and enforcement health care protections are validated as an integral part of social, cultural, political, or human rights. In order to secure sustainable human rights at the national level, there must be a strong civil society operating freely.[108]

Another illustration of the obstacles for implementing a human right to health or health protection is to be seen in the action of the WHO in revising the International Health Regulation in 2007 designed, as such, to set obligations for the 193 member states of the WHO in relation to the notification of infectious diseases at ports and airports and also to set maximum measures that countries may take during outbreaks of disease.[109] Although these new regulations require member states of the WHO to identify and respond to public health issues, they *do not* require the states to be proactive in addressing the conditions that foster disease. Indeed, the laws of member states of the WHO are generally only within the jurisdictional boundaries of the states. And, predictably, the states take quite different regulatory approaches to biotechnology and related public health issues. Our understanding of both health and health rights is shaped by contemporary definitions of disease and of health and also by our wealth or poverty, which in turn affects the social infrastructures that provide the necessary conditions for good health.[110]

Incentives to encourage compliance among the poorer countries need to be developed in order to ensure the enforcement and implementation of these new health requirements. Equitable incentive programs can be developed only from 'international consensus building and regulating harmonization only by engaging in dialogue that an

105 Smith, 'Human Rights and Bioethics' (2005) (n 16) 1320–1.

106 Smith, 'Human Rights and Bioethics' (2005) (n 16) 1301; Bhandri and Sykes, *Economic Dimensions in International Law* (n 61); and Steiner and Alston, *International Human Rights in Context* (n 55). See Steiner, Alston and Goodman, *International Human Rights in Context* (n 31) 302–7.

107 Smith, 'Human Rights and Bioethics' (2005) (n 16) 1320–1. Two landmark cases before the South African Constitutional Court decided in 2000 and 2002 respectively, *Government of the Republic of South Africa v Grootboom* 11 BCLR 1169 (CC) and *Minister of Health v Treatment Action Campaign* 10 BCLR 1033 (CC), gave a new interpretative gloss to the principle of progressivity by holding that while each citizen did not have an individual right to decent shelter or appropriate health, the government has an obligation to take these two broad constitutional rights declared in the South African Constitution seriously and to adopt reasonable programs which attempt to ensure their implementation for all citizens of these two social-economic rights. See C.R. Sunstein, *The Second Bill of Rights* (New York: Basic Books, 2004) 211 passim.

108 Bennett, 'Globalising Rights?' (n 28); and Smith, 'Bioethics and Human Rights' (n 90).

109 B.J. Bennett, *Health Law's Kaleidoscope: Health Law Rights* (Aldershot: Ashgate, 2008) ch 6.

110 Bennett, 'Globalising Rights?' (n 28).

understanding can be achieved on points of agreement and disagreement'.[111] From this can come, ideally, an international consensus, as the ethical challenges emerge and a common moral ground is found to guide the development of appropriate laws and policies to meet these challenges.

7. Conclusion

The work of the Bill and Melinda Gates Foundation, as well as that of countless NGOs and humanitarian groups toward combating world poverty and injustice, should be recognized as a synergistic force for not only advancing a transnational ethic supporting the notion of global health, but as a force for stabilizing impoverished Third World states with economic assistance.[112] Once stabilized, the states are then better equipped to work collectively toward accepting a shared level of responsibility for recognizing and providing health commensurate with other fundamental civil, social, and political rights.

The right of every human being to, in the words of the UN Bioethics Declaration, 'the highest attainable standard of health', calls for the need for informed and vigorous debate.[113] The recognition in an international instrument, even one that is non-binding and in need of further refinement, that such access is an aspect of contemporary and universal human rights, is a step in the right direction.

The nobility of purpose and the idealism behind the efforts of the United Nations[114]—and especially through the work of UNESCO to advance and protect human rights by building substantive and procedural frameworks for action—should be seen as sources for optimism and a pathway 'towards human progress and enlightenment'.[115] In a very positive way, specifically through its Universal Declarations on Bioethics and Human Rights, Genetic Data, and the Human Genome, the United Nations is promoting a new type of global constitutionalism in health-related rights.[116] The extent to which the members of the world community both ratify and pursue these efforts, and thereby show a willingness for legal change,[117] remains to be seen.[118]

111 Bennett, 'Globalising Rights?' (n 28).

112 Garrett, 'The Challenge of Global Health' (n 4); and 'The Birth of Philanthrocapitalism' (n 6).

113 M.D. Kirby, 'Human Rights and Bioethics: The Universal Declaration of Human Rights and UNESCO Universal Declaration of Bioethics and Human Rights' (2010) 25 *Journal of Contemporary Health Law and Policy* 325. See generally C. Foster, *Human Dignity in Bioethics and Law* (Oxford: Hart, 2011).

114 Kirby, 'Human Rights and Bioethics' (n 113) 325.

115 Kirby, 'Human Rights and Bioethics' (n 113) 325.

116 Smith, 'Bioethics and Human Rights' (n 90). See Foster, *Human Dignity in Bioethics and Law* (n 113) ch 7, analyzing the international instruments dealing specifically with Health Care Law and Bioethics. See also J. Waldron, 'How Law Protects Dignity' (2012) 71 *Cambridge Law Review* 200, 221, 222, referencing the influences of Art 3 of the Geneva Conventions; Art 7 of the ICCPR; and Art 3 of the ECHR as codifications of a commitment to protect and respect human dignity. See generally I.G. Cohen (ed), *The Globalization of Health Care: Legal and Ethical Issues* (Oxford: OUP, 2013); S. Jasanoff (ed), *Reframing Rights: Bioconstitutionalism in the Genetic Age* (Cambridge, MA: MIT Press, 2012).

117 Koh, 'How Is International Human Rights Law Enforced?' (n 86); and Kinney, 'The International Human Right to Health' (n 15); and Kinney and Clark, 'Provisions for Health and Health Care' (n 58). See generally M.D. Kirby, 'Law Reform as Ministering to Justice' in A.R. Blackshield (ed), *Legal Change: Essays in Honour of Julius Stone* (Sydney: Butterworths, 1983).

118 A note of positivism is seen in the work of Professor Laurence Gostin and his colleagues at the O'Neill Institute for National and Global Health Law, Georgetown University, in their efforts to strengthen global health law. See L.O. Gostin, 'A Framework Convention on Global Health: Health for All, Justice for All' (2012) 307 *Journal of the American Medical Association* 2087.

26

Environmental Sustainability and Global Health Law

The Case Study of Globalizing Artificial Photosynthesis

Tom A. Faunce, Anton Wasson, and Kim Crow

1. Introduction

The reality of anthropogenic climate change and its adverse global health and environmental impacts, biodiversity loss, pollution, and interference with the bio-chemical boundaries for safe occupation of the planet, highlight the importance of considering global human health and its governance in close connection with that of our biosphere. Yet jurisprudence related to global health remains fundamentally anthropocentric. Distributive justice and respect for human dignity, for example, are central to academic and policy debates over normative responses to climate change yet have a primary focus on the interests, responsibilities, and rights of human beings. The hypothesis explored here is that the normative basis of global health law, particularly as a result of the pressures first mentioned, is undergoing a shift in which environmental sustainability is granted equivalent status with distributive justice as a foundational social virtue. The increasing consideration being given to the granting of enforceable legal rights to ecosystems (wilderness areas, rivers, forests, valleys, for example) appears to be a manifestation of this normative transition.

The case study used here to explore this issue involves the potential global utilization of artificial photosynthesis technology in all human structures (roads, buildings, vehicles, for example). Large national research projects are now focused on utilizing a variety of approaches, including nanotechnology, to not only replicate but also improve upon the process of photosynthesis (in very basic and simplified terms the creation of hydrogen fuels and food using sunlight, water, and carbon dioxide). This new technology could have significant health impacts globally—not only adding atmospheric oxygen but reducing morbidity and mortality from lack of safe, accessible energy for heating, cooking, and transport, providing locally sourced hydrogen fuel and water (burning hydrogen produces a relatively small amount of fresh water), starch-based food and greenhouse gas mitigation (from atmospheric carbon dioxide reduction), as well as fertilizer (by fixing atmospheric nitrogen as ammonia). Our hypothesis is that the global roll-out of such 'green' technology is likely to be facilitated if governed by principles and instruments arising from a more non-anthropocentric, environmental sustainability-focused global health law. As will be explained, this may have health law reform implications ranging from domestic legal patent regimes to World Trade Organization (WTO) agreements, bilateral, regional, and international trade and investment agreements, the United Nations Millennium Development Goals, and a host of international conventions and declarations concerning climate change, the right to enjoy the benefits of science and its applications, the right to health and the concept of the common heritage of humanity.

2. Environmental Sustainability as a Foundational Social Virtue

Just as with human individuals, societies develop and maintain virtues through commitment (often overtly associated with conscience) to consistently implement, in the face of obstacles, principles applicable equally to the actions of most people. Legal institutions at community, national, and international levels are critical to this process. When running efficiently it results in a transparent and accountable governance framework known as the 'rule of law' which some jurisprudential scholars (in recent times notably John Rawls and Ronald Dworkin) influentially have linked to the ideal of a freely consented social contract. The consistent and predictable application of general principles, more specific rules, and rights derived from those foundational virtues, in turn sustains them and the society they characterize. Distributive justice, freedom, and equality are widely regarded as examples of foundational social virtues underpinning a normative system such as global health law.[1]

Yet the environmental context in which we debate the existence and application of such virtues and the principles derived from them is rapidly changing. Scientific evidence, for instance, now seems overwhelming that climate change is likely to have a devastating impact on the health of many societies, with more adverse impacts on vulnerable populations, other species, and continuing harm to the interests of future generations.

The notion of distributive justice, for instance, arguably underpins the notion of 'common but differentiated responsibilities' that itself forms the normative basis of a central document for global health law, the United Nations Framework Convention on Climate Change (UNFCCC).[2] The UNFCCC requires developed countries (Annex II states) to 'provide such financial resources, including for the transfer of technology, needed by developing country Parties to meet the agreed full incremental costs of implementing measures'[3] agreed between the developing countries and the financial mechanism of the convention, the Global Environment Facility (GEF).[4] All parties under the convention are to cooperate in the 'development, application and diffusion'[5] of technologies to combat climate change, including obligations to engage in technology transfer recognizing common but differentiated responsibilities and national and regional development priorities.[6] Indeed the extent to which developing countries need to meet their obligations under this agreement depends on the 'effective implementation by developed country Parties of their commitments under the Convention related to financial resources and transfer of technology and will take fully into account that economic and social development and poverty eradication are the first and overriding priorities of the developing country Parties'.[7]

[1] I. Kant, 'Principles of the Doctrine of Virtue' in M.J. Gregor (ed), *Collected Works* (San Francisco, CA: Harper & Row, 1996) 502. J. Rawls, *A Theory of Justice* (Harvard, MA: 1st edn, Harvard University Press, 1971). R. Dworkin, *Law's Empire* (Stanford, CA: 3rd edn, Stanford University Press, 2012). T.A. Faunce, *Who Owns Our Health* (Baltimore, MD: Johns Hopkins University Press, 2009).

[2] United Nations Framework Convention on Climate Change, opened for signature 9 May 1992, 1771 UNTS 107, S Treaty Doc No 102-38.

[3] UNFCCC (n 2) Art 4.3.

[4] UNFCCC (n 2) Art 11.

[5] UNFCCC (n 2) Art 4.1(c).

[6] UNFCCC (n 2) Art 4.1.

[7] UNFCCC (n 2) Art 4.7.

Under the Kyoto Protocol to the UNFCCC[8] (under which the greenhouse gas emission reduction targets for 2013–20 were by 2014 still to enter into force) the commitments are expanded to require diffusion of technology to all countries but with an emphasis on developing countries; all parties committing to:

> ... the promotion of effective modalities for the development, application and diffusion of, and take all practicable steps to promote, facilitate and finance, as appropriate, the transfer of, or access to, environmentally sound technologies, know-how, practices and processes pertinent to climate change, in particular to developing countries, including the formulation of policies and programs for the effective transfer of environmentally sound technologies that are publicly owned or in the public domain and the creation of an enabling environment for the private sector, to promote and enhance the transfer of, and access to, environmentally sound technologies.'[9]

One area identified as enabling such private and public sector technology transfer is the protection of intellectual property rights.[10] The Copenhagen Accord, a non-binding political agreement developed through the UNFCCC, established the Copenhagen Green Climate Fund and a mechanism to accelerate the development and transfer of renewable energy technology.[11]

Yet, significant jurisprudential difficulties have arisen in incorporating this combined global health threat (to human populations and their environment) into established jurisprudential theories of distributive justice. Theories focused on welfare components, sharing of resources or enhancing capabilities, while emphasizing principles of reciprocity, equality, priority, or sufficiency, struggle to deal with just access of populations to something as ubiquitous as the atmosphere and climate. Similarly, future generations and ecosystems, though their health is increasingly considered relevant in global health law debates, have a problematic status as ethical interest or legal rights holders under most established systems of distributive justice. Also problematic is the fact that human-driven climate change operates on a time scale beyond the experience of most contemporary policy-makers and its related equity issues are controversially framed in terms of economy-threatening national aggregate or per capita, historical industrial-related responsibilities for greenhouse gas emissions, severity of likely impacts (prolonged droughts in developing sub-tropical regions), or education and financial capacity to cope.[12]

Calls have been made for a new normative approach that more transparently and comprehensively encompasses our environmental duties and motivates people to respect them. Theorists supporting in this context the role of distributive justice, for example, could simply borrow appropriate bits and pieces from the normative foundations of contemporary environmental law—such as theories relating to the commons, public choice, welfare economics, and ecology. Likewise, they could draw upon aspects of cosmopolitan political theory, or promote incremental change based on new,

[8] Kyoto Protocol to the United Nations Framework on Climate Change UN Doc FCCC/CP/1997/7/Add. 1, Dec. 10, 1997; 37 ILM 22 (1998).

[9] Kyoto Protocol (n 8) Art 10(c).

[10] C. Hutchison, 'Does TRIPS Facilitate or Impede Climate Change Technology Transfer into Developing Countries?' (2006) 3 *University of Ottawa Law and Technology Journal* 524.

[11] UNFCCC (n 2).

[12] E.A. Page, *Climate Change, Justice and Future Generations* (Cheltenham: Edward Elgar, 2006). W. Steffen, 'A Truly Complex and Diabolical Problem' in J.S. Dryzek, R.S. Norgaard, and D. Schlosberg, *Climate Change and Society* (Oxford: OUP, 2011) 21.

globally democratic processes of adjudication or legislation.[13] A more elegant approach, it is argued here, is simply to accept that the situation requires the theoretical development of a non-anthropogenic foundational social virtue: environmental sustainability.

That environmental sustainability is a worthy candidate for such a foundational jurisprudential virtue already emerges, it can reasonably be claimed, in the first place from the widespread resonance in influential environmental policy lobby groups of so-called 'ecocentric' or 'biocentric' ethics. This is linked with so-called 'Gaia Theory' (which treats the processes underlying the biogeochemical homeostasis of the earth as akin to those of a single living entity), or 'Deep Ecology' (in which the interests and rights of the natural world are considered no less important than those of humanity) and finding soft-norm expression in documents like the Earth Charter or Earth Manifesto. Environmental sustainability, when articulated from such sources, appears as an emerging social virtue giving rise to two primary principles (the consistent application of which sustains the virtue itself). The first is that the flourishing and diversity of non-human life-forms should have intrinsic value requiring protection by policies and technologies that reduce the number of humans along with their demands on those other species. The second holds that human flourishing itself should require a deepening respect for right relationships with ecosystems that are reflected in the choices our species makes about the use of new technologies.

Such thinking suggests that the community of global health law scholars ought to begin consideration of including amongst that field's recognized foundational social virtues, one by which the planet is encouraged to be treated by both science and governance systems as a patient[14] and new technology facilitating environmental sustainability treated as a form of planetary medicine.[15] This might result in environmental sustainability being added to the standard bioethics canon of autonomy, nonmaleficence, beneficence, and justice in a new sub-specialty of 'planetary medicine' that linked the sciences of epidemiology, environmental safety, and a global expanded conception of physiology.[16] Issues of climate change, poverty, and lack of access to healthy food and fuel could then be viewed, not (as they have traditionally) as issues of distributive justice, but as global environment pathologies to be remedied in part by commitment to environmental sustainability amongst systems of global health law.

That the virtue of ecological sustainability has an inseparable connection with global health was an idea influentially propounded by ecoeconomists such as Ernest Schumacher (with his concept of 'small (and local) is beautiful') and Kenneth Boulding (with his idea of 'Spaceship Earth' as a closed economy requiring recycling of resources).[17] In doing

13 D. Jamieson, 'Ethics, Public Policy, Global Warming' in D. Jamieson (ed), *Morality's Progress: Essays on Humans, Other Animals and the Rest of Nature* (Oxford: Clarendon Press, 2003) 282; R. Cunningham, 'The Tragedy of (Ignoring) the Information Semicommons: A Cultural Environmental Perspective' (2010) 4 *Akron Intellectual Property Journal* 1; P.G. Harris, 'Reconceptualizing Global Governance' in J.S. Dryzek, R.S. Norgaard, and D. Schlosberg, *Climate Change and Society* (Oxford: OUP, 2011) 639; W.F. Baber and R.V. Bartlett, 'The Role of International Law in Global Governance' in *Climate Change and Society* (see previously) 652.

14 T. McMichael, 'The Biosphere, Health and "Sustainability"' (2002) 297 *Science* 1093; J. Lovelock, *Gaia, the Practical Science of Planetary Medicine* (London: OUP, 1991).

15 T.A. Faunce, 'Governing Planetary Nanomedicine: Environmental Sustainability and a UNESCO Universal Declaration on the Bioethics and Human Rights of Natural and Artificial Photosynthesis (Global Solar Fuels and Foods)' (2012) 6 *Nanoethics* 15.

16 T.L. Beauchamp and J.F. Childress, *Principles of Biomedical Ethics* (New York: OUP, 2012).

17 E.F. Schumacher, *Small is Beautiful: A Study of Economics as if People Mattered* (London: Random House, 2011); K.E. Boulding, 'The Economics of the Coming Spaceship Earth' in H. Jarrett (ed), *Environmental Quality in a Growing Economy* (Baltimore, MD: Johns Hopkins Press, 1966).

this, the former drew upon Buddhist ethical principles and virtues, while the latter relied upon those from the Quaker tradition. The economist Herman Daly similarly drew on the laws of thermodynamics and the tendency of the universe to greater entropy (dispersal of energy) to champion the idea of a steady state economy.[18]

The fundamental connection to environmental sustainability is also implicit in many of the central normative statements of global health law. Article 12 of the International Covenant on Economic, Social and Cultural Rights (ICESCR), for example, proclaims the 'right of everyone to the enjoyment of the highest attainable standard of physical and mental health'.[19] There are countless examples of threats to human health, as projected by this chapter, caused by the disruption of the sustainability of ecosystems, for example the contamination of water and food supply, and air pollution leading to acute respiratory diseases; and authoritative backing (through the General Comment on the Right to Health of the Committee on Economic, Social and Cultural Rights (CESCR), 'international assistance and cooperation, especially economic and technical') for States to satisfy obligations related to them.[20]

An issue that needs to be considered in this context is the relationship between 'environmental sustainability' and 'sustainable development'. Principle 1 of the Rio Declaration states that 'human beings are at the centre of concerns for sustainable development [and] they are entitled to a healthy and productive life in harmony with nature'.[21] The Stockholm Declaration affirms that a '[hu]man has the fundamental right to freedom, equality and adequate conditions of life, in an environment of quality that permits a life of dignity'.[22] The World Commission on Forests and Sustainable Development likewise explicitly states that the whole issue of forest ecosystems *is about people*. The report compiles the number of lives and livelihoods lost as a result of disruption in the forest ecosystem.[23]

In international law, the concept of sustainability wends back to human economic concerns in areas such as forestry and fisheries—'sustainability' meant the maintenance of the long-term productivity of these resources. The Convention on Wetlands of International Importance (Ramsar Convention) uses the phrase 'wise use' instead of sustainability. Sustainable utilization thus was defined as 'the human use of wetland so that it may yield the greatest continuous benefit to present generations while maintaining its potential to meet the needs and aspirations of future generations'.[24] The Brundtland Report, by the United Nations Commission on Environment and Development, defined sustainable development as 'meeting the needs of the present without compromising the ability of the future generations to meet their own needs'.[25]

18 T.A. Faunce, *Nanotechnology for a Sustainable World. Global Artificial Photosynthesis as the Moral Culmination of Nanotechnology* (Cheltenham: Edward Elgar, 2012).

19 International Covenant on Economic, Social and Cultural Rights, adopted 16 December 1966, entered into force 1 March 1976, 993 UNTS 3.

20 CESCR 'General Comment 14' in 'The Right to the Highest Attainable Standard of Health' (1994) UN Doc E/C.12.2000/4.

21 UNCED, 'Rio Declaration on Environment and Development' (1992) UN Doc A/CONF.151/26 (vol I).

22 UNGA, 'Declaration of the United Nations Conference on the Human Environment' (1972) UN Doc A/Conf.48/14/Rev 1.

23 E. Salim, O. Ullsten, and World Commission on Forests and Sustainable Development, *Our Forests, Our Future: Report of the World Commission on Forests and Sustainable Development* (Cambridge: CUP, 1999).

24 Convention on Wetlands of International Importance especially as Waterfowl Habitat, adopted 2 February 1971, entered into force 21 December 1975, 996 UNTS 245.

25 G.H. Brundtland, and World Commission on Environment and Development, *Our Common Future* (New York: OUP, 1987).

Judge Weeramantry of the International Court of Justice stated, in *Gabcikovo-Nagymaros Project (Hungary v Slovakia)*, that the principle of sustainable development, as formulated in the Brundtland Report, the Rio Declaration, and United Nations Agenda 21, forms part of the basic principle of law of civilized nations under Article 38(1) of the Statute of the International Court of Justice. He stated that damage to the environment could impair and undermine all the human rights spoken of in the United Nations Universal Declaration on Human Rights and other human rights instruments. Thus, he held, while governments have the right to initiate development projects for the benefit of their people, there is likewise a duty to ensure that those projects do not significantly damage the environment.[26] Such statements represented, as is characteristic of some of the great judicial dissents, a prescient and visionary jurisprudential extension of sympathy and understanding.

The judge found the principle of sustainable development supported by resolutions of the United Nations General Assembly, and various United Nations conventions (treaties binding under international law), such as the United Nations Convention to Combat Desertification in those Countries Experiencing Serious Droughts and/or Desertification, Particularly in Africa (UNCCD), the UNFCCC, and the Convention on Biological Diversity (CBD). The CBD, for the purpose of creating international legal norms, defines an ecosystem as a 'dynamic complex of plant, animal and micro-organism communities and their non-living environment interacting as a functional unit'.[27]

The majority in *Gabcikovo-Nagymaros Project (Hungary v Slovakia)*, while not going quite so far, also held:

> Throughout the ages, mankind has, for economic and other reasons, constantly interfered with nature. In the past, this was often done without consideration of the effects upon the environment. Owing to new scientific insights and to a growing awareness of the risks for mankind—for present and future generations—of pursuit of such interventions at an unconsidered and unabated pace, new norms and standards have been developed, set forth in a great number of instruments during the last two decades. Such new norms have to be taken into consideration, and such new standards given proper weight, not only when States contemplate new activities but also when continuing with activities begun in the past. This need to reconcile economic development with protection of the environment is aptly expressed in the concept of sustainable development.[28]

Sustainable development is likely to emerge reasonably soon as a principle of international customary law; environmental sustainability represents a much deeper and more complex jurisprudential challenge. A more ready-made way, however, in which environmental sustainability may appear in the normative foundations of global health law involves the precautionary principle. This emerged in German regulatory policy during the 1970s and rapidly spread through the international policy arena. The precautionary principle has now been incorporated into a number of specific laws on environmental protection relating to the ozone layer, climate change, biological

26 *Gabcikovo-Nagymaros Project (Hungary v Slovakia)* [1997] ICJ Rep 7.

27 S. Stec, 'Do Two Wrongs Make a Right? Adjudicating Sustainable Development in the Danube Dam Case' (1999) 29 *Golden Gate University Law Review* 317. Also supporting the norm of sustainable development, Judge Weeramantry held, were the preamble of the North American Free Trade Agreement between Canada, Mexico, and the United States, the preamble to the Marrakesh Agreement of 1994, establishing the World Trade Organization (WTO), as well as various key statements of the World Bank Group, the Asian Development Bank, the African Development Bank, the Inter-American Development Bank, and the European Bank for Reconstruction and Development.

28 *Gabcikovo-Nagymaros Project (Hungary v Slovakia)* [1997] ICJ Rep 7, 78.

diversity, and fisheries management; it explicitly extends to the protection of human health generally, notably in food safety.[29]

The precautionary principle was a philosophical challenge against policies and laws that demanded an often unrealistic level of scientific certainty about risks of marketing or otherwise introducing new technologies before recommending or implementing public health and environment protection measures. One well known international enunciation of the precautionary principle is found in Principle 15 of the Rio Declaration: 'Where there are threats of serious or irreversible damage, lack of full scientific certainty shall not be used as a reason for postponing cost effective measures to prevent environmental degradation.'[30] The development and application of the precautionary principle in connection with new technologies, however, is perceived as a contentious threat to foreign investment and multinational corporate profits, highlighting the disjunction between global public health objectives and the core corporate aim of maximizing shareholder profit.

The United Nations Millennium Development Goals more explicitly support recognition of environmental sustainability as a foundational social virtue alongside distributive justice and respect for human dignity.[31] These goals require nation states to:

Goal 1: Eradicate extreme poverty and hunger

Goal 2: Achieve universal primary education

Goal 3: Promote gender equality and empower women

Goal 4: Reduce child mortality

Goal 5: Improve maternal health

Goal 6: Combat HIV/AIDS, malaria and other diseases

Goal 7: *Ensure environmental sustainability* (emphasis added)

Goal 8: Develop a Global Partnership for Development

3. Introduction to Global Artificial Photosynthesis

Virtually all energy and food utilized by humans is derived from the sun through what is arguably life's greatest invention: photosynthesis (critically involving the capacity to store solar energy in transportable and readily transformable chemical bonds). Photosynthesis allows plants, algae, and some bacteria to capture photons and by using them to split water and reduce atmospheric carbon dioxide, to store that energy as biomass whilst liberating oxygen to build our protective and supporting atmosphere.

Photosynthesis is absolutely critical to the global health of human societies and their biosphere. Plants use photosynthesis to supply our energy as food (either directly or through livestock). Industrialization and human development (with all their positive benefits as well as detriments to global health) have been driven by the exploitation of 'archived photosynthesis' fuels (such as coal, oil, and natural gas) trapped geologically over billions of years. The use of these non-renewable resources of 'ancient photosynthesis' has assisted global human health, but at the same time is undermining it through the production of atmospheric greenhouse gases and pollution. A global public policy

[29] O. McIntyre and T. Mosedale, 'The Precautionary Principle as a Norm of Customary International Law' (1997) 9 *Journal of Environmental Law* 221.

[30] Rio Declaration (n 21) Principle 15.

[31] United Nations, 'Millennium Development Goals Report 2011' (New York, 2011).

consensus is developing that basing our economy on such 'archived photosynthesis' fuels is not consistent with basic norms supporting global human health, however they may be characterized.

Key challenges to meeting this threat involve shaping the governance conditions to encourage research and investment in renewable energy technologies. One of the most obvious sources for such sustainable energy is the vast nuclear reactor already positioned at a safe and workable distance from our planet. The average European consumption of primary energy (the energy of primary fuels, not including the energy in the food that they eat) is 125 kWh/day/person.[32] The 125 kWh/day of power required for a fulfilling standard of living is a quantitative target; it is the basic amount of energy that all people must have access to in an equal and just global society. Those presently enjoying access to that amount of energy are not doing so equitably, because those energy needs are being met through the consumption of fossil fuels. Humanity currently consumes 402 EJ of energy per year; by 2050 that is expected to rise to 590–1050 EJ/year. However, the amount of solar energy striking the earth is approximately 3.9×10^6 EJ/year.

With appropriate global governance, it should be possible to utilize this abundance of solar energy to meet our energy needs. Biofuel production represents one such attempt to sustainably utilize solar energy trapped as biomass as fuel; but it competes with food production for valuable land and water resources. Furthermore, it has been estimated that devoting 3000 m^2 per person[33] to biofuel production would generate only 36 kWh. Solar photovoltaic systems are also inefficient harvesters of this energy; 200 m^2 of solar photovoltaics per person, operating at 10 per cent efficiency, has been calculated as generating ~50 kWh/day.[34] These hypotheticals are not concerned with the safe and equitable processing, storage, or distribution of that energy.

Just and sustainable access to energy and food is not possible utilizing our current systems with the projected increases of human population. If the efficiency of natural photosynthesis can be improved and particularly if it can be engineered into all human-created structures on the surface of this planet, this equation can change. This is one of the great potential benefits of global artificial photosynthesis to global health and global health law. Researchers in nanotechnology and synthetic biology have already made great advances in improving upon or mimicking photosynthesis; with the aim of allowing the localized conversion of sunlight, water, and carbon dioxide into fuel for heating, cooking, lighting, and transport at low cost.[35] The capture of solar energy as fuel improves storage options for renewable energy.

Artificial photosynthesis could also allow each human structure to generate simple foodstuffs or to fertilize the soil about it through not only atmospheric carbon dioxide reduction but nitrogen fixation. Ammonia (NH_3) provides the bulk of the world's fertilizer but the Haber-Bosch process is energy intensive (requiring 1 to 2 per cent of the world's annual energy production). Some plants (legumes) enter into a symbiosis with nitrogen-fixing

32 D.J.C. Mackay, *Sustainable Energy—Without the Hot Air* (Cambridge: UIT Cambridge, 2008) 204.

33 The per capita land area of the Earth is ~21,805 m^2. Of the land area of Earth 13.1% is arable, 4.7% is permanent crops, and 26% is permanent pastures.

34 Mackay, *Sustainable Energy* (n 32) 41.

35 T.A. Faunce, W. Lubitz, A.W. Rutherford et al, 'Energy and Environment Policy Case for a Global Project on Artificial Photosynthesis' (2013) 6(3) *Energy and Environmental Science* 695; J. K. Hurst, 'In Pursuit of Water Oxidation Catalysts for Solar Fuel Production' (2010) 328 *Science* 315; T.A Faunce, 'Future Perspectives on Solar Fuels' in T. Wydrzynski and W. Hillier (eds), *Molecular Solar Fuels Book Series: Energy* (Cambridge: Royal Society of Chemistry, 2012) 506; T.A. Faunce, 'Towards Global Artificial Photosynthesis (Global Solar Fuels): Energy, Nanochemistry and Governance' (2012) 65 *Australian Journal of Chemistry* 557.

bacteria, called rhizobia. Rhizobia can convert atmospheric nitrogen into ammonia using a nitrogenase enzyme, a process that is energy intensive. The legume host provides the energy for this process through photosynthesis. Whilst directly genetically engineering nitrogenase into plants is impractical at present because the functioning of nitrogenase within the rhizobia is dependent on the bacteria being enclosed in a peribacteroid membrane within a specialized nodule, such limitations are not as much a barrier for a fully artificial photosynthetic system. Ammonia meets the US Department of Energy (DOE) 2015 H_2 storage target for H_2 based transport fuels. It can be blended with diesel for a fuel that releases H_2O and N_2 when combusted.[36]

The production of carbon-neutral hydrogen fuel by artificial photosynthesis is particularly relevant to the global health challenges facing humanity and its environment, because burning hydrogen produces fresh water as a by-product. Whether constructed for use in individual dwellings and structures or located in large plants (where the photon capture and water splitting are temporally and geographically separated), artificial photosynthesis systems could be used to provide food and fuel even on marginal lands, whilst actively reducing atmospheric carbon dioxide levels.

4. Governing Global Artificial Photosynthesis with Justice and Environmental Sustainability

Assuming that research in artificial photosynthesis ends up producing a safe, inexpensive, and practical device for globally distributed, personalized energy that can be made equitably available to citizens, the capacity of governments to promote and/or subsidize (or for industry to invest in this field) may depend to a large extent on the outcomes of debates about how domestic and international environmental and human rights law should interact with trade and investment law. Whether environmental sustainability comes to be recognized as being equally important as distributive justice as a foundational social virtue underpinning such normative systems is likely to be central to how such debates are resolved.

A critical aspect of this interaction is likely to involve the property rights regime and specifically patents, either over core aspects of the photosynthetic process or over central components of a successful artificial photosynthetic system. Enforceable patent rights will undoubtedly determine the trend towards innovation in this field and many large corporations seeking to invest in it will not risk doing so without a portfolio of hundreds of patents.[37] Unless appropriately regulated, the patent system may have a negative impact on scientific collaboration, as appears to have occurred with patents over synthetic organisms and proteins.[38]

Patents over the key components of artificial photosynthesis technology, such as antenna systems, reaction centers, water catalysts, carbon dioxide reduction, and nitrogen fixation components, will overlap, be hard to identify, fragmented in

36 R. Michalsky, B.J. Parman, V. Amanor-Boadu, and P.H. Pfromm. 'Solar Thermochemical Production of Ammonia from Water, Air and Sunlight: Thermodynamic and Economic Analyses' (2012) 42 *Energy* 251.

37 P. Drahos, 'Energy, Technology and Property: How they Fit Together' ANU Energy Change Open Day, 29 October 2012.

38 M. Blakeney, 'International Intellectual Property Jurisprudence after TRIPS' in D. Vaver and L. Bently (eds), *Intellectual Property in the New Millennium* (Cambridge: CUP, 2004) 3; M.K. Cho and D.A. Relman, 'Synthetic "Life", Ethics, National Security, and Public Discourse' (2010) 329 *Science* 38.

ownership, and be tactically broad.[39] Patent litigation will almost certainly result, especially as commercial competitors require access to each other's technology and 'patent trolls' seek to capitalize on uncertainty as they have in the field of biotechnology, tactically acquiring patents to profit from evolving research needs.[40] The patenting of photosynthesis is likely to be as controversial as the patenting of genes, as it is a process essential to life on earth.[41] There will be uncertainty as to whether patents encompass the products of artificial photosynthesis in addition to the processes and mechanisms.[42] A 'patent thicket' may emerge if the IP landscape of artificial photosynthesis becomes fragmented amongst multiple patent holders and research be hindered by the high cost of negotiating multiple licences, especially as each patent holder will seek to maximize the profitability of licensing access.[43]

One model for consideration, in terms of enhancing distributive justice and environmental sustainability as a balance to corporate monopoly rights in this area, involves the Open Innovation Network, which purchases patents related to the computer operating system Linux to ensure that they are not exploited.[44] Another option promoting longer-term environmental sustainability as a goal of innovation involves investing the core IP in a single patent pool to which all competitors could have access.[45] Patent pools may be utilized to overcome the problem of fragmented IP, but it is important that they don't exclude parties or they risk acting as cartels and violating anti-monopoly laws.[46]

An open source model for a publicly funded global artificial photosynthesis (GAP) project may be used to drive efficient outcomes. Publicly funded researchers could deposit their IP in an openly accessible repository to which private concerns could gain access in exchange for making their own IP accessible. Calls for public-private linkage grants could require private firms to specify the duration for which they would keep their IP closed, creating a bidding process where competing firms would lower that duration in order to gain access to linkage project materials.[47] Open source models include the Cambia's BiOS (Biological Open Source) initiative, the Initiative for Open Innovation by the Bill and Melinda Gates Foundation and the Lemelson Foundation, and the BioBricks Foundation.[48] Yet, it is unclear whether positing environmental sustainability as a foundational virtue for global health law would itself promote such endeavours to any greater or lesser extent than would reliance on distributive justice.

Another area where a more explicit acknowledgement of the normative importance of environmental sustainability could make a difference concerns the use of trade and investment law to restrict the development and implementation of renewable energy

39 G. van Overwalle, E. van Zimmeren, B. Verbeure, and G. Matthijs, 'Models for Facilitating Access to Patents on Genetic Inventions' (2006) 7 *Nature Reviews Genetics* 143.

40 B. Verbeure, 'Patent Pooling for Gene-based Diagnostic Testing: Conceptual Framework' in G. van Overwalle (ed), *Gene Patents and Collaborative Licensing Models* (Cambridge: CUP, 2009) 3.

41 L.J. Demaine and A.X. Fellmeth, 'Reinventing the Double Helix: A Novel and Nonobvious Reconceptualization of the Biotechnology Patents' (2002) 55 *Stanford Law Review* 303.

42 J. Calvert, 'Patenting Genomic Objects: Genes, Genomes, Function and Information' (2007) 16 *Science as Culture* 207.

43 J. Henkel and S.M. Maurer, 'Unbottling the Genes' (2009) 12 *Nature Biotechnology* 1095.

44 Verbeure, 'Patent Pooling' (n 40) 3.

45 Henkel and Maurer, 'Unbottling the Genes' (n 43).

46 J.A. Goldstein, 'Critical Analysis of Patent Pools' in G. van Overwalle (ed), *Gene Patents and Collaborative Licensing Models* (Cambridge: CUP, 2009) 50.

47 Henkel and Maurer, 'Unbottling the Genes' (n 43).

48 BIOS, <http://www.bios.net/daisy/bios/mta.html>; Initiative for Open Innovation, <http://www.openinnovation.org/daisy/ioi/home.html>; BioBrick Foundation, <http://bbf.openwetware.org/>.

technologies. In July 2011, for example, Texas-based Mesa Power Group LLC served Canada with an investor-state dispute settlement (ISDS) claim under the North American Free Trade Agreement's (NAFTA) Chapter 11 in connection with Ontario's solar feed-in tariff (FiT) program. Ontario's FiT program has also been challenged by Japan and the European Union under Article 2.1 of the WTO Agreement on Trade-Related Investment Measures (TRIMs Agreement), which restricts states' freedom to impose domestic content performance requirements despite exceptions relevant to the protection of the environment in paragraphs (b) and (g) of Article XX of GATT 1994.[49]

The Energy Charter Treaty (ECT) was signed in Lisbon in December 1994 with a Protocol on Energy Efficiency and Related Environmental Aspects (PEEREA) (both in force April 1998). The ECT was designed for the protection of foreign investments (national treatment or most-favoured nation treatment) and to provide non-discriminatory conditions for trade in energy materials, products, and energy-related equipment based on WTO rules and to ensure reliable cross-border energy transit flows through pipelines, grids, and other means of transport. It, too, could well be at the forefront of efforts by multinational corporations with substantial investments in the electricity grid, in centralized 'ancient photosynthesis' fuel supplies (coal, oil, and natural gas) to impede the development of competitive solar fuels technologies. A claim has already been brought against Spain, for example, under the ECT by a group of fourteen investors over that nation's retrospective cuts to solar energy tariffs. Foreign investors are also challenging the Italian government, under the ECT or bilateral investment treaties (BITs), over its efforts to roll back FiTs in the country's booming solar energy sector.[50]

Rebadging the International Centre for Trade and Sustainable Development (ICTSD) as the International Centre for Trade and Environmental Sustainability (ICTES) and requiring related dispute resolution proceedings to specifically address issues of environmental sustainability and reorganizing the WTO as the World Trade and Environmental Sustainability Organisation (WTESO), should be on the reform agenda for global health law. Such developments could have far-reaching implications for the engagement of the trade and investment law regime with the other components of a global social contract as represented, for example, by international human rights and international environmental law.

5. Global Artificial Photosynthesis (GAP) as Common Heritage of Humanity

Placing greater emphasis on environmental sustainability would undoubtedly assist in the transformation of various areas of public international law. One such example is that under which important features of our natural world, such as our natural and cultural heritage, the moon, outer space, the deep sea bed, and Antarctica are declared 'Common Heritage of Humanity'. Now that the molecular structure of natural photosynthesis is almost fully revealed, excessive patenting and its restrictions of access

[49] V. Font. 'The WTO v Ontario', 30 October 2012, *Renewable Energy World*, available at <http://www.renewableenergyworld.com/rea/news/article/2012/10/the-wto-vs-ontario-addressing-the-bigger-picture-of-trade-and-renewable-energy?cmpid=SolarNL-Tuesday-October30-2012> (accessed 4 November 2012). M. Sornarajah, 'A Law for Need or a Law for Greed?: Restoring the Lost Law in the International Law of Foreign Investment' (2006) 123 *International Environmental Agreements* 329.

[50] T.A.Faunce, 'Will International Trade Law Promote or Inhibit Global Artificial Photosynthesis?' (2011) 6 *Asian Journal of WTO and International Health Law and Policy* 313.

to information will not be far behind. This could be the right time to declare the molecular structure of photosynthesis 'Common Heritage of Humanity' under public international law.

If so, there would be five primary implications. First, artificial photosynthesis could not be legally owned and could not be appropriated by public or private concerns. Second, representatives of all nations would have to manage artificial photosynthesis on behalf of all. Third, all nations must share with each other the benefits of exploiting artificial photosynthesis, restraining the extent to which it can be exploited for profit, given the technique's status as a global public good. Fourth, no weaponry could be developed employing artificial photosynthesis technology. Fifth, artificial photosynthesis would have to be preserved for the benefit of future generations.[51]

Traditionally, the concept of 'common heritage' attached to a physical domain, a patch of wilderness, or a cultural artifact that could be physically or materially degraded, whereas the core component of artificial photosynthesis is likely to be knowledge. An international body could be established to ensure that the relevant knowledge was available to all and was preserved for future generations and their scientists. That same body may work to ensure that artificial photosynthesis technology is not being integrated into military platforms or interfered with as part of military operations. As with the human genome, common heritage status would not halt the application of all patents in this field, for example those that enhance the dissemination and improvement of the technology. One illustrative possibility is that the most successful version of artificial photosynthesis may rely upon a finite stock of a particular natural resource, perhaps as a key water-splitting catalyst. Sustainable management of that resource for future generations would then become the concern of the international governing body.

Establishing artificial photosynthesis as the common heritage of humanity might be analogous to existing claims seeking common heritage status for the genetic diversity of agricultural crops, biodiversity, or the atmosphere.[52] These claims are hard to establish. Article 1 of the UNESCO Universal Declaration on the Human Genome and Human Rights, is limited in the extent to which it claims common heritage status for the human genome, stating: 'The human genome underlies the fundamental unity of all members of the human family, as well as the recognition of their inherent dignity and diversity. In a symbolic sense, it is the heritage of humanity.'[53] Only Article 4 gives the human genome common heritage like status, stating: 'The human genome in its natural state shall not give rise to financial gains.'[54] As an alternative to common heritage status, artificial photosynthesis technology may be declared a global public good.

6. GAP and Safe Planetary Boundaries

Another manifestation of global health law based more firmly on environmental sustainability as well as societal virtues such as distributive justice, involves the potential for GAP to assist nation states with fulfilling enforceable obligations (for example under an international convention) concerning 'safe' planetary boundaries in terms of changes in land use and land cover; coastal and maritime ecosystems; stratospheric ozone

[51] Faunce, 'Governing Planetary Nanomedicine (n 15).

[52] T.A. Faunce, 'Governing Nanotechnology for Solar Fuels: Towards a Jurisprudence of Global Artificial Photosynthesis' (2011) 2 *Renewable Energy Law and Policy* 160.

[53] UNGA, Universal Declaration on the Human Genome and Human Rights (1998) UN Doc A/RES/53/152.

[54] Universal Declaration on the Human Genome and Human Rights (n 53) Art 4.

depletion; ocean acidification; chemical pollution; atmospheric aerosol loading; riverine flow; interference with nitrogen, carbon, and phosphorus cycles; climate change; global freshwater use; and biological diversity loss (terrestrial and marine).[55]

The role of global artificial photosynthesis (engineered into all human structures) could be to technologically ease the pressure on natural systems to remain vital contributors to our economy, allowing policy-makers the space to grant such ecosystems protected status. This approach to the development of global health law may be said to rest on differing branches of scientific enquiry related to environmental sustainability. These include ecological economics, global change research, and sustainability science, as well as research into resilience and its links to complex dynamics and self-regulation of living systems, emphasizing thresholds and shifts between states.[56] The call for such global environmental sustainability parameters to become legal boundaries parallels the movement to grant enforceable rights (through human guardians) to ecosystems.[57]

Shaping such planet physiological boundaries of environmental sustainability into enforceable norms of global health law to which GAP is addressed will be complicated, however, by many factors including that not all processes or subsystems on Earth have well-defined thresholds. Further, human actions that undermine the resilience of such processes or subsystems—for example land and water degradation—can increase the risk that thresholds will also be crossed in other processes, such as the climate system.[58]

7. Conclusion

The argument presented here is that global health law, particularly as it confronts challenges related to defining and making legally enforceable the safe boundaries for long-term human occupation of the Earth, should begin to develop an appreciation of environmental sustainability as a non-anthropocentric foundational social virtue of equal importance to distributive justice. Global artificial photosynthesis has been briefly examined as a case study of how this shift in normative understanding might receive a technological impetus to allow the development of normative instruments and concepts coherent with long-term stewardship of humanity over the earth. Positing environmental sustainability as a foundational social virtue alongside distributive justice in global health law is likely to enhance the focus of that system on utilizing technologies such as artificial photosynthesis to meet humanity's energy needs for this and future generations, while ensuring it dwells amongst a resilient ecosystem.

In this context an important point should be emphasized. In the past, technological developments have assisted the normative evolution of ideals (like human equality) into enforceable legal obligations by easing the economic pressures that required exploitation. May it not be that artificial photosynthesis, once engineered into every human structure, by taking the pressure off the natural environment to provide resources for us, will facilitate the recognition, in next generation global health law, that components of that environment are entitled to be protected by enforceable rights?

55 W. Steffen, P.J. Crutzen, and J.R McNeill, 'The Anthropocene: Are Humans now Overwhelming the Great Forces of Nature?' (2007) 36 *AMBIO: A Journal of the Human Environment* 614.

56 T.A. Faunce, 'Towards a Global Solar Fuels Project—Artificial Photosynthesis and the Transition from Anthropocene to Sustainocene' (2012) 49 *Procedia. Engineering* 348. T.A Faunce, S. Styring, M. Wasielewski et al, 'Artificial Photosynthesis as a Frontier Technology for Energy Sustainability'. (2013) 6 *Energy and Environmental Science* 1074.

57 Council of Canadians, Global Exchange, and Fundacion Pachamama, 'Does Nature Have Rights?: Transforming Grassroots Organizing to Protect People and the Planet' (San Francisco, 2010).

58 J. Rockström, W. Steffen, K. Noone, Å. Persson et al, 'A Safe Operating Space for Humanity' (2009) 461 *Nature* 472.

27

Bridging the Health/Law Divide in Global Health Law

The Role of Law Professors

Scott Burris

1. Introduction

This book bears the title *Law and Global Health*. The implication of an important connection between the two is not generally controversial. Advocates for a Framework Convention on Global Health argue that better governance through international law would improve the world's response to the health needs of billions of people.[1] The Global Commission on HIV and the Law identifies many ways in which laws and legal practices exacerbate the spread of AIDS.[2] The WHO Commission on the Social Determinants of Health, though few lawyers were involved in its work, treated policy as an important force for causing and reducing inequities.[3] The US Institute of Medicine has issued a string of reports over two decades emphasizing the important roles of law in public health.[4] Still, the claim that law matters to health is an empirical one—many, many empirical ones. It is important that this powerful influence be recognized, but from then on the important questions largely have to do with specifying the relationship in facts. The claim is also one that does little, no matter how often repeated, to erase the cultural gap that yawns between law and health.

Understanding and responding to how law influences health requires 'public health law research' (PHLR): scientific research on the relationship of laws and legal practices to public health.[5] In the US, the Public Health Law Research Program of the Robert Wood Johnson Foundation is supporting, through funding and methods work, the growth of a multi-disciplinary cohort of researchers to elucidate this complex relationship.[6] The program's goals include both empirically demonstrating the important connection between law and health, and bridging the divide between health and legal researchers. In this chapter, I will set out the conceptual and methodological elements

1 L. Gostin, 'Meeting Basic Survival Needs of the World's Least Healthy People: Toward a Framework Convention on Global Health' (2008) 96 *Georgetown Law Journal* 331.

2 Global Commission on HIV and the Law, 'Risks, Rights and Health' (New York, 2012).

3 World Health Organization Commission on Social Determinants of Health, 'Closing the Gap in a Generation: Health Equity through Action on the Social Determinants of Health' (Geneva, 2008).

4 Institute of Medicine, 'The Future of Public Health' (Washington, DC, 1988); Institute of Medicine, 'The Future of the Public's Health in the 21st Century' (Washington, DC, 2002); Institute of Medicine, 'For the Public's Health: Revitalizing Law and Policy to Meet New Challenges' (Washington, DC, 2011).

5 S. Burris, A.C. Wagenaar, J. Swanson, J.K. Ibrahim, J. Wood, and M.M. Mello, 'Making the Case for Laws that Improve Health: A Framework for Public Health Law Research' (2010) 88 *The Milbank Quarterly* 169.

6 S. Burris and E. Anderson, 'Making the Case for Laws that Improve Health: The Work of the Public Health Law Research National Program Office' (2011) 39 *Journal of Law, Medicine and Ethics* 15.

of PHLR, and then discuss the need for an empirical turn in global health law. The barriers are many, starting with the normative focus of much health law scholarship. Four key moves, which I prescribe in the second half of the chapter, would help. The first is for legal academics to give greater regard to the empirical elements of the legal scholarship they are already doing. The second is for legal academics to take a more frequent role in interdisciplinary empirical research on the effects of laws on health, something I argue is not as difficult as it may sound. The third is for health law academics to take a greater role in filling the gap in the availability of legal data for evaluation and policy monitoring. Finally, I urge health law academics to vigorously embrace the role of knowledge brokers between research and policy, bringing to bear both a sophisticated use of scientific evidence and a powerful normative vision.

2. Public Health Law Research in the United States

A 1961 article in the American Journal of Public Health described public health law as 'a subject which is treated rather infrequently in the public health literature'.[7] True at the time, but the seeds of change were already being planted. Beginning in areas like tobacco and injury control, lawsuits, product regulations, and behavioral rules began to be used more and more widely to reduce morbidity and mortality. Indeed, most of the items on the Centers for Disease Control and Prevention's (CDC) list of 'great public health achievements' depended to a greater or lesser degree on legal interventions.[8] Public health law research documented the effectiveness of such interventions as mandatory safety belts,[9] clean indoor air laws,[10] mandatory vaccination,[11] and childhood lead poisoning.[12] The empirical evaluation of law as a tool for improving public health was a consequence of wider use of law for this purpose, a dynamic that unfolded in a number of priority health areas, albeit sometimes slowly.[13] The CDC launched a public health law program that initially had funding to support research,[14] but it lost its research funding after only a few years. The National Institutes of Health have not recognized a distinct field of public health law research.

The National Program Office (NPO) for the RWJF Public Health Law Research Program began work to advance the field in 2009. Since then, it has issued five calls for proposals and funded over $12 million in investigator-initiated and NPO research projects. The program and its underpinnings are described elsewhere.[15] PHLR is rooted in epidemiology and the behavioral sciences of public health—sociology, social

[7] R.H. Hamlin, 'Public Health Law or the Interrelationship of Law and Public Health Administration' (1961) 51 *American Journal of Public Health and the Nation's Health* 1733, 1733.

[8] Centers for Disease Control and Prevention, 'Ten Great Public Health Achievements—United States, 2001–2010' (2011) 60 *Morbidity and Mortality Weekly Report* 619.

[9] D.J. Houston and L.E. Richardson, Jr, 'Getting Americans to Buckle Up: The Efficiency of State Seat Belt Laws' (2005) 37 *Accidents Analysis and Prevention* 1114.

[10] D.G. Meyers, J.S. Neuberger, and J. He, 'Cardiovascular Effect of Bans on Smoking in Public Places: A Systematic Review and Meta-Analysis' (2009) 54 *Journal of the American College of Cardiology* 1249.

[11] T.R. Wilson, D.B. Fishbein, P.A. Ellis, and S.A. Edlavitch, 'The Impact of a School Entry Law on Adolescent Immunization Rates' (2005) 37 *Journal of Adolescent Health* 511.

[12] K.S. Korfmacher, M. Ayoob, and R. Morley, 'Rochester's Lead Law: Evaluation of a Local Environmental Health Policy Innovation' (2012) 120 *Environmental Health Perspectives* 309.

[13] S. Burris and E. Anderson, 'Legal Regulation of Health-Related Behavior: A Half Century of Public Health Law Research' (2013) 9(1) *Annual Review of Law and Social Science* 95.

[14] R.A. Goodman, A. Moulton, G. Matthews et al, 'Law and Public Health at CDC' (2006) 55 *Morbidity and Mortality Weekly Report* 29.

[15] Burris and Anderson, 'Making the Case for Laws that Improve Health' (2011) (n 6); S. Burris, G.P. Mays, F.D. Scutchfield, and J.K. Ibrahim, 'Moving from Intersection to Integration: Public

psychology, anthropology, economics. The purpose of PHLR is to illuminate the relationship of laws and legal practices to the environments that structure health, the behaviors that embody health, and the level and distributions of outcomes that define public health in mortality and morbidity tables.[16] Though aspiring to the scientific rigor of the best health research, PHLR also draws on the theory and methods of the sociolegal research tradition. It assigns law the broad definition that has emerged from decades of sophisticated and theory-driven study of laws and legal systems from researchers in a variety of disciplines, embracing both 'laws on the books' and the attitudes and practices of those who enforce the law or are subject to its enforcement ('law on the streets').[17] For example, researchers have explained why people obey the law in terms of deterrence (ie the fear of sanctions), legitimacy (ie normative belief in the authority of the law-maker to set rules) and, more recently, the degree to which individuals experience encounters with law as procedurally fair.[18] Research in the 'law and society' tradition treats law less as a set of rules we consciously follow than a set of cultural beliefs and practices that shape how we see the world and that influence our behavior in ways of which we may not even be aware.[19] This perspective is essential to properly investigating how law shapes organizational and individual attitudes and behavior. The adoption of a strong vision of science was essential to both defining the core work of the project and speaking to the health scientists we needed to enlist. It was not intended to imply a judgment that scientific health law research is superior to 'merely' normative work, let alone that the two are incompatible. In fact, as I argue in this chapter, much of academic legal scholarship is empirical, if not scientific, and law professors have a critical role to play in advancing PHLR.

PHLR distinguishes three principal forms of public health law. 'Interventional public health laws' are enacted, or enforcement conducted, with the explicit aim of protecting and improving public health.[20] When it is deliberately used as a tool for promoting healthier environments or behaviors, law can and should be evaluated for effectiveness, in the same manner as any other form of public health intervention. This is probably the best recognized element of PHLR in the health research community, where empirical research on areas such as injury law and tobacco control is well established. 'Incidental public health laws' are enacted primarily for purposes other than promoting public health, but nonetheless have positive or negative consequences for health.[21] Studies examining the effect of criminal laws and the practice of criminal justice agencies on the spread of communicable disease exemplify incidental public health law research, showing how regimes intended to promote some sort of good can also have positive, or in this case significantly bad, health effects.[22] Laws or legal

Health Law Research and Public Health Systems and Services Research' (2012) 90 *The Milbank Quarterly* 375; Burris, Wagenaar et al, 'Making the Case for Laws that Improve Health' (2010) (n 5).

16 A.C. Wagenaar and S. Burris (eds), *Public Health Law Research: Theory and Methods* (San Francisco, CA: Wiley-Jossey Bass, 2013).

17 P. Ewick and S. Silbey, *The Common Place of Law: Stories from Everyday Life* (Chicago, IL: University of Chicago Press, 1998); S. Silbey, 'After Legal Conciousness' (2005) 1 *Annual Review of Law and Social Science* 323.

18 T.R. Tyler, *Why People Obey the Law* (New Haven, CT: Yale University Press, 1990).

19 Silbey, 'After Legal Conciousness' (n 17).

20 A.D. Moulton, S.L. Mercer, T. Popovic et al, 'The Scientific Basis for Law as a Public Health Tool' (2009) 99 *American Journal of Public Health* 17.

21 Burris, Wagenaar et al, 'Making the Case for Laws that Improve Health' (2010) (n 5).

22 T.M. Hammett, Z. Wu, T.T. Duc et al, '"Social Evils" and Harm Reduction: The Evolving Policy Environment for Human Immunodeficiency Virus Prevention among Injection Drug Users in China and Vietnam' (2008) 103 *Addiction* 137; R.A. Pollini, K.C. Brouwer, R.M. Lozada et al,

activities that have important unintended effects on population health can be studied; where necessary, they can be altered. Finally, 'infrastructural law' establishes the powers, duties, and features of public health agencies.[23] Research in this area explores how this baseline of authority shapes the outputs and outcomes produced by health agencies.[24] These categories, though inevitably fuzzy at their boundaries, usefully distinguish three distinct categories of investigation. Interventional public health law has been the best studied, while infrastructural law has been largely neglected within research on public health systems, and incidental health law has only now been defined as a topic worthy of intensive focus.

PHLR studies take a number of different forms. 'Policy-making studies' explore the determinants of health laws, rules, and decisions, typically through qualitative research.[25] 'Mapping studies' gather data (in the form of laws, regulations, and decisions) about the prevalence and distribution of specific laws,[26] what levels of government have relevant authority,[27] and variation in characteristics of the law across jurisdictions and over time.[28] 'Implementation studies' classically investigate the 'transformation process' that occurs as we move from the 'law on the books' enacted by the policy-maker to the 'law on the streets' actually put into practice by legal agents charged with enforcement.[29] 'Intervention studies', the core of PHLR, evaluate the effects of legal interventions—laws on the books, laws as implemented, or both—on health outcomes or key mediating factors that drive health outcomes.[30] Finally, what we call

'Syringe Possession Arrests are Associated with Receptive Syringe Sharing in Two Mexico-U.S. Border Cities' (2008) 103 *Addiction* 101; W. Small, T. Kerr, J. Charette, M.T. Schechter, and P.M. Spittal, 'Impacts of Intensified Police Activity on Injection Drug Users: Evidence from an Ethnographic Investigation' (2006) 17 *International Journal of Drug Policy* 85.

23 Burris, Wagenaar et al, 'Making the Case for Laws that Improve Health' (2010) (n 5).

24 P.D. Jacobson, J. Wasserman, A. Botoseneanu, A. Silverstein, and H.W. Wu, 'The Role of Law in Public Health Preparedness: Opportunities and Challenges' (2011) *Journal of Health Politics, Policy and Law* doi:10.1215/03616878-1538629; P.J.C. McCann, 'Agency Discretion and Public Health Service Delivery' (2009) 44 *Health Services Research* 1897.

25 C. Backtrom and L. Robins, 'State AIDS Policy Making: Perspectives of Legislative Health Committee Chairs' (1995) 10 *AIDS and Public Policy Journal* 238; E.A. Dodson, C. Fleming, T.K. Boehmer, D. Haire-Joshu, D.A. Luke, and R.C. Brownson, 'Preventing Childhood Obesity through State Policy: Qualitative Assessment of Enablers and Barriers' (2009) 30 *Journal of Public Health Policy* S161.

26 L.O. Gostin, Z. Lazzarini, V.S. Neslund, and M.T. Osterholm, 'The Public Health Information Infrastructure: A National Review of the Law on Health Information Privacy' (1996) 2755 *Journal of the American Medical Association* 1921; H.G. Hodge, Jr, A. Pulver, M. Hogben, D. Bhattacharya, and E.F. Brown, 'Expedited Partner Therapy for Sexually Transmitted Diseases: Assessing the Legal Environment' (2008) 98 *American Journal of Public Health* 238.

27 G.A Horlick, S.F. Beeler, and R.W. Linkins, 'A Review of State Legislation Related to Immunization Registries' (2001) 20 *American Journal of Preventive Medicine* 208.

28 J.F. Chriqui, K.M. Ribisl, R.M. Wallace, R.S. Williams, J.C. O'Connor, and R. el Arculli, 'A Comprehensive Review of State Laws Governing Internet and Other Delivery Sales of Cigarettes in the United States' (2008) 10 *Nicotine and Tobacco Research* 253; F.E. Shaw, K.L. McKie, C.A. Liveoak, and R.A. Goodman, 'Legal Tools for Preparedness and Response: Variation in Quarantine Powers among the 10 Most Populous U.S. States in 2004' (2007) 97 *American Journal of Public Health* S38; J.K. Wells, A.F. Williams, and M. Fields, 'Coverage Gaps in Seat Belt Use Laws' (1989) 79 *American Journal of Public Health* 332.

29 S.L. Percy, *Disability, Civil Rights, and Public Policy: The Politics of Implementation* (Tuscaloosa, AL: University of Alabama Press, 1989).

30 R.D. Foss, J.R. Feaganes, and E.A. Rodgman, 'Initial Effects of Graduated Driver Licensing on 16-Year-Old Driver Crashes in North Carolina' (2001) 286 *Journal of the American Medical Association* 1588; A. Harrell and B.E. Smith, 'Effects of Restraining Orders on Domestic Violence Victims' in E.S. Buzawa and C.G. Buzawa (eds), *Do Arrests and Restraining Orders Work?* (Thousand Oaks, CA: Sage Publications, 1996) 214.

'mechanism studies' advance the field by investigating *how* law has the effects it has.[31] Mechanism studies are important to improving regulatory design and enforcement, and strengthening causal inference in empirical research.[32] Many different designs, from qualitative ethnographies to randomized controlled trials, may be deployed in PHLR.[33]

PHLR has important links with health systems and services research. Although law has often been described as crucial to the effective operation of public health agencies, only a handful of researchers have empirically examined the relationship between law and public health system performance. The great potential of sociolegal research theories and methods to illuminate how actors in health systems use—or avoid—law has remained untapped, with key concepts like 'legal consciousness' entirely absent from the literature. An interdisciplinary review in the US suggested a research agenda built around three broad inquiries: (1) the structural role of law in shaping the organization, powers, prerogatives, duties, and limitations of public health agencies, and thereby their functioning and ultimately their impact on public health; (2) the mechanisms through which public health system characteristics influence the implementation of interventional public health laws; and (3) the individual and system characteristics that influence the ability of public health systems and their community partners to develop and secure enactment of legal initiatives to advance public health.[34]

In all this, we have pursued a strong commitment to interdisciplinarity, not just because it makes sense as an approach to good social science research, but more immediately as a way of trying to bridge the gap between law people and health people. I still find many people trained in health who see law as a strange and alien realm; they either ignore it as a possibly significant factor on health and health behavior, or abstract into a concept of 'policy' that is placed at the macrosocial level in multilevel models, without a sense of its constant operation in the immediate and everyday life.[35] For our part, lawyers doing empirical work are not generally oriented towards health outcomes—legal scholars study *law*—and academic health lawyers have focused largely on doctrinal and normative work. There are some excellent creators and wielders of empirical research in the health law community, but we are not immune from the general criticism of law professors that we have lost a clear sense of the distinction between normative and empirical claims, and have paid too little attention to the basic rules of scientific inference.[36] When it comes to deriving or supporting policy prescriptions with empirical data, we lawyers must often look to health scientists like bulls in the epistemic china shop. On both sides, there seems little sense that we ought to be talking to, and even working with, each other, let alone addressing the serious institutional barriers to collaboration.

Thus the various elements of our work coalesce around supporting teams of lawyers, health scientists, and legal and health practitioners by paying for research, supporting

31 M. Mello and T. Brennan, 'Deterrence of Medical Errors: Theory and Evidence for Malpractice Reform' (2002) 80 *Texas Law Review* 1595; A.C. Wagenaar, M.M. Maldonado-Molina, D.J. Erickson, L. Maa, A.L. Tobler, and K.A. Komro, 'General Deterrence Effects of U.S. Statutory DUI Fine and Jail Penalties: Long-Term Follow-up in 32 States' (2007) 39 *Accident Analysis and Prevention* 982.

32 S. Burris and A.C. Wagenaar, 'Integrating Diverse Theories for Public Health Law Research' in A.C. Wagenaar and S. Burris (eds), *Public Health Law Research: Theory and Methods* (San Francisco, CA: Wiley-Jossey Bass, 2013) 193.

33 Wagenaar and Burris, *Public Health Law Research* (n 16).

34 Burris, Mays, Scutchfield, and Ibrahim, 'Moving from Intersection to Integration' (n 15).

35 S. Burris, 'From Health Care Law to the Social Determinants of Health: A Public Health Law Research Perspective' (2011) 159 *University of Pennsylvania Law Review* 1649.

36 L. Epstein and G. King, 'The Rules of Inference' (2002) 69 *University of Chicago Law Review* 1.

stronger methods, and raising the profile for our collective efforts. Our aim is not to make every health law professor into an empirical researcher, nor to suggest that every health researcher devote herself entirely to the effects of law. In our imagined future, all social and behavioral researchers working in health will be able to detect when laws or legal practices may be present in an important way in the phenomena being studied; they will be willing and able to work with legal experts to properly theorize and measure the effects of law. Every health law scholar will be a competent consumer of scientific research, most will be team members in scientific research, and some will lead their own scientific research teams. And all this would be fundable, and rewarded professionally in law schools, schools of public health or medicine, and other schools and departments where policy evaluation is conducted. Such work would provide the evidence base for evidence-informed policy, and affirm the social value of facts, of rational analysis, to policy decisions.

2.1 Towards global PHLR

The gaps we seek to bridge in the US seem to be present in most places, even those that have achieved a significant level of development in academic health law and health research. While health law has emerged, despite some struggles, as a field, in Europe and elsewhere, health law remains primarily concerned with health law and practice, not empirical evaluation. Rigorous empirical research on the impact of laws on health remains rare, and the connection between academic legal research and health research tenuous or absent. The reasons for this are many, and most of them will be familiar to or unsurprising to the reader. I have already described the cultural differences. These are reflected in very tangible ways. Funding for health research, allocated from within the health culture, has not been allocated to research on law to a degree commensurate with law's impact on health. Many researchers in health feel that including law weakens a proposal in the eyes of proposal reviewers. In health law generally, barriers to more and better empirical research include lack of access to reliable data on the law and its implementation, the emphasis within law schools on sole-authored normative scholarship, the lack of supportive peers (and of rigorous peer review) in the legal academy, and limited or no training in empirical research during professional development.[37] An Institute of Medicine study of public health education lamented a parallel absence of legal education in schools of public health in the US.[38] The literature on barriers to health law outside the US is limited, and although there are important projects under way,[39] available papers do not lead me to believe that the barriers are substantially different elsewhere.[40]

[37] M.M. Mello and K. Zeiler, 'Empirical Health Law Scholarship: The State of the Field' (2008) 96 *Georgetown Law Journal* 649.

[38] K.M. Gebbie, L. Rosenstock, L.M. Hernandez, and Institute of Medicine Committee on Educating Public Health Professionals for the 21st Century, *Who Will Keep the Public Healthy? Educating Public Health Professionals for the 21st Century* (Washington, DC: National Academies Press, 2003).

[39] S.Y. Kim, Y. Lee, M. Sohn, and K. Hahm, 'Developing a Tool for Assessing Public Health Law in Countries' (2012) 24(5) *Asia-Pacific Journal of Public Health* 867.

[40] A. Attaran, T. Pang, J. Whitworth, A. Oxman, and M. McKee, 'Healthy by Law: The Missed Opportunity to Use Laws For Public Health' (2012) 379 *Lancet* 283; S. Gevers, 'Health Law in Europe: From the Present to the Future' (2008) 15 *European Journal of Health Law* 261; D. Tran, W. Zhengzhi, X. Fenglei, and S. Burris, 'Health Law Teaching and Research in Chinese Law Schools: Results of a Pre-SARS Survey' (2004) 18 *Temple International and Comparative Law Journal* 77.

The funding problem could be addressed by a funder investing in this field at the national or international level beyond the US. Over the years, some, like Ford and the Open Society Foundations, have provided significant funding for law and policy related activities, while others, notably Gates, have seemed to steer clear of our particular social technology. A few foundations fund rigorous reviews of evidence behind policy, for example the Beckley Foundation in its work on drug policy.[41] There has, however, been no focused and sustained support for measuring the effect of law on health. In the long run, integration with health research, rather than separate development, is the key to truly bridging the health/law divide. In the short and medium term, however, an emerging new subfield gets an obvious boost from dedicated funding. It thus remains important to advocate wherever we can for national funding agencies or major foundations to provide dedicated funding for public health law research. With more centers and funding, an international community of researchers can speed the improvement of methods and the sharpening of research agendas. The further development of the field anywhere, particularly the refinement of its tools and methods, provides levers to researchers everywhere. More funding, however, is not directly within our control as health lawyers (though it never hurts to ask). So I turn to a series of other more or less related steps we can take now to advance the cause.

2.1.1 Owning our empirical work

The first is simple, but essential: legal academia and our colleagues in health research can acknowledge the field: recognize the importance of building the evidence base for law in public health, do or support the work, spread the brand. Alas, this first simple step requires another, perhaps much harder one for us as individuals and as members of legal academic communities: taking ownership of the empirical work of law professors. I am not referring here simply to doing *scientific* empirical research on law's effects on health—ie studies using the falsifiable theories and explicit methods of social science within an established disciplinary tradition. There is a broader, more apt, definition of 'empirical' that encompasses much of our normal work, and suggests how we, as a group, have defined empiricism in a way that obscures just how much empirical analysis we do. Lee Epstein and Gary King, in an article that ought to be required reading for every law student and law teacher, offer this definition:

> The word 'empirical' denotes evidence about the world based on observation or experience. That evidence can be numerical (quantitative) or non-numerical (qualitative); neither is any more 'empirical' than the other. What makes research empirical is that it is based on observations of the world—i.e., data, which is just a term for facts about the world ... As long as the facts have something to do with the world, they are data, and as long as research involves data that is observed or desired, it is empirical.
>
> Under this definition of 'empirical,' assertions that 'the amount of theoretical and doctrinal scholarship ... overwhelms the amount of empirical scholarship,' [in the legal academy] ring hollow. For, as even the most casual reader of the nation's law reviews must acknowledge, a large fraction of legal scholarship makes at least some claims about the world based on observation or experience.[42]

41 B. Fischer, W. Hall, S. Lenton, P. Reuter, and R. Room, *Cannabis Policy: Moving Beyond Stalemate* (Oxford: OUP, 2008).

42 Epstein and King, 'The Rules of Inference' (n 36).

We in health law are particularly interested in questions of epidemiology and health behavior, and generally concern ourselves in part with matters of regulatory effectiveness. Even when we are purely concerned with the law on the books, our research may be empirical in the sense that the legal texts we are gathering and analyzing can be understood in empirical terms. When we collect laws or cases we are collecting data; when we attempt to make inferences about the world from the data we have collected, or from existing data (ie research studies) we are doing empirical analysis. Epstein and King argue that law professors do a great deal of empirical work, but because we don't acknowledge it as such, we get away with far too much sloppy practice.[43] Failing to recognize the empirical character of our work means making errors, and missing opportunities to do our work better and to communicate more effectively and credibly with colleagues in health.

Owning our empiricism takes practical form in how we use our tools and legal texts. First and foremost, 'theory' changes. In our normative work, we use 'theory' to name a framework for pulling together our ideas, or an idea we would like others to accept as persuasive. In empirical research, a theory is a proposition that can be falsified by the research and thus a means of identifying the important questions—generating hypotheses—for the study: for example judges in contract cases are becoming more likely to enforce shrink-wrap contracts. Thinking about our work as empirical, we become more conscious of the nature of the data. Cases are, in empirical terms, used as measures of something; we have to be clear about what that something is in order to know what, exactly, we are measuring. Are published cases a valid measure of the total decisional output of judges? Are they records of the actual motives or reasoning processes of judges deciding a particular case? Do they constitute the law, represent the law, serve as partial evidence of what the law is? The answers to questions like these tell us what set of phenomena in the world the cases are *about*. And since we are not looking at all cases, the means of selecting them largely determines whether the data we analyze and the inferences we make can be generalized to all cases that are about those things. This would entail something like a method that assured that all cases about the topic in question had an equal chance of being in the sample, and certainly would not be accomplished by a lawyer working back and across from a 'leading case'. A researcher attending to these considerations would be sure to do so explicitly, describing the research methods with sufficient specificity to allow others to reproduce the research. None of these steps is terribly difficult, but 'descriptive inference is not the near-trivial task' that so many of us seem to treat it as.[44] Causal inference is considerably more difficult, the challenge for all social scientists. Epstein and King reasonably abstain from suggesting that we law professors throw in the towel, advising instead that we make our 'questions as precise as possible, follow the best advice science has to offer about reducing uncertainty and bias, and communicate the appropriate level of uncertainty readers should have in interpreting' our results.[45] This is certainly the least we can do, and it is well within our training and capacity.

2.1.2 Participating in scientific studies

Aside from this dispositional shift towards greater consciousness of the time-honored standards of empirical analysis, taking ownership of empirical work could, for some of

43 Epstein and King, 'The Rules of Inference' (n 36).
44 Epstein and King, 'The Rules of Inference' (n 36).
45 Epstein and King, 'The Rules of Inference' (n 36) 27.

us, entail a greater willingness to take part in scientific research on the effects of laws and legal practices. Joining the enterprise as part of a team does not require the ability to design or conduct the research independently. A short course of reading[46] can equip the law professor with a conceptual grasp of the main elements of research and an insight into the empirical mind. In the interdisciplinary model, what law professors know already brings real value to the enterprise. Legal research is a skill, and doing it properly requires a solid understanding of the contexts of law: the structure of the particular legal regime (types and hierarchy of rules, role of courts, etc); the political and regulatory structure; the social context. We may take for granted the training required to do something as apparently straightforward as accurately identifying a particular kind of law across multiple jurisdictions for evaluation research.[47] In a broader sense, legal academics typically have a solid understanding of the prevailing theories of how law influences behavior (deterrence, procedural justice, legal consciousness), so that even if they are not trained to operationalize these theories for research purposes, they can collaborate with social scientists who are. As potential consumers and translators of scientific health law research, legal academics on research teams can help to focus the scientific work on questions of practical importance for which there might be an audience.

Though I encourage law professors to do empirical research because it is useful and rewarding, I don't expect that most will make this a major component of their professional work or identity, nor do I regard widespread participation as necessary to improving legal academia's contribution to empirical health law. This is not, in any case, the only way for a legal academic to take part in research. Here are two other important ways that law professors can help bridge the gap now.

2.1.3 Creating legal data and legal information

I have already alluded to lack of data as a barrier to legal and evaluation research, and to mapping studies as a way to fill this need. In federal systems, or in international work, it is often the lot of a law professor to 'survey' the law.[48] We use legal research to collect and then (at least to start with) describe the law of many jurisdictions. Examples in the US are many, but public health law pioneers have also conducted them in the EU[49] and Asia.[50] Global legal surveys include the Comparative Constitutions Project and the Campaign for Tobacco Free Kids' tobacco law website.[51] Georgetown's O'Neill Institute has built a database of decisional law in the health and human rights area.[52] Recent developments in methods and technology have made legal mapping more efficient and cost-effective. New ways of doing mapping studies have led to new ways of thinking about legal research within public health practice, monitoring, and

46 Wagenaar and Burris, *Public Health Law Research* (n 16).

47 C. LaFond, T.L. Toomey, C. Rothstein, W. Manning, and A.C. Wagenaar, 'Policy Evaluation Research. Measuring the Independent Variables' (2000) 24 *Evaluation Review* 92.

48 L.O. Gostin, 'Controlling the Resurgent Tuberculosis Epidemic. A 50-State Survey of TB Statutes and Proposals for Reform' (1993) 269 *Journal of the American Medical Association* 255.

49 R. Martin, A. Conseil, A. Longstaff, J. Kodo, J. Siegert, A.-M. Duguet, P. Lobato de Faria, G. Haringhuizen, J. Espin, and R. Coker, 'Pandemic Influenza Control in Europe and the Constraints Resulting from Incoherent Public Health Laws' (2010) 10 *BMC Public Health* 532.

50 Kim, Lee, Sohn, and Hahm, 'Developing a Tool for Assessing Public Health Law' (n 39).

51 Campaign for Tobacco Free Kids, 'Tobacco Control Laws' (2014), available at <http://www.tobaccocontrollaws.org/> (accessed 2 February 2014).

52 O'Neill Institute for National and Global Health Law, 'Global Health and Human Rights Database' (2014), available at <http://www.globalhealthrights.org/>.

evaluation. It is now possible to speak concretely about a global practice of 'policy surveillance' conducted in a consistent manner to serve a number of basic public health needs.

Jamie Chiriqui and colleagues explain:

> In public health, surveillance and reporting of disease are standard practices. According to the Centers for Disease Control and Prevention, 'public health surveillance is the ongoing, systematic collection, analysis, interpretation, and dissemination of data . . . Data disseminated by a public health surveillance system can be used for immediate public health action, program planning and evaluation, and formulating research hypotheses.' A logical extension of this definition would be for public health law and policy surveillance systems that involve the 'ongoing, systematic collection, analysis, interpretation and dissemination' of information about a given body of public health law and policy (e.g., tobacco control, cancer control, school health policy, built environment-related, food environment, HIV/AIDS, etc.).[53]

The key difference between traditional legal surveys and policy surveillance lies in the methods of collecting, analyzing, and disseminating legal data. As we and others from the empirical research side have conceptualized it, policy surveillance deploys an explicitly scientific method designed to make its methods transparent and the resulting data reproducible.[54] Creating the legal datasets that drive efficient policy surveillance is a matter of converting textual into numerical information, but the practice also depends upon a distinction between collecting and coding the apparent features of a legal text, on the one hand, and legal interpretation on the other. Though some degree of interpretation is inescapable in any coding exercise, researchers coding legal data quantitatively focus on objectively measurable features on the page—effective dates, regulated parties or actions, penalties—rather than attempting to capture what the terms mean as they might be applied to a particular set of facts or parties. Creating the data in a form scientists can use lowers the practical and cultural barriers to including legal variables in evaluation and epidemiological research. A quantitative measurement approach facilitates the collection of longitudinal data, both at the creation of the dataset and on an ongoing basis into the future, which shows policy stakeholders trends and allows more sophisticated research designs for evaluators.[55] It also allows machine coding and analysis, the easy publication of the data to websites, and the merging of legal data into other geocoded datasets and GIS platforms. PHLR has developed a prototype policy surveillance portal, LawAtlas, which includes coding software designed for collecting and coding laws, Workbench.[56] LawAtlas legal mapping studies have been published,[57] and evaluation research projects are now under way using LawAtlas data.

[53] J.F. Chriqui, J.C. O'Connor, and F.J. Chaloupka, 'What Gets Measured, Gets Changed: Evaluating Law and Policy for Maximum Impact' (2011) 39 (Suppl 1) *Journal of Law, Medicine and Ethics* 21.

[54] E. Anderson, C. Tremper, S. Thomas, and A.C. Wagenaar, 'Measuring Statutory Law and Regulations for Empirical Research' in A.C. Wagenaar and S. Burris (eds), *Public Health Law Research: Theory and Methods* (San Francisco, CA: Wiley-Jossey Bass 2013) 237.

[55] A.C. Wagenaar and K.A. Komro, 'Natural Experiments: Design Elements for Optimal Causal Inference' in A.C. Wagenaar and S. Burris (eds), *Public Health Law Research: Theory and Methods* (San Francisco, CA: Wiley-Jossey Bass 2013) 307.

[56] Public Health Law Research Program, 'LawAtlas: The Policy Surveillance Portal' (2012–14), available at <http://www.lawatlas.org> (accessed 18 November 2012).

[57] H.H. Harvey, 'Reducing Traumatic Brain Injuries in Youth Sports: Youth Sports Traumatic Brain Injury State Laws, January 2009–December 2012' (2013) 103(7) *American Journal of Public Health* 1249; J.K. Ibrahim, E.D. Anderson, S.C. Burris, and A.C. Wagenaar, 'State Laws Restricting

Policy surveillance conducted in this way can serve at least four important public health functions. As discussed, the work creates data that can immediately be used for evaluation. The data are also useful for less formal evaluation purposes. Policy is commonly an important tool for public health work, and so its enactment in jurisdictions and institutions large and small is an important implementation data point, and a useful practical guide to how well an agency's policy work is going. Yet health agencies are rarely actually tracking this, lacking either the tools or the belief such tracking is feasible, or both. Second, publishing policy surveillance data is a way of engaging, informing, and mobilizing stakeholders: if achieving wide coverage of smoke free laws is a priority, for example, it is important that the press, advocacy organizations, legislators, and the interested public know where they are in place and where they are not, what the trends are, and whether there are any obvious gaps or disparities. Third, with so many new and promising ideas coming from the local and national experimentation, policy surveillance is a way to diffuse innovation more quickly: potential adopters can find out what variants of policies are being implemented, and can readily get access to the texts themselves. Finally, we are seeing the potential to use the collection and coding of policies via a targeted form of public health agency crowdsourcing as a way to build interest in, and capacity to use, policy in the public health workforce. Each of these functions is valuable. Serving them with the same effort and system adds the considerable benefit of efficiency.

2.1.4 Evidence translation—and a bridge to the normative future

Law professors have an important role as knowledge brokers between research and policy. The literature on 'knowledge transfer' offers a number of evidence-based prescriptions for crossing the rocky terrain between research and policy.[58] Some of the advice is easier given than followed; some of it has the ring of an academic rediscovery of everyday practice; and some of it leaves the reader feeling that the conditions for evidence-based policy are impossible to satisfy. Whether we have been doing it all along or not, and regardless of whether it works in theory, the suggestion is that getting research into policy requires, in part, people who can transform bodies of data into ideas, linking information created by research to norms and values and hopes that (at least as much as data) drive policy decisions.[59] This sounds like a job for legal academics. One could go so far as to say that, at their most effective, they challenge the common notion that researchers cannot or should not engage normative concerns.

Though most of our individual ideas go nowhere most of the time, we do, as a collectivity, have an impact. We offer ideas that challenge mainstream notions about both our problems and the range of feasible solutions. We propose legal measures to improve public health, from local menu labeling ordinances[60] to international

Driver Use of Mobile Communications Devices: "Distracted-Driving" Provisions, 1992–2010' (2011) 40 *American Journal of Preventive Medicine* 659.

58 C. Mitton, C.E. Adair, E. McKenzie, S.B. Patten, and B. Waye Perry, 'Knowledge Transfer and Exchange: Review and Synthesis of the Literature' (2007) 85 *The Milbank Quarterly* 729.

59 J. Lavis, D. Robertson, J. Woodside, C. McLeod, and J. Abelson, 'How Can Research Organizations More Effectively Transfer Research Knowledge to Decision Makers?' (2003) 81 *The Milbank Quarterly* 221.

60 J.L. Pomeranz and K.D. Brownell, 'Legal and Public Health Considerations Affecting the Success, Reach, and Impact of Menu-Labeling Laws' (2008) 98 *American Journal of Public Health* 1578.

conventions on tobacco control.[61] In many of these instances, we are collaborators in devising and implementing broad strategies for health.[62] We add legal perspectives to health policy deliberations.[63] We take important public roles in assessing compliance with legal norms, as appointed officials—witness the work of Paul Hunt as the UN Special Rapporteur on the Right to Health[64]—and as scholars.[65] Though most of us will not have as high a level of public attention or influence as we'd like, we are the human infrastructure that supports the production of the stars, and anyone outside a winner-take-all world view will realize that most of us are actually performing humble but vital service in our particular areas—people who will do something or not, or do it in a particular way, because of something we have written or said.

Beyond the immediate task of translating research into policy today is the work of imagining worlds in which the legal conditions are more supportive of public health, the sort of work that Robert Cover captured in his image of law as a bridge to the normative future.[66] A neo-liberal political economy, which dominates many of our countries', does not seem to be good for traditional health strategies nor consistent with implementing new paradigms.[67] The recommendations of the Commission on the Social Determinants of Health are not likely to be taken up by the Tea Party. Austerity policies are decimating public health and social infrastructure. Deregulatory and starve-the-beast ideologies put undue faith in the market to manage externalities without collective oversight. On any given issue in this unfolding political story, we have more or less vigorous debate and political struggle. What we seem to lack are ideas big enough to challenge hegemonic neo-liberalism, or to offer new pathways once neo-liberalism collapses in autopoetic paralysis—as hegemonic ideas tend to do. The need for and the nature of new ideas about law will vary from place to place, but imagining alternative futures is a vital normative role for law professors.

This sort of imagining can certainly be done in deontological terms, and there is an inherent requirement of counterfactual thinking even in the most utilitarian essays in this genre. Still, for many of us, much of the time, the future we imagine is one in which regulations and other legal interventions that have been shown empirically to work are widely applied to problems whose dimensions have been reliably measured. (And also a world in which laws that do no good, or whose harms overwhelm the good they do, would be repealed.) The 'nomos' we imagine may be a product of normative analysis and preferences, but the actions we take within it are likely to depend to a greater or lesser degree on facts. In this role, law professors can suggest ways in which changes in how we think about the law can make it possible to apply evidence-informed measures to improve public health and welfare.[68]

61 R. Roemer, A. Taylor, and J. Lariviere, 'Origins of the WHO Framework Convention on Tobacco Control' (2005) 95 *American Journal of Public Health* 936.

62 C. Sunstein and R. Thaler, *Nudge: Improving Decisions About Health, Wealth, and Happiness* (New Haven, CT: Yale University Press, 2008); W.E. Parmet and R.A. Daynard, 'The New Public Health Litigation' (2000) 21 *Annual Review of Public Health* 437.

63 A. Faeh, 'Obesity in Europe: The Strategy of the European Union from a Public Health Law Perspective' (2012) 19 *European Journal of Health Law* 69.

64 S. Boseley, 'Paul Hunt: UN Special Rapporteur on the Right to Health' (2007) 370 *Lancet* 381.

65 M. Weait, *Intimacy and Responsibility—the Criminalisation of HIV Transmission* (Abingdon: Routledge-Cavendish, 2007).

66 R. Cover, 'The Supreme Court, 1982 Term—Foreword: Nomos and Narrative' (1983) 97 *Harvard Law Review* 4.

67 S. Burris, 'The Invisibility of Public Health: Population-Level Measures in a Politics of Market Individualism' (1997) 87 *American Journal of Public Health* 1607.

68 W. Parmet, *Populations, Public Health, and the Law* (Washington, DC: Georgetown University Press, 2009).

Getting our facts wrong, or interpreting them poorly, defeats much of the purpose, and certainly reduces the chances that we can get our allies in health to go along with our normative ideas. Getting our facts right—in Brandeis briefs, policy prescriptions, normative claims, or alternative futures—is a matter of properly reading existing scientific data. Many of us are consuming primary research literature much of the time, so this is not in itself a novel proposition or call for change. But there are important nuances that need attending to. Epstein and King find we often do just a terrible job interpreting empirical data. Every 'rule of inference' that a researcher must attend to in designing a study is a criterion a reader should apply to evaluate the study.[69] Attention to sampling and design goes a long way to forestalling unjustified generalization from limited data. Many sources are available that explain the important distinctions of design and statistical analysis.[70] Our tendency to elide these technical considerations in summarizing 'the facts' behind our claims is a petty vice, not a fundamental character flaw. Self-discipline and a short course of reading—reinforced by peer attention to this point—is enough to allow us to make the important distinctions related to design and methods. Most of us will not enter the lists about the relative advantages of random and fixed effects models, but we can appreciate the varying inferential value of case studies, cross-sectional observations, longitudinal quasi experiments, and randomized controlled trials.

Taking the science a bit more seriously is also important because it gives us a better chance to engage critically with a health research audience. Almost no research is perfect, and a good deal of research is flawed in ways that we can detect and help to remedy. If lawyers have not been involved, researchers may make fairly elementary mistakes in conceptualizing how legal systems work or what the law is. A critical gaze from the legal perspective can expose instances in which a whole line of research has ignored important questions.[71] There is much to critically monitor in how health research is prioritized, funded, and performed, but it does little good for the cause of better research for us to critically assess gaps and problems in the research literature in a law review article. Few of the readers will be planning to do research, and few of the researchers will be readers. It is important for us as health law scholars to devote some of our time to writing for and interacting with health researchers—and important for us as peers and senior professors to encourage our younger colleagues to do so.

Our normative engagement with the facts of the world should also include reflection on how we have defined 'health law'. There have been interesting debates about whether it should even be considered a field.[72] Assuming it is, we have, globally, quite a diversity of views about what it is and how it is institutionalized. In the US, for historical reasons, we have a strange division between public health law and health care law, reflecting a long (and we hope eroding) distinction between health care and public health. In Europe, health and health care are better integrated and so the line between health care and public health lawyers seems less stark. In Australia, Chris Reynolds and Michael Tooma have challenged the century-long habit of separating public health and

69 Epstein and King, 'The Rules of Inference' (n 36).

70 R.T. Katz, D.I. Campagnolo, G. Goldberg, J.C. Parker, Z.M. Pine, and J. Whyte, 'Critical Evaluation of Clinical Research' (1995) 76 *Archives of Physical Medicine and Rehabilitation* 82.

71 S. Burris, 'Law and the Social Risk of Health Care: Lessons from HIV Testing' (1998) 61 *Albany Law Review* 831.

72 M. Berman, 'Defining the Field of Public Health Law' (forthcoming 2014), 15 *DePaul Journal of Health Care Law*, available at <http://ssrn.com/abstract=2150723> (accessed 2 February 2014); E.R. Elhauge, 'Can Health Law Become a Coherent Field' (2006) 41 *Wake Forest Law Review* 365.

environmental law,[73] a particularly salient idea, given the predicted massive health effects of global climate change. Gostin's Framework Convention idea is a good example of how health law merges with development and global governance. All these instances point to the challenge of keeping our categories from binding us in the face of change.[74]

3. Conclusion

Thirty years ago, public health law was a moribund field in the US legal academy. Engagement with a titanic health shock, the HIV epidemic, brought it back to active life.[75] A growing cadre of academic health lawyers has made strides to institutionalize the discipline in law schools and schools of public health, and strategic interventions from the Centers for Disease Control and Prevention and the Robert Wood Johnson Foundation have supported both the broader field and the empirical project now advanced by PHLR in the US. A similar process is unfolding at the global level, as like-minded scholars from a variety of fields come together to figure out how to take law seriously in public health. The field needs more centers, more funding, and better integration with institutions and organizations that conduct public health research. What are we waiting for?

73 C. Reynolds, *Public and Environmental Health Law* (Annandale, NSW: Federation Press, 2011); M. Tooma, *Safety, Security, Health and Environment Law* (Annandale, NSW: Federation Press, 2009).

74 L. Gostin, 'Meeting Basic Survival Needs of the World's Least Healthy People' (n 1).

75 S. Burris and L.O. Gostin, 'The Impact of HIV/AIDS on the Development of Public Health Law' in R.O. Valdiserri (ed), *Dawning Answers: How the HIV/AIDS Epidemic Has Helped to Strengthen Public Health* (New York: OUP, 2003) 96.

28

International Law and Global Health

Geoffrey B. Cockerham and William C. Cockerham

1. International Law and Chronic Disease

This chapter examines why international law has largely ignored the causal factors associated with chronic diseases—despite the fact that human mortality throughout the world is largely due to chronic afflictions such as heart disease, cancer, stroke, and diabetes. The focus of global health governance has been almost exclusively on the control of infectious diseases since 1851 and the convening of the International Sanitary Conference in Paris to address worldwide health problems. The only major international legal response to chronic disease was in 2003 when the World Health Assembly of the World Health Organization adopted the Framework Convention on Tobacco Control (FCTC). The FCTC contains a number of regulations concerning tobacco use that states are obliged to follow and set a precedent for a global response to other chronic disease risk factors, namely poor diets, lack of physical activity, and alcohol use. However, these other risk factors have yet to be convincingly addressed in international law. Consequently, this chapter investigates why the only measures in international law pertaining to chronic disease currently exist for tobacco use and little else.

Our analysis of international legal action concerning chronic disease focuses on tobacco use, diet, exercise, and alcohol consumption. They constitute major risk factors for several chronic diseases or, alternatively, serve as preventive measures.[1] With the exception of smoking, which lacks any positive health benefits, the other three risk factors have a binary (positive or negative) function with respect to health. Lack of exercise can be harmful and exercise beneficial, diets can be either healthy or unhealthy, while moderate use of alcohol is healthier than excessive drinking or abstinence.[2] In each instance, the negative side of the practice constitutes a significant cause of chronic disease and premature death worldwide. Tobacco use and exposure to tobacco smoke, overweight and obesity, lack of physical activity, low fruit and vegetable consumption, and heavy drinking cause over 13 million deaths worldwide on an annual basis and this is projected to increase.[3] Fewer than half of these deaths were due to tobacco-related causes, yet tobacco stands largely alone as a target for the implementation of global legal action.

[1] W.C Cockerham, *Social Causes of Health and Disease* (Cambridge: 2nd edn, Polity Press, 2013).

[2] Cockerham, *Social Causes of Health and Disease* (n 1).

[3] E. Lee, 'The World Health Organization's Global Strategy on Diet, Physical Activity, and Health: Turning Strategy into Action' (2005) 60 *Food and Drug Law Journal* 569.

2. Analytic Framework

In order to explain the difference in the international legal response to tobacco compared to diet, physical activity, and alcohol, we apply an analytical framework utilizing elements of the norm dynamics and international legalization perspectives. Norm dynamics are based on a social constructionist view of international politics, while the legalization approach is primarily associated with rationalism. Social constructionism maintains that all knowledge is created through human interaction and interpretation and is the outcome of culturally specific processes leading to its creation.[4] The theory emphasizes the importance of norms that have, in turn, been identified as a fundamental feature of international interaction.[5] Norms are specific forms of behavior generally accepted as right and proper by a society that are used as standards intended to guide, regulate, or control conduct. They constitute an essential component of culture that helps to make social life possible. When they are codified, they become laws or other types of formal rules and regulations.

Rationalism maintains that knowledge is based on reason and provides the foundation for various theories of rational choice. These theories emphasize the pursuit of utility maximization by relevant actors, with the identities of the actors often being exogenous. An example is the way social systems are organized to influence individuals to act rationally and serve their own best interests within the constraints and enablements of their socio-economic position and in accordance with the resources available to them. While rationalism and constructionism are ontologically different, they are not mutually exclusive. The effect of law comes from both normative considerations as well as the calculated self-interests of actors.[6] Law begins as an idea, and then over time becomes widely accepted as a norm of behavior. Potentially, this norm may take a legal form whether it is a law, a legally binding contract, or a widely practiced custom. The eventual legal form that a norm may take could be based on rational calculation as well as being a social construction. Utilizing these two approaches, we examine the evolution of global health law in relation to chronic disease, as well as the constraints and costs that this process may pose on certain actors that are resistant to such regulation.

The norm dynamics approach we use to guide our analysis is based on the norm life cycle proposed by Finnemore and Sikkink.[7] The cycle is composed of three stages: (1) norm emergence, (2) norm cascade, and (3) norm internalization. The critical mechanism in the first stage of norm emergence is persuasion on the part of actors functioning as norm entrepreneurs. They try to persuade relevant authorities, which in the context of international politics would be national governments, to adopt their idea as a standard practice. Norm promoters at the international level need some type of organizational platform through which they advance their ideas. If the norm entrepreneurs are successful in their persuasion and reach a 'tipping point' when a critical mass of states accepts the norm, then the norm moves to the second stage of cascade in which it becomes broadly accepted. At this stage, the primary mechanism is socialization, where the authorities who have accepted the norm begin to socialize others into

[4] A. Horwitz, *Creating Mental Illness* (Chicago, IL: University of Chicago Press, 2002).

[5] A. Wendt, 'Anarchy is What States Make of It: The Social Construction of Power Politics' (1992) 46 *International Organization* 396.

[6] K. Abbott and D. Snidal, 'Hard and Soft Law in International Governance' (2000) 54 *International Organization* 421.

[7] M. Finnemore and K. Sikkink, 'Norm Dynamics and Political Change' (1998) 52 *International Organization* 887.

adopting the norm so that it moves in a cascade toward universal acceptance. If this socialization process achieves enough momentum, then at the far end of the norm cascade, the third stage of norm internalization is realized. When a norm becomes internalized in society at large, it reaches a point where it has been accepted as right and proper and taken for granted without further debate or the need to justify or rationalize it. A strongly internalized norm would be consistent with the international law concept of *jus cogens*, or a peremptory norm, which is a norm that is so powerful that it cannot be contravened by a contrary practice. Prohibitions against slavery and piracy are examples of norms that have received universal acceptance.

While the norm dynamics approach can explain how an idea will eventually be accepted as a standard of behavior at the international or global level, it does not specify the form that the norm will take. The literature on legalization is a useful supplement in this regard. Legalization refers to a concept that is a specific form of international institutionalization. It includes the elements of obligation, precision, and delegation. Obligation refers to the extent to which rules are binding actors, precision refers to the clarity and specificity of those rules, and delegation refers to the extent to which a third party has to interpret, apply, or adjudicate the rules.[8] The amount of each of the elements may vary in international institutions at relatively high, medium, or low levels.

In applying the concept of legalization to global health law, one key distinction is that of 'hard' law versus 'soft' law. Hard law would refer to a form of institutionalization with strong elements of legalization, while soft law refers to a form with weaker, or perhaps missing elements. Both forms share strengths and weaknesses. In terms of hard law, actors are able to make more credible commitments to the agreed upon rules, this increases the exposure and costs for noncompliance, and such rules would be more likely to be incorporated into domestic law. The weakness of pursuing a cooperative arrangement based on hard law is that it is costly to manage and enforce, and may require states to lose some sovereignty to a supranational authority. The strengths and weakness of soft law are in an opposite direction. Soft law provides a limited commitment, poses little or no cost for noncompliance, and would be unlikely to be incorporated into domestic law. At the same time, such an arrangement poses little cost to a state that makes such a commitment.[9] With a soft law arrangement, it is much easier to negotiate and to reach a compromise. This is, however, less likely to promote an effective policy change.

In taking these two differing approaches to understanding international legal arrangements into account, some interesting questions emerge. For instance, once a norm becomes internalized or generally accepted, how would that norm be represented in law? Would the norm remain as a shared understanding? Would it be recognized as a universal principle or a custom? Or would it have to be represented in a formal agreement with binding obligations? The purpose of this chapter is to apply these approaches and questions to global health in the area of chronic disease. In particular, we examine how norms have evolved in the key areas of international cooperation related to chronic disease, and how, or even if, they have manifested themselves in legal arrangements to address a global problem.

[8] K. Abbott, R.O. Keohane, A. Moravcsik, A.-M. Slaughter, and D. Snidal, 'The Concept of Legalization' (2000) 54 *International Organization* 401.

[9] Abbott and Snidal, 'Hard and Soft Law in International Governance' (n 6).

3. Tobacco

The genesis of an international legal response to the problem of tobacco began with the World Health Organization (WHO) in the 1970s. The World Health Assembly (WHA) passed its first resolution relevant to tobacco in 1970. Although this resolution did not address tobacco per se, it did state in its preamble that the WHA was aware of the significant effect smoking had on certain chronic diseases and it also requested, as an operative clause of the resolution, that the Director-General of the WHO should consider assembling an 'expert group to recommend further action that might be taken to discourage smoking'.[10] In 1979, a report by the WHO Committee on Smoking Control proposed that the WHA should contemplate invoking its power under Article 19 of the WHO Constitution to adopt an international convention addressing the tobacco epidemic.[11] Although the WHA had the legal power to produce a treaty, adoption would require a two-thirds vote, and the WHA had yet to invoke this power for an international agreement concerning health.

The WHA did not actively pursue a treaty-based solution during the 1980s, but the idea of such a solution became revitalized during the 1990s. The initial step was a meeting between two American academics Allyn Taylor and Ruth Roemer, who served as norm entrepreneurs. Taylor had published an article in 1992 in the American Journal of Law and Medicine. In her article, Taylor argued that the WHO should make greater use of its delegated legal authority to assist member states in strengthening their laws addressing health standards.[12] Roemer and Taylor together developed a proposal for an international regulatory response through the WHO to address tobacco control. They believed that tobacco would make a good test case because of its policy history in the WHO.[13] The proposal was presented to members of the WHO Secretariat and various international conferences.

At the 1994 World Conference on Tobacco and Health in Paris, Roemer drafted a resolution introduced by Judith Mckay, the director of the Asian Consultancy for Tobacco Control, calling for an international convention on tobacco control to be sponsored by the United Nations. Mckay had been a strong advocate for such a treaty and promoted this idea to the WHO and the United Nations Conference on Trade and Development (UNCTAD). A fair amount of pessimism was expressed in these organizations due to a perceived lack of support by some member states, as well as the expected strong opposition from tobacco companies.[14] Nevertheless, the resolution was approved at the Paris conference.

The next step in the process was to gain support in the WHA, which would have the authority to officially adopt a treaty on tobacco control. Canada, led by their delegate Jean Lariviere, took the lead in the WHA by drafting a resolution co-sponsored by Finland, Mexico, and Tanzania.[15] After negotiations, the WHA approved Resolution 48.11 in May 1995. This resolution, which referenced the one adopted in Paris,

10 World Health Assembly, 'Health Consequences of Smoking', WHA 23.32 (Geneva, 1970).

11 World Health Organization, 'History of the WHO Framework Convention on Tobacco Control' (Geneva, 2009).

12 A. Taylor, 'Making the World Health Organization Work: A Legal Framework for Universal Access to the Conditions for Health' (1992) 18 *American Journal of Law and Medicine* 301.

13 R. Roemer, A. Taylor, and J. Lariviere, 'Origins of the WHO Framework Convention on Tobacco Control' (2005) 95 *American Journal of Public Health* 936.

14 J. Mckay, 'The Making of a Convention on Tobacco Control' (2003) 81 *Bulletin of the World Health Organization* 551.

15 Roemer, Taylor, and Lariviere, 'Origins of the WHO Framework Convention' (n 13).

requested that the Director-General make a report to the WHA on the 'feasibility of developing an international instrument such as guidelines, a declaration, or an international convention on tobacco control'.[16] Roemer and Taylor followed up with a report on various options for the implementation of WHA48.11 that was presented to WHO two months later.[17]

Despite the relatively quick passage of time between the Roemer and Taylor proposals in 1993 and the passage of the WHA resolution in 1995, significant opposition to a legally binding convention still existed at the WHO. The adoption of an international convention would qualify as a 'hard law' response to an international health problem, which would require some clear legally binding obligations on member states. The WHO had not taken this approach in its history and so this strategy did not fit with its bureaucratic culture. As an intergovernmental organization, the WHO Secretariat had the purpose of serving its member states. Additionally, the organization was dependent on these states for financial support. Some WHO officials advocated that a 'soft law' approach would be a much more appropriate legal strategy, and a more politically acceptable approach to the tobacco issue. In this case, tobacco control could continue to addressed through WHA resolutions or, instead of a legally binding treaty, a non-binding code of conduct on tobacco could be adopted by the WHA or the United Nations General Assembly.[18] The WHO Executive Board, however, decided in early 1996 to endorse the treaty-based approach to tobacco even though the initiative faced opposition within the Secretariat. Following the Board's decision at the May 1996 meeting of the WHA, resolution WHA49.17 was passed. This resolution requested that the Director-General 'initiate the development of a framework convention in accordance with Article 19 of the WHO Constitution'.[19]

The buildup of momentum on the tobacco convention, however, slowed until 1998 due to a continued lack of support to continue to pursue the WHO's first treaty. At this time three key events took place that helped to push the convention to a formal negotiation stage. The first event was the choice of Gro Harlem Bruntlund from Norway as the new Director-General of the WHO. Upon assuming office, Bruntland made tobacco control and malaria key goals of her administration. In addition to her strong support for tobacco control, she was also a proponent of a legalistic approach to the issue. As a former Minister of Environmental Affairs, Bruntland was experienced with the treaty drafting process even though it was inconsistent with the culture of the WHO Secretariat.[20] She initiated the Tobacco Free Initiative (TFI) that was designed to raise global awareness of the health problems caused by tobacco, as well as to prepare and socialize member states into the potential acceptance of a treaty.

The strategy of the TFI was not only to gain the support of national governments, but also to work more with civil society organizations (CSOs), promote the cause with other intergovernmental organizations (IGOs), and form partnerships with organizations such as the Food and Agriculture Organization (FAO) and the United Nations Children's Fund (UNICEF).

16 World Health Assembly, 'An International Strategy for Tobacco Control', WHA48.11 (1995), available at <http://www.who.int/tobacco/framework/wha_eb/wha48_11/en/index.html>.

17 Roemer, Taylor, and Lariviere, 'Origins of the WHO Framework Convention' (n 13).

18 Roemer, Taylor, and Lariviere, 'Origins of the WHO Framework Convention' (n 13).

19 World Health Assembly, 'International Framework Convention for Tobacco Control', WHA49.17 (1996), available at <http://www.who.int/tobacco/framework/wha_eb/wha49_17/en/index.html>.

20 'International Framework Convention for Tobacco Control' (n 19).

These partnerships contributed to the second key event for tobacco control in 1998 that was collaboration between the WHO and the World Bank. The product of this relationship was the production of the World Bank report 'Curbing the Epidemic: Governments and Economics and the Economics of Tobacco Control'.[21] In this report, not only were the global trends and health consequences of smoking covered, but the report also showed the economic costs to national governments associated with smoking. The study found that in addition to improving the health of the population, tobacco control efforts would not significantly affect employment in most countries and the cost of a comprehensive tobacco program would be fairly affordable even in developing states. The economic analysis of the report proved to be very influential in the movement. Not only was tobacco control being addressed as a biomedical or a moral issue, but it was now supplemented with a cost-effective analysis utilizing statistics to indicate the economic benefits from such a policy. This evidence provided an effective counter-argument to the tobacco industry's position that increased tobacco regulation would be too harmful to national economies.[22]

The third key event of 1998 was the settlement between state governments and the tobacco industry in the US. The attorney generals of Mississippi and Minnesota brought lawsuits against major tobacco companies in 1994 to recover tobacco-related costs to their state's Medicaid programs. This lawsuit was soon joined by other states. A compromise was reached between four tobacco companies (Brown & Williamson, Lorillard, Philip Morris, and R.J. Reynolds) and forty-six state attorney generals in 1998. This settlement, known as the Master Settlement Agreement, provided that in return for the termination of the lawsuit, the prohibition of advertising directed at young people, and the disclosure of confidential industry documents, the tobacco companies agreed to pay $206 billion over twenty-five years as well as future payments based on the amount of cigarette sales made in the US by these companies.[23] The confidential documents were made available to the WHO as a result of this settlement. Using this information, a WHO panel of experts published a report in 2000, 'Tobacco Industry Strategies to Undermine Tobacco Control Activities at the World Health Organization'.[24] In this report, the WHO found that the tobacco industry had for years used financial influence by way of donations to political parties, distorted WHO research findings, and promoted the media and proxy lobbying groups to subvert the WHO in any tobacco-related activity.

The WHA approved a resolution establishing a working group and an intergovernmental negotiating body (INB) to begin to draft and negotiate a preliminary treaty in 1999. The draft of the text of the agreement was accepted by the WHA the following year, and approval was granted for the INB to begin negotiations for a final document. Transparency and civil society involvement was important in the WHO's strategy to gain acceptance of the framework convention. In October 2000, the WHO held its first public hearing on the convention, allowing the tobacco companies and civil society organizations to make testimonies on the agreement. Written and oral statements by over 160 different organizations were made publicly available.

21 P. Jha and F.J. Chaloupka, *Curbing the Epidemic: Governments and Economics and the Economics of Tobacco Control* (Washington, DC: World Bank, 1999).

22 J. Collin, 'Tobacco Politics' (2004) 47 *Development* 92.

23 S.A. Schroeder, 'Tobacco Control in the Wake of the 1998 Master Settlement Agreement' (2004) 350 New *England Journal of Medicine* 293.

24 T. Zeltner, D.A. Kessler, M. Anke, and F. Randera, 'Tobacco Industry Strategies to Undermine Tobacco Control Activities at the World Health Organization' (Geneva, 2000).

Treaty negotiations were somewhat contentious; they covered six INB sessions and were not concluded until February 2003. Collin identified three different coalitions that emerged over the course of the negotiations.[25] One was the Framework Convention Alliance (FCA), which was a group of civil society organizations that wanted an agreement with strong obligations requiring the implementation of significant tobacco control policies by member states. The second coalition was a group of governments from developed states, including much of the European Union, Canada, Australia, and New Zealand, who also supported a strong treaty, but with some flexibility for legal interpretation. The third was composed of states that were not in favor of a highly regulatory agreement, and expressed their desire for a limited approach. These states included the US, Germany, and Japan. The tobacco industry was not passive in the negotiation process and used their financial leverage to exert influence on certain states to favor a less restrictive treaty. In Germany, both the Christian Democratic Union/Christian Social Union and the Social Democratic Party received significant financial contributions from the tobacco industry.[26] Neither party favored a strong policy on tobacco regulation, and this position was reflected by Germany's negotiating stance on the framework convention. The industry also attempted to re-image itself as socially responsible by announcing its support for some control initiatives in an attempt to move states to accept a less restrictive agreement.

The WHA approved the final draft as the Framework Convention on Tobacco Control (FCTC) in May 2003. The treaty was signed by 168 states by June 2004, and came into effect in February 2005, after it had been ratified by forty states. As of June 2012, the FCTC has been signed by 175 states and ratified by 165 of those states, which makes it a legally binding agreement for the vast majority of countries in the world. Not only did it become the first international treaty on global health and the first treaty sponsored by the WHO, but the process of drafting, negotiation, signing, ratification, and entry into force was one of the fastest of any international treaty.[27]

Article 3 of the FCTC provides its objective, which is:

> To protect present and future generations from the devastating health, social, environmental and economic consequences of tobacco consumption and exposure to tobacco smoke by providing a framework for tobacco control measures to be implemented by the Parties at the national, regional and international levels in order to reduce continually and substantially the prevalence of tobacco use and exposure to tobacco smoke.[28]

The treaty provides for a number of different obligations for the states that agree to its terms. These obligations include the development of tobacco control policies and legislation, the provision of protection from tobacco commercial interests, and spending funds to implement the agreement. Policy areas that are covered in the FCTC included advertising, labeling of tobacco products, taxation, protection against exposure from tobacco smoke, sales practices, smuggling, legal liability, and research and surveillance on tobacco control.

The FCTC qualifies as a 'hard law' response to a global health problem. It is a document with a number of precise articles, and several of the articles in the agreement contain the highly obligatory phrase 'Each party shall' in describing the commitments

25 Collin, 'Tobacco Politics' (n 22) 91–6.

26 A.H. Cooper and P. Kurzer, 'Rauche ohne Feuer: Why Germany Lags in Tobacco Control' (2003) 21 *German Politics and Society* 24.

27 'History of the WHO Framework Convention on Tobacco Control' (n 11).

28 World Health Organization, 'WHO Framework Convention on Tobacco Control' (Geneva, 2003).

by the states. The FCTC also specifies under Article 30 that no reservations can be made to the agreement. The most significant limitation posed on the obligations stated in the treaty comes in Article 13 regarding a ban on tobacco advertising and promotion. As an exception to a ban, states were permitted to restrict advertising only in a way that did not conflict with its constitutional principles, which was a particular concern of the US in negotiations. Another suggested weakness of the treaty was the legal liability provisions under Article 19, which states: 'Parties shall consider taking legislative action or promoting their existing laws, where necessary, to deal with criminal and civil liability, including compensation where appropriate.' While this provision does not pose much of an obligation, Yach points out such a provision in addressing legal liability in an international convention is unusual and its inclusion should be viewed as a positive achievement.[29] A major omission from the final text of the treaty, other than briefly being mentioned in the preamble to the treaty, concerned trade in tobacco products. The FCTC did not address the trade issue even though many states supported its inclusion. High-income states with a strong policies of trade liberalization, such as the US and the UK, were able to avoid any mention of connection between tobacco consumption and trade in the main text of the treaty.[30]

Although the FCTC qualifies as a hard law response due to the significant levels of obligation and precision embodied in its text, it is weaker on the dimension of delegation. The FCTC articles relevant to delegation are Articles 23 to 25 that address institutional arrangements and Article 27 on dispute settlement. These articles provide for a Conference of Parties to oversee the convention, and cooperate with other IGOs. The WHO Secretariat would also serve as interim Secretariat until a permanent one for the FCTC is established. For the settlement of disputes, Article 27 permits parties to enter into an ad hoc arbitration process that would be directed by the Conference of Parties, but the only obligation for the parties is to settle their dispute by any appropriate means. Despite a very limited delegation of authority, the treaty is a very strong international response to a global health problem. Because treaty negotiations were completed so quickly in an area that has not historically been addressed by such a legalistic process at the international level, it is not surprising that delegation of authority was not much of a consideration in the process.

Returning to the analytic framework provided by norm dynamics, it would appear that tobacco has passed through the first stage of norm emergence and into the next stage of norm cascade resulting in a 'hard law' approach to the health problems of tobacco. It was possible to reach this far because norm entrepreneurs, such as Roemer and Taylor, were able to act as effective advocates in promoting tobacco control. They were able to gain support within the WHO Secretariat, as well as from member states such as Canada, that were willing to take a leadership role in drafting the first resolution in the WHA calling for an international legal instrument for tobacco control. The norm entrepreneurs had a sympathetic organizational platform in the WHO due to its history of debate on tobacco, strong scientific evidence supporting the need for action, and adverse public opinion directed toward the tobacco industry.

For tobacco control to successfully emerge as an international norm, WHO Director-General Bruntland used her office to advance the anti-tobacco agenda and push for a legalistic response to tobacco in spite of some resistance within the WHO due to the unusual step of a treaty-based approach and the bureaucratic culture of the

29 D. Yach, 'WHO Framework on Tobacco Control' (2003) 361 *Lancet* 611.

30 J. Collin, 'Global Health, Equity and the WHO Framework Convention on Tobacco Control' (2010) 17 *Global Health Promotion* 73.

organization. Perhaps even more significant than the cultural barrier, was the influence of neoliberalism which was widely accepted in the 1990s and emphasized the importance of the free market and a limited role for the state in economic affairs. The tobacco industry and some states, most notably the US, were not in favor of a tobacco control agreement because it would require some degree of market regulation and interference with personal choice. A major factor in overcoming neoliberalism was the Master Settlement with the tobacco industry that exposed it as unethical and manipulative. The harm to the public reputation of the industry encouraged it to move from a strongly adversarial position to acting in a supportive manner in order to portray itself as more socially responsible.

Finnemore and Sikkink observe that a norm only evolves from the emergence stage to the norm cascade stage once it reaches a certain threshold, which is met when either one-third of the states worldwide or the most influential states accept the norm.[31] This threshold was easily reached for tobacco control. As of June 2012, 165 states have ratified the FCTC. Even the US, which has yet to ratify the agreement, nevertheless signed it 2004. For the norm to continue to transition through the cascade stage, states need to be socialized by the norm and implement its practice without external or internal pressure. There is evidence this is taking place, as the WHO recently reported that some sixteen states had enacted comprehensive national smoke-free legislation between 2008 and 2010.[32] Also, the number of states with laws requiring 50 percent of the package displays to include health warnings increased from ten in 2007 to nineteen in 2010, while eleven states raised tobacco taxes to 75 percent of the purchase price between 2008 and 2010.[33] Conversely, the same report indicated that seventy-four states had no restrictions on tobacco advertising as of 2010.

It is therefore apparent that the norm of tobacco control is still in a relatively early phase of cascading. Although increasing numbers of states are adapting the FCTC to their legal systems, others are still being socialized into adopting its provisions. In the meantime, the use of tobacco products, primarily cigarettes, remains widespread by a majority of adult males in many countries, especially China, Russia, Japan, the Philippines, and others. The evolution of a norm during its life cycle is not inevitable and the norm on tobacco control is relatively new. Whether or not it reaches the third stage of norm internalization globally is uncertain, although the current direction is promising.

The next question relating to our analysis on tobacco control concerns when the tobacco control norm converts to a formal, legal response? The norm dynamics approach helps to explain when a norm begins, emerges, and then becomes accepted, but it does not directly explain the legal form the norm will take. The legalization approach, and its distinction between 'hard' and 'soft' law can provide insight into this process. According to Abbott and Snidal, states use a solution based on hard legalization to increase credible commitments, reduce transaction costs, and complete contracting.[34] Soft law is preferable when states are more concerned about sovereignty. In the case of tobacco control, the first step towards a hard law resolution was the emergence of a strong norm. The second step was whether states wanted to make a credible commitment to this issue despite the costs of sovereignty and managing the agreement.

31 Finnemore and Sikkink, 'Norm Dynamics and Political Change' (n 7) 901.

32 World Health Organization, 'WHO Report on the Global Tobacco Epidemic' (Geneva, 2011) 44.

33 'WHO Report on the Global Tobacco Epidemic' (n 32) 50.

34 Abbott and Snidal, 'Hard and Soft Law in International Governance' (n 6).

The combination of the scientific data on the harm caused by tobacco and the support of the WHO convinced states of the benefits, both to the health of their citizens and their economy of regulating tobacco. Much of the FCTC is aimed at the practices of the tobacco industry. When that industry lost credibility and the economic benefits of tobacco were jeopardized, the cost to states to regulate that industry was reduced. At this point, making a legal commitment to tobacco became a cost-effective state strategy. Once the tobacco control norm emerged, states made a decision to accept a hard law response out of a rational calculation. Nevertheless, states were still unable to make a commitment to restrict trade in tobacco products as such a restriction was deemed too costly despite the emergent norm.

4. Diet

The momentum gained from the tobacco initiative advanced greater awareness in the WHO of the potential for other legalistic responses to chronic disease, including health problems associated with poor diets. Diet as a global health problem had received little attention in international law. Previously, the WHO and the FAO had developed the Codex Alimentarius in 1963 to provide standards and recommended guidelines on food safety. The Codex, however, was restricted to safety standards and did not address issues concerning nutrition. The first step towards establishing a collective international response to dietary problems began in 1998, when the WHA passed Resolution WHA51.18, requesting the WHO Director-General to develop a global strategy for the prevention and control of non-communicable diseases (NCDs). Brundtland followed up in 2000, by outlining such a strategy to the WHA in May. She established three main objectives: (1) analyze the social, political, economic, and behavioral determinants of NCDs, especially among poor populations; (2) reduce exposure of population to risks factors for NCDs, citing tobacco, diet, and physical inactivity as the factors needing attention; and (3) improve health care for individuals suffering from NCDs. For implementation, Brundtland emphasized the importance of surveillance and health promotion, and encouraged member states to be engaged in this process by developing policy frameworks to address these objectives.[35] This strategy was formally adopted by the Assembly as Resolution WHA 53.17.

In order to examine the connection between poor diet and physical inactivity in relation to global health more carefully, the WHO and the FAO conducted a conference of health experts to discuss and analyze scientific evidence on these domains. This group, known as the Joint WHO/FAO Expert Consultation on Diet, Nutrition and the Prevention of Chronic Diseases, recommended greater consumption of fruits, vegetables, nuts, and whole grains, regular physical activity, and the reduction of fat, especially saturated and trans fat, salt, and sugar in diets. It suggests limits of sugar and saturated fat to be less than 10 percent of daily energy intake.[36]

Similarly to the strategy with tobacco control, once in possession of strong evidence, the WHO next sought to engage in discussions with member states, civil society organizations, and the food industry. Also as in the situation with tobacco, the WHO/FAO report produced a backlash from the private sector. The US sugar industry, along with soft drink corporations such as Coca-Cola and Pepsico, challenged

[35] World Health Organization, 'Non-Communicable Diseases in the South East Asia Region' (New Delhi, 2002).

[36] World Health Organization/Food and Agriculture Organization, 'Diet, Nutrition and the Prevention of Chronic Diseases' (Geneva, 2003).

the scientific evidence regarding the recommended standards for sugar consumption. They requested the US health secretary to ask the WHO to withdraw the report, and suggested that the US should consider withholding funds if it continued to support a scientifically-flawed study.[37] The backlash by the sugar industry was stronger than that of tobacco.[38] In contrast, the recommendations for physical activity did not meet the same kind of political resistance. Some companies in the private sector demonstrated willingness to support physical activity initiatives. Although in some instances it was apparent that this support was motivated by demonstrating social responsibility or to avoid stronger regulations for dietary standards.[39]

The WHO continued to pursue a draft for a Global Strategy on Diet, Physical Activity, and Health (DPAS) despite the strong objections from the sugar industry. Although the WHO viewed diet and tobacco both to be products associated with increased risks of chronic disease, it also viewed the two to be qualitatively different. Food, unlike tobacco, was not considered to be an inherently harmful product. It also viewed the food industry as a potential partner, and much less of an adversary than the tobacco industry.[40] Food corporations, especially the sugar industry, nevertheless, contended that food selection was an individual choice and should not be subject to regulation.

Before a draft of the DPAS was to appear before the WHO Executive Board in January 2004, the US Department of Health and Human Services sent a letter to the WHO, which was in support of the sugar industry's criticism of the WHO/FAO expert report. In response, Kaare Norum, one of the planners of DPAS, wrote an open letter to the US Secretary of the Department of Health and Human Services that backed the scientific findings of the report and pointed out the growing problem of obesity in the US. Global reaction to the letter helped to soften the position of the US at the WHO Executive Board meeting.[41] Key points of contention at the meeting consisted of the support some states gave to the sugar industry's position and concerns about the economic effect that restrictions on sugar consumption could place on sugar exporting nations. The Executive Board ultimately decided to approve a final draft of the report and provided it to the WHA for discussion at its meeting in May 2004.

The sugar industry continued to exert pressure against the DPAS, and especially the scientific findings of the WHO/FAO expert report. At the FAO Committee on Agriculture meeting in February 2004, the sugar industry challenged the composition of the expert group, as well as what it perceived to be a lack of consultation between the group and other relevant interests in its report. This assertion was backed by some developing countries at the meeting.[42] Before the WHA meeting in May 2004, the WHO Secretariat decided to de-emphasize the WHO/FAO expert report in its final draft of the DPAS due to the political pressure and it was not included or referenced in the document.[43] This final draft of DPAS was then approved by Resolution WHA57.17.

37 H. Ashraf, 'WHO's Diet Report Prompts Food Industry Backlash' (2003) 361 *Lancet* 1442; K.R. Norum, 'World Health Organization's Global Strategy on Diet, Physical Activity and Health: The Process Behind the Scenes' (2005) 49 *Scandinavian Journal of Nutrition* 83.

38 S. Boseley, 'Sugar Industry Threatens to Scupper WHO', *The Guardian*, 21 April 2003, 1.

39 K. Lee, 'Global Health Promotion: How Can We Strengthen Governance and Build Effective Strategies?' (2007) 21 *Health Promotion International* 42.

40 M. Chopra, S. Galbraith, and I. Darnton-Hill, 'A Global Response to a Global Problem: The Epidemic of Overnutrition' (2002) 80 *Bulletin of the World Health Organization* 952.

41 K. Norum, 'World Health Organization's Global Strategy' (n 37).

42 Norum, 'World Health Organization's Global Strategy' (n 37).

43 Norum, 'World Health Organization's Global Strategy' (n 37).

In contrast to tobacco control, the international response has been much more of a soft law approach. Although the norm of dietary restrictions certainly continued to emerge into the DPAS, the final product of negotiations is weak in comparison to the FCTC. The DPAS, as endorsed by the WHA, is not a legally binding agreement. It sets forth a series of guidelines for national governments to follow in regard to promoting diet and physical activity, but it does not establish any obligations to be undertaken by these governments. Rather, it sets up objectives to be achieved and provides recommendations, without including any language stating 'shall' in its text.[44] A lack of specificity is also evident in the DPAS. Because references to the WHO/FAO expert report were omitted, the section addressing dietary standards only contains language that individuals should 'limit the intake of free sugars' rather than the precise measure given in the report.[45]

In considering the soft law approach to diet, one consideration is whether the DPAS may eventually serve as a step towards a hard law approach. Yach et al have argued that a treaty-based approach would not be appropriate in addressing the problem of over-nutrition and obesity.[46] They suggest that, unlike tobacco, harm caused by food can be overcome by reduced consumption and physical activity. Therefore, regulation of the food industry would not necessarily be the best response. As an alternative, they propose a collaborative relationship with the food industry incorporating non-binding measures to set some standards in areas such as food labeling and advertising. Lee, however, suggests that a treaty-based response may be worth considering.[47] While she believes that the WHO must first take an incremental approach, which would focus on developing political support, having states make smaller commitments to the issue, and improving technical support and data sharing, which could lead to viable support for a treaty, as happened with tobacco.

As a global norm, diet and physical activity are in the first stage of norm emergence. It should be emphasized, however, that the fact that it is an emerging norm is a sign of progress in this area. Before the tobacco initiative began to gain momentum in the 1990s, any type of international diet control was more of an idea than anything resembling a norm. The success with tobacco created more awareness and motivation for the WHO and national health ministries to consider a more legalistic response to chronic disease, which soon led to diet and obesity as risk factors that needed more attention. Norm entrepreneurs were able to gain support relatively quickly in the WHO with the breakthrough of tobacco. Similarly to the situation with tobacco, scientific evidence showed a growing epidemic of obesity, especially in developing states. This led to a dialogue in the WHO about crafting an international response to the problem. The result of this process concluded with the DPAS. While the DPAS represented the emergence of norm related to diet and physical activity, it is a new norm that needs more of a broad-based consensus before it reaches a threshold to cascade.

However, as seen in the prevalence of food-borne infectious diseases, lapses in food safety, and rising rates of obesity among children and adults worldwide, profit-making

44 World Health Organization, 'Global Strategy on Diet, Physical Activity and Health' (Geneva, 2004).

45 'Global Strategy on Diet, Physical Activity and Health' (n 44).

46 D. Yach, C. Hawkes, J.E. Epping-Jordan, and S. Galbraith, 'The World Health Organization's Framework Convention on Tobacco Control: Implications for Global Epidemics of Food-related Deaths and Disease' (2003) 24 *Journal of Public Health Policy* 274.

47 Lee, 'The World Health Organization's Global Strategy' (n 3).

food producers and corporations cannot always be relied on to act in the public interest without legally binding regulation. This would suggest that some hard law measures would serve the public good if dietary problems and lack of physical activity causing chronic health ailments are to be fully addressed. When it comes to the activities of multinational food corporations, including the promotion of their products, such as the sugar-laden soft drink and cereal industry's advertising campaigns directed at children as well as adults, the causal role of these products in the onset and progression of chronic diseases is not addressed at the global level. The relevant norms have not evolved in enough strength to date to generate international legalization beyond the first stage of norm emergence.

There are several reasons for this. Among them is a lack of policy history concerning diet and physical activity at the WHO, the more invisible the physical harm caused by these risk factors, the strong backlash by the sugar industry, the more positive reputations of sugar and food corporations compared to tobacco companies, the WHO's collaborative approach with the food industry supporting self-regulation rather than an adversarial approach, a lack of support from critical states like the US, and a failure, unlike tobacco control, to overcome the contrary norm of neoliberalism as it relates to food choice.

The soft law approach to diet and physical activity is a rational response to a new, and relatively weak norm. Too few states have accepted the risks associated with dietary choice, so sufficient political will to assume the costs associated with a hard law, treaty-based response is lacking in the global community. Physical activity would be very difficult to regulate because it is dependent upon the personal choice and inclination of the individual. Diet, however, is like tobacco in that it is a consumable product that may be addressed through intervention with supply and demand. The main problem in creating a stronger norm for diet is that the causal connection between diet and chronic disease needs to be more generally recognized. A greater awareness of this link exists more than ever before, but because food is a necessary component of life and not an inherently 'bad' product like tobacco, an accepted norm on diet control is a much more challenging process.

5. Alcohol

Alcohol has a long history in the WHO, dating back to the early years of the organization. From 1950 to 1955, the WHO sought to define alcoholism and develop a program focusing on alcohol addiction as part of its Mental Health Unit. The program, however, was short-lived as the Unit became more focused on other topics by the late 1950s.[48] Alcohol received little attention from the WHO until the late 1960s, when it was brought back as part of the drug program.[49] Even with renewed emphasis, funding for research on the health effects of alcohol was limited. The US National Institute on Alcohol Abuse and Alcoholism (NIAAA) and the Nordic Council provided funding for the alcohol program, but their support was not supplemented with funds from the WHO's regular budget.[50] During the 1970s, the alcohol program

48 J. Moser, 'World Health Organization Activities Concerning Alcoholism' in R.E.Popham (ed), *Alcohol and Alcoholism* (Toronto: University of Toronto Press, 1970) 385.

49 R. Room, 'The World Health Organization and Alcohol Control' (1984) 79 *British Journal of Addiction* 85.

50 Room, 'The World Health Organization and Alcohol Control' (n 49).

only had two staff positions, in comparison with ninety-four staff positions for drug control in international agencies.[51]

Despite funding issues, the late 1970s and early 1980s witnessed a flurry of activity on alcohol based on scientific research. A significant accomplishment for the program was the WHO Expert Committee's report on 'Problems Related to Alcohol Consumption'.[52] This influential study was complemented by the adoption of Resolution WHA 32.40 by the World Health Assembly in 1979. This resolution stated that problems related to alcohol consumption constituted serious hazards for human health, welfare, and mortality, and therefore it was necessary for member states to pay greater attention to solving them.[53] In addition, the resolution called upon the states to take steps to reduce alcohol consumption among their population, especially vulnerable groups such as the young and pregnant women. It was the strongest language used, at this point in time, regarding the harmful effects of alcohol as an international problem by the WHA. The resolution also led to a technical discussion on alcohol consumption at the WHA in 1982, addressing concerns about international trade and its relationship to problems associated with alcohol. The discussions contributed to the formation by the WHO of a project to study the public health aspects of alcohol availability and examine the international features of the marketing and distribution of alcoholic products.

This activity led to the adoption of ResolutionWHA36.12 in 1983.[54] The focus of this resolution was its recommendation that national governments develop a comprehensive alcohol policy and consider the suggestions of the WHO's alcohol availability study. The resolution also asked the Director-General to include the WHO's program on alcohol-related problems as an integral part of its overall health strategy. Despite this request, however, little was accomplished during the remainder of the 1980s and funding for the study project on alcohol availability was canceled after one year without an explanation.[55]

In the 1990s, renewed interest in alcohol studies developed at the WHO and its Substance Abuse Department decided to initiate a worldwide database on alcohol and health. The Global Alcohol Database (GAD) was under way by 1996 and included information on alcohol consumption and health effects, production and trade of alcohol, as well as national alcohol policies. It was the first time such a comprehensive collection of information on alcohol had become available on a truly global scale.[56] The data from GAD contributed to some key studies on alcohol and health. In 1999, the WHO published its first 'Global Status Report on Alcohol', followed by subsequent reports on alcohol and its effects on young people, alcohol policy, and an updated report on the global status of alcohol in 2004.[57]

Building upon the momentum of these studies, as well as the progress made in the negotiations of the FCTC, the Nordic Council issued a declaration in 2004 calling for

[51] L. Pan and K. Bruun, 'Recent Developments in International Drug Control' (1979) 74 *British Journal of Addiction* 141.

[52] World Health Organization, 'Problems Related to Alcohol Consumption' (1980) 650 WHO Technical Report Series.

[53] World Health Assembly, 'Development of the WHO Programme on Alcohol-Related Problems', WHA 32.40 (1979).

[54] World Health Assembly, 'Alcohol Consumption and Alcohol-Related Problems: Development of National Policies and Programmes', WHA 36.12 (1983).

[55] R. McBride and J.F. Mosher, 'Public Health Implications of the International Alcohol Industry: Issues Raised by a World Health Organisation Project' (1985) 81 *British Journal of Addiction* 141.

[56] L. Gliksman and M. Rylett, 'The World Health Organization's Global Alcohol Database: Opportunities for Research and Support for Policy' (2009) 36 *Contemporary Drug Problems* 589.

[57] Gliksman and Rylett, 'The World Health Organization's Global Alcohol Database' (n 56).

more international cooperation among its members in addressing alcohol-related problems. The consensus among the Nordic states was demonstrated at the WHO Executive Board meeting in January 2005, with Iceland playing an important role in chairing the group.[58] At this meeting, the Executive Board agreed to submit a resolution on alcohol to the WHA; it was the first such resolution on alcohol since 1983. The primary issues in dispute during negotiations were the idea of pursuing a treaty-based solution, as in the case of tobacco, that would address alcohol and whether the WHO should pursue consultations with the alcohol industry. The treaty-based approach was supported by Pakistan and Thailand, but was strongly opposed by the US and was unable to achieve a consensus at the meeting. Similar coalitions were formed in regard to opening consultations with the private sector, as Pakistan and Thailand were joined by Russia, Nepal, and Tonga. These countries favored a strong policy by the WHO, while the US advocated involvement with the alcohol industry and received support from Australia, Guinea-Bissau, and the Maldives for this position.[59] The World Health Assembly nevertheless passed the final version of the resolution, WHA58.26, in May 2005 that requested member states to develop, implement, and evaluate effective strategies and programs to reduce the negative health and social consequences of alcohol use.[60] Much of the text, however, was aimed at the Director-General requesting the WHO to foster international cooperation to monitor and reduce the detrimental effects of alcohol consumption. In the preamble to WHA58.26, specific reference is made to the earlier resolution promoting the Global Strategy on Diet, Physical Activity and Health (DPAS).

The success of the movement in the WHO on DPAS, as well as the growing recognition and acceptance internationally of the problems caused by alcohol, led to a push for the WHO to endorse a similar strategy for alcohol as had been the case with diet and physical activity. In 2008, this effort culminated in the passage of WHA61.4, which approved negotiation for the drafting of a global strategy for alcohol by the Director-General working with member states, IGOs, NGOs, and the private sector in the process. As with the negotiation and drafting of DPAS, the WHO established a very transparent process with public hearings as well as roundtable meetings with members of the alcohol industry, NGOs and health professionals in 2008, and consultations with IGOs and UN agencies in 2009. The result was the adoption by the WHA of the Global Strategy to reduce the harmful use of alcohol in May 2010.

The international response to alcohol is very similar to the response to diet and physical activity. While alcohol consumption has a longer history at the WHO than diet and obesity, it has had inconsistent support. It did not become an emerging norm until after the growth in momentum of the international tobacco movement, as with the case with diet and obesity. The increased availability of scientific data, support from the WHO, and the political support of some states such as Sweden, Norway, Finland, Iceland, and Denmark of the Nordic Council have helped to develop this issue into an emerging norm, but it needs much more support from national governments before it reaches the next stage of a norm cascade. It did receive recognition by WHO member states in the form of the adoption of the Global Strategy to reduce the harmful use of alcohol. As with diet, however, the norm is still relatively new, and not strong enough

58 R. Room, 'Negotiating the Place of Alcohol in Public Health: The Arguments at the Interface' (2005) 100 *Addiction* 1396.

59 Room, 'Negotiating the Place of Alcohol in Public Health' (n 58).

60 World Health Assembly, 'Public-Health Problems Caused by Harmful Use of Alcohol', WHA 58.26 (2005).

for a sufficient number of states to conclude that a hard law response to alcohol consumption would be in their best interest.

The soft law approach that was agreed upon concluded with a set of guidelines that states were encouraged, but not obliged to follow. As with DPAS, no 'shall' language was included in the global strategy on alcohol document. There is some use of the word 'require', but it is employed in relation to phrases about achieving objectives that will require global, regional, and national levels of cooperation, concerted action by member states, effective global governance, and the appropriate engagement of all relevant parties.[61] None of the phrases in the document using the word 'require' establishes a specific obligation for member states. This lack of precision is another characteristic of the global strategy on alcohol. It provides a number of policy recommendations for states, but it does not provide set standards. In fact, the document observes that the measures should be implemented at the discretion of each member state, depending on national, religious, and cultural contexts within each country, national public health priorities, available resources, and in accordance with constitutional principles and international legal obligations—all of which serve to mitigate the overall weight of these recommendations.[62]

Although the international response to alcohol regulation has strengthened substantially over the last decade, a treaty-based solution is not in the foreseeable future. Similarly to diet and physical activity, a number of the provisions of the FCTC could be applicable to alcohol. A number of factors, however, distinguish the tobacco movement from alcohol, and that currently makes the same approach unsuitable under current circumstances. The first factor has to do with the alcohol industry. Like the tobacco industry, it has a strong and effective lobby. The alcohol industry, however, did not suffer the reputational cost that the tobacco industry did from the release of internal documents demonstrating duplicitous behavior.[63] Consequently, the WHO has also taken more of a self-regulation than adversarial approach to alcohol, similar to that adopted for diet and exercise and consistent with the neoliberal philosophy of the free market and free choice.

The second factor is NGO activities in regard to alcohol. NGOs in this policy area are weak because they have much less funding than anti-tobacco groups and are not supported financially by cancer and heart disease organizations, who focused their efforts on tobacco.[64] A third and possibly the most significant factor is the product itself. Studies on alcohol have not claimed that drinking is as strong a risk factor for chronic disease or premature death as tobacco. Moreover, the consumption of alcohol does not directly cause harm to bystanders as tobacco does with second-hand smoke. A major exception is found in Russia and some of the other states of the former Soviet Union, where the heavy episodic consumption of vodka with its high alcohol content has been directly linked to a significant increase in heart disease and premature mortality among working-class males.[65] This has caused a decline in male life expectancy that has been prevalent since the mid-1960s. Elsewhere, however, alcohol has not been viewed as more dangerous than tobacco, possibly because moderate drinking,

61 World Health Organization, 'Global Strategy to Reduce the Harmful Use of Alcohol' (Geneva, 2010).

62 'Global Strategy to Reduce the Harmful Use of Alcohol' (n 61).

63 S. Casswell and T. Thamarangsi, 'Reducing Harm from Alcohol: Call to Action' (2009) 373 *Lancet* 2247.

64 Casswell and Thamarangsi, 'Reducing Harm from Alcohol' (n 63).

65 W.C. Cockerham, 'The Intersection of Life Expectancy and Gender in a Transitional State: The Case of Russia' (2012) 34 *Sociology of Health and Illness* 943.

especially of red wine, has been found to reduce the risk of heart disease.[66] Also, alcohol is a much harder product to regulate due to its widespread popularity and use throughout the world.[67] In many countries, alcohol consumption is an accepted social custom deeply embedded in culture. This does not make its consumption a public good; rather it makes it difficult and perhaps impossible to outlaw.

6. Conclusion

Mortality from chronic diseases may reach as high as 75 percent of all deaths by 2020.[68] Norm dynamics and the rational choice-based approach of legalization are useful for an understanding of the nature of the international legal reaction to the growing global epidemic of chronic disease. The norm dynamic approach views norms as having a life cycle that evolves through different stages until ultimately they are accepted as an internalized standard of behavior. This life cycle does not become complete for all norms. Some norms remain in an emerging stage without enough acceptance to become internalized. Laws come from norms, but not all norms may be expressed in the form of law. The legalization approach can help to explain whether or not this transformation occurs for a particular norm. Once a norm is strong enough to be accepted by a critical mass of states, then states may make a rational calculus as to whether to accept the norm as hard law, which would be represented by an international treaty with precise legal obligations. The outcome of this calculus will derive from the perceived benefits of institutionalizing the norm as well as the costs for doing so. If a sizeable number of states decide that it is in their best interest to complete a clear and committed contract, then a hard law response may be in the offering.

In applying these approaches to the risk factors associated with chronic disease, it is apparent that the normative and legal evolution of tobacco control is quite different from that of diet and alcohol, even though they are all products that can be harmful for human consumption. The tobacco movement received much more support among national governments, civil society organizations, NGOs, and the WHO. Tobacco has been demonstrated to have a stronger harmful impact on health, and the powerful tobacco industry has been constrained by this data as well as the negative reputational effects stemming from their subversive practices. The norm of tobacco control became strong enough that states became convinced that international regulation of the product would be beneficial. This outcome was not the case with regard to diet and alcohol. The data regarding harm to health is not as strong in these areas. The consumption of sugary and salty foods and alcohol is also far more prevalent than tobacco globally. These norms are emerging, but they are in an early stage and will face greater challenges than tobacco before becoming accepted on a global scale. Without a generally accepted norm, a hard law response to these risk factors will not be forthcoming.

To reduce the burden of chronic disease through international law, a countervailing factor will always be neoliberalism. The regulation of consumable products will interfere with the free market as well as individual freedom of choice. Even the effect of tobacco control, which has had a much more measureable success than diet and alcohol regulation, has been mitigated by neoliberalism. The FCTC is largely designed

66 A.L. Klatsky, 'Moderate Drinking and Reduced Risk of Heart Disease' (1999) 23 *Alcohol Research and Health* 15.

67 Casswell and Thamarangsi, 'Reducing Harm from Alcohol' (n 63).

68 Lee, 'The World Health Organization's Global Strategy' (n 3).

to address the reduction of the demand for tobacco by directing attention to labeling, advertising, and taxes. Its silence, however, with regard to trade means that it has done little to address supply of the product. Tobacco control does provide a useful model for similar outcomes for diet and alcohol. The applicability of this model, however, will depend on the effectiveness of norm entrepreneurs to be advocates for the norms in these areas, the political will of IGOs, especially the WHO, to support a more legalistic response against the interests of transnational corporations, and ultimately the acceptance of member states that the risk factors of diet and alcohol are harmful enough to their population that enhanced regulation of these products outweighs the potential economic costs.

PART E

GOVERNANCE

29

Competition and Cooperation in Global Health Governance

The Impact of Multiple Framings

*Colin McInnes and Anne Roemer Mahler**

1. Introduction

For two decades the narrative that 'Health is Global'[1] has been developing, to such an extent that it may now be considered one of the dominant narratives in health policy and planning.[2] This is part of a broader *zeitgeist* concerning globalization and, as in other policy arenas, the implications appear profound.[3] The rapid spread of diseases such as SARS and 'swine flu', the globalized production of pharmaceuticals (including the emergence of international standards for intellectual property (IP) protection), the cross-national mobility of health professionals, and increased markets for harmful or unhealthy foodstuffs (including tobacco), raise questions for the governance of health and the development of health policy. Because if health is now global, traditional policy based largely on national agendas and governance mechanisms is inadequate. Rather new forms of global cooperation are required, what has become known as global health governance.[4]

However, despite considerable progress over the past decade in developing new governance mechanisms, including major legal instruments such as the Framework Convention on Tobacco Control and the much amended International Health

* The paper on which this chapter is based, drew on empirical work from a programme of research into global health governance, including work by other team members (Adam Kamradt-Scott, Kelley Lee, David Reubi, Simon Rushton, and Owain D. Williams). In particular it makes use of a bank of almost 300 interviews conducted as part of the program. These have informed this chapter but, for reasons of confidentiality, reference is not always directly made. We are grateful for the team's assistance in the project generally and for their comments on earlier drafts of the paper. All views expressed remain those of the authors. The research leading to these results has received funding from the European Research Council under the European Community's Seventh Framework Programme—Ideas Grant 230489 GHG.

1 Department of Health, 'Health is Global: A UK Government Strategy 2008–2013' (London, 2008).

2 For a discussion on the globalization narrative and health see C. McInnes and K. Lee, *Global Health and International Relations* (Cambridge: Polity Press, 2012).

3 Gro Harlem Brundtland, The 21st Special Session of the General Assembly for the Overall Review and Appraisal of the Implementation of the Programme of Action of the International Conference on Population and Development (New York, 1999) 2.

4 J. Youde, *Global Health Governance* (Cambridge: Polity Press, 2012); A. Kay and O. Williams (eds), *Global Health Governance: Crisis, Institutions and Political Economy* (London: Palgrave MacMillan, 2009); A. Cooper et al (eds), *Governing Global Health: Challenge, Response, Innovation* (Aldershot: Ashgate, 2007); R. Dodgson, K. Lee and N. Drager, 'Global Health Governance: A Conceptual Review', LSHTM/WHO Discussion Paper No 1 (2002), available at <http://whqlibdoc.who.int/publications/2002/a85727_eng.pdf> (accessed 10 September 2012).

Regulations (IHR), there is nevertheless a sense of disappointment and frustration that more has not been accomplished, especially given both the current and potential scale of problems faced.[5] A well-established range of factors have been identified as contributing to the failure of global health governance, including insufficient resources,[6] a lack of coordination between the multitude of actors and institutions involved,[7] market failure,[8] and the absence of political will.[9] This chapter, however, attempts an explanation that focuses on ideational factors and is broadly based in constructivist theory. For constructivists, the social world is one of our own making where the ideas we use shape our understanding of that world in a mutually constitutive relationship with material factors such as power and interests.[10] Specifically, in this chapter we use the concept of 'framing', whereby an issue is presented in such a way as to tie it into a broader set of ideas about the world, or 'socially constructed reality', and through this gain influence and policy purchase.[11] By linking an issue to a broader set of ideas and therefore contextualizing it in a specific way, frames suggest not only a particular way of understanding a problem but also imply a particular set of appropriate responses.

The concept of framing has been used extensively in the public policy literature,[12] although less so in public health.[13] The literature shows that framing is an essential component of political strategy because, if successful, frames can change the way issues are thought about and defined, and can affect perceptions of interest and appropriateness.[14] Frames can also be constitutive of meaning—ie they may move beyond being merely a tactical or presentational artifice to become a means of shaping the way in which a health issue is understood. The use of a particular frame may therefore begin as a tactic to gain attention and resources for a health issue, but may then become central to the construction of its meaning. The concept of framing highlights how contextualizing a health issue in a particular way opens up specific pathways of governance response while excluding others. The existing literature on global health governance has, to a limited extent, recognized the importance of frames in shaping policy development.[15] Yet, little attention has been paid to how different frames relate to

5 The scale of the problem can be measured in various ways, one example being WHO, 'Mortality and Burden of Disease Estimates for WHO Member States in 2004' (Geneva, 2009).

6 R. Dodgson, K. Lee, and N. Drager, 'Global Health Governance' (n 4).

7 K. Buse and A. Waxman, 'Public-Private Health Partnerships: A Strategy for WHO' (2001) 79 *Bulletin of the World Health Organization* 748.

8 P. Troullier, P. Olliaro, E. Torreele, J. Orbinski, R. Laing, and N. Ford, 'Drug Development for Neglected Diseases: A Deficient Market and a Public-Health Policy Failure' (2002) 359 *Lancet* 2188.

9 I. Kickbusch, 'Tackling the Political Determinants of Global Health' (2005) 331 *British Medical Journal* 246.

10 See eg N. Onuf, *World of our Making: Rules and Rule in Social Theory and International Relations* (Columbia, SC: University of South Carolina Press, 1989); J. Ruggie, *Constructing the World Polity: Essays on International Institutionalization* (London: Routledge, 1998) 33.

11 For an explanation of framing, see T. Gitlin, *The Whole World is Watching: Mass Media and the Making and the Unmaking of the New Left* (Berkeley, CA: University of California Press, 1980) 7.

12 See eg R.M. Entman, *Projections of Power: Framing News, Public Opinion and U.S. Foreign Policy* (Chicago, IL: University of Chicago Press, 2004); F. Fischer, *Reframing Public Policy: Discursive Politics and Deliberative Practices* (Oxford: OUP, 2003); J. Jerit, 'Issue Framing and Engagement: Rhetorical Strategy in Public Health Debates' (2008) 30 *Political Behavior* 1.

13 Exceptions include S. Rushton and O. Williams, 'Frames, Paradigms and Power: Global Health Policy-Making under Neoliberalism' (2012) 26 *Global Society* 147; L. Dorfman, L. Wallack, and K. Woodruff, 'More Than a Message: Framing Public Health Advocacy to Change Corporate Practices' (2005) 32 *Health Education and Behavior* 320.

14 M. Finnemore and K. Sikkink, 'International Norm Dynamics and Political Change' (1998) 52 *International Organization* 897.

15 Rushton and Williams, 'Frames, Paradigms and Power' (n 13); R. Labonté and M. Gagnon, 'Framing Health and Foreign Policy: Lessons for Global Health Diplomacy' (2010) 6 *Globalization*

Table 29.1 Summary of hypotheses

H1	The existence of multiple frames in global health governance can lead to competition between them
H2	Competition between frames can contribute to the failure of global health governance because it can lead to problems of policy coherence

one another. Often, different frames are used simultaneously to contextualize a policy issue in different ways. For instance, HIV/AIDS has been framed simultaneously as an issue of international security, development, and human rights. This chapter explores the effects of multiple framing on global health governance. Our core question is whether the framing of a particular health issue in multiple ways negatively affects global health governance.

In order to investigate this question we present two hypotheses about why the existence of multiple frames may negatively affect global health governance. The first hypothesis (H1) concerns the *relationship between the different frames*. We hypothesize that the existence of multiple frames in the same policy arena can lead to competition between them. Different frames imply different definitions of what the problem is and different ideas of what appropriate policy solutions may be. If the divergent views cannot be reconciled in the process of policymaking, or if one frame has not achieved dominance over others, a situation emerges in which problem definitions and policy solutions may compete with one another. Competing frames are then evident in policy documents (hence our later focus on such documents) and implementation. Our second hypothesis (H2) concerns the *effects of frame competition on governance*. We propose that competition between problem definitions and policy solutions can have negative effects on global health governance because it can create problems for policy coherence.

The remainder of the chapter investigates these hypotheses by means of three case studies: the global governance of HIV/AIDS,[16] tobacco control, and access to medicines in developing countries. These case studies are the subject of a wider programme of research.[17] They were chosen to balance the historic focus in global health governance on infectious disease with the emerging focus on non-communicable diseases seen at the end of the last decade. We first identify the key frames that were evident in the policy debates. We then analyse key policy documents for each issue area with regard to the problem definitions and policy solutions they imply. In particular, we analyse whether divergent problem definitions and policy solutions are reconcilable and can coexist or whether they are irreconcilable and compete with one another. We then investigate the implications that frame competition has had on how global health governance has been implemented in the three case studies.

and Health doi:10.1186/1744-8603-6-14; S. Rushton, 'Framing AIDS: Securitization, Development-ization, Rights-ization' (2010) 4 *Global Health Governance* 1; J. Shiffman, 'A Social Explanation for the Rise and Fall of Global Health Issues' (2009) 87 *Bulletin of the World Health Organization* 608; J. Shiffman and S. Smith, 'Generation of Political Priority for Global Health Initiatives: A Framework and Case Study of Maternal Mortality' (2007) 370 *Lancet* 1370.

16 We adopt this formulation rather than the more recent 'HIV and AIDS' for consistency with the documents used later.

17 See n * at the start of this chapter.

2. HIV/AIDS

Three key frames have dominated the political debate on HIV/AIDS in the last two decades: development, human rights, and security, with development being the most prominent.[18] The three frames define the 'problem' of HIV/AIDS in different ways. Framing HIV/AIDS as a development issue is based on the assumption that a vicious circle exists in which poor health is a key reason for poverty and, vice versa, poverty is a key determinant of poor health.[19] The security frame defines the 'problem' that the HIV/AIDS pandemic poses in quite different terms, namely as a threat to domestic stability and international peace and security. It has been argued that the HIV/AIDS pandemic threatens the stability of countries and regions, by 'hollowing out' the state,[20] threatening security forces,[21] and leading to economic downturn.[22] In addition, concerns have been raised about the impact of HIV/AIDS on international peacekeeping forces.[23] Finally, the human rights frame argues that 'when human rights are protected, fewer people become infected and those living with HIV and their families can better cope with HIV and AIDS'.[24] The protection of human rights therefore is essential to 'safeguard human dignity in the context of HIV'.[25]

To explore our first hypothesis we analyse how key UN documents reflect on the nature of the problem and present appropriate policy solutions:[26] UN Security Council Resolution 1308;[27] the Millennium Declaration;[28] the UN Secretary's report to the General Assembly ahead of the Millennium Summit, entitled, 'We the Peoples',[29] the United Nations General Assembly Special Session on HIV/AIDS (UNGASS) Declaration of Commitment on HIV/AIDS;[30] and the Political Declarations on HIV/AIDS of 2006 and 2011.[31] We use UN documents because of the central role UN agencies have played in the global response to the disease, though at the same time recognizing how other initiatives (such as the Global Fund and PEPFAR) have also played key roles.

18 Rushton, 'Framing AIDS: Securitization' (n 15).

19 K. Annan, 'We the Peoples: The Role of the United Nations in the 21st Century' (New York, 2000).

20 L. Garrett, 'HIV and National Security: Where Are The Links?' (New York, 2005).

21 R.L. Ostergard, 'Politics in the Hot Zone: AIDS and National Security in Africa' (2002) 23 *Third World Quarterly* 342.

22 D.M. Fox and J.S. Kassalow, 'Making Health a Priority of US Foreign Policy' (2005) 91 *American Journal of Public Health* 1555.

23 UNSC, UN Security Council Resolution 1308 (2000) on the Responsibility of the Security Council in the Maintenance of International Peace and Security: HIV/AIDS and International Peacekeeping Operations (Geneva, 2000); P. Tripodi and P. Patel, 'The Global Impact of HIV/AIDS on Peace Support Operations' (2002) 9 *International Peacekeeping* 51. For a more qualified view of these arguments, see C. McInnes and S. Rushton, 'HIV, AIDS and Security: Where Are We Now?' (2010) 86 *International Affairs* 225.

24 UNAIDS, 'International Guidelines on HIV/AIDS and Human Rights', consolidated version (Geneva, 2006) 16.

25 UNAIDS, 'International Guidelines' (n 24) 16.

26 In this we build on the work of one of our team members, Rushton, 'Framing AIDS: Securitization' (n 15).

27 UNSC Resolution 1308, 17 July 2000, available at <http://daccess-dds-ny.un.org/doc/UNDOC/GEN/N00/536/02/PDF/N0053602.pdf?OpenElement>.

28 UN, United Nations Millenium Declaration (Geneva, 2000), available at <http://www.un.org/millennium/declaration/ares552e.htm> (accessed 10 September 2012).

29 Annan, 'We the Peoples' (n 19).

30 UNGA, Declaration of Commitment on HIV/AIDS: 'Global Crisis—Global Action', S-26/2 (Geneva, 2001), available at <http://www.un.org/ga/aids/coverage/FinalDeclarationHIVAIDS.html> (accessed 11 September 2012).

31 UNGA, Political Declaration on HIV/AIDS, A/RES/60/262 (Geneva, 2006); UNGA, Political Declaration on HIV/AIDS, A/RES/65/277 (Geneva, 2011).

We find little evidence for competition between the problem definitions implied by the three frames. Rather, we find that they coexist next to one another and, in a few cases, even align with one another. UN Security Council Resolution 1308 focuses on HIV/AIDS almost exclusively from the perspective of international security.[32] While it makes hardly any mention of development and human rights, neither does it dispute those frames. In fact, it indirectly acknowledges them by referring to the need for HIV testing to be 'voluntary and confidential'—a key issue raised by human rights campaigners—and by referring to an earlier meeting of the UN Economic and Social Council meeting on HIV/AIDS. The Millennium Declaration[33] and the UN Secretary's report 'We the Peoples'[34] draw almost exclusively on the development frame. Yet, they do not dispute the problem definitions proposed by the security and human rights frames. In these documents, the different ways of framing the HIV/AIDS policy debate seems to be the manifestation of different organizational mandates rather than conflicting viewpoints of the problem and appropriate solutions.[35] This coexistence of different frames on HIV/AIDS is even more pronounced in the United Nations General Assembly Special Session on HIV/AIDS (UNGASS) Declaration of Commitment on HIV/AIDS[36] and the Political Declarations on HIV/AIDS from 2006 and 2011,[37] which combine the security, human rights, and development frames. For instance, the Declaration of Commitment states: 'We . . . [r]ecognize that HIV and AIDS constitute a global emergency, pose one of the most formidable challenges to the development, progress and stability of our respective societies and the world at large'.[38] The development frame is invoked in several other places, notably through reference to the Millennium Development Goals (MDGs).[39] The Political Declaration also frames HIV/AIDS as an important human rights concern when it affirms the need to work against stigma and discrimination.[40]

Thus in key documents on the global governance of HIV/AIDS we do not find evidence that the divergent problem definitions competed against one another. Rather they appear to coexist and are sometimes used to reinforce each other.[41] Similarly, the multiplicity of problem definitions does not seem to have created suggestions of policy solutions that are in competition with one another. The definition of HIV/AIDS as a development problem led to the integration of the issue into the emerging paradigm of international development policy, the MDGs, and the creation of institutions designed to address health issues within international development aid, such as the Global Fund to Fight AIDS, Tuberculosis and Malaria. Furthermore, the specific way in which HIV/AIDS was framed as a problem for development contributed significantly to the emergence of vertical, disease-specific programmes funded by national, international, and global donor agencies. Similarly, the framing of HIV/AIDS as a threat to security

32 See n 23. 33 UN, United Nations Millenium Declaration (n 28).

34 Annan, 'We the Peoples' (n 19).

35 This finding is also extensively supported by our interview data, see n * at the start of this chapter.

36 UNGA, Declaration of Commitment on HIV/AIDS (n 30).

37 UNGA, Political Declaration on HIV/AIDS (2006) (n 31); UN General Assembly, Political Declaration on HIV/AIDS (2011) (n 31).

38 UNGA, Declaration of Commitment on HIV/AIDS (n 30) para 7.

39 UNGA, Declaration of Commitment on HIV/AIDS (n 30) paras 13 and 18.

40 UNGA, Declaration of Commitment on HIV/AIDS (n 30) paras 11, 15, and 25.

41 An interesting example of this is the High-level Panel on Threats, Challenges and Change (2004) which states: 'Development and security are inextricably linked. A more secure world is only possible if poor countries are given a real chance to develop. Extreme poverty and infectious diseases threaten many people directly, but they also provide a fertile breeding-ground for other threats, including civil conflict': UN, 'A More Secure World: Our Shared Responsibility', Report of the Secretary-General's High Level Panel on Threats, Challenges and Change (Geneva, 2004) viii.

also promoted distinct policy responses. The operative paragraphs of UN Security Council Resolution 1308[42] promote specific actions with regard to UN peacekeeping personnel. The Secretary General is requested to provide training to help prevent the spread of the pandemic; member states are encouraged to increase cooperation on policies for prevention, testing, counselling and treatment for peacekeepers; and UNAIDS is encouraged to strengthen cooperation with member states on best practices.[43] Also the US Department of Defense's HIV/AIDS Prevention Program, which focuses on reducing the incidence of HIV/AIDS in (particularly African) militaries, can be seen as a response to the security framing of HIV/AIDS[44] and also UNAIDS' work with the UN's Department of Peacekeeping Operations.[45] Hence, the policy responses developed in response to the development and security frames do not always compete with one another. Indeed, some policies seem to have come about in response to a *combination* of both the development and the security frames. For instance it appears that security considerations contributed to the establishment of the US President's Emergency Plan for AIDS Relief (PEPFAR) alongside concerns for development and also religious ideas.[46]

Our analysis of key policy documents on the global governance response to HIV/AIDS found that multiple frames coexisted and sometimes even aligned without leading to frame competition. This does not mean, of course, that conflict between frames did not exist elsewhere. At the level of global policy, however (and specifically within the UN system, which played the key role in responding to the disease at the global level) the simultaneous framing of HIV/AIDS as a security, human rights, and development issue did not result in competition. Rather, it broadened the scope of the problem, thereby appealing to different audiences, and led to a range of complementary policy responses. The absence of frame competition at the level of global HIV/AIDS policy means that our second hypothesis, that frame competition can lead to problems of policy coherence, does not apply.[47] We therefore proceed straight to the second case study, tobacco control.

3. Tobacco Control

In the global debate on tobacco control, the use of tobacco has been framed in three main ways: as a health issue; in terms of human and civil rights; and in terms of its economic relevance.

The framing of tobacco use as a health issue has been promoted by proponents of tobacco control including the World Health Organization (WHO). In 1998, the then Director General of the WHO, Gro Harlem Brundtland, established the Tobacco Free Initiative (TFI), which defines tobacco use as a disease. On its website, the WHO

42 UN Security Council, Resolution 1308 'The Responsibility of the Security Council in the Maintenance of International Peace and Security: HIV/AIDS and International Peace-keeping Operations' (Geneva, 2000).

43 UN, 'A More Secure World' (n 41) paras 3–5.

44 Department of Defense, 'DoD HIV/AIDS Prevention Program' (Washington, DC, 2010), available at <http://www.med.navy.mil/SITES/NHRC/DHAPP/Pages/default.aspx> (accessed 11 September 2012); McInnes and Rushton, 'HIV, AIDS and Security' (n 23) 240–2.

45 UNAIDS, 'On the Front Line: A Review of Policies and Programmes to Address AIDS among Peacekeepers and Uniformed Services' (New York, 2005).

46 Fox and Kassalow, 'Making Health a Priority of US Foreign Policy' (n 22).

47 Though this may be the case with bilateral aid programmes such as PEPFAR, which may use different and/or competing framings because of different domestic constituencies and attitudes.

explains that the TFI was established to 'focus ... international attention, resources and action on the global tobacco *epidemic*'.[48] The TFI defines tobacco use as a disease that affects a large number of people with a 'massive toll of death, sickness and misery'.[49] The frame is also evident in the WHO Framework Convention on Tobacco Control (FCTC)[50] which recognizes 'that the spread of the tobacco epidemic is a global problem with serious consequences for public health'.[51] Moreover, the WHO identified the 'vector' responsible for the spreading of the disease as the tobacco industry.[52] The disease frame implies a specific pathway of policy response: intervention, specifically in the form of price measures (tax) and non-price measures such as advertising and marketing.[53]

Unsurprisingly, this way of framing tobacco use has been fiercely contested by the tobacco industry. Initially the industry denied the validity of evidence about the negative health consequences of smoking[54] and many companies still reject the evidence about the harmful effects of environmental tobacco smoke.[55] The industry has also contested the framing of tobacco use as a disease by developing a new frame that links tobacco use to human rights. In this frame, tobacco use is defined as part of an individual's right to choose the lifestyle they want without interference from government: 'smoking is a human right and should be respected according to the Declaration of Human Rights of the United Nations; ... Our aims are to: safeguard our fundamental rights as citizens'.[56] To promote this frame, tobacco companies have organized so called 'smokers' rights groups' in at least twenty-six countries.[57] The 'smokers' rights' frame therefore promotes a policy solution that contrasts with the one promoted by the disease frame, namely freedom from intervention. The rights-based frame promoted by the industry extended to the commercial rights of companies and consumers. In response to a proposed bill to ban tobacco advertising in Canada in the late 1980s, the industry ran an advertising campaign that invoked both civil and commercial rights:

> Whether or not you smoke, if you are a Canadian who cares about civil liberties you owe it to yourself to examine this issue and come to your own conclusions ... Bill C-51 denies tobacco manufacturers the right to provide information through advertising and the consumer the right to receive it. So the proposed legislation may well be a direct violation of the Charter of Rights.[58]

Similarly, commercial rights have been invoked in the industry's opposition to the proposal to introduce plain packaging: 'plain packaging ... would have the impact of

[48] Available at <http://www.who.int/tobacco/about/en/> (accessed 11 September 2012) (emphasis added).

[49] See n 48. For an even stronger condemnation see E. LeGresly, 'Understanding the Tobacco Industry. A "Vector Analysis" of the Tobacco Epidemic' (1999) 72 *Bulletin of Medicus Mundi Switzerland*, available at <http://www.medicusmundi.ch/mms/services/bulletin/bulletin199901/kap01/03legresley.html> (accessed 11 September 2012).

[50] WHO, 'Framework Convention on Tobacco Control' (Geneva, 2003).

[51] 'Framework Convention on Tobacco Control' (n 50) 1.

[52] J. Collin, K. Lee, and K. Bissell, 'The Framework Convention on Tobacco Control: The Politics of Global Health Governance' (2002) 23 *Third World Quarterly* 267. See also LeGresly 'Understanding the Tobacco Industry' (n 49); and 'Framework Convention on Tobacco Control' (n 50).

[53] 'Framework Convention on Tobacco Control' (n 50) v.

[54] See eg R. Cunningham, 'Smoke and Mirrors: The Canadian Tobacco War' (Ottawa, 1996).

[55] See eg <http://www.imperial-tobacco.com/index.asp?page=35> (accessed 11 September 2012).

[56] Tobacco International, 'Smokers Demand Rights' (1991), available at <http://legacy.library.ucsf.edu/tid/xof64c00> (accessed 11 September 2012).

[57] E.A. Smith and R.E. Malone, '"We Will Speak as the Smoker": The Tobacco Industry's Smokers' Rights Groups' (2006) 17 *European Journal of Public Health* 306.

[58] Cited in Cunningham, 'Smoke and Mirrors' (n 54) 72.

confiscating [Rothman's] trademark values'.[59] Here, the rights-based frame has been extended to include IP rights.

This framing of tobacco use (and production) as a human, civil, and commercial right has been contested by tobacco control advocates. This time, however, the competing frame is developed not by establishing a link to a new policy issue but by establishing a new link to the *same* policy issue, human rights. Tobacco control advocates opposed the idea that smokers have a human right to smoke by developing the competing frame that *non*-smokers have a human right to health, which means avoiding exposure to environmental smoke. In other words, the competing frame defines the link between tobacco use and human rights in a different way, namely that human rights extend equally to non-smokers, specifically their human right to health.[60] This frame is also reflected in the FCTC, which in its preamble refers to a series of rights, including 'the right of *everyone* to the enjoyment of the highest attainable standard of physical and mental health'.[61]

The third key frame used in the global debate on tobacco control links tobacco use to economic costs. The tobacco industry has long tried to avert tobacco control efforts by framing tobacco production and consumption as an important contributor to the economy (not least through employment) and to state revenue.[62] They argued that not only would the government lose tax revenue, without reducing tobacco consumption, but that these measures would also propel illegal activities.[63] More recently, the debate on the economic costs has shifted to tobacco companies arguing that plain packaging would hurt retailers, increase smuggling, and encourage counterfeiting.[64]

There is some evidence to suggest that the frame linking tobacco control to economic and tax revenue costs has been used successfully at several times and in several countries.[65] Yet, advocates of tobacco control, and particularly the TFI, have contested this frame. Gathering evidence from not only industrialized but also developing countries they were able to develop a counter-frame that presents tobacco use as detrimental to the economy. The counter-frame was launched purposefully and strategically by the TFI in order to mobilize support from ministries of finance for tobacco control efforts.[66] Providing evidence that the costs of tobacco use exceeded its benefits, even in developing countries, was crucial to garner support for the FCTC because the framing of tobacco as an important source of tax revenue had been very successful, especially with finance ministers.[67]

59 Cunningham, 'Smoke and Mirrors' (n 54) 137.

60 P.D. Jacobsen and A. Banerjee, 'Social Movements and Human Rights Rhetoric in Tobacco Control' (2005) 14 *Tobacco Control* ii45.

61 'Framework Convention on Tobacco Control' (n 50) (emphasis added).

62 R. Rosenblatt 'How Do Tobacco Executives Live with Themselves' (1994) *New York Times Magazine*, 41.

63 Philip Morris, 'Contraband Tobacco Estimates' (1992), File No 2073010095/2073010180/CONTRABAND TOBACCO ESTIMATE-920630, available at <http://legacy.library.ucsf.edu/tid/bgs57c00> (accessed 12 September 2012).

64 British American Tobacco, 'Plain Packaging' (2012), available at <http://www.bat.com/group/sites/uk__3mnfen.nsf/vwPagesWebLive/DO7J7DCZ?opendocument&SKN=1> (accessed 20 June 2012); A. Pandya, 'The Plain Packaging of Tobacco Products sets a Dangerous Precedent' (2012) *Institute of Economic Affairs Blog*, available at <http://www.iea.org.uk/blog/the-plain-packaging-of-tobacco-products-sets-a-dangerous-precedent> (accessed 20 June 2012).

65 Cunningham, 'Smoke and Mirrors' (n 54); L. Joosens, F.J. Chaloupka, D. Merriman, and A. Yurekli, 'Issues in the smuggling of tobacco products' in P. Jha and F.J. Chaloupka (eds), *Tobacco Control in Developing Countries* (Oxford: OUP, 2000) 393; 'Framework Convention on Tobacco' (n 50).

66 Authors' interviews with TFI representative (10 March 2010).

67 Authors' interviews with TFI representative (n 66).

So with regard to our first hypothesis (H1), that multiple frames lead to competition between them, we find mixed evidence.[68] Some of the frames used in the global debate on tobacco control have competed with one another in terms of the problem definitions and policy solutions they implied. We have found competition between frames that link tobacco use to different policy issues, such as health and human rights. We have also found competition between frames that link tobacco use to one single other policy issue, such as human rights. Here, competition emerged because the links that were established differed. While one frame defined tobacco use as a human right, namely the right to choose, the other defined tobacco use as a violation of a human right, namely the human right to health. In addition, we have found that the competing frames were linked to competing interests with regard to tobacco control, reinforcing the point made in the introduction concerning the mutually constitutive nature of interests and ideas. The alliance of competing frames with competing interests has greatly contributed to making the global governance of tobacco control a contested space. Yet, as in the case study on HIV/AIDS, we also find that some frames align well with one another. For instance, the frame defining tobacco use as a disease aligns well with the frame emphasizing the right to health of non-smokers. Also the policy solutions these two frames propose (intervention against the spread of a disease, and intervention to protect non-smokers) are compatible. So our research shows that multiple frames in global health can lead to competition but they do not have to.

With regard to H2, which suggests that competing frames can lead to problems of policy coherence, we find supporting evidence. In several countries, including Canada, Sweden, and the UK, competition between the frame that links tobacco use to economic costs and the one linking it to economic benefits seems to have contributed to policy incoherence. Tax increases were introduced with the argument that they could reduce the health burden and also economic costs created by smoking. Yet, after evidence was put forward suggesting that this also led to an increase in cigarette smuggling—and thereby a loss of government revenue—tax increases were withdrawn.[69]

These cases illustrate that frame competition can contribute to governance failure because it can trigger incoherent or inconsistent policies. However, competition between frames can be resolved. For example, the competition between the frame that defines tobacco use as overall beneficial to the economy and the one that defines tobacco use as overall costly was resolved when the latter became dominant. In the late 1990s, tobacco control rose on the global political agenda when Brundtland established the issue as one of WHO's priority areas. The WHO aligned with the World Bank to collect data on the economic costs of tobacco use. This data supported the framing of tobacco use as an overall cost to the economy and was communicated widely. The involvement of the World Bank in communicating this frame was crucial in order to reach key policymakers, particularly ministers of finance, many of whom were concerned about protecting revenues from tobacco tax and therefore tended to be sceptical about tobacco control policies. The involvement of the World Bank also facilitated the integration of data from developing countries and the responsiveness of governments from developing countries. The support both of finance ministries and of developing countries' governments were important preconditions for the conclusion of the FCTC. It also demonstrates that power hierarchies can help to resolve competition between frames and establish the dominance of one frame over another. We therefore

[68] This is also supported by our interview data, see n * at the start of this chapter.

[69] Cunningham, 'Smoke and Mirrors' (n 54); Joosens, Chaloupka, Merriman, and Yurekli, 'Issues in the smuggling of tobacco products' (n 65).

need to qualify H2. The risk of competition between frames contributing to governance failure is mitigated when power hierarchies establish dominant problem definitions and policy pathways.

We also need to qualify H2 in the light of another example, namely with regard to the integration of health concerns in trade negotiations. International trade agreements have been promoted by various business groups, including the tobacco industry, by invoking their civil right to economic freedom and their property rights over intangible assets, such as trademarks. This frame has also been used by governments from North America and the European Union in negotiating trade agreements.[70] Recently, however, competing frames on tobacco control have entered trade negotiations. Specifically the frame defining tobacco use as a disease and the frame that invokes the human right to health for non-smokers have been used by advocates of tobacco control to demand a change in international trade policies.[71] The alternative norms and ideas promoted by these frames appear to be contributing to policy change. Early in 2012, the US Trade Representative announced consultations about the possibility of introducing an 'exception' for the free trade of tobacco products in the Trans-Pacific Partnership trade agreement.[72] This example shows that competing frames do not inevitably lead to governance failure. They can facilitate policy change and, depending on one's perspective, this can improve policy. From a public health perspective, frame competition is improving trade policy. Yet, frame competition can also facilitate policy change for the worse (from the perspective of health outcomes). One such example is when attempts to strengthen tobacco control are challenged by tobacco companies and tobacco producing states who invoke the right to economic freedom and protection of (intellectual) property as codified in WTO and various bilateral trade agreements.[73]

To conclude, global tobacco control provides evidence in support of H1 that multiple frames can lead to frame competition. We also find evidence, however, that multiple frames do not have to lead to frame competition but that the problem definitions and policy solutions implied by different frames can coexist and even align. With H2, we find evidence that the existence of competing frames can contribute to problems of policy coherence. Yet, we also find evidence that power hierarchies can mitigate frame competition, which means that it does not necessarily lead to problems of policy coherence. Moreover, we find evidence that frame competition can spur policy change by introducing alternative problem definitions and policy proposals.

4. Access to Medicines

In the debate on access to medicines we have seen three key frames in operation: development, human rights, and IP rights. The framing of access to medicines as a development and human rights issue is based on the same arguments as those linking

70 J.S. Odell (ed.), *Negotiating Trade: Developing Countries in the WTO and NAFTA* (Cambridge: CUP, 2006).

71 T. Bollyky, 'Forging a New Trade Policy on Tobacco', Policy Innovation Memorandum No 7, (Washington, DC, 2011), available at <http://www.cfr.org/trade/forging-new-trade-policy-tobacco/p25658> (accessed 12 September 2012).

72 Office of the United States Trade Representative [hereafter USTR], 'Fact Sheet: TPP Tobacco Proposal', Washington, DC, May 2012, available at <http://www.ustr.gov/about-us/press-office/fact-sheets/2012/may/tpp-tobacco-proposal>. (hereinafter USTR, 'Fact Sheet: TPP Tobacco Proposal').

73 International Centre for Trade and Sustainable Development (ICTSD), 'Australian Cigarette Labelling Legislation Faces Renewed Controversy at WTO' (2011) 15 *Intellectual Property Programme*, available at <http://ictsd.org/i/news/bridgesweekly/117360/> (accessed 12 September 2012).

HIV/AIDS to development and human rights.[74] Access to medicines is framed as an important factor for health improvement in developing countries, and therefore as important to strengthen the virtuous circle of health and economic development. Access to medicines is also framed as an integral component of the human right to health. As in the case study on HIV/AIDS discussed previously, the problem definitions and policy pathways implied by these two frames do not compete with one another. Where competition has emerged, however, is around the framing of access to medicines as an issue of IP rights.

NGOs such as Knowledge Ecology International (KEI), Médecins Sans Frontières (MSF), Health Action International (HAI), and the Treatment Access Campaign (TAC), together with a range of developing countries (including Brazil, India, and South Africa), frame access to medicines not in a positive way but negatively in being linked to IP protection. In particular patent rights are presented as impeding access to medicines because they can be used to establish temporary monopolies for drugs and therefore lead to prices beyond the means of poor patients. Furthermore, they argue that the current system of medical innovation, which uses IP rights as an incentive to stimulate research and development (R&D) into new medicines, does not work with regard to medicines required by people in developing countries. They emphasize that IP is an effective incentive for innovation only in the presence of strong market demand. Hence, the weak purchasing power of most people in developing countries undermines the functioning of the IP-based system of medical innovation. Moreover, the IP-based innovation system prevents R&D into technologies that can adapt existing drugs to the conditions of resource-poor settings (through heat-resistant drug delivery systems, for example).[75] Hence, the frame that identifies IP protection as a key obstacle to access to medicines has two components: one focusing on access to *existing* drugs and one focusing on R&D for *new* drugs needed in resource-poor settings.

In contrast, the US government, the EU, and pharmaceutical companies that focus on R&D for new drugs, have developed a competing frame on the link between IP and access to medicines. This frame rejects the idea that IP protection prevents access, but focuses on other factors as more important constraints to access, such as distribution systems, healthcare systems, and government procurement policies.[76] Instead they emphasize the importance of IP for innovation. The International Federation of Pharmaceutical Manufacturers & Associations (IFPMA) maintains: 'Innovation is

[74] See eg Health Action International, Initiative for Health & Equity in Society, Knowledge Ecology International, Médecins Sans Frontières, Third World Network, 'An Essential Health and Biomedical R&D Treaty'. Submission to the WHO Consultative Expert Working Group on Research and Development: Financing and Coordination (2011) (On file with the authors).

[75] See eg Médecins Sans Frontières, Campaign for Access to Essential Medicines: TPP Issue Brief—September 2011, available at <http://www.msfaccess.org/sites/default/files/MSF_assets/Access/Docs/Access_Briefing_TPP_ENG_2011.pdf> (accessed 20 June 2012); WTO, 'Draft Ministerial Declaration Proposed by the Africa Group, Bangladesh, Barbados, Bolivia, Brazil, Cuba, Dominican Republic, Ecuador, Haiti, Honduras, India, Indonesia, Jamaica, Pakistan, Paraguay, Philippines, Peru, Sri Lanka, Thailand and Venezuela', WTO Doc IP/C/W/312; WT/GC/W/450 (Geneva, 2001); WTO, 'Submission by the Africa Group, Barbados, Bolivia, Brazil, Dominican Republic, Ecuador, Honduras, India, Indonesia, Jamaica, Pakistan, Paraguay, Philippines, Peru, Sri Lanka, Thailand and Venezuela to the TRIPS Council Discussion on Access to Medicines', WTO Doc IP/C/W/296 (Geneva, 2001).

[76] See eg International Federation of Pharmaceutical Manufacturers and Associations (IFPMA), 'The Changing Landscape on Access to Medicines' (Geneva, 2012), available at <http://www.ifpma.org/fileadmin/content/Publication/2012/IFPMA_Changing_Landscapes_Web.pdf> (accessed 20 June 2012); US Patent and Trademark Office, 'Patents and Health: Proposal by the Delegation of the United States of America', SCP/17/11 (Geneva, 2012) (On file with the authors).

vital in addressing the global health needs of today and tomorrow. Without constant research into and development of new medicines, many of today's health improvements may be jeopardized in the long run.'[77] Yet, they implicitly admit that the IP-based incentive system does not always work to stimulate R&D into new medicines: 'IFPMA and its members are open to the use of innovative finance mechanisms where there is demonstrable market failure.'[78]

Competition exists, therefore, at the level of problem definition: one frame emphasizes IP protection as a key obstacle to access to medicines in developing countries; the competing frame emphasizes the importance of IP for innovation and ultimately therefore access to improved medicines. These competing problem definitions lead to competing policy proposals: the first frame promotes a flexible interpretation of IP legislation that allows for competition from generic drugs.[79] Critics of this approach therefore argue that effective medicines do not always exist and that incentives to innovation are therefore required:

> Some of the public health issues facing developing and least developed countries (DC/LDCs) include neglected diseases, the spread of TB, malaria and HIV/AIDS, and availability of medicines to treat these and other ailments. There is no easy solution to these problems. Reducing patent protection is not likely to solve these thorny issues.[80]

The competing frame therefore promotes policy solutions that do not affect IP rights, such as company donations, preferential pricing, and capacity-building programmes.

With regard to increasing R&D for new drugs for developing countries, the difference between the policy pathways promoted by the two competing frames is less stark (as is also the case of access to existing drugs). Having recognized in principle that IP-based systems of medical innovation may not work without effective market demand, both frames agree on the need for more funding, especially from the public sector. Both frames also agree that partnerships between industry, government, and NGOs may help to increase R&D for neglected disease drugs. Differences exist, however, with regard to the types of partnerships that the two frames promote. The frame emphasizing the importance of IP for innovation, promoted by R&D-based companies, favours partnerships with limited interference in the licensing of IP rights and the pricing of products. An example of this is product development partnerships (PDPs). However, initiatives like the Medicines Patent Pool or prizes to reward successful R&D, which are strongly supported by KEI and MSF, are viewed with reservation by R&D-based companies.[81]

77 IFPMA, 'The Changing Landscape on Access to Medicines' (n 76) 47.

78 IFPMA, 'Innovative Financing' (Geneva, 2012), available at <http://www.ifpma.org/innovation/rd/innovative-financing.html> (accessed 11 September 2012).

79 See eg Médecins Sans Frontières, 'Campaign for Access to Essential Medicines' (n 75). Importantly, most NGOs and developing countries do not argue for the abolition of IP protection but for a 'system where new medicines have multiple producers, who each pay royalties to the patent holder, helping them not only to recoup their development costs but ensuring that people in developing countries have access', Médecins Sans Frontières, 'Access to Medicines: India Offers First Compulsory License' (2012), available at <http://www.doctorswithoutborders.org/press/release.cfm?id=5816&cat=press-release> (accessed 20 June 2012).

80 US Patent and Trademark Office, 'Patents and Health' (n 76).

81 M. Perez Pugatch, R. Chu, and D. Torstensson, 'Assembling the Pharmaceutical R&D Puzzle for Needs in the Developing World. An Assessment of New and Proposed Delinking Initiatives Aimed at Encouraging R&D into Neglected and Tropical Diseases and Specific Type II Diseases' (2012), 8, available at <http://www.ifpma.org/fileadmin/content/Publication/2012/Assembling_the_RD_puzzle_FINAL.pdf> (accessed 20 June 2012).

For our first hypothesis (H1), this case study supports our earlier findings that multiple framing can lead to competition but does not have to. The frames linking access to medicines to development and human rights do not compete with one another. Neither do they compete with the frame that identifies IP as a key obstacle to access. Yet, our analysis of how access to medicines has been framed as an issue of IP rights confirms that competing problem definitions and policy solutions can emerge through multiple framing. In fact, competition appears to be particularly fierce when different problem definitions emerge with regard to the same issue linkage. In a similar vein to the case study on tobacco control, frame competition has emerged that is based not on links to other policy issues, such as development and security, but by establishing different links between the same issues. In the case on tobacco, different links were established between tobacco use and human rights. Equally, different links were established between tobacco use and the economy. In the case on access to medicines, different links have been established between access and IP. Further, a new finding from this case study is that the degree of competition can vary between different elements of a frame. In the frames linking access to IP rights, competition is stronger with regard to access to *existing* drugs than with regard to R&D for *new* drugs.

Our second hypothesis (H2) suggests that competition between frames can contribute to governance failure. We analysed key policy documents in developing countries to see whether they reconciled the competing problem definitions and policy solutions promoted by the competing frames linking access to IP rights. These documents are: the Doha Declaration on the TRIPS Agreement and Public Health,[82] the report of the WHO Commission on Intellectual Property Rights, Innovation and Public Health (CIPIH),[83] the WHO Global Strategy and Plan of Action (GSPA),[84] the report of the WHO Consultative Expert Working Group on Research and Development: Financing and Coordination (CEWG),[85] and several bilateral and regional free trade agreements (FTAs) negotiated between the US and developing countries in the last ten years.[86]

The Doha Declaration reconciles the competition between the two frames by integrating key elements of both. On the one hand, the Doha Declaration repeatedly affirms the importance of IP protection for innovation and states: 'We recognize that intellectual property protection is important for the development of new medicines'[87] and 'reiterate[e] our commitment to the TRIPS Agreement'.[88] On the other hand, the Doha Declaration acknowledges the problem definition of the competing frame when it 'recognize[s] the concerns about its [intellectual property's] effects on prices'.[89] With regard to the policy solutions promoted by the two frames,

82 WTO, 'Declaration on the TRIPS Agreement and Public Health' (2001), available at <http://www.wto.org/english/thewto_e/minist_e/min01_e/mindecl_trips_e.htm> (accessed 11 September 2012) (Doha Declaration).

83 WHO, 'Commission on Intellectual Property Rights, Innovation and Public Health' (Geneva, 2006), available at <http://www.who.int/intellectualproperty/report/en/index.html> (accessed 11 September 2012) (CIPIH).

84 WHO, 'Global Strategy and Plan of Action on Public Health, Innovation and Intellectual Property' (Geneva, 2008), available at <http://www.who.int/gb/ebwha/pdf_files/A61/A61_R21-en.pdf> (accessed 11 September 2012) (GSPA).

85 WHO, 'Consultative Expert Working Group on Research and Development: Financing and Coordination' (Geneva, 2012), available at <http://www.who.int/phi/cewg_report/en/index.html> (accessed 11 September 2012) (CEWG).

86 For the texts of the Free Trade Agreement that the US has in force, see the website of the USTR at <http://www.ustr.gov/trade-agreements/free-trade-agreements>.

87 Doha Declaration (n 82) Art 3.

88 Doha Declaration (n 82) Art 4.

89 Doha Declaration (n 82) Art 3.

however, the Doha Declaration privileges one over the other because it provides for flexibilities in how TRIPS can be implemented, especially the right of governments to break patents and issue a compulsory licence to generic producers without the consent of the IP rights holder. It states: 'Each Member has the right to grant compulsory licences and the freedom to determine the grounds upon which such licences are granted.'[90]

Hence, the Doha Declaration resolves the competition between the two competing frames through two strategies: acknowledging important aspects of both frames and privileging the policy pathway of one over that of the other. One could argue that the competition between the two frames did not lead to governance failure because it did not prevent an international agreement on an important policy document. Yet, this verdict may look different if we include in our analysis the FTAs that the US has negotiated with various developing countries since 2000. Although the FTAs are not concerned predominantly with the issue of access to medicines but with increasing trade, their IP-related chapters do affect access to medicines in developing countries. Because the FTAs are not concerned directly with access to medicines, they perhaps unsurprisingly do not refer directly to the problem definitions put forward by either of the frames. Yet, in the policy pathway they establish, the FTAs clearly privilege policies promoted by the frame that emphasizes IP protection as key to innovation. Most FTAs negotiated by the US since 2000 contain provisions that go beyond the minimum standards for IP protection set out in TRIPS. While the FTAs do affirm their general commitment to the Doha Declaration, their IP-related provisions make it difficult for the signatories to apply some of the flexibilities provided for in the Declaration. For instance, data exclusivity may undermine the signatory governments' ability to use compulsory licensing. The reason for this is that data exclusivity concerns the protection of clinical test data while compulsory licensing applies only to the protection of patent rights. With regard to H2, our findings from these documents are therefore mixed. Both the Doha Declaration and the FTAs resolve the competition between the two frames by privileging the policy solution promoted by one frame over that of the other. The problem is, however, that they privilege conflicting policies. While the Doha Declaration emphasizes flexibilities in IP legislation, the FTAs raise standards of protection that limit the room for flexibilities. Competition between the two frames has been resolved *within* the policy documents, but it persists *between* them.

Within WHO, since 2003, several commissions and working groups have been established to address 'the question of appropriate funding and incentive mechanisms for the creation of new medicines and other products against diseases that disproportionately affect developing countries'.[91] The focus on policies to facilitate R&D for new medicines is important because, as demonstrated earlier, competition is less stark with regard to this issue than with regard to access to existing drugs. The documents we examined suggest that WHO's perspective and policies on R&D for new drugs have been gradually narrowing. The first WHO commission, CIPIH, included in its mandate considerations about access to existing drugs: 'innovation was pointless in the absence of favourable conditions for poor people in developing countries to access existing, as well as new, products. The price of medicines is an important factor in determining access, but so also are poverty and the lack of infrastructure for delivering health care to poor people'.[92] By bringing in the issue of access to existing drugs, and by

[90] Doha Declaration (n 82) Arts 4 and 5(b).
[91] CIPIH (n 83). [92] CIPIH (n 83) ix.

mentioning the issue of drug pricing, CIPIH indirectly acknowledges the frame that sees IP as a key obstacle to drugs. It seeks to resolve the competition with the competing frame that emphasizes the importance of other factors in impeding access to medicines by referring to poverty and the lack of infrastructure as other determinants of access. In addition, CIPIH supports the policy solutions promoted by the frame identifying IP as an obstacle to access. Not only does CIPIH state its support for the flexibilities mentioned in the Doha Declaration but it also calls on the governments of developing countries to make use of them.[93]

The Global Strategy and Plan of Action (GSPA), agreed two years later by the World Health Assembly (WHA), is more narrow in its mandate. It focuses almost exclusively on R&D for new drugs and aiming to 'provide a medium-term framework for securing an enhanced and sustainable basis for needs driven essential health research and development relevant to diseases which disproportionately affect developing countries'.[94] Six out of the eight sections ('Elements') of the GSPA focus on R&D for new drugs. Only Element 6 on 'Improving delivery and access' addresses the issue of access to existing drugs. While the GSPA mentions that '[i]nternational intellectual property agreements contain flexibilities that could facilitate increased access to pharmaceutical products by developing countries'[95], the section on 'Improving delivery and access' refers to the Doha Declaration only in so far as the Declaration 'need[s] to be considered for action by national authorities in the light of the circumstances in their countries'.[96] IP flexibilities are not referred to at all in the Action Points of Element 6.[97]

The most recent WHO working group on access, the Consultative Expert Working Group on Research and Development (CEWG), focuses even more narrowly on the issue of R&D for new drugs and does not mention the Doha Declaration at all.[98] The report states that: 'Our focus is on the needs of developing countries for new products (including medicines, vaccines and diagnostics).'[99] While it 'acknowledge[s] the importance of other relevant areas . . . to improve delivery and access to new and existing products',[100] the report makes only one reference to IP flexibilities, almost in passing.[101] The CEWG report does address the issue of access to existing drugs indirectly, however, when it discusses how to ensure that future drugs will be affordable once they are developed. To improve access to future drugs, the report suggests that the development costs be de-coupled from the price of the product, a concept that has become known as 'delinking'.[102]

Hence, the most contentious aspect in the competition between the two frames linking access to IP rights, access to existing drugs, has been increasingly left out in the WHO policy process. It can be argued that this has contributed to resolving the competition between the two frames in the WHO policy process and facilitated compromise with regard to the less contentious issue of R&D for new drugs. Here, differences in the problem definitions promoted by the two frames are not quite as significant since both frames acknowledge that IP-based incentive systems may not work when market demand is small.[103] Competition exists mainly with regard to the range of circumstances that require alternatives to the IP-based innovation system. R&D-based companies and US and EU governments seek to limit those circumstances to diseases disproportionately affecting developing countries, while NGOs and many developing countries emphasize the need for R&D into the special needs of

93 CIPIH (n 83) 120.
94 GSPA (n 84) 6.
95 GSPA (n 84) 6.
96 GSPA (n 84) 17.
97 GSPA (n 84) 18–19.
98 See generally CEWG (n 85).
99 CEWG (n 85) 8.
100 CEWG (n 85) 20–1.
101 CEWG (n 85) 38.
102 CEWG (n 85) 9.
103 CIPIH (n 83) 17; CEWG (n 85) 8.

resource-poor settings for all drugs. The WHO policy documents resolve this competition by acknowledging the importance of IP protection for innovation,[104] on the one hand, and extending the range of diseases for which alternative mechanisms are required,[105] on the other.

In summary, the WHO policy documents have resolved the competition between the two frames through a range of strategies, including acknowledging key elements of both frames, sidelining the most contentious issues, and supporting the policy pathways promoted by one frame over those promoted by the other. With regard to our second hypothesis (H2), we find that frame competition has not prevented agreement on key policy documents. At first glance, therefore, H2 does not seem to hold. Taking a closer or, in fact, broader look across the various global policies related to access to medicines in developing countries, however, we find that competition between frames has *not* been resolved. We have three groups of global policy documents that each take a different stance on access to existing drugs. The Doha Declaration confirms a specific set of flexibilities, several FTAs make the ability of governments to apply those flexibilities more difficult, and the WHO policy process has fallen increasingly silent on the issue. So while the competition between the two frames linking access to IP rights has been resolved *within* individual policy documents, it persists *between* them. With regard to H2 this means that competition between frames has contributed to the failure of global health governance because it has created a contradictory set of global policies with regard to access to medicines in developing countries.

5. Conclusion

This chapter was inspired by the observation that political debates on global health issues are often pervaded by different ways of defining the problem and, consequently, different ideas of appropriate policy solutions. This draws attention to the importance of ideas in policymaking, both as a carrier of meaning and as a strategic tool used to influence policy. The purpose of the chapter was to examine how different ideas about policy problems and solutions affect global health governance. We hypothesized that the existence of multiple frames can lead to competition between the problem definitions and policy solutions they promote (H1). Furthermore, we hypothesized that this competition can contribute to governance failure because it can lead to incoherent and even contradictory policies (H2).

The theoretical lens we use to investigate these hypotheses is social constructivism and in particular we use the concept of framing. This concept highlights that the way we think about policy problems and solutions is shaped by patterns of interpretation that contextualize an issue in specific ways, emphasizing certain aspects and de-emphasizing others. Importantly, framing enters political debates and decision-making both because it is used as a strategic tool to exert influence and as the result of unconscious patterns of thought. We investigated how different frames relate to one another and how they affect global health governance by means of three case studies, HIV/AIDS, tobacco control, and access to medicines in developing countries.

With regard to our first hypothesis (H1), that multiple frames lead to competition between them, we found mixed evidence. In all three case studies we found evidence that the existence of multiple frames does not necessarily lead to competition. This has

104 CIPIH (n 83) x; GSPA (n 84) 6; CEWG (n 85) 14.
105 CIPIH (n 83) 175–6; GSPA (n 84); CEWG (n 85).

been most obvious in the case of HIV/AIDS, where the human rights, development, and security frames largely coexist and even align in a mutually supportive manner. Also in the case studies on tobacco control and access to medicines we found that multiple frames existed without competing with one another. The frame defining tobacco use as a disease aligned well with the frame seeing tobacco use as infringing the human right to health of non-smokers. Both frames coexist with the frame identifying tobacco use as an overall cost to the economy. Also the policy solutions promoted by these three frames align well as they all suggest tighter regulation of tobacco use. We also observed multiple frames that do not compete with one another in the case study on access to medicines. Here the development and human rights frames align with one another and also with the frame identifying IP as a key obstacle to access to medicines. The problem definitions suggested by these frames differ—lack of access to medicines is seen as detrimental to development, as a human right violation, and as linked to IP protection. Yet, these different problem definitions are not mutually exclusive, nor are the policy solutions they imply. We also find that these frames were often used in parallel to mobilize the support of different audiences for a specific policy goal. This finding confirms insights from Shiffman[106] and Rushton's[107] work. Rushton writes: 'Indeed a strong argument could be made that part of the reason for the prioritisation of HIV is that it has been framed in multiple ways for different audiences.'[108] In that sense it can be argued that not only do multiple frames not necessarily lead to governance failure but that they may sometimes even contribute to successful governance. This may be the case when they are used to generate a broad basis of support for a specific policy pathway.

Yet we also found considerable evidence in support of H1 in the case studies on tobacco control and access to medicines. We identified competition between frames that create links to different policy issues. For instance, competition exists between the frames that link tobacco use to health and the frame that links tobacco use to human rights. We also identified competition within a frame which creates different links on the same policy: for example the link that established the use of tobacco as a human right (to choose) soon found itself in competition with the link that established the use of tobacco as a violation of a human right (to health). Similarly, in the case of access to medicines and IP, competition emerged about whether the link was about IP hampering access (through higher prices) or facilitating access (through innovation in the long-run). Although we did not specifically analyse the degree of competition within frames, there is some evidence to suggest that competition within frames that link to the same policy issue can be particularly fierce and difficult to reconcile in the process of policymaking.

With regard to our second hypothesis (H2), that competition between frames can contribute to incoherent and even contradictory policies, we find mixed evidence too. We find evidence that does not support the hypothesis because competition was resolved in the process of policymaking. The policy documents we analysed reflect different strategies by which frame competition has been resolved: recognizing key elements of the competing frames; sidelining the most contentious issues; and supporting the policy definition and/or policy solutions suggested by one frame over that suggested by the competing frame. Thus the ample evidence we find for the resolution of frame competition in policy documents seems to challenge H2. Yet, we also find

106 J. Shiffman, 'A Social Explanation for the Rise and Fall of Global Health Issues' (n 15).
107 Rushton, 'Framing AIDS: Securitization' (n 15).
108 Rushton, 'Framing AIDS: Securitization' (n 15) 15.

evidence in support of the hypothesis that frame competition can contribute to incoherent and contradictory policies. We find that this is the case especially when competition between frames is not resolved at the level of policymaking. One example is the persistent competition between the frame that identifies IP as a key obstacle to access to existing drugs and the frame that emphasizes the importance of other factors. As we have shown in our third case study, while competition between these two frames appears to be resolved within individual policy documents, it persists between them. This has led to a global governance of access to medicines in developing countries that is incoherent and in places contradictory.

Our study provided ample evidence that the existence of multiple frames does not present a problem for policy coherence in itself. Indeed, if problem definitions and policy solutions promoted by different frames are not in competition with one another they can help in the formation of broad coalitions. In this case, different frames can speak to the interests, values, and institutional mandates of different groups and mobilize their support for policy change in a certain direction. Even if frames compete with one another, however, the result does not necessarily have to be an incoherent policy approach. This is well illustrated by the case study on tobacco control. Competition between problem definitions and appropriate policy solutions was resolved in the process of policymaking when WHO and the World Bank rallied behind the frame that tobacco use is harmful to the economy and helped this frame become dominant in the global policy debate. The risk of competition between frames contributing to governance failure is therefore mitigated when power hierarchies establish dominant problem definitions and policy pathways. Yet, frame competition does seem to be problematic for governance if it cannot be resolved in the process of policymaking. This is illustrated in the case study on access to medicines. Competition between different interpretations of the role of IP in constraining access to medicines and, consequently, the importance of amending the global IP system has not been resolved. Rather, different international agreements pursue different policy approaches.

Frame competition is certainly not the only or even the most important factor leading to governance failure. In this chapter, we use the concept of framing to highlight the role that ideas play in shaping governance. While we focus on the concept of framing, our analysis also shows that the role of frames in policymaking is linked to other factors, such as interests and power. In the case studies on tobacco control and access to medicines we find that competition between frames is tied in with competition between material interests. The framing of tobacco use as a disease, infringing on the human right to health, and costly to the economy, threatens the profits of the tobacco industry, which has responded with various competing frames. Similarly, the framing of access to medicines as a problem linked to increased IP protection threatens the profits of R&D-based pharmaceutical companies, which equally responded by developing competing frames.

Furthermore, our research shows that the link between interests and frames does not run in one direction only, whereby interest groups rally around the frames that best suit their material interests. Rather, our case studies also reveal examples of frames shaping interests.[109] For instance, the frame that identified IP protection as an obstacle to access garnered support for a more flexible system of IP in the context of pharmaceutical innovation from groups that had initially been strictly opposed to it: the support of the

[109] This observation has been made by others as well. See eg Finnemore and Sikkink, 'International Norm Dynamics and Political Change' (n 14).

US government and the EU for the Doha Declaration on the TRIPS Agreement and Public Health cannot be explained without taking into account that government officials had understood better the link between IP protection and access to medicines in developing countries.[110] Also, the acknowledgement of many R&D-based pharmaceutical companies that the IP-based system of pharmaceutical innovation does not always work with regard to developing countries is difficult to explain without recourse to the frame that was initially introduced by NGOs.[111] This is not to say that new frames and ideas have led to a comprehensive change of interests, but they do seem to have contributed to an adjustment of interests.

By shaping how actors perceive their interests, framing can also affect power relations. One example to illustrate this point is the re-framing of tobacco use as overall costly to the economy, which was initially promoted by the WHO Tobacco Free Initiative and the World Bank. This frame helped to shift the perceptions of ministries of finance and governments concerning their interest with regard to tobacco control, and contributed to getting them on board to agree to the FCTC. Like the link between frames and interests, the link between frames and power also works in two directions. The emergence of new frames can change power relations, and existing power relations influence which frames become dominant.

The chapter highlights that the world views which lead to different interpretations of policy problems can compete with one another in the same way that material interests compete. It also shows that this competition can contribute to governance failure if the competition is not resolved in the process of policymaking. This finding does not mean that we consider contestation in itself a problem for governance. Rather, contestation about problem definitions and policy responses is at the core of politics and at the core of democratic governance. As we illustrate in the case studies on tobacco control and access to medicines, frame competition can be a positive element in the policy process because it can trigger policy change. Yet, governance requires contestation to be resolved—even if only temporarily—so that it can help to steer society in a specific direction, such as towards reducing HIV/AIDS infection rates, reducing tobacco use, and improving access to medicines. An essential aspect of the policymaking process, therefore, is to resolve conflict and find agreement on a course of action necessary to achieve these goals. Competition between problem definitions and policy pathways has to be resolved based on mechanisms that are considered widely legitimate. Hence, when competition between frames leads to incoherent policies it can be interpreted as a sign that a key aspect of policymaking, namely legitimate mechanisms of conflict resolution, is not working.

110 S. Sell and A. Prakash, 'Using Ideas Strategically: The Contest Between Business and NGO Networks in Intellectual Property Rights' (2004) 48 *International Studies Quarterly* 143.

111 A. Witty, 'New Strategies for Innovation in Global Health: A Pharmaceutical Industry Perspective' (2011) 30 *Health Affairs* 118.

30

The Interlocking World of Global Health Governance

The Tobacco Industry, Bilateral Investment Treaties, and Health Policy

*Hadii M. Mamudu**

1. Introduction

Trading of goods and services has been part of human endeavour, and since the mid-twentieth century, international trading has been governed by the General Agreement on Tariffs and Trade (GATT)/the World Trade Organization (WTO).[1] In 1948, the GATT emerged and through eight rounds of trade negotiations, tariff and non-tariff barriers to trade were reduced, especially among developed countries. The conclusion of the Uruguay round of trade negotiations, 1986–1994, resulted in the creation of the WTO in 1995 with the aim to further reduce barriers to trade. The underlying principles of this trading regime include trade without discrimination (ie most-favoured-nation), national treatment (ie treating foreigners and locals equally), free trade through negotiations, predictability through binding agreements and transparency, promoting fair competition, and encouraging economic development and reform.[2] The GATT/WTO provides for both first-instance and appellate dispute settlement mechanisms between states. The agreements under this trading regime provide some degree of flexibility for governments to promulgate and implement public health policies.[3,4,5] Nevertheless, Transnational Tobacco Companies (TTCs)

* I would like to thank the Department of Health Services Management and Policy and the College of Public Health for the logistical support for this research. Additionally, I would like to thank colleagues and students: Dr Sreenivas Veeranki, Yi He, David Kioko, Chika Ozodiegwu, Khuyen Nguyen, and Gary Johnson for painstakingly collecting data that supported this study. Finally, I would like to thank Dr Andrew Russell of Durham University, for taking time to review an initial draft of this chapter.

1 WTO, 'Understanding the WTO'. 2011, available at <http://wto.org/english/thewto_e/whatis_e/tif_e/understanding_e.pdf> (accessed 31 July 2012).

2 'Understanding the WTO' (n 1).

3 WTO, 'WTO Agreement and Public Health—a Joint Study by the WHO and the WTO Secretariat', Document No 02-4531 (Geneva, 2002).

4 M. Koivusalo, T. Schrecker, and R. Labonte, 'Globalization and Policy Space for Health and Social Determinants of Health' in R. Labonte, T. Schrecker, C. Packer, and V. Runnels (eds), *Globalization and Health: Pathways, Evidence and Policy* (New York: Routledge, 2009) 105.

5 J.N. Eckhardt, 'Balancing Interests in Free Trade and Health: How the WHO's Framework Convention on Tobacco Control Can Withstand WTO Scrutiny' *Duke Journal of Comparative and International Law* (2002) 12(1): 197.

have used and continue to use trade agreements against states' authority to protect public health.[6,7]

The multilateral agreements under the trading regime of the GATT/WTO have been supplemented by bilateral and multilateral trade/investment treaties around the world. The first bilateral investment treaty (BIT) was signed between Germany and Pakistan in November 1959,[8] and the number of BITs greatly increased in the 1980s and 1990s.[9,10,11] This worldwide proliferation of BITs has potential implications not only for domestic health policy but also global health governance[12,13] because evidence suggests that the liberalization of tobacco markets resulted in increased tobacco consumption.[14,15,16,17] Moreover, BITs primarily deal with economic concerns and rarely include issues involving market failures[18,19] that are entailed in tobacco use and advertising, marketing, and promotions, including information asymmetry and negative externalities produced through secondhand smoke (SHS) exposure and health care costs.[20] These issues are important in global tobacco control because tobacco use and associated morbidity and mortality[21,22,23,24,25] rates continue to increase amidst

6 A.L. Taylor, F.J. Chaloupka, E. Guindon, and M. Corbett, 'The Impact of Trade Liberalization on Tobacco Consumption' in P. Jha and F. Chaloupka (eds), *Tobacco Control in Developing Countries* (Oxford: OUP, 2000) 343.

7 WHO-TFI, 'Confronting the Tobacco Epidemic in the Era of Trade Investment and Liberalization' (2012), available at <http://whqlibdoc.who.int/publications/2012/9789241503723_eng.pdf> (accessed 29 July 2012).

8 R. Dolzer and M. Stevens, *Bilateral Investment Treaties* (The Hague: Kluwer Law International, 1996).

9 UNCTAD, 'Total number of Bilateral Investment Treaties Concluded', 1 June 2011, available at <http://unctad.org/sections/dite_pcbb/docs/bits_switzerland.pdf> (accessed 11 March 2012).

10 UNCTAD, 'What are BITs?' (2004), available at <http://www.unctadxi.org/templates/Page____1006.aspx> (accessed 9 March 2012).

11 UNCTAD, 'Bilateral Investment Treaties, 1959–1999' (2000), available at <http://www.unctad.org/en/docs/poiteiiad2.en.pdf> (accessed 9 March 2012).

12 WHO-TFI, 'Confronting the Tobacco Epidemic' (n 7).

13 A. Russell, M. Wainwright, and H.M. Mamudu, 'A Chilling Example? Uruguay, Philip Morris International and the WHO's Framework Convention on Tobacco Control' *Medical Anthropology* (2012) (In review).

14 F. Chaloupka and A. Laixuthai, 'US Trade Policy and Cigarette Smoking in Asia', NBER Working Paper Series, Paper 5543 1996 (April).

15 F.J. Chaloupka and R. Nair, 'International Issues in the Supply of Tobacco: Recent Changes and Implications for Alcohol' *Addiction* (2000) 95 (Suppl 4): S477.

16 Taylor et al, 'The Impact of Trade Liberalization' (n 6).

17 D.W. Bettcher, D. Yach, and G.E. Guindon, 'Global Trade and Health: Key Linkages and Future Challenges' *Bulletin of the World Health Organization* (2000) 78: 521.

18 K.J. Vandevelde, 'The Political Economy of Bilateral Investment Treaty' *American Society Journal of International Law* (1998) 92(4): 621.

19 Z. Elkins, A.T. Guzman, and B.A. Simmons, 'Competing for Capital: The Diffusion of Bilateral Investment Treaties, 1960–2000' *International Organization* (2006) 60(4): 811.

20 P. Jha and F. Chaloupka (eds), *Curbing the Epidemic: Government and the Economics of Tobacco Control* (Washington, DC: World Bank, 1999).

21 WHO, 'WHO Report on the Global Tobacco Epidemic, 2008: MPOWER Package' (Geneva, 2008).

22 WHO, 'WHO Report about Global Tobacco Epidemic, 2011: Warning about Dangers of Tobacco' (Geneva, 2011).

23 WHO, 'Global Burden of Disease: 2004 Update' (2008), available at <http://www.who.int/healthinfo/global_burden_disease/GBD_report_2004update_full.pdf> (accessed 28 June 2012).

24 V. Fuster and B.B. Kelly, 'Promoting Cardiovascular Health in the Developing World: A Critical Challenge to Achieve Global Health' (2010), available at <http://www.ncbi.nlm.nih.gov/books/NBK45693/pdf/TOC.pdf> (accessed 2 August 2012).

25 WHO, 'WHO Global Report: Mortality Attributable to Tobacco' (2012), available at <http://whqlibdoc.who.int/publications/2012/9789241564434_eng.pdf> (accessed 3 October 2012).

globalization of the tobacco industry.[26,27] This phenomenon mobilized governments for action against tobacco use through the World Health Organization (WHO) Framework Convention on Tobacco Control (FCTC),[28] the first negotiated international public health treaty by the WHO and the United Nations.[29,30] This study investigates the tobacco industry's role in the development of these BITs and how BITs were used to facilitate the spread of tobacco worldwide and undermine health policy and governance.

BITs exist in different forms, but they are generally referred to as:

> Agreements between two countries for the reciprocal encouragement, promotion and protection of investments in each other's territories by companies based in either country. Treaties typically cover... scope and definition of investment, admission and establishment, national treatment, most-favoured-nation treatment, fair and equitable treatment, compensation in the event of expropriation or damage to the investment, guarantees of free transfers of funds, and dispute settlement mechanisms, both state-state and investor-state.[31]

In this respect, BITs are qualitatively and substantively different from many agreements in inter-state relations, including the GATT/WTO. BITs purport to protect the flow of foreign direct investments (FDI) and economic cooperation through rights and guarantees. For this reason, BITs require that signatory parties should not only accord national treatment for parties' investments but also grant parties substantive rights to redress for the breach of the agreement.[32,33,34,35,36,37,38,39,40] Moreover, unlike the GATT/WTO agreements, where non-state entities do not have legal standing in dispute settlements, BITs provide for investor-state dispute settlement. These features make BITs unique because they not only provide more liberalized economic relations but also open up an avenue for the challenge of national policies (including those on health) that are considered against the interest of state parties and private investors. Since the mid-1960s these disputes have been mostly settled through international arbitration mechanisms at the World Bank's International Centre for Settlement of

26 D. Yach and D.W. Bettcher, 'Globalization of the Tobacco Industry Influence and New Global Response' *Tobacco Control* (2000) 9: 206.

27 WHO, 'Tobacco Industry Interference with Tobacco Control' (Geneva, 2008).

28 WHO, WHO Framework Convention on Tobacco Control (Geneva, 2003).

29 WHO, 'First Global Ministerial Conference on Non-communicable Disease Control: Moscow Declaration' (2011), available at <http://www.who.int/nmh/events/moscow_ncds_2011/conference_documents/moscow_declaration_en.pdf> (accessed 29 July 2012).

30 UNGA, Political Declaration of the High-level Meeting of the General Assembly on the Prevention and Control of Non-communicable Diseases (2011), available at <http://www.un.org/ga/search/view_doc.asp?symbol=A%2F66%2FL.1&Lang=E> (accessed 23 February 2012).

31 UNCTAD, 'Total number of Bilateral Investment Treaties Concluded' (n 9).

32 Dolzer and Stevens, *Bilateral Investment Treaties* (n 8).

33 Taylor et al, 'The Impact of Trade Liberalization' (n 6).

34 Elkins, Guzman, and Simmons, 'Competing for Capital' (n 19).

35 R. Dolzer, 'New Foundations of the Law of Expropriation of Alien Property' *American Journal of International Law* (1981) 75(3): 553.

36 M.S. Minor, 'The Demise of Expropriation as an Instrument of LDC Policy' *Journal of International Business Studies* (1994) 25(1): 177.

37 M. Sornarajah, *The International Law of Foreign Investment* (New York: CUP, 1994).

38 D.F. Vagts, 'Foreign Investment Risk Reconsidered: The View from the 1980s' *ICSID Review—Foreign Investment Law Journal* (1987) 2(1): 1.

39 L.E. Peterson and K.R. Gray, 'International Human Rights in Bilateral Investment Treaties and in Investment Treaty Arbitration' (2003), available at <http://www.iisd.org/pdf/2003/investment_int_human_rights_bits.pdf> (accessed 26 September 2012).

40 D. Bettcher and A.L. Taylor, 'Confronting the Tobacco Epidemic in an Era of Trade Liberalization' (2001).

Investment Disputes (ICSID)[41,42] and the UN Commission on International Trade Law (UNCITRAL).[43,44]

Although BITs allow more liberalized relations and a means for dispute settlements, they were rarely used against state policies until the 1980s.[45] Indeed, since the ICSID and UNCITRAL arbitration mechanisms emerged in the mid-1960s and mid-1970s to settle investor-state disputes, BITs were never used by any tobacco company (Table 30.1) to challenge states' policies.[46,47] The disputes involving tobacco control trade that emerged[48,49,50] were settled through state actors (with the tobacco industry influence) using mechanisms within the multilateral trading regime of GATT/WTO.[51,52,53,54,55] Thus, until recently,[56,57,58,59] although tobacco litigation occurred at the national level, tobacco trade-health conflicts in the international system were state-centric, which means that the TTCs could only act through states to influence the outcome and did not *directly* confront states.

This changed in 2010, however, when BITs emerged as a major issue in the governance of tobacco control with two high-profile cases. The first is the Philip Morris International (PMI) claim at ICSID against Uruguay's ban on brand stretching and requirements for rotating graphic health warnings on cigarette packages with an 80 per cent coverage area, based on a 1998 Switzerland-Uruguay BIT;[60,61,62] the second is the

41 ICSID, List of Concluded Cases (2012), available at <http://icsid.worldbank.org/ICSID/FrontServlet?requestType=GenCaseDtlsRH&actionVal=ListConcluded> (accessed 20 July 2012).

42 ICSID, List of Pending Cases (2012), available at <http://icsid.worldbank.org/ICSID/FrontServlet?requestType=GenCaseDtlsRH&actionVal=ListPending> (accessed 29 July 2012).

43 Peterson and Gray, 'International Human Rights' (n 39).

44 UNCITRAL, Arbitration Rules (revised 2010) (undated), available at <http://www.uncitral.org/uncitral/uncitral_texts/arbitration/2010Arbitration_rules.html> (accessed 17 October 2012); Investment Treaty Arbitration, Chronological, available at <http://www.italaw.com/awards/chronological> (Accessed 19 December 2012).

45 Peterson and Gray, 'International Human Rights' (n 39).

46 ICSID, List of Concluded Cases (n 41).

47 ICSID, List of Pending Cases (n 42).

48 Chaloupka and Laixuthai, 'US Trade Policy' (n 14).

49 Chaloupka and Nair, 'International Issues in the Supply of Tobacco' (n 15).

50 Taylor et al, 'The Impact of Trade Liberalization' (n 6).

51 D. Bettcher and I. Shapiro, 'Tobacco Control in an Era of Trade Liberalization' *Tobacco Control* (2001) 10(1): 65.

52 H. Chitanondh, 'Defeat in Trade—Victory in Health', Thailand Health Promotion Institute and the National Health Foundation (Bangkok, 2001).

53 C. Callard, H. Chitanondh, and R. Weissman, 'Why Trade and Investment Liberalization May Threaten Effective Tobacco Control Efforts' *Tobacco Control* (2001) 10: 68.

54 L. Eckhardt, S.I. Woodruff, and J.P. Elder, 'Related Effectiveness of Continued, Lapsed and Delayed Smoking Prevention Intervention in Senior High School Students' *American Journal of Health Promotion* (1997) 11: 418.

55 K. Lee, 'The Global Trade and Public Health Nexus: the Role of WHO' *New Solutions* (2003) 13(1): 61.

56 Koivusalo, Schrecker, and Labonte, 'Globalization and Policy Space' (n 4).

57 WHO-TFI, 'Confronting the Tobacco Epidemic' (n 7).

58 R. Labonte, K.S. Mohindra, and R. Lencucha, 'Framing International Trade and Chronic Disease' *Global Health* (2011) 7(1): 21.

59 R. Lencucha, 'Philip Morris versus Uruguay: Health Governance Challenged' *Lancet* (2010) 376: 852.

60 ICSID, *Philip Morris Brand Sarl (Switzerland), Philip Morris Products SA (Switzerland) and Abal Hermanos SA (Uruguay) v Oriental Republic of Uruguay* (ICSID Case ARB/10/7) (undated), available at <http://icsid.worldbank.org/ICSID/FrontServlet?requestType=CasesRH&reqFrom=ListCases&caseId=C1000&actionVal=viewCase> (accessed 28 March 2012).

61 LALIVE, Request for Arbitration (2010), available at <http://www.smoke-free.ca/eng_home/2010/PMIvsUruguay/PMI-Uruguay%20complaint0001.pdf> (accessed 28 March 2012).

62 T. Weiler, 'Philip Morris vs. Uruguay: An Analysis of Tobacco Control Measures in the Context of International Investment Law' (2010), available at <http://italaw.com/documents/WeilerOpinion-PMI-Uruguay.pdf> (accessed 11 March 2012).

Table 30.1 International disputes on trade/investment versus health

Dispute No	Date	Case	Nature of dispute
General Agreement on Trade and Tariffs, 1947–1994			
L/514-28S/100*	11 Jun 1981	*United States v Japan*	Japanese restraints on imports of manufactured tobacco from the United States
DS10/R-37s/200	7 Nov 1990	*United States v Thailand*	Restrictions on importation of and internal taxes on cigarettes
DS44/R*	7 Sep 1993	*(Argentina, Brazil, Canada, Chile, Colombia, El Salvador, Guatemala, Thailand and Zimbabwe) v United States*	Measures affecting the importation, internal sale, and use of tobacco
World Trade Organization, 1995–2012[†]			
DS227	1 Mar 2001	*Chile v Peru*	Taxes on cigarettes
DS300	28 Aug 2003	*Honduras v Dominican Republic*	Measures affecting the importation of cigarettes
DS302	8 Oct 2003	*Honduras v Dominican Republic*	Measures affecting the importation and internal sale of cigarettes
DS371	7 Feb 2008	*Philippines v Thailand*	Customs and fiscal measures on cigarettes from the Philippines
DS406	7 Apr 2010	*Indonesia v United States*	Measures affecting the production and sale of clove cigarettes
DS411	20 Jul 2010	*Ukraine v Armenia*	Measures affecting the importation and internal sale of cigarettes and alcoholic beverages
DS434	13 Mar 2012	*Ukraine v Australia*	Certain measures concerning trademarks and other plain packaging requirements applicable to tobacco products and packaging

DS435	4 Apr 2012	*Honduras v Australia*	Certain measures concerning trademarks, geographical indicators, and other plain packaging requirements applicable to tobacco products and packaging
DS441	18 Jul 2012	*Dominican Republic v Australia*	
DS458	3 May 2013	*Cuba v Australia*	
DS467	20 Sep 2013	*Indonesia v Australia*	
International Centre for Settlement of Investment Disputes (ICSID), 1966–2012			
ARB/95/1*	27 Apr 1995	*(Leaf Tobacco A Michaelides SA and Greek-Albanian Leaf Tobacco & Co SA) v Republic of Albania*	Tobacco manufacturing and warehousing
ARB/10/7	26 Mar 2010	*(Philip Morris Brand Sarl (Switzerland), Philip Morris Products SS (Switzerland) and Abal Hermanos SS (Uruguay) v Oriental Republic of Uruguay OR PMI) v Uruguay*	Uruguay's tobacco control measures ban brand stretching and require rotating graphic health warnings on cigarette packages with an 80% coverage area
United Nations Commission on International Trade Law (UNCITRAL), 1976–2012			
DFAT Case: 1107-F193	11 Nov 2011	*Philip Morris Asia v Australia*	Challenge to Australian plain packaging law

* Not tobacco control-related.

† WTO, 'Dispute Settlement: The Dispute: Index of Disputes Issues: Tobacco (2014), available at <http://wto.org/english/tratop_e/dispu_e/dispu_subjects_index_e.htm?id=G11#selected_subject>.

Sources: WTO Dispute Settlement System, at <http://www.wto.org/english/tratop_e/dispu_e/find_dispu_cases_e.htm#results>; ICSID Cases, at <http://icsid.worldbank.org/ICSID/FrontServlet>; UNCITRAL, at <http://www.uncitral.org/uncitral/uncitral_texts/arbitration/2010Arbitration_rules.html>.

Philip Morris Asia (PMA) claim at UNCITRAL against Australia's plain packaging law, based on a 1993 Hong Kong-Australia BIT.[63] While there are other investor-state disputes that have been settled by ICSID and UNCITRAL, these two tobacco-related cases are unprecedented and novel because they represent the first time TTCs have directly challenged states' policies in these international arbitration venues. Thus, this study explores TTCs' role in the development and spread of BITs in order to allow for better future BIT negotiations and governance in tobacco control. The chapter begins with an overview of BITs, then discusses how the tobacco industry used BITs to facilitate the spread of tobacco worldwide, and concludes with the implications of BITs for governance in tobacco control. BITs warrant global attention because thousands of them exist[64,65,66] and, as instruments to fight against the implementation of the FCTC, they have major implications for health policy and governance.[67,68]

2. Methods

This chapter utilizes a qualitative research approach[69] based on the collection and analysis of archival documents (published papers from three databases—PubMed, JStor, and Google Scholar; organizational documents from UNCTAD, WHO, World Bank's ICSID, UNCITRAL, and GATT/WTO; and tobacco industry documents—Legacy online library and tobaccodocuments.org). Standard method[70,71] was used between May and October 2012 to search for documents on BITs and the tobacco industry. The initial search terms were 'bilateral investment treaties AND tobacco', 'bilateral investment treaties AND [name of tobacco company]', and 'bilateral investment treaties AND tobacco control'. The retrieved documents were reviewed and evaluated to examine the role of the tobacco industry and their use of BITs to enhance the worldwide marketing and promotion of tobacco and against tobacco control.

3. Results

3.1 Bilateral investment agreements

The importance of BITs in inter-state relations became apparent in the 1950s when they were used to deal with issues that could not be addressed with customary international law and/or easily negotiated within the multilateral trading regime under the GATT. BITs originated from Europe in the late 1950s, when Germany signed treaties with Pakistan and the Dominican Republic in November and December

63 Australian Government, 'Investor-State Arbitration—Tobacco Plain Packaging' (2011), available at <http://www.ag.gov.au/Internationallaw/Pages/Investor-State-Arbitration—Tobacco-Plain-Packaging.aspx> (accessed 17 October 2012).

64 UNCTAD, 'Total number of Bilateral Investment Treaties Concluded' (n 9).

65 UNCTAD, 'Bilateral Investment Treaties, 1959–1999' (n 11).

66 UNCTAD, 'Bilateral Investment Treaties: 1995–2006' (2007), available at <http://unctad.org/en/Docs/iteiia20065_en.pdf> (accessed 25 June 2012).

67 WHO-TFI, 'Confronting the Tobacco Epidemic' (n 7).

68 Russell, Wainwright, and Mamudu, 'A Chilling Example?' (n 13).

69 C.K. Russell and D.M. Gregory, 'Evaluation of Qualitative Research Studies' *Evidence-Based Nursing* (2003) 6(2): 36.

70 R.E. Malone and E.D. Balbach, 'Tobacco Industry Documents: Treasure Trove or Quagmire?' *Tobacco Control* (2000) 9: 334.

71 S.J. Anderson, P.M. McCandless, K. Klausner, R. Taketa, and V.B. Yerger, 'Tobacco Documents Research Methodology' *Tobacco Control* (2011) 20: ii8.

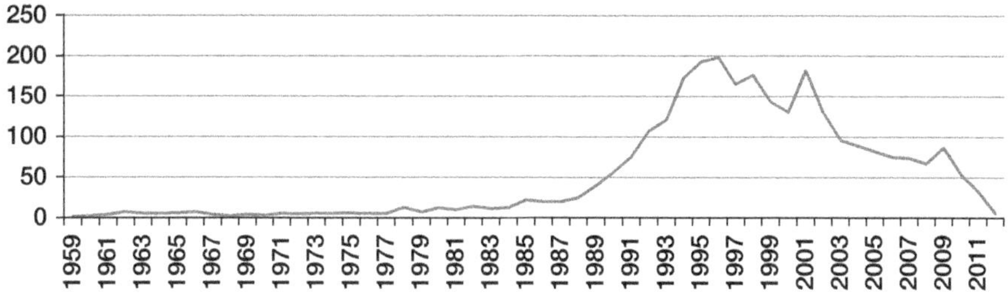

Fig. 30.1 The Growth of Bilateral Investment Treaties, 1959–2012

Sources: International Centre for Settlement of Investment Disputes (ICSID) and United Nations Conference on Trade and Development (UNCTAD).

1959. Since then, the number of BITs has grown to such an extent that by March 2012, there were over 2,808 BITs that involve over 177 countries.[72,73,74] The five countries with the largest number of BITs in the world were Germany (135), Switzerland (118), the United Kingdom (104), France (101), and the Netherlands (97). These BITs became the primary instruments for governing inter-state investment relations,[75,76] especially following the failed attempt by the Organization for Economic Cooperation and Development (OECD) to develop a multilateral agreement on investment (MAI) in the mid-1990s.[77] For this reason, Peterson and Gray argued, 'to the extent that flows of Foreign Direct Investment can be said to be governed at the global level, it is this quilt-work of bilateral treaties—and a handful of broader trade agreements with investment rules embedded in them—which will set the rules of the game'.[78]

Tables 30.2 and 30.3 illuminate BITs in the six WHO regions and by the level of economic development based on income. These tables show that most BITs exist between higher- and lower-income countries, and only a few among and between lower-income countries. The growth of BITs in the world displays more of a vertical relationship between developed and developing countries than horizontal relations among high-income or low- and middle-income countries. As such, there is an inherent power difference as the bargain is between two unequal parties, the powerful home country (developed) and the relatively weaker host country (developing).[79,80,81] This suggests the need to discern the rationale for the proliferation of BITs throughout the world.

BITs proliferated throughout the international system for several reasons, which include the failure to develop a broader multilateral investment treaty within the UN

72 UNCTAD, 'Bilateral Investment Treaties, 1959–1999' (n 11).

73 UNCTAD, 'Bilateral Investment Treaties: 1995–2006' (n 66).

74 ICSID, ICSID database of Bilateral Investment Treaties (undated), available at <http://icsid.worldbank.org/ICSID/FrontServlet> (accessed 31 July 2012).

75 Vandevelde, 'The Political Economy' (n 18).

76 Elkins, Guzman, and Simmons, 'Competing for Capital' (n 19).

77 E. Neumayer, 'Multilateral Agreement on Investment: Lessons for WTO for the Failed OECD-Negotiations' *Wirtschaftspolitische Blätter* (1999) 46(6): 618.

78 Peterson and Gray, 'International Human Rights' (n 39).

79 Vandevelde, 'The Political Economy' (n 18).

80 Elkins, Guzman, and Simmons, 'Competing for Capital' (n 19).

81 A. Guzman, 'Explaining the Popularity of Bilateral Investment Treaties: Why LDCs Sign Treaties That Hurt Them' *Virginia Journal of International Law* (1998) 38: 639.

system[82] and/or the OECD;[83] disagreement over customary international law standards for the treatment of foreign investors as expressed in the 'Hull Rule' that 'no government is entitled to expropriate private property, for whatever purpose, without provision for prompt, adequate, and effective payment therefore' (quoted in Elkins et al);[84] Western countries' fears of nationalization or arbitrary treatment at the hands of the governments of developing countries; and competitive pressure for FDI among countries, particularly low- and middle-income countries (LMICs).[85,86,87,88,89] Additionally, BITs among LMICs were facilitated by international organizations such as UNCTAD[90,91] and major capital exporting countries such as France and Germany[92] as a mechanism to enhance South-South cooperation and economic development. While these BITs are between sovereign, but mostly unequal states, the guarantee of investment protections and mechanisms for the settlement of grievances implies that they offer a way for the TTCs based in high-income countries to invest in LMICs and challenge domestic health policies that may impede the activities of investors. The expansive nature of BITs with no protection for market failures,[93] suggests that they provide protection for the TTCs. As such, there is the need to investigate TTCs' role in the development of these BITs to inform health policy and governance.

3.2 Tobacco industry and bilateral investment treaties

The TTCs recognized the significance of BITs by the late 1940s,[94,95,96] when British American Tobacco (BAT) became concerned about 'double taxation', which is a situation whereby TTCs and their subsidiaries simultaneously paid taxes to both home and host countries. Reports of BAT's annual meetings suggest it considered BITs as a means to provide 'relief' for the companies from this 'double taxation' and enhance their profits. In an address to the 47th Annual General Meeting of BAT on 12 May 1950, the Chairman said:

Very few countries have made any material reduction in the high rates of taxation imposed during the war [World War II], and it is therefore of the utmost importance that relief should be granted,

82 Vandevelde, 'The Political Economy' (n 18).
83 Guzman, 'Explaining the Popularity of Bilateral Investment Treaties' (n 81).
84 Elkins, Guzman, and Simmons, 'Competing for Capital' (n 19).
85 Dolzer and Stevens, *Bilateral Investment Treaties* (n 8).
86 Elkins, Guzman, and Simmons, 'Competing for Capital' (n 19).
87 Peterson and Gray, 'International Human Rights' (n 39).
88 Labonte, Mohindra, and Lencucha, 'Framing International Trade' (n 58).
89 B.M. Hoekman and M.M. Kostecki, *Political Economy of the World Trading System: The WTO and Beyond* (New York: 2nd edn, OUP, 2001).
90 Peterson and Gray, 'International Human Rights' (n 39).
91 UNCTAD, '29 Bilateral Investment Treaties signed by Least Developed Countries in Brussels' (2002), available at <http://archive.unctad.org/templates/webflyer.asp?docid=2914&intItemID=2022&lang=1> (accessed 7 October 2012).
92 Elkins, Guzman, and Simmons, 'Competing for Capital' (n 19).
93 Vandevelde, 'The Political Economy' (n 18).
94 D. Oppenheim, 'The Fifty-Third Annual General Meeting of British-American Tobacco Company Limited was held at Westminster, SWI' (1955), available at <http://legacy.library.ucsf.edu/tid/ahm64a99> (accessed 17 June 2012).
95 T. Winmill, 'The Forty-Seventh Annual General Meeting of British-American Tobacco Company Limited was held at Westminster, SWI' (1949), available at <http://legacy.library.ucsf.edu/tid/tgm64a99> (accessed 17 June 2012).
96 T. Winmill, 'The Forty-Ninth Annual General Meeting of British-American Tobacco Company Limited was held at Westminster, SWI' (1951), available at <http://legacy.library.ucsf.edu/tid/vgm64a99> (accessed 17 December 2012).

Table 30.2 Countries in the six WHO regions with bilateral investment treaties as of March 2012

Category	Countries (number of bilateral investment treaties)
Africa (AFR)	Algeria (48), Angola (8), Benin (14), Botswana (8), Burkina Faso (14), Burundi (7), Cameroon (16), Cape Verde (9), Central African Republic (4), Chad (14), Comoros (6), Côte d'Ivoire (10), Democratic Republic of Congo (15), Equatorial Guinea (8), Eritrea (4), Ethiopia (28), Gabon (12), Gambia (12), Ghana (26), Guinea (19), Guinea-Bissau (2), Kenya (12), Lesotho (3), Liberia (4), Madagascar (9), Malawi (5), Mali (17), Mauritania (19), Mauritius (27), Mozambique (24), Namibia (13), Niger (5), Nigeria (20), Republic of Congo (13), Rwanda (6), Sao Tome and Principe (1), Senegal (23), Seychelles (6), Sierra Leone (3), South Africa (46), Swaziland (4), Tanzania (15), Togo (4), Uganda (15), Zambia (12), Zimbabwe (30)
Americas/Pan American Health Organization (PAHO)	Antiqua and Barbuda (2), Argentina (73), Barbados (10), Belize (6), Bolivia (20), Brazil (16), Canada (29), Chile (51), Columbia (7), Costa Rica (19), Cuba (58), Dominica (2), Dominican Republic (16), Ecuador (19), El Salvador (21), Grenada (2), Guatemala (16), Guyana (8), Haiti (5), Honduras (10), Jamaica (15), Mexico (28), Nicaragua (18), Panama (20), Paraguay (23), Peru (32), St Lucia (2), St Vincent and the Grenadines (1), Suriname (3), Trinidad and Tobago (12), USA (47), Uruguay (30), Venezuela (28)
Europe (EUR)	Albania (42), Armenia (36), Austria (64), Azerbaijan (44), Belarus (58), Belgium (93), Bosnia (39), Bulgaria (68), Croatia (58), Czech Republic (80), Denmark (55), Estonia (27), Finland (71), France (101), Georgia (29), Germany (135), Greece (43), Hungary (58), Iceland (9), Israel (37), Italy (92), Kazakhstan (41), Kyrgyz Republic (28), Latvia (44), Lithuania (52), Macedonia (36), Malta (22), Moldova (39), Montenegro (17), Netherlands (97), Norway (15), Poland (62), Portugal (55), Romania (82), Russian Federation (71), San Marino (7), Serbia (48), Slovak Republic (54), Slovenia (38), Spain (76), Sweden (70), Switzerland (118), Tajikistan (31), Turkey (82), Turkmenistan (13), Ukraine (65), United Kingdom of Great Britain and Northern Ireland (104), Uzbekistan (49)
Eastern Mediterranean (EMR)	Afghanistan (3), Bahrain (31), Cyprus (27), Djibouti (7), Egypt (98), Iran (61), Jordan (53), Kuwait (58), Lebanon (50), Libya (31), Morocco (60), Oman (33), Pakistan (46), Qatar (49), Saudi Arabia (21), Somalia (2), Sudan (27), Syria (40), Tunisia (54), United Arab Emirates (38), Yemen (37)
Southeast Asia (SEAR)	Bangladesh (29), India (83), Indonesia (65), Korea, Democratic People's Republic of Korea (24), Myanmar (6), Nepal (6), Sri Lanka (28), Thailand (38), Timor-Leste (3)
Western Pacific (WPR)	Australia (24), Brunei Darussalam (7), Cambodia (21), China (127), Hong Kong* (15), Japan (18), Lao People's Democratic Republic (23), Malaysia (66), Mongolia (43), New Zealand (6), Papua New Guinea (6), Philippines (35), Republic of Korea (89), Singapore (40), Tonga (1), Vanuatu (2), Vietnam (57)

Note: Regional classification by the World Health Organization.

Sources: International Centre for Settlement of Investment Disputes (ICSID), United Nations Conference on Trade and Development (UNCTAD), and the World Health Organization.

*China resumed sovereignty in 1997 under the principle of one country, two systems. This institutional arrangement continues Hong Kong's prior international commitments, including BITs.

Table 30.3 Bilateral investment treaties signed by WHO regions as of March 2012 (n = 2808)

WHO Region (No of Countries)	Africa (AFR)	Americas/Pan American Health Organization (PAHO)	Eastern Mediterranean (EMR)	Europe (EUR)	Southeast Asia (SEAR)	Western Pacific (WPR)	Total
Africa (AFR)	81	22	90	286	16	53	548
Americas/Pan American Health Organization (PAHO)		95	24	320	18	60	517
Eastern Mediterranean (EMR)			105	387	39	76	607
Europe (EUR)				655	128	234	1017
Southeast Asia (SEAR)					15	51	66
Western Pacific (WPR)						53	53
Total	81	117	219	1648	216	527	2808

Note: Regional classification by the World Health Organization.

Sources: International Centre for Settlement of Investment Disputes (ICSID), United Nations Conference on Trade and Development (UNCTAD) and World Health Organization.

as soon as possible, from the double taxation at present suffered in so many cases. The Treaties already negotiated by our own Government have been of great value, but unfortunately, the negotiation of further bi-lateral treaties is proceeding very slowly and it is clear that in many cases such Treaties are most unlikely to be concluded. We therefore urge that our Government should grant full relief for overseas taxation, whether or not its action is reciprocated, so that enterprise may not be unduly discouraged and frustrated. By so doing our Government would only be following the example which has been set already by the [US] and by Canada.[97]

The efforts of TTCs to overcome the issue of 'double taxation' through BITs succeeded. According to an R.J. Reynolds' (RJR) annual report of 1976:

Other laws and actions affecting Sea-Land also received close attention during 1976. The company successfully worked to improve protection of American line carriers against taxation by foreign governments by updating provisions in bilateral treaties that provide reciprocal tax exemptions for U.S. ships and those of our trading partners.[98]

Since the late 1940s, BITs have evolved as a means for the TTCs to gain access to closed cigarette markets and protect their investments to maximize profits, especially as the TTCs recognized that the multilateral trade agreements of GATT/WTO did not wholly provide such protections.[99] The purpose of BITs for the TTCs had changed by the 1990s, as they increasingly became not only a means to access markets but also to counter states' policies, particularly after the 'Thai Case', which involved the

97 Winmill, 'The Forty-Ninth Annual General Meeting of BAT' (n 96).

98 RJRI, 'Annual Report R.J. Reynolds Industries, Inc.' (1976), available at <http://legacy.library.ucsf.edu/tid/hwp79d00> (accessed 17 June 2012).

99 F.A. Burke, (untitled) ['The Future Business Environment'] (1983), available at <http://legacy.library.ucsf.edu/tid/uzr13f00> (accessed 17 June 2012).

Table 30.4 Level of income of countries and bilateral investment treaties as of March 2012

Category	Countries (number of bilateral investment treaties)
Low-income economies	Afghanistan (3), Bangladesh (29), Benin (14), Burkina Faso (14), Burundi (7), Cambodia (21), Central African Republic (4), Chad (14), Comoros (6), Democratic People's Republic of Korea (24), Democratic Republic of Congo (15), Eritrea (4), Ethiopia (28), Gambia (12), Guinea (19), Guinea-Bissau (2), Haiti (5), Kenya (12), Kyrgyz Republic (28), Liberia (4), Madagascar (9), Malawi (5), Mali (17), Mauritania (19), Mozambique (24), Myanmar (6), Nepal (6), Niger (5), Rwanda (6), Sierra Leone (3), Somalia (2), Tajikistan (31), Tanzania (15), Togo (4), Uganda (15), Zimbabwe (30)
Lower-middle-income economies	Armenia (36), Albania (42), Bolivia (20), Belize (6), Cameroon (16), Cape Verde (9), Côte d'Ivoire (10), Djibouti (7), Egypt (98), El Salvador (21), Georgia (29), Ghana (26), Guatemala (16), Guyana (8), Honduras (10), India (83), Indonesia (65), Lao People's Democratic Republic (23), Lesotho (3), Moldova (39), Mongolia (43), Morocco (60), Nicaragua (18), Nigeria (20), Pakistan (46), Papua New Guinea (6), Paraguay (23), Philippines (35), Republic of Congo (13), Sao Tome and Principe (1), Senegal (23), Sri Lanka (28), Sudan (27), Swaziland (4), Syria (40), Timor-Leste (3) Tonga (1), Ukraine (65), Uzbekistan (49), Vanuatu (2), Zambia (12), Yemen (37)
Upper-middle-income economies	Algeria (48), Angola (8), Antiqua and Barbuda (2), Argentina (73), Azerbaijan (44), Belarus (58), Bosnia (39), Botswana (8), Brazil (16), Bulgaria (68), Chile (51), China (127), Columbia (7), Costa Rica (19), Cuba (58), Dominica (2), Dominican Republic (16), Ecuador (19), Gabon (12), Grenada (2), Iran (61), Jamaica (15), Jordan (53), Kazakhstan (41), Latvia (44), Lebanon (50), Libya (31), Lithuania (52), Macedonia (36), Malaysia (66), Mauritius (27), Mexico (28), Montenegro (17), Namibia (13), Panama (20), Peru (32), Romania (82), Russian Federation (71), Serbia (48), Seychelles (6), South Africa (46), St Lucia (2), St Vincent and the Grenadines (1), Suriname (3), Thailand (38), Tunisia (54), Turkey (82), Turkmenistan (13), Uruguay (30), Venezuela (28).
High-income economies	Australia (24), Austria (64), Bahrain (31), Barbados (10), Belgium (93), Canada (29), Croatia (58), Cyprus (27), Czech Republic (80), Denmark (55), Estonia (27), Finland (71), France (101), Germany (135), Greece (43), Hong Kong (15), Hungary (58), Iceland (9), Israel (37), Italy (92), Japan (18), Kuwait (58), Malta (22), Netherlands (97), New Zealand (6), Norway (15), Oman (33), Poland (62), Portugal (55), Qatar (49), Republic of Korea (89), San Marino (7), Saudi Arabia (21), Singapore (40), Slovak Republic (54), Slovenia (38), Spain (76), Sweden (70), Switzerland (118), Trinidad and Tobago (12), United Arab Emirates (38), United Kingdom of Great Britain and Northern Ireland (104), USA (47).

Note: This table is based on the World Bank's classification of countries by income, at <http://data.worldbank.org/about/country-classifications/country-and-lending-groups>.

Sources: International Centre for Settlement of Investment Disputes (ICSID, United Nations Conference on Trade and Development (UNCTAD), and World Bank.

US use of trade agreements to open the Thai cigarette market to the TTCs. This case illuminated the shortcomings of the reliance on the arbitration mechanisms provided by the GATT/WTO.[100,101] As a result, BITs became a vital tool for the

[100] RJR International, D.J. Albert, 'Thailand' (1990), available at <http://legacy.library.ucsf.edu/tid/wgf24d00> (accessed 17 December 2012).

[101] Brown & Williamson, R Pritchard, 'Five-Year Tobacco Environment' (1991), available at <http://legacy.library.ucsf.edu/tid/vsh30f00> (accessed 16 October 2012).

Table 30.5 Bilateral investment treaties signed by the level of income as of March 2012

	LIE	LMIE	UMIE	HIE	Total
LIE	138	311	380	306	1135
LMIE		138	392	346	876
UMIE			241	389	630
HIE				167	167
Total	138	449	1013	1208	2808

Note: This table is based on the World Bank's classification of countries by income, at <http://data.worldbank.org/about/country-classifications/country-and-lending-groups>.
Abbreviations: LIE—low-income economies; LMIE—lower-middle-income economies; UMIE—Upper-middle-income economies; HIE—high-income economies.
Sources: International Centre for Settlement of Investment Disputes (ICSID), United Nations Conference on Trade and Development (UNCTAD) and World Bank.

TTCs to use against tobacco control, especially with the development of the FCTC.[102,103,104,105]

3.2.1 BITs as an instrument to access international tobacco markets: 1950s–1990s

The historical importance of BITs to the TTCs has been their utilization to access closed tobacco markets, mostly in LMICs.[106,107] In making a business case for the industry's push for BITs, the Executive Vice President of Philip Morris (PM) said, in a December 1978 speech in support of the US BIT programme to a joint meeting of the World Affairs Council and the International Business Forum in Philadelphia:

> Bilateral investment treaties between the U.S. Government and individual developing countries also merit consideration. Several European nations already have signed such treaties. They define the treatment host governments will accord foreign investment, and include such guarantees as equitable treatment and protection consistent with international law, fair compensation and recourse to arbitration in the event of expropriation, and free transferability of capital.[108]

BITs emerged on top of the agenda of major TTCs in the 1970s and 1980s. In a reflection on the outlook of the US BITs programme in the 1980s, an October 1985 BAT document stated:

102 WHO-TFI, 'Confronting the Tobacco Epidemic' (n 7).

103 O'Neil Institute, 'Tobacco product regulation and WTO: *US—clove cigarettes*' (2011), available at <http://www.law.georgetown.edu/oneillinstitute/documents/2011-09-12_O%27Neill%20Institute%20Briefing%20Paper%20US%20-%20Clove%20Cigarettes.pdf> (accessed 23 February 2012).

104 H.M. Mamudu, R. Hammond, and S.A. Glantz, 'International Trade versus Public Health during the FCTC Negotiations, 1999–2003' *Tobacco Control* (2011) 20(1): e3.

105 WHO, 'International Trade and Health', Doc No A59/15 (2006), available at <http://apps.who.int/gb/ebwha/pdf_files/WHA59-REC1/e/Resolutions-en.pdf> (accessed 20 May 2012).

106 Mamudu, Hammond, and Glantz, 'International Trade versus Public Health' (n 104).

107 [RJR], 'Public Affairs Issues Inventory' (1986), available at <http://legacy.library.ucsf.edu/tid/jsg55a00> (accessed 17 June 2012).

108 H. Cullman, 'Interdependence: A Challenge to World Business'—Remarks by Hugh Cullman, Group Executive Vice President, Philip Morris Incorporated, at a joint meeting of the World Affairs Council and the International Business Forum (1978), available at <http://legacy.library.ucsf.edu/tid/mdu22d00> (accessed 17 June 2012).

The U.S. BIT programme has generated considerable interest among LDCs [less developed countries] seeking U.S. private investment, although many of the most attractive candidates elude it. Even so it can benefit MNCs [multinational corporations] both as a vehicle to solve current investment problems with a BIT candidate, as a means to provide clear ground rules for treatment of investment for at least 20 years in a BIT ratifying nation, and in the longer term, as a step toward building an international consensus on investment rules favourable to private enterprise.[109]

Similarly, RJR wrote in a 1985 report on major 'international tobacco' issues it faces, that: 'Of RJRTI's [RJR Tobacco International] 6 "major issues," only two issues are carry-overs from 1984: "international market access for tobacco" . . . The 4 newcomers include an additional trade concern, "bilateral investment treaties," . . .'[110] In a 1986 'confidential' document discussing RJR's positions on several tobacco-related issues, including the value of BITs for market penetration and lending support to the US BITs programme, it was pointed out that 'successful [BITs] negotiations would remove restrictions on foreign direct investment, and *ease RJR's entry into foreign markets*'[111] (emphasis added). For this reason, RJR chose to 'continue to support the [US] bilateral treaty programme by sharing our business experiences with treaty negotiators, and advocating ratification of treaties when they are before Senate in areas where we have or could have interest'.[112]

The TTCs used BITs to access international markets around the world, which started with those in Latin America and the Caribbean from the 1970s. The Tobacco Merchants Association (TMA) of the US 'Caribbean Initiative' set out to: 'Increase the number of Bilateral-Investment Treaties to ensure that US investors are treated no less favourably than host country investors and that the legal provisions concerning entry and duration of-investment are clear.'[113] At a meeting of BAT General Managers in San Pedro Sula, Honduras, in December 1972, it was 'agreed as group policy to suggest to governments that they include leaf tobacco in all bilateral agreements'.[114] The discussion at this meeting suggests that the managers planned to access the Honduras market through BITs with other countries, although Honduras has resisted the inclusion of tobacco in its BITs. It was:

Agreed that Marketing Managers of Companies participating in TORQUAY [a sampling scheme for tobacco leaf from El Salvador, Guatemala and Nicaragua to develop brands[115,116]] at next meeting in Guatemala will discuss possible interchange of cigarettes between Honduras, Nicaragua, El Salvador and Guatemala if Honduras returns to CACM [Central American Common Market] or when bilateral treaties are completed.[117]

109 [BAT], 'BATCo: Press Cuttings—Index' (1985), available at <http://legacy.library.ucsf.edu/tid/dnr55a99> (accessed 17 June 2012).

110 [RJR], ['RJR's Family Primary Concerns'] (1985), available at <http://legacy.library.ucsf.edu/tid/isg55a00> (accessed 17 June 2012).

111 [RJR], 'Federal Public Affairs Issues' (1986), available at <http://legacy.library.ucsf.edu/tid/swb35d00> (accessed 17 December 2012).

112 [RJR], 'Federal Public Affairs Issues' (n 111).

113 TMA, R.E. Scanlan, 'Special Report: The Caribbean Basin Initiative—What's at stake?' (1982), available at <http://legacy.library.ucsf.edu/tid/azu39b00> (accessed October 16 2012).

114 [BAT], 'CACM/Panama' (1972), available at <http://legacy.library.ucsf.edu/tid/nhr65a99> (accessed 20 June 2012).

115 JRC, 'Project Torquay: Sampling Scheme for Leaf Received from El Salvador, Nicaragua and Guatemala' (1973), available at <http://legacy.library.ucsf.edu/tid/cir65a99> (accessed 20 June 2012).

116 R.T. Hatch, 'Blending Procedures to be Carried Out in Central America on Project Torquay' (1972), available at <http://legacy.library.ucsf.edu/tid/eir65a99> (accessed 20 June 2012).

117 JRC, 'Project Torquay' (n 115).

Noticing the growth of bilateral agreements and other integration pacts in Latin America, BAT formed a working group to study the Andean Pact, Mercosur and the Mexican trilateral agreement to take several actions, including 'to produce a plan for lobbying the various trade agreements to represent BAT interests'.[118,119] The crux of this plan involved taking advantage of bilateral agreements, which were an integral part of the Latin American Integration Agreements. As a result, the General Managers of BAT in Central America countries (Costa Rica, El Salvador, Guatemala, Honduras, Nicaragua, and Panama) held a conference in July 1992 in Costa Rica and agreed to lobby governments on several trade-related issues, including bilateral tariff negotiations.[120]

The use of BITs as an instrument to access international tobacco markets peaked in the 1980s, when the US Cigarettes Export Association (USCEA) lobbied the US Trade Representative to use section 301 of the 1974 Trade Act and BITs to open tobacco markets in Asia.[121,122,123,124,125,126] From the late 1980s, BITs became an important component of the TTCs' strategies to access markets in the other regions of the world. In particular, in the late 1980s, the Commission on European Communities began BITs with countries in Central and Eastern Europe (CEE), which opened the CEE countries to tobacco.[127] These BITs created the opportunity for TTCs to penetrate CEE countries such as Hungary[128] and former Soviet countries such as Uzbekistan and Kazakhstan.[129,130,131,132,133] An Integral part of PM's 1990–1992 'long range plan' for the worldwide expansion of its activities (in Eastern Europe and the former Soviet

118 [BAT], 'Andean Pact: January 1992' (1992), available at <http://legacy.library.ucsf.edu/tid/blg90a99> (accessed 17 June 2012).

119 D.O. Laux, 'Andean Pact' (1991), available at <http://legacy.library.ucsf.edu/tid/alg90a99> (accessed 12 August 2012).

120 T. Wilson, 'CA GMs Conference, Costa Rica—5' (1992), available at <http://legacy.library.ucsf.edu/tid/yne28a99> (accessed 12 August 2012).

121 Chaloupka and Laixuthai, 'US Trade Policy' (n 14).

122 Taylor et al, 'The Impact of Trade Liberalization' (n 6).

123 Brown & Williamson, R. Pritchard, ['Letter to David Allvey of BAT Industries'] (1993), available at <http://legacy.library.ucsf.edu/tid/qpe43f00> (accessed 12 August 2012).

124 [No author], 'This Tariff Handicaps U.S. Manufacturers' Ability to Price Competitively in the Jat_nc_c m_rket. (1986), available at <http://legacy.library.ucsf.edu/tid/tln29b00> (accessed September 21 2012).

125 RJR, W.G.C. Mitchell, 'Re: Corporation Tobacco Issues' (1989), available at <http://legacy.library.ucsf.edu/tid/hye66b00> (accessed 13 July 2012).

126 D. Fried, 'Philip Morris Companies Inc.: Questions and Answers in Preparation for the Annual Meeting of Stockholders' (1990), available at <http://legacy.library.ucsf.edu/tid/kmq43a00> (accessed 12 September 2012).

127 Commission on European Communities, 'EC—East Europe: Relation with Control and Eastern Europe and the Commonwealth of Independent States' (1992), available at <http://legacy.library.ucsf.edu/tid/czb96a99> (accessed 12 September 2012).

128 P.C. Godby, 'Memo from Peter C Godby to Stuart Watterton enclosing brochure on "Investment and Privatisation in Central Europe"' (1991), available at <http://legacy.library.ucsf.edu/tid/tsk87a99> (accessed 12 September 2012).

129 D.J. Bishop, 'Letter from DJ Bishop to Abdoulla M Abdoukadirov regarding BAT project' (1994), available at <http://legacy.library.ucsf.edu/tid/etx87a99> (accessed 12 September 2012).

130 D.J. Bishop, 'Uzbekistan—Tobacco Taxes' (1994), available at <http://legacy.library.ucsf.edu/tid/ltx87a99> (accessed 12 September 2012).

131 D.J. Bishop, 'Uzbekistan—Tobacco Taxes' (1994), available at <http://legacy.library.ucsf.edu/tid/dtx87a99> (accessed 12 September 2012).

132 D.J. Bishop, 'Uzbekistan—Tobacco Taxes: Visit by DJ Bishop and CD Dufty—10–14 January 1994' (1994), available at <http://legacy.library.ucsf.edu/tid/mxs77a99> (accessed 12 September 2012).

133 D.J. Bishop, 'Uzbekistan' (1994), available at <http://legacy.library.ucsf.edu/tid/nmw37a99> (accessed 12 September 2012).

Union, the Middle East, Asia, and Africa) was to 'exploit existing bilateral trade agreements'.[134] In this respect, PM planned to enter into closed markets through countries where they have such agreements. Similarly, BAT's 1998–2000 strategy for the Southern Africa area was reliance on 'trading blocs' as well as bilateral trade agreements to enhance their activities in the region.[135]

The TTCs relied on state actors for BITs because such treaties involved inter-state negotiations. For this reason, they monitored governmental programmes on BITs and lobbied policymakers and politicians for them.[136,137,138] The efforts of the TTCs to persuade the US, the UK and the European Commission to engage in more BITs were mostly coordinated through the National Association of Manufacturers (NAMs).[139,140,141,142,143,144] In a February 1987 report, 'Brief Industry's Agenda', NAMs indicated that:

> Ten treaties to protect private investment in less developed countries (LDCs) were left unratified in the Senate Foreign Relations Committee at the end of the 99th Congress. Bilateral Investment Treaties (BITs) are necessary to minimize the overseas operating risks that firms face when investing in an LDC, and to encourage more open trade and investment policies. NAM will continue to press for [the US] Senate ratification of the ten BITs.[145]

Additionally, in the US, the tobacco industry activities on BITs were coordinated through the USCEA, which spearheaded the lobbying efforts to use bilateral trade agreements to liberalize tobacco trade around the world.[146,147]

In summary, BITs have been an essential aspect of TTCs' strategies to spread tobacco worldwide. As a result, they closely lobbied and monitored government programmes on BITs, such as those of the US,[148] and intervened whenever necessary. While BITs helped TTCs to access the international tobacco markets, they simultaneously helped them to overcome the issue of 'double taxation', and took advantage of associated benefits such as duty-free tobacco[149] to enhance their profit. As a 1993 BAT report opined, 'BIT develop[s] profitability through increased turnover'.[150] While the short-term goal for the TTCs in promoting BITs was market access, the long-term goal was to build international rules that favoured tobacco.

134 Philip Morris, 'Long Range Plan 1990–1992' (1989), available at <http://legacy.library.ucsf.edu/tid/zqh51b00> (accessed 7 October 2012).

135 [BAT], 'Southern African Area 1998–2000 Plan' (1998), available at <http://legacy.library.ucsf.edu/tid/nad65a99> (accessed 7 October 2012).

136 JRC, 'Project Torquay' (n 115).

137 Laux, 'Andean Pact' (n 119).

138 Bishop, 'Uzbekistan—Tobacco Taxes' (n 130).

139 Laux, 'Andean Pact' (n 119).

140 NAM, 'Brief in Industry's Agenda' (1987), available at <http://legacy.library.ucsf.edu/tid/yvg29b00> (accessed 16 October 2012).

141 NAM, 'Summary of Major 1988 Priorities Policy and Communications' (1988), available at <http://legacy.library.ucsf.edu/tid/rwg29b00> (accessed 16 October 2012).

142 NAM, 'Briefing: Weekly Summary of Legislative and Regulatory Developments' (1987), available at <http://legacy.library.ucsf.edu/tid/wvg29b00> (accessed 16 October 2012).

143 [NAM], 'AAk National Association of Manufacturers' (1987), available at <http://legacy.library.ucsf.edu/tid/oyg29b00> (accessed 16 October 2012).

144 [NAM], M.D. Lane, ['Computerized Association's Resource Index—CARI'] (1987), available at <http://legacy.library.ucsf.edu/tid/tyg29b00> (accessed 16 October 2012).

145 NAM, 'Summary of Major 1988 Priorities Policy' (n 141).

146 WHO, 'International Trade and Health' (n 105).

147 Brown & Williamson, R. Pritchard, ['1992 Progress against Objectives'] (1993), available at <http://legacy.library.ucsf.edu/tid/qpe43f00> (accessed 16 October 2012).

148 JRC, 'Project Torquay' (n 115).

149 Hatch, 'Blending Procedures' (n 116).

150 R. Brentnall, 'BIT Negotiations' (1993), available at <http://legacy.library.ucsf.edu/tid/cyj28a99> (accessed 16 October 2012).

3.2.2 BITs as an instrument against health policy and governance: 1990s to present

The entry of TTCs into markets around the world involved overcoming barriers such as tobacco control. TTCs recognized the limitations of the multilateral trading regime of GATT/WTO in the spread of tobacco in the 1980s and 1990s. Accordingly, the BAT Board pointed out, in a discussion on trade-related issues in a 1983 report on 'the future business environment':

> Although trade blocs will remain in being, national interests will be more important and national protectionism will tend to increase. GATT discussions will make only limited progress. The next round of talks [the Uruguay round] is unlikely to occur before 1985 and will have little impact before the end of the decade.[151]

This observed limitation became obvious with the GATT Panel ruling in 1990 in the Thai case,[152] which opened Thai cigarette markets to the TTCs, but at the same time provided a means for the Thai government to enact and implement more stringent tobacco control policies.[153] In an RJR letter that addressed the limitation of the GATT dispute settlement mechanism involving the Thai Case, it was stated:

> While not wishing to prejudice your respective assessments, it seems to me that owing to the GATT Dispute Settlement Report, the Thais now hold the upper hand and prospects for a market opening on favorable terms will largely depend on how the Thais decide to interpret the GATT decision and the actions they decide to undertake. In fact, there was some speculation on the part of the U.S. Government team that if the Thais are smart, they could take unilateral action and thereby undercut the bilateral process. The speculation was that the Thais could declare defeat on the import ban and announce that import licenses were now available to all interested foreign cigarette importers. Obviously strengthened by the GATT report, they would maintain a 55% ad valorem excise tax, the import duty, as well as maintain control of distribution and no advertising freedoms.[154]

As a result, RJR strongly advocated the use of BITs against the Thais' and other governments' policies, because the US could then directly challenge governments under section 301 of the 1974 Trade Act by issuing a threat of retaliation for trade discrimination. Additionally, a July 1991 Brown & Williamson letter discussing its 'international governmental activity' pointed out that 'the referral of recent trade issues to the GATT for resolution, e.g., Thailand, and the ineffectiveness of the GATT process, as compared to bilateral trade negotiations, does not bode well for the [section] 301 process as a tool for the industry to liberalize other markets'.[155] As noted earlier, this limitation has been enhanced with increasing consensus about the flexibility provided within the multilateral trading system of GATT/WTO and the development of the FCTC, which has elevated tobacco control higher on the global health agenda.[156,157]

151 I.W. Hughes and R. Salter, 'Future Business Environment B.A.T. Industries PLC' (1983), available at <http://legacy.library.ucsf.edu/tid/vzr13f00> (accessed 16 October 2012).

152 Chitanondh, 'Defeat in Trade-Victory in Health' (n 52).

153 Chitanondh, 'Defeat in Trade-Victory in Health' (n 52).

154 Brown & Williamson, R Pritchard, 'Five-Year Tobacco Environment' (n 100).

155 WHO-TFI, 'Confronting the Tobacco Epidemic' (n 7).

156 WHO, Moscow Declaration (n 27).

157 UNGA, 'Prevention and Control of Non-communicable Diseases' (n 28).

Since the Thai Case, while BITs continued to proliferate worldwide (see Figure 30.1) and trade disputes on tobacco emerged among states (see Table 30.1) with the support of the tobacco industry, they were not used to challenge tobacco control.[158] The TTCs maintained a low profile on the importance of BITs as instruments against tobacco control and covertly worked for them. However, two recent international cases, *PMI v Uruguay* and *PMA v Australia*, and threats of lawsuits from TTCs against countries for implementing tobacco control policies consistent with the FCTC,[159] provide evidence to support the TTCs' use of BITs to directly challenge states' health policymaking authority, making international investments a major issue currently confronting global health governance.[160]

First, the ICSID arbitration system has existed since the mid-1960s, but it was not used by TTCs to overtly and directly challenge states' ability or right to develop tobacco control policies.[161,162] In February 2010, however, while a domestic legal process that PMI eventually lost was under way in the Uruguayan court system,[163,164] PMI initiated another lawsuit under Article 36 of the ICSID Convention and Article 10 of the Swiss-Uruguay BIT.[165] As indicated earlier, PMI claimed that three tobacco control regulations implemented by Uruguay in 2009 violated the Swiss-Uruguay BIT and two multilateral treaties, WTO's Agreement on Trade Related Aspects of Intellectual Property Rights (TRIPS) and the Paris Convention for the Protection of Industrial Property (Paris Convention).[166,167] As Table 30.1 shows, this case represented the first use of BITs against tobacco control under the ICSID process,[168] and a dramatic shift in the value and the use of BITs for spreading tobacco worldwide. Despite the political solidarity shown by governments for Uruguay through the FCTC Conference of the Parties' Punta del Este Declaration on the Implementation of the WHO Framework Convention on Tobacco Control in November 2010,[169] the case was pending as of February 2014. This obstinate attitude despite a clear signal by states of their interests in defending sovereignty and fighting corporate interference in health policy and governance demonstrates the resolve of the tobacco industry to use BITs against tobacco control.

Second, although in the mid-1990s efforts by Canada to enact a plain packaging policy failed due to threats of lawsuits made by tobacco companies, the case did not rise to a formal litigation.[170,171,172,173,174] In December 2011, Australia became the first

158 UNCITRAL, Arbitration Rules (revised 2010)' (n 42).

159 S. Tavernise, 'Tobacco Firms' Strategy Limits Poorer Nations' Smoking Laws' (2013), available at <http://www.nytimes.com/2013/12/13/health/tobacco-industry-tactics-limit-poorer-nations-smoking-laws.html?hpw&rref=health&pagewanted=all&_r=0&pagewanted=print> (accessed 9 February 2014).

160 WHO-TFI, 'Confronting the Tobacco Epidemic' (n 7).

161 ICSID, List of Concluded Cases (n 41).

162 ICSID, List of Pending Cases (n 42).

163 Russell, Wainwright, and Mamudu, 'A Chilling Example?' (n 13).

164 Weiler, 'Philip Morris vs. Uruguay' (n 62).

165 ICSID, *Philip Morris* (n 60).

166 LALIVE, Request for Arbitration (n 62).

167 [BAT], 'BATCo: Press Cuttings—Index' (n 109).

168 [BAT], 'BATCo: Press Cuttings—Index' (n 109).

169 The FCTC Conference of the Parties, 'Decisions and Ancillary Documents' (2010), available at <http://apps.who.int/gb/fctc/PDF/cop4/FCTC_COP4_REC1.pdf> (accessed 28 March 2012).

170 [RJR], ['RJR's Family Primary Concerns'] (n 110).

171 C. Callard, N. Collishaw, and M. Swenarchuk, 'An Introduction to International Trade Agreements and their Impact on Public Measures to Reduce Tobacco Use: Physicians for a Smoke-Free Canada' (2001).

172 Physicians for Smoke-Free Canada, 'The Plot Against Plain Packaging' (2008), available at <http://www.smoke-free.ca/pdf_1/plotagainstplainpackaging-apr1'.pdf> (accessed 28 March 2012).

173 P. Crawford, 'Background on the Plain Packaging Debate in Canada' (1994), available at <http://legacy.library.ucsf.edu/tid/rer90a99> (accessed 23 October 2012).

174 R.G. Dearden, J.L. Katz, J.C. Luik, 'Plain Packaging and International Trade Treaties' (1998), available at <http://legacy.library.ucsf.edu/tid/fmh42c00> (accessed 23 October 2012).

country in the world to enact a plain packaging policy.[175] In response, the tobacco industry in the country (BAT, PM, Japan Tobacco International, and Imperial Tobacco) launched a lawsuit against the government of Australia for the violation of intellectual property rights and trademark rules,[176,177] which attracted a lot of global attention.[178,179,180,181,182,183,184] The tobacco industry lost the battle against the Australian government[185,186] in the domestic courts.[187,188] However, while the domestic litigation was in progress in the Australian High Court, PM Asia (PMA) moved its headquarters to Hong Kong to take advantage of a 1993 Hong Kong-Australia BIT, several months after the Australian government announced its intention to develop a plain packaging law.[189] Eventually, PMA filed a claim against Australia at UNCITRAL, establishing the first tobacco control case for UNCITRAL. Additionally, as of February 2014, five governments (Cuba, Dominican Republic, Honduras, Indonesia, and Ukraine) have filed claims against the Australian government using WTO dispute settlement mechanisms (see Table 30.1).[190] The strategic move by PMA to Hong Kong to take advantage of the BIT suggests that the tobacco industry perceives BITs as an opportunity not only to undo domestic health policy but also global health governance, generally.

In summary, since the 1990s, two routes for challenging tobacco control emerged within the international system—the GATT/WTO dispute settlement system and reliance on BITs through international arbitration. With the limitations of the GATT/WTO system in addressing international investment issues, the TTCs opted

175 Australian Government, Tobacco Plain Packing Act 2011—C2011A00148 (2011), available at <http://www.comlaw.gov.au/Details/C2011A00148> (accessed 16 October 2012).

176 High Court of Australia, *British American Tobacco Australasia Limited and ors v Commonwealth of Australia* (Case No S389/2011) (2012), available at <http://www.hcourt.gov.au/cases/case-s389/2011> (accessed 16 October 2012).

177 High Court of Australia, *JT International SA v Commonwealth of Australia* (Case No S409/2011) (2012), available at <http://www.hcourt.gov.au/cases/case-s409/2011> (accessed 16 October 2012).

178 M. Sweet, 'Tobacco Companies Launch Legal Action Against Plain Packaging' *British Medical Journal* (2011) 343: d4270.

179 A.D. Mitchell and D.M. Studdert, 'Plain Packaging of Tobacco Products in Australia: A Novel Regulation Faces Legal Challenge' *Journal of the American Medical Association* (2012) 307(3): 261.

180 S. Chapman, 'Legal Action by Big Tobacco against the Australian Government's Plain Packaging Law' *Tobacco Control* (2012) 21(2): 80.

181 B. Burton, 'Judges Grill Big Tobacco's Challenge to Australia's Law on Plain Tobacco Packaging' *British Medical Journal* (2012) 344: e2871.

182 M. Davison, 'Big Tobacco vs. Australia: Philip Morris Scores an Own Goal' (2012), available at <http://theconversation.edu.au/big-tobacco-vs-australia-philip-morris-scores-an-own-goal-4967> (accessed 16 October 2012).

183 S. Chapman, 'Big Tobacco Crashes at First Legal Hurdle on Plain Packaging' (2012), available at <http://theconversation.edu.au/big-tobacco-crashes-at-first-legal-hurdle-on-plain-packaging-8807> (accessed 16 October 2012).

184 WHO, 'Chan to the world: Stand with Australia' (2012), available at <http://www.who.int/mediacentre/news/releases/2012/tobacco_20120322/en/> (accessed 21 October 2012).

185 Reuters in Canberra, 'Tobacco Packaging: Cigarette Companies Lose Australian Court Case' (2012), available at <http://www.guardian.co.uk/business/2012/aug/15/tobacco-plain-packaging-australia-court/print> (accessed 16 October 2012).

186 M. Metherell, 'Big Tobacco Loses High Court Battle over Plain Packaging' (2012), available at <http://www.canberratimes.com.au/action/printArticle?id=3555683> (accessed 16 October 2012).

187 Burton, 'Judges Grill Big Tobacco's Challenge' (n 181).

188 Davison, 'Big Tobacco vs. Australia' (n 182).

189 The Australian government made its policy position on plain packaging known in April 2010. Philip Morris Asia acquired its interest in Philip Morris Australia in February 2011. And, in June 2011, Philip Morris filed a claim at UNCITRAL for the breach of the 1993 Australia-Hong Kong BIT.

190 Australian Government, 'Investor-State Arbitration' (n 63).

for BITs. The only BITs case conducted through the ICSID arbitration system as of February 2014 involved PMI and Uruguay,[191] and the only one conducted under UNCITRAL, involved PMA and the Australian government.[192,193] Thus, BITs have metamorphosed from being a mechanism to liberalize international tobacco market into an instrument for challenging tobacco control and states' authority to enact and implement health policies to protect their populations.

4. Discussion

The globalization of tobacco has contributed to the worldwide increase in tobacco use (over 1 billion smokers) and the incidence of non-communicable diseases (NCDs).[194,195] Globally, tobacco use and exposure to secondhand smoke kill over 6 million people annually,[196,197] with a cumulative total projected to reach 1 billion by the end of the twenty-first Century.[198] Central to the globalization of tobacco is trade liberalization,[199,200,201] which increased tobacco consumption in Asia,[202] Eastern Europe,[203,204] and other regions around the world.[205] While the multilateral trading regime of the GATT/WTO provided a major impetus for this globalization of tobacco, particularly with the inclusion of tobacco in the Uruguay round of talks (1986–1994) as an international tradable commodity, the process was enhanced by a plethora of BITs around the world (see Figure 30.1, and Tables 30.2 to 30.5).[206,207] This role of BITs has been noted for several years,[208,209] but recently emerged on the agenda of global health governance with the ICSID case *PMI v Uruguay* in February 2010,[210,211,212] and *PMA v Australian Government* at UNCITRAL in June 2011.[213] Indeed, the tobacco industry threats of lawsuits against African countries such as Gabon, Namibia, Togo, and Uganda, claiming that their tobacco control policies

191 ICSID, *Philip Morris* (n 60).

192 Australian Government, 'Investor-State Arbitration' (n 63).

193 UNCITRAL, Arbitration Rules (revised 2010) (n 44).

194 Fuster and Kelly, 'Promoting Cardiovascular Health' (n 24).

195 D. Yach, C. Hawkes, L. Gould, and K. Hoffman, 'Global Burden of Chronic Disease: Overcoming Impediments to Prevention and Control' *Journal of the American Medical Association* (2004) 291: 2616.

196 WHO, 'WHO Report about Global Tobacco Epidemic' (n 22).

197 S.S. Lim et al, 'A Comparative Risk Assessment of Burden of Disease and Injury Attributable to 67 Risk Factors and Risk Factor Clusters in 21 Regions, 1990–2010: A Systematic Analysis for the Global Burden of Disease Study 2010' *Lancet* (2012) 380: 2224.

198 WHO, 'WHO Report on the Global Tobacco Epidemic' (n 21).

199 Yach and Bettcher, 'Globalization of the Tobacco Industry Influence' (n 26).

200 WHO Framework Convention on Tobacco Control (n 28).

201 Bettcher and Taylor, 'Confronting the Tobacco Epidemic' (n 40).

202 Chaloupka and Laixuthai, 'US Trade Policy' (n 14).

203 A.B. Gilmore and M. McKee, 'Tobacco and Transition: An Overview of Industry Investments, Impact and Influence in the Former Soviet Union' *Tobacco Control* (2004) 13(2): 136.

204 A.B. Gilmore and M. McKee, 'Exploring the Impact of Foreign Direct Investment on Tobacco Consumption in the Former Soviet Union' *Tobacco Control* (2005) 14(1): 13.

205 Taylor et al, 'The Impact of Trade Liberalization' (n 6).

206 Taylor et al, 'The Impact of Trade Liberalization' (n 6).

207 Bettcher and Taylor, 'Confronting the Tobacco Epidemic' (n 40).

208 Taylor et al, 'The Impact of Trade Liberalization' (n 6).

209 R. Roemer, *Legislative Action to Combat the World Tobacco Epidemic* (Geneva: 2nd edn, WHO, 1993).

210 ICSID, *Philip Morris* (n 60).

211 LALIVE, Request for Arbitration (n 61).

212 [BAT], 'BATCo: Press Cuttings—Index' (n 110).

213 Australian Government, 'Investor-State Arbitration' (n 62).

contravene international trade rules, consolidates this strategy of using BITs to undermine tobacco control policy initiatives and innovation.[214] The study that formed the basis of this chapter used archival documents to analyse how the tobacco industry used BITs to increase the worldwide spread of tobacco in order to inform health policy and governance.

BITs originated in Europe, when Germany signed one with Pakistan in November 1959,[215] and proliferated worldwide in the virtual absence of multilateral treaties on investment (although some agreements entail investment rules).[216,217,218,219,220] By the early 1980s, the US had also become interested in BITs, which culminated in the creation of its BITs programme and the development of a model BIT.[221] This proliferation of BITs worldwide was due to several factors; one of which is the international competitive pressure for FDIs, especially among developing countries.[222,223] However, while developing countries enter into BITs anticipating FDIs and economic development,[224,225,226] the evidence on whether BITs improve economic development is still debatable.[227,228,229,230,231] But, unlike GATT/WTO and many regional trade agreements, BITs embody unique substantive rights for both state parties and investors.[232,233,234,235] Although these BITs were negotiated by sovereign states to demonstrate their commitment to foreign investment,[236,237] they were mostly negotiated between two unequal parties (developed versus developing) and at 'sovereignty costs', with the core terms being: mandatory dispute resolutions before an international arbitration body, a private right of action of investors, monetary compensation in the event of a violation, national treatment, and most-favoured-nation treatment.[238] Additionally, a typical BIT does not address

214 Tavernise, 'Tobacco Firms' Strategy Limits Poorer Nations' Smoking Laws' (n 159).

215 Dolzer and Stevens, *Bilateral Investment Treaties* (n 8).

216 Elkins, Guzman, and Simmons, 'Competing for Capital' (n 19).

217 UNCTAD, 'Total number of Bilateral Investment Treaties Concluded' (n 9).

218 Minor, 'The Demise of Expropriation' (n 36).

219 Sornarajah, *The International Law of Foreign Investment* (n 37).

220 Vagts, 'Foreign Investment Risk Reconsidered (n 38).

221 Prior to this time, the US had concluded friendship, commerce and navigation (FCN) treaties with several countries after World War II.

222 Elkins, Guzman, and Simmons, 'Competing for Capital' (n 19).

223 B.A. Simmons, F. Dobbin, and G. Garrett, 'Introduction: The International Diffusion of Liberalism' *International Organization* (2006) 60(4): 781.

224 Vandevelde, 'The Political Economy' (n 18).

225 Elkins, Guzman, and Simmons, 'Competing for Capital' (n 19).

226 Dolzer and Stevens, *Bilateral Investment Treaties* (n 8).

227 Vandevelde, 'The Political Economy' (n 18).

228 Sornarajah, *The International Law of Foreign Investment* (n 37).

229 Dolzer and Stevens, *Bilateral Investment Treaties* (n 8).

230 E. Neumayer and L. Spess, 'Do Bilateral Investment Treaties Increase Foreign Direct Development in Developing Countries?' *World Development* (2005) 33(10): 1567.

231 M. Hallward-Driemeier, 'Do Bilateral Investment Treaties Attract Foreign Direct Investment? Only a Bit... and They Could Bite' (2003), available at <http://www-wds.worldbank.org/external/default/WDSContentServer/IW3P/IB/2003/09/23/000094946_03091104060047/Rendered/PDF/multi0page.pdf> (accessed 9 December 2012).

232 Dolzer and Stevens, *Bilateral Investment Treaties* (n 8).

233 UNCTAD, 'What are BITs?' (n 10).

234 Elkins, Guzman, and Simmons, 'Competing for Capital' (n 19).

235 L.E. Peterson, 'Bilateral investment treaties and development policy-making', International Institute for Sustainable Development (Winnipeg, 2004).

236 Vandevelde, 'The Political Economy' (n 18).

237 Elkins, Guzman, and Simmons, 'Competing for Capital' (n 19).

238 Elkins, Guzman, and Simmons, 'Competing for Capital' (n 19).

issues of market failure,[239] which means that global health issues, such as increasing tobacco use in LMICs and NCDs worldwide[240] where there is enormous information asymmetry and negative externalities emanating from exposure to second-hand smoke,[241] fall outside the realm of such treaties because they are principally driven by economic concerns. Moreover, BITs usually accord foreign investments more rights and protections than domestic ones.[242] For these reasons, the TTCs were attracted to BITs because: 'Detailed inside [BITs] are provisions on treatment; expropriation/compensation; dispute settlement; capital transfers; performance requirements.'[243] TTCs started to push for BITs from the late 1940s in order to seek 'relief' from 'double taxation', which was several years before Germany signed the first BIT and countries such as the US became interested in them.[244] Since then, the importance of BITs to the TTCs has metamorphosed into an instrument to gain access to international tobacco markets and to challenge policies of states, including those on health.

The tobacco industry has played several, albeit negative roles in health policy and governance. These roles range from hiding scientific evidence on the dangers of tobacco use and the addictive nature of tobacco[245,246] and obfuscating the science on the harmful effects of tobacco use and exposure to second-hand smoke,[247,248,249] to undermining the work of individual scientists,[250,251] governmental organizations such as the WHO[252,253,254,255] and the World Bank,[256] and NGOs.[257,258] Additionally, during the FCTC negotiations, the tobacco industry unsuccessfully attempted to derail the process and worked to weaken the text of the

239 Vandevelde, 'The Political Economy' (n 18).

240 Bettcher and A.L. Taylor, 'Confronting the Tobacco Epidemic' (n 40).

241 Jha and Chaloupka, *Curbing the Epidemic* (n 20).

242 Elkins, Guzman, and Simmons, 'Competing for Capital' (n 19).

243 JRC, 'Project Torquay' (n 115).

244 Vandevelde, 'The Political Economy' (n 18).

245 J. Slade, L. Bero, P. Hanauer, D. Barnes, and S. Glantz, 'Nicotine and Addiction: The Brown and Williamson Documents' *Journal of the American Medical Association* (1995) 274: 225.

246 S.A. Glantz, D.E. Barnes, L. Bero, P. Hanauer, and J. Slade, 'Looking Through a Keyhole at the Tobacco Industry: The Brown and Williamson Documents' *Journal of the American Medical Association* (1995) 274(3): 248.

247 E. Ong and S. Glantz, 'Constructing 'Sound Science' and 'Good Epidemiology': Tobacco, Lawyers, and Public Relations Firms' *American Journal of Public Health* (2001) 91: 1749.

248 E. Ong and S. Glantz, 'Tobacco Industry Effort Subverting the International Agency for Research on Cancer's Secondhand Smoke Study' *Lancet* (2000) 355: 1253.

249 WHO, 'Committee of Experts Report on Tobacco Company Strategies to Undermine Tobacco Control Activities at the World Health Organization' (2000), available at <http://www.who.int/tobacco/en/who_inquiry.pdf> (accessed 5 December 2012).

250 H.M. Mamudu, M. Gonzalez, and S.A. Glantz, 'The Nature, Scope and Development of the Global Tobacco Control Epistemic Community' *American Journal of Public Health* (2011) 101(11): 2044.

251 A. Landman and S.A. Glantz, 'Tobacco Industry Efforts to Undermine Policy-relevant Research' *American Journal of Public Health* (2009) 99(1): 45.

252 WHO, 'Tobacco Industry Interference' (n 27).

253 Mamudu, Gonzalez, and Glantz, 'The Nature, Scope and Development of the Global Tobacco Control Epistemic Community' (n 250).

254 Landman and Glantz, 'Tobacco Industry Efforts to Undermine' (n 251).

255 WHO, 'Tobacco Industry Interference with Tobacco Control' (n 27).

256 H.M. Mamudu, R. Hammond, and S. Glantz, 'Tobacco Industry Attempts to Counter the World Bank Report Curbing the Epidemic and Obstruct the WHO Framework Convention on Tobacco Control' *Social Science and Medicine* (2008) 67(11): 1690.

257 H.M. Mamudu and S. Glantz, 'Civil Society and the Negotiation of the Framework Convention on Tobacco Control' *Global Public Health* (2009) 4: 150.

258 S.M. Carter, 'Mongoven, Biscoe & Duchin: Destroying Tobacco Control Activism from Inside' *Tobacco Control* (2002) 11: 112.

convention.[259,260,261,262,263,264] In this process, tobacco companies have developed several strategies against tobacco control, including direct lobbying, using front groups, paying academics, publishing industry-sponsored reports (for example economic impact studies), and creating corporate social responsibility programmes. Thus, the use of BITs against health policies conforms to the tobacco industry's strategies to undermine health policy and governance as several institutional developments within the UN system since the 1990s continue to diminish its influence. These institutional developments include the World Bank's decision not to support tobacco projects in 1991–92; the transfer of the UN tobacco control programme, the Focal Point, from the UN Conference on Trade and Development to the WHO in 1999; and the elevation of the WHO Tobacco or Health programme to the Tobacco-Free Initiative, a cabinet programme; development of the FCTC in 2003, which includes Article 5.3 and associated guidelines that effectively exclude the tobacco industry from the FCTC processes; and the UN Political Declaration on NCDs in 2011 that singled out the tobacco industry as a pariah enterprise that should not be involved in the health policy process.[265,266] It is possible that these increasing international collaborations in global health governance have limited options available to the TTCs to undermine tobacco control, which makes BITs an important alternative for them to challenge states in an increasingly unfavourable global environment for tobacco.

The TTCs lobbied their countries for BITs because they realized that the multilateral trading regime of GATT did not adequately provide mechanisms for access to international markets.[267,268] Alongside allies such as NAMs, the TTCs lobbied and supported BITs programmes in the US and Europe for access to markets in LMICs. The evidence in this study suggests that the TTCs would have found it difficult or not profitable to access international tobacco markets and extend their activities worldwide without BITs. While the GATT/WTO provided an international liberalized trading system, BITs provided direct access to markets and protections for investments that were difficult to achieve under the purview of GATT/WTO or any multilateral system. The TTCs expanded globally[269,270,271] and BITs assured them the security of their

259 Carter, 'Mongoven, Biscoe & Duchin' (n 258).

260 H.M. Mamudu, R. Hammond, and S.A. Glantz, 'Project Cerberus: Tobacco Industry Strategy to Create an Alternative to the Framework Convention on Tobacco Control' *American Journal of Public Health* (2008) 98(9): 1630.

261 H.M. Mamudu and S.T. Donley, 'Multilevel Governance and Shared Sovereignty: European Union, Members States, and the FCTC' *Governance* (2009) 22(1): 73.

262 H. Weishaar, J. Collin, K. Smith, T. Gruning, S. Mandal, and A. Gilmore, 'Global Health Governance and the Commercial Sector: A Documentary Analysis of Tobacco Company Strategies to Influence the WHO Framework Convention on Tobacco Control' *PLoS Medicine* (2012) 9(6): e1001249.

263 M. Assunta and S. Chapman, 'Health Treaty Dilution: A Case Study of Japan's Influence on the Language of the WHO Framework Convention on Tobacco Control' *Journal of Epidemiology and Community Health* (2006) 60: 751.

264 T. Gruning, H. Weishaar, J. Collin, and A.B. Gilmore, 'Tobacco Industry Attempts to Influence and Use the German Government to Undermine the WHO Framework Convention on Tobacco Control' *Tobacco Control* (2012) 21(1): 30.

265 UNGA, 'Prevention and Control of Non-communicable Diseases' (n 30).

266 P.A. Cairney, D.T. Studlar, and H.M. Mamudu, *Global Tobacco Control: Power, Policy, Governance and Transfer* (London: Palgrave Macmillan, 2011).

267 Sornarajah, *The International Law of Foreign Investment* (n 37).

268 W.H. Witherell, 'The OECD Multilateral Agreement on Investment' (1995), available at <http://unctad.org/en/docs/iteiitv4n2a2_en.pdf> (accessed 9 December 2012).

269 Bettcher, Yach, and Guindon, 'Global Trade and Health' (n 17).

270 Yach and Bettcher, 'Globalization of the Tobacco Industry Influence' (n 26).

271 G. Connolly, 'Worldwide Expansion of Transnational Tobacco Industry' *Journal of the National Cancer Institute Monograph* (1992) 12: 29–35.

investments and profits.[272,273,274] The broader ramification of the TTCs' penetration into markets under the protection of BITs is that states have become vulnerable to lengthy and costly legal battles.

While the use of BITs to change states' policies has prevailed in other issue areas,[275,276] they emerged as instruments for the TTCs to challenge tobacco control policies from the 1990s in all likelihood due to the disappointment with the GATT Panel's decision on the Thai Case, which opened the cigarette market, but simultaneously allowed the Thai government to enact stringent policies.[277,278] In the mid-1990s, tobacco companies threatened Canada with lawsuits over plain packaging, but the issue ended without a formal adjudication as Canada abandoned the policy.[279,280] Since then, while inter-state disputes over tobacco emerged through the GATT/WTO system (see Table 30.1),[281] there was no direct confrontation through international dispute settlement mechanisms between TTCs and states until February 2010, when PMI filed a claim at ICSID under the Swiss-Uruguay BIT,[282,283] and subsequently in June 2011, PMA against Australia at UNCITRAL under the Australia-Hong Kong BIT.[284] These direct lawsuits have broader implications because many LMICs do not have the resources to engage in a lengthy and costly legal battle with a wealthy tobacco industry,[285] which in turn undermines global health governance by dissuading states from enacting and implementing tobacco control policies such as those provided in the FCTC—ie the 'chilling effect' syndrome. How the current attacks on domestic health policies (ie tobacco control) will transform inter-state relations on investment is uncertain as the BIT cases are still pending at ICSID and UNCITRAL as of February 2014. It is also not certain how BITs will be reconciled with customary international law and a multitude of conventions and treaties, including the Vienna Convention on the Law of Treaties,[286] which requires that provisions of recent treaties supersede older ones, and public health treaties such as the FCTC (including declarations and guidelines)[287] and others such as the WTO[288] that gives states some degree of flexibility to protect public health.[289] Nonetheless, it is evident that BITs pose a challenge to global health governance in terms of reconciling them with domestic health policies and these international conventions and treaties pertaining to health in the face of the tobacco industry's judicial aggression.

272 Taylor et al, 'The Impact of Trade Liberalization' (n 6).

273 Bettcher, Yach, and Guindon, 'Global Trade and Health' (n 17).

274 [BAT], 'BATCo: Press Cuttings—Index' (n 109).

275 ICSID, List of Concluded Cases (n 41). 276 ICSID, List of Pending Cases (n 42).

277 H. Chitanondh, 'Defeat in Trade—Victory in Health' (n 52).

278 Callard, Chitanondh, and Weissman, 'Why Trade and Investment Liberalization' (n 53).

279 Physicians for Smoke-Free Canada, 'The Plot Against Plain Packaging' (n 172).

280 Crawford, 'Background on the Plain Packaging Debate' (n 173).

281 UNCITRAL, Arbitration Rules (revised 2010) (n 44).

282 ICSID, *Philip Morris* (n 60). 283 LALIVE, Request for Arbitration (n 61).

284 Australian Government, 'Investor-State Arbitration' (n 63).

285 Tavernise, 'Tobacco Firms' Strategy Limits Poorer Nations' Smoking Laws' (n 160) comment a26.

286 United Nations, Vienna Convention on the Law of Treaties (2005), available at <http://untreaty.un.org/ilc/texts/instruments/english/conventions/1_1_1969.pdf> (accessed 13 December 2012).

287 WHO Framework Convention on Tobacco Control (n 28).

288 WTO, 'Understanding the WTO: Basics' (undated), available at <http://www.wto.org/english/thewto_e/whatis_e/tif_e/fact4_e.htm> (accessed 28 March 2012).

289 M. Koivusalo and M. Rowson, 'The World Trade Organization: Implications for Health Policy' *Medicine, Conflict and Survival* (2000) 16(2): 175.

In summary, this study shows that BITs have been important to the TTCs in the globalization of tobacco. The TTCs used BITs to seek relief from 'double taxation', increase access to international tobacco markets, and challenge tobacco control policies. The issue has become the treatment of tobacco within BITs because they usually do not include protections for market failures.[290] Public health advocates have strongly argued for the exclusion of tobacco from such inter-state treaties and agreements for many years.[291,292,293,294] This proposal is possible because Honduras, a current party to the WTO claim against Australia over the plain packaging law, excluded cigarettes in BITs with neighbouring countries in the late 1970s and 1980s.[295,296] As indicated earlier, while trade in tobacco has existed for centuries,[297] it first became part of the multilateral trading regime of GATT/WTO through the Uruguay round of trade negotiations. This implies that it is within the power of states to exclude tobacco from inter-state investment/trade agreements, particularly if they wish to achieve policy coherence in global health governance as advocated by the World Health Assembly in its 2006 resolution, 'International Trade and Health',[298] and the United Nations Education, Science and Cultural Organization (UNESCO).[299] Alternatively, even if tobacco is included in investment/trade agreements, the right of investors to sue states, which is unique for BITs, should not be extended to the tobacco industry as the arbitration cases involving Uruguay and Australia, and threats of lawsuits using BITs have demonstrated that the TTCs are not good-faith actors and could involve states in costly legal battles over health policy and governance. Moreover, as of February 2014, BITs have been signed by 176 countries that are signatories to several multilateral treaties, including the WTO and the FCTC. In this respect, in the virtual absence of a multilateral treaty on investments,[300] it is incumbent upon states to reconcile their obligations under BITs and these multilateral treaties or re-initiate talks that could led to a multilateral treaty on investments that embodies protections for public health.

4.1 Limitations

This study has some limitations. First, the study depended solely on archival documents, which means that it is difficult to capture the entire context within which these

290 Vandevelde, 'The Political Economy' (n 18).

291 J.P. Wilkenfeld, 'Campaign for Tobacco-Free Kids. U.S. Should Protect Public Health and Exclude Tobacco From Proposed Free Trade Area of the Americas' (2003), available at <http://www.tobaccofreekids.org/press_releases/post/id_0710> (accessed 17 October 2012).

292 Campaign for Tobacco-Free Kids, 'Tobacco and Trade: Exclude Tobacco Products from Trade Agreements' (undated), available at <http://www.tobaccofreekids.org/what_we_do/federal_issues/trade/> (accessed 17 October 2012).

293 American Lung Association, ['Letter to the Advisory Committee on Tobacco Policy and Public Health'] (1997), available at <http://legacy.library.ucsf.edu/tid/uls97b00> (accessed 17 October 2012).

294 The Advisory Committee on Tobacco Policy and Public Health, 'Final Report' (1997), available at <http://legacy.library.ucsf.edu/tid/obd18b00> (accessed 17 October 2012).

295 JRC, 'Project Torquay' (n 115).

296 B. Selby, 'Visit of Ambassador' (1992), available at <http://legacy.library.ucsf.edu/tid/qgf28a99> (accessed 17 October 2012).

297 A. Brandt, *The Cigarette Century* (New York: Basic Books, 2007).

298 WHO, 'International Trade and Health', WHA59.26 (2006), available at <http://apps.who.int/gb/ebwha/pdf_files/WHA59-REC1/e/Resolutions-en.pdf> (accessed 20 May 2012).

299 UNESCO, '2012–2013 Draft Resolution' (2011), available at <http://unesdoc.unesco.org/images/0019/001919/191978e.pdf> (accessed 5 November 2012).

300 Vandevelde, 'The Political Economy' (n 18).

documents were produced. Second, the documents used for this chapter were based on those available on online databases and there is no way to determine that they constitute the full range of communication or activities on BITs. Third, the archival documents were internal communications of the tobacco industry and there is no independent means to validate the veracity of the statements made in them. Nevertheless, archival documents are a valid and standard means of providing insight into tobacco industry activities on a given subject matter.

5. Conclusion

The tobacco industry's use of the multilateral trading regime of GATT/WTO for the globalization of tobacco is limited for two major reasons—the lack of legal standing and some degree of flexibility provided for states to develop health policies. When this is coupled with the fact that the majority of countries in the world have signed and ratified the FCTC, the UN has endorsed implementation of the FCTC, and the FCTC has been cited in domestic litigation[301,302] and in WTO dispute settlements,[303] there are few venues left within the international system for the tobacco industry to pursue tobacco promotion and thwart health policy and governance. As such, BITs, for which TTCs have lobbied since the late 1940s, are one of the few options available for the tobacco industry to use against health policy and governance. Initially serving as a means to seek relief from 'double taxation', BITs have evolved into instruments for challenging health policies, as epitomized by the arbitration cases against Uruguay and Australia. Thus, while the economic development benefits of BITs are debatable, the indisputable evidence is that they arise at the cost of the states' sovereignty.[304] Legal analyses of the cases suggest that it is within the power of Uruguay[305] and Australia[306] to enact policies to protect the health of their populations. Politically, the FCTC Conference of the Parties adopted the Punta del Este in November 2010[307] in solidarity with Uruguay, and the WHO has strongly opposed the tobacco industry's efforts to undo Australia's plain packaging law.[308] While the outcomes of these cases are still uncertain, a loss for Philip Morris could possibly shut down the tobacco industry's effort to resort to these arbitration mechanisms provided under BITs to undermine health policy, while a loss by Uruguay or Australia would have broader implications since both Switzerland and Hong Kong have BITs with several other countries. Indeed, a loss by Uruguay or Australia could produce 'chilling effects', particularly on LMICs that are seeking to emulate Uruguay. In the long-run, it is possible to exclude tobacco from BITs because it is a 'global bad' that should not be protected by agreements between sovereign states. At a minimum, even if tobacco is

301 Australian Government, Tobacco Plain Packing Act 2011 (n 175).

302 Supreme Court of Appeal of South Africa, *BAT South Africa v Minister of Health* (2012), available at <http://www.saflii.org/za/cases/ZASCA/2012/107.pdf> (accessed 20 October 2012).

303 H. Jarman, J. Schmidt, and D.B. Rubin, 'When Trade Law Meets Public Health Evidence: The World Trade Organization and Clove Cigarettes' *Tobacco Control* (2012) 21(6): 596.

304 Elkins, Guzman, and Simmons, 'Competing for Capital' (n 19).

305 Weiler, 'Philip Morris vs. Uruguay' (n 62).

306 A.D. Mitchell and S.M. Wurzberger, 'Boxed In? Australia's Plain Tobacco Packaging Initiative and International Investment Law' *Arbitration International* (2011) 27(4): 623.

307 Russell, Wainwright, and Mamudu, 'A Chilling Example?' (n 13).

308 Australian Government, 'Investor-State Arbitration' (n 63); WHO, 'WHO welcomes landmark decision from Australia's High Court on tobacco plain packaging act' (2012), available at <http://www.who.int/mediacentre/news/statements/2012/tobacco_packaging_update/en/> (accessed 9 March 2014).

included in BITs, the protections for a private investor's right to sue states should not be extended to the tobacco industry. Above all, states should reconcile their obligations under BITs with customary international law and multilateral conventions and treaties by possibly developing a multilateral treaty on international investments that embodies protections for public health.

31

Mission (Im)possible?

The WHO as a 'Norm Entrepreneur' in Global Health Governance

*Obijiofor Aginam**

1. Introduction: Overview of the Argument

The World Health Organization (WHO) was established on 7 April 1948 when its Constitution, adopted by the International Health Conference held in New York in July 1946 and signed by sixty-one representatives of the participating nation-states, entered into force.[1] With 194 member states, the WHO is a specialized agency of the United Nations (UN) with a mandate, among twenty-one other functions, to 'act as the directing and co-ordinating authority on international health work'.[2] The WHO operates within the normative parameters of Westphalianism—a state-centric international system founded on the governance architecture constructed by the Treaty of Westphalia 1648.[3] Although the WHO Constitution made provisions for the organization to use innovative and fairly radical legal mechanisms (treaties, regulations, soft-law), those mechanisms have largely remained in the margins of the WHO's international health work in over six decades of its history. Although there was a significant improvement in the use of legal mechanisms, especially since the revision of the International Health Regulations (IHR 2005), and the entry into force of the WHO Framework Convention on Tobacco Control (FCTC) in 2005, this chapter argues that the WHO is yet to maximize its potentials as an effective and efficient 'norm entrepreneur' in the 'crowded' global health architecture that is now 'comprised of numerous and varied actors with competing values, interests, and motivations'.[4] In order to achieve its core objective of the 'attainment by all peoples of the highest possible level of health', and the twenty-two functions enumerated in its Constitution,

* This chapter is based on a presentation at the 'Law and Global Health Colloquium' hosted by University College London (UCL) Faculty of Laws, London, 2–3 July 2012. I would like to thank Dr Sarah Hawkes, and Professors Michael Freeman and Belinda Bennett for inviting me to the Colloquium, and the participants for their insightful comments on earlier drafts of this chapter.

1 World Health Organization, 'Basic Documents' (Geneva: 43rd edn, 2001) 1.

2 WHO Constitution, Art 2(a-v).

3 The Westphalian international system emerged from the Treaty of Westphalia 1648 that ended thirty years of war and conflict in Europe and led to the emergence of nation-states as the primary actors in international relations. Applied to public health diplomacy, membership of multilateral health organizations like the World Health Organization is open only to states, and only states can become parties to multilateral health treaties, conventions, and regulations negotiated under the auspices of those organizations.

4 M.W. Zacher and T.J. Keefe, *The Politics of Global Health Governance: United By Contagion* (New York: Palgrave MacMillan, 2008) 135. See generally, A.F. Cooper, J.J. Kirton, and T. Schrecker, 'Governing Global Health in the Twenty-First Century' in A.F. Cooper, J.J. Kirton, and T. Schrecker (eds), *Governing Global Health: Challenge, Response, Innovation* (Aldershot: Ashgate, 2007) 3–14.

the WHO should devise ways to re-invent its innovative legal/regulatory authority, and adapt this to the emerging and re-emerging health-related trends in an inter-dependent (and globalized) world. To buttress this point more succinctly, this chapter builds on the arguments of an earlier work that there is a 'structural imbalance' in the trade and public health mandates of the World Trade Organization (WTO) and WHO respectively. In this context, trade agreements—especially the Trade Related Intellectual Property Rights (TRIPS), General Agreement on Trade in Services (GATS), and the Agreement on Sanitary and Phytosanitary Measures (SPS)—legally enforced by the WTO would often trump public health imperatives including the human right to health.[5] Provocatively, the chapter explores the relevance of the WHO as an efficient and effective 'norm entrepreneur' in contemporary 'global health governance', a new paradigm that has transformed the governance architecture of public health from the classic Westphalian (inter-state) structure to a post-Westphalian governance architecture[6] characterized by the emergence of multiple actors: nation-states, international institutions, businesses and corporations, charitable foundations, civil society, non-governmental organizations (NGOs), and individuals (celebrities).

2. Overview of the Legal/Normative Authority of the WHO

The legal powers of the WHO fall into three categories: (1) treaty-making powers analogous to the conventional practice of treaty negotiation, adoption, and ratification by states in international law; (2) the authority to adopt legally-binding regulations analogous to legislative or quasi-legislative process in domestic law; and (3) the authority to adopt non-binding recommendations analogous to 'soft-law' in international law.

The WHO's conventional treaty-making powers—very similar to those of most multilateral institutions in the international system—are covered by Article 19 of its Constitution that provides as follows:

> ... the Health Assembly shall have the authority to adopt conventions or agreements with respect to any matter within the competence of the Organization. A two-thirds vote of the Health Assembly shall be required for the adoption of such conventions or agreements, which shall come into force for each Member when accepted by it in accordance with its constitutional processes.[7]

Although Article 19 is a conventional treaty-making authority that most international organizations derive expressly from their constitutions, charters, or other constituent instruments, some scholars, in the case of the WHO, argue that when combined with the WHO's ambitious objective of 'the attainment by all peoples of the highest possible level of health', and the organization's equally ambitious definition of health as 'a state of complete physical, mental, and social well-being and not merely the absence of

[5] O. Aginam, 'Health or Trade? A Critique of Contemporary Approaches to Global Health Diplomacy' (2010) 5(2) *Asian Journal of WTO and International Health Law and Policy* 355.

[6] On the transition from Westphalian to post-Westphalian governance architecture for global health, see D.P. Fidler, *SARS, Governance and Globalization of Disease* (New York: Palgrave Macmillan, 2004); D.P. Fidler, 'Constitutional Outlines for Public Health's "New World Order"' (2004) 77 *Temple Law Review* 247; O. Aginam, 'Between Isolationism and Mutual Vulnerability: A South-North Perspective on Global Governance of Epidemics in an Age of Globalization' (2004) 77 *Temple Law Review* 297; S. Bartsch, W. Hein, and L. Kohlmorgen, 'Interface: a Concept for the Analysis of Global Health Governance' in W. Hein, S. Bartsch, and L. Kohlmorgen, *Global Health Governance and the Fight Against HIV/AIDS* (New York: Palgrave MacMillan, 2007) 18; K. Lee, *The World Health Organization* (London and New York: Routledge, 2009) 99.

[7] WHO Constitution, Art 19.

disease or infirmity',[8] Article 19 provides the WHO with virtually limitless treaty-making power that surpasses any treaty powers possessed by the WHO's precursors: the Pan American Sanitary Bureau, the International Office of Public Health, and the Health Organization of the League of Nations.[9]

Article 21 of the WHO Constitution provides for an innovative norm-creating procedure—the power of the World Health Assembly (the WHO's highest policy making organ) to adopt legally binding regulations concerning:

(a) sanitary and quarantine requirements and other procedures designed to prevent the international spread of disease;

(b) nomenclatures with respect to diseases, cause of death, and public health practices;

(c) standards with respect to diagnostic procedures for international use;

(d) standards with respect to the safety, purity, and potency of biological, pharmaceutical, and similar products moving in international commerce;

(e) advertising and labeling of biological, pharmaceutical, and similar products moving in international commerce.[10]

Article 21 gives the World Health Assembly the authority to adopt regulations that could become legally binding without the positive act of consent by states as symbolized in the age-old treaty-making conventional practice of signature and subsequent ratification (consent to be bound) in international law. For regulations adopted under Article 21, there is a 'contracting out' procedure in Article 22. Such regulations shall come into force for all member states of the WHO after due notice has been given of their adoption by the Health Assembly, except for such members as may notify the WHO Director-General of a rejection or reservation(s) within the period specified in the notice. Articles 21 and 22 of the WHO Constitution have been described as creating a quasi-legislative procedure that constituted a radical departure from the conventional international treaty making practice in the late 1940s when the WHO was founded.[11]

Article 23 of the WHO Constitution gives the World Health Assembly the authority to adopt recommendations (soft-law) with respect to any matter within the competence of the organization. Although soft-law instruments, like recommendations and declarations, are not automatically legally-binding, international legal scholars agree that they have nonetheless catalyzed the evolution of rules of international law. As Szasz stated:

8 WHO Constitution, Preamble.

9 A leading exponent of this argument in the late 1990s is David Fidler. See D.P. Fidler, 'The Future of the World Health Organization: What Role for International Law' (1998) 31 *Vanderbilt Journal of International Law* 1079, 1087, arguing that 'the WHO is facing an international legal tsunami that will require a sea change in its attitude towards international law. WHO's lack of interest in international law does not reflect the historical experience of states and international health organizations prior to World War II. While WHO has been accused of focusing too little on international law, international relations prior to World War II were plagued by too much international health law'.

10 WHO Constitution, Art 21.

11 W.R. Sharpe, 'The New World Health Organization' (1947) 41 *American Journal of International Law* 509. For a study of the international legislative process of international organizations 'by which an increasingly substantial amount of international law is steadily being created', see P.C. Szasz, *Selected Essays on Understanding International Institutions and the Legislative Process* (Ardsley, NY: Transnational, 2001); E. Kwakwa, 'Some Comments on Rule-Making at the World Intellectual Property Organization' (2002) 12(1) *Duke Journal of International Law* 179.

. . . soft international law is not binding, though perhaps superficially it may appear to be so; nevertheless, international entities habitually comply with it, and it is this feature that makes it possible to categorize it as 'law'. . . . Soft law is usually generated as a compromise between those who wish a certain matter to be regulated definitively and those who, while not denying the merits of the substantive issue, do not wish to be bound by rigid and obligatory rules—perhaps because they fear they cannot obtain any necessary domestic legislative approval.[12]

In this sense, Malanczuk observed that soft laws—as guidelines of conduct—are 'neither strictly binding norms of law, nor completely irrelevant political maxims'.[13] Soft law instruments 'operate in a grey zone between law and politics',[14] and are considered a special characteristic of international law, especially on emerging economic and environmental issues.

In the Westphalian international system therefore, the relevance of international law in controlling the transnational spread of infectious and non-communicable diseases within the mandate of the WHO falls within the three broad categories of conventional treaty-making authority (Articles 19 and 20); regulatory authority (Articles 21 and 22), and non-binding soft-law authority (Article 23).

For most of its existence, the work of the WHO—as a multilateral institution with a mandate to coordinate international health work—has been dominated by medical and public health experts—physicians and epidemiologists. In the first five decades of its existence (1948–1998), the WHO largely relegated international legal mechanisms to the margins of its work. In the 1990s, the WHO's under-utilization of its enormous legal authority to use treaties, regulations, and soft-law in the pursuance of its objectives and functions became the subject of intense debate by (international) legal scholars, and physicians and epidemiologists. Tomasevski,[15] Taylor,[16] and Fidler,[17] all international legal scholars, were critical of the increased 'medicalization' of the WHO as a result of the organization's reluctance to use international legal mechanisms in its work. According to Fidler:

WHO was isolated from general developments concerning international law in the post-1945 period. This isolation was not accidental but reflected a particular outlook on the formulation and implementation of international health policy. WHO operated as if it were not subject to the normal dynamics of the anarchical society; rather, it acted as if it were at the center of a transnational Hippocratic society made up of physicians, medical scientists, and public health

12 See Szasz, *Selected Essays* (n 11) 26–7 citing T. Gruchall-Hesierski, 'A Framework for Understanding "Soft Law"' (1984) 30 *McGill Law Journal* 37; C.M. Chinkin, 'The Challenge of Soft Law: Development and Change in in International Law' (1989) 38 *International and Comparative Law Quarterly* 850.

13 P. Malanczuk, *Akehurst's Modern Introduction to International Law* (London and New York: 7th revd edn, Routledge, 1997) 54

14 Malanczuk, *Akehurst's Modern Introduction to International Law* (n 13).

15 K. Tomasevski, 'Health' in O. Schachter, and C.C. Joyner (eds), *United Nations Legal Order* Vol II (Cambridge: CUP, 1995) 859, 859, strongly critiquing the WHO's overt bias in favor of non-binding and non-legal norms built upon ethical rather than legal principles. Also observing that an important reason for the WHO's bias for non-binding rules is the traditional reluctance of the medical profession to submit itself to the rule of law. Beginning in the 18th century, medical associations developed codes of professional behavior. Self-regulation presumes the exclusion of lay persons, thus reinforcing the traditional paternalism of the medical profession, dating back to the Hippocratic Oath: the assumption that whatever a physician decides is, by definition, correct.

16 A.L. Taylor, 'Making the World Health Organization Work: A Legal Framework for Universal Access to the Conditions of Health' (1992) 18 *American Journal of Law and Medicine* 302.

17 Fidler, 'The Future of the World Health Organization' (n 9).

experts. The nature of this transnational Hippocratic society led WHO to approach international public health without a legal strategy.[18]

Similarly Taylor observed that:

> WHO's traditional reluctance to utilize law and legal institutions to facilitate its health strategies is largely attributable to the internal dynamics and politics of the organization itself. In particular, this unwillingness stems, in large part, from the organizational culture established by the conservative medical professional community that dominates the institution.[19]

The 'law versus medicine/epidemiology' debate is understandably influenced by the giant strides made by science in proving the germ theory correct. Once epidemiologists understood how humans were infected by disease, they automatically turned to diagnosis and healing, and not to international legal strategies and frameworks for solutions to public health problems. International legal scholars who are critical of the WHO's non-legal approaches to global health work recognize this viewpoint. As Fidler observed:

> The common argument used to explain WHO's antipathy towards international law is that WHO is dominated almost exclusively by people trained in public health and medicine, which produces an ethos that looks at global health problems as medical-technical issues to be resolved by the application of the healing arts. The medical-technical approach does not need international law because the approach mandates application of the medical and technical resource or answer directly at the national or local level.[20]

Science catalyzed the development of international health law in the 1890s because it provided the breakthrough needed to facilitate agreement by states on common rules and values.[21] But in the contemporary era, the antibiotic revolution impeded the development of international health law because doctors and public health officials go directly after microbes rather than seek recourse to international legal regimes on global health issues. It is therefore not surprising that in 1948, the very first year of the WHO's life, Sir Wilson Jameson, President of the first World Health Assembly, downplayed the relevance of 'international law' when he observed: 'Let us face the facts and refrain from a discussion of legal technicalities into which we, as an assembly of public health experts, are perhaps hardly competent to enter.'[22] In the six decades

18 D.P. Fidler, 'International Law and Global Public Health' (1999) 48 *University of Kansas Law Review* 1, 15.

19 Taylor, 'Making the World Health Organization Work' (n 16) 303. For a discussion of this theme in other seminal writings, see D.P. Fidler, *International Law and Infectious Diseases* (Oxford: Clarendon Press, 1999); D.P. Fidler, 'Return of the Fourth Horseman: Emerging Infectious Diseases and International Law' (1997) 81 *Minnesota Law Review* 788; O. Aginam, *Global Health Governance: International Law and Public Health in a Divided World* (Toronto: University of Toronto Press, 2005); A. Lakin, 'The Legal Powers of the World Health Organization' (1997) 3 *Medical Law International* 23; A. L'hirondel and D. Yach, 'Develop and Strengthen Public Health Law' (1998) 51 *World Health Statistics Quarterly* 79.

20 Fidler, 'The Future of the World Health Organization' (n 9) 1099.

21 For a discussion of the science and politics of the international sanitary conferences in the 19th century, see N. Howard-Jones, *The Scientific Background of the International Sanitary Conferences 1851–1938* (Geneva: WHO, 1975); N.M. Goodman, *International Health Organizations and Their Work* (London: Churchill Livingstone, 1977); D.P. Fidler, 'The Globalization of Public Health: The First 100 Years of International Health Diplomacy' (2001) 79(9) *Bulletin of the World Health Organization* 842; Fidler, *International Law and Infectious Diseases* (n 19); Aginam, *Global Health Governance* (n 19).

22 OR 13 1948 (Records of the First World Health Assembly, 1948) 77. Sir Wilson Jameson was responding to legal issues and reservations raised by US membership of the WHO.

following Sir Wilson Jameson's observation—corresponding also to the post-United Nations world order—the international system has transformed quite significantly in dynamic ways. First, the expansive definition of health in the WHO Constitution as 'a state of complete physical, mental and social well-being and not merely the absence of disease or infirmity' meant that the necessary linkages must be drawn between public health, and poverty, underdevelopment, human rights, food (in)security, food safety, climate, and other related environmental changes, natural disasters, wars and weapons of mass destruction, international trade agreements, and the multi-faceted dimensions of the phenomenon of globalization. On almost all of these issues, international law has created regimes and governance frameworks relevant to the WHO's public health mandate. In retrospect, the post-1945 decades since the establishment of the United Nations have witnessed the evolution of international legal mechanisms on human rights (including the right to health), global environmental issues (multilateral environmental agreements), international humanitarian laws, food and agriculture, and trade-related health concerns, among many others.[23] The WHO, due to the 'medicalization' of its public health mandate, missed out on most of these normative developments.

The second, and perhaps most remarkable, transformation of the international system relates to the emergence and re-emergence of transnational health issues that defy the sovereignty and geo-political boundaries of nation-states. These newly emerging and re-emerging issues are propelled by complex networks of the interdependence of nations, peoples, and markets in a globalizing world, and characterized by the increasing number of non-state actors involved in addressing them. Because the governance of these issues defies the classic Westphalianism, *global health governance* now offers a better framework to analyze and understand them. The transition from *international* to *global* health, or what has been characterized as 'post-Westphalian' governance architecture, poses a challenge to nation-states and intergovernmental organizations (IGOs) to adapt to a dynamic international system where they have to interact, or even compete with new (mostly non-state) actors to govern newly emerging and re-emerging global health issues that defy the geo-political boundaries of nation-states.

3. The Role and Relevance of the WHO in Global Health Governance Discourse

The transition from *international* to *global* health is a discourse that underscores three inexorably linked phenomena: (1) the increased vulnerability of geo-political boundaries to communicable and non-communicable disease threats; (2) the obsolescence of the distinction between national and international health in a globalized world; and (3) the multiple actors whose interests and power now shape the governance of emerging global health challenges.[24] Driven by the complex linkages between public health and

[23] See generally Fidler, *International Law and Infectious Diseases* (n 19).

[24] On 'global health governance', see generally D.P. Fidler, 'The Challenges of Global Health Governance', Working Paper, Council on Foreign Relations, May 2010; Cooper, Kirton, and Schrecker, *Governing Global Health: Challenge, Response, Innovation* (n 4); S. Harman, *Global Health Governance* (London and New York: Routledge: 2012); Hein, Bartsch, and Kohlmorgen, *Global Health Governance* (n 6); Aginam, *Global Health Governance* (n 19); Zacher and Keefe, *The Politics of Global Health Governance* (n 4).

the phenomenon of globalization,[25] global health governance refers to the dynamic interactions of nation-states, IGOs (such as the WHO), and non-state actors (civil society, charities, foundations, businesses, and corporations) in the regulatory, institutional, and policy frameworks and processes for the governance of global health.[26] Because the WHO is essentially characterized by Westphalian attributes as an IGO with membership open exclusively to nation-states,[27] what then should be the role of the organization in global health governance, especially with the emergence of non-state actors with varied and divergent interests on global health. Although the WHO has responded to this conundrum partly through its active participation in a number of public-private partnerships (PPPs) for global health,[28] this might complicate the role of the WHO as a norm entrepreneur in global health governance. Global PPPs for health are:

> Those collaborative relationships which transcend national boundaries and bring together at least three parties, among them a corporation (and/or industry association) and an intergovernmental organization, so as to achieve a shared health-creating goal on the basis of a mutually agreed and explicitly defined division of labour.[29]

As PPPs proliferate in global health governance to cover a number of health issues: malaria,[30] vaccines and immunization,[31] tuberculosis,[32] polio eradication,[33] leprosy,[34]

[25] The 'globalization of public health' refers to the cumulative impact of the cognitive, spatial, and temporal dimensions of global interdependence on public health across various regions and societies of the world. The globalization of the world's political economy creates opportunities for disease pathogens to travel transcontinental distances with the speed of a jet. On the globalization of public health, see K. Lee and R. Dodgson, 'Globalization and Cholera: Implications for Global Governance' (2000) 6 *Global Governance* 213; K. Lee, K. Buse, and S. Fustukian (eds), *Health Policy in a Globalising World* (Cambridge: CUP, 2002); D. Yach and D. Bettcher, 'The Globalization of Public Health, I: Threats and Opportunities' (1998) 88(5) *American Journal of Public Health* 735; D. Yach and D. Bettcher, 'The Globalization of Public Health, II: The Convergence of Self-Interest and Altruism' (1988) 88(5) *American Journal of Public Health* 738; G.H. Brundtland, 'Global Health and International Security' (2003) 9 *Global Governance* 417; G.H. Brundtland, 'Globalization as a Force for Better Health', Lecture, London School of Economics, London, 6 March 2001; D. Woodward et al, 'Globalization and Health: A Framework for Analysis and Action' (2001) 79(9) *Bulletin of the World Health Organization* 875; Fidler, 'The Globalization of Public Health: Emerging Infectious Diseases and International Relations' (1997) 5(1) *Indiana Journal of Global Legal Studies* 1; Fidler, *SARS, Governance and Globalization* (n 6).

[26] See n 24.

[27] On membership of the WHO, see WHO Constitution, Arts 3, 4, and 5.

[28] The literature on global PPPs for global health is quite voluminous. See K. Buse and A. Harmer, 'Power to the Partners?: The Politics of Public-Private Health Partnerships' (2004) 47(2) *Development* 49; K. Buse and G. Walt, 'Global Public-Private Partnerships: Part I—A New Development in Health?' (2000) 78(4) *Bulletin of the World Health Organization* 549; K. Buse and G. Walt, 'Global Public-Private Partnerships: Part II—What are the Issues for Global Governance?' (2000) 78(5) *Bulletin of the World Health Organization* 699; K. Buse and A. Waxman, 'Public-Private Partnerships: A Strategy for the WHO' (2001) 79(8) *Bulletin of the World Health Organization* 748; G. Pinet, 'Global Partnerships: A Key Challenge and Opportunity for Implementation of International Health Law' (2003) 22 *Medicine and Law* 561; O. Aginam, 'Global Governance' in S. Galea (ed), *Macrosocial Determinants of Population Health* (New York: Springer, 2007) 159; G. Adlide, A. Rowe, and J. Lob-Levyt, 'Public-Private Partnership to Promote Health: The GAVI Alliance Experience' in A. Clapham and M. Robinson (eds), *Realizing the Right to Health* (Swiss Human Rights Book, Vol 3) (Berne: ruffer and rub, 2009) 539.

[29] K. Buse and G. Walt, 'Globalisation and Multilateral Public-Private Partnerships: Issues for Health Policy' in K. Lee, K. Buse, and S. Fustukian (eds), *Health Policy in a Globalising World* (Cambridge: CUP, 2002) 41, 44.

[30] See Roll-Back Malaria Campaign; Medicines for Malaria Venture; and Multilateral Initiative on Malaria.

[31] Global Alliance for Vaccines and Immunization (GAVI).

[32] Stop TB; and Global Alliance for TB Drug Development.

[33] Global Polio Eradication Initiative.

[34] Global Alliance to Eradicate Leprosy.

HIV/AIDS,[35] trachoma,[36] and many others, questions have been raised concerning their legitimacy, fairness, effectiveness, accountability, and transparency.[37] It is in the context of these persistent questions that the role of the WHO as a norm entrepreneur in global health governance needs to be further explored and understood.

4. The WHO and Norm Entrepreneurship in Global Health Governance

In their widely cited work on the evolution of norms, Finnemore and Sikkink define a norm as 'a standard of appropriate behavior for actors with a given identity'.[38] Although the categories of norms differ across disciplines, 'the most common distinction is between regulative norms, which order and constrain behavior, and constitutive norms, which create new actors, interests, or categories of action'.[39] Finnemore and Sikkink identified the three stages in a norm's life cycle as: norm emergence, norm acceptance ('norm cascade'), and norm internalization.[40] Of the three stages of a norm's cycle, norm entrepreneurs play a critically important role in the first stage—norm emergence—through persuasion, when they 'attempt to convince a critical mass of states (norm leaders) to embrace new norms'.[41] There are two preconditions for a norm to successfully emerge: *norm entrepreneurs* (agents with strong notions about appropriate or desirable behavior in their community), and *organizational platforms* (a platform at the international level for norm promoters to promote their norms). While individuals—as in the widely cited case of Swiss national Henry Dunant and the norms of international humanitarian laws—are often credited with norm entrepreneurship, modern-day norm entrepreneurs would most likely work within the confines of an international organization to facilitate norm emergence. As Finnemore and Sikkink observed:

> . . . one prominent feature of modern organizations and an important source of influence for international organizations in particular is their use of expertise and information to change the behavior of other actors. Expertise, in turn, usually resides in professionals, and a number of empirical studies document the ways that *professional training of bureaucrats in these organizations helps or blocks the promotion of new norms* within standing organizations.[42]

35 Global Fund to Fight AIDS, Tuberculosis and Malaria, and the International Partnership for AIDS in Africa.

36 Global Elimination of Blinding Trachoma.

37 Buse and Walt, 'Globalisation and Multilateral Public-Private Partnerships' (n 29); O. Aginam, 'From the Core to the Peripheries: Multilateral Governance of Malaria in a Multi-cultural World' (2002) 3(1) *Chicago Journal of International Law* 87; G. Yamey, 'WHO in 2002: Faltering Steps Towards Partnerships' (2002) 325 *British Medical Journal* 1236; S. Bartsch, 'The Global Fund to Fight AIDS, Tuberculosis and Malaria' in W. Hein, S. Bartsch, and L. Kohlmorgen (eds), *Global Health Governance and the Fight Against HIV/AIDS* (New York: Palgrave MacMillan, 2007) 146.

38 M. Finnemore and K. Sikkink, 'International Norm Dynamics and Political Change' (1998) 52 (4) *International Organization* 887, 891, citing M. Finnemore, *National Interests in International Society* (Ithaca, NY: Cornell University Press, 1996) 22; P.J. Katzenstein, 'Introduction: Alternative Perspectives on National Security' in P.J. Katzenstein (ed), *The Culture of National Security: Norms and Identity in World Politics* (New York: Columbia University Press, 1996) 5; and A. Klotz, *Norms in International Relations: The Struggle Against Apartheid* (Ithaca, NY: Cornell University Press, 1995).

39 Finnemore and Sikkink, 'International Norm Dynamics' (n 38) 891 citing J.G. Ruggie, 'What Makes the World Hang Together? Neo-utilitarianism and the Social Constructivist Challenge' (1998) 52(4) *International Organization* 855.

40 Finnemore and Sikkink, 'International Norm Dynamics' (n 38) 895.

41 Finnemore and Sikkink, 'International Norm Dynamics' (n 38) 895.

42 Finnemore and Sikkink, 'International Norm Dynamics' (n 38) 899 (emphasis added).

Relating this to the WHO's role as either a norm entrepreneur or organizational platform for the promotion of new global health norms, it is arguable that the 'professional training of bureaucrats' in the organization largely 'blocks' instead of 'helps' the 'promotion of new norms'. As already stated, in over sixty years of its history, the WHO is known to have adopted only two legally-binding normative instruments: the International Health Regulations (IHR), and the Framework Convention on Tobacco Control (FCTC). The organization has historically neglected international law in its work by under-utilizing its enormous constitutional powers.[43]

5. The WHO, Norm Entrepreneurship, and the Revision of the IHR

The IHR (then known as 'International Sanitary Regulations') were adopted by the WHO in 1951 pursuant to Article 21 of its Constitution. In 1969, the WHO renamed the regulations the 'International Health Regulations', and slightly modified them twice in 1973 and 1981. The IHR represent one of the earliest legally-binding regulatory tools for global control of certain infectious diseases. As of 1997, the IHR were legally binding on virtually all of the WHO's member states. The IHR are a regulatory surveillance mechanism for the sharing of epidemiological information on the trans-boundary spread of three infectious diseases: cholera, plague, and yellow fever. The fundamental principle of the IHR was to ensure 'maximum security against the international spread of diseases with a minimum interference with world traffic'. To achieve this purpose, the IHR provided for binding obligations on the WHO member states to notify the organization of any outbreaks of cholera, plague, and yellow fever in their territories. Notifications sent by a Member State to the WHO are transmitted to all the other Member States, with details of acceptable public health measures to respond to such outbreaks.

The IHR lists maximum public health measures applicable during outbreaks and provides for rules applicable to international traffic and travel. These measures, among others, largely cover the requirements of health and vaccination certificates for travelers from areas infected by these three diseases to non-infected areas, as well as detailed health measures at airports and seaports in the territories of the WHO member states. Measures listed in the IHR are the maximum measures allowed in outbreak situations aimed to protect the country that suffers an outbreak against the risk of overreaction and unnecessary embargoes, which could be imposed by contiguous neighbors, trading partners, and other countries. These embargoes are often damaging economically, with severe consequences on tourism, traffic, and trade. By the 1990s, it became evident that the IHR had been unsuccessful as a global health regulatory tool. Chief among the reasons for IHR's ineffectiveness was the fear on the part of countries experiencing an outbreak of disease, specifically, of the potential for other nations to take excessive measures if an outbreak was reported to the WHO. Examples include the cholera epidemics in South America—first reported in Peru in 1991, which were estimated to have cost over $700 million in trade and other losses, and the 1994 plague outbreak in India that led to $1.7 billion of losses in trade, tourism, and travel as a result of excessive embargoes and restrictions imposed upon India by other countries.[44]

[43] See nn 14–18.

[44] A.L. Taylor, 'Controlling the Global Spread of Infectious Diseases: Toward a Reinforced Role for the International Health Regulations' (1997) 33 *Houston Law Review* 1348, stating that in the case of plague outbreak in India, such excessive measures included the closing of airports to aircraft that were arriving from India, barriers to importation of foodstuffs, and in many cases the return of Indian guest

The economic cost of disease outbreaks that are not subject to reporting obligations under the IHR was high. The outbreak of SARS, which first emerged in Southern China and spread rapidly to other countries, was reported to have 'rocked Asian markets, ruined the tourist trade of an entire region, nearly bankrupted airlines, and spread panic through some of the world's largest countries'.[45] In Canada, the economic cost of the SARS outbreak was estimated at $30 million daily. It is projected that China and South Korea each suffered $2 billion worth of SARS-related tourism and other economic losses. Visitor arrivals dropped drastically in Singapore, while Hong Kong carrier Cathay Pacific cut its weekly flights by 45 percent.[46] Apart from the likely economic embargoes, other reasons often cited for the ineffectiveness of the IHR include the WHO's relative inexperience in the creation and enforcement of norms and legal regimes; the IHR's inability to adapt to changing circumstances in international traffic, trade, and public health; and the IHR's limited coverage of only three diseases.

As the IHR had become ineffective, the forty-eighth World Health Assembly—in May 1995—passed a resolution calling on the Director-General of the WHO to start a process of IHR revision. Pursuant to this resolution, the WHO held an informal consultation of experts on IHR revision in December 1995.[47] The expert group proposed a range of amendments to the IHR, and in February 1998, the WHO circulated a provisional draft of the revised IHR to member states. The major amendments proposed by the consultation of experts focused on the expansion of diseases subject to the regulations beyond plague, yellow fever, and cholera to include immediate reporting of defined disease syndromes of urgent international importance as well as epidemiological information for their emergence, prevalence, and control, and the WHO's power to request information from member states based on information the WHO received from other reliable sources: the WHO Collaborating Centers, NGOs, mass media, other international organizations, and other non-member states. Previously, the WHO never had this power; it simply waited for a member state to notify it of an outbreak. The rationale behind this proposal is that few, if any, disease outbreaks can be hidden due to extensive global media networks. Innovations in communications technology have rendered state sovereignty irrelevant in disease outbreaks. Independent global outbreak monitoring sources now abound. Examples of these include the Global Public Health Information Network (GPHIN), an electronic surveillance system developed by Health Canada; Pro-MED, a private initiative of the Federation of American Scientists' Program for Monitoring Emergent Infectious Diseases that creates a global system of early detection and response to disease outbreaks; and PACNET, an internet-based information provider on disease outbreaks in the Pacific region. The implication of these innovations is that disease outbreaks can no longer be hidden under the veil of state sovereignty.

Despite the persuasive argument by some scholars[48] that credit the WHO secretariat with successful norm entrepreneurship on the revision and subsequent adoption

workers even though many of them had not lived in India for several years; L. Garret, 'The Return of Infectious Diseases' (1996) 75 Foreign Affairs 73, stating that India lost almost $2 billion as result of excessive measures following the plague outbreak.

45 'The Truth about SARS', *Time* (Canadian edn), 5 May 2003, 13.

46 'The Truth about SARS' (n 45) 13.

47 WHO, 'The International Response to Epidemics and Application of the International Health Regulations: Report of a WHO Informal Consultation', UN Doc WHO/EMC/IHR 96.1 (1995).

48 A. Kamradt-Scott, 'The WHO Secretariat, Norm Entrepreneurship, and Global Disease Outbreak Control' (2010) 1(2) *Journal of International Organization Studies* 72.

of the International Health Regulations (2005) (which officially entered into force on 15 June 2007), as a normative tool for global disease outbreak control, it is important to state that the process of IHR revision which started in 1995 was greatly impeded by WHO bureaucrats. As predominantly physicians, epidemiologists, and public health experts, WHO bureaucrats did not attach much importance to the IHR as a relevant tool in global infectious disease surveillance and control, neither was IHR revision high on the 'list of priorities' of the WHO Director-General Gro Harlem Brundtland in 1998 when she assumed office.[49] The emergence of IHR (2005) was catalyzed by a singular event; the outbreak and global spread of a new deadly and terrifying infectious disease—Severe Acute Respiratory Syndrome (SARS)—as opposed to a natural progression of IHR as a global disease control norm through the three stages of a norm's life cycle: norm emergence, norm cascade, and norm internalization. Before SARS, the IHR revision process was treated like an orphan in the WHO secretariat—starved of funds, manpower, and personnel.[50] As a result, the IHR became a toothless treaty that was relatively unknown to most WHO member states and ignored by WHO epidemiologists until the SARS outbreak. As Fidler rightly observed: 'WHO's indifference toward international law is also evident in the way the Member States of the Organization allowed the IHR to become irrelevant to the international spread of infectious diseases.'[51] Although the innovative provisions of IHR 2005 constitute a post-Westphalian departure from the Westphalian state-centric provisions of IHR 1969, and as such have been heralded by profound optimism within the relevant global health epistemic communities,[52] it is debatable whether the norm internalization stage of IHR 2005 will be effective.

6. The WHO, Norm Entrepreneurship, and the Framework Convention on Tobacco Control

The WHO Framework Convention on Tobacco Control (FCTC) directly implicates the organization as a norm entrepreneur in global health governance. In May 1999, the World Health Assembly adopted (by consensus) Resolution WHA52.18, urging the Director-General of the WHO to start a process of multilateral negotiations for the FCTC.[53] In its fifty-three-year history as of 1999, the FCTC process would be the WHO's first experience of using its treaty-making authority under Article 19 of its Constitution.

As a governance/regulatory tool, the FCTC was based on the evidence that tobacco use is one of the leading causes of preventable deaths, and a leading contributor to burdens of disease globally.[54] There are over 1 billion smokers in the world, and it was

[49] Kamradt-Scott, 'The WHO Secretariat, Norm Entrepreneurship' (n 48) 79.

[50] See the interviews of key IHR Team, cited by Kamradt-Scott, 'The WHO Secretariat, Norm Entrepreneurship' (n 48) 78–80.

[51] D.P. Fidler, 'International Law' in R. Smith, R. Beaglehole, D. Woodward, and N. Drager (eds), *Global Public Goods for Health* (New York: OUP, 2003) 178, 183–4.

[52] D.P. Fidler, 'From International Sanitary Conventions to Global Health Security: The New International Health Regulations' (2005) 4(2) *Chinese Journal of International Law* 325; M.G. Baker and D.P. Fidler, 'Global Public Health Surveillance under the New International Health Regulations' (2006) 12(7) *Emerging Infectious Diseases* 1058; C.-F. Lo, *A Commentary on the International Health Regulations (2005): A New Charter for Global Health Matters* (Taipei: Angle, 2010);

[53] World Health Assembly, Resolution WHA52.18, 'Towards a WHO Framework Convention on Tobacco Control' (Geneva: WHO, 1999).

[54] C.L Murray and A.D. Lopez (eds), *The Global Burden of Disease: A Comprehensive Assessment of Mortality and Disability From Diseases, Risk Factors in 1990 and Projected to 2020* (Cambridge, MA:

then estimated that about 4 million people die yearly from tobacco-related diseases. Although tobacco use is a leading cause of premature death in industrialized countries, the epidemic of tobacco addiction, disease, and death was rapidly shifting to developing countries.[55] Powerful and influential tobacco multinationals targeted growing markets in Latin America in the 1960s, the newly industrialized economies of Asia (Japan, the Republic of Korea, Taiwan, and Thailand) in the 1980s, and women and young persons in Africa in the 1990s.[56] As succinctly put by Fidler:

> Western tobacco companies succeeded in riding the waves of international trade law, liberal triumphalism and globalizing Western culture in penetrating the markets and lungs of millions of people in the developing world.[57]

In the late 1990s, a majority of smokers lived in developing countries (800 million); most were men (700 million) and 300 million were Chinese. At current levels of consumption, the tobacco epidemic is expected to kill up to 8.4 million people per year by 2020, with 70 percent of these deaths occurring in developing nations. If current consumption patterns remain unchecked, within the next thirty years tobacco use will be the leading cause of premature deaths worldwide.[58] Tobacco use is medically associated with a range diseases and fatal health conditions, including lung and bladder cancers, heart diseases, bronchitis and emphysema, and increased antenatal and pre-natal mortality.[59]

In May 1999, the World Health Assembly established a working group to analyze potential elements to be included in the tobacco treaty, and an Inter-Governmental Negotiating Body (open to the WHO's 191 member states) to negotiate and draft the proposed WHO Framework Convention on Tobacco Control and related protocols. The Tobacco Free Initiative of the WHO prepared background documents for the working group, enumerating possible elements to be covered by the Framework Convention and other elements of subsequent protocols. Draft elements of the Framework Convention included the preamble, principles and objectives, obligations, institutions, implementation mechanisms, law-making processes and final clauses (signatories, reservations, ratification, and withdrawal). Potential elements for subsequent related protocols include: cigarette prices and harmonization of taxes, measures against smuggling, duty-free tobacco products, tobacco advertising and sponsorship,

Harvard School of Public Health on behalf of the World Health Organization and The World Bank, 1996); C.L. Murray and A.D. Lopez, 'Alternative Projections of Mortality and Disability by Cause 1990–2020: Global Burden of Disease Study' (1997) 349 *Lancet* 1498.

55 Murray and Lopez, *The Global Burden of Disease* (n 54). See also A.L. Taylor, 'An International Regulatory Strategy for Global Tobacco Control' (1996) 21 *Yale Journal of International Law* 257, stating that the absence of effective domestic regulation of tobacco in developing countries has created a lucrative opportunity for transnational tobacco companies to target such countries. In many of the poorer states, aggressive tobacco promotion by the tobacco industry and Western states simply overwhelms underfunded national tobacco control efforts).

56 G.N. Connoly, 'Worldwide Expansion of the Transnational Tobacco Industry' (1992) 2 *Journal of the National Cancer Institute Monographs* 29.

57 D.P. Fidler, 'Neither Science Nor Shamans: Globalization of Markets and Health in the Developing World' (1999) 7 *Indiana Journal of Global Legal Studies* 191, 201.

58 A.L. Taylor and D. Bettcher, 'WHO Framework Convention on Tobacco Control: A Global Good for Public Health' (2000) 78(7) *The International Journal of Public Health* (Bulletin of the World Health Organization) 920, 923 citing C.L. Murray and A.D. Lopez, 'Assessing the Burden of Disease that can be Attributed to Specific Risk Factors' in *WHO Report of Ad Hoc Committee on Health Research Relating to Future Intervention Options, Investing in Health Research and Development* (Geneva: WHO, 1996).

59 Murray and Lopez, 'Assessing the Burden of Disease' (n 58).

reporting of toxic constituents of tobacco products, packaging and labeling, tobacco and agricultural policy, sharing of information.

The FCTC negotiating process went through different phases: Working Groups (1999–2000); Public Hearings (2000); and Intergovernmental Negotiating Body Sessions (2000–03). The Intergovernmental Negotiating Body (INB) on the WHO FCTC finalized its work on the first public health treaty under the auspices of the World Health Organization in February 2003. The WHO FCTC was adopted by the 56th World Health Assembly in May 2003, and was open for signature until 29 June 2004. The FCTC was signed by 168 states during this period, expressing their willingness to subsequently become Parties to the Convention. In accordance with Article 36 of the WHO FCTC, the Convention entered into force on 27 February 2005, ninety days after the fortieth State had acceded to, ratified, accepted, or approved it.[60] With 176 State Parties,[61] the FCTC has been widely accepted by WHO member states within a relatively short period. Regular sessions of the Conference of the Parties (COP) to the WHO FCTC are held every two years. The WHO FCTC authorizes the COP to adopt Protocols to the Convention.[62] After four years of negotiations, the first Protocol to the WHO FCTC—'Protocol to Eliminate Illicit Trade in Tobacco Products'—was adopted by the Parties to the FCTC at the 5th session of the COP on 12 November 2012.

Assessing the WHO FCTC through the three stages of a norm's life cycle: norm emergence, norm cascade, and norm internalization, it is clear that former Director-General of the WHO, Gro-Harlem Brundtland—as the FCTC norm entrepreneur—deployed her enormous global influence through persuasion to convince a critical mass of like-minded leaders and the WHO member states (as 'norm leaders') to support the FCTC process.[63] Brundtland, as FCTC norm entrepreneur, held very strong notions about the use of the FCTC as an effective tool in tobacco control, and utilized the WHO as an organizational platform at the international level to promote the norm. On the second stage of a norm's cycle, the rate of acceptance (norm cascade) of the FCTC within a relatively short period (176 Parties in under ten years) is remarkable. However, on norm internalization (the third stage), the WHO FCTC is likely to face serious obstacles and impediments. This is because the political economy of tobacco poses difficult regulatory and governance challenges due to a number of factors: the liberalization of global trade rules; the powerful influence and enormous wealth of tobacco multinationals, as evidenced by their aggressive marketing strategies in developing countries; the economic dependence of some developing world economies on tobacco farming as a foreign exchange earner;[64] and the complexity of harmonizing cigarette taxes, policies, and advertisements within domestic jurisdictions, and multilaterally.

Among these factors, the liberalization of global trade rules remains the most formidable challenge. The WHO FCTC could easily bump into the global trade arena where the World Trade Organization (WTO) now holds sway as a strict enforcer of trade agreements, norms, and rules such as 'national treatment', 'most favored nation', and many others. Although within the text of trade agreements there is an

60 Parties to the WHO Framework Convention on Tobacco Control, available at <http://www.who.int/fctc/signatories_parties/en/index.html> (accessed 26 February 2013).

61 As of 27 February 2013.

62 FCTC, Art 33.

63 Before she was appointed WHO Director-General, Gro-Harlem Brundtland had been the Prime Minister of Norway, and the Chair of the World Commission on Environment and Development (the 'Brundtland Commission') whose Report, entitled 'Our Common Future', shaped the global policy frameworks and discourse of sustainable development, including the Rio Earth Summit 1992.

64 Zimbabwe, Malawi, and Kenya are some of the African tobacco growing countries.

attempt to balance health and trade imperatives, in practice this balance raises policy complexities.[65] As a case in point, the recent decision by the Government of Australia to implement 'tobacco plain packaging', as legislated by the Tobacco Plain Packaging Act 2011, has been challenged by Phillip Morris Asia as a violation of the 1993 Hong Kong-Australia Bilateral Investment Treaty.[66]

As WHO member states continue to accept the WHO FCTC and its protocol(s), internalizing the terms of the convention in the legislative, legal, institutional, and policy frameworks of these states in the years ahead is likely to raise serious trade and investment questions, especially for developing and least-developed countries where tobacco conglomerates will continue to exploit the prevailing poverty and underdevelopment to their advantage. The WHO should devise effective strategies to counter this.

7. Postscript: the WHO, Norm Entrepreneurship, and Global Health Governance—the Way Forward

The role and relevance of the WHO as the 'directing and coordinating authority on international health work' has been challenged in complex ways by the dynamics of the globalization of public health. While the organization remains essentially a Westphalian institution with membership exclusively composed of nation-states, the trends, realities, and dynamics of the phenomenon of globalization have proven that the emerging and re-emerging global health issues defy the territorial boundaries of individual nation-states. Economic globalization has globalized communicable and non-communicable diseases and related threats. In an interdependent world, the globalization of public health constitutes one of the most critical challenges facing the contemporary Westphalian health governance architecture, which includes WHO and its member states. Globalization's challenge of public health Westphalianism has led to the concept of 'global health governance' that looks beyond state-centrism to identify the emerging, emergent, and other relevant non-state actors and stakeholders in the global health arena. The relationship between WHO and these emerging actors, whether in terms of the proliferating PPPs or other networks, is open to debate. However, most scholars agree that innovations are needed. As Cooper, Kirton, and Schrecker observed:

65 GATT, Art XX(b) (of 1994) provides that a trade-restricting measure necessary to protect human health is only justifiable if the measure does not 'constitute arbitrary or unjustifiable discrimination' between countries. On the balancing of public health and trade imperatives, see generally C. Blouin, J. Heymann, and N. Drager, *Trade and Health: Seeking Common Ground* (Montreal: McGill-Queen's University Press, 2007); WHO and WTO, 'WTO Agreements and Public Health: A Joint Study by the WHO and the WTO Secretariat' (Geneva: WHO/WTO, 2002); T. Kelly, *The Impact of the WTO: The Environment, Public Health and Sovereignty* (Cheltenham: Edward Elgar, 2007); C. Button, *The Power to Protect: Trade, Health and Uncertainty in the WTO* (Oxford: Hart Publishing, 2004); A.L. Taylor, D.W. Bettcher, and R. Peck, 'International Law and the International Legislative Process: The WHO Framework Convention on Tobacco Control' in R. Smith, R. Beaglehole, and N. Drager (eds.), *Global Public Goods for Health: Health Economic and Public Health Perspectives* (New York: OUP, 2003) 212; Aginam, 'Health or Trade?' (n 5).

66 In order to take advantage of launching an investment dispute under this BIT between Hong Kong and Australia, Phillip Morris Asia acquired Phillip Morris (Australia) Ltd on 23 February 2011. For a discussion of public health and tobacco plain packaging, see A.D. Mitchell, T. Voon, J. Liberman and G. Ayres (eds), *Public Health and Plain Packaging of Cigarettes: Legal Issues* (Cheltenham: Edward Elgar, 2012); A.D. Mitchell and T. Voon, 'Time to Quit? Assessing International Investment Claims Against Plain Tobacco Packaging in Australia' (2011) 14(3) *Journal of International Economic Law* 515.

These innovations will need to come in the realm of ideas, as the prevailing principles and norms that guide global health governance are redefined and reinvented for a comprehensively and instantaneously interconnected, complex world. They will be needed in the realm of institutions, where new rules, decision-making procedures, resources, and participants are required if the expectations and behavior of the world's countries and citizens are to converge on the reality, rather than just the ideal, of health for all. In both cases, the still dominant Westphalian model—now almost half a millennium old—of sovereign territorial states engaging in limited international cooperation for particular purposes is fast approaching the end of its useful life.[67]

Looking beyond the Westphalian model, the successor system will be carefully crafted to accommodate all the emergent relevant actors and stakeholders. According to Cooper, Kirton, and Schrecker;

Designing, developing and delivering the successor system will require the talents of many from national and sub-national governments, international institutions, healthcare professionals, philanthropists, the private sector, local communities, nongovernmental organizations (NGOs), faith groups, committed groups and victims from around the world.[68]

In both the contemporary (dominant) Westphalian model, and the imagined successor system with multiple actors and stakeholders, the possibility or otherwise of the WHO's mission as a norm entrepreneur would largely depend on how the organization innovatively deploys its legal and constitutional authorities to initiate new norms and craft a symbiotic and cooperative relationship with the new (non-state) actors in the global health arena.

[67] Cooper, Kirton, and Schrecker, 'Governing Global Health in the Twenty-First Century' (n 4) 4.
[68] Cooper, Kirton, and Schrecker, 'Governing Global Health in the Twenty-First Century' (n 4) 4.

32

Policy Space for Health in the Context of Emerging European Trade Policies

Meri Koivusalo and Nicola Watt

1. Overview

International trade agreements and their relationship with health policies have been discussed most prominently with respect to developing countries and, in particular, access to medicines. However, pharmaceutical policies are only one example of an area where policy concerns have emerged. Another area where health and trade policies have become discussed globally is that of public health policies with respect to alcohol, tobacco, and diet. In this chapter we will focus on three areas that have so far received less attention as negotiations have not made progress at global level: negotiation practices, services, and investments. These areas have become an increasingly prominent aspect of emerging bilateral and regional trade agreements. Just as attention has been drawn, in particular, to negotiations of free trade agreements (FTAs) and their relation to access to medicines,[1] trade negotiations in the field of services, investment, and government procurement can have implications for how governments regulate, subsidise, and provide health services within their countries.

This chapter argues that trade negotiations need to be considered not only as agreements across countries, balancing different national interests of negotiation parties, but also essentially as agreements that have implications for the powers and regulatory needs of public and international commercial sector actors. While trade agreements may not prohibit national regulation as such, they can set the broader framework for *how* governments may regulate, subsidize, and intervene in markets as part of their domestic policies. This is an issue that has been taken up already by the WHO in the area of public health policies and tobacco, as public health policies to reduce tobacco consumption have been challenged in the context of trade and investment agreements and trademarks.[2]

The implications of trade agreements for health are often discussed predominantly from the perspective of trade between rich and poor countries. However, the regulatory implications became apparent, and remain easier to understand, in the context of new and ongoing negotiations between rich countries. Examples are, the agreements negotiated between the European Union and Canada or the European Union and the United States, and World Trade Organisation (WTO) dispute settlement cases, such as Canada's challenge to asbestos regulation in the European Union and the lengthy case

[1] See eg C.M. Correa, 'Implications of Bilateral Free Trade Agreements on Access to Medicines' (2006) 84 *Bulletin of the World Health Organization* 399; S.K. Sell, 'TRIPs-plus Free Trade Agreements and Access to Medicines' (2007) 28 *Liverpool Law Review* 41.

[2] World Health Organization, 'Confronting the Tobacco Epidemic in a New Era of Trade and Investment Liberalisation' (Geneva, 2012).

on hormones and beef.[3] Health-related issues with respect to intellectual property rights and regulation, standard-setting, and trade in goods are likely to remain on the agenda of future trade negotiations between the European Union and the United States. However, this chapter focuses on the less well-understood area of negotiations for services, investment, and government procurement as part of new bilateral treaties between the European Union, Canada, and the United States as well as emerging plurilateral negotiations on services.[4] This focus also allows us to examine arguments of sovereignty and public accountability, as the European Commission negotiates trade and investment agreements on behalf of EU Member States, whereas a large share of regulatory measures, as well as the organization and financing of health systems, remain the responsibility of the Member States.

2. Policy Space for Health

Trade and investment agreements have implications for policy space for health. In discussing the implications of trade agreements in the context of national and global governance we will use the term national policy space to describe and explain the ways in which trade policies can restrict the scope and underlying assumptions of health policies that national governments can implement,[5] including, but not limited to, health services and equity. We have previously defined policy space as the 'freedom, scope, and mechanisms that governments have to choose, design, and implement public policies to fulfil their aims'.[6] Other policy priorities, commitments, and the degree of decentralization or federalization can and do restrict national policy space for decision-making.[7] Furthermore, the availability of policy space as such does not necessarily imply that this is used wisely or in favour of health priorities. However, it is important that governments understand fully the implications of trade policy commitments for the regulation and financing of health systems, so as to be able to balance these against the perceived gains for the private sector that drive negotiations in the first place.

The concept of policy space is as such part of trade-related language and has been used extensively in the context of trade and development policies, including the Sao Paulo Consensus from the 2004 United Nations Conference on Trade and Development and the Accra Declaration (2008):[8]

[3] While the disagreement on the matter has continued in principle, the EU and Canada have found a mutually agreeable solution in practice. The dispute settlement case was formally closed in 2011 with the acceptance of a Memorandum of Understanding concerning imports of beef not treated with hormones and increased duties applied by Canada on some EU products. Available at <http://www.wto.org/english/tratop_e/dispu_e/cases_e/ds48_e.htm> (accessed 10 February 2014).

[4] See eg European Commission,, 'The plurilateral agreement on services: at the starting gate', DG EXPO/B/PolDep/Note/2013_57 (2013); CETA agreement texts as of 2012 reflected these concerns in relation to negotiation methods as well as more comprehensive focus.

[5] In this chapter analysis is geared to focus on those parts of the agreements which are likely to have health concerns for health systems rather than seeking to have a broad focus on all aspects of given agreements.

[6] M. Koivusalo, T. Schrecker, and R. Labonte, 'Globalization and Policy Space for Health and Social Determinants of Health' in R. Labonte, T. Schrecker, C. Packer, and V. Runnels (eds), *Globalization and Health. Pathways, Evidence and Policy* (New York and Oxford: Routledge, 2009) 105.

[7] See Koivusalo, Schrecker, and Labonte, 'Globalization and Policy Space' (n 6); on decentralization and multilevel governance, see C. Charbit, *Governance of Public Policies in Decentralised Contexts* (Paris: OECD, 2011).

[8] UNCTAD, Accra Declaration (Geneva, 2008) 6, available at <http://unctad.org/en/Docs/iaos20082_en.pdf> (accessed 10 February 2014).

While development is the primary responsibility of each country, domestic efforts should be facilitated and complemented by an enabling international environment based on multilaterally agreed and applied rules. It is for each Government to evaluate the trade-off between the benefits of accepting international rules and commitments, and the constraints posed by the loss of policy space.

The implications of trade and investment agreements extend both to (a) how health systems are organized, financed and regulated; and (b) health protection and promotion policies affecting other sectors. WTO legal analysis of the implications of the General Agreement on Trade in Services (GATS) for national health policies, provides guidance on potential issues of concern.[9] The World Bank and OECD compilation of sectoral analyses also provides some insights on how domestic regulation requirements could affect national health systems.[10] If a government wishes to maintain maximum policy space for the regulation of its health system, including for measures which could discriminate against foreign providers in the market, the easiest way to secure this is to keep the services outside trade policy commitments.

This is what has happened in many countries and indeed, in the plurilateral 'request and offer' process in the wake of the WTO Hong Kong Ministerial conference, medical and hospital services were the only major areas which remained exempted, due to lack of interest.[11] On the other hand, this was not the case for health insurance. Furthermore, while GATS negotiations have been under broader scrutiny, the negotiation of bilateral treaties and investment treaties is not necessarily given as much attention with respect to implications for health systems.[12]

This implies that particular attention to such negotiations may be required, to ensure that governments fully understand the implications of commitments made in relation to health. While governments—as is the case of the GATS and WTO dispute settlement context—might be reluctant to challenge the health sector regulation of other governments for fear of retaliation, this may not be the case for corporate arbitration. Furthermore, the health sector is not merely a commercial sector, but has crucial importance for trade in other sectors, as direct economic costs—not even including those due to health and illness—can rise to billions, as has been the case with some recent epidemics, such as SARS, BSE, and E.Coli 0157.[13]

The articulation of issues regarding regulatory policy space takes place increasingly in the context of discussions concerning so called non-tariff barriers to trade (NTBs), which apply in particular to domestic regulation. For example, in the case of the European Union and the United States, tariff levels are already low. A non-tariff barriers impact assessment has estimated that reducing NTBs will be key for the transatlantic liberalization of trade, and as much as 80 per cent of potential gains could come from cutting costs imposed by bureaucracy and regulations as well as from

[9] See eg D. Fidler, C. Correa, and O. Aginam, 'Legal review of the General Agreement on Trade in Services (GATS) from health policy perspective' (Geneva: WHO, 2003), available at <http://www.who.int/trade/resource/gatslegalreview/en/index.html> (accessed 10 February 2014).

[10] D. Luff, 'Regulation of Health Services and International Trade Law' in A. Mattoo and P. Sauve (eds), *Domestic Regulation and Services Trade Liberalisation* (New York: World Bank and OUP, 2003) 191.

[11] R. Adlung, 'Trade in Healthcare And Health Insurance Services: The GATS as a Supporting Actor (?)', WTO Staff Working Paper ERSD 2009–15 (2009), available at <http://www.wto.org/english/res_e/reser_e/ersd200915_e.pdf> (accessed 10 February 2014).

[12] Adlung, 'Trade in Healthcare And Health Insurance Services' (n 11).

[13] See eg WHO, 'World Health Report'.(Geneva, 2007) 40, available at <http://www.who.int/whr/2007/07_chap3_en.pdf> (accessed 10 February 2014).

liberalizing trade in services and public procurement.[14] This is not only a matter for the European Union and United States, but as expressed by those making the assessment:

> Given that, collectively, the EU and the US would stand as the world's biggest trading block, there is a very real possibility that mutual agreement on regulations and standards would be adopted, partially, also by third countries. Thus, where the EU and the US act as a regulatory hegemony, there is scope for setting de facto common, global standards. This implies that the bilateral agreement will give EU and the US improved market access in third markets from reduced NTBs. In addition, there will be scope for reductions in NTBs amongst third countries, as they converge further on common standards.[15]

Health services and health systems are of importance as a sector, as substantial amount of private and public resources are spent on health. Where health care is publicly financed, but privately provided, it becomes a potential part of broader services markets, and the way in which national health systems subsidize health care provision is also affected by government procurement regulations. Furthermore, health-related regulatory measures in the field of health protection and promotion are of importance, as these affect the commercial prospects of international businesses, such as those in the tobacco, alcohol, and food industries.

3. Governance and Accountability

As new and more comprehensive trade and investment agreements are to be negotiated between the European Union and the United States and Canada, this necessitates a focus on multilevel governance within the European Union as well as on the potential consequences of trade-related commitments to Member States accountable for health systems organization and financing at national level. While the European Union has competence to engage in trade policy negotiations on behalf of the twenty-eight Member States, the Member States remain responsible for the organization and financing of health services. This creates a policy context where global multinational industries have a major interest in engaging with negotiations, as these might deliver benefits which could accrue in those Member States. In contrast, the organization of health systems varies across Member States, and in some cases responsibilities and accountability for the organization and financing of health systems may have been further shifted to the regional or local level.

The EU context of trade negotiations is a good example of the challenges of multilevel governance, as trade policies are decided at European level and health priorities at local level. The problem of 'constitutionalizing' trade and investment agreements has also been raised as a concern in relation to recent debates with respect to the international investment regime.[16] The capacity of governments to anticipate and understand the extent of commitments is important, in particular, when the context of trade negotiations changes from GATS-type 'positive' listing to a 'negative'

[14] J. Francois, 'Reducing Transatlantic Barriers to Trade and Investment: An Economic Assessment' (2013) 4, available at <http://trade.ec.europa.eu/doclib/docs/2013/march/tradoc_150737.pdf>. (accessed 10 February 2014).

[15] Francois, 'Reducing Transatlantic Barriers' (n 14) 26.

[16] This is reflected, for example, in the public statement on the international investment regime by thirty-five academics, see <http://www.osgoode.yorku.ca/public_statement> (accessed 15 October 2012), and critical literature concerning this role, see eg D. Schneiderman, *Constitutionalizing Economic Globalization. Investment Rules and Democracy's Promise* (Cambridge: CUP, 2007), G. van Harten, *Investment Treaty Arbitration and Public Law* (Oxford: OUP, 2007).

listing more in the style of the North American Free Trade Agreement (NAFTA), and includes new and more far-reaching measures to extend and solidify commitments, such as the use of horizontal commitments, a ratchet mechanism, and standstill requirements (see Box 32.1 at the end of this chapter).

4. European Union Role in Trade Negotiations

In principle, the European Commission has had the competence[17] to negotiate trade agreements with respect to tariffs and trade in goods since the establishment of the EEC in 1957, under Articles 110 and 116 of the Treaty of Rome,[18] but the interpretation of the general reference to trade resulted in disputes concerning competence in other areas of trade. The clarification of competence by the European Court of Justice in 1994[19] placed negotiations on services and intellectual property rights under shared competence. Shared competence remained until the Treaty of Nice was agreed in 2001.[20] The emphasis on negotiation in these areas was therefore ultimately limited by those Member States who could take more restrictive stances and in effect veto on the basis of national priorities.

The recognition of the importance of health, social, education, cultural, and audiovisual services was reflected in the fact that as part of the Nice Treaty negotiations, these were carved out to be left as subjects of shared competence.[21] This is in alignment with the fact that the European Commission did not have formal competence over the financing and organization of health services,[22] which remained with Member States. However, this was changed in the Lisbon Treaty,[23] which conferred upon the Commission competence for common commercial policy as it relates to services and foreign direct investment, but generally not aspects of investment protection and expropriation.[24] In commercial policy with respect to services trade, Member States were left to intervene only if there was a risk that negotiations might seriously undermine the organization and financing of their health care systems. This 'emergency brake' type measure was included in the treaty as a compromise, as a result of the lobbying of some

[17] Lisbon Treaty, Art 3(1e) sets out common commercial policy to the exclusive competence of the EU. Lisbon Treaty, Art 2(1): 'When the Treaties confer on the Union exclusive competence in a specific area, only the Union may legislate and adopt legally binding acts, the Member States being able to do so themselves only if so empowered by the Union or for the implementation of Union acts.' The division of competence between the EU and Member States is set out in Art 2, paras 1–6, available at <http://eur-lex.europa.eu/LexUriServ/LexUriServ.do?uri=OJ:C:2008:115:0047:0199:EN:PDF> (accessed 6 February 2014).

[18] Treaty of Rome (1957), Arts 110 and 116 establish common commercial policy, although the transitional period postponed the full implementation of this by twelve years.

[19] European Court of Justice, 'Competence of the Community to conclude international agreements concerning services and the protection of intellectual property—Article 228 (6) of the EC Treaty', Opinion 1/94 (1994), available at <http://eurlex.europa.eu/smartapi/cgi/sga_doc?smartapi!celexplus!prod!CELEXnumdoc&numdoc=61994V0001&lg=en> (accessed 6 February 2014).

[20] Treaty of Nice [2001] OJ C 80/1, available at <http://eur-lex.europa.eu/en/treaties/dat/12001C/pdf/12001C_EN.pdf> (accessed 14 October 2012).

[21] Treaty of Nice (n 20).

[22] Public Health Article (157) in the Amsterdam Treaty (1997), explicitly excluded powers on health services.

[23] Treaty of Lisbon [2007] OJ C 306/01, available at <http://eur-lex.europa.eu/JOHtml.do?uri=OJ:C:2007:306:SOM:EN:HTML> (accessed 14 October 2012).

[24] See eg M. Bungenberg, 'Going Global? The Common Commercial Policy after Lisbon' in C. Herrman and J.-P. Terhechte (eds), *European Yearbook of International Economic Law 2010* (Berlin and Heidelberg: Springer-Verlag, 2010) 123.

Member States, including Finland, the UK, and Sweden.[25] While this so-called 'emergency brake' clause still remains, the actual powers are limited, as the issue can only be raised late in the process, when the final stages of negotiations are to be approved.

5. Health as a Challenge in the Context of Multilevel Governance

EU trade interests are formed through policy initiatives with Member States and proposals by stakeholders, which have an important role in influencing actual trade policy stances and what can be seen as the interests of European industries and exporters. Woll[26] has noted that 'EU officials openly admit that trade policy is made to benefit business and aims to support the competitive position of European firms in the world economy'. This is not only the case for European trade policies, but also for trade policies within Member States. Dür[27] has emphasized the importance of domestic firms in understanding Member States' behaviour on trade policy. While non-governmental organizations can take part in trade negotiations and have been invited to consultations, they tend to focus on matters that concern developing countries (for example access to medicines) and are generally much less prepared to have more specific influence on negotiation stances than industry representatives. Indeed, their power has been described by researchers as 'inclusion without influence'.[28]

It can be argued that it is in the interest of the European Union to ensure that the wishes of Member States are respected in the process of trade negotiations, yet Commission trade negotiators rarely have the level of understanding of the functioning, organization, and financing of the twenty-eight Member States' national health care systems that would be required in practice. For example, this has been reflected in the split between publicly and privately funded health services in negotiations in the CARIFORUM (2008) agreement,[29] which does not reflect the difficulty faced by many countries in separating publicly and privately funded health services. The CARIFORUM agreement also resulted in new commitments for further liberalization of privately funded services for health tourism, which is not without its risks, such as the spread of hospital infections.[30]

Insurance-based health care systems ('Bismarck') and national health systems ('Beveridge') have different regulatory needs. Furthermore, the context of service provision has changed in many countries, with an increasing role for the commercial sector in the provision of publicly funded services. In order to manage the trade policy stances of twenty-eight Member States it makes sense for the Commission to seek more uniform

[25] M. Koivusalo, 'Constitutional Issues in European Health Policy and Practice' in K. Tuori and S. Sankari, *The Many Constitutions of Europe* (Aldershot: Ashgate, 2010) 263.

[26] C. Woll, 'Who Scripts European Trade Policies? Business-Government Relations in the EU-Canada Partnership Negotiations' in K. Hubner (ed), *Europe, Canada and the Comprehensive Economic Partnership* (London: Routledge, 2011) 41.

[27] A. Dür, 'Bringing Economic Interests Back into the Study of EU Trade Policy-Making' (2008) 10(1) *British Journal of Politics and International Relations* 27.

[28] D. De Bièvre and A. Dür, 'Inclusion without Influence? Civil Society Involvement in European Trade Policy' (2007) 27(1) *Journal of Public Policy* 79.

[29] CARIFORUM, CARIFORUM-EC Economic Partnership Agreement (EPA) (2012), available at <http://ctrc.sice.oas.org/Trade/CARIFORUM-ECEPA/CARIFORUM-ECEPA_e.asp> (accessed 5 January 2012).

[30] See eg K.K. Kumarasamy, M.A. Toleman, T.R. Walsh et al, 'Emergence of a New Antibiotic Resistance Mechanism in India, Pakistan, and the UK: a Molecular, Biological and Epidemiological Study' (2010) 10(9) *Lancet Infectious Disease* 597.

commitments for the European Union, including for health services. However, challenges remain in terms of how and on what basis common EU stances are agreed. Trade negotiators are often inclined to consider further liberalization of services as part of the progressive aims of trade negotiations,[31] with the consequence that it remains for the Member States to make the case for the further consideration of health, excluding health services, or keeping both public and private health services outside commitments that may have implications for domestic regulatory measures.

While Member States remain important for trade policies, the Lisbon Treaty not only expanded European Commission competence in trade policy, but also enhanced the role of the European Parliament in the process. This has been in the background of the more recent developments, for example, with respect to the Anti-counterfeiting Trade Agreement (ACTA) in the European Parliament, where the INTA Committee responsible for trade recommended that the European Parliament should reject the ACTA,[32] which the European Parliament did on 4 July 2012.[33] The European Parliament role in trade negotiations has therefore become more relevant and it has, for example, assessed and guided EU trade and investment treaty negotiations in ways that emphasize the role of health. For example, in the June 2008 resolution on European Union-Canada trade relations, article 12 calls for the investment chapter to respect the right of both parties to regulate, in particular in the areas of national security, the environment, public health, workers' and consumers' rights, industrial policy, and cultural diversity, as well as calling on the Commission to exclude from the scope of investment agreements sensitive sectors such as culture, education, national defence, and public health.[34] In the guidance on the European Union-India Free Trade Agreement (EU-India FTA), which is also still under negotiation, the European Parliament emphasized the importance of access to medicines and rejected data exclusivity.[35]

The European Union also has broader health-related commitments relating to the Lisbon Treaty, emphasizing the need to ensure a high level of health protection in all policies as articulated in Article 168.[36] In addition, the Council for the European Union has agreed on conclusions on the social determinants of health,[37] global health,[38] health

31 This is in practice reflected in the language of trade agreements, where 'ambitious' and 'more progressive' automatically imply deeper liberalization and broader sectoral coverage in trade agreements.

32 European Parliament, 'Parliament should say NO to ACTA, says International Trade Committee', Press release of 22 June 2012, available at <http://www.europarl.europa.eu/news/en/news-room/content/20120614IPR46889/html/Parliament-should-say-NO-to-ACTA-says-International-Trade-Committee> (accessed 6 February 2014).

33 European Parliament, 'European Parliament Rejects ACTA', Press release of 4 July 2010, available at <http://www.europarl.europa.eu/news/en/news-room/content/20120703IPR48247/html/European-Parliament-rejects-ACTA> (accessed 6 February 2014).

34 European Parliament, 'EU-Canada trade relations', texts adopted 8 June 2011, available at <http://www.europarl.europa.eu/sides/getDoc.do?pubRef=-//EP//TEXT+TA+P7-TA-2011-0257+0+DOC+XML+V0//EN&language=EN> (accessed 10 February 2014).

35 European Parliament, 'Free trade agreement with India', Resolution of 11 May 2011, available at <http://www.europarl.europa.eu/sides/getDoc.do?type=TA&reference=P7-TA-2011-0224&language=EN> (accessed 10 October 2012).

36 Treaty of Lisbon (2007), Art 168(1) on public health states: 'A high level of human health protection shall be ensured in the definition and implementation of all Union policies and activities'.

37 Council of the European Union, 'Council conclusions on equity and Health in All Policies: Solidarity in Health', Brussels, 8 June 2010, available at <http://www.consilium.europa.eu/uedocs/cms_data/docs/pressdata/en/lsa/114994.pdf> (accessed 14 October 2012).

38 Council of the European Union, 'Council conclusions on the EU role in Global Health', Brussels, 10 May 2010, available at <http://www.consilium.europa.eu/uedocs/cms_Data/docs/pressdata/EN/foraff/114352.pdf> (accessed 26 October 2012).

in all policies,[39] and policy coherence for development,[40] which could have wider relevance for decision-making. These represent common stances approved by EU Member State ministries. However, a crucial gap in trade negotiations often remains in terms of Member States' understanding of the health policy implications of trade policy commitments, as well as how national health policies relate to EU Treaty provisions and the requirements of internal markets.

6. Negotiation Process of More Comprehensive Trade and Investment Agreements

The aim of the European Union-Canada Free Trade Agreement (CETA) is to be the most comprehensive free trade agreement negotiated so far, bringing on the one hand elements of NAFTA and regulatory cooperation into the European Union, as well as shifting commitments in the area of government procurement and services trade to sub-national level in Canada. The focus on regulation and regulatory cooperation is also part of the broader 'transatlantic' trade agenda between the European Union and the United States.[41] In addition, negotiations have started on a plurilateral agreement on services (Trade in Services Agreement TiSA), enabling around twenty countries to take the services liberalization agenda further, building on the structure and basis of the General Agreement on Trade in Services (GATS).[42]

These new negotiations in the area of trade and investment have three distinct features: first, that these are negotiated, in particular, between high-income countries; second, they include new negotiation approaches and seek the further inclusion of sectors; and third, they have a comprehensive agenda, including investments and non-tariff barriers to trade, as well as the liberalisation of services and government procurement.

While EU-US negotiations are to begin, the CETA negotiations have introduced NAFTA-type negotiation on the basis of negative listing as well as the inclusion of investment protection to the negotiations (see Box 32.1). In contrast to GATS, where governments needed to know what they wanted to include, governments now need to know both current and future regulatory needs so as to know what they do not want to include as part of trade agreements. In other words, governments need to anticipate their future regulatory needs before negotiations. While this makes life easier for service providers and the commercial sector, it makes it much harder for governments as it increases the risk of commitments Outside Own Priority Setting (OOPS).[43] In other words it increases the risk that governments make commitments that are not in their national public interest, and that have not been fully thought through or prioritized within the sector.

[39] Council of the European Union, 'Council conclusions on Health in All Policies', Brussels, 30 November and 1 December 2006, available at <http://www.consilium.europa.eu/ueDocs/cms_Data/docs/pressData/en/lsa/91929.pdf> (accessed 10 February 2014).

[40] Council of the European Union, 'Council conclusions on policy coherence for development', Brussels, 14 May 2012, available at <http://www.consilium.europa.eu/uedocs/cms_data/docs/pressdata/EN/foraff/130225.pdf> (accessed 26 October 2012).

[41] Framework for advancing transatlantic economic integration between the European Union and the United States of America, Washington, DC, 30 April 2007, 2, available at <http://trade.ec.europa.eu/doclib/docs/2007/may/tradoc_134654.pdf> (accessed 26 October 2012).

[42] European Commission, 'The plurilateral agreement on Services: at the starting gate', DF EXPO/B/PolDep/Note/2013_57.

[43] Koivusalo, Schrecker, and Labonte, 'Globalization and Policy Space' (n 6) 110.

Bilateral agreements have sought different ways of cutting through and expanding commitments made as part of the GATS agreement, for example by adding new elements and distinctions for the inclusion and exclusion of services, as bilateral agreements largely aim to be more 'ambitious' than multilateral agreements, which are considered to form the 'basic level' of commitments. The reliance on language for the public services exception in GATS has also become less 'trustworthy' as it is now broadly agreed that the GATS exclusion for government procurement may no longer cover health services in many EU Member States where health services are publicly funded, but privately provided.[44]

New FTAs, such as CETA, have also included other more comprehensive negotiation measures, which can be seen as a response to Member States' previous lack of willingness to make further commitments (see Box 32.1). These include inclusion of commitments on the basis of existing legislation and ratchet, which implies that a sector is automatically included as part of the agreement as legislation changes. This is often complemented by standstill, ie a requirement of not introducing new regulations that are not compatible with provisions of the agreement. This is particularly challenging in health care, as in many countries health care provision has become 'liberalized' only recently, with relatively little regulation in place initially. In these cases it is likely that service provision is relatively 'under-regulated', such that new regulations are likely to limit commercial interests and markets in ways that could be challenged in the context of trade and investment agreements.

In some cases, governments may allow market access, but wish to retain scope for sovereignty in the regulation of health services. For example, Finland has liberal legislation on market access, but has wanted to maintain sovereignty in regulating health services. In other words, while market access is not restricted in practice, the government wishes to maintain policy space for regulation within the sector, irrespective of its impacts on foreign investors, markets, or service providers, and has not made commitments for market access in GATS. In contrast, the EU-Mexico FTA[45] led to problems for the health sector, as all sectors were to be included on the basis of their existing legislation, and specific negotiations had to be held later to ensure that this would not be a precedent for national commitments for the health sector in future.

The negotiation of association agreements initially brought in negative listing to EU trade negotiations, as generally these were applied to agreements with accession countries, which it was assumed would be part of European Union in the near future. However, the focus on negative listing, government procurement, and investment has since become part of more free-trade focused agreements with countries in the broader European region, such as Ukraine, but also with other countries, such as Canada. As new agreements tend to build on earlier negotiations and stances, there is also a challenge in reverting from more extensive negative listing approaches to a more narrow positive listing in the context of the most-favoured-nation principle (MFN)[46]

44 On articulation of the legal issues, see eg M. Krajewski, 'Public Services and Trade Liberalisation: Mapping the Legal Framework' (2003) 6(2) *International Journal of Economic Law* 341.

45 This was the case, for example, with Finland, which has not bound health services in trade agreements, although there is market access to the sector. EU and Mexico FTA, 'Economic partnership, political coordination and cooperation agreement between the European Community and its Member States, on the one part, and the United Mexican States, on the other part' [2000] OJ L276/45.

46 In the context of the WTO, MFN status is based on a principle that if a country improves the benefits that it gives to one trading partner, it has to give the same 'best' treatment to all the other WTO members so that they all remain 'most-favoured', see <http://www.wto.org/english/thewto_e/whatis_e/tif_e/fact2_e.htm> (accessed 10 February 2014).

if negotiations on the plurilateral agreement on services are to build on GATS. Precedence is important in trade negotiations as earlier stances are in general assumed to imply a willingness to commit the sector in future agreements as well. This implies that changes in government policies or losing focus on one trade agreement can make it more difficult to keep a sector out in future trade agreements.

Furthermore, the current negotiation priorities, both with respect to the EU-Canada FTA (CETA) as well as other negotiations on multilateral trade in services, seem to be geared towards standstill clauses and automatic liberalization on the basis of existing legislation. This applies not only to new bilateral agreements, but potentially also to the new negotiations on plurilateral agreements on services.[47] The European Commission has been given a negotiation mandate by the Council of the European Union. This was not an entirely smooth process as the European Parliament resolution on the negotiations on agreement on Trade in Services (TiSA), of 4 July 2013, pointed out that the Council accepted a mandate for negotiations, without first seeking the view of the European Parliament or conducting an impact assessment.[48] The consequence of the new more 'comprehensive' negotiation tactics is that Member States may not realize that sectors they never consciously committed as part of a trade agreement could still become governed on the basis of that agreement.

7. Increasingly Complex and Changing Context for Regulatory Measures

One important effect of the new negotiation practices in services is the narrowing of exclusionary criteria for health services cross-border trade, investments liberalization,[49] and different aspects of commitments.[50] Government procurement is also negotiated separately, although, in practice, it applies to service provision and purchasing for many countries. At the same time some regulatory aspects, such as commitments with respect to domestic regulation or investment protection (see Box 32.2 at the end of this chapter), can be negotiated as general horizontal commitments, requiring again separate policies for exclusion.[51]

One important aspect of excluding health services from GATS commitments was that these could be excluded from requirements for domestic regulation, to ensure national policy space for regulation and cost-containment. Understanding what is included and how to exclude crucial, sensitive sectors, such as the health sector, has

47 This is also the case with the negotiations on the plurilateral services agreement, which in 2014 covered twenty-three WTO members (the EU is one member). Negotiations were initiated in 2013 after exploratory negotiations. General information on the background to TiSA and negotiations can be found at the TiSA website (of the Australian government) at <https://www.dfat.gov.au/trade/negotiations/services/trade-in-services-agreement.html> (accessed 6 February 2014).

48 European Parliament resolution of 4 July on the opening of negotiations on a plurilateral agreement on services, available at <http://www.europarl.europa.eu/sides/getDoc.do?pubRef=-//EP//TEXT+TA+P7-TA-2013-0325+0+DOC+XML+V0//EN> (accessed 6 February 2014).

49 Investment liberalization has implications for regulation, as performance requirements set limits to what can be required from foreign investors.

50 Agreements may include national treatment, most-favoured-nation treatment, and market access commitments—some of these can be negotiated as horizontal commitments, while others remain optional, thus limiting the scope of options more narrowly. Specific exceptions may also imply that non-compliant legislation may remain in place, while other aspects, such as domestic regulation requirements, would otherwise apply to the whole sector.

51 As at 1 February 2013, the negotiations were continuing, and while this aspect had been discussed, it is so far unclear whither, and to what extent, the final provisions will include this.

become more difficult in the context of a 'new mix' of commitments. In addition, subsidies and taxation can be excluded from negotiations or included as general clauses with a more limited focus or requirements.

Furthermore, as commitments for the European Union in the context of trade policies may consist of a 'European' part and a 'national' part, this can further increase the vulnerability, if the European part is changed without compensatory changes to the national commitments.

Trade agreements can include an emphasis on the right to regulate. This is, however, often included in the preamble to the agreement.[52] While important in interpreting the agreement, the preamble is unlikely to carry equal weight in comparison to specific provisions and articles. The right to regulate can also be assigned only to those measures that conform to the agreement. While trade and investment agreements have implications for the way in which governments regulate, they do not need to lead to less regulation and, indeed, many require further regulation to be implemented in support of liberalization and competition. However, these agreements are likely to be more important for regulatory measures which seek to limit or ban commercial practices or affect in particular market opportunities for foreign service providers. While the legislation may in principle treat foreign and domestic providers equally, it can still discriminate against foreign providers in practice and become subject to trade disputes. Furthermore, banning of practices could be considered as setting restrictions in terms of a quota of zero for market access to providers, as was articulated in the case concerning online gambling at the WTO.[53]

Trade and investment negotiations affect national regulation through four main processes. First, through the extent to which market access and national treatment has been given for the sector;[54] second, in terms of how domestic regulation has been defined and addressed in the agreement;[55] third, in terms of how investment liberalization, performance requirements,[56] and government procurement have been defined, addressed, and included in the agreement; and fourth, through the extent to which investment protection is covered and what kinds of specific provisions for expropriation[57] have been included.

The potential impact on regulation and public policies is perhaps most recognized for investment liberalization, investor-state arbitration, and the protection of investors, including from expropriation by government (see Box 32.2). While the argument for investment treaties and arbitration for developing countries remains at best limited in terms of their positive impact on foreign investment, these have also attracted criticism as enabling 'treaty shopping' by multinational industries. The benefits of and need for investment treaties become even more ambiguous with respect to investment agreements between two rich countries. On the other hand, substantial concerns have been raised concerning the impact of investment arbitration and agreements for national policy-making

52 See eg General Agreement on Trade in Services (GATS) 1995.

53 WTO, *United States—Measures affecting the cross-border supply of gambling and betting services* WT/DS285/AB/R7, April 2005 (Geneva, 2005).

54 This will affect market banning of services provision as well as having implications for domestic regulation provisions in agreements, such as GATS.

55 Luff, 'Regulation of Health Services' (n 10).

56 See eg UNCTAD, 'Foreign direct investment and performance requirements. New evidence from selected countries' (2003), available at <http://unctad.org/en/Docs/iteiia20037_en.pdf> (accessed 6 February 2014).

57 See UNCTAD, 'Expropriation. A Sequel' (2012), available at <http://unctad.org/en/Docs/unctaddiaeia2011d7_en.pdf> (accessed 6 February 2014).

and accountability. These focus, in particular, on the possibility for investors to challenge and claim compensation for negative impacts arising as a result of public policy decisions or those made in public courts through a specific channel for arbitration.

Investor-state arbitration is a major element of the agreements and is of concern, for example, when the definition of investment is broad, ie it also covers portfolio, speculative, and short-term investments, no distinction is made between regulatory takings and legitimate public regulation, no exceptions from arbitration have been made, and provisions in the agreement are vague with respect to fair and equitable treatment, thus increasing potential grounds for investor-state claims. The number of investor-state arbitration proceedings has increased in recent years.[58] We also do not know to what extent the existence of the mechanism has inhibited the introduction of further regulatory measures that could have been challenged under investor-state dispute settlement. The effects of this type of 'regulatory chill' are not easy to measure. Experiences from environmental regulatory measures and expropriation suggest that the regulatory impact is more relevant for policies which more directly ban, exclude, or limit particular markets.[59]

Investment agreements have also emerged in the context of public health regulation, where the most high profile and prominent case is that challenging Australia's legislation on the plain packaging of cigarettes.[60] While most cases relate to public health regulation, the use of investment arbitration is not unknown in health care matters. Hall[61] has reported on a case where an investment agreement has been raised with respect to Poland's and Slovakia's backing of a privatization programme in health care. Investment agreements have also been taken up in the context of pharmaceutical policies in Canada.[62] Many investment agreements, including those negotiated by the European Union, would include intellectual property as a form of property and investment that can be expropriated.

The impacts of trade and investment agreements upon regulatory aspects of health care entail, for example, the following functions of relevance to health systems:

(1) the regulation of health professionals and health services;
(2) health care financing—cost-containment measures, cross-subsidies, and financing;
(3) pharmaceuticals, medical technology, and medical devices;
(4) access to information crucial to regulation, cost-containment, and licensing;
(5) public health measures, health protection, and health promotion;
(6) research and the collection of and access to data for health; and
(7) the training and qualifications of health professionals.

58 UNCTAD, 'Recent developments in investor-state dispute settlement (ISDS), UNCTAD IIA Issues Note, 1 May 2013 (Geneva, 2013), available at <http://unctad.org/en/PublicationsLibrary/webdiaepcb2013d3_en.pdf> (accessed 10 February 2014).

59 S. Baughen, 'Expropriation and Environmental Regulation: the Lessons of NAFTA Chapter 11' (2006) 18 *Journal of Environmental Law* 207.

60 The Australian government has made documents concerning the case available at <http://www.ag.gov.au/internationalrelations/internationallaw/pages/tobaccoplainpackaging.aspx> (accessed 10 February 2014).

61 D. Hall, 'Challenges to Poland and Slovakia Health Policy Decisions: Use of Investment Treaties to Claim Compensation for Reversal of Privatisation/Liberalisation Policies' (Greenwich: PSIRU, 2010), available at <http://gala.gre.ac.uk/2744/1/PSIRU_Report_9828_-_2010-02-H-tradelaw.pdf , (accessed 6 February 2014).

62 See eg B. Baker, 'Corporate Power Unbound: Investor-State Arbitration of IP Monopolicies on Medicines—Eli Lilly and the TPP', PIJIP Research Paper Series 5/2013, available at <http://digitalcommons.wcl.american.edu/research/36/> (accessed 10 February 2014).

8. Democratic Accountability and Regulatory Policy Space

While comments can be made with respect to the democratic deficit of governance within the European Union in general,[63] the negotiation of trade agreements which restrain national policy space for regulation and the redistribution of resources within health systems is of particular relevance to the European Union. As trade agreements form a global legal framework of governance, it is important to focus on how policies seeking to serve European investors may in practice limit the regulatory powers of European governments, while empowering multinational industries to shop, bargain, and act as stakeholders at the European level.[64] Furthermore there are already reports of the use of investment treaties for arbitration in the case of reversal of privatization programmes related to health care within the European Union.[65]

As European Member States remain responsible for the financing of health care for their citizens, the existence of an avenue to international arbitration for investors creates an important governance gap.[66] Furthermore, as industries and investors are likely to seek to influence European trade policies, agreements can become costly to Member States, but in ways that are not recognized until after commitments have been made. In the case of CETA, for example, there are clear common interests for both the European Union and Canada to keep health systems out of the agreement, in order to maintain scope for regulatory policy space within their respective national health care systems; however, there are emerging concerns with respect to the extent to which negotiations preserved promises of safeguarding sufficient health care exemptions and citizen interests in practice.[67] The European Union has sought exemption clauses for publicly funded services, but it is unclear to what extent earlier exemptions and definitions will be of relevance in the context of CETA negotiations.[68] Furthermore, should

63 The discussion on democratic deficit has been related to two phenomena: (1) the shift of powers from Member States to the European Union, and (2) exercise of powers and accountability by EU institutions other than European Parliament on matters which were previously addressed by national parliaments. For discussion on democratic deficit, see eg K. Featherstone, 'Jean Monnet and the "democratic deficit" in the European Union' (1994) 32 *Journal of Common Market Studies* 149.

64 See eg R. van Os and R. Knottnerus, 'Dutch Bilateral Investment Treaties. A Gateway to "Treaty Shopping" for Multinational Companies' (2011), available at <http://www.s2bnetwork.org/fileadmin/dateien/downloads/Dutch_Bilateral_Investment_Treaties.pdf> (accessed 10 February 2014).

65 Hall, 'Challenges to Poland and Slovakia Health Policy Decisions' (n 61).

66 This has been discussed, for example, in the public statement on the international investment regime, see (n 16), and critical literature concerning democratic accountability, investment treaties and arbitration, see eg Schneiderman, *Constitutionalizing Economic Globalization* (n 16); and van Harten, *Investment Treaty Arbitration* (n 16).

67 While agreement in principle was achieved on 18 October, the technical negotiations have been continuing. In Canada particular health service concerns have focused on lack of effective health and government procurement exemptions. See eg McBane, 'CETA Threats to Public Health Care in Canada', 28 January 2014, Remarks to the House of Commons Standing Committee on International Trade, available at <http://healthcoalition.ca/wp-content/uploads/2014/01/CETA-SEN2014.pdf> (accessed 6 February 2014); see also Canadian Labour Congress, 'How well is public health protected from Canada-EU Free Trade', March 2012, available at <http://www.canadianlabour.ca/sites/default/files/pdfs/ceta-and-health-care-2012-03-14-en.pdf> (accessed 6 February 2014). In the European Union, one of the main concerns with respect to health care is investment protection and whether this is included as part of the agreement. CETA has also raised broader concerns across the Atlantic. See eg 'Transatlantic Statement by nongovernmental organizations in European Union and Canada, including European Federation of Public Service Unions (EPSU): Stop the Corporate Giveaway! A transatlantic plea for sanity in the EU–Canada CETA negotiations', November 2013, available at <http://www.epsu.org/a/10004> (accessed 6 February 2014).

68 See eg Krajewski (2011), available at <http://www.epsu.org/IMG/pdf/Public_services_in_the_CETA_FINAL_with_cover.pdf> (accessed 6 February 2014).

investment protection provisions become part of CETA, this would undermine exemptions made with respect to publicly funded health services in terms of subjecting these to investment protection measures.[69]

Another aspect contributing to this governance gap is the lack of adequate accountability mechanisms to highlight issues with respect to health systems at the European level. Sustainability impact assessments have been poor in assessing health implications, showing a bias in assuming that the commercialization of health service provision will improve choice and thus the position of consumers in health care markets.[70] The impact assessment statement on the potential EU and US agreement states that in terms of social impact: 'The greater the extent of liberalisation proposed in the various policy options, the greater are the estimated welfare gains.' It notes stakeholder concerns at the harmonization of environmental and public health standards on the basis of the lowest common denominator, but considers that it is 'reasonable to assume' that social impacts with respect to standards and rights related to job quality, social inclusion and the protection of particular groups, gender equality, equal treatment and opportunities, non-discrimination, access to and effects on social protection, health and educational systems, as well as public health and safety will be 'broadly neutral'.[71] While impact assessments may not have brought up crucial health-related issues, the negotiation mandate for the Trade in Services Agreement (TiSA) negotiation was proposed by the Commission and accepted by the Council without any impact assessment.[72]

In order to be accountable for health to their citizens, governments have to have capacities to regulate and intervene in both publicly funded and private health care markets. The framework for the liberalization of services, government procurement, and investments, as well as the focus on regulatory measures in the new trade agreements, reaches far deeper into national policy-making than has been the case for tariff reductions. As tariffs are already low between high-income countries, expected benefits are to be gained from changes in domestic regulation and government procurement. Well-functioning health systems are important not only for trade in health services, but also for

[69] In spite of political agreement, the actual text on CETA had not been published by February 2014. It is also unclear to what extent investment protection provisions still remain under negotiation. On 3 December 2013, the European Union provided a document in support of investment protection provisions in the EU-Canada agreement: European Commission, 'Investment provisions in the EU-Canada agreement', available at <http://trade.ec.europa.eu/doclib/docs/2013/november/tradoc_151918.pdf> (accessed 6 February 2014). A crucial issue is the extent to which (a) core problems of investment protection measures would still remain, and (b) what is stated reflects negotiated outcome and practice. The May 2013 draft of the investment chapter has been seen as a move backwards, see N. Bernasconi-Osterwalder, 'The Draft Investment Chapter of the Canada-EU Comprehensive Economic and Trade Agreement: A Step Backward for the EU and Canada' (2013) 3(4) *IISD Investment Treaty News* 10, available at <http://www.iisd.org/pdf/2013/iisd_itn_june_2013_en.pdf> (accessed 6 February 2014). The Commission responses have also been seen more as lobby documents, see TNI, 'EU note is a lobby document and not objective or complete' (2014), available at <http://www.tni.org/article/eus-note-lobby-document-and-not-objective-or-complete> (accessed 6 February 2014).

[70] EU-Canada FTA SIA, 'Comprehensive Economic and Trade Agreement between EU and Canada' (2011) Draft final report March 2011, available at <http://trade.ec.europa.eu/doclib/docs/2011/march/tradoc_147755.pdf> (accessed 10 October 2012).

[71] European Commission, 'Impact assessment report on the future EU-US trade relations', Commission Staff Working Document SWD (2013)68 final, 50.

[72] European Parliament, European Parliament resolution of 4 July 2013 on the opening of negotiations on a plurilateral agreement on services (Strasbourg, 2013), available at <http://www.europarl.europa.eu/sides/getDoc.do?type=TA&reference=P7-TA-2013-0325&language=EN&ring=B7-2013-0314> (accessed 6 February 2014).

trade more broadly. A precautionary approach to services and investment liberalization is warranted. Perhaps the broadest and most important issue with respect to democratic decision-making relates to where and how public policy decisions are made. If trade and investment agreements and arbitration shift decision-making from open and more publicly accountable forums, towards those operating under commercial policy arbitration practices, there is a danger that not only will foreign investors have their own route for seeking justice, but that decisions that should be made publicly (for public accountability reasons) will be shifted away from public scrutiny. This was amongst the core concerns for an international group of researchers who issued a statement on the matter, drawing attention, amongst other issues, to the ways in which awards issued by international arbitrators against states have, in numerous cases, incorporated over-expansive interpretations, which have prioritized the protection of the property and economic interests of transnational corporations over states' right to regulate and peoples' right to self-determination, constituting a major reorientation of the balance between investor protection and public regulation in international law.[73]

9. National Health Policies in the Context of Negotiation of International Treaties

It can be claimed that in many areas, governments have substantial common *health policy* interests across countries, not only in relation to maintaining regulatory policy space within health systems or pharmaceutical policies,[74] but also with respect to non-communicable diseases and addressing the social determinants of health. Alcohol, tobacco, and occupational health exposures and legislation have all been dealt with under WTO dispute settlements. How, and on what basis, these are dealt with is crucially dependent on where, and from which perspective, discussions are held.

While carving out health services from the investment and trade agenda or negotiating a global framework agreement on policy space for health could provide a long-term solution, this broader policy discussion is unlikely in the context of the prevailing view of trade as a means to lower costs and solve personnel issues in health services. This view has been reflected, for example, in the emphasis of the benefits to rich countries from trade in health services and claims that, in the United States, health insurance inhibits trade in health services.[75] It is also likely that developing countries and emerging economies in the South will increase the pressure to liberalize health services and trade in health professionals, promoting trade in health services as part of their commercial policies and development strategy.

There are also proposals to bring health considerations into trade agreements. The European Union has utilized so-called 'social clauses' and references to the Doha Declaration as a means to include provisions that safeguard public health as part of bilateral agreements. However, this will not help to maintain scope for cost-containment, as ensuring the financial sustainability of health systems is not a matter of public health and safety, yet it is often the reason why governments restrict or limit

[73] G. van Harten and fifty-two signatories, 'Public Statement on the International Investment Regime', 31 August 2010, available at <http://www.osgoode.yorku.ca/public-statement/documents/Public%20Statement%20%28June%202011%29.pdf> (accessed 29 October 2012).

[74] M.T. Koivusalo, 'Common Health Policy Interests and the Shaping of Global Pharmaceutical Policies' (2010) 24 *Ethics and International Affairs* 395.

[75] A. Mattoo and R. Rathindran, 'How Health Insurance Inhibits Trade in Health Care Services' (2006) 25(2) *Health Affairs* 358.

market opportunities, for example, in restricting patient choice or giving special or exclusive rights to hospitals.[76] The EU approach to social clauses has also attracted criticism for not reaching far enough, remaining aspirational and not being enforceable, and lacking engagement with relevant civil society actors.[77] Furthermore, in the context of the investment agreement negotiated between the European Union and Canada, interest in securing the right to regulate through specific provisions has not been at the core of the EU agenda for most negotiations.[78] While there is scope for the incorporation of binding social provisions or provisions on corporate social responsibility commitments into trade agreements,[79] there is also a danger that voluntary and non-binding aspirational provisions 'encouraging' corporate social responsibility are used as if these could provide a counter-weight to the binding provisions on protection of investments.

EU stances have traditionally been restrictive with respect to global prospects for trade in health services and the protection of statutory social security—but as EU trade policies are evolving, this may not be the case in future. It is also clear that health tourism and the mobility of health professionals will be a part of future discussions as a result of pressures from low and middle-income countries. It was not necessarily anticipated that the liberalization of privately funded services and enabling of health tourism would have negative repercussions on publicly funded services. However, an example of the unexpected costs of trade in health services has emerged for health tourism in the form of hospital bacteria with high resistance to antibiotics in patients who have had operations in another country.[80] The potential costs to a country's health system of such infections spreading is not taken into account in the promotion of health tourism, although from a health policy point of view such risks could have been anticipated. It is also likely that the probability of outbreaks due to contaminated goods—most recently the EHEC outbreak in Germany resulting from imported fenugreek seeds[81]—will be affected by trade negotiations and resulting changes in scope and capacities of oversight and regulation by national authorities.

10. Conclusions

Legitimizing action to maintain policy space for health is a national, European, and global challenge, as the implications of trade agreements for the way in which governments can regulate become more evident. The challenge requires that health concerns and, in particular, common health and public policy interests across countries are taken

76 David Luff has discussed health care-related challenges in relation to domestic regulation, Luff, 'Regulation of Health Services' (n 10).

77 C. Scherrer, T. Greven, A. Leopold, and E. Molinari, 'An Analysis of the Relative Effectiveness of Social and Environmental Norms in Free Trade Agreements', EXPO/B/INTA/2008/62, Policy Department for External Policies (Brussels, 2009).

78 This is a situation which may change in the final agreement and a concern that has become reflected in a Commission document on investment protection in CETA negotiations, emphasizing the right to regulate. European Commission, 'Investment provisions in the EU-Canda free trade agreement' 3 December 2013, available at <http://trade.ec.europa.eu/doclib/docs/2013/november/tradoc_151918.pdf> accessed 6 February 2014).

79 UNEP, 'Corporate Social Responsibility and Regional Trade and Investment Agreements' (Geneva, 2011), available at <http://www.unep.ch/etb/publications/CSR%20publication/UNEP_Corporate%20Social%20Responsibility.pdf> (accessed 26 July 2012).

80 Kumarasamy, Toleman, Walsh et al, 'Emergence of a New Antibiotic Resistance' (n 30).

81 European Food Safety Authority, 'Tracing Seeds, in Particular Fenugreek (Trigonella Foenum-Graceum) Seeds, in Relation to the Shiga Toxin Producing E.Coli (STEC) O104:H2011 Outbreaks in Germany and France' (Parma, 2011), available at <http://www.efsa.europa.eu/en/supporting/doc/176e.pdf> (accessed 10 October 2012).

into account, not only as part of the negotiation of trade agreements, but also in terms of how these are negotiated. The use of more complex and extensive negotiation approaches makes it harder for governments to avoid unintended restrictions to national policy space.

A key prerequisite is the recognition that the negotiation of trade agreements affects the regulatory powers and policy space of national and local governments. This requires the recognition of potential conflicts of interest between the promotion of public interests and health policy priorities and those of commercial policy and trade. Furthermore, it is unlikely that action can be taken at national level only.[82] In practice, the changing context of trade negotiations would imply the need to strengthen the global legal framework for health as well as ensuring that negotiations held in other sectors recognize that the regulatory policy space for health is necessary at national, regional,[83] and global level. This requires not only a focus on the importance of health, but also scrutiny of the health policy-related content of commercial and trade policies.

Progress in this field will require new focus and skills in Ministries of Health, which need to recognize the implications of trade negotiations for the public administration burden of work, responsibilities, and human and financial resources. Furthermore, this awareness needs to result in global measures and the recognition of the scope and potential for global policy measures to secure health policy priorities. Otherwise there is a danger that common interests for health will be undermined by the priorities of multinational industries or strong national interest groups and proponents in favour of limiting the scope for national regulation and policy space for health.

Box 32.1 Listing and negotiation practices

Positive listing

- Used in negotiations of the General Agreement on Trade in Services (GATS), where governments actively opt-in sectors which they would like to include as part of trade agreements.
- Positive listing can include negative elements under broader service sectors, which may have been included as whole (for example other recreational services includes more narrow sub-sectors, such as gambling).[84]
- Positive listing makes it easier to leave sectors, such as health or social services, outside trade agreements.

Negative listing

- Used in the North American Free Trade Agreement (NAFTA). In this type of listing governments list in annexes services where legislation does not conform with treaty

(*Continued*)

[82] For clarity this could also imply federal, state, county, or local government-level decisions in some countries, depending on the context and focus of policy measures.

[83] This would apply also to the European Union, and as a level of governance would be comparable to cooperation, agreements, and policies decided and implemented between a more limited number of countries within or across regions.

[84] This was the situation in the WTO dispute settlement case between the United States and Antigua on Online Gambling: WTO. *United States—Measures affecting the cross-border supply of gambling and betting services* WT/DS285/AB/R7 April 2005.

Box 32.1 (Continued)

provisions as well as services for which they wish to reserve scope for any future measures or which they wish to keep wholly outside negotiations.

- In this type of listing, governments need to know what they would like to exclude and what their future regulatory needs are within a sector. It also makes it harder to exclude sectors, as the list of excluded services is often kept limited.

Negotiation choices to enhance negotiations

- *Horizontal commitments* cover more or less all sectors or services and do not require specific decisions to be made with respect to each sector or service unless exceptions within horizontal commitments can be made.
- *Stand-still requirements* imply that sectors are bound on the basis of existing legislation at the point of negotiation of the treaty within a sector, thus allowing existing (discriminatory) regulations, but not making new discriminatory regulations or making existing regulation tighter (more discriminatory). *Ratchet mechanisms* automatically include sectors on the basis of their legislation so that if governments change legislation, this may imply that a sector is included without the need for further negotiation.

Box 32.2 Investment liberalization and protection

Investment treaties as part of free trade agreements have in principle two functions: investment liberalization and investment protection. Investment liberalization commitments have relevance for the ownership of services as well as for contractual markets, as the return to public services from publicly-funded contractual markets becomes more difficult, both in terms of being against treaty commitments as well as in relation to potential claims that can be raised on the basis of arbitration and expropriation.

Investment liberalization

Investment liberalization includes both measures related to rights to establishment and foreign ownership within a country as well as treatment of investments in comparison to those of national investors.[85] Treatment of investors also includes additional requirements, such as performance requirements, which set limits to the requirements that governments can impose on foreign investors, for example in terms of employment of local people, technology transfer, or utilizing local sub-contractors or content in services or products.[86]

Investment protection

Perhaps the most controversial provision in investment treaties is related to investment protection and expropriation. Investment is usually defined broadly and includes intellectual

(Continued)

[85] Investment agreements can also include provisions in relation to the treatment of investors as well as those from the most favoured nation (MFN) on the basis of other bilateral or multilateral investment treaties.

[86] Performance requirements can differ between bilateral agreements. See eg the UNCTAD report on 'Foreign Direct Investment and Performance Requirements: New Evidence from Selected Countries' (New York and Geneva: United Nations, 2003), available at <http://unctad.org/en/docs/iteiia20037_en.pdf> (accessed 10 February 2014).

Box 32.2 (Continued)

property. Provisions which have formed a basis for claims in investment treaties have related to 'fair and equitable treatment', 'legitimate expectations of investor', and standards of 'full protection and security'.[87]

Expropriation

Expropriation articles in investment treaties allow foreign investors to claim compensation from governments through arbitration in relation to government measures which have resulted in direct or indirect expropriation. Indirect expropriation can include, for example, non-discriminatory public regulatory measures which affect investments made. Expropriation is best known in the context of Chapter 11 of NAFTA. The OECD (2004) legal analysis of expropriation recognizes concerns that relate to national regulatory policy space and 'to what extent a government may affect the value of property by regulation, either general in nature or by specific actions in the context of general regulations, for a legitimate public purpose without effecting a "taking" and having to compensate for this act'.[88]

Arbitration and investor-state dispute settlement (ISDS)

Investment treaties allow foreign investors to challenge measures made by national or local governments and make compensatory claims for losses. The additional channel for arbitration places foreign investors in a better position than national investors, which do not have this possibility. Arbitration through investment treaties is more associated with commercial arbitration with an often faster, but less open and accountable context for decision-making.[89] Furthermore, it can be used to challenge the decisions of public courts and democratically made policy decisions.

87 See eg UNCTAD, 'Investor-State Disputes Arising from Investment Treaties: A Review' (New York and Geneva: United Nations, 2005), available at <http://unctad.org/en/docs/iteiit20054_en.pdf> (accessed 10 February 2014).

88 OECD, '"Indirect Expropriation" and the "Right To Regulate" in International Investment Law', 2004/4 (Paris, 2004) 2.

89 On accountability and democratic governance, see Schneiderman, *Constitutionalizing Economic Globalization* (n 16); van Harten, *Investment Treaty Arbitration* (n 16). The transparency problems in the area have been reflected in the UNGA resolution and revision of UNCITRAL arbitration rules as these relate to transparency, see eg UNCITRAL, 'UNCITRAL rules on transparency in Treaty-based Investor-State Arbitration' (Vienna, 2014), available at <http://www.uncitral.org/pdf/english/texts/arbitration/rules-on-transparency/Rules-on-Transparency-E.pdf> (accessed 10 February 2014).

33

An Agenda for Normative Policy Analysis in the Study of Global Health Governance

*Benjamin Mason Meier**

While international health law was conceived as a means to protect independent state interests against global health threats, this paradigm of state power is increasingly being challenged by a new normative reality—with global health policy pursued as a means to realize a more just world. In seeking justice in an increasingly globalized world, norms are progressively framing global health governance. These norms for justice, collective understandings of 'right' and 'wrong', have become inherent in global health policy. Looking beyond calculations of state power interests in international health law, legal scholars must not ignore the expanding influence of normative frameworks for justice in global health policy.

Building from a long history of scholarship on international law as the basis of global norms, the past four decades have seen an unprecedented expansion of activity beyond legal norms, looking to policy in framing a normative agenda for justice in global health governance. In addressing global health (including the approaches, technologies, and systems that bear on the world's most pressing public health needs),[1] this global health governance describes the actors and norms that define global health policy in an increasingly globalized world.[2] With international legal scholars taking renewed interest in global health policy—driven by a recent rise of global health institutions and unprecedented levels of financial support—norms are proving increasingly relevant, if understudied, in framing global health governance.[3] As normative policy analysis has expanded in domestic health policy research,[4] a corresponding theoretical framework is necessary in global health policy, contributing to an understanding of how global health governance is both framing norms and being framed by norms.[5] Applied to global health governance, it will be necessary to understand the norms that bind together state and non-state actors (including non-governmental organizations, transnational corporations, and philanthropic groups) outside of the formal mechanisms of international

* The author is grateful to Scott Burris and Maria Stuttaford for their thoughtful comments on previous drafts of this chapter and to Kristen Brugh and Caitlin Pardue for their research assistance on normative policy analysis in global health governance.

1 L. Fried et al, 'Global Health is Public Health' (2010) 375 *Lancet* 535.

2 K. Buse, W. Hein, and N. Drager (eds), *Making Sense of Global Health Governance: A Policy Perspective* (New York: Palgrave Macmillan, 2009).

3 N.A. Szlezák et al, 'The Global Health System: Actors, Norms, and Expectations in Transition' (2010) 7 *PLoS Medicine*.

4 N. Kenny and M. Giacomini, 'Wanted: A New Ethics Field for Health Policy Analysis' (2005) 13(4) *Health Care Analysis* 247.

5 N. Kenny and C. Joffres, 'An Ethical Analysis of International Health Priority-Setting' (2008) 16 *Health Care Analysis* 145.

law. For international legal analysis to conceptualize this age of norms, it will be necessary to develop a research agenda on global health policy.

This chapter analyzes the expanding breadth of norms for justice in global health policy, advocating legal research on the impact of norms and outlining a research base for normative policy analysis in global health. Looking to international relations to conceptualize a theoretical foundation for this research, section 1 describes the realist foundations of international health law as a basis for communicable disease control and raises the constructivist challenge to this realist framework as a way of describing the growing influence of norms in global health. Section 2 chronicles the origins and evolution of the current 'age of norms', examining the principal norms for justice that now structure global health governance and outlining a research base for the study of norms in global health. With these norms supporting a focus on underlying determinants of health in a fragmented global health landscape, shifting legal analysis from international health law to global health policy, section 3 assesses the implications of normative policy analysis to the study of global health governance. This chapter concludes that there is a pressing imperative for international legal study to clarify the influence of norms for justice on global efforts to promote health. As these underlying norms determine both the reasoning by which policymakers seek justice in global health and the goals sought through policy advancement—answering 'why' there is a need for global health policy and 'what' it seeks to achieve—such normative policy analysis can seek to understand the process by which norms for justice are translated into policy for global health.

1. Conceptualizing Norms through Constructivist Theory

The application of normative policy analysis as a means of understanding changes in global health governance reflects a broader debate in international relations theory between realism and constructivism. Employing power against pandemic, the realist paradigm posits that states develop international law to serve national interests, controlling the spread of communicable disease through international legal cooperation.[6] Yet the realist paradigm, which for a century offered the predominant explanation of international affairs through state power, has been increasingly challenged by the growing influence of norms.[7] Viewing norms as both constraining and enabling action in global health—'constructing' the interests of state and non-state actors—the constructivist paradigm seeks to conceptualize the interactions between interests and institutions in the contemporary global system.[8] While power relations will continue to hold sway in global health governance, and often predominate in the international response to specific health threats threats, it is necessary to examine where the realist paradigm fails to describe global efforts to realize a more just world and how constructivist theory can conceptualize global health policy.

Grounded in realist theory, international relations scholars have long relied upon conceptualizations of power to elucidate state actions in international affairs, asserting that the paramount goal of the sovereign state is the pursuit of power.[9] Under this 'statist'

6 D.P. Fidler, 'The Globalization of Public Health: The First 100 Years of International Health Diplomacy' (2001) 79 *Bulletin of the World Health Organization* 842.

7 J. Checkel, 'The Constructivist Turn in International Relations Theory' (1998) 50 *World Politics* 324; A. Wendt, 'Anarchy Is What States Make of It: The Social Construction of Power Politics' (1992) 46 *International Organization* 391.

8 S.E. Davies, *Global Politics of Health* (Cambridge: Polity Press, 2010).

9 K.N. Waltz, *Theory of International Politics* (Reading, MA: Addison Wesley, 1979).

perspective, state power in international relations—as defined in political, military, and/or economic terms[10]—has framed the manner in which states set foreign policy in the pursuit of increased national security and economic advantage.[11] Harnessing this state power as a means to international cooperation, realism theorizes that international institutions exist only to the extent that they benefit powerful states.[12] Within the field of international relations, the realist paradigm has placed emphasis on the materialist premise that power relations are formed and maintained as states use material resources to compel other states to act in specified ways, looking to a 'rational actor' model to understand how powerful actors dominate the international negotiating process to meet their own self-interested objectives.[13] Applied to international health, realist scholarship has sought to explain the international response to those infectious diseases that threatened the trading interests of powerful states and, through mutual self-interest among the trading powers, led to the birth of international institutions to harmonize national regulations and compel international cooperation. While realist theory could conceptualize this cooperative international focus on infectious disease control,[14] with states largely focusing on specific transboundary disease threats that pose an existential threat to national material interests,[15] the singular application of realist theory appears increasingly incommensurate to contemporary health threats and global health governance.[16]

The ability of realist theory to conceptualize global efforts has been diminished by the expanding influence of norms for justice in global institutions. With globalization leading to a re-engagement with underlying economic, political, and social determinants of health, state power interests do not completely encompass this revitalized engagement with global health, as policy actors have operationalized norms as a basis to address those underlying determinants of health that do not impact state interests.[17] Where this concern for justice in global health does not comport with the statist model of the realist paradigm, international relations scholars have been constrained to addressing health issues in the limited contexts of epidemic control for select diseases.[18] Although states have continued at times to focus on disease prevention and health promotion as a means to economic development or national security,[19] these countervailing forces now appear in retrospect to have been isolated realist examples on a constructivist

[10] K. Lee, 'A Neo-Gramscian Approach to International Organization: an Expanded Analysis of Current Reforms to UN Development Activities' in J. MacMillan and A. Linklater (eds), *Boundaries in Question: New Directions in International Relations* (London: Pinter, 1995) 144.

[11] S. Krasner, 'State Power and the Structure of International Trade' (1976) 28 *World Politics* 317.

[12] S. Mercado, 'Towards a New Understanding of International Trade Policies: Ideas, Institutions and the Political Economy of Foreign Economic Policy' in J. MacMillan and A. Linklater (eds), *Boundaries in Question: New Directions in International Relations* (London: Pinter, 1995) 107.

[13] M. Barnett and R. Duvall, 'Power in International Politics' (2005) 59 *International Organization* 39; A. Wendt, *Social Theory of International Politics* (Cambridge: CUP, 1999).

[14] D.P. Fidler, *International Law and Infectious Diseases* (Oxford: Clarendon Press, 1999).

[15] D.P. Fidler, 'Caught Between Paradise and Power: Public Health, Pathogenic Threats, and the Axis of Illness' (2004) 35 *McGeorge Law Review* 45; E.A. Prescott, 'The Politics of Disease: Governance and Emerging Infections' (2007) 1 *Global Health Governance* 1; A. Price-Smith, *Contagion and Chaos* (Cambridge, MA: MIT Press, 2009).

[16] J. Youde, *Global Health Governance* (London: Polity Press, 2012); J.P. Ruger, *Global Health Justice and Governance* (Oxford: OUP, forthcoming).

[17] Davies, *Global Politics of Health* (n 8); J. Shiffman, 'Issue Attention in Global Health: The Case of Newborn Survival' (2010) 375 *Lancet* 2045.

[18] C. Thomas, 'On the Health of International Relations and the International Relations of Health' (1989) 15 *Review of International Studies* 273.

[19] G.H. Brundtland, 'Global Health and International Security' (2003) 9 *Global Governance* 419.

trajectory.[20] Through the collapse of traditional institutions for state cooperation and the creation of new institutions in a fragmented landscape for global health governance, norms have come to frame a more expansive vision of justice in global health.[21] Such global health efforts are no longer confined either to international legal frameworks or to the health sector, establishing a normative basis for a just world in a multilevel and multi-sectoral global health policy landscape.

Norms are collective understandings that have the capacity to shift the behaviors of a wider array of actors in global health.[22] These norms include certain shared ideas, values, attitudes, identities, and expectations that guide policymakers in choosing the most appropriate policy to meet the ideals of the global community.[23] Standardizing policymaking behavior, norms act by constraining or enabling the range of acceptable choices and actions, with normative theory categorizing norms as either:

- regulative norms, serving to order and constrain behavior;
- constitutive norms that create new options for available action; or
- evaluative or prescriptive norms, which provide a sense of 'oughtness' to shared ideas.[24]

Whereas the realist perspective attributes power to 'brute material forces', the constructivist paradigm holds that power is constituted by norms.[25] Thus, policy is both influenced by norms and influential in the development of norms, with norms internalized in policy outcomes and policymaking processes.[26]

In the same way that international relations theory employed realism to discuss power, it now looks to constructivism to describe norms. Situating ideas and discourse within a particular context, constructivism examines how the interests of actors are 'constructed', emphasizing the process of interaction among state and non-state actors such that interests are endogenous to the interactions between actors.[27] From this inherent endogeneity, creating a network of shared ideas, a model of governance emerges in which norms guide rule-governed, as opposed to power-driven, actions.[28] The constructivist paradigm is primarily focused on the formative role of these *ideational factors*, the most important of which 'are widely shared or "intersubjective" beliefs, which are not reducible to individuals, and these shared beliefs construct the

20 J. Youde, 'Enter the Fourth Horseman: Health Security and International Relations Theory' (2005) 6 *Whitehead Journal of Diplomacy and International Relations* 193.

21 B.M. Meier, 'Global Health Takes a Normative Turn: The Expanding Purview of International Health Law and Global Health Policy to Meet the Public Health Challenges of the 21st Century' in G.Z. Capaldo (ed), *The Global Community: Yearbook of International Law and Jurisprudence 2011* (Oxford: OUP, 2012).

22 J.T. Checkel, 'The Constructivist Turn in International Relations Theory' (1998) 50 *World Politics* 324; A. Harmer, 'Understanding Change in Global Health Policy: Ideas, Discourse and Networks' (2011) 6(7) *Global Public Health* 703.

23 J. Campbell, 'Ideas, Politics, and Public Policy' (2002) 28 *Annual Review of Sociology* 21.

24 M. Finnemore and K. Sikkink, 'International Norm Dynamics and Political Change' (1998) 52 *International Organization* 887.

25 Wendt, *Social Theory of International Politics* (n 13).

26 J. Goldstein and R. Keohane, 'Ideas and Foreign Policy: An Analytical Framework' in J. Goldstein and R. Keohane (eds), *Ideas and Foreign Policy: Beliefs, Institutions, and Political Change* (Ithaca, NY: Cornell University Press, 1993) 3.

27 J.T. Checkel, 'The Constructivist Turn in International Relations Theory' (1998) 50 *World Politics* 324.

28 Wendt, *Social Theory of International Politics* (n 13).

interests and identities of purposive actors'.[29] Thus, constructivist theory maintains that collective understandings of appropriate behavior, ie norms, have the ability to shape policy development and policymaker actions independent of structural constraints, such that international law and global governance are framed by ideas and values that exist apart from the distribution of state power.

Constructivism—both as a theoretical paradigm and as an empirical approach—considers these ideational factors as a basis for law and policy and describes the process through which ideas become 'socially causative', prompting action to realize the norm.[30] In this process of realizing norms, such ideational discourses evolve across time and space, emerging in particular communities, circulating domestically and internationally through the dissemination of ideas (stimulated in large part through globalized communications networks), and shaping global institutions that are continuously transformed by normative shifts. This 'normative life cycle' begins with *norm emergence* (where norm leaders, or 'norm entrepreneurs', work to persuade a critical mass to embrace a new norm), gains momentum through *norm cascade* (where states come to accept and maintain the norm), and becomes part of the social and political structure through *norm internalization* (where the norm becomes commonplace, is no longer an issue of public contention, and can achieve regulative status).[31] From this *norm internalization*, law and policy have come to reflect the negotiated codification of norms, advancing collective global ideas, discourses, and goals through governance institutions. Culminating in global governance, global norms may then 'trickle down' through incorporation in national law and practice, creating a feedback loop by which norms spread throughout the world.

Previous normative scholarship has looked to constructivism as a way of examining norms in international relations. As realist theory failed to explain the rise of new forms of governance following the Cold War, with the end of 'bipolar' international power struggles opening a space for collective global cooperation,[32] scholars sought to define the role of norms through constructivist international relations theory.[33] In an interconnected and rapidly globalizing world, constructivism (sometimes referred to as a 'globalist approach' to international relations) allowed scholars to examine changes in normative structures and analyze ideational shifts in international law and global policy.[34] Applied to global health, constructivist scholarship has examined, *inter alia*, how the World Health Organization (WHO) has diverged from state preferences in shaping global health policy[35] and how public-private partnerships are seeking to create new institutional mechanisms of global health governance.[36] From these specific examples, it is necessary to examine the contemporary role of constructivism as a theoretical paradigm for analyzing justice in global health policy—looking beyond

29 M. Finnemore and K. Sikkink, 'Taking Stock: The Constructivist Research Program in International Relations and Comparative Politics' (2001) 4 *Annual Review of Political Science* 393.

30 J.G. Ruggie, 'What Makes the World Hang Together? Neo-Utilitarianism and the Social Constructivist Challenge' (1998) 52(4) *International Organization* 855.

31 Finnemore and Sikkink, 'International Norm Dynamics' (n 24).

32 Wendt, *Social Theory of International Politics* (n 13).

33 Ruggie, 'What Makes the World Hang Together?' (n 30).

34 Checkel, 'The Constructivist Turn' (n 27).

35 N. Chorev, *The World Health Organization Between North and South* (Ithaca, NY: Cornell University Press, 2012).

36 A. Harmer, 'Understanding Change in Global Health Policy: Ideas, Discourse and Networks' (2011) 6 *Global Public Health* 703.

national governments and international organizations to encompass the non-state actors that are increasingly assuming authority in the global health landscape.

This chapter seeks to develop both a theoretical and methodological agenda for normative policy analysis in global health, outlining an empirical research program that encompasses both state and non-state actors in global health governance. Where ethicists have begun to consider the role of bioethics norms in creating a moral imperative for global health governance,[37] it is necessary to explore the implications of norms for justice in this constructivist turn in global health. Under a societal approach to constructivism, this study examines 'regulative global norms' for justice—norms ordering the behavior of global health actors, whether termed human rights, social justice, or health equity[38]—viewing the development of global health governance as indicative of an evolving set of global norms.[39] In this sense, global health policy reflects the negotiated codification of global norms already in existence, and reifies those norms until they are revised through normative evolution and subsequent policy advancements.[40] During this iterative process of normative change, both state and non-state actors harmonize individual norms (negotiating potentially conflicting norms) and advance these collective ideational goals in global health governance, with these global norms then incorporated in national law and internalized in public health practice.[41] It is only once we understand the role of these normative frameworks in global health that practitioners can develop effective policies to realize these norms, and researchers can analyze the impact of norms on global health governance.

2. The Age of Norms

As a basis for normative policy analysis, global health actors are moving beyond the communicable disease control regimes long prominent in international health law and working with normative frameworks to set an expansive agenda for disease prevention and health promotion. Beginning as early as the 1970s, there arose a renewed influence of norms in global health—focusing on underlying determinants of health in the developing world, raising awareness through global efforts to programmatize primary health care, taking hold in response to the horrors of a deepening HIV/AIDS pandemic, and enduring as a feature of the public health response to the insalubrious ramifications of globalization.[42] Despite realist justification for a brief focus on bioterrorism at the turn of the century,[43] the realist paradigm could not completely account for the shift from 'state security' to 'human security' that has come

37 S.R. Benatar, A.S. Daar, and P.A. Singer, 'Global Health Ethics: The Rationale for Mutual Caring' (2003) 79 *International Affairs* 107.

38 M. Finnemore, 'Are Legal Norms Distinctive' (1999) 32 *NYU Journal of International Law and Politics* 699.

39 Ruggie, 'What Makes the World Hang Together?' (n 30).

40 P. Alston, 'Conjuring Up New Human Rights: A Proposal for Quality Control' (1984) 78 *American Journal of International Law* 607.

41 C.O. Pannenborg, *A New International Health Order* (New York: Springer, 1979); M. Finnemore and K. Sikkink, 'International Norm Dynamics and Political Change' (1998) 52 *International Organization* 887.

42 Meier, 'Global Health Takes a Normative Turn' (n 21).

43 D.P. Fidler, 'Public Health and National Security in the Global Age: Infectious Diseases, Bioterrorism, and Realpolitik' (2003) 35 *George Washington International Law Review* 787; S.E. Davies, 'Securitizing Infectious Disease' (2008) 84 *International Affairs* 295.

to define the norms of a more expansive global health policy.[44] Breaking from the state-centric focus of the realist paradigm, refocusing global health away from select infectious diseases and toward those determinants of health that affect premature morbidity and mortality in the least developed countries, the constructivist paradigm is increasingly seen to explain the motivations and behaviors of state and non-state actors, with global governance institutions increasingly demonstrating the significance of various overlapping norms for justice in global health.[45] This new reality in global health governance encompasses norms for justice through an ideational focus on, among other normative frameworks, human rights, social justice, and health equity. While these interacting frameworks serve as examples of the transformational ideas now framing global health, such 'ontological frames'[46] highlight the confluence of norms as a basis for global solidarity in health. In this age of norms, during which norms have become a force for justice in global health, constructivism becomes a necessary theoretical paradigm for understanding the meaning, evolution, and impact of normative frameworks in global health governance.

2.1 Human rights

With states developing human rights under international law as a tool for public health, human rights stand as a 'civilizational standard'[47] and universally accepted normative framework to advance justice in global health.[48] Framing health disparities as 'rights violations', states have provided international standards by which to facilitate legal accountability for the progressive realization of human dignity.[49] In building from the expansive legal standards of the WHO Constitution and evolving through the United Nations' international legal institutions,[50] human rights law has sought to identify individual rights-holders and their entitlements and corresponding duty-bearers and their obligations,[51] empowering individuals to seek legal accountability for health efforts rather than serving as passive recipients of government benevolence.[52]

Codified seminally in the 1966 International Covenant on Economic, Social and Cultural Rights (ICESCR)—providing for 'the right of everyone to the enjoyment of the highest attainable standard of physical and mental health'[53]—the human right to

44 L. Axworthy, 'Human Security and Global Governance: Putting People First' (2001) 7 *Global Governance* 19; H. Feldbaum et al, 'Global Health and National Security: The Need for Critical Engagement' (2006) 22 *Medicine, Conflict and Survival* 192.

45 C. McInnes and K. Lee, *Global Health and International Relations* (Cambridge: Polity Press, 2012).

46 G.W. Brown, 'Distributing Who Gets What and Why: Four Normative Approaches to Global Health' (2012) 3 *Global Policy* 292.

47 J. Donnelly, 'Human Rights: A New Standard of Civilisation?' (1998) 74 *International Relations* 1.

48 S. Gruskin, 'Is There a Government in the Cockpit: A Passenger's Perspective on Global Public Health: The Role of Human Rights' (2004) 77 *Temple Law Review* 313.

49 L.O. Gostin and J.M. Mann, 'Towards the Development of a Human Rights Impact Assessment for the Formulation and Evaluation of Public Health Policies' (1994) 1 *Health and Human Rights* 58.

50 B.M. Meier, 'Global Health Governance and the Contentious Politics of Human Rights: Mainstreaming the Right to Health for Public Health Advancement' (2010) 46 *Stanford Journal of International Law* 1.

51 M. Robinson, 'What Rights Can Add to Good Development Practice' in P. Alston and M. Robinson (eds), *Human Rights and Development: Towards Mutual Enforcement* (New York: OUP, 2005) 25.

52 A.E. Yamin, 'Beyond Compassion: The Central Role of Accountability in Applying a Human Rights Framework to Health' (2008) 10 *Health and Human Rights* 1.

53 International Covenant on Economic, Social and Cultural Rights (ICESCR), GA Resolution 2200A (XXI), 993 (1966).

health has evolved in subsequent international instruments to offer detailed normative standards for justice in health.[54] Where scholars and practitioners long debated the normative legitimacy of social and economic rights,[55] the end of the Cold War brought with it a global consensus that all human rights are universal, indivisible, interdependent, and interrelated.[56] Memorializing such interconnected human rights and corresponding government duties, the UN Committee on Economic, Social and Cultural Rights (the institution charged with drafting official interpretations of, and monitoring state compliance with, the ICESCR)[57] issued a General Comment in 2000 to provide authoritative interpretation of the norms inherent in the human right to health.[58] The Committee clarified in General Comment 14 that the right to health depends upon a wide variety of interconnected rights to 'underlying determinants of health', beginning in preventive and curative health care and expansively encompassing underlying rights to food, housing, work, education, human dignity, life, nondiscrimination, equality, prohibitions against torture, privacy, access to information, and freedoms of association, assembly, and movement.[59] Based upon this evolution of health-related human rights, UN agencies, development organizations, and advocacy groups have increasingly invoked a 'rights-based approach to health' (grounded in the right to health and rights to various underlying determinants of health) as a means to operationalize international legal norms through advancements in global health governance.[60]

Galvanizing international institutions and reforming government practices, human rights now impact health through an expansive and reinforcing set of international treaties, regional instruments, and national laws and policies. At the international level, the United Nations has sought a cross-cutting commitment to 'mainstream' human rights in all programs, policies, and activities, with the WHO adopting this commitment as a way of incorporating key human rights principles in its health programming.[61] As states have incorporated health-related rights under national constitutions and laws,[62] this rights-based approach to health is explicitly shaping accountability for government efforts—framing the legal and policy environment, integrating core rights-based norms into policy and programming, and evaluating the implementation

[54] J. Tobin, *The Right to Health in International Law* (Oxford: OUP, 2012).

[55] P. Alston, 'The United Nations' Specialized Agencies and Implementation of the International Covenant on Economic, Social and Cultural Rights' (1979) 18 *Columbia Journal of Transnational Law* 83.

[56] United Nations, World Conference on Human Rights: Vienna Declaration and Programme of Action, Vienna, 14–25 June 1993.

[57] M. Craven, *The International Covenant on Economic, Social and Cultural Rights: A Perspective on Its Development* (Oxford: OUP, 1995).

[58] UN Committee on Economic, Social, and Cultural Rights, General Comment No 14, The Substantive Issues Arising in the Implementation of the International Covenant on Economic, Social, and Cultural Rights, UN Doc E/C.12/2000/4 (2000).

[59] General Comment 14 (n 58) para 11.

[60] H.K. Nielsen, *The World Health Organisation: Implementing the Right to Health* (Copenhagen: Europublishers, 1999) 37; L. Gable, 'The Proliferation of Human Rights in Global Health Governance' (2007) 35 *Journal of Law, Medicine and Ethics* 534; L. London, 'What Is a Human-Rights Based Approach to Health and Does It Matter?' (2008) 10 *Health and Human Rights* 65.

[61] W. Onzivu, '(Re)Invigorating the World Health Organization's Governance of Health Rights: Repositing an Evolving Legal Mandate, Challenges and Prospects' (2011) 4 *African Journal of Legal Studies* 225.

[62] E.D. Kinney and B.A. Clark, 'Provisions for Health and Health Care in the Constitutions of the Countries of the World' (2004) 37 *Cornell International Law Journal* 285; B.A. Simmons, *Mobilizing for Human Rights: International Law in Domestic Politics* (Cambridge: CUP, 2009).

of programs and budgets.[63] This rights-based approach has come to influence a wide range of national policy implementation efforts for underlying determinants of health,[64] and to assure this implementation, a global accountability regime has evolved to encompass treaty monitoring bodies, rights-based litigation, and 'naming and shaming' advocacy.[65] Given this development of health-related human rights and accountability for rights-based policy implementation, human rights now provide influential normative frameworks for justice in realizing public health pursuant to international law.

2.2 Social justice

Where the global community long failed to make health a political priority,[66] this tradition of neglect has begun to change, with normative frameworks for social justice elevating public health discourse in international affairs.[67] Addressing underlying determinants of health,[68] social justice seeks to ameliorate the harms that arise when social structures protect the powerful while unfairly burdening the vulnerable.[69] Social justice norms are now seen as a foundational justification for public health, structuring 'fairness' in preventing disease and promoting health.[70] In the context of global health, advocates have looked to health systems as a means to secure social justice as a normative framework for global health governance.[71]

Arising out of the failed revolutions of 1848, developing through the rise of social medicine, and speaking to contemporary global health governance,[72] the evolution of social justice frameworks for global health have achieved many of the goals of formal norm-setting without requiring the adoption of a treaty or the establishment of new institutions.[73] Where the United Nations was once thought to be solely the domain and tool of powerful states,[74] social justice norms have come to frame UN policy-making in a globalizing world[75] and thereby provide legitimacy for global health

63 G. Backman et al, 'Health Systems and the Right to Health: An Assessment of 194 Countries' (2008) 372 *Lancet* 2047.

64 A. Chapman, 'Globalization, Human Rights, and the Social Determinants of Health' (2009) 23 *Bioethics* 97.

65 J. Wolff, *The Human Right to Health* (New York: Norton, 2012).

66 K. Lee et al, *Health Impacts of Globalization: Toward Global Governance* (London: Palgrave Macmillan, 2003).

67 D.P. Fidler, 'Reflections on the Revolution in Health and Foreign Policy' (2007) 85 *Bulletin of the World Health Organization* 243; H. Feldbaum, K. Lee, and J. Michaud, 'Global Health and Foreign Policy' (2010) 32 *Epidemiologic Review* 82.

68 B. Jordan, *The New Politics of Welfare: Social Justice in a Global Context* (London: Sage Publications, 1998).

69 D.E. Beauchamp, 'Public Health as Social Justice' (1976) 13 *Inquiry* 3.

70 Beauchamp, 'Public Health as Social Justice' (n 69); L.O. Gostin and M. Powers, 'What Does Social Justice Require for the Public's Health? Public Health Ethics and Policy Imperatives' (2006) 25 *Health Affairs* 1053.

71 M. Rowson et al, 'The Global Health Watch: Mobilising Civil Society Around an Alternative World Health Report' (2004) 1 *PLoS Medicine* 31.

72 N. Krieger and A.-E. Birn, 'A Vision of Social Justice as the Foundation of Public Health: Commemorating 150 Years of the Spirit of 1848' (1998) 88 *American Journal of Public Health* 1603.

73 I. Kickbusch and P. Buss, 'Global Health Diplomacy and Peace' (2011) 25 *Infectious Disease Clinics of North America* 601.

74 H.J. Morgenthau, *Politics Among Nations: The Struggle for Power and Peace* (New York: Knopf, 1948).

75 Wendt, *Social Theory of International Politics* (n 13).

governance.[76] Through this normative framing of global health discourse, as policymakers both develop and implement normative frameworks, health has moved beyond rhetorical invocation and become a basis for global political action.[77] The 2000 Millennium Declaration,[78] followed by eight Millennium Development Goals (MDGs) to be met by 2015, has heralded widespread political attention to global health, focusing global policy on the 'vicious cycle' that links poverty and health.[79] Created as a social justice framework for a massive, global campaign to advance human development, four of the eight MDGs invoke improvements in health—including the reduction of maternal and infant mortality, the prevention of HIV infection, and the alleviation of poverty and hunger—with the MDGs seeking to address these specific health conditions through the influence of moral authority.[80] While criticized for advancing social justice frameworks in the absence of legal accountability,[81] these hortatory goals for global justice have nevertheless proven effective in creating specific benchmarks to implement national health policy and accountability mechanisms to evaluate public health outcomes.

This social justice agenda for political action in global health has continued to impact global health governance, with norms becoming increasingly prevalent and specific in framing the political statements of the global community.[82] Going beyond national self-interest, and piercing the veil of national sovereignty to prevent individual harm, UN proclamations increasingly emphasize the need for global cooperation to solve health harms in every country, with social justice rising as the impetus for mobilizing the global community to intervene to protect public health.[83] With an increasing need for independent institutions to allocate resources to the most deprived, the Global Fund to Fight AIDS, Tuberculosis and Malaria (Global Fund) was created in 2002 to manage funds for consultative projects developed by both public and private organizations,[84] with recent reforms allowing the Global Fund to target those with the greatest health needs, engage representatives from a wide variety of actors, and prevent national self-interest from impacting decision making and program management.[85] While improving health outcomes as a means to realize social justice is an explicit objective

76 R. Beaglehole and R. Bonita, 'Global Public Health: A Scorecard' (2008) 372 *Lancet* 1988; J. Shiffman, 'A Social Explanation for the Rise and Fall of Global Health Issues' (2009) 87 *Bulletin of the World Health Organization* 608.

77 Rowson et al, 'The Global Health Watch' (n 71).

78 United Nations Millennium Declaration, adopted 8 September 2000, GA Resolution 55/2, UN GAOR, 55th Session, Supp No 49, para 5, UN Doc A/RES/55/2 (2000).

79 L.P. Freedman, 'Achieving the MDGs: Health Systems as Core Social Institutions' (2005) 48 *Development* 19.

80 J.G. Ruggie, 'United Nations and Globalization: Patterns and Limits of Institutional Adaptation' (2003) 9 *Global Governance* 301; D. Hulme and S. Fukuda-Parr, 'International Norm Dynamics and "the End of Poverty": Understanding the Millennium Development Goals (MDGs)', BWPI Working Paper 96 (2009).

81 P. Alston, 'Ships Passing in the Night: The Current State of the Human Rights and Development Debate as Seen through the Lens of the Millennium Development Goals' (2005) 27 *Human Rights Quarterly* 755.

82 R. Horton, 'Health as an Instrument of Foreign Policy' (2007) 369 *Lancet* 806.

83 T.G.G. Weiss, *Thinking about Global Governance: Why People and Ideas Matter* (New York: Routledge, 2011).

84 G. Maciocco and A. Stefanini, 'From Alma-Ata to the Global Fund: The History of International Health Policy' (2007) 7 *Revista Brasileira de Saude Materno Infantil* 4.

85 P. Poore, 'The Global Fund to Fight AIDS, Tuberculosis and Malaria (GFATM)' (2004) 19 *Health Policy and Planning* 52; G.W. Brown, 'Multisectoralism, Participation, and Stakeholder Effectiveness: Increasing the Role of Nonstate Actors in the Global Fund to Fight AIDS, Tuberculosis, and Malaria' (2009) 15 *Global Governance* 169.

within global governance, these social justice norms are playing an underanalyzed role in prioritizing public health in international affairs,[86] highlighting the need for constructivist scholarship as states recommit themselves to normative goals in developing a post-2015 (post-MDG) global health agenda.[87]

2.3 Health equity

To alleviate systematic disadvantage as a means to achieve substantive equality,[88] health equity gives meaning to justice within socially stratified societies, framing the amelioration of disparities in health outcomes between more and less socially advantaged groups.[89] Although it is not possible to eliminate all global inequalities (both in opportunity and in outcome), inequity refers to those inequalities that are unjust, driven by structural unfairness in the global system. Where not all health inequalities can be thought of as inherently unjust, health equity focuses on the socially controllable factors that affect health, specifically the unfair distribution of resources that limits disadvantaged groups from achieving the highest attainable standard for health.[90] Equity in health thus requires a just distribution of the burdens and benefits of public health across society. Necessitating global intervention to realize a more just world, scholars have looked to inequity (within and between countries) based upon inequality in health expenditures,[91] in health outcomes,[92] in underlying determinants of health,[93] or in capability to be healthy.[94]

With equity now accepted as a normative framework for global health governance, the implementation of health equity has shifted policy discourse to establish the principles for prioritizing and distributing determinants of health. Because health exists on a gradient, both within and between countries, it has become possible to focus on the relatively unhealthy.[95] Within countries, this focus on health inequity has drawn policy attention to the needs of vulnerable populations—for example to the unequal social status of women, considering the implications of gender to access to health care, participation in health decision making, and reproductive health systems and seeking to alleviate these inequities through differential treatment (affirmative action or 'substantive equality') to prioritize women's health.[96] Between countries, health

[86] I. Kickbusch, 'Health in All Policies: Where to from Here?' (2010) 25 *Health Promotion International* 261.

[87] UNAIDS, UNICEF, UNFPA and WHO, 'Health in the post-2015 UN development agenda: Thematic Think Piece' (Geneva, 2012).

[88] P. Braveman, 'Health Disparities and Health Equity: Concepts and Measurement' (2006) 27 *Annual Review of Public Health* 167.

[89] P. Braveman and S. Gruskin, 'Defining Equity in Health' (2003) 57 *Journal of Epidomiology and Community Health* 254.

[90] N. Daniels, 'Equity and Population Health: Toward a Broader Bioethics Agenda' in A. Dawson (ed), *Public Health Ethics* (Cambridge: CUP, 2011) 191.

[91] M. Whitehead, 'The Concepts and Principles of Equity and Health' (1992) 22 *International Journal of Health Services* 429.

[92] S. Kumanyika, 'Health Disparities Research in Global Perspective: New Insights and New Directions' (2012) 33 *Annual Review of Public Health* 1.

[93] M. Marmot, 'Achieving Health Equity: From Root Causes to Fair Outcomes' (2007) 370 *Lancet* 1153.

[94] J.P. Ruger, 'Global Health Justice' (2009) 2 *Public Health Ethics* 261.

[95] E. Blas and A.S. Kurup (eds), 'Equity, Social Determinants and Public Health Programs' (Geneva: WHO, 2010).

[96] Marmot, 'Achieving Health Equity' (n 93), 'Gender Equity in Health: Debates and Dilemmas' (2000) 51 *Social Science and Medicine* 931.

inequity analysis seeks to apply a Rawlsian vision of justice at an international level,[97] looking to material wealth disparities as a basis of inequity and seeking to create a normative basis for international distributive justice.[98] Such normative frameworks for health equity have sought to prioritize the most marginalized through civil society participation at the national level and to justify mutual assistance as a basis for redistribution at the global level.[99]

Impacting global health governance toward those groups that experience social disadvantage,[100] with an understanding that health inequity is driven by underlying determinants of health and cannot be reduced by the health sector alone, actors have sought to develop multisectoral policy approaches to underlying determinants of health.[101] In meeting this imperative to address unjust disparities in status, resources, and power, the WHO Commission on Social Determinants of Health has attributed health inequities to the underlying circumstances in which people live, arguing 'for the ethical basis of action on social determinants of health[,] . . . the view that good health, fairly distributed, was a value in itself'.[102] The Commission has sought to apply this normative imperative to policy development, continuing the social movement for health equity coming out of the 1978 Declaration of Alma-Ata and employing its reports and political consultations to create plans for policy development and monitoring for health equity.[103] While a great deal remains to be done to address health equity on the global agenda and move health policy beyond health services,[104] steps are being taken to address equity through multisectoral action, encapsulated in the whole-of-government approach to health equity in the global governance initiative for Health in All Policies.[105]

It is in this political context, with a range of normative frameworks interacting to structure global health policy, that institutions have come together to realize public health in the twenty-first century. Reflecting on these overlapping ontological frameworks for human rights, social justice, and health equity—among myriad interconnected normative justifications for the global health response—global health policy development often begins by drawing on some combination of these normative frameworks to justify global action. As seen in the preamble to the 'working definition' of the Health in All Policies approach, the drafting committee for the 2013 Global Conference on Health Promotion noted that:

97 F. Peter and T. Evans, 'Ethical Dimensions of Health Equity' in T. Evans et al (eds), *Challenging Inequities in Health: From Ethics to Action* (New York: OUP, 2001).

98 A. Buchanan, 'Rawls's Law of Peoples: Rules for a Vanquished Westphalian World' (2000) 110 *Ethics* 697.

99 G. Ooms and R. Hammonds, 'Taking Up Daniel's Challenge: The Case for Global Health Justice' (2010) 12 *Health and Human Rights* 29; R. Labonte and T. Schrecker, 'Globalization and Social Determinants of Health: Promoting Health Equity in Global Governance' (2007) 3 *Globalization and Health*.

100 S.R. Benatar, S. Gill, and I. Bakker, 'Making Progress in Global Health: The Need for New Paradigms' (2009) 85 *International Affairs* 347.

101 N. Daniels, B.P. Kennedy, and I. Kawachi, 'Why Justice is Good for Our Health: The Social Determinants of Health Inequalities' (1999) 128 *Daedalus* 215.

102 M. Marmot et al, 'Building of the Global Movement for Health Equity: From Santiago to Rio and Beyond' (2012) 379 *Lancet* 181.

103 Commission on Social Determinants of Health, 'Closing the Gap in a Generation: Health Equity through Action on the Social Determinants of Health' (Geneva, 2008).

104 K. Lee, M. Koivusalo, E. Ollila, R. Labonte, C. Schuftan, and D. Woodward, 'Global Governance for Health' in R.N. Labonte (ed), *Globalization and Health: Pathways, Evidence and Policy* (London: Routledge, 2009) 289.

105 T. Ståhl et al, 'Health in All Policies: Prospects and Potentials' (Helsinki: Ministry of Social Affairs and Health, 2006).

Health in All Policies is a systemic and sustained approach to taking into account the impacts of public policies on health determinants and health systems across sectors, at the levels the decisions are made, in political, legislative and administrative processes, in order to realize health-related rights and to improve accountability for population health and health equity.[106]

Much like this example, norms are increasingly proving to be the tie that binds, bringing together state and non-state actors to address underlying determinants of health as a means to realize justice in global health. While norms are at times poorly elaborated or rhetorically conflated in global health governance, there is advantage in defining and delineating these norms in global health, analyzing how normative frameworks structure global health policy.

3. Implications of Normative Frameworks to Global Health Policy

Meeting an expanding set of global challenges to underlying determinants of health, normative frameworks are guiding global health policy efforts beyond traditional forms of international law. With international law bearing most directly on states, such legal constructs have limited effect on the global forces that increasingly structure public health,[107] with realism appearing insufficient to understand contemporary changes in statehood, international relations, and global health.[108] These limitations of international health law have moved global health governance beyond the purview of international legal constructs, engaging a diverse array of state and non-state actors through the rise of new policy institutions—institutions bound by their normative foundations and understood through the constructivist paradigm.

Where once the WHO reigned supreme over international health, the contemporary era lacks a strong institutional authority to coordinate every global initiative to prevent disease and promote health. Compounded by ongoing challenges to the power of the nation-state,[109] with realism unable to 'analyze changes in statehood and their implications for international relations',[110] the international system of governance no longer exerts the influence it once had on the public's health.[111] While this statist approach to governance is inherent in WHO's authority as an international organization,[112] it is simultaneously undermining WHO's constitutional mission to promote global health among an expanding range of non-state actors.[113] Filling this vacuum in global health governance, multilevel partnerships of governmental, intergovernmental, and

106 Action: SDH, 'Health in All Policies Approach' (Geneva, 2012), available at <http://www.actionsdh.org/Contents/Action/Governance/Building_governance/Health_in_All_Policies_approach3.aspx>.

107 R. Labonte and T. Schrecker, 'Globalization's Challenges to People's Health' in R.N. Labonte (ed), *Globalization and Health: Pathways, Evidence and Policy* (London: Routledge, 2009), 1.

108 O. Aginam, *Global Health Governance: International Law and Public Health in a Divided World* (Toronto: University of Toronto Press, 2005).

109 S. Strange, *The Retreat of the State: The Diffusion of Power in the World Economy* (Cambridge: CUP, 1996).

110 G. Sorensen, 'Big and Important Things in IR: Structural Realism and the Neglect of Changes in Statehood' in K. Booth (ed), *Realism and World Politics* (London: Routledge, 2011).

111 S. Moon et al, 'The Global Health System: Lessons for a Stronger Institutional Framework' (January 2010) *PLoS Medicine* 1, 2.

112 D.P. Fidler, 'After the Revolution: Global Health Politics in a Time of Economic Crisis and Threatening Future Trends' (2008) 2 *Global Health Governance*.

113 S.E. Davies, 'What Contribution Can International Relations Make to the Evolving Global Health Agenda?' (2010) 86 *International Affairs* 1167.

nongovernmental actors have arisen to address a multisectoral set of determinants of health.[114] These global health partnerships have complicated efforts to rely upon international law as a basis for the global health response.[115] Without steady institutional leadership or legal authority to coordinate this crowded and complex landscape—leading to what has been referred to generously as 'open-source anarchy,[116] less generously as a 'mosh pit'[117]—health advocates have turned to global health policy as a way of galvanizing a disparate set of actors to embrace shared norms for justice in global health.

Shifting governance from international health law to global health policy, partnerships have become particularly relevant in a landscape of scarce resources (and increased competition for those resources among an expanding set of actors), with partnerships for specific health priorities combining the efforts of inherently limited actors in achieving collective health goals. For example, in the aftermath of the politically-charged failure of WHO's malaria eradication effort in the 1950s and 1960s,[118] the contemporary Roll Back Malaria Partnership has brought together over 500 governmental, intergovernmental, and nongovernmental partners to create a coordinated global response, developing shared norms to articulate, carry out, and sustain this partnership to respond to malaria.[119] While these decentralized partnerships lack the hierarchical leadership structures and health systems focus of past efforts, the harmonizing force of normative frameworks allows for the combination of disparate actors in a single initiative.[120] Norms are influencing and binding the wide range of decentralized actors in this new global health architecture, and as a consequence of these changing global institutions for health, normative frameworks are playing a vital role in structuring global health policy.

Given the fragmentation of these uncoordinated initiatives (with each actor operating under independent motivations), policymakers seek shared norms for justice to coordinate these multilevel and multisectoral partnerships in the absence of international law.[121] Such norms 'act as a coalitional glue' in binding these actors together,[122] with policy making structured by an 'overlapping consensus' among state and non-state actors.[123] Moving beyond a state-centric approach—transitioning from international law driven by nation-states to 'soft law' binding the global community of state and non-state actors—norm-setting seeks to frame these new policy institutions to alter behaviors,

114 Szlezák et al, 'The Global Health System' (n 3).

115 B.M. Meier and A.M. Fox, 'International Obligations through Collective Rights: Moving from Foreign Health Assistance to Global Health Governance' (2010) 12 *Health and Human Rights* 61.

116 D.P. Fidler, 'Architecture amidst Anarchy: Global Health's Quest for Governance' (2007) 1 *Global Health Governance*.

117 K. Buse and A. Harmer, 'Global Health Partnerships: The Mosh Pit of Global Health Governance' in K. Buse, W. Hein, and N. Drager (eds), *Making Sense of Global Health Governance: A Policy Perspective* (Basingstoke: Palgrave Macmillan, 2009).

118 J. Siddiqi, *World Health and World Politics: The World Health Organization and the UN System* (Columbia, SC: University of South Carolina Press, 1995).

119 G.T. Keusch et al, 'The Global Health System: Linking Knowledge with Action—Learning from Malaria' (2010) 7 *PLoS Medicine*; see also R. Bruce Aylward et al, 'Global Health Goals: Lessons from the Worldwide Effort to Eradicate Poliomyelitis' (2003) 362 *Lancet* 909.

120 Szlezák et al, 'The Global Health System' (n 3).

121 G. Silberschmidt, D. Matheson and I. Kickbusch, 'Creating a Committee C of the World Health Assembly' (2008) 371 *Lancet* 1483.

122 Goldstein and Keohane, 'Ideas and Foreign Policy' (n 26) 12.

123 Ruger, *Global Health Justice and Governance* (n 16).

sustain funding, and coordinate efforts for justice in global health.[124] While there are legitimate concerns that these partnerships will enable states to shirk responsibility for the realization of health,[125] partnerships have nevertheless proven vital to global health governance, delineating shared norms to promote institutional responsibilities. No longer grounded in traditional legal institutions or traditional health sectors, this multilevel and multisectoral global health policy landscape is proving a focal point of normative frameworks to prevent disease and promote health as a means to global justice.

As parallel normative frameworks guide the range of discrete partnerships across the global health architecture, various scholars, practitioners, and advocates have sought to bring these multiple partnerships together under a singular normative framework for justice in global health. In accordance with these proposals—alternatively named an International Health Partnership, Public Health's New World Order, a Global Plan for Justice, a Global Health Constitution, or a Framework Convention on Global H-ealth—proponents seek a voluntary compact among states and their non-state partners in business, philanthropy, and civil society to redress global health harms under the normative auspices of human rights, social justice, and health equity.[126] While seeking to avoid the realist power constraints on international legal negotiations, these proposals often envision the WHO taking a leadership role through its constitutional mandate to develop norms and coordinate actors.[127] These proposals seek to reassert the WHO's institutional authority for normative development in global health to encompass the expanding sphere of global health policy, moving beyond 'vertical' partnerships for specific health priorities to address underlying determinants of health through 'diagonal' public health systems (combining horizontal and vertical approaches to health).[128] Supported by the institutionalization of a coordinated global health fund, proponents argue that the allocation of independent, predictable, and sustainable funding from state and non-state actors could be collected based upon financial targets and distributed to meet basic survival needs (as measured by poverty, morbidity, and premature mortality), with accountability mechanisms to assure compliance with established norms.[129] Where the WHO is presently thought to lack authority and direction in the new global health landscape,[130] proponents have looked to norms to provide legitimacy to WHO leadership, allowing it to coordinate the widening range of global health actors. Given these rapidly-evolving changes, constructivist scholarship provides a theoretical basis by which to analyze the roles, interests, and goals of state

124 A. Barnes and G.W. Brown, 'The Idea of Partnership within the Millennium Development Goals: Context, Instrumentality and the Normative Demands of Partnership' (2011) 32 *Third World Quarterly* 165.

125 D. Sridhar, S. Khagram, and T. Pang, 'Are Existing Governance Structures Equipped to Deal with Today's Global Health Challenges? Towards Systematic Coherence in Scaling-Up' (2008) 2 *Global Health Governance.*

126 L.O. Gostin, 'Redressing the Unconscionable Health Gap: A Global Plan for Justice' (2010) 4 *Harvard Law and Policy Review* 271.

127 L.O. Gostin, E.A. Friedman, G. Ooms, T. Gebauer, N. Gupta, D. Sridhar, W. Chenguang, J.-A. Røttingen, and D. Sanders, 'The Joint Action and Learning Initiative: Towards a Global Agreement on National and Global Responsibilities for Health' (2011) 8 *PLoS Medicine.*

128 G. Ooms et al, 'The "Diagonal" Approach to Global Fund Financing: A Cure for the Broader Malaise of Health Systems?' (2008) 4 *Globalization and Health.*

129 G. Ooms and R. Hammonds, 'Correcting Globalization in Health: Transnational Entitlements Versus the Ethical Imperative of Reducing Aid-Dependency' (2008) 1 *Public Health Ethics* 154.

130 R. Horton, 'Can WHO Survive?' (2012) 380 *Lancet* 1457; D. Legge, 'Future of WHO hangs in the balance' (2012) *British Medical Journal* 345.

and non-state actors and a new understanding of the contemporary operation of global health governance.

In the midst of a weakening international authority for global health, constructivism has the ability to capture the interests of state and non-state actors in the global community. Given a dearth of study on the norms that bind actors together and commit themselves to global health, normative policy analysis can move legal scholarship beyond an understanding of state power interests toward the study of global health policy. With no single normative approach providing a satisfactory account of global health governance, it is necessary for scholars to analyze areas where norms complement each other and where they conflict. Analyzed through the constructivist paradigm, it is possible to determine whether contemporary partnerships in global health governance are meeting norms for justice in global health policy. Through such scholarship, normative policy analysis can frame efforts to reform the global health landscape, set goals for global health progress, and evaluate efforts to realize justice in global health.

4. Conclusion

Global health governance is increasingly viewed as a means to a more just world, and these changes create an academic imperative for normative policy analysis in global health. In studying this shift toward normative frameworks as a basis for global health governance, it will be necessary to clarify what role norms play in the advancement of global health policy, how the influence of such norms can be measured through social scientific study, and what effects norm-driven policies have on global health. Applied to practice, such normative policy analysis can provide a basis for policymakers to reform institutions to meet normative goals, framing policy decisions to realize a more just world.

As global health policy finds justification across normative frameworks, the constructivist paradigm provides a basis to conceptualize the policy contexts and health issues correlated with particular normative frameworks. Given recent efforts to establish comprehensive normative frameworks for global health, it will be necessary to study the distinctions across normative frameworks before these frameworks can be harmonized across the global community. With these norms seeking to realize justice in global health, international legal research will be necessary to study the visions, goals, and consequences of these global health policies. Only through legal analysis of these normative frameworks will it be possible to understand why and how state and non-state actors come together in solidarity to address global health.

34

The Contributions of Science and Politics to Global Food Safety Law

Erik Millstone

1. Introduction and Agenda

One of the regulatory regimes that have been established to contribute to the protection of global public health focuses on the safety of internationally traded foodstuffs. The bulk of this chapter focuses on regimes that are used to regulate the safety of the food supply, though the analytical tools could equally be applied to the science-based regulation of other technologies such as mobile telecommunications or nuclear power plants. Prior to 1994, setting and enforcing food safety standards was the responsibility of individual national states and multilateral jurisdictions like the European Community; there was no statutory global regulatory regime. The treaties that established the World Trade Organization (WTO), however, were widely expected to create an integrated and unified global food safety regulatory system. Those involved in negotiating the treaties and advocating their adoption expected that a unified global regime would rapidly emerge and that it would contribute to improving food safety and enhancing aggregate economic welfare by diminishing or eradicating non-tariff barriers to trade that had arisen because of the differences between antecedent national regulatory regimes.

The WTO was established as a replacement for its predecessor, the General Agreement on Tariffs and Trade (GATT), which had been established in 1947. The GATT agreement had not, however, covered trade in food and agricultural commodities. The agricultural and food sectors were amongst those over which the individual national parties to GATT, such as the UK, France, Germany, Japan, and the US, were not willing to relinquish their control, partly because their domestic agricultural policies were based on subsidy programmes that discriminated against imports, and partly because those countries were not confident that other countries' food products were safe. The establishment of the WTO, and the inclusion of trade in agricultural and food products within its remit, was therefore widely expected in official and industrial circles to result in the creation of a single globally-harmonized food safety regulatory regime. The process of regulatory convergence was supposed to be accomplished in large part by relying on scientific knowledge and expertise to determine the existence, magnitude, and significance of food safety risks. Scientists were supposed to determine the technological conditions under which risks could be eradicated, or diminished to acceptable levels, and technical regulatory standards were supposed to be based on that knowledge. In practice, however, the project of achieving convergence has proved far more difficult to achieve than many had expected.

The four main questions that this paper addresses are:

- How have the national and international food safety legislative and regulatory regimes developed, and how might they evolve?

- How do scientific and policy considerations interact in, for example, food safety decision-making processes?
- Can science provide a definitive basis for international regulatory convergence?
- Under what conditions can science-based policy-making achieve and reconcile scientific and democratic legitimacy?

2. Terminological Clarification

Given that the use of terminology in the domains of legal studies and science policy do not always coincide, it is desirable to diminish ambiguity by explaining the meanings attributed to several of the key terms that are used in this chapter. In this context, the term 'policy' is used to refer to any and all decisions by institutions, such as governments and firms, which regularize and systematize their actions. Policy-making therefore includes *par excellence* legislation. While legal scholars and practitioners routinely refer, especially in the UK, to the contrast between primary and secondary legislation, the same contrast is referred to slightly differently by food industry employees and public officials with responsibility for setting, managing, and enforcing food safety standards; they use the term 'regulation(s)' to refer to secondary legislation. Science and technology policy analysts use the phrase 'regulatory policy' to refer to the entire regime of institutions, rules, and practices with which governments seek to regulate the products, processes, and practices of users of industrial technologies.

In the UK the primary legislation, such as the Food Safety Act 1990 and the Food Standards Act 1999, covering domains such as food safety, typically empower ministers to set regulations.[1] Those regulations provide specific rules that, for example, govern microbiological food safety and types of ingredients permitted in particular categories of products.[2] Primary legislation, in combination with the secondary regulations, together constitute the framework of rules that govern the production, distribution, and sale of foodstuffs.

There is, however, more to regulatory policy-making than passing laws and setting regulations. Stalin is reputed to have remarked that: 'To govern is not to write resolutions and distribute directives: to govern is to control the implementation of the directives.'[3] Policy outcomes are influenced by the ways in which laws and regulations are interpreted by so-called 'street level bureaucrats',[4] as well as by the ways in which they are interpreted by, for example, judges and juries. Judgments by, for example, trading standards officers or environmental health officers, about whether particular commercial activities are deemed to comply with legislation and regulations inevitably influence which activities are permitted, restricted, or forbidden, and which products can lawfully be produced, traded, and consumed. The phrase 'regulatory policy' is used in practice in those policy circles and amongst science and technology

[1] Food Safety Act 1990, see <http://www.legislation.gov.uk/ukpga/1990/16/contents>; Food Standards Act 1999, see <http://www.legislation.gov.uk/ukpga/1999/28/contents>.

[2] Food Safety (General Hygiene) Regulations 1995, see <http://www.hmso.gov.uk/si/si1995/Uksi_19951763_en_1.htm>; Food Hygiene (England) Regulations 2006, see <http://www.statutelaw.gov.uk/content.aspx?>; Food Standards Act 1999, see <http://www.legislation.gov.uk/ukpga/1999/28/contents>.

[3] Cf A. Jordan, 'The Implementation of EU Environmental Policy: A Policy Problem Without a Political Solution?' (1999) 17(1) *Environment and Planning C*, 69.

[4] M. Lipsky, *Street-Level Bureaucracy: Dilemmas of the Individual in Public Service* (New York: Russell Sage, 1980).

policy scholars to refer to all of the elements that together constitute regulatory regimes, and those include legislation, regulation, enforcement, and implementation.

One component of the complex regimes in which regulatory policy are established, maintained, and modified concerns the manner in which those regimes are portrayed to the public and to the commercial and/or industrial sector(s) governed by those regimes. In the following discussion one issue will be the extent to which official portrayals of food safety policy regimes have accurately represented their actual characteristics. The discussion will in particular suggest that official representations of policy-making systems have not always been accurate, let along comprehensive, and that important inaccuracies have concerned the roles played by scientific considerations, evidence, and advisers. An implication of the analysis is that unless and until official representations of the operations of regulatory regimes become less misleading, and consequently change their structures and procedures, the scientific and democratic legitimacy of policy processes and outcomes will remain problematic and contested.

3. The Evolution of Food Safety Regimes

Legislation and regulations to control food products to protect public health and welfare can be found in the statutes of classical Persia, Greece, and Rome, and in the laws of mediaeval and pre-industrial Europe.[5] With the formation in the eighteenth and nineteenth centuries of industrial nation states, centralized national regulations were often introduced, for example in respect of weights and measures, although in some cases, such as that of the German beer purity laws (*Reinheitsgebot*), pre-industrial legislation was sustained into the industrial era.

A brief period in the history of the UK, from 1815 to 1875, constituted an exception to the general rule that public authorities have regulated the production and sale of foodstuffs to protect public health and consumers' interests. In the aftermath of the Napoleonic Wars in 1815, and in the name of *laisez faire* political economy, the UK government repealed what were known as the 'Assize of Bread', which had regulated the composition of bread, as well as weights and measures. From 1815 until 1875 the welfare of British consumers was left to the less-than-tender mercies of the marketplace, and during those sixty years there was a marked deterioration in the quality and safety of the British food supply.[6] A new regulatory regime was eventually introduced, but only after a lengthy struggle between health professionals on the one hand and industrial interests on the other.[7] The sustained deterioration in the quality and safety of foods provoked the introduction of the Adulteration of Foods Act 1860. Much credit for provoking the adoption of that legislation has rightly been given to the medical journal *The Lancet*, although the resulting regulatory regime had a conspicuously light touch. While it empowered local authorities to appoint public analysts, it did not oblige them to do so, and stipulated that the cost of the analyses should be met by the people making a complaint.[8] It was not until 1875, when the Sale of Food and Drugs Act

5 See eg F.L. Hart, 'A History of the Adulteration of Food Before 1906' (1952) 7(1) *Food Drug Cosmetic Law Journal* 5; R. Tannahill, *Food in History* (London: Penguin, 1973); G.M. Burditt, 'The History of Food Law' (1995) 50 *Food and Drug Law Journal* 197.

6 J. Burnett, *Plenty and Want: A Social History of Diet in England from 1815 to the Present Day* (London: Scolar Press, 1979); R. Tannahill, *Food in History* (London: Penguin, 1988).

7 P. van Zwanenberg and E. Millstone, *BSE—Risk, Science and Governance* (Oxford: OUP, 2005) ch 3.

8 Ministry of Agriculture Fisheries and Food, 'Food Quality and Safety: A Century of Progress' (London: HMSO, 1976) 5.

became law, that local authorities were required to appoint public analysts and local inspectors were empowered to obtain samples for analysis, which allowed the provisions of the 1860 Act to be enforced. Those regulations were focused relatively narrowly on two dimensions, namely identity and purity; claims about the content of the products should be truthful, they should contain the ingredients as indicated by the claims of the sellers, and levels of contamination should be acceptably low; issues of toxicology and chemical safety were not regulated until the twentieth century.

During the twentieth century the scope of the regulation of national food systems grew by accretion, and they were variously extended to include controls on microbiological contamination as well as food additives, pesticides, and veterinary medicines, but the scope and substance of such regulatory regimes varied as between nation states. The shift from national regimes to an international regime began, albeit hesitantly in the 1960s. In 1963 member states of the UN Food and Agriculture Organisation (FAO) and of the World Health Organization (WHO) established the Codex Alimentarius Commission (or Codex for short). Codex was established to provide a set of uniform baseline food safety standards that could reconcile the aspiration to provide minimum standards of food safety with the aspiration to dismantle non-tariff barriers to international trade in food and agricultural products. The mere existence of national regulatory regimes does not constitute a barrier to trade, but the differences between the regimes do; those differences entail that products deemed to be in compliance with regulatory standards and acceptably safe in their home markets were not always deemed acceptable in export markets.

From 1963 until the end of 1994, Codex standards were only advisory, they had no statutory standing. With the creation of the World Trade Organization, however, Codex standards were formally adopted by the WTO and its member states, and deemed to constitute statutory minimum food safety standards for internationally traded foodstuffs.[9] The Agreement on Sanitary and Phytosanitary Measures (SPS), which is part of the set of treaties establishing the WTO, sought to prevent members from imposing trade-restrictive measures that are arbitrary or discriminatory by proposing to use science as a touchstone with which to distinguish between those measures that are consistent with the Agreement and those that are not, and to harmonize standards on those that are based on scientific assessments of risk.

The preamble to the SPS Agreement indicates that it is intended 'to further the use of harmonized sanitary and phytosanitary measures between Members, on the basis of international standards, guidelines and recommendations developed by the relevant international organizations, including the Codex Alimentarius Commission'. The crucial role of Codex is reiterated in paragraph 3(a) of Annex A: '. . . for food safety, the standards, guidelines and recommendations established by the Codex Alimentarius Commission relating to food additives, veterinary drug and pesticide residues, contaminants, methods of analysis and sampling, and codes and guidelines of hygienic practice'.

A key role for science is indicated in Article 3(3), which states:

> Members may introduce or maintain sanitary or phytosanitary measures which result in a higher level of sanitary or phytosanitary protection than would be achieved by measures based on the relevant international standards, guidelines or recommendations, if there is *a scientific justification*, or as a consequence of the level of sanitary or phytosanitary protection a Member determines to be appropriate in accordance with the relevant provisions of. . . Article 5. (emphasis added)

[9] Agreement on the Application of Sanitary and Phytosanitary Measures, Annex 1A-4 to Final Act Embodying the Results of the Uruguay Round of Multilateral Trade Negotiations, 15 April 1994, Art 3(1) (hereafter 'the SPS Agreement').

Since the WTO regime came into force in January 1995, any country has been able lawfully to exclude from its market imported products failing to meet Codex standards. On the other hand, if a country excludes from its market products that comply with Codex standards, the exporting country can make a formal complaint to the WTO, which will initiate a dispute procedure under which the onus is on the reluctant importer to show that its measure is based on a sufficient scientific risk assessment.[10]

The WTO treaties in effect presuppose that food safety standards can be set by reference to reliable and robust science, and that on such matters science, as it were, speaks with just one voice. The approach of the WTO and Codex is consequently vulnerable to evidence indicating that the relevant science is often characterized by problematic uncertainties, and/or evidence that different groups of experts provide competing assessments of risks, and/or evidence showing that, on its own, science is never sufficient to decide policy issues.[11]

4. The Evolution of Models of Science in Food Safety Policy-Making

4.1 A technocratic model

From 1963 until 1994 Codex operated relatively informally, and the organization's procedures and policies were substantially sheltered from public scrutiny. In that period Codex represented itself as operating what science and technology policy scholars have termed a 'technocratic' system, meaning that it sought to convey the impression that Codex standards were based on—and only on—scientific considerations, evidence, and expertise. A graphical representation of a technocratic system is provided in Figure 34.1.

A defining characteristic of this approach was that it portrayed scientific information as not just necessary for food safety policy-making but also as sufficient. That is to say, no other types of considerations, such as political, economic, or normative considerations, were acknowledged to have played any role or to have made any contribution to policy-making; policies were supposedly decided by reference to, and only to, scientific considerations. This model also therefore represented the science knowledge, the expert scientific advisers, and their risk assessments as if they were entirely independent of all political, economic, or normative considerations or influences. Technocratic models are implicit whenever claims are made to the effect that policies are based on, and only on, 'sound science'.[12]

Because the science underlying food safety policy-making is often uncertain, incomplete, and contested, the plausibility of technocratic models required ensuring that policy-making processes, such as those conducted by Codex, were concealed within

Fig. 34.1 The technocratic model: policy based on sound science

10 SPS Agreement, Arts 3(3) and 5(8).

11 Anon, 'Herringus Rufus', *The Lancet*, 21 December 1974, 1506; US National Academy of Sciences, 'Saccharin: a technical assessment of risks and benefits: Part 1', Committee for a Study of Saccharin and Food Safety Policy, 1978, US NAS, Washington, DC; Van Zwanenberg and Millstone, *BSE—Risk, Science and Governance* (n 7).

12 See eg Blair, *Hansard*, 18 June 2003.

closed, and consequently unaccountable, regimes. Technocratic portrayals of policy-making are only plausible in conditions where most of the evidence is confidential, scientific meetings are held in closed sessions, and policy-making bodies successfully contrive to be untroubled by legislative scrutiny, judicial oversight, or media reportage. Prior to 1994, scholarly discussions of Codex policy-making were almost entirely restricted to accounts provided by insiders; and they tended to be portrayed with technocratic narratives that were blandly reassuring but bereft of details, especially the important ones.[13] The few analyses of Codex policy-making by outsiders tended to be critical of the technocratic narratives and altogether less reassuring.[14]

More recently, however, technocratic models have been torpedoed below the water-line by the inescapable fact that scientific evidence and understanding is often incomplete, equivocal, and uncertain.[15] Science in policy contexts does not speak with unproblematic certainty or with one voice. Moreover, even if *per impossibile* all scientific uncertainties could be eliminated, science could still not decide food safety policy, or any other technology risk management policy issue either. As academic philosophers are wont to say: *You cannot derive an 'ought' from an 'is'*. They refer to the mistaken view that 'an ought may be derived from an is' as 'the naturalistic fallacy'.[16] Setting food safety standards is concerned with more than the existence and magnitude of risks, deciding regulations entails adjudicating the *acceptability* of possible risks (and uncertainties) in exchange for anticipated benefits, and those judgments are socially variable and value-laden. Consequently policy decisions on the regulation of technological risks such as those involved in food safety are not matters that science alone could ever decide.

13 See eg R. Truhaut, 'The Concept of the Acceptable Daily Intake: A Historical Review' (1991) 8(2) *Food Additives and Contaminants*; E. Poulsen, 'Rene Truhaut and the Acceptable Daily Intake: A Personal Note' (1995) 15 *Teratogenesis, Carcinogenesis and Mutagenesis* 273; S.C. Hathaway, 'Risk Assessment Procedures Used By the Codex Alimentarius Commission and its Subsidiary and Advisory Bodies' (1983) 4(4) *Food Control* 189; A. Huggett et al, 'Towards Internationally Acceptable Standards for Food Additives and Contaminants Based on the Use of Risk Analysis' (1998) 5 *Experimental Toxicology and Pharmacology* 227; G. Vettorazzi, 'International Perspectives for the Safety Evaluation of Pesticide Residues in Food: Toxicological Evaluation and Dietary Exposure' in A. Valverde and E. Gonzalez (eds), *Residuos de Plaguicidas* (Almería: Instituto de Estudios Almerienses, 1992), available at dialnet.unirioja.es as Dialnet-International Perspectives For The Safety Evaluation Of P-2245811-1.

14 P. Bereano, 'Harmony Or Havoc: Can The WTO, Biosafety Protocol And Codex Alimentarius Work Together?' (2006) 1(1) *Journal für Verbraucherschutz und Lebensmittelsicherheit* 70; D. McCrea, 'Report of the analysis of Codex documentation to aid the consumer decision-making process, Codex Committee on General Principles', commissioned by the Food Standards Agency, Completed March 2001; R. Lee, 'Agri-Food Governance and Expertise: The Production of International Food Standards' (2009) 49(4) *Sociologia Ruralis*, doi: 10.1111/j.1467-9523.2009.00493.x; L. Busch 'The Homiletics of Risk' (2002) 15 *Journal of Agricultural and Environmental Ethics* 17; L. Busch and C. Bain, 'New! Improved? The Transformation of the Global Agrifood System' (2009) 69 *Rural Sociology* 321; D. Winickoff and D. Bushey, 'Science and Power in Global Food Regulation: The Rise of the Codex Alimentarius' (2010) 35 *Science Technology Human Values* 356; V. Walker, 'Keeping the WTO from Becoming the "World Trans-science Organization": Scientific Uncertainty, Science Policy, and Factfinding in the Growth Hormones Dispute' (1998) 31 *Cornell International Law Journal* 251.

15 Anon, 'Herringus Rufus' (n 11) 1506; US National Academy of Sciences, 'Saccharin: a Technical Assessment of Risks And Benefits' (n 11); E. Millstone, 'How can scientific connoisseurship be socially useful and intellectually robust?', Report to the Science and Society Programme of the ESRC, February 2004, published in *Scientific Connoisseurs and Other Intermediaries: mavens, pundits and critics*, Appendix C, 30–47, ESRC, Science in Society Programme (Oxford, 2004), available at <http://www.insis.ox.ac.uk/fileadmin/InSIS/Scientific_Connoisseurship_Report.pdf>.

16 P.T. Geach, 'Good and Evil' (1956) 17(2) *Analysis* 33, doi: 10.1093/analys/17.2.33, see <http://analysis.oxfordjournals.org/content/17/2/33.extract>.

4.1.1 *Problems with and changes to the technocratic model*

As events unfolded, it was in the US that technocratic models were first widely seen as implausible and inadequate. Technocratic models were invoked in the US until the late 1960s, but they lost their plausibility as a consequence of the introduction of legislation providing for freedom of information regarding public authorities.[17] The initial 1966 legislation was adopted by Congress for reasons related to the conduct of the Vietnam War, and attempts by the administration to conceal a bombing campaign in Cambodia, but it had a substantial impact on science-based risk policy-making. The 1976 Act was a response to the Watergate scandal, and reinforced the impact of the 1966 Act.

Once the scientific evidence on which policies were supposedly based entered the public domain, the uncertainties could no longer be concealed or ignored. Uncertain science means that multiple interpretations of the available evidence can be equally plausible, authoritative, and scientifically legitimate, and any given body of scientific evidence can be consistent with a range of policy responses. The greater the conspicuous uncertainties the greater is the scope for what philosophers and sociologists of science have illuminatingly referred to as 'interpretative flexibility'.[18] In practice, research also showed that those who most enthusiastically articulated technocratic narratives were often amongst those best placed to know how misleading they were.[19]

4.2 The *Red Book* 'decisionist' model

One consequence of the evident shortcomings of the technocratic model was a recognition in the US that an alternative account was needed, not just for narrative purposes but as a basis for guiding processes of institutional reform. The alternative that emerged in the US was codified in 1983 in a report from the US National Research Council entitled 'Risk Assessment in the Federal Government: Managing the Process'.[20] The volume was bound in a bright red cover, so the model is often called the *Red Book* model. This model retained the assumption that risk policy-making starts from a scientific stage called a 'risk assessment', but supplements that activity with a subsequent stage, called 'risk management', during which non-scientific considerations make indispensable contributions. Those non-scientific considerations might include, for example, estimates of the costs and benefits of alternative policy options and political judgments about what can be accomplished and what would be acceptable to various interests and stakeholder groups. A graphic representation of this model is given in Figure 34.2. The importance of the *Red Book* model lies in large part in the fact that it has become a dominant contemporary official orthodoxy. It was first endorsed in the US, but then spread to the OECD and the EU, and in the late 1990s it was endorsed and adopted by the Codex Alimentarius Commission.

A defining feature of this model is that, while it supplemented science with non-scientific considerations as indispensible ingredients to policy-making, it portrayed the

17 US Freedom of Information Act 1966, 5 USC § 552; and the Government in the Sunshine Act, Pub L 94–409, 90 Stat 1241, enacted 13 September 1976, 5 USC § 552b.

18 S. Shapin, 'Why the Public Ought to Understand Science-in-the-Making' (1992) 1(1) *Public Understanding of Science* 27; P. van Zwanenberg and E Millstone, 'Beyond Sceptical Relativism: Evaluating the Social Constructions of Expert Risk Assessments' (2000) 25(3) *Science, Technology and Human Values* 259.

19 P. van Zwanenberg and Millstone, *BSE: Risk, Science And Governance* (n 7) chs 4–6.

20 Available at <http://www.nap.edu/openbook.php?isbn=0309033497> (accessed November 2012).

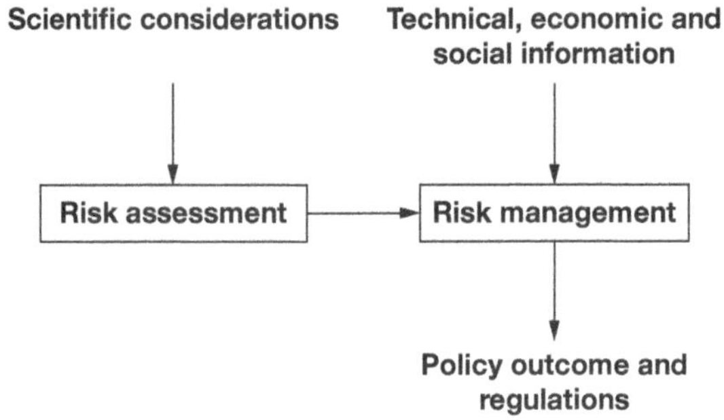

Fig. 34.2 The Red Book model: science first, policy-making second

science as influencing policy-making, but with the direction of influence going only one way; just as in the technocratic model, it portrays science as if it is entirely independent of all policy considerations. That is a crucial problem that will be addressed shortly. Before moving to that discussion, however, it is important to appreciate that one of the strengths of this model, when compared to its technocratic predecessor, is that it can accommodate some limited scientific uncertainties. If the scientists who acknowledge uncertainties are able to estimate (and agree on) the magnitude of those uncertainties, then risk management policy-makers can, for example, introduce quantitative 'safety factors' to take account of the uncertainties of those estimated magnitudes.[21]

For example, food additives are often regulated by reference to what is termed an 'acceptable daily intake' or ADI, which is specified in units of milligrams of a particular compound per kilogram of the body weight of the recipient.[22] ADIs are routinely derived from a so-called 'no effect level' (or NEL—also specified in mg/kg bw) obtained from an animal study, divided by a 'safety factor' (or SF). Therefore ADI = NEL/SF. It has often been suggested that the number '100' provides a suitable safety factor, supposedly because a factor of 10 can accommodate the difference between average laboratory animals and average humans, and a further factor of 10 to accommodate the variability within the human population. In practice the differences between rodents and humans and the variations within human populations can be far greater, moreover the proportion of safety factors actually applied coinciding with a figure of 100 is only a minority of cases. Selecting numerical values for an 'SF' is a decision point that has frequently been portrayed as if purely scientific, when in practice non-scientific considerations routinely influence the interpretation of scientific evidence.[23] Within the Codex system, ADIs for food additives are set by the Joint (WHO-FAO) Expert Committee on Food Additives (or JECFA), which is ostensibly a scientific body, but which routinely makes policy judgments that are portrayed as if they had been purely scientific.

The simplistic linear equation (ADI = NEL/SF) has often been modified when it suggested results that were problematic in policy or commercial terms. For example, when the equation has indicated an ADI that was too low to be industrially useful, a

[21] Commission of the European Communities, 'Food Additives and the Consumer' (Brussels, 1980) App I, 41–3.

[22] R. Truhaut, 'The Concept of an Acceptable Daily Intake: A Historical Review' (2001) 8(2) *Food Additives and Contaminants* 151.

[23] E Millstone, *Food Additives* (London: Penguin, 1986) ch 4, especially 86–95.

lower 'safety factor' has been invoked. Similarly if a 'no effect level' seems too low for industrial utility then advisory committees such as JECFA have sometimes chosen instead to set an ADI by reference to what they term a 'no observed adverse effect level' (or NOAEL). If the NEL is insufficiently high, some of the effects can be deemed not to be 'adverse', but merely as 'adaptations', and so discounted in favour of an NOAEL, if it is higher, so providing a larger numerical value for the ADI.

A corollary of adopting a simplistic approach of linear scaling with numerical safety factors, of course, is that if the magnitudes of the uncertainties are themselves uncertain then decision-making becomes increasingly problematic. In jurisdictions operating with *Red Book* models, such as the EU system and Codex, there are consequently pressures on scientific advisory panels with responsibility for risk assessments only to draw the attention of risk managers (and the general public too) to uncertainties for which estimates of their magnitudes can also be provided and only if future research might readily diminish those uncertainties; to others, blind eyes are turned.

I first attended a conference on food safety and toxicology in 1983, and on that occasion had an opportunity to ask the UK's then senior professor of toxicology a question that had puzzled me for a decade, namely: what is the relevance of mice and rats to humans? His answer was not one I had expected, but it was remarkably candid and honest. He replied: 'your guess is as good as mine'.[24] Thirty years later the extrapolative validity of laboratory data from experiments with rodents to the putative effects on humans remains no less uncertain; yet little or nothing has been done in the interim to diminish those uncertainties. Those chronic uncertainties are so problematic that they are almost never mentioned in toxicological circles or by official regulatory institutions.

4.2.1 The Red Book *model: orthodox but vulnerable*

As long as Codex standards had no legal authority, the Codex policy-making system was able to operate with processes that were opaque to almost all non-participants. Once it became clear, ie by about 1992, that the SPS agreement of the WTO treaty would assign a statutory authority to Codex standards in controlling the internationally-traded foodstuffs, Codex was compelled to clarify, formalize, and disclose its policy-making structures and procedures. That pressure was reinforced as it became clear that members of the WTO, especially the EU, would stipulate compliance with Codex standards within their own domestic regulatory frameworks.[25]

During the mid-1990s Codex made very little progress in that direction. A profound trigger of change, however, was the announcement in the British House of Commons on 20 March 1996 that, despite repeated previous reassurances that British beef was entirely safe, compelling evidence had emerged that BSE could transmit, and had transmitted, to humans.[26] This provoked changes to the institutional structures and processes with which food safety policies were made, for example, in the UK, France, Germany, and Japan, and also at EU level. Cases of a novel, distinct, and invariably fatal variant of Creutzfeld-Jakob Disease (CJD) that had emerged in the UK were almost certainly a consequence of consuming BSE-contaminated foodstuffs.[27] Food

24 Personal comment, University of Surrey, Guildford, 11 July 1983.

25 Corrigendum to Regulation (EC) 852/2004 of 29 April 2004 on the hygiene of foodstuffs [2004] OJ L139.

26 *Hansard*, 20 March 1996, vol 274, cols 375–387, available at <http://hansard.millbanksystems.com/commons/1996/mar/20/bse-health>.

27 van Zwanenberg and Millstone, *BSE: Risk, Science and Governance* (n 7) especially chs 6 and 8.

safety standards, and the institutions in which they were set, and by which they were enforced, then came under unprecedented scrutiny. Initially the scrutiny was most intense in the UK, but as evidence emerged from an inquiry of the European Parliament that the European Commission, and its advisory committees, had enthusiastically accepted and reiterated the UK's mistakenly reassuring narrative that BSE posed no threat whatsoever to public health, scrutiny spread to EU-wide decision-making.[28] Subsequently BSE emerged in cattle in other European countries, such as Germany and Austria, and countries further afield such as Japan, Canada, and the US, and in all those jurisdictions pressure increased for food safety policy-making to be reformed.

4.3 Developments at the Codex Alimentarius Commission

Codex could not be immune from those pressures; in fact the pressure on Codex became especially intense. As the global regulator of food safety, the divergences between different and separate national risk assessments, and related risk management regulations, posed very serious problems. In autumn 1996, the UK authorities asserted that British beef was then entirely safe, and therefore that all other Member States of the EU and Codex should accept imports of British beef. That view was, however, contested and protagonists turned to Codex and to the EU authorities to adjudicate those disputes. A few years later, the safety and acceptability of genetically modified (GM) foods, and their cultivation, erupted on to and up the public policy agenda. So intense were the disputes over agricultural biotechnology that the member states of Codex were unable to agree to include the control of these new technologies within the remit of Codex. Together those events compelled Codex—and consequently its member states and jurisdictions too—to clarify, formalize, and make more explicit its regulatory policy-making structures and procedures.

It was in those circumstances in the late 1990s therefore that Codex explicitly adopted and endorsed a *Red Book* model, and portrayed its structure and procedures as being organized in accordance with that model, even though doing so entailed implicitly repudiating its earlier technocratic narratives. The initial up-stream step, on the left-hand end of the model in Figure 34.2, is referred to as a 'scientific risk assessment', and responsibility for performing and delivering such assessments was explicitly assigned to expert scientific advisory bodies, which advised Codex 'risk management' committees.

Responsibility within Codex for assessments of the risks posed by food additives and contaminants was assigned to the WHO and FAO's Joint Expert Committee for Food Additives (or JECFA),[29] while the risks to consumers from pesticides were assigned to the WHO and FAO's Joint Meeting on Pesticide Residues (or JMPR).[30] The second down-stream stage has been termed 'risk management'; it is a stage at which scientific risk assessments are interpreted by risk management policy-makers by reference to sets of non-scientific considerations such as trade-offs between risks and benefits as well as issues such as costs and acceptability. In the Codex system responsibility for setting risk

28 European Parliament, 'Report on alleged contraventions or maladministration in the implementation of Community law in relation to BSE, without prejudice to the jurisdiction of the Community and national courts', Report of the Inquiry from a temporary committee into BSE, rapporteur: Manuel Medina Ortega, 7 February Doc EN\RR\319\319544 (Strasbourg, 1997).

29 See <http://www.fao.org/food/food-safety-quality/scientific-advice/jecfa/en/>.

30 See <http://www.who.int/foodsafety/chem/jmpr/en/index.html>.

management rules has been assigned to bodies such as the Codex Committee on Food Additives and Contaminants (CCFAC) and to the Codex Committee of Pesticides Residues (CCPR).[31] Similarly, food safety policy-making in the EU was structured so as to delegate responsibility for risk assessments to the Scientific Committee for Food, which in turn advised risk managers in the European Commission, then located in the Directorate General for Health and Consumer Protection (or DG-SANCO). Before the BSE crises of the late 1990s, responsibility for managing food safety risks at the EU level had been located in the Directorate General for the Internal Market. The formal adoption of a *Red Book* model did not, however, provide either Codex or the EU system with equilibrium or stability.

4.3.1 Flaws in the Red Book *model*

The attempt by Codex, the WHO, FAO and influential member states and jurisdictions, as well as the food and chemical industries, to characterize JECFA and the JMPR as purely scientific bodies, in whose deliberations non-scientific considerations played no part, always were problematic. Amongst the judgments that those bodies have provided since their inception were many cast in the form of quantitative figures for the ADIs of particular additives, contaminants, and pesticides. Codex and others have frequently tried to portray ADIs as if they were a type of natural constant, like the refractive index of water or the specific heat of copper, providing measurements of the relative toxicity of chemical compounds, where the more toxic a compound is the lower is its ADI.[32]

Given that setting an ADI entails making judgements of *acceptability*, it follows that ADIs are intrinsically normative; different social and economic groups with different interests and perspectives disagree about which risks are, and are not, acceptable. Choosing an ADI typically involves making trade-offs as between possible risks and anticipated benefits. JECFA's traditional practice has been to juxtapose aggregate risks against total benefits, but arguably a more objective analysis would be one that took account of circumstances in which those who bear most of the risks gain few, if any, benefits, while those who benefit most, may risk least.

Normative considerations have also influenced judgments made by JECFA on the crucial issue of how much data, and which sorts of data, are necessary and sufficient to enable JECFA to conduct its risk assessments and to assign ADIs to particular compounds. Over the years, the amounts of required data have increased, but only marginally. By the end of the twentieth century, JECFA would not attribute an ADI to a new compound without first receiving data from a long-term chronic-toxicity rodent-feeding study. Moreover, by then the convention had been adopted that such studies needed to administer a minimum of three doses of the test compound (at low, medium, and high doses), and to feed those doses to 50 males and 50 females, as well as a similar-sized control group that would receive the standard feed but with none of the compound being tested. In total, therefore, such studies required a minimum of 400 animals. That conventional figure is entirely arbitrary; if instead a minimum of 4,000

[31] NB some of the names of these bodies have changed as responsibilities have been marginally redefined. See <http://www.codexalimentarius.org/and http://www.codexalimentarius.org/committees-task-forces/en/>.

[32] Compounds that JECFA have presumed to be unproblematically safe when used in routine industrial practices, such as ascorbic acid or vitamin C, are assigned ADIs as 'not specified', meaning that no restrictions need be placed on their use.

or 40,000 animals were required the resulting study would provide far greater sensitivity and precision, but at higher cost to both funders and animals.

By choosing the figure of just 400 animals, and also only accepting evidence of a putative adverse effect if the result is 'statistically significant', in the conventional sense that there is less than one chance in 20 that the apparent effect was not a random phenomenon, entails that in practice such studies can only reliably detect adverse effects that occur in more than 20 per cent of the rodents. A strict scientific interpretation of an apparently negative result could at best mean only that, if the compound is harmful and if humans are sufficiently like rodents, then the compound is unlikely to cause harm to more than 20 per cent of consumers; such a study cannot properly be interpreted or represented as if demonstrating safety, nonetheless that is how JECFA routinely represents such results. Those practices reflect value-laden choices that serve some interests rather than others, and cannot properly be understood as purely scientific or objective. ADIs are therefore irredeemably hybrid judgments constructed out of both scientific and non-scientific considerations.

The approach taken by expert advisory bodies such as JECFA has therefore not been objective, socially neutral, or inevitable, and their chosen approach has depended on evaluative and normative considerations, even though such considerations routinely remained implicit. The fact that evidence also emerged showing that members of JECFA and JMPR, as well as the WHO's in-house senior toxicologist, were acting as paid consultants to some of the companies whose products they were asked to evaluate, reinforced the argument that the judgments emerging from, for example, JECFA and the JMPR were neither purely scientific nor socially or economically neutral.[33] The adoption by Codex of a *Red Book* model in the late 1990s represented a step forward, when compared to technocratic narratives, but it was insufficient to legitimate its status or authority.

Codex was, moreover, assailed by several more immediate practical problems as well as by the conceptual and theoretical issues discussed previously. Science—or more precisely the judgments of a group of expert scientific advisers—was supposed to provide a secure basis with which to achieve regulatory convergence, but the hoped-for convergence appeared to be elusive. The topics over which convergence was not achieved in the 1980s and 1990s included in particular beef from cattle treated with growth-promoting hormones and the synthetic hormone known in the EU as bovine somatotropin (or BST), which when injected into dairy cows increases milk yields per cow and per unit of feed. All of those compounds were first developed and approved in the US, and subsequently JECFA had deemed them acceptably safe, and they were and remain widely used in the US.[34] Several of the beef cattle growth promoting hormones had been judged acceptably safe in 1982 by the Lamming Committee, which advised the European Commission, as well as the EC Scientific Committee for Animal Nutrition in November 1982, the EC Scientific Committee for Food in February 1984, and a 1995 EC Scientific Conference on Growth Promotion in Meat Production. Nonetheless EU Member States and the Commission decided not to authorise

33 See eg T. Zeltner, D.A. Kessler, A. Martiny, and F. Randera, 'Tobacco Company Strategies to Undermine Tobacco Control Activities at the World Health Organization' (Geneva: WHO, 2000), available at <http://www.who.int/genevahearings/inquiry.html> (accessed 1 August 2003).

34 WHO, Technical Report Series 699, 1981; WHO, Technical Report Series 763, 1987; WHO, 'Toxicological Evaluation of Certain Veterinary Drug Residues in Food', Food Additives Series 23 (1988), available at <http://www.inchem.org/pages/jecfa.html> and from <http://www.who.int/foodsafety/chem/jecfa/publications/monographs/en/index.html>; WHO, 'Toxicological Evaluation of Certain Veterinary Drug Residues in Food', Food Additives Series 43 (2000).

their use because of high levels of public concern and resistance. Those decisions entailed that beef carcass meat from cattle treated with those hormones could not lawfully be imported into EC/EU markets.[35]

(a) The beef hormones dispute

After protracted but unsuccessful negotiations, the US government lost patience with the Europeans and took the EC/EU to a dispute at the WTO. In 1997, a WTO Dispute Panel found against the Europeans, and the WTO's Appellate Body confirmed most aspects of that Panel's judgment.[36] The US government then exercised its right to impose financial penalties, at the rate of some $160 million a year, on selected European imports, using the revenue to compensate US beef farmers for their lost sales.

The WTO Dispute Panel ruled against the EU, and that ruling was interpreted by some as implying that non-EU countries could compel the EU to accept their food and agricultural products, even if the European Commission was not convinced that those products were acceptable. The judgments of the WTO Dispute Panel and the Appellate Body were, however, rather more subtle and nuanced. The WTO Dispute Panel did not rule that the EU had no scientific evidence of risk, nor that the hormones are unproblematically safe, but concluded rather that the EU had not followed the rules concerning the requirements for, and conduct of, an appropriate science-based risk assessment. In practice, the EU did have some evidential grounds for its concerns about the safety of those hormones, but the data had not derived from studies of the consequences of consuming beef containing residues of growth hormones. They came instead from studies of the direct medical use of some of the hormones in pharmaceutical products and treatments. The WTO Dispute Panel ruled that those data were not sufficiently relevant to the alleged risk that the European measure was designed to control.

The European Commission responded not just by asking their expert advisers to assess the risks from eating beef produced using those hormones, but also by elaborating the questions that it wanted their advisers to answer in a way that widened the range of putative risks it wanted assessed. The US approach has been predicated on the assumption that, since the hormones in question are chemically similar to the animals' naturally occurring hormones, and since hormone residues in meat from cattle produced using hormone additives are similar to those found in traditionally-produced meat, their use poses no significant hazard. Moreover, they have argued that the use of growth-promoting hormones in the US grew noticeably after the early 1970s, but no adverse trends can be discerned from the US domestic public health epidemiological data.

Prior to the late 1990s, European risk assessors had framed their assessments in a similar way to that adopted in the US. Since the late-1990s, however, the European Commission has asked its risk assessors to consider issues that the US authorities had not raised. For example, it posed questions concerning the eventual environmental fate of the hormones that animals would excrete. That has not been considered a relevant issue in the US, and it had not previously been on the European agenda. Another

35 European Commission, 'Hormones in Bovine Meat: Background and History of WTO Dispute', 28 September 2001, see <http://ec.europa.eu/food/food/chemicalsafety/contaminants/hormones/aspects_en.htm> document available at http://ec.europa.eu/dgs/health_consumer/library/press/press57_en.pdf> (accessed 6 November 2012).

36 WTO, 'EC Measures Concerning Meat and Meat Products (Hormones) Complaint by the United States—Report of the Panel', WT/DS26/R/USA, 18 August 1997.

respect in which the scope of European risk assessments was widened was by asking the experts to assess the possible risks, not just to average consumers, but to especially vulnerable groups, in particular to pregnant women and pre-pubescent children; while in the US risks to those particular groups were not assessed by those advising the authorities. There is nothing in WTO statutes or case law to prevent a jurisdiction from extending the scope of its consideration of risks to aspects that had previously been beyond its purview.

In April 1999, the Scientific Committee on Veterinary Measures Relating to Public Health issued a report, which concluded that there was some evidence that several of the hormones may pose a risk to the health of vulnerable groups, and for the others there was insufficient evidence to be confident that they were acceptably safe.[37] On the strength of that revised risk assessment, the European Commission returned to the WTO Dispute Panel, and persuaded it that the EU's ban on those hormones and on meat from the US produced using those compounds, was compliant with the rules of the WTO, despite the divergence of the EU's assessment from those of both the USA FDA and JECFA. Since then, the EU has ceased to pay compensation and the US has abandoned its pursuit of the dispute.

(b) The rBST saga

Recombinant bovine somatotropin (or rBST), which in the US is termed bovine growth hormones (or BGH), has been used lawfully in the US since 1994. JECFA had also judged rBST to be acceptably safe first in 1993 and then again in 1997.[38] Its use has, however, never been deemed acceptable in the EC or EU. The rBST case is interesting in part because of a contrast it provides to the case of beef hormones discussed earlier. rBST is lawfully used in the US, but its use remains unlawful in the EU, yet the US has *not* initiated a WTO dispute over rBST. One widely held, but not universally accepted, view is that the European Commission learnt several lessons from the beef hormones case, which have subsequently been applied in the case of rBST. The way in which the European Commission dealt with rBST was, nonetheless, noticeably different in the mid-1990s, compared to the preceding period.

In March 1999 two separate official risk assessments of rBST were delivered to the European Commission, one that focused on the potential risks to human consumers of milk produced by cows treated with rBST and the other on the potential risks to the health and welfare of dairy cows receiving rBST treatment.[39]

The European Commission had specifically asked the Scientific Committee on Veterinary Measures relating to Public Health (SCVMPH) to 'assess the possible direct *and indirect* adverse effects on public health caused by the use of BST *under normal conditions*' (emphasis added). The inclusion of the word 'indirect' and the phrase 'under normal conditions' significantly extended the scope of the assessment beyond that

37 Scientific Committee on Veterinary Measures Relating To Public Health, 'Assessment of Potential Risks To Human Health From Hormone Residues in Bovine Meat and Meat Products', DG-SANCO, Doc XXIV/B3/SC4, 30 April 1999, available at <http://ec.europa.eu/food/fs/sc/scv/out21_en.pdf> (accessed 28 February 2013).

38 WHO, 'Evaluation of Certain Veterinary Drug Residues in Food', Technical Report Series 832, 1993, , 40–2; WHO, 'Toxicological Evaluation of Certain Veterinary Drug Residues in Food', Food Additives Series 41, 1998, 125–46.

39 European Commission's Scientific Committee on Veterinary Measures relating to Public Health, 'Report on Public Health Aspects of the Use of Bovine Somatotropin', 15–16 March 1999; European Commission's Scientific Committee on Animal Health and Animal Welfare, 'Report on Animal Welfare Aspects of the Use of Bovine Somatotrophin', 10 March 1999.

implied if they had been absent. In a parallel exercise, the Scientific Committee on Animal Health and Animal Welfare (SCAHAW) was 'asked to report on the incidence of mastitis and other disorders in dairy cows *and on other aspects of the welfare of dairy cows*' (emphasis similarly added).

When the US FDA and JECFA had previously assessed the risks of rBST they had, effectively, confined their focus to possible adverse effects on human consumers. They both acknowledged that there was evidence that the administration of rBST had a noticeable effect on mastitis in dairy cows, but discounted that evidence as having no direct bearing on the health of human consumers, to which their terms of reference supposedly confined them. US officials deemed the increased risk of mastitis in cows treated with rBST not to be a problem of 'veterinary health' but rather a problem of 'animal welfare', which could be mitigated by 'herd management' that in practice meant administering high doses of stronger antibiotics. In this way statistically significant adverse veterinary effects were retrospectively reclassified as not a health issue.[40]

The SCVMPH's risk assessment was inconclusive; the committee identified prima facie evidence of a possible hazard, but could not reliably estimate the probability or severity of adverse outcomes. If that had been the full extent of the evidence of risk it would almost certainly not have been sufficient to sustain a measure that permanently banned rBST from the EU.

In the event, however, the Scientific Committee on Animal Health concluded that: 'BST administration causes substantially and very significantly poorer welfare because of increased foot disorders, mastitis, reproductive disorders and other production related diseases. These are problems which would not occur if BST were not used and often results in unnecessary pain, suffering and distress.'[41] That scientific conclusion was judged by the European Commission, the US authorities, and the corporations seeking access to European markets as providing a sufficient basis for the EU to prevail in the event of a WTO dispute. Consequently the US authorities have declined to initiate a formal dispute at the WTO. While the use of rBST remains lawful and widespread in the US, it remains unlawful in the EU and in many other jurisdictions too.

The examples of beef and dairy hormones demonstrate that different jurisdictions can and do frame their risk assessments in different ways, and that a jurisdiction can adopt a measure that is more restrictive than that indicated by Codex and yet not be vulnerable to a WTO dispute, as long as a scientific risk assessment has been conducted, and as long as it provides a basis for the consequent measures adopted. Those examples also demonstrate that scientific risk assessments, whether performed at the Codex global level or at the level of national or regional jurisdictions, do not necessarily deliver regulatory convergence; science does not always and only speak with one voice. Different conclusions to scientific risk assessments can and will arise not just because different groups of experts may interpret scientific uncertainties in differing ways, but also because the questions posed to risk assessors by risk managers can and do diverge from one another.

The failure of Codex to deliver regulatory convergence became even more conspicuous in the late 1990s and early years of this century in the context of heated disputes concerning the safety and acceptability of GM foods. The disputes over food safety risk

40 E Millstone, 'Plagiarism or Protecting Public Health?' (1994) 371(6499) *Nature* 647.

41 Conclusions and Recommendations of the Scientific Committee on Animal Health and Animal Welfare on the Animal Welfare Aspects of the Use of Bovine Somatotrophin (adopted 10 March 1999), available in March 1999 at <http://europa.eu.int/comm/dg24/health/sc/scah/out21_en.html>.

assessments that erupted not just, for instance, between the EU and the US, but also within the EU as between Member States showed, amongst other things, that however attractive the *Red Book* model might have been to incumbent political and industrial interests, it was inadequate and irredeemably flawed.

Despite those problems, the EU explicitly invoked a *Red Book* model when it established the new European Food Safety Authority (EFSA) in January 2002. Responsibility for providing scientific risk assessments and advice to the European Commission, and to EU Member States, was assigned to EFSA, while responsibility for risk management was assigned to the European Commission and in particular its DG-SANCO, referred to earlier.

In practice those institutions have found the *Red Book* model a problematic characterization of their activities. Sometimes DG-SANCO has criticized EFSA for stepping over the line and making risk management judgments, while at others it has been keen for EFSA to make risk management judgments while wanting those judgments to be portrayed as if purely scientific. EFSA was supposed to be independent of both commercial and policy pressures, but given that only a very small minority of EFSA staff (five out of 351) have permanent contracts, DG-SANCO has managed to keep EFSA on a very tight rein.[42] As a DG-SANCO senior official revealingly commented: 'we want EFSA to be independent, but not out of control'.[43] *Red Book* models were also explicitly adopted when reforms to the institutions of food safety policy-making were introduced in, for example, France, Germany, Italy, Spain, and Japan, although no two of them interpreted or institutionalized the model in exactly the same way.[44]

4.4 Developments in Codex in the twenty-first century

In the early years of this century, and especially in the face of disputes over food safety standards of the sort discussed previously, Codex reached the point where its procedures and standards were struggling to be accepted as legitimate and authoritative.[45] This provoked a review and revision of a important document called the *Codex Procedural Manual.* The process by which Codex modified its procedural rules, implicitly rejecting the *Red Book* model in favour of what scholars have come to refer to as a 'co-dynamic model', is obscure but the outcome is both fascinating and important.

4.4.1 The co-dynamic model

Models of the co-dynamic type initially emerged in the work of sociologists of scientific knowledge and policy analysts earlier in the twentieth century.[46] The pivotal,

42 EFSA, 'Preliminary Budget and Establishment Plan 2013', available at <http://www.efsa.europa.eu/en/corporate/pub/bep13.htm>, see especially 10.

43 Personal comment, Brussels, 1999.

44 E. Millstone, 'Science, Risk and Governance: Radical Rhetorics and the Realities of Reform' (2009) 38(4) *Research Policy* 624, doi:10.1016/j.respol.2009.01.012.

45 See eg T. Lang, 'Diet, Health and Globalization: Five Key Questions' (1999) 58(2) *Proceedings of the Nutrition Society* 335, doi: 10.1017/S0029665199000452, published 28 February 2007; J. Clapp and D. Fuchs (eds), *Corporate Power in Global Agrifood Governance* (Cambridge, MA: MIT Press, 2009) especially ch 4, E. Smythe, 'In Whose Interests? Transparency and Accountability in the Global Governance of Food: Agribusiness, the Codex Alimentarius and the World Trade Organisation'; D.L. Post, 'The Precautionary Principle and Risk Assessment in International Food Safety: How the World Trade Organization Influences Standards' (2006) 26(5) *Risk Analysis* 1259.

46 D.E. Chubin and S. Restivo, 'The "Mooting" of Science Studies: Research Programmes and Science Policy' in K.D. Knorr-Cetina and M. Mulkay (eds), *Science Observed* (London: Sage

distinctive insight of a co-dynamic model is that it recognizes that scientific representations of risks, and for that matter of benefits too, are inevitably framed by some prior non-scientific judgments about, for example, what counts as a risk or as a benefit.

Funtowicz and Ravetz helpfully highlighted the contrast between science when used in controversial policy contexts and science as articulated and developed in supposedly 'normal' academic contexts; they coined the phrases 'regulatory science' and 'post-normal science' to refer to the former types of science.[47] As Funtowicz and Ravetz have explained, in regulatory science: 'facts are uncertain, values in dispute, stakes high and decisions urgent'.[48] In their analyses of the roles of regulatory science in the UK, scholars including Wynne, Levidow, and van Zwanenberg and Millstone, using slightly different vocabularies, have shown that up-stream, non-scientific framing assumptions, which are all too often taken for granted and so left implicit, are indispensable when seeking to understand and explain why different groups of scientists provide different, and sometimes contrary or even contradictory, representations of the risks that technologies and products might pose, as well as of the benefits that they might provide.[49] Analogous developments emerged in the US,[50] in France[51] and elsewhere.

The insight that scientific portrayals of risks (and benefits) are framed by prior up-stream non-scientific assumptions about what is important and what is valuable helps to explain the close correlations between competing scientific representations and the

Publications, 1983) ch 3; B. Wynne 'Uncertainty and environmental learning: reconceiving science and policy in the preventative paradigm' (1992) 2(2) *Global Environmental Change* 111; J. Abraham, 'Scientific Standards and Institutional Interests: Carcinogenic Risk Assessment of Benoxaprofen in the UK and US' (1993) 23 *Social Studies of Science* 387; S. Jasanoff, *The Fifth Branch: Science Advisors as Policy-Makers* (Cambridge, MA: Harvard University Press, 1990); S. Jasanoff and B. Wynne, 'Science and Decision-Making' in S. Rayner and E.L. Malone (eds), *Human Choices and Climate Change: Vol 1—The Societal Framework* (Columbus, OH: Battelle Press, 1998).

47 S.O. Funtowicz and J.R. Ravetz, 'Science for the Post-Normal Age' (1993) 25(7) *Futures* 739.

48 Funtowicz and Ravetz, 'Science for the Post-Normal Age' (n 47) 744.

49 B. Wynne, 'Risky Delusions: Misunderstanding Science and Misperforming Publics in the GE Crops Issue' in I.E.P. Taylor (ed), *Genetically Engineered Crops: Interim Policies, Uncertain Legislation,* (New York: Haworth Press, 2007); L. Levidow, S. Carr, D. Wield, and R. von Schomberg, 'European Biotechnology Regulation: Framing the Risk Assessment of a Herbicide-Tolerant Crop' (1997) 22 *Science, Technology and Human Values* 472; L. Levidow and S. Carr, (2007) 'GM Crops on Trial: Technological Development as a Real-World Experiment' (2007) 39(4) *Futures* 408; J. Murphy and L. Levidow, *Governing the Transatlantic Conflict over Agricultural Biotechnology: Contending Coalitions, Trade Liberalisation and Standard Setting* (London: Routledge, 2006); van Zwanenberg and Millstone, *BSE: Risk, Science and Governance* (n 7); E. Millstone, 'Can Food Safety Policy-Making be both Scientifically and Democratically Legitimated? If So, How?' (2007) 20 *Journal of Agricultural and Environmental Ethics* 483; doi: 10.1007/s10806-007-9045-x.

50 S. Jasanoff, (1987) 'Contested Boundaries in Policy-Relevant Science' (1987) 17 *Social Studies of Science* 195; Jasanoff, *The Fifth Branch* (n 46); Jasanoff and Wynne, 'Science and Decision-Making' (n 46); V. Walker, 'Keeping the WTO from Becoming the "World Trans-science Organization": Scientific Uncertainty, Science Policy, and Factfinding in the Growth Hormones Dispute' (1998) 31 *Cornell International Law Journal* 251; V. Walker, 'Transforming Science into Law: Transparency and Default Reasoning in International Trade Disputes' in W. Wagner and R. Steinzor (eds), *Rescuing Science from Politics: Regulation and the Distortion of Scientific Research* (Cambridge: CUP, 2006); S. Krimsky, 'The Funding Effect in Science and its Implications for the Judiciary' (2005) XIII(1) *Journal of Law and Policy* 43; S. Krimsky, 'Risk Assessment and Regulation of Bioengineered Food Products' (2000) 2 *International Journal of Biotechnology* 231; N. Oreskes, 'The Role of Quantitative Models in Science' in C.D. Canham, J.J. Cole, and W.K. Lauenroth (eds), *Models in Ecosystem Science* (Princeton, NJ: Princeton University Press, 2003) 13; N Oreskes, 'Science and Public Policy: What's Proof Got To Do With It?' (2004) 7(5) *Environmental Science and Policy* 369.

51 C. Marris and P.B. Joly, 'Between Consensus and Citizens: Public Participation in Technological Decision-Making in France' (1999) 12(2) *Science Studies* 3; P.B. Joly, C. Bonneuil, and C. Marris, 'Disentrenching Experiment? The Construction of GM-Crop Field Trials as a Social Problem in France' (2008) 33(2) *Science Technology and Human Values* 201.

socio-economic and cultural groups with which the different groups of scientists are aligned. It is not simply a matter of coincidence that scientists working in or for food companies frequently portray their employers' products as safe and wholesome, whereas representatives of consumer, environmental, or public health groups more often contest those representations.[52]

Policy analysts and sociologists of science have documented numerous examples of circumstances in which ostensibly scientific representations of risk and/or benefits have in practice been framed by socio-economic interests and contestable values. Consequently they have concluded that science has not provided, and cannot provide, neutral and uncontested foundations to which policy-making can be definitively anchored. Accepting that conclusion is tantamount to rejecting both the technocratic and *Red Book* models.

Figure 34.3 graphically represents a 'co-dynamic model'. This alternative is one that has become increasingly widely accepted by policy analysts, although less frequently by policy-makers, and even those who make statements implying they accept it, do not always then act accordingly—implementation remains partial and inconsistent.[53]

A key feature of this model, which distinguishes it from its predecessors, is that it represents specific risk assessments, not as detached from their socio-economic and historical contexts but as irredeemably located in particular circumstances, which have social, economic, and policy characteristics that influence the content and outcome of risk assessments. Scientific risk assessments are, as it were, sandwiched between up-stream framing considerations and down-stream interpretative judgments, both of which are different types of policy judgments. The up-stream framing assumptions are judgments about science rather than scientific judgments, that is to say they are not judgments that science itself, on its own, can settle. The model represents risk assessments as affected by the content and characteristics of particular types of high-level policy judgments. Those judgments are concerned with issues such as what is important and worthwhile, and how much of what kinds of evidence may be necessary and/or sufficient to sustain particular types of conclusions, for example about permitting, forbidding, or restricting products or processes.

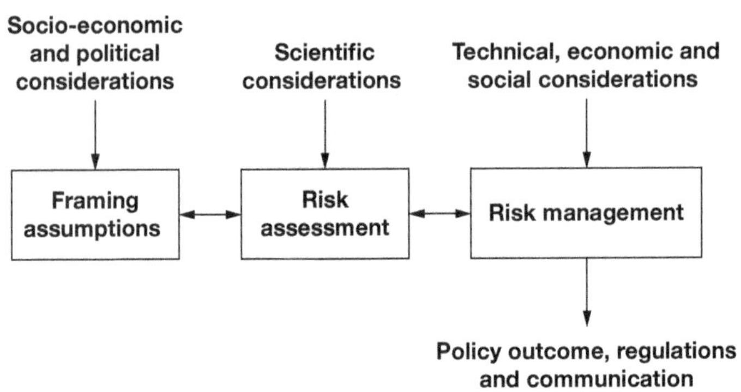

Fig. 34.3 The co-dynamic model

[52] See eg R. Walton, 'Aspartame Studies: Survey of Aspartame Studies: Correlation of Outcome and Funding Sources', available at <http://dorway.com/aspartame-the-bad-news-repost/peer-reviewed-aspartame-studies/>.

[53] E. Millstone, 'Can Food Safety Policy-Making be Both Scientifically and Democratically Legitimated?' (n 49); E. Millstone, 'Science, Risk and Governance' (n 44).

The advocates of the co-dynamic model do not argue that it is complete or exhaustive, but rather that it is more accurate and comprehensive than its predecessors, and they endorse the corollary that policy-making institutional structures and processes should be reformed to differentiate those distinct activities and to implement them in discrete stages of the policy-making process.

4.4.2 Clarifying the nature of the 'framing assumptions'

If the up-stream judgments, and those with policy responsibility for making those judgments, were to try telling risk assessors which conclusions they should reach, and which advice they should provide, then policy-makers would be making illegitimate intrusions into scientific matters, but policy-makers have a responsibility for framing the deliberations of the scientists by explicitly and clearly articulating which are the questions to which they want answers. To fulfil that responsibility they need to decide, and be explicit about, for example what is to count as 'harm' or 'a risk' or a 'benefit'? They should also take explicit responsibility for choosing those framing assumptions, and ensuring that they do guide the risk assessments that their expert advisers provide. Are the scientific advisers asked only to assess risks, or are they expected to trade possible 'risks' off against anticipated 'benefits? Judgments also need to be made about how much—of which kinds of—evidence is necessary to recommend permitting, restricting, or banning products or processes. Those too are judgments about science, but they are nonetheless normative ones that scientific considerations alone cannot settle. Responsibility for deciding those issues should lie with risk managers not with risk assessors, even if the assessors may contribute to the managers' deliberations before those managers take their decisions.

On this co-dynamic model, consequently, official expert representations of risks (and more generally scientific representations of risks) are understood to be hybrid judgments constructed out of combinations of both scientific and non-scientific considerations. However, too often historically, expert and official risk assessments have been mis-represented and portrayed as if they were purely scientific, as in the technocratic and *Red Book* models. The co-dynamic model assumes that it is not possible to conduct a scientific risk assessment unless and until some context-specific framing assumptions are adopted, either implicitly or explicitly. On this view scientists cannot, and therefore do not, assess risks as if they were suspended in a social, economic, historical, and cultural vacuum. Consequently, those adopting or advocating a co-dynamic model argue that the pretence that risk assessments are purely scientific should be abandoned, and instead frame-setting assumptions should be made explicit, and responsibility for selecting those assumptions should be explicitly assigned to, and located with, policy-makers such as government ministers, European Commissioners, and Codex risk management committees, but not with their scientific advisers.

4.4.3 The explanatory power of the co-dynamic model

Recognizing the important role of such upstream framing assumptions helps to explain the phenomenon discussed previously, namely the failure of the Codex Alimentarius Commission to achieve regulatory convergence amongst its member states over issues such as beef hormones and rBST, and the failure of EFSA to persuade the risk assessors of all EU Member States to share its assessments of the risk of eating and/or cultivating GM crops. Empirical studies have documented numerous examples in which the risk assessors of different jurisdictions have provided assessments that differed from each other. Research has also shown that although occasionally those differences arose because shared and agreed bodies of evidence were interpreted differently, more commonly the assessments differed because they have provided answers to different questions, not conflicting answers to a shared and agreed question or set of questions.[54]

An analysis of contrasting framing assumptions helps to explain why GM crops considered safe to cultivate and consume in countries such as the US are not deemed acceptably safe for either consumption or cultivation in several EU Member States.[55] Moreover, given the differences between the policies and judgments of individual EU Member States, the European Commission has conspicuously failed to achieve its goal of a single European market in either GM seeds or foods.[56]

4.5 Codex's ostensible endorsement of a co-dynamic model

While the co-dynamic model was widely adopted in the late twentieth century by scholars on both sides of the Atlantic, and in countries such as Australia and Japan, the governments of leading industrialized countries, and their counterpart institutions such as the European Commission and Codex, have remained wedded to versions of the *Red Book* model. In the early years of the twenty-first century, it was (rather unexpectedly) Codex that broke ranks with, for example, the US and the EU, and repudiated its previous adherence to a *Red Book* model in favour of a more co-dynamic understanding. This transition emerged in 2003 in a relatively obscure document, namely the 13th edition of the *Codex Procedural Manual*;[57] which did more than just adopt a co-dynamic model, it explicitly referred to what has been characterized earlier as the 'framing assumptions' guiding particular risk assessments, and coined a new phrase to refer to those framing assumptions by identifying them as 'risk assessment policy'. The *Codex Procedural Manual* refers to 'risk assessment policy' in the following terms:

> Determination of risk assessment policy should be included as *a specific component of risk management. Risk assessment policy should be established by risk managers in advance of risk assessment, in consultation with risk assessors and all other interested parties*... The mandate given by risk managers to risk assessors should be as clear as possible.[58] (emphasis added)

The *Procedural Manual* makes it clear that responsibility for setting risk assessment policies lies with risk managers, and stipulates that they should provide their risk

54 E. Millstone, P. van Zwanenberg, C. Marris, L. Levidow, and H. Torgersen, 'Science in Trade Disputes Related to Potential Risk: Comparative Case Studies', European Science and Technology Observatory Technical Report Series (2004), available at <http://esto.jrc.es/detailshort.cfm?ID_report=1203>.

55 L. Levidow, 'The Transatlantic Agbiotech Conflict: A Policy Problem and Opportunity for EU Regulatory Policies' in R. Falkner (ed), *The International Politics of Genetically Modified Food: Diplomacy, Trade and Law* (London: Palgrave Macmillan, 2006) 118; L. Levidow, 'Making Europe Unsafe for Agbiotech' in P. Atkinson, P. Glasner and M. Lock (eds), *The Handbook of Genetics and Society: Mapping the New Genomic Era* (London: Routledge, 2009); L. Levidow and S. Carr, *GM Food on Trial: Testing European Democracy* (New York and London: Routledge, 2009).

56 European Commission, 'Communication from the Commission to the European Parliament, the Council, the Economic and Social Committee and the Committee of the Regions on the Freedom for Member States to decide on cultivation of genetically modified crops', COM(2010) 380 final, Brussels, 13 July 2010, available at <http://ec.europa.eu/food/food/biotechnology/docs/communication_en.pdf>.

57 *Codex Alimentarius Commission Procedural Manual*, 13th edn, available at <http://www.codexalimentarius.org/procedures-strategies/procedural-manual/en/>.

58 *Codex Alimentarius Commission Procedural Manual* (n 57) App IV, paras 13–16.

assessors with a clear and explicit mandate *before* each and any risk assessment is conducted. Moreover, while risk assessors may contribute to deliberations about those risk assessment policies before the risk managers reach their risk assessment policy judgments, so too should *all* other interested parties, ie including representatives of consumers, environmental and public interest groups, as well as firms, trade associations, and trade unions. In other words, since 2003 Codex has repudiated the suggestion that scientific risk assessments can be constructed out of purely scientific considerations; Codex ostensibly acknowledged that they are hybrids, where the non-scientific factors frame and guide the scientific deliberations and risk assessment judgments.

A fact even more remarkable than the adoption by the Codex Alimentarius Commission of those risk assessment policy provisions, was the decision in 2007 by all 189 Codex member states to adopt precisely the same provisions in respect of their own domestic policy-making processes.[59] In 2007, therefore, governments representing over 90 per cent of the world's population (implicitly) abandoned the *Red Book* Model, in relation to food safety policy-making, in favour of a *co-dynamic* model—ie a model in which science and policy-making are understood as mutually influencing each other.

4.5.1 Codex and the inconsistent implementation of the risk assessment policy provisions

An empirical research project, entitled 'Risk-Assessment Policies: Differences Across Jurisdictions', supported by the EU's Institute for Prospective Technological Studies reported in 2008 that, while all Codex member states, as well as Codex itself, had committed themselves to adopting and implementing the provisions of the 13th edition of the *Codex Procedural Manual* in respect of their risk assessment policies, neither Codex itself, nor any of six leading member states covered by that research project (the UK, the US, France, Germany, Japan, and Argentina) were implementing their obligations comprehensively or consistently.[60] The study revealed at least three main types of inconsistencies in the implementation of the commitments in relation to risk assessment policy-making by those jurisdictions. First, within individual jurisdictions there were inconsistencies of practices and outcomes across types of products, processes, and risks. Second, there were inconsistencies within jurisdictions between what they had said they would do and how they actually behaved. Third, there were inconsistencies between countries regarding assessments and decisions concerning particular types of products, processes, and risks. Some risk managers, including government ministers and senior public officials, in every jurisdiction covered by that study were providing their risk assessors with some elements of a risk assessment policy, but none were providing comprehensive sets, and different groups of risk managers within jurisdictions were acting inconsistently with each other, and risk managers in

[59] CCGP, 'Report of the Codex Twenty-Fourth Session of the Codex Committee on General Principles, Paris, France, 2–6 April 2007 to the Codex Alimentarius Commission', Thirtieth Session, Rome, Italy, 2–7 July 2007, available 17 May 2007 at <http://www.codexalimentarius.net/download/report/681/al30_33e.pdf>.

[60] E. Millstone, P. van Zwanenberg, L. Levidow, A. Spök, H. Hirakawa, and M. Matsuo, 'Risk-Assessment Policies: Differences Across Jurisdictions', Institute for Prospective Technological Studies, Seville, Spain, EUR Number: 23259 EN, April 2008, available at <http://ipts.jrc.ec.europa.eu/publications/pub.cfm?id=1562>.

different jurisdictions dealing with common categories of potentially risky technologies were not providing risk assessment policy guidance that was consistent with each other.

4.5.2 Three main types of risk assessment policy considerations

The IPTS study, 'Risk-Assessment Policies: Differences Across Jurisdictions', also concluded that at least three main types of risk assessment policies, or sets of risk assessment policy issues, are salient in all relevant examples of science-based food safety policy-making; those types of issues were termed: *substantive*, *procedural*, and *interpretative* risk assessment policy issues. Each of those categories of risk assessment policy should be specified, by risk managers, before a scientific panel can initiate, or at any rate complete, a scientific risk assessment. In practice, however, many risk assessment policy issues of all three of those types are still in effect being decided by scientific risk assessors, rather than by risk managers.

Substantive risk assessment policy issues are those that concern scoping judgments, about what *counts* as a risk or a hazard and what should be (or can be) *discounted*? This type of risk assessment policy also includes judgments concerning what is deemed to count as relevant and necessary evidence. Are the experts expected to assess just 'risks' or assess both 'risks and benefits' and to trade likely risks and anticipated benefits off against each other? What counts as relevant evidence? Should evidence only be considered if it has been published in an academic journal or should unpublished data be included? Should unpublished data only be accepted if those providing it place it in the public domain? And what kinds of evidence (for example anecdotal) can be discounted?

An illustrative example of substantive risk assessment policy-making is provided by a category of food additives, namely emulsifiers. The risks of consuming emulsifiers have been and are being assessed in terms of their putative toxicity. If they are judged to be non-toxic by expert advisory panels they are deemed to be safe by panels of toxicologists and therefore acceptable. In practice, however, the main adverse impact of the industrial use of emulsifiers on public health is probably their contribution to the increasing prevalence of obesity, but that is not a toxicological effect it is a nutritional one, and nutritionists are rarely members of food safety expert panels. Emulsifiers in processed foods serve to keep oils and fats in emulsified suspensions, when they would otherwise not mix but settle in separate layers. The rising incidence of obesity in many countries has been directly linked to growing consumption of oils and fats, and the oil and fat content of modern diets has risen in part because of the unrestricted use of emulsifiers. Both food safety risk managers and risk assessors have assumed that the only risks from emulsifiers that deserve to be considered are toxicological ones. Since those selected to provide the risk assessments are toxicologists, it would be unrealistic to expect them to extend their considerations to issues concerning nutrition, as it is outside the scope of their expertise. If any group have responsibility and competence to address this issue, it is the risk managers, but they have conspicuously failed to engage with those considerations. In these contexts, the substantive risk assessment policies should be made explicit, and then revised, and consequently the range and types of expertise involved in providing risk assessments will need to be widened.

Procedural risk assessment policy issues concern judgments about the processes with which risk assessments should be conducted. For example should risk assessments take place in publicly open meetings or in closed sessions? How should the risk assessors cope with and respond to uncertainties? Do they respond differently to uncertainties that might readily be diminished with further studies, compared to those uncertainties that are likely to be more recalcitrant? Do they only report conclusions that are fully agreed by all members of the panels, or do they provide reports highlighting their differences as well as those matters on which they agree?

One of the fascinating developments that emerged from the UK's Food Standards Agency (FSA) in 2002 was a report entitled 'Review of Scientific Committees', which set out some of the clearest official procedural risk assessment policy in the English language.[61] The FSA subsequently endorsed and adopted the document, and consequently:

> Chairs of . . . advisory committees . . . [should ensure] that the proceedings of the committee . . . are properly documented . . . so that there is *a clear audit trail* showing how the committee reached its decisions . . . decisions should include an explanation of where differences of opinions have arisen during discussions and why conclusions have been reached . . . They should also explain *any assumptions and uncertainties* that are inherent in their conclusions.[62] (emphasis added)

These provisions are very sensible; they represented an attempt by FSA risk managers to provide explicit procedural risk assessment policy guidance to their risk assessors. If that guidance was being implemented, that would contribute substantially to improving the scientific and democratic legitimacy of the FSA's policy-making processes, so it is a matter of some disappointment that in practice those provisions are not being implemented by the risk assessors, and the FSA is failing to monitor or correct that failure to implement the Agency's policy.[63] Instead, uncertainties are being very selectively reported, and numerous procedural and interpretative assumptions remain implicit and unacknowledged.

At the EU level, expert committees that advise EFSA on the safety of consuming or cultivating GM foods and crops have been provided with extensive procedural guidance.[64] A curious feature in that case, however, is that instead of that procedural guidance having been provided by the relevant risk managers, ie DG-SANCO, it has been provided by EFSA to its own committees, ie to risk assessors from risk assessors; the risk managers have exempted themselves from taking responsibility for matters that they should have decided. That is inconsistent with the commitments adopted at Codex in 2007, and those shortcomings may well reinforce the reluctance of some EU Member States to accept EFSA's judgments.

Interpretative risk assessment policy concern judgments about how the evidence that is gathered should be interpreted? Experimental evidence does not interpret itself; the act of interpretation draws on assumptions, some of which are typically non-scientific. For example, what relevance to assessments of risks to human health should be ascribed to the results of studies on laboratory animals, or other model systems using, for example, microbiological or tissue culture methods? Should criteria of statistical significance be used to judge whether or not apparent differences between the groups are

61 Food Standards Agency, 'Review of Scientific Committees', April 2002, available at <http://webarchive.nationalarchives.gov.uk/20090903233850/http:/www.food.gov.uk/multimedia/pdfs/CommitteesReview.pdf>.

62 Food Standards Agency, 'Review of Scientific Committees' (n 61) 8, para 22.

63 E. Millstone, Review of Science in the Food Standards Agency, letter to Lenroy Wallace, Science Review Team, Government Office for Science, 19 May 2008, available at <http://www.bis.gov.uk/assets/goscience/docs/science-review-fsa/sussex-uni.doc>.

64 EFSA Panel on Genetically Modified Organisms (GMO), Guidance of the Scientific Committee/Scientific Panel On request from: European Commission and EFSA Question number: EFSA-Q-2008-089, EFSA-Q-2008-262, Adopted 21 October 2010, Published 12 November 2010: (2010) 8(11) *EFSA Journal* 1879, doi:10.2903/j.efsa.2010.1879.

deemed relevant and biologically significant? If so, which criterion or criteria should be used? If no statistically significant adverse effects are documented does this prove the test compound to be 'safe', 'acceptably safe', or likely not to cause adverse effects in more than, for example, 20 per cent of the population? Another issue of interpretative risk assessment policy concerns the relative attention given to possible false negatives as against possible false positives. The weight attributed to such possible errors is a normative judgment about science, rather than a purely scientific judgement.

Other interpretative risk assessment policy issues include, for example: How much evidence, and of which kinds, is necessary or sufficient for decisions about acceptance, rejection, or restrictions? What are the chosen benchmarks against which the evidence should be judged? How should uncertainties be interpreted? The US Food and Drug Administration has provided its risk assessors with relatively extensive guidance on how they should interpret evidence, although the FDA's reason for doing so have had more to do with protecting the agencies' decisions from judicial challenges than any concern for being compliant with its commitments at Codex.

The foregoing discussion reinforces the Codex requirement that risk managers should specify risk assessment policy framing assumptions to their risk assessors in advance of the conduct of any risk assessments. The fact that that requirement has, as Hamlet remarked, been 'more honoured in the breach than in the observance'[65] helps to explain some of the continuing instabilities in food safety regulatory systems.

5. Conclusions

This chapter has argued not merely that the co-dynamic model provides a far richer and more satisfactory set of analytical tools for understanding how food safety policies are set than its technocratic and *Red Book* predecessors. It also argued that this model provides more adequate and accurate explanations of the differences between the risk assessment and risk management policies of different jurisdictions. The chapter has also implied that if jurisdictions were to properly and comprehensively operationalize a co-dynamic model and if risk managers complied with the provisions of the Codex agreement of 2007, they could establish conditions under which the scientific and democratic legitimacy of their processes and decisions could be enhanced.

The chapter has also, in effect, argued that Codex stumbled blindly to the edge of a potentially beneficial watershed but then failed to step across it.

The discussion also indicated how the initial questions can be answered. The way in which national, regional, and global food safety legislative and regulatory regimes have evolved has been described and analysed, alongside the evolution in the ways in which those regimes have been portrayed and legitimated. The analysis shows that while the structures and procedures have become more sophisticated and less simplistic, they have not yet achieved equilibrium or legitimacy. Key sources of instability arise from the continued prevalence of arrangements under which responsibility for making key policy decisions continues to lie with scientific advisory panels, even though they have no democratic legitimacy and no competence to decide such issues.

The ways in which scientific and policy considerations interact, for example, in global food safety decision-making processes have been characterized, along with an account of the ways in which official portrayals of those interactions have been chronically misleading. The disparity between the ways in which they have been

65 W. Shakespeare, *Hamlet*, Act 1, Scene 4, Line 17.

interacting and the ways in which they could legitimately interact have been characterized by reference to a co-dynamic model and to key provisions of the thirteenth *Codex Alimentarius Commission Procedural Manual*. The discussion has shown how and why both 'technocratic' and *Red Book* model-based systems have always been misleading, despite their evident popularity with both policy-makers and their scientific advisory bodies.

The discussion has explained why, on its own, science cannot provide a definitive basis for international regulatory convergence. It does not follow, however, that regulatory convergence must be unobtainable, but it does show that such convergence cannot be obtained unless and until risk managers take explicit responsibility for their own risk assessment policy frameworks, and if convergence of those frameworks is achieved. That in turn provides some indication as to the alternative pathways along which global, regional, and national food safety regimes might evolve, as the risk assessment policy framing assumptions adopted within particular jurisdictions is a key determinant of their processes and outcomes. In the event that risk assessment policies are comprehensively articulated and legitimated by risk managers, but do not converge, the future might be one that could be characterized as 'sustainable diversity'. There would be little convergence, but those divergences would not occasion trade disputes at, for instance, the WTO or at the regional level with bodies such as the European Commission or the European Court of Justice. If the risk assessment policies were to converge then the resultant risk management policies and food safety standards could reasonably be expected to follow suit.

While the WTO and EU treaties were worded as if science alone could deliver convergence, it might well become increasingly clear that the key to unlocking the conundrum of the lack of convergence of food safety standards will require looking not just to science, but to a legitimate and well delineated coupling of both up-stream risk assessment policies with the subsequent assessments of food-borne risks. Until that happens, however, regulatory convergence will remain chimerical, and some communities will continue to endure lower standards of food safety than are available in other jurisdictions. WTO Dispute Panels will also not run out of cases.

Index